THE LAW OF DELICT IN SCOTLAND

Volume II

THE LAW OF DELICT
IN SCOTLAND

by

DAVID M. WALKER

M.A., LL.B.(Glas.), LL.B.(Lond.), PH.D., LL.D.(Edin.)
One of Her Majesty's Counsel in Scotland,
Of the Middle Temple, Barrister-at-Law,
Regius Professor of Law in the University of Glasgow

" I care not for the supposed dicta
of judges, however eminent, if
they be contrary to all principle."

Lord Mansfield, in *Sommersett's Case*
(1772) 20 St.Tr. 1.

Volume II

Published under the auspices of
THE SCOTTISH UNIVERSITIES LAW INSTITUTE

EDINBURGH
W. GREEN & SON LTD.
1966

First Published 1966

Printed in Great Britain
by
The Eastern Press, Ltd.,
of London and Reading

CONTENTS

VOLUME II
THE SPECIAL PART

v

THE SPECIAL PART

INTRODUCTION TO THE SPECIAL PART

THE Special Part of this book is concerned to some extent with examining the detailed applications of the general principles discussed in the General Part to particular circumstances, but particularly with those specialties and peculiarities which attach to delictual claims and liability in particular factual contexts and with the specialised principles which have developed in the context of particular kinds of claims.

As has been seen there are in the law of Scotland general principles of liability, so that this Special Part is not concerned with special or particular delicts having particular rules applicable to them only, but with the way in which the general principles have been developed and worked out and are applied in particular contexts and sets of circumstances. Only to a small extent, and even then mainly by reason of modern statutes, are there in Scots law special rules applicable only to a particular kind of delict. Similarly there are no nominate delicts in Scots law, and the names, such as trespass, defamation and passing-off are merely convenient labels to attach to delict in particular circumstances. They do not, as they did and to some extent still do in the Anglo-American common law, connote distinct delicts with their own characteristics.

To facilitate this detailed study it is necessary to group and classify the instances and sets of circumstances which give rise to delictual claims.

Possible classifications. Various classifications could be adopted [1] as the framework for discussion of the particular delicts. Thus one could [2] consider together all those delicts involving the mental element of intentional or malicious wrongdoing, and then those involving the mental element of inadvertence or carelessness. Again one could group individual delicts according to the agencies effecting the harm complained of, damage by persons, by animals, by vehicles, by ships, and so on, or the circumstances in which the harms were done, in social life, in business, on the streets, at sea, and so on. Or one could discuss all the delicts which are fundamentally instances and developments of liability under the *lex Aquilia*, such as assault or physical injury, of liability to the *actio injuriarum*, such as seduction and defamation, and of liability under statute or on other grounds.

The Roman law classification [3] into *furtum, rapina, damnum injuria datum* and *injuria* is artificial and quite unsatisfactory for modern use, even with the addition of the praetorian delicts, such as *metus* and *dolus*, and the quasi-delicts,[4] though it was accepted by Pothier [5] in substance.

---

[1] See also Holland, *Jurisprudence* (13th ed.), 33.
[2] As in *Glegg on Reparation*; this seems also the basis of the grouping of cases in the *Scots Digest* and *Faculty Digest* under the heads of Reparation and Negligence.
[3] Inst. IV, 1–4.
[4] Inst. IV, 5.
[5] *Traité des Obligations* (Evans' Trs.), § 116.

Grotius [6] and Van Leeuwen [7] grouped delicts according as they were directed against life, the person, freedom, honour and property, and this comes closer to a useful modern approach, classifying according to the particular interest of the victim which has been infringed.

The usual Anglo-American common law classification [8] is into (i) wrongs of intention: (a) on personality—assault and battery, false imprisonment; (b) on personality and substance—infringement of domestic relations, malicious prosecution, libel and slander; (c) on substance—trespass to land or chattels, conversion, interference with economic relations, deceit; (ii) negligence, and (iii) strict liability for the escape of dangerous agencies. Some authorities [9] take the view that no classification has met with general acceptance because the law of tort is " rather an unco-ordinated collection of remedies for misdoing which have developed haphazardly as they been brought before the court," and the Anglo-American emphasis has always been on tort as the law of wrongs.[10]

According to Stair [11] delicts or delinquences may be classed as (i) injury to the life, members or health of the person; (ii) injury to liberty; (iii) injury to fame, reputation and honour; (iv) injury to an object of affection; and (v) injury to goods and possessions. He further [12] distinguishes the general obligation by delinquence, pursued under the general name of damage and interest, and those of a special name and nature, which are chiefly these, assythment, extortion, circumvention, defraud of creditors, spuilzie, intrusion, ejection, molestation, breach of arrestment, deforcement, contravention and forgery.

Bankton [13] mentions the Roman classification only to reject it, and then [14] says: " Delinquencies, as they are civilly cognoscible with us, have their known names and titles in our law; and these are Assythment, Injury, Damage, Extortion, Circumvention, Spuilzie, Intrusion, Ejection, Molestation, Contravention of Lawborrows, Battery *pendente lite*, Breach of Arrestment, Deforcement, Escape of a Prisoner, Excessive and

---

[6] *Inleiding tot de Hollandsche Rechtsgeleertheyt* (trs. Lee as *Jurisprudence of Holland*), III, 33, 1.

[7] *Het Roomsch Hollandsch Recht* (trs. Kotzé, *Commentaries on the Roman-Dutch Law*), IV, 32, 9; *cf.* Van der Linden, *Rechtsgeleerd Practical en Koopmans Handboek* (trs. Juta, *Institutes of Holland*), I, 16, 1, amalgamates the third and fourth of these groups. See also Dernburg, *Pandekten*, § 129.

[8] See Holland, *Jurisprudence* (13th ed.), 330–335; Terry, *Leading Principles of Anglo-American Law*, § 524–541; Wigmore, " Responsibility for Tortious Acts: Its History " (1893) 7 H.L.R. 315, 383, 441; Wigmore, " The Tripartite Division of Torts " (1894) 8 H.L.R. 200; Wigmore, " A General Analysis of Tort Relations " (1894) 8 H.L.R. 377; Smith, " Tort and Absolute Liability—Suggested Changes in Classification " (1916) 30 H.L.R. 241, 319, 409; Isaacs, " Quasi-delict in Anglo-American Law " (1922) 31 Yale L.J., 571; Seavey, " Principles of Torts " (1942) 56 H.L.R. 72; Prosser, 24; Winfield, 17; Salmond, 30.

[9] Clerk and Lindsell, 11.

[10] *Cf.* Clerk and Lindsell, 23, " The most usual classification of torts is according to the wrong committed."

[11] I, 9, 4. At the fourth heading Stair uses the phrase " the fourth *interest* that may be damnified."

[12] I, 9, 6.

[13] I, 10, 2.

[14] I, 10, 13.

Deceitful Gaming, Forgery of Writings, and Perjuries." These individual wrongs are discussed *seriatim*, but he refers [15] to " The next interest is one's Fame and Reputation . . . " which shows an appreciation that the fundamental matter in delict is the protection of personal interests.

Erskine [16] lays down that " every fraudulent contrivance, or unwarrantable act, by which another suffers damage, or runs the hazard of it, subjects the delinquent to reparation . . . Wrongs may arise, not only from positive acts of trespass or injury, but from blameable omission or neglect of duty . . . no person ought to be subjected to the reparation of damage, who has not by some culpable act or omission been the occasion of it." His brief account seems therefore to distinguish only between deliberate and inadvertent wrongs.

Hume [17] discussed separately obligations *ex delicto* and *quasi ex delicto*. The former were cases of deliberate wrongs, the latter included two different sorts of cases, where a man was " made liable as a quasi-delinquent for the consequences of his own negligence or inadvertency which, where it is prejudicial to others, the law considers as approaching to or savouring of a delinquency," [18] and cases of " deviations, on considerations of expediency chiefly, from that natural rule, observed in our practice, ' *culpa tenet suum auctorem* '—that each man is liable for his own fault, and no one for that of another," cases, in short, of vicarious liability.[19]

Bell [20] distinguishes between delict—an offence committed with an injurious, fraudulent or criminal purpose,[21] and quasi delict—gross negligence or imprudence, though it should bear no such character of fraud, malice or criminal purpose as to subject the person to criminal cognisance, is, as a ground for an action of damages, held as a delict, to the effect of making the person guilty of the imprudence or negligence liable to indemnify the person who suffers by the fault.[22]

More [23] likewise considered obligations arising from delinquency, or from quasi-delinquency, but the specific cases discussed, breach of professional duty, breach of contract, slander and libel, nuisance, personal injury, assault and assythment, invasion of exclusive privileges, spuilzie and illegal use of diligence has begun to approximate to a classification on the basis of the interests infringed.

The classification adopted. Stair's classification with minor modifications is on the whole the most satisfactory and it is proposed hereinafter to treat successively of liability imposed in various circumstances by law, whether for breach of common law duty or of statutory duty, for

[15] I, 10, 21.
[16] III, 1, 13.
[17] *Lectures*, III, 120 and 186.
[18] *Ibid.*, 186.
[19] *Ibid.* 187.
[20] *Prin.*, §§ 543 *et seq.*
[21] § 544.
[22] § 553.
[23] *Lectures*, I, 331.

loss, injury or damage caused to an individual by invasion of his legally recognised interests of personality or of substance. An interest is a demand or desire which human beings either individually or in groups seek to satisfy, of which, therefore, the ordering of human relations in civilised society must take account.[24]

Interests of personality [25] include the interest of the individual (a) in personal physical integrity—the immunity of the body from direct or indirect injuries,[26] the immunity of the body or will from coercion,[27] the immunity of the mind and nervous system from injury,[28] and the immunity of feelings and susceptibilities, such as the desire for privacy [29]; (b) in the familial relationships [30]; (c) in honour and reputation [31]; and (d) in freedom of belief and opinion.[32]

Interests of substance [33] include rights in land [34] and corporeal things,[35] to incorporeal rights,[36] to freedom of industry and contract,[37] and to advantages promised by contract and economically advantageous relations with other individuals.[38]

This approach based on the interest of the victim which has been infringed is consonant with the view already propounded that the law of delict is intended to protect various interests rather than to penalise certain kinds of conduct.[39]

The difficulties of any grouping according to the interest of the pursuer which has been infringed are, first, that several nominate delicts or means of causing harm may all infringe any one interest,[40] secondly, that one actual wrong may infringe more than one interest, as where a person is physically hurt, has a relation killed, and has his vehicle damaged, all in one street accident, and, thirdly, that it is difficult to formulate precisely what legal rights a person enjoys for the protection of particular interests.

[24] Pound, *Introduction to the Philosophy of Law*, 42, 107; *Interpretations of Legal History*, 158.
[25] See further Pound, " Interests of Personality " (1915) 28 H.L.R. 343, 445, and in *Selected Essays*, 87; Pound, " Individual Interests in the Domestic Relations " (1916) 14 Mich. L.R. 177; Pound, *Social Control Through Law*; Stone, *The Province and Function of Law*, Chap. 21; Prosser, 12.
[26] Chaps. 15, 16, 17 and 18.
[27] Chap. 20.
[28] Chap. 19.
[29] Chap. 21.
[30] Chap. 22.
[31] Chaps. 23 and 24.
[32] Chap. 25.
[33] Stone, *op. cit.*, 527.
[34] Chap. 27.
[35] Chap. 28.
[36] Chap. 29.
[37] Chap. 26.
[38] Chap. 26.
[39] Street classifies the interests protected by the English law of tort as (a) personal and proprietary interests; (b) reputation; (c) economic relations; (d) family relations; (e) interference with judicial process; and (f) miscellaneous. But there is an overriding grouping of invasion of interests into intentional invasions, negligent invasions, and invasions of strict liability, all of interests in persons or property, before dealing with the other interests protected.
[40] For this reason the kinds of conduct discussed in Chaps. 15, 16, 17 and 18 may infringe either the interest of the individual in his personal physical integrity, or if he is killed, the interest of certain surviving relatives in unimpaired familial relations with the deceased.

Furthermore it has to be borne in mind that some of the interests in question are in some circumstances secured by other legal means, such as by equitable remedies or criminal procedure. Nevertheless it is thought that a classification on the basis of the interests infringed is on the whole the most satisfactory, and where one delict or one mode of committing that delict is relevant to more than one interest, the main discussion is under the heading of the predominant interest.

Classification by interests infringed also implies that relationships of legal obligation existing by reason of the commission of delict are considered primarily from the standpoint of the pursuer; the treatment, that is, deals primarily with a person's rights of action *ex delicto* for harmful acts or omissions a, b and c, rather than with a person's liability for x, y and z.[41] The emphasis, that is, is on the question, Can a person injured by another's conduct in circumstances a, b or c claim?, rather than on the question, Is a person liable to another for injury caused to that other in circumstances a, b or c?, on the pursuer's right *in personam* rather than on the defender's duty *in rem*.

[41] *Cf.* Clerk and Lindsell, 13 *et seq.*, where torts are classified as breaches of rights (a) of the person, (b) of property, though recognising that some torts may infringe both kinds of rights.

CHAPTER 15

INFRINGEMENTS OF THE INTEREST IN PHYSICAL IMMUNITY FROM WILFUL HARM

1. Assault
2. Rape
3. Intentional Mental Harm
4. Contravention of Lawburrows
5. Deforcement
6. Breach of Arrestment
7. Battery *pendente lite*

A PERSON has a legally protected interest in the immunity of his person both from wilful insult or affront, and from actual wilful harm or injury. " Everyone who lives under the protection of the law has an absolute right to the safety of his person; and wherever this right is invaded, there is in civil law a provision for redress of the injury, as well as in penal law a punishment for the crime." [1]

The claim for reparation for the infringement of the legally protected interest in immunity from wilful affront is of the nature of an *actio injuriarum*. The requisite *animus injuriandi* is presumed if the circumstances fall within the category of what the law recognises as an intentional injury, and no further proof of malicious intention is necessary.[2] The essence of the wrong is *injuria*, affront or insult (*contumelia*), and no actual harm need be proved to justify an award of solatium, though if actual injury or patrimonial loss is sustained, it justifies greater compensation under the principle of the *actio legis Aquiliae*.[3]

The principal specific wrongs which fall under this head are assault, rape, and intentional mental harm. Assault is classified by Bankton [4] as injury by facts, " as beating, or other atrocious usage of one's person," as distinct from injury by words or writing, or verbal injuries, though both groups of injury equally hurt a person's interest in his fame and reputation.[5]

1. ASSAULT

Assault [6] is an overt physical act intended to insult or affront or harm another, done without lawful justification or excuse.[7] Assault is a real

[1] Bell, *Prin.*, § 2028; *cf.* § 543; Stair, I, 9, 4; I, 10, 22.
[2] Bell, *Prin.*, § 2032.
[3] *Macnaughton* v. *Robertson*, Feb. 17, 1809, F.C.
[4] I, 10, 22.
[5] On the distinction based on Roman law, between real and verbal injuries, see further Chap. 23.
[6] Generally Bankton, I, 10, 22; Bell, *Prin.*, § 2032; Hume, *Lect.*, III, 120; More, *Lect.*, I, 347.
[7] Bell, *Prin.*, § 2032. It is unnecessary to aver that an assault was " wrongful," that being inherent in the notion: *Wilson* v. *Bennett* (1904) 6 F. 269.

injury, tending to the disgrace of the person assaulted, and the worst kind of *injuria*, closely akin to defamation.[8] Originally the remedy was by an action for assythment.[9] The claim for damages is not merely for damage sustained, but *in solatium* for affront and insult,[10] and it is not discharged by the application of criminal sanctions.[11] Hence solatium can be claimed even where no actual injury is or can be proved.[12]

Bankton distinguished between an assault, as by holding up the fist, or any weapon, against one in a threatening manner, which is a real injury because it tends much to the person's disgrace who is so used, and battery, by striking one, which is a high injury to his person, and more or less atrocious, according to the circumstances of the case.[13] This useful distinction, though accepted in English law, has subsequently usually [14] been ignored in Scotland and the term assault applied to cases of actual physical harm as well as to cases of affront or threat.

Intention. The requisite *animus injuriandi* is inferred from proof of the deliberate doing of the acts. Other or further proof of malice is unnecessary.[15] In some older cases evidence has been admitted of conduct showing malice, such as previous assaults,[16] but it is incompetent to prove that the defender was notoriously quarrelsome.[17] If, however, the defender's conduct were involuntary or uncontrolled it could not be said to be deliberate, or done *animo injuriandi*.[18] Reckless but unintentional conduct causing harm, such as the discharge of firearms at poachers, does not amount to assault for criminal purposes,[19] but may do so for civil purposes; in *MacDonald* v. *Robertson* [20] it was held that wilfully to discharge a loaded gun, without lawful excuse, such as self-defence, at or in the direction of another person, who is or may very well be within range of the gun, whether he be a poacher or not, is wrongful if injury be caused thereby.

8 Bankton, I, 10, 22; *cf.* Mackenzie, *Crim.L.*, I, 30, 1, 3.

9 Bankton, I, 10, 35.

10 Bell, *Prin.*, § 2032; *Cruickshank* v. *Forsyth* (1747) Mor. 4034; *Anderson* v. *Marshall* (1835) 13 S. 1130.

11 Bell, *supra*; the award of damages is compensation not punishment: *Hyslop* v. *Miller* (1816) 1 Mur. 43, 54; *Lang* v. *Lillie* (1826) 4 Mur. 82, 86; *Muckarsie* v. *Dixon* (1848) 11 D. 4, 5.

12 *Beatson* v. *Drysdale* (1819) 2 Mur. 151, 153.

13 I, 10, 22.

14 The phrase " assault and battery " is found in *Kerr & Shaw* v. *Hay* (1774) Mor. 7420; *Mair* v. *Shand* (1778) Mor. 7421, and in Jury Court cases, *e.g.*, *Lang* v. *Lillie* (1826) 4 Mur. 82. There was also formerly the crime of battery *pendente lite*; see Ersk. IV, 4, 37, and s. 7, *infra*.

15 *Cf.* the case of defamation, where similarly the requisite *animus injuriandi* is presumed from deliberate conduct,

16 *Macdonnell* v. *Macdonald* (1813) 2 Dow 66.

17 *Haddaway* v. *Goddard* (1816) 1 Mur. 151; *Bannerman* v. *Fenwicks* (1817) 1 Mur. 252; *Hall* v. *Otto* (1818) 1 Mur. 444; *Lang* v. *Lillie* (1826) 4 Mur. 86; *McFarlane* v. *Young* (1824) 3 Mur. 412.

18 *Cf. Morriss* v. *Marsden* [1952] 1 All E.R. 925.

19 *H.M.A.* v. *Phipps* (1905) 4 Adam 616.

20 (1910) 27 Sh.Ct.Rep. 103; contrast negligent shooting case of *Stephen* v. *Buchan* (1906) 23 Sh.Ct.Rep. 165.

Transferred intention. If a defender intends to assault one person and accidentally harms another, the other may probably sue for assault as if the assault had been intended for him, the defender's wrongful intention against the second person being deemed transferred against the person actually injured. Thus if A throws a bottle at B and hits C, C can sue.[21]

Aggravation of assault. An assault may be aggravated by the gravity of the injuries inflicted,[22] the enormity of the insult or affront,[23] the fact that it was committed in a public place *coram populo*,[24] or accompanied with abuse.[24]

Affronts, i.e., notional assaults. Assault covers primarily conduct affronting the pursuer, as by spitting at him,[25] or in his face,[26] or riding a horse at a pedestrian so as to put him in danger and reasonable alarm, even without touching him,[27] or discharging a gun at a person [28] or using abusive language and threatening behaviour and thereby inducing fright and ill-health.[29] It is not necessary that the pursuer be struck or caused any physical harm, if he be put in dread or apparent danger of bodily harm,[30] but words, or coming forward, or furious looks have been stated not to be an assault.[31] To snatch papers from a person may be an assault.[32] To kiss a woman against her will, or make any sign or gesture of an immodest nature which affronts her is likewise an assault: so, *a fortiori*, is any attempted or actual fondling or handling of a woman.[33]

It is an assault to hold up the fist, or any weapon, against one in a threatening manner.[34] Similarly it would be an assault to present a fire-arm at a person within range in a manner causing apprehension,[35] though he should not be wounded, even if it be unloaded or not cocked,[36] unless the person threatened actually knows that the weapon is not loaded,[37] or that it is a dummy or otherwise incapable of being fired,[38] or to pursue him with an uplifted whip,[39] or otherwise to threaten harm.

It would not be an assault to shake a fist or lift a knife or other weapon if the complainer were out of range or so protected, *e.g.*, on the other

[21] *Cf.* Prosser, 33.
[22] *Cf. Kerr* v. *Anderson* (1837) 15 S. 928.
[23] *Gordon* v. *Stewart* (1842) 5 D. 8.
[24] *Thom* v. *Graham* (1835) 13 S. 1129.
[25] *Ewing* v. *Earl of Mar* (1851) 14 D. 314 (and sequel, 330).
[26] *Tullis* v. *Glenday* (1834) 13 S. 698.
[27] *Ewing, supra*, 315; *cf. Cook* v. *Neville* (1797) Hume, 602.
[28] *Macnaughton* v. *Robertson*, Feb. 17, 1809, F.C.; *MacDonald* v. *Robertson* (1910) 27 Sh.Ct.Rep. 103.
[29] *Stedman* v. *Henderson* (1923) 40 Sh.Ct.Rep. 8.
[30] *Hyslop* v. *Staig* (1816) 1 Mur. 22. *Cf. Lurie* v. *N.B.Ry.*, 1917, 2 S.L.T. 59.
[31] *Lang* v. *Lillie* (1826) 4 Mur. 82, 86; *cf. Read* v. *Coker* (1853) 13 C.B. 850.
[32] *Robson* v. *Hawick School Board* (1900) 2 F. 4, 11.
[33] *Hill* v. *Fletcher* (1847) 10 D. 7; *cf. Moorov* v. *H.M.A.*, 1930 J.C. 68. See also *Nash* v. *Sheen* [1953] C.L.Y. 3726 (application to hair of " tone-rinse " without consent) and *R.* v. *Kobi*, 1912 T.P.D. 1106 (indecent exposure an assault).
[34] Bankt., I, 10, 22.
[35] *Ewing* v. *Mar* (1851) 13 D. 314, 315.
[36] *Osborn* v. *Veitch* (1858) 1 F. & F. 317.
[37] *H.M.A.* v. *Morison* (1842) 1 Broun 394.
[38] *R.* v. *St. George* (1840) 9 C. & P. 483; *secus, Blake* v. *Barnard* (1840) 9 C. & P. 626.
[39] *Martin* v. *Shoppee* (1828) 3 C. & P. 373.

side of railings, as to have no reasonable ground for apprehension of harm, but it would if the assailant were advancing and would have reached the complainer if not stopped.[40] Nor do violent gestures and opprobrious words spoken *in rixa* amount to assault or defamation.[41] It has been doubted whether sending a challenge to fight is relevant to infer damages.[42]

It is probably not essential that the pursuer knew of the affront at the time it was committed. A person asleep or under an anaesthetic may be affronted or assaulted, even though the wrong be not appreciated till afterwards.[43]

Actual assaults (batteries). " Battery, by striking one, is a high injury to his person, and is more or less atrocious, according to the circumstances of the case." [44] It is clearly an assault where the complainer is actually struck and any form of physical harm, pain or injury caused, however slight or transient, as where his hat was knocked off,[45] or his nose pulled,[46] or a kick caused a broken leg,[47] or one hit another with a milk can,[48] or a baton,[49] or a blow caused a fractured jaw with much pain and inconvenience,[50] or caused the effusion of blood,[51] or a broken nose,[52] or a broken bone,[53] or the complainer was thrown into the harbour,[54] or knocked down by persons riding furiously,[55] or pushed off a moving vehicle,[56] ejected from premises,[57] or shot by an irate farmer,[58] or injured by a stone thrown.[59] In such cases damages may include elements not

[40] *Stephens* v. *Myers* (1830) 4 C. & P. 349.
[41] *Mackintosh* v. *Squair* (1868) 40 S.Jur. 561.
[42] *Hyslop* v. *Staig* (1816) 1 Mur. 22; *Hyslop* v. *Miller* (1816) 1 Mur. 54; *Armstrong* v. *Vair* (1823) 3 Mur. 315.
[43] *Cf. Restatement*, § 18. *Cf.* also the crime of clandestine injury to women, of having connection with a woman while she was asleep: *H.M.A.* v. *Sweenie* (1858) 3 Irv. 109.
[44] Bankt., I, 10, 22.
[45] *Jamieson* v. *Corrie* (1833) 11 S. 1027.
[46] *Gordon* v. *Stewart* (1842) 5 D. 8.
[47] *MacGregor* v. *Murphy* (1895) 11 Sh.Ct.Rep. 85.
[48] *Houston* v. *McIndoe*, 1934 S.C. 362.
[49] *Wilson* v. *Bennett* (1904) 6 F. 269; *cf. Jardine* v. *Lang*, 1911, 2 S.L.T. 494.
[50] *McGregor* v. *Shepherd* (1946) 62 Sh.Ct.Rep. 139.
[51] *Falconer* v. *Cochran* (1837) 15 S. 891; *Reekie* v. *Norrie* (1842) 5 D. 368; *McGeever* v. *McFarlane* (1951) 67 Sh.Ct.Rep. 48.
[52] *Forgie* v. *Henderson* (1818) 1 Mur. 410.
[53] *Gordon* v. *O'Hara*, 1931 S.C. 172.
[54] *Beaton* v. *Drysdale* (1819) 2 Mur. 151.
[55] *McLachlan* v. *Monach* (1823) 2 S. 590. For further examples see *Wighton* v. *Bisset* (1799) Hume, *Lect.*, III, 122; *Jaffery* v. *Stedman* (1800), *ibid.*; *Hyslop* v. *Miller* (1815) 1 Mur. 43; *Haddaway* v. *Goddard* (1816) 1 Mur. 148; *Bannerman* v. *Fenwicks* (1817) 1 Mur. 249; *Forgie* v. *Henderson* (1818) 1 Mur. 410; *Hall* v. *Otto* (1818) 1 Mur. 442; *Henry* v. *Evans* (1820) 2 Mur. 329; *Scott* v. *Scougall* (1821) 4 Mur. 42; *Mackie* v. *Wight* (1822) 3 Mur. 23; *Lang* v. *Lillie* (1826) 4 Mur. 82; *Miles* v. *Finlayson* (1829) 5 Mur. 84; *Jamieson* v. *Corrie* (1833) 11 S. 1027; *Ball* v. *Longlands* (1834) 12 S. 934; *Anderson* v. *Broom* (1834) 14 S. 1131; *Hynds* v. *Singer Sewing Machine Co.*, 1909, 2 S.L.T. 127; *Gordon* v. *O'Hara*, 1931 S.C. 172; *Marco* v. *Merrens*, 1964 S.L.T. (Sh.Ct.) 74.
[56] *Bryce* v. *Glasgow Tramways Co.* (1898) 6 S.L.T. 49; *Stevenson* v. *Glasgow Corpn.*, 1922 S.L.T. 185. *Cf. McGraw* v. *Edinburgh Tramways* (1891) 28 S.L.R. 256; *Hanlon* v. *G.S.W. Ry.* (1899) 1 F. 559; *Docherty* v. *Glasgow Tramways* (1894) 2 S.L.T. 406; *Peebles* v. *Cowan* 1915, 1 S.L.T. 363.
[57] *Gillespie* v. *Hunter* (1898) 25 R. 916.
[58] *MacDonald* v. *Robertson* (1910) 27 Sh.Ct.Rep. 103.
[59] *Russell* v. *Kerr* (1888) 4 Sh.Ct.Rep. 312.

only for *solatium*, but for consequential absence from work, loss of earnings, and medical expenses.[60]

The assault need not have been conduct intended to cause harm; thus it has been held an assault forcibly to remove a passenger from a train,[61] and it would be if one engaged in a frolic touches or pushes another to his injury.[62] Even though one assailant be averred to have taken a more prominent part in the assault than the other the trials should not be separated,[63] and they should indeed be sued jointly and severally.[64]

Physical contact is not necessary; thus it would be assault to throw pepper in another's face, as much as to hit with a stick, or to injure by shooting,[65] or to throw a stone which hits another.[66]

But mere obstruction, if lawful, as by standing in a place so that the complainer cannot enter, is not an assault.[67] Nor is it an assault to turn a person out of a room without violence.[68]

An assault by deliberately driving a vehicle against a person, or deliberately driving off dragging a person who had tried to stop the vehicle, is an assault and a " liability which is required to be covered by a policy of insurance " under the Road Traffic Act, 1960, ss. 203 and 207, and the Motor Insurers' Bureau is liable to satisfy an unsatisfied decree obtained against the driver.[69]

Characters of parties. In many cases evidence has been tendered that one or other of the parties was violent or quarrelsome. Evidence as to the defender has been held incompetent [70] and competent.[71] Evidence as to the pursuer's own character has frequently been admitted,[72] particularly where specific incidents are pleaded on record,[73] but sometimes rejected.[74]

Indirect assault. It is doubtless equally an assault deliberately to do any act such as to take away a person's clothes, which results in the person's being affronted, or put in a state of alarm, or physically hurt,

---

[60] Hume, *Lect.*, III, 120, 121; *McNaughton* v. *Robertson*, Feb. 17, 1809, F.C.; *Houston* v. *McIndoe*, 1934 S.C. 362; *cf. McGregor* v. *Shepherd* (1946) 62 Sh.Ct.Rep. 139.
[61] *Harris* v. *N.B.Ry.* (1891) 18 R. 1009 (£25 damages for " indignity and detention "); *cf. Glover* v. *L.S.W.Ry.* (1867) L.R. 3 Q.B. 25; *Seymour* v. *McLaren* (1828) 6 S. 969 (ejection from theatre); *McDiarmid* v. *Barrie* (1902) 18 Sh.Ct.Rep. 47 (assault on trespasser).
[62] *Reid* v. *Mitchell* (1885) 12 R. 1129.
[63] *Anderson* v. *Barr and Cavens* (1847) 9 D. 929.
[64] *Bannerman* v. *Fenwicks* (1817) 1 Mur. 253; *cf. McLachlan* v. *Monach* (1823) 2 S. 506.
[65] *Macnaughton* v. *Robertson*, Feb. 17, 1809, F.C.
[66] *Russell* v. *Kerr* (1888) 4 Sh.Ct.Rep. 312.
[67] *Innes* v. *Wylie* (1844) 1 C. & K. 257.
[68] *Brown* v. *Gibson-Craig* (1834) 13 S. 697.
[69] *Hardy* v. *Motor Insurers' Bureau* [1964] 2 All E.R. 742; *cf. D.P.P.* v. *Smith* [1961] A.C. 290.
[70] *Haddaway* v. *Goddard* (1816) 1 Mur. 151.
[71] *Macdonnell* v. *Macdonald* (1813) 2 Dow. 66; *Jamieson* v. *Main* (1830) 5 Mur. 120.
[72] *Jamieson, supra.*
[73] *Bannerman* v. *Fenwicks* (1817) 1 Mur. 249; *McFarlane* v. *Young* (1824) 3 Mur. 412; *Walker* v. *Ritchie* (1836) 14 S. 1128.
[74] *Hall* v. *Otto* (1818) 1 Mur. 444; *Lang* v. *Lillie* (1826) 4 Mur. 85

as by pulling away his chair,[75] or the ladder on which he is standing,[76] or striking his horse whereby it throws him,[77] or throwing an object at or near him, even without striking him, or violently stopping the horse he is riding,[78] or daubing with filth a towel a person is expected to use.[79]

Medical examination and treatment. It is an assault for a medical practitioner to examine or treat a person unless that person, or the person's parent or guardian, has freely consented, expressly or by conduct, to the examination or treatment in question.[80] It is sufficient consent if the complainer's conduct was such as to give rise to a reasonable belief that he consented.[81] In case of serious emergency consent may probably be dispensed with.[80] Consent extorted by violence, fear or fraud is no consent, but consent unwillingly given, or under an erroneous notion of law, is valid consent.[82] An unauthorised operation is subject to the same principles.

Freedom from torture, search, etc. It seems certain, though not vouched by any modern authority, that the police may not apply any kind of torture or physical pressure to obtain information from a suspect, or to extract a confession. Such would be an assault. Heavy damages would be recoverable if such conduct were proved.[83] An action of damages for assault and maltreatment has been sustained at the instance of a prisoner against the governor and turnkeys of a jail.[84]

The police have no right to infringe the persons of suspects by searching their persons unless they consent or unless they have been apprehended; only thereafter may it be done.[85] The same is the rule in respect of taking fingerprints [86]; after apprehension but before committal to prison the police may at common law take fingerprints without any warrant,[87] and after committal to prison there is statutory warrant for taking fingerprints.[88]

Physical tests. The application of any kind of physical test to the person, or the taking of anything from the individual's person, with a

[75] *Hopper* v. *Reeve* (1817) 7 Taunt. 698.
[76] *Collins* v. *Renison* (1754) Sayer 138.
[77] *Dodwell* v. *Burford* (1670) 1 Mod. 24; *cf. H.M.A.* v. *Keay* (1837) 1 Swin. 543.
[78] *H.M.A.* v. *Kennedy* (1854) 1 Irv. 533.
[79] *Restatement,* § 18.
[80] *Thomson* v. *Devon* (1899) 15 Sh.Ct.Rep. 209; *Marshall* v. *Curry* [1933] 3 D.L.R. 260 (Wright, *Cases,* 101).
[81] *R.* v. *Flattery* (1877) 2 Q.B.D. 410; *R.* v. *Donovan* [1934] 2 K.B. 498; *O'Brien* v. *Cunard S.C. Co.* (1891) 154 Mass. 272 (Wright, *Cases,* 93). *Cf. Thomson* v. *Devon* (1899) 15 Sh.Ct.Rep. 209.
[82] *Latter* v. *Bradell* (1881) 50 L.J.Q.B. 448.
[83] *Cf.* the High Court's reluctance to admit evidence of " confessions " obtained by moral pressure or influence: *H.M.A.* v. *Aitken,* 1926 J.C. 83; *H.M.A.* v. *Rigg,* 1946 J.C. 1. *Chalmers* v. *H.M.A.,* 1954 J.C. 66; contrast *Manuel* v. *H.M.A.,* 1958 J.C. 41.
[84] *McFarlane* v. *Young* (1824) 3 Mur. 408, 415.
[85] *Jackson* v. *Stevenson* (1897) 24 R.(J.) 38; *Adair* v. *McGarry,* 1933 J.C. 72, 78, 89; *McGovern* v. *H.M.A.,* 1950 J.C. 33, 36.
[86] *Adamson* v. *Martin,* 1916 S.C. 319, 326; *Adair* v. *McGarry, supra; cf. McGovern* v. *H.M.A., supra.*
[87] *Adair* v. *McGarry, supra.*
[88] Renton and Brown, 33.

view to obtaining evidence for use in a criminal case against that person, may be an actionable wrong unless the individual is cautioned and charged and his consent properly obtained. In *Reid* v. *Nixon*; *Dumigan* v. *Brown*,[89] evidence obtained by a police doctor from a motorist who had neither been cautioned nor charged, nor had he given his consent, was held incompetent. The High Court of Justiciary laid down certain principles [90]: the suspect should be charged, cautioned, and his consent specifically obtained, and he should be warned that the results of the tests may be given in evidence, that he need not submit, and may summon a doctor of his own choice to make independent tests. If consent is refused, no examination or test may be made, but the doctor may observe. Observation is not an infringement of physical integrity. These principles have been held to apply only to the offence of driving a vehicle while under the influence of drink. In *Forrester* v. *H.M. Advocate*,[91] it was held that in the case of an ordinary common law crime an examination, in the presence of the police, by a doctor of a person who had been arrested, charged and cautioned, was competent and evidence thereof admissible, though he did not consent. In the same way the court has refused to ordain a defender to submit to a blood test with a view to determining paternity of a child.[92]

Assault combined with other wrong. Assault is frequently in fact combined with defamation,[93] as where one man, under provocation, violently assaulted another and called him the greatest blackguard in the country,[94] or where one called another a damned, low, mean puppy and a blackguard, and struck him.[95] Similarly, assault has been combined as a ground of action with wrongful apprehension, imprisonment and detention.[96]

Vicarious liability for assault. An assault committed by an employed person, if at the time acting in the course of his employment, infers liability of his employer in the usual way [97]; the employer is not liable for an assault resulting from a private quarrel.[98]

---

[89] 1948 J.C. 69; see also *Farrell* v. *Concannon*, 1957 J.C. 12; *McKie* v. *H.M.A.*, 1958 J.C. 24.

[90] While laid down primarily as a guide to the admissibility of evidence in such cases, the principles seem relevant also to the question of a claim for infringement of personal integrity.

[91] 1952 J.C. 28, following *Adair* v. *McGarry*, 1933 J.C. 72.

[92] *Whitehall* v. *Whitehall*, 1958 S.C. 252; *cf. Imre* v. *Mitchell*, 1958 S.C. 439.

[93] Hume, *Lect.*, III, 163.

[94] *Thom* v. *Graham* (1835) 13 S. 1129.

[95] *Anderson* v. *Marshall* (1835) 13 S. 1130; see also *Porter* v. *Smith* (1788) Hume 591; *Tullis* v. *Crichton* (1850) 12 D. 867; *Short* v. *Haggart* (1904) 20 Sh.Ct.Rep. 44.

[96] *e.g., Hyslop* v. *Staig* (1816) 1 Mur. 15.

[97] *Bryce* v. *Glasgow Tramways* (1898) 6 S.L.T. 49; *Hynds* v. *Singer Sewing Machine Co.*, 1909, 2 S.L.T. 127; *Downie* v. *Connell Bros.*, 1910 S.C. 781; *Jardine* v. *Lang*, 1911, 2 S.L.T. 494; *Wood* v. *N.B.Ry.* (1899) 1 F. 562; *Lurie* v. *N.B. Ry.*, 1917, 2 S.L.T. 59; *Stevenson* v. *Glasgow Corpn.*, 1922 S.L.T. 185. *Cf. Warren* v. *Henlys* [1948] 2 All E.R. 935.

[98] *Gillespie* v. *Hunter* (1898) 25 R. 916; *cf. Power* v. *Central S.M.T. Co.*, 1949 S.C. 376.

Death resulting from assault. If death results from an assault a claim lies at the instance of the deceased's surviving relatives for assythment.[99]

Defences: Justifications. It has been stated [1] that where an assault is proved, the only defence is a justification, the onus of proving which lies on the defender, but this does not settle what may be justifications.

Conduct which would otherwise be an assault is excusable and not actionable if there is justification by official duty, or absolute necessity, or self-defence,. or the defence of one's wife, or child, or property, or excuse by unavoidable accident.[2] It is no justification that the conduct was intended as a joke, or was not intended to cause harm,[3] or affected the pursuer only by mischance, or was an incorrect mode of doing something proper.[4] To explain the origin of what happened is not to justify it.[5]

Unavoidable accident. A merely accidental application of force to another, as by bumping into him in the street, is clearly not an assault [6] (though it might in some circumstances amount to negligent physical injury), nor is force which is inevitable in the circumstances, as where policemen hold back a crowd, or people jostle one another when entering or leaving a place of entertainment, even though some actual physical hurt be sustained. A woman who interfered with a constable who was handling a refractory prisoner and got pushed aside and injured was held to have no claim.[7]

Provocation. A person is not entitled to complain of assault if he provoked it, as by holding up his fist in a threatening manner, or touching the other's body in a particular way, or twisting the neck-cloth of the other, even though the provocation was greatly less than the assault committed.[8] But no merely verbal provocation whatever will justify a blow.[9] Verbal injury is no justification, but will mitigate the damages.[10] A defence on the ground of provocation must be based on proof of specific acts, not merely an averment that the pursuer is of a quarrelsome disposition.[11]

Conduct in retaliation for an assault may itself be actionable if it goes beyond self-defence,[12] and a person who renews an affray after it

---

[99] *Milne* v. *Thomson* (1841) 3 D. 1163; and see Chap. 22, *infra.*
[1] *Beaton* v. *Drysdale* (1819) 2 Mur. 151, 153; *cf. Reekie* v. *Norrie* (1842) 15 S.Jur. 151.
[2] Bell, *Prin.,* § 2032.
[3] *Cf. Reid* v. *Mitchell* (1885) 12 R. 1129.
[4] *Miles* v. *Finlayson* (1829) 5 Mur. 84.
[5] *Gordon* v. *Stewart* (1842) 5 D. 8.
[6] Bell, *Prin.,* § 2032. *Cf. Bourhill* v. *Young,* 1942 S.C.(H.L.) 78, 92, *per* Lord Wright.
[7] *Hall* v. *Watson* (1896) 12 Sh.Ct.Rep. 117.
[8] *Young* v. *Allison* (1820) 2 Mur. 231; see also *Robertson* v. *Hill* (1824) 3 S. 383; *Seymour* v. *McLaren* (1828) 6 S. 969. *Cf. Hallowell* v. *Niven* (1843) 5 D. 759.
[9] *Anderson* v. *Marshall* (1835) 13 S. 1130; *cf. Seymour* v. *McLaren* (1828) 6 S. 969; *Brown* v. *Gibson-Craig* (1834) 13 S. 697; *Falconer* v. *Cochran* (1837) 15 S. 891.
[10] Bell, *Prin.,* § 2032; *Thom* v. *Graham* (1835) 13 S. 1129; *Anderson, supra; Falconer, supra; Gordon* v. *Stewart* (1843) 5 D. 8.
[11] *Macfarlane* v. *Young* (1824) 3 Mur. 412.
[12] *Dowie* v. *Douglas* (1822) 1 Sh.App. 125; *cf. Hyslop* v. *Miller* (1816) 1 Mur. 53.

has terminated is liable in damages.[13] Cross-actions may be brought arising out of the one incident.[14]

Self-defence. A person may legitimately use force in defence of his person, or that of his wife or child,[15] or probably of any other equally close relative or even of any stranger in danger, but greater latitude is permissible in defence of self, wife or child than in defence of a stranger.[16] The force or measures used in defence must not be disproportionate to the assault threatened or made, nor more than necessary for self-protection,[17] and weapons are not justifiable in parrying an assault with fists. But the court will not examine too critically the reaction of a person assaulted.[18] If the circumstances do not justify reasonable apprehension of danger to life or limb, the use of force is not defence but an assault.[19]

Protection of property. In the same way the ejection of a trespasser, believed to be poaching, is not an assault unless unnecessary violence has been employed.[20]

Making lawful arrest or preventing crime. A person may legitimately use physical force to effect arrest if in the circumstances arrest was lawful,[21] or to prevent the completion of a crime in course of commission. Excessive use of force is unjustifiable and an assault.[22]

Necessity. The use of physical force may be necessary to restrain a person from doing harm to himself or third parties,[23] or doing malicious damage to property, or to save him from some danger. A trespasser who declines to remove himself on being asked to do so, may be removed by force, so long as that used is not disproportionate to the resistance offered. But excessive force is an assault.[24] Violence used by an hotel-keeper or his servants in removing an objectionable person from the premises is not an assault unless used in a degree that is excessive or unnecessary.[25]

Consent. Consent, or *volenti non fit injuria*, negatives any claim for assault, so long as the consent has been freely and voluntarily given. In the case of taking fingerprints it has been pointed out that if the person is young, and untrue representations are made to him by those in authority as to their legal rights, the court will be slow to draw the inference of

---

[13] *Robertson* v. *Hill* (1824) 3 S. 383.
[14] *Pirie* v. *Meikle* (1874) 2 R. 40.
[15] Bankton, I, 10, 23; Bell, *Prin.*, § 2032.
[16] *Blades* v. *Higgs* (1861) 10 C.B.(N.S.) 713.
[17] *Hallowell* v. *Niven* (1843) 5 D. 759.
[18] *Cf. Owens* v. *H.M.A.*, 1946 J.C. 119; *Crawford* v. *H.M.A.*, 1950 J.C. 67.
[19] *McDiarmid* v. *Barrie* (1901) 18 Sh.Ct.Rep. 47.
[20] *Bell* v. *Shand* (1870) 7 S.L.R. 267.
[21] As to the legality or illegality of arrests in various circumstances, see Chap. 20, *infra.*
[22] *Cf. Woods* v. *Cooper* (1928) 44 Sh.Ct.Rep. 294.
[23] *Cf. Knight* v. *Inverness District Board of Control*, 1920, 2 S.L.T. 157.
[24] *Anderson* v. *Barr and Cavens* (1847) 9 D. 929.
[25] *Cook* v. *Paxton* (1910) 48 S.L.R. 7. *Cf. Wallace* v. *Mooney* (1885) 12 R. 710.

consent.[26]   Consent covers cases of medical or surgical treatment, and the examination of suspected criminals.[27]   Consent is implied where a person allows himself to be treated without objection taken at the time, so long as this absence of objection is not induced by any misrepresentation.[28]   It is also implied where a person takes part in a lawful sport or game in which trivial injury is reasonably incidental and unavoidable,[29] so long as his participation is voluntary,[30] but this does not extend to injuries which result from conduct going beyond the fair playing of the game.   Hence deliberate fouling is an assault.[31]   Injuries caused in an illegal sport such as prize-fighting would not give rise to any claim for assault.[32]

Consent is presumed to those ordinary contacts which are inevitable in life in crowded communities, or not normally objected to, such as tapping on the shoulder to attract attention.[33]

Persons in official positions.   Persons, such as police, ticket collectors, stewards at meetings, and others holding some official positions have no privilege to commit what would otherwise be an assault,[34] but to make a relevant case of assault against a police officer on duty, it is necessary to aver either that the order which he was seeking to enforce was outwith the scope of his duty,[35] or that force was unnecessary, in that the pursuer was willing to comply with the order, or that the force used was manifestly in excess of the requirements of the case.[36]   The matter of excessive or unnecessary force has similarly been held to be the criterion in such cases as restraining a patient in a mental hospital,[37] removing an objectionable person from hotel premises,[38] and removing from a train a passenger who had no ticket.[39]   Similarly the captain of a ship has authority over the crew and passengers and is not liable for the forcible arrest of a passenger unless malice and lack of probable cause be proved.[40]

[26] *Adamson* v. *Martin*, 1916 S.C. 319, 329, *per* Lord Salvesen.
[27] *Cf. Reid* v. *Nixon*, 1948 J.C. 68.
[28] *Thomson* v. *Devon* (1899) 15 Sh.Ct.Rep. 209.
[29] *Christopherson* v. *Bare* (1848) 11 Q.B. 473.
[30] *Reid* v. *Mitchell* (1885) 12 R. 1129, 1132.
[31] *Leslie* v. *Harvie* (1627) Pitmedden on *Mutilation*, s. 10; *Crawford* v. *Scot* (1631) Pitmedden, s. 192 (both cases of assythment for injuries in wrestling matches).
[32] *Cf. R.* v. *Coney* (1882) 8 Q.B.D. 534.
[33] *Coward* v. *Baddeley* (1859) 4 H. & N. 478.
[34] *Wilson* v. *Bennett* (1904) 6 F. 269; *cf. McFarlane* v. *Young* (1824) 3 Mur. 412 (prison officer); *Baillie* v. *Edinburgh Corpn.* (1906) 14 S.L.T. 344; *Wood* v. *N.B.Ry.* (1899) 1 F. 562; *Woods* v. *Cooper* (1927) 44 Sh.Ct.Rep. 294; *Daniels* v. *Whetstone Entertainments* [1962] C.L.Y. 1140. See also *Hynds* v. *Singer Sewing Machine Co.*, 1909, 2 S.L.T. 127.
[35] *Cf. Lennox* v. *Rose* (1824) 2 S. 650; *Wallace* v. *Mooney* (1885) 12 R. 710. See also *Grant* v. *Harper*, Feb. 6, 1810, F.C.
[36] *Mason* v. *Orr* (1901) 4 F. 220; see also *Baillie* v. *Edinburgh Mags.* (1906) 14 S.L.T. 344.
[37] *Knight* v. *Inverness District Board of Control*, 1920, 2 S.L.T. 157.
[38] *Cook* v. *Paxton* (1910) 48 S.L.R. 7.
[39] *Highland Ry.* v. *Menzies* (1878) 5 R. 887; *MacRaild* v. *N.B.Ry.* (1902) 10 S.L.T. 348; *cf. Harris* v. *N.B.Ry.* (1891) 18 R. 1009; *Gillespie* v. *Hunter* (1898) 25 R. 916; *Maxwell* v. *Caledonian Ry.* (1898) 25 R. 550; *Hanlon* v. *G.S.W.Ry.* (1899) 1 F. 559; *Wood* v. *N.B. Ry.* (1899) 2 F. 1.
[40] *Coutts and Park* v. *MacBrayne*, 1910 S.C. 386.

Corporal punishment. Reasonable chastisement of a child by his parent, or other person *in loco parentis*,[41] or a schoolteacher,[42] is not an actionable assault, but if the punishment is excessive in extent,[43] or an improper instrument is used, or a sensitive part of the body touched,[44] the conduct may be held an assault. Similarly the interests of discipline on board ship may justify a blow,[45] as will authorised corporal punishment in prison.

Compensatio injuriarum. A plea of *compensatio injuriarum*, namely, that the pursuer was himself guilty of a similar assault to that of which he complains, can only be given effect to in a counterclaim, and not by a plea in defence.[46] Subject to that, it is competent for each party to sue the other, and for compensation to operate once the damages have been quantified.[47] Thus a claim for assault has been met by a counterclaim for enticement,[48] and a claim for slander met by a counterclaim for assault.[49]

2. RAPE

As a head of reparation rape is an aggravated assault, which is actionable by the woman on her own behalf [50] and, if she has a husband, also by him as being an interference with his domestic relations.[51] The claim is a pure *actio injuriarum*, the conduct being a gross affront to the pursuer. The elements of the delict are thought to be the same as those of the crime of rape, namely, some degree of penetration of the female body by the male organ, but not necessarily full penetration nor rupture of the hymen, still less emission of semen, and also that the connection was obtained by force, in the total absence of consent on the part of the woman [52] with resistance maintained till she was exhausted or overcome.[53] The gravity

---

[41] *Wight* v. *Burns* (1883) 11 R. 217.

[42] *Ewart, infra*; *Scorgie, infra*; *Skewis* v. *Adams* (1914) 30 Sh.Ct.Rep. 217.

[43] *Muckarsie* v. *Dickson* (1848) 11 D. 4; *Ryan* v. *Fildes* [1938] 3 All E.R. 517; *cf. Stevenson* v. *Borthwick* (1895) 15 Sh.Ct.Rep. 200.

[44] *Ewart* v. *Brown* (1882) 10 R. 163 (boy struck on head with pointer); *Scorgie* v. *Lawrie* (1883) 10 R. 610 (girl struck on hand with cane); *Ryan* v. *Fildes* [1938] 3 All E.R. 517 (boy struck on ear and made deaf). See also *Stevenson* v. *Borthwick* (1899) 15 Sh.Ct.Rep. 200; *Skewis* v. *Adams* (1914) 30 Sh.Ct.Rep. 217.

[45] *Reekie* v. *Norrie* (1842) 5 D. 368; *Wight* v. *Burns* (1883) 11 R. 217 (master chastising apprentice); *cf. Downie* v. *Connell Bros.*, 1910 S.C. 781.

[46] *Tullis* v. *Crichton* (1850) 12 D. 867; *Bertram* v. *Pace* (1885) 12 R. 798; *McDiarmid* v. *Barrie* (1902) 18 Sh.Ct.Rep. 47.

[47] *Dick* v. *Small* (1835) 13 S. 1134; *Tullis, supra.*

[48] *McGeever* v. *McFarlane* (1951) 67 Sh.Ct.Rep. 48.

[49] *Pirie* v. *Meikle* (1874) 2 R. 40.

[50] *Armstrong* v. *Thomson* (1894) 2 S.L.T. 70; *A.* v. *B.* (1895) 22 R. 402; *E. T.* v. *T. B. M.* (1905) 21 Sh.Ct.Rep. 156. See also a case of assault with intent to rape, *Hill* v. *Fletcher* (1847) 10 D. 7; *cf.* also *A.* v. *C.* (1919) 35 Sh.Ct.Rep. 166.

[51] *Black* v. *Duncan*, 1924 S.C. 738; see also Chap. 22, *infra.*

[52] If the woman was a virgin and consented a claim may lie for seduction instead of for rape, and if she were married a claim may lie at the instance of her husband for adultery, or for enticement.

[53] Hume, I, 302; Alison, I, 209.

of the wrong is enhanced by resultant pregnancy [54] or physical injury or shock resulting to the woman.

Consent is a defence, but consent to intercourse impetrated by force [55] or fear,[56] by drink or drugs,[57] or a trick or fraud,[58] or by personation [59] is not true consent. For the purposes of the criminal law it is, though criminal, not rape to take advantage of a woman while she is asleep,[60] but it is thought that, regarding such facts as a delict, the rule may be different, for the essence of the civil wrong is the affront to personality, whereas the essence of the crime is obtaining intercourse by force and against her will.

A woman of any age may complain civilly of rape, and her claim is not excluded by her bad character,[61] though this is very relevant to her credibility as a witness. Averments that the defender is of a licentious disposition and had on other occasions attempted to ravish other women are irrelevant.[62]

A married woman cannot sue her husband for rape,[63] because she is presumed by entering into matrimony to have consented to intercourse with her husband so long as they are married [64] and not separated by decree of judicial separation.[65] Commencing divorce proceedings does not import revocation of the wife's implied consent.[66] But a divorced husband can rape his former wife.[67]

Conduct similar to but falling short of rape may amount to an indecent assault for which damages may be claimed as for any other assault, the indecency being a material factor to be included in the assessment of damages.[68]

Rape may be pleaded as a defence to an action of divorce for adultery but the onus is on the wife to establish that she was raped rather than that she consented.[69]

3. INTENTIONAL MENTAL HARM

It appears now to be recognised that intentional conduct likely to cause, and in fact causing, harm by way of nervous shock is actionable.[70] The

[54] As in *Black* v. *Duncan*, 1924 S.C. 738; *Armstrong, supra.*
[55] *H.M.A.* v. *Mackenzie* (1828) Syme 323.
[56] Hume, I, 302; Alison, I, 211.
[57] *H.M.A.* v. *Logan*, 1936 J.C. 100.
[58] *Cf. R.* v. *Case* (1850) 1 Den. 580.
[59] *H.M.A.* v. *Montgomery*, 1926 J.C. 2.
[60] *H.M.A.* v. *Sweenie* (1858) 3 Irv. 109; *H.M.A.* v. *Thomson* (1872) 2 Coup. 346.
[61] Hume, I, 304; Alison, I, 214; *H.M.A.* v. *Yates and Parkes* (1851) J. Shaw, 528.
[62] *A.* v. *B.* (1895) 22 R. 402.
[63] *Cf.* Hume, I, 306; Alison, I, 218.
[64] *R.* v. *Clarence* (1888) 22 Q.B.D. 23.
[65] *R.* v. *Clarke* [1949] 2 All E.R. 448.
[66] *R.* v. *Miller* [1954] 2 Q.B. 282.
[67] *R.* v. *Sharpless* [1957] C.L.Y. 846.
[68] *Cf. Hill* v. *Fletcher* (1847) 10 D. 7 (assault with intent to rape); *A.* v. *C.* (1919) 35 Sh.Ct. Rep. 166.
[69] *Redpath* v. *Redpath and Mulligan* [1950] 1 All E.R. 600.
[70] See Magruder, " Mental and Emotional Disturbance in the Law of Torts " (1936) 49 H.L.R. 1033; Prosser, " Intentional Infliction of Mental Suffering: A New Tort " (1939) 37 Mich.L.R. 874; see also Chap. 19, *infra.*

precise limits and conditions of this ground of action are not settled, but it is possibly fair to formulate the law as being that there is a duty not deliberately to do anything which will naturally or probably cause harm by way of nervous shock to anyone foreseeably likely to be affected by the conduct in question.

Mere fright or shock is possibly not enough [71] without some physical consequence of the shock or fright,[72] but if such be proved, damages are recoverable, as where a practical joker sent a false message to a lady that her husband had been seriously injured and caused her serious illness,[73] or a detective falsely told a woman that she had been corresponding with an enemy spy.[74] It has been held that there was no relevant averment of breach of duty *ex delicto* where a lodger committed suicide in his lodgings, to the shock of the proprietor of the house.[75] The courts have several times, without discussing the precise ground of decision, allowed persons a claim for the making of an unauthorised post-mortem examination of a deceased relative, and these decisions also may be justifiable on this principle.[76] In one doubtful English case [77] shock at the accidental upsetting of the coffin containing the body of a relative was held actionable; deliberate interference with or desecration of the body would have been a stronger case.[78]

4. CONTRAVENTION OF LAWBURROWS

This ancient wrong [79] is not obsolete. Lawburrows is caution to keep the law and a person fearing harm to himself [80] or his family [81] at the instance of another may petition the sheriff court, or J.P. court, and the court may order the defender to grant a bond of caution or to find caution not to harm the petitioner under a penalty fixed by it. The procedure is now regulated by the Civil Imprisonment Act, 1882.[82] Failing caution, warrant may be sought for the defender's arrest and imprisonment till he finds caution as ordered. Parties could be taken bound to find mutual caution.[83]

[71] *Dulieu* v. *White* [1901] 2 K.B. 669, 673; *Behrens* v. *Bertram Mills Circus, Ltd.* [1957] 2 Q.B. 1, 27; *Schneider* v. *Eisovitch* [1960] 2 Q.B. 430.
[72] *Stedman* v. *Henderson* (1923) 40 Sh.Ct.Rep. 8.
[73] *Wilkinson* v. *Downton* [1897] 2 Q.B. 57.
[74] *Janvier* v. *Sweeney* [1919] 2 K.B. 316.
[75] *Anderson* v. *McCrae* (1930) 47 Sh.Ct.Rep. 287; see also *A.* v. *B.* (1906) 12 S.L.T. 830; both decisions are doubtful.
[76] *Pollok* v. *Workman* (1900) 2 F. 354; *Conway* v. *Dalziel* (1900) 3 F. 918; *Hughes* v. *Robertson*, 1913 S.C. 394.
[77] *Owens* v. *Liverpool Corpn.* [1939] 1 K.B. 394, criticised in *Bourhill* v. *Young*, 1942 S.C. (H.L.) 78.
[78] *Cf. Dewar* v. *H.M.A.*, 1945 J.C. 5 (theft of coffin lids said to be " inhuman disrespect for the dead [and] callous indifference to the feelings of the living "; could relatives have sued if they had discovered this practice at the time?).
[79] Stair, I, 9, 30; IV, 48, 1; Bankt. I, 10, 157; Ersk. IV, 1, 16; see also Dobie, *Sheriff Court Practice*, 510.
[80] Lawburrows Act 1429, c. 129.
[81] Lawburrows Act 1581, c. 117.
[82] See also *Mackenzie* v. *Maclennan*, 1916 S.C. 617.
[83] *Balbegno* v. *Lauriston* (1624) Mor. 8031.

If the defender contravenes the court's decree not to harm the petitioner, the latter may sue him and his cautioner, if any, in an action of
contravention of lawburrows craving forfeiture of the caution. The
concurrence of the procurator-fiscal is necessary, but the action is a civil
one, craving forfeiture of the penalty provided. One-half of the sum goes
to the Crown, one-half to the pursuer. The pursuer does not need to
prove any damage resulting from the act of contravention.[84]

Contravention has been held incurred where the defender pursued
the petitioner with a drawn sword, though he did not strike him,[85] or
struck him on the breast,[86] or violently entering on possession of lands,[87]
or uttered injurious words and spitting in the complainer's face,[88] or
intromitting with teind sheaves,[89] or sowing land not pertaining to the
person doing so.[90]

But contravention was held not constituted by boasting and chasing,
without any harm or damage[91]; or merely pasturing cattle on the complainer's lands, without also herding them[92]; or knocking off and jumping
on a man's hat and threatening others, the bond being not to harm in
body[93]; or letting water from a pit flood another's pit[94]; or taking horses
from the pursuer's tenant.[95] Contravention is not sustained upon any
illegal deed where the matter of right is doubtful.[96]

The action for contravention is elided by the pursuer's forgiveness or
passing from the offence,[97] but that does not elide the ordinary action of
damages for any injury done.[98] Nor does friendship and familiarity with
the party charged after caution has been found discharge the lawburrows,
unless that be done by writ.[99] In one case[1] the Lords assoilzied the
defender from the action of contravention, but sustained the summons
as an action for reparation.

Proceedings for contravention are not exclusive of any other remedy
competent for the wrong in question. Even if the pursuer has forgiven

---

[84] Bankt. I, 10, 166; *Strangs* v. *Sandilands* (1591) Mor. 8024.
[85] *McKie* v. *McKie* (1607) Mor. 8029.
[86] *Bruce* v. *Laird of Clackmanan* (1609) Mor. 8030.
[87] *Muirhead* v. *Laird of Barsinok* (1616) Mor. 8031.
[88] *A.* v. *B.* (1629) Mor. 8033.
[89] *Hepburn* v. *Tenants of Douglas* (1630) Mor. 8034.
[90] *Laird of Whittingham* v. *The Lady* (1631) Mor. 8034.
[91] *Wallace* v. *Laird of Hayning* (1604) Mor. 8027.
[92] *Shaw* v. *Wilkieson* (1604) Mor. 8027; cf. *Anderson* v. *Galbraith* (1616) Mor. 8031.
[93] *Constable of Dundee* v. *Flescheour* (1605) Mor. 8028.
[94] *Anderson* v. *Blackwood* (1629) Mor. 8033.
[95] *Grant* v. *Grant* (1632) Mor. 8036; *Lindsay* v. *Denniston* (1633) Mor. 8040.
[96] Stair, I, 9, 30; *Strangs* v. *Sandilands* (1591) Mor. 8024. Cf. *Brock* v. *Rankine* (1874) 1 R.
991.
[97] Bankt. I, 10, 173; *Somerville* v. —— (1607) Mor. 8028; *King's Advocate* v. *Lindsay*
(1633) Mor. 8038.
[98] *Somerville, supra; Anderson* v. *Blackwood* (1629) Mor. 8033.
[99] *A.* v. *B.* (1628) Mor. 8032.
[1] *Wemyss* v. *Stuart* (1633) Mor. 8037.

the conduct, or been killed,[2] the public prosecutor may insist criminally in a complaint based on assault or breach of the peace.[3]

5. DEFORCEMENT

Deforcement is the wrong of forcibly preventing an officer of law or his assistants from executing a legal warrant of a competent court. Such conduct is criminal,[4] but also civilly actionable.[5] The officer must be duly commissioned, and be performing his duty in a lawful manner, and, if requested, exhibit his warrant. Deforcement protects the writs of every court which require to be served.[6] In its civil aspect an action lies against all who have interposed to save the debtor from diligence. The claim is for payment of the debt due and damages.

There need not have been any actual assault (*i.e.*, battery) so long as there has been a show of violence or any sort of actual violence, such as would overcome the constancy of a man of ordinary firmness, courage and determination,[7] used towards the officer in the execution of his duty and designed to prevent its accomplishment.

The conduct must have actually prevented the execution of the warrant; there is no deforcement if he succeeds, despite resistance,[8] or if the defenders did not stop him but he desisted from the attempt.[9]

6. BREACH OF ARRESTMENT

This is a wrong of the same nature as deforcement, punishable criminally as a contempt of court and of the authority of the law, but also actionable civilly.[10] The wrong consists in an arrestee deliberately disregarding the arrestment used in his hands and paying the sum, or delivering the goods arrested, to the common debtor. The punishment included escheat of moveables, out of which the debt of the arrestee and damages were paid, and the criminal proceedings were competent in the Court of Session or the High Court of Justiciary. The civil action is for payment of the debt, so far as attached, again, and formerly for damages also, or for damages amounting to the sum secured by the arrestment and wrongly paid away.[11] If the value of the fund or subject arrested cannot be ascertained, the claim is for the amount of the arrester's debt.[12] The arrestee

---

[2] *The King* v. *Balfour* (1545) Mor. 8024.

[3] Bankt. I, 10, 173; *The King* v. *Crichton* (1517) Mor. 8023; *Treasurer* v. *Sinclair* (1561) Mor. 8024; *Sheriff of Forrest* v. *Turnbull* (1613) Mor. 7898; *Robertson* v. *Ross* (1873) 11 M. 910.

[4] Hume, I, 396; Alison, I, 505.

[5] Stair, I, 9, 29; IV, 49, 1; Mack. IV, 4, 17; Bankt. I, 10, 190; Ersk. IV, 4, 32; Ross's *Lect.*, I, 338; *McConnell* v. *Brew* (1907) 23 Sh.Ct.Rep. 261.

[6] *H.M.A.* v. *McLean* (1886) 14 R.(J.) 1; 1 White 232.

[7] *H.M.A.* v. *Hunter* (1860) 3 Irvine 518; *H.M.A.* v. *Nicolson* (1887) 1 White 307.

[8] *Hunter*, *supra*.

[9] *McConnell* v. *Brew* (1907) 23 Sh.Ct.Rep. 261.

[10] Stair, I, 9, 29; IV, 50, 30; Bankt., I, 10, 190; Ersk., III, 6, 14; IV, 4, 36; Hume, *Lect.*, VI, 112; cases in Morison, p. 984 *et seq.*; See also *Inglis & Bow* v. *Smith & Aikman* (1867) 5 M. 320.

[11] *Grant* v. *Hill* (1792) Mor. 786; *McEwen* v. *Blair & Morrison* (1822) 1 S. 313.

[12] *Macarthur* v. *Bruce* (1760) Mor. 803.

will not be liable in second payment if he could not, when he paid the common debtor, have known of the arrestment.[13]

7. BATTERY PENDENTE LITE

This wrong was committed by a party to a cause who slew, wounded or otherwise invaded his adversary at any period between the execution of the summons and the full execution of the decree, or who was accessory to such invasion.[14] By Acts now repealed the punishment of the crime was the loss of the cause.[15]

This wrong, though in existence till the end of the 18th century,[16] is probably now obsolete, such conduct being punishable criminally and actionable civilly at common law.

[13] *Laidlaw* v. *Smith* (1841) 2 Robin. 490.
[14] Bankt., I, 10, 179; Ersk., IV, 4, 37.
[15] See cases in Morison, 1367 *et seq.*
[16] *Annand* v. *Ross* (1790) Mor. 1379; *Cadell* v. *Morthland* (1799) Mor. 16789.

CHAPTER 16

LIABILITY FOR NEGLIGENTLY
CAUSING PHYSICAL INJURY OR DEATH

1. Road Accidents
2. Railway Accidents
3. Shipping Accidents
4. Aircraft Accidents
5. Accidents Arising out of Employment
6. Dangerous Premises
7. Roads and Streets
8. Dangerous Goods
9. Damage done by Animals
10. Persons Professing Special Skills
11. Miscellaneous Cases

" THE law protects personal safety, not only against malice and crime, but also against negligence and gross disregard of the safety and interests of others." [1]

To cause physical injury to a person by a negligent act or omission is an infringement of his legal interest in the immunity of his body from such invasion, and is actionable by him. To cause death to a person by a negligent act or omission is an infringement of the legal interest of certain classes of relatives not to suffer infringement of their interest in the continuance of unimpaired familial relations with the deceased, and is actionable by them. [2]

Any particular negligent act or omission may by harm to one victim infringe either of these interests but not both, but the duties of care and the breaches of duty are the same, whichever interest has been infringed. It is necessary to examine the circumstances in which the courts have held that conduct inferred fault and amounted to breach of duty to an injured person, or by killing him, to the relatives of the person killed.

While the general principles of liability for negligent harm apply to all cases, particular sets of rules have developed in relation to accidents arising in some particular sets of circumstances and these have accordingly to be discussed separately.

1. ROAD ACCIDENTS

Persons using the highway, whether on foot, leading, riding or driving animals, or driving any kind of mechanically or electrically propelled vehicle must take reasonable care for the safety of their passengers, other road users in vehicle or on foot, and persons so near as to be within

---

[1] Bell, *Prin.*, § 2030.
[2] The relatives' claim is considered further in Chap. 22, *infra*.

the area of danger of harm if they fail to take reasonable care.[3]   Liability depends on the ordinary principles of negligence and the person sued is liable only if he has failed in some respect to take the care deemed reasonable in the circumstances and has thereby caused the harm complained of.

In view of the known volume of traffic on modern roads " reasonable care " is a fairly high standard.   It is common experience that many drivers and pedestrians are not careful and a road-user must guard against the obvious and common kinds of follies which other road-users commonly commit.[4]

Rule of the road—vehicles.   The rule of the road is that vehicles, including horsed vehicles, powered vehicles and pedal-driven vehicles, approaching each other from opposite directions must each move on the driver's own left or near-side of the road so as to allow the other vehicle to pass on the driver's right.[5]   Failure to do so is prima facie evidence of negligence.[6]   In anticipation of meeting other vehicles it is accordingly advisable at all times to keep to the left of the centreline of the road, particularly when approaching corners, crests of hills and at other places where an oncoming vehicle may come into sight suddenly and at close range.[7]   Where a collision occurs the vehicle which was not on its own proper side of the road is prima facie to blame.[8]   The rules of the road are flexible, not absolute,[9] but a driver going on to the wrong side of the road must take greater care than if he were to keep to his proper side,[10] and driving on the wrong side may mislead another vehicle into adopting a dangerous course of action.[11]

Rule of the road—animals and pedestrians.   The rule of keeping to the left applies to animals being ridden or driven as much as to mechanically propelled vehicles.[12]   But in the case of led animals the common law rule, affirmed by the Highway Code, is that the animal should be led along the right-hand or off-side of the road, *i.e.,* facing oncoming traffic, with the man leading the animal walking on its left-hand or near-side, and therefore between the animal and oncoming and passing vehicles.[13]   But if an animal is being led along the near-side, an overtaking vehicle should pull well over to the other side when passing it.[14]

---

[3] *Bourhill* v. *Young,* 1942 S.C.(H.L.) 78; *King* v. *Phillips* [1953] 1 Q.B. 429.
[4] *L.P.T.B.* v. *Upson* [1949] A.C. 155; *Berrill* v. *Road Haulage Executive* [1952] 2 Lloyd's Rep. 490.
[5] Traffic Regulation (Scotland) Act, 1772, s. 8 (now repealed), affirming common law. This section was fenced with a penalty and may have imposed a public duty only.   See also *Nuttall* v. *Pickering* [1913] 1 K.B. 14 and Highway Code, para. 17.
[6] *Duncan* v. *Wilson,* 1940 S.C. 221.
[7] See observations in *Barty* v. *Harper,* 1922 S.C. 67.
[8] But in *Barty, supra,* the proximate cause of the accident was held to be the failure of the vehicle which was on its proper side to stop; see also *Wallace* v. *Bergius,* 1915 S.C. 205.
[9] *Christie* v. *Glasgow Corpn.,* 1927 S.C. 273, 276; *cf. Clay* v. *Wood* (1803) 5 Esp. 44.
[10] *Pluckwell* v. *Wilson* (1832) 5 C. & P. 375.
[11] *Wallace* v. *Bergius,* 1915 S.C. 205.
[12] *Turley* v. *Thomas* (1837) 8 C. & P. 103.
[13] See *Umphray* v. *Ganson Bros.,* 1917 S.C. 371, and Highway Code, paras. 64–69.
[14] *Umphray, supra.*

Where there is no pavement for pedestrians there is no rule, but it is usually considered wise for pedestrians to walk on the right and thus to face oncoming traffic.[15]

The Highway Code. By the Road Traffic Act, 1930, s. 45, now Road Traffic Act, 1960, s. 74, the Minister of Transport is required to prepare and issue a code known as the Highway Code, comprising such directions as appear to him proper for the guidance of persons using the roads. Various editions have appeared from time to time.[16] In large part the Highway Code reproduces pre-existing common law and the custom of road users. By section 74 (5) of the Act it is provided that: " A failure on the part of any person to observe a provision of the Highway Code shall not of itself render that person liable to criminal proceedings of any kind, but any such failure may in any proceedings (whether civil or criminal, and including proceedings for an offence under this Act) be relied upon by any party to the proceedings as tending to establish or to negative any liability which is in question in those proceedings."

The effect of this has been explained as follows: " The code is not binding as a statutory regulation; it is only something which may be regarded as information and advice to drivers. It does not follow that, if they fail to carry out that which is provided for by the code, they are necessarily negligent. It only provides that they may be found to be negligent if they do not carry out the provisions of the code. Nor is it sufficient excuse for them to say, in answer to a claim for negligence: ' We did everything that is provided for in the code.' "[17] In short, compliance will not necessarily exculpate, non-compliance will not necessarily inculpate, either civilly or criminally.

Road Traffic Acts and Orders. Numerous statutes and orders made thereunder regulate the construction, fittings and use of motor-vehicles on roads and, apart from any issue of criminal liability for breach of the statutory provision, failure to comply with the regulations is a matter to be considered in the determination of negligence. But compliance does not relieve drivers from their common law obligations to take reasonable care, to take common-sense action in emergencies, and to take appropriate action outside the Highway Code and the regulations in circumstances where it becomes essential in the interest of safety.[18] Failure to comply with regulations does not, at least in most cases, give a right of action for breach of statutory duty to an injured person.[19] The fact that a vehicle was not lit as required by statute may, however,

---

[15] *Cf.* Highway Code, para. 3.
[16] The current edition is that of 1960.
[17] *Croston* v. *Vaughan* [1938] 1 K.B. 540, *per* Greer L.J. (where held that intention to stop signalled by stop-light only was evidence of negligence, as not complying with Code).
[18] *Croston* v. *Vaughan* [1938] 1 K.B. 540, *per* Scott L.J.; *cf. Winter* v. *Bristol Tramways and Carriage Co.* (1917) 86 L.J.K.B. 240, 936.
[19] *Badham* v. *Lambs* [1946] K.B. 45; *Clarke* v. *Brims* [1947] K.B. 497; *Winter* v. *Cardiff R.D.C.* [1950] 1 All E.R. 819; *Barkway* v. *South Wales Tpt. Co.* [1950] A.C. 185; *cf. Balmer* v. *Hayes*, 1950 S.C. 477.

be used as a make-weight in establishing a case of common law fault.[20]

Traffic signs. By the Road Traffic Act, 1960, s. 14, a driver must observe traffic signs (defined by section 51) and signals and the directions of a police officer on duty. A white line painted on the road is not a traffic sign within this provision, but only a helpful indication of the road which may best be followed.[21] Accordingly to cross it is prima facie evidence of negligence and no more.

Other traffic signs are distinguished by the Highway Code as those which must be observed,[22] those which warn,[23] and those which inform.[24] Those which require to be observed must be obeyed strictly.[25]

(a) Mechanically-propelled vehicles

Duty of driver generally. The duty of the driver of a vehicle on the highway is generally to manage his vehicle with reasonable care, and not do, or omit to do, anything which the driver could reasonably foresee might injure any person or animal [26] whom he might reasonably have anticipated to be injured by his failure to take care.[27] This duty is owed to pedestrians and other road-users within sight and the range of possible harm, to the drivers of and passengers in other vehicles similarly situated, and to passengers in the driver's own vehicle. The same degree of care is due when driving in a private avenue to which the public have access as on the public road.[28]

Liability depends on negligence in the management of the vehicle and is not established merely by the happening of an accident.[29] It is evidence of negligence when a pedestrian walking in the roadway is struck from behind, neither party knowing more about it,[30] and there has been said to be a strong presumption of negligence against a driver who runs down a person in daylight.[31] A driver is bound to anticipate that other road-users do not always take proper care, and have regard to experience of other drivers' carelessness.[32]

No liability for inevitable accident. A driver is not liable if an accident happens by reason of inevitable accident, not attributable in any way or

20 *Isbister* v. *J. & T. Smith*, 1948 S.L.T.(Notes) 8.
21 *Evans* v. *Cross* [1938] 1 K.B. 694.
22 *e.g.*, Halt at Major Road Ahead; 30 m.p.h. speed limit.
23 *e.g.*, Cross-roads; School.
24 *e.g.*, route signs, place name signs, car park signs.
25 *Tolhurst* v. *Webster* [1936] 2 All E.R. 1020; *Anderson* v. *St. Andrew's Ambulance Assn.*, 1943 S.C. 248; *Buffel* v. *Cardox* [1950] 2 All E.R. 878.
26 *Graham* v. *Edinburgh Tramways*, 1917 S.C. 7.
27 *Bourhill* v. *Young*, 1942 S.C.(H.L.) 78; *King* v. *Phillips* [1953] 1 Q.B. 429.
28 *Bowie* v. *Shenkin*, 1934 S.C. 459.
29 *Alexander* v. *Phillip* (1899) 1 F. 985; *cf. Holmes* v. *Mather* (1875) L.R. 10 Ex. 261; *Gayler & Pope* v. *Davies* [1924] 2 K.B. 75; *Milliken* v. *Glasgow Corpn.*, 1918 S.C. 857 is an unsatisfactory decision.
30 *Page* v. *Richards*, reported in *Tart* v. *Chitty* [1933] 2 K.B. 453.
31 *Clerk* v. *Petrie* (1879) 6 R. 1076; *Snee* v. *Durkie* (1903) 6 F. 42; *cf. Martin* v. *Ward* (1887) 14 R. 814.
32 *L.P.T.B.* v. *Upson* [1949] A.C. 155.

his fault, as where he died at the wheel,[33] or, doubtless, had a stroke [34] or a fit,[35] unless this might have been anticipated.[36] But a driver was held negligent when he lost control when a fly entered his eye.[37]

It is, however, fault on a driver's part to drive while under the influence of drink or a drug,[38] or when overcome by sleep,[39] and to cause harm in consequence. A lesser incapacity than would justify conviction for driving while under the influence of drink [40] will be a relevant averment of fault.[41]

Where one vehicle is crossing at a junction in obedience to a light signal and another crosses at right-angles in obedience to a policeman's signal, neither driver may be guilty of negligence, each having acted in reliance on signals which he was entitled to follow.[42]

Emergencies. In circumstances of emergency the question is whether the driver acted reasonably or not. Thus to brake suddenly when a dog darts across in front of a bus may be reasonable and passengers who fall in consequence have then no claim for negligence,[43] or a sudden stop may not have been reasonable, in which case it is legally negligent.[44] The sudden stopping of a public service vehicle causing injury to a passenger raises a prima facie case of negligence and the onus is on the driver to justify his conduct.[45]

Dangerous conditions. In dangerous conditions, as of fog or ice, reasonable care demands much greater precautions than usual, particularly with heavy and laden vehicles, and there is normally a duty to reduce speed, but it is questionable if vehicles must stop solely to eliminate the risk of skidding or collision.[46]

Defective condition of vehicle. Reasonable care must be taken that a vehicle is maintained in proper condition, so that it can be safely driven.[47] Hence an owner must take the steps a careful owner would to have his vehicle kept in proper repair, so as to be safe to drive. While the liability is not absolute [48] it is evidence of negligence if a vehicle becomes uncontrollable by reason of defective steering,[49] or a wheel comes off,[50] or a tyre bursts,[51] or the brakes pull violently to one side.[52]

33 *Ryan* v. *Youngs* [1938] 1 All E.R. 522.
34 *Waugh* v. *Allan,* 1964 S.L.T. 269 (H.L.).
35 *Hill* v. *Baxter* [1958] 1 Q.B. 277.
36 *Balmer* v. *Hayes,* 1950 S.C. 477.
37 *Johnston* v. *N.C.B.,* 1960 S.L.T.(Notes) 84.
38 *Armstrong* v. *Clark* [1957] 2 Q.B. 391; *cf. Watmore* v. *Jenkins* [1962] 2 Q.B. 572.
39 *Kay* v. *Butterworth* (1945) 61 T.L.R. 452.
40 R.T.A., 1960, s. 6.
41 *Bark* v. *Scott,* 1954 S.C. 72.
42 *Wilson* v. *West,* 1947 S.C. 198.
43 *Parkinson* v. *Liverpool Corpn.* [1950] 1 All E.R. 367.
44 *Sutherland* v. *Glasgow Corpn.,* 1951 S.C.(H.L.) 1.
45 *Sutherland, supra.*
46 *Laurie* v. *Raglan Building Co.* [1942] 1 K.B. 152; *Daborn* v. *Bath Tramways* [1946] 2 All E.R. 333; *Burton* v. *West Suffolk C.C.* [1960] 2 All E.R. 26.
47 *Phillips* v. *Britannia Hygienic Laundry Co.* [1923] 1 K.B. 539; [1923] 2 K.B. 832; *Stewart* v. *Hancock* [1939] 2 All E.R. 578.   48 *Roberts* v. *Wallis* [1958] 1 Lloyd's Rep. 29.
49 *Hutchins* v. *Mander* (1920) 37 T.L.R. 72.   50 *Phillips, supra.*
51 *Barkway* v. *South Wales Transport Co.* [1950] A.C. 185.
52 *R.* v. *Spurge* [1961] 2 All E.R. 688.

Duty to passengers. A driver, *e.g.*, of a hired car or taxi, who takes a person as a fare-paying passenger must take reasonable care for the safety of the passenger and of anything he brings with him in the vehicle, and this duty is contractual as well as delictual.[53] A gratuitous passenger by invitation is owed a similar duty *ex delicto* only.[54] The duty covers not only the driving, but care to see that a door is not closed on the passenger's fingers.[55] Hence an injured passenger may have a claim against both his own driver and the other vehicle concerned.

A passenger is not identified with his driver so as to have his claim reduced or barred by the driver's contributory negligence in a question with another vehicle, save where the passenger had the right and duty to control the driver's driving,[56] or where the driver was acting as agent for the passengers.[57]

Duty to persons given lifts. A person who gives another a " lift " or casual gratuitous carriage must take reasonable care not to cause the other injury by negligent driving. He is not liable for unknown defects in his vehicle but only for those of which he knows, and should warn the passenger of a danger known to him but unknown to the passenger.[58] In *Dann* v. *Hamilton* [59] a passenger, injured by reason of the negligent driving of a driver whom the passenger knew to be under the influence of drink, was held not barred from claiming damages by his acceptance of the lift in the knowledge of the driver's state. A similar view has been taken in Scotland,[60] but subsequently a different view has been adopted, that accepting a lift in such circumstances justified a plea of *volenti non fit injuria* or of contributory negligence.[61]

The driver of a vehicle, such as a milk-lorry or a dust-cart, on which fellow-employees commonly ride, must take reasonable care for their safety in his driving.[62]

Duty to pedestrians. A driver must at all times take reasonable care for the safety of pedestrians within the area of potential danger from his vehicle.[63]

Where the pavement is obstructed, so that a pedestrian may be expected to step into the roadway, greater care should be taken.[64]

---

[53] As to delictual duty see Occupiers' Liability (Scotland) Act, 1960 ss. 1 (3) and 2.
[54] *Paterson* v. *Gardiner*, 1924 S.L.T. 63.
[55] *Hett* v. *Mackenzie*, 1939 S.C. 350.
[56] *Lampert* v. *Eastern National Omnibus Co.* [1954] 2 All E.R. 719; *cf. Trust Company* v. *de Silva* [1956] 1 Lloyd's Rep. 309.
[57] *Scarsbrook* v. *Mason* [1961] 3 All E.R. 767.
[58] *Lowys* v. *Barnett & Dunbar* [1945] 2 All E.R. 555.
[59] [1939] 1 K.B. 509.
[60] *Bankhead* v. *McCarthy*, 1963 S.C. 263.
[61] *McCaig* v. *Langan*, 1964 S.L.T. 121.
[62] *Davies* v. *Swan Motor Co.* [1949] 2 K.B. 291; *cf. Jones* v. *Livox Quarries* [1952] 2 Q.B. 608 (where passenger's presence unknown to driver).
[63] *Bourhill* v. *Young*, 1942 S.C.(H.L.) 78; *King* v. *Phillips* [1953] 1 Q.B. 429.
[64] *Adamson* v. *Roberts*, 1951 S.C. 681.

Duty to persons in other vehicles. A driver also owes a duty of care to persons in other vehicles which are so close that they may be injured by his failure to take reasonable care.[65]

Moving off from rest. A driver must take care when moving off from rest and give signals of his intention to do so. He is under no duty to persons in the vicinity unless he ought reasonably to have anticipated danger to others through his failure to take care,[66] but particular care should be taken if there are children in the vicinity, or if the vehicle is to be reversed.[67]

Speed. A driver of a vehicle should drive at a speed which is reasonable in the circumstances, having regard to the weather, visibility, condition, and extent of use of the road, the amount and kind of traffic on it or which might reasonably be expected.[68] A lesser speed is accordingly reasonable where other road-users are present or may be anticipated. Whether speed was excessive or not in particular circumstances is entirely a question of fact in each case.[69] A public service vehicle is not justified in proceeding at a speed which causes risk of harm to other road-users merely in order to try to maintain its schedule.[70] Vehicles being used for fire brigade, ambulance or police purposes are exempted from speed limits if the observance of those provisions would be likely to hinder the use of the vehicle for the purpose for which it is being used on that occasion,[71] but this does not affect the civil liability of the driver for injuries caused by negligence.[72]

The maximum speeds of certain classes of vehicles are limited by statute [73] and, apart from criminal consequences, it is prima facie negligence on the driver's part to exceed those limits.[74]

It is an offence to drive a vehicle at a speed in excess of the maximum permitted for that road,[75] and is also probably prima facie negligence to do so.[76]

Range of vision. It is also evidence of negligence, but not a rule that it is negligence,[77] if a driver drives at such a speed as not to be able to

---

65 *Bourhill* v. *Young*, 1942 S.C.(H.L.) 78 (where accepted that Young in breach of duty to persons in car with which he collided).
66 *Connelly* v. *Hemphill*, 1948 S.L.T.(Notes) 13 (H.L.).
67 *Cf. King* v. *Phillips* [1953] 1 Q.B. 429; *Carney* v. *Smith*, 1953 S.C. 19.
68 *Foster* v. *Rintoul* (1891) 28 S.L.R. 636; *French* v. *Mitchell* (1901) 9 S.L.T. 219; *Cowan* v. *Robertson*, 1941 S.C. 502.
69 *Miller* v. *Liverpool Coop. Socy.* [1940] 4 All E.R. 367; *Hurlock* v. *Inglis* [1963] C.L.Y. 2349.
70 *Daly* v. *Liverpool Corpn.* [1939] 2 All E.R. 142.
71 R.T.A., 1960, s. 25.
72 *Gaynor* v. *Allen* [1959] 2 Q.B. 403.
73 R.T.A., 1960, s. 24 and Sched. I.
74 *Kingman* v. *Seager* [1939] 1 K.B. 397; *Durnell* v. *Scott* [1939] 1 All E.R. 183; *Bracegirdle* v. *Oxley* [1947] 1 All E.R. 126.
75 R.T.A., 1960, s. 19. The speed is normally 30 m.p.h., but 40 m.p.h. or 50 m.p.h. in certain cases.
76 *Cf. Tribe* v. *Jones* (1961) 105 S.J. 931; *Barna* v. *Hudes Merchandising Corpn.* (1962) 106 S.J. 194.
77 *Stewart* v. *Hancock* [1940] 2 All E.R. 427; *Cowan* v. *Robertson*, 1941 S.C. 502; *Morris* v. *Luton Corpn.* [1946] 1 K.B. 114; *White* v. *McKean*, 1948 S.L.T. 210; *secus, Griffiths* v. *Alexander*, 1941 S.L.T. 66.

pull up within the limits of his vision, as in darkness or fog or where vision is limited by dazzle from lights or other cause. In a number of cases drivers have been held negligent when they were unable to pull up in time when an obstruction came within their range of vision.[78]

Lookout. The driver of a vehicle must maintain a good lookout all round for other traffic, pedestrians and traffic signs and other warnings, particularly at crossings and other places of obvious danger, in darkness or bad visibility [79] and particularly if joining a main road or reversing.[80] Circumstances inferring failure to keep a good lookout are evidence of negligence.[81] In some cases an accident has been held attributable either to having driven at a speed too great to check within the limits of vision, or to having failed to keep a good lookout, as where a driver has had to brake suddenly and consequently caused injury to a passenger.[82]

Vehicle lights. Vehicles must carry certain minimum prescribed lights and have them illuminated during hours of darkness so as to give warning of their presence on the road and direction of movement.[83] Breach of the statutory duty to exhibit the required lights does not by itself give a person injured in consequence of a breach of the statutory duty any claim of damages,[84] but failure to exhibit proper lights is evidence of negligence, because common prudence and custom dictate the showing of lights, and their absence may mislead another driver and prevent him taking necessary precautions,[85] or fail to show up a pedestrian.[86] Failure to exhibit the lights required by statute may be founded on as part of a case of common law fault.[87]

Where a vehicle was provided with a tail-light which later, without the driver's knowledge and without negligence on his part, went out, the owner was held not liable when a following vehicle ran into it.[88] It is,

---

[78] *Tart* v. *Chitty* [1933] 2 K.B. 453; *Page* v. *Richard and Draper* (1920) referred to therein; *Baker* v. *Longhurst* [1933] 2 K.B. 461; *Evans* v. *Downes* [1933] 2 K.B. 465n.; *Tidy* v. *Battmann* [1934] 1 K.B. 319, followed in *Scott* v. *McIntosh*, 1935 S.C. 199; *Stewart* v. *Hancock* [1940] 2 All E.R. 427; *Griffiths* v. *Alexander*, 1941 S.L.T. 66; *Cowan* v. *Robertson*, 1941 S.C. 502; *McGeown* v. *Greenock Motor Services, Ltd.*, 1943 S.C. 33; *Drew* v. *Western S.M.T. Co.*, 1947 S.C. 222; *Henley* v. *Cameron* [1948] W.N. 468; *Hill-Venning* v. *Bezzant* [1950] 2 All E.R. 1151; *Harvey* v. *Road Haulage Executive* [1952] 1 K.B. 120. The dictum of Scrutton L.J. in *Baker* v. *Longhurst* [1933] 2 K.B. 461, 468, was overruled in *Morris* v. *Luton Corpn.* [1946] K.B. 114.

[79] *Drew* v. *Western S.M.T. Co.*, 1947 S.C. 222.

[80] *Muir* v. *L.N.E.Ry.*, 1946 S.C. 216; see also *McKnight* v. *General Motor Carrying Co.*, 1936 S.C. 17.

[81] *Grant* v. *Glasgow Dairy Co.* (1881) 9 R. 182; *Muir* v. *L.N.E.Ry.*, 1946 S.C. 216; *Randall* v. *Tarrant* [1955] 1 All E.R. 600.

[82] *Mars* v. *Glasgow Corpn.*, 1940 S.C. 202; *O'Hara* v. *Central S.M.T. Co.*, 1941 S.C. 363; *Ballingall* v. *Glasgow Corpn.*, 1948 S.C. 160.

[83] Road Transport Lighting Act, 1957, and R.T. Lighting (Amendment) Act, 1958.

[84] *Clarke* v. *Brims* [1947] K.B. 497; *West* v. *David Lawson, Ltd.*, 1949 S.C. 430; *Dawrant* v. *Nutt* [1960] 3 All E.R. 681.

[85] *Pressley* v. *Burnett*, 1914 S.C. 874; *Tait* v. *Trotter*, 1917 S.C. 378; *Winter* v. *Bristol Tramways and Carriage Co., Ltd.* (1917) 86 L.J.K.B. 240; *Baker* v. *Longhurst* [1933] 2 K.B. 461; *Dawrant* v. *Nutt* [1906] 3 All E.R. 681. See also *Jones* v. *Price* [1963] C.L.Y. 2316.

[86] *Gibson* v. *Milroy* (1879) 6 R. 890.

[87] *Isbister* v. *J. & T. Smith*, 1948 S.L.T.(Notes) 8.

[88] *Maitland* v. *Raisbeck* [1944] K.B. 689; *Shave* v. *Lees* [1954] 3 All E.R. 249; *Sieghart* v. *B.T.C.* [1956] C.L.Y. 5961.

however, negligent to have a tail-light obscured, *e.g.*, by a lowered tail-board.[89] Substitute lighting, *e.g.*, the lamp in a miner's cap instead of a cycle lamp, may be held adequate, but it must be proved to be a reasonably adequate warning to other road-users, and the onus of proof of adequacy is on the user of the substitute lighting.[90]

Headlights. It will also prima facie be negligent not to have or to use adequate lights to enable the driver to see traffic or any obstruction in front, so as to be able to stop in time or avoid the obstruction.[91] Thus it may be negligent not to use headlights even in a lit street, if the street lighting is poor, and greater care is necessary when rounding a bend when the beam from lights is not illuminating the path to be traversed by the vehicle.[92] Where a vehicle collides with an unlit obstruction invisible up to the moment of collision, the driver is not necessarily at fault; the fault may be solely that of the person who left the obstruction unlit.[93]

A driver who is dazzled by the lights of approaching vehicles may be negligent if he drives on when he cannot see properly and runs into something: he should slow down or stop. It may also be negligent in particular circumstances for the other driver not to have dipped his headlights if that may prevent the dazzled driver from seeing some obstruction.

Audible warnings. Audible warning of approach, as by sounding a horn,[94] is a precaution of small importance and does not give any right of way or by itself satisfy the requirement of taking reasonable care.[95] Failure to do so is not evidence of negligence though it may be a factor to be taken into account in the determination of negligence.[96]

Driver's signals. Drivers should give the customary and recommended signals by hand or electrical means before altering speed or direction, and failure to do so is evidence of negligence.[97] It has been held negligent to fail to give a hand signal of intention to slow down, even though a stop light fitted to the vehicle was working and indicated the application of the brakes.[98] The signal from one driver to another to pass does not absolve the passing driver from taking care, and the driver of the overtaken vehicle may be liable for signalling a following vehicle to pass when it was not safe to do so.[99] He may also be liable, if, in the knowledge that another vehicle is overhauling him, he signals his intention to turn right and then

89 *Drew* v. *Western S.M.T. Co.*, 1947 S.C. 222.
90 *Connachan* v. *S.M.T. Co.*, 1946 S.C. 428.
91 *Provek* v. *Winnipeg, Selkirk and Lake Winnipeg Ry.* [1933] A.C. 61.
92 *McGeown* v. *Greenock Motor Services Co.*, 1943 S.C. 33.
93 *Scott* v. *McIntosh*, 1935 S.C. 199.
94 Every vehicle must have a horn which is in working order: Motor Vehicles (Construction and Use) Regulations, 1951 (S.I. 1951 No. 2101). It is an offence to sound the horn at night (11.30 p.m.–7 a.m.) in a built-up area.
95 *Clerk* v. *Petrie* (1879) 6 R. 1076; see also *Docherty* v. *Watson* (1884) 21 S.L.R. 449.
96 *Wintle* v. *Bristol Tramways and Carriage Co., Ltd.* (1917) 86 L.J.K.B. 240; *McGeown* v. *Greenock Motor Services Co.*, 1943 S.C. 33.
97 *Davies* v. *Swan Motor Co.* [1949] 2 K.B. 291; as to the duty of the driver of a left-hand drive vehicle see *Daborn* v. *Bath Tramways Motor Co.* [1946] 2 All E.R. 333.
98 *Croston* v. *Vaughan* [1938] 1 K.B. 540.
99 *White* v. *Broadbent* [1958] Crim.L.R. 129.

turns right without ascertaining whether his signal had been seen and appreciated.[1]

White lines. A white line was formerly not a traffic sign, but a helpful indication of the road which may best be followed,[2] but is now covered by the Road Traffic Act, 1960, s. 51 (1); to drive slightly over the white line is not necessarily negligent.[3]

A double white line is, however, a traffic sign which must be obeyed,[4] and to have an accident by crossing it is prima facie negligence.

Traffic lights. It is an offence to disobey a traffic light signal,[5] and it is also negligent driving.[6] A driver who is crossing with the lights is under no duty to look out for traffic crossing against the lights,[7] though if he does observe such traffic he must take reasonable care to avoid a collision and do everything reasonably in his power to avert the consequences of any subsequent emergency of which he receives, or ought to have received, due warning.[8] It is not necessarily contributory negligence to go on when the light has changed from green to amber but it is too late, in the driver's view, to stop with safety.[9] Fire-engines,[10] ambulances and police cars are not entitled to disregard traffic lights.

Police signals. Similar principles apply to hand signals given by policemen directing traffic. In a case where a collision occurred, one driver having entered the crossing in reliance on traffic lights and the other having proceeded against the lights in obedience to a signal from a constable, it was held that neither driver had been guilty of negligence, both having entered the crossing in response to signals which they were entitled to obey and there being nothing to suggest to either the emergence of some unseen danger.[11] A driver should not rely on signals given by an unauthorised person and his reliance will be no defence if it would have been negligence to proceed in the absence of such signals.

Emerging from gateway or side road. The driver of a vehicle emerging from a gateway, yard or other entry less than a side-road should take great care to ascertain if the road is clear before entering the street.[12]

---

[1] *Sorrie* v. *Robertson*, 1944 J.C. 95.

[2] *Evans* v. *Cross* [1938] 1 K.B. 694.

[3] *Kirk* v. *Parker* (1938) 60 Ll.L.R. 129; see also *Baker* v. *Market Harborough Industrial Coop. Socy.* [1953] 1 W.L.R. 1472.

[4] Traffic Signs Regs. and General Directions, 1957 (S.I. 1957 No. 13, amended by S.I. 1959 No. 761).

[5] R.T.A., 1960, s. 14.

[6] *Eva* v. *Reeves* [1938] 2 K.B. 393.

[7] *Eva* v. *Reeves* [1938] 2 K.B. 393; *Revie* v. *Ever Ready Co.*, 1947 S.N. 9; *McLelland* v. *Stewart* (1955) 71 Sh.Ct.Rep. 337.

[8] *Wilson* v. *West*, 1947 S.C. 198; *Kennedy* v. *Glasgow Corpn.* (1954) 70 Sh.Ct.Rep. 239.

[9] *McBurnie* v. *Central S.M.T. Co.*, 1939 S.C. 66.

[10] *Ward* v. *L.C.C.* [1938] 2 All E.R. 341; *cf. Watt* v. *Herts. C.C.* [1954] 2 All E.R. 368.

[11] *Wilson* v. *West*, 1947 S.C. 198.

[12] *Campbell* v. *Train*, 1910 S.C. 556; see also *Macandrew* v. *Tillard*, 1909 S.C. 78; *Robertson* v. *Wilson*, 1912 S.C. 1276; *McAllester* v. *Glasgow Corpn.*, 1917 S.C. 430.

It may be negligent in some cases not to have the driver's mate dismount to signal to the driver.[13]

Road junctions and roundabouts. At road junctions the vehicle on the major road has the right of way over a vehicle on, or turning out of, the minor road, but both drivers must exercise caution.[14] The rule is not inflexible and a departure from it is not in all cases necessarily negligent.[15] In some cases both roads are equally major roads, in which case neither driver has any right of precedence.[16] If in such a case a collision takes place prima facie both drivers have been negligent.[16]

It is an offence to disobey either the Slow, Major Road Ahead, or Halt at Major Road Ahead, signs [17] and also evidence of negligence.[18] The driver on the major road is not, however, thereby absolved from any duty of taking care to avoid collision with a vehicle entering from a side road,[19] though greater care is expected from the driver emerging from the side road than from the driver continuing along the main road.[20]

At roundabouts there is no settled order of precedence though it is suggested that vehicles already proceeding round the central island, *i.e.*, approaching from the right, should be accorded precedence by those entering on the circuit round the central island.

Obstructions in the roadway. A driver mustbeprepared for obstructions in the highway such as heaps of road-metal, or stationary or broken-down vehicles, and it is prima facie negligence to run into such an obstruction.[21] But the person or body responsible for the obstruction must take reasonable steps to prevent the obstruction being a danger to road-users, unless he should have statutory authority for it conferring on him absolute immunity,[22] and will be liable if a driver runs into it because it has been left unlighted or unmarked, unless the lights should fail without negligence on the part of the authority responsible for the obstruction,[23] or

---

[13] *Miller* v. *Liverpool Co-op. Soc.* [1940] 4 All E.R. 367.

[14] See *Macandrew* v. *Tillard*, 1909 S.C. 78; *Campbell* v. *Train*, 1910 S.C. 475; *Robertson* v. *Wilson*, 1912 S.C. 1276; *McAllester* v. *Glasgow Corpn.*, 1917 S.C. 430; *McNair* v. *Glasgow Corpn.*, 1923 S.C. 398; *Hutchison* v. *Leslie*, 1927 S.C. 95; *Anderson* v. *St. Andrew's Ambulance Assocn.*, 1943 S.C. 248; *Browne* v. *Central S.M.T. Co.*, 1949 S.C. 9; *Lang* v. *London Transport Executive* [1959] 3 All E.R. 609.

[15] *McNair, supra.*

[16] *Baker* v. *Market Harborough Industrial Co-op. Soc.* [1953] 1 W.L.R. 1472; *France* v. *Parkinson* [1954] 1 All E.R. 739.   [17] R.T.A., 1960, s. 14.

[18] See *Tolhurst* v. *Webster* (1936) 53 T.L.R. 174; *Anderson S. C. Andrew's Ambulance Assocn.*, 1943 S.C. 248; *Browne* v. *Central S.M.T. Co.*, 1949.*St* v. 9; *Buffel* v. *Cardox (G.B.), Ltd.* [1950] 2 All E.R. 878n.; *Lang* v. *London Transport Executive* [1959] 3 All E.R. 609.

[19] *Hutchison* v. *Leslie*, 1927 S.C. 95; *McNair* v. *Glasgow Corpn.*, 1923 S.C. 397; *Browne, supra*; *Lang, supra*; *Cockburn* v. *Scottish Motor Omnibus Co.*, 1964 S.L.T.(Notes) 7.

[20] *Hutchison, supra*; *Lang, supra.*   [21] *Randall* v. *Tarrant* [1955] 1 All E.R. 600.

[22] *Great Central Ry.* v. *Howlett* [1916] 2 A.C. 511.

[23] *Scott* v. *McIntosh*, 1935 S.C. 199; *Greenwood* v. *Central Service Co.* [1940] 2 K.B. 447; *Foster* v. *Gillingham Corpn.* (1942) 111 L.J.K.B. 364; *Ware* v. *Garston Haulage Co.* [1944] K.B. 30; *Maitland* v. *Raisbeck* [1944] K.B. 689; *Fisher* v. *Ruislip & Northwood U.D.C.* [1945] K.B. 584; *Whiting* v. *Middlesex C.C.* [1948] 1 K.B. 162; *Henley* v. *Cameron* (1948) 65 T.L.R. 17; *Hill-Venning* v. *Beszant* [1950] 2 All E.R. 1151; *Harvey* v. *Road Haulage Executive* [1952] 1 K.B. 120; *Parish* v. *Judd* [1960] 3 All E.R. 33; *West* v. *Lawson*, 1949 S.C. 430. See also *Sieghart* v. *B.T.C.* [1956] C.L.Y. 5961. *Cf. Drew* v. *Western S.M.T. Co.*, 1947 S.C. 222.

if an accident is caused by failure to regulate the traffic at the point of obstruction.[24]

A driver must be on his guard for animals which stray on to the road; the owner is not at fault in not preventing them doing so.[25] But where a person drives animals on, or on to, the highway, he must take reasonable thought for other road users, including drivers of vehicles.

Persons crossing the road. Drivers of vehicles must take reasonable care for the safety of persons crossing the highway, and guard against such possibilities as their stopping or turning back,[26] or their being unable to move with normal speed,[27] or their not looking.[28]

Pedestrian crossings. At points in streets marked as pedestrian crossings [29] drivers must accord priority to pedestrians on the crossing and should accordingly approach such crossings at such a speed as to be able to pull up if a pedestrian is proceeding to cross. The driver is not civilly subject to an absolute liability, but must take all reasonable care to give precedence to pedestrians on the crossing.[30] The result of the regulations is that if a pedestrian is injured by a vehicle on a crossing, apart from criminal consequences, it indicates prima facie negligence by the driver, and if the driver can see by the exercise of reasonable care, that there is a pedestrian on the crossing, it is not a defence to prove that the pedestrian did not look before starting to use the crossing.[31] But the driver is not liable if a pedestrian suddenly steps on to a crossing so as to give the driver no opportunity of avoiding a collision and the driver was driving with reasonable care, having regard to the presence of the crossing,[32] or if a pedestrian changes her mind and runs back in front of the vehicle, which was being driven carefully.[33] A pedestrian standing on a refuge in the middle of the street is not " on " a crossing.[34]

Where a pedestrian crossing is controlled by traffic lights, a policeman or a school crossing patrol,[35] both drivers and pedestrians must obey the controlling directions, and a pedestrian crossing against the lights will be at least contributorily negligent if there is an accident.[36] If lights

---

[24] *Nitt* v. *Wimpey* [1951] C.L.Y. 4058.
[25] *Heath's Garage, Ltd.* v. *Hodges* [1916] 2 K.B. 370; *Fraser* v. *Pate*, 1923 S.C. 748; *Hughes* v. *Williams* [1943] 1 K.B. 574; *Searle* v. *Wallbank* [1947] A.C. 341; *Brock* v. *Richards* [1951] 1 K.B. 529.
[26] *McLean* v. *Bell*, 1932 S.C.(H.L.) 21; *Kayser* v. *L.P.T.B.* [1950] 1 All E.R. 231.
[27] *Daly* v. *Liverpool Corpn.* [1939] 3 All E.R. 142.
[28] *Muir* v. *L.N.E.Ry.*, 1946 S.C. 216.
[29] Pedestrian Crossings Regulations, 1954 (S.I. 1954 No. 370); in a criminal court, the duty is absolute: *Hughes* v. *Hall* [1960] 2 All E.R. 504.
[30] *Cf. Leicester* v. *Pearson* [1952] 2 Q.B. 668; *Watson* v. *Wright*, 1940 J.C. 32.
[31] *Bailey* v. *Geddes* [1938] 1 K.B. 156; *Gibbons* v. *Kahl* [1956] 1 Q.B. 59.
[32] *Bailey* v. *Geddes* [1938] 1 K.B. 156; *Knight* v. *Sampson* [1938] 3 All E.R. 309; *Chisholm* v. *L.P.T.B.* [1939] 1 K.B. 426; *Sparks* v. *Edward Ash, Ltd.* [1943] K.B. 223; *L.P.T.B.* v. *Upson* [1949] A.C. 155.
[33] *Kayser* v. *L.P.T.B.* [1950] 1 All E.R. 231.
[34] *Wilkinson* v. *Chetham-Strode* [1940] 2 K.B. 310.
[35] Acting under the School Crossing Patrols Act, 1953.
[36] See *L.P.T.B.* v. *Upson* [1949] A.C. 155; *Gibbons* v. *Kahl* [1956] 1 Q.B. 59.

change while a pedestrian is actually crossing, he is entitled to be allowed to complete his crossing, at least as far as any central refuge or island, but it will be negligence in such a case to leave the refuge without taking due care for his own safety.[37]

One vehicle meeting another head-on. Such vehicles should keep to their respective near-sides and pass off-side to off-side. If necessary one vehicle should slow or stop to allow the other to pass,[38] and one may even need to reverse to a passing-place to allow the other to pass. Which should stop or reverse is regulated by custom and road manners rather than by law but, prima facie, the smaller or lighter or more manoeuvrable vehicle should get out of the way and, on a hill, the vehicle descending should make way for the vehicle ascending. If there is a collision in the highway and there is no evidence against one driver rather than the other, the proper inference is that both are equally to blame.[39] Where a driver, faced with an oncoming vehicle on its wrong side of the road, himself at the last minute turned to his wrong side in an attempt to avoid a collision, his action in such a position of difficulty was held not to amount to contributory negligence.[40]

One vehicle following another. The following vehicle should not approach so close as not to be able to pull up safely if the leading vehicle has to slow or stop suddenly. The respective liabilities of the two vehicles depend on the circumstances and whether there was need or justification for the leading vehicle to stop suddenly or without warning.[41] But that it may have to do so is a contingency which the following driver must guard against and it is some evidence of negligence if he is unable to stop.[42] Similarly a following vehicle should not be driven so close behind another as to be unable to pull up if a person falls or jumps off the leading vehicle, or if a child running after it falls.[43]

Where one vehicle is following another by arrangement, the leader owes a duty of care to the follower not to mislead him or lead him into danger.[44]

One vehicle overtaking another going the same way. At common law, and also under the Highway Code, the overtaking vehicle must pass on the right-hand or off-side of the vehicle being passed, except where the driver of the vehicle being overtaken has indicated his intention to turn right.

37 *Wilkinson* v. *Chetham-Strode* [1940] 2 K.B. 310; *McGeown* v. *Greenock Motor Services Co.*, 1943 S.C. 33.
38 *Barty* v. *Harper*, 1922 S.C. 67.
39 *Baker* v. *Market Harborough Industrial Co-op. Soc.* [1953] 1 W.L.R. 1472; *France* v. *Parkinson* [1954] 1 W.L.R. 581; *cf. Bray* v. *Palmer* [1953] 1 W.L.R. 1455.
40 *Wallace* v. *Bergius*, 1915 S.C. 205.
41 *Valentine* v. *Central S.M.T. Co.* (1951) 67 Sh.Ct.Rep. 56.
42 *Mars* v. *Glasgow Corpn.*, 1940 S.C. 202; *Brown & Lynn* v. *Western S.M.T. Co.*, 1945 S.C. 31; *Initial Services, Ltd.* v. *Central S.M.T. Co.* (1953) 69 Sh.Ct.Rep. 307; *cf. Sharp* v. *Avery* [1938] 4 All E.R. 85; *Neilson* v. *Pantrini*, 1947 S.C. (H.L.) 64.
43 *Auld* v. *McBey* (1881) 8 R. 495.
44 *Sharp* v. *Avery* [1938] 4 All E.R. 85; *Smith* v. *Harris* [1939] 3 All E.R. 960.

This rule does not necessarily apply at roundabouts, or on one-way roads, or when overtaking tramcars. The driver of the overtaking vehicle should see that it is safe to do so, particularly if visibility is poor, and he should not overtake at or near a corner or bend, a road junction, [45] a pedestrian crossing, when approaching the brow of a hill or a hump-backed bridge, where the road narrows or when to overtake would force other vehicles to swerve or reduce speed. The overtaking driver may do so only when he can do so without causing danger to other traffic.[46] The driver of the overtaken vehicle, if turning right, must signal his intention and also observe whether his signal has been appreciated before turning.[47]

Before moving to his off-side preparatory to overtaking a driver should signal his intention to do so, and not do so if he might obstruct other traffic following him. Having overtaken, a driver should not return sharply to his near-side, in front of the overtaken vehicle. A driver ready to be overtaken should give the appropriate signal, and not accelerate or swerve to his off-side while being overtaken.[48] Special care must be taken when passing a vehicle marked " Left hand drive. No signals." [49]

Animals should be passed slowly and without avoidable noise, and allowed ample room.

Tramcars may be overtaken on either side, but if being overtaken on the near-side the driver of the overtaking vehicle must watch for passengers about to alight or even jumping off, for prospective passengers on the roadway as the tram approaches a stopping-place, and for the operations connected with reversing direction at a terminus.[50]

Skidding. The fact that a vehicle skids is neutral and neither establishes that the driver was driving negligently nor exculpates him if he has collided with another vehicle or thing, or a person.[51] The skid cannot, however, be considered in isolation, but in the light of the whole circumstances.[52] It may, depending on the road conditions prevailing at the material time, be some evidence of negligent driving,[52] but it may be attributable to inevitable accident and be quite consistent with his having exercised all due care, or have been caused by the negligence of a third party.[53] The fact that the weather and road conditions are such as to make a vehicle liable to skid does not make it a nuisance to use the vehicle on the road,[54] though it does impose on the driver an enhanced duty of care in his handling of the vehicle. A driver has been held not negligent when on an

---

[45] *Dorrington* v. *Griff Fender* [1953] 1 All E.R. 1177.
[46] *Leaver* v. *Pontypridd U.D.C.* (1911) 76 J.P. 31; *Umphray* v. *Ganson*, 1917 S.C. 371.
[47] *Sorrie* v. *Robertson*, 1944 J.C. 95.
[48] *Milliken* v. *Glasgow Corpn.*, 1918 S.C. 857.
[49] *Daborn* v. *Bath Tramways Co.* [1946] 2 All E.R. 333.
[50] See *Christie* v. *Glasgow Corpn.*, 1927 S.C. 273.
[51] *Laurie* v. *Raglan Building Co.* [1942] 1 K.B. 152.
[52] *McGregor* v. *Dundee Corpn.*, 1962 S.C. 15; see also *Henderson* v. *Mair*, 1928 S.C. 1.
[53] *Hunter* v. *Wright* [1938] 2 All E.R. 621; *Browne* v. *De Luxe Car Services* [1941] 1 K.B. 549; *Burron* v. *West Suffolk C.C.* [1960] 2 All E.R. 26.
[54] *Wing* v. *L.G.O.C.* [1909] 2 K.B. 650; *Parker* v. *L.G.O.C.* (1909) 101 L.T. 623.

icebound road his vehicle skidded partly over the centre of the road and was run into by a lorry.[55]

Mounting the pavement: overturning. Where a vehicle mounts the pavement and collides with a person or object there, that fact is by itself evidence of negligent driving, and that even though it is shown that the vehicle skidded on to the pavement.[56] Similarly for the vehicle to overturn is evidence of negligence on the driver's part.[57]

Tyre bursting. An accident caused by a tyre-burst is prima facie indicative of fault.[58] A tyre-burst is in itself neutral since it may or may not be due to negligence, but the inference of negligence is likely to be drawn unless the defenders show that the burst could not have been foreseen or prevented by reasonable care and diligence.[59]

Similarly the defence of latent defect, where a road wheel collapsed and caused an accident, failed, there being insufficient evidence in the circumstances to displace the prima facie inference of fault.[60]

Loading. Reasonable care must be taken to see that a vehicle is properly loaded and the load properly lashed and secured. Accordingly, there is prima facie negligence if the load or part of it falls or is knocked off and injures any person on the highway.[61] But *res ipsa loquitur* does not necessarily apply, particularly where there has been possible meddlesome interference by the pursuer.[62] It may also be negligence to discover that the load is leaking and not to try to warn other road-users of danger.[63]

Opening vehicle doors. Reasonable care must be taken before opening a door to avoid striking a pedestrian, cyclist, or another vehicle[64]; conversely a vehicle should not, if possible, pass another, stationary, vehicle so close as to be in danger of colliding if a door is opened.

A person should not close a door at a time when other persons are in close proximity without ascertaining that he can do so with safety, and it may be negligent to take no precautions.[65]

Parking. It may be negligent *vis-à-vis* an employer for a driver to park his vehicle unlocked or unattended, whereby it is stolen.[66] *Vis-à-vis*

---

[55] *Gibson, Mercer & Co.* v. *Partridge* (1957) 73 Sh.Ct.Rep. 233.
[56] *Walton* v. *Vanguard Motorbus Co.* (1908) 25 T.L.R. 13; *Barnes U.D.C.* v. *L.G.O.C.* (1908) 100 L.T. 115; *McGowan* v. *Stott* (1923) 99 L.J.K.B. 357; *Ellor* v. *Selfridge* (1930) 46 T.L.R. 236; *Liffen* v. *Watson* (1939) 161 L.T. 351; *Laurie* v. *Raglan Building Co.* [1942] 1 K.B. 152; *N.S. Hydro Electric Board* v. *Townsley* (1952) 68 Sh.Ct.Rep. 137; *Wells* v. *Beattie's Bakeries, Ltd.* (1953) 69 Sh.Ct.Rep. 134.
[57] *Halliwell* v. *Venables* (1930) 99 L.J.K.B. 353; *Verney* v. *Wilkins* [1962] C.L.Y. 2651.
[58] *Barkway* v. *South Wales Tpt. Co.* [1950] A.C. 185.
[59] *Elliot* v. *Young's Bus Service*, 1945 S.C. 445.
[60] *Ritchie* v. *Western S.M.T. Co.*, 1935 S.L.T. 13.
[61] *Connelly* v. *L.M.S.Ry.*, 1940 S.C. 477; *Farrugia* v. *G.W.Ry.* [1947] 2 All E.R. 565; see also *Milliken* v. *Glasgow Corpn.*, 1918 S.C. 857.
[62] *Connelly, supra.*
[63] *Pope* v. *Fraser* (1939) 55 T.L.R. 324.
[64] *Shears* v. *Matthews* [1948] 2 All E.R. 1064; *Watson* v. *Lowe* [1950] 1 All E.R. 100; *Jones* v. *Prothero* [1952] 1 All E.R. 434; *cf. Eaton* v. *Cobb* [1950] 1 All E.R. 1076.
[65] *Hett* v. *Mackenzie*, 1939 S.C. 350.
[66] *W.L.R. Traders* v. *British and Northern Shipping Agency* [1955] 1 Lloyd's Rep. 554; *Fulwood House* v. *Standard Bentwood Chair Co.* [1956] 1 Lloyd's Rep. 160.

other road users it may be negligence to park in a place which narrows the road or obscures the view.[67]

Vehicles left unattended. It is an offence [68] to leave a vehicle on any road in such a position or in such condition or in such circumstances as to be likely to cause danger to other persons using the road, and such conduct may also amount to negligence, as where a vehicle was left on a slope with only a block of wood under a wheel to hold it,[69] or a lorry was left at the top of a steep street with the engine running and without precautions to secure it,[70] or a car was left on a steep hill and after some time, for an unexplained reason, ran down the hill.[71] Merely to leave a vehicle unattended is no evidence of negligence because, if properly parked, it cannot move by itself.[72] But it may be negligent to leave a vehicle by the roadside at night without lights, particularly if it could have been parked on the verge.[73]

If a vehicle is left unattended in a safe and proper place, the owner is not liable if a horse shies at it and gets out of control,[74] interfering third parties seek to move it and do damage,[75] or if children climb thereon and are injured.[76] It may be otherwise if the place is dangerous or unsuitable or if the intervention of children or other persons seems likely,[77] or if the vehicle is left in a condition, *e.g.*, in gear and with brakes not applied, which might cause an accident even without interference.[78]

(b) Omnibuses, trolley-buses and tramcars

In general the duties of care incumbent on the drivers of such vehicles towards other persons on the road are the same as those owed by the drivers of other mechanically or electrically propelled vehicles, though the frequency with which such vehicles start and stop, come in to the pavement and move out again requires particular care. Certain specialties apply, however, to tramcars.[79]

---

[67] *Brockhurst* v. *War Office* [1957] C.L.Y. 2388; *Murray* v. *Park Bros. (Liverpool)* [1959] C.L.Y. 2222.

[68] R.T.A., 1960, s. 16.

[69] *Martin* v. *Stanborough* (1924) 41 T.L.R. 1.

[70] *Hambrook* v. *Stokes* [1925] 1 K.B. 141.

[71] *Parker* v. *Miller* (1926) 42 T.L.R. 408.

[72] *Ruoff* v. *Long* [1916] 1 K.B. 148; *McCusker* v. *Armstrong*, 1946 S.N. 113.

[73] *Henley* v. *Cameron* [1949] L.J.R. 989; *Hill-Venning* v. *Beszant* [1950] 2 All E.R. 1151; *cf. Harvey* v. *Road Haulage Executive* [1952] 1 K.B. 120; *Parish* v. *Judd* [1960] 3 All E.R. 33.

[74] *Macfarlane* v. *Colam*, 1908 S.C. 56.

[75] *Ruoff* v. *Long* [1916] 1 K.B. 148.

[76] *Donovan* v. *Union Cartage Co.* [1932] 2 K.B. 7.

[77] *Rawsthorne* v. *Orley* [1937] 3 All E.R. 902; *Culkin* v. *McFie* [1939] 3 All E.R. 613; *Flemington Trust* v. *Brown & Lynn* (1953) 69 Sh.Ct.Rep. 108; *Creed* v. *McGeoch* [1955] 3 All E.R. 123.

[78] *McCusker, supra.*

[79] As to accidents arising from defects in construction of tramway cars see *Cass* v. *Edinburgh Tramways*, 1909 S.C. 1068; *Suttie* v. *Edinburgh Tramways*, 1910, 1 S.L.T. 125; *Gibb* v. *Edinburgh Tramways*, 1912 S.C. 580; *Adams* v. *Lanarkshire Tramways Co.*, 1918, 1 S.L.T. 244.

Unlike other road vehicles tramcars run on fixed rails and have no liberty to deviate from their fixed path. Other vehicles meeting or passing them or crossing their paths must accordingly take account of this.[80] Trolley-buses have freedom of movement limited by the length of their trolley-poles. Other vehicles, not using flanged wheels, may also use the part of the roadway in which the tramway track is laid, except at places where the trams have a private track, separate from the roadway.[80] The fact that trams have priority in the use of the part of the road containing the tracks does not in any way exempt drivers from the common law obligation to take reasonable care not to injure persons lawfully using the highway.[81] A tramdriver must therefore beware of animals [82] and other traffic [83] and be satisfied that there is adequate clearance before he overtakes another vehicle.[84]

Other vehicles may pass a tramcar either on its near or on its offside, and a tramdriver must be prepared for this.[85] It has been observed that they should do so on the nearside, not the offside,[86] but special care must be taken if so doing as intending passengers may step on to the roadway as the tram approaches, and passengers may jump off,[87] or even be thrown off,[88] while the tram is in motion, while passing a tramcar on the offside takes the overtaking vehicle on to its wrong side of the road in face of any oncoming traffic.

Duties of drivers to their passengers. Apart from the duties of care incumbent on the drivers of public service vehicles towards other persons on the road the carrier and his driver owe duties of care to their passengers. This is to carry with due care.[89] The duties are the same, whether the carriage is gratuitous or for reward,[90] and whether regarded as arising *ex contractu*, from an implied term in the contract of carriage, or *ex delicto*, from the passengers' being within the ambit of reasonable foresight of harm.[91] A driver is not necessarily at fault if he starts his vehicle before a passenger is aboard, in that he may be entitled to rely on

---

[80] *Ogston* v. *Aberdeen District Tramways* (1896) 24 R.(H.L.) 8.
[81] *Rattee* v. *Norwich Electric Tramway Co.* (1902) 18 T.L.R. 562; *cf. Brocklehurst* v. *Manchester Tramways Co.* (1886) 17 Q.B.D. 118; *McKendrick* v. *Stewart & McDonald*, 1934 S.N. 4.
[82] *Rattee, supra; Downing* v. *Birmingham and Midland Trams* (1888) 5 T.L.R. 40; *Craig* v. *Glasgow Corpn.*, 1919 S.C.(H.L.) 1.
[83] *McDermaid* v. *Edinburgh Tramways* (1884) 12 R. 15; *Shields* v. *Glasgow Corpn.*, 1917, 2 S.L.T. 156; *Taylor* v. *Dumbarton Tramways*, 1918 S.C. 96; *Craig* v. *Glasgow Corpn.*, 1919 S.C. (H.L.) 1; *McKendrick* v. *Stewart & McDonald*, 1934 S.N. 4.
[84] *Leaver* v. *Pontypridd U.D.C.* (1911) 56 S.J. 32; *Milliken* v. *Glasgow Corpn.*, 1918 S.C. 857.
[85] *Christie* v. *Glasgow Corpn.*, 1927 S.C. 273.
[86] *Ramsay* v. *Thomson* (1881) 9 R. 140; *Jardine* v. *Stonefield Laundry Co.* (1887) 14 R. 839.
[87] *McSherry* v. *Glasgow Corpn.*, 1917 S.C. 156.
[88] *Watt* v. *Glasgow Corpn.*, 1919 S.C. 300; *Stewart* v. *Glasgow Tramways* (1883) 21 S.L.R. 47.
[89] *Readhead* v. *Midland Ry.* (1869) L.R. 4 Q.B. 379; *Barkway* v. *South Wales Transport* [1950] A.C. 185; *Sutherland* v. *Glasgow Corpn.*, 1951 S.C.(H.L.) 1.
[90] *Lygo* v. *Newbold* (1854) 9 Ex. 302, 305, *per* Parke B; *Austin* v. *G.W.Ry.* (1867) L.R. 2 Q.B. 442; *Hyman* v. *Nye* (1881) 6 Q.B.D. 685; *Smith* v. *Turnbull* (1895) 2 S.L.T. 549; *Karavias* v. *Callinicos* [1917] W.N. 323; *Harris* v. *Perry* [1903] 2 K.B. 219; *Ritchie* v. *Western S.M.T. Co.*, 1935 S.L.T. 13; *Lewys* v. *Burnett and Dunbar* [1945] 2 All E.R. 555; *Elliot* v. *Young's Bus Service*, 1945 S.C. 445.
[91] *Cf. Austin* v. *G.W.Ry., supra; Foulkes* v. *Metropolitan Ry.* (1880) 5 C.P.D. 157.

his conductor's bell signal,[92] nor because the vehicle bounces on its springs and a passenger falls.[93]

Who are passengers. The category of passengers to whom the carrier owes duties of care clearly covers all who have entered into contractual relations with the carrier by boarding his vehicle as fare-paying travellers, but also persons who have not yet paid or even do not intend to pay the fare, or who intend to pay only part of the due fare.[94]

Avoidance of " contracting-out." By statute [95] a contract for the conveyance of a passenger in a public service vehicle is void so far as it purports to negative or restrict liability in respect of the death of or injury to a passenger while being carried in, entering or alighting from the vehicle.

Provision of roadworthy vehicle. Carriers of passengers are not under an absolute liability to provide a safe and roadworthy vehicle but must take reasonable care to do so. What is reasonable in the circumstances is a high degree of care, " the duty of exercising all vigilance to see that whatever is required for the safe conveyance of their passengers is in fit and proper order." The carrier is not, however, liable for " a disaster occasioned from a latent defect in the machinery which they are obliged to use, which no human skill or care could either have prevented or detected." [96]

This implies a duty to undertake regular inspections of the vehicle in accordance with the practice of reasonably careful carriers,[97] and the happening of an accident is evidence of negligence on the carrier's part which can be countered by proof that all reasonable skill and care were used to discover and remedy defects, or that the failure was due to a latent defect in the vehicle which was not attributable to the carrier and could not have been detected by any reasonable exercise of skill and care.[98] There is no liability if the accident was caused by defect or failure in a part of the vehicle supplied by a reputable manufacturer, *e.g.,* fracture of a road-spring, the defect being latent *quoad* the carrier.[99]

The vehicle operators are also liable for faults in construction which amount to failure to take reasonable and practicable precautions for the safety of their passengers.[1] When a bus was operated with the doors

---

[92] *O'Hare* v. *Scottish Omnibuses, Ltd.,* 1957 S.L.T.(Notes) 14, not followed in *McLaughlin* v. *Glasgow Corpn.* (1963) 79 Sh.Ct.Rep. 172.

[93] *Bias* v. *Lowland Motorways, Ltd.* (1957) 73 Sh.Ct.Rep. 288.

[94] *Vosper* v. *G.W.Ry.* [1928] 1 K.B. 340 (passenger travelling first-class with third-class ticket entitled to recover for loss of luggage).

[95] Road Traffic Act, 1960, s. 151.

[96] *Readhead* v. *Midland Ry.* (1869) L.R. 4 Q.B. 379.

[97] *Bremner* v. *Williams* (1824) 1 C. & P. 414; *Elliot* v. *Young's Bus Service,* 1945 S.C. 445; *Barkway* v. *South Wales Transport Co., Ltd.* [1949] 1 K.B. 54 [1950] A.C. 185.

[98] *Mathieson* v. *MacNeill,* 1948 S.L.T. (Notes) 24.

[99] *Donnelly* v. *Glasgow Corpn.,* 1953 S.C. 107, as overruled and explained by *Davie* v. *New Merton Board Mills* [1959] A.C. 604.

[1] *Cass* v. *Edinburgh & District Tramways Co.,* 1909 S.C. 1068; *Adams* v. *Lanarkshire Tramways Co.,* 1918, 1 S.L.T. 244; *Suttie* v. *Edinburgh & District Tramways Co.,* 1910, 1 S.L.T. 125; *cf. Gibb* v. *Edinburgh & District Tramways Co.,* 1912 S.C. 580.

open, the owners were held liable to a passenger who fell out in respect of the failure to provide a central pillar on the platform, and that notwithstanding that the vehicle had a certificate of fitness issued in respect of it.[2]

Safe driving. Passengers have a claim if they are injured by the negligent management of the vehicle, as where the vehicle is driven recklessly, producing fear of an accident,[3] or brushed against a tree,[4] or started prematurely [5] or suddenly, throwing the passenger off,[6] or accelerated,[7] or the passenger is thrown down when the vehicle stops suddenly,[8] or thrown off the platform [9] or out of the door [10] or otherwise hurt [11] when the vehicle swerves. A sudden swerve is evidence of negligent driving,[12] as is sudden braking, but the mere fact that a passenger falls from the platform or doorway is a neutral fact.[13] A jolt or swerve must be out of the ordinary to be actionable.[14] A person who jumps from the step while the vehicle is in motion will usually be held at least partly to blame for his own injuries, even if done by reason of fear of being thrown off.[15] The driver is not necessarily in fault if intending passengers crowd forward and one has a foot run over.[16]

A passenger is not entitled to travel on the step [17] and it may, depending on the circumstances, amount to contributory negligence for him to descend to the step before the vehicle has stopped, or almost stopped,[18] but there is no rule that such conduct is negligent.[19]

A conductor or conductress is responsible for signalling to the driver to stop, and to go on,[20] and should exercise reasonable care that such

[2] *Wyngrove's C.B.* v. *Scottish Omnibuses, Ltd.,* 1965 S.L.T. (Notes) 55.
[3] *Walker* v. *Pitlochry Motor Co.,* 1930 S.C. 565.
[4] *Radley* v. *L.P.T.B.* [1942] 1 All E.R. 433; *Hale* v. *Hants & Dorset Motor Services* [1947] 2 All E.R. 628.
[5] *Holland* v. *North Metropolitan Tramway Co.* (1886) 3 T.L.R. 245; *Annand* v. *Aberdeen District Tramways Co.* (1890) 17 R. 808; *Spindlow* v. *Glasgow Corpn.,* 1933 S.C. 580; *Wilkie* v. *L.P.T.B.* [1947] 1 All E.R. 258; *Davies* v. *Liverpool Corpn.* [1949] 2 All E.R. 175.
[6] *Geeves* v. *L.G.O.C.* (1901) 17 T.L.R. 249; *Clarke* v. *Edinburgh Tramways,* 1914 S.C. 775; *Maitland* v. *Glasgow Corpn.,* 1947 S.C. 20; *Mackenzie* v. *Aberdeen Mags.* (1950) 66 Sh. Ct.Rep. 13.
[7] *Stewart* v. *Glasgow Tramways Co.* (1883) 21 S.L.R. 47.
[8] *Mars* v. *Glasgow Corpn.,* 1940 S.C. 202; *Ballingall* v. *Glasgow Corpn.,* 1948 S.C. 160; *Sutherland* v. *Glasgow Corpn.,* 1951 S.C.(H.L.) 1; *cf. Parkinson* v. *Liverpool Corpn.* [1950] 1 All E.R. 367; *McMinigal* v. *Glasgow Corpn.* (1957) 73 Sh.Ct.Rep. 172.
[9] *O'Hara* v. *Central S.M.T. Co.,* 1941 S.C. 363; *Watt* v. *Glasgow Corpn.,* 1919 S.C. 300; *Gray* v. *Glasgow Corpn.,* 1926 S.C. 967; *Baxter* v. *Aberdeen Mags.,* 1933 S.L.T. 447; *Grant* v. *Alexander,* 1937 S.L.T. 572.
[10] *Folkes* v. *N. London Ry.* (1892) 8 T.L.R. 269; *Jude* v. *Edinburgh Corpn.,* 1943 S.C. 399; *Allam* v. *Western S.M.T. Co.,* 1944 S.L.T. 100; *Johnstone* v. *Western S.M.T. Co.,* 1954 S.L.T.(Notes) 16.
[11] *Doonan* v. *S.M.T. Co.,* 1950 S.C. 136; *Baxter* v. *Mags. of Aberdeen,* 1933 S.L.T. 447.
[12] *O'Hara, supra; Doonan, supra; Baxter, supra.*
[13] *Johnstone* v. *Western S.M.T. Co.* (1955) 105 L.J. 762.
[14] *Law* v. *Alexander* (1951) 67 Sh.Ct.Rep. 5.
[15] *McSherry* v. *Glasgow Corpn.,* 1917 S.C. 156.
[16] *McNally* v. *Tait,* 1923 S.L.T. 46; *cf. Degan* v. *Dundee Corpn.,* 1940 S.C. 457.
[17] *McSherry* v. *Glasgow Corpn.,* 1917 S.C. 156.
[18] *McSherry, supra; Stewart* v. *Glasgow Tramways & Omnibus Co.* (1883) 21 S.L.R. 47; *Watt* v. *Glasgow Corpn.,* 1919 S.C. 300; *Caldwell* v. *Glasgow Corpn.,* 1936 S.C. 490; *cf. Askew* v. *Bowtell* [1947] 1 All E.R. 883.
[19] *Grant* v. *Alexander,* 1937 S.L.T. 572.   [20] *Clarke* v. *Edinburgh Tramways,* 1914 S.C. 775.

signals are given only when it is safe to do so, but is not automatically in fault if absent from the platform when the vehicle has to stop or start.[21] The conductor is under no general duty to prevent passengers from standing on the platform where they are in danger of being thrown off into the roadway.[22] The vehicle operator will not be liable for an accident caused by the conductress having acted out of deliberate malice, in furtherance of a private quarrel.[23] In some circumstances a driver and conductor may be in fault in not stopping at the proper stopping-place, as where a rush of people attempting to board a tram, which did not stop, caused a passenger on the platform to fall to the road,[24] or in failing to warn a passenger that where the vehicle had halted was not a stop.[25] The opening of a bus door by the driver before the vehicle had stopped has been held not by itself to be an invitation to alight.[26]

Statutory formulation of common law duty of care. The Occupiers' Liability (Scotland) Act, 1960, s. 1, provides that a person having control of any vehicle owes to persons entering thereon the duty (s. 2) of taking such care as in all the circumstances of the case is reasonable to see that the passenger will not suffer injury or damage by reason of any danger which is due to the state of the vehicle or to anything done or omitted to be done in relation to it and for which the person in control is in law responsible. This duty may be extended, restricted, modified or excluded by agreement.

(c) Horse-drawn vehicles

The same general principles apply to horse-drawn as to mechanically propelled vehicles, but particular care has to be taken having regard to the danger of the horse becoming restive, being startled, or moving of its own volition.[27] There is a presumption of fault if a horse drawing a vehicle runs away and knocks down a person in daylight in a public street.[28]

It is prima facie negligence if a horse-drawn vehicle is left unattended and the horse bolts,[29] or if children play with the animal and are injured

---

21 *Gray* v. *Glasgow Corpn.*, 1926 S.C. 967; *Mottram* v. *South Lancs. Tpt. Co.* [1942] 2 All E.R. 452; *cf. McKendrick* v. *Stewart & McDonald*, 1934 S.N. 4. But see *Davies* v. *Liverpool Corpn.* [1949] 2 All E.R. 175.

22 *Rodger* v. *Alexander* [1951] C.L.Y. 4427.

23 *Power* v. *Central S.M.T. Co.*, 1949 S.C. 376.

24 *Buchanan* v. *Glasgow Corpn.*, 1919 S.C. 515.

25 *Prescott* v. *Lancashire Tpt.* [1953] 1 All E.R. 288; *cf. Baird* v. *S. London Tramways Co.* (1886) 2 T.L.R. 756.

26 *Fraser* v. *Alexander*, 1964 S.L.T.(Notes) 79.

27 See *Wakeman* v. *Robinson* (1823) 1 Bing. 213; *North* v. *Smith* (1861) 10 C.B.(N.S.) 572; *Simson* v. *L.G.O.C.* (1873) L.R. 8 C.P. 390; *Burlain* v. *Bilezikdji* (1889) 5 T.L.R. 673; *Macfarlane* v. *Colam*, 1908 S.C. 56.

28 *Snee* v. *Durkie* (1903) 6 F. 42; *cf. Shaw* v. *Croall* (1885) 12 R. 1186.

29 *McEwan* v. *Cuthill* (1897) 25 R. 57; *Hendry* v. *McDougall*, 1923 S.C. 378; *Gayler & Pope, Ltd.* v. *Davies* [1924] 2 K.B. 75; *Cutler* v. *United Dairies* [1933] 2 K.B. 297; *Haynes* v. *Harwood* [1935] 1 K.B. 1, 46; *cf. Aldham* v. *United Dairies* [1940] 1 K.B. 507; *McCairns* v. *Wordie* (1901) 8 S.L.T. 354; *McIntosh* v. *Waddell* (1896) 24 R. 80.

by it,[30] or even if a passer-by struck the horse and caused it to do damage,[31] but not if the horse is unyoked.[32] Reasonable care must be taken to tether the horse securely and in a place where it will not cause damage, and, where it is tethered in a yard, care must be taken that it does not stray on the street.[33] It is not negligent to unload a cart without having a person to hold the horse's head,[34] nor to look out for pedestrians in the vicinity before removing a nose-bag.[35]

Negligence has also been inferred where a horse ran away in consequence of the breaking of a chain-stay of the cart and did damage.[36]

(d) Cycles

The same general principles apply to cyclists as to mechanically propelled vehicles though the Highway Code contains warnings applicable specially to cyclists. The cyclist is in fault if he does not have his bicycle under such control as to be able to stop and avoid an accident which he should have been able to avoid.[37] Cyclists must give signals of intention to turn and, in particular circumstances, may be in fault if they do not look round before turning across the line of traffic.[38] They must carry adequate lights or, at very least, substitute lighting giving adequate warning of their presence on the road.[39]

(e) Animals

A person leading or driving animals onto or along the highway must take reasonable care to keep them under control and prevent them causing damage to persons using the highway or to property on or adjacent thereto,[40] and must take reasonable precautions, as by carrying a light after dark,[41] to warn other road-users of the presence of the animals. Thus the owner of animals has been held liable where a heifer tossed a pedestrian,[42] where a cow trampled on a pedestrian,[43] where a cow was allowed to wander into the path of a car,[42] and where a colt was not secured and ran across the road.[44] But he is not liable if the animal breaks loose, if he has used the precautions which are usual and reasonably safe in the circumstances, even though other methods are

---

[30] Lynch v. Nurdin (1841) 1 Q.B. 29.
[31] Illidge v. Goodwin (1831) 5 C. & P. 190; Haynes v. Harwood, supra.
[32] Donovan v. Union Cartage Co. [1933] 2 K.B. 71.
[33] Deen v. Davies [1935] 2 K.B. 282; cf. Smith v. Wallace (1898) 25 R. 761; Milne v. Nimmo (1898) 25 R. 1150.
[34] Hayman v. Hewitt (1789) Peake's Add.Cas. 170.
[35] Hogg v. Cupar District Cttee., 1912, 1 S.L.T. 57; cf. Shaw v. Croall (1885) 12 R. 1186.
[36] Welsh v. Lawrence (1818) 2 Chit. 262, expld. in Phillips v. Britannia Laundry Co. [1923] 1 K.B. 539, 550.
[37] Foster v. Rintoul (1891) 28 S.L.R. 636.
[38] Dalziel v. Callan (1948) 64 Sh.Ct.Rep. 259.
[39] Connachan v. S.M.T. Co., 1946 S.C. 428.
[40] Pinn v. Rew (1916) 32 T.L.R. 451.
[41] Highway Code, §§ 64–69; it is not, by itself, negligence not to carry a light; Catchpole v. Minster (1913) 109 L.T. 933; Turner v. Coates [1917] 1 K.B. 670.
[42] Turnbull v. Wieland (1917) 33 T.L.R. 144; Ludlam v. Peel (1939) 83 S.J. 832.
[43] Phillips v. Nicoll (1884) 11 R. 592.
[44] Turner v. Coates, supra.

well known and more secure.[45] He may be liable if an animal escapes from its stable, having been insecurely tethered.[46]

Where an animal, being driven along the road, strays into an adjacent building and there does damage, it is evidence of negligence against the drovers.[47]

The same principles apply to dogs; the owner is liable only if he has been negligent in allowing the dog to be loose, or if he should have known from the dog's habits that it was liable to wander so as to be a danger to other road-users.[48]

Liability for harm caused by animals straying on the roadway. There is no duty on an occupier of land in the country to fence his land or premises securely under pain of incurring liability to anyone injured by reason of the presence of a harmless animal on the roadway.[49] This rule is traditional [50] and any other might be unduly onerous on farmers. "The motorist must put up with the farmer's cattle: the farmer must endure the motorist." [51]

A landowner is accordingly under no liability if animals are allowed to come or to be on the road, and they are involved in a collision with road-users.[52] Thus landowners have been held not liable where fowls collided with a cyclist,[53] a sow caused a horse to shy and collide with a car,[54] cows collided with a cyclist,[55] a horse crossing the road collided with a bicycle,[56] sheep escaped and collided with a car,[57] a horse broke out of a field and injured a person on the road,[58] horses emerged from a farm and collided with a car,[59] a cyclist ran into a horse grazing by the highway,[60] frightened calves escaped and collided with a cyclist,[61] a horse

---

[45] *Harper* v. *G.N.S.Ry.* (1886) 13 R. 1139.

[46] *Deen* v. *Davies* [1935] 2 K.B. 282.

[47] *Tillett* v. *Ward* (1882) 10 Q.B.D. 17; *Gilligan* v. *Robb*, 1910 S.C. 856; *Gayler and Pope* v. *Davies* [1924] 2 K.B. 75; *cf. Cameron* v. *Hamilton's Auction Marts, Ltd.* (1955) 71 Sh.Ct.Rep. 285.

[48] *Jones* v. *Owen* (1871) 24 L.T.(N.S.) 587; *Milligan* v. *Henderson*, 1915 S.C. 1030; *Hines* v. *Tonsley* (1926) 70 S.J. 732; *Pitcher* v. *Martin* [1937] 2 All E.R. 918. See also *Burns* v. *Western S.M.T. Co.* (1955) 71 Sh.Ct.Rep. 232.

[49] *Hadwell* v. *Righton* [1907] 2 K.B. 345 (fowls upsetting cyclist); *Higgins* v. *Searle* (1909) 25 T.L.R. 301 (sow causing horse to shy); *Jones* v. *Lee* (1911) 28 T.L.R. 92; *Heath's Garage, Ltd.* v. *Hodges* [1916] 2 K.B. 370 (sheep); *Carswell* v. *Ramage*, 1919, 2 S.L.T. 268; *Fraser* v. *Pate*, 1923 S.C. 748; *Sinclair* v. *Muir*, 1933 S.N. 42, 62; *Turner* v. *Coates* [1917] 1 K.B. 670; *Hughes* v. *Williams* [1943] 1 K.B. 574; *Searle* v. *Wallbank* [1947] A.C. 341; *Brock* v. *Richards* [1951] 1 K.B. 529 (horses); *Wright* v. *Callwood* [1950] 2 K.B. 515 (calves).

[50] *Searle, supra; Brock, supra.*

[51] *Searle, supra,* at 361, *per* Lord du Parcq.

[52] *Fraser* v. *Pate*, 1923 S.C. 748; *Brackenborough* v. *Spalding U.D.C.* [1942] A.C. 310.

[53] *Hadwell* v. *Righton* [1907] 2 K.B. 345.

[54] *Higgins* v. *Searle* (1909) 100 L.T. 280.

[55] *Ellis* v. *Banyard* (1911) 106 L.T. 51; *cf. Milne* v. *MacIntosh* (1952) 68 Sh.Ct.Rep. 301.

[56] *Jones* v. *Lee* (1911) 106 L.T. 123.

[57] *Heath's Garage, Ltd.* v. *Hodges* [1916] 2 K.B. 370.

[58] *Carswell* v. *Ramage*, 1919, 2 S.L.T. 268.

[59] *Hughes* v. *Williams* [1943] K.B. 574.

[60] *Searle* v. *Wallbank* [1947] A.C. 341.

[61] *Wright* v. *Callwood* [1950] 2 K.B. 515.

jumped the hedge and landed on a motor-cyclist,[62] or a stirk emerged from a side-road and collided with a motor cyclist.[63]

This, however, must be regarded as an exception, and in general the owner of an animal will be liable if he negligently [64] allows a beast to do harm while on the roadway, or by its coming there.[65]

Thus there is liability for harm resulting from driving animals along the road if the drover has them under insufficient control,[66] or has insufficient strength and experience to manage them,[67] or otherwise there is evidence of negligence.[68] In *Harpers* v. *G.N.S. Ry.*[69] the majority view [70] was that a person conveying a bull through the streets of a town was not liable to pedestrians for damage caused by its breaking loose unless fault were established, and that there was no liability if the custodier of the bull used the precautions which are usual and reasonably safe in the circumstances even though there were other methods known ... liability clearly depended on *culpa*, which was

... in accordance with the usual principle the owner of the animals will be liable if the animals were *ferae naturae*, or if, being *mansuetae naturae*, they have acted in a way contrary to their ordinary nature or have previously given indication of particular vice, which requires him to take precautions.[71]

There is liability too if the animal is known to have special or dangerous characteristics, so that harm is reasonably foreseeable.[72]

Liability may also exist if animals escape from land to such an extent as to cause an obstruction on the highway,[73] or if an animal is negligently allowed to stray on the road and causes damage to other road-users.[74]

---

[62] *Brock* v. *Richards* [1951] 1 K.B. 529.

[63] *Milne* v. *MacIntosh* (1952) 68 Sh.Ct.Rep. 301.

[64] *Hammack* v. *White* (1862) 11 C.B.(N.S.) 588; *Manzoni* v. *Douglas* (1880) 6 Q.B.D. 145 *Aldham* v. *United Dairies, Ltd.* [1940] 1 K.B. 507.

[65] *Ellis* v. *Banyard* (1911) 28 T.L.R. 122; *Wright* v. *Callwood* [1950] 2 K.B. 515; *Lathall* v. *Joyce* [1939] 3 All E.R. 854.

[66] *Karrigan* v. *Edgar* (1888) 4 Sh.Ct.Rep. 83; *Smith* v. *Swan* (1888) 4 Sh.Ct.Rep. 162; *Pinn* v. *Rew* (1916) 32 T.L.R. 451; *cf. Turnbull* v. *Wieland* (1916) 33 T.L.R. 143; *Catchpole* v. *Minster* (1913) 30 T.L.R. 111 (no duty when driving sheep at night to carry light) probably could not be supported today.

[67] *Milligan* v. *Wedge* (1840) 12 Ad. & El. 737; *Brown* v. *Fulton* (1881) 9 R. 36; *Gilligan* v. *Robb*, 1910 S.C. 856; *Lanark Plate Glass Mutual Protection Soc.* v. *Capie* (1908) 24 Sh. Ct.Rep. 156.

[68] *Phillips* v. *Nicoll* (1884) 11 R. 592; *Harpers* v. *G.N.S.Ry.* (1886) 13 R. 1139; *cf. Walker* v. *Bowie* (1888) 4 Sh.Ct.Rep. 188; *Smith* v. *Scott* (1923) 39 Sh.Ct.Rep. 105; *Cessford* v. *Young*, 1933 S.L.T. 502.

[69] (1886) 13 R. 1139; *cf. Tillett* v. *Ward* (1882) 10 Q.B.D. 17.

[70] Dissenting, L.J.C. Moncreiff, who favoured strict liability; the precautions, in his view, must be absolutely efficient.

[71] *Milligan* v. *Henderson*, 1915 S.C. 1030.

[72] *Shanks* v. *Cartha Athletic Club* (1924) 40 Sh.Ct.Rep. 89; *Ellis* v. *Banyard* (1911) 28 T.L.R. 122; *cf. Deen* v. *Davies* [1935] 2 K.B. 282; *Aldham* v. *United Dairies, Ltd.* [1940] 1 K.B. 507; *Brock* v. *Richards* [1951] 1 K.B. 529; *Searle, supra*, at p. 360.

[73] *Ellis* v. *Banyard* (1911) 28 T.L.R. 122; *cf. Cunningham* v. *Whelan* (1917) 52 Ir.L.T.R. 67.

[74] *Deen* v. *Davies* [1935] 2 K.B. 282.

In the streets of an inhabited area in particular, moreover, the owner of an animal is liable for negligent harm done by the animal to person or property.[75] Negligence must be established.

If a horse is left unattended in a public street and it bolts, that may be prima facie evidence of negligence on the part of the owner,[76] even if the bolting has been provoked by the mischievous act of a third party, if that was foreseeable.[77] So, too, where a horse was left unattended and attacked a passer-by, it being found that the driver should have known that the horse was likely to do harm.[78]

(f) Riding animals

The rider of a horse has been held not to be negligent merely by reason of trying a horse whose temperament was unknown in a frequented thoroughfare,[79] but it is negligence to spur a horse on when it was within kicking distance of a pedestrian,[80] and probably also to gallop it on a busy road, or otherwise to ride without due regard for the safety of other road-users.

(g) Pedestrians

A pedestrian has the same right to use a road as have vehicles[81]; he is entitled to expect that the drivers of vehicles will show reasonable consideration and take reasonable care for his safety,[82] but on the other hand he must take reasonable care for his own safety and show reasonable consideration for vehicle drivers.

There has been said to be a strong presumption of negligence against a driver who runs down a pedestrian in daylight,[83] though it has been observed in the case of a child that the onus was on the pursuer to prove fault and not on the driver to prove inevitable accident.[84]

In the interests of their own safety pedestrians should use the footpath where there is one[85] and, where there is none, should walk on the right

[75] *Tillett* v. *Ward* (1882) 10 Q.B.D. 17; *McEwan* v. *Cuthill* (1897) 25 R. 57; *McGavin* v. *Wordie* (1901) 8 S.L.T. 354; *Hendry* v. *McDougall*, 1923 S.C. 378; *Gayler & Pope* v.*Davies* [1924] 2 K.B. 75; *Haynes* v. *Harwood* [1935] 1 K.B. 146; *Ballantyne* v. *Hamilton*, 1938 S.L.T. 468; *cf. Shaws* v. *Croall* (1885) 12 R. 1186; *Gray* v. *N.B.Ry.* (1890) 18 R. 76; *Smith* v. *Wallace* (1898) 25 R. 761; *Cutler* v. *United Dairies, Ltd.* [1933] 2 K.B. 297.
[76] *Milligan* v. *Wedge* (1840) 12 A. & E. 737; *Templeman* v. *Haydon* (1852) 12 C.B. 507 (defective cart); *Simpson* v. *L.G.O.C.* (1873) L.R. 8 C.P. 390; *Brown* v. *Fulton* (1881) 9 R. 36; *Shaws* v. *Croall* (1885) 12 R. 1186; *Smith* v. *Walker, supra*; *Milne* v. *Nimmo* (1898) 25 R. 1150; *Wilson* v. *Wordie* (1905) 7 F. 927; *Hogg* v. *Cupar Dist. Cttee.*, 1912, 1 S.L.T. 57; *Tillett* v. *Ward* (1882) 10 Q.B.D. 16.
[77] *Illidge* v. *Goodwin* (1831) 5 C. & P. 190; *Haynes, supra*.
[78] *Aldham* v. *United Dairies (London), Ltd.* [1940] 1 K.B. 507.
[79] *Hammack* v. *White* (1862) 11 C.B.(N.S.) 588.
[80] *North* v. *Smith* (1861) 10 C.B.(N.S.) 572.
[81] Except in the case of motorways, where pedestrians may be banned, and where there is a footpath, when pedestrians must use it.
[82] *Boss* v. *Litton* (1832) 5 C. & P. 407; *Gibson* v. *Milroy* (1879) 6 R. 890; *Craig* v. *Glasgow Corpn.*, 1919 S.C.(H.L.) 1.
[83] *Clerk* v. *Petrie* (1879) 6 R. 1076; *Snee* v. *Durkie* (1903) 6 F. 42; see also *Anderson* v. *Blackwood* (1886) 13 R. 443; *French* v. *Mitchell* (1901) 9 S.L.T. 219.
[84] *Alexander* v. *Phillips* (1899) 1 F. 985.
[85] Highway Code, § 1; *McKechnie* v. *Couper* (1887) 14 R. 345 (where pavements, pedestrian entitled to walk in road and vehicles bound to keep clear) must be qualified to this extent under modern conditions of traffic.

of the road to face oncoming traffic. When walking on the pavement pedestrians should not walk next to the kerb with their backs to traffic proceeding in the same direction, nor step off the pavement or even put a foot in the gutter without looking. Such conduct might amount to contributory negligence or even full responsibility for any resulting harm.[86] A person who steps from the kerb owes a duty to traffic approaching him within risk of collision to exercise due care,[87] and a driver may reasonably expect that a pedestrian will be walking on the footpath, so that, especially at dusk or in the dark, an injured pedestrian may be debarred from recovery.[88]

Pedestrians owe duties of care to each other, particularly in relation to the management of umbrellas, prams, trolley-baskets and parcels. But there is no liability for unforeseeable harm, or harm attributable to an unknown disability.[89]

Adults should take reasonable care of children so as to prevent them running out in the roadway,[90] or kicking a ball into the roadway,[91] thereby causing accidents to drivers or motor-cyclists.

Pedestrians should similarly keep proper control of dogs, and may be liable if a dog's lead trips a pedestrian.[92]

2. RAILWAY ACCIDENTS

The railway authority owes duties of care *ex lege* to third parties, to passengers whom it is carrying under contract, and to its own employees, arising out of its operation of railway services. The duties of the last kind are also dealt with, in so far as they arise from the employment relationship, under the heading of Employment Accidents.

The duty of care is fundamentally to take reasonable care to provide and maintain safe stations, permanent way and rolling-stock, and to maintain a safe system of operation of trains. In view of the obvious risks reasonable care demands a high standard of foresight and precautions, but nevertheless liability is for negligence and the railway authority is not an insurer against harm. The occurrence of a collision or other accident does not *ipso facto* impose liability,[93] but is strong prima facie evidence of negligence in some respect. If an accident occurs by reason of the breakdown of the plant of the railway the presumption is that it is the fault of the railway authority.[94] If a train goes off the lines, or a collision occurs,

---

[86] *Adamson* v. *Roberts*, 1951 S.C. 681.

[87] *Nance* v. *British Columbia Electric Ry.* [1951] A.C. 601, 611.

[88] *Tidy* v. *Battman* [1934] 1 K.B. 319; *Scott* v. *McIntosh*, 1935 S.C. 199; *McKnight* v. *General Motor Carrying Co.*, 1936 S.C. 17. As to blackout conditions, see *Franklin* v. *Bristol Tramways* [1941] 1 K.B. 255; *Cowan* v. *Robertson*, 1941 S.C. 502; *Sparks* v. *Ash* [1943] K.B. 223; *McGeown* v. *Greenock Motor Services*, 1943 S.C. 33.

[89] *Guthrie* v. *Creagh*, 1949 S.L.T.(Notes) 42; *cf. Bourhill* v. *Young*, 1942 S.C.(H.L.) 78, 92.

[90] *Carmarthenshire C.C.* v. *Lewis* [1955] A.C. 549.

[91] *Hilder* v. *Associated Portland Cement Mfrs.* [1961] 3 All E.R. 709.

[92] *Pitcher* v. *Martin* [1937] 3 All E.R. 918; *cf. Jones* v. *Owen* (1871) 24 L.T. 587.

[93] *Bird* v. *G.N.Ry.* (1858) 28 L.J.Ex. 3; *Ferus* v. *N.B.Ry.* (1872) 9 S.L.R. 652.

[94] *Watson* v. *N.B.Ry.* (1876) 3 R. 637.

that raises a prima facie case of negligence,[95] but it may be rebutted by proof that the accident was caused by the wrongful act of a third party,[96] or by a latent defect in the rolling-stock.[97] Matters were formerly somewhat complicated by the existence of different companies, sometimes with running powers over each other's lines.

It has been held that it is the duty of the railway authority to warn intending passengers, before they enter into the contract of carriage, of the existence of circumstances inferring unusual risk, and that, if it failed to do so, the authority might be liable to passengers for injury caused by accidents for which it might otherwise not have been responsible.[98]

(a) Permanent way and rolling-stock

The duty with reference to permanent way and rolling-stock requires the provision and maintenance of safe engines, carriages and track. It is negligent to run a train on rails known to be defective,[99] or to allow the line to become defective,[1] or to run a coach with a defective footboard.[2] The railway authority is not responsible for injury done by sparks from engines, so long as those engines are of good design and construction, and all reasonable precautions and safeguards are used to minimise the risk of sparks causing damage or injury.[3]

The prima facie inference of negligence may be rebutted by proof of a latent defect in rolling-stock,[4] or by proof that a collision was caused by the wrongful act of a third party.[5]

Fencing the line. The railway authority is bound to erect and maintain fences along the line " for the accommodation of the owners and occupiers of lands adjoining the railway "[6] ; accordingly loss due to the breach of this duty is actionable only at the instance of such owners or occupiers and not by the general public.[7] The railway authority is thus not liable if cattle straying on the highway get on the line by reason of defective fencing and are killed,[8] nor if the cattle stray from a field not adjoining the railway,[9] nor if a person in a train is injured by a collision between the train and straying cattle,[10] nor if the fence would have been

---

[95] *Skinner* v. *L.B. & S.C.Ry.* (1850) 5 Ex. 787.
[96] *Latch* v. *Rumner Ry.* (1858) 27 L.J.Ex. 155.
[97] *Readhead* v. *Midland Ry.* (1869) L.R. 4 Q.B. 379.
[98] *Jarvie* v. *Caledonian Ry.* (1875) 2 R. 623.
[99] *Pym* v. *G.N.Ry.* (1861) 2 F. & F. 619.
[1] *Smyth* v. *Caledonian Ry.* (1897) 24 R. 488.
[2] *Stewart* v. *Caledonian Ry.* (1870) 8 M. 486.
[3] *Murdoch* v. *G.S.W.Ry.* (1870) 8 M. 768; *Port-Glasgow and Newark Sailcloth Co.* v. *Caledonian Ry.* (1893) 20 R.(H.L.) 35.
[4] *Readhead* v. *Midland Ry.* (1869) L.R. 4 Q.B. 379.
[5] *Latch* v. *Rumner Ry.* (1858) 27 L.J.Ex. 155.
[6] Railways Clauses Consolidation (Scotland) Act, 1845, s. 60. See also *Brown* v. *Edinburgh & Glasgow Ry.* (1864) 2 M. 875; as to fencing disused line, see *Simpson* v. *Caledonian Ry.* (1878) 5 R. 525.
[7] *Dawson* v. *Midland Ry.* (1872) L.R. 8 Ex. 8; *Archibald* v. *N.B.Ry.* (1883) 21 S.L.R. 60.
[8] *M.S. & L.Ry.* v. *Wallis* (1854) 14 C.B. 213; *Luscombe* v. *G.W.Ry.* [1899] 2 Q.B. 313.
[9] *Ricketts* v. *E. & W. India Docks Co.* (1852) 12 C.B. 160; contrast *Sharrod* v. *L.N.W.Ry.* (1849) 4 Ex. 580.
[10] *Buxton* v. *N.E.Ry.* (1868) L.R. 2 Q.B. 549.

adequate for normal circumstances and is inadequate only under unusual conditions.[11]

Bridges, embankments, culverts and cuttings. These must all be maintained in reasonably safe condition, and collapse is evidence of negligence, which can be rebutted by showing that there was no negligence in any respect in construction or maintenance and that the most approved methods and materials were used.[12] It is not sufficient to show that competent engineers were employed, nor that the collapse was due to exceptional weather, because precautions must be taken against even exceptional weather.[13] But there is no liability for not taking precautions which would avail against weather so exceptional as to be *damnum fatale.*

Where the railway passes underneath a highway the railway authority must maintain a bridge and approaches over the line, and it is liable if the surface is not perfectly maintained, so that damage is caused to passing traffic,[14] or if the bridge is not reasonably safe for pedestrians.[15]

Where the railway passes over a highway the bridge must allow statutorily specified clearance, but the main duty to ensure the safety of the passage, in the case of a passage made under a railway after its formation, is on the road authority.[16]

Level-crossings. At a level-crossing over a highway the railway authority must take reasonable care to minimise the danger created thereby, the actual measures depending on the circumstances.[17] It will be liable if a vehicle passing over is damaged by the defective condition of the crossing,[18] and the crossing and any necessary approaches must be kept in good repair [19] but need not be reconstructed periodically to suit changing traffic conditions. Unless there are special circumstances there is no duty at common law to fasten gates or post a watchman to tell pedestrians when it is safe to cross and when dangerous.[20] There is no general duty to light crossing gates, and hence no liability to a person who runs into the gates by reason of their being unlit,[21] but there may be where a level-crossing is replaced by other constructions.[22]

[11] *Cooper* v. *Railway Executive* [1953] 1 All E.R. 477.
[12] *Grote* v. *Chester and Holyhead Ry.* (1848) 2 Ex. 251.
[13] *G.W.Ry. of Canada* v. *Braid* (1863) 1 Moo.P.C.(N.S.) 101; *cf. Greenock Corpn.* v. *Caledonian Ry.,* 1917 S.C.(H.L.) 56, see also *Withers* v. *North Kent Ry.* (1858) 27 L.J.Ex. 417.
[14] Railways Clauses Consolidation (Scotland) Act, 1845, s. 39; *Swain* v. *Southern Ry.* [1939] 2 K.B. 560.   [15] *Lay* v. *Midland Ry.* (1875) 34 L.T. 30.
[16] *McFee* v. *Broughty Ferry Police Commrs.* (1890) 17 R. 764.
[17] *Smith* v. *L.M.S.Ry.,* 1948 S.C. 125; *Lloyds Bank, Ltd.* v. *Railway Executive* [1952] 1 All E.R. 1248.
[18] *Hendrie* v. *Caledonian Ry.,* 1909 S.C. 776; *Oliver* v. *N.E.Ry.* (1874) L.R. 9 Q.B. 409.
[19] *Bell* v. *Caledonian Ry.* (1902) 4 F. 431; *Hertfordshire C.C.* v. *G.E.Ry.* [1909] 2 K.B. 403; criticised in *Sharpness New Docks Co.* v. *Att.-Gen.* [1915] A.C. 654; under the Railways Clauses Consolidation Act, 1845, s. 16, there is no liability to repair the approaches: *West Lancashire R.D.C.* v. *L. & Y.Ry.* [1903] 2 K.B. 394; for Scotland, *cf.* Railways Clauses Consolidation (Scotland) Act, 1845, s. 40.
[20] *Stubley* v. *L.N.W.Ry.* (1865) L.R. 1 Ex. 13; *Hendrie, supra.*
[21] *L.N.E.Ry.* v. *Frost* (1935) not reported, referred to in *Law* v. *Railway Executive* (1949) 65 T.L.R. 288.
[22] *Law, supra.*

Where a railway crosses a public carriage road on the level the railway authority must by statute erect and maintain good and sufficient gates across the road, and employ persons to open and shut them.[23] If the railway crosses a bridleway, the authority must erect and maintain good and sufficient gates, and if it crosses a footway, good and sufficient gates or stiles on each side of the railway. The authority is liable if a person is injured, having got on to the line by reason of the absence of a gate or stile,[24] or if the gates are left open and the gatekeeper does not warn pedestrians.[25] The gates are to protect the public from the railway, not conversely, so that an engine-driver, injured by a motorist's negligence in not closing a gate and letting it swing, could sue the motorist, but not the railway authority.[26] Similarly the railway authority is liable if an animal strays on to the road and is killed on the line by reason of defective gates [27] or fencing.[28]

Apart from statute, the railway authority is under no duty to employ a gatekeeper at a level-crossing,[29] but where a gatekeeper is required by statute and is not present, a third party should not open a gate; if he does so and is injured, the railway authority is not liable.[30]

The railway authority must take reasonable care in the management of crossings to avoid causing injury to members of the public, as by misleading them into thinking it was safe to cross,[31] or by carelessness.[32] While there is no obligation on an engine-driver to sound his whistle or horn before every level crossing [33] it may be evidence of negligence in particular circumstances not to do so.[34]

The driver of a wheeled vehicle should comply with the warnings of the Highway Code [35] when crossing at a level-crossing, and may be

---

[23] Railways Clauses Consolidation (Scotland) Act, 1845, s. 40; *Woods* v. *Caledonian Ry.* (1886) 13 R. 1118; and see *Hendrie* v. *Caledonian Ry.*, 1909 S.C. 776. A lodge must be erected at the crossing: Railways Clauses Act, 1863, s. 6: see also Road and Rail Traffic Act, 1933, ss. 42, 48, 49. As to crossing over private road, see *Macpherson* v. *Callander and Oban Ry.* (1887) 25 S.L.R. 474.

[24] *Williams* v. *G.W.Ry.* (1874) L.R. 9 Ex. 157.

[25] *Stapley* v. *L.B. & S.C.Ry.* (1865) L.R. 1 Ex. 21; *Woods* v. *Caledonian Ry.* (1886) 13 R. 1118. *Cf. Lunt* v. *L.N.W.Ry.* (1866) L.R. 1 Q.B. 277; *N.E.Ry.* v. *Wanless* (1874) L.R. 7 H.L. 12.

[26] *Knapp* v. *Railway Executive* [1949] 2 All E.R. 508.

[27] *Charman* v. *S.E.Ry.* (1888) 21 Q.B.D. 524; *Fawcett* v. *York and N. Midland Ry.* (1851) 16 Q.B. 610.

[28] *Barclay* v. *G.N.S.Ry.* (1882) 10 R. 144; *Parkinson* v. *Garstang and Knott End Ry.* [1910] 1 K.B. 615.

[29] *Cliff* v. *Midland Ry.* (1870) L.R. 5 Q.B. 258; *Stubley* v. *L.N.W.Ry.* (1865) L.R. 1 Ex. 13; *Newman* v. *L.S.W.Ry.* (1890) 7 T.L.R. 138; *Hendrie* v. *Caledonian Ry.*, 1909 S.C. 776; *cf. Bilbee* v. *L.B. & S.C.Ry.* (1865) 18 C.B.(N.S.) 584.

[30] *Wyatt* v. *G.W.Ry.* (1865) 34 L.J.Q.B. 204.

[31] *Lunt* v. *L.N.W.Ry.* (1866) L.R. 1 Q.B. 277; *Stapley* v. *L.B. & S.C.Ry.* (1865) L.R. 1 Ex. 21.

[32] *N.E.Ry.* v. *Wanless* (1874) L.R. 7 H.L. 12; *Smith* v. *S.E.Ry.* [1896] 1 Q.B. 178; *Mercer* v. *S.E. & C.Ry.* [1922] 2 K.B. 549.

[33] *Ellis* v. *G.W.Ry.* (1874) L.R. 9 C.P. 551; *Ireland* v. *N.B.Ry.* (1882) 10 R. 53; *Newman* v. *L.S.W.Ry.* (1890) 7 T.L.R. 138.

[34] *Gilchrist* v. *Ballochney Ry.* (1850) 12 D. 979; *Dublin, etc., Ry.* v. *Slattery* (1878) 3 App.Cas. 1155; *James* v. *G.W.Ry.* (1867) L.R. 2 C.P. 634n.; *Russell* v. *Caledonian Ry.* (1879) 7 R. 148; *Gray* v. *N.E.Ry.* (1883) 48 L.T. 904; *Jenner* v. *S.E.Ry.* (1911) 105 L.T. 131. See also *Bain* v. *British Railways Board*, 1964 S.L.T.(Notes) 92.

[35] Reg. 39.

contributorily negligent if he has not taken reasonable care for his own safety.[36] He should stop, look and listen, and take particular care in fog.[37]

Accommodation crossings. At an accommodation crossing, provided for the convenience of adjacent lands, the railway authority need not at common law take such precautions as it must under statute at a public level-crossing, but it must do all that could reasonably be required in the way of warnings, whistles, and so forth, to reduce the danger to people using the crossing.[38] If it is known that the public use a private crossing, the railway authority must take reasonable care to make the crossing safe.[39] There is no duty to provide a watchman.[40] An engine-driver approaching such a crossing must take reasonable care but is under no duty to drive at a speed such that he can stop within the limit of his vision.[41] A similar duty of reasonable care has been held incumbent where a temporary level-crossing was constructed to enable timber to be transported across the line,[42] and where a railway crossed a public right of way, which was not a public highway.[43]

Footpaths crossing line. Where the tracks cross a footpath, a gate or stile must be provided.[44] It has been held in particular circumstances that, where the gate had negligently been left unlocked, it was an invitation to a pedestrian to cross the line, so that he was entitled to damages when he was knocked down by a train.[45]

To cross the railway at an unauthorised place, even in the claimed exercise of a right of way, may be a trespass.[46]

Yards and sidings. Reasonable care, by way of warning, whistling or lookout men, must be exercised in yards and sidings where shunting takes place, and the failure to do so is evidence of negligence.[47] But

---

36 *Skelton* v. *L.N.W.Ry.* (1867) L.R. 2 C.P. 631; *Stubley* v. *L.N.W.Ry.* (1865) L.R. 1 Ex. 13, *Ellis* v. *G.W.Ry.* (1874) L.R. 9 C.P. 55; *Davey* v. *L.S.W.Ry.* (1883) 12 Q.B.D. 70; *French* v. *Hills Plymouth Co.* (1908) 24 T.L.R. 644.

37 *Hazell* v. *B.T.C.* [1958] 1 All E.R. 116; *Kemshead* v. *B.T.C.* [1958] 1 All E.R. 119.

38 *Grant* v. *Caledonian Ry.* (1870) 9 M. 258; *Russell* v. *Caledonian Ry.* (1879) 7 R. 148; *Fryer* v. *N.B.Ry.* (1908) 15 S.L.T. 886; *Knight* v. *G.W.Rly.* [1943] 1 K.B. 105; *Lloyds Bank, Ltd.* v. *Railway Executive* [1952] 1 All E.R. 1248.

39 *Smith* v. *Smith and Railway Executive* [1948] W.N. 276 (Notice " Beware of the trains " held inadequate); *cf. Lloyds Bank, Ltd.* v. *B.T.C.* [1956] 3 All E.R. 291.

40 *Liddiatt* v. *G.W.Ry.* [1946] K.B. 545.

41 *Knight* v. *G.W.Ry.* [1943] 1 K.B. 105; *Hazell* v. *B.T.C.* [1958] 1 All E.R. 116; *Kemshead* v. *B.T.C.* [1958] 1 All E.R. 119.

42 *Anderson* v. *MacDonald* (1954) 104 L.J. 762.

43 *Smith* v. *L.M.S.Ry.*, 1948 S.C. 125.

44 Railways Clauses Consolidation (Scotland) Act, 1845, s. 52; *cf. Stubley* v. *L.N.W.Ry.* (1865) L.R. 1 Ex. 13; *Bilbee* v. *L.B. & S.C.Ry.* (1865) 18 C.B.(N.S.) 584.

45 *Gillespie* v. *G.S.W.Ry.* (1906) 14 S.L.T. 85; *Mercer* v. *S.E. & Chatham Ry. Managing Cttee.* [1922] 2 K.B. 549; *cf. Skelton* v. *L.N.W.Ry.* (1867) L.R. 2 C.P. 631. See also *Ellis* v. *G.W.Ry.* (1874) L.R. 9 C.P. 551; *Jenner* v. *S.E.Ry.* (1911) 27 T.L.R. 445; *Davey* v. *L.S.W. Ry.* (1883) 12 Q.B.D. 70.

46 *Caledonian Ry.* v. *Walmesley*, 1907 S.C. 1047.

47 *Russell* v. *Caledonian Ry.* (1879) 7 R. 148; *Duthie* v. *Caledonian Ry.* (1898) 25 R. 934; *Grant* v. *G.W.Ry.* (1898) 14 T.L.R. 174; *Paul* v. *G.E.Ry.* (1920) 36 T.L.R. 344; *Moore* v. *N.B.Ry.*, 1923 S.L.T. 128; *Edwards* v. *L.M.S.Ry.*, 1928 S.C. 471; *Jones* v. *G.W.Ry.* (1930) 47 T.L.R. 39; *Ross* v. *Railway Executive*, 1948 S.C.(H.L.) 58; *cf. Wyllie* v. *Caledonian Ry.* (1871) 9 M. 463; *Smith* v. *Highland Ry.* (1888) 16 R. 57; *Adams* v. *G.S.W. Ry.* (1894) 2 S.L.T. 277; *Malley* v. *L.M.S.Ry.*, 1944 S.C. 129; *Cahill* v. *Mersey Docks & Harbour Board* (1948) 81 Ll.L.R. 329; see also *Smyth* v. *Caledonian Ry.* (1897) 24 R. 488.

persons lawfully present must not run unnecessary risks and cannot recover if they walk into obvious danger.[48] Where lines are in a dockyard there is no obligation to shut the dock gates, which open on to a public street, before commencing shunting operations.[49] Whether sidings on private ground adjacent to the main line require to be fenced is a question of circumstances.[50] A fireman should, if he observes a person about to cross the line in front of the engine, warn the driver.[51]

The statutory obligation as to erecting gates at level-crossing applies only to public railways and not to private lines or sidings.[52] There is a common law duty to take reasonable precautions, but no more [53] but a higher duty is owed where children are known to frequent the siding.[54]

Lookout and speed. An engine-driver does not owe the same duties as a car-driver to maintain a lookout for persons or obstructions in his path. A driver was held not negligent when he ran down some cows, though he had been running at a speed at which, owing to mist, he could not pull up within the limits of his vision.[55] But the driver must take all reasonable steps that he can to ensure that, consistently with maintaining his schedule and watching for signals, he can stop if there is an obstacle ahead,[56] and in special circumstances failure to keep adequate lookout has been held negligent.[57]

(b) Stations and other premises

The railway authority owes a duty *ex contractu* to ticket-holding passengers to maintain its stations and other premises ancillary to the contract of carriage in reasonably safe condition.[58] It also owes to persons who resort to stations as intending passengers, ticket-holders, senders or consignees of goods, or while seeing friends off or awaiting their arrival, the duties owed by the occupiers of dangerous premises to those resorting thereto as invitees.[59] Such premises must therefore be kept reasonably safe for persons using them with reasonable care and in the ordinary way.[60] But there is no liability to persons using them in an unreasonable

---

[48] *Ross, supra.*
[49] *Clark* v. *N.B.Ry.,* 1912 S.C. 1.
[50] *Waugh* v. *City of Glasgow Union Ry.* (1883) 20 S.L.R. 585.
[51] *Anderson* v. *Railway Executive,* 1955 S.L.T.(Notes) 48.
[52] *Matson* v. *Baird* (1877) 5 R. 87; (1878) 5 R.(H.L.) 211.
[53] *Morran* v. *Waddell* (1883) 11 R. 44.
[54] *Haughton* v. *N.B.Ry.* (1892) 20 R. 113; *Innes* v. *Fife Coal Co.* (1901) 3 F. 335; *Crannie* v. *Glengarnock Iron & Steel Co.* (1908) 16 S.L.T. 434.
[55] *Knight* v. *G.W.Ry.* [1943] K.B. 105; *Jones* v. *P.L.Authy.* [1954] 1 Lloyd's Rep. 489.
[56] *Trznadel* v. *B.T.C.* [1957] 3 All E.R. 196.
[57] *Slater* v. *Clay Cross* [1956] 2 Q.B. 264; *Braithwaite* v. *South Durham Steel Co.* [1958] 3 All E.R. 161; *Videan* v. *B.T.C.* [1963] 3 All E.R. 860. See also *Ferguson* v. *N.B.Ry.* 1915 S.C. 566.
[58] *Stewart* v. *Caledonian Ry.* (1870) 8 M. 486; *Protheroe* v. *Railway Executive* [1951] 1 K.B. 376.
[59] *Wilson* v. *N.B.Ry.* (1873) 1 R. 172; *Watkins* v. *G.W.Ry.* (1877) 37 L.T. 193; *Norman* v. *G.W.Ry.* [1915] 1 K.B. 584; *Stowell* v. *Railway Executive* [1949] 2 K.B. 519; *cf. Tough* v. *N.B.Ry.,* 1914 S.C. 291. And see now Occupiers' Liability (Scotland) Act, 1960.
[60] *Schlarb* v. *L.N.E.Ry.* [1936] 1 All E.R. 71; *Tomlinson* v. *Ry. Executive* [1953] 1 All E.R. 1.

way,[61] and persons other than travellers may be excluded from stations, in which case, if they enter, they do so as trespassers,[62] nor is there liability for an unforeseeable injury.[63] The standard of care, whether the duty is based on an implied term of the contract of carriage, on or the duty to maintain reasonably safe premises for persons whom it could be foreseen are likely to resort thereto, appears to be the same. There is no liability unless there is negligence.[64]

Safety of platforms.—Reasonable care must be taken to maintain platforms in safe condition; thus the railway authority has been held liable where it had failed to take care and persons were injured by slipping on a patch of oil on the platform,[65] tripping on a crack between paving stones,[66] tripping over the casing of signal levers,[67] slipping on snow on the platform.[68]

While the presence of such dangers as oil,[69] snow, banana skins, and the like is some evidence of negligence on the authority's part, in some cases, as when snow has been falling, the presence of the hazard on the platform should be anticipated and an injured passenger may be guilty of contributory negligence, or the harm may be attributable to inevitable accident.

But there is no liability for obvious dangers, such as the protruding base of a weighing machine which a passenger tripped over,[70] or caked snow,[71] or a lift accessible to and allowed to be operated by the public.[72]

Platforms must be lit so that passengers can see their way about[73] and reasonable precautions taken, by way of warning signs and barriers, that persons do not fall off the platforms on to the line. This is of particular importance in darkness[73] or fog.[74]

Reasonable precautions must be taken by the provision of adequate staff and barriers, to control crowds of passengers, so as to prevent such accidents as passengers being pushed off the platform,[75] but there is no liability if there is a sudden rush of passengers, resulting in injury to one.[76]

[61] *Rigg* v. *M.S. & L.Ry.* (1866) 14 W.R. 834.
[62] *Perth General Station Cttee.* v. *Ross* (1897) 24 R.(H.L.) 44; *Wood* v. *N.B.Ry.* (1899) 2 F. 1; *cf. N.B.Ry.* v. *Mackintosh* (1890) 17 R. 1065; *Shevlin* v. *L.M.S.Ry.*, 1927 S.N. 124.
[63] *Murchison* v. *L.M.S.Ry.*, 1932 S.N. 72.
[64] *Toomey* v. *L.B. & S.C.Ry.* (1857) 3 C.B.(N.S.) 146; *Murchison, supra.*
[65] *Stowell* v. *Railway Executive* [1949] 2 K.B. 519; *Blackman* v. *Railway Executive* [1954] 1 W.L.R. 220.
[66] *Protheroe* v. *Railway Executive* [1951] 1 K.B. 376.
[67] *Sturges* v. *G.W.Ry.* (1892) 8 T.L.R. 231.
[68] *Tomlinson* v. *Railway Executive* [1953] 1 All E.R. 1 (no failure in care—claim failed).
[69] *Blackman* v. *Railway Exeuctive* [1953] 2 All E.R. 323.
[70] *Cornman* v. *E.C.Ry.* (1859) 4 H. & N. 781; *Blackman* v. *L.B. & S.C.Ry.* (1869) 17 W.R. 769.
[71] *Brackley* v. *Midland Ry.* (1916) 85 L.J.K.B. 1596.
[72] *Wilson* v. *G.S.W.Ry.*, 1915 S.C. 215.
[73] *Martin* v. *G.N.Ry.* (1855) 16 C.B. 179; *Bryce Ewing* v. *S.E.Ry.* (1892) 8 T.L.R. 679; *cf. Roe* v. *G.S.W.Ry.* (1889) 17 R. 59.
[74] *L.T. & S.Ry.* v. *Paterson* (1913) 29 T.L.R. 413 (criticised in Beven, *Negligence*, II, 1187); *Schlarb* v. *L.N.E.Ry.* [1936] 1 All E.R. 71.
[75] *Hogan* v. *S.E.Ry.* (1873) 28 L.T. 271; *McGregor* v. *Glasgow District Subway Co.* (1901) 3 F. 1131; *Fraser* v. *Caledonian Ry.* (1902) 5 F. 41; *cf. MacArthur* v. *Glasgow Subway Ry.*, 1922 S.L.T. 32.
[76] *McCallum* v. *N.B.Ry.*, 1908 S.C. 415; *Cannon* v. *M.G.W.Ry. of I.* (1876) 6 L.R.Ir. 199.

The authority is not liable for failing to see an intoxicated passenger safely off the platform at which he has arrived.[77]

Approaches to stations. The duties of reasonable care cover also approaches to stations, such as stairs and pathways, and internal communications, such as crossings or bridges from one platform to another. Liability has been established where an intending passenger slipped on entrance steps which were worn and dangerous with caked snow,[78] or a passenger fell over a projecting bolt protruding above the level of a pathway.[79]

But there is no liability without negligence; the fact that a person slips on steps which many people daily used safely is not proof of negligence,[80] nor is the fact that a woman caught her heel in a small space on an escalator.[81]

If a bridge or crossing is provided a passenger who jumps down on the rails, to cross from one platform to another, and is injured, has no claim.[82] A passenger using a crossing between platforms is entitled to warning of approaching trains [83] but must take reasonable care for his own safety and not run unnecessary risks or flout obvious dangers.[84] The absence of a bridge throws a greater onus on the railway authority to take care for the safety of the public.[85]

Entrances, exits and other routes to, from, and in stations must be adequately signposted and lit; a passenger has been held to have a good claim where he passed through an open unlighted wicket gate in the belief that it was the exit and fell down an unfenced stair.[86] A station should be fenced so that the public may not be misled into injury by seeing a place unfenced and taking that, as the shortest way, to the station.[87] There is no duty to keep private parts of stations, such as porters' rooms, safe for even drunk men.[88]

Refreshment rooms and other facilities. It is part of the business duty of the railway authority to provide food for passengers, certainly at major stations, and it cannot act so as to deprive itself of the facilities for doing so.[89] It is doubtful if the authority would be liable in damages

---

[77] *McCormick* v. *Caledonian Ry.* (1904) 6 F. 362; *Cuthill* v. *N.B.Ry.* (1908) 15 S.L.T. 785.
[78] *Osborne* v. *L.N.W.Ry.* (1888) 21 Q.B.D. 220; *G. Central Ry.* v. *Hewlett* [1916] 2 A.C. 511; *Letang* v. *Ottawa Electric Ry.* [1926] A.C. 725; *cf. Brackley* v. *Midland Ry.* (1916) 85 L.J.K.B. 1596; *Burton* v. *M.S. & L.Ry.* (1876) 40 J.P. 664.
[79] *Bloomstein* v. *Railway Executive* [1952] 2 All E.R. 418.
[80] *Crafter* v. *Metropolitan Ry.* (1866) L.R. 1 C.P. 300.
[81] *Alexander* v. *City & South London Ry.* (1928) 44 T.L.R. 450.
[82] *Wilby* v. *Midland Ry.* (1876) 35 L.T. 244.
[83] *Dublin, Wicklow and Wexford Ry.* v. *Slattery* (1878) 3 App.Cas. 1155; *Brown* v. *G.W.Ry.* (1885) 1 T.L.R. 614; *Wright* v. *Midland Ry.* (1885) 1 T.L.R. 406; *Crowther* v. *L. & Y.Ry.* (1889) 6 T.L.R. 18; *Dallas* v. *G.W.Ry.* (1893) 9 T.L.R. 344.
[84] *Walker* v. *Midland Ry.* (1866) 14 L.T. 796; *Davey* v. *L. & S.W.Ry.* (1883) 12 Q.B.D. 70.
[85] *Thomson* v. *N.B.Ry.* (1876) 4 R. 115.
[86] *McKeever* v. *Caledonian Ry.* (1900) 2 F. 1085; contrast *Calder* v. *N.B.Ry.*, 1922 S.L.T. 395.
[87] *Burgess* v. *G.W.Ry.* (1858) 32 L.T.(o.s.) 76.
[88] *Murchison* v. *L.M.S.Ry.*, 1932 S.N. 72.
[89] *County Hotel & Wine Co.* v. *L.N.W.Ry.* [1918] 2 K.B. 251.

for failing to do so. It has been held that lavatory accommodation and cloakrooms may be ordered as " facilities " under the Railway and Canal Traffic Act, 1854, s. 2.[90]

Misconduct of railway staff. The railway authority is liable for misconduct of railway staff on platforms, as by their throwing parcels out of a train and injuring a passenger, leaving a carriage door open so that it strikes a passenger,[91] letting a trunk fall from a barrow on top of a passenger,[92] flagging a train to start while a carriage door was still open.[93] But there is no negligence in not looking after a drunken passenger unless he is obviously liable to do himself harm.[94]

Unless there has been some fault imputable to the railway authority or its servants, there is, however, no liability, as where a stray dog bit a passenger on the platform.[95]

Ejection of passengers. It is not misconduct to remove from a train a passenger who does not have a proper ticket for the journey, so long as no unnecessary force is used,[96] but it may be if the passenger is willing to pay any excess due to rectify the ticket held,[97] or if one passenger is sought to be expelled for a fault possibly not his.[98]

Left luggage offices. Where such offices are provided the railway authority incurs the liabilities of a custodier for reward towards depositors.

The receipt issued commonly seeks to limit liability for the loss of articles left for custody, but such limitation may not be applicable if the authority is itself in breach of contract.[99]

(c) System of operation

The system of operation covers the management of trains, the driving,[1] and the general arrangements for the safe and comfortable transport of passengers. The basic principle is that the railway authority is bound to take reasonable care and to use the best precautions in known practical use for securing the safety and convenience of its passengers.[2] It must take due care, which involves a high degree of care and imposes

[90] *Singer Mfg. Co.* v. *L.S.W.Ry.* [1894] 1 Q.B. 833; *Metropolitan Water Board* v. *L.B. & S.C. Ry.* [1910] 2 K.B. 890.
[91] *Thatcher* v. *G.W.Ry.* (1893) 10 T.L.R. 13; *Toal* v. *N.B.Ry.*, 1908 S.C.(H.L.) 29; *Burns* v. *N.B.Ry.*, 1914 S.C. 754; *Hare* v. *B.T.C.* [1956] 1 W.L.R. 250.
[92] *Tabbutt* v. *Bristol & Exter Ry.* (1870) L.R. 6 Q.B. 73.
[93] *Anderson* v. *G.S.W.Ry.* (1881) 18 S.L.R. 627.
[94] *McCormick* v. *Caledonian Ry.* (1904) 6 F. 362; *Cuthill* v. *N.B.Ry.* (1908) 15 S.L.T. 785.
[95] *Smith* v. *G.E.Ry.* (1866) L.R. 2 C.P. 4.
[96] *Highland Ry.* v. *Menzies* (1878) 5 R. 887; *MacRaild* v. *N.B.Ry.* (1902) 10 S.L.T. 348.
[97] *Brahan* v. *Caledonian Ry.* (1895) 2 S.L.T. 552.
[98] *Harris* v. *N.B.Ry.* (1891) 18 R. 1009.
[99] *Handon* v. *Caledonian Ry.* (1880) 7 R. 966; contrast *Lyons* v. *Caledonian Ry.*, 1909 S.C. 1185. See further *Alexander* v. *Railway Executive* [1951] 2 K.B. 882.
[1] On the driver's duty of lookout see *Lloyds Bank, Ltd.* v. *B.T.C.* [1956] 3 All E.R. 291, 294, 298; *Trznadel* v. *B.T.C.* [1957] 3 All E.R. 196n.
[2] *Ford* v. *L.S.W.Ry.* (1862) 2 F. & F. 730.

the duty of exercising all vigilance to see that whatever is required for the safe conveyance of passengers is in fit and proper order.[3]

Trains should be operated as quietly as is reasonably practicable and the railway authority has been held liable where a spark from an engine injured a passenger leaving the station,[4] an engine blew off steam at a crossing and thereby frightened a horse,[5] or frightened cattle by noisy shunting.[6] But there is no duty not to blow off steam in a station though that may frighten animals on the road outside,[7] nor to refrain from whistling.[8] It is, however, improper operation to put on steam so violently while passing a platform that sparks are emitted from the chimney and injure persons on the platform.[9]

Statutory formulation of common law duty of care to passengers. The Occupiers' Liability (Scotland) Act, 1960, s. 1, provides that a person having control of any vehicle owes to persons entering thereon the duty (s. 2) of taking such care as in all the circumstances of the case is reasonable to see that the passenger will not suffer injury or damage by reason of any danger which is due to the state of the vehicle or to anything done or omitted to be done in relation to it and for which the person in control is in law responsible. This duty may be extended, restricted, modified or excluded by agreement.

Starting and stopping. The train should not be started or stopped suddenly, save in emergency, but with reasonable care. A sudden or violent starting[10] or stopping[11] which causes injury to a passenger is prima facie evidence of negligence.[10] In such a case the railway authority has " to show both that they acted reasonably and properly in suddenly stopping the train and also that the cause which led to the necessity of stopping the train was not brought about by any negligence upon their part." [11] Hence they were liable where a train was stopped suddenly to avoid running down a person crossing the line and the plaintiff was injured by being thrown from his seat, because they failed to show that the presence of the person on the line was not due to any negligence on the company's part.[11] It is similarly evidence of negligence if a train stops for sufficiently long to appear to be finally stopped and then moves forward with a jerk,[12] or if it is run into the buffers and stopped with a jerk,[13] or if, at an intermediate stop, sufficient time is not given to alight.[14]

---

3 *Readhead* v. *Midland Ry.* (1869) L.R. 4 Q.B. 379, 393.
4 *Atherton* v. *L.N.W.Ry.* (1905) 21 T.L.R. 671.
5 *M.S.J. & A.Ry.* v. *Fullarton* (1863) 14 C.B.(N.S.) 54.
6 *Sneesby* v. *L. & Y.Ry.* (1875) 1 Q.B.D. 42.
7 *Simkin* v. *L.N.W.Ry.* (1888) 21 Q.B.D. 453.
8 *Glancy* v. *G.S.W.Ry.* (1898) 25 R. 581.
9 *Gray* v. *Caledonian Ry.*, 1912 S.C. 339.
10 *Metropolitan Ry.* v. *Delaney* (1921) 90 L.J.K.B. 721.
11 *Angus* v. *L.T. & S.Ry.* (1906) 22 T.L.R. 222, *per* L.C. Loreburn.
12 *L.N.W.Ry.* v. *Hellawell* (1872) 26 L.T. 557; *Langton* v. *L. & Y. Ry.* (1886) 3 T.L.R. 18; *Stockdale* v. *L. & Y.Ry.* (1863) 8 L.T. 289; *Goldberg* v. *G. & S.W.Ry.*, 1907 S.C. 1035.
13 *Burke* v. *M.S. & L.Ry.* (1870) 22 L.T. 442.
14 *Anderson* v. *G.S.W.Ry.* (1881) 18 S.L.R. 627.

A passenger must, however, take reasonable care for his own safety and may be [15] negligent if he stands in an open carriage doorway while the train is still in motion,[16] or attempts to board [17] or leave [18] the train then.

Means of boarding and alighting from trains. Reasonably safe and sufficient means of access must be provided at places where trains stop for passengers to board or alight from trains.[19] It is evidence of fault on the railway authority's part if the platform provided is not high enough, or too far from the doors of the carriages,[20] and a passenger is injured thereby.[21] But the facilities need be sufficient only for normal persons and there is no special duty to have regard to passengers suffering from disabilities or peculiarities.[22] Nor need there always be an unvarying distance between platform and step.[22] Sufficient time must be allowed for passengers to alight.[23]

Entering or leaving a train while it is moving. A passenger who attempts to get into or out of a train while it is moving is in general failing to take care for his own safety, but not if he is justifiably ignorant of the fact that it is moving.[24] He must also take care for persons on the platform, that they are not injured by the carriage door being open temporarily while the train is moving.[25]

Entering guard's van. A passenger is not entitled to enter or travel in the guard's van without permission, and has no claim for injuries incurred while so entering without permission.[26]

Leaning out of windows. It is dangerous for passengers to lean out of carriage windows when a train is in motion, and a passenger who does so and strikes his head is prima facie the author of his own harm. Where a passenger, feeling unwell, put her head out and was struck by a mail-bag hanging from an automatic pick-up apparatus at the side of the track, it was held that the arrangement was not one from which danger was to be anticipated.[27]

Stopping short of, or overshooting, platform. The railway authority is not automatically in fault if a train stops short of, or overshoots, a platform,[28] and any person boarding or alighting when it is so stopped does

---

[15] *Hall* v. *London Tramways Co.* (1896) 12 T.L.R. 611.
[16] *Langton, supra; Folkes* v. *North London Ry.* (1892) 8 T.L.R. 269.
[17] *Avis* v. *G.E.Ry.* (1892) 8 T.L.R. 693.
[18] *Metropolitan Ry.* v. *Wright* (1886) 11 App.Cas. 152.
[19] *Robson* v. *N.E.Ry.* (1876) 2 Q.B.D. 85; *Henderson* v. *L.M.S.Ry.,* 1935 S.C. 734.
[20] *Cockle* v. *L. & S.E.Ry.* (1872) L.R. 7 C.P. 321.
[21] *Stewart* v. *Caledonian Ry.* (1870) 8 M. 486; *Foulkes* v. *Metropolitan Ry.* (1880) 5 C.P.D. 157; *Wharton* v. *L. & Y.Ry.* (1888) 5 T.L.R. 142; *Manning* v. *L.N.W.Ry.* (1907) 23 T.L.R. 222.
[22] *Henderson* v. *L.M.S.Ry.,* 1935 S.C. 734.
[23] *Anderson* v. *G.S.W.Ry.* (1881) 18 S.L.R. 627.
[24] *Roe* v. *G.S.W.Ry.* (1889) 17 R. 59.
[25] *Booker* v. *Wenborn* [1962] 1 All E.R. 431.
[26] *Thompson* v. *N.B.Ry.* (1882) 9 R. 1101.
[27] *Pirie* v. *Caledonian Ry.* (1890) 17 R. 1157.
[28] *Potter* v. *N.B.Ry.* (1873) 11 M. 664.

so at his own risk.[29] But if a passenger is expressly or impliedly invited
to board or alight in such circumstances, and he does so without
negligence but is injured, he can recover.[30] It is the duty of the railway
servants to warn passengers of the dangers, if they see them about to
alight off the platform or in other dangerous circumstances,[31] and to
render assistance if passengers do, or have to, alight off the platform.[32]
A porter's calling out the name of the station as the train comes in is not
an invitation to alight as soon as the train has stopped,[33] but if this is
followed by a stop long enough to appear to be stopping for that station,
it may be held to be an invitation.[34]

There is an invitation to alight if a porter opens the carriage door,[35]
particularly if this is combined with calling the station name, but an
alighting passenger must still take reasonable care for his own safety
and not alight without looking.[36]

Conversely, there is clearly no invitation to alight if passengers are
warned to keep their seats, and a passenger who alights in defiance of a
warning has no claim.[37] A passenger who failed to hear such a warning
has been held entitled to recover.[38]

Carriage doors. The railway servants should take reasonable care to
see that carriage doors are properly closed before a train leaves a station.[39]
The opening of a door by itself while the train is in motion is prima facie
evidence of negligence on the part of someone, and so long as it can be
shown that none of the passengers interfered with it, the inference must
be that it had not been properly secured by railway servants.[40] But the
mere opening of a door in a corridor coach is not evidence of negligence
against the railway.[41] Nor is the fall of a carriage window in its channels
any evidence of negligence.[42] A passenger has been held barred where
he fell out while trying to close a door which repeatedly flew open, since
he was doing what was obviously dangerous.[43]

[29] *Harrold* v. *G.W.Ry.* (1866) 14 L.T. 440; *Siner* v. *G.W.Ry.* (1869) L.R. 4 Ex. 117; *Owen*
     v. *G.W.Ry.* (1877) 46 L.J.Q.B. 486; *Muirhead* v. *N.B.Ry.* (1884) 11 R. 1043; *McAulay*
     v. *G.S.W.Ry.* (1896) 23 R. 845; *Abbott* v. *N.B.Ry.*, 1916 S.C. 306.
[30] *Foy* v. *L.B. & S.C.Ry.* (1865) 18 C.B.(N.S.) 225 (train too long for platform); *Robson* v.
     N.E.Ry. (1876) 2 Q.B.D. 85; *Neilson* v. *N.B.Ry.*, 1907 S.C. 272.
[31] *Potter* v. *N.B.Ry.* (1873) 11 M. 664; *Aitken* v. *N.B.Ry.* (1891) 18 R. 836; *McGinty* v.
     L.M.S.Ry., 1939 S.C. 361.
[32] *Potter, supra; Abbott, supra.*
[33] *Lewis* v. *L.C. & D.* (1873) L.R. 9 Q.B. 66; *Plant* v. *Midland Ry.* (1870) 21 L.T. 836.
[34] *Cockle* v. *L. & S.E.Ry.* (1872) L.R. 7 C.P. 321; *Weller* v. *L.B. & S.C.Ry.* (1874) L.R. 9
     C.P. 126; *Bridges* v. *North London Ry.* (1874) L.R. 7 H.L. 213.
[35] *Praeger* v. *Bristol and Exeter Ry.* (1871) 24 L.T. 105.
[36] *Sharpe* v. *Southern Ry.* [1925] 2 K.B. 311; *London, Tilbury & Southend Ry.* v. *Glancock*
     (1902) 19 T.L.R. 305.
[37] *Anthony* v. *Midland Ry.* (1908) 100 L.T. 117.   [38] *Rose* v. *N.E.Ry.* (1876) 2 Ex.D. 248.
[39] *Cooper* v. *Caledonian Ry.* (1902) 4 F. 880; *Fowler* v. *N.B.Ry.*, 1914 S.C. 866; *Inglis* v.
     L.M.S.Ry., 1941 S.C. 551; *Brookes* v. *L.P.T.B.* [1947] 1 All E.R. 506.
[40] *Cooper, supra; Fowler, supra; Inglis, supra; Warburton* v. *Midland Ry.* (1870) 21 L.T.
     835; *Gee* v. *Metropolitan Ry.* (1873) L.R. 8 Q.B. 161; *Richards* v. *G.E.Ry.* (1873) 28 L.T.
     711; *Cassidy* v. *N.B.Ry.* (1873) 11 M. 341; *Dudman* v. *N.L.Ry.* (1886) 2 T.L.R. 365;
     Hamer v. *Cambrian Ry.* (1886) 2 T.L.R. 508.
[41] *Easson* v. *L.N.E.Ry.* [1944] K.B. 421; *O'Connor* v. *B.T.C.* [1958] 1 All E.R. 558.
[42] *Murray* v. *Metropolitan Ry.* (1873) 27 L.T. 762.
[43] *Adams* v. *L. & Y.Ry.* (1869) L.R. 4 C.P. 739, criticised in *Gee, supra.*

Doors must be shut carefully, and warning should be given if a passenger is getting in or out, or is close to the door [44]: there is no need to give warning if the passengers are seated,[45] but it is negligent to slam a door without giving a passenger a reasonable chance to alight or without taking reasonable care to see that it is safe to shut the door.[46]

It is evidence of negligence against the railway authority if a train starts and a passenger who has alighted is struck by a door left open.[47]

In a train with automatic doors it is negligence to start it with a jerk, so that a passenger's hand is caught as the sliding door shuts.[48] The doors of such trains must be closed before the train starts.[49]

Overcrowding. The railway authority should prevent persons getting into carriages already full, and will be liable if passengers are injured by overcrowding.[50] This liability has been held not to extend to a passenger having his hand trapped when the carriage door was shut,[51] nor to being assaulted,[52] or robbed [53] by other passengers, nor to being caught in a rush to leave the train and injured,[54] these not being the natural results of overcrowding. Passengers are not entitled to enter or travel in the guard's van and a passenger who sustains injury while trying to enter there has no claim against the railway authority.[55]

Collisions. Though liability for injuries sustained in a collision depends on proof of negligence, the circumstances normally give rise to an inference of fault, the whole undertaking being under the management of the one railway authority.[56] Running into the buffers at a terminus is evidence of negligence.[57]

But such an inference is not irrebuttable; it may be rebutted by proof that the accident arose from the wilful and wrongful act of a stranger,[58] or of another passenger,[59] or, doubtless, from *damnum fatale.*

---

[44] *Richardson* v. *Metropolitan Ry.* (1868) L.R. 3 C.P. 374n.; *Fordham* v. *L.B. & S.C.Ry.* (1869) L.R. 4 C.P. 619; *Atkins* v. *S.E.Ry.* (1885) 2 T.L.R. 94; *Murray* v. *L.M.S.Ry.*, 1948 S.L.T. (Sh.Ct.) 30.

[45] *Drury* v. *N.E.Ry.* [1907] 2 K.B. 322; *Benson* v. *Furness Ry.* (1903) 88 L.T. 268; *cf. Metropolitan Ry.* v. *Jackson* (1877) 3 App.Cas. 193.

[46] *Bird* v. *Railway Executive* [1949] W.N. 196.

[47] *Toal* v. *N.B.Ry.*, 1908 S.C.(H.L.) 29; *Burns* v. *N.B.Ry.*, 1914 S.C. 754; *Hare* v. *B.T.C.* [1956] 1 All E.R. 578.

[48] *Metropolitan Ry.* v. *Delaney* (1921) 90 L.J.K.B. 721.

[49] *Brookes* v. *L.P.T.B.* [1947] 1 All E.R. 506.

[50] *Metropolitan Ry.* v. *Jackson* (1877) 3 App.Cas. 193.

[51] *Metropolitan Ry., supra.*

[52] *Pounder* v. *N.E.Ry.* [1892] 1 Q.B. 385.

[53] *Cobb* v. *G.W.Ry.* [1894] A.C. 419.

[54] *Machen* v. *L. & Y.Ry.* (1918) 88 L.J.K.B. 371.

[55] *Thompson* v. *N.B.Ry.* (1882) 9 R. 1101.

[56] *Carpue* v. *L. & B.Ry.* (1844) 5 Q.B. 747; *Skinner* v. *L.B. & S.C.Ry.* (1850) 5 Ex. 787; *Ayles* v. *S.E.Ry.* (1868) L.R. 3 Ex. 146; see also *Ferus* v. *N.B.Ry.* (1872) 9 S.L.R. 652; *Watson* v. *N.B.Ry.* (1876) 3 R. 637.

[57] *Burke* v. *M.S. & L. Ry.* (1870) 22 L.T. 442.

[58] *Latch* v. *Rumner Ry.* (1858) 27 L.J.Ex. 155; *Daniel* v. *Metropolitan Ry.* (1871) L.R. 5 H.L. 45.

[59] *E.I.Ry.* v. *Kalidas Mukerjee* [1901] A.C. 396.

Similarly if an accident happens by reason of a defect in a carriage, the onus is on the railway authority to show that due skill and care were exercised in the manufacture and testing of the vehicle.[60]

Injury from weather. Travellers in bad weather must take certain risks and have no claim for illness or injury resulting from exposure to cold or other weather conditions, at least in the absence of gross neglect by the railway servants or of attempts by them to clear the line or otherwise alleviate the conditions.[61] But there may be liability if intending passengers are not warned of a blockage on the line or other circumstances inferring unusual risk on the journey.[62]

Injuries caused by other passengers. The railway authority's servants should take reasonable care to prevent a person joining a train if he is known to be, or seems likely to be, a nuisance or a danger to other travellers, as by reason of drink, expressed intention, or other apparent sign.[63] So too they should take reasonable steps to preserve order in trains and to remove disorderly persons therefrom. But the authority is not liable if one passenger wilfully or negligently injures another when the danger of this was not reasonably foreseeable,[64] and an authority has been held not liable for refusing to delay a train so that a gang who had robbed a passenger might be detained and searched.[65]

3. SHIPPING ACCIDENTS

The operators of ships owe duties of care to their passengers, to persons who come near or on board the ship in the course of repairing, refitting, loading or unloading her, to legitimate visitors on board, to persons on wharves and other vessels, and to members of the crew, to take reasonable care not to cause them personal injury by defect in the condition of the vessel or danger arising from lack of reasonable care in her navigation or management. The duties of operators of ships to their own crew fall under the heading of Employment Accidents.

General duty of care to persons coming on board. The Occupiers' Liability (Scotland) Act, 1960, s. 1, restating the common law, imposes on, *inter alios*, persons occupying or having control of any vessel, in relation to any person entering thereon, the duty (s. 2) of taking such care as in all the circumstances of the case is reasonable to see that the person will not suffer injury or damage by reason of any danger due to the state of

---

[60] *Manser* v. *Eastern Counties Ry.* (1860) 3 L.T. 585; *Holton* v. *L.S.W.Ry.* (1885) Cab. & E. 542.

[61] *Mathieson* v. *Caledonian Ry.* (1903) 5 F. 511.

[62] *Jarvie* v. *Caledonian Ry.* (1875) 2 R. 623.

[63] *Pounder* v. *N.E.Ry.* [1892] 1 Q.B. 385 (criticised in *Cobb* v. *G.W.Ry.* [1894] A.C. 419 and by Beven, *Negligence*, II, 1198–1201); *Murgatroyd* v. *Blackburn Tramways* (1887) 3 T.L.R. 451.

[64] *E. Indian Ry.* v. *Kalidas Mukerjee* [1901] A.C. 396; *cf. Palsgraf* v. *Long Island Railroad*, 248 N.Y. 339 (1928) (person on platform injured by explosion of fireworks dropped by passenger boarding train: railroad company not liable).

[65] *Cobb* v. *G.W.Ry.* [1894] A.C. 419.

the vessel or to anything done or omitted to be done on it and for which the occupier is in law responsible, though this duty may be restricted, modified or excluded by agreement.

This duty will cover all the foregoing categories, except persons on wharves or other vessels, though in the case of passengers it is no more than is implied by the contract of carriage, and in the case of crew no higher than is implied in the contract of employment, and it does not relieve the person having control of a ship of any higher duty owed to any particular class of persons under any statute or rule. The defence of *volenti non fit injuria* remains competent under the statute.

(a) Duties to passengers

The operators of passenger ships [66] owe to their passengers duties of care *ex lege* as persons who are within the ambit of reasonable foresight of harm from various possible dangers, duties implied by the contract of carriage, and statutory duties imposed by the Merchant Shipping Acts, 1894–1964. The contract of carriage may, and frequently does, contain conditions limiting or purporting to limit the liability of the carrier for damage, injury or other loss occurring to the passenger in prescribed circumstances.[67]

Common law liability. Apart from contract, liability depends on negligence. The shipowner does not absolutely warrant the seaworthiness of his ship for the voyage but is liable for loss of life or personal injury only if he has failed to exercise due diligence and care to make his ship seaworthy. He must also exercise reasonable skill and foresight to carry the passenger in safety, including making reasonable provision of food,[68] and having regard for the safety,[69] comfort [70] and accommodation [71] of the passengers during the voyage.

Statutory liability. The statutory duties imposed on shipowners are too numerous and detailed to be listed.[72] A passenger injured in consequence of the breach of one of these statutory duties has an action of damages based thereon for his loss.[73]

---

[66] Defined (Merchant Shipping Act, 1894, s. 267; Merchant Shipping (Safety Convention) Act, 1949, s. 26) as steamers that take more than 12 passengers, apart from the crew. Special forms of contract are compulsory in the case of emigrant ships and of steerage passengers.

[67] See Chap. 10, *supra*; *Henderson* v. *Stevenson* (1875) 2 R.(H.L.) 71; *Hood* v. *Anchor Line*, 1918 S.C.(H.L.) 143.

[68] *Young* v. *Fewson* (1837) 8 C. & P. 55, 57.

[69] *Andrews* v. *Little* (1887) 3 T.L.R. 544.

[70] *Andrews, supra.*

[71] *Adderley* v. *Cookson* (1809) 2 Camp. 15.

[72] See particularly Merchant Shipping (Safety and Load Lines Convention) Act, 1932; Merchant Shipping (Safety Convention) Act, 1949, and, generally, Temperley's *Merchant Shipping Acts* (6th ed.); Halsbury's *Laws of England*, tit. " Shipping and Navigation," part 4.

[73] *Rudd* v. *Elder Dempster & Co.* [1933] 1 K.B. 566.

Access to the ship. The shipowners owe a duty to take reasonable care to provide safe means for boarding the ship.[74] Thus they will be liable if a vessel casts off before the gangway is withdrawn so that an intending passenger falls into the water,[75] or if the gangway collapses.[76]

Safety on board. A duty of reasonable care is also incumbent on shipowners for the safety of passengers while on board, and shipowners have been held liable where there was no ladder provided for the passenger in an upper berth, and she was injured,[77] or where a porthole glass was not properly secured and injured a passenger's hand,[78] or where the floor of an alleyway had been washed down without warning to the passengers of its being slippery,[79] or a passenger fell down an unguarded opening in the saloon.[80]

Injuries sustained during voyage. If a passenger suffers personal injury during a voyage a distinction must be drawn, for the purposes of assigning liability, between any causes of the injury which are the responsibility of the shipowners, such as unlighted or unfenced hatchways, slippery companion ladders, defective tackle or bad seamanship, and any causes which are not their responsibility, such as heavy weather. In some cases both factors may contribute towards an injury, and in such a case the question may arise whether the shipowners and their servants did what was reasonably practicable, as they must, to avoid or minimise the damage caused by natural phenomena.

Claims have arisen where vessels have grounded or been wrecked and injuries been sustained in consequence.[81]

Personal injuries arising from ship collision. If the ship in which a passenger is travelling is involved in collision and he suffers death or personal injury he has a claim against the shipowner, even though the other ship was entirely to blame, based on a breach of the implied term of safe carriage in his contract of passage.[82] If a shipowner has to pay damages to one of his passengers, he can recover the sum paid in the damages claimed from the ship in fault, as being a natural, probable and direct consequence of that ship's fault.

The Merchant Shipping Act, 1894, ss. 502–503, amended by the Merchant Shipping (Liability of Shipowners and Others) Act, 1958, permits shipowners, charterers, managers of the ship, and the master

---

74 *John* v. *Bacon* (1870) L.R. 5 C.P. 437; *Grieve* v. *Turbine Steamers* (1903) 11 S.L.T. 379; *Cameron* v. *L.M.S.Ry.* (1936) 54 Ll.L.R. 95; *Adler* v. *Dickson* [1955] 1 Q.B. 158.
75 *Monaghan* v. *Buchanan* (1886) 13 R. 860.
76 *Adler* v. *Dickson, supra.* Contrast *O'Brien* v. *Arbib,* 1907 S.C. 975, where pursuer was on board as licensee only. *Cf. Williamson* v. *N. of Scotland S.N. Co.,* 1916 S.C. 554.
77 *Andrews* v. *Little & Co.* (1887) 3 T.L.R. 544.
78 *Jones* v. *Oceanic S.N. Co.* [1924] 2 K.B. 730.
79 *Beaumont-Thomas* v. *Blue Star Line* [1939] 3 All E.R. 127.
80 *Taylor* v. *P. & O.S.N. Co.* (1869) 21 L.T. 442.
81 *Hood* v. *Anchor Line,* 1918 S.C.(H.L.) 143; *cf. Henderson* v. *Stevenson* (1875) 2 R.(H.L.) 71.
82 *Lewis* v. *Laird Line,* 1925 S.L.T. 316; *Reavis* v. *Clan Line Steamers,* 1925 S.C. 725.

and crew, to limit their liability in respect of claims for loss of life or personal injury suffered by any person on board and any property on board the ship, provided that the loss occurred without the actual fault or privity of the persons claiming limitation.[83]

Joint and several liability of ships. Where a person on board a vessel suffers loss of life or personal injury owing to the fault of that vessel and of any other vessel or vessels, the liability of the owners of the vessels is joint and several, and action may be brought against both or all vessels.[84] The one owner has a claim for contribution against the other.[85]

(b) Injuries to stevedores or others working about a ship

The liability of shipowners to persons not their own employees who come on board or work about the ship, as when painting or repairing it, loading or unloading, depends partly on common law principles of negligence and partly on special statutory duties of care. The Occupiers' Liability (Scotland) Act, 1960, now states the basic duty of care incumbent at common law on the owner or charterer.[86]

At common law the shipowners must take reasonable care for the safety of stevedores, workmen and others whom they reasonably foresee as likely to come on board. Thus they may have been held liable for injuries caused by the fall of a stanchion while cargo was being discharged,[87] or a defective rope,[88] or defective loading tackle,[89] for failure to provide a safe means of descent into the hold,[90] or a safe means of access to the vessel from the quay,[91] for defective scaffolding used in repairing the ship,[92] or leaving a hatchway open and unlighted,[93] or failing to make sure that the place where a workman was to work was reasonably safe.[94]

Statutory liability to workmen. The Factories Act, 1961, s. 175 (2), includes within the expression " factory " premises, whether or not they are factories under the general definition thereof, including " (i) any yard or dry dock (including the precincts thereof) in which ships or vessels are constructed, reconstructed, repaired,[95] refitted, finished or

83 See, *e.g.*, *Leadbetter* v. *Dublin and Glasgow S.P. Co.*, 1907 S.C. 538.
84 Maritime Conventions Act, 1911, s. 2.
85 *Ibid.* s. 3.
86 As to who is liable, see *McCallum* v. *Connell* (1901) 9 S.L.T. 276; *McLauchlan* v. *Hogarth*, 1911 S.C. 522; *Wright* v. *Anchor Line*, 1920, 1 S.L.T. 265.
87 *McLachlan* v. *SS. Peveril Co.* (1896) 23 R. 753.
88 *Traill* v. *A/S Dalbeattie* (1904) 6 F. 798.
89 *Walker* v. *Olsen* (1882) 9 R. 946.
90 *Chadwick* v. *Elderslie SS. Co.* (1898) 25 R. 730; *cf. Wood* v. *Mackay* (1906) 8 F. 625.
91 *Adamson* v. *McGuiness* (1907) 14 S.L.T. 672; *cf. Waterson* v. *Murray* (1884) 11 R. 1036; *Leeson* v. *Gardner*, 1947 S.L.T. 264; *Jordan* v. *Court Line*, 1947 S.C. 29.
92 *Davison* v. *Henderson* (1895) 22 R. 448.
93 *Burns* v. *Henderson* (1905) 7 F. 697; *Grant* v. *Sun Shipping Co.*, 1948 S.C.(H.L.) 73.
94 *Grant* v. *Sun Shipping Co.*, 1948 S.C.(H.L.) 73.
95 This includes painting with anti-fouling composition: *Day* v. *Harland & Wolff, Ltd.* [1953] 2 All E.R. 387; *Hurley* v. *Saunders* [1955] 1 All E.R. 833; but not internal painting: *Taylor* v. *Ellerman's Wilson Line* [1952] 1 Lloyd's Rep. 144. See also *Gardiner* v. *The Admiralty*, 1964 S.L.T. 194 (H.L.).

broken up," [96] and the person who regulates and controls the work which is done in such premises is accordingly the " occupier " of a " factory " for the purposes of the Act, and liable if the requirements of the Act are not implemented and injury results to a person on the premises.

Application of Factories Act to docks and ships. By section 125 (1) specified provisions of the Factories Act, 1961, apply to every dock,[97] wharf [98] or quay (including any warehouse [99] belonging to the owners, trustees or conservators of the dock, wharf or quay, and any line or siding used in connection with and for the purposes of the dock, wharf or quay and not forming part of a railway or tramway) and every other warehouse (not forming part of a factory) in or for the purposes of which mechanical power is used, as if it were a factory and as if the person having the actual use or occupation of it [1] were the occupier of a factory.

By section 125 (3) other specified provisions apply to the process of loading, unloading,[2] or coaling any ship in any dock, harbour or canal, and to all machinery or plant used in these processes, as if the premises were a factory.

Section 125 (6) applies other provisions of the Act to every warehouse [99] mentioned in section 125 (1) as if it were a factory.

Application of Factories Act to ships under repair. Specified provisions of the Factories Act, 1961, apply to any work carried out in a harbour or wet dock in constructing, reconstructing, repairing, refitting, painting, finishing or breaking up a ship or in scaling, scurfing or cleaning boilers, or certain other specified operations, and for the purposes of these provisions, a ship is to be deemed a factory and any person undertaking the work to be deemed the occupier of a factory.[3]

Docks Regulations. The Docks Regulations, 1934,[4] apply with certain exceptions to the processes of loading, unloading, moving and handling goods in, on or at any dock, wharf or quay, and the processes of loading, unloading and coaling any ship in any dock, harbour or canal.

Shipbuilding Regulations. The Shipbuilding and Ship-repairing Regulations, 1960,[5] apply (a) as respects work carried out in any of the

---

[96] This covers shipbuilding yards, and fitting-out basins within the precincts or perimeter thereof: *Smith* v. *Cammell Laird & Co., Ltd.* [1940] A.C. 242; and public dry docks, *i.e.*, not part of a shipbuilding yard. A vessel under repair in a public wet dock has been held not to be a " factory ": *Bowman* v. *Ellerman Lines*, 1953 S.L.T. 271; and a vessel under repair and made fast to the repairer's jetty has been held not to be a factory: *Chatburn* v. *Manchester Dry Dock Co.* (1950) 83 Ll.L.Rep. 1.

[97] " Dock " means the solid structure, not the water space; a ship in dock is not necessarily a factory under the Act: *Houlder* v. *Griffin* [1905] A.C. 220.

[98] See *Haddock* v. *Humphrey* [1900] 1 Q.B. 609; *Ellis* v. *Cory* [1902] 1 K.B. 38.

[99] *Green* v. *Britten & Gilson* [1904] 1 K.B. 350; *McEwan* v. *Perth Mags.* (1905) 7 F. 714.

[1] See *Merrill* v. *Wilson* [1901] 1 K.B. 35; *Carrington* v. *Bannister* [1901] 1 K.B. 20; *Raine* v. *Jobson* [1901] A.C. 404; *Reid* v. *Anchor Line* (1903) 5 F. 435.

[2] See *Lysons* v. *Knowles* [1901] A.C. 79; *Manchester Ship Canal* v. *D.P.P.* [1930] 1 K.B. 547.

[3] Factories Act, 1961, s. 126.

[4] S.R. & O. 1934 No. 207.

[5] S.I. 1960 No. 1932; replacing Shipbuilding Regulations, 1931.

operations in a shipyard in the case of a ship or vessel whether or not the shipyard forms part of a harbour or wet dock; (b) as respects work carried out in any of the operations in a harbour or wet dock in the case of a ship (but not in the case of a vessel other than a ship) not being work done by the master or crew, on a trial trip, in raising or removing a sunk or stranded ship, or on a ship which is not under command to bring it under command.

(c) Duties to legitimate visitors

The duty of care under the Occupiers' Liability (Scotland) Act, 1960, is owed to such a person as an officer's wife, permitted to come on board to see her husband,[6] and doubtless to such persons as pilots and customs officers, and to any other legitimate visitor.

(d) Injuries to persons on wharves or other ships

The shipowners must take reasonable care so to manage their ship that it does not cause death or personal injury to persons on quays or wharves, or in other vessels. Hence they will be liable if, by negligence, their vessel collides with a wharf or another vessel and causes injury or death thereon,[7] or where a person standing on the quay is knocked down by a mooring rope.[8]

4. AIRCRAFT ACCIDENTS

Operators of aircraft similarly owe duties of care to their passengers, their crew and to persons on the ground or in other aircraft, and are liable if injury is caused by negligence in the maintenance or operation of their aircraft. A high standard of care is demanded in view of the serious harm which may flow from an accident in or about aircraft.

(a) Safety of airfields

At common law operators of aircraft must take reasonable care to protect the public and intending passengers from being injured by aircraft. Thus where a visitor to an airfield was led to a dangerous position and killed by a revolving propeller the operators were held liable[9]; similarly where a plane was flown too close to the ground and a woman was killed, it was said that damages were recoverable.[10]

---

[6] O'Brien v. Arbib, 1907 S.C. 975.

[7] Haglund v. Russell (1882) 9 R. 958; The Bernina (1888) 13 App.Cas. 1; Carse v. N.B. Steam Packet Co. (1895) 22 R. 475; Kendrick v. Burnett (1897) 25 R. 82; Leadbetter v. Dublin and Glasgow Steam Packet Co., 1907 S.C. 538; Rodger v. Glen-Coats, 1913, 1 S.L.T. 434.

[8] Clark v. Glasgow, etc., Steam Packet Co. (1901) 3 F. 991; cf. Craig v. Aberdeen Harbour Commrs., 1909 S.C. 736, where harbour authorities, and not the moving vessel, were held liable in the circumstances.

[9] Waring v. East Anglian Flying Services, Ltd. [1951] W.N. 553.

[10] Billings v. Reed [1944] 2 All E.R. 415, 417 (the actual decision was on a point of wartime legislation).

(b) Safety of passengers

Statutory formulation of common law duty of care to passengers. The Occupier's Liability (Scotland) Act, 1960, s. 1, imposes on the person having control of any aircraft the duty to persons entering thereon of (s. 2) taking such care as in all the circumstances of the case is reasonable to see that the person does not suffer injury or damage by reason of any danger due to the state of the aircraft or to anything done or omitted to be done on it and for which in law the person in control is responsible. This duty may be extended, restricted, modified or excluded by agreement, and yields to any higher standard of duty imposed by particular legislation.

Liability to passengers in the aircraft. The liability to such persons depended formerly on general principles of negligence, the duty of the carrier being to carry with due care.[11] Thus where a plane crashed immediately after taking-off the owners were held liable to injured passengers.[12] These principles probably still apply to a gratuitous carriage or a special hiring, as of an air-taxi or pleasure flight. In cases regulated by common law, it is competent for carrier and passenger to make a contract completely excluding liability for death or injury arising out of the carriage and if the terms are clear and unambiguous they will receive effect.[13]

Liability now depends in practically every case on the Carriage by Air Act, 1932, to be replaced by the Carriage by Air Act, 1961 (which applies only to international carriage as therein defined [14]) [15], and the Carriage by Air (Non-International Carriage) (United Kingdom) Order, 1952, supplemented by the carrier's own conditions of carriage, which usually are based on the General Conditions of Carriage of the International Air Transport Association. An attempt to contract-out of the rules is void.

The air carrier must issue a passenger ticket, otherwise he is, in general, not entitled to avail himself of the provisions of the Act which exclude or limit his liability,[16] and it must state specified particulars, including that the carriage is subject to the rules relating to liability established by the convention.

Statutory liability. The air carrier is liable for damage sustained in the event of the death or wounding of a passenger or any other bodily injury suffered by a passenger, if the accident which caused the damage

---

[11] *Ludditt* v. *Ginger Coote Airways, Ltd.* [1947] 1 All E.R. 328.

[12] *Fosbroke-Hobbes* v. *Airwork, Ltd.* [1937] 1 All E.R. 108.

[13] *McKay* v. *Scottish Airways*, 1948 S.C. 254.

[14] On this see *Grein* v. *Imperial Airways* [1937] 1 K.B. 50; *Phillipson* v. *Imperial Airways* [1939] A.C. 332.

[15] This was passed to give effect to the Warsaw Convention of 1929, amended at The Hague in 1955, which is reproduced in the Schedule to the Act. The 1952 Order applies the same conditions, with slight modifications, to non-international carriage.

[16] 1961 Act, Sched. I, Art. 3 (2): *secus* under the Order: see Sched. I, para. 2 thereof.

so sustained took place on board the aircraft or in the course of any of the operations of embarking or disembarking.[17]

The carrier is not liable if he proves that he and his agents have taken all necessary measures to avoid the damage or that it was impossible for him or them to take such measures.[18] If the carrier proves that the damage was caused by or contributed to by the negligence of the injured person the court may, in accordance with the provisions of its own law, exonerate the carrier wholly or partly from his liability.[19]

Limitation of liability. The liability of the carrier for each passenger is limited to 250,000 francs,[20] unless by special contract a higher limit of liability is agreed.[21] Any provision tending to relieve the carrier of liability or to fix a lower limit than that which is laid down in the Warsaw Convention is null and void.[22]

The limitation is not to apply if the passenger can prove that the damage which he suffered was caused by the wilful misconduct of the carrier or his servants or agents.[23] To establish wilful misconduct a pursuer must satisfy the court that the person who did the act knew at the time that he was doing something wrong and yet did it nevertheless, or that he did it recklessly, not caring whether he did the right thing or not, regardless of the effects of his conduct on the safety of the aircraft and of the passengers.[24]

The right to damages is extinguished if the action is not brought within two years from the date of arrival, or from the date on which the aircraft ought to have arrived, or from the date on which the carriage stopped.[25] This provision is not to be read as applying to proceedings for contribution between wrongdoers, but an action for contribution is not to be brought after two years from the time when judgment is obtained against the person seeking contribution.[26]

Liability for death of passenger. In the event of a passenger's death liability extends to those persons who are entitled, apart from the Act, to sue the carrier (whether for patrimonial damage or *solatium* or both) in respect of the death.[27]

Compulsory insurance. It is an offence to fly, or cause or permit any other person to fly, an aircraft, unless there is in force (a) a policy of insurance covering all liability which the owner of the aircraft may incur

17 1961 Act, Sched. I, Art. 17; 1952 Order, Sched. III, Art. 17.
18 1961 Act, Sched. I, Art. 20; 1952 Order, Sched. III, Art. 20 (1).
19 1961 Act, Sched. I, Art. 21; 1952 Order, Sched. III, Art. 21.
20 Defined: 1961 Act, Sched. I, Art. 22 (5); 1952 Order, Sched. III, Art. 22 (5).
21 1961 Act, Sched. I, Art. 22 (1); 1952 Order, Sched. III, Art. 22 (1).
22 1961 Act, Sched. I, Art. 23; 1952 Order, Sched. III, Art. 23.
23 1961 Act, Sched. I, Art. 25; 1952 Order, Sched. III, Art. 25.
24 *Horabin* v. *B.O.A.C.* [1952] 2 All E.R. 1016.
25 1961 Act, Sched. I, Art. 29; 1952 Order, Sched. III, Art. 29.
26 1961 Act, ss. 5 and 11.
27 1961 Act, s. 11 (b) referring to Sched. I, Art. 17. The 1932 Act gave entitlement to damages to those entitled under the [English] Fatal Accidents Acts, 1846–1959.

in respect of loss or damage caused to persons or property on land or water by, or by any person in, or any article or person falling from, the aircraft while in flight, taking off or landing, or (b) an undertaking by an authorised giver of securities to make good any failure by the owner of the aircraft to discharge any such liability. This does not apply to aircraft owned by a local or police authority or being used for police purposes.[28]

(c) Liability to crew

The liability of owners of aircraft to the crew of the aircraft is regulated by the ordinary principles of the liability of employer to employee.

(d) Statutory liability to persons on land or water

The Civil Aviation Act, 1949, s. 40 provides: " (2) Where material loss or damage [29] is caused to any person or property on land or water by, or by a person in, or an article or person falling from, an aircraft while in flight, taking off [30] or landing, then unless the loss or damage was caused or contributed to by the negligence of the person by whom it was suffered, damages in respect of the loss or damage shall be recoverable without proof of negligence or intention or other cause of action, as if the loss or damage had been caused by the wilful act, neglect, or default of the owner of the aircraft:

Provided that where material loss or damage is caused as aforesaid in circumstances in which:

(a) damages are recoverable in respect of the said loss or damage by virtue only of the foregoing provisions of this subsection; and

(b) a legal liability is created in some person other than the owner to pay damages in respect of the said loss or damage;

the owner shall be entitled to be indemnified by that other person against any claim in respect of the said loss or damage."

Section 40 appears to have no application to aircraft belonging to or exclusively employed in the service of Her Majesty,[30a] which are accordingly regulated by common law subject, in appropriate circumstances, to the alterations made by the Crown Proceedings Act, 1947.

The effect of this section is generally to impose an absolute liability on the owner of the aircraft, unless he can prove contributory negligence, the onus of proof of which is on him,[31] and even though the loss or damage had been caused by wrongful act, default or neglect of a third party, or by *damnum fatale*. The section applies only, however, to damage to person or property on land or water, and does not apply to crew or passengers

[28] Civil Aviation Act, 1949, s. 43.
[29] Defined by s. 63 as including, in relation to persons, loss of life and personal injury.
[30] See *Blankley* v. *Godley* [1952] 1 All E.R. 436n.
[30a] s. 61 (1), made applicable to Part IV of the Act by s. 49 (3).
[31] *Cubitt* v. *Gower* (1933) 47 Ll.L.R. 65.

in the aircraft, nor to persons in any other aircraft, and to damage caused by " persons in,[32] or an article or person falling from " an aircraft, and not by the aircraft itself, *e.g.*, crashing.

Where section 40 applies, *res ipsa loquitur* can be invoked, as where an aircraft took off and crashed before it had gained height.[33] The liability is imposed on the owner of the aircraft but if an aircraft has been hired out for a period exceeding fourteen days, and no operative member of the crew of the aircraft is in the employment of the owner, the hirer is subject to the liability as if he were owner.[34]

The Act does not cover liability for loss or damage caused by a person other than the owner of the aircraft, such as a hirer for a period of less than fourteen days, in which case liability depends on negligence.

Limitation of liability. A person who, or whose estate, is liable to pay damages by reason of loss or damage which is caused on any one occasion to persons or property on land or water by, or by a person in, or an article or person falling from, an aircraft while in flight, taking off or landing, may limit his or his estate's total liability to pay damages by reason of the loss or damage in accordance with Schedule V to the Civil Aviation Act, 1949. Limitation cannot be claimed in any case in which it is proved that the loss or damage was attributable to that person's wilful misconduct, or to wilful misconduct on the part of any of his servants or agents unless it is proved that the loss or damage occurred without his actual fault or privity.[35]

When several claims are made or apprehended, application may be made to the Court of Session, and that court may assess the liability to pay damages, and determine whether, and if so, to what amount, it can be limited under this section, dealing separately, if need be, with such of the claims as are in respect of loss of or damage to property and, if the liability can be so limited, may distribute the amount thereof among the several claims on the following principles:

(a) if the claims are solely in respect of loss of life or personal injury or solely in respect of loss of, or damage to, property, the amount of the liability shall be distributed rateably;

(b) if there are claims under both heads, half of the total amount of liability shall be appropriated, so far as necessary, to life claims and distributed rateably among them, and the other half distributed rateably among all other claims, including life and injury claims so far as they exceed the appropriation already made.[36]

It is further provided that nothing in section 40 or 42 is to affect the operation of the Carriage by Air Act, 1932, or any contract for the carriage

---

32 *Quaere*; does this include damage caused by the negligence of the *pilot* in the plane?

33 *Fosbroke-Hobbes* v. *Airwork, Ltd.* [1937] 1 All E.R. 108.

34 Civil Aviation Act, 1949, s. 49 (2).

35 Civil Aviation Act, 1949, s. 42 (1).

36 s. 42 (4).

of passengers or goods by air in so far as the contract provides for determining or limiting the liability of the carrier thereunder. This limitation accordingly does not apply to passengers.

(e) Aircraft collisions

Damage or injury to a person in an aircraft in flight, caused by aerial collision, is not covered by section 40 of the 1949 Act, and liability therefore depends on proof of common law negligence on the part of the pilot of the other aircraft, possibly combined with negligence by the injured person's own pilot and for any radio operators, ground control staff, and other personnel who may have been concerned. In many cases proof of negligence may be extremely difficult, and the principle of res ipsa loquitur may require to be invoked, though if, as is not unlikely, all persons in both planes are killed, it is difficult to see how even this principle could apply.

In the case of collisions over any part of the United Kingdom the observance or non-observance of the Rules of the Air prescribed in the Air Navigation Order, 1960, Sched. II, as amended, is of importance.

5. ACCIDENTS ARISING OUT OF EMPLOYMENT

The liability of an employer to pay damages to an employee who sustains personal injuries in the course of the employment may arise on various grounds, on the ground of breach by the employer of one or more of the duties of care for the safety of his employees imposed directly on him by common law, or on the ground of his vicarious liability at common law for the acts and omissions of other employees, acting in the course of and within the scope of their employment, or on the ground of breach by the employer of one or more of various statutory duties of care imposed on him by Act of Parliament or regulations made thereunder. On the facts of a particular case any one or two or all three of these grounds may be founded on. Claims founded on both common law fault (whether direct liability or vicarious liability) and a breach of statutory duty should be distinguished in the pursuer's pleadings both in averments and in pleas in law,[37] and a court should approach the questions of common law fault and breach of statutory duty independently.[38] In addition an accident arising out of employment may give a right of action against the occupier of the premises (if other than the employer) on which the accident occurred, if it were attributable to the premises or the occupier's fault.

The present state of the law requires some explanation by reference to its historical development, because older cases are properly comprehensible only in the light of the former law, and because social and economic beliefs and legal doctrines now obsolete account for much of the form of the modern law.

[37] Keenan v. Glasgow Corpn., 1923 S.C. 611.
[38] Chipchase v. British Titan Products, Ltd. [1956] 1 Q.B. 545.

Liability of Employer to Injured Employee

Common law duty of care. In Scots law it was early recognised that an employer must take reasonable care for the safety of his employees, and that he was liable to them for injuries caused where he was himself in fault.[39] Similarly it was recognised that an employer was vicariously liable for the wrongs done by his employees not only to third persons but to his other employees.[40] But in these earlier cases the courts tended to uphold defence pleas of *volenti non fit injuria* and contributory negligence (which was then a complete defence) more readily and liberally than they would today.[41]

Common employment. Though the doctrine that an employer was vicariously liable for the wrongs of his employees, done to third parties, had been accepted in Scotland by the early nineteenth century, it was held in England in *Priestley* v. *Fowler* [42] that, while the master might be liable to an injured servant for personal fault, he was not liable vicariously to an injured servant for an injury caused by another servant, with whom the plaintiff was engaged in common employment. This principle was extended [43] to fellow employees doing different work and, quite unjustifiably, extended to Scotland by the House of Lords,[44] reversing the Court of Session, and applied even to cases where the fellow employees were very different in point of station and duties.[45] The doctrine did not elide the personal liability of the other employee.[46]

---

[39] *Hislop* v. *Durham* (1842) 4 D. 1168; *Macaulay* v. *Buist* (1846) 9 D. 245 (" to see that all the necessary precautions are taken, which human foresight can suggest " (249, Lord Fullerton)); *Sneddon* v. *Addie* (1849) 11 D. 1159 (" He is bound to strict diligence, because life is concerned " (1161, Lord Mackenzie)); *Whitelaw* v. *Moffat* (1849) 12 D. 434 (" the defenders . . . were bound to establish that they took every precaution "); *McNeill* v. *Wallace* (1853) 15 D. 818 (" it is the paramount duty of coalmasters, and persons engaged in such undertakings, to provide in every way for the safety of the workmen in their employment, against the risks and dangers which such employment involves " (L.J.C. Hope, 819)); *Dixon* v. *Rankin* (1852) 14 D. 420, 423, 425, 427; *Paterson* v. *Wallace* (1854) 1 Macq. 748; *Marshall* v. *Stewart* (1855) 2 Macq. 30 (" A master is liable for accidents occasioned by his neglect towards those whom he employs."); *McNaughton* v. *Caledonian Ry.* (1858) 21 D. 160; *cf. Clark* v. *Armstrong* (1862) 24 D. 1315.

[40] *Sword* v. *Cameron* (1839) 1 D. 493; *Dixon* v. *Rankin* (1852) 14 D. 420; *Nisbett* v. *Dixon* (1852) 14 D. 973; *Gray* v. *Brassey* (1852) 15 D. 135; *Baird* v. *Addie* (1854) 16 D. 490; *O'Byrne* v. *Burn* (1854) 16 D. 1025; *McNaughton* v. *Caledonian Ry.* (1857) 19 D. 271; *Cook* v. *Duncan* (1857) 20 D. 180. But in *Paterson* v. *Monkland Iron Co.* (1851) 13 D. 1270, the court had questioned whether a master was liable for an injury caused to one servant by the fault or negligence of another; so too in *Gray* v. *Brassey* (1853) 15 D. 135; see also *Lennan* v. *Addie & Miller* (1857) 21 D. 1382n.

[41] *MacNeill* v. *Wallace* (1853) 15 D. 818; *Paterson* v. *Wallace* (1855) 17 D. 623; *Sutherland* v. *Monkland Rys.* (1857) 19 D. 1004; *Lawson* v. *Gray* (1860) 22 D. 710; *O'Neill* v. *Wilson* (1858) 20 D. 427; *Cook* v. *Bell* (1857) 20 D. 137; *Crichton* v. *Keir & Crichton* (1863) 1 M. 407.

[42] (1837) 3 M. & W. 1.

[43] *Hutchinson* v. *York, Newcastle & Berwick Ry.* (1850) 5 Ex. 343.

[44] *Bartonshill Coal Co.* v. *Reid* (1858) 3 Macq. 266; *Bartonshill Coal Co.* v. *McGuire* (1858) 3 Macq. 300. *Priestley* v. *Fowler* had been cited and not followed in *Dixon* v. *Rankin* (1852) 14 D. 420.

[45] *Wright* v. *Roxburgh and Morris* (1864) 2 M. 748; *Macfarlane* v. *Caledonian Ry.* (1867) 6 M. 102; *Wilson* v. *Merry & Cuninghame* (1868) 6 M.(H.L.) 84; *Leddy* v. *Gibson* (1873) 11 M. 304; see also review of authorities in *Woodhead* v. *Gartness Mineral Co.* (1877) 4 R. 508.

[46] *Wright* v. *Roxburgh and Morris, supra.*

The worst injustices of the doctrine were mitigated by the Employers' Liability Act, 1880,[47] and the Workmen's Compensation Acts of 1897 and subsequent years,[48] and by the development of liability for breach of statutory duties designed to protect safety and health.[49] But the doctrine had still to be applied, and was held to cover two men working on a common task, though they had different masters,[50] and two employees so related that the negligence of one to the other was an ordinary risk of the employment,[51] but not where the employer's manager ordered a man to do work out of his ordinary line [52] or two employees were so separate that the one ran no greater risk from the negligence of the other than he did from negligence of third parties,[53] nor where the injured man had been allocated to the employment under a Government scheme.[54] The doctrine was finally abolished by the Law Reform (Personal Injuries) Act, 1948, s.1 (1). The result is to restore the authority of Scottish decisions prior to the imposition on Scotland of the doctrine of common employment.

The development of the employer's personal duty. The unfairness of many of the decisions which had to be given so long as the doctrine of common employment subsisted forced the courts to develop formulations of the personal duties of care incumbent on the employer (as distinct from the employer's liability vicariously for the breach of duty of a fellow-servant), a task which the Scottish courts had begun before the regrettable decisions in the *Bartonshill* cases.[55] Thus it was held in *Sword* v. *Cameron* [56] that an employer was liable where he had failed to provide a safe system of work, and in *Paterson* v. *Wallace* [57] the law was said to be that a man employing a servant in work, particularly of a dangerous character, was " bound to take all reasonable precautions that there shall be no extraordinary danger incurred by the workman," and in *Brydon* v. *Stewart* [58] that the master was " bound to exercise due care in order to have his tackle and machinery in a safe and proper condition, so as to

[47] Repealed, as no longer necessary, by the Law Reform (Personal Injuries) Act, 1948, s. 1 (2).
[48] Repealed and replaced by the National Insurance (Industrial Injuries) Acts, 1946–1964.
[49] Early cases were *Coe* v. *Platt* (1851) 6 Ex. 752; (1852) 7 Ex. 460, 923; *Clarke* v. *Holmes* (1862) 7 H. & N. 937; *Edgar* v. *Law & Brand* (1871) 10 M. 236; see also *Stewarts* v. *Scottish N.E.Ry.* (1866) 1 S.L.R. 251; the competency of such an action was assumed in *Baddeley* v. *Earl Granville* (1887) 19 Q.B.D. 423 and decided in *Groves* v. *Lord Wimborne* [1898] 2 Q.B. 402; it was also held that neither common employment nor *volenti non fit injuria* was a defence in such a case.
[50] *Johnson* v. *Lindsay* [1891] A.C. 371.
[51] *Miller* v. *Glasgow Corpn.*, 1947 S.C.(H.L.) 12.
[52] *Stark* v. *McLaren* (1871) 10 M. 31. *Cf. McAulay* v. *Brownlie* (1860) 22 D. 975.
[53] *The Petrel* [1893] P. 320; *Radcliffe* v. *Ribble Motor Services* [1939] A.C. 215; *Metcalfe* v. *L.P.T.B.* [1939] 2 All E.R. 542; *Neilson* v. *Pantrini*, 1947 S.C.(H.L.) 64; *Lancaster* v. *L.P.T.B.* [1948] 2 All E.R. 796; *Healy* v. *L.P.T.B.* [1948] W.N. 132.
[54] *Mullen* v. *Sloan*, 1947 S.C. 720; *Kelly* v. *Spencer*, 1949 S.C. 143.
[55] *Bartonshill Coal Co.* v. *Reid* (1858) 3 Macq. 266; *Bartonshill Coal Co.* v. *McGuire* (1858) 3 Macq. 300.
[56] (1839) 1 D. 493.
[57] (1854) 1 Macq. 748: it was also pointed out that, if the duty of taking precautions were entrusted to a manager, the company would be responsible for the manager's negligence.
[58] (1855) 2 Macq. 30.

protect the servant against unnecessary risks." The extent of the employer's personal obligation was several times restated by the House of Lords.[59]

After the *Bartonshill* decisions [55] the master was several times held liable for injury caused by the fault of managers or foremen, who were not at first regarded as fellow-servants,[60] or by the fault of independent contractors employed by the master.[61]

This development received its definitive statement in *English* v. *Wilsons & Clyde Coal Co.*,[62] where the master's obligation was said to be threefold, the provision of a competent staff of men, adequate material, and a proper system and effective supervision,[63] an obligation not absolute but fulfilled by the exercise of due care and skill, but personal to the employer in that it was not fulfilled by entrusting its fulfilment to employees, even though selected with due care and skill, but one which he had to perform by himself or his delegates. " I think the whole course of authority consistently recognises a duty, which rests on the employer and which is personal to the employer, to take reasonable care for the safety of his workmen, whether the employer be an individual, a firm, or a company, and whether or not the employer takes any share in the conduct of the operations. The obligation is threefold, as I have explained. Thus the obligation to provide and maintain proper plant and appliances is a continuing obligation. It is not, however, broken by a mere misuse or failure to use proper plant and appliances due to the negligence of a fellow servant, or a merely temporary failure to keep in order or adjust plant and appliances, or a casual departure from the system of working, if these matters can be regarded as the casual negligence of the managers, foremen, or other employees." [64]

The modern law. With the abolition of the doctrine of common employment the fact that the wrongdoer is in common employment with the injured person is no bar to the latter's claim, and the latter may freely sue the wrongdoer, or the employer as vicariously liable for the wrongdoer. While, for the same reason, the stress on the duties of care incumbent on the employer personally and non-delegable, is no longer necessary, the formulations of the duty of care in such cases as *English* v.

---

[59] *e.g., Wilson* v. *Merry & Cuninghame* (1868) 6 M.(H.L.) 84, 89, *per* L.C. Cairns; *Weems* v. *Mathieson* (1861) 4 Macq. 215, 226, *per* Lord Wensleydale; *Smith* v. *Baker* [1891] A.C. 325, 353, *per* Lord Watson.

[60] *Cook* v. *Duncan* (1857) 20 D. 180; *Hardie* v. *Addie* (1858) 20 D. 553; *McAulay* v. *Brownlie* (1860) 22 D. 975; *McMillan* v. *McMillan* (1861) 23 D. 1082; *Stark* v. *McLaren* (1871) 10 M. 31; *Somerville* v. *Gray* (1863) 1 M. 768.

[61] *Baird* v. *Addie* (1854) 16 D. 490; *Gregory* v. *Hill* (1869) 8 M. 282; *cf. Woodhead* v. *Gartness Mineral Co.* (1877) 4 R. 469.

[62] 1937 S.C.(H.L.) 46, approved *Winter* v. *Cardiff R.D.C.* [1950] 1 All E.R. 819.

[63] *Ibid.* 60, *per* Lord Wright, quoting Lord McLaren in *Bett* v. *Dalmeny Oil Co.* (1905) 7 F. 787, 796, approved by Lord Shaw in *Black* v. *Fife Coal Co.* 1912 S.C.(H.L.) 33, 50, and in *McMullan* v. *Lochgelly Iron Co.*, 1933 S.C.(H.L.) 64, 80.

[64] *Ibid.* 65, *per* Lord Wright, citing as illustrations *Wilson* v. *Merry & Cuninghame* (1868) 6 M.(H.L.) 84; *Hedley* v. *Pinkney & Sons S.S. Co.* [1894] A.C. 222 and *Griffiths* v. *London and St. Katherine Dock Co.* [1884] 12 Q.B.D. 493.

Wilsons & Clyde Coal Co.,[65] remain important and useful general statements of the duties of care of the employer. The rule that those duties could not be delegated to a manager so as to rid the employer of liability is still the law but is now irrelevant, for even if the duty could be delegated, the employer would now be vicariously liable for the manager's or foreman's default. The modern law, which is as favourable to workmen as it was unfavourable a century ago, has been further altered generally in the workman's favour by the Law Reform (Contributory Negligence) Act, 1945, whereby an injured man is not disabled from recovering by his own partial contribution to the causation of the accident, but merely suffers a diminution of damages in proportion to the degree in which he is held himself in fault.

Independently of these changes in common law, large numbers of stringent statutory duties have been imposed on employers.[66]

It remains convenient, accordingly, to discuss separately the cases in which the employer is held liable for personal fault, those in which he is liable vicariously for the fault of an employee, and those in which he is held liable for breach of a statutory duty.

(a) The employer's personal duty of care

" The whole course of authority consistently recognises a duty which rests on the employer, and which is personal to the employer, to take reasonable care for the safety of his workmen, whether the employer be an individual, a firm, or a company, and whether or not the employer takes any share in the conduct of the operations." [67] " The duty of an employer towards his servant is to take reasonable care for his servant's safety in all the circumstances of the case." [68] " But we can at least return to the simple question which is at the bottom of it all: ' Has the employer taken reasonable care for the safety of the workman?' a question which can only be answered in each case by a consideration of all its circumstances." [69]

In some cases the law is still stated in an earlier formulation,[70] that the employer must not expose his employees to unnecessary risk [71] or unreasonable risk.[72] This formulation certainly does not today imply that an employer may with impunity expose his workmen to risks inherent in the work or to reasonable risks, and it is less satisfactory that the formulation which requires the exercise of due care.

[65] 1937 S.C.(H.L.) 46.
[66] See Chap. 18, *infra.*
[67] *English* v. *Wilsons & Clyde Coal Co.*, 1937 S.C.(H.L.) 46, 65, *per* Lord Wright.
[68] *Paris* v. *Stepney Borough Council* [1951] A.C. 367, 384, *per* Lord Oaksey, approved in *Cavanagh* v. *Ulster Weaving Co.* [1960] A.C. 145.
[69] *Davie* v. *New Merton Board Mills* [1959] A.C. 604, *per* Viscount Simonds.
[70] Found in *Hutchinson* v. *York, Newcastle & Berwick Ry.* (1850) 5 Ex. 343; *Bartonshill Coal Co.* v. *Reid* (1858) 3 Macq. 266.
[71] *Smith* v. *Baker* [1891] A.C. 325, 362.
[72] *Street* v. *British Electricity Authority* [1952] 2 Q.B. 399, 406; *Latimer* v. *A.E.C., Ltd.* [1952] 2 Q.B. 701, 708; *Harris* v. *Bright's Asphalt Contractors, Ltd.* [1953] 1 Q.B. 617, 626; *Drummond* v. *British Building Cleaners, Ltd.* [1954] 3 All E.R. 507, 512; *Rands* v. *McNeil* [1955] 1 Q.B. 253, 257.

This general duty of care comprehends in particular, but is not limited to, " the provision of a competent staff of men, adequate material, a proper system, and effective supervision." [73] The duty is " to take reasonable care, and to use reasonable skill, first, to provide and maintain proper machinery, plant, appliances, and works; secondly, to select properly skilled persons to manage and superintend the business and thirdly, to provide a proper system of working." [74] These aspects of the employer's duty are not independent heads of liability but only manifestations of the employer's duty to take reasonable care.[75]

Standard of duty. The duty is to take reasonable care,[76] not absolutely to ensure safety, and it has been observed that it is desirable that the courts be vigilant " to see that the common law duty owed by a master to his servants should not be gradually enlarged until it is barely distinguishable from his absolute statutory obligations." [77] So, too, the courts have deprecated treating the relationship of employer and skilled workman as equivalent to that of a nurse and imbecile child.[78] Nevertheless " reasonable care " requires a high standard of care and diligence,[79] higher than that required of an occupier of premises to an invited visitor.[80] The failure of plant, in the absence of explanation, is itself evidence of inadequate care in relation thereto.[81]

An employer has been held to have discharged the duty of reasonable care when he took, and followed, the advice of officials of the National Coal Board whom the employers were entitled to regard as experts,[82] and not to have been in fault where an employee was killed, having interfered with a furnace which he had no right to touch, and which had operated safely for years.[83]

In considering whether due care has been taken, the known peculiarities of any particular workman are relevant, so that greater care must be taken where there is risk of greater injury.[84] So, too, greater precautions are necessary at particularly dangerous stages in operations and if the persons concerned are proverbially reckless.[85]

---

[73] *Bett* v. *Dalmeny Oil Co.* (1905) 7 F. 787, 790, *per* Lord McLaren, approved in *Black* v. *Fife Coal Co.*, 1912 S.C.(H.L.) 33, 50; *McMullen* v. *Lochgelly Iron Co.*, 1933 S.C.(H.L.) 64, 80, and *English* v. *Wilsons & Clyde Coal Co.*, 1937 S.C.(H.L.) 46, 60, *per* Lord Wright.

[74] *English, supra*, 66, *per* Lord Maugham; *cf. Vaughan* v. *Ropner & Co., Ltd.* (1947) 80 Ll.L.R. 119, 121.

[75] *Wilson* v. *Tyneside Window Cleaning Co.* [1958] 2 Q.B. 110, 121, 123.

[76] *Smith* v. *Baker* [1891] A.C. 325, 362; *Williams* v. *Birmingham Battery Co.* [1899] 2 Q.B. 338; *English, supra*; *Paris* v. *Stepney B.C., supra.*

[77] *Latimer* v. *A.E.C., Ltd.* [1953] A.C. 643, 658, *per* Lord Tucker; *cf. Chipchase* v. *British Titan Products* [1956] 1 Q.B. 545.

[78] *Smith* v. *Austin Lifts* [1959] 1 All E.R. 81 (H.L.), *per* Viscount Simonds.

[79] *Winter* v. *Cardiff R.D.C.* [1950] 1 All E.R. 819.

[80] *London Graving Dock* v. *Horton* [1951] A.C. 737; *Christmas* v. *General Cleaning Contractors* [1952] 1 K.B. 141.

[81] *Macaulay* v. *Buist* (1846) 9 D. 245; *Whitelaw* v. *Moffat* (1849) 12 D. 434.

[82] *Szumczyk* v. *Associated Tunnelling Co., Ltd.* [1956] 1 All E.R. 126.

[83] *Brophy* v. *Bradfield & Co., Ltd.* [1955] 3 All E.R. 286.

[84] *Paris* v. *Stepney B.C.* [1951] A.C. 367 (duty to provide goggles for one-eyed workman, though possibly no such duty to man with two eyes).

[85] *Paterson* v. *Wallace* (1854) 1 Macq. 748.

Implement of the duty or failure to do so must be judged by reference to the state of knowledge reasonably available and methods accepted at the time and not in the light of subsequent developments and advances in knowledge and technique.[86]

Personal nature of duty. The duty of care is personal to the employer and he cannot rid himself of liability by instructing a manager, safety officer or other subordinate to take precautions.[87] Nor could he, even prior to 1948, rely on the defence of common employment. Since 1948 the employer is in any event vicariously liable for a failure by such a subordinate. " If the master fails in any of these primary duties [*i.e.*, to select competent staff, to furnish adequate materials, and to establish a safe system of working] and injury is caused to his servant thereby, the master is liable to his servant as for personal fault, and cannot avail himself of the plea of collaborateur or fellow servant. The principle underlying this liability is that these primary duties of a master are of so paramount a kind in the interest of the servant's safety that he cannot be held to be excused by the delegation of these duties to his servants, no matter how competent or how carefully selected, so as to relieve himself of personal responsibility if accident and injury should occur owing to any of the duties being neglected. On the other hand, duties that do not fall within this paramount class may properly be delegated and, where in such a case the injury arises through the negligence of the servant to whom the delegation is made, a plea of fellow servant may competently arise in answer to a claim." [88] It follows that where the defender is a company the directors are not personally in fault unless they were actually aware of the danger alleged, or had not selected competent staff or provided proper plant or a proper system.[89]

The employer can, however, rid himself of liability in the case where tools, machinery or materials used are normally and necessarily obtained from an outside supplier, who is in law an independent contractor, where the employer has obtained them from one who is reasonably believed to be a reputable and competent supplier of goods of that kind, and the damage is attributable to a defect in the goods supplied which was not discoverable by any reasonable examination. Thus employers were held not liable to a workman injured by a particle of metal flying off a tool which the employers had purchased from reputable suppliers, was apparently in good condition, but was in fact dangerous by reason of its negligent manufacture by reputable makers.[90] Similarly, an employer

---

[86] *Ebbs* v. *Whitson* [1952] 2 Q.B. 877; *Szumczyk* v. *Associated Tunnelling Co., Ltd.* [1956] 1 All E.R. 126; *Graham* v. *Co-operative Wholesale Soc.* [1957] 1 All E.R. 654; *Richards* v. *Highway Ironfounders, Ltd.* [1957] 2 All E.R. 162.

[87] *Wilson* v. *Merry & Cuninghame* (1868) 6 M.(H.L.) 84; *McKillop* v. *N.B.Ry.* (1896) 23 R. 768; *Macdonald* v. *Udston Coal Co.* (1896) 23 R. 504; *Bain* v. *Fife Coal Co.*, 1935 S.C. 681; *English* v. *Wilsons and Clyde Coal Co.*, 1937 S.C.(H.L.) 46.

[88] *Thomson* v. *Edinburgh Collieries Co., Ltd.*, 1934 S.C. 217, 221, *per* L.J.C. Aitchison.

[89] *Thomson, supra*; *cf. Wright* v. *Dunlop & Co.* (1893) 20 R. 363.

[90] *Davie* v. *New Merton Board Mills* [1959] A.C. 604.

was held not liable to an employee when he was injured by the failure of a vehicle hired out by a reputable firm to another firm, for whom the injured man's employer was performing services under contract. The defect would not have been discovered save by dismantling and thorough inspection, and in the circumstances the employer was under no duty to carry out such an inspection as would have revealed the defect.[91]

(1) The duty with reference to competent staff

In view of the abolition of the doctrine of common employment the employer's duty to appoint competent staff is of less importance than formerly, since he is now vicariously liable for the consequences to other employees of their incompetence, but many such cases could be treated, as formerly, as instances of the employer's personal failure in his duty to provide competent staff.

The duty is to take reasonable care by appointing to all posts persons adequately qualified, trained and experienced, to be able to discharge their duties competently and safely, and to deal with foreseeable happenings.[92] The employer does not warrant that members of his staff are competent, nor is he, or they, automatically in fault because some mishap occurs. " The servant . . . has a right to understand that the master has taken reasonable care to protect him from such risks by associating him only with persons of ordinary skill and care." [93] It has been held sufficient to render an action relevant to aver that the defender had knowingly selected an incompetent and inexperienced driver,[94] or entrusted the signals to an inexperienced signalman,[95] or employed a negligent and incompetent foreman.[96]

The duty is breached where the men in question had no knowledge of, or experience in, dangers foreseeable in the employment, such as carbon monoxide in a pit,[97] where injury results from operations being managed by an unskilled manager-foreman.[98]

There is probably a prima facie breach of this duty in every case where a person is employed to perform any task, and does not possess any requisite qualification, such as a mine manager's certificate.[99]

The duty covers also the provision of an adequate number of men to do the job in question, so that it may be fault if a man is sent single-handed to do a job and is injured because he has no, or no adequate, help.[1]

[91] Sullivan v. Gallagher & Craig, 1959 S.C. 243.
[92] Wilson v. Merry & Cuninghame (1868) 6 M.(H.L.) 84.
[93] Hutchinson v. York, Newcastle and Berwick Ry. (1850) 5 Ex. 343, 353, per Alderson B.; cf. Tarrant v. Webb (1856) 18 C.B. 797.
[94] McCarten v. McRobbie, 1909 S.C. 1020; cf. Mackay v. John Watson, Ltd. (1897) 24 R. 383.
[95] Morton v. Edinburgh & Glasgow Ry. (1864) 2 M. 589.
[96] Flynn v. McGaw (1891) 18 R. 554.
[97] Black v. Fife Coal Co., 1912 S.C.(H.L.) 33.
[98] Stark v. McLaren (1871) 10 M. 31.
[99] This is quite apart from any criminal liability incurred thereby. Cf. Ferguson v. N.B.Ry., 1915 S.C. 566.
[1] Hardaker v. Huby [1962] C.L.Y. 2076.

The duty extends not merely to the appointment of competent employees, but to adequate supervision and direction of them. Hence an employer is in fault if he, or his manager or foremen, have failed to prevent workmen using a wrong or dangerous method, or have allowed them to neglect safety precautions. He is also in fault if by failure in supervision safety instructions, whether statutory or private, are not observed.

In *Smith* v. *Crossley Bros.*[2] two apprentices seriously injured a third by a practical joke. The court held that their conduct could not reasonably have been foreseen and that the defendants had not been in breach of their duty of supervision. But in *Hudson* v. *Ridge Mfg. Co.*[3] it was held to have been breach of the duty to provide competent workmen to have continued in employment a man who had habitually indulged in horseplay and had been warned repeatedly to desist; the source of danger should have been removed. And in *Ryan* v. *Cambrian United Dairies*[4] employers were held at fault in employing a man who was known to be vicious and dangerous and who attacked and injured a fellow-servant. But frivolity may be outside the scope of a man's employment and hence render his employer not liable for injuries to a fellow-employee.[5]

(2) *The duty with reference to adequate plant and materials*

The employer's duty is to provide and maintain proper machinery, plant,[6] appliances, and works.[7] The duty covers all kinds of tools, fixed machinery, vehicles and working materials, and the premises [8] in which to do the job.

The duty of provision is peculiarly that of the master rather than of the servant. The master, however, " does not warrant the soundness of the plant, and if there is a latent defect which could not be detected on reasonable examination, or if in the course of working plant becomes defective and the defect is not brought to the master's knowledge, and could not by reasonable diligence have been discovered by him, the master is not liable, and further, a master is not bound at once to adopt the latest improvements and appliances." [9]

But there is no liability merely because apparatus slips and someone is injured, if there has been neither neglect to provide proper apparatus, nor defect therein.[10]

---

[2] (1951) 95 S.J. 655; [1951] C.L.Y. 2329.
[3] [1957] 2 Q.B. 348.
[4] [1957] C.L.Y. 2424.
[5] *Sidwell* v. *British Timken* (1962) 106 S.J. 243; [1962] C.L.Y. 1137; contrast *Vale* v. *Furness Withy* [1962] 2 Lloyd's Rep. 298.
[6] See *Haston* v. *Edinburgh Street Tramways Co.* (1887) 14 R. 621; *Fraser* v. *Hood* (1887) 15 R. 178.
[7] *McNeil* v. *Wallace* (1853) 15 D. 818; *Weems* v. *Mathieson* (1861) 4 Macq. 215; *English* v. *Wilsons & Clyde Coal Co.*, 1937 S.C.(H.L.) 46, 66, *per* Lord Maugham.
[8] See *Johnson* v. *Mitchell* (1885) 22 S.L.R. 698; *Macleod* v. *Caledonian Ry.* (1885) 23 S.L.R. 68; *Moore* v. *Ross* (1890) 17 R. 796; *Jeffrey* v. *Donald* (1901) 9 S.L.T. 199.
[9] *Toronto Power Co., Ltd.* v. *Paskwan* [1915] A.C. 734, 738, *per* Sir Arthur Channell; *cf.* *Weems* v. *Mathieson* (1861) 4 Macq. 215; *Ovington* v. *McVicar* (1864) 2 M. 1066, 1072; *Bain* v. *Fife Coal Co.*, 1935 S.C. 681.
[10] *Watt* v. *Neilson* (1888) 15 R. 772; the facts of this case might have raised a case of faulty system.

Where the work contemplated is done on other persons' premises, such as painting or window cleaning, it is still the employer's duty to provide such apparatus as ladders and tools which the employee normally requires to use in the doing of the job.[11]

Even at common law, care in relation to plant requires that guards on dangerous apparatus, such as circular saws, be provided,[12] or other precautions taken to obviate foreseeable dangers.[13]

Provision of plant by outside supplier. Where the employer has obtained the plant from a reputable supplier of goods of that kind he has discharged his duty and is not liable if by reason of a latent defect attributable to the maker's negligence but not discoverable by any reasonable examination, the plant fails and causes injury to an employee.[14] It may be otherwise if the plant requires inspection or test after delivery, or if it has been built to the employer's specification and the injury is attributable to defect in the specification,[15] and it almost certainly is otherwise if it is " a case of acquiring a dilapidated truck from some dubious source." [16] In a case of latent defect the onus is on the workman to prove that the makers were not reputable manufacturers upon whose skill the employers were entitled to rely.[17]

Nor is the employer liable if the work involves sending his men to do something on the premises of another and an employee is injured by reason of a defect in the other's premises which the employer had no reason to suspect; he is not in such a case under a duty to inspect the other's premises to see if they are safe.[18]

But the injured employee may have a claim directly against the maker or supplier of the plant which caused the injury.[19]

The employer is, moreover, liable for a defect in plant supplied or constructed by a third party, if the latter were not competent or experienced in that kind of work, if the defect were discoverable by any kind of examination which was reasonable in the circumstances, or if it had been supplied to the instructions or specification or under the supervision of the employer.[20]

11 *Cf. General Cleaning Contractors, Ltd.* v. *Christmas* [1953] A.C. 180.

12 *Harriman* v. *Martin* [1962] 1 All E.R. 225.

13 *Harvey* v. *Singer Mfg. Co.,* 1960 S.C. 155.

14 *Davie* v. *New Merton Board Mills, Ltd.* [1959] A.C. 604; overruling *Donnelly* v. *Glasgow Corpn.,* 1953 S.C. 107, and approving *Mason* v. *Williams & Williams, Ltd.* [1955] 1 All E.R. 808; followed in *Sullivan* v. *Gallagher & Craig,* 1959 S.C. 243; *cf. McInulty* v. *Primrose* (1897) 24 R. 442.

15 *Ibid., per* Lord Tucker.

16 *Sullivan, supra,* 260, *per* L. J. C. Thomson.

17 *McMillan* v. *B.P. Refinery (Grangemouth), Ltd.,* 1961 S.L.T.(Notes) 79.

18 *Wilson* v. *Tyneside Cleaning Co.* [1958] 2 Q.B. 110, 121. In such a case the workman may have a claim against the occupier of the premises under the Occupiers' Liability (Scotland) Act, 1960.

19 *Donoghue* v. *Stevenson,* 1932 S.C.(H.L.) 31; *cf. Edwards* v. *Hutcheon* (1889) 16 R. 694; *Sullivan* v. *Gallagher & Craig,* 1959 S.C. 243.

20 *Thomson* v. *Wallace,* 1933 S.N. 15 (defective scaffolding); *cf. Muir* v. *Moy Hammerton, Ltd.,* 1947 S.N. 190.

Employer's duty in relation to premises. In relation to premises the duty clearly involves fencing and lighting dangers, the provision of necessary ladders and ancillaries,[21] the avoidance of slippery floors, obstacles thereon, and unsafe doors, fittings and furniture, and generally of taking reasonable care to maintain the premises in a condition free from any concealed danger of which the employer is or ought to be aware.[22] There has been held to be a duty to fence off an area of floor under repair, even though the employee was making an unnecessary deviation in going into the dangerous area,[23] and to provide a handrail for steps,[24] and not to allow a floor to become slippery and dangerous.[25]

Circumstances inferring breach of duty. Breach of the duty to provide safe plant and appliances is inferred (a) where there is a total failure to provide necessary plant; (b) where any plant supplied is inadequate, defective, or otherwise dangerous; and (c) where improvements or modifications have not been adopted.

(a) TOTAL FAILURE TO PROVIDE NECESSARY PLANT. Instances of this are the failure to provide a ladder,[26] or planks for a staging,[27] or a guard-rail at the edge of a roof,[28] or boards on a lower part of a roof to arrest the fall of a workman.[29]

The court has, however, dismissed on relevancy actions of this kind where the plant desiderated by the pursuer in his pleadings was, as a matter of common knowledge and experience, unnecessary.[30]

(b) PROVISION OF INADEQUATE OR DEFECTIVE PLANT. The happening of an accident to a workman which is unexplained or unascertained does not raise a presumption that it was caused by a defect in the machinery or plant for which the employer was responsible. The pursuer must prove that the cause of the accident was some defect for which the employer was responsible, though it is not necessary to show the precise nature of the defect.[31] The supply of a vicious horse to a vanman has been held to be defective plant,[32] as has the sending to sea of a vessel not properly equipped.[33] The failure of shipowners to provide essential spare ropes has been held negligent.[34] So has the provision by the railway authority

---

[21] *Williams* v. *Birmingham Battery Co.* [1899] 2 Q.B. 338.
[22] *Cole* v. *de Trafford* [1918] 2 K.B. 523.
[23] *Murray* v. *R. S. McColl*, 1947 S.N. 13; *cf. Lowe* v. *Waygood Otis, Ltd.*, 1947 S.N. 57.
[24] *Kimpton* v. *Steel Co. of Wales* [1960] 2 All E.R. 274.
[25] *Davidson* v. *Handley Page, Ltd.* [1945] 1 All E.R. 235.
[26] *Williams* v. *Birmingham Battery & Metal Co.* [1899] 2 Q.B. 338.
[27] *Lovell* v. *Blundells and Crompton & Co.* [1944] 1 K.B. 502.
[28] *Pratt* v. *Richards* [1951] 2 K.B. 208.
[29] *Harris* v. *Brights Asphalt Contractors* [1953] 1 Q.B. 617.
[30] *Loughney* v. *Caledonian Ry.* (1902) 4 F. 401.
[31] *Macaulay* v. *Buist* (1846) 9 D. 245; *Macfarlane* v. *Thomson* (1884) 12 R. 232; *Stanforth* v. *Burnbank Foundry Co.* (1887) 24 S.L.R. 722.
[32] *Robertson* v. *Thomas's, Ltd.* (1907) 15 S.L.T. 32; *Richardson* v. *Beattie*, 1923 S.L.T. 440. *Cf. Bowater* v. *Rowley Regis Corpn.* [1944] 1 K.B. 476.
[33] *Tyrrell* v. *Paton & Hendry* (1905) 8 F. 112; *Gordon* v. *Pyper* (1892) 20 R.(H.L.) 23.
[34] *Vaughan* v. *Ropner & Co., Ltd.* (1947) 80 Ll.L.R. 119.

to their men of a wagon with a hole in the floor thereof.[35] But an employer is not liable to his workmen for a defect in a wagon sent to be loaded and not part of the employer's plant at all,[36] nor if ordinary appliances prove unsuitable in the circumstances and no request is made for other appliances.[37] There is authority for the view that failure to use properly plant supplied may amount to " defective plant." [38]

(c) FAILURE TO ADOPT IMPROVEMENTS. The failure to use the most modern type of plant, or to adopt the latest modifications or improvements, is not negligence by itself, but is a factor to be taken into account and it may amount to negligence in the circumstances of the case.[39] The question is whether the failure to adopt the improvement is a failure to take reasonable care, and the antiquity of the plant used and that method of doing the work is a relevant factor. In particular it may be negligence not to adopt an improvement after an accident which could have been prevented thereby.[40]

Duty to maintain. The duty extends also to current maintenance; " The obligation to provide *and maintain* proper plant and appliances is a continuing obligation. It is not, however, broken by a mere misuse of, or failure to use, proper plant and appliances, due to the negligence of a fellow servant, or a merely temporary failure to keep in order or adjust plant and appliances, or a casual departure from the system of working, if these matters can be regarded as the casual negligence of the manager, foremen or other employees." [41]

The detailed requirements of maintenance necessarily vary from case to case, according to the nature of the plant used, but will normally involve regular inspection and testing, periodical maintenance and overhauls, and replacement of parts found to be worn, faulty or unserviceable. Some guidance may be got from the principle of the general practice of the reasonable man. If a defect is reported, or otherwise becomes known to the management and no repair or replacement is effected, that is clearly failure to maintain.[42] On the other hand, the master of a trawler has been held not in fault in failing to inspect the work of competent engineers in derusting a windlass mechanically sound but affected in a material part by rust.[43]

---

35 *McDonald* v. *B.T.C.* [1955] 3 All E.R. 789.
36 *Robinson* v. *Watson* (1892) 20 R. 144.
37 *Ramsay* v. *Robin, McMillan & Co.* (1889) 16 R. 690.
38 *Robertson* v. *Kinneil Coal Co.*, 1932 S.C.(H.L.) 14; see also *Connell* v. *James Nimmo & Co.*, 1924 S.C.(H.L.) 84.
39 *Dynen* v. *Leach* (1857) 26 L.J.Ex. 221; *Mitchell* v. *Patullo* (1885) 23 S.L.R. 207; *McGill* v. *Bowman* (1890) 18 R. 206; *Toronto Power Co.* v. *Paskwan* [1915] A.C. 734.
40 *Toronto Power Co., supra.*
41 *English* v. *Wilsons & Clyde Coal Co.*, 1937 S.C.(H.L.) 46, 65, *per* Lord Wright. *Cf. Smith* v. *Baker* [1891] A.C. 325, 362, and, under statute, *Crane* v. *William Baird & Co.*, 1935 S.C. 715.
42 *Cf. McLaughlan* v. *Colin Dunlop & Co.* (1882) 20 S.L.R. 271.
43 *McLeod* v. *Hastie*, 1936 S.C. 501.

Circumstances inferring breach of duty to maintain. Such circumstances can be grouped under the heads of (a) failure to remedy known defects; (b) failure to discover unknown defects; and (c) delay or failure to effect repairs or replacement.

(a) FAILURE TO REMEDY KNOWN DEFECTS. It is fault on the employer's part not to take proper steps to remedy a known defect or cure a known and continuing dangerous condition of the plant.[44]

(b) FAILURE TO DISCOVER UNKNOWN DEFECTS. The failure to discover an unknown defect which has caused an accident is imputable as fault of the employer only if the defect could have been discovered by the exercise of reasonable care, and by any testing or inspections which were customary and proper. " It is not sufficient . . . to prove that the employer's machinery broke down while being put to an ordinary use. The pursuer must prove that the cause of the breakdown of the machinery could have been discovered and remedied if a reasonable inspection of the machinery had been made by the employer." [45]

The failure to inspect and examine equipment periodically in search of defects and thereby to discover patent defects is also fault.[46]

(c) DELAY OR FAILURE TO EFFECT REPAIRS OR REPLACEMENT. An employer can be held liable only if he has delayed unreasonably or totally failed to repair or replace, after the need for such action had come to his notice, or should reasonably have been discovered by inspection or testing. " A merely temporary failure to keep in order or adjust plant or appliances " [47] does not infer breach of duty. Thus a completely unexplained failure which had caused an accident before it was discovered and could be rectified imported no liability at common law.[48]

(3) *The duty with reference to a proper system of working*

The employer's duty to establish and maintain a proper system of working is probably the widest and most general aspect of his duty of care. The purpose of a proper system of working is to exclude avoidable dangers and to minimise unavoidable risks, and the employer's faith in the impeccability of his servants is no substitute for such a system.[49] " System " is, broadly, the " practice and method adopted in carrying on the master's business of which the master is presumed to be aware." [50]

---

[44] *Henderson* v. *Carron Co.* (1889) 16 R. 633.

[45] *Gavin* v. *Rogers* (1889) 17 R. 206; *cf. Whitelaw* v. *Moffat* (1849) 12 D. 434 (no sufficient inspection).

[46] *Murphy* v. *Phillips* (1876) 35 L.T. 477; *Marney* v. *Scott* [1899] 1 Q.B. 986; *Szuca* v. *Balfour Beatty,* 1953 S.L.T.(Notes) 6; *Kerr* v. *Cook,* 1953 S.L.T.(Notes) 23.

[47] *English* v. *Wilsons & Clyde Coal Co.,* 1937 S.C.(H.L.) 46, 65, *per* Lord Wright.

[48] *Millar* v. *Galashiels Gas Co.,* 1949 S.C.(H.L.) 31.

[49] *Kerr* v. *Glasgow Corpn.,* 1945 S.C. 335, 350.

[50] *English* v. *Wilsons & Clyde Coal Co.,* 1936 S.C. 883, 904, *per* L.J.C. Aitchison.

This normally implies that the work consists of a series of similar operations and the concept of system is not easily applied to a case where only a single act of a particular kind is to be performed. But a proper system of operation is necessary even though the particular work undertaken is of an unusual kind.[51] Where the system or mode of operation is complicated or highly dangerous or prolonged or involves a number of men performing different functions, it is naturally a matter for the employer to take the responsibility of deciding what system shall be adopted.[52]

" The phrase ' defective system of working' has never been comprehensively defined, but in general, and in the practice of the Scottish courts since *Smith* v. *Baker & Sons*,[53] it has been taken to include defects of a relatively permanent and continuous kind (whether in fact he has or has not knowledge)—as distinct from defects of a transitory kind which may emerge in the day's working, and which are normally not part of the regular system or method of working. Thus a defect in the layout of a railway system was held to be a defective system in *McKillop* v. *N.B. Ry.*[54] Again, if mineowners were to conduct their mining operations in a way contrary to recognised safe mining practice, thereby exposing their servants to danger and injury, they would be liable as for personal negligence by their use of a defective system of working." [55]

" The duty of an employer to provide a safe system of working for his employees is relative to and arises out of the circumstances of the particular case; it is not an absolute duty, and whether in the circumstances of each particular case the duty exists, and, if so, the extent of the obligations, must be measured by the standard of reasonable foresight." [56] The duty is owed not only to employees but to the employees of another who have been " lent " to the occupier of the premises or other person responsible for the system.[57]

The duty with regard to " system " involves the organisation, layout and planning of the work, the choice of persons to do it and their numbers and equipment, their direction and supervision, the timing of operation, the co-ordination of departments, stages or tasks, the provision of warnings, guard-rails, lighting, and the taking of precautions against the weather, fire, floods and other foreseeable risks. System may include " the physical layout of the job,—the setting of the stage, so to speak—the sequence in which the work is to be carried out, the provision in proper cases of warnings and notices and the issue of special instructions. A system may be adequate for the whole course of the job or it may have to be modified or improved to meet circumstances which arise; such modifications or improvements appear to me equally to fall under the head of system." [58]

[51] *McMullan* v. *Collins* [1950] C.L.Y. 4781.
[52] *Winter* v. *Cardiff R.D.C.* [1950] 1 All E.R. 819.
[53] [1891] A.C. 325.
[54] (1896) 23 R. 768.   [55] *Bain* v. *Fife Coal Co.*, 1935 S.C. 681, 692, *per* L.J.C. Aitchison.
[56] *Grace* v. *Stephen & Sons*, 1952 S.C. 61, 66, *per* L.J.C. Thomson.
[57] *Garrard* v. *Southey & Co.* [1952] 1 All E.R. 597.
[58] *Speed* v. *Thomas Swift & Co., Ltd.* [1943] K.B. 557, 563, *per* Lord Greene M.R. See also *Colfar* v. *Coggins & Griffiths (Liverpool), Ltd.* [1945] A.C. 197.

" System " has been held not to extend to the provision of transport after the conclusion of the day's work; it is confined to " system of work " or " system or method of conducting the work." [59]   Whether or not a safe system of working has been provided is in each case a question of fact and previous decisions are, at best, guiding examples.[60]

System normally involves taking usual, or obvious, precautions.   Consideration of whether certain facts amount to faulty system or not may raise the issue of whether the defender took, or failed to take, the precautions usual and normal in such circumstances or precautions which were so obviously wanted that it would be folly in anyone in the defender's position to neglect such precautions.[61]   An employer is not obliged to render his premises safe by extraordinary means involving great expense or the adoption of the latest scientific improvements, but to take the precautions which ordinarily would be taken in the circumstances,[62] nor is failure to observe the common practice conclusive of negligence, particularly if alternative precautions are provided.[63]   In many cases a pursuer alleging faulty system must be able to indicate a practicable alternative, but in many other cases it is enough to point to the danger inherent in the method of working.[64]

Faulty system and casual negligence.   For the purpose of attaching liability a distinction must be taken between mishaps attributable to faulty system, and those attributable to merely casual negligence of individual employees, for which the employer is not liable, at least on this ground of fault.[65]   To be chargeable as faulty system the conduct must have sprung from some defect in the organisation of getting the job done, not something merely incidental to the doing.   Thus where a plumber's mate dropped a hammer through a skylight and injured a cement worker, this was purely casual negligence.[66]   Similarly it was not faulty system to send a heavy voltage regulator on a lorry, not lashed down, though a rope was provided and there was a competent foreman in charge.[67]

---

[59] *Ramsay* v. *Wimpey & Co.*, 1951 S.C. 692.
[60] *Qualcast* v. *Haynes* [1959] A.C. 743.
[61] *Sneddon* v. *Summerlee Iron Co.*, 1947 S.C. 555, founding on *Morton* v. *Dixon*, 1909 S.C. 807; *cf. Macdonald* v. *Udston Coal Co.* (1896) 23 R. 504; *Gallagher* v. *Balfour, Beatty & Co., Ltd.*, 1951 S.C. 712; *Cavanagh* v. *Ulster Weaving Co.* [1960] A.C. 145.
[62] *Gallagher, supra*, 716, *per* L.P. Cooper, citing *Murdoch* v. *Mackinnon* (1885) 12 R. 810; *McGill* v. *Bowman* (1890) 18 R. 206; *Murray* v. *Merry & Cuninghame* (1890) 18 R. 815 and *Paris* v. *Stepney Borough Council* [1951] A.C. 367.
[63] *Brown* v. *Rolls-Royce, Ltd.*, 1960 S.C.(H.L.) 22.
[64] *Dixon* v. *Cementation Co.* [1960] 3 All E.R. 417; *Robertson* v. *Guardbridge Paper Co.*, 1961 S.L.T. (Notes) 10; *Brander* v. *Spencer*, 1964 S.L.T. (Notes) 14.
[65] He may be liable vicariously: see, *e.g., Lindsay* v. *Connell*, 1951 S.C. 281.
[66] *Maguire* v. *Russell* (1885) 12 R. 1071; contrast *Murphy* v. *Bladen* (1906) 14 S.L.T. 250; *cf. Padbury* v. *Holliday* (1912) 28 T.L.R. 494.
[67] *Winter* v. *Cardiff R.D.C.* [1950] 1 All E.R. 819.

So too the employer is not bound to ensure that nobody makes a mistake in the course of using the system, as by using a wrong rope,[68] nor that some other person will not do something which causes an accident to the employee.[69]

Lord Justice-Clerk Aitchison sought to draw the distinction in this way [70]: " What is system and what falls short of system may be difficult to define . . . but, broadly stated, the distinction is between the general and the particular, between the practice and method adopted in carrying on the master's business of which the master is presumed to be aware and the insufficiency of which he can guard against, and isolated or day to day acts of the servant of which the master is not presumed to be aware and which he cannot guard against; in short, it is the distinction between what is permanent or continuous on the one hand and what is merely casual and emerges in the day's work on the other hand." So too it has been said [71]: " There is a sphere in which the employer must exercise his discretion and there are other spheres in which foremen and workmen must exercise theirs."

Thus in *Grace* v. *Stephen* [72] a workman was injured because a cable had been left lying across a set of rails. This was held not to be faulty system in the absence of averment or proof that cables were commonly left lying or that the employers knew or ought to have known that they were left lying; it was a casual and incidental happening. In *Milliken* v. *Rome* [73] a plank had been removed from the entrance to a building under construction, and a labourer fell and was injured. The removal was held to be casual negligence, and not a fault in the system of working.

Modification of system. A system of working safe in some conditions may be unsafe in others, and it is part of the duty to adapt the system to changes in circumstances [74]; the duty must be considered in relation to the particular circumstances of each job.[75] Employers must instruct workmen as to what precautions they should take in particular circumstances to make the system of working as reasonably safe as it can be made.[76]

Abuse of system. It does not suffice for employers to establish a proper and safe system of working if they do not try to ensure that it is adhered to. If the system is abused or ignored, the case becomes equivalent to

---

68 *O'Melia* v. *Freight Conveyors, Ltd.* [1940] 4 All E.R. 516; contrast *Speed* v. *Thomas Swift* [1943] 1 K.B. 557.
69 *Holt* v. *Rhodes* [1949] 1 All E.R. 478.
70 *English* v. *Wilsons & Clyde Coal Co.*, 1936 S.C. 883, 904; affd. 1937 S.C.(H.L.) 46; passage approved in *Speed* v. *Thomas Swift* [1943] K.B. 557, 563, *per* Lord Greene M.R.
71 *Winter* v. *Cardiff R.D.C.* [1950] 1 All E.R. 819.
72 1952 S.C. 61.
73 1952 S.L.T. (Notes) 56.
74 *Porter* v. *Port of Liverpool Stevedoring Co., Ltd.* [1944] 2 All E.R. 411.
75 *Speed* v. *Thomas Swift & Co.* [1943] K.B. 557, 562–563; *Holt* v. *Rhodes* [1949] 1 All E.R. 478; *Winter* v. *Cardiff R.D.C.* [1950] 1 All E.R. 819.
76 *General Cleaning Contractors* v. *Christmas* [1953] A.C. 180.

one of no, or faulty, system.[77]   But the failure of employees to adhere to the system in the face of constant protests by the employers may be an abuse for which only the workmen are to blame.[78]

Regard for peculiarities of individual workmen.   The employer's duty of care is owed to each individual workman, and in organising the system of working the employer must have regard to any known infirmities, weaknesses or peculiarities of particular individuals.   It may therefore be faulty system to put a particular man on a certain task,[79] or not to provide him with goggles, even though it was not the practice to provide normal men engaged in similar work with goggles, because he was one-eyed and therefore risked total blindness if his eye were injured.[80]   Where the employers are unaware of the peculiarity of a particular workman, such as his susceptibility to fits, their fault may be reduced by the work-man's contributory negligence in failing to disclose his disability.[81]   The duty to the employee who is susceptible to an industrial disease does not extend to refusing to employ him in work involving a risk of that disease; if the employee knows there is a risk and decides to take it there is no breach of duty by the employer if the employee contracts the disease.[82] Similarly the fact that an employee is of low intelligence is relevant to the standard of duty owed him by his employer.[83]

Dangers of carelessness.   The duty to establish and maintain a safe system includes the duty to take precautions against carelessness in execution of the work engendered by familiarity with its risks.   " It is well known to employers that their workpeople are very frequently, if not habitually, careless about the risks which their work may involve. It is . . . for that very reason that the common law demands that em-ployers should take reasonable care to lay down a reasonably safe system of work.   Employers are not exempted from this duty by the fact that their men are experienced and might, if they were in the position of an employer, be able to lay down a reasonably safe system of work them-selves.   Workmen are not in the position of employers.   Their duties are not performed in the calm atmosphere of a boardroom with the advice of experts.   They have to make their decisions on narrow sills and other places of danger where the dangers are obscured by repetition." [84]   " Where a practice of ignoring an obvious danger has grown up I do not think it is reasonable to expect an individual workman to take the initiative

---

[77] *Henderson* v. *John Watson, Ltd.* (1892) 19 R. 954.
[78] *Andrews* v. *Colvilles, Ltd.*, 1947 S.N. 10; *cf. Ramsay* v. *Wimpey*, 1951 S.C. 692; *Williams* v. *Liverpool Stevedoring Co.* [1956] 2 All E.R. 69.
[79] *Cf. Gibson* v. *Nimmo* (1895) 22 R. 491.
[80] *Paris* v. *Stepney B.C.* [1951] A.C. 367; *Heapy* v. *Cheshire C.C.* [1955] C.L.Y. 1895.
[81] *Cork* v. *Kirby Maclean & Co.* [1952] 2 All E.R. 402.
[82] *Withers* v. *Perry Chain Co.* [1961] 3 All E.R. 676.
[83] *Baxter* v. *Woolcombers* [1963] C.L.Y. 2320.
[84] *General Cleaning Contractors, Ltd.* v. *Christmas* [1953] A.C. 180, 189, *per* Lord Oaksey; *cf. McNeil* v. *Wallace* (1853) 15 D. 818; *Clifford* v. *Challen* [1951] 1 K.B. 495; *Drummond* v. *British Building Cleaners* [1954] 3 All E.R. 507.

in devising and using precautions. It is the duty of the employer to consider the situation, to devise a suitable system, to instruct his men what they must do and to supply any implements that may be required." [85] If, however, a reasonably safe system has been provided the employer is not bound to see that nobody makes a mistake in the course of using the system,[86] and the relationship of employer and skilled workman has been said not to be reduced to that of nurse and imbecile child.[87]

Supervision and enforcement. An important element in any system of working is the provision of adequate supervision and means to try to secure that the system is enforced. A system not put into operation or not enforced is no system.[88] Thus it is not enough to provide cream for protection against dermatitis if it is kept locked up, and the foreman does nothing to encourage men to use it,[89] or not to take any steps to compel foundry workers to wear masks.[90]

Supervisory staff should keep on the lookout for such faults in system as articles unsafely stacked.[91]

But the employer is not bound " through his foreman, to stand over workmen of age and experience every moment they are working and every time that they cease work, in order to see that they do what they are supposed to do. That is not the measure of duty at common law. The duty is to take reasonable care and so to carry on his operations as not to subject those employed by him to unnecessary risk." [92] " If [the employer] does all that is reasonable to ensure that his safety system is operated he will have done all that he is bound to do." [93]

Instructions. One aspect of system of work is the giving to a workman of adequate instructions on the use of tools or machinery; thus it has been held negligent to fail to instruct a man to use a milling machine with the hood down over the cutter,[94] or to fail to supply, and instruct the use of, goggles when using a carborundum wheel.[95] Similarly it would be faulty system to set a driver the test of driving a vehicle of unusual construction without any steps being taken to see that he can fulfil the duty.[96]

It is equally an aspect of faulty system to fail to give a foreman adequate instructions about warning his gang of approaching danger,[97] or not

[85] *General Cleaning Contractors, Ltd., supra,* 194, *per* Lord Reid.
[86] *O'Melia* v. *Freight Conveyors, Ltd.* [1940] 4 All E.R. 516.
[87] *Smith* v. *Austin Lifts* [1959] 1 All E.R. 81 (H.L.).
[88] *Reid* v. *Colvilles, Ltd.,* 1959 S.L.T.(Notes) 6.
[89] *Clifford* v. *Challen* [1951] 1 K.B. 495.
[90] *Crookall* v. *Vickers-Armstrong* [1955] 2 All E.R. 12.
[91] *Andrews* v. *Colvilles, Ltd.,* 1947 S.N. 10.
[92] *Woods* v. *Durable Suites* [1953] 2 All E.R. 391, 395; *per* Singleton L.J. (where plaintiff had ignored warnings about precautions against dermatitis). *Cf. Wilson* v. *British Railways Board,* 1964 S.L.T.(Notes) 102.
[93] *General Cleaning Contractors, Ltd.* v. *Christmas* [1953] A.C. 180, 194, *per* Lord Reid.
[94] *Quinn* v. *Horsfall & Bickham, Ltd.* [1956] 2 All E.R. 467, 473.
[95] *Nolan* v. *Dental Mfg. Co.* [1958] 2 All E.R. 449.
[96] *Winter* v. *Cardiff R.D.C.* [1950] 1 All E.R. 819, 822.
[97] *Redpath* v. *L.N.E.Ry.,* 1944 S.C. 155, 171.

adequately to warn a greaser not to oil certain dangerous machines while in motion,[98] or not to warn a new boy assistant not to cross a railway by the metals.[99]

The duty of giving instructions as to the safe performance of a job is not implemented by giving him a copy of relevant Regulations and telling him to comply with them.[1]

Where the job is simple it is not necessarily a fault on the employer's part not to give instructions, but to leave it to the foreman or workman on the spot.[2]

Particularly in the case of more experienced and responsible employees, employers are not under any duty to provide a foreman watching constantly to ensure that instructions in regard to safety are implemented.[3]

Safe access to place of work. Reasonable care for the safety of the employee includes the provision of safe means of access to the workplace,[4] but if this is done the employer is not liable if the employee is injured when approaching by another, unsafe, route.[5] But the common law standard of safe access is less stringent than that demanded by the Factories Act.[6]

This aspect of safe system covers also reasonable precautions for the safety of workpeople entering and leaving the premises before and after the day's work.[7]

Safety of premises. It would be faulty system to require a workman to work in a space which is inadequate and dangerous.[8] It may amount to faulty system to require workmen to continue working in premises rendered dangerous, as by flooding, but not necessarily if this is a merely transient and exceptional condition. If the risk is inconsiderable it is not necessarily faulty system.[9]

But to permit the continuance for any length of time, or the permanent existence, of any obvious or apparent danger such as a slippery patch on the floor or protruding parts of machinery can well be faulty system.[10]

---

[98] *Lewis* v. *High Duty Alloys, Ltd.* [1957] 1 All E.R. 740.

[99] *Robinson* v. *Smith & Son* (1901) 17 T.L.R. 423.

[1] *Barcock* v. *Brighton Corpn.* [1949] 1 K.B. 339.

[2] *Winter* v. *Cardiff R.D.C.* [1950] 1 All E.R. 819; *cf. Parkes* v. *Smethwick Corpn.* [1957] 121 J.P. 415.

[3] *Woods* v. *Durable Suites, Ltd.* [1953] 2 All E.R. 391; *Qualcast (Wolverhampton), Ltd.* v. *Haynes* [1959] A.C. 743.

[4] *Sheppey* v. *Shaw* [1952] 1 T.L.R. 1272; *Milliken* v. *Rome*, 1952 S.L.T.(Notes) 56.

[5] *Ashdown* v. *Williams* [1957] 1 Q.B. 409.

[6] *Waters* v. *Rolls-Royce, Ltd.*, 1960 S.L.T.(Notes) 91.

[7] *Cf. Bell* v. *Blackwood Morton & Co.*, 1960 S.C. 11; *Lee* v. *John Dickinson* [1960] C.L.Y. 1160; but see *Ramsay* v. *Wimpey*, 1951 S.C. 692; *McLaughlin* v. *Scott's Shipbuilding Co.*, 1960 S.L.T.(Notes) 58.

[8] *Bain* v. *Fife Coal Co.*, 1935 S.C. 681; *cf. Braithwaite* v. *S. Durham Steel Co.* [1958] 3 All E.R. 161.

[9] *Davies* v. *De Havilland Aircraft Co., Ltd.* [1950] 2 All E.R. 582; *Latimer* v. *A.E.C., Ltd.* [1953] A.C. 643.

[10] *Paine* v. *Colne Valley Electricity Co.* [1938] 4 All E.R. 803; *cf. Kerr* v. *Glasgow Corpn.*, 1945 S.C. 335.

It is not necessarily faulty system to fail to inspect premises not occupied or controlled by the employer but on or in which the employer sends his men to do work,[11] though where the job involves obvious dangers, as in window-cleaning, the employer should consider what safety precautions could be taken and instruct his men to use them.[12]

Fencing dangers. At common law the duty to fence machinery was not readily imposed[13] and seems to have demanded averment and proof that fencing was practicable and customary on that kind of machine, or so obviously necessary that it was folly not to have it. It is thought that the courts would exact a more stringent standard even at common law today. But other dangers should also be fenced at common law, such as unlit openings in the decks of ships.[14]

Supporting earth. System involves taking precautions to shore-up exposed faces of earth or stone to prevent their falling on workmen.[15]

Similarly it is common law fault not to have the roof of a mine properly supported,[16] or not to have the roof of a tunnel inspected regularly.[17]

Inadequate signalling system. The provision of a proper system for signalling or communicating between *e.g.* the man operating a crane and the men in a ship's hold, or between an engineman and the pit bottom, is necessary.[18]

Inadequate warning system. Where work has to be done in the intervals between recurring dangers, a system of warning against the approach of danger is essential. Examples of this kind of faulty system include: failure to warn a platelayer of the approach of a train[19]; failure to warn foundrymen that old iron was being broken up[20]; failure to provide a signalman to warn persons working that shunting was taking place[21]; and where railwaymen working on the permanent way had only one lookout who failed to notice that a train was coming in each direction.[22]

---

11 *Taylor* v. *Sims* [1942] 2 All E.R. 375; *Cilia* v. *James & Sons* [1954] 2 All E.R. 9; *cf. Hughes* v. *McGoff and Vickers, Ltd.* [1955] 2 All E.R. 291.
12 *Drummond* v. *British Building Cleaners, Ltd.* [1954] 3 All E.R. 507.
13 See, *e.g., Ross* v. *Thomson & Co.* (1882) 20 S.L.R. 46; *Little* v. *Paterson* (1890) 28 S.L.R. 64; *Cameron* v. *Walker* (1898) 25 R. 449; *Hosie* v. *Walker,* 1907 S.C. 134; *Morton* v. *Dixon,* 1909 S.C. 807; *Reid* v. *British Basket Co.,* 1913, 2 S.L.T. 201. See also *Murray* v. *Merry & Cuninghame* (1890) 17 R. 815. The duty was recognised in *Darby* v. *Duncan* (1861) 23 D. 529; *Edwards* v. *Hutcheon* (1889) 16 R. 694; *Stewart & Co.* v. *London and Midland Ins. Co.,* 1916, 2 S.L.T. 189.
14 *Forsyth* v. *Ramage & Ferguson* (1890) 18 R. 21; *Thomson* v. *Scott* (1897) 25 R. 54; *Jamieson* v. *Russell* (1892) 19 R. 898; *cf. Burns* v. *Henderson* (1905) 7 F. 697; *Gray* v. *Thomson* (1889) 17 R. 200. *Cf.* also *Grantham* v. *N.Z. Shipping Co.* [1940] 4 All E.R. 258 (failure to fence edge of ship's deck); *Morris* v. *West Hartlepool S.N. Co.* [1956] A.C. 552.
15 *Pollock* v. *Cassidy* (1870) 8 M. 615; *cf. McInally* v. *King's Trs.* (1886) 14 R. 8.
16 *Stewart* v. *Coltness Iron Co.* (1877) 4 R. 952; *McMullen* v. *Newhouse Coal Co.* (1896) 23 R. 759.
17 *Gallagher* v. *Balfour Beatty & Co.,* 1951 S.C. 712.
18 *Murdoch* v. *Mackinnon* (1885) 12 R. 810; *Johnson* v. *Beaumont* [1953] 2 All E.R. 106.
19 *Redpath* v. *L.N.E.Ry.,* 1944 S.C. 154; *cf. Duthie* v. *Caledonian Ry.* (1898) 25 R. 934.
20 *McGuire* v. *Cairns* (1890) 17 R. 540.
21 *Bremner* v. *McAlpine* (1907) 15 S.L.T. 106.
22 *Dyer* v. *Southern Ry.* [1948] 1 K.B. 608.

Instruction as to safety precautions. An element of safe system is to ascertain what safety precautions can be taken in relation to the kinds of work undertaken by the employer and to instruct workmen to use such precautions and safe methods as may be available; failure to do so may infer liability.[23]

Protective clothing or prophylactics. In many cases the employer's failure has consisted in not supplying or not ensuring the use of protective headgear, goggles, respirators, gloves, etc., or of protective or barrier creams.[24] Examples include: allowing work at a grinding machine without goggles, these having been put in the foreman's office and the workman not knowing where they were, and not drawing the attention of the workmen to the need to use goggles nor informing them where they were kept [25]; not providing goggles for a workman who was already one-eyed [26]; failing to insist on foundry workers wearing protective spats or boots [27]; failing to warn, encourage and exhort workmen to wear masks when it was appreciated that the process exposed workmen to a material risk of contracting silicosis [28]; failing to have safety belts available nearer than at the main office, half a mile away.[29]

Similarly employers have been held liable where the work involved danger of dermatitis and they had not provided proper washing facilities,[30] but conversely where the danger of dermatitis was unknown,[31] or not reasonably anticipated.[32]

The employer was held not liable where instruction was given of the danger of dermatitis and barrier cream was provided but the employee, without the employer's knowledge, did not observe the precautions fully and contracted dermatitis,[33] nor was he where barrier cream was not provided but adequate washing facilities were provided,[34] nor where protective clothing had, to the employee's knowledge, been made available but not used.[35]

---

23 *O'Byrne* v. *Burn* (1854) 16 D. 1025; *Drummond* v. *British Building Cleaners, Ltd.* [1954] 3 All E.R. 507; see also *Woods* v. *Durable Suites Ltd.* [1953] 2 All E.R. 391.

24 *Adamson* v. *Bickle Bros.* [1957] C.L.Y. 2426; *Hardy* v. *Briggs Motor Bodies* [1957] C.L.Y. 2427.

25 *Finch* v. *Telegraph Construction and Maintenance Co.* [1949] 1 All E.R. 452, where it was said that to leave it to each man to ask for goggles if he wanted them was not a system of working at all.

26 *Paris* v. *Stepney B.C.* [1951] A.C. 367.

27 *Qualcast* v. *Thorpe* [1955] C.L.Y. 1896.

28 *Crookall* v. *Vickers-Armstrong, Ltd.* [1955] 2 All E.R. 12; *Balfour* v. *Beardmore*, 1956 S.L.T. 205.

29 *Roberts* v. *Dorman Long & Co.* [1953] 2 All E.R. 428.

30 *Gardiner* v. *Motherwell Machinery & Scrap Co.*, 1961 S.C.(H.L.) 1. *Cf. Clifford* v. *Challen* [1951] 1 K.B. 495.

31 *Coleman* v. *Harland & Wolff* [1951] 2 Lloyd's Rep. 76; *cf. Harman* v. *Mitcham Works* [1955] C.L.Y. 1894.

32 *O'Neil* v. *Railway Executive* (1952) 68 Sh.Ct.Rep. 260.

33 *Woods* v. *Durable Suites, Ltd.* [1953] 2 All E.R. 391; *cf. Wilson* v. *Glasgow Corpn.* (1901) 9 S.L.T. 133.

34 *Brown* v. *Rolls-Royce, Ltd.*, 1960 S.C.(H.L.) 22.

35 *Qualcast (Wolverhampton), Ltd.* v. *Haynes* [1959] A.C. 743.

Faulty co-ordination of branches of work. Examples of this include: setting off a blasting charge before other workmen could get away to safety [36]; a crane swinging stones over the heads of other workmen working in a cutting.[37]

Layout of premises. Faulty system may consist in the layout of the premises in question, such as placing a water-tank where it obstructed the view of an engine-driver,[38] or parking vehicles so that they created a blind corner,[39] or siting a steam crane so near the edge of a quarry that cinders from the firebox fell and ignited a blasting charge on the quarry face.[40]

Dangerous layout of work. Examples of this are: where a man painting a door was thrown from his ladder by the unexpected opening of another door [41]; where a cleaner in a bus depot was struck by another vehicle, there being no time to prevent it coming too close [42]; where buses were so parked as to create an artificial blind corner where a collision took place.[43]

Inadequate lighting or ventilation. The failure to provide adequate lighting, which may cause an employee to trip over something,[44] or may cause him eye strain at work, is undoubtedly a defect in system.

Apart from statutory duty, there is little doubt that failure to provide proper ventilation or to take steps to maintain reasonably clean air in a workshop would be faulty system.[45] The failure at common law to provide ventilation of a mine to enable inspection to be made of the working place after shots had been fired has been held irrelevant where no causal connection was averred between the failure and the accident which had happened.[46] There is no breach of duty if the employers did not know, nor ought they to have known, that particular dust in the working atmosphere was dangerous.[47]

Inadequate tackle. " System " includes the provision where necessary of tackle, such as planks, ropes, chocks and so on, necessary to enable a particular job to be done. The court has dismissed as irrelevant a case based on inadequate supply of tackle when it was a matter of common knowledge and experience that the tackle desiderated by the pursuer

---

36 *Sword* v. *Cameron* (1839) 1 D. 493.
37 *Smith* v. *Baker* [1891] A.C. 325.
38 *McKillop* v. *N.B.Ry.* (1896) 23 R. 768, 772.
39 *Kerr* v. *Glasgow Corpn.*, 1945 S.C. 335.
40 *Grant* v. *Drysdale* (1883) 10 R. 1159.
41 *Spencer* v. *Green and Silley Weir, Ltd.* (1947) 80 Ll.L.R. 217.
42 *Calvert* v. *London Transport Executive* [1949] W.N. 341.
43 *Kerr* v. *Glasgow Corpn.*, 1945 S.C. 335.
44 *Farnham* v. *New Bank Coal Co.* (1896) 23 R. 722; *cf. Grant* v. *Sun Shipping Co.*, 1948 S.C.(H.L.) 73.
45 *Cf. Quinn* v. *Cameron & Roberton*, 1957 S.C.(H.L.) 22; *Nicholson* v. *Atlas Steel Foundry & Engineering Co., Ltd.*, 1957 S.C.(H.L.) 44.
46 *Park* v. *Wilsons and Clyde Coal Co.*, 1926 S.N. 141 (not discussed in 1929 S.C.(H.L.) 38).
47 *Graham* v. *C.W.S.* [1957] 1 All E.R. 654.

was unnecessary,[48] but held an employer liable where tackle for a job was inadequate, even though if those engaged on the work had looked around they would have found proper materials.[49]

Defective tackle. It is clearly part of " system " to provide sufficient ropes, slings or other tackle for the job to be done and to have it of adequate strength. But the employer is not liable if, having done so, a defective rope is somehow substituted for a good rope supplied by the employer.[50]

The employer is liable if tackle, such as scaffolding, is supplied by a third party and fails by reason of a defect which would have been apparent to a reasonably skilled person inspecting it.[51]

Akin to defective tackle is the supply of a vehicle the steering of which operated in the direction opposite to that of other such vehicles owned by the employer.[52]

Misuse of tackle. It may be faulty system to use apparatus for a purpose for which it was not intended,[53] or to use it badly, as, for example, to lift a load quickly so that it swung and injured another workman.[54]

Instruction of young and inexperienced workers. At common law it is defective system to employ young or inexperienced workers without full and careful instruction in how best to do their jobs, and in the dangers to be guarded against.[55]

But the employer is still liable if instruction is given, but is insufficient or if the instructions are allowed to be disobeyed.[56]

Use of workmen outside their line of work. It may be faulty system to employ men to do what is outside their line of work, certainly if no steps are taken to ascertain whether it can be done safely.[57]

Workman where he had no business to be. It is no defence that the workman, when injured, was where he had no business to be and would not have been injured but for that.[58]

Devolution of duty on workman himself. An experienced workman may in some circumstances reasonably be left to organise his own work, and if in such a case he chooses to adopt a dangerous method he alone

---

[48] *Loughney* v. *Caledonian Ry.* (1902) 4 F. 401.
[49] *Rees* v. *Cambrian Wagon Works* (1946) 62 T.L.R. 512.
[50] *O'Melia* v. *Freight Conveyors, Ltd.* [1940] 4 All E.R. 516.
[51] *Macdonald* v. *Wyllie & Son* (1898) 1 F. 339; *cf. Davison* v. *Henderson & Co.* (1895) 22 R. 448.
[52] *Kabango* v. *Renfrew Stevedoring Co.*, 1949 S.L.T.(Notes) 33.
[53] *Welsh* v. *Moir* (1885) 12 R. 590; *cf. Bruce* v. *Barclay* (1890) 17 R. 811.
[54] *Staveley Iron Co.* v. *Jones* [1956] A.C. 627.
[55] *Grizzle* v. *Frost* (1863) 3 F. & F. 622; *Gibson* v. *Nimmo* (1895) 22 R. 491.   *Cf. King* v. *John Brown & Co.*, 1952 S.L.T.(Notes) 63.
[56] *Cribb* v. *Kynoch, Ltd.* [1907] 2 K.B. 548; *Young* v. *Hoffman Mfg. Co.* [1907] 2 K.B. 646; *Olsen* v. *Corry and Gravesend Aviation, Ltd.* [1936] 3 All E.R. 241; *cf. Lewis* v. *High Duty Alloys, Ltd.* [1957] 1 All E.R. 740.
[57] *Stark* v. *McLaren* (1871) 10 M. 31; *Robertson* v. *Brown* (1876) 3 R. 652.
[58] *Whitelaw* v. *Moffat* (1849) 12 D. 434.

will be responsible for his injuries. This principle will normally apply only where the operation is fairly simple [59] and in the case of a man with the experience and the capacity to choose his mode of working, and the degree of danger inherent in the work is very relevant.[60] The principle is perhaps more readily applied in the case of workmen, such as painters, who have normally to be sent out singly or in small parties to do work on another's premises and cannot so readily or continuously be supervised. Similarly the duty may be devolved on a foreman or chargehand on the spot.[59]

It is not, however, enough to tell a workman not to do anything dangerous, nor merely to tell him to read the Regulations, without trying to ensure that he does appreciate the dangers and comply with the Regulations.[61]

(b) The employer's vicarious liability

The abolition of the doctrine of common employment [62] has restored the vicarious liability of the employer to one employee for injury caused him by the fault of another employee. He is as much liable for harm done by one employee, acting in the course of his employment, to another employee as he would be for the same harm done to a stranger.[63] It is incompetent by contract to exclude or limit this liability.[64] In effect this restores the law as it stood prior to the imposition on Scotland of the doctrine of common employment,[65] and reinstates pre-1858 decisions (*i.e.*, cases prior to *Bartonshill Coal Co.* v. *Reid*) as good law.

The question whether the employer is vicariously liable or not is determined by the same considerations, whether the injured person is another employee or a third party.[66] The cases turn very much on their own facts.

The scope of employment in this context has been held to include an apprentice (who had no driving licence and was not an authorised driver) moving a vehicle by driving it and causing a fellow employee fatal injuries [67]; and also one employee jostling another when the workers were rushing down the stairs after the hooter had sounded at the end of the day's work.[68]

[59] *Winter* v. *Cardiff R.D.C.* [1950] 1 All E.R. 819.
[60] *Martin* v. *Dalzell & Co., Ltd.* [1956] 1 Lloyd's Rep. 94; *Winstanley* v. *Athel Line, Ltd.* [1956] 2 Lloyd's Rep. 424.
[61] *Barcock* v. *Brighton Corpn.* [1949] 1 K.B. 339.
[62] Law Reform (Personal Injuries) Act, 1948, s. 1 (1).
[63] *Lindsay* v. *Connell & Co.*, 1951 S.C. 281; *Baxter* v. *Colvilles, Ltd.*, 1959 S.L.T. 325.
[64] 1948 Act, s. 1 (3).
[65] By *Bartonshill Coal Co.* v. *Reid* (1858) 3 Macq. 266.
[66] See further Chap. 5, *supra*.
[67] *Mulholland* v. *William Reid & Leys*, 1958 S.C. 290.
[68] *Bell* v. *Blackwood Morton & Sons, Ltd.*, 1960 S.C. 11; *cf. Brydon* v. *Stewart* (1855) 2 Macq. 30, 36; *Tunney* v. *Midland Ry.* (1866) L.R. 1 C.P. 291; *Weaver* v. *Tredegar Iron and Coal Co.* [1940] A.C. 955, 966; *Staton* v. *N.C.B.* [1957] 1 W.L.R. 893.

If, however, the act of the fellow employee which causes the harm was done outwith the course of his employment, as, for example, striking a match in a coal mine to light a cigarette and thereby causing an explosion,[69] the employers are not liable vicariously to fellow employees injured thereby.

The modes in which vicarious liability may be incurred are too numerous to mention, and probably cover every kind of harm caused by negligence on the part of the employee towards his fellow employee, so long always as the wrongdoer was at the time acting in the course of his employment.

Casual negligence. The employer is vicariously liable for even casual or isolated acts of negligence by one employee which cause harm to another, provided the acts are still within the course of the employment.[70]

Vicarious liability not co-extensive with personal liability. It is noteworthy that an employer may be held vicariously liable though not himself personally liable on another ground, *e.g.*, faulty system. Conduct by an employee which is a mere casual departure from a safe system of working does not make the employer liable directly, but if the employee has, in the course of his employment, been negligent towards another employee and causes him injury, the employer will be liable vicariously. In *Winter* v. *Cardiff R.D.C.*,[71] the defendants loaded a heavy voltage regulator on a lorry; a competent chargehand was in charge and though a rope was provided to lash the regulator to the lorry it was not used. When the lorry was rounding a bend the regulator fell off the lorry, knocking the plaintiff off also and injuring him. It was held that the defendants had not provided an unsafe system of working, but that the negligence complained of was truly that of a fellow employee. The defendants were not liable directly, but, *semble*, would have been liable vicariously.

Personal liability of wrongdoer. The inability to bring, or failure of, an action against an employer because, in the circumstances, he was not vicariously liable, does not absolve the wrongdoing employee, and he remains personally liable, if fault can be established, though he is not usually worth suing. There is no doubt that one employee owes duties of care while at work to fellow employees as much as to third parties, whether or not his conduct would in the circumstances render the employer liable vicariously.[72]

Employer's right of indemnity. Where an employer is rendered liable vicariously for a wrong actually committed by an employee, he is entitled

---

[69] *Kirby* v. *N.C.B.*, 1958 S.C. 514.
[70] *Lindsay* v. *Connell & Co.*, 1951 S.C. 281, 285.
[71] [1950] 1 All E.R. 819. (The accident happened in the days of the common employment rule.)
[72] *Cf. Lees* v. *Dunkerley Bros.* [1911] A.C. 5; *Lonbach* v. *Cooptimists Entertainment Syndicate* (1926) 43 T.L.R. 30; *Lister* v. *Romford Ice and Cold Storage Co.* [1957] A.C. 555.

to claim indemnity from the employee against the damages and expenses which he has had to pay.[73] But this is a right often not worth pursuing and likely to provoke trouble if too readily invoked.

Contributory negligence. An injured employee's own failure to take reasonable precautions for his own safety is a competent defence, formerly completely,[74] and now to the effect of abating damages,[75] both in cases of alleged personal fault of the employer, and in cases of vicarious liability for the fault of a fellow employee.

Volenti non fit injuria. This is similarly a competent defence both in cases of employer's alleged personal fault and of employer's vicarious liability for alleged fault, but in modern practice the court would have to be convinced by the clearest evidence that the injured person had truly voluntarily undertaken to run the risk of injury and to release the employer from the duty of taking care in relation thereto.

(c) The employer's statutory duties

Employers are also subject to numerous duties imposed by statute for the safety, health and welfare of employees, for the breach of many of which a civil claim lies. This topic is discussed in Chapter 18.

The imposition of a statutory duty does not, in the absence of express words or clear implication, abrogate or supersede an employer's common law duties to take reasonable care for the safety of his workmen. It is cumulative therewith, and may in range of precautions and standard of care go beyond any duties recognised at common law, but does not automatically exclude them.[76] When the court is considering a common law claim it cannot take into account statutory regulations which nearly apply, but in fact do not apply.[77]

Liability of Third Parties to Injured Employees

Where in the course of employment an employee is necessarily working outside his employer's premises, he may suffer injury by reason of the fault of some person other than his employer or fellow employees. To put the matter in another way, a third party employing a contractor may become liable *ex delicto* to the contractor's men directly, if one is injured or killed by the fault of the third party. Thus a contractor's or sub-contractor's employee may complain of injuries sustained on board a

---

[73] *Weld-Blundell* v. *Stephens* [1919] 1 K.B. 520, 536; *Ryan* v. *Fildes* [1938] 3 All E.R. 517; *Jones* v. *Manchester Corpn.* [1952] 2 Q.B. 852; *Semtex, Ltd.* v. *Gladstone* [1954] 2 All E.R. 206; *Lister* v. *Romford Ice and Cold Storage Co.* [1957] A.C. 555; and see Chap. 12 *supra*.

[74] *McNaughton* v. *Caledonian Ry.* (1858) 21 D. 160.

[75] Law Reform (Contributory Negligence) Act, 1945.

[76] *Matuszczyk* v. *N.C.B.*, 1953 S.C. 8.

[77] *Chipchase* v. *British Titan Products Co.* [1956] 1 Q.B. 545.

ship being built or tested by the defender by reason of the defender's alleged fault [78] and a sub-contractor's man may complain of injuries caused by the fault of the principal contractor.[79]

(a) *Third party's dangerous premises.* If an employee of employer A, in the course of his employment, goes on the premises of B, B owes to the employee the duty of reasonable care which he owes to any legitimate visitor under the Occupiers' Liability (Scotland) Act, 1960.[80] At common law it had been held that when engineers employed a firm of carters to do work in connection with a contract undertaken by them, the engineers were bound to take reasonable care that their premises were in a condition safe for the carter's employees, and were liable to the widow of one killed.[81] Similarly a proprietor of premises has been held liable to a plasterer's employee for injuries sustained on the premises by reason of the fault of a joiner's employee, engaged in a different bit of the same operation on the premises.[82] A dock labourer may have a claim against the owners of the ship on which he is injured while employed.[83] An injured workman, employed by A, injured on B's premises by the fault of C, another firm engaged by B, has been held to have no remedy against C; his claim lies against B.[84] Unless the employer is in occupation and has control of the third party's premises he is under no duty to his own men to see that the premises are reasonably safe.[85]

In some cases the occupier of the premises and another party may both be liable, or possibly liable.

Where a dock labourer in the course of his employment was working on board a ship, he fell through a hatchway left unlit by ship repairers who had been working on the vessel. The House of Lords held the ship-owners liable for failing to make sure that the place where the labourer was to work was reasonably safe, and the ship repairers also liable for

[78] *e.g., Hobson* v. *Bartram* [1950] 1 All E.R. 412; *Mace* v. *Green and Silley Weir* [1959] 2 Q.B. 14.

[79] *Mulready* v. *Bell* [1953] 2 All E.R. 215.

[80] On this Act see p. 589, *infra.* Under the pre-1960 law a workman employed by A and entering on B's premises to work there was classed as an invitee of B: *Indermaur* v. *Dames* (1866) L.R. 1 C.P. 274; *Oliphant* v. *Johnstone & Macleod* (1894) 21 R. 531; *London Graving Dock* v. *Horton* [1951] A.C. 737. He might be a licensee on parts of B's premises which he did not need to, but was allowed to, visit: *Bolch* v. *Smith* (1862) 7 H. & N. 736; *Jacobs* v. *L.C.C.* [1950] A.C. 361; or a trespasser if he went to a place where he had no right to be: *Hillen* v. *I.C.I. (Alkali), Ltd.* [1936] A.C. 65.

[81] *Muirhead* v. *Watt & Wilson* (1895) 3 S.L.T. 71.

[82] *Sally* v. *Dumbar* (1899) 6 S.L.T. 322. See also *Gregory* v. *Hill* (1869) 8 M. 282; *Maguire* v. *Russell* (1885) 12 R. 1071; *Carlin* v. *Clan Line Steamers*, 1937 S.L.T. 190; *Macdonald* v. *Wyllie* (1898) 1 F. 339.

[83] *Jordan* v. *Court Line*, 1947 S.C. 29; *Leeson* v. *Gardner*, 1947 S.L.T. 264; *cf. Jerred* v. *Roddam Dent & Son* [1948] 2 All E.R. 104.

[84] *Campbell* v. *A. & D. Morrison* (1891) 19 R. 282. The reasoning is not satisfactory, depending on the premiss that C's breach of contract with B cannot also be a delict against A, which *non sequitur*. Would A's man not have had a claim against C today? See also *Nelson* v. *Scott, Croall & Sons* (1892) 19 R. 425.

[85] *Taylor* v. *Sims & Sims* [1942] 2 All E.R. 375; *Cilia* v. *James* [1954] 2 All E.R. 9; *Durie* v. *Main*, 1958 S.C. 48; *Gemmill* v. *Macdonald*, 1964 S.L.T.(Notes) 9.

leaving the hatch uncovered and unlit. The independent acts of negligence had in combination caused the accident.[86]

Again where a window cleaner fell from an upper window he sued the occupiers of the premises for danger therein and also his employers for not providing a safe system of working. The occupiers were dismissed from the action but the employers were held liable for breach of duty.[87] In another case, however,[88] it was held to be fault on the employers' part not to have enquired of the occupiers as to the possibility of attaching safety belts to transoms above windows.

A variant of this ground of liability is the case of the employee of A injured on A's premises by the fault of a servant of B, whose men were working there under contract with A. A claim lies against B,[89] and probably against A also. Thus where a man working on a ship was injured by an explosion, caused by the escape of an inflammable mixture from a cylinder brought there by another set of workmen, the latter's employer was held liable.[90]

But where an employee of C, employed as sub-contractors by B to do work preliminary to repairs being done by B on A's premises was injured by the collapse of the part of the premises he was working on, it was held that B was not liable, not knowing of the danger, and the pursuer not being an employee or invitee of B.[91]

The liability of the principal for dangerous premises, which result in injury to his contractor's employee, now depends on the Occupiers' Liability (Scotland) Act, 1960. Under the corresponding English Act a skilled man sent by his employer B to do blasting for A failed in his claim against A when it was held that A had not been in breach of his duty to take reasonable care for the plaintiff's safety.[92]

(b) *Third party's dangerous machinery or appliances.* If an employee of employer A, in the course of his employment, necessarily uses machinery, tackle, equipment or appliances provided by B for the use of A and his men, where reliance is placed on B's care in selection, inspection or fitting, then B owes a duty of care to A's employees to take reasonable care that they will not be injured by any defect in B's equipment of which B knew or reasonably should have known. This is simply an example of the general principle that the supplier is liable to the ultimate user, if

---

[86] *Grant* v. *Sun Shipping Co.*, 1948 S.C.(H.L.) 73; see also *Simpson* v. *Paton* (1896) 23 R. 590; *McLachlan* v. *S.S. Peveril Co.* (1896) 23 R. 753; *Taylor* v. *Cairn Line*, 1928 S.N. 123.

[87] *General Cleaning Contractors* v. *Christmas* [1953] A.C. 180; *cf. Bates* v. *Parker* [1953] 2 Q.B. 231; *Wilson* v. *Tyneside Window-Cleaning Co.* [1958] 2 Q.B. 110, where action against employers failed.

[88] *Drummond* v. *British Building Cleaners* [1954] 3 All E.R. 507; see also *Kerner* v. *Amalgamated Window and General Cleaning Contractors* [1954] C.L.Y. 2284; *Pullar* v. *Window Clean, Ltd.*, 1956 S.C. 13; *Heggie* v. *Edinburgh and Leith Window Cleaning Co.*, 1959 S.L.T. 30.

[89] *Gorman* v. *Morrison* (1885) 12 R. 1073; *Leitch* v. *Howie*, 1927 S.L.T. 186.

[90] *Beckett* v. *Newalls Insulation Co.* [1953] 1 All E.R. 250.

[91] *Leckie* v. *Caledonian Glass Co.*, 1957 S.C. 89; see also *Welsh* v. *Mackenzie* (1958) 74 Sh.Ct.Rep. 44.

[92] *Savory* v. *Holland, Hannen & Cubitts (Southern)* [1964] 3 All E.R. 18.

injured by a defective article.[93] The occurrence of an accident, without satisfactory explanation, suggests that the equipment was defective and that the supplier is liable.[94] Thus in *Heaven* v. *Pender* [95] dockowners supplied staging for the use of shipowners and a painter employed by the shipowners was injured because of a defect therein and recovered damages from the dockowners. In *Traill* v. *A/S Dalbeattie* [96] a stevedore's labourer was killed owing to a defect in a rope supplied to him by shipowners to be used in the discharge of the ship, and a claim on the ground of failure to inspect the rope was held relevant. So, too, in *Oliver* v. *Saddler & Co.*[97] stevedores supplied to porters a defective sling and were held liable for the death of a porter killed when the sling broke.

Where a colliery employee was injured by reason of a defect in a railway wagon, the coalmasters were held not liable, the wagon not being part of their plant, but merely sent to be loaded under a contract of carriage with the railway company.[98] When a stevedore goes on board a ship to discharge a cargo he does not owe any general duty of care to his employees to inspect the ship and its equipment to see that they are in a safe condition. If, however, there are suspicious facts or indications of insecurity coming to his actual knowledge, he should investigate the possible danger and, if necessary, take precautions.[99]

Where on the other hand one railway company gratuitously allowed its wagons to be used for particular traffic and an employee of another company was killed, owing to a defect in a wagon brake, while it was being so used, the owning company was held to have owed no duty to employees of the second company to see that the wagons were in proper order.[1] Similarly where workmen used plant without authority they were held to have no claim against the owner of the plant, as it had not been intended for their use.[2]

The broad principle of *Donoghue* v. *Stevenson* was applied also in *Denny* v. *Supplies and Transport Co., Ltd.*[3] where men from one firm of stevedores unloaded timber into barges which were towed to a quay where men from a second firm of stevedores unloaded the timber onto lorries. An employee of the second firm was injured while taking timber out of the barge, it having been badly loaded by the first firm's men, and was held to have a right of action against the first firm.

---

[93] *Donoghue* v. *Stevenson*, 1932 S.C.(H.L.) 31.
[94] *Walker* v. *Olsen* (1882) 9 R. 946.
[95] (1883) 11 Q.B.D. 503. *Cf. Thomson* v. *Wallace*, 1933 S.N. 15; *Muir* v. *Moy Hammerton, Ltd.*, 1947 S.N. 190; *Jordan* v. *Court Line*, 1947 S.C. 29.
[96] (1904) 6 F. 798. *Cf. Carlin* v. *Clan Line*, 1937 S.L.T. 190.
[97] 1929 S.C.(H.L.) 94. See also *Edwards* v. *Hutcheon* (1889) 16 R. 694.
[98] *Robinson* v. *John Watson, Ltd.* (1892) 20 R. 144.
[99] *Durie* v. *Main*, 1958 S.C. 48.
[1] *Caledonian Ry.* v. *Warwick* (1897) 24 R.(H.L.) 1; *cf. Kemp & Dougall* v. *Darngavil Coal Co.*, 1909 S.C. 1314.
[2] *Nicolson* v. *Macandrew & Co.* (1888)15 R. 854; *Watson* v. *McLeish & McTaggart* (1898) 25 R. 1028.
[3] [1950] 2 K.B. 374; distinguished on the facts, in *Twiss* v. *Rhodes and Mersey Docks and Harbour Board* [1951] 1 Lloyds' Rep. 333.

Responsibility assumed by contractor. The third party is not, however, liable to his contractor's workmen if under the contract, or in fact, the contractor has assumed the responsibility of choosing, or setting up, or examining the apparatus used by his men. Thus in *Shaw* v. *West Calder Oil Co.*,[4] the lessees of a shale pit contracted with A to work the shale for them, A to supply and maintain machinery, etc., and to satisfy himself that the shaft and fittings were safe. It was held that workmen employed by A, who sustained injuries caused by the defective state of a rope, could not recover from the lessees. Similarly in *McGill* v. *Bowman & Co.*,[5] a coalmaster employed a contractor to sink a pit, the coalmaster supplying the equipment but the contract providing that the contractor should satisfy himself as to the condition and strength of all materials and tackle provided. When an accident occurred by the fall of certain plant brought about by the neglect of the contractor's pitheadman, the coalmaster was held not liable.[6]

Some older cases on this topic cannot now be supported, having been decided on the basis that conduct might be a breach of contract and was therefore not a delict.[7]

(c) *Third party's dangerous system.* An employee may have an action against a third party by whose dangerous system of working he has been injured, while in the course of his employment, but it must be clear that the fault was on the part of the third party, rather than of his own employer.[8] Thus a drover employed by a cattle-dealer was injured when a train ran into the truck on which he was working; he recovered damages from the railway company.[9] A cooper's man, injured when staves being loaded on a contractor's lorry rolled back, by reason of the fault of the carter, recovered damages from the contractor.[10] A dock labourer may have a claim if no hatchmouthman is posted to transmit signals to a cranedriver.[11] An employee of the owner of a factory has a claim against contractors working therein by whose fault he has been injured.[12]

(d) *Third party delivering dangerous things.* If an employee of employer A, in the course of his employment, has entrusted to him by B for carriage or some similar purpose, something dangerous, B owes him a duty to take reasonable care to warn him of the dangers attaching to the thing.

Thus dangerous goods must not be entrusted for carriage without warning,[13] nor highly inflammable goods delivered without proper marking or warning.[14]

---

4 (1872) 9 S.L.R. 254.
5 (1890) 18 R. 206.   6 See also *Robertson* v. *Russell* (1885) 12 R. 634.
7 *Campbell* v. *A. & D. Morrison* (1891) 19 R. 282.
8 *Robertson* v. *Russell* (1885) 12 R. 634; cf. *Breslin* v. *Clyde Quarries, Ltd.* (1905) 7 F. 557; *Murphy* v. *Bladen* (1906) 14 S.L.T. 250.
9 *Wyllie* v. *Caledonian Ry.* (1871) 9 M. 463; *Congleton* v. *Angus* (1887) 14 R. 309.
10 *Smyth* v. *Turnbull* (1890) 17 R. 877.
11 *Stewart's Exrx.* v. *Clyde Navigation Trs.*, 1946 S.C. 317.   12 *Ward* v. *Revie*, 1944 S.C. 325.
13 *Farrant* v. *Barnes* (1862) 11 C.B.(N.S.) 553; *Bamfield* v. *Goole and Sheffield Transport Co.* [1910] 2 K.B. 94.
14 *Macdonald* v. *MacBrayne*, 1915 S.C. 716; *Philco Radio* v. *Spurling* [1949] 2 All E.R. 882; cf. *Anglo-Celtic Shipping Co.* v. *Elliott and Jeffery* (1926) 42 T.L.R. 297.

(e) *Third party instructing hazardous operation.* Where a third party employs an independent contractor to perform a hazardous operation he is liable for injury or harm caused by the contractor's negligence in the course thereof, not merely to third parties but also to the contractor's servants.[15]

6. Dangerous Premises

The liability *ex delicto* of the occupiers of land, buildings or other private premises to persons who come on these premises and are injured by defects or dangers encountered thereon is a " special subhead of the general doctrine of negligence."[16] Liability to persons who have not entered the premises but are injured by reason of their dangerous state depends on general principles of negligence,[17] and liability to persons who have not entered but are injured by the escape of something dangerous from the premises depends on one of the principles of strict liability.[18] Liability to persons who come on premises in pursuance of a contract with the occupier depends on terms implied into the contract.[19] The present head covers cases protected by the law of delict only.

Development of Scottish law. Prior to 1929 the Scottish courts had recognised that the strictness of the duty of care incumbent on the occupier of premises varied according to the circumstances in which the injured party had entered on the premises, and the extent of his right, or lack of it, to enter. The extent of right, and consequently the stringency of the duty of care, and the question whether care sufficient in the circumstances had been shown, were in each case questions of fact to be determined with regard to the circumstances of the case. [20]

In 1929, however, the House of Lords, in *Dumbreck* v. *Addie and Sons (Collieries) Ltd.,*[21] imposed on Scotland the much more rigid principles which had developed in English law by the gradual hardening into distinctions of law of what had been only differences of fact and consequent differences in the application of a general duty of reasonable care. These principles were that persons coming on premises had to be treated as falling into one or other of three classes or categories of visitors, to each of which different standards of care had as a matter of law to be shown. It was said there by Viscount Dunedin [22]: " I cannot do better than preface my remarks by a quotation from the exceedingly comprehensive and able judgment pronounced by Lord Sumner, at that time Hamilton L.J., in the case of *Latham* v. *Johnson* [23]:

---

15 *Anderson* v. *Brady & Ross*, 1964 S.L.T.(Notes) 11.
16 *Muir* v. *Glasgow Corporation*, 1943 S.C.(H.L.) 3, 13, *per* Lord Wright.
17 *e.g.*, *Moffat* v. *Park* (1877) 5 R. 13; *Caminer* v. *Northern & London Investment Trust* [1951] A.C. 88; *Robertson's Tutor* v. *Glasgow Corpn.*, 1950 S.C. 502.
18 Chap. 17, *infra.*
19 See Employment Accidents, *supra*, and Miscellaneous Cases, *infra.*
20 On the pre-1929 Scottish law see particularly *Shillinglaw* v. *Turner*, 1925 S.C. 807, 816–817, *per* L. P. Clyde; see also Lord Sands' formulation of the occupier's duty of care, at p. 820.
21 1929 S.C.(H.L.) 51.　　　　　　　　　　　　　　　22 *Ibid.* at p. 58.
23 [1913] 1 K.B. 398, 410.

' Where a question arises, not between parties who are both present in the exercise of equal rights *inter se*, but between parties of whom one is the owner or occupier of the place and the other, the party injured, is not there as of right, but must justify his presence there if he can, the law has long recognised three categories of obligation. In these the duty of the owner or occupier to use care, if it exists at all, is graduated distinctly, though never very definitely measured . . . Contractual obligations of course stand apart. The lowest is the duty to a trespasser. More care, though not much, is owed to a licensee—more again to an invitee . . . The owner of the property is under a duty not to injure the trespasser wilfully; " not to do a wilful act in reckless disregard of ordinary humanity towards him "; but otherwise a man " trespasses at his own risk." On this point Scotch law is the same. In English and Scotch law alike, when people come on the lands of others for their own purposes without right or invitation, they must take the lands as they find them, and cannot throw any responsibility upon the person on whose lands they have trespassed: *per* Lord Kinnear, *Devlin* v. *Jeffray's Trustees*.[24] The rule as to licensees, too, is that they must take the premises as they find them, apart from concealed sources of danger; where dangers are obvious they must run the risk of them. In darkness where they cannot see whether there is danger or not, if they will walk they walk at their peril.'

" With every word of this passage I agree and I agree that it is the law of Scotland as well as that of England.[25] What I particularly wish to emphasise is that there are the three different classes—invitees, licensees, trespassers . . . Now the line that separates each of these three classes is an absolutely rigid line. There is no half-way house, no no-man's land between adjacent territories. When I say rigid, I mean rigid in law. When you come to the facts it may well be that there is great difficulty— such difficulty as may give rise to difference of judicial opinion—in deciding into which category a particular case falls, but a judge must decide and, he having decided, then the law of that category will rule and there must be no looking to the law of the adjoining category. I cannot help thinking that the use of epithets, ' bare licensees,' ' pure trespassers ' and so on, has much to answer for in obscuring what I think is a vital proposition, that, in deciding cases of the class we are considering, the first duty of the tribunal is to fix once and for all into which of the three classes the person in question falls."

Accordingly, after and in consequence of that decision, in cases of alleged occupier's liability to a visitor for injuries caused by the state of the premises, Scottish courts had to answer two questions: into which of these three categories was the pursuer to be placed, and, secondly, what was the accepted legal formulation of the duty of care owed to a person entering in that capacity, before they could determine liability. The

---

24 (1903) 5 F. 130.
25 It is impossible to discover what authority Lord Dunedin conceived there was for this proposition.

accepted legal formulations of the different duties of care were drawn almost exclusively from the English cases, dated from the mid-nineteenth century, in which formulations of the duties had been developed applicable to the different categories.

Not merely was this a subversion of the common law of Scotland but it gave rise to many narrow and difficult arguments on categorisation, particularly as between invitee and licensee. The insistence on labels, categories and rigidly distinct compartmentation obscured fundamental principles and produced results exhibiting the worst characteristics of purely mechanical jurisprudence.[26]

The categories, in later cases, showed a great tendency to shade into one another and similar facts were sometimes differently categorised as between Scotland and England and at different times.[27] There was also a noticeable tendency to treat judicial formulations of a duty of care as canonical and to accord them the deference, and the casuistic interpretation, usually reserved for statutes.[28]

The categories of visitors and the duties thereto. The strict categorisation of visitors, as developed in English law and under the influence of *Dumbreck* v. *Addie's Collieries*,[29] accepted since 1929 in Scots law also, was into (i) invitees, who came on the premises by the invitation, express or implied, of the occupier; (ii) licensees, who came by the tolerance or with the leave, licence or permission of the occupier; and (iii) trespassers, who came without any right, invitation or permission and whose presence, if known, was objected to. A trespasser, if his trespasses were tolerated, might be held to have become a licensee.

To invitees the occupier's duty was to take reasonable care to prevent damage from unusual danger the existence of which he knew or ought to have known,[30] including danger from such acts of third parties as could reasonably be foreseen,[31] and from the actings of independent contractors.[32]

To licensees, the duty of care was not to make the premises safe but merely to warn the licensee of any concealed danger on the premises of which the occupier actually knew,[33] or, as it was sometimes put, not

---

[26] *Cf.* Pound, " Mechanical Jurisprudence " (1908) 8 Col.L.R. 605.

[27] *e.g., Ellis* v. *Fulham B.C.* [1938] 1 K.B. 212 (child injured in paddling pool in park held to be licensee); *Plank* v. *Stirling Mags.,* 1956 S.C. 92 (child injured on chute in park held to be invitee).

[28] *London Graving Dock* v. *Horton* [1951] A.C. 737. See also criticisms of the categorisation in *McPhail* v. *Lanarkshire C.C.,* 1951 S.C. 301, 314, 319; *Mooney* v. *Lanarkshire C.C.,* 1954 S.C. 245, 250; *Plank, supra,* 104.

[29] 1929 S.C.(H.L.) 51.

[30] *Indermaur* v. *Dames* (1866) L.R. 1 C.P. 274, 287; *Whitby* v. *Burt, Boulton and Hayward, Ltd.* [1947] K.B. 918; *London Graving Dock* v. *Horton* [1951] A.C. 737.

[31] *Simons* v. *Winslade* [1938] 3 All E.R. 774; *Hobson* v. *Bartrams, Ltd.* [1950] 1 All E.R. 412.

[32] *Cox* v. *Coulson* [1916] 2 K.B. 177; *Wilkinson* v. *Rea, Ltd.* [1941] 1 K.B. 688; *Thomson* v. *Cremin* (1941) 1956 S.L.T. 357.

[33] *Latham* v. *Johnson* [1913] 1 K.B. 398; *Fairman* v. *Perpetual Investment Building Soc.* [1923] A.C. 74; *Mersey Docks and Harbour Board* v. *Proctor* [1923] A.C. 253; *Coleshill* v. *Manchester Corpn.* [1928] 1 K.B. 776; *Coates* v. *Rawtenstall Corpn.* [1937] 3 All E.R. 602; *Ellis* v. *Fulham B.C.* [1938] 1 K.B. 212; *Sutton* v. *Bootle Corpn.* [1947] K.B. 359; *Mackin* v. *Glasgow Corpn.,* 1949 S.C. 468; *Pearson* v. *Lambeth B.C.* [1950] 2 K.B. 353.

knowingly to lead the licensee into a trap, even if created by a third party.[34] Apart from that the licensee had to accept the premises as they were.

To trespassers, the occupier owed no duty of care to keep his premises safe or to give warning of hidden dangers,[35] but only to refrain from intentionally harming them [36] and from acting with indifference to the consequences to trespassers of whose presence he knew or ought to have known.[37]

The Occupiers' Liability (Scotland) Act, 1960. This Act [38] supersedes the common law categories for the purpose of determining the care which an occupier of premises is required to show towards persons entering on the premises in respect of dangers which are due to the state of the premises or to anything done or omitted to be done on them and for which he is in law responsible.

Effect of the Act generally. The most general effect of the Act is that it is no longer necessary to categorise a visitor as an invitee, licensee or trespasser, (which might, and often did, involve lengthy consideration of the cases laying down the criteria for deciding that issue), nor to determine from those cases the precise legal formulation of the duty of care applicable to a visitor of the relevant category, and then to determine whether that duty had or had not in the circumstances been implemented. Each case must be treated wholly as a question of fact, the degree of entitlement the visitor had to come on the premises being no more than a factor to be considered in determining whether or not the occupier had taken reasonable care for his safety.

Interests protected by the Act. At common law the special principles governing occupier's liability seem in Scotland to have protected the individual against personal injury only. The Act expressly covers " injury or damage occasioned to persons *or property*," and this represents a formal change from the common law, though it is doubtful if it has made any difference in substance or effect. In *Caledonian Ry.* v. *Greenock Sacking Co.*[39] the tenant of a store which collapsed was held liable to a carrier for the loss of a horse killed by the fall of the building. Such a case would now come under the Act.

On whom duty incumbent. The common law still determines the person on whom in relation to any premises a duty to show care towards persons

---

34 *Ellis* v. *Fulham B.C.* [1938] 1 K.B. 212.
35 *Grand Trunk Ry. of Canada* v. *Barnett* [1911] A.C. 361; *Conway* v. *Wimpey* [1951] 1 All E.R. 56; *Young* v. *Box* [1951] 1 T.L.R. 789.
36 *Ilott* v. *Wilkes* (1820) 3 B. & Ald. 304; *Hardy* v. *C.L.Ry.* [1920] 3 K.B. 459; *Dumbreck* v. *Addie's Collieries*, 1929 S.C.(H.L.) 51; *Hillen* v. *I.C.I.(Alkali), Ltd.* [1934] 1 K.B. 455.
37 Hart, " Injuries to Trespassers " (1931) 47 L.Q.R. 92; *Mourton* v. *Poulter* [1930] 2 K.B. 183; *Excelsior Wire Rope Co.* v. *Callan* [1930] A.C. 404.
38 Passed to give effect to the First Report of the Law Reform Committee for Scotland (Cmnd. 88, 1957); it came into force on September 2, 1960. It corresponds to, but is not identical with, the [English] Occupiers' Liability Act, 1957.
39 (1875) 2 R. 671.

entering thereon is incumbent.[40] At common law liability attaches to occupancy and control of premises, rather than to ownership, because the person who is in actual occupation and possession of the premises has the power of supervision and control, of permitting or forbidding entry, the knowledge of the condition of the premises and the responsibility for noticing and removing or guarding against dangers.[41] Attention is accordingly directed to the liability of the " occupier," whether or not he is also owner. Title to the premises is not an essential element, but is a factor in determining whether or not the defender had possession and control.[42] The Act [43] refers to the care which a person must take " by reason of such occupation or control " of premises.

Who are " occupiers." The term " occupier " includes any person or body in actual possession, physical control and beneficial occupation of premises, whether owner,[44] tenant,[45] heritable creditor in possession,[46] trustee in bankruptcy,[47] but possibly not licensee.[48] Contractors who take possession of premises while working therein may be " occupiers," [49] and the category includes a person having the concession of a fairground though not having any lease,[50] the committee running a race meeting,[51] a cricket club,[52] a contractor engaged in converting a ship in a dry dock,[53] a local authority in respect of a requisitioned house,[54] but Post Office engineers working on and under the roadway are not " occupiers " thereof,[55] nor are house factors " occupiers ".[56]

Knowledge of the identity of the occupier of premises is a " material fact of a decisive character " within the meaning of the Limitation Act, 1963, ss. 1 and 7, justifying an extension of the time within which an action may be brought.[57]

The Act binds the Crown (s. 4), but no further than is competent under the Crown Proceedings Act, 1947. This statutory liability accordingly applies to Crown premises, and Crown vessels, vehicles and aircraft.

---

[40] s. 1 (2).
[41] *Devlin* v. *Jeffray's Trs.* (1902) 5 F. 130; *Hartwell* v. *Grayson, Rollo and Clover Docks Ltd.* [1947] K.B. 901, 915, 917.
[42] *Murdoch* v. *A. & R. Scott*, 1956 S.C. 309.
[43] s. 1 (1).
[44] *Mellon* v. *Henderson*, 1913 S.C. 1207; *Mathieson's Tutor* v. *Aikman's Trs.*, 1910 S.C. 11.
[45] *Caledonian Ry.* v. *Greenock Sacking Co.* (1875) 2 R. 671; *Devlin* v. *Jeffray's Trs.* (1902) 5 F. 130; *Kennedy* v. *Shotts Iron Co.*, 1913 S.C. 1143; *McIlwaine* v. *Stewart's Trs.*, 1914 S.C. 934.
[46] *Baillie* v. *Shearer's J.F.* (1894) 21 R. 498.
[47] *Cf. Meigh* v. *Wickenden* [1942] 2 K.B. 160.
[48] *Cf. Foster* v. *Newhaven Harbour Trs.* (1897) 61 J.P. 629.
[49] *Smith* v. *Cammell Laird & Co.* [1940] A.C. 242; *Rippon* v. *P.L.A. and Russell & Co.* [1940] 1 K.B. 858; *Wilkinson* v. *Rea, Ltd.* [1941] 1 K.B. 688; *Billings* v. *Riden* [1958] A.C. 240.
[50] *Humphreys* v. *Dreamland (Margate), Ltd.* [1930] All E.R.Rep. 327.
[51] *Glass* v. *Paisley Race Committee* (1902) 5 F. 14; *McSourley* v. *Paisley Mags.* (1902) 10 S.L.T. 86; *cf. Adair* v. *Paisley Mags.* (1904) 12 S.L.T. 105.
[52] *Duncan* v. *Perthshire Cricket Club* (1904) 12 S.L.T. 635.
[53] *Hartwell* v. *Grayson Rollo and Clover Docks, Ltd.* [1947] K.B. 907.
[54] *Hawkins* v. *Coulsdon and Purley U.D.C.* [1954] 1 Q.B. 319; *Greene* v. *Chelsea B.C.* [1954] 2 Q.B. 127.
[55] *Hughes* v. *Lord Advocate*, 1963 S.C.(H.L.) 31.
[56] *Skelton* v. *Welsh*, 1964 S.L.T.(Notes) 12.
[57] *Clark* v. *Forbes Stuart (Thames Street)* [1964] 2 All E.R. 282.

What are " premises." " Premises " primarily means buildings, or land or other heritable subjects. The Act uses the phrase " land or other premises," but does not define " premises."

In England it had been held at common law that the principles of occupiers' liability applied not only to landed property, but to appliances attached to or situated on the premises, such as slings,[58] ladders,[59] a lift,[60] and scaffolding,[61] and suggested that they applied to such moveables as trains,[62] cars,[63] aeroplanes [64] and ships.[65]

It is not clear whether the Scottish courts were prepared at common law to apply these special principles to any kind of moveable property, and they declined to do so in *Carney* v. *Smith*,[66] where, however, the accident resulted from alleged negligence of the driver and not from any defect in the construction of the vehicle itself. The special principles of occupiers' liability were not relied on in cases of defects in the vehicles themselves.[67] Section 1 (3) of the Act, however, extends the occupiers' liability to notional premises.

Application of rules to notional premises. The statutory provisions apply not only, as did the superseded rules, to heritable property, but also to certain notional kinds of premises. They apply (s. 1 (3)) " in like manner and to the same extent as they do in relation to an occupier of premises and to persons entering thereon;

(a) in relation to a person occupying or having control of any fixed or moveable structure, including any vessel, vehicle or aircraft, and to persons entering thereon; and

(b) in relation to an occupier of premises or a person occupying or having control of any such structure and to property thereon, including the property of persons who have not themselves entered on the premises or structure."

The interpretation of these words seems apt to give rise to many controversies and in default of authority only suggestions can be offered.[68]

Notional premises (a). Section 1 (3) (*a*), as well as covering heritable property and vessels,[69] vehicles [70] or aircraft,[71] seems habile to cover any kind of moveable property on which a visitor may come, such as a

---

58 *Oliver* v. *Saddler*, 1929 S.C.(H.L.) 94.
59 *Woodman* v. *Richardson* [1937] 3 All E.R. 866.
60 *Haseldine* v. *Daw* [1941] 2 K.B. 343.
61 *Pratt* v. *Richards* [1951] 2 K.B. 208.
62 *Readhead* v. *Midland Ry.* (1869) L.R. 4 Q.B. 379, 385.
63 *Haseldine, supra*, 358.
64 *Fosbroke-Hobbes* v. *Airwork, Ltd.* [1937] 1 All E.R. 108.
65 *Duncan* v. *Cammell Laird* (1943) 171 L.T. 186, 190; [1946] A.C. 410; *London Graving Dock* v. *Horton* [1951] A.C. 737.
66 1953 S.C. 19.
67 e.g., *Donnelly* v. *Glasgow Corpn.*, *Henderson* v. *Glasgow Corpn.*, *Ross* v. *Glasgow Corpn.*, 1953 S.C. 107.
68 The wording of the [English] Occupiers' Liability Act, 1957 (s. 1 (3)) is much clearer.
69 See sec. 3 of this chapter, *supra*.
70 See sec. 1, *supra*.
71 See sec. 4, *supra*.

ladder, scaffold,[72] crane, gangway, or floating dock, and probably in effect does no more than restate the common law. It probably covers not only the fare-paying passenger, but the friend or guest conveyed gratuitously.[73]

Notional premises (*b*). Section 1 (3) (*b*) is more obscure; it seems to impose liability on an occupier of premises *stricto sensu*, or a person occupying or having control of any fixed or moveable structure, including any vessel, vehicle or aircraft, for injury or damage to property thereon, including the property of persons who have not themselves entered on the premises or structure.

This provision seems to impose liability *ex lege*, *e.g.*, on the depositary for goods deposited in his premises, on the person having control of a vessel, vehicle or aircraft for luggage or cargo loaded therein for transport, and on the porter on whose trolley any goods are carried. It covers both the case of goods or luggage accompanied by the owner, and the case of goods not so accompanied. The words seem habile to cover animals in transit.

The liability under section 1 (3) (*b*) is presumably for damage to the property while in or on the occupier's " premises "[74]; it is not clear whether it imposes liability for total destruction, *e.g.*, by fire, or for loss, *e.g.*, by theft. It is not clear how this liability interacts with, *e.g.*, hotel-keepers' liability,[75] or with contractual liability of carriers, warehousemen and others, or with the special liability of a common carrier.[76]

Section 1 (3) (*b*) certainly represents a very wide extension of the concept of " occupiers' liability " for " dangerous premises " as hitherto understood in Scotland, and it is questionable whether it has added anything of value to the law, whether, that is, the duty (s. 2 (1)) to take " such care as in all the circumstances of the case is reasonable " is any greater or other than is already imposed in relation to property by other principles of law, such as by implied terms of contract.

Particularly in view of the formulation of the duty of care (s. 2 (1)) in terms appropriate to premises *stricto sensu*, *i.e.*, heritable property, its extended application to notional premises, particularly by section 1 (3) (*b*), seems singularly infelicitous.

Who are " visitors." The duty of care under the Act is owed to " persons entering on the premises." This clearly covers all who would, under the former principles, have been classed as invitees, or as licensees, and probably also those classed as trespassers, though the care due to the last class may not be as high as to the others. It probably cannot, however, be said that no duty is owed to trespassers.

[72] *Cf. Nicolson* v. *Macandrew* (1888) 15 R. 854.
[73] *Cf. Paterson* v. *Gardiner*, 1924 S.L.T. 63.
[74] *Cf.* The long title of the Act . . . " liability of occupiers and others for injury or damage to persons or property . . ."
[75] See, *e.g., Burns* v. *Royal Hotel (St. Andrews), Ltd.*, 1956 S.C. 463 and Hotel Proprietors Act, 1956.
[76] See Chap. 8, *supra*.

" Visitors " includes such persons as guests, clients or customers on business,[77] intending passengers at railway stations,[78] persons at stations to see their friends away,[79] workmen admitted to do some work,[80] stevedores working on ships,[81] persons permitted to come on board ship,[82] contractors doing work on the occupiers' premises,[83] firemen who have come to extinguish a fire,[84] a policeman investigating a possible burglary,[85] persons calling to collect brock for pigs,[86] or to make a complaint,[87] or to collect articles from a carrier,[88] persons visiting at a hospital [89] or a patient therein,[90] persons in a hotel or public-house,[91] persons allowed to play on particular premises,[92] and persons allowed to help on particular premises,[93] carriers who come to deliver or remove goods,[94] spectators at a sport,[95] sanitary inspectors examining premises under reconstruction.[96]

Right to enter the premises. Under the pre-1960 law the question whether a pursuer had a legal right to enter the premises, and whether it was right of invitation, express or implied, or right of licence or permission, frequently arose and, possibly most frequently, the questions whether an invitee had gone beyond the scope of the invitation and rendered himself merely a licensee or even a trespasser,[97] or a person prima facie a trespasser had by tolerance of his trespasses acquired a tacit licence.[98] With the assimilation of the duties owed to invitees and to licensees this question is of reduced importance. It may be of relevance only if the courts take the view that " reasonable care in all the circumstances " implies a higher standard to those invited or permitted to enter than to those whose presence is unwanted and who would, if discovered,

---

77 *Brady* v. *Parker* (1887) 14 R. 783; *Dolan* v. *Burnett* (1896) 23 R. 550; *Somerville* v. *Hardie* (1896) 24 R. 58.
78 *Mackeever* v. *Caledonian Ry.* (1900) 2 F. 1085; *Fraser* v. *Caledonian Ry.* (1902) 5 F. 41.
79 *Tough* v. *N.B.Ry.*, 1914 S.C. 291; *Burns* v. *N.B.Ry.*, 1914 S.C. 754.
80 *Indermaur* v. *Dames* (1867) L.R. 2 C.P. 311; *Paterson* v. *Kidd's Trs.* (1896) 24 R. 99.
81 *McLachlan* v. *Peveril S.S. Co.* (1896) 23 R. 753; *Chadwick* v. *Elderslie S.S. Co.* (1898) 25 R. 730; *Grant* v. *Sun Shipping Co.*, 1948 S.C.(H.L.) 73.
82 *O'Brien* v. *Arbib*, 1907 S.C. 975.
83 *Bates* v. *Parker* [1953] Q.B. 231; *Smith* v. *Austin Lifts* [1959] 1 All E.R. 81.
84 *Merrington* v. *Ironbridge Metal Works* [1952] 2 All E.R. 1101; *Hartley* v. *Mayoh* [1954] 1 Q.B. 383.
85 *Great Central Ry.* v. *Bates* [1921] 3 K.B. 578.
86 *Smillies* v. *Boyd* (1886) 14 R. 150.
87 *White* v. *France* (1877) 2 C.P.D. 308.
88 *Wylie* v. *Caledonian Ry.* (1871) 9 M. 463.
89 *Weigall* v. *Westminster Hospital* (1936) 52 T.L.R. 310.
90 *Lindsey C.C.* v. *Marshall* [1937] A.C. 97.
91 *Cairns* v. *Boyd* (1879) 6 R. 1004; *Mackie* v. *Macmillan* (1898) 36 S.L.R. 137; *Walker* v. *Midland Ry.* (1886) 2 T.L.R. 450; *Greenlees* v. *Royal Hotel, Dundee* (1905) 7 F. 382.
92 *Cooke* v. *Midland G.W.Ry. of I.* [1909] A.C. 229; *Mackenzie* v. *Fairfield Shipbuilding Co.*, 1913 S.C. 213; *Taylor* v. *Glasgow Corpn.*, 1922 S.C.(H.L.) 1; *McKinlay* v. *Darngavil Coal Co.*, 1923 S.C.(H.L.) 34; *Boyd* v. *Glasgow Iron & Steel Co.*, 1923 S.C. 758.
93 *Ross* v. *McCallam's Trs.*, 1922 S.C. 322.
94 *Caledonian Ry.* v. *Greenock Sacking Co.* (1875) 2 R. 761; *Daily* v. *Allan* (1885) 12 R. 841.
95 *Duncan* v. *Perthshire C.C.* (1904) 12 S.L.T. 635.
96 *Fleming* v. *Eadie* (1898) 25 R. 500.
97 e.g., *Hillen* v. *I.C.I.* [1936] A.C. 65; *Pearson* v. *Coleman* [1948] 2 K.B. 359; *Videan* v. *B.T.C.* [1963] 2 All E.R. 860.
98 *Lawrie* v. *Earl of Wemyss*, 1930 S.N. 120; *Breslin* v. *L.N.E.Ry.*, 1936 S.C. 816; *Edwards* v. *Ry. Executive* [1952] A.C. 737; *Phipps* v. *Rochester Corpn.* [1955] 1 Q.B. 450.

be warned off the premises, in which case a broad distinction arises between those who may be expected to come and who are lawfully on the premises and those not expected and not entitled to be on the premises at all. To the former group a higher standard of care may be owed.

Persons present " as of right." The older cases sometimes regarded persons entering " as of right " as a separate category,[99] and sometimes classed them as invitees or licensees.[1] The phrase " as of right " was truly meaningless, ignoring the issue of: what right; right of invitation, of licence, or of any other degree? It is submitted that under the 1960 Act there is no warrant for treating such persons as a separate category. Such persons as policemen and officials in the exercise of a legal duty or power to enter premises, are clearly owed a reasonably high standard of care.

But such a person who exceeded his statutory or common law powers of entry was at common law merely a trespasser,[2] and this fact might still justify a lower standard of care.

Persons present on public property. Another group of pursuers sometimes treated separately in the past were members of the public entering on premises publicly owned and existing for the public benefit such as parks, libraries, museums, public lavatories, public offices, and so on. While it is now irrelevant to discuss whether such persons are invitees or licensees it is certain that local authorities and other bodies in occupation of public property, such as parks, must take reasonable care for the safety of visitors, and many cases decided before the 1960 Act will still give guidance on what duties of care should be taken. Thus it will doubtless still be negligent to have poisonous berries growing in an accessible part of a Botanic Garden,[3] though not necessarily to have a river in a public park unfenced,[4] or a pond in a park unfenced and unattended.[5]

It is submitted that there is no longer any warrant for regarding such persons as in a separate category or owed any exceptional duty.

Occupier's duty of care under statute. The Act provides: section 2 (1) " The care which an occupier of premises is required, by reason of his occupation or control of the premises, to show towards a person entering thereon in respect of dangers which are due to the state of the premises

---

[99] e.g., *Taylor* v. *Glasgow Corpn.*, 1922 S.C.(H.L.) 1, 4, *per* Lord Atkinson—" not merely as a licensee, but as of right." *Cf. Plank* v. *Stirling Magistrates*, 1956 S.C. 92, 116, *per* Lord Mackintosh. See generally Paton, " Liability of an Occupier to Those Who Enter as of Right " (1941) 19 Can.B.R. 1; Prosser, " Business Visitors and Invitees " (1941) 19 Can.B.R. 357; Friedmann, " Liability to Visitors of Premises " (1943) 21 Can.B.R. 859; Wallis-Jones, " Liability of Public Authorities as Occupiers of Dangerous Premises " (1949) 65 L.Q.R. 367.

[1] *McPhail* v. *Lanarkshire C.C.*, 1951 S.C. 301.

[2] *G.C.Ry.* v. *Bates* [1921] 3 K.B. 578 (policeman entering warehouse held trespasser); *Darling* v. *Att.-Gen.* [1950] 2 All E.R. 793; *Stroud* v. *Bradbury* [1952] 2 All E.R. 76.

[3] *Taylor* v. *Glasgow Corpn.*, 1922 S.C.(H.L.) 1.

[4] *Stevenson* v. *Glasgow Corpn.*, 1908 S.C. 1034.

[5] *Hastie* v. *Edinburgh Mags.*, 1907 S.C. 1102.

or to anything done or omitted to be done on them and for which the occupier is in law responsible shall, except in so far as he is entitled to and does extend, restrict, modify or exclude by agreement his obligation towards that person, be such care as in the circumstances of the case is reasonable to see that that person will not suffer injury or damage by reason of any such danger."

This subsection in substance restores the pre-1929 Scottish common law rules, as exemplified in such cases as *McKinlay* v. *Darngavil Coal Co.*,[6] where Lord Dunedin said: " The duty in each particular case is deducible from, and referable to, the particular circumstances of the case," and *Shillinglaw* v. *Turner*,[7] where Lord President Clyde said: " Most of those duties (whereof the breach constitutes negligence) arise simply out of the relation into which the complexities of social life bring the defender with the pursuer. Those relations are infinitely various, and in Scotland we have been slow and unwilling to classify and categorise them. This has been extensively done in England; . . . The plan we follow may be thought to err on the side of looseness, but it has the advantage of adaptability to the constantly varying materials with which it is devised to deal."

The general concept of reasonable care in this context was well expressed by Lord Sands in *Shillinglaw* v. *Turner*,[8] in this passage: " I shall venture to formulate what I conceive to have been the understanding of the law of Scotland in relation to the obligation of proprietors as regards the safety of persons using their property as follows: Where a proprietor devotes the use of his property to a certain purpose, he is responsible if, through his negligence in allowing the property to be in a dangerous condition to those using it, injury is suffered by a person exercising ordinary care, whose lawful presence on and use of the premises must have been contemplated by the proprietor in view of the purpose to which his premises were devoted." This formulation implies that a lesser duty is owed to trespassers than to lawful visitors.

The subsection thus generally restores the authority of pre-1929 Scottish decisions, before the strict classification of the pursuer as invitee, licensee or trespasser became so important. In these older cases, while a general distinction was recognised between visitors invited to come on the premises,[9] visitors permitted to be on the premises,[10] and visitors

---

6 1923 S.C.(H.L.) 34, 37.

7 1925 S.C. 807, 816.

8 1925 S.C. 807, 820.

9 See, *e.g.*, *Wylie* v. *Caledonian Ry.* (1871) 9 M. 463; *Cairns* v. *Boyd* (1879) 6 R. 1004; *Smillies* v. *Boyd* (1886) 14 R. 150; *Brady* v. *Parker* (1887) 14 R. 783; *Dolan* v. *Burnet* (1896) 23 R. 550; *Maclachlan* v. *Peveril* (1896) 23 R. 753; *Somerville* v. *Hardie* (1896) 24 R. 58; *Paterson* v. *Kidd's Trs.* (1896) 24 R. 99; *Chadwick* v. *Elderslie S.S. Co.* (1898) 25 R. 730; *Mackie* v. *Macmillan* (1898) 36 S.L.R. 137; *McKeever* v. *Caledonian Ry.* (1900) 2 F. 1085; *McCulloch* v. *Clyde Navigation Trs.* (1903) 5 F. 1149; *Paterson* v. *Gardner*, 1924 S.L.T. 63.

10 *e.g.*, *Brownlie* v. *Tennant* (1854) 16 D. 998; *Robertson* v. *Adamson* (1862) 24 D. 1231; *McMartin* v. *Hannay* (1872) 10 M. 411; *Messer* v. *Cranston* (1897) 25 R. 7; *Johnstone* v. *Stewart* (1897) 25 R. 103; *Devlin* v. *Jeffray's Trs.* (1902) 5 F. 130; *Collumb* v. *Turners*

with no right to be on the premises,[11] the categorisation was not so rigid nor the different duties to members of the different categories so clearly differentiated as in English law.

Different duty under English Act. The English Act [12] imposes on an occupier towards all his visitors a " common duty of care " defined as " a duty to take such care as in all the circumstances of the case is reasonable to see that the visitor will be reasonably safe in using the premises for the purposes for which he is invited or permitted by the occupier to be there." While the words down to " reasonable " are the same the duty is not identical with that imposed by the Scottish Act and decisions on the English Act must therefore not be accepted unquestioningly in Scotland.

What is " reasonable care " ? The three strictly distinguished categories of visitors on premises have no longer any existence in Scots law, and there is no longer any need to categorise visitors. But the precise degree of care which " in all the circumstances of the case is reasonable " will still, it is thought, depend in part on the extent of the legal right, if any, which the visitor had to come on the premises because that materially affects the occupier's foresight of possible harm, and it is thought that " reasonable care " towards persons invited, expressly or impliedly, or permitted to come on the premises will still be materially higher than towards trespassers, who have neither invitation nor permission nor any other legal right to come on the premises, and whose presence, if known, would be objected to and not tolerated. They come, if at all, unasked and unwanted. In short the existence of some legal right for coming on the premises is a material factor among " all the circumstances of the case."

In the case of visitors invited or permitted they must be reasonably guarded from known dangers, and probably also from any dangers which a careful occupier should have known of and appreciated as dangerous and taken precautions against. The standard is not necessarily the same for all legitimate visitors.

Again the age of the foreseeable visitors is a relevant factor and the duty may be higher if the presence of children is to be anticipated. A higher

(1908) 15 S.L.T. 845; *Mackenzie* v. *Fairfield Shipbuilding Co.,* 1913 S.C. 213; *Tough* v. *N.B.Ry.,* 1914 S.C. 291; *Burns* v. *N.B.Ry.,* 1914 S.C. 754; *Ross* v. *McCallum's Trs.,* 1922 S.C. 322; *Taylor* v. *Glasgow Corpn.,* 1922 S.C.(H.L.) 1; *McKinlay* v. *Darngavil Coal Co.,* 1923 S.C.(H.L.) 34; *Boyd* v. *Glasgow Iron & Steel Co.,* 1923 S.C. 758; *Shillinglaw* v. *Turner,* 1925 S.C. 807; *Edwards* v. *L.M.S.Ry.,* 1928 S.C. 471; *Cooke* v. *Forfar Mags.,* 1932 S.L.T. 255.

[11] *e.g., Balfour* v. *Baird* (1857) 20 D. 238; *Ferguson* v. *Laidlaw* (1871) 8 S.L.R. 333; *Nicolson* v. *Macandrew* (1888) 15 R. 854; *Ross* v. *Keith* (1888) 16 R. 86; *Devlin* v. *Jeffray's Trs.* (1902) 5 F. 130; *Macdonald* v. *Caldwell,* 1914, 2 S.L.T. 334; *Cummings* v. *Darngavil Coal Co.* (1903) 5 F. 513; *Edwards* v. *L.M.S.Ry.,* 1928 S.C. 471; *Dumbreck* v. *Addie's Collieries,* 1929 S.C.(H.L.) 51; *Lawrie* v. *Earl of Wemyss,* 1930 S.N. 120.

[12] Occupiers' Liability Act, 1957, s. 2 (1) and (2); see *Roles* v. *Nathan* [1963] 2 All E.R. 908.

duty may be owed in the case of an intoxicated person,[13] or a blind or infirm person,[14] where such a person's presence was, or should have been, foreseen as possible.

The Act does not lay down any criteria for determining what is reasonable care, and it will accordingly be entirely a question of fact to be decided in the circumstances of each case.[15] But in determining whether or not reasonable care has been taken cases decided prior to the Act may still be of use. Thus it seems clear that reasonable care for the safety of persons invited to come or permitted to come on the premises requires that the condition of premises should be inspected regularly,[16] no traps, hidden dangers or allurements should be permitted,[17] floors should not be overloaded,[18] warnings should be given of known dangers,[19] normal and customary gates and barriers should be maintained to prevent persons falling into holes or stepping into areas of danger,[20] and obvious dangers should be fenced,[21] materials should not be stacked dangerously,[22] or vehicles on the premises operated carelessly,[23] lifts should be maintained in proper repair,[23a] and lift shafts should be guarded,[24] stairs and their railings should be kept in safe condition,[25] doors and gates should be safe and not fall,[26] dangerous places must be adequately lighted,[27] doors leading to prohibited or unsafe parts of premises locked,[28] vicious dogs should be kept under control,[29] and so on.

The duty probably does not require precautions against obvious risks, particularly if the visitor did not require to go to the place in question,[30] nor the elimination of dangers unknown and not readily discoverable.[31]

---

13 *Morrison* v. *Haggarty* (1956) 72 Sh.Ct.Rep. 335.
14 *Cf. Haley* v. *London Electricity Board* [1964] 3 All E.R. 185.
15 Contrast section 2 (3) of the English Act which mentions certain circumstances relevant to the duty of care required.
16 *Dolan* v. *Burnet* (1896) 23 R. 550; *Paterson* v. *Kidd's Trs.* (1896) 24 R. 99; *Duncan* v. *Perthshire Cricket Club* (1904) 12 S.L.T. 635; *Collumb* v. *Turners, Ltd.* (1908) 15 S.L.T. 845; *MacDonald* v. *Reid's Trs.*, 1947 S.C. 726.
17 *Greenlees* v. *Royal Hotel, Dundee* (1905) 7 F. 382; *Taylor* v. *Glasgow Corpn.*, 1922 S.C. (H.L.) 1.
18 *Caledonian Ry.* v. *Greenock Sacking Co.* (1875) 2 R. 671.
19 *Roles* v. *Nathan* [1963] 2 All E.R. 908 (under English Act of 1957).
20 *Brady* v. *Parker* (1887) 14 R. 783; *Somerville* v. *Hardie* (1896) 24 R. 58; *Greenlees* v. *Royal Hotel, Dundee* (1905) 7 F. 382.
21 *McFeat* v. *Rankin's Trs.* (1879) 6 R. 1043; *Gavin* v. *Arrol & Co.* (1889) 16 R. 509; *Royan* v. *McLennan* (1889) 17 R. 103.
22 *Messer* v. *Cranston* (1897) 25 R. 7.
23 *Tough* v. *N.B.Ry.*, 1914 S.C. 291.
23a *Oliphant* v. *Johnstone & Macleod* (1894) 21 R. 531.
24 *Brady* v. *Parker* (1887) 14 R. 783; *Greenlees* v. *Royal Hotel, Dundee* (1905) 7 F. 382; *cf. Millar* v. *Galashiels Gas Co.*, 1949 S.C.(H.L.) 31.
25 *McMartin* v. *Hannay* (1872) 10 M. 411; *Fulton* v. *Anderson* (1884) 22 S.L.R. 100; *Grant* v. *Fleming*, 1914 S.C. 228; *Shillinglaw* v. *Turner*, 1925 S.C. 807.
26 *Daily* v. *Allan* (1885) 12 R. 841; *Findlay* v. *Angus* (1887) 14 R. 312.
27 *Brady* v. *Parker* (1887) 14 R. 783; *Fleming* v. *Eadie* (1898) 25 R. 500; *cf. Gaunt* v. *McIntyre*, 1914 S.C. 43; *Feachan* v. *Glasgow Subway Co.*, 1922 S.C. 519.
28 *Cairns* v. *Boyd* (1879) 6 R. 1004; *cf. Findlay* v. *Angus* (1887) 14 R. 312; *Mackie* v. *Macmillan* (1898) 6 S.L.T. 222; *Burns* v. *Steel Co. of Scotland* (1893) 21 R. 39.
29 *Smillies* v. *Boyd* (1886) 14 R. 150.
30 *Kelly* v. *State Line S.S. Co.* (1890) 27 S.L.R. 707.
31 *Davidson* v. *Aberdeen Mags.*, 1919, 2 S.L.T. 213.

There may be no duty not to deposit on land materials which are safe but may become dangerous if ignited.[32]

In the case of trespassers [33] it is thought that, as prior to the 1960 Act, " reasonable care " imposes no general positive duty of lighting, fencing or warning but still imposes the negative duty of refraining from doing them any deliberate harm.[34]

But there is also authority at common law in Scotland for requiring in exceptional circumstances some precautions against readily foreseeable harm happening even to trespassers. In *Black* v. *Cadell* [35] a person fell into an unfenced pit situated four feet from the road on which he was walking, and damages were given, but this was an exceptional case on its facts and, while consistent with the modern law rather than with the 1929–1960 rule (that no positive duty of care at all was owed to a trespasser), is not authority for imposing generally on a landowner a duty to fence dangers on his land against trespassers.[36] It has been explained [37] that the duty of an owner of land to fence pitfalls in the proximity of a public road does not apply to natural features, however dangerous they may be and however close to a public road, but only to such artificial dangerous features as an excavation, and probably only to such excavations as substantially adjoin the highway. Also, where trespass is so regular as to appear to be tolerated, the occupier may be under a duty to trespassers in respect of non-obvious dangers such as the intermittent operation of machinery.[38] Again, where trespass is readily foreseeable and indeed likely, as in the case of a building site, or premises being demolished,[39] the duty of reasonable care may import the need to fence the more treacherous and serious dangers, against reasonable probabilities though not against fantastic possibilities.[40] But the trespasser must probably still take the risk if he goes among dangers obvious to a reasonable person of his age. It has been held that the owners of an electric transformer which was incompletely fenced were not liable in damages to a boy who was electrocuted, since there were warning notices and on the unfenced side of the transformer there was a sheer drop of eight feet to the railway lines. There was no obligation to fence so that no member

---

[32] *Johnstone* v. *Lochgelly Mags.*, 1913 S.C. 1078.

[33] On the word " trespasser " in this kind of case see *Dumbreck* v. *Addie's Collieries*, 1928 S.C. 547, 554, *per* L. P. Clyde.

[34] *Ferguson* v. *Laidlaw* (1871) 8 S.L.R. 333; *Sinnerton* v. *Merry & Cuninghame* (1886) 13 R. 1012; *Ross* v. *Keith* (1888) 16 R. 86; *Paton* v. *United Alkali Co.* (1894) 22 R. 13; *Prentice* v. *Assets Co.* (1890) 17 R. 484; *Devlin* v. *Jeffray's Trs.* (1902) 5 F. 130; *Holland* v. *Lanarkshire Middle Ward District Cttee.*, 1909 S.C. 1142; *Macdonald* v. *Caldwell*, 1914, 2 S.L.T. 334; *Melville* v. *Renfrewshire C.C.*, 1920 S.C. 61; *Dumbreck* v. *Addie's Collieries*, 1929 S.C.(H.L.) 51.

[35] (1804) Mor. 13905; (1812) 5 Paton 567.

[36] *Prentice* v. *Assets Co.* (1890) 17 R, 484, 488, 492, explaining *Black, supra* and *Hislop* v. *Durham* (1842) 4 D. 1168. In *McFeat* v. *Rankin's Trs.* (1879) 6 R. 1043 the injured person was not a trespasser. Contrast also *Sinnerton* v. *Merry & Cuninghame* (1886) 13 R. 1012; *Paton* v. *United Alkali Co.* (1894) 22 R. 13; *Melville* v. *Renfrewshire C.C.*, 1920 S.C. 61.

[37] *Dumbreck* v. *Addie's Collieries*, 1928 S.C. 547, 552, *per* L.P. Clyde.

[38] *Dumbreck, supra,* 554.

[39] *Donald* v. *William Dixon, Ltd.*, 1936 S.L.T. 429; *Miller* v. *S.S.E.B.*, 1958 S.C.(H.L.) 20.

[40] *Fardon* v. *Harcourt-Rivington* (1932) 146 L.T. 391, 392, cited in *Miller, supra.*

of the public could not get past the barrier, particularly an agile and determined trespasser. The boy had deliberately made up his mind to overcome the obstacle.[41]

Relevance of kind of danger to duty of care. The standard of care demanded in a particular case may be affected by the nature of the danger on the land. Thus a distinction has been drawn [42] between sources of danger arising from physical features of the ground—whether natural or artificial—such as a precipice or an excavation, natural water or an artificial pond; and sources of danger arising from mechanical and similar contrivances. " The former are presumed from their own character to constitute obvious and usual dangers against which people, be they adults or children, must protect themselves; while the latter are in their very nature calculated to do harm, and, although the dangers presented by them are perfectly obvious to those who have created them, they may not be at all obvious to those, whether adults or children, who come upon them unawares, or are suddenly subjected to the risks attendant upon them when set in motion." [43]

Again a special duty of care may be incumbent where there is a special invitation to a part of the premises, over and above that already given or implied.[44]

Conditions to be guarded against. Older cases still give guidance as to the kind of conditions and dangers which an occupier, in the performance of his duty of taking reasonable care, must guard against. These include dangers unlit or unfenced,[45] dangers suspected or known as possible even if not actually known,[46] and dangers which may develop if the premises are not periodically examined for defects,[47] dangers which arise only occasionally as when wagons on a railway siding are shunted.[48]

It is questionable, however, if the dangers to be guarded against include such as vicious animals [49]; it is doubtful if a vicious dog is a " danger . . . due to the state of the premises " though its presence unleashed might be " anything done or omitted to be done on [the premises] and for which he is in law responsible " (section 1 (1)).

Greater care for particular classes of visitors. The duty of " reasonable care " probably, as in other contexts, imports a duty to take greater care where children or infirm persons are known to come, or should reasonably be expected,[50] and particularly if there is anything of the

---

41 *McGlone* v. *British Railways Board,* 1964 S.L.T.(Notes) 85.
42 *Dumbreck* v. *Addie's Collieries,* 1928 S.C. 547, 552, *per* L. P. Clyde.
43 Citing *Stevenson* v. *Glasgow Corpn.,* 1908 S.C. 1034, 1044; *Holland* v. *Lanarkshire Middle Ward District Cttee.,* 1909 S.C. 1142, 1149.
44 *Hopper* v. *L.M.S.Ry.,* 1948 S.L.T.(Notes) 25.
45 *Grant* v. *Sun Shipping Co.,* 1948 S.C.(H.L.) 73.
46 *Ellis* v. *Fulham B.C.* [1938] 1 K.B. 212; *Pearson* v. *Lambeth B.C.* [1950] 2 K.B. 353.
47 *Griffiths* v. *Smith* [1941] A.C. 170.
48 *McKeown* v. *L.N.E.Ry.,* 1931 S.N. 27.
49 Cf. *Smillies* v. *Boyd* (1886) 14 R. 150; *Lowery* v. *Walker* [1911] A.C. 10.
50 But see *Grant* v. *Fleming,* 1914 S.C. 228, 232, 238.

nature of a hidden danger or trap, which might not be as apparent to such persons as to normal adults,[51] or anything of the nature of an allurement or particularly tempting to children, such as a railway turntable [52] or a climbable tree [53] or pylon,[54] or bright red berries on a bush,[55] or a stationary unhorsed van,[56] or a cement mixer.[57]

But this duty should not be stretched to impose something approaching a duty of insurance on occupiers, because inquisitive and adventurous children can come to harm on nearly every kind of premises [58]; in the case of child-trespassers at common law the courts have denied that the duty of care is any higher towards a child than towards an adult.[59]

In the case of children it is relevant to consider the age and mentality of the children whose presence was, or should have been, known, since a danger which may be obvious to an adult might not be evident to a child.[60] Also warning notices may be inadequate, certainly for children too young to read or heed such warnings, and more positive safety measures may be required. A child of seven has been held not to have become a trespasser merely because, in the absence of a public lavatory, she sought a secluded spot to relieve herself and thereby came within the area of risk from a fierce animal.[61]

Modified or enhanced standard. The occupier's duty to a person entering his premises may be extended, restricted, modified or excluded by agreement.[62] This would appear to preserve the possibility of limitation or exclusion of liability by conditions on a ticket,[63] to exclude modification or exclusion by mere notice or warning,[64] and to require the assent of the visitor or user of the premises. It is doubtful if the exclusion of the liability of the Transport Commission to holders of platform tickets [65] could be called an exclusion " by agreement." Modification or exclusion

---

51 *Cf. Gibson* v. *Glasgow Police Commrs.* (1893) 20 R. 466; *Fryer* v. *Salford Corpn.* [1937] 1 All E.R. 617; *Morley* v. *Staffordshire C.C.* [1939] 4 All E.R. 92; *Sutton* v. *Bootle Corpn.* [1947] K.B. 359; *Winter* v. *Cardiff Corpn.* [1950] 1 K.B. 514.
52 *Cooke* v. *Midland G.W.Ry. of Ireland* [1909] A.C. 229. *Cf. Railroad Co.* v. *Stout,* 17 Wall. 657 (U.S.Sup.Ct.) (1873).
53 *Buckland* v. *Guildford Gas Light & Coke Co.* [1948] 2 All E.R. 1086.
54 *McLaughlin* v. *Antrim Electricity Supply Co.* [1941] N.I. 23.
55 *Taylor* v. *Glasgow Corpn.,* 1922 S.C.(H.L.) 1.
56 *Donovan* v. *Union Cartage Co.* [1933] 2 K.B. 71.
57 *Shields* v. *Smith,* 1948 S.L.T.(Notes) 24; contrast *Miller* v. *McDonald* [1948] C.L.Y. 4597.
58 *Morley* v. *Staffordshire C.C.* [1939] 1 All E.R. 92; *cf. Pearson, infra.*
59 *Dumbreck* v. *Addie's Collieries,* 1929 S.C.(H.L.) 51; *cf. Liddle* v. *Yorkshire C.C.* [1934] 2 K.B. 101; *Adams* v. *Naylor* [1944] K.B. 750; *Walder* v. *Hammersmith B.C.* [1944] 1 All E.R. 490; *McLaughlin, supra*; *Edwards* v. *Railway Executive* [1952] A.C. 737.
60 *Forbes* v. *Aberdeen Harbour Commrs.* (1888) 15 R. 323 (danger to boy of 7; no danger to boy of 16); *Morley* v. *Staffordshire C.C.* [1939] 4 All E.R. 92; see also *Hastie* v. *Edinburgh Mags.,* 1907 S.C. 1102; *Stevenson* v. *Glasgow Corpn.,* 1908 S.C. 1034.
61 *Pearson* v. *Coleman Bros.* [1948] 2 K.B. 359, distinguishing *Dumbreck, supra.*
62 s. 2 (1). The English Act, s. 2 (1) says " . . . by agreement *or otherwise.*"
63 *e.g., Williamson* v. *N. of S.S.N. Co.,* 1916 S.C. 554; *Hood* v. *Anchor Line,* 1918 S.C.(H.L.) 143.
64 Contrast *Ashdown* v. *Williams* [1957] 1 Q.B. 409, still good law under the English Act.
65 B.T.C. Passenger Charges Scheme, 1953, para. 32 (*b*).

is possible only where the occupier is entitled to modify the standard, and not, for example, in the case of passengers in public service vehicles.[66]

Section 2 (2) of the 1960 Act preserves, unimpaired by the Act, any higher standard of care incumbent on an occupier by virtue of any enactment or rule of law imposing special standards of care on particular classes of persons, such as the duties on the occupier of a factory at common law and under statute to maintain safe premises for his employees, which are frequently of a higher standard than merely reasonable care.

Defence of acceptance of risk. By Section 2 (3) the 1960 Act does not impose on an occupier any obligation to a person entering on his premises " in respect of risks which that person has willingly accepted as his; and any question whether a risk was so accepted shall be decided on the same principles as in other cases in which one person owes to another a duty to show care." Under this subsection the defence of *volenti non fit injuria* may competently be adduced in suitable circumstances. In *London Graving Dock* v. *Horton* [67] H. was employed by a firm employed by L.G.D. to do work in the hold of a ship. L.G.D. provided the necessary staging for the workmen, consisting of boards placed on angle irons. H. stepped on an angle iron, slipped and was injured. His claim for damages failed on the ground, *inter alia*, that H. had fully appreciated the danger and continued at work in that knowledge and that this was sufficient to free L.G.D. from liability, not on the ground of *volenti non fit injuria*, but on the ground that H.'s knowledge of the danger was equivalent to the discharge of the duty of care by giving H. adequate warning. But similar facts might give rise to a plea of *volenti non fit injuria*. A fireman entering premises to extinguish a fire is not normally *volens* as to any danger on the burning premises,[68] nor is a person who goes on premises to attempt to save life or property from serious danger.[69]

Liability of occupier for independent contractors. The Scottish Act does not, as the English Act does,[70] deal with the case of damage to a visitor by the faulty execution of any work of construction, maintenance or repair by an independent contractor employed by the occupier. Is it then sufficient in Scotland for the occupier to show that he had employed an independent contractor reasonably believed to be competent, and had satisfied himself, so far as he could, that the work had been properly done? There is English authority that that is sufficient at common law

[66] Road Traffic Act, 1960, s. 151.
[67] [1951] A.C. 737. (The decision is overruled by the English Act, s. 2 (4) (*a*), so far as it decided that notice to or knowledge of the risk by an injured person, provided he recognised the full significance of the risk, would exculpate the occupier.) See also *Fleming* v. *Eadie* (1898) 25 R. 500; *Forbes* v. *Aberdeen Harbour Commrs*. (1888) 15 R. 323; *Galt* v. *Watson*, 1931 S.N. 26.
[68] *Merrington* v. *Ironbridge Metal Works* [1952] 2 All E.R. 1101.
[69] *Baker* v. *Hopkins* [1959] 3 All E.R. 225; see further Chap. 10.
[70] Occupiers' Liability Act, 1957, s. 2 (4) (*b*).

in some cases to exculpate the occupier.[71] In *Cremin* v. *Thomson* [72] however, a Scottish appeal, the House of Lords held that an occupier could not rid himself of his obligation to an invitee by entrusting its performance to independent contractors, however reputable or generally competent. It seems that *Cremin* v. *Thomson* [72] is overruled by the English Act [70] though not by the Scottish, but *Cremin* will not probably stand along with *Davie* v. *New Merton Board Mills*,[73] and it is submitted that it should be treated as superseded.[74] In any event under the Act the occupier's duty is to take reasonable care and to impose liability for the fault of a competent independent contractor would be insurance rather than reasonable care. In *Fulton* v. *Anderson* [75] the proprietor of a tenement, the stair of which collapsed, was held liable, but the repair thereto executed by him previously had been done without consulting any skilled person. It may be that in some cases the occupier will be liable for the fault of his independent contractor and in other cases he will not.[76] He probably is if he has given the contractor inadequate or faulty instructions and retained control over the work.[77]

Personal liability of contractors. Quite apart from the liability of the occupiers of premises, independent contractors doing work on the premises of another, though not having full occupation of these premises, may be liable directly to persons injured on the premises by reason of the contractor's acts or omissions. This liability does not depend on the 1960 Act but on the more general principle of liability for those whom a person should reasonably have foreseen as likely to be injured by his conduct.[78]

Liability of other non-occupiers. The 1960 Act does not apply to dangers caused by persons who are not " occupiers " of the premises in question, but third parties to the relationship of occupier and visitor. Such a third party, such as a contractor working on the highway adjacent to the premises, must at common law take reasonable care for the safety of persons going to and from the premises so that their passage thereto may not be rendered perilous.[79] This principle was applied in *Billings* v. *Riden*,[80] and it was made clear that such liability is independent of that of

---

[71] *Haseldine* v. *Daw* [1941] 2 K.B. 343; *Wilkinson* v. *Rea* [1941] 1 K.B. 688; *Woodward* v. *Mayor of Hastings* [1945] K.B. 174. *Cf. Davie* v. *New Merton Board Mills* [1959] A.C. 604; see also *Walsh* v. *Holst* [1958] 3 All E.R. 33.

[72] (1941) 71 Ll.L.R. 1; 1956 S.L.T. 357; *sub nom. Thomson* v. *Cremin* (1941); [1953] 2 All E.R. 1185; [1956] 1 W.L.R. 103n. See also *Sandeman* v. *Duncan's Trs.* (1897) 4 S.L.T. 336; 5 S.L.T. 21; *Brown* v. *Keay* (1902) 9 S.L.T. 442; *Wolfson* v. *Forrester*, 1910 S.C. 675; *MacDonald* v. *Reid's Trs.*, 1947 S.C. 726.

[73] *Supra.*

[74] See also *Green* v. *Fibreglass, Ltd.* [1958] 2 All E.R. 521.

[75] (1884) 22 S.L.R. 100.

[76] *Cf. Riverstone Meat Co.* v. *Lancashire Shipping Co.* [1961] A.C. 807; *MacDonald* v. *Reid's Trs.*, 1947 S.C. 726.

[77] *Boyle* v. *Glasgow Corpn.*, 1949 S.C. 254.

[78] *Miller* v. *S.S.E.B.*, 1958 S.C.(H.L.) 20; *cf. Davis* v. *St. Mary's Demolition Co.* [1954] 1 All E.R. 578. See also *Boyle* v. *Glasgow Corpn.*, 1949 S.C. 254; *Knight* v. *Demolition and Construction Co.* [1954] 1 All E.R. 711; *Creed* v. *McGeoch* [1955] 3 All E.R. 123.

[79] *Mooney* v. *Lanarkshire C.C.*, 1954 S.C. 245.

[80] [1958] A.C. 240.

occupier to visitor. "A person executing works on premises . . . is under a general duty to use reasonable care for the safety of those whom he knows or ought reasonably to know may be affected by or lawfully in the vicinity of his work." [81]

If by reason of contractors' operations on the premises in question the visitor trespasses on adjacent premises and is there injured, he has no claim against the contractors even if they encouraged or instigated the trespass.[82]

The liability of the occupier of adjacent premises for injury caused on the premises in question depends not on the 1960 Act but on general principles of negligence and possibly on the principle of strict liability for the escape of dangerous things from the defender's premises to other premises.[83]

SPECIAL CASES OF OCCUPIER'S LIABILITY— LANDLORD AND TENANT

A common case of persons coming on premises is the case of a tenant, his family, friends, lodgers, and so on, coming on to premises let to him. A specialty is introduced by the fact that the tenant is in contractual relations with the landlord and may be able to rely on express or implied terms of the lease, whereas his family and friends cannot do so but must rely on the principles of delictual liability if injured.

The lease implies a warrandice by the landlord that the subject of let is reasonably fit for the purpose for which it is let,[84] so that a house must be reasonably fit to live in, a shop to trade in, and so on. Furthermore, a landlord is bound at common law, in the case of urban leases, to put the subjects at entry into, and to maintain them during the lease in, a tenantable or habitable condition.[85] The obligation is not a warranty against defects,[86] and these must be brought to the landlord's notice to enable him to remedy them.[87] The landlord is not liable for exceptional encroachments of the elements,[88] nor for deterioration from the fault of the tenant himself,[89] nor for defect arising from the fault of a third party,[90] nor for *damnum fatale* or pure accident.

Accordingly harm befalling a tenant, but not his family or others, and attributable to breach of the landlord's contractual duty to remedy

---

[81] *Ibid.* 263–264, *per* Lord Somervell.
[82] *Ibid.* 262, *per* Lord Keith.
[83] On the latter principle, see Chap. 17.
[84] Ersk. II, 6, 39; Bell, *Prin.*, § 1253; Rankine, *Leases*, 240.
[85] Bankton, I, 20, 15; II, 9, 20; Ersk. II, 6, 43; *Dickie* v. *Amicable Property Investment Bldg. Soc.*, 1911 S.C. 1079.
[86] *Hampton* v. *Galloway & Sykes* (1899) 1 F. 501; *Dickie, supra.*
[87] *Baikie* v. *Wordie's Trs.* (1897) 24 R. 1098; *Irvine* v. *Caledonian Ry.* (1902) 10 S.L.T. 363.
[88] *Wolfson* v. *Forrester*, 1910 S.C. 675.
[89] *McLellan & Kerr* (1797) Mor. 10134.
[90] *Allan* v. *Robertson's Trs.* (1891) 18 R. 932; *Wolfson, supra*; *Brown* v. *Keay* (1902) 9 S.L.T. 442; *Sandeman* v. *Duncan's Trs.* (1897) 4 S.L.T. 336, 5 S.L.T. 21; see also *Menzies* v. *Whyte* (1888) 15 R. 470.

a known defect may give rise to a claim of damages *ex contractu*.[91] The tenant's claim may be barred by remaining in occupation in the knowledge of the defect.[92]

Statutory condition of fitness for habitation. The Housing (Scotland) Act, 1950, s. 3,[93] implies into any contract for letting for human habitation a house at a rent not exceeding £26 per annum, notwithstanding any stipulation to the contrary, a condition that the house is at the commencement of the tenancy, and an undertaking that the house will be kept by the landlord during the tenancy, in all respects reasonably fit for human habitation. The landlord has a right of entry, after giving notice, to view the state and condition of the house. The landlord is liable only when notice of latent defects has been given to him by the tenant.[94] It is thought that this section protects not merely tenants but those whom a landlord should reasonably foresee might use the house.

The standard of reasonable fitness for human habitation is stringent. In *Morgan* v. *Liverpool Corpn.*[95] it was said: " if the state of repair of a house is such that by ordinary usage damage may naturally be caused to the occupier, either in respect of personal injury to life or limb or injury to health, then the house is not in all respects reasonably fit for human habitation." In *Summers* v. *Salford Corpn.*[96] it was held that a broken sash cord on a window was a breach of the section, and in *McCarrick* v. *Liverpool Corpn.*[97] a claim for injuries sustained because of the defective condition of the stone steps was excluded only by failure to notify the landlord.

Claims ex delicto at common law. So far as the tenant himself is concerned it has been held that, since he is in contractual relations with the landlords, the law of invitor and invitee did not apply.[98] This seems doubtful and there seems no reason for saying that the existence of a contractual duty excludes the existence of a duty *ex lege*, though the latter would not in fact impose any greater onus on the landlord. There is, however, some authority for the contrary view, that the law of invitee, licensee and trespasser applies only to persons coming on property otherwise than in the course of contractual relationship.[99]

So far as concerns injury to the tenant's family, friends and others, they are not parties to the contract of lease and a claim can be brought only *ex delicto*, and fault must be relevantly averred and proved,[1] but,

---

91 *Maitland* v. *Allan* (1896) 4 S.L.T. 121.
92 *Webster* v. *Brown* (1892) 19 R. 765; *Proctor* v. *Cowlairs Co-operative Soc.*, 1961 S.L.T. 434.
93 This replaces earlier legislation in similar terms. It applies also (s. 4) to houses occupied by workmen engaged in agriculture.
94 *Morgan* v. *Liverpool Corpn.* [1927] 2 K.B. 131; *McCarrick* v. *Liverpool Corpn.* [1947] A.C. 219 (decided on corresponding sections of English Acts).
95 [1927] 2 K.B. 131, 145, *per* Atkin L.J.
96 [1943] A.C. 283.
97 [1947] A.C. 219.
98 *Proctor* v. *Cowlairs Co-operative Soc.*, 1961 S.L.T. 434.
99 *London Graving Dock* v. *Horton* [1951] A.C. 737.
1 *Irvine* v. *Caledonian Ry.* (1902) 10 S.L.T. 363.

when relevant averments were made, a tenant's wife,[2] or servant,[3] or child,[4] or guest,[5] have been held to have an action against the landlord, for injury caused by such defects as defective drains.[6]

In *Cameron* v. *Young*[7] the House of Lords, in a claim for damages by a tenant's wife and children in respect of illness due to the insanitary condition of a house, laid down that the landlord's liability was contractual only and that he owed no duty to the tenant's family and friends who were mere licensees of the landlord. This decision is vitiated by the same fallacy as pre-*Donoghue* v. *Stevenson* cases, that non-existence of a contractual duty imports total non-existence of any duty, and on general principles of delict a landlord must surely have in reasonable contemplation that a tenant's wife, family and friends as well as the tenant will use the let house and may be injured by its defective condition.

Apart from the change brought about by the Occupiers' Liability (Scotland) Act, 1960, *Cameron* v. *Young*[7] is inconsistent with *Donoghue* v. *Stevenson*,[8] and is also distinguishable in that only breach of contract was averred, for which the tenant's wife and family clearly could not sue. It should therefore now be ignored as a bad decision.

Statutory provisions. The Occupiers' Liability (Scotland) Act, 1960, now provides:

" Section 3 (1). Where premises are occupied or used by virtue of a tenancy under which the landlord is responsible for the maintenance or repair of the premises, it shall be the duty of the landlord to show towards any persons who or whose property may from time to time be on the premises the same care in respect of dangers arising from any failure on his part in carrying out his responsibility aforesaid as is required by virtue of the foregoing provisions of this Act to be shown by an occupier of premises towards persons entering on them.[9]

(2) Where premises are occupied or used by virtue of a sub-tenancy, the foregoing subsection shall apply to any landlord who is responsible for the maintenance and repair of the premises comprised in the sub-tenancy.

(3) Nothing in this section shall relieve a landlord of any duty which he is under apart from this section.[10]

---

[2] *McNee* v. *Brownlie's Trs.* (1889) 26 S.L.R. 590; *Hall* v. *Hubner* (1897) 24 R. 875.

[3] *Kennedy* v. *Bruce*, 1907 S.C. 845.

[4] *Blair* v. *Brown*, 1930 S.L.T. 504; *Grimes* v. *Middleton*, 1931 S.L.T. 84.

[5] *Gaunt* v. *McIntyre*, 1914 S.C. 43.

[6] *Henderson* v. *Munn* (1888) 15 R. 859; *McNee* v. *Brownlie's Trs.* (1889) 26 S.L.R. 590; *Baikie* v. *Wordie's Trs.* (1897) 24 R. 1098; *cf. N.B. Storage and Transit Co.* v. *Steele's Trs.*, 1920 S.C. 194.

[7] 1908 S.C.(H.L.) 7, following English authorities, particularly *Cavalier* v. *Pope* [1906] A.C. 428, and overruling *Hall* v. *Hubner* (1897) 24 R. 875 and, by implication, *Kennedy* v. *Bruce*, 1907 S.C. 845. This principle has been followed repeatedly since, *e.g.*, *Malone* v. *Laskey* [1907] 2 K.B. 141; *Dunster* v. *Hollis* [1918] 2 K.B. 795; *Kennedy* v. *Shotts Iron Co.*, 1913 S.C. 1143; *Shillinglaw* v. *Turner*, 1925 S.C. 807; *Otto* v. *Bolton* [1936] 2 K.B. 36; *Howard* v. *Walker* [1947] K.B. 860; *Ball* v. *L.C.C.* [1949] 2 K.B. 159; *Johnston* v. *Glasgow Corpn.* (1950) 66 Sh.Ct.Rep. 177.

[8] 1932 S.C.(H.L.) 31.   [9] For these see Dangerous Premises, *supra.*

[10] *e.g.*, under the Housing (Scotland) Act, 1950, s. 3.

(4) For the purposes of this section, any obligation imposed on a landlord by any enactment by reason of the premises being subject to a tenancy shall be treated as if it were an obligation imposed on him by the tenancy, ' tenancy ' includes a statutory tenancy which does not in law amount to a tenancy [11] and includes also any contract conferring a right of occupation,[12] and ' landlord ' shall be construed accordingly.

(5) This section shall apply to tenancies created before the commencement of this Act as well as to tenancies created after its commencement."

The position of tenant, tenant's wife, family, friends and lodger *vis-à-vis* the landlord is accordingly assimilated to the position of visitor *vis-à-vis* occupier under section 2 of the Act, and a landlord must show towards all of them, " except in so far as he is entitled to and does extend, restrict, modify or exclude by agreement his obligations towards that person . . . such care as in all the circumstances of the case is reasonable to see that that person will not suffer injury or damage by reason of any such danger," *i.e.*, dangers due to the state of the premises or to anything done or omitted to be done on them and for which the occupier is in law responsible. It has been held that a tenant's daughter injured by a cracked pane of glass in a bathroom door had relevantly averred a breach of section 3 (1),[13] but after proof it was held [14] that the defenders were not liable, because the house had not by reason of the defect ceased to be reasonably fit for human habitation.

It appears to be competent to modify or exclude the liability and this could *vis-à-vis* the tenant be done in the lease, but such an exclusion would not bind the tenant's wife or children, still less his lodger or visitors, as not being parties to the lease. It might, however, be done by separate contracts with such third parties.

If by the terms of the lease the landlord is not responsible for the maintenance or repair of the premises, the landlord is not subject to the statutory duty.

It would seem accordingly that the landlord is liable *ex contractu* to his tenant, and also liable *ex delicto* to anyone who legitimately comes into the let property and is injured there by any defect or danger which could by the exercise of reasonable care have been discovered or eliminated, such as defective drainage.[15] This again is consistent with older Scottish common law.[16]

Parts of premises retained in landlord's possession. Where the landlord retains parts of premises, such as the close and common stairway,[17]

---

11 *i.e.*, under the Rent Restrictions Acts.
12 *e.g.*, a licence to occupy for a limited period.
13 *Haggarty* v. *Glasgow Corpn.*, 1963 S.L.T.(Notes) 73.
14 1964 S.L.T.(Notes) 95.
15 *Cf. McNee* v. *Brownlee's Trs.* (1889) 26 S.L.R. 590; *Maitland* v. *Allan* (1896) 4 S.L.T. 121; *Henderson* v. *Nimmo* (1902) 10 S.L.T. 394; *Dickie* v. *Amicable Property Investment Co.*, 1911 S.C. 1079; *cf. Baikie* v. *Wordie's Trs.* (1897) 24 R. 1098.
16 *McMartin* v. *Hannay* (1872) 10 M. 411; see also *Young* v. *Campbell*, 1924 S.C. 157, 162, *per* Lord Sands.
17 *McMartin* v. *Hannay* (1872) 10 M. 411; *Fulton* v. *Anderson* (1884) 22 S.L.R. 100; *Hamilton* v. *Nimmo* (1902) 10 S.L.T. 394; *Mechan* v. *Watson*, 1907 S.C. 25; *Grant* v. *McClafferty*,

or a lift,[18] in his own possession he is under a duty to maintain these parts in reasonably safe condition for all whom he should reasonably foresee would be likely to use those common parts, tenants, their families and friends, postmen, message-boys, tradesmen, canvassers and so on. Hence the landlord is liable where he has permitted a state of disrepair to arise which has caused injury,[17] but not for an obvious danger. Hitherto since *Dumbreck* v. *Addie*,[19] the standard of duty in such cases has been defined as that owed to a licensee, so that there has been no liability for obvious dangers, but only for concealed dangers or traps.[20] Under the 1960 Act the duty will be that owed by occupier to legitimate visitor.

At common law a landlord was probably under no duty to light a common close or stairway,[21] but the Burgh Police (Scotland) Act, 1892, s. 104, imposes a duty on owners of common stairs to provide lamps on them, and a duty on occupiers to light them,[22] and under the 1960 Act such a duty might well be an element of reasonable care. Local authorities may, however, have such a statutory duty under local Acts and an action lies for injuries caused by breach of the statutory duty.[23]

Landlord's liability under law of neighbourhood. A landlord may also be liable, not *qua* landlord but *qua* occupier or proprietor of adjacent property, to his tenant and any person in the tenant's property for damage or injury suffered by reason of the landlord's operations. Thus where a coal company by working coal caused a subsidence on the surface which brought down a ceiling in a house owned by them and tenanted by an employee and injured the tenant's visitor, he was held to have a good claim against the coal company.[24]

7. ROADS AND STREETS

The principal difficulty facing a person injured on a road or street (including pavements and bridges) by reason of some defect in the condition thereof or a danger thereon [25] is to ascertain what person or body is responsible for the control, management and maintenance of

1907 S.C. 201; *Kennedy* v. *Shotts Iron Co.*, 1913 S.C. 1143; *Mellon* v. *Henderson*, 1913 S.C. 1207; *Gaunt* v. *McIntyre*, 1914 S.C. 43; *Grant* v. *Fleming*, 1914 S.C. 228; *McIlwaine* v. *Stewart's Trs.*, 1914 S.C. 934; *Buchanan* v. *Lilley*, 1923 S.L.T. 125; *Campbell* v. *Young's Trs.*, 1926 S.N. 64; *Blair* v. *Brown*, 1930 S.L.T. 504; *Galt* v. *Watson*, 1931 S.N. 26; *Grimes* v. *Middleton*, 1931 S.L.T. 84.

18 *Mathieson's Tutor* v. *Aikman's Trs.*, 1910 S.C. 11; *cf. Greenlees* v. *Royal Hotel, Dundee* (1905) 7 F. 382.

19 1929 S.C.(H.L.) 51.

20 *Young* v. *Campbell*, 1924 S.C. 157; *Shillinglaw* v. *Turner*, 1925 S.C. 807; *Blair* v. *Brown, supra*; *Galt* v. *Watson, supra*; *Grimes* v. *Middleton, supra*; *Mackin* v. *Glasgow Corpn.*, 1949 S.C. 468.

21 *Gaunt* v. *McIntyre*, 1914 S.C. 43; *Devine* v. *London Housing Society* [1950] 2 All E.R. 1173.

22 *Byrne* v. *Tindal's Exrx.*, 1950 S.C. 216.

23 *Mackin* v. *Glasgow Corpn.*, 1949 S.C. 468; *Ghannan* v. *Glasgow Corpn.*, 1950 S.C. 23; contrast *Hutson* v. *Edinburgh Corpn.*, 1948 S.C. 668.

24 *McCormick* v. *Fife Coal Co.*, 1931 S.C. 19.

25 Injuries caused by the conduct of another road-user come under Road Accidents, sec. 1, *supra*.

the road in question, and for creating or permitting the particular defect or danger complained of. Responsibility does not depend automatically on ownership of the solum of the road or street, but on possession and control, which may, but need not, flow from property.[26] Liability for injury depends on failure to take adequate steps to guard, maintain or repair the road or street in question. Persons engaged on operations on roads, streets and pavements must take reasonable care not to endanger road users, including persons of abnormal susceptibilities, such as blind persons, if their presence is or should be foreseen.[27]

Trunk roads. Trunk roads, designated in the schedules to the Trunk Roads Acts, 1936 and 1946, are the responsibility for management and maintenance of the Secretary of State for Scotland (till 1956 the Minister of Transport), though a local authority may be employed as his agents to carry out maintenance work.

Special roads. These are intended for specified classes of traffic and are provided by the Secretary of State or by the local authority, under statutory schemes.[28]

Roads in counties. The responsibility for management and control of public roads and bridges in counties is vested in the county councils.[29] Their right is one of control and maintenance, not of property in the *solum*, such control as is necessary for securing the public interest in free and easy passage.[30] A road authority may be liable in damages for injury, damage or loss caused by its failure to maintain a road in a reasonably safe condition for road-users, as where it allows a heap of stones to encroach on the road,[31] or a heap of road scrapings to be collected in front of cottages,[32] or the surface to become slippery and dangerous.[33] It is liable for the obstruction of a highway by snow only if there had been failure to do what was reasonable in the circumstances to clear the road.[34] There is no liability if in emergency the authority has failed to maintain what is normally a sufficient and unobstructed road; the duty is only to see that, so far as possible, roads are maintained unobstructed and passable.[35] There may be liability for not shutting up an old road if it is dangerous and injury is sustained by going on it.[36]

---

[26] *Laurie* v. *Aberdeen Mags.*, 1911 S.C. 1226; *Laing* v. *Paull & Williamsons*, 1912 S.C. 196.
[27] *Haley* v. *London Electricity Board* [1964] 3 All E.R. 185.
[28] Special Roads Act, 1949.
[29] Local Government (Scotland) Act, 1889, s. 11, replacing county road trustees under Roads and Bridges (Scotland) Act, 1878, s. 11; *Perth and Kinross C.C.* v. *Crieff Mags.*, 1934 S.C.(H.L.) 1.
[30] *Galbreath* v. *Armour* (1845) 4 Bell 374; see also *Stewartry Dairy Assocn., Ltd.* v. *Kirkcudbright Town Council*, 1956 S.L.T. 341.
[31] *Mackay* v. *Waddell* (1820) 2 Mur. 201; *Cromar* v. *Haddingtonshire C.C.* (1902) 9 S.L.T. 437.
[32] *Nelson* v. *Lanarkshire C.C. Lower Ward District Cttee.* (1891) 19 R. 311.
[33] *W. Alexander & Son* v. *Dundee Corpn.*, 1950 S.C. 123; *cf. Aitken* v. *Douglas* (1836) 14 S. 204.
[34] *Cameron* v. *Inverness C.C.*, 1935 S.C. 493.
[35] *Cameron, supra; cf. Crombie* v. *Balfour* (1838) MacF. 155.
[36] *McLachlan* v. *Wigtownshire Road Trs.* (1827) 4 Mur. 216.

The road authority must erect parapet walls, mounds or fences along the sides of all bridges, embankments or other dangerous parts of the highway.[37]

The road must be kept sufficiently fenced, and a claim lies for injuries sustained by reason of inadequate fencing.[38] The same applies to bridges.[39] It is a question of circumstances whether a particular place is so dangerous as to require it to be fenced.[40]

Parts of the road which are undergoing repair should be adequately fenced.[41]

There is a duty to inspect trees bordering the road, and it may be negligent not to observe a danger and have it removed.[42] The road authority may require the proprietor of lands bordering on a public road to remove a barbed wire fence which was a danger to persons and animals using the road.[43]

A farmer has been held liable at common law and under the Roads and Bridges (Scotland) Act, 1878, for permitting an obstruction of the road, in the form of a farm gate swinging across the road, which caused an accident.[44]

Private roads in counties. The responsibility is incumbent on the owner of the lands whose private road is in issue. He probably owes the duty of care of an occupier to a visitor, under the Occupiers' Liability (Scotland) Act, 1960, to anyone who comes on his private road for a legitimate purpose, *e.g.*, to deliver goods to his house, but a lesser duty to anyone who comes by mistake [45] or by deliberate trespass.

Public roads and streets in burghs. The presumption is that the *solum* of a street in a burgh [46] *ad medium filum* belongs so far as *ex adverso* of adjacent property, to the adjacent owner.[47] At least in royal burghs, where the property cannot be traced to be in anyone else, it belongs to the Crown.[48] But at common law the management and maintenance of streets in royal burghs was vested in the magistrates and town council.[49] The Roads and Bridges (Scotland) Act, 1878, ss. 11 and 47, vested the management and maintenance of highways and bridges within burghs

---

37 Roads and Bridges (Scotland) Act, 1878, s. 123, incorporating General Turnpike Act, 1831, s. 94; *Greer* v. *Stirlingshire Road Trs.* (1882) 9 R. 1069; *cf. Harris* v. *Leith Mags.* (1881) 8 R. 613; *Johnstone* v. *Glasgow Mags.* (1885) 12 R. 596.
38 *Watson* v. *Scott* (1838) MacF. 140; *Strachan* v. *Aberdeen District Cttee.* (1894) 21 R. 915. See also *Horsburgh* v. *Sheach* (1900) 3 F. 268.
39 *Greer* v. *Stirlingshire Road Trs.* (1882) 9 R. 1069; *Murray* v. *Lanarkshire Middle Ward County Road Trs.* (1888) 15 R. 737; *McIntyre* v. *Lochaber District Cttee.* (1901) 4 F. 188.
40 *Fraser* v. *Rothesay Mags.* (1892) 19 R. 817.
41 *Watson* v. *Scott* (1838) MacF. 140; *cf. Millar* v. *Road Trs.* (1828) 4 Mur. 563.
42 *Brierley* v. *Midlothian C.C. Suburban District Cttee.*, 1921, 1 S.L.T. 192; *Costello* v. *Midlothian C.C.*, 1946 S.N. 103.
43 *Elgin County Road Trs.* v. *Innes* (1886) 14 R. 48.
44 *Taylor* v. *Laird* (1952) 68 Sh.Ct.Rep. 207.
45 *Ross* v. *Keith* (1888) 16 R. 86; *Prentice* v. *Assets Co.* (1890) 17 R. 484; *Paton* v. *United Alkali Co.* (1894) 22 R. 13; *Melville* v. *Renfrewshire C.C.*, 1920 S.C. 61.
46 On the distinction between roads and streets, see *Threshie*, *infra*, 281.
47 *Dobbie* v. *Ayr Mags.* (1898) 25 R. 1184.
48 *Miller & Dalrymple* v. *Swinton* (1740) Mor. 13527.
49 *Threshie* v. *Annan Mags.* (1845) 8 D. 276.

in the burgh local authority. In the case of small burghs this responsibility,[50] so far as relating to classified roads,[51] was transferred to the
county council by the Local Government (Scotland) Act, 1929, s. 2,[52] but
a small burgh remains the authority for all public streets and unclassified
roads [50] in the burgh. Large burghs are authorities for all public streets
and, where they have undertaken the adoptive powers of the Roads and
Streets in Police Burghs (Scotland) Act, 1891, s. 2, for both classified and
unclassified highways [51] within the burgh. Under the Burgh Police Act,
1903, s. 104 (replacing 1892 Act, s. 128), the town council has the sole
charge and control of the carriageway of all the public streets within the
burgh and the footways thereof and also of all public footpaths, and all
such public streets, footways and footpaths are, for the purposes of
such charge and control, vested in the town council. Under s. 188 of the
same Act a hole made in the street must be lighted and fenced or enclosed
by the authority or contractor causing the excavation to be made.[53]
In many cases the position of the local authority is further defined by
private legislation. It has long been settled that the public authority
having the control and management of the public roads is liable for
injury caused by neglect of the duty to maintain in a reasonably safe
condition.[54]

Local authority's responsibility. The local authority is bound to
maintain [55] and repair its highways and may be liable for injury or loss
caused by its failure to maintain a road in a reasonably safe condition
for traffic, *e.g.*, for allowing a road to become slippery and dangerous.[56]
At the junction between the areas of two road authorities the rights of
an injured person are not affected by any private arrangement between
the authorities as to maintenance.[57] Liability has been imposed for
permitting a road to be used when a bridge spanning it was so low as
not to permit a person safely to drive a cab under it,[58] for damage caused
by heaps of stones left in the roadway [59] a stone left in the roadway,[60]
a trestle left there,[61] heaps of rubbish [62] or road sweepings.[63]

[50] On the extent of the powers of the county council, see *Fife County Council* v. *Lord Advocate*,
1950 S.L.T. 386.
[51] The Secretary of State is empowered to classify roads as main roads, connecting roads,
and unclassified roads: Ministry of Transport Act, 1919, s. 17, as amended.
[52] *Feeley* v. *Burgh of Milngavie* (1953) 69 Sh.Ct.Rep. 300.
[53] *McIntyre* v. *Gallacher*, 1962 J.C. 20.
[54] *Innes* v. *Edinburgh Mags.* (1798) Mor. 13189; *Dargie* v. *Forfar Mags.* (1855) 17 D. 730;
18 D. 343; *Kerr* v. *Stirling Mags.* (1858) 21 D. 169; *Virtue* v. *Alloa Police Commrs.* (1873)
1 R. 285.
[55] On this word see *Lanark C.C.* v. *N.C.B.*, 1948 S.C. 698.
[56] *Alexander* v. *Dundee Corpn.*, 1950 S.C. 123; *Western S.M.T. Co.* v. *Greenock Mags.*
1958 S.L.T.(Notes) 50. See also *Scott* v. *Glasgow Police Commrs.* (1895) 21 R. 466.
[57] *Gray* v. *St. Andrews & Cupar District Committees*, 1911 S.C. 266.
[58] *McFee* v. *Broughty Ferry Police Commrs.* (1890) 17 R. 764; *cf. Lewys* v. *Burnett* [1945]
2 All E.R. 458.
[59] *Findlater* v. *Duncan* (1839) McL. & Rob. 911, as modified by *Virtue, infra.*
[60] *Dargie* v. *Forfar Mags.* (1855) 17 D. 730.
[61] *Virtue* v. *Alloa Police Commrs.* (1873) 1 R. 285.
[62] *Stephen* v. *Thurso Police Commrs.* (1876) 3 R. 535.
[63] *Nelson* v. *Lanark Lower Ward C.C.* (1891) 19 R. 311; *cf. Barton* v. *Kinning Park Commrs.*
(1892) 29 S.L.R. 329.

The liability is for failing to take reasonable care to maintain the streets and pavements in a safe condition.[64] Members of the public are entitled to expect that no temporary obstructions, such as heaps of stones [65] or rubbish, or dangers, such as projecting flagstones, defective sewer gratings or holes, will be permitted without fencing, lighting or other adequate warning.[66] By inference the responsible authority must inspect periodically to discover defects and dangers.[67]

Hence claims have been brought where a vehicle overturned on a heap of stones left unlit in the roadway,[68] or unfenced,[69] where a woman fell over a heap of road sweepings in the dark,[70] where a woman broke her leg in a gutter grating,[71] where a person was injured by reason of subsidence of the pavement,[72] or by the tilting of the metal cover of a cellar opening,[73] or by falling on an uneven road when alighting from a tramcar,[74] or by tripping over a loose flagstone,[75] or by falling into the unguarded opening of a water-hydrant,[76] or by falling into the basement area of a building, the railings having been broken by a car.[77]

Duty to fence. A road or street should be fenced where there is an adjacent danger, such as a stream.[78]

Where authorities open manholes in streets or pavements they must take precautions for the safety of the public by fencing but are not liable to persons who do not look where they are going.[79] It is negligence to open a manhole and leave about unguarded ropes, lamps and other allurements to small boys,[80] or to open a trench in the street and leave it unfenced and unlit at night.[81]

Duty to light. Local authorities must light streets and other public places in burghs [82] and will be liable if an accident results from a more than temporary failure to light. An authority has been held liable for

---

[64] *Cf. Wisely* v. *Aberdeen Harbour Commrs.* (1887) 14 R. 445; *McFee, supra.*
[65] *Almeroth* v. *Chivers* [1948] 1 All E.R. 53.
[66] *Doran* v. *Glen* (1900) 8 S.L.T. 199; *Higgins* v. *Glasgow Corpn.* (1901) 4 F. 94; *Carson* v. *Kirkcaldy Mags.* (1901) 4 F. 18.
[67] *Rush* v. *Glasgow Corpn.,* 1947 S.C. 580.
[68] *Findlater* v. *Duncan* (1837) 15 S. 1304; (1838) 16 S. 1150; revd. (1839) 1 Rob. 911; *Cromar* v. *Haddingtonshire C.C.* (1902) 9 S.L.T. 437; *cf. Almeroth* v. *Chivers* [1948] 1 All E.R. 53.
[69] *Watson* v. *Scott* (1838) MacF. 140.
[70] *Nelson* v. *Lanark C.C., Lower Ward District Cttee.* (1891) 19 R. 311; *cf. Virtue* v. *Alloa Police Commrs.* (1873) 1 R. 285; *Stephen* v. *Thurso Police Commrs.* (1876) 3 R. 535; *Barton* v. *Kinning Park Commrs.* (1892) 29 S.L.R. 329.
[71] *Higgins* v. *Glasgow Corpn.* (1901) 4 F. 94.
[72] *Laurie* v. *Aberdeen Mags.,* 1911 S.C. 1226; *cf. Bauchnan* v. *Glasgow Corpn.,* 1923 S.C. 782.
[73] *Laing* v. *Paull & Williamsons,* 1912 S.C. 196.
[74] *Low* v. *Glasgow Corpn.,* 1917 S.C. 160.
[75] *Dargie* v. *Forfar Mags.* (1855) 17 D. 730; *Baillie* v. *Hutton* (1894) 21 R. 498.
[76] *McKibbin* v. *Glasgow Corpn.,* 1920 S.C. 590.
[77] *Stevenson* v. *Edinburgh Mags.,* 1934 S.C. 226.
[78] *Barrie* v. *Kilsyth Police Commrs.* (1898) 1 F. 194.
[79] *Adams* v. *Aberdeen Mags.* (1884) 11 R. 852; *cf. McKibbin* v. *Glasgow Corpn.,* 1920 S.C. 590.
[80] *Hughes* v. *Lord Advocate,* 1963 S.C.(H.L.) 31.
[81] *Sanderson* v. *Paisley Burgh Commrs.* (1899) 7 S.L.T. 255.
[82] Burgh Police (Scotland) Act, 1892, s. 99; County Road Trustees under the 1878 Act had not powers to light roads: *Lanarkshire Lower Ward County Road Trs.* v. *Kelvinside Estate Trs.* (1886) 14 R. (H.L.) 18.

breach of a continuing duty to keep lighted a bollard at the end of a refuge in the street, which the plaintiff had run into,[83] and contractors for failure adequately to light a heap of earth left by them in the roadway.[84]

Duty to keep free from ice and snow. The road authority should, *inter alia*, take reasonable precautions, by sweeping and sanding roads, to prevent them from becoming dangerous by reason of ice and snow. This obligation must be interpreted reasonably and drivers and pedestrians cannot expect ice and snow to be cleared perfectly, or from all roads at once. Thus there has been no liability where the pursuer averred that the road had been icebound for only twelve hours.[85]

There is no liability for the presence of ice on a pavement caused by the overflow from a fountain freezing unless the local authority knew of the overflow or had neglected to repair it.[86]

It has been held in England that a road authority was under no duty to warn road users of a danger—ice—which they had not created.[87]

Duty to inspect for other defects. There may be a duty to inspect trees which overhang a road and have them lopped if necessary.[88] But if the trees grow on private land fronting on the road, the frontager must act as a reasonable and prudent landowner and may be liable if a tree should have been suspected or found to be liable to fall.[89]

Responsibility for pavements. Local authorities have power,[90] and are now under a duty, to provide footpaths by the side of roads wherever these are deemed necessary or desirable.[91] At common law burgh magistrates were liable for obstructions on public streets and pavements.[92]

In burghs the local authority may require the frontagers [93] on any public street to make pavements, which must thereafter be maintained by the council,[94] and may undertake the maintenance of all pavements in the burgh, having first caused the frontagers to have them put in a sufficient state of repair.[94] In small burghs responsibility for the pavement lies on the county council as highway authority.[95] Local authorities

---

83 *Polkinghorn* v. *Lambeth B.C.* [1938] 1 All E.R. 339; *Fisher* v. *Ruislip-Northwood U.D.C.* [1945] K.B. 584; *Whiting* v. *Middlesex C.C.* [1948] 1 K.B. 162.
84 *White* v. *McKean*, 1948 S.L.T. 210.
85 *Gordon* v. *Inverness Town Council*, 1957 S.L.T.(Notes) 48.
86 *O'Keefe* v. *Edinburgh Corpn.*, 1911 S.C. 18.
87 *Burton* v. *West Suffolk C.C.* [1960] 2 All E.R. 26.
88 *Brierley* v. *Midlothian C.C. Suburban District Cttee.*, 1921, 1 S.L.T. 192; *Costello* v. *Midlothian C.C.*, 1946 S.N. 103. Cf. *Hale* v. *Hants & Dorset Motor Services* [1947] 2 All E.R. 628.
89 *Caminer* v. *London and Northern Investment Trust* [1951] A.C. 88; *Lambourn* v. *London Brick Co.* [1950] C.L.Y. 2738.
90 Roads and Bridges (Scotland) Act, 1878, s. 45.
91 Road Traffic Act, 1930, s. 58.
92 *Innes* v. *Edinburgh Mags.* (1798) Mor. 13189; *Dargie* v. *Forfar Mags.* (1855) 17 D. 730.
93 On these see *Campbell* v. *Edinburgh Mags.* (1891) 19 R. 159.
94 Burgh Police (Scotland) Act, 1892, ss. 141–142.
95 *Feeley* v. *Burgh of Milngavie* (1953) 69 Sh.Ct.Rep. 300; *Thomson* v. *Angus C.C.*, 1958 S.L.T. 208; 1961 S.L.T. 436.

do not always or automatically assume responsibility for the maintenance of pavements when they assume responsibility for the carriageway,[96] but yet it has been held that they may be liable to an action by a pedestrian injured because of a defective pavement by virtue of their general responsibility for the state of the streets in the burgh.[97] It has been held that under the relevant Glasgow private Act, the Corporation of Glasgow is under a statutory duty to see that even a private foot-pavement bordering on a public street, though not taken over by the corporation, was kept in proper repair.[98]

There must be fault, such as permitting a fountain to be defective and let water overflow and form ice; the authority is not at fault if there is a merely temporary or unknown defect.[99] It is fault, at least in relation to a blind person, to have the cover off a water-hydrant and a pipe attached, the whole being unfenced.[1] A frontager, even if his titles include the *solum* of the pavement, is not necessarily bound to maintain in a safe condition hatches placed in the pavement for sanitary purposes.[2] If the pavement has not been taken over by the local authority, the owner of the *solum* is liable.[3]

In Glasgow, where there is relevant private legislation, the corporation has a duty to inspect a private footpath even though it has not vested in the corporation,[4] and a statutory duty to see that it is kept in proper repair,[5] while the opinion has been expressed that it has also a common law duty to see that pavements not taken over are kept reasonably safe, a duty not discharged merely by serving a notice on the frontagers,[6] nor by making a mere visual inspection for patent defects.[7] The corporation is under no duty to inspect back courts and remedy defects therein.[8]

Liability of frontagers. A frontager's liability to a person injured on the street or pavement depends on possession and control[9]; he is liable if he causes a danger on the pavement,[10] as where a bus company, which

96 *Cumnock Mags.* v. *Murdoch*, 1910 S.C. 748.
97 *Higgins* v. *Glasgow Corpn.*, 1920, 2 S.L.T. 71; *Keenan* v. *Glasgow Corpn.*, 1923 S.C. 611; *Rush* v. *Glasgow Corpn.*, 1947 S.C. 580; *Black* v. *Glasgow Corpn.*, 1958 S.C. 260; *cf. Gray* v. *Glasgow Corpn.*, 1915, 2 S.L.T. 203; *Macpherson* v. *Glasgow Corpn.* (1948) 64 Sh.Ct.Rep. 217.
98 *Kinnell* v. *Glasgow Corpn.*, 1950 S.C. 573.
99 *O'Keefe* v. *Edinburgh Corpn.*, 1911 S.C. 18; *cf. Christie* v. *Glasgow Corpn.* (1899) 7 S.L.T. 27; *Gordon* v. *Inverness Town Council*, 1957 S.L.T.(Notes) 48 (road ice-bound 12 hours only).
1 *McKibbin* v. *Glasgow Corpn.*, 1920 S.C. 590; *cf. McEwen* v. *Lowden* (1881) 19 S.L.R. 22.
2 *Keeney* v. *Stewart*, 1909 S.C. 754; *Mitchell* v. *Watt*, 1935 S.C. 104.
3 *Baillie* v. *Shearer's J.F.* (1894) 21 R. 498; *cf. Doran* v. *Glen* (1900) 8 S.L.T. 199.
4 *Rush* v. *Glasgow Corpn.*, 1947 S.C. 580; *Dickie* v. *Glasgow Corpn.* (1951) 67 Sh.Ct.Rep. 90; *Black, supra.*
5 *Kinnell* v. *Glasgow Corpn.*, 1950 S.C. 573.
6 *McQueen* v. *Glasgow Corpn.* (1953) 69 Sh.Ct.Rep. 332.
7 *Rush, supra.*
8 *Monaghan* v. *Glasgow Corpn.*, 1955 S.C. 80.
9 *Laurie* v. *Aberdeen Mags.*, 1911 S.C. 1226.
10 *e.g., Shearer* v. *Malcolm* (1898) 35 S.L.R. 924; *cf. Turner* v. *Maclachlan*, 1909, 1 S.L.T. 342.

habitually washed vehicles at night and allowed the water to drain over the pavement into the gutter, failed to anticipate the onset of frost or to take precautions against the formation of ice on the pavement on which a pedestrian slipped and was injured,[11] or a frontager placed a stepping-stone in front of his property,[12] or allowed a strip of his ground bordering on the pavement and on which people walked to get out of level there-with.[13]   Frontagers having a coal-chute or cellar-door let into the pavement are liable if they leave it open, not properly fastened or otherwise dangerous,[14] but they are not liable for the safety of hatches placed in the pavement for sanitary purposes.[15]   A frontager whose titles include the *solum* of the pavement is not automatically relieved of liability by the fact that a local authority has the control and management of the street and pavement, and he may still be liable to pedestrians injured by his neglect of maintenance.[16]

There is at common law no duty on frontagers not to have premises with a door or gate opening on a street when that door is harmless while unopened. The only liability is on a person who carelessly opens such a door and so causes harm.[17]   Nor is a frontager bound to provide a gate which will stand up to misuse, as by children swinging on it, particularly if he does not know of this practice,[18] nor to avoid placing on his land objects which may frighten animals.[19]   But there is liability if a door is insecurely fixed and falls out on a passer-by.[20]

The owner of a butcher's shop has been held liable where a pedestrian slipped on a piece of fat on the pavement outside the shop, the inference being that the fat had been put on the pavement or carried out on a customer's shoe.[21]

A frontager has no common law authority to litter or obstruct the pavement in the course of operations on his premises, but may do so, so far as reasonable and necessary, only if he takes precautions, by warning, fencing and lighting, for the safety of pedestrians. Thus it may be negligence, or a nuisance, to have a compressor pipe-line running across the pavement.[22]

Private streets.   A street privately maintained, but available for *de facto* use by the public,[23] or at least a section of the public, is a private

---

11 *Lambie* v. *Western S.M.T. Co.*, 1944 S.C. 415.
12 *Shearer* v. *Malcolm, supra.*
13 *Laurie, supra; cf. McEwen* v. *Lowden* (1881) 19 S.L.R. 22.
14 *Laing* v. *Paull & Williamsons*, 1912 S.C. 196; *Daniel* v. *Rickett Cockerell* [1938] 2 K.B. 322.
15 *Keeney* v. *Stewart*, 1909 S.C. 754.
16 *Baillie* v. *Shearer's J.F.* (1894) 21 R. 498.
17 *Evans* v. *Edinburgh Mags.*, 1916 S.C.(H.L.) 149; *cf. Murphy* v. *Smith* (1886) 13 R. 985.
18 *McMurray* v. *Glasgow School Board.*, 1916 S.C. 9.
19 *Gibson* v. *Stewart* (1894) 21 R. 437.   20 *Beveridge* v. *Kinnear* (1883) 11 R. 387.
21 *Dollman* v. *Hillman* [1941] 1 All E.R. 355.
22 *Farrell* v. *Mowlem* [1954] 1 Lloyd's Rep. 437; contrast *Trevett* v. *Lee* [1955] 1 All E.R. 406.
23 *Magistrates of Edinburgh* v. *N.B. Ry.* (1904) 6 F. 620; see also *Millar's Trs.* v. *Leith Police Commissioners* (1873) 11 M. 932; *Kinning Park Police Commrs.* v. *Thomson* (1877) 4 R. 528; *Hope* v. *Edinburgh Road Trust* (1878) 5 R. 694; *Neilson* v. *Borland, King & Shaw* (1902) 4 F. 599; *Dunfermline Magistrates* v. *Rintoul*, 1911 S.C. 737; *Greenock Corpn.* v. *Bennett*, 1938 S.C. 563.

street and subject to the statutory provisions relevant thereto, though, unless the public have any legal right to use the street, the owner may resume possession for his exclusive use, when it will cease to be a private street.[24] The local authority has a limited control over public streets and may have them levelled, paved, drained and completed at the expense of the frontagers.[25] Even though the local authority has possession and control, the frontagers may still be liable to persons injured as a result of the condition of the street.[26]

It may also require frontagers to make the street up to a proper standard of construction,[27] and the local authority may then, on application, take it over as a public street,[27] and it is then maintainable by the local authority.

Paths other than public footpaths. In *Taylor* v. *Saltcoats Mags.*[28] a person fell on an embankment which, though frequented by the public, was not a public street or footpath within the meaning of the Burgh Police (Scotland) Act, 1892, and the local authority was held to be under no duty to maintain it in a safe condition.

Operations in streets by statutory undertakers. The Public Utilities Street Works Act, 1950, makes uniform provision for the breaking up and opening of streets by statutory undertakers, by providing a Street Works Code,[29] which regulates the work of undertakers [30] taken on their initiative, and a code in Part II of the Act which regulates operations initiated by road, bridge or transport authorities of their own which may affect the undertaker's works, or require works to be done by them to facilitate the street works, or give them an opportunity to make improvements in their undertaking.

Section 8 (1) imposes on undertakers executing or who have executed any code-regulated works [31] the duty of securing that, so long as the street or controlled land is open, it is adequately fenced and guarded, that traffic signs are placed and, where so directed, operated and lighted, that no greater width or length of any street on controlled land than is reasonably necessary is open or broken up at any one time, that there is no greater obstruction of traffic on any street or interference with the normal use of controlled land than is reasonably necessary, and that any spoil or other material not required for the execution of the works or of the

---

24 *Kinning Park Police Commrs.* v. *Thomson* (1877) 4 R. 528; *Glasgow Corpn.* v. *Caledonian Ry.*, 1909 S.C.(H.L.) 5; *cf. Wallace* v. *Dundee Police Commrs.* (1875) 2 R. 565; *Carson* v. *Kirkcaldy Mags.* (1902) 4 F. 18.
25 Burgh Police (Scotland) Act, 1903, s. 104; Burgh Police (Scotland) Act, 1892, s. 137.
26 *McClement* v. *Kirkintilloch Mags.*, 1962 S.L.T.(Notes) 91.
27 Burgh Police (Scotland) Act, 1892, s. 133, as amended by Burgh Police (Scotland) Act, 1902, s. 104. See also *Alloa Mags.* v. *Wilson*, 1913 S.C. 6; *Stewartry Dairy Association, Ltd.* v. *Kirkcudbright Town Council*, 1956 S.L.T. 341.
28 1912 S.C. 880.
29 Contained in ss. 3–14 of and Scheds. I, II and III to the Act.
30 Defined in s. 1 (2).
31 Defined in s. 1 (5).

reinstatement and making good is carried away as soon as is reasonably practicable. Failure to implement these duties is an offence (s. 8 (3)), without prejudice to civil liability (s. 20 (1)).

By section 36 (14) a local authority is not to be liable for any loss, injury or damage arising from the execution of any undertakers' works in any street.

In *McNair* v. *Dunfermline Corpn.*[32] a pedestrian who had tripped in a cavity in the pavement in the dark and been injured sued the burgh corporation. The defenders blamed the Scottish Gas Board, alleging failure to carry out their duties under the 1950 Act. It was held, *inter alia,* that section 36 (14) did not affect the ordinary liability of the local authority for the safety of the streets.

It has been held that in a small burgh the duties of the town council to keep pavements swept and free of rubbish and snow [33] do not limit or supersede the liability of the county council as highway authority,[34] so that a pedestrian who had fallen on packed snow and ice on the pavement of a street in a small burgh was entitled to sue the county council.[35]

The duty is one of reasonable care to maintain safe pavements, and this has been held not to have been breached by a flagstone projecting less than half an inch above the level of the pavement.[36]

Damage on highway by fault of person not on highway. A person lawfully using the highway is entitled to recover from anyone who, not being himself on the highway, negligently causes injury to him there. Thus a pedestrian can recover if struck by a golf-ball driven from a tee dangerously near the highway [37]; or if struck by the fall of a tree growing on adjoining land, if the tree should have been lopped or the owner had otherwise failed to act as a prudent estate manager and to show reasonable consideration for the safety of possible passers-by.[38]   The road authority has been held liable where, although a tree which fell on persons using the road was growing on private ground, it had been rendered unstable by operations undertaken for widening the road and it should have been apparent to any surveyor or roadman that there was in consequence an imminent risk of the tree falling on to the road.[39] So too a passer-by injured by the collapse of a building,[40] or the fall of snow from a roof,[41] or the fall of a brick from a building,[42] or a cricket

32   1953 S.C. 183.
33   Burgh Police (Scotland) Act, 1892, s. 116.
34   Under Local Government (Scotland) Act, 1929, s. 2.
35   *Thomson* v. *Angus County Council,* 1958 S.L.T. 208.
36   *MacDonald* v. *Argyll C.C.* (1953) 69 Sh.Ct.Rep. 345.
37   *Castle* v. *St. Augustine's Links, Ltd.* (1922) 38 T.L.R. 615; *McLeod* v. *St. Andrews Magistrates,* 1924 S.C. 960.
38   *Caminer* v. *Northern and London Investment Trust, Ltd.* [1951] A.C. 88; see also *Cunliffe* v. *Bankes* [1945] 1 All E.R. 459; *Costello* v. *Midlothian C.C.,* 1946 S.N. 103.
39   *Mackie* v. *Dunbartonshire C.C.,* 1927 S.C.(H.L.) 99; *cf. Brierley* v. *Midlothian C.C.,* 1921, 1 S.L.T. 192; *Costello, supra.*
40   *Wringe* v. *Cohen* [1940] 1 K.B. 229.
41   *Slater* v. *Worthington Cash Stores* [1941] 1 K.B. 488.
42   *Walsh* v. *Holst* [1958] 3 All E.R. 33.

ball hit out of the ground,[43] or in a collision in smoke billowing across the road from a bonfire in defendant's garden,[44] or by falling on ice formed on the pavement from water draining over it from a garage,[45] may have a claim if the danger should reasonably have been foreseen as possible and a real risk, and could have been prevented.[46]

The local authority was held not liable where a pursuer, who had known there were holes in the road, tripped over a hole less than two inches deep which the local authority had noticed but had decided did not constitute an immediate danger.[47]

Nor is it liable because the footpath is obscured by a projecting house which prevented pedestrians and vehicles from seeing each other.[48]

Whether a road authority is liable for the existence of a hole in the road or such a danger as a grating sunk below the general level of the gutter is very much a question of position and degree.[49]

8. DANGEROUS GOODS

Many kinds of corporeal moveable property are liable, at least in some circumstances, to cause injury to another, and a distinction has sometimes been drawn between " dangerous goods " and others, supposedly non-dangerous.

In English cases the tortious liability of a person who supplied or entrusted to another a thing " dangerous in itself " is frequently spoken of as settled, whereas there was no such rule in the case of things ordinarily safe.[50] Lord Wright has said: " A distinction has been drawn in some cases between things intrinsically dangerous or dangerous *per se* and other things which are not dangerous in the absence of negligence. The correctness or value of the distinction has been doubted by eminent judges.[51] I think, however, that there is a real and practical distinction between the two categories. Some things are obviously and necessarily dangerous unless the danger is removed by appropriate precautions. These things are dangerous *per se*. Other things are only dangerous where there is negligence." [52]

---

43 *Bolton* v. *Stone* [1951] A.C. 850.
44 *Rollingson* v. *Kerr* [1958] C.L.Y. 2427; *cf. Holling* v. *Yorkshire Traction* [1948] 2 All E.R. 662.
45 *Lambie* v. *Western S.M.T.*, 1944 S.C. 415.
46 Liability might also arise under the *actio de effusis vel dejectis* principle, on which see Chap. 8.
47 *Goodwin* v. *Dunbarton C.C.* (1953) 69 Sh.Ct.Rep. 318.
48 *McKenzie* v. *Musselburgh Mags.* (1901) 3 F. 1023.
49 *Higgins* v. *Glasgow Corpn.* (1901) 4 F. 94. See also *Law* v. *Glasgow Corpn.*, 1917 S.C. 160.
50 See distinction drawn in *Longmeid* v. *Holliday* (1851) 6 Ex. 761; *Blacker* v. *Lake and Elliott* (1912) 106 L.T. 533; *Wray* v. *Essex C.C.* [1936] 3 All E.R. 97; *Burfitte* v. *Kille* [1939] 2 K.B. 743; *Ball* v. *L.C.C.* [1949] 2 K.B. 159.
51 *e.g., Hodge* v. *Anglo-American Oil Co.* (1922) 12 Ll.L.R. 183, *per* Scrutton L.J.; see also Goodhart, " Dangerous Things and the Sedan Chair " (1949) 65 L.Q.R. 518, criticising *Ball* v. *L.C.C.* [1949] 2 K.B. 159, now overruled in part by *Billings* v. *Riden* [1958] A.C. 240.
52 *Muir* v. *Glasgow Corpn.*, 1943 S.C.(H.L.) 3, 18. But see *Beckett* v. *Newalls Insulation Co., Ltd.* [1953] 1 All E.R. 250, where Singleton L.J. denied the existence of a category of dangerous things.

There is, however, no authority in Scotland for the recognition of a separate category of "inherently dangerous" goods which impose special standards of care on possessors or suppliers, and Lord Atkin [53] regarded the distinction as an unnatural one so far as used to serve to distinguish the existence or non-existence of a legal right. On the contrary all goods have dangerous potentialities, but some more so than others, and the degree of care which has to be taken must be proportioned to the danger which is known, or reasonably should be known, to inhere in the particular goods in question. " There is, so to speak, an element of danger in every chattel—it may break, it may be defective in such a way as to allow of misuse, and the result may be injury; but I think there must always be found somewhere the element of negligence on his part to make the owner of a chattel liable for that injury." [54] The reasonable man is more careful with a loaded gun than with a stick,[55] with petrol than with water, and with radio-active material than with a stone. " What that duty [of care] is will vary according to the subject-matter of the things involved. It has, however, again and again been held that in the case of articles dangerous in themselves, such as loaded firearms, poisons, explosives, and other things *ejusdem generis*, there is a peculiar duty to take precaution imposed upon those who send forth or install such articles when it is necessarily the case that other parties will come within their proximity." [56] Whereas in England the distinction whether a particular thing fell into one class or the other was one of law,[57] in Scotland it is always one of fact, though it may be [58] that the more dangerous a thing is the wider the circle to whom the duty of care is owed.

Categories of cases. There are two groups of cases of liability for moveables which have caused harm; the first includes the cases of possessors of goods for harm done by them, of retailers of goods for harm done to the purchaser, and of donors, lenders or lessors of goods for harm done to donees, borrowers or hirers thereof. In some such cases liability *ex delicto* co-exists with liability *ex contractu*.[59] The second group includes cases where the person responsible for the harmful quality of the goods and the person injured are not related contractually, so that no claim *ex contractu* is possible, but in the view of the law the person responsible should reasonably have contemplated the use of the goods by such a person as was injured, and should have taken precautions against the happening of that kind of injury; such cases include the liability of the manufacturer of goods to the ultimate consumer, the liability of installers or repairers of goods to users, and the liability of consignors of goods to ultimate users.[60]

[53] *Donoghue, supra,* 54.
[54] *Oliver* v. *Saddler,* 1929 S.C.(H.L.) 94, 103, *per* Lord Dunedin.
[55] *Cf. King* v. *Pollock* (1874) 2 R. 42.
[56] *Dominion Natural Gas Co.* v. *Collins* [1909] A.C. 640.
[57] *Blacker* v. *Lake and Elliot* (1912) 106 L.T. 533.
[58] *Per* Lord Atkin in *Donoghue, supra,* 54–55.
[59] Sub-heads (a), (b) and (c), *infra.*   [60] Sub-heads (d), (e), (f), (g) and (h), *infra.*

(a) *Liability of possessor of dangerous thing.* Under the general principle of liability the person in possession and control in public [61] of any moveable property, which it is reasonably foreseeable may do injury to another person, must take reasonable precautions against such injury, by lighting, fencing, warning, guarding or otherwise, and is liable in reparation if an injury occurs which is attributable to his failure to take such reasonable care. The standard of care and the precautions requisite depend on the circumstances and on the degree of danger involved. Thus persons have been held liable for leaving an oil cake crusher unguarded and unfenced in the market place of a county town where young children habitually resorted for amusement,[62] for letting out a threshing mill inadequately guarded, whereby the farmer's daughter was injured,[63] for leaving a vehicle unattended in a crowded street and then driving it away without looking to see whether, as had happened, a child had been playing under it,[64] for leaving petrol in a pail normally filled with water and in fact, mistakenly used for water,[65] for leaving an open barrel of a poisonous substance at an open doorway where children were in the habit of standing.[66] There might be fault in putting out something dangerous as rubbish.[67]

The possessors of firearms must take care that they do not injure other people. Thus it is negligent to leave a loaded gun where it may go off by accident or by the intervention of another person and injure someone,[68] but the possessor is not liable if he had taken precautions, and had reasonable cause to believe that the gun was unloaded and safe.[69] It may be negligent in some circumstances to leave explosives at the site of works in the public street when persons can get within the barricaded area and steal them with consequent injury.[70] Similarly, in the use of a hazardous instrument such as a blowlamp, the standard of reasonable care is very high.[71]

Where, however, the thing is not dangerous in itself, such as a barrow left in a lane, there is no liability merely because a child has interfered with it and been hurt,[72] nor is there where the thing is quite obviously

---

[61] If the injured person had to come on another's premises before coming within the area of danger, the principles of occupier's liability for dangerous premises apply.

[62] *Campbell* v. *Ord & Maddison* (1873) 1 R. 149; contrast *McGregor* v. *Ross & Marshall* (1883) 10 R. 725 where precautions adequate but frustrated by unknown person.

[63] *Edwards* v. *Hutcheon* (1889) 16 R. 694; cf. *Reilly* v. *Greenfield Coal Co.*, 1909 S.C. 1328.

[64] *Morrison* v. *McAra* (1896) 23 R. 564.

[65] *Ross* v. *McCallum's Trs.*, 1922 S.C. 322.

[66] *Fitzpatrick* v. *Melville*, 1926 S.L.T. 478. See also *Duff* v. *National Telephone Co.* (1889) 16 R. 675; *McLelland* v. *Johnstone* (1902) 4 F. 459.

[67] *Pattendon* v. *Beney* (1934) 50 T.L.R. 204.

[68] *Lynch* v. *Nurdin* (1841) 1 Q.B. 29; cf. *Dixon* v. *Bell* (1816) 5 M. & S. 198; *Donaldson* v. *McNiven* [1952] 1 All E.R. 1213.

[69] *King* v. *Pollock* (1874) 2 R. 42. Cf. *Galloway* v. *King* (1872) 10 M. 788, where pursuer was trespasser.

[70] *McWilliam* v. *Hunter & Clark*, 1926 S.L.T. 676.

[71] *Gilmour* v. *Simpson*, 1958 S.C. 477; cf. *Nautilus S.S. Co.* v. *Henderson*, 1919 S.C. 605 (oxy-acetylene burner).

[72] *Duff* v. *National Telephone Co.* (1889) 16 R. 675.

dangerous, such as a coke brazier at the site of road works.[73] Vehicles left unattended in the streets are not dangerous unless there is something specially attractive about the load or otherwise which invites interference, or unless they have not been properly parked, so that interference is foreseeably likely to cause harm, e.g., by making the vehicle run away.[74]

(b) *Liability of retailer of goods.* The retailer of goods is under a contractual liability to the buyer of goods from him, if the goods are in breach of warranty.[75] He is liable to the buyer both for latent defects and for defects discoverable on reasonable examination [76]; while the difference does not affect his liability to the buyer, it does affect the retailer's right of recourse against the wholesaler and eventually against the manufacturer. The retailer will also be liable *ex delicto* for harm caused by any defect of which he knew or reasonably should have known.[77]

The retailer is under no liability *ex delicto* to a buyer injured by defect in the goods, if the defect were unknown to the retailer and it was impossible or not reasonably practicable for the retailer to examine the goods and discover the defect. This will cover all cases where discovery of the defect could have been made only by chemical or other tests,[78] or by destroying the packaging or sealed condition in which the goods were intended to reach the buyer. Such examination is not commercially practicable or to be expected. Thus a grocer could not examine the contents of a tin of salmon,[79] or a cafe proprietor the contents of an opaque bottle stopped with a crown cork.[80]

Retailer's delictual liability. A retailer may, however, be liable if examination of a kind reasonably practicable could have been made by him, and either was not made, or was made and did not uncover a discoverable defect. Thus a retailer who sells holed or " blown " tinned foods which turn out to be poisonous would presumably be liable,[81] and a dealer in secondhand cars will be liable for selling a car with a readily discoverable defect.[82] A retailer will also be liable if he knew of the dangers inherent in the thing sold, and gives no warning or no adequate warning on the container of the thing's dangerous characteristics.[83]

---

[73] *McLelland* v. *Johnstone* (1902) 4 F. 459.
[74] *Cf. Hendry* v. *McDougall*, 1923 S.C. 378; *Ballantyne* v. *Hamilton*, 1938 S.L.T. 468.
[75] Sale of Goods Act, 1893, s. 14; *cf. Wallis* v. *Russell* [1902] 2 I.R. 585; *Chaproniere* v. *Mason* (1905) 21 T.L.R. 633; *Frost* v. *Aylesbury Dairy Co.* [1905] 1 K.B. 608; *Jackson* v. *Watson* [1909] 2 K.B. 193.
[76] *Randall* v. *Newson* (1877) 2 Q.B. 102; *Myers* v. *Brent Cross Service Co.* [1934] 1 K.B. 46; *Grant* v. *Australian Knitting Mills* [1936] A.C. 85. *Cf. Thompson* v. *Sears*, 1926 S.L.T. 221.
[77] *Cf. Webber* v. *McCausland* (1948) 98 L.J. 360.
[78] *Grant* v. *Australian Knitting Mills* [1936] A.C. 85.
[79] *Gordon* v. *McHardy* (1903) 6 F. 210.
[80] *Donoghue* v. *Stevenson*, 1932 S.C.(H.L.) 31.
[81] The person using such tins would possibly be guilty of contributory negligence or barred by the *volenti* principle.
[82] *Andrews* v. *Hopkinson* [1957] 1 Q.B. 229.
[83] *Devilez* v. *Boots Pure Drug Co.* [1962] C.L.Y. 2015.

A retailer is not obliged to examine goods for defects if he has bought from a manufacturer of repute, unless there is anything to put him on his guard,[84] but if he has obtained them from an unusual or doubtful source,[85] he probably should examine them or samples of them, the precise duty depending on the source of the goods, the possibility of defect and the kind of harm anticipated.[86]

Retailer's liability for own fault. A retailer may also be liable if damage is caused by goods sold and the defect is attributable to his fault, as by having stored them until they have gone bad, or having allowed them to be contaminated by dirt, damp or vermin, or where the retailer is also manufacturer and there has been a fault in the manufacture which is liable to cause harm. He may also be liable where he has had to do something to the goods apart from the distribution of them, as where a chemist, instructed to test the product before use, attached the wrong label to it.[87] Where a customer tendered a bottle to a chemist to be filled with nitric acid and, by reason of the presence in the bottle of traces of some other substance, there was effervescence and persons were injured, the court was unable, in the absence of evidence of usual precautions, to say whether the chemist had failed in any duty of care as to examination of the bottle.[88]

Again, a retailer may be liable if he sells [89] or delivers [90] to a person goods of a dangerous character without taking adequate precautions to see that the dangerous character of the goods is appreciated or warning the recipient, or if the retailer has read the manufacturer's instructions but failed to apply them or bring them to the customer's notice.[91] A retailer may also be liable if he supplies goods in containers inadequate for them, having regard to the potentially dangerous quality of the goods; thus suppliers of petrol were held liable for harm caused by supply in a barrel not reasonably fit for the purpose, which burst and caused a fire.[92]

(c) *Liability of donor, lender or lessor.* A person who gives, lends or hires out goods to another may similarly owe a duty *ex contractu* to the donee, borrower, or hirer, and a wider duty *ex lege* to all who may foreseeably be affected, including such as the hirer's employees, to take reasonable care not to give, loan or let on hire goods which may cause damage.[93] The delictual liability is to take reasonable care to examine and to warn of any known defects, which might make the goods dangerous

---

84 *Gordon* v. *McHardy* (1903) 6 F. 210, 212, *per* L.J.C. MacDonald; *Mason* v. *Williams* [1955] 1 All E.R. 808; *cf. Davie* v. *New Merton Board Mills* [1959] A.C. 604.
85 *e.g.,* a purchase of bankrupt's stock, or goods salvaged from a fire or other catastrophe.
86 *Watson* v. *Buckley* [1940] 1 All E.R. 174. In such cases it might be advisable to sell the goods expressly free of all warranties.
87 *Kubach* v. *Hollands* [1937] 3 All E.R. 907.
88 *Muir* v. *Stewart,* 1938 S.C. 590.
89 *Yachuk* v. *Oliver Blais Co.* [1949] A.C. 386.
90 *Cf. Philco Radio* v. *Spurling* [1949] 2 K.B. 33.
91 *Holmes* v. *Ashford* [1950] 2 All E.R. 76.
92 *Marshall* v. *R.O.P., Ltd.,* 1938 S.C. 773.
93 *Fraser* v. *Fraser* (1882) 9 R. 896.

or unfit for any reasonably contemplated purpose.[94]   The standard of care may be rather less in the case of gift or gratuitous loan than in the case of letting on hire. There is no liability for defects unless the owner, having regard to the nature of the goods and his knowledge of their age, condition and previous use, should have known of or at least suspected them.[95]   Thus in *Heaven* v. *Pender*,[96] a dockowner lent a staging to a shipowner to be used by employees of the firm engaged to paint the ship. An employee having been injured by reason of the breaking of a defective rope, the dockowner was held liable for not having taken reasonable care as to the state of the articles lent. In *Oliver* v. *Saddler* [97] stevedores gratuitously permitted a porterage company to use their rope slings and were held liable when a sling broke and caused the death of an employee of the porterage company; the stevedore's employee had failed to discover the defect in the sling which broke. In *Andrews* v. *Hopkinson* [98] the hirer of a secondhand car taken on hire-purchase recovered damages from the seller for delivering a car having a defect discoverable by reasonable diligence, but not found, which caused him personal injuries. In *Sullivan* v. *Gallagher & Craig* [99] the lessor of a truck was held liable to the driver (an employee of a firm using the hired vehicle) for a defect attributable to faulty maintenance.

No liability is incurred merely because the article causes injury or damage while in use, and there must be evidence of negligence on the part of the owner. Still less is there liability if the article is misused, or used in an uncontemplated way, or overloaded.[1]

Where the article given, lent or hired is not intended to be used at once and there is a reasonable opportunity for examination by the donee, borrower or hirer, the owner is not liable, because the donee, borrower or hirer can, and should, inspect for himself and will be at least contributorily negligent if damage is caused by a discoverable defect. Where the C.R. lent wagons to the G.S.W.R. for the last stage of a journey and an employee of the latter was killed by a defect in a wagon, the C.R. were held not to be under any duty to ensure that the wagons were in proper order for the last stage.[2]

There is, however, no liability if the goods given, lent or hired are supplied to the borrower or hirer's specifications, or are inspected and passed by him as fit for his purposes. In that event the hirer, and not the

---

[94]   *Clarke* v. *Army & Navy Co-operative Soc.* [1903] 1 K.B. 155; *White* v. *Steadman* [1913] 3 K.B. 340.

[95]   *Marshall* v. *Sellactite & British Uralite, Ltd.* (1947) 63 T.L.R. 456; *Johnson* v. *Croggan* [1954] 1 All E.R. 121.

[96]   (1883) 11 Q.B.D. 503; see also *Elliott* v. *Hall* (1885) 15 Q.B.D. 315; *Hawkins* v. *Smith* (1896) 12 T.L.R. 532; (all approved in *Donoghue* v. *Stevenson*, 1932 S.C.(H.L.) 31).

[97]   1929 S.C.(H.L.) 94; see also *Traill* v. *A/S Dalbeattie* (1904) 6 F. 798.

[98]   [1957] 1 Q.B. 229.

[99]   1959 S.C. 243.

[1]   *McKinstry* v. *Johannes (Owners)* (1935) 52 Ll.L.R. 339.

[2]   *Caledonian Ry.* v. *Warwick* (1897) 25 R.(H.L.) 1; distinguished in *Oliver* v. *Saddler*, 1929 S.C.(H.L.) 94 and explained in *Donoghue* v. *Stevenson*, 1932 S.C.(H.L.) 31.

lessor, is the person liable to an employee or third party injured by the failure of the thing.[3] The defect must be one which proper inspection would have revealed.[4]

Similarly there is no liability on a proprietor of premises if goods, such as planks, ladders, etc. are taken and used by a contractor's workmen without authority.[5]

(d) *Liability of manufacturer to ultimate consumer.* The delictual liability of a wide variety of persons for harm caused by putting into the hands of an ultimate consumer or user goods made or supplied by them which are liable to, and which actually do, cause harm is based on the general principle which is well stated in the speeches in *Donoghue* v. *Stevenson*,[6] namely, that a person " must take reasonable care to avoid acts or omissions which [he] can reasonably foresee would be likely to injure . . . persons who are so closely and directly affected by [his] act that [he] ought reasonably to have them in contemplation as being so affected when [he is] directing [his] mind to the acts or omissions which are called in question."

This principle applies equally whether the goods are normally safe, or inherently dangerous, but the degree of care which is " reasonable " will vary very greatly in proportion to the potentially dangerous qualities of the thing in question in each particular case. Cases of this class prior to 1932 are frequently vitiated by the fallacy that if the manufacturer owed no contractual duty to the ultimate consumer he necessarily also owed no duty *ex lege*.[7] *Donoghue's* case [6] shattered this fallacy, re-emphasising that duty *ex lege* was independent of duty *ex contractu*, and could well be owed to a wide range of ultimate consumers of manufactured goods.

Duty of manufacturer to consumer. If there is a contractual relationship between manufacturer and consumer the latter may have a claim, if the goods are defective, under the Sale of Goods Act, 1893, s. 14. Where there is a chain of successive purchasers each may claim in turn under s. 14 from the person who sold to him for the damages he has had to pay to the person who bought from him, and for any expenses reasonably incurred in defending the claim.[8]

Independently of contract, " a manufacturer of products, which he sells in such a form as to show that he intends them to reach the ultimate consumer in the form in which they left him with no reasonable possibility of intermediate examination, and with the knowledge that the

---

[3] *Shaw* v. *West Calder Oil Co.* (1872) 9 S.L.R. 254; *McGill* v. *Bowman* (1890) 18 R. 206; *cf. Robertson* v. *Russell* (1885) 12 R. 634.

[4] *Gavin* v. *Rogers* (1889) 17 R. 206; *cf. Milne* v. *Townsend* (1892) 19 R. 830.

[5] *Nicolson* v. *Macandrew* (1888) 15 R. 854; *Watson* v. *McLeish & McTaggart* (1898) 25 R. 1028: see also *Barron* v. *Walker & Dick* (1906) 14 S.L.T. 668.

[6] 1932 S.C.(H.L.) 31, 44, *per* Lord Atkin.

[7] *e.g.*, judgments of Lords Ormidale and Anderson in *Mullen* v. *Barr & Co.*, 1929 S.C. 461 (overruled by *Donoghue, supra*).

[8] *Kasler & Cohen* v. *Slavonski* [1928] 1 K.B. 78; *Biggin* v. *Permanite* [1951] 2 K.B. 314.

absence of care in the preparation or putting up of the products will result in an injury to the consumer's life or property, owes a duty to the consumer " to take reasonable care in their manufacture so that they can be used or consumed in the manner intended with safety.[9]

To whom duty owed. The manufacturer owes the duty of care to the person ultimately injured, where the goods had been obtained by that person for his or her own use,[10] or where the goods had been sold to another in the contemplation that that other would use the goods on such a person as the ultimate victim, without any probability of intermediate examination.[11]

Standard of care. Liability is for negligence, the onus of proof of which is on the injured pursuer, but a high standard of care is demanded, more particularly with the potentially more dangerous kind of things, and the bare happening of an injury is some evidence of lack of due care in preparing the product, sufficient to throw on the manufacturer the onus of satisfying the court that he used all due care in its preparation. The pursuer is not obliged to prove exactly how, or where in the process of manufacture, the flaw occurred.[12]

Intermediate examination. The qualification as to intermediate examination of the product is important and the manufacturer will not be liable if any defect in the product was reasonably discoverable, and should have been discovered, by an intermediate wholesaler or retailer. It has been suggested [13] that it should not be reasonable " possibility " of intermediate examination, but reasonable " probability," that would elide liability, because a purchaser from a reputable manufacturer is normally entitled to rely on the manufacturer's skill and care, and should not be barred because no examination was made though such was reasonably possible. The point is truly whether examination or testing was probable or contemplated, and a manufacturer cannot escape merely by showing that examination was technically possible and would have revealed the defect before it did harm.[14] Thus where manufacturers supplied a defective chisel to employers, who issued it to a workman, they were liable to the workman when it splintered and injured him, because, though it might have been possible, it was not reasonably contemplated that the employers would examine and test the tool, and

[9] *Donoghue* v. *Stevenson*, 1932 S.C.(H.L.) 31, 57, *per* Lord Atkin.
[10] e.g., *Grant* v. *Australian Knitting Mills, Ltd.* [1936] A.C. 85.
[11] e.g., *Parker* v. *Oloxo* [1937] 3 All E.R. 524; *Watson* v. *Buckley* [1940] 1 All E.R. 174.
[12] *Donoghue, supra,* 72; *Grant* v. *Australian Knitting Mills, Ltd.* [1936] A.C. 85; *Lockhart* v. *Barr,* 1943 S.C. (H.L.) 1; *Basted* v. *Cozens and Sutcliffe* [1954] 2 All E.R. 753n.; *Mason* v. *Williams and Williams* [1955] 1 All E.R. 808.
[13] *Paine* v. *Colne Valley Electricity Supply Co.* [1938] 4 All E.R. 803; *Haseldine* v. *Daw* [1941] 2 K.B. 343, 376.
[14] On this ground *Dransfield* v. *British Insulated Cables, Ltd.* [1937] 4 All E.R. 382 must be treated as wrongly decided; on this see *Herschtal* v. *Stewart & Ardern, Ltd.* [1940] 1 K.B. 155, *per* Tucker J.; *Haseldine* v. *Daw* [1941] 2 K.B. 343, 376, *per* Goddard L.J.; 54 L.Q.R. 59.

they were not in fault in not doing so.[15] On the other hand the National Coal Board, as suppliers of coal, were not liable to a person injured by an explosion in the fireplace, since the retailers of the coal could, and should, reasonably have inspected the coal for explosives therein.[16]

Kind of goods covered by principle. The kind of goods held covered include scaffolding[17] food and drink,[18] water,[19] clothing,[20] cosmetics,[21] vehicles,[22] lifts,[23] a kiosk,[24] a tombstone,[25] a hot water bottle,[26] parts of buildings,[27] a barge loaded with timber,[28] an electrical installation in a building.[29]

Kind of defects covered by principle. The defect may be in the design,[30] or a failure in the course of the manufacturing process,[31] or in the inadequacy of the container,[32] or in a misleading label or description on the container,[33] or in the assembly or repair of goods,[34] or the reconditioning of a car,[35] or the loading of a barge,[36] or in the connections of an electrical installation.[37]

Where inspection contemplated. Where it is reasonably contemplated that the manufactured goods will be inspected, tested or examined before use, the manufacturer will still be liable for damage caused by a defect attributable to his fault, though it should have been, but was not, discovered by the examination; but the injured person's primary remedy is

---

15 *Mason* v. *Williams and Williams* [1955] 1 All E.R. 808; *Davie* v. *New Merton Board Mills* [1959] A.C. 604.

16 *Nicholson* v. *N.C.B.* (1952) 68 Sh.Ct.Rep. 161; see also *Lusk* v. *Barclay* (1953) 69 Sh.Ct.Rep. 53.

17 *Heaven* v. *Pender* (1883) 11 Q.B.D. 503.

18 *Donoghue* v. *Stevenson*, 1932 S.C.(H.L.) 31; *Daniels* v. *White* [1938] 4 All E.R. 258; *Barnett* v. *Packer & Co., Ltd.* [1940] 2 All E.R. 575 (wire in sweet); *Lockhart* v. *Barr*, 1943 S.C.(H.L.) 1; *Norton* v. *Reid* (1954) 70 Sh.Ct.Rep. 133.

19 *Barnes* v. *Irwell Valley Water Board* [1939] 1 K.B. 21; *Read* v. *Croydon Corpn.* [1938] 4 All E.R. 631.

20 *Grant* v. *Australian Knitting Mills, Ltd.* [1936] A.C. 85; *Mayne* v. *Silvermere Cleaners* [1939] 1 All E.R. 693.

21 *Parker* v. *Oloxo* [1937] 3 All E.R. 524; *Watson* v. *Buckley, Osborne, Garrett & Co., Ltd.* [1940] 1 All E.R. 174; contrast *Holmes* v. *Ashford* [1950] 2 All E.R. 76; *cf. George* v. *Skivington* (1869) L.R. 5 Ex. 1.

22 *Herschtal* v. *Stewart and Ardern, Ltd.* [1940] 1 K.B. 155; *Andrews* v. *Hopkinson* [1957] 1 Q.B. 229.

23 *Haseldine* v. *Daw* [1941] 2 K.B. 343.

24 *Paine* v. *Colne Valley Electricity Supply Co.* [1938] 4 All E.R. 803.

25 *Brown* v. *Cotterill* (1934) 51 T.L.R. 21.

26 *Steer* v. *Durable Rubber Co.* [1958] C.L.Y. 2250.

27 *Gallagher* v. *McDowell* [1961] N.I. 26; *Sharp* v. *Sweeting* [1963] 2 All E.R. 455.

28 *Denny* v. *Supplies and Transport Co.* [1950] 2 K.B. 374.

29 *Hartley* v. *Mayoh* [1954] 1 Q.B. 383.

30 *Hindustan S.S. Co.* v. *Siemens Bros. & Co., Ltd.* [1955] 1 Lloyd's Rep. 167.

31 *Donoghue* v. *Stevenson*, 1932 S.C.(H.L.) 31; *Grant* v. *Australian Knitting Mills, Ltd.* [1936] A.C. 85; *Daniels & Daniels* v. *White* [1938] 4 All E.R. 258.

32 *Donoghue, supra; cf. Bates* v. *Batey & Co.* [1913] 3 K.B. 351.

33 *Kubach* v. *Hollands* [1937] 3 All E.R. 907; *Watson* v. *Buckley, Osborne Garrett & Co., Ltd.* [1940] 1 All E.R. 174.

34 *Malfroot* v. *Noxal* (1935) 51 T.L.R. 551; *Haseldine* v. *Daw* [1941] 2 K.B. 343; *Howard* v. *Furness Houlder, Ltd.* [1936] 2 All E.R. 781; *Stennett* v. *Hancock* [1939] 2 All E.R. 578.

35 *Herschtal* v. *Stewart and Ardern, Ltd.* [1940] 1 K.B. 155; *Andrews* v. *Hopkinson* [1957] 1 Q.B. 229.

36 *Denny* v. *Supplies and Transport Co.* [1950] 2 K.B. 374.

37 *Hartley* v. *Mayoh* [1954] 1 Q.B. 383.

against the retailer who should have examined the goods and discovered the defect, for having failed to do so. Thus the retailer of foods packed in polythene bags is liable if he fails to notice that the goods have become soft and bad.

The question is not whether intermediate inspection is possible, but whether it is reasonably practicable and was reasonably contemplated by the original manufacturer.[38]

Consumer's knowledge of defect. If the consumer or user, by examination or otherwise, has acquired knowledge of the defect in the manufactured thing, and nevertheless uses it, his claim, if he has been injured, may fall to be rejected on the principle of *volenti non fit injuria* or reduced by the operation of contributory negligence.[39] It is a question of circumstances and of causation. Thus where an employee of the buyers of a crane noticed that it was defective when assembling it, but nevertheless worked it without having the defects remedied, the manufacturers were held not liable for his death.[40] But knowledge of a danger is no defence if the injured party had no alternative but to accept the danger.[41]

Supervening defect. The manufacturer is not liable when the defect has been caused by something not attributable to his fault but supervening after he has issued the goods.[42] Thus the lapse of time since manufacture,[43] natural deterioration, damage from other causes, wear and tear, and the extent of any maintenance and repair since manufacture are all relevant.[44]

Injury due to consumer's idiosyncrasy. The manufacturer is not liable to an ultimate consumer who sustains injury only by reason of some idiosyncrasy or peculiarity and if a consumer of normal sensitivity would not have sustained any injury,[45] particularly where the consumer knew but did not disclose her abnormal sensitivity.[46]

Unusual use. The liability attaches only where the manufactured thing is used or consumed in the manner and for the purpose intended, and not if it is used in some uncontemplated way, or for some unusual purpose. Thus if a jack is supplied for a small car but used to jack up a loaded lorry, there can be no claim if it collapses under a weight it was never made to bear. It may be a narrow question in particular circumstances

[38] *Grant* v. *Australian Knitting Mills, Ltd.* [1936] A.C. 85; *Haseldine* v. *Daw* [1941] 2 K.B. 343, 376.

[39] *Grant* v. *Australian Knitting Mills, Ltd.* [1936] A.C. 85, 105, *per* Lord Wright; *London Graving Dock* v. *Horton* [1951] A.C. 737, 750, *per* Lord Porter, *obiter*.

[40] *Farr* v. *Butters Bros.* [1932] 2 K.B. 606.

[41] *Denny* v. *Supplies and Transport Co.* [1950] 2 K.B. 374; *Twiss* v. *Rhodes* [1951] 1 Lloyd's Rep. 333.

[42] *Donoghue* v. *Stevenson*, 1932 S.C.(H.L.) 31, 72, *per* Lord Macmillan.

[43] *Evans* v. *Triplex Safety Glass Co.* [1936] 1 All E.R. 283.

[44] *Cf.* the hypothetical case envisaged in *Grant* v. *Australian Knitting Mills* [1936] A.C. 85, 107, of the ship's rudder breaking after some years of use.

[45] *Griffiths* v. *Conway* [1939] 1 All E.R. 685; contrast *Mayne* v. *Silvermere Cleaners, Ltd.* [1939] 1 All E.R. 693; *cf. Board* v. *Hedley* [1951] 2 All E.R. 431.

[46] *Ingham* v. *Emes* [1955] 2 Q.B. 366.

whether a use or manner of use is such as to be uncontemplated or not. In *Kubach* v. *Hollands* [47] the makers of a chemical which exploded in a school classroom had had no notice of the use intended, and were held not liable.

Neglect of instructions or warnings. A manufacturer may be freed from liability if he has warned the ultimate consumer, or even an intermediary who applies the goods to the ultimate consumer, or required precautions to be taken or instructions followed, and these have not been complied with.[48] But a warning is not sufficient to exculpate the supplier if the recipient is a child or otherwise not competent to appreciate the warning.[49]

(e) *Liability of installers.* A delictual duty is incumbent on persons who instal any kind of apparatus in premises, or modify, repair or deal with it once installed, to take reasonable care that the apparatus is properly and safely installed, or repaired, so that it will not be a source of danger to persons who live or work in the premises and use the apparatus.[50] Where the installers are, as is usual, skilled tradesmen, the liability can alternatively be rested on the principle *spondet peritiam artis* in the case where the injured person was the employer of the installers. In *Eccles* [50] a builder's workman was killed by an electric shock; his father sued the electricians and the owners of the building, and the former were held not liable in view of the pursuer's averments that the latter had an opportunity to make, and a duty of making, intermediate inspection of the electrician's work (under the principle of *Donoghue* v. *Stevenson* [51]). But in a case where there were no such averments there is little doubt that the former's duty would be held to extend to third parties who might be injured by defect in the apparatus installed.

The intermediate inspection, if it is to exculpate the negligent installer, must have been practicable and probable, and by a person competent to discover a defect. It is submitted that if tradesmen carelessly instal dangerous apparatus in A's house, they are not exempted from liability to A's friend, injured by the apparatus, merely because A, technically unskilled, saw the work when done and did not reject it as defective. Such unskilled inspection is no inspection.

Boilers. In *Ball* v. *L.C.C.*,[52] the defendants installed a hot water boiler in the kitchen of a house; it had no safety-valve and by reason thereof exploded and injured the tenant's daughter. It was held that a boiler without a safety-valve was not a " dangerous thing," and that no

---

[47] [1937] 3 All E.R. 907.
[48] *Holmes* v. *Ashford* [1950] 2 All E.R. 76.
[49] *Burfitt* v. *Kille* [1939] 2 K.B. 743.
[50] *Eccles* v. *Cross & McIlwham*, 1938 S.C. 697 (doubted by Lord Denning in *Miller* v. *S.S.E.B.*, 1958 S.C.(H.L.) 20, 39); see also *Muir* v. *Moy Hammerton, Ltd.*, 1947 S.N. 190; *Hartley* v. *Mayoh* [1954] 1 Q.B. 383.
[51] 1932 S.C.(H.L.) 31.
[52] [1949] 2 K.B. 159.

duty was owed to the injured daughter, the defendants having no contract with her. The decision has been overruled by the House of Lords [53] and seems to be clearly wrong.

Gas. A person who instals gas fittings or appliances is liable to anyone injured by reason of his negligence in conducting the operation, unless there was reasonable probability of the installation being inspected by an intermediate person. Examples include such cases as where a builder sold a house which was equipped with a gas boiler fitted with a special burner which required no flue if properly regulated. It was wrongly regulated and the purchaser and his wife were killed by gas [54]; or where a landlord, on being told that the tenant would not require a gas fire, removed it and the tap, so that when the gas was turned on at the meter it filled the room and killed the tenant [55]; or where a gas-fitter made a temporary connection from which gas escaped, exploded, and injured a person on the premises.[56]

In such cases it is not necessarily a defence to show that the immediate cause of the damage was the negligence of the injured person or of a third party in using a lighted candle trying to discover the leak,[57] though the conscious act of another volition in the form of deliberate interference by the injured person may be a defence.[58]

Electricity. A person installing electrical apparatus is similarly liable to a third party who is injured by reason of his defective work if there is no reasonable probability of intermediate inspection.[59]

Machinery. A similar duty of reasonable care towards foreseeable users rests on those who instal or repair machinery of any kind. In *Haseldine* v. *Daw*,[60] D. employed engineers to adjust, clean and lubricate periodically the mechanism of a lift. By reason of the failure of an employee of the engineers correctly to replace a part, the lift fell to the bottom of the well and injured a passenger therein, who recovered damages from the engineers. *Billings* v. *Riden*,[61] though dealing with different circumstances, seems to justify the general proposition that a person, not in occupation of premises, who causes them to be dangerous to

---

[53] *Billings* v. *Riden* [1958] A.C. 240.

[54] *Bottomley* v. *Banister* [1932] 1 K.B. 458 (builder held not liable as installation part of realty and no duty owed in respect of it to purchaser; this *ratio* seems unsound).

[55] *Davis* v. *Foots* [1940] 1 K.B. 116; *cf. Travers* v. *Gloucester Corpn.* [1946] 2 All E.R. 506.

[56] *Parry* v. *Smith* (1879) 4 C.P.D. 325.

[57] *Parry, supra; Burrows* v. *March Gas Co.* (1872) L.R. 7 Ex. 96.

[58] *Bottomley* v. *Banister* [1932] 1 K.B. 458.

[59] *Cf. Eccles* v. *Cross & McIlwham*, 1938 S.C. 697; *Paine* v. *Colne Valley Electricity Supply Co.* [1938] 4 All E.R. 803. (In both cases held that there was probable inspection by the customer intervening between installer and ultimate victim.) See also *Waddell's C.B.* v. *Lindsay*, 1960 S.L.T.(Notes) 23.

[60] [1941] 2 K.B. 343.

[61] [1958] A.C. 240, overruling *Malone* v. *Laskey* [1907] 2 K.B. 141 and criticising *Ball* v. *L.C.C.* [1949] 2 K.B. 159 (where landlord had installed domestic boiler not fitted with safety valve which exploded and injured tenant's daughter).

persons who might be expected lawfully to visit them, is under a duty to all such persons to take such care as in all the circumstances is reasonable to ensure that visitors are not exposed to danger by his actions.

(f) *Liability of repairer.* A person who undertakes to repair a defective thing clearly undertakes contractually a duty to show reasonable knowledge, skill and care in effecting the repair and hence will be liable if the repaired article again becomes defective and causes harm in such a way, or within such a period, as evidences improper repair.

Independently of contract a similar duty of care is owed *ex lege* to all who might reasonably foreseeably be harmed by the insufficiency of the repair,[62] including users other than the person who instructed the repair, and bystanders.[63]

(g) *Liability of consignor of goods.* A person who delivers goods to a carrier for transport should take reasonable care to ensure that they can be carried and unloaded without damage to persons or property with which the goods are likely to come in contact during the transit. Thus the consignor may be liable to a man injured when unloading dangerously stowed cargo.[64]

Dangerous goods (which includes things dangerous in themselves, things dangerous by defective manufacture or packing,[65] and things unfit to be carried in the manner contemplated) which require special care in handling, demand that reasonable notice be given, as by labelling and declaration to the carrier, and the consignor will be liable for damage caused by his failure to give due notice.[66] The consignor is liable, in the case of dangerous goods, even if he neither knew that the goods were dangerous nor was negligent in failing to discover this fact.[67]

The liability certainly extends to damage to the carrier's vehicle, and to injury to his employees, but also covers damage to other goods carried, as by contamination by fumes, leakage or mixing,[68] and injury to the consignees of other goods contaminated in transit by the dangerous goods, and even to injury to purchasers from the consignees of the contaminated goods.[69]

---

[62] *Malfroot* v. *Noxal* (1935) 51 T.L.R. 551; *Howard* v. *Furness Houlder Line, Ltd.* [1936] 2 All E.R. 781; *Herschtal* v. *Stewart and Ardern, Ltd.* [1940] 1 K.B. 155; *Haseldine* v. *Daw* [1941] 2 K.B. 343; *Malone* v. *Laskey* [1907] 2 K.B. 141, to a contrary effect, has been overruled by *Billings* v. *Riden* [1958] A.C. 240. The older cases, such as *Winterbottom* v. *Wright* (1842) 10 M. & W. 109; and *Earl* v. *Lubbock* [1905] 1 K.B. 253, are good decisions on contract, but are not consistent with *Donoghue* v. *Stevenson*, 1932 S.C.(H.L.) 31, so far as concerns the wider duty owed *ex delicto*.

[63] *Stennett* v. *Hancock* [1939] 2 All E.R. 578, doubted *obiter* in *Shave* v. *Rosner* [1954] 2 All E.R. 280, 282.

[64] *Denny* v. *Supplies and Transport Co.* [1950] 2 K.B. 374; *Wickens* v. *Associated Portland Cement Co.* [1951] 1 Lloyd's Rep. 162.

[65] *Marshall* v. *R.O.P., Ltd.*, 1938 S.C. 773.

[66] *Farrant* v. *Barnes* (1862) 11 C.B.(N.S.) 553; *Cramb* v. *Caledonian Ry.* (1892) 19 R. 1054.

[67] *Bamfield* v. *Goole and Sheffield Transport Co.* [1910] 2 K.B. 94; *cf. Burley* v. *Stepney Corpn.* [1947] 1 All E.R. 507.

[68] *Farrant* v. *Barnes, supra*; *G.N.Ry.* v. *L.E.P. Transport Co.* [1922] 2 K.B. 742.

[69] *Cramb* v. *Caledonian Ry.* (1892) 19 R. 1054.

If the carrier delivers goods to the consignee in the same condition as he received them, he is not liable to the consignee if the latter is injured by reason of the goods being defective, as the carrier is a mere agent for carrying. If on the other hand, he does not deliver the goods in the same condition as he received them, and the goods have deteriorated or been damaged by the carrier's negligence, so as to be unfit or unsafe for the contemplated use by the consignee, and the carrier knows or reasonably should have known of this change of condition,[70] he may be liable to the consignee for injury or damage caused by the goods being used for any contemplated purpose, if he has failed to give the consignee adequate warning of the observed or suspected deterioration. So, too, the carrier may be liable for misdelivery, as where he delivers too much, or the wrong kind of thing,[71] or to the wrong person,[72] and foreseeable damage [73] ensues in consequence.

(h) *Liability of builders.* The principle of liability to the ultimate user has also been applied in Northern Ireland and England to the builders of houses, so that a builder has been held liable to an occupier injured by a fault in construction which the landlord could not reasonably be expected to have discovered by examination.[74] There seems to be, as yet, no Scottish authority for applying the principle to defects in heritage.

9. Damage Done by Animals

While in certain circumstances the owner of an animal may be under a strict liability to take effectual precautions to keep it under control, with resultant liability if it gets out of control and does harm, even though no negligence be proved,[75] this is not exclusive of liability for harm caused by negligence, and the owner of an animal may be held liable for negligence in not properly controlling it where he might or could not have been held strictly liable. Thus where a defendant allowed two dogs coupled together to run about the roadway and the coupling chain caught the plaintiff's legs and pulled him down, the defendant was held liable for negligence.[76] Where a cow being driven from market entered a house and caused the inmate a nervous shock only negligence was alleged.[77] Where a bull had not previously exhibited any dangerous propensity known to the defenders (and accordingly the defenders had not been

---

[70] In *Cramb* v. *Caledonian Ry.* (1892) 19 R. 1054, the carrier did not know. *Cf. Taylor* v. *Union Castle Steamship Co.* (1932) 48 T.L.R. 249.

[71] *Macdonald* v. *Macbrayne*, 1915 S.C. 716.

[72] *Philco Radio* v. *Spurling* [1949] 2 All E.R. 882.

[73] *Cf. Cunnington* v. *G.N.Ry.* (1883) 49 L.T. 392.

[74] *Gallagher* v. *McDowell, Ltd.* [1961] N.I. 26; *Sharpe* v. *Sweeting* [1963] 2 All E.R. 455.

[75] On strict liability for animals see Chap. 17; on liability for straying animals see Chap. 27.

[76] *Jones* v. *Owen* (1871) 24 L.T.(N.S.) 587; *Pitcher* v. *Martin* (1937) 53 T.L.R. 903; *cf. Fardon* v. *Harcourt-Rivington* (1932) 48 T.L.R. 215; *Aldham* v. *United Dairies* [1940] 1 K.B. 507; *Brackenborough* v. *Spalding U.D.C.* [1942] A.C. 310.

[77] *Gilligan* v. *Robb*, 1910 S.C. 856.

saddled with knowledge of its dangerous propensities so as to make them strictly liable if it did harm) [78] it was held that the defenders could still be liable if negligence on their part were proved.[79]

A person who brings an animal on to, or drives one on, a public road, must take reasonable care for the safety of persons and property on and adjacent to the road. Thus liability has been held established where an excited cow became unmanageable when being led along the street and trampled a pedestrian,[80] or an inexperienced boy driving a cow set a dog at the cow which became frightened, entered a house and frightened the occupier,[81] or a lorryman left his horse and cart unattended and the horse bolted and injured a woman,[82] or the driver of a pony and van let it escape on to the street.[83]

Conversely, there was no liability where a person was injured by a bull which was being taken through the streets when those in charge had taken the usual and reasonable safety precautions and it escaped because of a latent defect, the ring in its nose breaking,[84] or where a docile horse, yoked to a cab, ran off for no apparent reason,[85] or a horse yoked to a vehicle suddenly backed the vehicle into an old woman,[86] or a horse bolted from a yard into the street, no specific negligence being averred.[87]

Liability for failure to take reasonable care that an animal does not do harm may be incurred to strangers,[88] and also to employees of the animal's owner.[89]

In the case of damage by animals not to persons but to property, as by trampling down or eating another's crops, apart from the Winter Herding Act,[90] liability probably must depend on negligence. Thus liability for allowing an animal being driven along the street to enter a building properly depends on negligence.[91]

In *Milligan* v. *Henderson*,[92] where a lady cyclist was injured by a fall when a dog ran out from behind an oncoming wagonette and caused her to fall, the owner was held not liable for the result of the dog's behaviour as the dog had not previously shown, and the defender consequently

[78] On this rule see Chap. 17.
[79] *Henderson* v. *John Stuart (Farms), Ltd.*, 1963 S.C. 245.
[80] *Phillips* v. *Nicoll* (1884) 11 R. 592.
[81] *Gilligan* v. *Robb*, 1910 S.C. 856.
[82] *McEwan* v. *Cuthill* (1897) 25 R. 57. *Cf. McIntosh* v. *Waddell* (1896) 24 R. 80; *McCairns* v. *Wordie* (1901) 8 S.L.T. 354.
[83] *Milne* v. *Nimmo* (1898) 25 R. 1150. See also *Clelland* v. *Robb*, 1911 S.C. 253; *Brown* v. *Fulton* (1881) 9 R. 36; *Wilson* v. *Wordie* (1905) 7 F. 927; *Gray* v. *N.B.Ry.* (1890) 18 R. 76; *Hendry* v. *McDougall*, 1923 S.C. 378; *Richardson* v. *Beattie*, 1923 S.L.T. 440; *Ballantyne* v. *Hamilton*, 1938 S.L.T. 468.
[84] *Harpers* v. *G.N.S.Ry.* (1886) 13 R. 1139.
[85] *Shaw* v. *Croall* (1885) 12 R. 1186.
[86] *Hogg* v. *Cupar District Cttee.*, 1912, 1 S.L.T. 57.
[87] *Smith* v. *Wallace* (1898) 25 R. 761; *cf.* *Carswell* v. *Ramage*, 1919, 2 S.L.T. 268; *Cessford* v. *Young*, 1933 S.L.T. 502.
[88] *Renwick* v. *Von Rotberg* (1875) 2 R. 855; *Phillips* v. *Nicoll* (1884) 11 R. 592.
[89] *Henderson, supra.*
[90] Act 1686, c. 11.
[91] *Gilligan* v. *Robb*, 1910 S.C. 856; *Cameron* v. *Hamilton's Auction Marts, Ltd.* (1955) 71 Sh.Ct.Rep. 285 seems to have been argued on the wrong principle (of strict liability).
[92] 1915 S.C. 1030.

had no knowledge of, any vicious or dangerous propensities. The case was argued on the issue of the defender's strict liability and he was rightly held not liable on this ground. But there might have been liability for negligence in controlling the dog, quite independently of strict liability, but this was not averred or argued. Lord Justice-Clerk Scott Dickson seems, however, to be in error in stating [93] that a pursuer cannot succeed " unless there is proof of the defender's previous knowledge of the propensity." This is true only of strict liability; it ignores the possibility (which was admittedly not averred or argued) of liability for failing to keep reasonable control of the dog, independently of its propensities and of the owner's knowledge thereof. Lord Johnston, however,[94] who dissented, clearly thought that there might have been liability for negligence, and the pursuer might have had greater success if she had founded her case on negligence rather than on strict liability.

Exceptionally, even though there be negligence, the occupier of farmland adjacent to a public road is not liable if his tame animals escape on to the highway.[95] There is no duty at common law to prevent ordinary tame farm animals escaping on to the highway, and even though such escape subjects the owner to a statutory penalty, that does not confer on an injured person a claim for breach of statutory duty.[96]

10. PERSONS PROFESSING SPECIAL SKILLS

Personal injuries or death are sometimes caused by the failure of a person who is a member of a recognised profession, or a skilled tradesman, to show the degree of skill and care reasonably to be expected of such a person. Such a person will normally owe a duty arising by implication from the contract with the person consulting or instructing him, and owed to that person only, to take reasonable care and show a reasonable standard of knowledge and skill, but, in some cases, particularly where personal injuries are a possible consequence of failure to take proper care, may also owe a wider duty *ex lege*, to persons whom he should reasonably have contemplated as being affected by his actings, to take care that such a person does not suffer loss, injury or damage by his failure to take reasonable care. Thus a doctor owes a duty *ex contractu* to the person, such as a parent, who calls him in, and also a duty *ex lege* to the patient.[97]

The duties incumbent in particular circumstances on different kinds of persons of special skill are considered in Chap. 30.

11. MISCELLANEOUS CASES

In other miscellaneous cases the precise duties of persons in particular situations have been considered.

[93] p. 1037.
[94] pp. 1041, 1045.
[95] *Heath's Garage, Ltd.* v. *Hodges* [1916] 2 K.B. 370; *Fraser* v. *Pate*, 1923 S.C. 748; *Sinclair* v. *Muir*, 1933 S.N. 42, 62.
[96] *Sinclair, supra.*
[97] *Edgar* v. *Lamont*, 1914 S.C. 277.

(1) *Education authorities and schools.* An education authority, or board of governors of a school, may be liable either personally, for its own fault, or vicariously, for the fault of teachers or other employees in the course of their employment.[98] An education authority must take reasonable care to provide reasonably safe premises,[99] and its teachers must show towards pupils the care which would be exercised by a reasonably careful parent.[1] But teachers cannot be Argus-eyed nor always supervising, nor can they insure children from harm.

The Education (Scotland) Act, 1946, s. 20, authorises the Secretary of State for Scotland to prescribe the standards of premises, furnishing and equipment of schools and other educational establishments [2] and education authorities must secure that their establishments conform thereto.

Under similar English legislation a boy has been held entitled to recover for injuries sustained when he caught his foot in the asphalt of the playground,[3] or put his hand through a glass panel in a door,[4] a girl whose hand was caught by a door with a too strong spring,[5] and a master injured by the bursting of heating apparatus.[6]

Travelling to and from school. Where vehicles are provided to transport children to and from school, the education authority must exercise reasonable care for the safety of children using the vehicle and supervision over them, and will be liable where a child is injured by reason of the lack of supervision and protection.[7]

But where children make their own arrangements for travel the responsibility of the teachers for supervision commences only when the children arrive and ends when they leave.[8]

In and about the classroom. A teacher should not leave dangerous articles, such as chemicals, lying about in places to which children have access,[9] but he cannot be expected to analyse chemicals supplied for use in the school to see if they are dangerous.[10] The dangerous quality of articles depends on the nature of the thing, and the age of the pupils

---

98 For the latter class, see also Chap. 30, *infra,* s.v. " School teachers."
99 The principles discussed under the heading of Dangerous Premises apply; see also *Cormack* v. *School Board of Wick* (1889) 16 R. 812; *Davies* v. *School Board of Kilbirnie,* 1911, 2 S.L.T. 371; *Cahill* v. *West Ham Corpn.* (1937) 81 Sol.Jo. 630; *Ralph* v. *L.C.C.* (1947) 63 T.L.R. 546; *Lyes* v. *Middlesex C.C.* [1963] C.L.Y. 2426; *Reffell* v. *Surrey C.C.* [1964] 1 All E.R. 743.
1 *Williams* v. *Eady* (1893) 10 T.L.R. 41; *Jackson* v. *L.C.C.* (1912) 28 T.L.R. 359; *Shepherd* v. *Essex C.C.* (1913) 29 T.L.R. 303; *Ricketts* v. *Erith B.C.* (1944) 113 L.J.K.B. 269; *Ralph* v. *L.C.C.* (1947) 63 T.L.R. 546.
2 See the School Premises (Standards and General Requirements) (Scotland) Regulations, 1959 (S.I. 1959 No. 1096).
3 *Ching* v. *Surrey C.C.* [1910] 1 K.B. 736.
4 *Lyes* v. *Middlesex C.C.* [1963] C.L.Y. 2426.
5 *Morris* v. *Carnarvon C.C.* [1910] 1 K.B. 840.
6 *Abbott* v. *Isham* (1920) 90 L.J.K.B. 309.
7 *Shrimpton* v. *Hertfordshire C.C.* (1911) 104 L.T. 145; *Ellis* v. *Sayers Confectioners* [1963] C.L.Y. 2347.
8 *Cf. Jeffery* v. *L.C.C.* (1954) 119 J.P. 45.
9 *Williams* v. *Eady, supra; Shepherd* v. *Essex C.C., supra.*
10 *Kubach* v. *Hollands* (1937) 53 T.L.R. 1024 (impure chemicals supplied).

likely to find it or use it.[11]   An inference of fault is not inevitable merely
because a pupil attacks another with a knife used for handicrafts and taken
from a drawer,[12] or with scissors during a handicraft period,[13] nor because
children have an unsupervised period during which one is injured.[14]

It has been held negligent for a teacher to send a thirteen-year-old
girl to poke the fire and draw the damper in a grate unfamiliar to her,[15]
or to fail to provide a guard for a gas cooker used by a girl of eleven,[16]
or to fail to provide a guard for a circular saw used in a woodwork class,
when the suggested guard was a recognised method of guarding saws,[17]
though not to send a boy from one room to another carrying an oilcan
with a long spout which injured another boy's eye when he came round
a corner and ran into it,[18] nor to require a pupil of 14 to carry a pot of
hot tea whereby he was scalded,[19] nor to allow a class of ten-year-olds to
carry along with their knitting, knitting needles with exposed ends.[20]
In this case it was held that a teacher had no duty to warn a child of
that age of such an obvious danger as the exposed ends of knitting
needles, and there was no averment that the children did not appreciate
the danger, or that there was any practice for teachers to ensure that
such needles were made safe when not in use, as by fitting corks to the
ends.

In gymnasium and at games.   Children must be supervised in the
gymnasium and when playing games, to ensure that there is no horseplay and that exercises are not done and games are not played in a
dangerous way.[21]   There is no liability for injury in the course of games
played in a proper way.[22]   Nor is there liability for the casual negligence
or unexpected act or frolic of one pupil against another,[23] nor where
children run from the gymnasium to the dressing room and one puts her
hand through a glass panel in a door, there being no reason to anticipate
that happening.[24]   Games should not be permitted in an unsuitable place.

---

[11] *Williams, supra*; *cf. Chilvers* v. *L.C.C.* (1916) 32 T.L.R. 363 (toy soldiers held to be
ordinary playthings for children of five, and not dangerous) and contrast *King* v. *Ford*
(1816) 1 Stark. 421 (possession of fireworks without supervision negligent).

[12] *Suckling* v. *Essex C.C.* [1955] C.L.Y. 1844; *cf. Driscoll* v. *Gratton Wilson* [1954] C.L.Y.
2239.

[13] *Ellesmere* v. *Middlesex C.C.* [1956] C.L.Y. 6025.

[14] *Harris* v. *Guest* [1960] C.L.Y. 2146.

[15] *Smith* v. *Martin* [1911] 2 K.B. 775.

[16] *Fryer* v. *Salford Corpn.* [1937] 1 All E.R. 617.

[17] *Smerknich* v. *Newport Corpn.* (1912) 76 J.P. 454.

[18] *Wray* v. *Essex C.C.* [1936] 3 All E.R. 97.

[19] *Cooper* v. *Manchester Corpn.* [1959] C.L.Y. 2260.

[20] *MacDonald's Tutor* v. *Inverness C.C.*, 1937 S.C. 69.

[21] *Gibbs* v. *Barking Corpn.* [1936] 1 All E.R. 115; *Gillmore* v. *L.C.C.* [1938] 4 All E.R. 331;
Ralph v. *L.C.C.* (1947) 63 T.L.R. 546.

[22] *Jones* v. *L.C.C.* (1932) 48 T.L.R. 577; *Cahill* v. *West Ham Corpn.* (1937) 81 S.J. 630;
Wright v. *Cheshire C.C.* [1952] 2 All E.R. 789.

[23] *Gow* v. *Glasgow Education Authority*, 1922 S.C. 260; *Clarke* v. *Bethnal Green B.C.* (1939)
55 T.L.R. 519; *cf. Camkin* v. *Bishop* [1941] 2 All E.R. 713 (boys doing farm work on
half-holiday).

[24] *Skinner* v. *Glasgow Corpn.*, 1961 S.L.T. 130; *cf. Cahill, supra*; *Ralph, supra*.

In playground. Children should be reasonably supervised in the playground, though this supervision need not be continuous,[25] so that there was no liability when a pupil hit a golf-ball through a doorway from the playground,[26] nor when a child fired an arrow from a bow and hit another child,[27] nor where boys jumped on a lorry delivering coke, causing it to tip and injure another boy,[28] nor where a boy injured another by throwing a piece of coke taken from a heap in the playground,[29] nor where one child injured another at play,[30] nor where a child was injured by an ordinary toy soldier,[31] nor where a child clambered up a waterpipe on to a glass roof through which he fell,[32] nor where a child used a prohibited bat in playing rounders.[33]

Boarding schools and school hostels. More extensive duties are incumbent on the school authority and on the teacher in the case of boarding schools and school hostels, and to a substantial extent the authority and the teacher are *in loco parentis,* [34] but even so owe no higher standard of precautions than would be observed by a reasonable parent.[35] There has been held inadequate supervision, where a child of seven at a holiday home climbed a tree by a ladder left accessible for the children and jumped down.[36]

School excursions and outside activities. Reasonable supervision and precautions are necessary where parties go out from school for an excursion or outside activities, but it is not necessarily negligence to allow a party of older children to go unsupervised.[37] " Boys of fourteen and sixteen at a public school are not to be treated as if they were infants at crèches, and no headmaster is obliged to arrange for constant and perpetual watching out of school hours." [38] Similarly, where boys visited a zoo and one was injured by trespassing and provoking a lion, it was held not negligent for those in charge to allow boys to split up into unsupervised groups.[39]

Liability to third parties. While a child is at school the teacher is *in loco parentis* to the extent that the authority may be liable to a third

---

[25] *Gow* v. *Glasgow Education Authority,* 1922 S.C. 260; *Rawsthorne* v. *Ottley* [1937] 3 All E.R. 902.
[26] *Langham* v. *Wellingborough School* (1932) 101 L.J.K.B. 513.
[27] *Ricketts* v. *Erith B.C.* (1944) 113 L.J.K.B. 269; see also *Clark* v. *Monmouthshire C.C.* [1954] C.L.Y. 2240.
[28] *Rawsthorne* v. *Ottley* [1937] 3 All E.R. 902.
[29] *Rich* v. *L.C.C.* [1953] 2 All E.R. 376; contrast *Jackson* v. *L.C.C.* (1912) 28 T.L.R. 359, distinguished in *Rich* as a decision on the facts. See also *Smith* v. *Hale* [1956] C.L.Y. 5940.
[30] *Gow, supra.*
[31] *Chilvers* v. *L.C.C.* (1916) 32 T.L.R. 363.
[32] *Jeffrey* v. *L.C.C.* [1954] C.L.Y. 2241.
[33] *Price* v. *Carnarvonshire C.C.* [1960] C.L.Y. 2145.
[34] *MacDonald's Tutor* v. *Inverness C.C.,* 1936 S.C. 69, 77.
[35] *Gow* v. *Glasgow Education Authority,* 1922 S.C. 260, 267.
[36] *Peters* v. *Hill* [1957] C.L.Y. 2367.
[37] *Camkin* v. *Bishop* [1941] 2 All E.R. 713 (boy injured while party working on farm on half-holiday: no liability).
[38] *Ibid.* 716, *per* Goddard L.J. See also *Trevor* v. *Inc. Froebel Institute* [1954] C.L.Y. 2238.
[39] *Murphy* v. *Zoological Society* [1962] C.L.Y. 68.

party injured by reason of the teacher's failure adequately to supervise the child; thus the authority was held liable where a child of four was left unattended, left the classroom and got out on to the road, where a lorry driver, trying to avoid the child, ran into a telegraph pole and was killed.[40]

(2) Hospital authorities

The liability of hospital authorities for their premises and personnel has been materially affected by the National Health Service (Scotland) Act, 1947, which transferred most hospitals to the control of Boards of Management acting subject to the overriding control of Regional Hospital Boards. The principles of law formerly applicable may, however, still apply to hospitals of a public character (as distinct from proprietary nursing homes) which have not been " nationalised " and maintained from public funds or brought under a Board of Management.[41]

Liability of hospital management. The managers of a hospital are certainly liable for injury caused by their employment of inadequate or unskilled staff,[42] provision of bad or inadequate equipment, defective system of operation, or other defaults attributable to the management of the hospital,[42] rather than to the premises themselves or lack of professional skill or care on the part of professional staff.

They will be liable, on the ordinary principles of liability for dangerous premises, for injury caused by defect or deficiency in the premises amounting to failure to take reasonable care for the safety of patients and visitors.[43] Under the Occupiers' Liability (Scotland) Act, 1960, patients and visitors are lawfully on the premises and are owed the duty of reasonable care for the safety of the premises. The hospital owes to child patients the duty of discipline and supervision owed by a schoolteacher or a parent and is not liable for injuries resulting from forbidden and unforeseeable capering.[44]

Within the sphere of medical and surgical treatment it has been held in England [45] that where the post-operative condition was markedly worse than before, the circumstances raised a prima facie case of negligence against the hospital authority, and that it was not necessary for the plaintiff to prove that a particular doctor or nurse was negligent, when all the persons by whom he was treated were servants of the defendants. Such a prima facie inference may, however, be rebutted by showing that it was consistent with, or not attributable to, any failure in due skill, care and attention, or was attributable to misadventure or risks not reasonably foreseeable and preventable.[46]

---

40 *Carmarthenshire C.C.* v. *Lewis* [1955] A.C. 549.
41 *e.g.,* Erskine Hospital for Ex-Service Men.
42 *e.g., Jones* v. *Manchester Corpn.* [1952] 2 Q.B. 852 (authority negligent in leaving administration of dangerous anaesthetic to inexperienced doctor without adequate supervision).
43 *e.g., Weigall* v. *Westminster Hospital* [1936] 1 All E.R. 232; *Slade* v. *Battersea Group Hospital Cttee.* [1955] 1 All E.R. 429.
44 *Gravestock* v. *Lewisham Hospital Cttee.* [1955] C.L.Y. 1853.
45 *Cassidy* v. *Ministry of Health* [1951] 2 K.B. 343.
46 *Roe* v. *Ministry of Health* [1954] 2 Q.B. 66.

Liability of hospitals for nurses. The view was formerly held that public hospitals were not liable for negligence by nurses while engaged in the exercise of professional skill and functions, so long as reasonable care had been taken by the hospital authorities to employ competent nurses,[47] but that they were liable for negligence by nurses engaged in merely ministerial or administrative duties " such as, for example, attendance of patients in the wards, the summoning of medical aid in cases of emergency, the supply of proper food, and the like." [48] The distinction between professional and ministerial duties was vague and unworkable, and ill related to the variety of functions which a nurse on duty may have to perform.

In more recent cases the distinction between professional duties and merely ministerial duties has been recognised as untenable, and hospital authorities have been held liable for negligence of nurses on the hospital staff, acting in the course of their employment, whatever the precise nature of the default.[49]

Liability of hospitals for physicians and surgeons. It was formerly accepted as law that public hospitals were not only not liable for any negligence of consultant physicians and surgeons, but not even liable for the negligence of physicians and surgeons employed by the hospital authority while acting in the discharge of their professional functions, so long as the hospital authority had taken reasonable care to employ competent persons.[50] They were, however, liable for acts not done in the exercise of professional duty, but merely administrative or ministerial.

The justifications for this exception to the principle of *respondeat superior* were said to be that the hospital managers could not control the skilled staff in matters of professional knowledge and discretion,[51] and that they set out only to provide premises to which the sick could resort and submit themselves to professional ministrations, much of which was voluntary and gratuitous.[52]

This view is no longer accepted, particularly since hospitals have been entrusted to public boards of management and supported by the State.

---

[47] *Hillyer* v. *St. Bartholomew's Hospital* [1909] 2 K.B. 820; *Smith* v. *Martin* [1911] 2 K.B. 775; *Reidford* v. *Aberdeen Mags.*, 1933 S.C. 276; *Strangways-Lesmere* v. *Clayton* [1936] 2 K.B. 11; *Lindsey C.C.* v. *Marshall* [1937] A.C. 97.

[48] *Hillyer, supra*, at p. 829, *per* Kennedy L.J.

[49] *Wardell* v. *Kent C.C.* [1938] 2 K.B. 766; *Voller* v. *Portsmouth Corpn.* (1947) 203 L.T.J. 264; *Fox* v. *Glasgow S.W. Hospitals Board*, 1955 S.L.T. 337. The cases of *Strangways-Lesmere* v. *Clayton* [1936] 2 K.B. 11, and, possibly, of *Dryden* v. *Surrey C.C.* [1936] 2 All E.R. 535 would now be decided differently. See also Goodhart, " Hospitals and Trained Nurses " (1938) 54 L.Q.R. 553, and *Gold* v. *Essex C.C.* [1942] 2 K.B. 293.

[50] *Evans* v. *Liverpool Corpn.* [1906] 1 K.B. 160; *Hillyer* v. *St. Bartholomew's Hospital* [1909] 2 K.B. 820; *Foote* v. *Greenock Hospital*, 1912 S.C. 69; *Scottish Insurance Commrs.* v. *Edinburgh R.I.*, 1913 S.C. 751; *Reidford* v. *Aberdeen Mags.*, 1933 S.C. 276.

[51] Reason given in *Hillyer, supra*; doubted by L.J.C. Alness in *Lavelle* v. *Glasgow R.I.*, 1932 S.C. 245; criticized by Lord Wright in *Lindsey C.C.* v. *Marshall* [1937] A.C. 97, 122.

[52] See *Cassidy* v. *Ministry of Health* [1951] 2 K.B. 343, 359, *per* Denning L.J., *Macdonald* v. *Glasgow Western Hospitals Board*, 1954 S.C. 453.

Hospital boards are now liable for the professional negligence of physicians and surgeons employed by them even in matters of professional knowledge, skill or discretion,[53] and even if they are employed only part-time.[54]

Hospital boards are also liable for the professional negligence of consultants and visiting physicians and surgeons, if they are employed by the hospital board part-time,[55] but voluntary hospitals are not liable for consultants and visiting staff.[56]

In the case of private nursing homes, the managers will be liable for damage caused by defective premises or equipment, and failure on the part of nurses or other employed staff, but not for visiting physicians and surgeons.[57]

Where something goes far wrong in the course of an operation or other hospital treatment, the facts raise a prima facie case of negligence against the hospital authorities and their servants. It is not for the pursuer to show exactly what went wrong or who was to blame, but for the defenders to displace the prima facie case made against them.[58] To raise this prima facie case it is probably not enough to say that no cure has been effected, but where the post-treatment condition is worse than before the inference may be drawn.[59]

(3) Prisons

The Secretary of State for Scotland, and the governors and staff of a prison or other corrective establishment, must take reasonable care that persons in their custody do not do harm to other persons in the prison, or outside. Thus actions have been brought by a prisoner attacked by a fellow-prisoner in a prison,[60] by a person injured at work in a prison,[61] by a boy injured at an approved school,[62] and by a person seriously assaulted by a mental defective released on licence from a criminal lunatic institution.[63] But a prisoner is not a servant or employee of the Secretary of State, so that averments of fault based on that relationship are irrelevant.[64]

---

[53] *Collins* v. *Hertfordshire C.C.* [1947] K.B. 598; *Cassidy* v. *Ministry of Health* [1951] 2 K.B. 343; *Jones* v. *Manchester Corpn.* [1952] 2 Q.B. 852; *Macdonald* v. *Glasgow Western Hospitals Board*, 1954 S.C. 453.

[54] *Roe* v. *Minister of Health* [1954] 2 Q.B. 66.

[55] *Hayward* v. *Edinburgh R.I. Management Board*, 1954 S.C. 453; *Razzell* v. *Snowball* [1954] 3 All E.R. 429; *Higgins* v. *N.W. Metropolitan Hospital Board* [1954] 1 W.L.R. 414.

[56] *Gold* v. *Essex C.C.* [1942] 2 K.B. 293; *Collins* v. *Hertfordshire C.C.*, *supra*; *Cassidy* v. *Ministry of Health*, *supra*.

[57] *Powell* v. *Streatham Manor Nursing Home* [1935] A.C. 243.

[58] *Cassidy* v. *Ministry of Health* [1951] 2 K.B. 343.

[59] In *Roe* v. *Minister of Health* [1954] 2 Q.B. 66, negligence was disproved, the worse post-operative state being due to misadventure, unknown and unforeseen.

[60] *Ellis* v. *Home Office* [1953] 2 Q.B. 135; *D'Arcy* v. *Prison Commrs.* [1955] C.L.Y. 1907.

[61] *Pullen* v. *Prison Commrs.* [1957] 3 All E.R. 470; *Davis* v. *Prison Commrs.* [1963] C.L.Y. 2866.

[62] *Smith* v. *Hale* [1956] C.L.Y. 5940.

[63] *Holgate* v. *Lancashire Mental Hospitals Board* [1937] 4 All E.R. 19.

[64] *Keatings* v. *Secretary of State for Scotland* (1961) 77 Sh.Ct.Rep. 113.

(4) *Playing games*

A participant in a game is in general barred from claiming damages for injuries received incidentally in his participation therein, on the principle of *volenti non fit injuria*.[65] But he has not undertaken to run the risk of deliberate injuries, as by fouling or hacking, and proof of such conduct would amount to assault and justify damages. Nor has he undertaken the risk that other competitors or participants would not observe the rules and normal procedures.[66]

The promotors of a sport or game to which the public are admitted owe spectators a duty to take reasonable care for their safety but do not guarantee their safety.[67]

A spectator is owed a duty of care by participants, the standard of which depends on the standard of conduct which the sport or game permits or involves, and a spectator takes the risk of injury done him by participants in the course of the sport or game, even though resulting from an error of judgment, provided it is not reckless or deliberate. Thus a spectator injured by a horse at a horse show has no claim.[68]

A person, not himself participating as player or spectator, can claim damages if the conduct which caused his injury was in the circumstances negligent. In *Ward* v. *Abraham*[69] a child, sitting in the pursuer's back green, was struck by a cricket ball hit from a neighbouring green belonging to one of the defenders. The action was dismissed as irrelevant on the ground that it was not necessarily illegal to play cricket in a back green, and that it was not averred that the game was being played in an illegal manner. This ground is not satisfactory: the issue was not the illegality or legality of the game or the manner of its playing, but whether the playing, being legal, was in the whole circumstances foreseeably likely to cause injury or damage. In *Bolton* v. *Stone*[70] the plaintiff had been hit by a cricket ball which passed over a fence seven feet high, seventeen feet above the pitch, and seventy-eight yards from the batsman, to strike the plaintiff 100 yards from the batsman. Balls had occasionally been hit into the highway before, though nobody had ever previously been hit.

It was held that the defendants were not liable because the risk of damage was so small that a reasonable man was entitled to think it right to refrain from taking steps to prevent the danger. In considering this, account should be taken, not only how remote the chance was that a person might be struck, but also how serious the consequences were likely to be if he were struck, but not the difficulty of remedial measures.

---

[65] *Murray* v. *Harringay Arena, Ltd.* [1951] 2 K.B. 529.
[66] *Anthony* v. *Braine* [1956] C.L.Y. 5935.
[67] *Meldrum* v. *Perthshire Agricultural Soc.* (1948) 64 Sh.Ct.Rep. 89; *cf. Hall* v. *Brooklands Auto-Racing Club* [1933] 1 K.B. 205; *Murray* v. *Harringay Arena, supra*; *O'Dowd* v. *Frazer-Nash* [1951] W.N. 173; *Brand* v. *Hibernian F.C.* [1951] C.L.Y. 4273; *Callaghan* v. *Killarney Race Co.* (1956) 90 I.L.T. 134.
[68] *Wooldridge* v. *Sumner* [1962] 2 All E.R. 978.
[69] 1920 S.C. 299.
[70] [1951] A.C. 850.

" If cricket cannot be played on a ground without creating a substantial risk, then it should not be played there at all." [71]

A local authority or other proprietors of a golf course may be liable if it has permitted play at places where there is a reasonably foreseeable substantial danger of persons being hurt, as where a foot-path crosses the line of play or a hole runs alongside a public road.[72]

[71] *Cf.* the case of a person injured by a golf-ball driven from the adjacent golf-course: in *Castle* v. *St. Augustine's Links, Ltd.* (1922) 38 T.L.R. 615 recovery was permitted on the ground of public nuisance. See also *Cleghorn* v. *Oldham* (1927) 43 T.L.R. 465.
[72] *McLeod* v. *St. Andrews Magistrates*, 1924 S.C. 960.

CHAPTER 17

STRICT LIABILITY FOR CAUSING PHYSICAL INJURY OR DEATH

> 1. Quasi-Delicts
> 2. Liability for Animals
> 3. Nuisance
> 4. Escape of Dangerous Thing

IT is difficult to say precisely in what circumstances a defender will be held liable for physical injury caused neither wilfully nor negligently but in circumstances importing strict liability, *i.e.*, where liability to make reparation is imposed for risk created or by legal presumption of culpa rather than on proof thereof, where the duty is not merely to take reasonable precautions but to take effective precautions, subject only to limited defences. It is equally difficult to say whether, if a person is killed by a breach of a duty of strict liability, his surviving relatives have any claim for the loss caused them by the death.

Such strict liability may arise in Scots law in at least some of the circumstances covered by the Roman quasi-delicts[1]; and also in some circumstances justified on other grounds.

1. QUASI-DELICTS

The concept of the quasi-delicts properly so called has been discussed already.[2] If it is accepted that at least some of these Roman categories have been accepted in Scots law it seems possible to hold a defender strictly liable for injury or death caused by *res positae vel suspensae* or by *res ejectae vel diffusae*. In *Gray* v. *Dunlop*[3] it is submitted that the court could, and should, have found liability under the latter principle.

2. LIABILITY FOR ANIMALS

Without prejudice to possible liability for negligence, *i.e.*, for failing to take reasonable precautions to prevent harm being done by his animal,[4] the owner of an animal is frequently subject to strict liability for his animals, *i.e.* he is bound to take not merely reasonable, but effectual, precautions to keep them under control and is liable if they escape from control and do harm, even without proof of negligence.[5]

---

[1] *i.e.*, quasi-delicts properly so called, as distinct from the later Scottish use of the term quasi-delict as covering cases of negligence. See further Chap. 8.

[2] Chap. 8, *supra.*

[3] (1954) 70 Sh.Ct.Rep. 270.

[4] On liability under this head see Chap. 16, sec. 9, *supra.*

[5] See also generally Williams', *Liability for Animals*; *Report of Committee on Civil Liability for Animals* (Cmd. 8746, 1953) and Twelfth Report of Law Reform Committee for Scotland (Cmnd. 2185, 1963).

Liability is strict where the owner had, or is deemed by law to have had, knowledge of the dangerous propensities of the animal, because in such circumstances he should have taken greater care than merely that reasonable care, failure to take which is held to be legal negligence. The effect in most cases is to absolve the pursuer from the need to aver and prove negligence; he can rely on the fact that the animal was not in fact kept safe as sufficient to impose liability. The effect on the defender is to impose a duty to take not merely reasonable precautions but effectual precautions against harm.

There is ample authority for the view that this strict liability for injury done by one's animal applies to cases of personal injury, both to direct personal injury, as by biting or goring,[6] and to indirect personal injury, as by causing one person to drop something on another's foot,[7] or by causing a collision.[8] Strict liability for animals also applies to cases of a relative claiming for the death of a person caused by a dangerous animal.[9] It applies as between master and servant [10] as well as between master and third party.

It probably does not apply to damage done by animals straying on to another's land, a case largely covered by the Winter Herding Act, 1686, nor to animals straying on or from roads and damaging property, and in any case where the requisites for strict liability are not established, a claim founded on proven negligence remains competent.[11]

Strict liability depends on prior knowledge. Stair [12] justifies the strict liability by anterior accession, " by connivance in foreknowing and not hindering those, whom they might and ought to have stopped, and that either specially in relation to one singular delinquence, or generally in knowing and not restraining the common and known inclination of the actors towards delinquencies of that kind, as when a master keeps outrageous and pernicious servants or beasts. And therefore in many cases, even by natural equity, the master is liable for the damage done by his beast. As is clearly resolved in the Judicial law,[13] in the case of the pushing ox, which if it was accustomed to push beforetime, the owner is liable for the damage thereof, as being obliged to restrain it; but if not, he is free. So the like may be said of mastiffs and other dogs, if they be accustomed to assault men, their goods and cattle and be not destroyed or restrained, the owner is liable."

Prior to *Fleeming* v. *Orr* [14] the law of Scotland does not seem to have been settled and that judgment still left the law in some doubt, but as

---

[6] *Burton* v. *Moorhead* (1881) 8 R. 892.
[7] *Fraser* v. *Bell* (1887) 14 R. 811.
[8] *Milligan* v. *Henderson*, 1915 S.C. 1030.
[9] *Clelland* v. *Robb*, 1911 S.C. 253.
[10] *Clark* v. *Armstrong* (1862) 24 D. 1315; *Daly* v. *Arrol Bros.* (1886) 14 R. 154; see also *Henderson* v. *John Stuart* (Farms), Ltd., 1964 S.C. 245; cf. *Brock* v. *Copland* (1794) 1 Esp. 203; *Barnes* v. *Lucille* (1907) 96 L.T. 680; *Rands* v. *McNeil* [1955] 1 Q.B. 253.
[11] *Henderson* v. *John Stuart* (Farms), Ltd., 1964 S.C. 245.
[12] I, 9, 5.
[13] Exodus, xxi, 28 *et seq.*   [14] (1855) 2 Macq. 14; 18 D.(H.L.) 21; reversing 15 D. 486.

subsequently interpreted, it seems to have been settled that the laws of Scotland and of England were to the same general effect, that, apart from cases where there is proven failure to take reasonable care, *scientia*, proved or imputed, was necessary,[15] and the law has since been generally understood in that sense.[16]

In *Henderson* v. *John Stuart (Farms) Ltd.*,[17] which was decided as a case of negligent keeping of an animal and not of strict liability, Lord Hunter expressed the view, *obiter*, that when Scottish judges have expressed opinions to the effect that the law of Scotland is the same as, or similar to, the law of England, they must have had in mind practical results in the particular circumstances under consideration rather than underlying principles. But he seems to treat the strict liability as a species of *culpa*, the fault consisting not in failure to take reasonable care, but in failure to restrain or confine, rather than a species of liability for risk, similar to though not necessarily identical with the English *scienter* action.

The principles at present accepted can be regarded as consistent with the principle of liability only for fault,[18] for unjustifiable and reasonably foreseeable harm, the function of the proof of vicious propensities of a tame animal or of the imposition of imputed knowledge of dangerous propensities of a wild animal being to establish that such harm was reasonably foreseeable. In *McIntyre* v. *Carmichael*[19] the owner of a dog which worried sheep was held liable on the ground of *culpa*, having been certiorated of the animal's propensity by a prior instance of worrying. But the fault does not lie in failure to take reasonable care, but in failure to confine effectually so that it seems better to regard the principles as a case of liability for risk, the owner being certiorated of the risk by actual or imputed knowledge. The standard of care demanded is not reasonable care but effectual precautions and there may be liability with only technical fault.

In Scots law, the principles are also justifiable on the basis of the *actio de pauperie* under which a person who suffered damage through the unnatural vice of a domesticated animal, acting from innate vice or excitement or *contra naturam sui generis*, had an action against the owner,[20] while an action also lay for damage done by a wild beast in captivity.[21]

---

[15] *Milligan* v. *Henderson*, 1915 S.C. 1030, 1035, *per* L.J.C. Scott Dickson; *Fraser* v. *Pate*, 1923 S.C. 748.

[16] See *Clark* v. *Armstrong* (1862) 24 D. 1315; where L.J.C. Inglis (p. 1320) did not " apprehend that there is any substantial difference between the laws of Scotland and England on the point." *McIntyre* v. *Carmichael* (1870) 8 M. 570; *Renwick* v. *Von Rotberg* (1875) 2 R. 855; *Cowan* v. *Dalziels* (1878) 5 R. 241; *Murray* v. *Brown* (1881) 19 S.L.R. 253; *Burton* v. *Moorhead* (1881) 8 R. 892; *Smillie* v. *Boyd* (1886) 14 R. 150; *Fraser* v. *Bell* (1887) 14 R. 811; *McDonald* v. *Smellie* (1903) 5 F. 955; *Gordon* v. *Mackenzie*, 1913 S.C. 109.

[17] 1964 S.C. 245, 247–248.

[18] It seems from *Fleeming* v. *Orr* (1853) 15 D. 486 (revd. 2 Macq. 14) that Scots law was formerly understood by at least some judges to rest on actual or presumed negligence.

[19] (1870) 8 M. 570.

[20] Dig. 9, 1, 1, 3; Voet, IX, 1, 4.

[21] Inst. 4, 9, pr.; Dig. 9, 1, 1, 10; but see Buckland, 603.

The English rules, stated to be like the Scottish ones by the House of Lords,[22] are known as "the *scienter* action" because of the need to prove, or attach to the owner imputed knowledge of, the kind of animal's dangerous habits, and of the old English form of declaration which stated that the defendant was liable "*quod canem scienter retinuit . . .*".

"The reason why by the English law it is necessary to allege and prove the *scientia* is, that in the case of an animal *mansuetae naturae* the presumption is that no harm will arise from leaving it at large. Starting from that presumption, it follows that there cannot be blame or negligence in the owner merely from his allowing liberty to an animal which has not by nature the propensity to cause mischief. Blame can only attach to the owner when, after having ascertained that the animal has propensities not generally belonging to his race, he omits to take proper precautions to protect the public against the ill consequences of those anomalous habits, and, therefore, according to English law, it is necessary to aver and prove this knowledge on the part of the owner. But after all, the *culpa* or negligence of the owner is the foundation on which the right of action against him rests, though the knowledge of the owner is the medium, and the only medium, through which we in England arrive at the conclusion that he has been guilty of neglect—and in that sense it is said that *scientia* is the gist of the action."[23] In *Clark* v. *Armstrong*,[24] Lord Justice-Clerk Inglis observed that in English practice a more specific averment of *scientia* on the part of the owner, or knowledge of the vicious propensities and habits of the animal may be required than is necessary in Scottish pleading.

"The law of Scotland will not, any more than that of England, make a master responsible for injury done by a domestic animal unless it be an animal of unusually vicious habits and propensities, and known to the owner to be so."[25]

Parties liable. The owner of the animal is liable, unless he has committed the care of the animal to another for a substantial time and for the latter's own behoof and the custodier is trustworthy and fully aware of the precautions necessary. He is certainly liable if the animal is in his personal custody, and even so long as he retains substantial control over its custody, whether exercising that by himself or by another, the actual custodier, if he has full knowledge of the animal's nature, is also liable, possibly more so than the owner.[26]

The owner's knowledge. Strict liability depends on the owner's knowledge of the dangerous or mischievous propensities of that animal, and his failure, in the light of that knowledge, to have kept effective control

---

[22] *Fleeming* v. *Orr* (1855) 2 Macq. 14.
[23] *Fleeming* v. *Orr* (1855) 2 Macq. 14, 23, *per* L.Ch. Cranworth.
[24] (1862) 24 D. 1315, 1320.
[25] *Clark* v. *Armstrong* (1862) 24 D. 1315, 1320, *per* L.J.C. Inglis, citing Stair, I, 9, 5.
[26] *Cowan* v. *Dalziels* (1877) 5 R. 241.

of the animal and prevented it doing what it has done. The owner's knowledge may be of either of two kinds, actual knowledge, based on experience, information from others, or observation of the particular animal; or imputed knowledge, which is ascribed by law to the owners of animals of various kinds, that these are of a dangerous nature. Accordingly there has developed a distinction between tame or domesticated animals, where actual knowledge of the dangerous propensities of that particular beast must be proved, and dangerous animals, where knowledge of the dangerous propensities of the species is imputed by law to the owner, whether or not he actually knew of them and whether or not the particular beast did have the dangerous propensities attributed to its species. Hence an owner is not liable for an unlikely, unforeseen or improbable act of an animal of a species *domitae naturae*, though he is liable for the act of such an animal if it is, or should have been, actually known to be dangerous; and he is liable for any harmful act of an animal of a species *ferae naturae*, whether probable or not, and whether or not he knew that that animal was dangerous.

" A person who keeps an animal with knowledge (*scienter retinuit*) of its tendency to do harm is strictly liable for damage it does if it escapes; he is under an absolute duty to confine or control it so that it shall not do injury to others. All animals *ferae naturae*, that is all animals which are not by nature harmless, such as a rabbit, or have not been tamed by man and domesticated, such as a horse, are conclusively presumed to have such a tendency, so that the *scienter* need not in their case be proved. All animals in the second class *mansuetae naturae* are conclusively presumed to be harmless until they have manifested a savage or vicious propensity; proof of such a manifestation is proof of *scienter* and serves to transfer the animal, so to speak, out of its natural class into the class of *ferae naturae*." [27] " The distinction between those animals which are *ferae naturae* by virtue of their genus and those which become so by the exhibition of a particular habit seems to me to be this: that in the case of the former it is assumed (and the assumption is true of a really dangerous animal such as a tiger) that whenever they get out of control they are practically bound to do injury, while in the case of the latter the assumption is that they will only do injury to the extent of the propensity which they have peculiarly manifested. It would not be at all irrational if the law were to recognise a limited distinction of this sort while holding that both classes of animals are governed by the same *scienter* rule." [28]

The distinction is not properly between wild and tamed species of animals, but between " those which, according to the experience of mankind are not dangerous to man, and those others which are dangerous." [29]

---

[27] *Behrens* v. *Bertram Mills Circus, Ltd.* [1957] 2 Q.B. 1, 13–14, *per* Devlin J.
[28] *Ibid.* 18, *per* Devlin J.
[29] *Fraser* v. *Pate*, 1923 S.C. 748, 751, *per* Lord Ashmore; *Behrens* v. *Bertram Mills Circus, Ltd.* [1957] 2 Q.B. 1, 14.

The law concerns itself with the class of animal, not the particular one, and the harmful or harmless label falls to be attached not by reference to the particular beast's training and habits, but by reference to the general habits of the species to which it belongs. Thus a circus animal, even if tamed, is still classed as one of its species.[30] " The law ignores the world of difference between the wild elephant in the jungle and the trained elephant in the circus." [31]

Animals domitae naturae. In the case of animals *domitae naturae* or *mansuetae naturae* it must be shown that the owner actually knew [32] that the particular animal [33] had previously shown a dangerous or vicious tendency, of the kind complained of, by committing, or attempting,[34] an act of the same harmful kind. To that extent the old maxim, that every dog is allowed one worry with impunity [35] is justified, for the first exhibition of vice known to the owner serves merely to fix the owner with knowledge of the animal's vicious propensity in that direction. One previous act exhibiting vice is sufficient [36] and it does not matter that it took place a considerable time before,[37] but it must be an act exhibiting the same kind of viciousness as is later in issue,[38] and a tendency to attack,[39] and it is not enough if a dog merely exhibited fierceness when defending its master's property, for that is natural for a dog and not, by itself, evidence of vice,[40] nor probably that a dog has snapped if its bone is threatened, which also is a natural reaction.

Knowledge of vice is not attached by showing that the animal has done something in accord with the natural instincts of its species. Thus it has been held not enough to show that a cat trespassed and killed pigeons, but necessary to establish that the damage was due to a special propensity, beyond that common to cats, and that the owner was aware of that.[41] Unbroken fillies which knocked down a plaintiff were held not to be vicious but merely playful, and it was not established that they had any vicious propensity to the knowledge of the owners.[42]

---

30 *Behrens, supra* (immaterial that circus elephant in fact tame).
31 *Ibid.* 14, *per* Devlin J.
32 *Mason* v. *Keeling* (1700) 12 Mod. 332, 335.
33 *Tallents* v. *Bell* [1944] 2 All E.R. 474.
34 *Worth* v. *Gilling* (1866) L.R. 2 C.P. 1 (chained dog running to limit of chain in attempts to bite).
35 *Cf. Fleeming* v. *Orr* (1853) 15 D. 486, 487, *per* Lord Cockburn (revd. 2 Macq. 14); *Burton* v. *Moorhead* (1881) 8 R. 892, 895, *per* L.J.C. Moncrieff. The observation of L.J.C. Macdonald in *Gordon* v. *Mackenzie*, 1913 S.C. 109, 111, that evidence of *subsequent* attacks was admissible as showing a vicious disposition, seems unfounded.
36 *Charlwood* v. *Greig* (1851) 3 C. & K. 46; *cf. McIntyre* v. *Carmichael* (1870) 8 M. 570; *Gould* v. *McAuliffe* [1941] 2 All E.R. 527.
37 *Sarch* v. *Blackburn* (1830) 4 C. & P. 297.
38 *Osborne* v. *Chocqueel* [1896] 2 Q.B. 109 (dog biting goats); *Glanville* v. *Sutton & Co.* [1928] 1 K.B. 571 (horse biting horses). *Cf. Worth, supra* (general tendency to run at humans).
39 *Fitzgerald* v. *Cooke Bourne (Farms), Ltd.* [1964] 1 Q.B. 249.
40 *Sycamore* v. *Ley* [1932] All E.R.Rep. 97.
41 *Buckle* v. *Holmes* [1926] 2 K.B. 125; *cf. Manton* v. *Brocklebank* [1923] 2 K.B. 212; *Tallents* v. *Bell and Goddard* [1944] 2 All E.R. 474.
42 *Fitzgerald* v. *Cooke Bourne (Farms)* [1963] 3 All E.R. 36.

The actual knowledge of a servant [43] who has the control and management of the animal, or of a relative [44] is imputed to the owner, and it is also sufficient if a third party had conveyed to the owner credible information of his animal's vicious nature.[45] The owner may also be held liable even if the servant owned the animal, if he used it in the course of his employment.[46] It is a question of fact whether a servant has sufficient charge of an animal to make his knowledge the master's knowledge.[47]

An owner has been held fixed with knowledge by warning people not to go near a dog,[48] or that a particular bull would run at anything red.[49]

Liability attaches not only to owners but to persons having possession and control,[50] even to persons allowing animals to resort to their premises,[51] but not where animals have merely strayed on to premises.[52]

The classes of animals recognised as *domitae naturae* include those which are harmless by their very nature, such as rabbits, hares, pheasants, grouse and partridges, and those which are accepted by long experience to be generally and as a race harmless, such as cats,[53] dogs,[54] fowls,[55] sheep,[56] horses,[57] cattle,[58] bulls,[59] sows,[60] camels,[61] rams.[62]

But liability has attached, despite the generic classification, for such particular animals as a mischievous ram,[63] a fierce bull,[64] an easily infuriated cow,[65] a kicking horse,[66] a vicious horse,[67] vicious and dangerous

---

43 *Baldwin* v. *Casella* (1872) L.R. 7 Exch. 325; *Cowan* v. *Dalziels* (1877) 5 R. 241. *Cf.* *Applebee* v. *Percy* (1874) L.R. 9 C.P. 647.
44 *Gladman* v. *Johnson* (1867) 36 L.J.C.P. 153.
45 *Soames* v. *Barnardiston* (1689) 6 St.Tr. 1063; *McIntyre* v. *Carmichael* (1870) 8 M. 570, 574.
46 *Knott* v. *L.C.C.* [1934] 1 K.B. 126.
47 *Colget* v. *Norris* (1886) 2 T.L.R. 471.
48 *Judge* v. *Cox* (1816) 1 Stark. 285; *secus, Sycamore* v. *Ley* [1932] All E.R.Rep. 97.
49 *Hudson* v. *Roberts* (1851) 6 Exch. 697.
50 *Knott* v. *L.C.C.* [1934] 1 K.B. 126, 141.
51 *McKone* v. *Wood* (1831) 5 C. & P. 1.
52 *Smith* v. *G.E.Ry.* (1866) L.R. 2 C.P. 4.
53 *Clinton* v. *Lyons* [1912] 3 K.B. 198; *Buckle* v. *Holmes* [1926] 2 K.B. 125.
54 *Fleeming* v. *Orr* (1855) 2 Macq. 14; *Renwick* v. *Von Rotberg* (1875) 2 R. 855; *Filburn* v. *People's Palace and Aquarium Co., Ltd.* (1890) 25 Q.B.D. 258, 260; *Milligan* v. *Henderson*, 1915 S.C. 1030. The breed does not matter: *Tallents* v. *Bell and Goddard* [1944] 2 All E.R. 474.
55 *Hadwell* v. *Righton* [1907] 2 K.B. 345.
56 *Heath's Garage, Ltd.* v. *Hodges* [1916] 2 K.B. 345; *Fraser* v. *Pate*, 1923 S.C. 748.
57 *Hammack* v. *White* (1862) 11 C.B.(N.S.) 588; *Cox* v. *Burbidge* (1863) 13 C.B.(N.S.) 430; *Jones* v. *Lee* (1911) 28 T.L.R. 92; *Bradley* v. *Wallaces* [1913] 3 K.B. 629; *Glanville* v. *Sutton* [1928] 1 K.B. 571; *Coyle* v. *Bald* (1920) 36 Sh.Ct.Rep. 83; *Magee* v. *L.N.E.Ry.* (1929) 45 Sh.Ct.Rep. 220. *Cf. Manton* v. *Brocklebank* [1923] 2 K.B. 212 (mare biting horse).
58 *Ellis* v. *Banyard* (1911) 28 T.L.R. 122.
59 *Clarke* v. *Armstrong* (1862) 24 D. 1315; *Hudson* v. *Roberts* (1851) 6 Exch. 697; *Lathall* v. *Joyce* [1939] 3 All E.R. 854.
60 *Higgins* v. *Searle* (1909) 100 L.T. 280.
61 *McQuaker* v. *Goddard* [1940] 1 K.B. 687.
62 *Jackson* v. *Smithson* (1846) 15 M. & W. 563.
63 *Ibid.*
64 *Blackman* v. *Simmons* (1827) 3 C. & P. 138; *Hudson* v. *Roberts* (1851) 6 Exch. 697; *Harpers* v. *G.N.S.Ry.* (1886) 13 R. 1139. *Cf. Mitchell* v. *Langlands and Scott* (1885) 2 Guthrie 465.
65 *Phillips* v. *Nicoll* (1884) 11 R. 592.
66 *Clelland* v. *Robb*, 1911 S.C. 253.
67 *R.* v. *Dant* (1865) 10 Cox C.C. 102; *Walker* v. *Hall* (1876) 40 J.P. 456; *Lowery* v. *Waerlt* [1911] A.C. 10.

dogs,[68] a mischievous monkey,[69] a bull trespassing and serving cows in an adjacent field.[70]

The tendency of sheep to stray on the highway is not a vicious or mischievous propensity.[71]

The same strict duty exists to guard against even a temporary mischievous propensity of particular animals, such as the tendency of bullocks to be wild when being unloaded from the railway,[72] or the tendency for a normally tame dog, confined in a motor-car, to be possessive and attack a person interfering with its car.[73]

Animals ferae naturae. Conversely, in the cases of animals *ferae naturae*, the owner is held by law bound to know that the particular beast, by reason of belonging to a particular species, may do harm if not controlled, and he is liable if harm results, without need for proof of actual knowledge of dangerous propensities, and without further proof of negligence. The extent of the category of animals *ferae naturae* is a matter of law [74] and has been held to include monkeys,[75] boars,[76] lions,[77] bears,[78] elephants,[79] ferrets,[80] and zebras.[81] For the purposes of this rule " wild animals " probably include only animals dangerous to mankind [82]; animals dangerous only to other animals or to property are probably excluded.

Liability attaches not for the mere keeping of the animal, which is not in any way wrongful, but for letting it get out of control and do damage; there is no liability if it is kept under control.[83]

It is no defence that the animal acts out of fright and that the damage does not result from any savagery in its nature,[84] so long as it does result from its getting out of control.

Liability is for failure to keep under control, not for negligence. Apart from the question of actual or imputed knowledge of the propensities

---

[68] *Renwick* v. *Von Rotberg* (1875) 2 R. 855; *Cowan* v. *Dalziel* (1877) 5 R. 241; *Burton* v. *Moorhead* (1881) 8 R. 892; *Smillies* v. *Boyd* (1886) 14 R. 150; *Daly* v. *Arrol* (1886) 14 R. 154; *Fraser* v. *Bell* (1887) 14 R. 811; *Macdonald* v. *Smellie* (1903) 5 F. 955; *Baker* v. *Snell* [1908] 2 K.B. 825; *Rennett* v. *G.N.S.Ry.*, 1909, 2 S.L.T. 328; *Gordon* v. *Mackenzie*, 1913 S.C. 109.

[69] *May* v. *Burdett* (1846) 9 Q.B. 101.

[70] *Harvie* v. *Turner* (1916) 32 Sh.Ct.Rep. 267.

[71] *Heath's Garages, Ltd.* v. *Hodges* [1916] 2 K.B. 370; *cf. Shanks* v. *Cartha Athletic Club* (1924) 40 Sh.Ct.Rep. 89; *Lawson* v. *Barclay* (1924) 40 Sh.Ct.Rep. 202; *Paterson* v. *Aitchison* (1933) 49 Sh.Ct.Rep. 216.

[72] *Howard* v. *Bergin* [1925] 2 I.R. 110.

[73] *Sycamore* v. *Ley* [1932] All E.R. Rep. 97.

[74] *McQuaker* v. *Goddard* [1940] 1 K.B. 687, 700.

[75] *May* v. *Burdett* (1846) 9 Q.B. 101.

[76] *Hennigan* v. *McVey* (1881) 9 R. 411.

[77] *Pearson* v. *Coleman Bros.* [1948] 2 K.B. 359.

[78] *Besozzi* v. *Harris* (1858) 1 F. & F. 92; *Wyatt* v. *Rosherville Gardens Co.* (1886) 2 T.L.R. 282.

[79] *Filburn* v. *People's Palace and Aquarium Co., Ltd.* (1890) 25 Q.B.D. 258; *Behrens* v. *Bertram Mills Circus, Ltd.* [1957] 2 Q.B. 1.

[80] *Nicol* v. *Summers* (1921) 37 Sh.Ct.Rep. 77.

[81] *Marlor* v. *Ball* (1900) 16 T.L.R. 239.

[82] *Buckle* v. *Holmes* [1926] 2 K.B. 125, 129; *McQuaker, supra*, 695.

[83] *Knott* v. *L.C.C.* [1934] 1 K.B. 126; *Behrens, supra*, 19.

[84] *Behrens, supra*.

of the class of animals in question, it must be shown that the owner failed to keep it under control. What control was necessary depends partly on the species of animal in question, but it is not necessary to prove negligence or failure to take reasonable care to keep the animal under control. Liability is strict in that, if the necessary knowledge exists, the owner will be liable if the animal in fact gets out of control and does harm, whether or not he took reasonable steps to keep it in,[85] and even though the immediate cause of the harm is the intervention of a third party.[86] "When the ferocity of the dog is quite well known[87] to the owner his obligation is not one of reasonable care, but not to keep the dog at all, unless he does it in such a way as to make it perfectly secure . . . the owner of the dog keeps it entirely at his own risk . . . he must restrain, and, if he does not, he will be responsible for its acts."[88] "If a dog is known to be vicious, then there is an obligation on the owner of the dog to keep it in proper restraint."[89] The question is solely whether the precautions taken or control exercised were effectual, not whether they were reasonable or not. The keeper is not responsible for the consequences if e.g., an elephant slips or stumbles, unless there was a failure of control, even temporarily.[90]

Damage to person. This strict liability covers all cases of the animal in question doing harm to a person, as by kicking or biting, or upsetting a person from a cycle, and also cases of indirect personal damage, such as from a fall when running away from a dangerous animal.[91]

Damage to property. Under these principles, liability has frequently been imposed in cases of dogs worrying sheep,[92] or dogs chasing horses,[93] or cats killing poultry.[94] But cats are less frequently or easily controlled than dogs and probably must be allowed more freedom to range,[95] though at owner's risk if they kill poultry, which it is in the nature of cats to do.[96]

---

[85] *Burton* v. *Moorhead* (1881) 8 R. 892; *Behrens* v. *Bertram Mills Circus, Ltd.* [1957] 2 Q.B. 1, 13.

[86] *Baker* v. *Snell* [1908] 2 K.B. 825 (servant inciting savage dog to attack plaintiff).

[87] The same applies in cases of other kinds of animals where the knowledge is imputed.

[88] *Burton* v. *Moorhead* (1881) 8 R. 892, 895, per L.J.C. Moncrieff; cf. 896, per Lord Young: " he keeps it at his own risk . . ." " The risk shall be entirely his, and the precautions he takes must be effectual. If they are not, the owner is responsible." Cf. also *Gordon* v. *Mackenzie*, 1913 S.C. 109, 111, per Lord Dundas.

[89] *Smillies* v. *Boyd* (1886) 14 R. 150, 153, per Lord Justice-Clerk Moncreiff.

[90] *Behrens* v. *Bertram Mills Circus, Ltd.* [1957] 2 Q.B. 1, 19.

[91] *Behrens* v. *Bertram Mills Circus, Ltd.* [1957] 2 Q.B. 1, 17–18, per Devlin J. Cf. *Wormald* v. *Cole* [1954] 1 Q.B. 614.

[92] *Barr* v. *McIsaac & Kemp* (1864) 1 Guthrie 498; *Smith* v. *Hurll* (1885) 1 Sh.Ct.Rep. 246; *Turners* v. *McLaren* (1887) 3 Sh.Ct.Rep. 57; *Duncan* v. *Rodger* (1891) 7 Sh.Ct.Rep.313; *Howison* v. *White* (1892) 8 Sh.Ct.Rep. 318; *Jackson* v. *Drysdale* (1896) 12 Sh.Ct.Rep. 224; *Stevenson* v. *Hunter* (1898) 14 Sh.Ct.Rep. 149; *Lyon* v. *Craig* (1901) 17 Sh.Ct.Rep. 9; later cases fall properly under the Dogs Act, 1906.

[93] Cf. *Arneil* v. *Paterson*, 1931 S.C.(H.L.) 117; *Belford* v. *Reid* (1912) 28 Sh.Ct.Rep. 12.

[94] *Allan* v. *Reekie* (1906) 22 Sh.Ct.Rep. 57; *Peden* v. *Charleton* (1906) 22 Sh.Ct.Rep. 91; *Turner* v. *Simpson* (1913) 29 Sh.Ct.Rep. 81.

[95] *Brown* v. *Soutar* (1914) 30 Sh.Ct.Rep. 314.

[96] *Turner, supra*; secus, *Buckle* v. *Holmes* [1926] 2 K.B. 125, where held an owner was not liable where his cat, following the common instincts of its kind, killed fowls and pigeons.

Some cases suggest that these principles apply also to damage done by animals to or on another's heritable property.[97]   Where an excited cow being taken to the auction mart escaped into the public street, climbed a stairway above a shop and fell through the upper floor into the shop and in its struggles turned on a tap, flooded the shop and damaged goods therein, the auctioneers were held not liable on the ground that the harm which had befallen was not a natural and probable consequence of any negligence on their part, but the action was held relevant against the farmer for, it was averred, knowing of the cow's vicious propensity and failing to warn the auctioneers.[98] It is probable that this particular case should have been dealt with as an instance of common law liability for negligence or for trespass by animals rather than as a case of strict liability for damage to property.[99]

Nature of damage done.   The *actio de pauperie* and the modern Scottish action lie only for physical damage to person or animal; the barking of dogs [1] or the smell of cattle [2] may give rise to an action for nuisance but do not justify a claim under these special rules. But physical damage probably includes not only bites and kicks but transmission of a contagious disease.[3]

Defences. The defender is not liable if the pursuer teased or provoked the animal or was materially imprudent or negligent in approaching or handling it, on the basis of *volenti non fit injuria* or of contributory negligence.[4] Nor is he liable if the animal is still under control, *e.g.*, on a chain,[5] or in its stall,[6] nor if the pursuer had no right to be where the animal harmed him.[7] Nor, again, if the injury complained of is too remotely connected with any initial fault, such as allowing an excited dog to escape.[8] It is not a defence that the immediate cause of the damage done by a dangerous animal is the intervening wrongful act of a third party who has frightened the animal,[9] though it is a defence that the animal was properly secured and improperly let loose and urged to

---

[97] *Smith* v. *Scott* (1923) 39 Sh.Ct.Rep. 105.

[98] *Cameron* v. *Hamilton's Auction Marts, Ltd.* (1955) 71 Sh.Ct.Rep. 285.

[99] *Cf. Milligan* v. *Wedge* (1840) 12 A. & E. 737; *Tillett* v. *Ward* (1882) 10 Q.B.D. 17; *Gilligan* v. *Robb*, 1910 S.C. 856; *Lathell* v. *Joyce* [1939] 3 All E.R. 854.

[1] *Cf. Leeman* v. *Montagu* [1936] 2 All E.R. 1677.

[2] *Cf. Aldred's Case* (1610) 9 Co. 576.

[3] *Cf. Theyer* v. *Parnell* [1918] 2 K.B. 333.

[4] *Daly* v. *Arrol Bros.* (1886) 14 R. 154; *Campbell* v. *Wilkinson* (1909) 43 I.L.T. 237; *Gordon* v. *Mackenzie*, 1913 S.C. 109; *Lee* v. *Walkers* (1939) 162 L.T. 189; *Sycamore* v. *Ley* [1932] All E.R.Rep. 97; *Sylvester* v. *Chapman* (1935) 79 Sol.Jo. 777; *Behrens* v. *Bertram Mills Circus, Ltd.* [1957] 2 Q.B. 1, 20–21.

[5] *Daly, supra.*

[6] *Rands* v. *McNeil* [1955] 1 Q.B. 253; *Behrens* v. *Bertram Mills Circus, Ltd.* [1957] 2 Q.B. 1, 19.

[7] *Blackman* v. *Simmons* (1827) 3 C. & P. 138; *Sarch* v. *Blackburn* (1830) 4 C. & P. 297; *Hudson* v. *Roberts* (1851) 6 Exch. 697;   *cf. Lowery* v. *Walker* [1911] A.C. 10, and see also *Pearson* v. *Coleman Bros.* [1948] 2 K.B. 359.

[8] *Gray* v. *N.B.Ry.* (1890) 18 R. 76.

[9] *McEwan* v. *Cuthill* (1897) 25 R. 57; *Baker* v. *Snell* (1908) 2 K.B. 825; *Illidge* v. *Goodwin* (1831) 5 C. & P. 190; *Haynes* v. *Harwood* [1935] 1 K.B. 146; *Behrens, supra*, 21–25.

mischief by another person.[10] It is not a defence that the owner took reasonably sufficient precautions. " I think the precautions must be effectual, and not only reasonably sufficient, in the sense that though they were not effectual the owner was morally excusable. The reason of our judgment is that ineffectual precautions are no defence to an action for injuries done to a person, where he lawfully was, by a ferocious animal." [11] *Damnum fatale* is doubtless a defence, as when lightning severs the chain securing a tiger.[12]

Statutory liability—The Dogs Acts. The Dogs Act, 1906,[13] makes the owner of a dog liable in damages for injury done by that dog to any " cattle," defined (s. 7) as including horses, mules, asses, sheep, goats and swine, or poultry,[14] without proof of previous mischievous propensity in the dog, or knowledge thereof by the owner, or proof that the injury was attributable to neglect on the owner's part. In cases to which it applies, this statutory liability supersedes the common law but the common law still applies to injuries to mankind by dogs. This statutory liability is apparently absolute,[15] so that the only proof required is of the causation of the injury by the defender's dog. Awards of damages have several times been made under this Act in cases of sheep-worrying.[16] It has been held to be no defence that the animals injured were trespassing at the time they were injured.[15] Where two or more dogs engage jointly in sheep-worrying their owners are jointly and severally liable.[17]

3. INJURY CAUSED BY NUISANCE

Nuisance consists in so using one's heritable property as to cause continuing or repeated serious disturbance or material inconvenience to, and interference with, the enjoyment or use of adjacent property by another person.[18] It is unnecessary to prove either intention to harm, or fault or lack of reasonable care.[19] Nuisance is usually confined to harm to property or the enjoyment thereof, but may in some cases be applicable to personal injury also. It would seem strange if a defender were liable without proof of negligence for inconvenience or discomfort caused by,

10 *Fleeming* v. *Orr* (1855) 2 Macq. 14.
11 *Burton* v. *Moorhead* (1881) 8 R. 892, 896, *per* Lord Young.
12 *Cf. Nichols* v. *Marsland* (1875) L.R. 10 Ex. 255, 260, *per* Bramwell B.
13 This replaces the Dogs (Scotland) Act, 1863, under which it was doubtful whether fault had to be proved or liability was strict; see *McIntyre* v. *Carmichael* (1870) 8 M. 570; *Murray* v. *Brown* (1881) 19 S.L.R. 253. The Dogs Act, 1871, deals only with criminal liability for keeping a dangerous dog or not keeping it under proper control. The Dogs (Protection of Livestock) Act, 1953, makes worrying livestock a criminal offence.
14 Extended to poultry by the Dogs (Amendment) Act, 1928, s. 1 (1). " Poultry," is defined in s. 1 (2) thereof. Tame rabbits are not " cattle ": *Tallents* v. *Bell and Goddard* [1944] 2 All E.R. 474.
15 *Grange* v. *Silcock* (1897) 77 L.T. 340.
16 *A.B.* v. *C.D.* (1911) 27 Sh.Ct.Rep. 212; *Belford* v. *Reid* (1912) 28 Sh.Ct.Rep. 12; *Balfour* v. *Duncan* (1949) 66 Sh.Ct.Rep. 40; *Riach* v. *Neish* (1950) 66 Sh.Ct.Rep. 286.
17 *Arneil* v. *Paterson*, 1931 S.C.(H.L.) 117.
18 See generally, Chap. 27, *infra.*
19 *Sedleigh-Denfield* v. *O'Callaghan* [1940] A.C. 880, 897; *Read* v. *Lyons* [1947] A.C. 156, 183.

say, pollution of the atmosphere or discharge of sewage, and not liable for injury resulting therefrom save on proof of negligence. Nuisance certainly covers " serious disturbance to or substantial inconvenience to [a] neighbour," [20] and the line between disturbance, inconvenience or discomfort to a person and personal injury to him is vague. In *Fleming* v. *Hislop*,[21] a remedy was given " although the evidence does not go to the length of proving that health is in danger," and a case of actual personal injury seems merely a stronger case than the ordinary one of discomfort rather than a totally different kind of infringement of interest. But there seems to be no clear Scottish authority for damages for personal injury caused by nuisance.

In *Evans* v. *Edinburgh Magistrates* [22] a person going along a lane was struck by a garden door which opened outwards. The claim against the proprietor was based on negligence, and failed, but Lord Skerrington observed [23] that " if the pursuer had alleged that other persons passing along the lane had collided with the door prior to the occasion in question and that this was known to the owner of the premises . . . the owner might properly be found liable." This probably does not mean more than that previous instances would fix the proprietor with knowledge of a risk which it would be negligence on his part to ignore or not to rectify, though nuisance was not argued and it is possible that repeated collisions with pedestrians might have led to the door being held a nuisance. In *Gray* v. *Dunlop* [24] the sheriff-substitute accepted the relevancy of averments of personal injury caused by nuisance and held that the pursuer would have been entitled to succeed if he showed that the incident complained of was part of a practice, the existence of which was known or ought to have been known to the defenders.

In *Ware* v. *Garston Haulage Co.*[25] an unlighted vehicle was left unattended on the highway and a cyclist collided with it; it was held a nuisance and the owner was held liable for the injuries without proof of negligence. In *Bolton* v. *Stone*,[26] where a person outside a cricket ground was hit by a ball struck with an exceptional, though not wholly unprecedented, stroke from the wicket 100 yards away, a claim founded on negligence or on nuisance failed on both heads, it being admitted that if the big hit out of the ground did not infer liability for negligence, it could not for nuisance. While the criteria of liability in nuisance for personal injury were not clarified, none of their Lordships rejected as incompetent the possibility of a claim for personal injuries caused by nuisance. If the hitting of the ball out of the ground had been a sufficiently common occurrence it could probably have been held a nuisance in view of the

---

[20] *Watt* v. *Jamieson*, 1954 S.C. 56, 58, *per* L.P. Cooper.
[21] (1886) 13 R.(H.L.) 43, 45.
[22] 1915 S.C. 895; affd. 1916 S.C.(H.L.) 149.
[23] *Ibid*. 904.
[24] (1954) 70 Sh.Ct.Rep. 270; see pp. 294, 641, *supra*.
[25] [1944] K.B. 30; contrast *Maitland* v. *Raisbeck* [1944] K.B. 689.
[26] [1951] A.C. 850.

potential danger to passers-by,[27] and if in those circumstances one had been struck, it is difficult to see why a claim based on nuisance should have failed.

There are, however, some dicta suggesting that nuisance is confined to injuries to property and interests therein,[28] and the law would be clearer if this were settled beyond question.

The law is clearly uncertain on this point and it may be that if the defender's conduct amounts to a nuisance he is liable also for personal injuries (as distinct from discomfort or inconvenience) directly resulting from the nuisance though he would not be liable for personal injuries thus caused save on proof of negligence if they did not also amount to a nuisance, as where the conduct was isolated and not continuing.

4. STRICT LIABILITY FOR ESCAPE OF DANGEROUS THING

A more stringent liability than merely to take reasonable care not to cause foreseeable harm is, for reasons of public policy, imposed on persons who have introduced to or accumulated on their premises dangerous substances which are obviously liable to do serious harm if they escape. If such a dangerous substance does escape and do harm, it is no defence that all reasonable precautions had been taken. In Scots law this liability seems to depend on the recognition by the court of circumstances which require peculiar care, and a willingness to presume fault if harm results.[29] It is an instance of liability for the creation of an obvious risk of harm. This principle is certainly applicable in cases of damage to property, but it is undecided whether it applies also to personal injuries or death. In the leading case,[30] however, Lord Justice-Clerk Hope said: " When an operation is made which involves great risk to the safety *of life* and of property, the condition on which alone that can be allowed which causes such risk is complete protection." In a later case [31] Lord Patrick said, obiter: " If a quarrymaster using the utmost care fires a blast in his quarry whereby the skull of a neighbour is fractured, neither reason nor public policy nor, in my opinion, the law of Scotland dictates that his dependants should not recover damages from the quarrymaster, notwithstanding that they cannot prove the quarrymaster to have been guilty of negligence." The application of the principle to injuries or death has accordingly been judicially envisaged and not ruled out of account.

---

27 Cf. Castle v. St. Augustine's Links (1922) 38 T.L.R. 615.
28 Cunard v. Antifyre, Ltd. [1933] 1 K.B. 551; Spicer v. Smee [1946] 1 All E.R. 489, 493; and see Newark, " The Boundaries of Nuisance " (1949) 65 L.Q.R. 480. The leading case on nuisance, Sedleigh-Denfield v. O'Callaghan [1940] A.C. 880, states the principles in terms of interference with enjoyment of land or premises; see also Watt v. Jamieson, 1954 S.C. 56.
29 See further Chap. 27, infra, where the principle is examined in detail, and Thirteenth Report of the Law Reform Committee for Scotland (Cmnd. 2348, 1964).
30 Kerr v. Earl of Orkney (1857) 20 D. 298, 302; passage approved in Caledonian Ry. v. Greenock Corpn., 1917 S.C.(H.L.) 56, 60, per L.C. Finlay.
31 Western Silver Fox Ranch v. Ross and Cromarty C.C., 1940 S.C. 601, 605.

There is some doubt in England also whether the analogous principle of *Rylands* v. *Fletcher* [31a] applies to personal injuries or only to damage to property.[32] It has been applied to personal injuries [33] and this doubt is probably unfounded.[34] But the basic maxim is *sic utere tuo ut alienum non laedas*, not *alium*,[35] and it might conduce to legal simplicity to restrict the principle to injury to property. " Its place [the *Rylands* v. *Fletcher* principle] as I understand, is in that branch of the law of property which has regard to the rights and liabilities of neighbourhood." [36]

On principle there is no reason for not giving damages under this principle for personal injuries. In the first place it would seem absurd if liability for an explosion or dam-burst causing personal injuries and also damage to property had to be based on one principle—negligence— as regards the injuries and on another, more stringent—strict liability— as regards the damage to property. The law should be at least as solicitous for the protection of the individual's person as for his property. In the second place there is the English authority for the application of the corresponding principle of English law to personal injuries or death.

There is, however, no direct Scottish decision, and at least some dicta against this. In *Paterson* v. *Lindsay* [37] a gardener working in a garden was injured by a stone from a blasting shot fired on adjacent property. The defender was held liable for fault, so that strict liability was not considered, though the sheriff would have given damages even though negligence had not been proved.[38] In *Snedden* v. *Nimmo* [39] a colliery company periodically discharged hot water from boilers into a ditch, and the pursuer's child fell in and was scalded to death. The claim was dismissed as irrelevant, as the pursuer had not averred that the defenders were either proprietors or tenants of the ground traversed by the footpath and no ground of liability arising from ownership or occupancy was disclosed. The pursuer clearly rested his case on fault, but the possibility of strict liability might appropriately have been considered.

In *Reynolds* v. *Lanarkshire Tramways Co.*[40] a passenger on the platform of an electric tramcar, holding on to the rods which supported the roof, averred that he had received an electric shock which threw him off the car and caused him injuries. It was held that he had failed to prove that the shock, though established, was caused by the negligence of the

---

[31a] (1868) L.R. 3 H.L. 330.
[32] *Read* v. *Lyons* [1947] A.C. 156, 171, *per* Lord Macmillan.
[33] *Miles* v. *Forest Rock Granite Co.* (1918) 34 T.L.R. 500; *Shiffman* v. *Order of St. John* [1936] 1 All E.R. 557; *Hale* v. *Jennings Bros.* [1938] 1 All E.R. 579 (the latter two being doubtful cases); *Perry* v. *Kendricks Transport Co.* [1956] 1 W.L.R. 85.
[34] Charlesworth, 258; the *Restatement*, s. 519, recognises liability for harm caused by " ultra-hazardous activity " to " person, land or chattels." *Cf.* Prosser, 536.
[35] As noted in *Read* v. *Lyons* [1947] A.C. 156. This maxim was founded on by Lord President Inglis in *Laurent* v. *Lord Advocate* (1869) 7 M. 607, 610.
[36] *Reynolds* v. *Lanarkshire Tramways Co.* (1908) 16 S.L.T. 230, 232, *per* Lord Dundas.
[37] (1885) 13 R. 261.
[38] Note, at p. 263, citing *Rylands* v. *Fletcher* (1868) L.R. 3 H.L. 330 and a ferocious animal case: *Burton* v. *Moorhead* (1881) 8 R. 892.
[39] (1903) 5 F. 1036.
[40] (1908) 16 S.L.T. 230 (O.H.).

defenders. The *Rylands* v. *Fletcher* principle was prayed in aid, but Lord Dundas thought that its place was in the law of property and inapplicable to the case.

In *McLaughlan* v. *Craig* [41] gas escaped from a service pipe in a tenement of houses and exploded, injuring a tenant and his property, and an attempt was made to saddle the proprietors with liability on the basis of strict liability. This failed on the ground that it was held not to be a case for the application of the principle of strict liability at all [42]; if the proprietors were to have been liable it would have had to be on some ground of negligence. But nothing was said by the court about differentiation between grounds of liability for personal injury and for property damage.

While therefore there is no actual decision, or even clear authority for the view, that strict liability may exist for personal injuries, none of the cases have been appropriate directly to raise the issue for decision and all have been decided on other grounds, leaving intact the general issue of whether, in a case to which the principle of strict liability does apply, it applies equally to personal injuries as to damage to property.

It is submitted that in appropriate circumstances strict liability for personal injuries or death, independently of fault, should be recognised. The circumstances appropriate for application of this principle are that the defender should have brought on to or accumulated on land which he occupied some dangerous substance, such as fire, water or explosives, not naturally there, which imports an obvious risk of harm to persons outside that land if the substance escapes, and that it should have escaped and directly caused personal injuries or death. It has been held in England that a nationalised gas undertaking was not liable under the *Rylands* v. *Fletcher* principle for personal injuries resulting from an escape of gas since it did not collect and distribute the gas " for its own purposes " within the rule of that case.[43] But no doubts were cast on the possibility of such a liability for injuries in an appropriate case.

Conclusions. It is clearly uncertain whether, under some of the heads of strict liability, a pursuer may claim damages for personal injuries without proving wilful or negligent conduct on the part of the defender and the law awaits further elucidation in many respects. But it seems clear that common law liability cannot be restricted to wilful or negligent wrongs. At least in the case of injury by animals there certainly may be strict liability.

---

[41] 1948 S.C. 599.
[42] There was no " escape " from the defender's land to the land of another.
[43] *Dunne* v. *N.W. Gas Board* [1963] 3 All E.R. 916.

CHAPTER 18

STATUTORY LIABILITY FOR CAUSING PHYSICAL INJURY OR DEATH

1. Factories Act
2. Mines and Quarries Act
3. Offices, Shops and Railway Premises Act
4. Agriculture (Safety, Health and Welfare Provisions) Act
5. Merchant Shipping Acts
6. Air Navigation Orders
7. Railways Acts
8. Road Traffic Acts
9. Radioactive Substances Acts
10. Police and Municipal Acts

THE general requisites for the existence of liability to a common law action for damages founded on breach of a statutory duty, alone or conjoined with a claim founded on breach of a common law duty, have already been discussed.[1] The present chapter deals with the leading principles of the main statutes which have been held to impose statutory duties, breaches of which, causing personal injuries or death, have been held to give a civil remedy. Full citation and consideration of the cases decided on sections of particular statutes and regulations must be sought in the textbooks and commentaries on the several bodies of legislation. Even where there has been breach of a statutory duty the pursuer may fail if the breach was not the proximate cause of the injury sustained by him.[2]

Interaction with common law. Unless there are clear words excluding common law liability, liability for breach of a statutory duty intended to protect individuals from personal injuries or death is cumulative with common law liability and not exclusive thereof. Consequently even if there be no breach of statutory duty, the defenders' conduct may amount to breach of common law duty.[3]

1. FACTORIES ACT

The Factories Act, 1961, replacing and extending earlier legislation, makes extensive provisions for, *inter alia*, the health, safety and welfare of persons employed in and about factories. The Act is analysed and

---

[1] *Supra*, Chap. 9. See also Fricke, " Juridical Nature of the Action upon the Statute " (1961) 76 L.Q.R. 240.
[2] *Maxwell* v. *Baird*, 1933 S.L.T. 64. See also *Gardiner* v. *Motherwell Machinery and Scrap Co.*, 1961 S.C.(H.L.) 1; *McWilliams* v. *Sir William Arrol & Co.*, 1962 S.C.(H.L.) 70.
[3] See *e.g., Franklin* v. *Gramophone Co.* [1948] K.B. 542.

annotated in specialised works [4] to which reference must be made. Considerations of space forbid more than general observations on the Act and its interpretation in relation to the law of delict.

" Factory " is extensively defined (s. 175) and the Act must be complied with within the boundaries of every place within the definition. Premises may be a "factory" though incomplete,[5] though only one person is employed,[6] and though entirely in the open air.[7] A canteen,[8] the back room of a shop,[9] and a consulting engineer's premises [10] may be "factories." Premises in which factory machinery is oiled and tested may be part of the factory.[11] A prison workshop is not a factory,[12] nor is a water pumping station.[13]

The Act applies where an injured person has only part of his body within the boundary of the factory and that part is injured by a breach of the Act within the boundary.[14] An earlier Factories Act has been held not to apply to an accident on a British ship while at sea.[15]

A person is " employed in manual labour " for the purposes of the Act if that is the substantial purpose of his employment.[16] He is not " employed " if he is injured while working on a private job after hours.[17]

Enforcement of the Act. Breach of the manifold duties imposed by the Act is punishable by criminal prosecution but in the case of many, but not all, sections of the Act, it has been held that a person injured by reason of the failure to implement the statutory duty has a cause of action based on that failure. All the main provisions designed to ensure health (ss. 1–11), safety from personal injuries, contained in Part II of the Act (ss. 12–56) and welfare (ss. 57–62) give the injured person an action of damages for breach of statutory duty.[18] Certain limited defences are made available to the occupier of a factory by section 161 (3) but

4 See Samuels, *Factory Law* (7th ed.); Redgrave, *Factories, Truck and Shops Acts* (20th ed.); *Encyclopaedia of Factories, Shops and Offices Law and Practice*; See also Munkman, *Employer's Liability* (5th ed.); Mansfield Cooper, *Outlines of Industrial Law* (4th ed.); Samuels, *Industrial Law* (6th ed.); Fridman, *Modern Law of Employment*.

5 *Ward* v. *Coltness Iron Co.*, 1944 S.C. 318; *Barrington* v. *Kent Rivers Catchment Board* [1947] 2 All E.R. 782; *Street* v. *British Electricity Authy.* [1952] 2 Q.B. 399.

6 *Griffith* v. *Ferrier*, 1952 J.C. 56; *McDonald* v. *Ferrier*, 1955 S.L.T. (Notes) 74.

7 *Back* v. *Dick, Kerr & Co.* [1906] A.C. 325. *Cf. Hosking* v. *De Havilland* [1949] 1 All E.R. 540.

8 *Luttman* v. *I.C.I.* [1955] 3 All E.R. 481; contrast *London Co-op Soc.* v. *Southern Essex Assessment Cttee.* [1942] 1 K.B. 53; *King* v. *Magnatex* [1951] C.L.Y. 1382; *Thomas* v. *B.T.H. Co.* [1953] 1 All E.R. 29.

9 *McLeavy* v. *Liptons* [1959] C.L.Y. 1284.

10 *Stanger* v. *Hendon B.C.* [1948] 1 K.B. 571.

11 *Thurogood* v. *Van den Berghs* [1951] 2 K.B. 537.

12 *Pullin* v. *Prison Commrs.* [1957] 3 All E.R. 470.

13 *Longhurst* v. *Guildford, etc., Water Board* [1961] 3 All E.R. 545; contrast *Newton* v. *Stanning* [1962] 1 All E.R. 78.

14 *Hunter* v. *Glenfield and Kennedy*, 1947 S.C. 536.

15 *Collins* v. *Anchor Line*, 1939 S.L.T. 301.

16 *Joyce* v. *Boots Cash Chemists (Southern)* [1950] 2 All E.R. 719.

17 *Napieralski* v. *Curtis* [1959] 2 All E.R. 426.

18 See *e.g.*, *Nicholson* v. *Atlas Steel Foundry*, 1957 S.C. (H.L.) 44 (breach of health section); *John Summers & Sons* v. *Frost* [1955] A.C. 740 (safety section); *Reid* v. *Westfield Paper Co.*, 1957 S.C. 218 (welfare section). Breach of statutory provisions as to *e.g.*, hours of work, will not necessarily give rise to a civil claim.

these afford no defence to a civil claim.[19]   The Act is intended to prevent accidents to workmen and should be construed so as to further that end.[20]

Persons protected.   The provisions of the Factories Act exist to protect everyone who is legitimately on the premises,[21] including an independent contractor's servants,[22] but not a person who is neither " employed " nor " working on the premises." [23]

Whom bound by duties.   The duties imposed by the Act are incumbent on the occupier [24] of the " factory " as the person prima facie liable, though certain sections [25] make the owner liable.   More than one person may be an " occupier " of one premises for different purposes.[26]   An independent contractor working in a factory may be a notional occupier for certain purposes.[27]   Apart from exceptional cases a factory has only one occupier.[28]

The duties of care are not in general imposed on the workman, and even if a duty is so imposed, breach would not necessarily disentitle the workman from suing in respect of the defender's breach.[29]

Standard of duty.   In many cases it has been held that the duty, except in so far as qualified in the Act itself, is an absolute obligation, not to be qualified by considerations of practicability.[30]   Thus in cases based on breach of the duty to fence machinery securely (ss. 12, 13 and 14) the duty is absolute and the only defences are to show that there was in fact no breach of duty or that the workman's own conduct was entirely [31] the cause of the harm.   Similarly the duty to keep a hoist or lift " properly maintained " [32] is absolute and breach is established by proof of the failure of the lift, though unexplained.[33]

In other cases the duty is merely that of taking reasonable care against foreseeable risks.[34]

---

[19] *Riddell* v. *Reid,* 1942 S.C.(H.L.) 51; *Gallagher* v. *Dorman Long & Co., Ltd.* [1947] 2 All E.R. 38; *Harrison* v. *N.C.B.* [1951] A.C. 639, 657.

[20] *Norris* v. *Syndic* [1952] 2 Q.B. 135.

[21] *Kelly* v. *Glebe Sugar Refining Co.* (1893) 20 R. 833; *Ward* v. *Coltness Iron Co.,* 1944 S.C. 318; *cf. Whitby* v. *Burt, Boulton & Hayward, Ltd.* [1947] K.B. 918; *Lavender* v. *Diamints, Ltd.* [1949] 1 K.B. 585; *Massey Harris-Ferguson* v. *Piper* [1956] 2 All E.R. 722; *C.P.Ry.* v. *Bryers* [1958] A.C. 485; contrast *Hartley* v. *Mayoh* [1954] 1 Q.B. 383.

[22] *Kerr* v. *Cook,* 1953 S.L.T.(Notes) 23.

[23] *Napieralski* v. *Curtis* [1959] 2 All E.R. 426.

[24] On the term " occupier " see *Ramsay* v. *Mackie* (1904) 7 F. 106, 109; *Wearings* v. *Kirk & Randall* [1904] 1 K.B. 213; *Turner* v. *Courtaulds* [1937] 1 All E.R. 467; *Wilkinson* v. *Rea* [1941] 1 K.B. 688; *Meigh* v. *Wickenden* [1942] 2 K.B. 160; *Cox* v. *Cutler* [1948] 2 All E.R. 665.

[25] ss. 121–122, 163.

[26] *Rippon* v. *P.L.A.* [1940] 1 K.B. 858.

[27] *Whalley* v. *Briggs Motors* [1954] 2 All E.R. 193.

[28] *Smith* v. *Cammell Laird* [1940] A.C. 242.   [29] *McCafferty* v. *Brown,* 1950 S.C. 300.

[30] *Davies* v. *Owen* [1919] 2 K.B. 39; *Pugh* v. *Manchester Dry Dock Co.* [1954] 1 W.L.R. 389; *Summers* v. *Frost* [1955] A.C. 740.

[31] *e.g., Rushton* v. *Turner Bros. Asbestos Co., Ltd.* [1959] 3 All E.R. 517.

[32] s. 22 (1).

[33] *Millar* v. *Galashiels Gas Co.,* 1949 S.C.(H.L.) 31; *cf. Whitehead* v. *James Stott* [1949] 1 K.B. 358.

[34] *e.g., McCarthy* v. *Daily Mirror Newspapers* [1949] 1 All E.R. 801 (1937, s. 43 = 1961, s. 59); *cf. Barr* v. *Cruickshank* (1958) 74 Sh.Ct.Rep. 218; *Marshall* v. *Babcock & Wilcox,* 1961 S.L.T. 259.

Duties qualified by practicability. In some cases, however, the statutory duty is qualified by " so far as is reasonably practicable." [35] The burden of proving that prevention is not reasonably practicable lies on the factory-occupier.[36] Liability depends on whether the degree of risk outweighs the steps necessary to eliminate the risk.[37] The tendency of earlier cases was to construe the duty of provision and maintenance of safe means of access as a continuing one [38] but it was held in *Levesley* v. *Firth & Brown* [39] that there was no breach of duty where there was a merely transient source of danger. In other cases the duty is to take " all practicable measures," [40] which is a higher duty [41] and involves not only providing safety apparatus but taking energetic measures to see that they are used.[42] The practicability of precautions has to be judged by reference to the state of knowledge at the time, particularly that of the scientific experts.[43] " Practicable " measures impose a stricter standard than " reasonably practicable," [44] and this in turn is a higher standard than " reasonable care " [45]; or the duty may be " except in so far as . . . impracticable." [46]

The principal duties. The principal duties for breach of which an action lies relate to health, safety from accidents, and welfare.

Health. There are duties [47] as to cleanliness,[48] avoidance of overcrowding, the maintenance of temperature and ventilation,[49] lighting and drainage.

Safety. Duties are imposed [50] to fence securely prime movers, transmission machinery and every dangerous part of any machinery, as to lifting apparatus, means of access, means of escape in case of fire and as to other dangers. The seller of the machinery is not liable to an injured person under the Act, nor liable to relieve the factory occupier if a successful claim is made for injury from unfenced machinery.[51]

---

[35] *e.g.*, s. 29 (1) (provision of safe means of access to working places); and see *Sharp* v. *Coltness Iron Co.*, 1937 S.C.(H.L.) 68; *Thomson* v. *Irving*, 1961 S.L.T. 14.
[36] *McCarthy* v. *Coldair* [1951] 2 T.L.R. 1226.
[37] *McCarthy* v. *Coldair* [1951] 2 T.L.R. 1226; *cf. Edwards* v. *N.C.B.* [1949] 1 K.B. 704; *Marshall* v. *Gotham* [1954] A.C. 360.
[38] *Callaghan* v. *Kidd* [1944] K.B. 560; *Alison* v. *Bruce*, 1951 S.L.T. 399.
[39] [1953] 2 All E.R. 866; see also *Latimer* v. *A.E.C.* [1953] A.C. 643; *Thomas* v. *Bristol Aeroplane Co.* [1954] 2 All E.R. 1.
[40] *e.g.*, s. 63 (1); see *Crookall* v. *Vickers-Armstrong* [1955] 2 All E.R. 12; *Gregson* v. *Hicks Hargreaves* [1955] 3 All E.R. 507; *Balfour* v. *Beardmore*, 1956 S.L.T. 205; *Richards* v. *Highway Ironfounders* [1957] 2 All E.R. 162.
[41] *Lee* v. *Nursery Furnishings* [1945] 1 All E.R. 387.
[42] *Crookall* v. *Vickers-Armstrong* [1955] 2 All E.R. 12.
[43] *Adsett* v. *K. and L. Steelfounders* [1953] 2 All E.R. 320; *Richards, supra.*
[44] *Moorcroft* v. *Powells* [1962] 3 All E.R. 741; *Fern* v. *Dundee Corpn.*, 1964 S.L.T. 294.
[45] *Edwards* v. *N.C.B.* [1949] 1 K.B. 704; *Marshall* v. *Gotham* [1954] A.C. 360.
[46] *Buchan* v. *Hutchison*, 1953 S.L.T. 306.
[47] ss. 1–11.
[48] See *Carroll* v. *N.B. Locomotive Co.*, 1957 S.L.T.(Sh.Ct.) 2.
[49] *Ebbs* v. *Whitson* [1952] 2 Q.B. 877; *Nicholson* v. *Atlas Steel Foundry*, 1957 S.C.(H.L.) 44; *Ashwood* v. *Steel Co. of Scotland*, 1957 S.C. 17; *Graham* v. *C.W.S., Ltd.* [1957] 1 All E.R. 654.
[50] ss. 12–56.
[51] *Biddle* v. *Truvox Engineering Co.* [1952] 1 K.B. 101.

Fencing dangerous machinery. Fencing must be completely safe, not merely moderately or reasonably safe [52]; nor is it sufficient that the fencing provided is the best-known type, or the standard type for the kind of machine [53]; and it must give protection against negligence and misuse, ill-advised conduct, frivolity, indolence, folly and recklessness.[54] The test of whether it has been " securely fenced " or not is whether an accident is reasonably foreseeable.[55] The fencing of a transmission belt has been held intended to prevent persons from coming into contact with the machinery, so that there was no breach when a belt broke and an end struck a workman.[56] Nor is the duty of fencing applicable to dangerous machinery made in the factory, but only to machinery used in manufacturing the factory product.[57] Nor does it extend to preventing tools held in the operator's hand coming into contact with the machinery.[58]

In *John Summers & Sons, Ltd.* v. *Frost* [59] the House of Lords held that the obligation to fence securely, except in so far as qualified by the Act itself, is an absolute obligation, not to be qualified by considerations of practicability, so that if dangerous machinery cannot be fenced securely its use is prohibited [60]; that a dangerous part is securely fenced if, and only if, the presence of the fence effectively protects the workman and makes it no longer dangerous within the meaning of that word as used in the section in question; and that a part may be dangerous although it is dangerous only to a careless or inattentive workman.

" *Dangerous* " *machinery.* The test of whether machinery is " dangerous," so as to require fencing is that of reasonable foresight, if, that is, danger may be reasonably anticipated from the use of it without protection.[61] The question of danger is one of fact and much depends on the

---

[52] *Souter* v. *Steel Barrel Co., Ltd.* (1935) 33 L.G.R. 376; *Chasteney* v. *Michael Nairn & Co., Ltd.* [1937] 1 All E.R. 376; *Findlay* v. *Newman, Hender & Co., Ltd.* [1937] 4 All E.R. 58; *Burns* v. *Terry* [1951] 1 K.B. 454.
[53] *Dennistoun* v. *Greenhill* [1944] 2 All E.R. 434.
[54] *Blenkinsop* v. *Ogden* [1898] 1 Q.B. 783; *Pursell* v. *Clement Talbot, Ltd.* (1914) 111 L.T. 827; *Vowles* v. *Armstrong Siddeley Motors, Ltd.* [1938] 4 All E.R. 796; *Wraith* v. *Flexible Metal Co.* [1943] K.B. 24; *Lyon* v. *Don Bros., Buist & Co.*, 1944 J.C.1; *Smith* v. *Chesterfield Co-operative Soc.* [1953] 1 All E.R. 447.
[55] *Burns, supra.*
[56] *Carroll* v. *Barclay*, 1948 S.C.(H.L.) 100. *Cf. Kilgollan* v. *Cooke* [1956] 2 All E.R. 294; *Close* v. *Steel Co. of Wales* [1961] 2 All E.R. 953; *Eaves* v. *Morris Motors* [1961] 2 Q.B.385.
[57] *Parvin* v. *Morton Machine Co.*, 1952 S.C.(H.L.) 9.
[58] *Sparrow* v. *Fairey Aviation Co.* [1962] 3 All E.R. 706.
[59] [1955] A.C. 740.
[60] *Cf. Davies* v. *Owen* [1919] 2 K.B. 39; *Mackay* v. *Ailsa Shipbuilding Co.*, 1945 S.C. 414; *Pugh* v. *Manchester Dry Docks Co.* [1954] 1 All E.R. 600. This seems an unreasonable interpretation: if Parliament wished dangerous machinery of all or any kinds not to be used at all, it could, and should, have prohibited their use expressly. The obligation is surely one to fence securely, consistently with still being able to use the machine, with liability resulting if a workman sustains injury. The result seems to be to impose liability for every accident resulting from the use of the machinery, but in a very clumsy and silly way, and probably to subject to a criminal penalty every time the machine is used, even safely! The statutory pursuit of safety seems designed to drive machinery out of use. And see *Gough* v. *N.C.B.* [1959] 2 All E.R. 164, 169: " Parliament cannot have intended altogether to prevent the winning of coal, and that nothing in the [Mines and Quarries] Act can be read in such a way as to produce this result."
[61] *Hindle* v. *Birtwhistle* [1897] 1 Q.B. 192, 195. *Cf. Hull* v. *Colvilles* [1949] C.L.Y. 4651; *Smithwick* v. *N.C.B.* [1950] 2 K.B. 335; *John Summers & Sons* v. *Frost* [1955] A.C. 740.

circumstances of each case.[62] The fact that an inspector has seen the machine frequently and not required it to be fenced is relevant.[63]

Similarly " safe " requires the elimination of almost all danger: " ' safe ' means safe for all contingencies that may reasonably be foreseen, unlikely as well as likely, possible as well as probable " [64] or " free from any danger which is both appreciable and foreseeable." [65]

The duty to fence dangerous machinery covers machinery used for production, and not machinery being produced in the factory [66]; it has also been interpreted as a duty to keep the workman out of the machinery, not to protect him from parts of material or machinery ejected by the machine.[67] It may, however, be different where such ejection is so common as to be a normal incident.[68] It may be that the duty is only to fence against foreseeable methods of encountering the danger, and not against unforeseeable approaches.[69]

Fencing may be removed when machinery is being repaired, so far as necessary for that purpose.[70] A fence which is insecure or moves so as to cause injury amounts to a failure to fence.[71]

Danger in relation to careless or foolish conduct. When considering whether a particular part of any machinery is or is not dangerous, regard must be had not only to the ordinary course of operations, but to the inadvertent or indolent conduct of the careless or inattentive worker,[72] deliberate misconduct contrary to orders, such as putting a hand into the machine,[73] a workman playing the fool,[74] and any other conduct which is foreseeable. Responsibility extends to everything except conduct of the incalculable individual who does not only what is unlikely or forbidden but what is unforeseeable.

It is no defence to show that the machinery had long been used safely, or that the factory inspector had made no complaint, or that the

---

[62] *Carr* v. *Mercantile Produce, Ltd.* [1949] 2 K.B. 601.

[63] *Mitchell* v. *N.B. Rubber Co.*, 1945 J.C. 69.

[64] *McCarthy* v. *Coldair* [1951] 2 T.L.R. 1226.

[65] *Moodie* v. *Furness Shipbuilding Co.* [1951] 2 Lloyd's Rep. 600, 605. See also *Sheppey* v. *Shaw* [1952] 1 T.L.R. 1272; *Moncrieff* v. *Swan Hunters* [1953] 2 Lloyd's Rep. 149; *Clayton* v. *Russell* [1953] 2 Lloyd's Rep. 692.

[66] *Parvin* v. *Morton Machine Co.*, 1952 S.C.(H.L.) 9.

[67] *Nicholls* v. *Austin* [1946] A.C. 493; *Carroll* v. *Barclay*, 1948 S.C.(H.L.) 100; *Kilgollan* v. *Cooke* [1956] 2 All E.R. 294; *Bullock* v. *Power* [1956] 1 All E.R. 498; *Close* v. *Steel Co. of Wales* [1961] 2 All E.R. 953. Contrast *Hoare* v. *Grazebrook* [1957] 1 All E.R. 470

[68] *Hindle* v. *Birtwistle* [1897] 1 Q.B. 192; *Carroll, supra*; *Dickson* v. *Flack* [1953] 2 Q.B. 464; *cf. Kinder* v. *Camberwell B.C.* [1944] 2 All E.R. 315.

[69] *Burns* v. *Terry & Sons* [1951] 1 K.B. 454.

[70] *Richard Thomas & Baldwins* v. *Cummings* [1955] A.C. 321; see also *Lewis* v. *High Duty Alloys* [1957] 1 All E.R. 740; *Knight* v. *Leamington Spa Courier* [1961] 2 Q.B. 253.

[71] *Rutherford* v. *Glanville* [1958] 1 All E.R. 532.

[72] *Mitchell, supra*; *Trott* v. *Smith* [1957] 3 All E.R. 500; *cf. Blenkinsop* v. *Ogden* [1898] 1 Q.B. 783.

[73] *Chasteney* v. *Michael Nairn & Co.* [1937] 1 All E.R. 376; *Wood* v. *L.C.C.* [1940] 2 K.B. 642 (revd. on another point, [1941] 2 K.B. 232); *Smith* v. *Chesterfield & Dist. Co-operative Soc., Ltd.* [1953] 1 All E.R. 447; *Rushton* v. *Turner Bros.* [1959] 3 All E.R. 517. *Cf. Smithwick* v. *N.C.B.* [1950] 2 K.B. 335. In *Carr* v. *Mercantile Produce Co.* [1949] 2 K.B. 601 (a prosecution for contravention of s. 14 (1)) the finding of fact seems unjustified.

[74] *Cottrell* v. *Vianda S.S. Co.* [1955] 2 Lloyd's Rep. 450.

machinery would not have been dangerous if the employee concerned had obeyed instructions or been careful or attentive.[75] " In considering whether machinery is dangerous, it must not be assumed that everyone will always be careful. A part of a machine is dangerous if it is a possible cause of injury to anybody acting in a way in which a human being may reasonably be expected to act in circumstances which may be reasonably expected to occur." [76]

Lifting apparatus. Similarly the obligation of proper maintenance of a hoist or lift (s. 22 (1)) is absolute, and a breach is inferred by the failure, even for an inexplicable reason, of any part of the apparatus: " maintained " denotes continuance in a state of working efficiency.[77] Other examples of absolute duty are those relating to the safety of lifting tackle.[78]

Floors, stairs and means of access. There is a duty to keep floors, stairs, etc., properly maintained and, so far as reasonably practicable, free from obstruction and from any substance likely to cause persons to slip.[79] In each case the safety of the floor, etc., is a question of degree falling to be decided on the particular facts of the case.[80] There is also a duty, so far as reasonably practicable, to provide and maintain safe means of access to working places.[81]   This is more exacting than the common law standard,[82] but is not breached by the existence of a merely transient source of danger.[83] It is owed not only to employed persons, but to independent contractors, such as window cleaners, and their employees, and to access both outside and inside the premises.[84] It is a continuing duty.[85] There is no breach of duty if a place provides secure foothold in all normal circumstances though a man might be thrown off by a wholly abnormal occurrence.[86] The duty to provide safe means of access covers means of access over a thing being worked upon, such as the deck of a boat under repair.[87]

---

[75] *Sutherland* v. *Jas. Mills, Ltd., Executors* [1938] 1 All E.R. 283; *Mitchell* v. *N.B. Rubber Co.,* 1945 J.C. 69.
[76] *Walker* v. *Bletchley Flittons* [1937] 1 All E.R. 170, 175, *per* du Parcq J.; approved in *John Summers* v. *Frost* [1955] A.C. 740.
[77] *Millar* v. *Galashiels Gas Co.,* 1949 S.C.(H.L.) 31; *cf. Whitehead* v. *James Stott* [1949] 1 K.B. 358.
[78] s. 26; *Reilly* v. *William Beardmore & Co.,* 1947 S.C. 275; *Gledhill* v. *Liverpool Abattoir Utility Co.* [1957] 3 All E.R. 117; *McNeil* v. *Dickson and Mann,* 1957 S.C. 345; *Milne* v. *Wilson,* 1960 S.L.T. 162.
[79] s. 28; see also *Hosking* v. *De Havilland* [1949] 1 All E.R. 540; *Latimer* v. *A.E.C.* [1953] A.C. 643; *Harrison* v. *Metro-Vickers* [1954] 1 All E.R. 404; *Tate* v. *Swan, Hunters* [1958] 1 All E.R. 150; *Newberry* v. *Westwood* [1960] 2 Lloyd's Rep. 37.
[80] *Payne* v. *Weldless Steel Tube Co.* [1956] 1 Q.B. 196.
[81] s. 29. *Ginty* v. *Belmont Building Supplies* [1959] 1 All E.R. 414; as to alternative routes, see *Donovan* v. *Cammell Laird* [1949] 2 All E.R. 92 (no duty where workman chooses other than safe route).   As to visiting the toilet, see *Rose* v. *Colvilles,* 1950 S.L.T.(Notes) 72. See also *Ross* v. *Associated Portland Cement Mfrs.* [1964] 2 All E.R. 452.
[82] *Waters* v. *Rolls-Royce, Ltd.,* 1960 S.L.T.(Notes) 91.
[83] *Levesley* v. *Firth & Brown* [1953] 2 All E.R. 866; *cf. Latimer* v. *A.E.C.* [1953] A.C. 643; *Thomas* v. *Bristol Aeroplane Co.* [1954] 2 All E.R. 1.
[84] *Lavender* v. *Diamints* [1949] 1 K.B. 585. *Cf. Barrie* v. *Carntyne Steel Castings Co.* [1949] C.L.Y. 4650; *Wigley* v. *British Vinegars* [1962] 3 All E.R. 161.
[85] *Alison* v. *Bruce,* 1951 S.L.T. 399.
[86] *Tinto* v. *Stewarts & Lloyds, Ltd.,* 1962 S.L.T. 314.
[87] *Gardiner* v. *Admiralty Commrs.,* 1964 S.L.T. 194.

Boilers and air receivers. Boilers, steam containers and air receivers must be soundly constructed and properly maintained (ss. 32–38). A motor-tyre and wheel is not an " air receiver " within the meaning of these sections.[88]

Welfare provisions. Sections 57 to 62 impose duties in the interests of welfare generally, such as the provision of washing facilities, breach of which may give rise to an action.[89]

Health, safety and welfare (special provisions). Duties are also imposed in relation to particular kinds of factories and processes, including the prevention of impurities in the air [90] and the protection of eyes in certain processes.[91] In this context an employer must keep abreast of discoveries and developments in his industry and take measures to counter what come to be recognised as dangers.[92]

Special applications and extensions of Factories Act. By sections 120 to 132 the Factories Act or parts thereof is applied to various kinds of premises not covered by the definition of " factory," including docks, wharves and warehouses and to work carried out on a ship in a harbour or wet dock.

Dangerous trades regulations. Under section 76 the Minister may certify that any manufacture, machinery, plant, equipment, appliance, process or description of manual labour is dangerous, if satisfied that it involves risk or bodily injury to employees, or any class of them, and may make special regulations in such cases. Many such sets of regulations have been made.[93] Among those which have most often come before the courts are the Building Regulations, the Docks Regulations, the Electricity Regulations, the Shipbuilding Regulations and the Woodworking Machinery Regulations. Many are very far-reaching and in effect provide a code of safety precautions in themselves, and such regulations may

---

[88] *Friel* v. *East Kilbride Dairy Farmers, Ltd.,* 1948 S.L.T.(Notes) 23.

[89] *McCarthy* v. *Daily Mirror* [1949] 1 All E.R. 801; *Reid* v. *Westfield Paper Co.,* 1957 S.C. 218. *Cf. Coote* v. *Eastern Gas Board* [1953] 1 Q.B. 594; *Adsett* v. *K. & L. Steelfounders* [1953] 2 All E.R. 320; *Gardiner* v. *Motherwell Machinery Co.,* 1961 S.C.(H.L.) 1.

[90] s. 63; see *Crookall* v. *Vickers-Armstrong* [1955] 2 All E.R. 12; *Richards* v. *Highways Ironfounders* [1955] 3 All E.R. 205; *Carmichael* v. *Cockburn,* 1955 S.C. 487; *Balfour* v. *Beardmore,* 1956 S.L.T. 205; *Wardlaw* v. *Bonnington Castings,* 1956 S.C.(H.L.) 26; *Quinn* v. *Cameron & Roberton,* 1957 S.C.(H.L.) 22; *Ashwood* v. *Steel Co. of Scotland,* 1957 S.C. 17.

[91] s. 65; see *Finch* v. *Telegraph Construction Co.* [1949] 1 All E.R. 452; *Whalley* v. *Briggs Motor Bodies* [1954] 2 All E.R. 193; *Daniels* v. *Ford Motor Co.* [1955] 1 All E.R. 218; *Nolan* v. *Dental Mfg. Co.* [1958] 2 All E.R. 449. See also *Leighton* v. *Harland & Wolff,* 1953 S.L.T.(Notes) 36; *Hunter* v. *Singer Mfg. Co.,* 1953 S.L.T.(Notes) 85.

[92] *Graham* v. *C.W.S.* [1957] 1 All E.R. 654; *cf. Morton* v. *Dixon,* 1909 S.C. 807. See also *Richards* v. *Highway Ironfounders* [1957] 2 All E.R. 162.

[93] By Sched. 6, para. 2, regulations made under earlier Factories Acts have been continued in force. For a list see Samuels, *Factory Law* (7th ed.).
The text of these regulations can be found in *Factory Orders* (H.M.S.O.) and in the *Encyclopaedia of Factories, Shops and Offices Law and Practice.*

supersede the provision of the Act entirely,[94] or in part.[95] In many cases breach has been held to give a civil action.[96]

Defences—Contracting out. It is impossible to contract out of the Factories Act even where the occupier is contracting with an independent contractor.[97]

Fault of independent contractor. It is generally no defence that the accident was attributable to the fault of an independent contractor employed by the defender.[98]

Latent defect. Where the duty is absolute, it is no defence that the accident was caused by latent defect in the machinery or apparatus concerned.[99] Where the duty is less, such as to do what is practicable, proof that the accident was due to latent defect may be a defence.

Delegation of duty to injured pursuer. In some cases it has been held that an employer could validly delegate, and had delegated, the observance of a statutory duty to the employee who subsequently complained of breach of that statutory duty.[1] The employer cannot delegate merely by employing the person to do the job, nor by telling him to be careful, and there must be clear evidence of delegation, in a respect where it is reasonable and indeed necessary to give the man on the spot some discretion. The defence has accordingly usually failed.[2] The clearest cases for delegation are such as to keep the guard of a power saw adjusted or to move ladders or crawling boards as required.[3] For valid delegation it is essential that the person to whom performance of the duty has been delegated was fully and appropriately qualified to perform it, and that it must be made clear to him that a duty imposed by statute is being delegated to him.[4]

Pursuer's own wilful default. An injured person's claim may be defeated by his own breach of section 143, which prohibits the misuse by employees of things provided under the Act for their health, safety or welfare and requires employees to use appliances provided for these

---

[94] *Miller* v. *Boothman* [1944] 1 All E.R. 333; *Franklin* v. *Gramophone Co.* [1948] 1 K.B. 542.
[95] *Benn* v. *Kamm* [1952] 2 Q.B. 127; *Automatic Woodturning Co.* v. *Stringer* [1957] A.C. 544.
[96] See *e.g., Leeson* v. *Gardner*, 1947 S.L.T. 264; *Grant* v. *Sun Shipping Co.*, 1948 S.C.(H.L.) 73; *Stewart's Exrx.* v. *Clyde Navigation Trs.*, 1946 S.C. 317; *Carvil* v. *Hay*, 1955 S.C. 1 (Docks Regulations); *Riddell* v. *Reid*, 1942 S.C.(H.L.) 51 (Building Regulations).
[97] *Lavender* v. *Diamints* [1949] 1 K.B. 585.
[98] *Hosking* v. *De Havilland* [1949] 1 All E.R. 540; *Dooley* v. *Cammell Laird* [1951] 1 Lloyd's Rep. 271; *Mulready* v. *Bell* [1953] 2 Q.B. 117.
[99] *Whitehead* v. *Stott* [1949] 1 K.B. 358; *Millar* v. *Galashiels Gas Co.*, 1949 S.C.(H.L.) 31. See also *McNeil* v. *Dickson and Mann*, 1957 S.C. 345.
[1] *Smith* v. *Baveystock* [1945] 1 All E.R. 531; *Barcock* v. *Brighton Corpn.* [1949] 1 K.B. 339; *Johnson* v. *Croggan* [1954] 1 All E.R. 121; *Ginty* v. *Belmont Building Supplies, Ltd.* [1959] 1 All E.R. 414.
[2] *Vyner* v. *Waldenberg* [1946] 1 K.B. 50; *Cakebread* v. *Hopping* [1947] 1 K.B. 641; *Gallagher* v. *Dorman Long* [1947] 2 All E.R. 38; *Beal* v. *Gomme* (1949) 65 T.L.R. 543; *Manwaring* v. *Billington* [1952] 2 All E.R. 747; *Davison* v. *Apex Scaffolds* [1956] 1 Q.B. 551; *Jenner* v. *Allen West* [1959] 2 All E.R. 115.
[3] *Gallagher, supra; Beal, supra.*
[4] *Nicolson* v. *Patrick Thomsons, Ltd.*, 1964 S.L.T. 171.

purposes.[5] The duty to do so is absolute.[6] Employed persons further (s. 143 (2)) must not wilfully and without reasonable cause do anything likely to endanger themselves or others. This covers perverse meddling with the apparatus, not mere touching or misplacing something,[7] still less mere mistake on the worker's part.[8]

Similarly it has been held that, even if an employee had been in breach of statutory duty in working at a machine without being fully instructed about it, this would not necessarily have disentitled him from suing in respect of a breach by his employers of that same section.[9]

Contributory negligence. In an action founded on breach of statutory duty the contributory negligence of the injured person is a defence.[10] His claim may accordingly be defeated in whole or in part if his own fault was the sole real cause,[11] or a materially contributing cause,[12] of the accident.

Volenti non fit injuria. This defence is not competent in an action based on breach of statutory duty.[13]

2. MINES AND QUARRIES ACT

The Mines and Quarries Act, 1954, replacing earlier legislation [14] prescribes *inter alia* requirements as to safety, health and welfare of employees in mines [15] and quarries.[16] No provision of the Act, of any order made thereunder or of regulations is to be construed as derogating from any rule of law with respect to the duties owed by masters to their servants (including, in particular, the duty to provide a safe system of working).[17] It has long been settled that breach of the statutory provisions, at least of those designed to protect safety, gives an injured person a civil remedy.[18] The safety provisions are not confined to the avoidance of injury by direct contact with machinery.[19]

[5] *Ginty* v. *Belmont Building Supplies* [1959] 1 All E.R. 414.
[6] *Norris* v. *Syndic Mfg. Co.* [1952] 2 Q.B. 135.
[7] *Charles* v. *Smith* [1954] 1 All E.R. 499. *Cf.* " serious and wilful misconduct " of workman: *George* v. *Glasgow Coal Co.*, 1908 S.C. 846; affd. 1909 S.C.(H.L.) 1. See also *Morris* v. *Boase Spinning Co.* (1895) 22 R. 336.
[8] *Pringle* v. *Grosvenor* (1894) 21 R. 532.
[9] *McCafferty* v. *Brown*, 1950 S.C. 300.
[10] *Caswell* v. *Powell Duffryn* [1940] A.C. 152; *Barnes* v. *Southhook Potteries*, 1947 S.N. 6.
[11] *Manwaring* v. *Billington* [1952] 2 All E.R. 747; *Norris* v. *Moss* [1954] 1 All E.R. 324; *Rushton* v. *Turner* [1959] 3 All E.R. 517.
[12] *Norris* v. *Syndic Mfg. Co.* [1952] 2 Q.B. 135; *Jenner* v. *West* [1959] 2 All E.R. 115; *McMath* v. *Rimmer* [1961] 3 All E.R. 1154.
[13] *Wheeler* v. *New Merton Board Mills* [1933] 2 K.B. 669.
[14] Principally the Coal Mines Act, 1911, the Metalliferous Mines Regulation Acts, 1872–75, the Quarry (Fencing) Act, 1887, and the Quarries Act, 1894. Cases decided under these Acts may still be of value. " Mine " and " quarry " are defined by s. 180.
[15] ss. 22–97.
[16] ss. 108–115.
[17] s. 193.
[18] *Baddeley* v. *Earl Granville* (1887) 19 Q.B.D. 423: *Bett* v. *Dalmeny Oil Co.* (1905) 7 F. 787; *David* v. *Britannic Merthyr Coal Co.* [1909] 2 K.B. 146; *Black* v. *Fife Coal Co.*, 1912 S.C.(H.L.) 33; *M'Mullan* v. *Lochgelly Iron Co.*, 1933 S.C.(H.L.) 64; *Caswell* v. *Powell Duffryn* [1940] A.C. 152. Under earlier legislation no duty was held owed to non-employees: *Sinnerton* v. *Merry & Cuninghame* (1886) 13 R. 1012; *Hamilton* v. *Hermand Oil Co.* (1893) 20 R. 995.　　　　　　　　　　[19] *Boryk* v. *N.C.B.*, 1959 S.C. 1.

Duties under the Act are imposed on the " owners " of mines and quarries, which term includes the Crown and Government departments [20]; the " owner " is the person for the time being entitled to work the mine or quarry, or his contractor.[21]

The owner of a mine or quarry is not absolved from liability to pay damages in respect of a contravention, by a person employed by him, of a provision of the Act, of an order made thereunder or of regulations, or a requirement imposed by a notice served under the Act by an inspector, by reason only that the provision contravened expressly imposed on that person a duty or requirement or expressly prohibited that person from doing a specified Act.[22] This apparently imposes liability both personal and vicarious on owners for breaches of statutory duty.[23]

Standard of duty. The duty imposed by some sections of the 1954 Act is absolute and continuing, in which case the owner is liable on proof of injury caused by breach of duty.[24] " The word ' absolute ' in this connexion has become part of the dictionary of the law. Sometimes the word ' continuing ' is substituted for it. Either word means that, in effect, the employer warrants that the machine or other equipment which he is obliged to maintain will never be out of order." [25] But under other sections it is less: under section 48 (duty to keep the roof secure), it is a duty to take all such steps as care, skill and experience may suggest as necessary for keeping it secure, and if, despite such steps, the roof falls, there is no breach of duty.[26] Machinery is " dangerous " if it may reasonably be foreseen to be a source of injury to persons in the vicinity.[27]

Defence of impracticability. It is a defence to an action of damages, in so far as based on a contravention of a provision of the Act, an order thereunder or regulations, or a requirement imposed by a notice served by an inspector, or a condition attached to an exemption, consent, approval or authority granted by the Minister or an inspector, to prove that it was impracticable to avoid or prevent the contravention.[28] " Impracticable " seems to connote a more limited defence than " not reasonably practicable " under the Coal Mines Act, 1911, s. 102 (8), and a more objective standard.[29] It is much more than merely extremely

---

[20] s. 179; *cf. McLaughlan* v. *N.C.B.*, 1953 S.L.T.(Notes) 31.

[21] s. 181.

[22] s. 159. *Cf. Alford* v. *N.C.B.*, 1952 S.C.(H.L.) 17.

[23] It accordingly supersedes such cases as *Harrison* v. *N.C.B.* [1951] A.C. 639.

[24] s. 81 (1)—duty of properly maintaining all parts and working gear of mining machinery: *Hamilton* v. *N.C.B.*, 1960 S.C.(H.L.) 1. *Cf. Edwards* v. *N.C.B.* [1949] 1 K.B. 704, security of travelling roads (1911 Act); *Close* v. *N.C.B.*, 1951 S.C. 578; *Walsh* v. *N.C.B.* [1955] 3 All E.R. 632; see also *Grant* v. *N.C.B.*, 1956 S.C.(H.L.) 48.

[25] *Hamilton, supra*, 6, *per* Viscount Simonds.

[26] *Mazs* v. *N.C.B.*, 1958 S.C. 6; *Brown* v. *N.C.B.* [1962] A.C. 574.

[27] *Smithwick* v. *N.C.B.* [1950] 2 K.B. 335.

[28] s. 157.

[29] On impracticability, see *Marshall* v. *Gotham Co.* [1952] 2 All E.R. 1044; *Jackson* v. *N.C.B.* [1955] 1 All E.R. 145; *Lomax* v. *Beckermet Mining Co.* [1960] C.L.Y. 1998; *Morris* v. *N.C.B.* [1963] 3 All E.R. 644.

inconvenient,[30] but less than impossible.[31] The onus of establishing the defence is on the owners, and the burden is a heavy one; the owners must explain in detail what they did and show why the Act could not be complied with.[32] If the duty was imposed on a subordinate, such as an agent, the owners must prove that it was impracticable for him to avoid or prevent the contravention.[33]

The defence (under the 1911 Act) succeeded in *Sharp* v. *Coltness Iron Co.*,[34] where machinery was exposed for a brief period while being tested after repair, in *Marshall* v. *Gotham Co., Ltd.*,[35] where the roof of a gypsum mine collapsed owing to a rare geological fault, in *Jackson* v. *N.C.B.*,[36] where pit props were dislodged by an abnormal explosion, and in *Burns* v. *N.C.B.*[37] It is doubtful whether the same decisions would be arrived at under the 1954 Act in view of the changed wording. More frequently the defence has failed.[38]

3. OFFICES, SHOPS AND RAILWAY PREMISES ACT

The Offices, Shops and Railway Premises Act, 1963, establishes standards for the health, safety and welfare of employees in those kinds of premises [39] very similar to those laid down by the Factories Act, 1961. There is power under many sections to make regulations.[40] It is accordingly probably safe to infer that breach of the requirements of the Act will give rise to liability in damages, quite apart from criminal liability. The duty of securing compliance is generally upon the occupier of the premises,[41] but where buildings are owned by one and parts let to others,[42] or owned in parts by different persons,[43] the responsibility in respect of common parts and the sanitary conveniences and washing facilities rests on the owner of the building or part of the building concerned rather than on the occupier.[42] Parts of the Act bind the Crown.[44]

The Minister of Labour or the local authority having power to enforce the Act may grant certain limited exemptions from the operation of the Act. Enforcement is by the local authority, save that local authority and certain other public premises are the responsibility of the factory inspectorate, while fire provisions come under the local fire authority.[45]

30 *Cf. Murray* v. *Merry & Cuninghame* (1890) 17 R. 815.
31 *Jayne* v. *N.C.B.* [1963] 2 All E.R. 220.
32 *Crane* v. *William Baird & Co.*, 1935 S.C. 715; *Edwards* v. *N.C.B.* [1949] 1 K.B. 704.
33 *Cf. Crane, supra; Yelland* v. *Powell Duffryn* [1941] 1 K.B. 154.
34 1937 S.C.(H.L.) 68; see also *Park* v. *Wilsons and Clyde Coal Co.*, 1928 S.C. 121 (not adverted to in 1929 S.C.(H.L.) 38).   35 [1954] A.C. 360.
36 [1955] 1 All E.R. 145.
37 1957 S.C. 239: see also *Mullen* v. *N.C.B.*, 1957 S.C. 202.
38 *e.g. Bain* v. *Fife Coal Co.*, 1935 S.C. 681; *Crane* v. *William Baird & Co.*, 1935 S.C. 715; *Caulfield* v. *Pickup, Ltd.* [1941] 2 All E.R. 510; *Edwards* v. *N.C.B.* [1949] 1 K.B. 704; *Gough* v. *N.C.B.* [1959] A.C. 698.
39 All as defined in s. 1, but subject to the exceptions in ss. 2 and 3.
40 See particular s. 20.
41 s. 63.
42 s. 42.
43 s. 43.
44 s. 83.
45 s. 52.

The standard of the duty imposed by the Act would appear to vary, but, on the analogy of cases under the Factories Act, may be absolute in some cases.[46] In some cases the duty is the qualified one of taking steps " so far as is reasonably practicable." [47]

By s. 67 it is a defence to a criminal charge under the Act to prove that the person used all due diligence to secure compliance with the provision of the Act or regulations thereunder which is charged. But this will be no defence to an action for damages, unless the injured employee himself caused the breach of statutory duty and was injured in consequence.[48]

4. AGRICULTURE (SAFETY, HEALTH AND WELFARE PROVISIONS) ACT

The Agriculture (Safety, Health and Welfare Provisions) Act, 1956, empowers provision by regulations for the protection of workers employed in agriculture against risks of bodily injury or injury to health arising out of a wide range of circumstances. The Act applies to persons working on agricultural holdings and there is power (s. 19) to exclude the operation of certain provisions of the Factories Acts, in whole or in part, from specified agricultural premises. Contravention of the regulations is an offence but regulations intended to protect workers' safety or health are probably not exclusive of a civil remedy in addition. It is a defence (s. 16) for a person charged with a contravention of a provision of the Act or of regulations thereunder to prove that he used all due diligence to secure compliance with that provision. Thus a boy whose foot was trapped when pushing a sheaf into the aperture of a threshing machine was held entitled to recover.[49] The Agriculture (Poisonous Substances) Act, 1952, also contains provisions designed to protect the health of farm-workers.

5. MERCHANT SHIPPING ACTS

Provisions for ensuring the safety and health of persons employed on merchant ships is made in the Merchant Shipping Acts, 1894 to 1964, and regulations made thereunder.[50] These fall under the general headings of safety provisions applicable to all ships, provisions enacted in the interest of the crew and special provisions as to passengers and emigrant ships (the last category not being here relevant).

General safety precautions. It is an offence to send to sea a British ship " in such an unseaworthy state that the life of any person is likely

---

[46] e.g., ss. 16, 17.
[47] e.g., ss. 6 (3), 16 (1), and cf. Hall v. Fairfield Shipbuilding Co., 1963 S.L.T. 37.
[48] Gallagher v. Dorman Long & Co., Ltd. [1947] 2 All E.R. 38.
[49] Holdman v. Hamlyn [1943] K.B. 664: cf., Jones v. Richards [1955] 1 All E.R. 463 (under Threshing Machines Act, 1878, repealed by 1956 Act).
[50] See Temperley's Merchant Shipping Acts (6th ed.) 1963.

to be thereby endangered.[51] It is a defence if the shipowner was ignorant of the unseaworthy state of the vessel and had used all reasonable means to make and keep her seaworthy.[52] " Unseaworthy " for these purposes connotes the unfitness of the vessel to encounter the ordinary perils of the sea.

There is an implied obligation in every contract of service with a seaman that the owner, master and every agent charged with the loading of the ship, or the preparing of the ship for sea, or the sending of the ship to sea, shall use all reasonable means to ensure the seaworthiness [53] of the ship for the voyage at the time when the voyage commences, and to keep her in a seaworthy condition for the voyage during the voyage.[54]

No ship may go to sea without a certificate of safety.[55]

The Merchant Shipping (Safety Convention) Act, 1949, and the Merchant Shipping Act, 1964, make applicable to British ships the safety requirements of the International Conventions for the Safety of Life at Sea, of which the 1960 one came into force in May, 1965.

Health of crew. Statutory provision is made with regard to accommodation on board ship, the carrying of provisions, water and medical supplies.[56] An action lies at the instance of a seaman against the owners for injury arising from failure to provide a sufficient supply of medicines.[57]

Statutory provision is made for the marking of load lines and the prevention of overloading, for the provision of boats and life-saving appliances, signals and lights, and for the prevention of collisions at sea.[58] In addition members of the crew might have a claim against the shipowners if injury or damage is caused them by the misconduct or incompetency of a certificated officer.

6. AIR NAVIGATION

Statutory provisions [59] in general prohibit the flying of aircraft registered in or within the United Kingdom unless there is in force in respect of it a certificate of airworthiness, and for any public transport aircraft to fly unless a certificate of safety is in force.[60] Breach of such provisions may give a right of action for damages.[61] But the liability of carriers by air to passengers, or to persons not in the aircraft are mainly regulated by the Carriage by Air Act, 1961, and the Civil Aviation Act, 1949.

[51] M.S.A., 1894, s. 457.
[52] *R.* v. *Freeman* (1875) I.R. 9 C.L. 527, 532.
[53] On this see *Hedley* v. *Pinkey & Sons S.S. Co.* [1894] A.C. 222; *Gillies* v. *Cairns* (1905) 8 F. 174; *McLeod* v. *Hastie*, 1936 S.C. 501.
[54] M.S.A. 1894, s. 458. See *Waddle* v. *Wallsend Shipping Co., Ltd.* [1952] 2 Lloyd's Rep. 105.
[55] M.S.A., 1949, s. 12.
[56] M.S.A., 1894, ss. 198–210.
[57] *Couch* v. *Steel* (1854) 3 E. & B. 402.
[58] M.S.A., 1894, ss. 418–424; 427–450.
[59] Air Navigation Order, 1960, Arts. 10, 66.
[60] *Ibid.* Art. 15.
[61] *Cf. Dominion Air Lines, Ltd.* v. *Strand* [1933] N.Z.L.R. 1; *Hesketh* v. *Liverpool Corpn.* [1940] 4 All E.R. 429.

7. RAILWAYS ACTS

Safety on some railway premises is dealt with by the Offices, Shops and Railway Premises Act, 1963. The Prevention of Accidents Rules 1902, made pursuant to the Railway Employment (Prevention of Accidents) Act, 1900, imposes duties of care, particularly for the benefit of men working on the permanent way, such as to provide adequate lookout and warning of oncoming traffic.[62] The obligations of at least part of the rules are absolute.[63]

8. ROAD TRAFFIC ACTS

Legislation regulating road traffic is normally framed in terms *ex facie* importing only criminal liability for breach. But some provisions have been held to confer a civil right of action if breached, while others have been held to impose public duties only. The former category includes running down a pedestrian on a controlled crossing,[64] and permitting another to drive while uninsured.[65]

The latter class includes: selling a car with defective brakes [66]; failing to have a rear light on a car lit [67]; having a vehicle not properly maintained [68]; having tyres not properly maintained [69]; obtaining a driving licence without disclosing a physical defect [70]; failure to insure [71]; driving in excess of the speed limit [72]; while holding a provisional licence, driving unaccompanied and causing an accident.[73]

Failure to conform to the requirements of the Highway Code is not breach of statutory duty, though such failure may be relied upon as tending to establish civil liability.[74]

9. RADIOACTIVE SUBSTANCES ACTS

The U.K. Atomic Energy Authority is under a statutory duty to ensure that no ionising radiations from anything on any premises occupied by them, or from any waste discharged (in whatever form) on or from any premises occupied by them, cause any hurt to any person or any damage

---

[62] See *e.g. Thomson v. Baird* (1903) 6 F. 142; *Ferguson v. N.B.Ry.*, 1915 S.C. 566; *Vincent v. S.Ry.* [1927] A.C. 430; *Hutchinson v. L.N.E.Ry.* [1942] 1 K.B. 481; *Redpath v. L.N.E. Ry.*, 1944 S.C. 154; *L.N.E.Ry. v. Berriman* [1946] A.C. 278; *Dyer v. S.Ry.* [1948] 1 K.B. 608; *Judson v. B.T.C.* [1954] 1 All E.R. 624; *Reilly v. B.T.C.* [1956] 3 All E.R. 857; *Cade v. B.T.C.* [1958] 2 All E.R. 615.
[63] *Vincent, supra; Redpath, supra.*
[64] *L.P.T.B. v. Upson* [1949] A.C. 155.
[65] *Monk v. Warbey* [1935] 1 K.B. 75; *Houston v. Buchanan*, 1940 S.C.(H.L.) 17. *Cf. Corfield v. Groves* [1950] 1 All E.R. 488.
[66] *Badham v. Lambs* [1946] K.B. 45.
[67] *Clarke v. Brims* [1947] K.B. 497; *West v. Lawson*, 1949 S.C. 430.
[68] *Winter v. Cardiff R.D.C.* [1950] 1 All E.R. 819.
[69] *Barkway v. S. Wales Transport Co.* [1950] A.C. 185.
[70] *Balmer v. Hayes*, 1950 S.C. 477.
[71] *Fleming v. McGillivray*, 1946 S.C. 1.
[72] *Barna v. Hudes Merchandising Corpn.* (1962) 106 S.J. 194.
[73] *Verney v. Wilkins* (1962) 106 S.J. 879.
[74] R.T.A., 1960, s. 74. On the duties to obey " Halt " and " Slow " signs see *Anderson v. St. Andrew's Ambulance Association*, 1943 S.C. 248.

to any property, whether he or it is on any such premises or elsewhere.[75] This appears to be a completely absolute obligation. The Authority may grant nuclear site licences to persons to instal and operate plants using atomic energy, and such persons shall [76] ensure that no ionising radiations cause any hurt to any person or any damage to any property whether that person or property is on the site or elsewhere. The licensee must [77] make provision, by insurance or otherwise, for sufficient funds to be available to ensure that all claims established against the licensee are satisfied up to prescribed amounts. The disposal of radioactive waste is also regulated by statute.[78] Whether any of these provisions give rise to civil liability is undecided.

10. POLICE AND MUNICIPAL ACTS

Numerous statutory duties are imposed by the Burgh Police Acts and the local legislation of particular burghs; some of these, particularly duties in relation to pavements and lighting common stairs, have been prayed in aid in cases arising from accidents on such premises.

Lighting of common stairs. The duty imposed by the Burgh Police (Scotland) Act, 1892, s. 104, on the owners of common stairs to supply and maintain means of lighting them under penalty, if broken, confers a civil right of action.[79] Where the duty is on the local authority under s. 105, it is liable for injuries attributable to its failure to implement its duties.[80]

So, too, property owners and local authorities have been held liable for failure to implement statutory obligations, under private Acts, to light common stairs.[81]

Lighting of streets. Local legislation commonly imposes statutory duties to light streets; such an obligation has been held not to be absolute but only to do all that is reasonably possible to maintain the lighting.[82]

Drainage of streets. Local authorities are frequently also under statutory duty to provide drainage. This has been held to be an absolute duty to provide effective drainage with consequent liability in damages for harm done to property by overflow and, doubtless, also for personal injury.[83]

[75] Atomic Energy Authority Act, 1954, s. 5 (3).
[76] Nuclear Installations (Licensing and Insurance) Act, 1959, s. 4; as to government departments, see s. 9.
[77] *Ibid.*, s. 5 (1). But see now Nuclear Installations (Amendment) Act, 1965.
[78] Radioactive Substances Act, 1960.
[79] *Byrne* v. *Tindal's Exrx.*, 1950 S.C. 216.
[80] *Driscoll* v. *Partick Burgh Commrs.* (1900) 2 F. 368, 370 *per* L.O. Kincairney, approved in *Baikie* v. *Glasgow Corpn.*, 1919 S.C.(H.L.) 13; see also *Jackson* v. *Glasgow Corpn.*, 1928 S.C. 37.
[81] *Gaunt* v. *McIntyre*, 1914 S.C. 43; *Gemmell* v. *Glasgow Corpn.*, 1945 S.C. 287; *Ghannan* v. *Glasgow Corpn.*, 1950 S.C. 23; contrast *Hutson* v. *Edinburgh Corpn.*, 1948 S.C. 668. *Caldwell* v. *Glasgow Corpn.*, 1920 S.C. 242, and *Jackson* v. *Glasgow Corpn.*, 1928 S.C. 37, depend mainly on emergency conditions.
[82] *Keogh* v. *Edinburgh Mags.*, 1926 S.C. 814.
[83] *Hanley* v. *Edinburgh Mags.*, 1913 S.C.(H.L.) 27 (local Act); *St. George Cooperative Soc.* v. *Glasgow Corpn.*, 1921 S.C. 872 (Local Act and Public Health Acts); *Brownlie* v. *Barrhead Mags.*, 1925 S.C.(H.L.) 41 (Burgh Police Act).

Paving of streets and pavements. It is frequently a difficult question of interpretation to say whether sections of public general or of local legislation have imposed actionable statutory duties on local authorities or on frontagers to make and maintain safe the surface of roads and pavements, and precisely what these duties are. Under the Burgh Police Act, 1892, where a local authority has taken over a pavement it alone is responsible for its maintenance and repair.[84] Most cases, however, have turned on the terms of local Acts. Thus it has been held that a town council has been put in statutory possession of a pavement so as to be liable for its dangerous condition [85]; in other circumstances that the local authority had a statutory duty to call on the owners of a pavement not owned by it to remedy a defect therein [86]; again, it has been held that a local authority had control of the pavements of public streets though these had not been taken over by the authority and were accordingly liable for breach of a statutory duty to keep them in proper repair.[87]

A local authority has been held liable where it had failed to give the frontagers notice to remedy a defect [88] and where it had failed to make such adequate inspection of the pavements as would have disclosed a danger.[89]

Even the owner of a private street, habitually used by the public, may be under a statutory duty to make the roadway safe for public use or to prevent the public from using it.[90]

A local authority's statutory power to require the proprietor of land adjoining a street to repair the footpath, when it is private, has been held mandatory and implying a duty of inspection, with liability for failure to do so.[91] On the other hand a statutory power to require the proprietor of a tenement to repair a drain in the back court thereof has been held to be no more than permissive and not to imply any duty of systematic inspection on the local authority.[92]

Other provisions. In *Pullar* v. *Window Clean, Ltd.*[93] it was held that breach of a statutory duty to construct windows so that they could be cleaned from the inside gave no right of action to an injured window-cleaner.

---

[84] *Mitchell* v. *Watt*, 1935 S.C. 104. *Cf.* as to street, *Carson* v. *Kirkcaldy Mags.* (1901) 4 F. 18. See also *Taylor* v. *Saltcoats Mags.*, 1912 S.C. 880.
[85] *Laurie* v. *Aberdeen Mags.*, 1911 S.C. 1226; *Laing* v. *Paull & Williamsons*, 1912 S.C. 196; *Gray* v. *Glasgow Corpn.*, 1915, 2 S.L.T. 203; *Buchanan* v. *Glasgow Corpn.*, 1923 S.C. 782; *Chalmers* v. *Glasgow Corpn.*, 1924 S.L.T. 54.
[86] *Higgins* v. *Glasgow Corpn.*, 1920, 2 S.L.T. 71, on which see *Monaghan* v. *Glasgow Corpn.*, 1955 S.C. 80; *cf. Christie* v. *Glasgow Corpn.* (1899) 7 S.L.T. 27.
[87] *Keenan* v. *Glasgow Corpn.*, 1923 S.C. 611; *Kinnell* v. *Glasgow Corpn.*, 1950 S.C. 573. *Cf. Boyle* v. *Glasgow Corpn.*, 1937 S.N. 1.
[88] *Armour* v. *Glasgow Corpn.*, 1959 S.C. 197.
[89] *Rush* v. *Glasgow Corpn.*, 1947 S.C. 580.
[90] *Carson* v. *Kirkcaldy Mags.* (1901) 4 F. 18.
[91] *Black* v. *Glasgow Corpn.*, 1958 S.C. 260 (sequel 1959 S.C. 188).
[92] *Monaghan* v. *Glasgow Corpn.*, 1955 S.C. 80.
[93] 1956 S.C. 13.

Under the Burgh Police Act, 1892, as modified, a person who fell on packed snow and ice on the pavement of a classified road in a small burgh has been held to have a right of action against the county council as highway authority,[94] and persons injured by the fall of a racecourse stand have been held entitled to sue the local authority for having failed to inspect the stand.[95]

[94] *Thomson* v. *Angus C.C.*, 1958 S.L.T. 208.
[95] *Adair* v. *Paisley Mags.* (1904) 12 S.L.T. 105; *Phin* v. *Paisley Mags.* (1904) 12 S.L.T. 109.

CHAPTER 19

INFRINGEMENTS OF THE INTEREST IN MENTAL INTEGRITY

1. Nervous Shock caused Deliberately
2. Nervous Shock caused Negligently
3. Death caused by Shock

MANY of the kinds of conduct which may harm a person physically may in addition, or alternatively, injure his nervous system, sensibilities or mental health. It was recognised much later than in the case of physical injury that the individual had legal interests in his mental integrity as much as in his physical integrity which deserved recognition and protection, and that claims on the ground of nervous shock and disturbance alone were competent,[1] though difficulties of proof were greater than in the case of purely physical lesions, which are normally more visible and more readily evaluated as injuries. The first cases recognised were where physical injury was done but damages were allowed also for shock and fright caused incidentally thereto.[2] Only later were damages given for shock without physical lesion. " Physical impact or lesion is not a necessary element in the case of recovery of damage in ordinary cases of tort." [3]

" The crude view that the law should take cognisance only of physical injury resulting from actual impact has been discarded, and it is now well recognised that an action will lie for injury by shock sustained through the medium of the eye or the ear without direct contact. The distinction between mental shock and bodily injury was never a scientific one, for mental shock is presumably in all cases the result of, or at least accompanied by, some physical disturbance in the sufferer's system. And a mental shock may have consequences more serious than those resulting from physical impact. But in the case of mental shock there are elements of greater subtlety than in the case of an ordinary physical injury, and these elements may give rise to debate as to the precise scope of legal liability." [4]

---

[1] The competency of claims founded only on shock without physical impact or lesion was probably settled only in *Brown* v. *John Watson, Ltd.*, 1914 S.C.(H.L.) 44, where the contrary view of the Privy Council in *Victorian Ry. Commrs.* v. *Coultas* (1888) 13 App.Cas. 222 was declared no longer of guiding authority. See also Parry, " Nervous Shock as a Cause of Action in Tort " (1926) 41 L.Q.R. 297.

[2] *e.g., Dulieu* v. *White* [1901] 2 K.B. 669.

[3] *Brown, supra,* 51, *per* Lord Shaw.

[4] *Bourhill* v. *Young* 1942 S.C.(H.L.) 78, 87, *per* Lord Macmillan. See also Magruder, " Mental and Emotional Disturbances in the Law of Torts " (1936) 49 H.L.R. 1033. Prosser, "Intentional Infliction of Mental Suffering: A New Tort " (1939) 37 Mich.L.R. 874.

1. NERVOUS SHOCK CAUSED DELIBERATELY

A person who without legal justification intentionally causes fright, nervous injury or emotional distress to another, or who intentionally acts in such a way that nervous injury is a foreseeable or natural and probable consequence, is liable for the distress and bodily harm directly resulting from his conduct. Similarly it is an assault to confront a person with express or implied threats of violence.[5] This principle can be justified as a development of the *actio injuriarum*; it is as much actionable deliberately to shock a person as to affront or insult or assault him physically.

In *Wilkinson* v. *Downton*[6] the defendant, in the execution of what he seems to have regarded as a joke, falsely represented to the plaintiff that he was charged by her husband with a message to the effect that her husband had suffered an accident, had had both legs broken, and that she was to go to bring him home. The plaintiff suffered a violent shock to her nervous system, producing vomiting and other more serious and permanent physical consequences, at one time threatening her reason, and entailing weeks of suffering and incapacity. She was held entitled to recover on the ground that the defendant had " wilfully done an act calculated to cause physical harm to the plaintiff—that is to say, to infringe her legal right to personal safety, and had in fact thereby caused physical harm to her . . . This wilful *injuria* is in law malicious, although no malicious purpose to cause the harm which was caused nor any motive of spite is imputed to the defendant." [7]

In *A.* v. *B.'s Trustees*[8] a lodger committed suicide in furnished lodgings and this caused nervous shock and severe upset to the landlady. The decision that she had a cause of action against the lodger's trustees turned partly on breach of an implied term of contract, but can be justified on the principle of the *actio injuriarum*; the authorities cited were mainly cases of negligent causation of nervous shock.

Similarly in *Janvier* v. *Sweeney*[9] a private detective made false statements to a woman in order to obtain some letters from her; the plaintiff claimed to have sustained a severe shock and resulting neurasthenia, and was held entitled to recover.

Shock to feelings by unauthorised post-mortem examination of relative. It has been accepted that, if a defender has caused hurt feelings by conducting an unauthorised post-mortem examination of a deceased person, he is liable to the relatives of the deceased *in solatium* for their hurt feelings.[10] The unauthorised retention of organs of the body examined is another and more serious wrong.[11] In *Pollok*[10] it was said

---

[5] Bankton, I, 10, 22.
[6] [1897] 2 Q.B. 57.
[7] *Ibid. per* Wright J.
[8] (1906) 13 S.L.T. 830.
[9] [1919] 2 K.B. 316.
[10] *Pollok* v. *Workman* (1900) 2 F. 354; *Conway* v. *Dalziel* (1901) 3 F. 918; *Hughes* v. *Robertson*, 1913 S.C. 394.
[11] *Conway, supra*, 922.

in argument that the action was of the nature of an action of assythment, which is possibly correct.

In *Pollok* [10] the question of title to sue was raised and the action was dismissed on the ground that all the parties interested in the claim should sue in the one action, which is consistent with the view that this is a kind of action of assythment.[12]   But this right of action could equally, or better, be sustained on the ground that this is an *actio injuriarum*, for affront, shock and hurt feelings to the surviving relatives. The question of what relatives are entitled to sue for this wrong is uncertain, whether those entitled to pursue an assythment,[13] or those entitled to pursue an *actio utilis legis Aquiliae* for the death of a relative,[13] or some other group.

Other cases of shock by deliberate affront. In view of the generality of the *actio injuriarum* other sets of circumstances may yet be recognised as justifying reparation, if substantial shock has been caused deliberately or in circumstances where that is a natural and probable consequence of what has been deliberately done.[14]   Many kinds of practical jokes could thus be actionable. So, too, could insults or abuse or affronts, if causing the requisite degree of shock to the nervous system.[15]

2. NERVOUS SHOCK CAUSED NEGLIGENTLY

The view was formerly held that " damage arising from mere sudden terror unaccompanied by any actual physical injury but occasioning a nervous or mental shock " could not be considered a natural consequence of negligent conduct and was therefore too remote to justify liability,[16] but " the case [16] can no longer be treated as a decision of guiding authority " [17] and it is now recognised that there may be liability for shock caused negligently without any physical impact or lesion.[18] It is probable now that any kind of conduct which would have given rise to liability if it had caused physical injury will equally give rise to liability if it causes nervous shock. There is now recognised, that is, a duty to take reasonable care not to cause shock to persons within the ambit of the duty, as much as a duty not to cause physical injury.[19] The factors to be considered in determining liability are the same in each case. " On principle, the distinction between cases of physical impact or lesion being

---

[12] Following *Darling* v. *Gray* (1892) 19 R.(H.R.) 31, a decision on title to sue in the extended *actio legis Aquiliae* for the death of a relative, on which see Chap. 22.

[13] See Chap. 22, *infra.*

[14] The activities of the resurrectionists might have been actionable under this principle.

[15] *Cf. Finburgh* v. *Moss's Empires, Ltd.*, 1908 S.C. 928 (woman shocked by being wrongly called a prostitute and ejected from theatre; held actionable as slander).

[16] *Victorian Ry. Commrs.* v. *Coultas* (1888) 13 App.Cas. 222 (P.C.)

[17] *Brown* v. *John Watson, Ltd.*, 1914 S.C. (H.L.) 44; *cf. Pugh* v. *L.B.S.C.Ry.* [1896] 2 Q.B. 248; *Dulieu* v. *White* [1901] 2 K.B. 669; *Cooper* v. *Caledonian Ry.* (1902) 4 F. 880; *Bell* v. *G.N.Ry. of Ireland* (1890) 26 L.R. Ir. 428.

[18] *Bourhill* v. *Young*, 1942 S.C.(H.L.) 78.

[19] *Hambrook* v. *Stokes* [1925] 1 K.B. 141, 158, *per* Atkin L.J. See also Prosser, 346; Havard, " Reasonable Foresight of Nervous Shock " (1956) 19 M.L.R. 478.

necessary as a ground of liability for damage caused seems to have nothing in its favour—always on the footing that the causal connection between the injury and the occurrence is established. If compensation is to be recovered under the statute [20] or at common law in respect of an occurrence which has caused dislocation of a limb, on what principle can it be denied if the same occurrence has caused unhinging of the mind? " [21]

What kinds of mental shocks are actionable. Liability does not exist for any of the numerous but transitory and trivial emotional shocks and frights to which individuals are subjected in daily life, as by hearing a sudden loud noise [22] or realisation of a narrow escape from accident. To justify liability the shock must be substantial in degree and effect and cause mental upset or disturbance to the nervous system persisting well after the immediate incident which provoked it has passed, " an actual physical disorder of the nervous constitution of the body, producing in consciousness an intellectual or emotional stress, and resulting, or capable of resulting, in incapacity in varying degree." [23] " When the term ' shock ' is used in [cases] it is not in the sense of mental reaction but in a medical sense as the equivalent of nervous shock." [24] In *Auld* v. *Barony Parish* [25] defenders were held not liable when a boarded-out lunatic frightened a child, though the decision did not turn on the triviality of the shock. Annoyance and discomfort are also insufficient to found a claim.[26]

Nervous shock as well as physical lesion. It is quite clear that if by the defender's fault a pursuer is caused physical injury, damages can be claimed for nervous shock accompanying or following on the physical injury, subject to the ordinary limitations imposed by the principles of remoteness of injury and remoteness of damage.

Physical lesion unnecessary. It is now settled that a pursuer has a good ground of action if he suffers shock, *i.e.*, material disturbance of the functioning of the nervous system, even without any physical injury, from a happening, such as a vehicle accident. " It is now quite clearly and definitely settled that shock may be good ground of action, even where the pursuer is unable to aver any outward physical or visible hurt." [27] The question is usually whether the pursuer in such a case was within the ambit of the duty of care.[27a]

Duty affected by relationship of parties. Some cases [28] suggest that criteria may differ according as the pursuer was shocked in the safety of

[20] This was a Workmen's Compensation case.
[21] *Brown* v. *John Watson, Ltd.*, 1914 S.C.(H.L.) 44, 51, *per* Lord Shaw.
[22] *e.g.*, the one o'clock gun at Edinburgh Castle, instanced by Lord Robertson in *Bourhill* v. *Young*, 1941 S.C. 395 at 407.
[23] *Bourhill* v. *Young*, 1941 S.C. 395, 432, *per* L.J.C. Aitchison.
[24] *Behrens* v. *Bertram Mills Circus, Ltd.* [1957] 2 Q.B. 1, 28, *per* Devlin, J.
[25] (1897) 5 S.L.T. 3.   [26] *Soutar* v. *Mulhern*, 1907 S.C. 723.
[27] *Cowie* v. *L.M.S.Ry.*, 1934 S.C. 433, 437, *per* L.J.C. Aitchison.
[27a] *Bourhill* v. *Young*, 1942 S.C.(H.L.) 78; *King* v. *Phillips* [1953] 1 Q.B. 429.
[28] *e.g.*, *Walker* v. *Pitlochry Motor Co.*, 1930 S.C. 565, 568–569, *per* Lord Mackay.

his home, while in contractual relations, especially of carriage, with the wrongdoer, on the public streets, or otherwise situated. But these distinctions have not been developed.

Standard of sensitivity. In all cases it is particularly important to judge the pursuer by the standard of the ordinary individual, not by the standard of a person predisposed to nervous shock or any other idiosyncrasy or in an abnormal state of body or mind.[29] If, however, breach of duty is established, then the defender must be held to have taken the victim as he found him, and he may be liable for unforeseen consequences.[30]   " If the record contained nothing more than a case of an excessively invalid and neurotic person . . . receiving shock injuries because of her exceptional condition, I should have thought it right . . . to throw the case out." [31]   If, however, there is reasonable notice of unusual conditions of health inferring unusual susceptibility there may be a higher duty of care, and in this context shock caused by invasion of the home [32] may be in a different category for there persons of the tenderest susceptibilities may be.[33]

Shock arising from fear for oneself. It is now well settled that a claim is relevant if nervous shock is caused by the fear of immediate bodily injury to the pursuer himself.[34]   " It is now well settled that persons who are so situated [in relation to the place where a careless act is done that they stand in danger of bodily injury], and whose nervous shock is caused by reasonable apprehension of immediate bodily injury, have a good claim in law for reparation." [35]   " It is clear that the action will lie for injury by shock whenever a person is placed in reasonable fear of immediate injury to himself, provided that the defendant could reasonably have foreseen the risk and ought to have guarded against it." [36]

Reasonableness of fear. A claim for shock arising from fear for oneself is relevant only if the court regards the fear as reasonable in the circumstances. This is really the same question as asking whether the pursuer's injuries " were the natural and reasonable result " [37] of the allegedly negligent conduct, or " so likely to result from what he did

---

[29] *Wilkinson* v. *Downton* [1897] 2 Q.B. 57.
[30] *Walker* v. *Pitlochry Motor Co.*, 1930 S.C. 565, 569; *Graham* v. *Paterson*, 1938 S.C. 119, 131; *Bourhill* v. *Young*, 1942 S.C.(H.L.) 78.
[31] *Walker, supra,* 569, *per* Lord Mackay. *Cf. Cooper* v. *Caledonian Ry.* (1902) 4 F. 880, 882, *per* Lord Stormonth Darling: "that the fright resulting from the negligent act might reasonably arise in a mind of average intelligence and strength."
[32] *e.g., Dulieu* v. *White* [1901] 2 K.B. 669; *Gilligan* v. *Robb,* 1910 S.C. 856.
[33] *Walker, supra,* 569.
[34] *Bell* v. *G.N.Ry.* (1890) 26 L.R.Ir. 428; *Dulieu* v. *White* [1901] 2 K.B. 669; *Cooper* v. *Caledonian Ry.* (1902) 4 F. 880; *Wallace* v. *Kennedy* (1908) 16 S.L.T. 485; *Gilligan* v. *Robb,* 1910 S.C. 856; *Fowler* v. *N.B.Ry.,* 1914 S.C. 866; *Campbell* v. *Henderson,* 1915 1 S.L.T. 419; *Ross* v. *Glasgow Corpn.,* 1919 S.C. 174; *Brown* v. *Glasgow Corpn.,* 1922 S.C. 527; *Cowie* v. *L.M.S.Ry.,* 1934 S.C. 433, explained in *Bourhill* v. *Young,* 1941 S.C. 395, 401.
[35] *Bourhill, supra,* 399 *per* Lord Robertson.
[36] *King* v. *Phillips* [1953] 1 Q.B. 429, *per* Hodson L.J., founding on *Bourhill* v. *Young.*
[37] *Ross* v. *Glasgow Corpn.* 1919 S.C. 174, 177, *per* L.P. Strathclyde.

that a reasonable man . . . ought to have foreseen that the injury would result from what he did." [38] If the fear of personal harm, alleged to have brought on the nervous shock complained of, was in the view of the court unreasonable, the claim falls to be dismissed on the ground of remoteness of injury, the tests applied being those of remoteness of injury. [39] As it was put in another case [40] the fright resulting from the allegedly negligent conduct must be such as might reasonably arise in a mind of average intelligence and strength.

Shock arising from event causing fear for another. In several cases it has been laid down that actionable nervous shock must be occasioned by reasonable apprehension of immediate personal bodily injury. [41] But this cannot be taken as a rigid limitation of the liability. There may be liability for shock occasioned by reasonable fear for another. [42] In *Hambrook* v. *Stokes* [43] the executor of a woman was held entitled to damages for nervous shock caused by apprehension for the safety of her children, which shock actually caused her death. In that case negligence was admitted, so that no question arose as to breach of duty or not. *Hambrook* [43] was only a majority decision of the Court of Appeal and the dissenting judgment of Sargant L.J. has generally been preferred in Scotland. [44] It was held that a woman who suffered a severe nervous shock, resulting in her death, from fear for the safety of her children, on hearing a runaway motor lorry bumping down a steep street in which her children were, though out of her sight, had a right of action. Sargant L.J. would have limited liability to shock arising from fear of immediate personal injury to herself. This decision was considered unsound authority for Scotland in *Currie* v. *Wardrop*. [45]

In *Currie* v. *Wardrop* [45] a woman was walking by the side of a road arm in arm with her fiancé when he was knocked down from behind by a vehicle. The woman did not appear to have been herself struck but she was pulled to the ground and suffered severely from shock. A majority of the Second Division held that the trial judge had been correct in instructing the jury not to discriminate between the shock suffered by the pursuer due to apprehension for her own safety and that due to anxiety for her fiancé. The jury had in fact found that the woman's shock from fear for her own safety had been aggravated by anxiety for the safety of her companion. The case is not, therefore, clear authority for the view

[38] *Ibid.* 179, *per* Lord Mackenzie.
[39] *Ross, supra, passim.*
[40] *Cooper* v. *Caledonian Ry.* (1902) 4 F. 880; *cf. Brown* v. *Glasgow Corpn.*, 1922 S.C. 527; *Bell* v. *G.N.Ry. of Ireland* (1890) 26 L.R.Ir. 428.
[41] *Wallace* v. *Kennedy* (1908) 16 S.L.T. 485; *Campbell* v. *Henderson*, 1915, 1 S.L.T. 419; *Ross* v. *Glasgow Corpn.*, 1919 S.C. 174; *Brown* v. *Glasgow Corpn.* 1922 S.C. 527; *Cowie* v. *L.M.S.Ry.* 1934 S.C. 433.
[42] See Goodhart, " Shock Cases and the Area of Risk " (1953) 16 M.L.R. 14; " Emotional Distress and the Unimaginative Taxicab Driver " (1953) 69 L.Q.R. 347.
[43] [1925] 1 K.B. 141.
[44] *Cf. Currie* v. *Wardrop*, 1927 S.C. 538; *Bourhill* v. *Young*, 1942 S.C.(H.L.) 78. *Hambrook* was distinguished in *King* v. *Phillips* [1953] 1 Q.B. 429.
[45] 1927 S.C. 538.

that shock arising from apprehension for the safety of another is actionable, and the dissenting judges thought that the jury should have been directed to disregard the aggravation, *i.e.*, the shock from fear for her friend. Also, as the Lord Justice-Clerk observed, what affected the pursuer was not shock caused by apprehension of harm to her friend, but shock when she saw what had befallen him.

Nor is *Currie* [45] clear authority for the view that reasonable fear of immediate bodily harm to another is not actionable, and such fear is very likely to cause nervous shock where the person endangered is a relative or person with whom there are strong emotional ties.

In *Owens* v. *Liverpool Corpn.*[46] mourners were held entitled to damages for shock when a tram-car collided with the hearse and caused the coffin to be overturned, although there was no apprehension or sight of injury to a human being. The House of Lords in *Bourhill* v. *Young* [47] reserved opinions on the soundness of *Hambrook* [48] and *Owens*,[46] and indicated that these cases reached the high water mark of claims of this character, and indeed possibly went too far, particularly *Owens*.[46] More recently it has been held in England [49] that a person not himself endangered by the defendants' carelessness can recover when he sustained nervous shock by fear of the consequences to his fellow-workmen, out of his sight.

The position seems to be that *Hambrook* [48] is special in that liability, *i.e.*, breach of duty, was admitted; *Currie* [50] is not a clear authority, and *Owens* [46] probably goes too far. There seems to be no Scottish case as yet in which shock brought about by fear for another by itself has been held actionable. It seems certain, too, that if an event causing fear for the safety of another is actionable, the fear must be natural and reasonable, as for a close relative who is reasonably believed to have been involved or possibly involved.

Shock from seeing or hearing harm being caused to another. The question may also arise whether nervous shock is actionable when caused by seeing or hearing the actual infliction of harm to another, though without any fear of immediate bodily injury to the pursuer himself. This is not clearly settled.

No satisfactory distinction can be drawn between seeing and hearing accidents or other events giving rise to nervous shock, and the issue in both cases is whether there can be any duty to a person who merely sees or hears something which causes him or her nervous shock, as distinct from the person who is sufficiently close to have a reasonable fear of bodily harm from the incident, or, possibly, of bodily harm to a relative, or possibly even to another person.

[46] [1939] 1 K.B. 394.
[47] 1942 S.C.(H.L.) 78.
[48] [1925] 1 K.B. 141.
[49] *Dooley* v. *Cammell Laird & Co.* [1951] 1 Lloyd's Rep. 271.
[50] 1927 S.C. 538.

In *Brandon* v. *Osborne, Garrett & Co.*[51] a wife, reasonably believing that her husband was in danger from glass falling from the roof, exerted herself instinctively to try to pull him out of the way and strained her own leg and precipitated a recurrence of thrombosis. Her action was held not to amount to contributory negligence and she was awarded damages for the consequences to her, though she herself sustained no direct physical injury. If instead of thrombosis she had brought on a recurrence of nervous shock, should she not equally have recovered? Probably she should, particularly since it was found that, though not in fact injured, she also was in danger of physical harm from the glass.

In *Smith* v. *Johnson*[52] a man was negligently killed by the defendant in the sight of the plaintiff and the plaintiff became ill from the shock of seeing this. This was held to be too remote an injury to make the conduct actionable, and it can also be explained[53] on the basis that there was no evidence of breach of legal duty of care towards the plaintiff or in regard to him. In *Campbell* v. *James Henderson, Ltd.*[54] a pursuer was held not entitled to damages when shocked by seeing her brother run over by the defenders' fault. Similarly in *Brown* v. *Glasgow Corpn.*[55] it was indicated that shock from the sight of an accident, and apart from apprehended injury to the pursuer, was not a good ground of action, though the pursuer had a cause of action in her own fear that she might be run into and injured.

Owens v. *Liverpool Corpn.*[56] almost certainly goes too far. A negligently driven tram-car collided with a hearse and the coffin was overturned and in danger of being ejected into the road. Relatives who saw the accident were shocked in varying degrees. The Court of Appeal held that there was liability if real injury had genuinely been caused by shock from apprehension even as to something less important than human life, for example, the life of a beloved dog. The House of Lords in *Bourhill*[57] criticised the decision, and it should probably not be followed.

In *Bourhill* v. *Young*[57] a pregnant woman suffered a nervous shock by, she alleged, having heard, and seen at least the consequences of, a fatal road accident. The courts disposed of the case on the basis that the defender had owed no duty of care to her and dicta on the present point were only obiter.[58] Lord Justice-Clerk Aitchison in the Court of Session,[59] however, thought that no distinction could be drawn between

---

[51] [1924] 1 K.B. 548.
[52] Not reported, cited in [1897] 2 Q.B. 61.
[53] *Per* Lord Porter, in *Bourhill* v. *Young*, 1942 S.C.(H.L.) 78, 95.
[54] 1915, 1 S.L.T. 419.
[55] 1922 S.C. 527, 532, *per* Lord Hunter.
[56] [1939] 1 K.B. 394.
[57] 1942 S.C.(H.L.) 78.
[58] See, however, Lord Robertson at 1941 S.C. 395, 399, indicating that if a pregnant woman looking out of the window saw a window cleaner fall to his death from a house opposite, she would have no right of action.
[59] 1941 S.C. 395, 432, *et seq.* See also *Brown* v. *Glasgow Corpn.*, 1922 S.C. 527, 532, *per* Lord Hunter, who thought that the sight of a street accident might well unnerve a pregnant woman but would not be a good ground of action unless there was real fear of injury to the pursuer herself.

shock arising from fear for oneself, and shock due to what one sees or hears, and he would have given damages.

In *King* v. *Phillips*,[60] where a mother suffered nervous shock from seeing from a window her child endangered by a vehicle which negligently reversed into him in the street some seventy yards away, the Court of Appeal held that the driver had owed no duty of care to the mother or, *per* Denning L.J., that he had owed such a duty but the shock suffered by the mother was too remote a head of damage to be recoverable. In the view of Denning L.J., while a bystander who suffers shock by witnessing an accident from a safe distance cannot recover, " if the bystander is a mother who suffers from shock by hearing or seeing, with her own unaided senses, that her child is in peril, then she may be able to recover from the negligent party, even though she was in no personal danger herself." [61]   And in *Schneider* v. *Eisovitch* [62] Paull J. observed that " It cannot be doubted . . . that if the plaintiff had not herself been injured but had seen her husband killed the resultant shock would have been actionable." In *McLinden* v. *Richardson*,[63] however, a mother averred that as she went into the street to meet her child she heard screaming and, rushing into the street, she saw the defender's van reversing and her child, torn and bleeding, under the van. In consequence she sustained nervous shock. The court allowed a proof before answer on these averments. Again in *Boardman* v. *Sanderson*,[64] where D. ran his car onto S.'s foot, and P., S.'s father, heard screams, ran up and suffered shock on seeing what had happened, it was held that a plaintiff could sue for shock caused by negligent harm to a third party, though not present when the accident happened but within earshot.

It is submitted accordingly that a person has a good cause of action if he or she is present and actually sees or hears an accident in which a close relative, or, possibly, even a friend, or, even possibly, anyone, sustains physical injury, certainly where the claimant was sufficiently close to be himself or herself within the danger area, and possibly even if present but outside that area and himself or herself in no danger of physical harm or shock from the harmful agency. If the claimant is not present, but sees or hears only from a distance, as from a window, he may be outwith the ambit of the duty.

If this formulation is sound it may require limitation in particular cases by the principle of *volenti non fit injuria*, as where a mother deliberately watches her son participating in speedway racing and he is injured by the negligence of a fellow-competitor.

Shock on hearing report of accident. It seems certain, both on the grounds of ambit of duty and of remoteness of injury, that if a person,

60 [1953] 1 Q.B. 429.
61 Citing and approving *Hambrook* v. *Stokes, supra.*
62 [1960] 2 Q.B. 430.
63 1962 S.L.T. (Notes) 104.
64 [1964] 1 W.L.R. 1317.

such as a relative of one killed, sustains shock on hearing a report of an accident, that is not a ground of action against the person responsible for the accident. The duty to take care not to kill or injure does not, if breached, import liability to a person not present who is shocked when told of the accident. " A wife or mother who suffers shock on being told of an accident to a loved one cannot recover damages from the negligent party on that account." [65] The person communicating such a report might, however, be liable if he did not take reasonable care to break the news as gently as possible.[66] In *Bourhill* v. *Young* [67] Lord Robertson considered the case of a person shocked by reading in the newspapers an accurately detailed account of a harrowing accident and indicated that there would be no duty on the newspapers not to shock, nor on the injured persons not to be injured, nor on those causing their injuries, towards the shocked reader. The same principle would doubtless apply to television or newspaper photographs. In *Gray* v. *Sun Publishing Co.*[68] defendants were held not liable for having negligently published an untrue statement that the plaintiff's husband and children had been killed in an accident, and thereby caused the plaintiff severe shock.

In *Schneider* v. *Eisovitch* [69] the plaintiff was rendered unconscious in a car accident and her husband was killed. When she recovered consciousness she was told of her husband's death and sustained a new, serious and continuing shock, independent from that caused her by the physical injury in the accident. It was held that damages for the shock were recoverable as a direct consequence of the defendant's negligence which had caused the husband's death. Paull J. held that " the fact that the defendant by his negligence caused the death of the plaintiff's husband does not give the plaintiff a cause of action for the shock caused to her, but the plaintiff having a cause of action for the negligence of the defendant may add the consequences of shock caused by hearing of her husband's death when estimating the amount recoverable on her cause of action." It seems, therefore, that in the learned judge's view, if the wife had not herself been present and been injured, she would have had no claim for the shock caused by the news. Her only claim was consequential on that for her own injuries, caused by the same negligence.

Shock on hearing report about oneself. A person making a report about the health or condition of another must take reasonable care as to the mode of communication and may be liable if shock is caused thereby. In *Furniss* v. *Fitchett* [70] a husband sought from a doctor a certificate about his wife's health. The certificate stated that the wife

---

[65] *King* v. *Phillips* (1954) 1 Q.B. 429, *per* Denning L.J., *obiter*. *Wilkinson* v. *Downton* [1897] 2 Q.B. 57 is different, as the communication was deliberately false and the action was against the reporter.

[66] *Cf.* the occasion when a village policeman, charged to tell a woman that her husband had been killed, did so in the phrase: " Mrs. X., your man's dead."

[67] 1941 S.C. 395, 399.

[68] (1952) 2 D.L.R. 479 (British Columbia C.A.).

[69] [1960] 2 Q.B. 430.

[70] (1958) N.Z.L.R. 396; (1958) C.L.Y. 2284.

exhibited symptoms of paranoia. When this was put to the wife in matrimonial proceedings she suffered severe shock, and recovered damages on the ground that the doctor had known that the publication of the report was likely, and would be harmful to the wife, and that he was accordingly in breach of duty.

Conclusions on extent of duty not to cause nervous shock. Apart from the clear case of the duty not to cause a person nervous shock by putting him or her in reasonable fear of immediate personal bodily harm to him or herself, and, at the other extreme, the apparent absence of any liability to a person shocked on hearing the report of an accident to another, the extent of the duty not to cause nervous shock is still uncertain, and the cases of persons shocked by fear of injury to close relatives, or other persons, or by the sight or sound of an actual injury to another, or by the sight of what has happened, are still not clear. The cases, moreover, cannot always be clearly segregated. Can a clear distinction really be drawn for the purposes of actionability between the cases of (a) a mother shocked by fear of immediate personal harm to herself, (b) shocked by fear of her child being injured or killed, (c) shocked by hearing an accident in which, as she had feared, her child was injured or killed, and (d) shocked by seeing her child injured or killed before her eyes? [71] The first is certainly actionable, the rest are uncertain and are not, as yet, recognised as actionable.

Consequences of nervous shock. If a pursuer by the defender's fault sustains nervous shock, damages are recoverable for all natural and direct consequences of the shock, such as miscarriage induced thereby,[72] or even death caused thereby,[73] or serious physical illness,[74] or loss of employment and continuing ill-health.[75]

3. DEATH CAUSED BY SHOCK

It is settled law that if an intentional or negligent physical injury, instead of merely causing injury to the victim (which, if he survived, would give him a cause of action), causes his death, certain surviving relatives have an independent right of action for the loss caused to them by the death.[76] While there is no clear authority there seems no good ground for contending that it would be otherwise if death were caused by nervous shock, without any physical lesion. It is submitted that if, in the circumstances, the deceased would have had a right of action if he had survived, his entitled relatives equally have a right of action if the shock caused his death.[77]

---

[71] Cases based on example taken by Atkin L.J. in *Hambrook* v. *Stokes* [1925] 1 K.B. 141.
[72] *Dulieu* v. *White* [1901] 2 K.B. 669; (child born an idiot); *Brown* v. *Glasgow Corpn.*, 1922 S.C. 527; and *per* L.J.C. Aitchison (dissenting) in *Bourhill* v. *Young*, 1941 S.C. 395, 436.
[73] *Hambrook* v. *Stokes* [1925] 1 K.B. 141.
[74] *Wilkinson* v. *Downton* [1897] 2 Q.B. 57.
[75] *Walker* v. *Pitlochry Motor Co.*, 1930 S.C. 565.
[76] See Chap. 22, *infra*.
[77] *Cf. Hambrook, supra; Blaikie* v. *B.T.C.*, 1961 S.C. 44 (death from coronary thrombosis precipitated by strain); see also *Carslake* v. *Devos* [1959] C.L.Y. 876.

CHAPTER 20

INFRINGEMENTS OF THE INTEREST IN FREEDOM OF ACTION

1. Physical Detention
2. Wrongful Apprehension
3. Wrongful Imprisonment
4. Force or Fear—Intimidation
5. Circumvention and Fraud
6. Seduction

THE individual's moral personality is entitled to the respect of others equally with the integrity of his physical person, and he is entitled to the protection of the law against being unjustifiably threatened, coerced or overcome by force of any kind. His individual interest in the free exercise of his will is recognised and secured.[1] This interest may be infringed in many ways, and all are outrages on personality giving rise to *actiones injuriarum*.

1. PHYSICAL DETENTION

The slightest interference with the personal liberty of an individual which is not warranted by law will justify an *actio injuriarum* for *solatium*. " By the law of this country no man can be restrained of his liberty without authority in law." [2] Thus where an hotel manager locked a guest in an hotel room until she would apologise for an alleged insult, conduct described as " an outrage," [3] damages were held recoverable,[4] and where a person who, as subsequently transpired, was innocent, was detained in a locked room for three hours by a pawnbroker and then given into custody on suspicion of having offered to pawn stolen goods, a trial was allowed and it was observed that even probable cause for doing so would not have justified three hours' detention.[5]

To amount to detention the complainer must have been totally detained, and prevented from free movement in all directions. It is not detention, *e.g.*, if a road is blocked but it is open to go round by another way.[6] Nor is it unjustifiable detention if the complainer is seeking escape from a place in breach of contract; having contracted to enter and stay in the premises to do the job he is not entitled to be released on demand.[7]

1 Pound, " Interests of Personality," in *Selected Essays*, p. 100 *et seq.*
2 *Herd* v. *Weardale Steel Co.* [1915] A.C. 67, *per* Viscount Haldane L.C.
3 1908 S.C. 200, 206, *per* Lord Low.
4 *Mackenzie* v. *Cluny Hill Hydropathic Co.*, 1908 S.C. 200.
5 *Mackenzie* v. *Young* (1902) 10 S.L.T. 231.
6 *Bird* v. *Jones* (1845) 7 Q.B. 742.
7 *Herd* v. *Weardale Steel Co., Ltd.* [1915] A.C. 67 (miners striking and wishing to leave mine: short delay not detention).

Nor again is it unjustifiable detention to hold a person to conditions, such as paying a fee, which he impliedly accepted on entering, before allowing him to emerge.[8] Thus the passenger in a train or aircraft has no claim for detention if he is locked in until the end of the journey, because he entered on the journey impliedly accepting that this would happen. A bus passenger cannot complain if he is not allowed to leave till he has paid his fare. A student cannot complain if he is not allowed to leave while the lecture is in progress.

Detention caused inadvertently, as by locking an employee in the strong-room, imposes no liability, unless possibly for negligence, if such can be proved and actual harm be sustained.[9]

A person may be " detained " without any actual physical confinement if prevailed upon to stay where he is, or to go somewhere else, by reasonable apprehension of being seized and compelled if he does not acquiesce, as where a customer in a shop, wrongly accused of shoplifting, went with a shop-detective to a room to be searched " in order to prevent the necessity of actual force being used." [10] Again he may be detained even if too ill to move, so that he could not have escaped even if he would.[11]

A person may be detained without his knowing it, while asleep or drunk or unconscious or a lunatic, though damages would be affected by the complainer's knowledge or not of his detention. He might be imprisoned by having the key of a door turned against him, so that he is imprisoned although he does not know that the key has been turned.[12]

It is probably not wrongful detention if there is a way of escape open which any reasonable man would have appreciated as such, and could have used without undue risk. Thus it will not be detention if there is another door, which is unlocked; secus if the window is open but escape could be effected only by clinging to a string-course of masonry or descending a rone-pipe.

Necessity. Any person may probably be justified in exceptional circumstances in detaining a person against his will and without any legal warrant if that seems necessary in the circumstances, if, *e.g.,* the person seems likely to do serious harm to himself or others.[13] But any such detention must not be continued any longer than seems absolutely necessary, unless some legal warrant for longer detention be obtained.

Detention as a person of unsound mind. " Groundless confinement of a person in a lunatic asylum will give a good foundation for an action

---

[8] *Robinson* v. *Balmain New Ferry Co.* [1910] A.C. 295; *Herd, supra.*
[9] *Restatement,* s. 35, Ill. 1.
[10] *Meering* v. *Graham-White Aviation Co.* (1919) 122 L.T. 44; *cf. Conn* v. *Spencer* [1930] 1 D.L.R. 805 (Brit. Columbia).
[11] *Grainger* v. *Hill* (1838) 4 Bing.N.C. 212.
[12] *Meering* v. *Graham-White Aviation Co.* (1919) 122 L.T. 44 (C.A.). *Secus, Restatement,* ss. 35, 42; *Herring* v. *Boyle* (1834) 1 C.M. & R. 377.
[13] Thus a drunken person could be detained in his own interests until he recovers reasonable sobriety.

of damages." [14]   Detention on this ground is justified if the alleged incapax has been admitted to a mental hospital in pursuance of an application for admission under the Mental Health (Scotland) Act, 1960, s. 24, accompanied by two medical recommendations and approved by the sheriff, or under an emergency recommendation made under s. 31. If authority for detention is not renewed it lasts for not more than one year; if renewed, the authority subsists for a further period of one year, and thereafter for periods of two years at a time.[15]

A person liable to detention in a hospital under the Mental Health Act, 1960, who absents himself without leave, fails to return from any period of leave of absence, or absents himself without permission from a place where he is required to reside, may be taken into custody and returned to the hospital by any mental health officer, officer on the staff of the hospital, constable or any person authorised in writing by the hospital board of management.[16]   But a patient shall not be taken back into custody after the expiry of certain prescribed periods and if still at liberty he thereupon ceases to be liable to detention or guardianship.[17]

Parties liable for wrongful detention. All parties who have been involved in causing the wrongful detention may be sued, though the grounds of liability and the requisites for relevancy of a claim vary. A family solicitor who advised the insane person's mother to apply for a warrant to have him detained has been sued and was held not privileged, the sole issue being whether he acted " wrongfully, the pursuer not being insane." [18] Even if a solicitor acted wrongfully in initiating an application for admission, *e.g.*, if the complainer were not insane, a material point is whether his action " caused " any wrongful detention, since any detention requires consideration of the case by medical men and the sheriff, whose interventions may more properly be regarded as the real and proximate cause of any detention.[19]

Doctors who have examined the alleged lunatic and granted medical certificates may be liable, for granting certificates " without due inquiry and examination." [20]   They owe him a duty to take care not unjustifiably to cause his detention.[21]   No wrong is done if the doctors acted in the full belief, in the exercise of their skill and judgment, that the complainer was in a state of insanity requiring detention, if they proceeded with due deliberation, and made due inquiry, applied their minds to the case and proceeded with fair caution and acted in good faith, but it would be a wrong if they were not qualified practitioners, if they knew the pursuer

---

14 Bell, *Prin.*, § 2042.
15 Mental Health (Scotland) Act, 1960, s. 39 (2).
16 *Ibid.* s. 36 (1).
17 *Ibid.* s. 36 (3).
18 *Mackintosh* v. *Fraser* (1859) 21 D. 783; (1860) 22 D. 421; (1863) 1 M.(H.L.) 37; *cf. Strang* v. *Strang* (1849) 11 D. 379.
19 See *Harnett* v. *Bond* [1925] A.C. 669; *De Freville* v. *Dill* (1927) 43 T.L.R. 702.
20 *Strang* v. *Strang* (1849) 11 D. 378; *Mackintosh* v. *Fraser* (1860) 22 D. 421, 422.
21 *De Freville* v. *Dill* (1927) 43 T.L.R. 702.

not to be insane, or if they made no examination of him at all, but granted the certificate haphazard, or if they did not apply their minds to the question of whether he was insane or not, but at the solicitation of some person granted the certificate without having formed any opinion at all. That the medical certificates were, in the view of other authorities, incorrect in recommending detention is not sufficient to impose liability, unless it can be shown that they were not granted in bona fide, or, possibly, were so wildly inaccurate that no competent medical officers could reasonably have given them, because otherwise medical officers might be liable for a mere mistaken opinion or diagnosis.[22]

The managers of a mental hospital may be sued for having " wrongfully and illegally " detained the pursuer,[23] which may be constituted by failure to conform to any of the statutory requirements, as by detaining without a warrant [24] or after authority for discharge had been granted. " The only circumstances which would go to establish an illegal detention would be these—either that they were not proper medical certificates, or that there was no warrant from the sheriff, or that he was detained after there had been a proper authority for his discharge, or that the place into which he was received was not a legally licensed asylum." [25]

The sheriff might be sued at common law if he had acted outwith his jurisdiction or made an order which was irregular.[26]

Conspiracy to confine wrongfully has been alleged and an action has been brought against parents, their solicitor, certifying doctors and the asylum manager, all jointly and severally,[27] though in a later case separate issues were allowed against each defender.[28] Malice need not now [29] be averred in any case.

Statutory protection. Under the Mental Health (Scotland) Act, 1960, s. 107,[30] no person is liable, whether on the ground of want of jurisdiction [31] or on any other ground, to any civil or criminal proceedings to which he would have been liable apart from the section, in respect of any act purporting to be done in pursuance of the Act or any regulations thereunder, unless the act was done in bad faith or without reasonable care. To make a relevant case today, accordingly, express averments of bad faith or absence of reasonable care are necessary.

---

[22] *Mackintosh* v. *Fraser, supra,* 22 D. at 422; *Everett* v. *Griffiths* [1921] 1 A.C. 631; *Harnett* v. *Bond* [1925] A.C. 669; *Harnett* v. *Fisher* [1927] A.C. 573; *De Freville* v. *Dill* (1927) 43 T.L.R. 702; *cf. Buxton* v. *Jayne* [1960] 2 All E.R. 688.

[23] *Mackintosh* v. *Smith and Lowe* (1864) 2 M. 389, 1261; (1865) 3 M.(H.L.) 6. (Wrongful treatment while under detention is a separate matter.)

[24] *Strang* v. *Strang* (1849) 11 D. 378.

[25] *Mackintosh, supra* (H.L.) 13, *per* Lord Chelmsford.

[26] *Mackintosh* v. *Arkley* (1868) 6 M.(H.L.) 141.

[27] *McCosh* v. *McCosh* (1832) 10 S. 579.

[28] *Strang* v. *Strang* (1849) 11 D. 378.

[29] *Dickie* v. *Dickie* (1825) 3 Mur. 509, 514.

[30] Superseding generally similar protective sections, *viz.,* Lunacy (Scotland) Act, 1866, s. 24; Mental Deficiency and Lunacy (Scotland) Act, 1913, s. 73.

[31] This would apply to the sheriff granting a warrant for detention; *cf. Mackintosh* v. *Arkley* (1868) 6 M.(H.L.) 141.

Reasonable detention by parents. A parent,[32] or guardian,[33] or person *in loco parentis*, or one to whom parental authority is deemed to be delegated, such as a school teacher, may detain and restrict the free movement of a child or young person or ward so far as this is reasonable and necessary in the interests of discipline and training or the ward's own safety. In every case it will be a question of circumstances whether the detention was or was not reasonably necessary. No case challenging detention of this kind seems to be recorded, but it is thought that to render such a claim relevant it would have to be averred that the detention went substantially beyond what was reasonable or necessary, and that it was not imposed bona fide in the interest of the child or ward.

Imprisonment by ship's master. The master of a merchant ship is entitled at common law to arrest and confine in a reasonable manner and for a reasonable time any seaman or other person on board ship if he has reasonable cause to believe, and does in fact believe, that the arrest and confinement are necessary for the preservation of order and discipline, or for the safety of the vessel or persons or property on board.[34] This power extends over members of the crew,[35] and passengers,[36] but the master is liable if he had no reasonable cause for believing, or did not in fact believe, the detention was necessary,[35] or if he acted maliciously and without probable cause.[37]

2. WRONGFUL APPREHENSION

Arrest or apprehension of a person for criminal wrongdoing is a grave outrage if it is not legally justifiable, and accordingly it justifies an *actio injuriarum* claiming *solatium*.

Arrest under warrant. Warrant to arrest a person suspected of a crime is normally granted by a judge, sheriff or magistrate to whom a petition has been presented, signed by a procurator fiscal or Crown counsel, craving such a warrant. In emergency, a warrant may be granted without a written petition.[38] The warrant must name the person to be arrested and a general warrant is illegal.[39]

---

[32] On a parent's power of custody of a child see generally *Fraser on Parent and Child* (3rd ed.), 76; on a tutor's power, p. 283; and on a curator's power, p. 469.

[33] Under the Mental Health (Scotland) Act, 1960, s. 25, a person may be received into guardianship on medical recommendations, approved by the sheriff; the guardian, who may be the local health authority, a person chosen by that authority, or any other person accepted as suitable, has the powers (s. 29 (4)) of a father over a pupil child, but he has no power to intromit with property (s. 29 (5)), nor to administer corporal punishment (s. 29 (6)). Regulations may be made as to the exercise of powers by guardians (s. 33 (1)). A person under guardianship who absents himself without leave may be taken into custody and returned to his guardian, unless certain prescribed periods of liberty have elapsed (s. 36 (2) and (3)). The period of guardianship is limited (s. 39).

[34] *Hook* v. *Cunard S.S. Co.* [1953] 1 All E.R. 1021.

[35] *Hook, supra.*

[36] *Aldworth* v. *Stewart* (1866) 4 F. & F. 957; *cf. Lundie* v. *MacBrayne* (1894) 21 R. 1085.

[37] *Coutts & Park* v. *MacBrayne*, 1910 S.C. 386.

[38] *Hume on Crimes*, II, 77; Alison, II, 121; Macdonald's *Criminal Law* (5th ed.), 198; Renton and Brown's *Criminal Procedure* (3rd ed.), 31.

[39] *Leach* v. *Money* (1765) 19 St.Tr. 1002.

A warrant cannot authorise arrest outside the area for which the granter has judicial authority and for which the warrant accordingly runs, unless it is endorsed by a sheriff or magistrate of the area in which the arrest is to be effected.[40] A warrant of the High Court of Justiciary requires no endorsation anywhere in Scotland, and a warrant granted by a sheriff against a person charged with a crime within that sheriffdom may be executed at any place in Scotland without backing or endorsation, if executed by a messenger-at-arms or officer of the court where it was issued,[41] but otherwise it must be endorsed by the sheriff of the sheriffdom in which it is to be executed.

In border counties [42] a constable can execute without endorsation within any of the counties a warrant for the apprehension of a criminal accused or convicted of a crime committed in the county for which the constable is appointed, in the same way as he could have in his own county.[43]

A constable executing a warrant of arrest must inform the person of the charge against him and, if requested, show, but not hand over, his warrant.[44] He should bring the prisoner before a sheriff or magistrate as quickly as possible.[45]

The existence of a warrant is sufficient authority for any police constable taking into custody the person sought and detaining him till the arrival of the officer in possession of the warrant, particularly if there is any likelihood that the wanted person will try to escape.[46]

Arrest without warrant. " It is a general rule of our law that no one in this country, man or woman, is to be deprived of his or her liberty without a warrant from a magistrate. That is the general rule, which no doubt is subject to certain pretty well-defined exceptions." [47]

A suspect may be arrested without a warrant, but if this is done, a petition is presented and a warrant obtained as soon thereafter as possible.[48] Arrest without warrant must always be regarded as exceptional and as conduct requiring justification.[49] In general the question is one of the circumstances of each case and, in particular, whether the person making the arrest had reasonable grounds for believing that, if he did not act but delayed, the ends of justice would be harmed, as by the commission of a crime or the escape of a criminal.[50] If this belief is challenged it is probably sufficient to show facts which would create

---

[40] Hume, II, 78; Alison, II, 124; Macdonald, 198; Renton and Brown, 35.
[41] Sheriff Courts (Scotland) Act, 1838, s. 25.
[42] Northumberland, Cumberland, Berwick, Roxburgh or Dumfries.
[43] Police (Scotland) Act, 1956, s. 5.
[44] Hume, II, 79; Macdonald, 199.
[45] Hume, II, 80; Alison, II, 129; *Crawford* v. *Blair* (1856) 2 Irv. 511; *Macdonald* v. *Lyon* (1851) J. Shaw 516; *Maitland* v. *Douglas* (1861) 24 D. 193.
[46] Renton and Brown, 35.
[47] *Leask* v. *Burt* (1893) 21 R. 32, 36, *per* Lord Young.
[48] *Peggie* v. *Clerk* (1868) 7 M. 89, 93, *per* Lord Deas.
[49] Hume, II, 75; Alison, II, 116; Macdonald, 197; Renton and Brown, 31; *Beaton* v. *Ivory* (1887) 14 R. 1057; *Shields* v. *Shearer*, 1914 S.C.(H.L.) 33.
[50] Hume, II, 75–76; *Peggie* v. *Clerk, supra.*

a reasonable suspicion in the mind of a reasonable man, but not merely to allege that the arrester himself reasonably suspected. The test, that is, is objective.[51]

A magistrate, such as a sheriff,[52] a police officer, or other officer of law, acting within his own area of jurisdiction,[53] is entitled to arrest without a warrant:

(1) if he sees a crime committed or finds a person in the act of committing, or attempting to commit, a serious crime [54];

(2) if he finds any person under suspicious circumstances with goods in his possession which the officer knows to have been stolen, and for the possession of which the person cannot account in any way consistent with innocence, and if there is a probability that the criminal will escape if immediate action is not taken [55];

(3) if he is informed by an injured person, or by a credible eye witness, that any person has just committed, or attempted to commit, a serious crime, and the suspect is escaping or there is a danger that the criminal will escape if immediate action is not taken [56];

(4) if he sees, or receives direct information from credible eye witnesses that a person is committing a breach of the peace, or an outrage, or threatening violence, and if there is a danger that the person may do injury to himself or others if he is not immediately arrested [57];

(5) if a criminal is hiding and the officer is credibly informed that he is about to abscond [58];

(6) if a suspected individual is reputed to live by crime or has no fixed residence or known honest livelihood [58];

(7) if in the circumstances there is statutory power to arrest without a warrant.[59]

If a person charged by another with crime is a householder or person of respectability and generally law abiding, apprehension without warrant is unjustifiable unless there are reasonable grounds for supposing that he means to abscond.[60]

In the case of offences against children and young persons, a constable may without warrant take into custody (a) any person who within his view commits such an offence if the constable does not know

---

51 *Broughton* v. *Jackson* (1852) 18 Q.B. 378, 385; *Hogg* v. *Ward* (1858) 27 L.J.Ex. 443.
52 *Beaton* v. *Ivory* (1887) 14 R. 1057.
53 *Leask* v. *Burt* (1893) 21 R. 32.
54 Hume, II, 75–76; Alison, II, 117; *Peggie* v. *Clerk, supra*; *Jackson* v. *Stevenson* (1897) 24 R.(J.) 38, 40.
55 Hume, *supra*; Alison, *supra*.
56 Hume, *supra*; Alison, *supra*; *Leask* v. *Burt, supra*; *Jackson* v. *Stevenson* (1897) 24 R.(J.) 38; *H.M.A.* v. *McGuigan*, 1936 J.C. 16.
57 Hume, *supra*; *McVie and Linch* v. *Dykes* (1856) 2 Irv. 429; *Jackson* v. *Stevenson* (1897) 24 R.(J.) 38.
58 *Peggie* v. *Clerk, supra*.
59 For powers, see *Index to the Statutes in Force*, s.v. Arrest.
60 *Peggie, supra*.

and cannot ascertain his name and address; and (b) any person who has committed, or whom he has reasonable cause to believe to have committed, any such offence if the constable does not know and cannot ascertain his name or address or has reasonable ground for believing that he will abscond.

In the case of serious crime an officer may also without warrant break open doors and enter premises in the course of apprehending the suspect, provided he first disclosed his identity to those within, and demanded, and was refused, access.[61]

In the case of minor offences, arrest without warrant is undesirable unless there is danger of the offence being repeated, or the suspect escaping or doing injury to himself or to others.[61]   An officer may not break open premises in the case of breach of the peace unless there is a disturbance actually proceeding.[62]

In all cases an officer may demand the assistance of bystanders to apprehend an offender.[63]

A judge, sheriff, magistrate or justice of the peace who actually witnesses a crime may without warrant arrest the offender, or orally order arrest in any case where immediate complaint is made to him by persons who know the facts and the identity of the offender.[64]

A private citizen who actually witnesses a crime may without warrant arrest the offender,[65] but may not do so on suspicion or on information.[66] He may not enter premises and may intervene to stop a breach of the peace, but may not arrest.[67]   A person attacked in the street, or having his pocket picked, may arrest the aggressor without warrant.[68]

A person arresting without warrant must at once take the person arrested to a police station or before a magistrate,[69] and must inform the person arrested of the true ground of the arrest, though this need not be formulated in technical terms, and need not be done at all if the reason for the arrest is quite obvious in the circumstances,[70] or if it cannot be done at all at the time, e.g., if there is a scuffle or melee.

These principles are not as clear as they might ideally be and give scope for much honest misinterpretation,[71] and both police and citizens deserve legal protection, even if an arrest was unjustified, if it was in the circumstances made in bona fide and on reasonable grounds.

---

[61] Cf. Dumbell v. Roberts [1944] 1 All E.R. 326.
[62] Hume, II, 80; Alison, II, 117–118.
[63] Hume, II, 76; Alison, supra; cf. R. v. Brown (1841) C. & Mar. 314.
[64] Hume, II, 76–77; Alison, II, 119–120; Macdonald, 197; Renton and Brown, 32–33; Alison, loc. cit., suggests that in certain cases the victim of a crime may arrest upon information.
[65] Leask v. Burt (1893) 21 R. 32; Lundie v. MacBrayne (1894) 21 R. 1085; Somerville v. Sutherland (1899) 2 F. 185, 188.
[66] Cf. Walters v. W. H. Smith & Son, Ltd. [1914] 1 K.B. 595.
[67] Hume, supra; Alison, supra.
[68] Leask v. Burt (1893) 21 R. 32, 36.
[69] Hume, supra; Alison, II, 117–118; John Lewis & Co. v. Tims [1952] A.C. 676.
[70] Christie v. Leachinsky [1947] A.C. 573.
[71] e.g., What are " serious crime " and " minor offences " in the principles above stated; it may be very difficult in marginal cases.

Similar principles apply to actions directed against other parties than the police, who may have instructed or authorised the apprehension, such as a sheriff,[72] a procurator-fiscal,[73] or a ship's captain.[74]

Conditions of liability for wrongful arrest. " A constable . . . must make up his mind on what he sees (or hears on credible information) whether to arrest or not, and if he does arrest in good faith, the law will protect him, whether his opinion at the time of the guilt of the person arrested prove accurate or not." [75]

Where apprehension by the police is being challenged as wrongful it is normally necessary to aver not merely that this conduct was legally unjustifiable or malicious, but that it was done " maliciously and without probable cause," and to aver and prove facts and circumstances from which the court or jury may legitimately infer that the defender was not acting in the bona fide discharge of his duty but was actuated by a malicious motive.[76] " The presumption in favour of a public officer that he is doing no more than his duty and doing it honestly and bona fide is a very strong one, and certainly ought not to be overcome by the simple use of the word 'malice'." [77] The court has to decide in each case whether the averments of malice are sufficient, if proved, to justify a court or jury in holding that the arrest was not done in bona fide.[78] An averment of malice in general terms may be sufficient as between private individuals,[79] but a mere formal averment would not suffice to take a case out of the privilege which belongs to sheriffs, magistrates and senior police officers.[80]

Malice and want of probable cause. These are distinct elements and averment or proof of one is not averment or proof of the other. Malice (or malice in fact [81]) is malevolence or ill-will, which may co-exist with highly probable cause, not with absence of it. Probable cause is *probabilis causa*, a case capable of proof, or at least prima facie satisfactory to the mind.[82]

If there is no probable cause for the conduct in question, malice may be inferred from that fact.[83] Malice may also be inferred from the facts that the arrest was made with unnecessary violence, accompanied by abusive language, or by physical restraint uncalled for in the circumstances,[84] or from recklessness in arresting.[85]

---

[72] *Beaton* v. *Ivory* (1887) 14 R. 1057.
[73] *McPherson* v. *McLennan* (1887) 14 R. 1063; *Walker* v. *Brander*, 1920 S.C. 840.
[74] *Coutts* v. *David MacBrayne, Ltd.*, 1910 S.C. 386.
[75] *Jackson* v. *Stevenson* (1897) 24 R. (J.) 38. *Cf. Dallison* v. *Caffery* [1964] 2 All E.R. 610.
[76] *Beaton* v. *Ivory* (1887) 14 R. 1057; *Young* v. *Glasgow Mags.* (1891) 18 R. 825; *Leask* v. *Burt* (1893) 21 R. 32; *Hill* v. *Campbell* (1905) 8 F. 220.
[77] *Beaton, supra*, 1061, *per* L.P. Inglis. *Cf.* Lord Shand at p. 1063.
[78] See, *e.g., Young* v. *Glasgow Mags.* (1891) 18 R. 825; *Malcolm* v. *Duncan* (1897) 24 R. 747.
[79] *Beaton, supra*, 1061.
[80] *Young, supra*, 829.
[81] See *Shields* v. *Shearer*, 1914 S.C.(H.L.) 33, 34, *per* L.Ch. Haldane; 35, *per* Lord Dunedin.
[82] *Cf. Hill* v. *Thomson* (1892) 19 R. 377.
[83] *Macdonald* v. *Fergusson* (1853) 15 D. 545.
[84] *Young* v. *Glasgow Mags.* (1891) 18 R. 825, 829.   [85] *Shields, supra*, 37, *per* Lord Shaw.

If it is admitted or proved that the pursuer was convicted on the charge for which he was arrested, that normally negatives want of probable cause and, therefore, whether or not there was malice, the pursuer's action for wrongful arrest must fail.[86] If, however, a person were arrested in circumstances which clearly did not justify arrest at all, the fact that he was subsequently convicted should not bar an action for wrongful arrest, though it would bar an action for malicious prosecution.

Whether there is probable cause or not is a question for the trial judge,[87] but whether malice should be inferred in the circumstances or not is a question for the jury.[88]

It has been held unnecessary to include malice and want of probable cause in the issue for the jury in a case of alleged wrongful apprehension without warrant, where the pursuer's averments disclosed a case of such prima facie wrongful and unreasonable conduct that, if these averments were proved, the actings of the constables could not possibly be regarded as privileged and protected.[89] Nor was it considered necessary to put malice in issue in a case where constables, empowered by statute to arrest without warrant a person " reasonably suspected " of having committed crime, did arrest without a warrant and maintained that they had bona fide suspected the pursuer of a crime and had considered that they had reasonable grounds of suspicion, and were therefore protected by the terms of the local Act authorising arrest in such circumstances; the question for the jury was only whether or not the defenders had had reasonable grounds of suspicion for their apprehension of the pursuer.[90]

Search. A constable, having arrested a person, may search him, but may not search him previously to find evidence to determine whether to arrest or not. He has no authority to search the person of a man when there is no sufficient ground for apprehending and no warrant to search.[91] Wrongful search may therefore be a further outrage, additional to wrongful arrest.

Detention after arrest. An arrested person may, immediately after he has been brought before a magistrate for examination on declaration, apply to the magistrate or sheriff to be liberated on bail.[92] All crimes and offences, except murder and treason, are bailable and a magistrate or sheriff may at his discretion, admit to, or refuse a person, bail,[93] but the court must grant bail unless of the opinion that, looking to the public interest and to securing the ends of justice, there is good reason why

[86] *Hill* v. *Campbell* (1905) 8 F. 220.
[87] *Fraser* v. *Hill* (1853) 1 Paterson 232, 235; *Craig* v. *Peebles* (1876) 3 R. 441.
[88] *Auld* v. *Shairp* (1875) 2 R. 940, 958; *Ritchie* v. *Barton* (1883) 10 R. 813.
[89] *Harvey* v. *Sturgeon*, 1912 S.C. 974. Cf. *Leask* v. *Burt* (1893) 21 R. 32.
[90] *Shields* v. *Shearer*, 1914 S.C.(H.L.) 33; (" wrongfully and illegally ").
[91] *Jackson* v. *Stevenson* (1897) 24 R.(J.) 38, 40, 42.
[92] Criminal Procedure (Scotland) Act, 1887, s. 18.
[93] Bail (Scotland) Act, 1888, s. 2.

bail should not be granted; this right of refusal is not limited to cases where the court thinks there is a danger of the accused absconding.[94] The prosecutor is entitled to be heard thereon, and the court will not readily disregard his objections.[95] Applications for bail must be disposed of within twenty-four hours. The application for bail may be renewed after commitment for trial, and either party may appeal to the High Court against the grant or refusal of bail.

It is accordingly wrongful detention for a sheriff or magistrate to refuse to consider an application for bail, or to fix the amount of bail at a sum wholly unreasonable in the circumstances, and such that the accused could not possibly find it, and thereby to condemn him to remain in prison pending trial. If the sole ground of complaint were the demanding of allegedly excessive bail, it is only in the most extreme cases and on the clearest averments of bad faith that the court is ever likely to allow investigation of alleged wrongful detention by refusal of bail, since the magistrate or sheriff is given an unfettered discretion and may in many circumstances justifiably set bail at a high figure.[96]

3. WRONGFUL IMPRISONMENT

A person who in the exercise of judicial powers causes another to be imprisoned, or to suffer a similar deprivation of liberty [97] is doing what, if unjustifiable, is a grave wrong justifying solatium in an *actio injuriarum*.

Judges of the High Court are immune from any such action.[98] " The principle is clear and the decisions are emphatic. The principle is that such judges are the King's judges directly, bound to administer the law between his subjects, and even between his subjects and himself. To make them amenable to actions of damages for things done in their judicial capacity, to be dealt with by judges only their equals in authority and by juries, would be to make them not responsible to the King, but subject to other considerations than their duty to him in giving their decisions, and to expose them to be dealt with as servants not of him but of the public. Accordingly, the remedy in this case, if they flagrantly offend against duty, is not by proceedings in any court, but only by addresses to the Crown from the Houses of Parliament." [99]

But it is otherwise in the case of inferior courts and magistrates. " Where a magistrate, professing to sit as such, and dealing with a case which he has no jurisdiction to deal with at all, commits what is an undoubted wrong upon a citizen, both by principle and practice, he is

---

[94] *Mackintosh* v. *McGlinchy*, 1921 J.C. 75; *cf. Young* v. *H.M. Advocate*, 1946 J.C. 5.

[95] *Mackintosh, supra*; *A.B.* v. *Dickson*, 1907 S.C.(J.) 111; *H.M.A.* v. *Saunders*, 1913 S.C.(J.) 44; *Macdonald* v. *Clifford*, 1952 J.C. 22.

[96] The protection clause of the Summary Jurisdiction Act, 1954 (s. 75) may be relevant in such a case.

[97] This covers both imprisonment or detention by way of sentence, and also detention in custody pending inquiries, as in *McPhee* v. *Macfarlane's Exor.*, 1933 S.C. 163.

[98] *Taaffe* v. *Downes* (1813) 3 Moo.P.C. 36n.

[99] *McCreadie* v. *Thomson*, 1907 S.C. 1176, 1182, *per* L.J.C. Macdonald.

held liable for the wrong done ",[1] and the same is the rule where a magistrate acts in excess of his jurisdiction.[2]

Liability arises only when an *ultra vires* sentence has been carried into effect. " It is not for what he has ordered, but for what he has caused another to suffer that he is amenable to the law. That he has pronounced an illegal sentence is not sufficient to subject him to damages if nothing has been done upon it. But when it has been carried out so that the wrong has been made effective, then he may be answerable." [3]

Accordingly in the case of judges of the inferior courts a pursuer must show that the judge pronounced a sentence which was *ultra vires*, and that he suffered loss of liberty thereunder. Where the judge's conduct has been *ultra vires* it is not necessary to aver or prove malice.[4]

The court has, however, indicated that it should not be supposed that any *culpa levissima* would warrant damages against a judge,[5] and a magistrate will not be made liable for having made an error in statutory interpretation, as to his powers, when his conduct was reasonable and in accordance with practice. A mistake must be a glaring one, or irregularity gross, for there to be liability.[6]

Even if *intra vires*, an inferior judge's conduct in causing imprisonment is actionable, but any judge or magistrate is presumed to be acting in good faith, and the clearest and most explicit averments and proof of malice and lack of probable cause would be essential.[7]

Statutory protections. Judges of inferior courts may rely on the statutory protection conferred by the Summary Jurisdiction (Scotland) Act, 1954, s. 75, and earlier provisions.[8] Such a protection will cover a magistrate only so long as he does not act *ultra vires*; but a magistrate does not necessarily act outside his powers because he makes an honest mistake in applying the law.[9]

Imprisonment following on complaint. Where imprisonment results from a complaint made by an officer of a public body, an action may lie against the body if it has adopted a wrong course of procedure, but there must be specific averments of malice and lack of probable cause.[10] Mere irregularity in procedure will not suffice. If the matter is not challenged there is probably no onus on the sheriff or other magistrate to ascertain whether or not the preliminary procedure has been regularly carried through.

Liability of procurator-fiscal, police or complainer. An individual who complains, the police who investigate, and the procurator-fiscal who

1 *Ibid.* 1183.
2 *Ibid.* 1183–1184; *Groome* v. *Forrester* (1816) 5 M. & S. 314.
3 *Ibid.* 1184; *Barton* v. *Bricknell* (1850) 13 Q.B. 393.
4 *Strachan* v. *Stoddart* (1828) 7 S. 4, 6; *McCreadie, supra,* 1186; *Bell, Prin.,* § 2038.
5 *McCreadie, supra.*
6 *McPhee* v. *Macfarlane's Exor.,* 1933 S.C. 163, 169.
7 *Watt* v. *Thomson* (1870) 8 M.(H.L.) 77; *Watt* v. *Ligertwood* (1874) 1 R.(H.L.) 21.
8 See Chap. 13, *supra.*
9 *McPhee, supra.*
10 *Macaulay* v. *North Uist School Board* (1887) 15 R. 99.

prosecutes are all free of liability for wrongful imprisonment, in that the act which " causes " the imprisonment is that of the sheriff or magistrate, not that of the other persons. In any event the conduct of such persons would have to be shown to be malicious and lacking in probable cause to be actionable, and in the cases of the procurator-fiscal and the police malicious in a high degree.

An individual may be liable if he has made a false accusation or given false information upon which a prosecution has proceeded, but only if malice and lack of probable cause be shown.[11]

Imprisonment under executive order. In wartime wide powers have been entrusted by Parliament to the executive which have placed serious restrictions on personal freedom. Apart from the political responsibility of the Minister concerned to Parliament, the validity of the executive order may be challenged by action for declarator and/or for damages for wrongful detention.[12] The validity of the order turns on the interpretation of the power conferred and on the terms of its exercise. In *R.* v. *Halliday, ex parte Zadig,*[13] Z was interned by order of the Home Secretary under Regulation 14B made under the Defence of the Realm Consolidation Act, 1914, and the Regulation was held *intra vires* and adequate to justify the detention. In *Liversidge* v. *Anderson,*[14] L was detained under an order made by A under Regulation 18B of the Defence (General) Regulations issued under the Emergency Powers (Defence) Act, 1939. The order was held valid and the detention justified.[15] A similar view was taken in other cases.[16] The exigencies of wartime justify restrictions not tolerable in peacetime, and it is always for the detaining authority to justify the detention on a fair construction of the empowering legislation.

4. FORCE OR FEAR—INTIMIDATION

The Roman law wrong of *metus,* of unlawfully overcoming the will of another, with its distinct action of reparation for injury resulting therefrom [17]—*actio quod metus causa*—has not been fully adopted in Scots law, though the quasi-contractual obligation of restitution, the equitable action of reduction and other remedies exist to prevent one party enjoying an advantage over another obtained by force.

11 *Arbuckle* v. *Taylor* (1815) 3 Dow's App. 160; *Young* v. *Leven* (1822) 1 Sh.App. 179; *Sheppeard* v. *Fraser* (1849) 11 D. 446; *Dallas* v. *Mann* (1853) 15 D. 746; *Thomson* v. *Adam* (1865) 4 M. 29; *Rae* v. *Linton* (1875) 2 R. 669; *Green* v. *Chalmers* (1878) 6 R. 318.
12 This was the form of action in *Liversidge* v. *Anderson* [1942] A.C. 206.
13 [1917] A.C. 260.
14 [1942] A.C. 206.
15 The very wide interpretation given in this case to the phrase " If the Secretary of State has reasonable cause to believe . . . " was severely criticised, and said not to be a general rule as to the construction of the phrase, in *Nakkuda Ali* v. *Jayaratne* [1951] A.C. 66.
16 *Greene* v. *Home Secretary* [1942] A.C. 284; *Budd* v. *Anderson* [1943] K.B. 642 (and *cf.* *R.* v. *Home Secretary, ex p. Budd* [1942] 2 K.B. 14).
17 Dig. IV, 2, 1; IV, 2, 14, 3 and 5; IV, 2, 16, 2.

Stair [18] and Bankton [19] both refer to extortion as a known kind of delinquency and the action by reason of fear has been prayed in aid in South Africa,[20] so that there is no good reason in principle why, independently of restitution, a person coerced should not in Scots law recover damages for the wrong done him by having had pressure put on him,[21] and recover damages for the loss sustained if restitution is impossible.

Stair [22] lays down that " extortion signifies the act of force, or other means of fear, whereby a person is compelled to do that which, of his proper inclination, he would not have done. It doth also imply the obligation of the injurer to the injured to repair his loss and damage by such acts. Things so done are said to be done *vi majori* or *metus causa*, by force or fear." Having referred to the *actio quod metus causa*, he observes that " The delinquence done by extortion obliges to reparation ... our customs go much along with the course of the civil law in this ... and it is competent, either by way of action, or sometimes by exception ... "

In modern practice reduction and restitution *in integrum* are usually sought alone but it is thought that these remedies are not exclusive.

In *Macpherson* v. *Ettles* [23] it was held that to require a person unnecessarily to find caution would not only entitle him to set aside the obligation but would justify a claim of damages for extorting it. Equally clear, it would seem, in the case where a person is induced by force and fear to sign a cheque which is cashed or grant a deed which is used before the granter recovers his liberty of action. His claim would be not only for reduction of the document signed but for damages in compensation for what he had been induced to give up. Thus a person blackmailed is entitled to recover what he has paid. Where a landlord threatens a tenant to evict him unless a sum of money is paid, that is clearly criminal [24] but a civil claim would also seem to lie for the recovery of any money paid and for any loss sustained in consequence.

In *Brown* v. *Murray* [25] a police officer, acting on the information of the proprietor of the official race cards for a race meeting, and apprehensive of a possible breach of the peace, went to the shop of the publisher of an unofficial and inaccurate racecard and by strong remonstrances, though without express threats of criminal proceedings, induced him to stop the sale of them. The shopkeeper sued him for damages representing his loss of profits, but was held not entitled to damages, as the action was held justifiable as preventing what might reasonably have resulted in a breach of the peace. The actionability of the conduct does not seem to have been questioned.

[18] I, 9, 6.
[19] I, 10, 13.
[20] Voet, IV, 2, translator's note.
[21] Bell, *Law Dictionary*, s. v. Extortion, says that acts and deeds extorted by force or fear may be reduced " and the offender, besides, may be subjected in damages."
[22] I, 9, 8.
[23] (1787) Hailes, 1021.
[24] *Silverstein* v. *H.M. Advocate*, 1949 J.C. 160.   [25] (1874) 1 R. 776.

It seems clear that threats of personal violence to the pursuer, or a relative, threats of damage to his property, threats of vexatious litigation or of giving unfounded information to the police, may all amount to coercion or intimidation.[26] Threats of anything which may in the circumstances legitimately be done, such as to do diligence on a decree, or to sue for money owed, are permissible pressure and not actionable coercion or intimidation. Pressure stemming from superior economic power is not illegitimate, such as the pressure one contracting party may put on another.[27]

Loss from intimidation of third party by defender. The threats may be directed against a third party and thereby do harm to the pursuer, as where the defender by threats induced customers not to deal with the pursuer, and he thereby loses business.[28] In *Tarleton* v. *McGawley*[29] the defendant, by firing cannon at them, deterred natives from trading with the plaintiff's ship, whereby he lost trade; this was held actionable. These cases have been held to amount to the tort of intimidation.

In *Hewit* v. *Edinburgh Lathsplitters' Association*[30] it was held to be an actionable wrong for members of a union to obtain the pursuer's dismissal from various employments by threats that they would strike unless he were dismissed. More recently it has been held in England that the tort of intimidation had been committed where the defendants harmed the plaintiff by putting pressure on a third party (by threatening to break a contract with him), and the third party, under pressure, dismissed and thus caused the loss to the plaintiff of which he complained.[31] Such cases, however, belong to the chapter of the law where the pursuer complains of economic loss, rather than of personal coercion or intimidation.

5. CIRCUMVENTION AND FRAUD

" Circumvention signifieth the act of fraud, whereby a person is induced to a deed or obligation by deceit. It is called *dolus malus* . . . The Roman praetors . . . did give this of fraud, *Quae dolo malo facta esse dicentur* . . . *judicium dabo* . . . reparation [was] given to the injured to the single value only . . . We have in this also resumed the sentence of the civil law, because it is most equitable and expedient." [32] " Fraud gives remedy by reparation to all that are damnified thereby, against the actor of the fraud, either by annulling of the contract . . . or by making up the damage sustained by the fraud, at the option of the injured." [33]

Fraud is a delict in that the individual's free will is overborne by a deliberately false representation of fact, without which he would not have

26 *Cf. Allen* v. *Flood* [1898] A.C. 1, 105, *per* Lord Watson.
27 *Cf. Silverstein* v. *H.M.A.*, 1949 J.C. 160, 163.
28 *Cf. Garret* v. *Taylor* (1620) Cro.Jac. 567.
29 (1794) Peake, 270.
30 (1906) 14 S.L.T. 489.
31 *Rookes* v. *Barnard* [1964] 1 All E.R. 367; see further Chap. 26, *infra.*
32 Stair, I, 9, 9–11.
33 *Ibid.* I, 9, 14.

acted as he did. Fraud consists in " a false representation made by the defendant knowingly, or without belief in its truth, or recklessly, careless whether it be true or false, with the intention that the plaintiff should act in reliance upon the representation, which causes damage to the plaintiff in consequence of his reliance upon it." [34] The constituent elements of fraud are discussed mostly in cases where reduction of a contract is sought on the ground of fraud.

It is now settled that damages may be recovered for being induced fraudulently to contract, though the contract is not reduced.[35] Fraud is normally an infringement of interests of substance, in that it normally affects the individual by leading him into a financially detrimental situation,[36] as by inducing an unprofitable contract, but it may also be an infringement of the individual's freedom of action and may equally induce an individual to act to the detriment of some aspect of his personality. Fraud may, for example, lead a man into a situation where he suffers personal injuries.

Thus in *Wilkinson* v. *Downton* [37] the defendant caused the plaintiff serious nervous shock by a false representation, intended to be acted on, and in fact acted on, that the plaintiff's husband had been seriously injured. This could be treated as fraudulent misrepresentation. In *Burrows* v. *Rhodes*,[38] B, induced by fraudulent misrepresentations to join unwittingly in an illegal enterprise (the Jameson raid into the Transvaal in 1895), in which he was wounded, lost a leg and suffered loss of earnings, was held to have a good right of action against R. for damage suffered in consequence of entering on the illegal enterprise. This principle would not necessarily apply, even though the representations were fraudulent, to a case where the pursuer knew, or reasonably should have known, that what he was being persuaded to do was clearly criminal, such as to take part in a bank robbery; in such a case *ex turpi causa non oritur actio*.

Circumvention, fraud and deceit may also be the ground of action of a woman led astray, in circumstances where a claim founded on seduction [39] is not competent.

Negligent misrepresentation. Liability for negligent misrepresentation causing personal injury is undecided, but there is no good ground in principle for denying the possibility of such liability.[40] It is submitted that there is a duty to take reasonable care in making statements, reliance on which, if they are unfounded, is foreseeably likely to result in personal injuries or death or economic loss. In the main English authorities [41] an

---

[34] *Derry* v. *Peek* (1889) 14 App.Cas. 337, 374, *per* Lord Herschell, L.C.
[35] *Smith* v. *Sim*, 1954 S.C. 357.
[36] For this reason it is discussed further in Chap. 26.
[37] [1897] 2 Q.B. 57; so, too, in *Janvier* v. *Sweeney* [1919] 2 K.B. 316.
[38] [1899] 1 Q.B. 816.
[39] See further, section 6, *infra*.
[40] See full discussion, in relation to injuries to substance, in Chap. 26, *infra*.
[41] *Candler* v. *Crane, Christmas & Co.* [1951] 2 K.B. 164; *Hedley Byrne & Co.* v. *Heller and Partners* [1964] A.C. 465.

injury to personal substance, patrimonial loss, was alone in issue and a ground faintly adumbrated for the majority decision against liability in *Candler* [41] was that the principle of *Donoghue* v. *Stevenson* [42] did not give a remedy for an injury to substance but was confined to cases of physical injury, This suggests that liability for personal injury caused by negligent misrepresentation would have been more favourably considered by the court. It is submitted that personal injury is *a fortiori* of injury to substance, and, that subject to the conditions suggested by Denning, L.J.,[43] liability may exist. It is submitted, for example, that if the manufacturers of a patent medicine or tinned food negligently misrepresented on the label or accompanying literature the nature of the contents or dose and thereby induced a person to consume, whereby he is injured, the principle of *Donoghue* would apply. So, too, if the manufacturers or repairers of a vehicle or aircraft negligently represented it as safe, there would be liability if it were not and injury resulted.[44]

Innocent misrepresentation. Probably no liability exists to make reparation for personal injury resulting from misrepresentation quite innocent and not amounting to negligent misrepresentation, because there is clearly absent that element of circumvention or *dolus* or negligence demanded by all the authorities. But where personal injury is possible it would be extremely difficult to satisfy a court that a misrepresentation was innocent and not inferring liability rather than negligent.

6. SEDUCTION

Seduction may be regarded as a special instance of circumvention. It consists in obtaining sexual relations with a virgin by fraud, circumvention, guile, misrepresentations or other persuasive practices and deflowering her. It differs from fornication and adultery, which are fully consensual, and from indecent assault and rape, where the woman's consent is wholly absent. The wrong consists in overcoming the will by means other than force, and causing loss of virginity. There is no remedy for a voluntary surrender of virtue. The popular use of the word " seduce " differs from its legal sense; the popular sense means no more than intercourse; in the legal sense " seduction " implies that consent to intercourse was induced by arts or deceit.[45] Though the action is frequently regarded as an *actio injuriarum*, and certainly has affinities therewith, it cannot properly be regarded as based on *injuria* since the consent of the woman, albeit obtained by deceit or circumvention, is necessary, and an *injuria* implies no consent.[46]

The wrong is actionable at the instance of the woman debauched, and is wholly different from the English action, which lies at the instance

[42] 1932 S.C.(H.L.) 31.
[43] [1951]2 K.B. 164, 179.
[44] *Cf.* instances referred to by Denning L.J., in *Candler, supra*, 179, of the negligent analyst of food, and the negligent inspector of lifts.
[45] *Cathcart* v. *Brown* (1905) 7 F. 951, 953.
[46] Grotius, *Jurisprudence of Holland*, 3, 35, 8.

of the girl's father for loss of services caused him by her seduction.[47] The claim by a husband against another man who has led his wife astray, though sometimes called " seduction," [48] is properly enticement, and a different wrong.[49]

It is essential that the pursuer was a virgin when seduced [50] and not married, widowed or previously unchaste, though subsequent unchastity or marriage to another [51] do not bar the action. This is because the essence of the wrong is not the intercourse, but the woman's loss of her virginity.[45] Consequently though a woman previously unchaste, or married, or widowed, may in fact be led astray and beguiled into consenting to intercourse, as distinct from indulging in fully voluntary intercourse, she has no right of action for seduction, not having lost her virginity by reason of the defender's having cheated her of it.[52] Her right of action would properly be for loss caused by circumvention and fraud.

It follows also that a woman can only once sue for seduction; if she is subsequently led astray again she would have to sue for loss caused by circumvention and fraud, or possibly for breach of promise.

But unchastity subsequent to the seduction complained of, or marriage to another, will not bar the action, though both will weigh heavily against substantial damages as indicating that the girl did not value her virginity or that its loss had not harmed her matrimonial prospects. It is not necessary to put in issue that the pursuer was previously " a person of virtuous conduct and untainted character," [53] but if a pursuer does not make herself out to be such, she is not entitled to damages.[54] It does not, however, seem always to have been appreciated that the action was competent only to women who were virgins prior to the seduction.[55]

By Moses' judicial law, a man who seduced a woman was bound *stupratam aut dotare aut nubere* [56] and this was the rule of the canon law,[57] and the Roman-Dutch law,[58] but in modern Scottish practice an award of damages is the sole remedy; the damages are not so much solatium as

---

[47] See, e.g., *Rosses* v. *Bhagvat Sinhjee* (1891) 19 R. 31.
[48] e.g., *Macdonald* v. *Macdonald* (1885) 12 R. 1327.
[49] Chap. 22, *infra.*
[50] Grotius, *supra*; McKerron, 194; van Leeuwen, 4, 36, 2. *Cf. Gairdin* v. *Lammye* (1543) Fraser on *Husband and Wife*, I, 501; " *quia seduxit defloravit et dormivit cum dicta Agnete,* she being at the time a virgin."
[51] *Kay* v. *Wilson's Trs.* (1850) 12 D. 845, 847; *Rosses, supra.*
[52] Voet, 48, 5, 4; van der Linden, 1, 16, 4; applied in South Africa, *van Staden* v. *Rudy,* 1908 E.D.C. 7.
[53] *Linning* v. *Hamilton* (1748) Mor. 13909, 13911; *McCandy* v. *Turpy* (1826) 5 S. 527; *Walker* v. *McIsaac* (1857) 19 D. 340.
[54] Voet, 48, 5, 4, says that there is a presumption that an unmarried girl is a virgin, that she consequently need not prove this, and that the onus of disproof is on the defender.
[55] *Walker, supra,* 341, *per* L. J. C. Hope; " even if it should turn out that the pursuer's conduct early in life was not correct." Such a fact would properly result in dismissal of the action. The pursuer had in fact expressly averred that she had lost her virginity by the defender's conduct.
[56] *Hislop* v. *Ker* (1696) Mor. 13908, referring to Exodus, 22, 16–17. *Nubere* is bad Latin; the proper verb is *ducere.*
[57] *Linning* v. *Hamilton* (1748) Mor. 13909, 13912.
[58] Grotius, *Jurisprudence of Holland,* 3, 3, 35, 8; Voet, 48, 5, 3; van Leeuwen, 4, 37, 6; van der Linden, 1, 16, 4.

" *in compensationem ipsius dotis.*" [59] If, however, the defender can, and elects to, marry the girl, that probably elides her right of action. That he cannot, by reason of being married already, does not bar the action, even if the girl knew that.

It is essential that the woman establish that her scruples were overcome and her consent obtained by deceit, wiles or artful practices.[60] She has no claim if she were truly the seducing party, or readily consented to an invitation to intercourse, or did not believe a false representation made to her,[61] nor, probably, if she demanded payment or other benefit as the price of her virginity, as distinct from accepting presents pressed on her. Seduction is *stuprum fraudulentum.*[62] No damages are due to the woman if the couple have given way to mutual desires, or if it appears that the woman led the man astray—*volenti non fit injuria.*

Means of seduction. Seduction consists of " any artful practices or false insinuations held out to entrap a resolute chastity; any deliberate plan to corrupt the principles or inflame the passions of an inexperienced female; or even any long and persevering solicitations after repeated repulse and resistance." [63] " To make out seduction in the legal sense it must be established that the parties did not meet on equal terms, and that the woman was unfairly treated by the defender. What has to be negatived is the *prima facie* view that, where a man and a woman commit an act of immorality, both are free and willing consenters." [64]

The means allegedly used to overcome her reluctance must be set out in the pleadings and in the issue.[65] The circumstances implying fraudulent conduct which justify an action of damages have been classified [66] into four groups: " (1) Where there has been a promise to marry and connexion has taken place on the faith of the promise. The great majority of the reported cases fall under this head, and the underlying principle is that possession of the woman has been obtained by means of a fraudulent promise to marry. It is well settled that, in cases of this nature damages may be craved and issues proposed, both as regards the breach of promise and also the ensuing seduction. In the latter issue the seductive arts employed require to be specifically set forth.[67] (2) Where there has been courtship with apparent intention to marry, and, on the faith of this,

---

[59] *Gairdin* v. *Lammye* (1543) Fraser on *Husband and Wife*, I, 501.
[60] Fraser, *Husband and Wife* (2nd ed.) I, 501; Hume, *Lect.* III, 132; *Linning* v. *Hamilton* (1748) Mor. 13909; *Stewart* v. *Menzies* (1837) 15 S. 1198; *Gray* v. *Brown* (1878) 5 R. 971; *Gray* v. *Miller* (1901) 39 S.L.R. 256; *Murray* v. *Fraser*, 1916 S.C. 623.
[61] *Sassen* v. *Campbell* (1826) 2 W. & Sh. 309, 333; *Murray, supra.*
[62] *Hislop* v. *Ker* (1696) Mor. 13908; *Linning* v. *Hamilton, supra.*
[63] *Stewart* v. *Menzies* (1873) 15 S. 1198, 1199, *per* Lord Jeffrey.
[64] *Reid* v. *Macfarlane*, 1919 S.C. 518, 522, *per* Lord Skerrington.
[65] *Stewart* v. *Menzies, supra*; *Forbes* v. *Wilson* (1868) 6 M. 770; *Gray* v. *Brown* (1878) 5 R. 971; *Cathcart* v. *Brown* (1905) 7 F. 951.
[66] *Murray* v. *Fraser*, 1916 S.C. 623, 625, *per* Lord Anderson.
[67] Citing *Forbes* v. *Wilson* (1868) 6 M. 770; *Cathcart* v. *Brown* (1905) 7 F. 951. Also *McCandy* v. *Turpy* (1826) 5 S. 527; *Walker* v. *McIsaac* (1857) 19 D. 340; *Paton* v. *Brodie* (1858) 20 D. 258.

connexion has taken place, an action of damages for seduction will lie. In this case the courtship is presumed to have been fraudulently conducted in order to obtain possession of the woman [68] . . . (3) Where the woman is in a position of dependence, as when she is in domestic service, and fraudulent practices have been employed, she is entitled to recover damages for seduction. The dominant consideration here is the position of dependency, whereby her freedom of will is restricted, and her consent influenced by the ascendancy of her master.[69] (4) Where the parties stand in an independent relationship to one another, an action will lie if the woman's consent has been obtained by means of fraudulent circumvention." [70]

These categories are not exhaustive or exclusive. Thus surrender to persistent solicitations is seduction.[71] In one or two cases other averments have been held adequate, such as " threats, solicitations and masterful ascendancy over the pursuer," or " artful practices, continued solicitations and the exercise of authority and force over " the pursuer,[72] ascendancy and influence coupled with the story that anything the defender might do would not harm her.[73] This last representation has been expressly held unnecessary.[74] In a narrow case [75] it was held sufficient to aver that the defender took advantage of his authority and influence as the girl's employer, and professed sincere affection for her and represented that he would do her no harm. It seems therefore that where the relationship between pursuer and defender was that of servant and master or a similar relationship inferring moral ascendancy on the defender's part, that fact is relevant and goes a considerable way to amount to seduction: " Seduction may also be effected by the aid of such dominating influence as might be exercised by a master towards his servant or, it may be, by a doctor towards his patient or a pastor towards a member of his flock, or the like." [76] " It is settled that seduction may be effected by the aid of such dominating influence as that of a master over his servant." [77]

Proof that consent has been obtained by arts and deceit is still necessary even if the pursuer is below sixteen, the age of legal consent under the Criminal Law Amendment Act, 1885, s. 5. Seduction is not presumed,

---

[68] Citing *Linning* v. *Hamilton* (1748) Mor. 13909; *Gray* v. *Brown* (1878) 5 R. 971. Also *Kay* v. *Wilson's Trs.* (1850) 12 D. 845.

[69] Citing *Buchanan* v. *McNab* (1785) Mor. 13918; *Gray* v. *Miller* (1901) 39 S.L.R. 256; *Brown* v. *Harvey*, 1907 S.C. 588. Also *McCandy* v. *Turpy* (1826) 5 S. 527; *Rosses* v. *Bhagvat Sinhjee* (1891) 19 R. 31.

[70] Citing Fraser on *Husband and Wife*, I, 500–505.

[71] *Linning* v. *Hamilton, supra*; cases of *Castlelaw* v. *Agnew* (1719) Ferg.Cons.Rep. 125; *Cameron* v. *Cameron* (1814) *ibid.*, 139; *Black* v. *Nicoll* (1781); *Moliere* v. *Macdowal* (1790); and *Bennet* v. *Ninian* (1808) in Fraser, *Husband and Wife*, I, 503.

[72] *Gray* v. *Miller* (1901) 39 S.L.R. 256.

[73] *Brown* v. *Harvey*, 1907 S.C. 588; *Reid* v. *Macfarlane*, 1919, S.C. 518.

[74] *Murray* v. *Fraser*, 1916 S.C. 623, 632, *per* L.J.C. Scott Dickson.

[75] *MacLeod* v. *MacAskill*, 1920 S.C. 72.

[76] *Murray* v. *Fraser, supra*, 633 *per* Lord Dundas; *cf. R.* v. *Flattery* (1877) 2 Q.B.D. 414; *R.* v. *Williams* [1923] 1 K.B. 340 (intercourse obtained by representations of performing surgical operation).

[77] *Reid* v. *Macfarlane*, 1919 S.C. 518, 520, *per* Lord Mackenzie.

and the man is not liable civilly in such a case merely on proof of the intercourse [78]; such a doctrine would merely be an encouragement to precocious female immorality.[79]

The youth of the girl is an important element in considering whether she had willingly resigned herself or been circumvented by the fraud of her paramour. " The weight to be given to this element will be greater or less according to her precise age between the limits of twelve and sixteen; and will depend in each case, upon the state of her physical development, upbringing, character and knowledge or ignorance of sexual relations. In the case of a very young girl, for example, a girl of twelve or thirteen, who was proved to have had connexion with a man of mature years, there would, in my opinion, be a presumption in fact (which could only be displaced by positive evidence) that she had been the victim of seduction; and the same result would follow if it were proved that a girl below sixteen was as ignorant of sexual matters as a child generally is." [80]

Pregnancy alone is not a ground of action: " The Lords found a woman's being got with child was no ground of action for damages, else a hundred such processes would be intented by whores; as also they thought that every promise and insinuation of marriage was not sufficient to found this action." [81] By itself pregnancy gives rise only to a claim for affiliation and aliment.

Combined claims. An action for seduction may competently be combined with a conclusion for breach of promise of marriage.[82] Separate issues are proper, with separate claims of damages under each head.[83] It may also be combined with a claim for inlying expenses and aliment for an illegitimate child.[84]

Prior to the abolition of marriage by promise *subsequente copula*,[85] the question was liable to arise whether there had not been intercourse on the faith of a promise of marriage, thereby constituting actual marriage, and destroying any claims for breach of promise and for seduction. Thus an action might be brought for declarator of marriage and for adherence, or alternatively for breach of promise and seduction.[86] But this is no longer competent.

Mora. Though the point does not seem to have been discussed it seems clear that delay on the woman's part to make a claim will be regarded unfavourably. Just as an accusation of rape is sometimes the

[78] *Murray* v. *Fraser, supra.*
[79] *Cf. Murray, supra,* 635, *per* Lord Salvesen.
[80] *Murray* v. *Fraser,* 1916 S.C. 623, 636, *per* Lord Salvesen.
[81] *Hislop* v. *Ker* (1696) Mor. 13908.
[82] *Forbes* v. *Wilson* (1868) 6 M. 770.
[83] *Cathcart* v. *Brown* (1905) 7 F. 951.
[84] *Rosses* v. *Bhagvat Sinhjee* (1891) 19 R. 31; *Brown* v. *Harvey,* 1907 S.C. 588; *MacLeod* v. *MacAskill,* 1920 S.C. 72.
[85] Marriage (Scotland) Act, 1939, s. 5.
[86] *McCandy* v. *Turpy* (1826) 5 S. 527; *Paton* v. *Brodie* (1857) 20 D. 258.

reaction of hysteria and remorse after fornication, a claim for seduction
may be brought after consensual intercourse, and such a claim, if at all
seriously delayed, must be critically examined.

Condonation. If a woman be seduced by a man and subsequently they
marry, her right of action may still exist but she is likely to be held to have
condoned the wrong to her; it is in any event unlikely that her evidence
of seduction would be accepted.

Damages. The damages in a case of seduction are in compensation
to the woman for her hurt feelings, defloration and possibly being prejudiced in the marriage market in consequence. Heavier damages are due
if she has been made pregnant. No patrimonial loss need be proved.
Regard must be had to the pursuer's age, condition in life, the defender's
position, his conduct towards her, and the degree of resistance or acquiescence displayed.

Seduction of man by woman. Though there is nothing about the male
comparable to a woman's loss of her virginity, an action by a man for
being persuaded, tricked and beguiled into having intercourse is conceivable. Such would not, however, be a claim for seduction, but for
enticement or adultery.[87]

Action by husband of woman. Where a married woman has intercourse
with a man other than her husband, the husband has a right of action
against the other man, and this is frequently mis-called a claim for
seduction. It does not in fact depend at all on whether the wife was led
astray, beguiled or ensnared by the other man, still less on whether she
was a virgin; it depends solely on the fact of her intercourse with the
other man, and she may have been willing and even eager. Such claims
are properly called cases of enticement or adultery, not seduction, and
are dealt with under these headings.[88]

[87] *Infra,* Chap. 22.
[88] *Infra.* Chap. 22.

CHAPTER 21

INFRINGEMENTS OF THE INTERESTS IN
IMMUNITY OF FEELINGS

1. Infringement of Privacy
2. Breach of Confidence
3. Interference with Domestic Relations

THE law has not yet fully recognised the interest which an individual has that his private and personal affairs shall not be pried into and disclosed to outsiders. " Such an interest is the basis of the disputed legal right of privacy. It is a modern demand, growing out of the conditions of life in the crowded communities of today, and presents difficult problems. The interest is clear. Such publicity with respect to private matters of purely personal concern is an injury to personality. It impairs the mental peace and comfort of the individual and may produce suffering much more acute than that produced by a mere bodily injury. But as the injury is mental and subjective, the difficulties already considered must, at least, confine legal securing of the interest to ordinary sensibilities. Here as in many other cases, in a weighing of interests, the oversensitive must give way. For over and above the difficulties in mode of proof and in applying legal redress, social interests in free speech and dissemination of news have also to be considered. On such grounds, no doubt, a legal right to privacy which fully secures this interest has not been recognised anywhere. For the most part the interest has been secured incidentally, as it were, by taking account of infringement thereof as an element of damage where well-recognised legal rights have also been violated, rather than by establishing a legal right of privacy a violation whereof should constitute a cause of action. But while the law is slow in recognising this interest as something to be secured in and of itself, it would seem that the aggressions of a type of unscrupulous journalism, the invasions of privacy by reporters in competition for a " story," the activities of photographers, and the temptation to advertisers to sacrifice private feelings to their individual gain call upon the law to do more in the attempt to secure this interest than merely take incidental account of infringements of it. A man's feelings are as much a part of his personality as his limbs. The actions that protect the latter from injury may well be made to protect the former by the ordinary process of legal growth. The problems are rather to devise suitable redress and to limit the right in view of the interests involved." [1]

[1] Pound, *Interests of Personality* (1912) 28 H.L.R. 343, 445, and *Selected Essays*, 87, 106–108.

1. INFRINGEMENT OF PRIVACY

The need for legal recognition of an enforceable right to privacy was cogently argued in America in 1890 [2] and since then has been recognised to a varying degree by legislatures and courts there.[3] In England it has not been expressly recognised [4] and in Scotland the issue has not been thoroughly discussed in any reported case. But the absence of precedent does not mean that the wrong does not exist or is not redressible. It is open to consider the problem on principle.

On what principle actionable. It is submitted that the principle of the *actio injuriarum* would justify a Scottish court in giving a remedy for infringement of privacy [5]; the kinds of conduct which amount to such infringement are certainly affronts to personality likely to cause hurt feelings and if the pursuer is aggrieved a remedy should be given. The difficulty is to reconcile the individual's desire to be left alone in peace with what is in many cases a legitimate interest on the part of another person or of the public in certain of his affairs.

Cases raising the problem. The kind of cases which have raised the problem of whether the law does or does not recognise the right of privacy include the publication of a photograph taken surreptitiously and without consent,[6] the use of a person's name or title or photograph or other reference to or representation of him in an advertisement without his consent,[7] the unauthorised use of a person's name in bogus testimonials published in advertisements,[8] and the publication of a biography of a distinguished person without that person's permission, knowledge or co-operation, and against his wishes.[9] The essence of the wrong consists in bringing the name, characteristics, appearance or facts relating to the pursuer into public notice without the consent of the pursuer or legal justification.

A remedy is particularly necessary against over-zealous journalists or photographers who may make an intolerable nuisance of themselves and intrude most objectionably on a person's private life. At the same time the activities of people in public positions are to some extent a matter of legitimate public interest.

---

[2] Warren and Brandeis, " The Right to Privacy " (1890) 4 H.L.R. 193; *Selected Essays*, 122.

[3] Green " The Right of Privacy " (1932) 27 Ill.L.R. 237; Nizer, " The Right to Privacy: A Half Century of Development " (1941) 39 Mich.L.R. 526; Feinberg, " Recent Developments in the Law of Privacy " (1948) 48 Col.L.R. 712; see generally Prosser, Chap. 22; *Restatement*, s. 867. See also Gutteridge and Walton, " The Comparative Law of the Right of Privacy " (1931) 47 L.Q.R. 208, 219.

[4] Winfield, " The Right to Privacy " (1931) 47 L.Q.R. 23; Neill " The Protection of Privacy " (1962) 25 M.L.R. 393.

[5] A Bill, entitled The Right of Privacy Bill was introduced in the House of Lords in 1961 and obtained a second reading, but was subsequently dropped.

[6] *Manola* v. *Stevens and Myers* (1890) cited in Warren and Brandeis, *loc. cit.*; *Pollard* v. *Photographic Co.* (1888) 40 Ch.D. 345, *arguendo.*

[7] *Cf. Tolley* v. *Fry* [1931] A.C. 333.

[8] *Cf. Mazatti* v. *Acme Products, Ltd.* [1930] 4 D.L.R. 601 (Wright, Cases, 699).

[9] Circumstances alleged in " Sunday Telegraph " review.

Incidental redress. Redress can be, and has several times been, given for what is in substance an infringement of the right of privacy, incidentally to some other claim. In *Monson* v. *Tussaud* [10] the plaintiff's portrait model was exhibited, without his consent, in the defendant's waxwork gallery. In the circumstances it was held a libel. In *Tolley* v. *Fry & Sons* [11] an amateur golfer complained of an advertisement of the defendants' chocolate which included a caricature of him, depicted as playing golf with a packet of the defendants' chocolate protruding from his pocket, and a limerick containing his name, averring that it was libellous, as representing that he had prostituted his reputation as an amateur for advertising purposes. It was held that the advertisement was defamatory. This remedy is necessarily restricted to circumstances where the advertisement is, expressly or by innuendo, defamatory. On the other hand, in *Blennerhassett* v. *Novelty Sales Services, Ltd.* [12] where B, without his knowledge or consent, was accidentally ridiculed in an advertisement, the action failed since it would not reasonably have been thought to refer to a living person and was in any event not capable of a defamatory meaning.

Again, in *Pollard* v. *Photographic Co.*, [13] the court restrained a photographer from selling or exhibiting copies of a picture which he had, for consideration, taken of the plaintiff and supplied to her, on the ground that sale and exhibition were a breach of implied contract and a breach of confidence. But it was admitted in argument that a person who took a picture " on the sly " might sell or exhibit it without being in breach of contract. [14] In all these cases the facts permitted of a remedy being given or refused on other legal grounds. But what if no action would lie on contract, or for defamation, or on other recognised grounds?

In *Corelli* v. *Wall*, [15] where defendants published and sold, without the plaintiff's consent, postcards depicting imaginary incidents in her life, an injunction was refused, as the cards were not libellous and the plaintiff had not established any legal right to restrain the publication of a portrait of herself made without her authority and which, though professing to be her portrait, was totally unlike her. The plaintiff was certainly a well-known authoress and at that time a public figure, but it was accepted that the sale of the postcards was a matter of grave annoyance to her, and as the cards had no relevance to the sphere of public life in which she moved, it is thought that an infringement of privacy existed and could have been enjoined.

In *Williams* v. *Settle* [16] the defendant, who had taken photographs at the plaintiff's wedding, subsequently sold one to a newspaper for

---

[10] [1894] 1 Q.B. 671.
[11] [1931] A.C. 333.
[12] (1933) 175 L.T.J. 393; Wright, *Cases*, 701. Such facts might have justified an action for convicium in Scotland.
[13] (1888) 40 Ch.D. 345.
[14] *Cf. Sports & General Press Agency* v. *" Our Dogs " Publishing Co.* [1916] 2 K.B. 880.
[15] (1906) 22 T.L.R. 532. Contrast *Dunlop Rubber Co.* v. *Dunlop* [1921] 1 A.C. 367, where publication by company of portrait of D., falsely representing him as foppish old gentleman, was restrained as libellous.   [16] [1960] 1 W.L.R. 1072.

publication when the plaintiff's father-in-law was murdered. Damages were awarded, nominally for infringement of copyright in the photograph, but the conduct was said to be " in total disregard not only of the legal rights of the plaintiff regarding copyright but of his feelings and his sense of family dignity and pride." This comes very close to recognising an actionable right of privacy.

A remedy has several times in other cases been granted by invoking the principles of copyright [17] or of breach of contract or of confidence.[18] In some cases too it would probably be possible in Scotland to give a remedy on the ground of convicium, if the pursuer was brought into hatred, contempt or ridicule by the publication complained of.

In *White* v. *Dickson* [19] the court declined to interdict a proposed publication of correspondence between the parties, the recipient having a legitimate interest to publish and there being no reason to anticipate outrage or invasion to reputation and private feelings, but reserved the possibility of liability in damages for injury done by the publication. Such liability might well, it is thought, include liability for feelings hurt by invasion of privacy. Again, in *MacColl* v. *MacColl* [20] the pursuer in a divorce case intercepted and opened a letter from the defender to her paramour and had a photostat copy made.[21] Such conduct could well be actionable as infringement of privacy, though whether the damages claimed could include a claim for consequential loss by being divorced in consequence of what was in the letter being adduced in evidence seems more doubtful.

Telephone tapping. The practice of tapping telephone wires [22] and thus overhearing matter being communicated seems similarly to be an infringement of privacy, even though the information obtained thereby may be admissible in evidence.[23] Since, however, such tapping requires the co-operation of Post Office engineers it is questionable if there is any remedy. "The position may well be that the Crown has no power conferred by law to tap telephones but that the citizen has no means of redress if the Crown does authorise tapping of his calls." [24] In America in *Rhodes* v. *Graham* [24a] damages were given for this as being an invasion of privacy.

---

[17] *Dodsley* v. *McFarquhar* (1775) 5 B.S. 509; *Cadell and Davies* v. *Stewart* (1804) Mor.Appx. Literary Property, No. 4; 5 Pat. 493; *Gee* v. *Pritchard* (1818) 2 Swans. 402; *Prince Albert* v. *Strange* (1849) 2 De G. & Sm. 652. *Cf. Caird* v. *Sime* (1887) 14 R.(H.L.) 37.

[18] *Yovatt* v. *Winyard* (1820) 1 Jac. & W. 394; *Abernethy* v. *Hutchinson* (1824) 3 L.J.Ch. 209.

[19] (1881) 8 R. 896, citing Bell, *Com.* I, 111.

[20] 1946 S.L.T. 312 (sequel 1948 S.C. 500); see also *Rattray* v. *Rattray* (1897) 25 R. 315, and Crown Proceedings Act, 1947, s. 9.

[21] The Committee on The Interception of Communications (Cmnd. 283, 1957) refers to an opinion by Lord Chancellor Campbell that interception of mail was illegal at common law.

[22] The competency of this was considered in The Report of the Committee of Privy Councillors appointed to inquire into the Interception of Communications (Cmnd. 283, 1957).

[23] *Re Marrinan* [1957] C.L.Y. 2747.

[24] Street, *Freedom, The Individual and the Law* (1963) p. 37.

[24a] (1931) 238 Ky. 225.

Examination of persons detained under suspicion of crime. Privacy is involved in the case where a person is detained by the police on suspicion of having committed a crime, and the issue has arisen of whether taking the finger-prints of such a person, without his consent or a warrant, is an undue invasion of his liberties. It was held that at common law it was not an actionable invasion of liberty for the police to do so without a warrant, and it was indicated that the same applied to examination of his person and clothing.[25]

Where on the other hand a person has not been apprehended but charged with crime and liberated on bail, photographs and finger-prints may not be taken without consent, and to do so is illegal and actionable.[26] Nor in such a case may a person be searched, or have his finger-prints taken or scrapings taken from under his fingernails.[27] And a person merely charged cannot be subjected to medical examination without his consent, though he may be observed medically.[28]

Wrongful search of premises. The clearest case of infringement of privacy is where a wrongful or unwarranted search is made of the com-plainer's premises, and such facts are recognised as wrongful. In the absence of a warrant such a search by police or others is clearly wrongful, unless in cases of extreme urgency [29] as also if the terms of any warrant issued do not cover what is actually done.[30] If there is a warrant in existence but it was granted outwith the granter's jurisdiction,[31] or was in general terms,[32] it is unjustifiable and the granter is responsible for the wrong done thereby, without any question of malice and lack of probable cause.[33] Even if such a search is warranted a procurator-fiscal instructing it will be liable in damages if he can be shown to have acted maliciously and without probable cause. If search is consented to, things found during the search may be seized and evidence relating thereto is admissible; no question of infringement of privacy arises.[34] A search warrant may, however, be granted, and search thereunder will consequently not be actionable, though the persons whose premises are searched have been neither charged nor apprehended.[35]

Besetting and watching property. In *Robertson* v. *Keith* [36] a woman complained that the chief constable had subjected her house to con-tinuous watch over a period, and thereby damaged her reputation and

[25] *Adair* v. *McGarry*, 1933 J.C. 72.
[26] *Adamson* v. *Martin*, 1916 S.C. 319.
[27] *McGovern* v. *H.M. Advocate*, 1950 J.C. 33.
[28] *Reid* v. *Nixon*, 1948 J.C. 68; see also *Forrester* v. *H.M. Advocate*, 1952 J.C. 28; *Farrell* v. *Concannon*, 1957 J.C. 12; *McKie* v. *H.M. Advocate*, 1958 J.C. 24.
[29] *H.M. Advocate* v. *McGuigan*, 1935 J.C. 16.
[30] *H.M. Advocate* v. *Turnbull*, 1951 J.C. 96.
[31] *Sawers* v. *McCrone* (1835) 13 S. 443.
[32] *Entick* v. *Carrington* (1765) 19 St.Tr. 1063.
[33] *Bell* v. *Black and Morrison* (1865) 3 M. 1026.
[34] *H.M. Advocate* v. *Hepper*, 1958 J.C. 39.
[35] *Stewart* v. *Roach*, 1950 S.C. 318, disapproving *MacLauchlan* v. *Renton*, 1911 S.C.(J.) 12, 14.
[36] 1936 S.C. 29.

business. The watch was in fact for a detective who was thought to be associating with the pursuer. The action did not expressly charge invasion of privacy, but " wrongful and illegal actings " and also alleged defamation. In the result the defender's actings were held privileged in the absence of averments and proof of malice and lack of probable cause, but similar conduct by a non-privileged defender would probably have been actionable on both grounds.

Limits to claim for infringement of privacy. In considering a claim for infringement of privacy, countervailing social interests have to be weighed. Freedom of speech and of the Press, the reasonable interest of individuals in the lives and deeds of persons prominent in the community, or " in the news," and the public interest in government, the administration of justice, and so on, all militate against the existence of an unqualified " right to be left alone." But there is a difference between those who seek publicity, and those who are unwillingly dragged into notoriety, *e.g.* relatives of a person murdered, and there should be some limits to Press intrusions. So too, where heritage is involved, a person cannot reasonably be heard to complain if another should stand where he can see into the complainer's garden, or build his house where he will be able to overlook the complainer's property. But persistent " snooping " or " noseyness " may be another matter from the possibility of accidental or incidental observation,[37] and a person should surely not have to submit to whatever attentions the Press direct at him or her without possibility of remedy.[38] Watching a house persistently may be a nuisance,[39] or defamatory,[40] and a " peeping Tom " is committing a breach of the peace.[41] These kinds of conduct should certainly be recognised as forms of invasion of privacy and actionable, unless justified in the circumstances.

2. BREACH OF CONFIDENCE

Akin to prying into one's private affairs is the wrong of disclosing information about a third party in breach of confidence, of an undertaking or obligation not to do so. It may cause an individual acute hurt to feelings, grief or shame, and may harm his reputation and business or other interests if a person discloses information about him to a third party, or parties, or to persons generally. A difficulty about legal redress is that it may require even wider publication of the matters desired to be kept secret to enable a court to grant a remedy.

---

[37] *Cf. Victoria Park Racing Co.* v. *Taylor* (1937) 58 C.L.R. 479, discussed in 54 L.Q.R. 319.

[38] *Cf. Melvin* v. *Reid* (1931) 112 Cal.App. 285 (Prosser and Smith, *Cases and Materials on Torts,* 1084) where a reformed prostitute, living respectably, complained of an un-authorised film of her life, using her name, which exposed her to obloquy, contempt and ridicule. She was held to have a good cause of action. In Scotland would this have been actionable as convicium? See Chap. 23.

[39] *Lyons* v. *Wilkins* [1899] 1 Ch. 255.

[40] *Robertson* v. *Keith,* 1936 S.C. 29.

[41] *Raffaeli* v. *Heatly,* 1949 J.C. 101.

There seems little doubt that such conduct is actionable under the principle of the *actio injuriarum*; if the information disclosed is derogatory an action may lie for convicium or defamation.[42] Even if true and accurate a claim may lie for breach of confidence.

The main issue is whether the circumstances were such as to raise a duty on the defender's part to keep confidence and maintain secrecy about the information which he is alleged to have disclosed. Such a duty does arise in many circumstances.[43] In some contracts of employment it is an express term that the employee will observe the prohibitions of the Official Secrets Acts.

In most cases of the employment of persons of professional standing, it is an implied term that the practitioner will not, save under legal compulsion, disclose information which comes to his knowledge in the course of the employment. Thus an accountant will be held liable for communicating to the Inland Revenue, unasked, information obtained from papers put in his possession.[44]

The duty of confidence probably exists also in any case where one person communicates information to another with the request that the latter do not publish it further, agreement to this becoming contractual if the second person does not demur to receiving the information.

Such a duty of confidence also exists in some cases where there is no contract of employment, as in the relationship between clergyman and parishioner. It is submitted that it would be actionable for a clergyman, save under legal compulsion, to disclose information given him by a parishioner making confession or seeking advice.[45] The same probably applies to information given to a friend whom one consults, though not in his professional capacity, and possibly even to information given to a journalist.

3. INTERFERENCE WITH DOMESTIC RELATIONS

The commonest case giving rise to a claim for hurt feelings is where a third party has, wilfully or negligently, caused the death of a person bound to the pursuer by ties of blood or marriage and thereby caused the pursuer grief and pained feelings, with or without patrimonial loss. These, and related cases, are dealt with in Chapter 22.

---

42 See further Chap. 23, *infra*.
43 *Mushets* v. *Mackenzie* (1899) 1 F. 756 (no duty to keep secret "character" given by former employer); *Fulton* v. *Stubbs* (1903) 5 F. 814 (no duty on creditors to preserve silence about creditors' meeting at which debtor offered composition); *Neuman* v. *Kennedy* (1905) 12 S.L.T. 763.
44 *Brown's Trs.* v. *Hay* (1898) 25 R. 1112. See also *Watson* v. *McEwan* (1905) 7 F.(H.L.) 109 (doctor); *Garner* v. *Garner* (1920) 36 T.L.R. 196; *C.* v. *C.* [1946] 1 All E.R. 562 (doctors); *Wheeler* v. *Le Marchant* (1881) 17 Ch.D. 675 (solicitor); *Tournier* v. *National Provincial and Union Bank of England* [1924] 1 K.B. 461 (banker).
45 *Cf. Broad* v. *Pitt* (1828) 3 C. & P. 518.

CHAPTER 22

INFRINGEMENTS OF THE INTERESTS IN THE DOMESTIC RELATIONS

1. Enticement
2. Adultery
3. Rape
4. Loss of Consortium
5. Physical or Mental Injury to Relative
6. Assythment
7. Death of Relative caused Negligently
8. Statutory Action under Carriage by Air Acts
9. Slander of deceased Relative

EVERY person has a legally recognised and protected interest in the continuance unimpaired of his domestic relations, that is, to be allowed to continue living with his or her spouse, and with his or her parents or children without interference from a third party. Certain infringements of this interest are recognised as actionable delicts.

1. ENTICEMENT

Enticement of wife

A husband has a right of action against anyone, whether a stranger or a member of her own family,[1] who entices his wife to leave him, and thus to violate her duty of adhering to and consorting with her husband.[2] The main propositions applicable to a case of this kind were set out in *Adamson* v. *Gillibrand* [3] as follows:

1. A person who entices a wife away from her husband so as to deprive him of her society is prima facie liable.
2. Threats overbearing her will infer liability.
3. Advice or approval regarding her own wish or intention to leave her husband, given by a friend or stranger in good faith does not subject to liability.[4]
4. A husband has no claim if ill-treatment justifies the wife's departure or if the wife represents this to be so and this is believed and acted on.
5. The wife's parents are liable as much as a stranger though a lesser degree of misconduct or ill-usage would justify a parent's action in receiving back a daughter on grounds of natural affection, if in good faith.[5]

---

[1] *Duncan* v. *Cumming* (1714) 5 B.S. 104 (her father); *Adamson* v. *Gillibrand*, 1923 S.L.T. 328 (her mother).
[2] Compare the action for inducing breach of contract.
[3] 1923 S.L.T. 328; *cf. Place* v. *Searle* [1932] 2 K.B. 497, 517, *per* Greer L.J.
[4] *Cf. Smith* v. *Kaye* (1904) 20 T.L.R. 261.
[5] *Cf. Gottlieb* v. *Gleiser* [1955] C.L.Y. 2694.

714

Clearly the enticement need not be for adultery or immoral purposes; it need not be by a male person at all; it may be by a relative; and it may in particular circumstances be justifiable. In every case it will be necessary to show that the wife's natural wish and legal duty to adhere to her husband were overcome, and it is not enough to prove that she left her husband voluntarily (whether justifiably or not) and was then taken in by a relative or friend. It is clear also that a claim for enticement would probably fail if in the circumstances the wife had already been relieved of her obligation to adhere to the husband, as where he was guilty of adultery, desertion or cruelty, if, in short, she had reasonable grounds for non-adherence. As it was put in an English case [6]: " It is the duty of the wife to reside and consort with her husband. This is a duty which she owes to him, and a person who procures, entices or persuades her to violate this duty commits a wrong towards the husband for which he is entitled to recover damages; unless the person who procured, enticed or persuaded her acted from ' principles of humanity,' to protect her from her husband's ill-treatment, in which case no action can be maintained, even though it should turn out that the wife's allegation was unfounded."

There seems to be no authority for founding an action on harbouring of a spouse, in the absence of enticement to leave his or her spouse.[7]

Enticement of wife for adultery. The husband also has an action where another man entices his wife away from her adherence to him, for the purpose of adultery and illicit cohabitation.[8] By analogy with the claim competent to a virgin personally for being led astray and tricked into surrendering her virtue,[9] this claim by the husband is frequently miscalled a claim for seduction.[10]

It appears, however, that, unlike cases of seduction of virgins, in cases of enticement of wives, it is unnecessary to condescend in detail on the arts, wiles, promises and contrivances employed to attach the woman's affections and subdue her principles.[11] Indeed there may have been none, but rather persuasion or even threats. Hume [12] states that if the criminal conversation (*i.e.*, the adultery) is proved, " the seduction of the woman is thence presumed in respect of the natural character of the sex " so that the onus of proof is rather on the defender. This is inaccurate in that proof of adultery is not an essential of enticement, and it is questionable if enticement by the man would always be inferred today from proven adultery; wife and paramour might be equally guilty and the wife not at all reluctant. The only differences between an action on the ground of

---

6 *Place* v. *Searle* [1932] 2 K.B. 497, 517, *per* Greer L.J.
7 *Winchester* v. *Fleming* [1957] 3 All E.R. 711; sequel [1958] 3 All E.R. 51n.
8 As to liability for adultery without enticement from adherence, see s. 2, *infra.*
9 *Supra,* Chap. 20.
10 As in *Baillie* v. *Bryson* (1818) 1 Mur. 317; *Glover* v. *Samson* (1856) 18 D. 609; *Macdonald* v. *Macdonald* (1885) 12 R. 1327. Hume, *Lect.* III, 130, also sanctions the transferred use of the word " seduction."
11 Contrast Hume, *Lect.* III, 131 (enticement) with III, 132 (seduction); see also *Glover* v. *Samson* (1856) 18 D. 609; *Macdonald* v. *Macdonald* (1885) 12 R. 1327.
12 *Lect.* III, 131.

enticement of, and one founded on adultery with, the pursuer's wife are that, if enticement is founded on, evidence must be led that the defender took steps to alienate the wife's affections and induce or persuade her to leave, which justifies heavier damages than does a case of simple adultery where erring wife and paramour are equally guilty and the wife's diversion from adherence to her husband was quite voluntary,[13] and that in enticement proof of actual adultery is not essential, it being sufficient to establish that the paramour caused the wife to abandon her husband. An impotent man could be held liable for enticement, but not for adultery. Sometimes it is not clear in particular cases whether the ground of action is adultery or enticement.[14] The basis of the action for adultery [15] is *concubitus*, but of that for enticement is encouragement to desert, whether there be proven *concubitus* or not.

Enticement of husband. It has been held in England [16] that an action lies at the suit of a wife whose husband has been enticed away and this has been followed in Scotland, in a case where it was held necessary to make averments of deliberate attempts to entice a reluctant male to give up his wife and commit adultery with the defender.[17]

Enticement of child. It is probable that any third party who entices a pupil or minor child to leave his parent or other person having lawful custody of him is liable in damages. A claim may lie even against a parent not entitled to custody who seeks to entice the child out of the custody of the parent lawfully entitled thereto. In English law the basis of the action is for depriving the parent of the child's services,[18] but in Scots law the basis of the claim is probably interference with the natural parental rights to custody and upbringing.[19] In *Delaney* v. *Stirling* [20] an action of damages had been brought against the directors of an institution for destitute children for having illegally detained the pursuer's children (who had been voluntarily left there), and a sum of £100 was paid in settlement of the claim. The father's subsequent action against the superintendent of the institution for damages for loss of the children was in the circumstances held barred by the terms of the discharge he had granted to the directors, but no question was raised as to the competency of the claim.

Such a claim would certainly be incompetent if the custody of the child has been judicially awarded to some person other than the pursuing

---

[13] *Baillie* v. *Bryson* (1818) 1 Mur. 317, 334, 336–337; *cf. Francis* v. *Francis* [1959] C.L.Y. 956.
[14] *Ker* v. *Renton* (1792) Hume, *Lect.* III, 131; *Maxwell* v. *Montgomery* (1787) Mor. 13919; *Paterson* v. *Bone* (1803) Mor. 13920; *Baillie* v. *Bryson* (1818) 1 Mur. 317.
[15] s. 2, *infra.*
[16] *Gray* v. *Gee* (1923) 39 T.L.R. 429; *Newton* v. *Hardy* (1933) 149 L.T. 165; approved *Place* v. *Searle* [1932] 2 K.B. 497; *Best* v. *Samuel Fox & Co.* [1952] A.C. 716; *Welton* v. *Broadhead* [1958] C.L.Y. 3297.
[17] *McGeever* v. *McFarlane* (1951) 67 Sh.Ct.Rep. 48 (miscalled a case of seduction).
[18] *Lough* v. *Ward* [1945] 2 All E.R. 338.
[19] Fraser, P. & Ch. 76; *cf. Hutchinson* v. *Hutchinson* (1890) 18 R. 237; *Edgar* v. *Fisher's Trs.* (1893) 21 R. 325; *Begbie* v. *Nichol*, 1949 S.C. 158.
[20] (1893) 20 R. 506; see also *Delaney* v. *Edinburgh Children's Aid* (1889) 16 R. 753; *Delaney* v. *Colston* (1891) 19 R. 8.

parent, and would doubtless fail if the defender could show that he had bona fide and justifiably taken the child from the possession of a parent or parents to save it from serious moral or physical dangers. Such a course would, however, only be reasonable in dire emergency and pending an application to have the child's custody regulated by the court.

The enticement may be of a child or young person of either sex, and need not be for sexual purposes. It would be actionable to persuade or assist a boy to run away to go to sea, as much as to procure or attempt to procure a girl to leave her home to become a prostitute.[21]

2. ADULTERY

Adultery[22] with a woman is a grave wrong to the feelings, honour and reputation of the husband of the woman concerned and gives rise to an *actio injuriarum* at his instance against his wife's paramour.[23] This right of action does not require proof of enticement away from her husband, nor of seductive arts, nor of interference with matrimonial life. It depends simply on infringement of the right of spouses to have sexual access to each other exclusively, and on wrongful carnal intercourse.[24] The claim may be made in an action of divorce at the husband's instance in which the adultery is founded on and the other man is cited as co-defender,[25] provided that the Court of Session has jurisdiction, under the rules applicable to divorce, to dissolve the marriage, and also has jurisdiction over the co-defender under the rules applicable to petitory actions for damages.[26] Alternatively, the claim may be made by separate action of damages.

It is probably essential to prove that the defender (paramour) knew, or at least in the circumstances reasonably should have known, at the time of the connection, that the woman was already married.[27] This is because *dolus* is an element of the *injuria*, and it is absent if the paramour believed, or reasonably thought, that he was merely indulging in fornication, rather than adultery, and was ignorant that he was infringing the husband's matrimonial rights. But failure to inquire as to the woman's status does not amount to bona fide or reasonable belief that she was unmarried.

The claim is not barred merely because the spouses were living apart by agreement or judicially separated, they being still husband and wife, though adultery in such circumstances would probably justify lesser

---

21 An offence under the Criminal Law Amendment Act, 1885, s. 1. Compare the offence of abduction of a girl under 18 with intent to have carnal knowledge of her, under s. 7.

22 As to what adultery is see *MacLennan* v. *MacLennan*, 1958 S.C. 105; *sed quaere.*

23 Fraser, *Husband and Wife*, II, 1203; *Steedman* v. *Coupar* (1743) Mor. 7337; *Kirk* v. *Guthrie* (1817) 1 Mur. 271.

24 *Baillie* v. *Bryson* (1818) 1 Mur. 317, 334.

25 *Fraser* v. *Fraser and Hibbert* (1870) 8 M. 400.

26 *Fraser* v. *Fraser and Hibbert* (1870) 8 M. 400.

27 Voet 48, 5, 8; this rule is established in Scotland so far as concerns the paramour's liability for expenses: *Miller* v. *Simpson* (1863) 2 M. 225; *Laurie* v. *Laurie*, 1913, 1 S.L.T. 117; *Heggie* v. *Heggie*, 1917, 2 S.L.T. 246. In *Kydd* v. *Kydd* (1864) 2 M. 1074, on an issue of divorce, such proof was not held essential.

damages.[28] It will, however, be barred, equally with a claim for divorce of the offending wife, if there has been connivance [29] or collusion.[30]

This claim may be brought without having taken any proceedings against the wife for divorce,[31] or after having obtained decree of divorce on the ground of her adultery,[32] or even if the wife's adultery has been condoned,[33] or if she has died.[34] But condonation may be very relevant to the question of damages as diminishing the pursuer's loss.[33] There need be no enticement of the wife; she may have continued to live with her husband, but that does not elide the wrong of her paramour.

In all cases the basis of the claim *ex delicto* is the disgrace and dishonour to the husband's marriage-bed, the affront to his feelings, honour and reputation, and the hurt to his family life.[35] Regard must also be had in assessing damages to the husband's loss of his wife's society, to her value as a wife, including her private fortune,[36] her assistance to him in business,[37] her capacity as a housekeeper, the comfort and companionship she provided in the home and her qualities as a wife and mother of a family.[38]

The measure of damages may be increased where the paramour had acted dishonourably towards the husband or the husband and wife had previously lived happily on affectionate terms.[39] Conversely, damages may be diminished if the wife had been of bad character, or the husband had shown no affection or regard for the wife, or had misconducted himself with other women,[40] or had connived at the adultery.[41]

Adultery gives the injured spouse no right of action *ex delicto* against the erring spouse; the only remedies are consistorial, by way of action for separation or divorce.

Wife's action against husband's paramour. There appears to be no reported authority for giving a wife an action against a woman who has committed adultery with the pursuer's husband, but there is no ground in principle for refusing it, particularly if the other woman is capable of paying damages and if her wealth and manner of life contributed to any

---

[28] *Cf. Laurie* v. *Laurie*, 1913, 1 S.L.T. 117, where no damages claimed and expenses against co-defender refused.

[29] *Donald* v. *Donald* (1863) 1 M. 741; *Wemyss* v. *Wemyss* (1866) 4 M. 660; *Thomson* v. *Thomson*, 1908 S.C. 179; *Gallagher* v. *Gallagher*, 1928 S.C. 586.

[30] *Fairgrieve* v. *Chalmers*, 1912 S.C. 745; *Riddell* v. *Riddell*, 1952 S.C. 475.

[31] *Maxwell* v. *Montgomery* (1787) Mor. 13919; *Paterson* v. *Bone* (1803) Mor. 13920; Fraser, *Husband and Wife*, II, 1204.

[32] *Steedman* v. *Coupar* (1743) Mor. 7337; *Baillie* v. *Bryson* (1818) 1 Mur. 317; *Glover* v. *Samson* (1856) 18 D. 609.

[33] *Collins* v. *Collins* (1882) 10 R. 250, 258; *Macdonald* v. *Macdonald* (1885) 12 R. 1327.

[34] *Stocker* v. *Stocker* [1917] P. 264; *Kent* v. *Atkinson* [1923] P. 142.

[35] Fraser, *Husband and Wife*, II, 1203; *Baillie* v. *Bryson* (1818) 1 Mur. 317; *Wilton* v. *Webster* (1835) 7 C. & P. 198; *Evans* v. *Evans* [1899] P. 195; *Butterworth* v. *Butterworth* [1920] P. 126.

[36] *Evans, supra.*

[37] *Keyse* v. *Keyse* (1886) 11 P.D. 100; *Stedman* v. *Stedman* (1744) Mor. 13909.

[38] *Butterworth* v. *Butterworth* (1920) P. 126.

[39] *Baillie, supra.*

[40] *Baillie, supra.*

[41] *Henderson* v. *Syme* (1803) Hume, *Lect.* I, 167; Fraser, *H. & W.* II, 1205.

material extent to inducing the adultery. In view of the modern recognition of the equality of the sexes it would be only reasonable to hold, as in England,[42] and South Africa [43] that each spouse has a cause of action against a third party who, without justification, interferes with relations between the spouses.

Wife's action against her own paramour. Nor is there any authority for a wife claiming damages from her own paramour on the ground of being led astray by him and consequently being divorced by her husband, and thereby losing the status and advantages of being his wife, doubtless on the ground that *ex hypothesi* she was a consenting party and that *volenti non fit injuria* or that *ex turpi causa non oritur actio.*

3. RAPE

The rape of a married woman is not only a grave personal wrong to her, actionable by her,[44] but is also a wrong to her husband justifying an *actio injuriarum* at his instance; the wrong consists in the gross affront to the husband, the hurt to his feelings, the violation of the husband's right to the exclusive possession of his wife's person, and the dishonour done to his marriage-bed by the other man.[45] If such a case is held established heavy damages are justified, but much less heavy damages if it appears that the intercourse was not rape but merely adultery, the wife being then a consenting party and *particeps criminis.* The constituent elements of rape or indecent assault for this purpose are doubtless the same as those which constitute the corresponding crimes. An extract conviction is probably competent evidence. The husband obviously has no remedy, consistorial or otherwise, against his wife if she was raped or indecently assaulted, she being free of blame.

An attempt to rape a married woman similarly gives the husband an action,[46] and the same principle doubtless applies to an indecent assault falling short of rape or attempted rape.

4. LOSS OF CONSORTIUM

The term " consortium " [47] has sometimes been used for the complex " bundle of rights some hardly capable of precise definition," [48] including mutual comfort and society, affection, assistance, services, and sexual relations. " Companionship, love, affection, comfort, mutual services, sexual intercourse—all belong to the married state. Taken together they make up the consortium . . . " [49]

---

42 *Place* v. *Searle* [1932] 2 K.B. 497, 512, *per* Scrutton L.J. *Cf. Gray* v. *Gee* (1923) 39 T.L.R. 429; *Newton* v. *Hardy* (1933) 49 T.L.R. 522; *McGeever* v. *McFarlane* (1951) 67 Sh.Ct. Rep. 48.
43 *Foulds* v. *Smith*, 1950 (1) S.A. 1 (A.D.).
44 *Supra*, Chap. 15.
45 *Black* v. *Duncan*, 1924 S.C. 738; *cf. Long* v. *Long and Johnson* (1890) 15 P.D. 218.
46 *Colonel Charteris* (1723) Hume II, 123, explained in *Black, supra.*
47 Fridman, " Consortium as an ' Interest ' in the Law of Torts " (1954) 32 Can.B.R. 1065.
48 *Best* v. *Samuel Fox & Co., Ltd.* [1952] A.C. 716, 736 *per* Lord Reid.
49 *Best, supra* [1951] 2 All E.R. 116, 125, *per* Birkett L.J.

The problem is whether one spouse has a right of action against a third party whose negligent conduct has unjustifiably caused the pursuer to lose enjoyment of consortium with his or her spouse, as where by the third party's negligence the husband is injured and rendered impotent and the wife thereby loses at least elements of the consortium she formerly enjoyed with her husband. In an English appeal on such facts,[50] the House of Lords held that the wife, who alleged interference with her consortium with her husband, loss of the opportunity of marital relations and of further children, and ill-effects on her health, had no right of action; in converse circumstances the husband would have had a right of action [51] but this was an anomalous right, a survival of the proprietary right a husband formerly had in his wife and her services, which should not be extended. In any event, consortium was an indivisible whole, and the wrong alleged merely interfered with it in part and did not wholly destroy it. There is no authority for any such right of action, by either spouse, in Scotland. Certain definite and deliberate interferences with consortium, such as enticement, adultery and rape, are recognised wrongs, as are the total destructions of consortium effected by causing the death of the other spouse deliberately or negligently, but interference or partial destruction, particularly as a mere consequence of negligent conduct, gives no right of action. The recognition of a right of action for the loss of some elements of consortium would be a dangerous innovation.

Loss of consortium as consequential damage. There seems to be no authority either in which it has been held that an admissible element of damage consequential on direct personal injuries was loss of consortium sustained by the injured person's spouse. If the injured person suffers, as part of his injuries, loss of the ability to give his spouse love and companionship, or to enjoy the companionship and love of his spouse, that is an element of his claim of damages, but the wrong to him seems to create no right of action in his spouse, or in him for the loss sustained by the other spouse. Thus a man rendered impotent or paralysed has a claim therefor, and account is taken in the damages awarded to him of the consequential inability to enjoy some of the normal incidents of married life, but the accident gives his wife no action and nothing can be added to the husband's damages in respect of the wife's loss.

Loss of consortium in consequence of breach of contract. If a third party has been in breach of contract with the pursuer, it is a possible consequence that the pursuer may have lost the consortium of his spouse completely or for a period. It has been held in England that damages may be recovered for this loss as damages for breach of contract, provided that the loss was, on ordinary principles of remoteness of damage in contract, such as arises in the ordinary course of events and thus not too remote. In *Jackson* v. *Watson* [52] the defendant sold to the plaintiff tinned

---

[50] *Best* v. *Samuel Fox & Co., Ltd.* [1952] A.C. 716.
[51] *Cf. McNeill* v. *Johnstone* [1958] 3 All E.R. 16.   [52] [1909] 2 K.B. 193.

salmon which was unsound and poisonous [53]; the plaintiff's wife died from
food poisoning, and it was held that the plaintiff could recover for the
loss of his wife's services as a natural consequence of the defendant's
breach of contract. If she had been made ill, he could have recovered
for expenses and outlays incurred in consequence, but probably not for
loss of consortium.

5. PHYSICAL OR MENTAL INJURY TO RELATIVE

No action lies at the instance of an individual on the ground of physical
or mental injury, however severe, done to a close relative. The only
possible ground of action is for pecuniary loss actually sustained by the
pursuer himself, in the form of expenses or outlays, in consequence of
the injury to the relative, and that only in a case where such outlays by
or other pecuniary loss to the pursuer are foreseeable.[54] Thus where a
wife is injured and the husband has to pay for medical treatment and is
put to the expense of employing a housekeeper by reason of his wife's
inability to undertake her ordinary household duties, which she normally
performed gratuitously and as her part of the marriage partnership, not
under any contract, he can recover these outlays,[55] as part of the increased
cost of supporting her; but he can recover nothing by way of solatium to
himself for the wife's injuries, even if he has suffered acutely by seeing
them.[56] Nor is any claim competent for the loss of services which were
actually, or could well have been, performed for the pursuer by the injured party under contract.[57] Thus a husband can recover nothing if, by
reason of his wife's injuries caused by a third party, he loses his wife's
services as secretary, because secretarial work is something which she
actually does, not as her part of the matrimonial partnership but under
contract, or which she could equally well have done under contract.[58]
Nor could he recover if his secretary, not being his wife, were injured.[59]
Similarly where a husband and wife dancing partnership was broken by
the wife's death, which was due to the defendant's fault, no damages were
recoverable for the loss of the wife as dancing partner, but only as wife.[60]
No damages could have been recovered if his dancing partner had been a
lady other than his wife. A wife rendered unconscious in an accident has

---

[53] This was a breach of s. 14 (1) of the Sale of Goods Act, 1893.
[54] Cf. Murphy v. Baxter's Bus Services, 1962 S.C. 589; Thomson v. Angus C.C., 1962 S.C. 590.
See also Robertson v. Glasgow Corpn. 1965 S.L.T. 143; Edgar v. Postmaster-General,
1965 S.L.T. 158; sed quaere.
[55] McBay v. Hamlett, 1963 S.L.T. 18.
[56] Cf. Kirkpatrick v. Anderson, 1948 S.C. 251, approved in Nicolson v. Cursiter, 1959 S.C.
350. The wife, of course, has her own right of action for solatium for her own injuries,
and she could therein claim for medical expenses and the cost of a housekeeper, and
reimburse her husband if he had in the first instance made these outlays: Murphy, supra;
Thomson, supra.
[57] Reavis v. Clan Line Steamers, 1925 S.C. 725, 739.
[58] Quin v. Greenock Tramways, 1926 S.C. 544.
[59] Allan v. Barclay (1864) 2 M. 873; Reavis, supra; Gibson v. Glasgow Corpn., 1963 S.L.T.
(Notes) 16.
[60] Burgess v. Florence Nightingale Hospital [1955] 1 Q.B. 349.

been held not entitled to damages for anxiety at the injuries to her husband in the same accident,[61] but entitled to damages for nervous shock on being later told, in hospital, of her husband's death in the same accident.[62]

Similar considerations apply as between parent and child. In *Soutar* [63] the court allowed a proof as to outlays and expenses arising from the illness of the pursuer's daughter, which was caused by the defender's fault, but rejected as irrelevant a claim for annoyance and anxiety caused to the pursuer by his daughter's illness.

But different considerations arise where the defender's fault causes the death of one or more of certain close relatives.

6. Assythment

Assythment formerly signified the obligation to make reparation, and the reparation itself, for slaughter, mutilation and other injuries to the members or health of the body,[64] chiefly pursued by the wife, children or nearest of kin of the party slain. Latterly it was confined to cases where death resulted, a claim by a surviving person for injuries being brought under the name of damages for assault. It was " pecuniary amends to the kinsmen of the deceased, in solatium partly of their patrimonial loss, and partly of their grief and distress on the occasion." [65]

Assythment " was a species of atonement, in addition to the vindication of public law, for the injury done to the survivors of the deceased, a kind of retributive justice in the way of compensation for the loss and suffering caused, and I rather think there is no instance where such a claim has been sustained except in the case of a crime. Unless the act complained of is one which could be prosecuted as a crime, there is no authority for holding that the person who has committed it is liable in proper assythment." [66]

" The claim of assythment properly applies only where murder has been committed and where the delinquent is liable to be tried criminally for the offence and to suffer a capital punishment. In the event of his escaping such punishment, the claim for assythment is competent against him." [67] According to Hume a panel convicted, not of murder but only of culpable homicide, was liable in assythment to the widow and children or other next-of-kin of the deceased [68] and later authorities [69] do not limit assythment to cases of murder but allow it in any case where death has been caused by criminal conduct.

[61] *Wood* v. *Miller*, 1958 S.L.T. (Notes) 49.
[62] *Schneider* v. *Eisovitch* [1960] 2 Q.B. 430.
[63] *Soutar* v. *Mulhern*, 1907 S.C. 723; *cf. Quin, supra.*
[64] *Quoniam Attachiamenta*, c. 69; Balfour, *Prac.* 516, s.v. Assythment; Stair, I, 9, 7; Bankton, I, 10, 14; Hume, *Lect.*, III, 128. For the history, see Kames, *Historical Law Tracts*, V, 2; Walker, " Solatium " (1950) 66 J.R. 144; and Lord Deas' note in *Greenhorn* v. *Addie* (1855) 17 D. 860.
[65] Hume, *Lect.*, III, 128; *Moodie* v. *Stewart* (1741) 5 B.S. 709, approved in *Black* v. *N.B. Ry.*, 1908 S.C. 444, 452, *per* L.P. Dunedin.
[66] *Eisten* v. *N.B. Ry.* (1870) 8 M. 980, 986, *per* Lord Ardmillan.
[67] More, *Lect.*, I, 348; *cf.* Bell, *Prin.*, § 2029.   [68] *Comm.*, I, 286; *Lect.*, III, 129.
[69] Bell, *Prin.*, § 2029; *Eisten* v. *N.B. Ry.* (1870) 8 M. 980; *Horn* v. *N.B. Ry.* (1878) 5 R. 1055.

Assythment was formerly recoverable in the High Court of Justiciary, or modified in the Court of Exchequer,[70] but latterly was regarded as also competent in the Court of Session.[71] Some nineteenth-century cases do not clearly distinguish between assythment and reparation for negligence as the cause of action.[72]

It was and is competent only where the wrongdoing which caused the death was criminal,[71] and as negligent wrongdoing has almost completely replaced criminal wrongdoing, assythment has been almost completely superseded by the claim for solatium and patrimonial loss based on the extended *actio legis Aquiliae*.[73] Assythment remains, however, competent and is indeed the proper remedy where the wrongdoing is criminal, *e.g.*, has given rise to a prosecution for murder, culpable homicide, or causing death by reckless or dangerous driving.[74]

" If the action had been laid against an individual defender in Scotland, through whose fault and negligence it was said to have occurred, so that the defender would, in a criminal suit, have been liable to a charge of culpable homicide, that would have been a very different case and I do not at present see any reason to doubt that the law of assythment would have been applicable to such a case." [75] There is no reason to believe that assythment, indicated as still competent in 1870,[75] has since become incompetent. In the case of death caused by negligent conduct, not punishable or at least not punished criminally, the appropriate action is, however, the claim of damages by way of solatium and patrimonial loss which has to some extent sprung out of or been engrafted on the old law of assythment, or the principles on which that law was founded,[76] and to some extent developed independently.[77]

The claim to assythment is extinguished if the wrongdoer suffers the capital penalty,[78] but not if he is pardoned or his crime remitted, and consequently the wife or executors of the deceased, who were entitled to the assythment, had to grant letters of slains,[79] acknowledging that they had received satisfaction, or otherwise to concur in soliciting for the pardon before it could be obtained.[80] Nor is it extinguished if a verdict

---

70 Stair, I, 9, 7, Hume, *Lect.*, III, 128; Hume, *Comm.*, I, 285; II, 500.
71 Hume, *Lect.*, III, 128; Bell, *Prin.*, § 2029; *Greenhorn* v. *Addie* (1855) 17 D. 860, 862; *Black* v. *N.B. Ry.*, 1908 S.C. 444, 453. In *Morton, infra*, criminal proceedings were taken; see *H.M.A.* v. *Paton and McNab* (1845) 2 Broun 525.
72 *Hislop* v. *Durham* (1842) 4 D. 1168; *Morton* v. *Edinburgh and Glasgow Ry.* (1845) 8 D. 288; *Greenhorn, supra; Maclean* v. *Russell, Macnee & Co.* (1849) 12 D. 1035; contrast *Elder* v. *Croall* (1849) 12 D. 1040.
73 For some time the actions seem to have stood side by side: *Black* v. *N.B. Ry.*, 1908 S.C. 444, 453, *per* L.P. Dunedin.
74 R.T.A., 1960, s. 1.
75 *Eisten* v. *N.B. Ry.* (1870) 8 M. 980, 984, *per* Lord Deas.
76 *Dow* v. *Brown* (1844) 6 D. 534; *Greenhorn* v. *Addie* (1855) 17 D. 860, 862; *Eisten* v. *N.B. Ry.* (1870) 8 M. 980.
77 *Black* v. *Cadell* (1804) Mor. 13905; *Brown* v. *Macgregor*, Feb. 26, 1813, F.C.; More, *Lect.*, I, 346, 348; and see Sect. 7, *infra*.
78 *Machargs* v. *Campbell* (1767) Mor. 12541.
79 For form, see Dallas's *Styles* (1697), 655.
80 Ersk., IV, 4, 105; Hume, *Comm.*, I, 285; II, 499–500; Bell, *Prin.*, § 2029.

of less than murder be returned and a punishment less than death be exacted,[81] nor by a general indemnity granted by Parliament.[82]

Title to sue. The classes of persons entitled to claim assythment were and are not clearly settled. It certainly extended to the widow and legitimate children [83]; bastard children were doubtful.[84] Failing widow and children the nearest of kin were entitled.[85] Collaterals could claim,[86] and it has been hinted [87] that title to sue was co-extensive with those relatives who might have prosecuted if the Crown did not do so. All entitled relatives had to concur in one action. [88] A claim could be brought even though the deceased had accepted satisfaction for injuries in his lifetime.[89]

Parties liable. Assythment was both a solatium and indemnification for damage.[90] This reparation was due by the person who had committed the homicide, even where there was no criminal conviction for the homicide, as where the delinquent had fled or been outlawed,[91] or where there had been a conviction for murder but no death penalty had been imposed,[92] or where the criminal had obtained a royal pardon,[93] or the homicide was not punishable by death, as in the case of culpable homicide,[94] or there was a general indemnity by Parliament.[95] There being, in general, no vicarious liability for crime, assythment will not lie against a wrongdoer's employer, or otherwise vicariously.

Where the delinquent was found guilty of murder and executed, it was held that no claim for assythment was competent, either because penal actions do not transmit against heirs,[96] or because the criminal was held to have given full satisfaction by his death both to the public and to the party injured.[97]

---

[81] *Blair* v. *Montgomerie* (1556) Balf. *Prac.* 518; *Stewart* v. *Story* (1785) 5 B.S. 646.
[82] Ersk., IV, 4, 106; Bell, *Prin.*, § 2029.
[83] Balf., *Prac.* 516; Stair, I, 9, 7; Bankt., I, 10, 15; Hume, *Comm.*, I, 284; Hume, *Lect.*, III, 128; Bell, *Prin.*, § 2029; *Guild* v. *Home* (1605) Mor. 13903; *Black* v. *Cadell* (1804) Mor. 13905; (1812) 5 Paton 567.
[84] Contrast *Forrest* v. *Clerkington* (1542) Mor. 13903 with *Montgomery* v. *Barclay* (1555) and *Falconer* v. *Maxwell* (1555) Balf., *Prac.* 516.
[85] Bankt., I, 10, 15; Hume, *Comm.*, I, 286; *Lect.*, *loc. cit.*
[86] Stair, I, 9, 7; Hume, *Comm.*, I, 284; *Machargs* v. *Campbell* (1767) Mor. 12541.
[87] *Greenhorn* v. *Addie* (1855) 17 D. 860, 866.
[88] *McCartnay* v. *C.* (1541) Balf., *Prac.* 517.
[89] *Drew* v. *Horne* (1611) Mor. 13904.
[90] Balf., *Prac.* 516; *Moodie* v. *Stewart* (1741) 5 B.S. 709; *Stewart* v. *Story, supra*; Bell, *Prin.*, § 2029.
[91] Ersk., IV, 4, 105; More, *Lect.*, I, 347; *Stewart, Lady Leithhall* v. *Earl of Fife* (1768) Mor. 13904; Maclaurin, 718; 1 Hailes, 206; Kames, Sel. Dec. 330.
[92] *Machargs* v. *Campbell* (1767) Mor. 12541 and 13904; Maclaurin, 673; Kames, Sel. Dec. 326; Rem. Dec. 253; Feb. 27, 1767, F.C.
[93] *Keay* v. *McNeill*, Feb. 15, 1717; Hume, I, 284–285; Hume, *Lect.*, III, 129.
[94] *Stewart* v. *Story* (1785) 5 B.S. 646; Hume, I, 286; Hume, *Lect.*, III, 129; Bell, *Prin.*, § 2029.
[95] Ersk., IV, 4, 106; Bell, *Prin.*, § 2029.
[96] More, *Lect.*, I, 348.
[97] *Machargs* v. *Campbell* (1767) as explained by Kames, Sel. Dec. 326. (Also Maclaurin, 673; Mor. 12541 and 13904; Feb. 24, 1767, F.C.) Hume, *Comm.*, I, 284; Hume, *Lect.*, III, 129; Bell, *Prin.*, § 2029.

7. DEATH CAUSED NEGLIGENTLY

(The so-called actio injuriarum)

Where, by the fault or negligence of one person, not amounting to criminal wrong, the death of another person has been caused, certain of the surviving relatives of the deceased have at common law a right of action against the wrongdoer for reparation for the unjustified interference with their interest in the continuance of unimpaired domestic relations with the deceased. The interest protected by this right of action is both one of emotion and sentiment, and one of substance, so that the action lies for either or both of being caused grief at the death, and of pecuniary loss in consequence thereof.

This right of action was fully recognised only at the end of the eighteenth century [98] and during much of the nineteenth century co-existed with the action for assythment,[99] coming largely to replace it as negligent killing, particularly in road and industrial accidents, came so largely to supersede deliberate or criminal killing. Indeed many mid-nineteenth-century cases founded on negligent killing are miscalled actions of assythment.[1]

By a gross misunderstanding of Roman law this action has been commonly called judicially an *actio injuriarum* or even "the" *actio injuriarum*.[2] This is a complete misuse of the Roman term which was, and is, properly confined to cases of *deliberate* personal affront or outrage. The true basis of this action is the *utilis actio legis Aquiliae*,[3] as developed by the later commentators, with the addition of a claim for solatium taken over from the older action of assythment [4] (quite unconnected with the claim for solatium competent in the Roman law in an *actio injuriarum* properly so-called).

The underlying principle of such cases, apart from their historical origin, is somewhat difficult to state. It can be put on the basis that the defender, by unjustifiably causing the death of one person, has indirectly done an injury to that person's surviving close relatives, even though he did not know them or even know of their existence, or on the basis that a defender has imputed to him by the law, whether in fact he had it or not, foresight and knowledge of the fact that a person who may be killed by his negligence may have certain surviving relatives so closely related as to

---

[98] *Gardner* v. *Fergusons* (1795), not reported; see Green's *Encyclopaedia*, XII, 517; *Black* v. *Cadell* (1804) Mor. 13905; (1812) 5 Paton 567; *Brown* v. *McGregor*, Feb. 26, 1813, F.C.

[99] See, *e.g.*, *Hislop* v. *Durham* (1842) 4 D. 1168; *Morton* (*Cooley's Factor*) v. *Edinburgh & Glasgow Ry.* (1845) 8 D. 288; *Elder* v. *Croall* (1849) 12 D. 1040; *Greenhorn* v. *Addie* (1855) 17 D. 860.

[1] *e.g.*, *McLean* v. *Russell* (1849) 11 D. 1035; *Lenaghan* v. *Monkland Iron Co.* (1857) 19 D. 975; *McNaughton* v. *Caledonian Ry.* (1857) 19 D. 271; 21 D. 160.

[2] *e.g.*, *Eisten* v. *N.B. Ry.* (1870) 8 M. 980, 984, *per* L.P. Inglis; *Black* v. *N.B. Ry.*, 1908 S.C. 444, 453, *per* L.P. Dunedin; *Quin* v. *Greenock Tramways*, 1926 S.C. 544, 546, *per* L.P. Clyde.

[3] *Stewart's Exrx.* v. *L.M.S. Ry.*, 1943 S.C.(H.L.) 19, 39, *per* Lord Macmillan; McKechnie, in *Introduction to Scottish Legal History* (Stair Society), 274, 276–277. See also Grotius, *Jurisprudence of Holland*, III, 33, 2; Stair, I, 9, 4.

[4] *Greenhorn* v. *Addie* (1855) 17 D. 860; *Black* v. *N.B. Ry.*, *supra*; Walker, "Solatium" (1950) 62 J.R. 144.

suffer grief and/or financial loss by reason of the death. By such a fiction a defender can be held liable to the surviving relatives directly, having caused them reasonably foreseeable harm by unjustifiably infringing their interest in the continued life of and their domestic relationship with the deceased. The action is common and undoubtedly competent in the case of death negligently caused, and is possibly competent even where the death was caused deliberately and in circumstances amounting to a criminal wrong, since the *actio legis Aquiliae* was not confined to wrongs done *culpa* but extended also to wrongs done *dolo*, though in this case assythment is equally competent, and, if there has been a prosecution, more correct. The right of action has been called a " peculiarity in our system." [5]

Statement of principle. The leading case is *Eisten* v. *N.B. Ry.*,[6] where Lord President Inglis laid down the law as follows: " In the law of Scotland ... a claim of this kind is sustained at the instance of a wife for the death of her husband, a husband for the death of his wife, a parent for the death of his child, and a child for the death of his parent, when the death has been caused by delict or *culpa*. And it is equally true that this claim may be maintained, although the party raising the action cannot qualify any direct pecuniary loss by the death of his relative. It appears to me that the true foundation of this claim is partly nearness of relationship between the deceased and the party claiming on account of the death, and partly the existence during life, as between the deceased and the claimant, of a mutual obligation of support in case of necessity. On these two considerations in combination our law has held that a party standing in one of these relations to the deceased may sue an action like this for solatium, where he can qualify no real damage, and for pecuniary loss in addition, where such loss can be proved."

The recognition on this principle of rights of action at the instance of relatives has been criticised as " trench[ing] somewhat closely upon the province of the legislature," [7] and as not resting " upon any definite principle capable of extension to other cases which may seem to be analogous, but constitut[ing] an arbitrary exception from the general law which excludes all such actions, founded in inveterate custom, and having no other ratio to support it." [8] It is submitted that the principle has better historical antecedents, in assythment and the *actio legis Aquiliae*, than Lord Watson conceded, and that, despite Lord Watson, there is both analogy with and historical derivation from assythment.

Elements of claim. The claim accordingly is a composite one which partakes of two elements and entitled parties who have a title to sue claim for either or for both, though in the particular circumstances of a case either element of claim may be valueless or of a merely nominal value, and

---

[5] *Eisten, supra,* 984.
[6] (1870) 8 M. 980, approved repeatedly, *e.g., Quin* v. *Greenock Tramways*, 1926 S.C. 544.
[7] *Darling* v. *Gray* (1891) 19 R.(H.L.) 31, *per* Lord Watson.
[8] *Clarke* v. *Carfin Coal Co.* (1891) 18 R.(H.L.) 63, 65; see also Lord President Cooper in *McKay* v. *Scottish Airways*, 1948 S.C. 254, 263.

the court or jury may competently award nothing under either head.[9] The two elements are solatium, compensation for pain and grief suffered by reason of the death of the deceased, and patrimonial loss, or pecuniary loss actually sustained by reason of the loss, in consequence of the death, of financial support actually being afforded by the deceased and likely to continue, or likely to be afforded by him in the case of need therefor. " *Solatium*, borrowed from the action of assythment, has in the *actio injuriarum* [sic] come to mean reparation for feelings—in short all reparation which is not comprehended under the heading of actual patrimonial loss." [10] It does not cover injury to the pursuer's health, but only compensation for grief and distress.[11]

The claim for solatium has several times been affirmed to be a separate *jus actionis*, and not merely an element in a single claim of damages for loss caused by the death,[12] though it is common practice to claim for each pursuer a lump sum covering both elements of the composite claim and for the judge or jury to award a single lump sum covering both elements. The preferable practice is, however, to separate the elements and this has advantages for the parties and particularly for an appellate court reviewing an award of damages.[13]

The patrimonial loss complained of must spring from relationship, not contract.[14] Hence nothing can be recovered for the loss of a son, as manager of his mother's business,[15] nor for the loss of a wife, as professional dancing partner, but only as wife.[16] It must be based on the loss of the financial support which was actually being afforded to the pursuer by the deceased prior to his death,[17] or at least loss of a contingent right of support exigible from the deceased in case of future need.[18] If support was actually being afforded, and is lost by the death, a claim lies under this head, even though the survivor has other resources and is not left wholly unsupported.[19] A claim is likewise competent if support was actually being afforded though the payments were made voluntarily and the recipient was not in actual need of support.[20]

Relatives for whose death one can claim. The question of which relatives of a deceased can sue in respect of his death, or for which relatives' deaths a given pursuer can competently sue, has been discussed under

[9] *Rankin* v. *Waddell*, 1949 S.C. 555 (no award of solatium); *McKinlay* v. *Glasgow Corpn.* 1951 S.C. 495 (no award for patrimonial loss).
[10] *Black* v. *N.B. Ry.*, 1908 S.C. 444, 453, *per* L.P. Dunedin. *Cf. Dow* v. *Brown* (1844) 6 D. 534, *per* L.J.C. Hope: " Our law recognises the broad general ground of solatium for loss of happiness, status, comfort or patrimonial interests."
[11] *Kirkpatrick* v. *Anderson*, 1948 S.C. 251; *Nicolson* v. *Cursiter*, 1959 S.C. 350.
[12] *Naftalin* v. *L.M.S.Ry.*, 1933 S.C. 259, 264, 269, 272; *McElroy* v. *McAllister*, 1949 S.C. 110; *Hewitt* v. *West's Gas Improvement Co.*, 1955 S.C. 162, 167.
[13] *Hewitt, supra,* 167, *per* Lord Carmont.
[14] *Cf. Sykes* v. *N.E.Ry.* (1875) 44 L.J.C.P. 191.
[15] *Quin* v. *Greenock Tramways Co.*, 1926 S.C. 544.
[16] *Burgess* v. *Florence Nightingale Hospital* [1955] 1 Q.B. 349.
[17] *e.g., Quin, supra.*
[18] *Sagar* v. *N.C.B.*, 1955 S.C. 424.
[19] *Cruickshank* v. *Shiels*, 1953 S.C.(H.L.) 1.
[20] *Dickson* v. *N.C.B.*, 1957 S.C. 157.

the heading of title to sue.[21]   It has been said that the title of any relative to sue in respect of death of another is an anomaly, not based on any precise legal principle, and that the decisions should not be extended by analogy.[22]   This seems unsound; historically, this action derives much from assythment,[23] and something from the extended *actio legis Aquiliae*, though the classes of relatives entitled to pursue an assythment were wider; philosophically, the principle of " mutual obligation of support " is a convenient indication of what relatives can reasonably be regarded as having had an interest infringed by the death of the deceased, and statute has now extended the classes of relatives entitled to sue beyond those recognised when the action was novel.

The cases fall into two groups, (a) one spouse suing for loss due to the death of the other, and (b) a person suing for loss due to the death of an ascendant or descendant.[24]   It is now settled that a pursuer can sue for the death of his wife,[25] or of her husband.[26]   An " unmarried wife " or mistress has probably no claim for her " husband's " death,[27] though her children may claim for their father's death.[28]   A wife living in adultery with another man has probably no claim,[29] but she probably retains her claim if her husband has left her because of her adultery.[30]   A spouse judicially separated may still be entitled to sue.   A former wife cannot sue, even though holding a maintenance order from the English courts.[31]   A separated wife who is not willing to adhere is not entitled to aliment [32] and may not be entitled to sue.   A widow may sue though she has remarried since the deceased's death [33] or even begun to cohabit with another man [34] though such circumstances will be relevant to damages.[35]   A spouse contemplating a divorce or petition for nullity has still a claim.[36]

So, too, a pursuer may claim for the death of either parent,[37] or any grandparent, if the intervening parents are both dead and also any other grandparents with a prior liability to support the pursuer in case of

---

21 Chap. 3, *supra.*
22 *Clarke* v. *Carfin Coal Co.* (1891) 18 R.(H.L.) 63, 65, *per* Lord Watson; *cf. Darling* v. *Gray* (1892) 19 R.(H.L.) 31.
23 Walker, " Solatium " (1950) 62 J.R. 144.
24 *Eisten* v. *N.B.Ry.* (1870) 8 M. 980, 984.
25 *e.g., McKinlay* v. *Glasgow Corpn.*, 1951 S.C. 495.
26 *e.g., Blaikie* v. *B.T.C.*, 1961 S.C. 44.
27 *Cf. Phipps* v. *Cunard White Star* [1951] 1 T.L.R. 359.
28 Law Reform (Misc. Prov.) (Sc.) Act, 1940, s. 2 (2).
29 *Cf. Jack* v. *Jack*, 1962 S.C. 24; *Stimpson* v. *Wood* (1888) 4 T.L.R. 589.
30 *Cf. Donnelly* v. *Donnelly*, 1959 S.C. 97.
31 *Hemmens* v. *B.T.C.*, 1955 S.L.T. (Notes) 48.
32 *Beveridge* v. *Beveridge*, 1963 S.L.T. 248.
33 *Cf. Mead* v. *Clarke, Chapman & Co.* [1956] 1 All E.R. 44.
34 *Donnelly* v. *Glasgow Corpn.*, 1949 S.L.T. 362.
35 *Cf. Curwen* v. *James* [1963] 2 All E.R. 619.
36 *Haxton* v. *Edinburgh and Glasgow Ry.* (1863) 35 Sc.Jur. 596.
37 *Rankin* v. *Waddell*, 1949 S.C. 555 (father's death); *McRae* v. *Glasgow Corpn.*, 1915, 2 S.L.T. 94 (mother's death—father alive but insane); *Mill* v. *Dundas*, 1919, 2 S.L.T. 65 (death of mother); *Kelly* v. *Glasgow Corpn.*, 1951 S.C. (H.L.) 15 (death of mother); Law Reform (Misc.Prov.) (Sc.) Act, 1940, s. 2 (2) (title of illegitimate to sue for death of either parent); see also *Moorcraft* v. *Alexander*, 1946 S.C. 465 (posthumous child).

need [38]; a parent [39] or both parents [40] may sue for the death of a child, legitimate,[41] illegitimate [42] or adopted,[43] or of a grandchild if the intervening parents were dead.[44] No claim lies as between stepparents and stepchild.[45]

Claims are also competent by any combination of relatives who are each individually entitled to sue, all combining in one action with separate conclusions for damages for each,[46] such as husband and children,[47] mother, wife and children,[48] and wife and children.[49]

No claim lies for either solatium or patrimonial loss for the death of a brother, sister or more remote collateral, even though grief may have been felt and loss of support experienced, there being no legally recognised mutual obligation of support between collaterals.[50] Nor, it seems, does a claim lie for the death of any relative such as a stepchild,[50a] or daughter-in-law,[50b] or parent-in-law,[50c] between whom and the pursuer there existed in life no legal obligation of support in case of necessity.

It is not competent to investigate relationship in the reparation action. Hence where marriage or legitimacy is in doubt such matters must be elucidated by separate process.[50d]

Single action only competent. All the relatives of the deceased who have a title to sue must concur in one action, even though their claims are formally separate and distinct, with a separate conclusion for damages for each pursuer,[51] and when the court or jury is considering damages it must consider all the claims together as related parts of a family claim.[52] If some entitled relatives refuse to concur or cannot be found this should be averred and they should be called as defenders for their interest.[53]

---

[38] *Cooper* v. *Fife Coal Co.*, 1907 S.C. 564; *Ewart* v. *R. & W. Ferguson*, 1932 S.C. 277; see also *Gay's Tutrix* v. *Gay's Tr.*, 1953 S.L.T. 278.

[39] *Eisten* v. *N.B.Ry.* (1870) 8 M. 980, 984; *Horn* v. *N.B.Ry.* (1878) 5 R. 1055 (father); *Weems* v. *Mathieson* (1861) 4 Macq. 215 (widowed mother).

[40] Law Reform (Damages and Solatium) (Sc.) Act, 1962, s. 1, overruling *Laidlaw* v. *N.C.B.*, 1957 S.C. 49; *Kelly* v. *Nuttall*, 1965 S.L.T. 178; and see, further, Chap. 3, *supra*.

[41] *e.g.*, *Horn, supra*. As to legitimated child see *McLean* v. *Glasgow Corpn.*, 1933 S.L.T. 396. A child cannot be legitimated after its death for this purpose: *McNeill* v. *McGregor* (1901) 4 F. 123.

[42] Law Reform (Damages and Solatium) (Sc.) Act, 1962, s. 2.

[43] Law Reform (Misc.Prov.) (Sc.) Act, 1940, s. 2 (1).

[44] *Hanlin* v. *Melrose* (1899) 1 F. 1012.

[45] *MacDonald* v. *MacDonald* (1846) 8 D. 830.

[46] *Gray* v. *Caledonian Ry.*, 1912 S.C. 339.

[47] *Mill* v. *Dundas*, 1919, 2 S.L.T. 65.

[48] *Thomson* v. *Donaldson*, 1922 S.L.T. 66.

[49] *Slorach* v. *Kerr*, 1921 S.C. 285.

[50] *Eisten* v. *N.B.Ry.* (1870) 8 M. 980.

[50a] *Macdonald* v. *Macdonald* (1846) 8 D. 830.

[50b] *Hoseason* v. *Hoseason* (1870) 9 M. 37; *Mackay* v. *Mackay's Trs.* (1904) 6 F. 936.

[50c] *McAllan* v. *Alexander* (1888) 15 R. 863; *Hanlin* v. *Melrose* (1898) 1 F. 1012.

[50d] *Lenaghan* v. *Monkland Iron Co.* (1857) 19 D. 975; *McLean* v. *Glasgow Corpn.*, 1933 S.L.T. 396. *Cf. Wallace* v. *Fife Coal Co.*, 1909 S.C. 682; contrast *McDonald* v. *McKenzie* (1891) 18 R. 502; *Johnstone* v. *Spencer*, 1908 S.C. 1015.

[51] *Gray* v. *Caledonian Ry.*, 1912 S.C. 339.

[52] *Patterson* v. *L.M.S. Ry.*, 1942 S.C. 156; *Kelly* v. *Glasgow Corpn.*, 1951 S.C.(H.L.) 15, 20; *Pellow* v. *Lord Advocate*, 1953 S.L.T. (Notes) 41.

[53] *Smith* v. *Wilsons & Clyde Coal Co.* (1893) 21 R. 162; *Grant* v. *Wood Bros.* (1902) 10 S.L.T. 296; *Pollok* v. *Workman* (1900) 2 F. 354; *Slorach* v. *Kerr*, 1921 S.C. 285; *Kinnaird* v. *McLean*, 1942 S.C. 448.

This rule has two purposes, to prevent the defender from being harassed by a multiplicity of actions, and to bring before the court the whole claims at one time, so that they may be considered together as inter-related claims.[54]

Independence of claim. The claim by the relatives is an independent one, not one derived by succession from the deceased,[55] nor one benefiting his executry and, the elements of loss for which damages are claimed are losses sustained by the surviving relatives personally, not by the deceased. Damages recovered belong to the relatives not to the estate. Indeed a claim of this kind brought by the relatives is inconsistent with a claim vested in the deceased, by virtue of his having suffered injuries later causing his death, claiming for the suffering and loss caused by these injuries, action for which is continued after his death by his executor. Though in particular circumstances both such claims may be possible, as where the executor is also a, or the, surviving relative, only one can be prosecuted to the exclusion of the other.[56]

The right to institute proceedings for solatium for personal injuries does not transmit on an injured person's death to the deceased's executor,[57] but the right to raise an action for patrimonial loss to the estate incurred between the injury and the death does.[58] If the injured person raised an action and then died, his executor can continue these proceedings and recover for the benefit of the estate the damages which the injured person could himself have recovered.[59] It is not sufficient that the injured person merely intimated a claim before his death.[60] If the injured person were killed instantaneously, or were injured and died subsequently but before he had himself raised an action for damages, the only claim competent is by any entitled surviving relatives.

An executor may abandon an action commenced by the deceased before his death, in which case the entitled relatives may competently sue for solatium and patrimonial loss.[61] Whether this is wise in a particular case depends on issues of title to sue, in that a person who is executor may not have a title to sue, qua relative,[62] and on the differences in the elements of damages an executor and entitled relatives are respectively entitled to recover.[63] But no person may claim both as executor

54 *Kelly, supra.*
55 *Neilson* v. *Rodger* (1854) 16 D. 325, 330; *Darling* v. *Gray* (1892) 19 R.(H.L.) 31; *Davidson* v. *Sprengel*, 1909 S.C. 566; *McKay* v. *Scottish Airways*, 1948 S.C. 254.
56 *Darling, supra; Bruce* v. *Stephen*, 1957 S.L.T. 78.
57 *Bern's Exor.* v. *Montrose Asylum* (1893) 20 R. 859; *Stewart's Exrx.* v. *L.M.S.Ry.*, 1943 S.C.(H.L.) 19, 25.
58 *Smith* v. *Stewart & Co.*, 1961 S.C. 91.
59 *Neilson* v. *Rodger* (1853) 16 D. 325; *Darling* v. *Gray* (1892) 19 R.(H.L.) 31; *Reid* v. *Lanarkshire Traction Co.*, 1933 S.C. 416.
60 *Smith* v. *Stewart & Co.*, 1960 S.C. 329, overruling *Leigh's Exrx.* v. *Caledonian Ry.*, 1913 S.C. 838, and *McAlpine* v. *N.C.B.* (1951) C.L.Y. 4368.
61 *Bruce* v. *Stephen*, 1957 S.L.T. 78.
62 Thus a sister may be an executor, and may be a, or the sole, beneficiary under the deceased's will or intestacy, but she has no title to sue *qua* relative: *Stewart's Exrx.* v. *L.M.S.Ry.*, 1943 S.C.(H.L.) 19.
63 *Reid* v. *Lanarkshire Traction Co.*, 1933 S.C. 416; Sequel, 1934 S.C. 79.

and as an entitled relative claiming solatium; the two claims are inconsistent and cannot both be pursued.[64]

The claim is, however, a derivative claim in that it springs from a wrong to the deceased, a breach of a duty owed to him primarily and actionable by the relatives only if the deceased was killed or has died from his injuries and cannot himself sue.[65]

Survival of right of action. The right of action for solatium and patrimonial loss passes to the entitled relative's executor on his or her death,[66] but the executor can recover only such damages as the entitled relative could have recovered had he survived, and these are limited in amount by the fact of the short period of survivance.[67]

Grounds of action and defences. Though their action is wholly independent and not derivative, the relative's action is founded on a breach of a duty of care owed by the defender not to them but to the deceased, and any of the grounds of liability which might be founded on in an action for personal injuries, if only injury has been caused, are equally grounds of liability in an action by a relative if death has been caused.[68] The defender's conduct complained of must be such that the deceased, if he had survived, could himself have sued. Moreover the defender may adduce against the relative any defence which he could have adduced if the deceased had been merely injured and not killed, and had himself sued personally for his injuries.[69] Thus it is a defence that no duty was owed to the deceased, or that there had been no breach of any duty owed to him. Again the deceased's contributory negligence, either total [70] or partial,[71] is a defence; so is his voluntary assumption of the risk which killed him,[72] acceptance by the deceased of compensation in full of all claims arising from injury,[73] unless this was done under essential error [74] or induced by fraud,[75] acceptance of conditions in a ticket which would have barred a claim by the deceased himself if he had survived,[76] or his

---

[64] *Darling* v. *Gray* (1891) 19 R.(H.L.) 31; *Stewart's Exrx.* v. *L.M.S.Ry.* 1943 S.C.(H.L.) 19; *Bruce* v. *Stephen, supra.*

[65] *Horn* v. *N.B.Ry.* (1878) 5 R. 1055, 1061; *MacNamara* v. *Laird Line,* 1948 S.C. 265.

[66] *Kelly* v. *Glasgow Corpn.,* 1951 S.C.(H.L.) 15. *Cf. Hunter* v. *L.M.S. Ry.,* 1939 S.L.T. 297.

[67] *Kelly* v. *Glasgow Corpn.,* 1949 S.C. 496, 499–500; see also *Nevay* v. *B.T.C.,* 1955 S.L.T. (Notes) 28.

[68] *Horn* v. *N.B.Ry.* (1878) 5 R. 1055, 1061.

[69] *Armsworth* v. *S.E.Ry.* (1871) 11 Jur. 758; *Coldrick* v. *Partridge, Jones & Co.* [1910] A.C. 77; *Walpole* v. *Canadian Northern Ry.* [1923] A.C. 113.

[70] *Tucker* v. *Chaplin* (1848) 2 C. & K. 730; *Paterson* v. *Wallace* (1854) 1 Macq. 748; *McNaughton* v. *Caledonian Ry.* (1858) 21 D. 160; *Senior* v. *Ward* (1859) 1 E. & E. 385; *Pym* v. *G.N.Ry.* (1862) 2 B. & S. 759.

[71] Law Reform (Contributory Negligence) Act, 1945, s. 1 (4); *Lever* v. *Greenock Motors,* 1949 S.C. 88.

[72] *Degg* v. *Midland Ry.* (1857) 26 L.J.Ex. 171; *Dynen* v. *Leach* (1857) 26 L.J.Ex. 221; *Williams* v. *Birmingham Battery Co.* [1899] 2 Q.B. 338; *D'Urso* v. *Sanson* [1939] 4 All E.R. 26; *Baker* v. *Hopkins* [1958] 3 All E.R. 147.

[73] *Read* v. *G.E.Ry.* (1868) L.R. 3 Q.B. 555.

[74] *Huckle* v. *L.C.C.* (1910) 27 T.L.R. 112.

[75] *Lee* v. *L. & Y.Ry.* (1871) 6 Ch.App. 527; *Hirschfeld* v. *L.B. & S.C.Ry.* (1876) 2 Q.B.D.1.

[76] *Haigh* v. *R.M.S.P. Co.* (1883) 52 L.J.Q.B. 640; *The Stella* [1900] P. 161; *Mackay* v. *Scottish Airways,* 1948 S.C. 254; *McNamara* v. *Laird Line,* 1948 S.C. 260.

having contracted not to claim compensation for injury or death,[77] or the lapse of time which would bar the deceased's claim before his death,[78] or acceptance of a contract of employment whereby the deceased had agreed to look only to a particular fund for compensation if killed or injured.[79] It has been held in England [80] under the corresponding statutory procedure that where a deceased had agreed merely to limit the damages recoverable if he were injured, an action lies without limitation if he is killed. It seems that any rule of law, and proof of any facts, which would have gone to exclude or minimize a claim by the deceased himself if he had survived, may be proponed in defence to an action by the deceased's relatives for loss caused them by the death.

It is also competent to propone in defence any plea valid against the pursuer personally, such as that he was himself *sciens* and *volens*, so that *volenti non fit injuria* applied to bar a claim by a father for the death of his child, when the father had known of and acquiesced in the position of the gas-bracket which set the child's clothing on fire and caused her death.[81] Similarly if a father were driving his son in a car involved in an accident and the father sued the other driver for the son's death, it would be relevant to plead in defence the contributory negligence of the father. It may also be a defence if the pursuer has elected to accept benefits under a pension scheme to which the deceased had contributed.[82]

Differences in heads of damages. The heads of damages recoverable by an entitled relative are solatium to the relatives for grief and the pain of bereavement caused them by the death, patrimonial loss, namely compensation for the loss of the natural support which the deceased had afforded to the pursuer or might in future have afforded or continued to afford, and outlays and expenses incurred in connection with the death.[83] The loss to be compensated is that sustained by the relative, not by the deceased.

On the other hand in a claim by an executor the loss to be compensated is that sustained by the deceased and his estate, not by the executor or by any surviving relatives. The heads of damages recoverable by an executor carrying on the deceased's action are [84] compensation for the pain and suffering sustained by the deceased down to the date of death,[85] patrimonial loss sustained by him for the same period, and expenses and disbursements caused him.[86] A modest award is competent for the

---

[77] *Griffiths* v. *Earl Dudley* (1882) 9 Q.B.D. 357.
[78] *Williams* v. *Mersey Docks and Harbour Board* [1905] 1 K.B. 804.
[79] *Griffiths* v. *Earl Dudley* (1882) 9 Q.B.D. 357.
[80] *Nunan* v. *Southern Ry.* [1924] 1 K.B. 223.
[81] *Davidson* v. *Sprengel*, 1909 S.C. 566; see also *Innes* v. *Fife Coal Co.* (1901) 3 F. 335, where pursuer had caused death of his own child.
[82] *Smith* v. *B.E.A.* [1951] 2 K.B. 893.
[83] *Eisten* v. *N.B.Ry.* (1870) 8 M. 980; *Quin* v. *Greenock Tramways*, 1926 S.C. 544.
[84] *McEnanay* v. *Caledonian Ry.*, 1913, 2 S.L.T. 293 (sequel to *Leigh's Exrx.* v. *Caledonian Ry.*, 1913 S.C. 838).
[85] *Reid* v. *Lanarkshire Traction Co.*, 1934 S.C. 79; *Rose* v. *Ford* [1937] A.C. 826.
[86] *McEnanay, supra; cf. Neilson* v. *Rodger* (1853) 16 D. 325.

shortening of the deceased's life.[87] Nothing is recoverable for prospective loss of earnings or future outlays.[88] Moreover in an executor's action any sum recovered by way of damages falls into the deceased's estate, is liable to death duties, and passes to those entitled under the deceased's will or under the rules of intestacy.

Analogy with English statutory claim. The Scottish common law action at the instance of a relative for solatium and patrimonial loss is the counterpart of and generally analogous to the English statutory action given by the Fatal Accidents Acts, 1846 to 1959. While the actions are roughly comparable there are many material points of difference and cases decided under the English Acts are not always safe guides in Scottish practice. The principal points of difference are: The English action is brought by the executor or administrator of the deceased, failing whom, by any beneficiary, for the benefit of specified relatives; no compensation is allowed for the grief or mental sufferings of relatives, *i.e.*, no solatium; and a deduction from damages must be made if beneficiaries under the Acts are entitled to any share in the deceased's estate and damages have been recovered by the estate under the (English) Law Reform (Married Women and Tortfeasors) Act, 1934, for loss of expectation of life, pain and suffering and other loss to the estate.

8. STATUTORY ACTION UNDER CARRIAGE BY AIR ACTS

Under the Carriage by Air Act, 1932, Second Schedule, as amended by the Fatal Accidents Act, 1959, an action to enforce liability of a carrier by air might be brought by the personal representative of a passenger killed or by any person for whose benefit the liability was enforceable.[89] The Act governed " international carriage " as defined in the Schedule, and was extended to internal carriage by the Carriage by Air (Non-international Carriage) (U.K.) Order, 1952.[90] Only one action was permitted in the United Kingdom in respect of the death of any one passenger, and every such action, by whomsoever brought, was for the benefit of all such entitled persons as are domiciled in the United Kingdom, or, not being domiciled there, express a desire to take the benefit of the action. The liability was for the benefit of " such of the members of the passenger's family as sustained damage by reason of his death." [91]

When the Carriage by Air Act, 1961, is brought into force it repeals the 1932 Act. It provides as regards Scotland (s. 11) that in the Convention scheduled to the Act, reference to the liability of a carrier for

---

[87] *McMaster* v. *Caledonian Ry.* (1885) 13 R. 252; *McEnanay, supra; Reid, supra; Rose, supra; Benham* v. *Gambling* [1941] A.C. 157.
[88] *McEnanay, supra; Reid, supra.*
[89] This action was analogous to and modelled on the (English) Fatal Accidents Acts, 1846 to 1959.
[90] S.I. 1952, No. 158.
[91] Second Schedule, para. 2; see also para. 1, as substituted by Fatal Accidents Act, 1959, s. 1 (5). See also *Preston* v. *Hunting Air Transport* [1956] 1 Q.B. 454 (claim by children for widowed mother's death).

damage sustained in the event of the death of a passenger (Art. 17) shall be construed as including liability to " such persons as are entitled, apart from this Act, to sue the carrier (whether for patrimonial damage or solatium or both) in respect of the death." A claim is competent accordingly to those who could sue at common law in Scotland, as amended by statutes. The carrier's liability is limited to 250,000 francs, unless a higher limit is agreed upon.

The Carriage by Air (Supplementary Provisions) Act, 1962, does not directly affect this matter further.

9.   SLANDER OF DECEASED RELATIVE

The question has been raised whether surviving relatives can sue for a defamatory statement about a deceased relative, which has caused them mental suffering, if not pecuniary loss. It is difficult to see why they should not, as such a statement may be acutely hurtful, and possibly also patrimonially harmful. But the only case in point is inconclusive and, if correct, decides the matter in the negative. It cannot be said to be a satisfactory state of the law which allows slander to be published of the dead with impunity, unless, probably, it should by implication slander the living relatives. It could be very hurtful to a widow for it to be said untruly that her late husband had been a drunkard, though it probably does not imply any aspersion on her.

In *Broom* v. *Ritchie* [92] the widow and children of a man who died in a hotel sued a newspaper for having untruly stated that the deceased had committed suicide. A majority of the court held that the slander gave the surviving relatives no right of action, when it contained no implied imputations on them. Lord Young, however, thought that such a claim was competent, though the present claim was irrelevant. The Lord Justice-Clerk's ground of decision [93]—" An aspersion on a person after death cannot, I hold, give right to anyone else to recover damages as for a wrong done to the deceased "—misses the point, which is whether the conduct can be regarded as a direct wrong to the surviving relatives. Lord Trayner also speaks of relatives bringing the deceased's action, which they were not seeking to do, and this judgment also misses the mark.

It is thought accordingly that the disapproval in *Broom* of the older case of *Walker* v. *Robertson*,[94] where a son was awarded damages *in solatium* for the hurt to his feelings caused by an attack on his deceased father's character, is unsound, though the second ground of disapproval,[95] that Walker, senior, had sued and the action been continued to verdict by his son before the son had sued in his own interest, seems valid. But ignoring that specialty *Walker* seems a good authority, and the reasons of the majority in *Broom* against allowing the action seem ill-founded.

[92] (1904) 6 F. 942.
[93] p. 945.
[94] (1821) 2 Mur. 508.
[95] *Broom, supra*, 946.

CHAPTER 23

INFRINGEMENTS OF INTERESTS IN HONOUR AND
REPUTATION—VERBAL INJURIES

1. Verbal Injury
2. Convicium
3. Defamation (or Libel or Slander)
4. Defences to an Action for Defamation

A PERSON has a legally recognised interest in the preservation of his own self-esteem and honour from unjustifiable attacks, and this has come to be extended to include an interest in his own reputation and good name in the eyes of others.[1] A claim for *solatium*, of the nature of an *actio injuriarum*, accordingly lies against a person who unjustifiably impugns a person's honour and self-esteem, and a claim for patrimonial loss lies in addition where his public reputation has been impugned as well.

The wrong is variously called verbal injury, convicium, defamation, slander and libel in the Scottish books and cases. The wrong, or possibly rather wrongs, are the counterpart of the connected torts of libel and slander in English law, but these terms, springing from very different historical sources and courses of development, have technical connotations in English law which are absent in Scots law. In Scots law libel and slander are frequently used interchangeably for each other and for defamation,[2] whereas in English law slander denotes the oral communication of an idea derogatory to the self-esteem or reputation of an individual, and libel the communication of such an idea in writing or other permanent form.[3]

In earlier Scottish practice actions for defamation were dealt with chiefly by the commissaries, who imposed fine or imprisonment, and the requirement of making recantation by palinode, as well as making an award of damages *in solatium* to the complainer.[4]

Bases of right of action. The modern Scottish action has two bases: the first is the Roman *actio injuriarum* which gave *solatium* as reparation for *contumelia*, affront to personality in the shape of *convicium*, insult or derogatory communication to a man, harmful to his feelings and self-esteem. Such an action would lie without the need of communication of the remarks to any person other than the insulted hearer. " Any

---

[1] Generally Stair I, 9, 4; Mackenzie, *Crim.L.*, Tit 30; Bankt. I, 10, 24 and 34; Ersk. I, 5, 30; IV, 4, 80; Hume, *Lect.*, III, 133; *Crim.L.* I, 340; Bell, *Prin.*, §§ 2043–2057.
[2] See the examination of the terms in Borthwick, *Libel and Slander*, Chap. 1.
[3] See generally *Gatley on Libel and Slander*; Clerk and Lindsell, Chap. 20; Pollock, Chap. 37; Salmond, Chap. 12; Winfield, Chap. 11; Street, Chaps. 15–17.
[4] Borthwick, *Libel and Slander* (1826), Chap. 2.

imputation on a man's good name may be sued . . . even where the scandal
is of such a nature that it cannot be the occasion of any pecuniary loss;
it is sufficient to say, I am hurt in my character." [5]   " Our law says that a
man may have damages for injury done to his feelings."   " The law of
Scotland recognises the claim of a person to recover damages for a
slanderous statement made in a letter written to himself and not communicated to anyone else . . . verbal statements, amounting to slander,
made to a man outwith the presence of others will also afford a good
ground for an action of damages." [6]   In the same way words or conduct
may be injurious and actionable by what they imply, as where immoral
overtures are made to a virtuous woman.

    This basis of action, being an *actio injuriarum*, necessarily required
proof of *animus injuriandi*, though that will today be inferred from proof
that the accusation was false and of defamatory quality without more.[7]

    The other basis of action is for harm to a person's public reputation,
his standing in the eyes of others, causing him thereby potential or actual
patrimonial loss, which necessarily postulates that the statement complained of has been published to some person or persons other than the
complainer himself.   This basis of action is of the nature of an *actio
utilis legis Aquiliae*, and requires either *animus injuriandi* or *culpa*, followed
by loss,[8] so that it would be actionable, provided loss was anticipated, or
followed, to say incorrectly, either deliberately or without having made
due inquiry, that a person was insolvent.

    In modern practice the two bases seem to have coalesced, or at least
the distinction has been lost sight of, particularly now that the requirement
of *animus injuriandi* is satisfied by proof of the utterance of a statement
which is untrue and derogatory,[9] and does not now bulk largely in the
cases.[10]

1.   Verbal Injury

In the institutional writers defamation is usually discussed under the
head of verbal injury [11]; verbal injury [12] was contrasted with real injury,
such as by assault (*i.e.*, threat of force) or battery (*i.e.*, striking).   " A
verbal injury is, when words are spoken to or concerning one, whereby he
is defamed, whether they affect his life, liberty, estate, reputation, trade

---

[5] Kames, *Law Tracts*, 225.
[6] *Mackay* v. *McCankie* (1883) 10 R. 537, 539, *per* L.P. Inglis; *cf.* Borthwick, 189; *Hutchison*
v. *Naismith* (1808) Mor.Appx. Delinquency, No. 4; *McCandies* v. *McCandie* (1827)
4 Mur. 198; *Brown* v. *Wason* (1838) McFarlane 114; *Bryson* v. *Inglis* (1844) 6 D. 363;
Kennedy v. *Baillie* (1855) 18 D. 138; *Stuart* v. *Moss* (1888) 13 R. 299.
[7] Voet, 47, 10, 20; Vinnius, *ad Inst.* 4.4.1; Ersk. IV, 4, 80.
[8] *Craig* v. *Hunter*, June 29, 1809, F.C.
[9] This seems to have been accepted since *Tytler* v. *Macintosh* (1823) 3 Mur. 239.
[10] In *Rose* v. *Robertson* (1803) Hume 614, a statement that the minister had got drunk was
held not sufficient to indicate such an *animus injuriandi* as to found an action of damages.
So too *Gardner* v. *Marshall* (1803) Hume 620. Both were cases of reporting current rumour.
Buchan v. *Walch* (1857) 20 D. 222, was at least partly founded on defamation, and the
judges desiderated an averment of malice which was absent.
[11] See also Stair, I, 9, 4; Mackenzie, *Criminal Law*, Tit. 30.
[12] *i.e.*, *injuria verbis*: Dig. 47.10.15.

or profession, or charge him with a foul disease whereby his character is blemished." [13] " Injuries are either verbal or real. . . . A verbal injury, when it is pointed against a private person, consists in the uttering of contumelious words, which tend to vilify his character, or render it little or contemptible. . . . The *animus injuriandi* which is of the essence of this crime, being an act of the mind, must be inferred from presumptions; and, in general, it is presumed from the injurious words themselves, especially where they are made use of to hurt one in his moral character, or to fix some particular guilt upon him; as if one should give his neighbour the name of thief, cheat, liar, etc." [14]

" Verbal injuries—those which affect a person in his good name and reputation . . . these injuries are of two kinds, either written or spoken." [15] " Papers which . . . tended, in a general way, to vilify and depreciate, and hold out to ridicule or contempt, are actionable." [16] It is essential " in either kind of injury, written or spoken, that the defender appear to have been actuated by an *animus injuriandi*. But in the ordinary case . . . this is rather to be understood in a limited and qualified sense, and not in the most obvious or favourable construction for the party charged, as if it were necessary for the pursuer to instruct a special and deliberate malice—a *malus animus*—a precise and injurious purpose—directed against him in particular. It is rather to be understood in a negative sense, as a means of defence in those cases where it can be clearly shown by evidence on the part of the defender, both that there was no sort of purpose to injure, and that in truth no harm did, or was at all likely to ensue." [17] " But saving such cases,[18] the *animus injuriandi* is commonly and must be presumed from the words themselves, if they are uttered seriously, and are naturally of a bad and unfavourable meaning and must, if believed, prove prejudicial to the complainer." [19] " In those matters which so nearly touch the interests of third parties—affect them so deeply in their enjoyment of life—it is not sufficient to be free of pure wilful malice. On such occasions, in the estimation of law, supine negligence—gross indiscretion—rash and precipitate proceedings—are equivalent to malice. The maxim of the Roman law applies, *culpa lata equiparatur dolo.* Gross disregard and indifference of the rights of a neighbour binds to reparation just as a purpose to injure one's neighbour would do." [20] " It thus appears on the whole, that in the ordinary case and in the civil action of damages the requisite *animus injuriandi* is not to be received as a clear—special— malice propense against the party injured; so far from it, that a person may be liable in damages to one who is not even known to him, either personally or by name. 'Tis sufficient, the defender have so conducted

[13] Bankt. I, 10, 24; and see also I, 10, 34; *cf.* Ersk. IV, 4, 81.
[14] Ersk. IV, 4, 80.
[15] Hume, *Lect.* III, 133; *cf. Comm. on Crimes,* I, 340.
[16] *Ibid.* 140.
[17] *Ibid.* 141–142.
[18] *i.e.,* cases of privilege.
[19] *Ibid.* 146.
[20] *Ibid.* 149.

himself, though owing to rashness only, or levity, and indiscretion, as to occasion harm, or the risk of harm, to the complainer." [21]

Borthwick,[22] writing of the defamation of private individuals, says that this is technically known in the law of Scotland by the designation of verbal injury, which comprehends calumny expressed both by means of libel and of slander properly so called. He affirms [23] that "not merely the character and the estate, but also the happiness of individuals, is protected by the law of Scotland from the attacks of calumny. . . . All such disparagement, though it may have no effect in blackening a man's moral character, is, by our law, accounted injurious and actionable." Furthermore,[24] " it need hardly be added that all charges which affect one's patrimonial estate or moral character, are still more entitled to redress by the Scots law."

Verbal injury in its true sense. It seems accordingly that in the institutional and other older writers verbal injury was *injuria verbis*, an affront to personality by words, and that this was the generic term, within which fall the modern species of convicium, defamation, and malicious or injurious falsehood.[25] Verbal injury was punishable criminally, and also gave rise to a claim of damages,[26] but since the eighteenth century the civil remedy has superseded the criminal. In the early nineteenth century reports of cases of defamation are frequently called " verbal injury " in this generic sense. But the term verbal injury has come in the later nineteenth century to be used not as the generic term, including defamation and other species, but for a species, possibly the only species, of wrong to reputation other than defamation, so that the modern discussion of the subject has tended to deal with defamation and verbal injury.[27] In short the true view is that verbal injury is the genus, and it comprises three species, convicium, defamation (or libel or slander), and malicious or injurious falsehood. But since the mid to late nineteenth century the general understanding has been that there are two species, defamation and verbal injury (including malicious or injurious falsehood), of an innominate genus, which is probably wrongs to honour and reputation, though not recognised as such in the books and cases.

Modern misinterpretation of " verbal injury." In *Paterson* v. *Welch* [28] the pursuer claimed damages on the ground that the defender had falsely attributed to him a particular statement, with the intention of injuring the pursuer in the opinion of the citizens of the town in which they lived,

---

[21] *Ibid.* 152, citing *Finlay* v. *Ruddiman* (1763) Mor. 3436; *Jardine* v. *Creech* (1776) Mor. 3438; *cf. Hulton* v. *Jones* [1910] A.C. 20.
[22] *Treatise on the Law of Libel and Slander as applied in Scotland* (1826), 148.
[23] p. 183.
[24] p. 187.
[25] Guthrie Smith, *Damages*, 240 distinguishes defamation or slander, words false but not slanderous followed by damage, convicium, and slander of title as four forms of verbal injury. In the present book the second and fourth are grouped under malicious falsehood.
[26] Ersk. IV, 4, 81.
[27] *Cf.* Cooper's book on *Defamation and Verbal Injury.*
[28] (1893) 20 R. 744.

and that he had in fact so injured the pursuer. Lord President Robertson, with the concurrence of Lords Adam and McLaren, held that the pursuer had no ground of action on the head of slander, for having been stated by the defender to have said that some of the inhabitants of the burgh were of worse morals than another class, and that the one would corrupt the other if they were brought together, but that the pursuer had a ground of action for verbal injury. " When speech is ascribed to A by B, A will have an action if (1) the statement of B is false; (2) the statement was made with a design to injure; and (3) injury has resulted." [29] The question was whether the statements " were false, and were made with the design of exposing, and did expose, the pursuer to public hatred and contempt, to his loss, injury and damage." [30]

It is apparent that the court in fact allowed an issue on the ground of convicium,[31] and quite properly so, but the case seems subsequently to have been regarded, quite wrongly, as laying down that verbal injury was a kind of wrong distinct from slander.[32] Thus in *Waddell* v. *Roxburgh*,[33] where there were allegations of securing a contract " in a mean and contemptible manner," the court allowed an issue for slander but refused one modelled on that allowed in *Paterson*, and the report epitomises this in the phrase that: " The pursuer was not entitled to an issue of verbal injury." *Paterson* v. *Welch* was explained,[34] though the distinction between slander and the other form of action (for the words " verbal injury " are not used by the court) is not made clear.

In *Waugh* v. *Ayrshire Post, Ltd.*[35] W. sued a newspaper for having published an anonymous letter purporting to come from him and representing him as anxious to shed Roman Catholic blood. The Lord Ordinary allowed an issue not of slander but of convicium, of publishing the letter " with the design and with the result of holding up the pursuer to public hatred and contempt, to his loss, injury and damage," but the First Division reversed him and allowed an issue of falsely and calumniously representing that the pursuer had incited to riot and bloodshed, *i.e.*, an issue of slander. *McLaughlan* v. *Orr, Pollock & Co.*[36] was also a case of convicium, where in the circumstances the court refused an issue. In *Lever Bros.* v. *Daily Record (Glasgow), Ltd.*[37] Lord President Dunedin assumed for the purposes of the case that there could be " an action for verbal injury [38] which is not strictly to be designated as an action of

---

[29] *Ibid.* 749, *per* L.P. Robertson.
[30] *Ibid.* 750 (terms of issue approved for trial).
[31] As to convicium, see next section.
[32] Possibly partly because the headwords of the rubric of the report read " Reparation—Slander—Verbal injury—Issues."
[33] (1894) 21 R. 883. None of the judges mentions " verbal injury."
[34] *Ibid.* p. 886, *per* Lord Kinnear, Lords McLaren and Adam concurring.
[35] (1893) 21 R. 327. See also *Burns* v. *Diamond* (1896) 3 S.L.T. 256, where it was held that a charge of having changed his religion did not expose a man to public hatred and contempt.
[36] (1894) 22 R. 38. Again no mention of " verbal injury " in opinions.
[37] 1909 S.C. 1004, 1008.
[38] In the institutional sense of *injuria verbis*.

slander." That is correct, but the action other than slander is truly convicium, another species of verbal injury, and not verbal injury itself.[39] By *Andrew* v. *Macara* [40] the misunderstanding of " verbal injury " by the reporters (not the judges) reaches finality. The rubric states: " In an action of damages for verbal injury, on the ground that the defender had, with the design of exposing the pursuer to public hatred, falsely attributed to him certain statements. . . ." Lord Justice-Clerk Scott Dickson [41] said: " It is therefore quite plain that the pursuer in the issues he originally proposed recognised that there was a distinction between an action for slander on the one hand and an action of damages for verbal injury, as it is shortly called, on the other.[42] The pursuer founded on . . . *Paterson* v. *Welch* [43] and accepted the view which the Lord President expressed in that case, namely, that an issue of holding up to public hatred and contempt is not an issue founded on slander at all. Observations have been made upon *Paterson's* case in subsequent cases, but I do not think it has ever been overruled or that the view expressed by the Lord President has ever been declared to be unsound." [44]

In *Lamond* v. *Daily Record (Glasgow), Ltd.* [45] a variety artiste complained of an article in a newspaper containing a pretended interview with her as calculated to injure the pursuer in her profession. Lord Constable explained in his charge to the jury the substance of defamation and continued: " But then there is another class of case where somebody says or writes about another something which is not defamatory in the ordinary sense of the term, but which is still likely to do injury either to his business or to his property. That is called a case of verbal injury. In such a case, if a person complains, it is necessary for him to prove that the statement is false, and it is necessary for him to establish that he has suffered damage as the result of the statement." But the issue, as adjusted by Lord Blackburn, is substantially one of slander rather than of anything else, and it is thought that he should have allowed the proposed issue which complained of being held up to public hatred, ridicule and contempt. Lord Constable's explanation of the law to the jury was crystallising the misunderstanding of " verbal injury " reached in *Andrew* v. *Macara*,[46] as a species of action distinct from an action for slander, and possibly also drawing on memories of the other group of cases (slander of property, slander of business) sometimes thought of as also cases of so-called " verbal injury," but truly cases of malicious falsehood,[47] the third species within the genus verbal injury (in its institutional sense).

---

[39] Again the phrase " Slander—Verbal injury " appears in the rubric.
[40] 1917 S.C. 247.
[41] *Ibid.* 250–251.
[42] This seems to be the first occasion on which a judge, as distinct from the reporter, used the phrase " verbal injury " as something distinct from slander.
[43] (1893) 20 R. 744.
[44] The view is, of course, not unsound; it has simply been misunderstood and miscalled " verbal injury " instead of, as it should have been, *convicium.*
[45] 1923 S.L.T. 512.
[46] 1917 S.C. 247.
[47] On these see Chap. 26.

Other cases of " verbal injury." Another group of cases are commonly said to fall within modern " verbal injury." These are cases of so-called " slander of title " and " slander of property." Examination of the cases usually cited under these heads indicates that these cases have been decided on the incautious citation of English authority where the two heads mentioned are the main heads of the wrong of malicious or injurious falsehood, which is a wrong to a man's economic interests and only indirectly and inferentially to his reputation. The presence of the word " slander " is merely confusing. This group of cases may and, it is submitted, should properly be treated as a third species of the genus verbal injury (in the proper, institutional, sense of that term) and is more conveniently discussed in the context of economic harms.[48]

The Defamation Act, 1952, and verbal injury. The Defamation Act, 1952, seems unfortunately to have been drafted on the assumption that verbal injury (in the modern sense) was part of Scots law. Section 14 substitutes for section 3 (which relates to actions under English law for " slander of title, slander of goods or other malicious falsehood ") a similar section for Scots law to the effect that: " In any action for verbal injury it shall not be necessary for the pursuer to aver or prove special damage if the words on which the action is founded are calculated to cause pecuniary damage to the pursuer."

If the explanation of verbal injury (including slander of title and slander of property) given in the foregoing pages is accepted, this section is redundant and unnecessary. It should, in any event, not be taken as parliamentary affirmation of the existence of a distinct action for verbal injury in Scots law, but must be taken as inserted under the misapprehension, hitherto common, that such was the law. The modern, mistaken, view that verbal injury is a ground of action distinct from defamation should be disregarded, and the doctrines of slander of title and slander of property should similarly be recognised as unnecessary importations, incautiously made from English law and not really connected with defamation at all.

Modern position of verbal injury. The modern position is accordingly that the name verbal injury is seldom used in its institutional sense of *injuria verbis*, but the terms defamation, libel and slander are used indifferently and, in the case of the latter two words, without the technical connotations of English law, while convicium has been largely forgotten and the term verbal injury has in the present century been misunderstood and applied to cases which should properly be classed as cases of convicium, and to the categories of slander of title and slander of property, which belong properly to the sphere of wrongs to property. Defamation (or libel or slander) is the common form of wrong to self-esteem or reputation and has been developed in detail and applied in many cases. But

[48] *Infra*, Chap. 26.

convicium is not obsolete,[49] and may be a valuable protection in circumstances where an action for defamation is inappropriate. In defamation the question is whether the defender falsely, calumniously and maliciously communicated to, or of and concerning, the pursuer an idea defamatory of him to his loss, injury and damage, and in convicium it is whether the defender falsely, or probably even truly, and maliciously communicated of and concerning the pursuer an idea calculated to bring him into public hatred, ridicule and contempt and caused him loss, injury or damage thereby.

2. CONVICIUM

In Roman law convicium was sometimes used as a term for defamation but sometimes with the special sense of vituperation or abuse, and, in this sense, of reviling or insulting or abusing a person in odium or disparagement of him,[50] it has passed into Scots law. It is convicium " if in defiance of the good morals of the civic community he abuses or reviles some other definite, but not indefinite, person so as to arouse ill will and contempt against such person, or causes that to be done." " Even the shouting and imputing of that which involves no baseness can involve a wrong of this type. Instances would be if a person in order to create ill will against another taunts him with poverty, or with some natural defect. . . ." [51]

Convicium is accordingly, though equally an *injuria*, a form of verbal injury (in the institutional, not the modern, sense), distinct from defamation; it consists in reviling and unflattering remarks which, if true, would render a man contemptible. " To hurt another's feelings by in this manner holding up to general amusement or ridicule such physical defects is generally held to be an injury as much when this is done verbally as when it is done in a caricature." [52]

Erskine,[53] having laid down that injuries are either verbal or real, continues: " A verbal injury when it is pointed against a private person, consists in the uttering of contumelious words, which tend to vilify his character, or render it little or contemptible. As one may be sensibly hurt by reproachful words, though they should have no tendency to blacken his moral character, sarcastical nicknames and epithets, or such other strokes of satire, are accounted injurious: And even taunting one with the deformity of his person or other natural defect, where it is accompanied with any ill-natured expression, that may place him in a ridiculous light; though it is agreed by all, that infirmities of that sort imply no real reproach, either in themselves, or in the just opinion of mankind. The *animus injuriandi*, which is of the essence of this crime, being an act of the

---

[49] It was applied in *Murray* v. *Beaverbrook Newspapers*, 1957, not reported.
[50] Dig. 47, 10, 15; Voet, 47, 10, 8; de Villiers, 85.
[51] Voet, 47, 10, 8.
[52] de Villiers, 97–98.
[53] IV, 4, 80.

mind, must be inferred from presumptions; and, in general, it is presumed from the injurious words themselves, especially where they are made use of to hurt one in his moral character, or to fix some particular guilt upon him; as if one should give his neighbour the name of thief, cheat, liar, etc. ... But where the injurious reflections are frequently repeated in private companies, or bandied about in whispers to confidents, the offence grows up to the crime of slander and defamation." Erskine accordingly clearly distinguished between verbal injury by sarcasm, satire, taunting, or showing up as ridiculous and the more serious verbal injury of slander or defamation which involves blackening a man's moral character, and this was recognised in many cases. So, too, Hume [54] states: " redress may be had for the imputation even of mere defects and misfortunes, such as are attended with no manner of blame, if they are such as to expose the person to ridicule, or derision, and thus tend to exclude the individual from society, or to depreciate or degrade him there. Thus it would be an actionable scandal, to propagate the story against a woman of her being affected with a cancer, or scrophula, or other loathsome disease, or of her having been insane, or being of a family who are liable to that affliction—or to raise the report against a man, that he is castrated, or impotent, or incurably diseased or the like." Borthwick similarly [55] states: " Our law holds that one may be sensibly hurt in his feelings, or in his fortune, by reproachful imputations, by sarcastical nicknames and epithets, and even by taunting allusions to the deformity of his person, or other natural defects, when these are accompanied by any ill-natured expression that may place him in a ridiculous light. All such disparagement, though it may have no effect in blackening a man's moral character, is, by our law, accounted injurious and actionable."

" Relevant ground for a claim of damages . . . is always afforded by the publication of such articles as, whether they contain defamatory statements or not, by causelessly holding a man up to the ridicule of the public, and exposing his habits in a ludicrous and absurd light to their gaze, may render a man of ordinary feeling nervous and uncomfortable . . ." [56] While one attack may not be actionable, a series of persistent and repeated attacks intended to hold a person up to public contempt is actionable.[57]

In *Cunningham* v. *Phillips* [58] Lord Deas said: " I am not disposed to doubt that there are some kinds of injurious publications, for which, according to our law, there may be a relevant claim of damages, although there is no slander. Examples of such a claim are afforded by cases in which some physical deformity or secret defect, such, for instance, as that peculiar defect in respect of which marriage may be annulled, is wantonly and offensively paraded before the public. Other examples

[54] *Lect.* III, 139–140; *cf.* Borthwick, 185.
[55] p. 183.
[56] *Sheriff* v. *Wilson* (1855) 17 D. 528, 530, *per* L.J.C. Hope.
[57] *Sheriff, supra*; *Cunningham, infra*, 929, *per* Lord Ardmillan.
[58] (1868) 6 M. 926, 928.

might also be given, and, in such cases, the truth may often be an aggravation of the offence and injury." In these remarks the judge had convicium
in mind.

So, too, Lord Young remarked in *Macfarlane* v. *Black* [59]: " It was
suggested when these issues were discussed, as part of the general argument
on the relevancy of the action that possibly the case was *of another category*,
that in which a party complains of being injuriously held up in a series
of attacks to public hatred, contempt and ridicule," but an issue on
these lines was not proceeded with and the case was fought as one of
defamation rather than convicium.

" The claim in such cases [of attack on character] may either take
the form of an issue of damages founded on specific misrepresentation
. . . or where no specific charge has been made the pursuer may be entitled
to an issue of holding up to public hatred, ridicule and contempt. But I
venture to think that an issue in the last mentioned form ought not to be
granted except where the libel imputes moral depravity of some kind . . .
it being for the jury to say whether the purpose of the libel was to exhibit
the pursuer as having laid himself open not merely to ridicule but to
the odium of his associates and fellow citizens." [60]

Where the ground of action is convicium rather than defamation
the issue is one of " holding up to public hatred, contempt and ridicule "
as well as or instead of wounding the pursuer's feelings and degrading
him in the estimation of society.[61]

Requisites of action for convicium. It is submitted that an action of
damages for convicium lies where the defender has (a) maliciously, (b)
communicated of and concerning the pursuer an idea, which may be
either true or false (the falsity not being an essential of the action and
the truth no defence), (c) calculated to bring him into public hatred,
contempt or ridicule, and has thereby caused him loss, injury or damage.
The requisite malice or *animus injuriandi* or " design of exposing . . . the
pursuer to public hatred and contempt " [62] may be inferred from the
idea communicated and the circumstances, and no proof of express or
actual malice (malevolence, spite or ill will) need be adduced. The
idea communicated need not be defamatory [63]; thus an action for convicium would lie, it is submitted, for saying of a man that he was an atheist,
or sexually impotent, or suffered from a contagious disease, or believed
that socialists should be shot, or criminals castrated, or otherwise attribut-
ing views or conduct which, though not defamatory of him, would
probably lead him to be hated, ridiculed or treated with loathing or contempt. It might well be convicium falsely to attribute to a scholar authorship

[59] (1887) 14 R. 870, 874.
[60] *McLaughlan* v. *Orr, Pollock & Co.* (1894) 22 R. 38, 43, *per* Lord McLaren.
[61] *Sheriff, supra,* 532; *cf.* issues in *McLaren* v. *Ritchie* (1856), not reported, quoted in
   Macfarlane v. *Black* (1887) 14 R. 870, 873; *Cunningham* v. *Phillips* (1868) 6 M. 926;
   Paterson v. *Welch* (1893) 20 R. 744; *McLaughlan* v. *Orr, Pollock & Co.* (1894) 22 R. 38.
[62] *Paterson* v. *Welch* (1893) 20 R. 744, 750.
[63] On what ideas are defamatory, see Sect. 3, *infra*.

of a bad and discreditable book. Nor, it is submitted, is it essential that the ideas or views be attributed falsely, though false attribution is worse than true attribution, and in many cases a man would not object to having truly ascribed to him views which he held, even though they rendered him unpopular or even ridiculed.

Truth as a defence to convicium. Proof of the factual truth of the alleged imputation is a defence in an action for defamation, but there has been great difference of opinion whether the maxim *veritas convicii non excusat* is still good law. On principle it should be good law; for the purpose of the action for damages for convicium is to protect from abuse or vilification or ridicule rather than from unfounded aspersions on moral character or business credit. If a man who is sexually impotent is taunted with his impotence to his acute embarrassment, contempt, ridicule and hurt, he would be remediless if *veritas convicii* is a defence. So, too, a true imputation of homosexuality may lead a man to be condemned, ridiculed or hated as much as a false imputation. A man can be acutely hurt and injured in reputation by having some long-forgotten but true peccadillo raked up and used to bring him into contempt and ridicule.

According to Voet, [64] " if it is clear that what was imputed is true, not even then is he who makes the imputation always excused from the commission of a wrong "; while Erskine [65] states that certain injurious expressions amount " to an aggravated case of wrong, but not nowadays to the crime of slander, the distinction of the Roman law [66] being now ignored in our practice, *except to the effect of allowing no defence of veritas.*" Hume [67] indicates that the maxim *veritas convicii non excusat* applies in the semi-criminal claim for verbal injury, though not in the civil action for defamation. Guthrie Smith also [68] held that since convicium might often lead to public disturbance, while the truth of the libel was a good plea in all other cases, in this case the maxim applied: *veritas convicii non excusat.*

The older authorities are conflicting.[69] In later cases the phrase *veritas convicii* seems rather to have been used as connoting the truth of the imputation, *i.e.*, of the alleged slander, and not to have been used in its strict sense, of abuse as distinct from slander.[70] In *Mackellar,*[71] where the older cases were discussed, it was settled that *veritas* could be proved in defence, but despite the use of the phrase *veritas convicii*, the case was one of slander, not of convicium proper, and it is no authority

---

[64] Voet, 47, 10, 9.
[65] *Prin.* IV, 4, 45 (21st ed. (1911), p. 753).
[66] *i.e.*, between slander and convicium.
[67] *Lect.*, III, 156.
[68] *Damages*, 241.
[69] See *Macdonald* v. *Macdonald*, June 2, 1813, F.C.; *Dyce* v. *Kerr*, July 9, 1816, F.C.; and cases in *Mackellar, infra.*
[70] *i.e.*, convicium as distinct from slander.
[71] *e.g., Friend* v. *Skelton* (1855) 17 D. 548, 553; *Mackellar* v. *Duke of Sutherland* (1859) 21 D. 222, 227.

for a case of convicium. It is submitted that in a case of convicium proper, the maxim *veritas convicii non excusat* still embodies the true view of the law.

In *Cunningham* v. *Phillips*,[72] a case of convicium, Lord Deas said that truth might often be an aggravation of the injury, which suggests that he regarded it as no defence.

In *Paterson* v. *Welch* [73] it was averred by the pursuer that the statement ascribed by the defender to him was false, and the falsity was said by the court to be an essential element of the claim of damages. But the defender could equally well have vilified the pursuer, *animo injuriandi*, and brought him into public hatred and contempt by ascribing *truly* to him opinions which were unpopular and such as to arouse feelings of animosity against him.[74] The false ascription was not an essential of the action, but rather an aggravation of the defender's wrongful conduct.

Examples of convicium. Convicium has been the ground of action where a series of paragraphs, notices and letters were published in a newspaper making the pursuer appear ludicrous and addicted to gluttony [75]; where newspaper articles ridiculed the pursuer and made a fool of him [76]; where a newspaper held the pursuer up in a series of attacks to public contempt and odium [77]; where a person attributed to another a very unpopular, and possibly slanderous, opinion about a particular class of the community [78]; where a newspaper made fun of the supposed peculiarities of manner, indiscretions of speech and assumptions of autocratic authority on the pursuer's part [79]; where a newspaper attributed to the pursuer a desire to have bloodshed [80]; where a person had attributed to the pursuer the statement that soldiers went into the trenches in World War I to have an easy time [81]; and where a pretended newspaper interview with a variety artiste falsely attributed to her views on the prohibition of alcohol then in force in the U.S.A. and the consequent failure of her tour.[82]

3. DEFAMATION (OR LIBEL OR SLANDER)

" Slander is a defamatory statement maliciously made to the injury of another." [83] Defamation (or libel or slander) is the wrong of communicating, either deliberately or, in the case of communication to third

---

[72] (1868) 6 M. 926, 928.
[73] (1893) 20 R. 744.
[74] *e.g.*, the opinion that all trade unionists were scoundrels who should be suppressed by force, or that his own employees were just fools.
[75] *Sheriff* v. *Wilson* (1855) 17 D. 528.
[76] *Cunningham* v. *Phillips* (1868) 6 M. 926.
[77] *Macfarlane* v. *Black* (1887) 14 R. 870, referring to *McLaren* v. *Ritchie* (1856), not reported. The pursuer elected to go to trial on an issue of slander.
[78] *Paterson* v. *Welch* (1893) 20 R. 744; *cf. Waddell* v. *Roxburgh* (1894) 21 R. 883.
[79] *McLaughlan* v. *Orr, Pollock & Co.* (1894) 22 R. 38: action dismissed.
[80] *Waugh* v. *Ayrshire Post, Ltd.* (1893) 21 R. 327: issue of slander allowed in Inner House. *Cf. Lever Bros.* v. *Daily Record (Glasgow), Ltd.*, 1909 S.C. 1004, where issue of convicium disallowed as redundant.
[81] *Andrew* v. *Macara*, 1917 S.C. 247.
[82] *Lamond* v. *Daily Record (Glasgow), Ltd*, 1923 S.L.T. 512.
[83] *Shaw* v. *Morgan* (1888) 15 R. 865, 870, *per* Lord Young. Lord Kinnear, in *Russell* v. *Stubbs, Ltd.*, 1913 S.C.(H.L.) 14, 19, mentions as the approved definition of an actionable

parties, without due care, and without legal justification, to, or to third parties of and concerning, a person, a statement of fact, meaning or idea which is false or incorrect in fact and derogatory in its nature, to his loss, injury and damage.[84] If communicated to the pursuer only, it can hurt him in his feelings only and justifies a claim by him for solatium only. If communicated to third persons of and concerning the pursuer it may do so, and may also lower his reputation in the eyes of others and cause him actual pecuniary loss, justifying a claim for solatium and for patrimonial loss actual or anticipated.

Some general statements do not distinguish defamation from convicium; thus Lord Kinnear said [84]: " All actionable words which are either injurious to the character or credit of the person of whom they are spoken, or which expose the person with reference to whom they are uttered to public hatred and contempt, are defamatory or slanderous words." This statement is acceptable only if " defamatory or slanderous " is used in a broad sense, meaning " verbally injurious."

The issue for the jury in a defamation action [85] is whether the defender " falsely and calumniously stated of and concerning the pursuer " words carrying a defamatory imputation " to the loss, injury and damage of the pursuer."

The two elements of affront to the pursuer's feelings and damage to his reputation frequently both arise in one action, justifying awards both of solatium and of damages for patrimonial loss.

Defenders. Defamation is essentially a wrong committed by persons, rather than associations or corporations. An action of defamation against the executive committee of a trade union as individuals is not barred by the Trade Disputes Act, 1906, s. 4.[86]

Requisites of action. To make good a claim of damages for defamation a pursuer must aver and establish (a) the communication to him, or to others of and concerning him, of a meaning which is factually incorrect; (b) which is hurtful to his private feelings and self-esteem or derogatory to his reputation, *i.e.*, defamatory; and (c) which was made *animo injuriandi* or, in the case of injury to his public reputation, negligently and harmfully, or, as it is now more usually said, maliciously.

These requisites require individual examination.

Provinces of judge and jury. The respective provinces of judge and jury in defamation actions are no different from other actions *ex delicto.* It is for the court to determine as a matter of law, having heard argument on the relevancy of the pursuer's pleadings, whether the words are capable

libel that the statement holds the pursuer up to hatred, contempt or ridicule or conveys an imputation injurious to him in his trade. The first part of this dictum seems to proceed either on English authority, or on forgetfulness of convicium.

[84] *Waddell* v. *Roxburgh* (1894) 21 R. 883.

[85] Contrast the issue in an action based on convicium (falsely called verbal injury).

[86] *National Union of Bank Employees* v. *Murray*, 1948 S.L.T.(Notes) 51.

in the circumstances of bearing a meaning defamatory of the pursuer.[87] The case must be left to the jury if the words are so capable, even though the words might also bear an innocent interpretation.[88] It is also for the court to determine, where the words are *ex facie* innocent or meaningless, whether there has been relevantly averred a secondary, defamatory, meaning when the words are read in the circumstances in which they were uttered or written and with reference to the context in which they appear.[89] If defamation is relevantly averred, the pursuer is entitled to an inquiry to ascertain whether or not he has sustained damage thereby,[90] and the wrong does not cease to be actionable because the damage sustained is trivial.[91]

If in the view of the court the words complained of are, taken in their natural or ordinary sense, meaningless or innocent, or if there are no adequate averments of facts and circumstances which could reasonably have induced persons, to whom words prima facie innocent were uttered, to understand them in a secondary or defamatory sense. the court must dismiss the action as irrelevant.[92]

If the court holds the pursuer's case relevant, it remains to satisfy the jury that the words were used, that they did refer to the pursuer, that in the circumstances they did contain an imputation, and were accordingly defamatory of the pursuer.[93] If the words are capable of a defamatory meaning, taken in their natural or ordinary sense, the judge must leave it to the jury to decide whether the words were so understood on the occasion when they were used.[94]

Requisites of Defamation

(a) Communication of False Idea

Communication to the pursuer. A statement, written or oral, may be actionable even though not generally published, but communicated only to the pursuer himself. If it affronts him and damages his feelings and self-esteem, an action for solatium, of the nature of an *actio injuriarum*, lies.[95] " Our law says that a man may have damages for injury done to his

---

87 *Capital and Counties Bank* v. *Henty* (1882) 7 App.Cas. 741, 744; *Leon* v. *Edinburgh Evening News*, 1909 S.C. 1014, 1020; *Adam* v. *Ward* [1917] A.C. 309, 329, *per* Lord Dunedin; *Russell* v. *Stubbs, Ltd.*, 1913 S.C.(H.L.) 14, 20.
88 *Turner* v. *M.G.M. Pictures* [1950] 1 All E.R. 449.
89 *Smith* v. *Walker*, 1912 S.C. 224, 228, *per* Lord Kinnear.
90 *Cassidy* v. *Connochie*, 1907 S.C. 1112.
91 *Shaw* v. *Burns*, 1911 S.C. 537.
92 *Mulligan* v. *Cole* (1875) L.R. 10 Q.B. 549; *Ruel* v. *Tatnell* (1880) 43 L.T. 507; *Capital and Counties Bank* v. *Henty* (1882) 7 App.Cas. 741; *Nevill* v. *Fine Art Co.* [1897] A.C. 68; *Frost* v. *London Joint Stock Bank* (1906) 22 T.L.R. 760; *Beswick* v. *Smith* (1907) 24 T.L.R. 169; *Russell* v. *Stubbs, Ltd., supra.*
93 *Adam* v. *Ward* [1917] A.C. 309, 329, *per* Lord Dunedin; *Russell* v. *Stubbs, Ltd.*, 1913 S.C.(H.L.) 14.
94 *Capital and Counties Bank* v. *Henty* (1882) 7 App.Cas. 741, 777, *per* Lord Blackburn; *Hart* v. *Wall* (1877) 2 C.P.D. 146; *Ritchie* v. *Sexton* (1890) 17 R. 680; affd. 18 R.(H.L.) 20; *Cooney* v. *Ederlain* (1897) 14 T.L.R. 34; *Hunter* v. *Ferguson* (1906) 8 F. 574; *James* v. *Baird*, 1916 S.C.(H.L.) 158, 163; *Gray* v. *Jones* [1939] 1 All E.R. 798, 803; *Turner* v. *M.G.M. Pictures* [1950] 1 All E.R. 449.
95 Borthwick, 189.

feelings . . . The law of Scotland recognises the claim of a person to recover damages for a slanderous statement made in a letter written to himself and not communicated to anyone else, and therefore we must, I think, in consistency hold that verbal statements, amounting to slander, made to a man outwith the presence of others will also afford a good ground for an action of damages." [96]

But " although the law of Scotland sustains, in certain circumstances, an action of damages for libellous expressions contained in a letter addressed to the party himself, it by no means follows that the statements in such a letter will always found an action of damages, because they would do so if published to the world, or addressed and sent to a third party. [The defender] . . . was entitled, in my opinion, to write to the pursuer in the terms which he did . . . provided only he did so in good faith, which must here be assumed; but it does not at all follow that he would have been equally entitled, in whatever good faith, erroneously and unnecessarily, to have written in the same terms of and concerning the pursuer to a third party. He might be privileged in the one case and not in the other; or free from all liability in the one case, and not in the other." [97] A person, that is, may be legally entitled to communicate a matter to a person himself, which he would not be entitled to communicate to others.

In a case of communication to the pursuer alone, must the communication be deliberate? The action being an *actio injuriarum, animus injuriandi* should be required. The requisite *animus injuriandi* probably refers to the deliberate making of the defamatory statement rather than to its deliberate communication to the pursuer, so that if a secretary finds in her employer's case a manuscript note addressed to herself intimating her dismissal for immorality, that reason, if false, would be actionable, the writing having been done *animo injuriandi*, though no communication to her had been made, whether or not *animo injuriandi*. But if her employer orally attributed immorality to her, it should not be actionable if that imputation were made merely without having made due inquiry rather than intentionally or deliberately (*i.e., animo injuriandi*).

Where defamatory matter is communicated to the pursuer alone, the pursuer cannot complain so far as loss is attributable to publicity of the aspersion because the pursuer is himself the author of any publicity given to the alleged slander.[98] He cannot therefore claim for damage to his public reputation, but only for hurt feelings.

Communication by the defender. The pursuer must aver and prove, if it is not admitted, that it was the defender who uttered, or wrote, or

---

[96] *Mackay* v. *McCankie* (1883) 10 R. 537, 539, *per* L.P. Inglis; similar expressions by other judges; *Ramsay* v. *MacLay* (1890) 18 R. 130; *cf. Hutchison* v. *Naismith* (1808) Mor.App. Delinquency, No. 4; *McCandies* v. *McCandie* (1827) 4 Mur. 198; *Brown* v. *Wason* (1838) McFarlane 114; *Bryson* v. *Inglis* (1844) 6 D. 363; *Kennedy* v. *Baillie* (1855) 18 D. 138; *Stuart* v. *Moss* (1888) 13 R. 299.
[97] *Kennedy* v. *Baillie* (1855) 18 D. 138, 157, *per* Lord Deas.
[98] *Will* v. *Sneddon, Campbell & Munro*, 1931 S.C. 164.

otherwise originated the statement complained of. In the case of anonymous letters the defender must be identified as the writer by *comparatione
literarum* or otherwise, and evidence of the defender's motive may be
led in supplement of other evidence of authorship.[99] Letters to persons
other than the pursuer may properly be pleaded and proved for the
purpose only of helping to prove that the letters complained of were in
the defender's handwriting.[1] In the case of oral slander the defender
must be identified as the utterer of the slander by the evidence of
hearers. This may be extremely difficult in the case of oral slander by
telephone.

Words alleged must be proved. No question of what words were used
normally arises in the case of written libel, but in the case of oral slander
the pursuer must prove that there were uttered the words averred by him
in his pleadings and complained of as defamatory, or at least all material
parts of them, or words substantially to the same effect and conveying
practically the same meaning to the mind of a reasonable man.[2] But the
pursuer fails if the words proved to have been uttered differ materially
from those alleged on record, though the court may allow amendment at
the bar so long as this will not amount to altering the whole basis of the
action. The pursuer also fails if he proves that the words alleged were
uttered, but it is also established that they had some addition or qualification not averred which materially changes their meaning.[3]

Communication " of and concerning " the pursuer. Where the communication has been made to a third party, the court must be satisfied
that the communication complained of was made " of and concerning "
the pursuer or pursuers: *si incertae personae convicium fiat nulla executio
est.*[4] Does the communication, that is, clearly refer to the pursuer and
besmirch his character? It is for the jury to say whether the pursuer or
pursuers are the persons who would be understood as the persons referred
to.[5]

Words must relate to the pursuer. The pursuer must aver and prove
that the words complained of as defamatory were published to him, or
to others of and concerning him, and his action must fail unless he can
show that the alleged imputation related to him.[6] There is no difficulty
where the pursuer is named expressly or otherwise clearly designated,
as by reference to his office,[7] in the defamatory context.

---

[99] *Melville* v. *Crichton* (1820) 2 Mur. 277; *Home* v. *Sandie* (1832) 10 S. 508; *Menzies* v.
  Goodlet (1835) 13 S. 1136; *MacTaggart* v. *MacKillop*, 1938 S.C. 847.
[1] *Swan* v. *Bowie*, 1948 S.C. 46.
[2] *Tournier* v. *National Provincial Bank* [1924] 1 K.B. 461.
[3] *Orpwood* v. *Barkes* (1827) 4 Bing N.C. 261.
[4] Dig. 47, 10, 15.
[5] *Hulton* v. *Jones* [1910] A.C. 20; *Browne* v. *Thomson*, 1912 S.C. 359, 362.
[6] *Caldwell* v. *Munro* (1872) 10 M. 717; *A.* v. *B. & Co.* (1898) 25 R. 951; *Lawrence* v. *Newberry*
  (1891) 64 L.T. 797; *Fournet* v. *Pearson* (1897) 14 T.L.R. 82; *Sadgrove* v. *Hole* [1901]
  2 K.B. 1.
[7] *Beattie* v. *Mather* (1860) 22 D. 952.

Where, however, the pursuer is not expressly named or otherwise clearly identified, as where he is referred to by initials,[8] or a nickname, or not named at all, the pursuer must aver and prove that the defamatory statement was understood as referring to him [9]; he must satisfy the court that the words are capable of referring to him, as an identifiable individual, and satisfy the jury that the words do so refer [10]; and the evidence of persons who so understood the statement, as relating to the pursuer and as being defamatory of him, is competent and necessary.[11] Evidence is also competent of facts and circumstances known to persons hearing the words complained of from which it can reasonably be inferred that they understood the words to refer to the pursuer.[12]

If the defamation is done by means other than words it is competent and necessary to elicit from witnesses what they understood by the pictures, signs or other defamatory matter and to whom they understood the idea communicated to refer.

Reference to pursuer by mistake. A pursuer has a good ground of action if he shows that defamatory matter was considered by others to refer to him, even though by mistake on the defenders' part. In *Outram* v. *Reid* [13] a wine and spirit merchant recovered damages from the publishers of the Glasgow Herald, which had published a notice, abbreviated from the Edinburgh Gazette, of the bankruptcy of a wine and spirit merchant of his name, but had not included the address. He established that the statement, true of another, had been understood as referring to him, and had caused him loss of business and damage to credit. In *Wragg* v. *Thomson* [14] a pursuer was allowed an issue on averments that a newspaper paragraph was slanderous and related to one of his name. The same applies even though the statement understood to refer to the pursuer was not intended to, and did not in fact, refer to any real person at all.[15] The originator of the statement, that is, runs the risk of its being mistakenly understood to refer to the pursuer.

Such cases may not be covered by the Defamation Act, 1952, s. 4 (5), which protects the innocent publisher of defamatory matter if he did not intend to publish it of and concerning the pursuer, did not know of circumstances by virtue of which they might be understood as defamatory of the pursuer, and exercised all reasonable care in relation to the

---

[8] *Jardine* v. *Creech* (1776) Mor. 3438.
[9] *Godfrey* v. *Thomsons* (1890) 17 R. 1108; *Waugh* v. *Ayrshire Post* (1894) 21 R. 326; *Webster* v. *Paterson*, 1910 S.C. 459, 469.
[10] *Braddock* v. *Bevins* [1948] 1 K.B. 580.
[11] *Bourke* v. *Warren* (1826) 2 C. & P. 307; *Smith* v. *Gentle* (1844) 6 D. 565; *Broome* v. *Gooden* (1845) 1 C.B. 728; *Hulton* v. *Jones* [1909] 2 K.B. 444; [1910] A.C. 20; *Cassidy* v. *Daily Mirror* [1929] 2 K.B. 331; *Hough* v. *London Express* [1940] 2 K.B. 507; *Jozwiak* v. *Sadek* [1954] 1 All E.R. 3.
[12] *Capital and Counties Bank* v. *Henty* (1882) 7 App.Cas. 741.
[13] (1852) 14 D. 577; *cf. Cassidy* v. *Daily Mirror Newspapers, Ltd.* [1929] 2 K.B. 331; *Newstead* v. *London Express Newspaper, Ltd.* [1940] 1 K.B. 377.
[14] 1909, 2 S.L.T. 409; *cf. Finlay* v. *Ruddiman* (1763) Mor. 3436; *Harkness* v. *Daily Record (Glasgow), Ltd.*, 1924 S.L.T. 759; *Harper* v. *Provincial Newspapers, Ltd.*, 1937 S.L.T. 462.
[15] *Hulton* v. *Jones* [1910] A.C. 20.

publication.[16]   In *Outram* [13] and these other cases there had not been all reasonable care, but a situation is conceivable in which the section would afford a defence.

Reference to a number of people. Questions of difficulty arise where the statement in question is applicable to a number of people, whether it is " of and concerning " each one sufficiently to be actionable by each one as being an infringement of each one's legally protected interest in his reputation. In *Shearlock* v. *Beardsworth* [17] damages were awarded to the commanding officer of a regiment for expressions defamatory of the regiment, presumably on the basis that he represented it, but possibly on the basis that aspersions on a unit necessarily reflect on the commanding officer.

In later cases the question has been treated as one of whether the defamation of a class or group in general terms amounted by implication to slander of the individual members of the class or group. Only if it did, is it actionable by them individually.[18]

In *Browne* v. *Thomson*,[19] seven clergymen sued individually in one action for having been libelled in an article published by the defenders which alleged that the " Roman Catholic religious authorities " had abused their religious influence. Lord President Dunedin said [20]: " if a certain set of people are accused of having done something, and if such accusation is libellous, it is possible for the individuals in that set of people to show that they have been damnified, and it is right that they should have an opportunity of recovering damages as individuals "; and Lord Kinnear [21]: " It is a question of fact for the jury whether, holding the article to be libellous, it applies to the persons now complaining. That is a question of fact, and each of the pursuers must satisfy the jury that he is hit by the language of which they all complain. It might very well be that one might succeed and another might fail, but the question is one of fact."

Sometimes the context of the statement complained of excludes the pursuer from the group defamed,[22] but a group reference may be capable of being read as defaming a particular pursuer.[23]

More than one pursuer can sue together for a single alleged slander applicable to each of them, but there must be separate conclusions, and separate issues [24]; where the slander is applicable only to one person,

---

[16] On s. 4 see *Ross* v. *Hopkinson* [1956] C.L.Y. 5011.
[17] (1816) 1 Mur. 196; said in *Broom* v. *Ritchie* (1904) 6 F. 942, 946, to be a doubtful decision.
[18] *Macphail* v. *Macleod* (1895) 3 S.L.T. 91; *Wardlaw* v. *Drysdale* (1898) 25 R. 879; *Webster* v. *Paterson*, 1910 S.C. 459; *Briggs* v. *Amalgamated Press*, 1910, 2 S.L.T. 334; *Browne* v. *Thomson & Co.*, 1912 S.C. 359; *Couper* v. *Balfour*, 1914 S.C. 139; *cf. A.* v. *B. & Co.* (1898) 25 R. 951.
[19] 1912 S.C. 359.
[20] p. 363.
[21] p. 363.
[22] *A.* v. *B. & Co.* (1898) 25 R. 951; *Couper* v. *Balfour of Burleigh*, 1914 S.C. 139.
[23] *Briggs* v. *Amalgamated Press*, 1910, 2 S.L.T. 334.
[24] *Graeme* v. *Cunningham* (1765) Mor. 13923; *Scotlands* v. *Thomson* (1776) Mor.App. Delinquency, No. 3; *Young* v. *Inglis* (1801) Hume 608; *Henderson* v. *Henderson* (1855) 17 D. 348; *Harker* v. *Mowat* (1862) 24 D. 701; *Ritchies* v. *Barton* (1883) 10 R. 813; *Mitchell* v. *Grierson* (1894) 21 R. 367.

two or more persons may sue, if it may apply to one of them.[25] Two pursuers have been allowed to sue in one action for alleged slanderous statements made regarding them on different occasions and at different places where they were husband and wife and the wrongs complained of arose out of one and the same matter.[26]

Defamation of a class or group. If a defamatory statement is uttered of and concerning an indeterminate class or group of persons, such as lawyers or Scotsmen, neither the group nor any individual member or members of the group may sue.[27]

If, on the other hand, the class or group is sufficiently determinate and small, so that the defamation can reasonably be regarded as being defamation of each individual member of that group, then any or all of the members of the group may sue.[28] " The crucial question in these cases in which an individual plaintiff sues in respect of defamation of a class or group of individuals is whether on their true construction the defamatory words were published of and concerning the individual plaintiff. Unless this can be answered in the affirmative, he has no cause of action." [29] Under this principle actions have been allowed by the members of a presbytery,[30] and by seven Roman Catholic clergymen defamed as a group.[31]

Individual members of a limited company cannot sue, either independently or with the company, for defamation which tends to depreciate the company's business or honour,[32] but where defamatory statements were made about an unincorporated company, a person who was a partner and manager thereof and was named in the statements was held entitled to sue.[33]

It has also been held that a chartered society may sue for verbal injury.[34]

In general, where defamatory matter is published of a group, the larger the group, the smaller is the chance that any one, or all, of the group will be able to show that the matter was understood as personally defamatory of him or them. Thus a statement that the M.P. for a constituency " and her friends in A " took a certain attitude was held to refer to political supporters in A and to be a mere generalisation which could not be referred to any identifiable individual.[35]

[25] *Mitchell, supra.*
[26] *Golden* v. *Jeffers,* 1936 S.L.T. 388.
[27] *Eastwood* v. *Holmes* (1858) 1 F. & F. 347; *McFadyen* v. *Spencer* (1892) 19 R. 350, 353–354; *Wardlaw* v. *Drysdale* (1898) 25 R. 879; *Campbell* v. *Ritchie,* 1907 S.C. 1097; *O'Brien* v. *Eason* [1913] Ir.L.T. 266; *Campbell* v. *Wilson,* 1934 S.L.T. 249 (members of association).
[28] *Browne* v. *Thomson,* 1912 S.C. 359.
[29] *Knupffer* v. *London Express* [1944] A.C. 116, 123, *per* Lord Russell of Killowen; *cf.* *Braddock* v. *Bevins* [1948] 1 K.B. 580.
[30] *Macphail* v. *Macleod* (1895) 3 S.L.T. 91.
[31] *Browne* v. *Thomson,* 1912 S.C. 359; on this case see Lord Mackay in *Campbell* v. *Wilson,* 1934 S.L.T. 249. [32] *Campbell* v. *Wilson,* 1934 S.L.T. 249.
[33] *Hustler* v. *Watson* (1841) 3 D. 366; *cf.* *Williams* v. *Allan* (1841) 3 D. 600, where another partner and manager also sued, though not mentioned by name.
[34] *Society of Solicitors* v. *Robertson* (1781) Mor. 13935.
[35] *Braddock* v. *Bevins* [1948] 1 K.B. 580, applying *Knupffer* v. *London Express Newspaper* [1944] A.C. 116.

The distinction must be kept clear between defamation directed against the corporation or body and that directed against individuals, though as officers of the body.[36] It is quite clear that a corporation or other body may be defamed as a corporate entity, by aspersions on its financial or commercial reputation.[37]

Defamation of individual within a class. Where defamatory words appear to cast imputations on a class or group, it may be shown that in fact they truly point to one or more determinate individuals, and in such a case an action will lie at the instance of the individual or individuals. " Where a class is described it may very well be that the slander refers to a particular individual. This is a matter of which evidence is to be laid before the jury, and the jurors are to determine whether, when a class is referred to, the individual who complains that the slander applied to him is, in point of fact, justified in making such complaint . . . whether a man is called by one name, or whether he is described by a pretended description of a class to which he is known to belong, if those who look on, know well who is aimed at, the very same injury is inflicted, the very same thing is in fact done as would be done if his name and Christian name were ten times repeated." [38]

In *McFadyen* v. *Spencer & Co.*[39] the pursuer averred that he and three other men were sent to do a job on the defenders' vessel, that the defender then sent his employers a bill for whisky found to be missing after the job had been done saying that " your men had taken it," and that he had thereby been slandered as being a thief. The court held that the communication was privileged and, no malice having been averred, the pursuer's case was irrelevant. It was observed, however,[40] that " it cannot be said that the defenders were making an accusation of theft against any individual workmen " so that the action could have been dismissed on the ground that there was no imputation against the pursuer and he had no title to sue. So too in *Wardlaw* v. *Drysdale* [41] an intemperate letter to a newspaper directed against publicans was held not to be an attack on two publicans as individuals.

Defamation of corporate bodies. " It is not disputed that an action of damages, for reparation of injury inflicted by slander, may be competently raised by the incorporation, if there be relevant grounds of action." [42] A corporation has no feelings to be hurt but has a trade or

---

[36] *Dumfries Fleshers* v. *Rankin,* Dec. 10, 1816 F.C.; *Selkirk* v. *Rankin* (1819) 2 Mur. 128; *Hustler* v. *Watson* (1841) 3 D. 366.

[37] See, further, *infra.*

[38] *Le Fanu* v. *Malcolmson* (1848) 1 H.L.Cas. 637.

[39] (1892) 19 R. 350.

[40] 353, *per* L.J.C. Macdonald.

[41] (1898) 25 R. 879.

[42] *North of Scotland Banking Co.* v. *Duncan* (1857) 19 D. 881, 885, *per* L.O. Ardmillan; cf. *Society of Solicitors* v. *Robertson* (1781) Mor. 13935; *Incorporation of Fleshers of Dumfries* v. *Rankine,* Dec. 10, 1816, F.C.; *British Legal Life Assce. Co., Ltd.* v. *Pearl Life Assce. Co. Ltd.* (1887) 14 R. 818; *South Hetton Coal Co.* v. *Northeastern News* [1894] 1 Q.B. 133; *D. & L. Caterers, Ltd.* v. *D'Ajou* [1945] K.B. 364.

business reputation which may be damaged or ruined, as by the imputation that it is insolvent,[43] or corrupt,[44] or fraudulent,[45] or by aspersions on its products,[46] or that it provides insanitary houses for employees [47] or refuses to abide by a conciliation board wages award.[48] It therefore cannot recover solatium, but can recover damages for loss of business, actual or potential.

A non-profit-making corporation similarly probably has a public reputation to protect, as has a municipal corporation.[49]

Quasi-corporations. Quasi-corporations are in a similar position; thus a trade union can sue as an entity for an unjustified disparagement of its activities,[49a] or for an imputation of " rigging " a ballot of its members,[50] and a firm for defamation of the firm as an entity.[51]

Defamation by implication. A statement directly defamatory of A may by implication cast aspersions on B's credit or character. To stigmatise A as illegitimate casts by implication an imputation on A's parents and possibly also on his brothers and sisters.[52] To stigmatise X as a " crooked lawyer " or a " bogus physician " [53] implies an imputation on X's professional partners. But in such a case it would be necessary to aver an innuendo, stating plainly what defamatory meaning the pursuer claims the statement carried of and concerning him, as distinct from its obvious defamatory meaning of and concerning the person directly referred to.

Similarly, defamation of individuals as office-bearers or committee of management may amount to slander of the corporation or institution they represent.[54] A distinct innuendo is necessary. Defamation of a partner in a firm may likewise imply defamation of the firm as an entity.

In *North of Scotland Banking Co.* v. *Duncan* [55] Lord Deas, in a dissenting judgment, sought to distinguish two classes of cases, " cases in which the party slandered is the party seeking reparation, and cases in which reparation is sought by a party who says he is injured in consequence of another party having been slandered. In the former it is enough to prove that the slanderous words of and concerning the pursuer were uttered —the falsehood and malice being presumed. In the latter it is necessary, I think, to aver and to prove malice, or, what is substantially the same

---

43 *Metropolitan Saloon* v. *Hawkins* (1859) 4 H. & N. 87.
44 *South Hetton Coal Co.*, *supra.*
45 *British Legal Life Assce. Co.*, *Ltd.* v. *Pearl Life Assce. Co.*, *Ltd.* (1887) 14 R. 818.
46 *British Empire Machine Co.* v. *Linotype* (1899) 81 L.T. 331.
47 *South Hetton Coal Co.*, *supra.*
48 *Holdsworth* v. *Associated Newspapers*, *Ltd.* [1937] 3 All E.R. 872.
49 *Bourne* v. *Marylebone Corpn.* [1908] W.N. 52; *cf. Mayor of Manchester* v. *Williams* [1891] 1 Q.B. 94, doubted in *Willis* v. *Brooks* [1947] 1 All E.R. 191.
49a *N.U.G.M.W.* v. *Gillian* [1946] K.B. 81.
50 *Willis* v. *Brooks* [1947] 1 All E.R. 191.
51 *Le Fanu* v. *Malcolmson* (1848) 1 H.L.Cas. 637, 669; *cf. McVean* v. *Blair* (1801) Hume 609.
52 *Cf. Symmond* v. *Williamson* (1752) Mor. 3435; *Broom* v. *Ritchie* (1904) 6 F. 942, 946, *per* L.J.C. Macdonald.
53 *Cf. Chisholm* v. *Grant*, 1914 S.C. 239.
54 *North of Scotland Banking Co.* v. *Duncan* (1857) 19 D. 881.
55 (1857) 19 D. 881, 887.

thing, an intent to injure the pursuer. It is quite easy to conceive that one party may be injured by a slander directed against another . . . A slander against one member of a family may injure the other members—for instance, to attack the character of one daughter may deeply injure another daughter, but unless the latter alleges that the slander was intended to injure her she cannot claim damages." No authority was cited for this proposition so far as demanding proof of malice, and it seems to be unwarranted,[56] while it omits the requirement of an innuendo, which seems essential.

In *Finburgh* v. *Moss' Empires, Ltd.*[57] a husband and wife visited a theatre; an official, acting under a mistake, scrutinised them and stated that the woman was a bad character and must leave the theatre; when the husband sought to explain that the lady was his wife he was told by the manager that he had heard that story before; later it was stated that she was a notorious prostitute. This accusation was false, and the wife's claim for defamation was held relevant. The husband also sued, alleging that he was by implication accused of associating with a notorious prostitute and of trying to pass her off as his wife. The court dismissed this action as too far-fetched. Lord Ardwall said [58]: " Now, it is said, that by calling his wife a prostitute the defender's servants impliedly accused him of being an associate of prostitutes. I do not think that this presents a relevant case of slander. The fact that a woman has erroneously been called a prostitute, or that a man has been called a swindler or a thief, will not entitle the relatives or friends of such a person, however near or intimate, to raise actions for slander because forsooth the accusation made against their relative or friend implies that they are the relatives or friends of a person of bad character. In my opinion a person who has uttered a slander is, as a general rule, only liable for the direct damage caused thereby to the person of and concerning whom the slander has been written or uttered, and any damage that may have been caused to other persons through the utterance of such slander is too remote and consequential to infer liability against the alleged slanderer." So far as concerns husband and wife and close relations this dictum seems too strong and there is force in the Lord Ordinary's view [59] that there was an imputation on the husband's character also, particularly when he was told that the manager had heard the story before that the lady was her escort's wife. It is thought that this dictum should be treated as too general. To accuse a respectable man of associating with a notorious prostitute and trying to pass her off as his wife, as happened in this case, is a serious imputation. But, subject to that, Lord Ardwall's general principle seems sound, that a defender will be liable only to persons directly

---

[56] The judgment is promoted by *Cooper on Defamation* (p. 83) to be a distinct head of verbal injury, the slander of A through the slander of B. There seems to be no justification for this at all.

[57] 1908 S.C. 928.

[58] *Ibid.* 941.

[59] p. 934.

defamed, and not to those remotely or indirectly affected by implication. It is highly questionable whether the friends who accompanied the Finburghs to the theatre could have sued, as being impliedly stamped as companions of a prostitute.

Defamation of a deceased person. In Roman and Roman-Dutch law an *injuria* immediately affecting one person might be regarded as immediately affecting another who was intimately related to him. Thus where a defamatory statement was made concerning one now deceased, his heirs might be entitled to bring an *actio injuriarum*,[60] and so might his widow and children.[61]

This principle has not, however, been generally followed in Scots law. In general, defamation is *actio personalis quae moritur cum persona* and an executor would not have a title to sue unless he clearly averred patrimonial loss.[62] Defamatory words of and concerning a deceased do not give surviving relatives any right of action for *solatium*, unless the defamation is such in its nature as to affect their reputations also.[63] " If a slander be uttered and directed against the character of a deceased person, from which it is a necessary implication that others are directly injured, as, *e.g.*, that his children are stamped as bastards, there can be no doubt that action would be competent as for wrong although indirectly done through aspersion of the deceased." [64] Lord Young, however, stated, *obiter*,[65] that if a person were defamed and died " an action would be competent at the instance of his widow or his children, not only where the injury affected his person, but also where it affected his reputation . . . I am of opinion that the widow and children of a dead man whose character has been defamed are not only interested to clear the character of the deceased, but it is their duty to take such measures as are necessary to clear his character and to seek solatium for the injury done to their own feelings . . . And where a widow for herself and her pupil children resorts, in the discharge of a reasonable and proper duty, to an action to clear the character of the deceased husband and father, I think that solatium for injury to the feelings of the pursuer is as proper an element in fixing and awarding damages as it would be in an action brought at the dead man's own instance." This opinion does not seem ever to have been applied and rests on the hypothesis that just as to cause the death of the husband hurts the wife's feelings, so to defame her late husband hurts her feelings.

---

60 D. 47, 10, 1, 4 and 6; Inst. 1, 6, 1.

61 Voet, 47, 10, 5.

62 *Cf. Smith* v. *Stewart & Co.*, 1961 S.C. 91.

63 *Broom* v. *Ritchie* (1904) 6 F. 942. In *Tullis* v. *Crichton* (1850) 12 D. 867, an action was brought for assault and slander and, the pursuer having died, the action was insisted in by the tutor-at-law to his child. The point of title to sue seems to have passed by unnoticed, but it is hard to see that the child had any title.

64 *Broom, supra*, 946, *per* L.J.C. Macdonald. *Walker* v. *Robertson* (1821) 2 Mur. 508, was not followed by the Lord Ordinary, and rejected by the L.J.C. See also *Watsons* v. *Smeaton* (1805) Hume 624.

65 *Ibid.* 948, founding on analogy with the principle of *Eisten* v. *N.B.Ry.* (1870) 8 M. 980, 984.

This possibly goes too far,[66] but at least some defamatory imputations on a deceased could be very hurtful to the surviving relatives, and probably should be actionable.

None of the dicta in *Broom* v. *Ritchie* deal directly with the case where the defamation of the deceased has caused the surviving relatives pecuniary loss,[67] and in such a case, as where a person has falsely published that A died insolvent and A's widow wished to carry on, or to sell, A's business, it is thought that a claim would lie if probable or actual damage to the business could be shown. This point is still quite open, but it is thought that a claim is competent in such a case.

If a person has been defamed and then died, his executor can carry on any action raised by the deceased before his death,[68] but, probably, for damages for patrimonial loss only and not for such solatium as the deceased might have recovered. An executor could probably initiate a claim only if he averred and proved patrimonial loss to the estate.[69]

It is accordingly unsound to imagine that defamation of the deceased may be expressed with impunity. " Even a matter of history may be a subject for claiming damages, if it is injurious to descendants." [70]   The concept of defamation by implication might be utilised to give surviving relatives a claim in some cases.

Matter communicated. The matter communicated and complained of must be of fact, not of belief or opinion, though a statement of belief or opinion may be as actionable as a statement of fact, if it is merely a cloak for a defamatory imputation. But a statement which is truly one of belief or opinion as to some matter of fact truly stated is not defamatory, even if hurtful.[71] " The expression of an opinion as to a state of facts truly set forth is not actionable, even when that opinion is couched in vituperative or contumelious language." [72]   Strong disapprobation is not necessarily defamatory,[73] and a person's conduct,[74] or the system within which he operates [75] may be criticised without necessarily impugning that person's character or competence.

---

[66] But an unauthorised post-mortem on her husband's body gives the widow a claim for solatium: *Pollok* v. *Workman* (1900) 2 F. 354; *Conway* v. *Dalziel* (1908) 3 F. 918; *Hughes* v. *Robertson*, 1913 S.C. 394.

[67] The L.O. (p. 943) posed the question whether the widow could claim where the statement " caused her mental suffering, but not pecuniary loss "; the L.J.C. (p. 945) said: " . . . where solatium only is in question," and it seems implicit in Lord Young's opinion that he would have allowed a claim if injury to business could be shown.

[68] *Broom, supra*, 945, *per* L.O. Kincairney (" . . . the person defamed or his executor in his right ").

[69] *Cf. Auld* v. *Shairp* (1874) 2 R. 191; *Smith* v. *Stewart & Co.*, 1961 S.C. 91.

[70] *Walker* v. *Robertson* (1821) 2 Mur. 516, 519. In *Tullis* v. *Crichton* (1850) 12 D. 867 on the pursuer's death his child, through a tutor-at-law, insisted in the action; the justification for this is obscure.

[71] *Archer* v. *Ritchie* (1891) 18 R. 719, 727; *Meikle* v. *Wright* (1893) 20 R. 928; *Bruce* v. *Ross* (1901) 4 F. 171, 176. *Cf. Campbell* v. *Ferguson* (1882) 9 R. 467.

[72] *Archer, supra.*

[73] *Bruce, supra*; *cf. Munro* v. *Mudie* (1901) 9 S.L.T. 91.

[74] *Neilson* v. *Johnston* (1890) 17 R. 442.

[75] *Langlands* v. *John Leng & Co.*, 1916 S.C.(H.L.) 102.

The dividing line is, however, narrow and a statement of opinion, *e.g.*, that an author's book is a poor one, may come very close to imputing to him professional incompetence.

Means of conveying defamatory imputation. Liability is imposed only where there is deliberate or negligent communication by one person to another,[76] of and concerning the pursuer, of an idea which is false in fact and defamatory of the pursuer, in any way by which an idea or a meaning can be communicated. Most commonly defamation is effected by words, written or otherwise marked on paper, or spoken. Broadcasting by means of wireless telegraphy is equivalent to written defamation,[77] and the same is probably true of words recorded on magnetic tape and played over. Where " words " are mentioned hereafter, other means of communicating ideas are included.[78] Among other means of communicating possibly defamatory ideas which have been recognised are questions,[79] allegory,[80] quotation,[81] hypothesis,[82] letters,[83] newspaper advertisements or intimations,[84] newspaper bills,[85] newspaper headlines,[86] in precognitions [87] in a notarial protest objecting to banns of marriage,[88] by posting the name of the party defamed,[89] in statements from the pulpit,[90] photographs,[91] pictures,[92] cartoons,[93] placards,[94] caricatures,[95] or cinematograph [96] or television pictures [97] of a person. It may also be done by conduct,[98] such as setting up an effigy,[99] chalking marks on a

---

[76] Who may himself be the pursuer, and need not be a third party.

[77] Defamation Act, 1952, s. 1 (section not applicable to Scotland) defines broadcast statements as publication in permanent form, *i.e.*, as libel rather than slander, but it is undoubted that broadcasting may convey defamatory imputations.

[78] *Cf.* Defamation Act, 1952, s. 16 (1): " Any reference . . . to words shall be construed as including a reference to pictures, visual images, gestures and other methods of signifying meaning."

[79] *Lockhart* v. *Cumming* (1852) 14 D. 452; *Carmichael* v. *Cowan* (1863) 1 M. 204; *Scott* v. *Johnston* (1885) 12 R. 1022; *McKercher* v. *Cameron* (1892) 19 R. 383.

[80] *Mackie* v. *Lawson* (1851) 13 D. 725.

[81] *Sexton* v. *Ritchie* (1891) 18 R.(H.L.) 20.

[82] *Hamilton* v. *Hope* (1826) 4 Mur. 222.

[83] *Stuart* v. *Moss* (1886) 13 R. 299.

[84] *McLean* v. *Bernstein* (1900) 8 S.L.T. 42; *Morrison* v. *Ritchie* (1902) 4 F. 645; *Wood* v. *Edinburgh Evening News*, 1910 S.C. 895.

[85] *Archer* v. *Ritchie* (1891) 18 R. 719.

[86] *Gudgeon* v. *Outram* (1889) 16 R. 183.

[87] *Harper* v. *Robinsons* (1821) 2 Mur. 383.

[88] *Hendersons* v. *Henderson* (1855) 17 D. 348.

[89] *Mackay* v. *Campbell* (1832) 11 S. 1031.

[90] *McIntosh* v. *Flowerdew* (1851) 13 D. 726; *Williamson* v. *Umphray* (1890) 17 R. 905; *Selbie* v. *Saint* (1891) 18 R. 88.

[91] *Garbett* v. *Hazell, Watson & Viney* [1943] 2 All E.R. 359 (collocation of legend and pictures); *Thaarup* v. *Hulton Press* (1943) 169 L.T. 309.

[92] *Du Bost* v. *Beresford* (1810) 2 Camp. 511; *Monson* v. *Tussauds* [1894] 1 Q.B. 678; *Drysdale* v. *Earl of Rosebery*, 1909 S.C. 1121, 1123.

[93] *Spider's Web* v. *Pearson* (1953) cited in Gatley, 20.

[94] *Archer* v. *Ritchie* (1891) 18 R. 719, 727.

[95] *Smith* v. *Wood* (1813) 3 Camp. 323; *Dunlop* v. *Dunlop Co.* (1920) 1 Ir.R. 280; *Tolley* v. *Fry* [1931] A.C. 333.

[96] *Youssoupoff* v. *M.G.M.* (1934) 50 T.L.R. 581.

[97] *Ahmed* v. *Associated Rediffusion* (1963) C.L.Y. 2014.

[98] *Kennedy* v. *Allan* (1848) 10 D. 1293; *Drysdale* v. *Earl of Rosebery*, 1909 S.C. 1121.

[99] *Monson* v. *Tussauds* [1894] 1 Q.B. 671; *cf. Corelli* v. *Wall* (1906) 22 T.L.R. 532.

gate [1] or pavement,[2] circulating a letter,[3] burning a person in effigy,[4] fixing an object or sign on his house,[5] attaching a nick-name to certain premises, [6] having premises watched by the police,[7] by sounds,[8] signs [9] or gestures,[10] by a bank refusing or failing to honour a customer's cheque when there were funds available to honour the cheque,[11] by filing a photograph and finger-prints among criminal records,[12] prosecuting a person,[13] the pronouncing of a sentence of excommunication,[14] the presentation of a petition to the licensing justices,[15] the action of a society in expelling a member,[16] or in any other way by which an idea can be communicated.

Publication. While the words complained of as defamatory must have been published to the pursuer himself, they need not have been published any more widely to render them actionable.[17] A defender is liable if a defamatory statement is made inadvertently, as by a letter sent to the pursuer by mistake.[18] But the wider the publication the more the pursuer is likely to be, and to feel, injured, so that the extent of publication is relevant to damages.[19] The original utterer or publisher of defamatory matter is the person primarily liable, as he has originated the harm. In an action against a newspaper for innocently publishing a defamatory notice,[20] communicated to it by a person unknown, Lord Kincairney said: " There can be no doubt that the pursuers . . . would doubtless recover exemplary damages from the mean scoundrel who sent the advertisements, if they could discover him . . ."

It is questionable, however, whether a defamatory idea put on paper but not disclosed to anyone would ground an action, if it were found by the person defamed, say, in the writer's desk. Such might be held to be

---

1 *Tarpley* v. *Blabey* (1836) 2 Bing.N.C. 437.
2 *Haylock* v. *Sparke* (1853) 1 E. & B. 471.
3 *Kennedy* v. *Allan* (1848) 10 D. 1293; *cf. McDonald* v. *McDonald* (1803) Borthwick, 388; *N. of Scotland Bank* v. *Duncan* (1857) 19 D. 881; *Richards* v. *Chisholm* (1860)22 D. 215; *Waugh* v. *Ayrshire Post, Ltd.* (1894) 21 R. 326.
4 *Eyre* v. *Garlick* (1878) 42 J.P. 68.
5 *Jefferies* v. *Duncombe* (1809) 2 Camp. 3 (suspending lamp in front of house, " intending to mark it as a bawdy-house.")
6 As where a female students' hostel was referred to as The Brothel.
7 *Robertson* v. *Keith*, 1936 S.C. 29.
8 *Gregory* v. *Duke of Brunswick* (1843) 6 M. & G. 953.
9 *Gutsole* v. *Mathers* (1836) 1 M. & W. 495, 501 (deaf and dumb language); *cf. Drysdale* v. *Earl of Rosebery*, 1909 S.C. 1121, 1123.
10 *Cook* v. *Cox* (1814) 3 M. & S. 110, 114 (holding up empty purse); *Drysdale, supra.*
11 *Marzetti* v. *Williams* (1830) 1 B. & A. 415; *Rolin* v. *Steward* (1854) 14 C.B. 595; *King* v. *B.L.Co.* (1899) 1 F. 928; *Wilson* v. *United Counties Bank* [1920] A.C. 102; see also *Fleming* v. *Bank of New Zealand* [1900] A.C. 577; *Plunkett* v. *Barclays Bank* [1936] 2 K.B. 107; *Gibbons* v. *Westminster Bank* (1939) 55 T.L.R. 888; *Davidson* v. *Barclays Bank* [1940] 1 All E.R. 316; *Pyke* v. *Hibernian Bank* [1950] Ir.R. 195.
12 *Adamson* v. *Martin*, 1916 S.C. 319.
13 *Craig* v. *Peebles* (1875) 3 R. 441.
14 *Dunbar* v. *Skinner* (1849) 11 D. 945.
15 *Keay* v. *Wilsons* (1843) 5 D. 407.
16 *Murdison* v. *Scottish Football Union* (1896) 23 R. 449.
17 *Mackay* v. *McCankie* (1883) 10 R. 537; *secus* in English law.
18 *Outram* v. *Reid* (1852) 14 D. 577; *Gordon* v. *Stubbs* (1895) 3 S.L.T. 10.
19 See *Gillie* v. *Labno* (1949) C.L.Y. 4792.
20 *Morrison* v. *Ritchie* (1902) 4 F. 645, 647.

inadvertent publication. It is publication nonetheless because a party communicates the matter to the party defamed in breach of confidence.[21]

Repetition. Each publication or repetition of a defamatory statement is a fresh and separate wrong,[22] and each person who repeats is liable in the same way and to the same extent as the person who originated the defamatory imputation.[23] Thus a newspaper is liable for repeating by publishing a slander communicated by an individual to it.[24] It is no defence that the defamatory statement was received from another disclosed person,[25] not even if it were honestly believed to be true,[26] or was merely being republished,[27] or transmitted.[28] " The existence of a slanderous report, or its prevalent currency, is no justification for repeating it. Each repetition is a new injury to the party slandered . . . He is entitled to prosecute any person propagating the slander, and if such party can prove that he did not originate the slander . . . still that circumstance can only operate in mitigation of the amount of damages due." [29]

It is no defence that the defamatory matter was stated as hearsay, or current rumour, unless the rumour were honestly believed by the defender to be true and the occasion of the repetition was also privileged.[30] Nor is it a defence that the defamatory imputation, though expressed, was coupled with expressions of doubt or disbelief or otherwise disclaimed, nor that the source of the imputation is given.[31] A newspaper cannot plead privilege as a defence to a claim for slander if it refuses to disclose the name of the writer of an anonymous letter to the editor which it has published.[32]

The fact that a defender has merely repeated in bona fide a current report or had transmitted apparently reliable information will however be a factor in mitigation of damages,[33] particularly if, the statement not being *ex facie* defamatory, the repeater discloses his source.[34]

---

21   *McCandies* v. *McCandie* (1827) 4 Mur. 197.
22   *Winn* v. *Quillan* (1899) 2 F. 322.
23   *Gibson* v. *Cheap* (1823) 1 Sh.App. 459; *Marshall* v. *Renwick* (1834) 13 S. 1127; *Watts* v. *Fraser* (1835) 7 C. & P. 369; *Browne* v. *McFarlane* (1889) 16 R. 368; *Cunningham* v. *Duncan* (1889) 16 R. 383; *A.B.* v. *Blackwood* (1902) 5 F. 25; *Marchant* v. *Ford* [1936] 2 All E.R. 1510.
24   *Morrison* v. *Ritchie* (1902) 4 F. 645; *cf. Finlay* v. *Ruddiman* (1763) Mor. 3436; *Jardine* v. *Creech* (1776) Mor. 3438 and Appx. Delinquency, No. 1.; *Drew* v. *Mackenzie* (1862) 24 D. 649, 662; *Neilson* v. *Johnston* (1890) 17 R. 442.
25   *Fair* v. *Barclay* (1834) 12 S. 565; *McPherson* v. *Daniels* (1829) 10 B. & C. 263; *De Crespigny* v. *Wellesley* (1829) 5 Bing. 392; *Tidman* v. *Ainslie* (1854) 10 Ex. 63.
26   *Tidman* v. *Ainslie, supra.*
27   *Lewis* v. *Walter* (1821) 4 B. & Ald. 605.
28   *Macdonald* v. *Martin,* 1935 S.C. 621, 641.
29   *Marshall* v. *Renwick* (1835) 13 S. 1127; see also *Gibson* v. *Cheap* (1823) 1 Sh.App. 459; *Fair* v. *Barclay* (1834) 12 S. 565; *Lowe* v. *Taylor* (1843) 5 D. 1261; *Richards* v. *Chisholm* (1860) 22 D. 215; *Ogilvy* v. *Paul* (1873) 11 M. 776; *Milne* v. *Walker* (1894) 21 R. 155.
30   *Watkin* v. *Hall* (1868) L.R. 3 Q.B. 396.
31   *Morrison* v. *Ritchie* (1902) 4 F. 645, 652.
32   *Brims* v. *Reid* (1885) 12 R. 1016; *McKerchar* v. *Cameron* (1892) 19 R. 383.
33   *Macculloch* v. *Litt* (1851) 13 D. 960; *Paul* v. *Jackson* (1884) 11 R. 460.
34   *Browne* v. *MacFarlane* (1889) 16 R. 368; *Cunningham* v. *Duncan* (1889) 16 R. 383, 390.

Further repetitions of a slander by one defender is relevant to damages.[35]

Exceptions. The repetition of a defamatory imputation may be justifiable if the hearer, believing it to be true, repeats it on a privileged occasion.[36]

Persons, such as librarians, booksellers or newsagents, who transmit or disseminate slanderous matter are not liable for publishing it by repetition unless they could, by the exercise of reasonable care, have been aware of the defamatory matter and have refrained from circulating it.[37] Persons such as carriers or porters are not liable, having no concern with the contents at all.

Nor is slander necessarily deemed repeated by clerks or typists who merely act as the defender's hands or mouth, nor by post-office clerks transmitting telegrams.[38] A solicitor may be liable for repeating slander, even on the client's instructions, if he has adopted the statements as his own[39]; *secus* if he confined himself to communicating facts or opinions by his client's instructions.[40]

A person is not guilty of repetition by " concurring and adopting " the defamatory statement of another, unless he has done something amounting to uttering it himself, though not necessarily with doing so in so many words. But presence and absence of dissent at hearing a slander does not amount to repetition.[41]

In other cases a party may be liable but will be entitled to ask that damages be mitigated in the circumstances. Cases of this include repetition in *bona fide* of a current report or on the basis of apparently reliable information and the repetition of matter not *ex facie* defamatory, certainly where the informant is disclosed or cannot be traced.[42]

Liability of original defamer for repetition by another. The person who initiates a defamatory statement is liable for the natural and probable consequences of the original publication thereof, but not, at least prima facie, for unauthorised republication or repetition of the defamation by persons to whom it was published.[43] The question is whether the repetition was a natural and foreseeable consequence, or such as to be a *novus actus interveniens* in the causal connection between initial utterance and ultimate harm. Hence a person making a complaint to the proper authority will not prima facie be liable if the authority propagates the slander

---

35 *Morrison* v. *Ritchie* (1902) 4 F. 645, 647.
36 *McPherson* v. *Daniels* (1829) 10 B. & C. 263, 271.
37 *Emmens* v. *Pottle* (1885) 16 Q.B.D. 354; *Vizetelly* v. *Mudie* [1900] 2 Q.B. 170; *cf. Morrison* v. *Ritchie* (1902) 4 F. 645, 651.
38 *Evans* v. *Stein* (1904) 7 F. 65.
39 *Crawford* v. *Adams* (1900) 2 F. 987; *cf. Wilson* v. *Purvis* (1891) 18 R. 72.
40 *Crawford, supra*, 997.
41 *Jack* v. *Fleming* (1891) 19 R. 1.
42 *Browne* v. *MacFarlane* (1889) 16 R. 368; *Cunningham* v. *Duncan* (1889) 16 R. 383, 390; *Morrison* v. *Ritchie* (1902) 4 F. 645.
43 *Ward* v. *Weeks* (1830) 7 Bing. 211; *Clarke* v. *Morgan* (1877) 38 L.T. 354; *Weld-Blundell* v. *Stephens* [1920] A.C. 956; *Bradstreets* v. *Mitchell* [1933] 1 Ch. 190.

rather than taking up the complaint without unnecessary publicity. In *Williamson* v. *Umphray and Robertson*,[44] R. was instructed by U. to appear to oppose the grant of a licence to W., and read to the licensing court a letter received from U., defamatory of W. W. was held entitled to an issue against U. only, and not R., as on the pursuer's averments R. was acting only as agent. " The letter of the defender U., being a confidential communication to his agent R. would never have come to the knowledge of the pursuer W. . . . unless either the agent had violated the confidentiality by publishing it without the authority of the client, or the client had authorised its publication. In the former case the agent would have been responsible to the pursuer and to his client. In the latter case (which on the averments of the pursuer is the case actually before us), the client alone is responsible for the publication." [44] The former case could have been treated as one of *novus actus interveniens*.

Exceptions. But the original publisher will be liable if he intends or authorises republication of the defamatory matter,[45] as where defamatory matter is deliberately communicated to the Press.[46]

He will also be liable if repetition is the natural and probable consequence of his publication.[47] This is a matter for determination by the court, as a matter of law, having regard to the circumstances. The original defamer will be liable if repetition was foreseeable and might reasonably have been anticipated.[48]

Again, the original publisher will be liable if the person to whom the defamation was published was under a social, moral or legal duty to repeat or republish the matter to a third person, provided he was aware of the circumstances giving rise to the duty of repetition at the time he initiated the defamation.[49]

Original defamer or repeater protected by privilege. The originator of a defamatory statement which has been repeated will not be liable if, when he made the defamatory statement, he was protected by privilege, and in such a case only the repeater can be liable, unless indeed the repetition was also and separately protected by privilege. The originator is not protected merely by the fact that a repetition may have been privileged,[50] if the original publication was not privileged. So, too, the repeater can escape liability only if privilege attached on the occasion and in the circumstances in which he repeated the defamation; he cannot rely on privilege attaching to the initial publication.

---

[44] (1890) 17 R. 905, 913, *per* L.P. Inglis.
[45] *Gibson* v. *Cheap* (1823) 1 Sh.App. 459; *Speight* v. *Gosnay* (1891) 60 L.J.Q.B. 231, 232; *Ratcliffe* v. *Evans* [1892] 2 Q.B. 524, 530; *Morrison* v. *Ritchie* (1902) 4 F. 645.
[46] *Bond* v. *Douglas* (1836) 7 C. & P. 626; *R.* v. *Cooper* (1846) 8 Q.B. 533; *Whitney* v. *Moiguard* (1890) 24 Q.B.D. 630.
[47] *Speight* v. *Gosnay, supra.*
[48] *Lynch* v. *Knight* (1861) 9 H.L.C. 592, 600; *Weld-Blundell* v. *Stephens* [1920] A.C. 956.
[49] *Derry* v. *Handley* (1867) 16 L.T.(N.S.) 263; *Speight* v. *Gosnay, supra.*
[50] *e.g.,* if stated in judicial pleadings.

Defamation by agent. A person is not relieved from responsibility merely because he was acting as agent for another when he communicated the defamatory matter. Thus a solicitor is liable for defamatory matter in letters,[51] unless he wrote under express instructions from the client. Even in this case he will be liable, equally with the client, if he adopted or approved the defamatory statements.[52] The client is not liable for defamatory matter communicated by the agent without his authority or instructions.[53]

Similarly a husband is not liable for slander uttered by his wife unless he joined in or authorised or ratified it.[54]

An action of defamation against the executive committee of a trade union as individuals is not barred by the Trade Disputes Act, 1906, s. 4; they may be liable as agents though their principal, the union, is statutorily protected.[55]

Falsity. It is essential that the words complained of be false and untrue in fact, since a person cannot complain of, as being defamatory, another saying to or of him what is true in fact.[56] The pursuer must accordingly aver that the defender communicated the defamatory idea " falsely." [57] But he is not called on to *prove* the falsity of the imputation. " When a libel is produced . . . the law presumes falsehood and from thence infers malice." [58] If the words are defamatory in their nature and plain meaning the law will presume in the pursuer's favour that they are false, unless and until the defender proves the contrary. " There are cases too in modern days (of which *McNeill* v. *Rorison*, Nov. 12, 1847, and *Burnaby* v. *Robertson*, March 3, 1848, may be selected as instructive examples), in which it is taken for granted as too clear to admit of dispute, that wherever a defender is charged with defamation—*i.e.*, with falsely and calumniously defaming the defender—the falsehood is presumed, and does not require to be proved on the part of the pursuer; but it is open to the defender to aver and prove the truth of the alleged slander, to the effect of a complete defence against the action." [59] " In the absence of an issue of *veritas*, the presumption will be that he did not [act corruptly]." [60]

Even where a communication contains a substantially accurate statement of facts, the jury may find for the pursuer if satisfied that the representation was in substance false and calumnious.[61]

---

[51] *Wilson* v. *Purvis* (1891) 18 R. 72.
[52] *Crawford* v. *Adams* (1900) 2 F. 987.
[53] *Watsons* v. *Smeaton* (1805) Hume 624; *Yeo* v. *Wallace* (1868) 5 S.L.R. 253.
[54] *Martin* v. *Murray* (1803) Hume 619; *Barr* v. *Neilsons* (1868) 6 M. 651; *Milne* v. *Smiths* (1893) 20 R. 95; *Scorgie* v. *Hunter* (1872) 9 S.L.R. 292; *Hook* v. *McCallum* (1905) 7 F. 528.
[55] *N.U. Bank Employees* v. *Murray*, 1948 S.L.T.(Notes) 51.
[56] *e.g.*, *Cook* v. *Gray* (1891) 29 S.L.R. 247.
[57] *Campbell* v. *Ferguson* (1882) 9 R. 467; *Meikle* v. *Wright* (1893) 20 R. 928.
[58] *Scott* v. *McGavin* (1821) 2 Mur. 484.
[59] *Mackellar* v. *Duke of Sutherland* (1859) 21 D. 222, 229, *per* L.J.C. Inglis.
[60] *Hunter* v. *Ferguson* (1906) 8 F. 574, 578, *per* Lord Stormonth-Darling.
[61] *James* v. *Baird*, 1916 S.C. 510 (revd. on another point, 1916 S.C.(H.L.) 158).

If a statement is true in fact and not defamatory, it matters not that it was communicated maliciously, with the design and result of injuring the pursuer in his business.[62]

The truth of the alleged imputations may appear from the pursuer's own pleadings, in which case the action may be dismissed *de plano*,[63] or the truth may be tabled in defence, by the plea of *veritas*,[64] and sustained on the evidence.

(b) Defamatory Quality of Idea Communicated

The idea communicated must be accepted by the court as defamatory before they will regard the action as relevant to go to a jury. It must be such, that is, as conveys an imputation on the moral character of the pursuer,[65] or is injurious to the character or the credit of the pursuer,[66] or assails the pursuer's character or credit,[66] or ascribes to him conduct of a dishonourable or immoral kind,[67] or is a false statement about a man to his discredit,[68] or " tends to lower the plaintiff in the estimation of right-thinking members of society generally." [69]

The criterion is *arbitrium boni viri*, " the view which would be taken by the ordinary good and worthy subject of the King," [70] " the opinion of any fair-minded reader." [71] " The question is . . . what the words used would convey to an ordinary reader, reading the articles as articles in newspapers are usually read." [72]

If the words tend to expose the pursuer to hatred, ridicule or contempt, they amount to convicium rather than slander.[73]

It is incorrect to define " defamatory " as including any element of tendency to injure a person in his office, profession or trade, because at least some statements may be made with such a tendency which are not defamatory. Thus to say falsely and deliberately that X has given up business is likely to injure his business, but conveys no necessary imputation against character or credit.[74] But it might be actionable as so-called verbal injury (*i.e.*, malicious falsehood).[75]

Defamatory quality a question of law. The defamatory quality of the communication complained of is in the first place a question of law to be

---

[62] *Parlane* v. *Templeton* (1896) 4 S.L.T. 153.
[63] *Carson* v. *White*, 1919, 2 S.L.T. 215.
[64] On which see, *infra*.
[65] *Archer* v. *Ritchie* (1891) 18 R. 719, 727.
[66] *Waddell* v. *Roxburgh* (1894) 21 R. 883, 886.
[67] *Paterson* v. *Welch* (1893) 20 R. 744, 749.
[68] *Scott* v. *Sampson* (1882) 8 Q.B.D. 491, 503, *per* Cave J., adopted in *Youssoupoff* v. *M.G.M.* (1934) 50 T.L.R. 581, 585.
[69] *Sim* v. *Stretch* (1936) 52 T.L.R. 669; *cf. Tolley* v. *Fry* [1930] 1 K.B. 467.
[70] *Byrne* v. *Deane* [1937] 1 K.B. 818, 833, *per* Slesser L.J.
[71] *Boal* v. *Scottish Catholic Printing Co.*, 1907 S.C. 1120.
[72] *Hunter* v. *Ferguson & Co.* (1906) 8 F. 574, 578, *per* L.J.C. Macdonald.
[73] *Supra*, p. 744. The definition of libel by Parke B. in *Parmiter* v. *Coupland* (1840) 6 M. & W. 105, 108, resting on " hatred, ridicule or contempt " is unsuitable for Scotland and has been criticised in England as too narrow.
[74] *Ratcliffe* v. *Evans* [1892] 2 Q.B. 524.
[75] On this aspect of verbal injury, see Chap. 26, *infra*.

determined by debate on the relevancy of the pursuer's pleadings. The court must be satisfied that the particular communication can be held to fall within the legal category of " defamatory," before it is justified in allowing an issue to go to a jury. If the idea communicated was not, in the court's view, fairly capable of conveying a defamatory imputation, the action falls to be dismissed as irrelevant.[76] If more than one defamatory meaning is alleged and such are alleged to be inferred from the natural and ordinary meaning of the words used, the court must rule whether the words are capable of bearing each of the defamatory meanings.[77] The ordinary and natural meaning of words complained of may include any implication or inference which a reasonable reader or hearer without special knowledge might draw from them, and it is for the jury to decide whether such a person might draw that inference.[78]

Standard of opinion by which defamatory quality judged. The opinion by which to consider whether a statement is defamatory or not is objective, *i.e.*, the question is not whether the pursuer considers his self-esteem has been damaged or his reputation harmed, but whether the statement is regarded by the court, as representing the general view of society, as being such as, if proved, is fairly capable of hurting the pursuer or degrading the pursuer in the estimation of others. Thus the misdescription of a person tried for a licensing offence as a " prisoner," though he was not technically such, is not libellous because it does not impute guilt or anything else defamatory.[79]

Secondly, the court, in exercising its controlling function at the relevancy stage, tries to apply the standard of opinion of " right-thinking members of society generally." The question is: would reasonably careful, prudent, fairminded and judicious individuals regard such a statement as disparaging.

" Words are not defamatory, however much they may damage a man in the eyes of a section of the community, unless they also amount to disparagement of his reputation in the eyes of right-thinking men generally. To write or say of a man something that will disparage him in the eyes of a particular section of the community but will not affect his reputation in the eyes of the average right-thinking man is not actionable within the law of defamation." [80] Words, that is, are not defamatory if they tend to bring the pursuer into lower esteem only within a particular section or class of society,[81] particularly if its standards are lower than that reasonable average held by " right-thinking " persons.[82]

[76] *Russell* v. *Stubbs, Ltd.*, 1913 S.C.(H.L.) 14; *Adam* v. *Ward* [1917] A.C. 309, 329.
[77] *Rubber Improvement* v. *Daily Telegraph* [1964] A.C. 234.
[78] *Jones* v. *Skelton* [1963] 3 All E.R. 952.
[79] *Leon* v. *Edinburgh Evening News, Ltd.*, 1909 S.C. 1014; *secus, Davidson* v. *Anderson* (1905) 12 S.L.T. 679.
[80] *Tolley* v. *Fry* [1930] 1 K.B. 467, 479, *per* Greer L.J.
[81] *Clay* v. *Roberts* (1863) 8 L.T. 397; *Miller* v. *David* (1874) L.R. 9 C.P. 118; *Myroft* v. *Sleight* (1921) 90 L.J.K.B. 853.
[82] *Maure* v. *Pigott* (1869) Ir.R. 4 C.L. 54 (priest charged with being informer against criminals); *Byrne* v. *Deane* [1937] 1 K.B. 818.

Censure. Quite apart from any question of privilege, words of censure or rebuke are not necessarily defamatory, particularly in certain circumstances and relations of parties, such as clergyman and parishioner, master and servant, master and pupil. Thus to say to a person: " You are the cause of the trouble; you are a bad influence " is not defamatory unless some particular moral fault, or evil influence, amounting to a material imputation on character, is charged.[83]

Sarcasm. Similarly, statements held in the circumstances to be merely sarcastic are not defamatory.[84]

Excessively strong expressions. A person is not liable for defamation if he uses an extravagant or excessively strong expression which, in its strict sense, is defamatory. Thus where a report described persons convicted of catching wild birds as " thieves," it was held that this could not reasonably be held to amount to a charge of theft.[85] The word " thief " was only an abusive epithet, " a rather extravagant term of abuse." In the same way to call a man a liar may in the circumstances be no more than a strong denial and not an accusation of habitual mendacity.[86]

Abuse or slang. Similarly, words are not defamatory if the words used, though their literal and grammatical meaning is defamatory, were used as slang or abuse or vehement criticism. " To accuse a man of committing a fraud is a slander; but if slang is used it must be taken according to its ordinary meaning. Here it is nothing else than slang; and calling a man a fraud does not mean that he has committed a fraud. All that is meant is that he is not nearly so good as he pretends to be; . . . the ordinary slang expression of calling a person a fraud does not mean that the person has committed a fraud in the legal sense of the term. Therefore, to call a man a liar and a fraud is not slanderous. It is abusive language which may or may not be deserved, but it is not slanderous." [87]

Context. The proper meaning of words used may depend on the context in which they were used. If the alleged slander is in a letter, the court must look at the correspondence of which it is part.[88] On the one hand words prima facie defamatory may be shown to have been uttered in jest, or with a secondary and innocent meaning,[89] or to have been neither intended nor understood in a defamatory sense.[90]

---

[83] *Rooney* v. *McNairney*, 1909 S.C. 90; *cf. McNeill* v. *Forbes* (1883) 10 R. 867.
[84] *Bell* v. *Haldane* (1894) 2 S.L.T. 320.
[85] *Campbell* v. *Ritchie*, 1907 S.C. 1097.
[86] *Watson* v. *Duncan* (1890) 17 R. 414; *Christie* v. *Robertson* (1899) 1 F. 1155.
[87] *Agnew* v. *British Legal Life Assce. Co., Ltd.* (1906) 8 F. 422, 428, *per* L.P. Dunedin. *Cf. Somerville* v. *Buchanan* (1801) Hume 608; *Mackintosh* v. *Squair* (1868) 5 S.L.R. 635; *Grierson* v. *Harvey* (1871) 43 Sc.Jur. 190; *Jameson* v. *Bonthrone* (1873) 11 M. 703; *Cockburn* v. *Reekie* (1890) 17 R. 568; *Watson* v. *Duncan* (1890) 17 R. 404; *Macdonald* v. *Rupprecht* (1894) 21 R. 389; *Christie* v. *Robertson* (1899) 1 F. 1155; *Mackay* v. *Grant* (1903) 11 S.L.T. 380.
[88] *Smyth* v. *Mackinnon* (1897) 24 R. 1086, 1091.
[89] *Hankinson* v. *Bilby* (1847) 16 M. & W. 442.
[90] *McNeill* v. *Forbes* (1883) 10 R. 867; *Christie* v. *Robertson* (1899) 1 F. 1155.

On the other hand words prima facie innocent may be shown to carry a defamatory meaning, having regard to the context in which they appear.[91] Thus an announcement in the Births column of a newspaper was recognised as defamatory only when it appeared that the " parents " had been married only two months.[92]

In several cases publication of a photograph has been held defamatory only because, in the context or in the circumstances in which it is published, it conveys a defamatory imputation.[93] Again, where an accused, who had been acquitted, sued a newspaper whose report of the case was headed " . . . *Prisoners* Acquitted," on the ground that he had never been apprehended nor been a prisoner, it was held that the word " prisoners " was not used in its strict sense and was in the circumstances not defamatory.[94]

Relevance of time and place. The defamatory nature or not of a statement may sometimes depend on the time and place of its expression, and on the state of opinion and public feeling at the time. What was not formerly defamatory may be so now, and conversely; what is defamatory in one place may not be so in another. " In the time of Elizabeth it was actionable to call a person a witch, for witchcraft was then a statutory offence.[95] In the time of Charles II it was actionable to call a person a Papist and to say that he went to Mass,[96] though it was held otherwise in the reign of James I,[97] and in the existing state of law[98] and opinion in England no action would lie for such a statement at the present day." [99] Accordingly, old authorities as to whether a word is or is not defamatory should not be blindly followed, but weighed by contemporary standards.[1]

Words in foreign language. Words in any language other than English, and possibly even words in a dialect of Scots or English, require to be averred as having been uttered in the language used and to have an English translation set out in the same way as an innuendo, and it has to be proved that the words in the language concerned actually were spoken and that the English meaning of the words is what the pursuer avers the meaning to be.[2]

Questions of the proper translation may arise and also of the overtones and connotations of a particular foreign word, which may be absent

---

[91] *Foulger* v. *Newcomb* (1867) L.R. 2 Ex. 327; *Russell* v. *Notcutt* (1896) 12 T.L.R. 195; *Cassidy* v. *Daily Mirror* [1929] 2 K.B. 331.

[92] *Morrison* v. *Ritchie* (1902) 4 F. 645; *cf. Wood* v. *Edinburgh Evening News*, 1910 S.C. 895 (a very doubtful decision, irreconcilable with *Morrison*).

[93] *Garbett* v. *Hazell, Watson & Viney* [1943] 2 All E.R. 359.

[94] *Leon* v. *Edinburgh Evening News*, 1909 S.C. 1014.

[95] *Rogers* v. *Cravat* (1597) Cro.Eliz. 571.

[96] *Row* v. *Clargis* (1683) Sir Thos.Raym. 482; *Walden* v. *Mitchell* (1692) 2 Vent. 265. During the penal centuries, it was a crime to say or to hear Mass in England.

[97] *Ireland* v. *Smith* (1610) 2 Brown. & Gold. 166.

[98] *Cf. Bourne* v. *Keane* [1919] A.C. 815; *Re Cans* [1934] Ch. 162.

[99] Gatley, 23.

[1] *Cf. Beith's Trs.* v. *Beith*, 1950 S.C. 66.

[2] *Bernhardt* v. *Abrahams*, 1912 S.C. 748; *cf. Matheson* v. *Mackinnon* (1832) 10 S. 825; *Martin* v. *McLean* (1844) 6 D. 981; *McLaren* v. *Robertson* (1859) 21 D. 183; *Anderson* v. *Hunter* (1891) 18 R. 467.

from its English counterpart, in which case, if the pursuer relies on a connotation as defamatory, an innuendo will be necessary.

Defamatory words and phrases. In considering what words and phrases and other imputations have been held to be defamatory and to make a case relevant for trial by jury, a distinction falls to be taken between words and phrases which have previously been, or are, in an unprecedented case, accepted as openly and *ex facie* defamatory, and other words and phrases which are *ex facie* innocent or ambiguous but convey a defamatory meaning only if further facts and circumstances are averred and established, which shed a different light on the words and convert the innocent into the imputation. " In all actions for libel, whether the writing complained of does or does not contain words or expressions clearly actionable, it is the duty of the pursuer to state on record what he understands, and undertakes to show, is the true meaning of the writing taken as a whole. But in such cases there is room for a distinction. Where the words or expressions used are in their natural or ordinary sense not actionable, and where the pursuer undertakes to prove or infer from extrinsic facts that they were intended to be used in a non-natural sense, he is bound to state on record the extrinsic facts from which the inference is to be drawn. This is illustrated and very clearly established by the cases of *Broomfield* [3] and of *Brydone* [4]; but in other cases where a non-natural meaning is not sought to be ascribed to particular words or expressions, and the pursuer merely alleges that the writing, though not free from ambiguity, is yet according to its fair construction a libel on his conduct and reputation, he is not necessarily required to state extrinsic facts from which to infer the construction for which he contends. All that is required of him in such cases is to state distinctly the libellous meaning which he attaches to the writing." [5] " With regard to the actionable nature of the words complained of, the agreement that " blackguard " and " person of bad character " are not actionable without innuendo, is perfectly new to me. The rule of the law of Scotland is, that words spoken or written (for in this respect the law of Scotland recognises no distinction) casting imputations on moral character, are relevant to ground an action of damages. If imputations, however general, are made upon the moral character, in words distinctly importing such a charge, these words are clearly actionable." [6]

(i) *Words ex facie defamatory*

A large number of words have been recognised in past cases as being defamatory in their ordinary and natural meaning or *ex facie* defamatory,[7]

---

3 *Broomfield* v. *Greig* (1868) 6 M. 563.
4 *Brydone* v. *Brechin* (1881) 8 R. 697.
5 *Sexton* v. *Ritchie & Co.* (1890) 17 R. 680, 685, *per* L.P. Inglis; *cf.* Lord Shand at pp. 691–692, Lord McLaren at p. 696.
6 *Brownlie* v. *Thomson* (1859) 21 D. 480, 485, *per* L.J.C. Inglis.
7 See the directory of such words in *Cooper on Defamation*, pp. 291–334 and in Gatley, pp. 25–41.

and accordingly to be relevant grounds for actions of damages. Unprecedented cases may be decided by analogy with cases already decided, or by reference to the overriding general criterion of whether or not they would tend to lower the pursuer in the estimation of right thinking members of society generally. Such words as " adulterer," " whore," " crook," " racketeer " need no explanation of their defamatory quality. The ordinary and natural meaning of words complained of may include any implication or inference which a reasonable reader or hearer without any special knowledge might draw from them, it being for the jury to decide whether such a person might draw that inference.[8]

Interpretation of allegedly defamatory words. Unless the pursuer seeks to prove that the words bear in the circumstances some special or extended meaning, words and phrases must be given their normal and natural meaning, the meaning which persons of normal intelligence would naturally give to those words.[9] This is not a matter for evidence, but a matter eminently for the jury.[10] There is no rule that, if the words are capable, by some stretching or unusual construction, of bearing an innocent meaning, that meaning should be given them.[11] " The standard to be applied by the court . . . is the presumed intelligence of the reasonable man. . . . Would a reasonable man, reading the publication complained of, discover in it matter defamatory of the pursuer ? Or, put otherwise, the question is, What meaning would the ordinary reader of the newspaper put upon the paragraph which the pursuer complained of? " [12]

The words alleged to be defamatory must be considered as a whole,[13] and in their context. Thus the whole of a correspondence, in which an allegedly defamatory letter is a part, must be read,[14] and the heading of a newspaper paragraph as well as the text.[15]

(ii) *Words not defamatory in natural sense—Innuendo*

No difficulty arises where a pursuer establishes the publication to, or of and concerning, him of words *ex facie* defamatory, understood in their plain, ordinary and natural meaning. But if the words are not defamatory in their ordinary and natural meaning, or are in a code or slang, the pursuer must, if he is to succeed, aver and prove that the words used had a connotation which was defamatory in the circumstances. This attribution of a special meaning to the words, which sense must be averred and

---

[8] *Jones* v. *Skelton* [1963] 3 All E.R. 952.
[9] *Hankinson* v. *Bilby* (1847) 16 M. & W. 442, 445; *Capital and Counties Bank* v. *Henty* (1882) 7 App.Cas. 742, 745, 772, 788; *Gray* v. *Jones* [1939] 1 All E.R. 798.
[10] *Hobbs* v. *Tinling* [1929] 2 K.B. 1; *Hough* v. *London Express* [1940] 2 K.B. 507.
[11] *Hunter* v. *Ferguson* (1906) 8 F. 574.
[12] *Duncan* v. *Scottish Newspapers*, 1929 S.C. 14, 20, *per* Lord Anderson.
[13] *Australian Newspapers* v. *Bennett* [1894] A.C. 284, 288, *per* Lord Herschell L.C.; *Wardlaw* v. *Drysdale* (1898) 25 R. 879; *Campbell* v. *Ritchie*, 1907 S.C. 1097, 1099, 1101, *per* Lord Stormonth-Darling.
[14] *Smyth* v. *Mackinnon* (1897) 24 R. 1086.
[15] *Leon* v. *Edinburgh Evening News*, 1909 S.C. 1014; *Grand Theatre (Glasgow)* v. *Outram*, 1908 S.C. 1018n.

proved, is called the innuendo. "If a statement complained of is not slanderous in itself, the pursuer, if he is to succeed, must endeavour to innuendo the language used, so as to extract from it a defamatory imputation." [16]

In a case of this kind the pursuer must aver that the defender communicated to him, or of and concerning him to others, a statement which in the surrounding circumstances was capable of conveying, was intended to convey, and was understood by some hearers as conveying, an idea with a factually false and defamatory imputation. Innuendo is a matter of fact, to be averred specifically [17] and proved.[18]

"An innuendo ought to be an averment that words which in their ordinary acceptation are not libellous had, in the circumstances in which they were used, a specified libellous meaning, or that they had a libellous application not otherwise obvious. The pursuer must therefore define with precision the specific meaning which he ascribes to language not obviously libellous. . . ." [19] "In all actions for libel it is the duty of the pursuer to state on the record what he understands, and undertakes to show, is the true meaning of the writing taken as a whole. If he proposes to put upon words that are apparently harmless a defamatory meaning by reading them with some special application, then it is his duty to allege the extrinsic circumstances which he says prove that defamatory meaning; . . . that is the duty of the pursuer, and it is not the duty of the court." [20]

"It is for the pursuer of an action to state definitely the meaning which he alleges that the article or words complained of bear, and to put that meaning in issue, and thereafter the court determines whether there is any issuable matter and approves or disapproves, or it may vary or adjust, the issues proposed for the trial." [21] A party is bound by the innuendo set out in the pleadings, and cannot put a new meaning on a libel at the trial.[22]

An innuendo must be supported by averments of circumstances which support that special meaning: "a party is not entitled to innuendo anything that may serve the purposes of a particular action of damages. There must be some solid ground stated with reference to the innuendo upon which the action is to hang or can be put." [23] In short a pursuer cannot aver; the defender said X; he thereby intended to convey that I was dishonest; he must also aver facts and circumstances from which the court can reasonably infer that the defender, in saying X, could have intended to convey an imputation of dishonesty. And he must then prove

---

[16] *Duncan* v. *Associated Scottish Newspapers*, 1929 S.C. 14, 21, *per* Lord Anderson.
[17] *Smith* v. *Walker*, 1912 S.C. 224.
[18] *James* v. *Baird*, 1916 S.C.(H.L.) 158, 166, *per* Lord Kinnear.
[19] *Murdison* v. *Scottish Football Union* (1896) 23 R. 449, 463, *per* Lord Kinnear.
[20] *James* v. *Baird*, 1916 S.C.(H.L.) 158, 165, *per* Lord Kinnear, approving *Sexton* v. *Ritchie* (1890) 17 R. 680, 685; *cf. Russell* v. *Stubbs, Ltd., infra.*
[21] *Russell* v. *Stubbs, Ltd.*, 1913 S.C.(H.L.) 14, 24, *per* Lord Shaw.
[22] *McCandies* v. *McCandie* (1827) 4 Mur. 198.
[23] *Caldwell* v. *Monro* (1872) 10 M. 717, 728, *per* Lord Cowan. *Cf. Richards* v. *Chisholme* (1859) 22 D. 215.

those facts and circumstances and that the defender's statement was understood in the circumstances as conveying that imputation.[24]

Innuendo must make words defamatory. It is not sufficient to aver an innuendo which makes more clear the statement complained of, if it does not also make it out to be defamatory. An innuendo which merely translates the statement into other language effects nothing. Thus it has been held that a statement " Your housekeeper has been accusing me of charging you for more milk than I supplied " would bear an innuendo of false accusations, but that the innuendo was not defamatory.[25] Where an innuendo merely paraphrased and did not add anything to the statement complained of, the action was held irrelevant for lack of any averment making clear that the word in question was slanderous in the circumstances.[26] An innuendo was rejected where there was no specification of the nature of the conduct founded on which justified the innuendo that it was done for a reason derogatory to the pursuer's reputation.[27]

Importance of careful averment of innuendo. The averments of innuendo deserve careful attention as particular words may be held incapable of sustaining the innuendo sought to be put upon them, in which case the action will fall to be dismissed, though they might have been capable of sustaining another innuendo.[28] Moreover the innuendo must be reasonably specific, and an innuendo of a vague character is unlikely to be sustained.[29]

Court's function in considering innuendo. The function of the court is to determine, " whether or not the words or thing complained of by the pursuer are reasonably susceptible of bearing the innuendo put upon them by the pursuer." [30] " The duty falls upon the court to ascertain . . . whether the innuendo proposed with regard to the words used is warranted on the principle that it is a reasonable, natural or necessary inference from the words used." [31] If in the view of the court the statement is not reasonably capable of sustaining the innuendo, the action is irrelevant.[32] " The court has with reference to this innuendo to apply the same standard of the presumed intelligence of the reasonable man, and has to determine whether the suggested innuendo is reasonable, whether, that is to say, it can reasonably be extracted from the language used." [33] " If the words will fairly bear the innuendo which is put on them, we are not to weigh the words in very nice scales." [34]

---

[24] *Smith* v. *Walker,* 1912 S.C. 224; *James* v. *Baird,* 1916 S.C.(H.L.) 158.
[25] *Paton* v. *Edine* (1898) 6 S.L.T. 191.
[26] *Gardner* v. *Robertson,* 1921 S.C. 132.   [27] *Cairns* v. *L.M.S.Ry.,* 1930 S.N. 123.
[28] *Barclay* v. *Manuel* (1902) 10 S.L.T. 450; *cf. Lyal* v. *Henderson,* 1916 S.C.(H.L.) 167.
[29] *Dobson* v. *A.S.R.S.* (1901) 8 S.L.T. 378.
[30] *Duncan* v. *Associated Scottish Newspapers,* 1929 S.C. 14, 19, *per* Lord Ormidale; *cf. Fraser* v. *Morris* (1888) 15 R. 454; *Smith* v. *Walker,* 1912 S.C. 224.
[31] *Langlands* v. *John Leng & Co.,* 1916 S.C.(H.L.) 102, 109, *per* Lord Shaw.
[32] *Capital and Counties Bank* v. *Henty* (1882) 7 App.Cas. 741, 744; *Wood* v. *Edinburgh Evening News,* 1910 S.C. 895; *Smith, supra; Langlands* v. *John Leng & Co., supra.*
[33] *Duncan, supra,* 21, *per* Lord Anderson; *cf. Hunter* v. *Ferguson* (1906) 8 F. 574, 579.
[34] *Fraser, supra,* 456, *per* L.J.C. Moncreiff.

The test whether a proposed innuendo can be supported by the bare words used has been said [35] to be: " Is the meaning sought to be attributed to the language alleged to be libellous one which is a reasonable, natural or necessary interpretation of its terms? It is productive, in my humble judgment, of much error and mischief to make the test simply whether some people would put such and such a meaning upon the words, however strained or unlikely that construction may be. The interpretation to be put on language varies infinitely. It varies with the knowledge, the mental equipment, even the prejudices, of the reader or hearer; it varies—and very often greatly varies—with his temperament or his disposition, in which the elements, on the one hand, of generosity or justice, or, on the other, of mistrust, jealousy, or suspicion, may play their part. To permit, in the latter case, a strained and sinister interpretation, which is thus essentially unjust, to form a ground for reparation, would be, in truth, to grant reparation for a wrong which had never been committed." More recently the opinion has been expressed [36] that the test for an innuendo is not merely whether the statement can bear the construction averred, but whether, taken in conjunction with the circumstances in which it is alleged to have been made, it gives reasonable grounds for an inference that an attack on the pursuer's character was intended.

In several cases the court has refused an issue where the innuendo sought to be put on the words was held to be too vague to amount to any real imputation,[37] or where the words did not admit of the innuendo alleged.[38] Similarly the action is irrelevant if the proposed innuendo does not add anything to a statement *ex facie* not necessarily slanderous, or merely paraphrases it. A proper innuendo makes clear the slanderous point of an otherwise non-defamatory statement.[39]

Jury's function with regard to innuendo. If the court has approved an issue in which certain words are innuendoed as defamatory, it has held that the words are fairly capable, in the circumstances averred, of being understood in a defamatory sense. The jury's function is to determine in fact whether the words complained of were communicated by the defender, of and concerning the pursuer, in the surrounding circumstances averred, and whether they were, in those circumstances, in fact understood by some persons as bearing the defamatory sense averred in the innuendo.[40] If they were not in fact so understood, the fact that they are capable in law of being so understood does not justify a verdict for the pursuer.[41]

---

[35] *Russell* v. *Stubbs, Ltd.*, 1913 S.C.(H.L.) 14, 23, *per* Lord Shaw; citing *Capital and Counties Bank* v. *Henty* (1880) 5 C.P.D. 514, 541; (1882) 7 App.Cas. 741, 746, 782, 788, 790. See also *Langlands* v. *John Leng & Co.*, 1916 S.C.(H.L.) 102.
[36] *Gollan* v. *Thompson Wyles Co.*, 1930 S.C. 599, *per* L.P. Clyde and Lord Morison.
[37] *Mathieson* v. *Scottish Trade Protection Soc.* (1898) 25 R. 683; *Costa* v. *Lumley* (1907 15 S.L.T. 230. *Cf. Ewart* v. *McLaren* (1894) 2 S.L.T. 325; *Cairns* v. *L.M.S.Ry.*, 1930 S.N. 123.
[38] *Mackenzie* v. *Anderson* (1900) 7 S.L.T. 469.
[39] *Gardner* v. *Robertson*, 1920 S.C. 132.
[40] *Russell* v. *Stubbs, Ltd.*, 1913 S.C.(H.L.) 14.
[41] *Bernhardt* v. *Abrahams*, 1912 S.C. 748.

Ambivalent words. Some words and phrases may be susceptible of two possible meanings, one, whether *ex facie* or as innuendoed by the pursuer, being defamatory, the other harmless. In such a case it is a question of fact for the jury to say which meaning the words did convey in the particular case.[42] Similarly an innuendo that the pursuer was represented as guilty of " immoral conduct " has been criticised as bad by reason of vagueness.[43]

Cases where innuendo necessary. It is impossible to list or to imagine all the circumstances in which an innuendo is necessary, but guidance can be obtained from decided cases. " If the primary meaning of the writing be inoffensive—but the pursuer sets forth extrinsic facts which he says interpret the writing, and impress upon it a secondary and defamatory meaning—a question of relevancy is raised, and it is for the court to determine whether the facts stated are such as to entitle the pursuer to have the case sent to a jury on an issue setting forth the innuendo or secondary meaning which he undertakes to prove . . . If the writing is ambiguous—that is to say, if there are two meanings apparent to any intelligent person, one of these being inoffensive and the other defamatory, . . . it is for the jury to say . . . which of these is the true meaning of the publication." [44]

Innuendo bringing out point of imputation. An innuendo has frequently been averred so as to bring out clearly what imputation the pursuer contends was made against him by a statement not clearly defamatory; thus a newspaper article headed " Fire at Ayr Farina Mills—Singular conduct of the Manager " was innuendoed as representing that the manager had tried to prevent the fire being extinguished [45]; a letter as meaning that the pursuer had put forward an unfounded claim under an insurance policy [46]; a question by a shop assistant as meaning that the pursuer had fraudulently tendered a farthing for a half-sovereign [47]; a statement by a ticket collector as meaning that the pursuer had knowingly defrauded the railway company [48]; a statement to a banker as meaning that the pursuer had dishonestly appropriated trust money to his own uses [49]; a letter to the cautioners for an executrix as meaning that the pursuer would dishonestly appropriate trust funds [50]; statements that a man spat at his country, remained seated during the playing of the national anthem, and would honour every country but his own, as meaning that he was disloyal.[51]

---

[42] *Russell* v. *Stubbs, Ltd.*, 1913 S.C.(H.L.) 14.
[43] *Ewart* v. *McLaren* (1894) 2 S.L.T. 325; *cf. Mathieson* v. *Scottish Trade Protection Soc.* (1898) 5 S.L.T. 291; 25 R. 683.
[44] *Sexton* v. *Ritchie* (1890) 17 R. 680, 696, *per* Lord McLaren.
[45] *Gudgeon* v. *Outram* (1888) 16 R. 183.
[46] *Oliver* v. *Laidlaw* (1895) 3 S.L.T. 142.
[47] *McLeod* v. *Ure & Young*, 1915, 1 S.L.T. 151 (innuendo not sustained).
[48] *Cumming* v. *G.N.S.Ry.*, 1916, 1 S.L.T. 181.
[49] *Smyth* v. *Mackinnon* (1897) 24 R. 1086.
[50] *Stewart* v. *Hannah* (1905) 8 F. 107.
[51] *Moffat* v. *London Express Newspapers, Ltd.*, 1950 S.L.T. (Notes) 46.

Words in foreign language. If the words complained of were spoken in a foreign language, an innuendo is necessary stating their meaning in English.[52]

Innuendo giving substance of statements. Where the tenor of an article or long statement is allegedly defamatory, an innuendo is necessary " to gather together the expressions which really are of a slanderous character, and which appear to give colour to the whole article, and so to bring before a jury in a condensed form the substance of that which is complained of." [53] Similarly where the defender, a medical practitioner, had stated that the pursuer's bread was injurious to health and unfit for food, an issue was allowed on the innuendo that the pursuer, in violation of the law, kept adulterated bread and flour in his premises.[54]

Innuendo identifying pursuer as person defamed. If the statement complained of does not clearly refer to the pursuer, an innuendo must be averred and evidence led to connect the pursuer with the person mentioned in the defamatory statement by nickname, fictitious name, description or otherwise.[55] The claim will fail if the jury is not satisfied that the pursuer was the person defamed. Thus if a landlord is spoken of in an article as " Shylock " the pursuer must aver an innuendo connecting himself with the landlord thereby designated and averring what imputation he contends is conveyed by the appellation.

Inoffensive words. If words prima facie inoffensive are to be sued on as defamatory there must be an innuendo setting out the facts and circumstances which interpret the writing and impress upon it a secondary and defamatory meaning.[56] Thus to publish that twins had been born to a couple can be defamatory only if there is an innuendo of pre-marital intercourse, based on averments that they had been married only two months.[57]

Ambiguous statements. An ambiguous statement which may be defamatory in one of its senses is actionable only if explained by an innuendo. The jury has to decide which is the true meaning. An illustration is an ironical attack.[58]

" The statement complained of being then susceptible of two meanings —one of them inoffensive and one defamatory—it is incumbent on the

---

[52] *Matheson* v. *Mackinnon* (1832) 10 S. 825 (Gaelic); *Martin* v. *McLean* (1844) 6 D. 981; *McLaren* v. *Robertson* (1859) 21 D. 183; *Anderson* v. *Hunter* (1891) 18 R. 467; *Bernhardt* v. *Abrahams*, 1912 S.C. 748.
[53] *Neilson* v. *Johnston* (1890) 17 R. 442, 448, *per* L.P. Inglis. See also *Macrae* v. *Sutherland* (1889) 16 R. 476; *Turnbull* v. *Oliver* (1891) 19 R. 154.
[54] *Broomfield* v. *Greig* (1868) 6 M. 563.
[55] *Fournet* v. *Pearson* (1897) 14 T.L.R. 82; *Sadgrove* v. *Hole* [1901] 2 K.B. 1; *Bruce* v. *Odhams Press* [1936] 1 K.B. 697; *Hough* v. *London Express* [1940] 2 K.B. 507.
[56] *Sexton* v. *Ritchie* (1890) 17 R. 680, 696, *per* Lord McLaren.
[57] *Morrison* v. *Ritchie* (1902) 4 F. 645; contrast *Wood* v. *Edinburgh Evening News, Ltd.,* 1910 S.C. 895, where it was held that the advertisement for a wet-nurse, required at the home of persons married only five months, would not sustain an innuendo of ante-nuptial fornication. *Sed quaere.*
[58] *Sexton* v. *Ritchie* (1890) 17 R. 680, 696, *per* Lord McLaren.

pursuer to state clearly, and to put before the jury, the slanderous meaning which he attaches to it. In other words, he must innuendo it." [59]

At the trial evidence may be led of the way in which hearers or readers understood the words.[60]

Slang, provincial or technical words. No innuendo is necessary for slang words in wide general use but it is for a word or phrase restricted in use to a particular section of the community and which requires explanation before the court and an average jury would appreciate the imputation allegedly conveyed. The same is the case for provincialisms or dialect words, and for technical terms.[61] This must be supported by evidence of the meaning of the word from those conversant with its slang or other use who understood it in a defamatory sense.

Innuendo placed on actings. An innuendo may be based on the context in which a photograph, effigy or similar reproduction is placed. Thus the effigy of Monson in Madame Tussauds was innuendoed as defamatory because it was placed among the effigies of convicted murderers.[62] But while there may be a wrong by actings alone, the question is always " whether the innuendo sought to be put upon such actings can in truth reasonably be drawn from them " [63]; if the actings are clearly within the defender's legal rights it is difficult to make them sustain an innuendo that the actings conveyed a defamatory imputation.[63] Where, on the other hand, the actings (the taking of a person's fingerprints) were unwarranted and illegal it was rather easier to have them read as bearing a defamatory imputation.[64]

Innuendo from surrounding circumstances. Any concomitant circumstances which colour an otherwise innocuous statement about the pursuer and make it defamatory must, if relied on as doing so, be averred and proved.[65] But the pursuer must specifically aver the facts and circumstances which would give the phrase complained of a slanderous meaning and which he wishes to prove for that purpose.[66]

Innuendo from voice or other facts. A statement may take on a different shade of meaning from the speaker's tone of voice,[67] from his attitude, or gestures accompanying the statement, and a statement, verbally inoffensive, may thereby become actionable. An innuendo is then essential, and may be very difficult to aver and prove with sufficient precision.

[59] *Gardner* v. *Robertson,* 1921 S.C. 132, 140, *per* Lord Ormidale.
[60] *Barnett* v. *Allen* (1858) 3 H. & N. 376.
[61] *Ibid.*
[62] *Monson* v. *Tussauds* [1894] 1 Q.B. 671.
[63] *Drysdale* v. *Earl of Rosebery,* 1909 S.C. 1121.
[64] *Adamson* v. *Martin,* 1916 S.C. 319.
[65] *Morrison* v. *Ritchie* (1902) 4 F. 645. In *Wood* v. *Edinburgh Evening News, Ltd.,* 1910 S.C. 895, the court held that the words complained of would not bear the innuendo put on them by averment of concomitant circumstances.
[66] *Smith* v. *Walker,* 1912 S.C. 224.
[67] *e.g.,* The sergeant-major's statement to the clumsy recruit: " You're a splendid soldier."

(iii) *Defamatory imputations*

Imputation of guilt of crime. It is defamatory falsely to impute to the pursuer guilt of a crime or offence.[68] There need not have been intent to do so: even a misdescription of a person may impute guilt.[69] The crime imputed need not be indictable [70] and the defamation may indeed be only a general imputation of criminality rather than a specific charge,[71] and is probably defamatory even though for technical reasons a charge could not relevantly be brought.

Such imputations are actionable not because of any danger that they provoke a prosecution but because of the damage to reputation.[72]

Instances [73] include imputations of murder,[74] fraud,[75] theft,[76] forgery,[77] cruelty to animals,[78] contravention of public health Acts,[79] neglect of children,[80] housebreaking,[81] procuring abortion,[82] and brothel-keeping.[83]

Imputation of criminal intention or attempt. Though a criminal intention does not *per se* amount to a crime, it may be defamatory to impute such an intention, because it is discreditable in a person to harbour such intentions, and reflects on his character.[84]

It is certainly defamatory to impute having attempted to commit a crime, attempt being itself criminal,[85] or having made preparations for the commission of a crime.

---

[68] Hume, *Lect.* III, 134; *Monson* v. *Tussauds* [1894] 1 Q.B. 671 (murder); *cf. Clark* v. *Gray* 1951 S.L.T.(Notes) 60.

[69] *Davidson* v. *Anderson* (1905) 12 S.L.T. 679; *Harkness* v. *Daily Record (Glasgow), Ltd.,* 1924 S.L.T. 759.

[70] *e.g., Buchan* v. *N.B.Ry.* (1894) 21 R. 379 (evading railway fare); *Nelson* v. *Irving* (1897) 24 R. 1054 (poaching); *Cook* v. *Spence* (1897) 4 S.L.T. 295 (poaching); *Davidson, supra* (police offence); *Handasyde* v. *Hepworth* (1907) 15 S.L.T. 180; *Leon* v. *Edinburgh Evening News,* 1909 S.C. 1014 (licensing offence); *Jardine* v. *N.B.Ry.,* 1923 S.L.T. 55 (defrauding railway).

[71] *Webb* v. *Beavan* (1883) 11 Q.B.D. 609; *Cockburn* v. *Reekie* (1890) 17 R. 568; *Campbell* v. *McLachlan* (1896) 4 S.L.T. 143; *Christie* v. *Robertson* (1899) 1 F. 1155; see also *Abinet* v. *Fleck* (1894) 2 S.L.T. 30.

[72] *Gray* v. *Jones* (1939) 55 T.L.R. 437.

[73] For fuller list see *Cooper on Defamation,* pp. 35–41.

[74] *Paul* v. *Jackson* (1884) 11 R. 460; *Harkness* v. *Daily Record (Glasgow), Ltd.,* 1924 S.L.T. 759.

[75] *Gudgeon* v. *Outram* (1888) 16 R. 183; *Godfrey* v. *Thomson* (1890) 17 R. 1108; *Oliver* v. *Laidlaw* (1895) 3 S.L.T. 142; *Smyth* v. *Mackinnon* (1897) 24 R. 1086; *Ellis* v. *National Free Labour Assocn.* (1905) 7 F. 629; *Green* v. *Reid* (1905) 7 F. 891; *Stewart* v. *Hannah* (1905) 8 F. 107; *Agnew* v. *British Legal Life Insce. Co.* (1906) 8 F. 422; *Costa* v. *Lumley* (1907) 15 S.L.T. 230; *Boal* v. *Scottish Catholic Printing Co.,* 1907 S.C. 1120; *Webster* v. *Paterson,* 1910 S.C. 549; *Quigley* v. *Brown,* 1913, 1 S.L.T. 61; *Cumming* v. *G.N.S.Ry.* 1916, 1 S.L.T. 181.

[76] *Wilson* v. *Purvis* (1890) 18 R. 72; *Reid* v. *Moore* (1893) 20 R. 712; *Kennedy* v. *Henderson* (1903) 11 S.L.T. 156; *Campbell* v. *Ritchie,* 1907 S.C. 1097; *McAdam* v. *City & Suburban Dairies,* 1911 S.C. 430; *Adams* v. *Templeton,* 1913, 2 S.L.T. 241; *Neville* v. *C. & A. Modes,* 1945 S.C. 175; *cf. Mitchell* v. *Steele* (1874) 11 S.L.R. 364; *Allen* v. *Blair* (1895) 3 S.L.T. 126.

[77] *Logan* v. *Weir* (1872) 10 S.L.R. 22; *Mackay* v. *McCankie* (1883) 10 R. 537.

[78] *Campbell* v. *McLachlan* (1896) 4 S.L.T. 143.

[79] *Broomfield* v. *Greig* (1868) 6 M. 563.

[80] *Rae* v. *S.S.P.C.C.,* 1924 S.C. 102 (innuendo rejected).

[81] *Faulks* v. *Park* (1855) 17 D. 247.

[82] *A.B.* v. *C.D.* (1904) 7 F. 72; 13 S.L.T. 159 (H.L.).

[83] *Mason* v. *Tait* (1851) 13 D. 1347.

[84] *Macdonald* v. *Macdonald,* June 2, 1813, F.C.; *Ogilvie* v. *Scott* (1835) 14 S. 729; *cf. Waugh* v. *Ayrshire Post* (1893) 21 R. 326.

[85] *Oliver* v. *Laidlaw* (1895) 3 S.L.T. 142.

Suspicions of crime. Words which import that the speaker has suspicions as to the complainer having committed some crime are probably
actionable if they amount to a positive imputation and not merely a
vague doubt.[86] It does not matter if the statement is disguised as an
expression of opinion, or personal view, or speculation. Thus a defender
has been held liable for publishing an advertisement importing that a
warrant of a criminal nature had been issued to apprehend two persons,
and that they had absconded.[87]

Criminal imputations as abuse. Words which *ex facie* carry an imputation of criminality are not defamatory if intended and understood as
mere abuse.[88] This is clear where the words are spoken *in rixa*, in the
heat of a quarrel, but even in cold blood such words must not necessarily
be understood as anything more than vulgar abuse.[89]

Imputations against honesty. An imputation against honesty is actionable; this includes an imputation of cheating or other dishonesty[90]; of
passing off inferior goods as those of another[91]; of obtaining a contract
by deceit[92]; of evading payment of debts[93]; of being of a generally
dishonourable character[94]; of being guilty of hypocrisy, deceit and
treachery[95]; of acting corruptly[96]; of deceiving the public[97]; and of
neglect of duty.[98]

Imputations on moral character generally. " If imputations, however
general, are made upon the moral character, in words distinctly importing
such a charge, these words are clearly actionable." [99] If the words do not
impute any particular moral fault they may not be actionable, particularly where the words complained of—" You are a source of evil . . ."—
were spoken by priest to parishioner as censure.[1]

Imputations of unchastity or sexual immorality. Words are defamatory
if they clearly impute to a pursuer of either sex[2] unchastity or sexual

[86] *Cf. Stewart* v. *Hannah* (1905) 8 F. 107; *Boal* v. *Scottish Catholic Printing Co.*, 1907 S.C. 1120.
[87] *Lawrie* v. *Campbell* (1800) Hume 606.
[88] *Agnew* v. *British Legal Life Assce. Co.* (1906) 8 F. 422; *Campbell* v. *Ritchie*, 1907 S.C. 1097.
[89] *e.g.*, to say that " the boss is a bugger " is not necessarily an imputation of guilt of sodomy.
[90] *Donaldson* v. *Lord Perth* (1800) 4 Pat. 112; *Thom* v. *Cameron* (1813) Hume 646; *Landles*
    v. *Gray* (1816) 1 Mur. 79; *cf. Paterson* v. *Shaw* (1830) 8 S. 573; *Ross* v. *Ronald* (1834)
    12 S. 936; *Grant* v. *Smith* (1837) 15 S. 558 (imputation of acting with partiality as arbiter);
    contrast *McNeil* v. *Carruthers* (1868) 5 S.L.R. 220; *Dun* v. *Bain* (1877) 4 R. 317; *Ramsay*
    v. *McLay* (1890) 18 R. 130; *Hunt* v. *Paton* (1904) 12 S.L.T. 553; *Agnew* v. *British Legal
    Life Assce. Co.* (1906) 8 F. 422; *McAdam* v. *City and Suburban Dairies*, 1911 S.C. 430.
[91] *Webster* v. *Paterson*, 1910 S.C. 459. *Cf. Adams* v. *Scottish Agricultural Publishing Co.*,
    1926 S.L.T. 255.
[92] *Stuart* v. *Moss* (1885) 13 R. 299.
[93] *Williamson* v. *Maclean*, 1909, 2 S.L.T. 268.
[94] *Macrae* v. *Sutherland* (1889) 16 R. 476; *Turnbull* v. *Oliver* (1891) 19 R. 154.
[95] *Griffen* v. *Divers*, 1922 S.C. 605.
[96] *Langlands* v. *John Leng & Co.*, 1916 S.C.(H.L.) 102.
[97] *Johnston* v. *Dilke* (1875) 2 R. 836.
[98] *Cockburn* v. *Reekie* (1890) 17 R. 568.
[99] *Brownlie* v. *Thomson* (1859) 21 D. 480, 485, *per* L.J.C. Inglis. *Cf.* Hume, *Lect.* III, 137.
[1] *Rooney* v. *McNairney*, 1909 S.C. 90.
[2] *Richardson* v. *Walker* (1804) Hume 623; *Milne* v. *Smiths* (1893) 20 R. 95 (" a seducer of
    girls ").

immorality.[3] This extends to imputations of pre-marital intercourse,[4] of having had illicit intercourse with the defender,[5] of adultery,[6] of associating with a prostitute and attempting to pass her off as one's wife,[7] of being a prostitute,[8] of having fathered a bastard,[9] or given birth to one,[10] of cohabiting with a man as his wife,[11] of " want of proper womanly delicacy," [12] of immodest or indelicate conduct,[13] or of " keeping a disreputable house." [14]

Other cases which would doubtless fall under this heading would be imputations of homosexuality [15] or lesbianism [16]; and it may be defamatory to publish of a woman that she has been raped,[17] as this may cause her to be shunned or avoided, even though there was no turpitude on her part.

Imputations of improper or disgraceful conduct. It is actionable falsely to impute to a person conduct which is regarded in society generally,[18] or in the class of society in which the pursuer moves,[19] as improper, disgraceful or discreditable. Some such cases might be treated as convicium rather than defamation.

Thus it has been held actionable to post a man as " destitute of the feelings or spirit of a gentleman," [20] or as a coward and scoundrel,[18] to state that an excise officer exacted duties illegally,[21] or informed against another,[22] to call a man a liar,[23] to represent that a man acted deceitfully and treacherously to his trade colleagues,[24] to say that a girl lacked " proper womanly delicacy," [25] or that a woman was immodest and indecent, without natural or proper womanly delicacy of mind or action,[26] or that a man desecrated the Sabbath,[27] or that an officer ordered his troops to surrender,[28] or a person was addicted to drunkenness and

---

3 See also cases collected in *Cooper on Defamation*, pp. 44–45.
4 *Morrison* v. *Ritchie* (1902) 4 F. 645; *Wood* v. *Edinburgh Evening News*, 1910 S.C. 895 (doubtful case).
5 *Gilmour* v. *Hansen*, 1920 S.C. 598.
6 *Cleland* v. *Mack* (1829) 5 Mur. 70; *Rankin* v. *Simpson* (1859) 21 D. 1057.
7 *Finburgh* v. *Moss's Empires*, 1908 S.C. 928 (husband's action failed).
8 *Finburgh, supra* (wife's action successful). *Cf. McNeill* v. *Forbes* (1883) 10 R. 867.
9 *C.* v. *M.*, 1938 S.L.T. 369.
10 *Chattell* v. *Daily Mail* (1901) 18 T.L.R. 165.
11 *Cassidy* v. *Daily Mirror* [1929] 2 K.B. 331.
12 *A.B.* v. *Blackwood* (1902) 5 F. 25.
13 *Cuthbert* v. *Linklater*, 1935 S.L.T. 94, explaining *A.B.* v. *Blackwood, supra.*
14 *Brydon* v. *Brechin* (1881) 8 R. 697.
15 *Richardson, supra.*
16 *Cf. Kerr* v. *Kennedy* [1942] 1 K.B. 409.
17 *Youssoupoff* v. *M.G.M.* (1934) 50 T.L.R. 581, 584, *per* Scrutton L.J. Query: in Scotland would this not be convicium rather than defamation?
18 *Menzies* v. *Goodlet* (1835) 13 S. 1136.
19 *Cf. Macfarlane* v. *Black* (1887) 14 R. 870; *Milne* v. *Smiths* (1893) 20 R. 95.
20 *Mackay* v. *Campbell* (1833) 11 S. 1031.
21 *Leven* v. *Young* (1818) 1 Mur. 364; 1 Sh.App. 179.
22 *Graham* v. *Roy* (1851) 13 D. 634.
23 *McLaren* v. *Robertson* (1859) 21 D. 183; *Milne* v. *Walker* (1893) 21 R. 155; *Neill* v. *Henderson* (1901) 3 F. 387.
24 *Griffen* v. *Divers*, 1922 S.C. 605.
25 *A.B.* v. *Blackwood* (1902) 5 F. 65.
26 *Cuthbert* v. *Linklater*, 1935 S.L.T. 95.
27 *Lowe* v. *Taylor* (1845) 7 D. 117; *Macfarlane* v. *Black* (1887) 14 R. 870.
28 *Gordon* v. *John Leng & Co.*, 1919 S.C. 415.

falsehood,[29] or not a trustworthy administrator of a bequest,[30] or that a person had been drunk when injured,[31] or that an Irishman was an informer to the Crown for money,[32] or that a claimant was attempting to extort money,[33] that a solicitor was a " dirty low scum," [34] or that a jockey was guilty of " pulling " horses to prevent them winning.[35]

Again in many cases actions for defamation have been founded on imputations of a wide variety of conduct, which is neither criminal nor immoral but in a general way disgraceful, or falling below what seems a standard of proper and honourable conduct. Under this head [36] would fall such cases as to say that a man is a disgusting brute,[37] or a woman an improper character,[38] or a man of questionable character,[39] or a scoundrel,[40] or two-faced.[41]

Some such cases might well, depending on the circumstances, be treated as mere expressions of abuse or anger and not as defamatory imputations at all.

But it is not enough to impute merely lack of manners, ignorance of etiquette or the accepted code of conduct, coarseness or other social fault which does not really go to character at all. Thus to say that it was mean of a man to do something has been held incapable of sustaining an innuendo of cheating [42]; and similarly in cases of imputation of mercenary motives,[43] and to accuse a person of circulating statements of an incriminatory character and of being the author of lewd and immoral language has been held irrelevant.[44] To impute the use of bad language is not necessarily defamatory.[45]

Imputations of financial unsoundness or insolvency. Injury to business standing or commercial credit is a wrong for which reparation is granted.[46] Regard must be had to the pursuer's position and his profession or business.[47] It is accordingly defamatory of a person unjustifiably to allege that he is unable to pay his debts,[48] or has gone away without paying his debts,[49] or is insolvent or bankrupt.[50] Other actionable

---

[29] *Aird* v. *Kennedy* (1851) 13 D. 775; *cf. Oliver* v. *Laidlaw* (1895) 3 S.L.T. 142.
[30] *Falconer* v. *Docherty* (1893) 20 R. 765.
[31] *Oliver* v. *Laidlaw* (1895) 3 S.L.T. 142.
[32] *Winn* v. *Quillan* (1899) 2 F. 322.
[33] *Edmondson* v. *Cartner* (1905) 13 S.L.T. 78.
[34] *Shepherd* v. *Elliot* (1895) 3 S.L.T. 115.
[35] *Breasley* v. *Odhams Press* [1963] C.L.Y. 2001.
[36] See further cases collected in *Cooper on Defamation*, pp. 47–57.
[37] *Croucher* v. *Inglis* (1889) 16 R. 774.
[38] *McCulloch* v. *Litt* (1851) 13 D. 334.
[39] *Macleod* v. *Marshall* (1891) 18 R. 811.
[40] *White* v. *Clough* (1848) 10 D. 332.
[41] *Cunningham* v. *Duncan* (1889) 16 R. 383.
[42] *Fraser* v. *Morris* (1888) 15 R. 454.
[43] *Godfrey* v. *Thomson* (1890) 17 R. 1108.
[44] *Milne* v. *Smiths* (1892) 20 R. 95.
[45] *Murdison* v. *Scottish Football Union* (1896) 23 R. 449.
[46] *A.B.* v. *C.D.* (1904) 7 F. 22, 25, *per* Lord McLaren; Ersk. IV, 4, 81; Hume, *Lect.* III, 134.
[47] *A.B.*, *supra*, 24, *per* L.P. Dunedin.
[48] *Stubbs* v. *Russell*, 1913 S.C.(H.L.) 14.
[49] *O'Brien* v. *Clement* (1846) 16 M. & W. 159.
[50] *McBean & Co.* v. *Blair* (1801) Hume 609; *Outram* v. *Reid* (1852) 14 D. 577.

statements to the same general effect have been that the pursuers were hard-up,[51] or had been " cleaned out and lost his all," [52] or that a bank had "stopped payment," [53] or was "in liquidation," [54] or was "not worth £5," [55] or was once in pecuniary difficulties,[56] or were in financial difficulties.[57]

An inference of financial unsoundness is readily drawn from the appearance of a name in the list of persons against whom decrees in absence have passed, and the unjustified publication of names has frequently been held actionable as defamatory.[58] Much depends on the terms of any headings, warnings or explanatory notes which accompany the list of names.[59] Thus a prefatory note that publication of a name does not import any inability to pay has been held to preclude an innuendo that the inclusion of the name imputed insolvency,[60] but not to preclude the innuendo that it imputed that the person was not creditworthy.[61]

It is similarly defamatory falsely to impute insolvency, financial unsoundness or lack of creditworthiness to a firm or company,[62] such as to say that a bank has stopped payment,[63] or gone into liquidation,[64] or otherwise to create distrust and alarm about its credit.[65]

It is defamatory for a bank not to honour a customer's cheque if there were funds wherewith to meet it,[66] and it may be defamatory to return it to the payee marked " Refer to drawer " or in similar terms.[67] In the case of a deposit account with a merchant bank damages require proof of special agreement or of special damage sustained.[68]

It is not necessarily defamatory to say that a company is about to be taken over by a rival.[69]

51 *Wright & Greig* v. *Outram* (1889) 16 R. 1004.
52 *A.B.* v. *C.D.* (1904) 7 F. 22.
53 *Forster* v. *Lawson* (1826) 3 Bing. 451; *N. of S. Banking Co.* v. *Duncan* (1857) 19 D. 881.
54 *L. & N. Bank* v. *George Newnes* (1900) 16 T.L.R. 76.
55 *Cousland & Taylor* v. *Cuthill* (1830) 5 Mur. 148.
56 *Cox* v. *Lee* (1869) L.R. 4 Ex. 284, 288.
57 *Bayne & Thomson* v. *Stubbs, Ltd.* (1901) 3 F. 408; *Robertson* v. *J. M. Scott* (1903) 10 S.L.T. 575.
58 *Andrews* v. *Drummond & Graham* (1887) 14 R. 568; *Crabbe & Robertson* v. *Stubbs* (1895) 22 R. 860; *McLintock* v. *Stubbs* (1902) 5 F. 1; *Hunter & Co.* v. *Stubbs* (1903) 5 F. 920; *Barr* v. *Musselburgh Merchants' Association*, 1912 S.C. 174; *Russell* v. *Stubbs*, 1913 S.C.(H.L.) 14; *Mazure* v. *Stubbs*, 1919 S.C.(H.L.) 112; *cf. Taylor* v. *Rutherford* (1888) 15 R. 608; *Rarity* v. *Stubbs* (1893) 1 S.L.T. 74.
59 *Andrews, supra; Hunter, supra; Russell, supra; Mazure, supra.*
60 *Russell, supra.*
61 *Mazure, supra.*
62 *Capital & Counties Bank* v. *Henty* (1882) 7 App.Cas. 741.
63 *Forster* v. *Lawson* (1826) 3 Bing. 451.
64 *L. & N. Bank* v. *Newnes* (1900) 16 T.L.R. 76.
65 *N. of Scotland Banking Co.* v. *Duncan* (1857) 19 D. 881.
66 *Marzetti* v. *Williams* (1830) 1 B. & A. 415; *Rolin* v. *Steward* (1854) 14 C.B. 595; *King* v. *B.L. Bank* (1899) 1 F. 928; *Fleming* v. *Bank of New Zealand* [1900] A.C. 877; *Wilson* v. *United Counties Bank* [1920] A.C. 102.
67 *Capital & Counties Bank* v. *Henty* (1882) 7 App.Cas. 741; *Allen* v. *L.C. & W. Bank* (1915) 84 L.J.K.B. 1286; *Flach* v. *L. & S.W. Bank* (1915) 31 T.L.R. 334; *Barber* v. *Deutsche Bank London Agency* [1919] A.C. 304; *Plunkett* v. *Barclays Bank* [1936] 2 K.B. 107; *Davidson* v. *Barclays Bank* [1940] 1 All E.R. 316.
68 *Gibb* v. *Lombank Scotland*, 1962 S.L.T. 288.
69 *General Accident Insce. Corpn.* v. *Miller* (1902) 9 S.L.T. 510.

Not all statements of indebtedness defamatory. It is not, however, necessarily defamatory falsely to say that a person has borrowed money, or got a personal loan, or an overdraft, or money from a building society, because these statements, even if true, do not imply unwillingness or inability to repay these advances according to their terms.[70]

Nor is it necessarily defamatory falsely to say that a person has declined to pay an account, because there may be good grounds for disputing liability or amount, nor to refuse to make a loan, on discovering that representations made by the prospective borrower were incorrect.[71] Nor is it necessarily defamatory to say that a person is poor [72] or has lost his money, but it may be.[73]

Imputations against public character. Imputations against a man's character as a public figure in the community may likewise be actionable.[74] Instances include charges that a man was unfit for the office of professor [75]; that a candidate for Parliament was a scoffer at religion,[76] or had enjoyed the hospitality of political opponents [77]; that a candidate for municipal office had gone bankrupt dishonestly and disreputably [78]; that a candidate for office in a Good Templar Lodge had been guilty of sharp practice [79]; that a J.P. was unfaithful to his public trust [80]; that a town councillor had been guilty of wilful falsehood and dishonesty,[81] or acted corruptly for his own benefit,[82] or, possibly, had been guilty of bribery [83]; that a member of a school board had been guilty of dishonourable conduct [84]; that an architect had acted unfairly in the exercise of a quasi-judicial function [85]; that clergymen had abused their religious influence [86]; that a parish minister, trustee of a charitable trust, was not a trustworthy trustee and administrator [87]; that a political lecturer had sacrificed his political principles to secure an audience [88]; that a sanitary inspector had endeavoured to discredit another official and recklessly spent public money in doing so [89]; that a candidate for a local authority post had been guilty of misconduct unfitting him for the post [90]; that the

---

70 *R.* v. *Coughlan* (1865) 4 F. & F. 316; *McCann* v. *Edinburgh Roperie* (1889) 28 L.R.Ir. 24.
71 *Robertson* v. *John M. Scott*; *Robertson* v. *Taylor* (1903) 10 S.L.T. 575.
72 *McLaren* v. *Robertson* (1859) 21 D. 183, 186.
73 *A.B.* v. *C.D.* (1904) 7 F. 22.
74 Hume, *Lect.* III, 136; see also cases in *Cooper on Defamation*, pp. 68–75.
75 *Auld* v. *Shairp* (1875) 2 R. 940.
76 *Macfarlane* v. *Black* (1887) 14 R. 870.
77 *Westwood* v. *John Leng & Co.*, 1923 S.L.T. 725 (innuendo rejected).
78 *Bruce* v. *Leisk* (1892) 19 R. 482.
79 *Archer* v. *Ritchie* (1891) 18 R. 719 (proposed innuendo rejected).
80 *Mitchell* v. *Grierson* (1894) 21 R. 367.
81 *Coghill* v. *Docherty* (1881) 19 S.L.R. 96.
82 *Hunter* v. *Ferguson* (1906) 8 F. 574.
83 *Gardner* v. *Robertson*, 1921 S.C. 132.
84 *Lyal* v. *Henderson*, 1916 S.C.(H.L.) 167.
85 *Crawford* v. *Adams* (1900) 2 F. 987; *cf. Langlands* v. *John Leng & Co.*, 1916 S.C.(H.L.) 102.
86 *Browne* v. *Thomson*, 1912 S.C. 359.
87 *Falconer* v. *Docherty* (1893) 20 R. 765.
88 *Godfrey* v. *Thomson* (1890) 17 R. 1108 (issue refused on facts).
89 *Neilson* v. *Johnston* (1890) 17 R. 442.
90 *Campbell* v. *Weir*, 1924 S.L.T. 14 (innuendo rejected).

chairman of a parish council had been misreported as having failed in a previous action to prove that statements made about him were untrue [91]; or that a chief constable had been a party to graft and corruption.[92]

Imputations against professional honour or competence. It is defamatory falsely to disparage a man in respect of his office, profession, trade or vocation in any way which reflects on his official, professional or commercial honour or reputation.[93]

Thus it is defamatory to impute to a person unfitness for his office or profession by reason of ignorance, bad character or by reason of any dishonest or disgraceful conduct in the exercise of the office or profession, or neglect of the duties of his office, or improper conduct therein. It has been held defamatory to say of a barrister that he knows no law,[94] or of a solicitor that he has been guilty of " sharp practice," [95] or fraudulent actings,[96] or been in breach of professional confidence,[97] or given his client's interests away,[98] or been influenced by thought of his own gain only,[99] or that he has been suspended,[1] or is a quack,[2] or struck off the roll.[3]

It is defamatory to say of a medical practitioner that he was guilty of gross professional negligence or unskilfulness in treatment,[4] or caused the death of a patient,[5] or that he is a quack.[6]

It is defamatory of a clergyman to say that he had been guilty of dishonourable conduct unbecoming the character and sacred profession of a minister,[7] but not that he was insubordinate, careless, and neglectful of his duties, inefficient, and unfit for his position,[8] or that he was guilty of immorality or drunkenness, or used to preach sedition, lies or false doctrine, or attacked parishioners personally from the pulpit,[9] or desecrated part of his church.[10]

Other instances of imputations against persons in their professional capacities include saying that a colonel had ordered a surrender and thereby failed in his duty as a soldier,[11] that a schoolmaster was unfit for

---

[91] *Duncan* v. *Associated Scottish Newspapers,* 1929 S.C. 14 (innuendo rejected).
[92] *Macdonald* v. *Martin,* 1935 S.C. 621.
[93] See generally Hume, *Lect.* III, 136, and cases in *Cooper on Defamation,* pp. 61–75.
[94] *Palmer* v. *Boyer* (1594) Cro.Eliz. 342; *Bankes* v. *Allen* (1616) 1 Roll.Abr. 54; *cf. Balfour* v. *Wallace* (1853) 15 D. 913; *Sharp* v. *Wilson* (1868) 5 S.L.R. 444.
[95] *Boydell* v. *Jones* (1838) 4 M. & W. 446; *cf. Archer* v. *Ritchie* (1891) 18 R. 719.
[96] *Bayne* v. *Macgregor* (1862) 24 D. 1126.
[97] *Moore* v. *Jerell* (1833) 4 B. & A. 870; *cf. Woodgate* v. *Ridout* (1865) 4 F. & F. 202.
[98] *Kelly* v. *O'Bierne* (1909) 127 L.T. 214.
[99] *MacRostie* v. *Ironside* (1849) 11 D. 74.
[1] *Clarkson* v. *Lawson* (1830) 4 M. & P. 356.
[2] *Wakley* v. *Healey* (1849) 7 C.B. 591; *cf. Chisholm* v. *Grant,* 1914 S.C. 239.
[3] *Blake* v. *Stevens* (1865) 11 L.T. 543.
[4] *Simmers* v. *Morton* (1900) 8 S.L.T. 285.
[5] *Stevens* v. *Kitchener* (1887) 4 T.L.R. 159.
[6] *Long* v. *Chubb* (1831) 5 C. & P. 55; *Collins* v. *Carnegie* (1834) 1 A. & E. 695; *Hunter* v. *Sharpe* (1866) 4 F. & F. 983; *Dakhyl* v. *Labouchere* [1908] 2 K.B. 325n.; *cf. Chisholm* v. *Grant,* 1914 S.C. 239.
[7] *Barclay* v. *Manuel* (1902) 10 S.L.T. 450.
[8] *Barclay, supra.*
[9] *Edwards* v. *Bell* (1824) 1 Bing. 403.
[10] *Kelly* v. *Sherlock* (1866) L.R. 1 Q.B. 686.
[11] *Gordon* v. *John Leng & Co.,* 1919 S.C. 415.

his post,[12] that an inspector of poor was unfit for a public position owing to his drunken habits,[13] that an accountant was unfit for the office of trustee on a debtor's estate,[14] that a newspaper proprietor wrote offensive articles of a disgraceful character for his paper,[15] that a farmer worked a farm carelessly and unskilfully,[16] that an engineer was grossly incompetent and lacking in skill as such,[17] that an editor was a libellous journalist,[18] that a publisher was guilty of deceiving the public,[19] that an architect was incompetent to restore a building,[20] or to attribute to an author work not his,[21] to say that an actor cannot act [22] or that an actress's performance was vulgar,[23] and even to bill an artiste in a position in the programme inferior to that of lesser artistes,[24] or that a schoolmaster had treated a pupil brutally.[25]

Criticism by a master of an employee's skill or competence, if moderate and merely an honest expression of opinion, is not actionable,[26] but a skilled tradesman may have his reputation damaged in much the same way as a professional man.[27] To instruct an estate factor to hand over his books and papers may be no more than is lawful, and not actionable.[28]

In the case of a person engaged in trade it is defamatory falsely to impute anything to him, the natural consequence of which is to injure his trade,[29] such as the use of false measures,[30] overcharging at a hotel,[31] knowingly [32] selling unwholesome goods,[33] or committing a breach of the conditions of a liquor licence,[34] or conducting the business in a disorderly and illegal manner,[35] or being guilty of shebeening,[36] or supplying as " certified milk " milk of an inferior quality.[37]

---

[12] *McKercher* v. *Cameron* (1892) 19 R. 383.
[13] *Tait* v. *Morrison*, 1913, 2 S.L.T. 325.
[14] *Oliver* v. *Barnet* (1895) 3 S.L.T. 163.
[15] *A.* v. *B.* (1899) 36 S.L.R. 533.
[16] *Dun* v. *Bain* (1877) 4 R. 317; *McKeand* v. *Maxwell* (1896) 3 S.L.T. 321.
[17] *Slack* v. *Barr*, 1918, 1 S.L.T. 133.
[18] *Wakley* v. *Cooke* (1849) 4 Ex. 511.
[19] *Johnston* v. *Dilke* (1875) 2 R. 836.
[20] *Botterill* v. *Whytehead* (1879) 41 L.T. 588.
[21] *Lee* v. *Gibbins* (1892) 67 L.T. 263; *Ridge* v. *English Illustrated* (1913) 29 T.L.R. 592; *cf.* *A.* v. *B.* (1899) 36 S.L.R. 533.
[22] *Duplany* v. *Davis* (1886) 3 T.L.R. 184.
[23] *Cooney* v. *Edevain* (1897) 14 T.L.R. 34.
[24] *Russell* v. *Notcutt* (1896) 12 T.L.R. 195.
[25] *Wright* v. *Steel*, 1909, 2 S.L.T. 265.
[26] *Munro* v. *Mudie* (1901) 9 S.L.T. 91; *cf. Dobson* v. *A.S.R.S.* (1901) 8 S.L.T. 378; *Brown* v. *Edinburgh Mags.*, 1907 S.C. 256.
[27] *Slack* v. *Barr*, 1918, 1 S.L.T. 133 (engineer); *Bryant* v. *Edgar*, 1909 S.C. 1080 (shop manager); *cf. Vallance* v. *Ford* (1903) 10 S.L.T. 555 (skirt cutter); *Pybus* v. *Mackinnon* (1908) 15 S.L.T. 1066 (estate agent); *McDonald* v. *McLachlan*, 1907 S.C. 203 (shepherd).
[28] *Drysdale* v. *Earl of Rosebery*, 1909 S.C. 1121.
[29] *Riding* v. *Smith* (1876) 1 Ex.D. 91.
[30] *Prior* v. *Wilson* (1856) 1 C.B.(N.S.) 95.
[31] *Macrae* v. *Wicks* (1886) 13 R. 732.
[32] *Broomfield* v. *Greig* (1868) 6 M. 563; *Adams* v. *Scottish Agricultural Co.*, 1926 S.L.T. 255.
[33] *Evans* v. *Harlow* (1844) 5 Q.B. 624; *Solomon* v. *Lawson* (1846) 8 Q.B. 823.
[34] *Menzies* v. *Macdonald* (1899) 1 F. 977.   [35] *Meikle* v. *Wright* (1893) 20 R. 928.
[36] *Lumsden* v. *West Lothian Printing and Publishing Co.* (1905) 7 F. 1006; *cf. Cook* v. *Gray* (1891) 29 S.L.R. 247.
[37] *Lord Hamilton of Dalzell* v. *Glasgow Dairy Co.*, 1931 S.C.(H.L.) 67.

Where there are imputations against business standing, the claim is irrelevant in the total absence of averments of patrimonial loss.[38]

Imputations against legitimate birth. It is possibly defamatory falsely to say of a person that he is illegitimate,[39] or to imply that fact. The same imputation will, with greater justification, give his father or mother a right of action.[40]

Imputations of disease. There is considerable English authority to the effect that it is actionable falsely to impute to a person that he suffers from any contagious or infectious disease which may cause him to be less highly esteemed, or shunned or excluded from society as a person with whom it is unsafe to associate, whether the disease be contracted by accident or indiscretion.[41]   In Scottish practice such an imputation might be slanderous,[42] or might be, and is probably more likely to be, actionable as convicium.[43]   But false allegations of insanity have been held actionable.[44]   An imputation that a person was facile and not in a fit state of mind to contract marriage has been held slanderous.[45]

But an imputation of disease of mind or body which carries no implication of misconduct, or is not likely to cause the person to be shunned or regarded with hatred, ridicule or contempt, would seem not to be actionable at all, either as slander or as convicium. It is a misfortune, and no disgrace or dishonour attaches to one so afflicted.

(c) *The Mental Element in Liability*

The standard averment in defamation actions is that the defender published the statement complained of " calumniously," or sometimes " maliciously." These words are for present purposes synonymous.[46] If the word malice is used it has to be appreciated that it may mean merely the deliberate communication of what is defamatory (sometimes called malice in law), or communication made deliberately, with malevolence, spite or other injurious motive (sometimes called malice in fact). Malice in the latter sense need be averred and proved only in cases of qualified privilege and certain other cases; in the ordinary case of defamation malice in the former sense only is relevant, and this is sufficiently established by the proof of publication of matter injurious to the credit or

---

38 *Thompson* v. *Fifeshire Advertiser*, 1936 S.N. 56.
39 It is not very clear why this should be defamatory, as a person's illegitimate birth is a misfortune for which he is in no way responsible, and it is not a circumstance which would justify any rational person in shunning or despising him or thinking less of him. Again such a statement might be convicium rather than defamation.
40 *Stephen* v. *Paterson* (1865) 3 M. 571.
41 Gatley, 57; *Carslake* v. *Mapledoram* (1788) 2 T.R. 473; *Watkin* v. *Hall* (1868) L.R. 3 Q.B. 396; *Riding* v. *Smith* (1876) 1 Ex.D. 91.
42 *A.* v. *B.*, 1907 S.C. 1154 (erroneous statement that pursuer had V.D.).
43 See *Cunningham* v. *Phillips* (1868) 6 M. 926, especially opinion of Lord Deas.
44 *Mackintosh* v. *Weir* (1875) 2 R. 877.
45 *Henderson* v. *Henderson* (1855) 17 D. 348.
46 *McLean* v. *Bernstein* (1900) 8 S.L.T. 42.   See also de Villiers, " Malice in the English and Roman Law of Defamation " (1902) 17 L.Q.R. 388.

reputation of the pursuer.[47] " But saving such cases [of privilege], the *animus injuriandi* is commonly and must be presumed from the words themselves, if they are uttered seriously, and are naturally of a bad and unfavourable meaning and must, if believed, prove prejudicial to the complainer. It will not therefore at all answer the defender's purpose to allege, if the words are bad, and naturally tend to the pursuer's prejudice, that he had no special ill will to him, but was actuated by an aversion to vice, or a zeal for reformation, or some other the like innocent or even laudable motive." [48] " It thus appears, on the whole, that in the ordinary case and in the civil action of damages the requisite *animus injuriandi* is not to be received as a clear—special—malice propense against the party injured; so far from it, that a person may be liable in damages to one who is not even known to him, either personally or by name. Tis sufficient, the defender have so conducted himself, though owing to rashness only, or levity, and indiscretion, as to occasion harm, or the risk of harm, to the complainer." [49] " The communication not being privileged, the pursuers are not bound to aver or prove malice; malice is presumed." [50] There need be no further express or actual malice or *animus injuriandi*.[51]

" According to the Scottish practice, when the words are in themselves false and calumnious and are put in issue, general malice is assumed from the fact of their being false and calumnious, and that being so, there is no necessity upon either party to refer specifically to malice. But the necessity to insert specific reference to malice arises in this way, that although a slander or libel may be false and calumnious in its terms, nevertheless it may have been used on an occasion which was privileged, in the sense that the person who uttered it had the right, erroneously and even falsely, to make his statement. In such circumstances malice enters a Scottish record by way of a suggestion by the pursuer that the privilege which the defender pleads disappears in consequence of the special malice which is averred; . . . if the record is in that state, namely, that the defender pleads privilege and the pursuer counters it by a special plea of specific malice, the case approaches the jury in this situation, that, if in the course of the enquiry before them it does appear that the occasion was privileged, then the pursuer is entitled to prove as matter of fact circumstances going to the malice which would rebut the privilege." [52]

---

[47] *Tytler* v. *Macintosh* (1823) 2 Mur. 241. The dictum of L.J.C. Inglis in *Mackellar* v. *Duke of Sutherland* (1862) 24 D. 1124 seems to confuse the two senses of malice, though in the result he did not misstate the law when he said that " the words . . . being in themselves defamatory and actionable, the law presumes . . . the motive of the person speaking or writing them to be malicious." *Cf.* Hume, *Lect.* III, 141–142.

[48] Hume, *Lect.* III, 146; *cf. ibid.*, 141.   [49] *Ibid.* 152.

[50] *Morrison* v. *Ritchie* (1902) 4 F. 645, 650, *per* Lord Moncreiff.

[51] Hume *Lect.*, III, 146; Borthwick, 190; *cf. Outram* v. *Reid* (1852) 14 D. 577. In older cases there had to be more than mere communication to justify an inference of *animus injuriandi*, *e.g.*, repetition: *Edwards* v. *Macintosh* (1823) 3 Mur. 379; and an action did not lie in the absence of facts indicating *malus animus* or *animus injuriandi*, *e.g.*, *Rose* v. *Robertson* (1803) Hume 614; *Gardner* v. *Marshall* (1803) Hume 620; *Melville* v. *Crichton* (1820) 2 Mur. 277.

[52] *Langlands* v. *John Leng & Co.*, 1916 S.C.(H.L.) 102, 109, *per* Lord Shaw.

It follows that even if words *ex facie* defamatory have been uttered, if they have been uttered *in rixa*, in the heat of a squabble and not intended to be taken seriously, nor even deliberately used, they may be held not to have been uttered maliciously at all, nor with even the slightest *animus injuriandi*, nor used in a defamatory sense,[53] and hence may be held not actionable.[54] In the same way words *ex facie* defamatory may be used as mere terms of general abuse, and not with any defamatory intent at all.[55] It is questionable if these pleas apply to other than spoken words.

But even though uttered *in rixa* words may be held to have been deliberately used, in which case there is adequate *animus injuriandi* to render them defamatory.[56]

Malice in case of hurt to pursuer's feelings. The action for hurt to the pursuer's self-esteem being an *actio injuriarum* for pure *solatium*, an essential element of liability is *animus injuriandi*, as in the Roman and Roman-Dutch law.[57] In modern practice, while it is still necessary to aver that the defender communicated the defamatory matter " calumniously " or " maliciously," the existence of *animus injuriandi* is presumed from the fact that the defender was responsible for communicating matter which was false and defamatory,[58] so that " calumniously " or " maliciously " means no more than " deliberately " or " intentionally." The case is, of course, even clearer if there is distinct evidence of *animus injuriandi*.

It would appear to follow that proof that there was truly no *animus injuriandi* would exculpate a defender, but since the allegation of malice has become non-traversable, and an irrebuttable inference from proof of deliberate communication, this is no longer so.[59] Malice is only the intention presumed when a wrongful act is done without legal justification or excuse,[60] and it is presumed from the mere act of deliberately communicating defamatory matter. " If a man in mere gossip utter a slander, the law assumes that he did so maliciously, and he must answer accordingly for it. Malice is imputed to him without any evidence but the making of the statement." [61] But in the case of claims for solatium alone, it would not suffice that the imputation was made negligently and not deliberately [62]; " where a person sues, not for reparation of damage but

---

53 Hume, *Lect.* III, 142; Bell, *Prin.*, § 2044; Borthwick, 190; *Watson* v. *Duncan* (1890) 17 R. 404, 408.
54 *e.g. Cockburn* v. *Reekie* (1890) 17 R. 568; *Christie* v. *Robertson* (1899) 1 F. 1155.
55 *Cockburn, supra.*
56 *Mackay* v. *Grant* (1903) 41 S.L.R. 18.
57 De Villiers, 26–29.
58 Voet 47, 10, 20; Matthaeus, *De Criminibus*, 47, 4, 1, 10; Vinnius ad Inst. 4, 4, 1.
59 Formerly evidence of no *animus injuriandi* exculpated; see *Rose* v. *Robertson* (1803) Hume 614; *Gardner* v. *Marshall* (1803) Hume 620.
60 " Malice in common acceptation means ill-will against a person, but in its legal sense it means a wrongful act, done intentionally, without just cause or excuse ": *Bromage* v. *Prosser* (1825) 4 B. & C. 247, 255, *per* Bayley J. *Cf. McPherson* v. *Daniels* (1829) 10 B. & C. 263, 272; *Harris* v. *Arnott* (*No. 2*) (1890) 26 L.R.Ir. 55, 75; *Adam* v. *Ward* [1917] A.C. 309, 318.   61 *Shaw* v. *Morgan* (1888) 15 R. 865, 870.
62 See *Graeme and Skene* v. *Cunningham* (1765) Mor. 13923, *per* Lord Kames; Borthwick, 192–193.

for a *solatium* on account of the pain and distress inflicted by a verbal injury. There, a tincture of malignity may seem to be essential to the pursuer's success; and indeed injuries which are capable of occasioning this sort of vexation, must generally be attended with circumstances of that character." [63] " I conceive, however, that to authorise an award of this sort, *in solatium* of distress and vexation of mind, where no damage could possibly ensue—that the malignant and injurious intent, the bitter and reproachful spirit—must appear on the writing—, a purpose to vex and disquiet, and inflict a suffering on the object of the charge." [64]

Malice in case of hurt to pursuer's reputation. In the case of harm to public reputation by the publication of defamatory matter to third parties, which is an *actio utilis legis Aquiliae* rather than a pure *actio injuriarum*,[65] the matter complained of may have been published either *animo injuriandi, i.e.*, intentionally or recklessly, or *culpa, i.e.*, unintentionally but without taking reasonable care.[66] Where there is no *animus injuriandi* but only *culpa* there must be proof of some actual loss.[67] " In those matters which so nearly touch the interest of third parties—affect them so deeply in their enjoyment of life—it is not sufficient to be free of pure wilful malice. On such occasions, in the estimation of law, supine negligence, gross indiscretion, rash and precipitate proceedings are equivalent to malice. The maxim of the Roman law applied *culpa lata equiparatur dolo.* Gross disregard and indifference of the rights of a neighbour binds to reparation just as a purpose to injure one's neighbour would do." [68] In *McLean* v. *Bernstein and Daily Record (Glasgow), Ltd.*,[69] an action against a person who had inserted an advertisement in a paper, and the paper itself, Lord Stormonth-Darling said: " In the case of the newspaper it would be absurd to attribute anything of that kind [actual and conscious malice] to its publishers, and accordingly the case against them is founded on negligence. It is the malice of a kind which arises from a reckless statement—a statement made without due inquiry . . . But it does not at all make negligence necessary as a matter of pleading, because the short and sufficient averment by the pursuer is made that the advertisement was published falsely and calumniously. Calumniously, of course, means maliciously, and the malice which is inferred against the two defenders differs, as I have said, in quality; but it is malice and not negligence."

Similarly, in *Morrison* v. *Ritchie* [70] a couple who had been married only two months complained of the publication in the " Births " column

---

[63] Hume, *Lect.* III, 153.
[64] *Ibid.* 156.
[65] See *infra*, p. 790.
[66] *Outram* v. *Reid* (1852) 14 D. 577, 579, *per* Sheriff Alison, who held that *culpa levis* (slightly blameable omission) was enough to import liability. The Lord Ordinary (Wood) (p. 580) held it to be " culpable negligence." The First Division upheld both views.
[67] *Craig* v. *Hunter*, June 29, 1809, F.C.; *Outram, supra.*
[68] Hume, *Lect.* III, 149; *cf. Graeme and Skene* v. *Cunningham* (1765) Mor. 13923, *per* Lord Kames; Borthwick, 192–193.
[69] (1900) 8 S.L.T. 42.   [70] (1902) 4 F. 645.

of a newspaper of an entry referring to them, which had been inserted by some third party. The newspaper was ignorant of the facts which made the entry defamatory, and could not be said to have published it deliberately or *animo injuriandi*. But it could not show absence of *culpa*. Lord Moncreiff said [71]: " The communication not being privileged, the pursuers are not bound to aver or prove malice; malice is presumed. . . . The pursuers do not admit . . . that the defenders exercised due care to ascertain the genuineness of the information; and accordingly the defenders would in any case have had to satisfy the jury that they were free from blame."

" The defenders . . . take what they consider sufficient precautions to ensure the genuineness of these advertisements. But these precautions . . . only consist in their requiring the name and address of the sender, which may be purely fictitious. . . . The question remains, upon whom is the loss consequent upon a false notice being published to fall? Upon [the pursuers] or upon the defenders, who . . . without having succeeded in obtaining an effectual security for the genuineness of the notices, have given the libel such wide publicity? " [72] In *Wood* v. *Edinburgh Evening News, Ltd.*[73] an *ex facie* innocent advertisement in a newspaper was alleged to be defamatory. Lord Salvesen, with whom Lord Kinnear concurred, reserved his opinion as to how far a newspaper could be made responsible without averments of negligence for the publication of a prima facie innocent advertisement. It seems proper in such a case accordingly to aver that no reasonable or sufficient enquiries as to accuracy were made before publication.

In the case of the original utterer of a defamatory statement failure to inquire or take reasonable precautions before making it is equivalent to the *animus injuriandi* or " malice " sufficient to ground an action.

Accordingly, if the defender has communicated a slander it matters not that the defender did not intend the words used to bear a defamatory meaning,[74] or did not intend to injure the pursuer's reputation,[75] or that the words were uttered inadvertently,[76] or by way of a jest,[77] or were not intended to refer to the pursuer,[78] or to any living person at all.[79]

Even proof of a good motive, or an honest belief that the words were true,[80] is not a defence, though such facts may go in mitigation of damages.

---

[71] *Ibid.* 650.
[72] *Ibid.* 650. *Cf.* Lord Kames's interlocutor in *Finlay* v. *Neil and Ruddiman* (1763) Borthwick 191 (not in report in Mor. 3436); see also 5 B.S. 575.
[73] 1910 S.C. 895.
[74] *Nevill* v. *Fine Art Co.* [1895] 2 Q.B. 156.
[75] *Hulton* v. *Jones* [1910] A.C. 20.
[76] *Blake* v. *Stevens* (1864) 11 L.T. 543; *Shepheard* v. *Whitaker* (1875) L.R. 10 C.P. 502; *Tompson* v. *Dashwood* (1883) 11 Q.B.D. 43; *Morrison* v. *Ritchie* (1902) 4 F. 645.
[77] *Donoghue* v. *Hayes* (1831) Hayes Exch. 265; *Capital and Counties Bank* v. *Henty* (1882) 7 App.Cas. 741, 772.
[78] *Hulton* v. *Jones* [1910] A.C. 20; *Cassidy* v. *Daily Mirror* [1929] 2 K.B. 331; *Newstead* v. *London Express* [1940] 1 K.B. 377.
[79] *Hulton* v. *Jones, supra.*
[80] *Watkin* v. *Hall* (1868) L.R. 3 Q.B. 396; *Hulton* v. *Jones* [1910] A.C. 20, 23-24, *per* Lord Loreburn L.C.

Statutory defence where defamation unintentional. In cases of unintentional defamation, the defender now has, by the Defamation Act, 1952, s. 4, a defence if, and only if, the statutory conditions are satisfied and he makes an offer of amends under that section.[81]

Loss, injury or damage. Every defamatory communication is by Scots law actionable *per se*, sounding at least in an award of solatium for hurt feelings and lowered self-esteem,[82] or in an award of Aquilian damages for the loss proved or presumed from an unjustly disparaged reputation, or in both such awards, and there is no need to prove any actual or resulting damage.[83] An action cannot be dismissed merely on the ground that the pursuer has *ex facie* of the pleadings suffered no actual damage or loss. If slander is relevantly averred the question whether there has or has not been damage to the pursuer, at least in feelings, cannot be decided without inquiry into the facts.[84] " If a slander has been uttered the pursuer is prima facie entitled to some damages, or, at all events, to an apology." [85] Proven defamation therefore always justifies at least a small award of damages.[86] But to justify an award of more substantial damages for injury to reputation, there must be proof of actual damage or at least of circumstances in which some loss, injury and damage may be considered to have followed or to be likely to follow from the stained reputation.[87] Thus there may be proof of a general loss of professional earnings or business profits consequent on the defamation.[88]

Evidence in aggravation of damages. The pursuer may in aggravation of damages give evidence of the circumstances in which the defamation was published,[89] or that the defender repeated the slander after warning,[90] or of the circulation of the journal in which publication was made,[91] or that the defender knew that repetition and republication elsewhere would follow,[92] and generally of the defender's whole conduct in the matter.[93] The defender's conduct of the case in court may be held to aggravate damages, but not the way in which his counsel has conducted the case, unless it be shown that in so doing counsel was acting on the

---

[81] See further p. 795, *infra*, on this defence.
[82] See Hume, *Lect.* III, 155, citing *Naismith* v. *Hutchison*, May 18, 1808 F.C. and Hume, 614; *Lovi* v. *Wood* (1802) Hume 613.
[83] In England only libel is actionable *per se*; slander is not actionable without proof of special (*i.e.*, actual) damage, except in certain exceptional cases where special damage is presumed.
[84] *Cassidy* v. *Connochie*, 1907 S.C. 1112.
[85] *Cassidy, supra,* 1116, *per* Lord Stormonth-Darling.
[86] *Fletcher* v. *Wilsons* (1885) 12 R. 683.
[87] *Cf.* Bankt. I, 10, 24 and 28; Hume, *Lect.* III, 154–155; Borthwick, 190–191.
[88] *Cf. Ingram* v. *Lawson* (1840) 6 Bing.N.C. 212; *Rose* v. *Groves* (1843) 5 M. & Gr. 613; *Evans* v. *Harries* (1856) 1 H. & N. 251; *Ritchie* v. *Barton* (1883) 10 R. 813; *Boal* v. *Scottish Catholic Printing Co.*, 1908 S.C. 667.
[89] *Scotlands* v. *Thomson* (1776) 2 Hailes 716; *Cunningham* v. *Duncan* (1889) 16 R. 383, 387; *Morrison* v. *Ritchie* (1902) 4 F. 645.
[90] *Morrison, supra.*
[91] *Gathercole* v. *Miall* (1846) 15 M. & W. 319.
[92] *Whitney* v. *Moignard* (1890) 24 Q.B.D. 630.
[93] *Praed* v. *Graham* (1889) 24 Q.B.D. 53, 55.

express instructions of his client.[94] An attempt to establish the defence of
veritas involves the repetition and attempted substantiation of the imputation and, if unsuccessful and particularly if apparently unjustified,
may go in aggravation of damages.[95]

Evidence of the pursuer's good character is unnecessary and irrelevant
in aggravation of damages; his character is presumed unblemished,[96]
but if the imputation is of the pursuer's general bad character, evidence
of general good character is admissible in rebuttal,[97] and such evidence
is also competent if the defender has led evidence of the pursuer's general
bad character in mitigation of damages.[98]

Evidence in mitigation of damages. In mitigation of damages the
defender may prove the absence of *animus injuriandi* other than that
inferred from the making of the statement held to be defamatory,[99]
the fact that the defender merely transmitted the statement, or repeated
a general report,[1] or published it in circumstances not suggestive of its
being inaccurate or defamatory,[2] or published, or offered to publish, an
apology,[3] or published information received from a reliable source, such
as a newspaper's regular correspondent.[4] If, in the last instance, the correspondent is not disclosed, the publisher cannot prove facts of which
the publisher was ignorant which might have influenced the correspondent's judgment,[5] nor can he prove that the correspondent was not
motivated by malice.[6] It is also relevant to show that the pursuer's
reputation had been affected by factors other than the defender's defamation,[7] or that the pursuer's conduct had provoked the statement
complained of.[8]

The pursuer in a slander action necessarily puts his character in issue,
and it is a relevant defence to aver and prove that his character was such
as did not suffer damage by the statement complained of. Evidence of
the pursuer's general bad character or bad reputation in the respect which
is in issue is therefore admissible,[9] but not evidence of rumours that he had

---

94 *James* v. *Baird*, 1916 S.C. 510, 526, 529, explaining *Praed, supra* (reversed 1916 S.C.(H.L.)
   158 on another point).
95 *Warwick* v. *Foulkes* (1844) 12 M. & W. 507; *Simpson* v. *Robinson* (1848) 12 Q.B. 511;
   Caulfield v. *Whitworth* (1868) 18 L.T.(N.S.) 527.
96 *Cornwall* v. *Richardson* (1825) Ry. & M. 305; *Guy* v. *Gregory* (1840) 9 C. & P. 584.
97 *Hobbs* v. *Tinling* [1929] 2 K.B. 1.
98 *Bate* v. *Hill* (1823) 1 C. & P. 100.
99 *Lowe* v. *Taylor* (1844) 7 D. 117; *White* v. *Clough* (1847) 10 D. 332; *Paul* v. *Jackson* (1884)
   11 R. 460; *Cunningham* v. *Duncan* (1889) 16 R. 383.
1 *Macculloch* v. *Litt* (1851) 13 D. 960; *Paul, supra*.
2 *Browne, infra*; *Morrison* v. *Ritchie* (1902) 4 F. 645.
3 *Morrison, supra*, 652.
4 *Browne* v. *MacFarlane* (1889) 16 R. 368; *Cunningham, supra*.
5 *Browne, supra*; *Morrison* v. *Smith* (1897) 24 R. 471, 476.
6 *Browne, supra*.
7 *McDonald* v. *Begg* (1862) 24 D. 685.   8 *Tullis* v. *Crichton* (1850) 12 D. 867, 872.
9 *Hyslop* v. *Staig* (1816) 1 Mur. 15; *Scott* v. *McGavin* (1821) 2 Mur. 484; *Walker* v. *Robertson*
   (1821) 2 Mur. 508; *Tytler* v. *Mackintosh* (1823) 3 Mur. 263; *Kingan* v. *Watson* (1828)
   4 Mur. 485; *Scott* v. *Sampson* (1882) 8 Q.B.D. 491; *G.* v. *M.*, 1923 S.C. 1; *Hobbs* v. *Tinling* [1929] 2 K.B. 1; *Dingle* v. *Associated Newspapers* [1961] 2 Q.B. 162; *Plato Films* v.
   Speidel [1961] A.C. 1090; *cf. Bern's Exor.* v. *Montrose Asylum* (1893) 20 R. 859, 863;
   McDonald v. *Begg* (1862) 24 D. 685.

done what was alleged, nor of particular acts of misconduct as tending to reveal his character,[10] nor of general bad character in respects not in issue, nor of bad character subsequent to the time which is in issue.[11] If notice is given on record the pursuer may be cross-examined as to specific instances of misconduct even though it is incompetent to lead evidence to establish them.[12] Where libel has been published on a privileged occasion and subsequently repeated on a non-privileged occasion, the former publication cannot be founded on in mitigation of damages as having already damaged the pursuer's reputation,[13] nor can damages be mitigated because other contemporaneous publications contained the same libel.[14]

Tenders in defamation actions. A tender in a defamation case must not only offer a sum of money in full of the conclusions of the summons, but also contain a complete judicial [15] retractation of the statement complained of,[16] so as to clear the pursuer's character as much as a verdict for him would do.[17] It must, that is, be a withdrawal with apology and admission that the aspersion is unfounded.[18] A retractation without tender of a sum as damages amounts to a verdict by consent for the pursuer, and consequently entitles him to expenses.[19] A tender without retractation is of no value.[20] But it is competent to tender, retracting the statement complained of as innuendoed by the pursuer, without admission that the defender made the statement,[21] or without admission that it will bear the innuendo the pursuer has put upon it.[19]

Issues and counter-issues. The matters raised by the issue for the pursuer submitted to the jury are whether the statement was communicated by the defender to, or of and concerning, the pursuer, whether it was false and calumnious, whether taken in its natural meaning or as innuendoed it conveyed a stated imputation, to the pursuer's loss, injury and damage.

The defender may, if his pleadings justify it, raise by counter-issue the defences of lack of intent to defame, pursuer's authority, *rixa, veritas,* absolute privilege, qualified privilege, fair retort, or fair comment.

4. DEFENCES TO AN ACTION FOR DEFAMATION

The following defences are competent:

(1) Denial of having made or repeated the statement objected to.

10 *Scott* v. *Sampson* (1882) 8 Q.B.D. 491; explained *Hobbs* v. *Tinling* [1929] 2 K.B. 1; *Wood* v. *Cox* (1888) 4 T.L.R. 652; *C.* v. *M.,* 1923 S.C. 1.
11 *Thompson* v. *Nye* (1850) 16 Q.B. 175; *C.* v. *M.,* 1923 S.C. 1.
12 *C.* v. *M.,* 1923 S.C. 1, 5.
13 *Dingle, supra.*
14 *Associated Newspapers* v. *Dingle* [1962] 2 All E.R. 737.
15 *Curror* v. *Martin* (1839) 11 Sc.Jur. 463; *Arrol* v. *King* (1855) 18 D. 98; *Lawson* v. *Ferguson* (1866) 38 Sc.Jur. 528; *Malcolm* v. *Moore, supra.*
16 *Bisset* v. *Anderson* (1847) 10 D. 233; *Faulks, infra.*
17 *Faulks* v. *Park* (1854) 17 D. 247.
18 *Malcolm* v. *Moore* (1901) 4 F. 53.
19 *Hunter* v. *Russell* (1901) 3 F. 596.
20 *Faulks, supra,* 250; *Sproll* v. *Walker* (1899) 2 F. 73.
21 *Arrol, supra; cf. Mitchells* v. *Nicoll* (1890) 17 R. 795.

(2) Denial that it refers to the pursuer, or was capable of referring to, or being understood to refer to, the pursuer.

(3) Denial that the words convey any defamatory imputation, or were capable of bearing or being understood to bear, any defamatory imputation.

(4) Proof that the communication of defamation was unintentional, coupled with an offer of amends.

(5) Proof that the statement was authorised by the pursuer or with his consent.

(6) Proof that the words were uttered in heat as mere abuse.

(7) Proof of the truth of the statement complained of.

(8) Proof that the statement was made in circumstances of absolute privilege.

(9) Proof that the statement was made in circumstances of qualified privilege (including the plea of " fair retort ").

(10) Proof that the statement was to be regarded as fair comment on a matter of public interest.

Three other pleas require prior consideration, provocation, common report, and *compensatio injuriarum*.

Provocation. Provocation [22] is not a defence if defamation has been uttered, but is a factor relevant in mitigation of damages,[23] and evidence of provocative circumstances is admissible for that purpose.[24]   The plea is distinct from *compensatio injuriarum* though both may arise in one set of circumstances.[25]   The facts alleged to amount to provocation should be averred.[26]   Without a counter-issue of *veritas*, a defender may not prove the truth of an imputation, either as a defence or in mitigation of damages, but a defender may lead evidence disclosing something less than *veritas*, such as circumstances which amount to provocation or conduct on the part of the pursuer of such a nature as to lead to the slander though not to justify it, and this is material on the question of damages.[27]   If the matter of provocation cannot be distinguished from that of *veritas*, evidence is not admissible without a counter-issue.[27]

Common report. The fact that the alleged defamatory statement was commonly reported in the country, or in the district, was formerly a defence, so long as there was no evidence of *animus injuriandi* nor of resultant harm.[28]   In modern practice repetition of even common report is not a defence, but may be pleaded in mitigation of damages.[29]

22 See Borthwick, 303–306.
23 *Scotlands* v. *Thomson* (1776) Mor.App.Delinquency, 3; *Ogilvie* v. *Scott* (1835) 14 S. 729.
24 *Bryson* v. *Inglis* (1844) 6 D. 363.
25 *Tullis* v. *Crichton* (1850) 12 D. 867.
26 *Muller* v. *Robertson* (1853) 15 D. 661.
27 *Paul* v. *Jackson* (1884) 11 R. 460.
28 Borthwick, 291–303; *Rose* v. *Robertson* (1803) Hume 614; *Gardner* v. *Marshall* (1803) Hume 620.
29 *Durham* v. *Mair* (1796) Hume 599; *McKennal* v. *Wilson* (1806) Hume 628; *Scott* v. *McGavin* (1821) 2 Mur. 484, 487; *Marshall* v. *Renwicks* (1834) 13 S. 1127, 1129; *Macculloch* v. *Litt* (1850) 13 D. 960.

Compensatio injuriarum. The principle of *compensatio injuriarum* was that a defender should not be compelled to pay damages to a pursuer, if the pursuer was liable in as great, or greater, damages to the defender for a similar wrong, which was proponed as a defence and counter-claim.[30] In older cases,[31] the plea was hardly distinguishable from provocation, and the mutual claims were tried in one action.

As explained in *Tullis* v. *Crichton*,[32] the plea is not a defence or justification or palliation, but a plea " that the pursuer is not to obtain a decree to enforce damages due to him, if the reparation due by him for another wrong is such that it totally extinguishes the claim for damages—or is to obtain his decree only for the difference." It is not that one injury compensates another, but that one sum is to be set off against another once each injury, if proved, has been quantified in monetary damages. Unless the incidents are inseparable, as where both happened *in rixa*, separate actions must be brought.[33] The defender's counter-action may show provocation and so reduce the damages. In *Tullis* the opinion was expressed that action and counter-action should be tried by the same jury and the principle of compensation could then apply as between the two verdicts as it could between two liquid debts.

Defences Proper

(1) *Denial of making the statement complained of*

It is obviously a defence for the defender to deny having made or repeated or otherwise communicated the statement complained of as defamatory. This is a pure question of fact, and the onus is on the pursuer to establish utterance or other communication. Where the defender denies having made the slander, as where the slander is contained in an anonymous letter, evidence as to the defender's motive for the making of the slander, though insufficient to identify him with the writer, may be relevant for the jury's consideration on the matter along with any other evidence adduced to establish or disprove authorship of the letter.[34] It is similarly a defence to show that any statement made by the defender differs so materially from that complained of on record as to be substantially a different statement. But an amendment of record may be allowed by the court, which would counter this latter plea.

(2) *Denial that it refers to the pursuer*

The pursuer has to aver adequately, and to prove, that the statement he complains of refers to him, or at least was reasonably capable of

---

30 See Borthwick, 279–291.
31 *Porteous* v. *Izat* (1781) Mor. 13937; *Robertson* v. *Falconer* (1798) Hume 603; *Robertson* v. *Rose* (1801) Borthwick 340; *Lovi* v. *Wood* (1802) Hume 613; *Forbes* v. *Young* (1805) Hume 627; *McGuffie* v. *McDonell* (1809) Hume 638; *Hyslop* v. *Miller* (1816) 1 Mur. 43; *Goddard & Co.* v. *Haddaway* (1816) 1 Mur. 156; *Edwards* v. *Macintosh* (1823) 3 Mur. 369; *Gilchrist* v. *Dempster* (1823) Borthwick 433.
32 (1850) 12 D. 867, 871, *per* L.J.C. Hope, followed in *Bertram* v. *Pace* (1885) 12 R. 798. Cf. *Edwards* v. *Macintosh* (1823) 3 Mur. 369, 387.
33 *Hyslop, supra.*
34 *MacTaggart* v. *MacKillop*, 1938 S.C. 847. Cf. *Melville* v. *Crichton* (1820) 2 Mur. 277.

referring to him or of being understood as referring to him, and was so understood. He must, that is, show that the derogatory idea was applicable to him. If this is denied, and the pursuer fails to prove it, his action fails. Thus in *Hulton* v. *Jones* [35] the plaintiff proved that certain persons had actually thought that *he* was the Artemus Jones whose discreditable conduct was reported in the defendants' article. In a case of fairly general reference, the defender may succeed in a denial that it refers to the pursuer; whether it refers to another determinate person or not is irrelevant.

(3) Denial that the words were defamatory

This is in the first place an issue of law, to be debated as a question of relevancy. If the defender's arguments convince the court that the words complained of do not in their reasonable sense convey any defamatory meaning, or are not reasonably capable of being understood, in the way the pursuer seeks to interpret them, as bearing any defamatory innuendo, the defender succeeds on relevancy and the pursuer's case falls to be dismissed.

Even if the court holds as a matter of law that the words are capable of conveying a defamatory meaning, the pursuer must then satisfy the jury, as a matter of fact, that the words were actually used and were understood in the defamatory sense and conveyed a derogatory imputation. The defender succeeds if he satisfies the jury that none of the witnesses in fact understood the words in a defamatory sense.

(4) Proof that defamation was unintentional

At common law it had been held that defamation while drunk, but followed, when the defender was informed of the language (which he had forgotten and probably had not intended), by an offer of apology in any terms to be fixed by the company present, gave no proper ground of action,[36] and it might still be held vexatious, if not groundless, to sue for unintentional defamation promptly assuaged by apology.

The defence now known was introduced by the Defamation Act, 1952, s. 4. If a defender claims that he published allegedly defamatory matter innocently in relation to the person defamed, he may escape liability if and only if the statutory conditions are satisfied. The onus of this defence is entirely on the defender. Accordingly while the earlier decisions on unintentional defamation [37] stand, a defender now has a conditional statutory defence in such circumstances.

The Act [38] provides:

" s. 4 (1). A person who has published words alleged to be defamatory of another person may, if he claims that the words were published by

[35] [1910] A.C. 20.
[36] *Ewart* v. *Mason* (1806) Hume 633; *cf. Campbell* v. *Menzies* (1855) 17 D. 1132.
[37] *Outram* v. *Reid* (1852) 14 D. 577; *Wragg* v. *Thomson*, 1909, 2 S.L.T. 409; *Hulton* v. *Jones* [1910] A.C. 20; *Harkness* v. *Daily Record*, 1924 S.L.T. 759; *Cassidy* v. *Daily Mirror* [1929] 2 K.B. 331; *Harper* v. *Provincial Newspapers, Ltd.*, 1937 S.L.T. 462; *Newstead* v. *London Express* [1940] 1 K.B. 377.
[38] As modified in application to Scotland by s. 14 (c).

him innocently in relation to that other person, make an offer of amends under this section; and in any such case—

(a) if the offer is accepted by the party aggrieved and is duly performed, no proceedings for defamation shall be taken or continued by that party against the person making the offer in respect of the publication in question (but without prejudice to any cause of action against any other person jointly responsible for that publication);

(b) if the offer is not accepted by the party aggrieved, then, except as otherwise provided by this section, it shall be a defence, in any proceedings by him for defamation against the person making the offer in respect of the publication in question, to prove that the words complained of were published by the defender innocently in relation to the pursuer and that the offer was made as soon as practicable after the defender received notice that they were or might be defamatory of the pursuer, and has not been withdrawn."

It is provided [39] that words are to be treated as published " innocently " only if " (a) the publisher did not intend to publish them of and concerning [the pursuer], and did not know of circumstances by virtue of which they might be understood to refer to him; or (b) the words were not defamatory on the face of them, and the publisher did not know of circumstances by virtue of which they might be understood to be defamatory of [the pursuer]."

Paragraph (b) of subsection (1) does not apply in relation to the publication by any person of words of which he is not the author unless he proves that the words were written by the author without malice.[40]

An offer of amends under the section means [41] an offer " (a) in any case, to publish or join in the publication of a suitable correction of the words complained of, and a sufficient apology to the party aggrieved in respect of those words; (b) where copies of a document or record have been distributed by or with the knowledge of the person making the offer, to take such steps as are reasonably practicable on his part for notifying persons to whom copies have been so distributed that the words are alleged to be defamatory of the party aggrieved."

An offer of amends must [42] be " expressed to be made for the purposes of this section, and must be accompanied by a written declaration signed by that person specifying the facts relied upon by the person making it to show that the words in question were published by him innocently in relation to the party aggrieved; and for the purposes of a defence [in the case where the offer of amends is not accepted] no evidence, other than evidence of facts specified in the written declaration, shall be admissible on behalf of that person to prove that the words were so published." A

---

[39] Defamation Act, 1952, s. 4 (5). See also *Ross* v. *Hopkinson* [1956] C.L.Y. 5011.
[40] *Ibid.* s. 4 (6).
[41] *Ibid.* s. 4 (3).
[42] *Ibid.* s. 4 (2).

defender may not lead evidence of facts in the declaration unless notice of his intention to do so has been given in the defences to the action.[43]

Where an offer of amends has been accepted any issue as to the steps to be taken in fulfilment of the offer falls, failing agreement, to be determined by the Court of Session or the sheriff, as the case may be, which decision shall be final.[44]

(5) *Proof that statement was authorised by the pursuer or with his consent*

A pursuer cannot, on the principle *volenti non fit injuria*, complain of, as being defamatory of him, a communication referring to him which has been authorised by him, or by another person with his consent, or in any way expressly or impliedly assented to by him.[45] A defender can accordingly escape liability by clear and unequivocal proof of assent or authority. In its nature this defence is more likely to be applicable to cases of exhibition of photographs and the like, rather than to cases of oral or written statements. In *Cook* v. *Ward*,[46] however, the plaintiff sued a newspaper for having published a story which the plaintiff had told against himself at a party. It was not established that he had authorised publication, but if he had, his action must have failed. Where a person gives an interview to a newspaper or television reporter he must probably be held to have assented impliedly to publication thereof.

(6) *Proof that the words were uttered in heat, as abuse*

The defender may escape liability by proving that the words complained of were uttered *in rixa*, as an angry retort[47] in the heat of a squabble or altercation, and were not in such circumstances intended to convey, and did not in fact convey, the defamatory meaning which these words by themselves would convey in their natural sense if uttered deliberately.[48] The words, that is, are not defamatory if in the circumstances not meant to be, and not understood to be, taken seriously. Probably the basis is that the circumstances elide any inference of *animus injuriandi*. Even in an altercation, however, a defamatory imputation may be made, so that it is not enough to prove the squabble, but " it is a very relevant consideration, when weighing the evidence to consider that the words were spoken in heat, for the purpose of finding out the true sense in which the words were used."[49] " The question is whether the words were used in a defamatory sense, or whether they were not mere intemperate expressions used in anger or in the heat of discussion, not intended to impute and not

---

43 *Ibid.* s. 14 (c).
44 *Ibid.* s. 4, as applied by s. 14 (d).
45 *Monson* v. *Tussauds* [1894] 1 Q.B. 671, 691, 697; *Chapman* v. *Lord Ellesmere* [1932] 2 K.B. 431; *Cookson* v. *Harewood* [1932] 2 K.B. 478n.; *cf. Russell* v. *Duke of Norfolk* [1949] 1 All E.R. 109.
46 (1830) 4 Mor. & P. 99.
47 It is distinct from the privilege of " fair retort " on which see, *infra.*
48 *Shand* v. *Finnie* (1802) Hume 612; *McCrae* v. *Stevenson* (1806) Hume 631; *Harper* v. *Fernie* (1810) Hume 643; *Reid* v. *Scott* (1825) 4 S. 5.
49 *Christie* v. *Robertson* (1899) 1 F. 1155, 1157, *per* Lord McLaren.

really imputing falsehood as a characteristic of the pursuer." [50] "It is a condition of [the pursuer's] right to damages that the words complained of were applied to him in a defamatory sense, and the sense in which the words were really used is to be ascertained, as in any other case of construction, from the context and the history of the case or 'surrounding circumstances.' " [51] The defence has no place if a definite charge is made against another: "giving such point in regard to time and circumstances as to lead those who were present to believe that the charge was seriously made, it is no defence that the words were spoken in heat." [52]

The defence of *rixa* is common only in cases of oral slander, and it is less appropriate to written libel,[53] because writing implies some deliberation, even if a man is angry.[54] It is completely elided if the words used *in rixa* are subsequently deliberately repeated,[55] or if the defender called on others to witness his words.[55] Such facts justify an inference of *animus injuriandi* sufficient to found an action.

It is particularly appropriate where the words used are capable of conveying a defamatory imputation if taken seriously, but are also words of common vulgar abuse frequently uttered in the heat of anger or quarrels, such as "liar," [56] "bastard," "bugger," [57] "tart," "damned bitch," [58] "whore," [59] and frequently strengthened by vituperative epithets.[60]

The defence is particularly strong if an apology is subsequently offered.[61]

(7) *Truth of the statement*

By definition defamation is the publication of matter which is, *inter alia*, false. It is accordingly a complete defence to prove that the statement complained of is true,[62] since an individual cannot complain of there being communicated to, or of and concerning, him what is factually true, even though it be malicious,[63] or may cause him hurt feelings or loss of reputation. Any such loss is *damnum absque injuria*.[64] Where a defender has

---

[50] *Watson* v. *Duncan* (1890) 17 R. 404, 407, *per* Lord McLaren.
[51] *Ibid*. 408, *per* Lord McLaren.
[52] *Christie* v. *Robertson* (1899) 1 F. 1155, 1157, *per* Lord McLaren.
[53] The defence was upheld in *Lovi* v. *Wood* (1802) Hume 613, a case of written defamation.
[54] What if a man comes back to his office in a fury, and dictates a defamatory letter, which he signs as soon as typed, before his anger has cooled?
[55] *Mackay* v. *Grant* (1903) 41 S.L.R. 18.
[56] *McCrae* v. *Stevenson* (1806) Hume 631; *Watson* v. *Duncan* (1890) 17 R. 404; *Christie* v. *Robertson* (1899) 1 F. 1155; *Mackay* v. *Grant* (1903) 41 S.L.R. 18.
[57] *Grahame* v. *McKenzie* (1810) Hume 641.
[58] *Shand* v. *Finnie* (1802) Hume 612.
[59] *Somerville* v. *Buchanan* (1801) Hume 608; *Gibson* v. *Douglas* (1810) Hume 639; *Harper* v. *Fernie* (1810) Hume 643; *Reid* v. *Scott* (1825) 4 S. 5.
[60] See also cases collected in *Cooper on Defamation*, pp. 95–96.
[61] *Ewart* v. *Mason* (1806) Hume 633.
[62] *Inglis* v. *Calder* (1790) Hume 594; *Scott* v. *McGavin* (1821) 2 Mur. 484; *Hamilton* v. *Hope* (1826) 4 Mur. 222; *Mitchell* v. *Thomson* (1828) 7 S. 458; *Wilson* v. *Weir* (1862) 24 D. 67; *Wallace* v. *Mooney* (1885) 12 R. 710; *Cook* v. *Gray* (1891) 29 S.L.R. 247; *Buchan* v. *N.B.Ry.* (1894) 21 R. 379.
[63] *Buchan*, *supra*.
[64] *McPherson* v. *Daniels* (1829) 10 B. & C. 263.

published a defamatory statement, "the falsehood is presumed and does not require to be proved on the part of the pursuer; but it is open to the defender to aver and prove the truth of the alleged slander, to the effect of a complete defence against the action." [65] The onus of proof is on the defender.[66] If the truth of the imputation appears from the pursuer's own pleadings, his action must be dismissed as irrelevant.[67]

The plea of *veritas* may be tabled notwithstanding a denial of having made the statement complained of [68]; there is no inconsistency, though the pleas are necessarily alternative, *veritas* being in issue only if the statement is proved to have been made. Nor is the plea excluded by the fact that the defender had, on a former occasion, written a letter of apology, admitting that similar statements then made were false, and undertaking not to repeat them.[69]

A defender seeking to plead *veritas* must aver specifically facts which, if proved, will justify the statement alleged to be slanderous and establish the truth of the imputation, and table a plea-in-law to that effect.[70] If the imputation is in general terms, the defender must aver and prove specific instances which justify the general imputation. A more general averment of the truth of the imputation will be dismissed as lacking in specification and irrelevant.[71] A general imputation is not generally justified by proof of one or two specific instances.[72]

The standard of proof required to establish the defence is the balance of probabilities, though in the case of a serious imputation the standard may be high.[73]

A plea of *veritas* must be sufficiently wide to justify, if it is made out, the literal language of the defamatory statement and also any inferences which follow naturally in the context from the literal terms used.[74] Thus to call a man a poacher connotes that he poached at least once but carries also the natural implication that he did so habitually; hence a plea of one conviction for poaching was held an inadequate plea of *veritas*.[75]

---

[65] *Mackellar* v. *Duke of Sutherland* (1859) 21 D. 222, 229, per L.J.C. Inglis. Similarly *McNeill* v. *Rorison* (1848) 10 D. 15; *Burnaby* v. *Robertson* (1848) 10 D. 855.

[66] *Gibsons* v. *Marr* (1823) 3 Mur. 261.

[67] *Campbell* v. *Ferguson* (1882) 9 R. 467; *Carson* v. *White*, 1919, 2 S.L.T. 215.

[68] *Mason* v. *Tait* (1851) 13 D. 1347; *Burnet* v. *Gow* (1896) 24 R. 156, 157, *per* L.O. Kincairney.

[69] *R.* v. *S.*, 1914 S.C. 193. But if the action had been founded on the defender's breach of her undertaking not to repeat admitted slanders, the plea of *veritas* would have been irrelevant.

[70] *McNeill* v. *Rorison* (1848) 10 D. 15; *Rankin* v. *Simpson* (1859) 21 D. 1057; *McIver* v. *McNeill* (1873) 11 M. 777; *Fletcher* v. *Wilson* (1885) 12 R. 683; *Macleod* v. *Marshall* (1891) 18 R. 811; *H.* v. *P.* (1905) 8 F. 232.

[71] *McRostie* v. *Ironside* (1850) 12 D. 74; *McDonald* v. *Begg* (1862) 24 D. 685; *Hunter* v. *MacNaughton* (1894) 21 R. 850; *Hamilton* v. *Wright* (1895) 3 S.L.T. 10; *Goodall* v. *Forbes*, 1909 S.C. 1300.

[72] *Milne* v. *Walker* (1894) 21 R. 155; *Powell* v. *Long* (1896) 23 R. 534; *Burnet* v. *Gow* (1896) 24 R. 156; *cf. Fletcher, supra.*

[73] *Andrew* v. *Penny*, 1964 S.L.T.(Notes) 24.

[74] *O'Brien* v. *Bryant* (1846) 16 M. & W. 168; *Wakley* v. *Cooke* (1849) 4 Ex. 511; *Bishop* v. *Latimer* (1861) 4 L.T.(N.S.) 775; *Digby* v. *Financial News* [1907] 1 K.B. 502; *Sutherland* v. *Stopes* [1925] A.C. 47; *Burton* v. *Board* [1929] 1 K.B. 301.

[75] *Brownlie* v. *Thompson* (1851) 21 D. 480; *cf. Fletcher* v. *Wilson* (1885) 12 R. 683.

The facts averred in support of the counter-issue must meet the defamation in its fair meaning.[76]

A plea of *veritas* may be tabled in respect only of part of the slander complained of, if separable from the rest,[77] but a partial plea or partial proof of the truth of one imputation is valueless. It may also be taken to the effect of denying the innuendo placed on the statement complained of, even though the statement is admitted to have been made.[78]

In the absence of a plea of *veritas*, averments directed to justifying the imputation are irrelevant.[79]

Belief not enough to sustain plea of veritas. To succeed in a plea of *veritas*, the defender must prove not merely that he honestly and reasonably believed the statement to be true, but that it was true in actual fact,[80] and that whether the statement was expressed as belief or as fact, as direct statement or as reported hearsay or repeated rumour.[81] Where the imputation is of crime it is not enough to prove that there was suspicion,[82] or that the pursuer had a reputation for offences of the kind imputed.[83]

Proof of exact truth. To establish the defence of *veritas* the defender must justify exactly the imputation he has conveyed.[84] It is not enough to establish the truth of facts, justifying an imputation of the same general character.[85]

Proof of one instance or example does not generally justify an imputation of general bad conduct or character in that respect.[86] Thus to show that a person once told a falsehood does not justify the imputation that he is a " liar," [87] but by common usage a person who has committed one murder is called a murderer and such an appellation would accordingly be justifiable by proof of one instance. Regard must be had accordingly to common understanding and usage of the word complained of and to whether the expression is justified by the instances proved.

Truth of whole imputation. At common law a defender has to prove the truth of all the material statements in the defamatory matter complained of, justifying everything contained in the defamatory statement

---

[76] *Bertram* v. *Pace* (1885) 12 R. 798; *Burnet* v. *Gow* (1896) 24 R. 156; *British Workman* v. *Stewart* (1897) 24 R. 624.

[77] *McNeill* v. *Rorison* (1848) 10 D. 15; *Mackellar* v. *Duke of Sutherland* (1859) 21 D. 222.

[78] *Henderson* v. *Russell* (1895) 23 R. 25.

[79] *C.* v. *M.*, 1923 S.C. 1.

[80] *Peters* v. *Bradlaugh* (1884) 4 T.L.R. 467.

[81] *Douglas* v. *Chalmers* (1785) 3 Paton 26; *McPherson* v. *Daniels* (1829) 10 B. & C. 263; *De Crespigny* v. *Wellesley* (1829) 5 Bing. 392; *Brodie* v. *Blair* (1833) 12 S. 941; *Marshall* v. *Renwicks* (1834) 13 S. 1127; *Watkin* v. *Hall* (1868) L.R. 3 Q.B. 396; *Cookson* v. *Harewood* [1932] 2 K.B. 478n.

[82] *Mountney* v. *Watton* (1831) 3 B. & Ad. 673.

[83] *Wood* v. *Earl of Durham* (1888) 21 Q.B.D. 501.

[84] *McKennal* v. *Wilson* (1806) Hume 608; *Burnet* v. *Gow* (1896) 24 R. 156; *Wernher, Beit* v. *Markham* (1901) 18 T.L.R. 763.

[85] *Maisel* v. *Financial Times, Ltd.*, (*No. 2*) [1915] 3 K.B. 336; *Sutherland* v. *Stopes* [1925] A.C. 47.

[86] *Wakley* v. *Cooke* (1849) 4 Ex. 511; *Bishop* v. *Latimer* (1861) 4 L.T.(N.S.) 775.

[87] *Milne* v. *Walker* (1893) 21 R. 155; *cf. Brownlie* v. *Thompson* (1851) 21 D. 480; *Fletcher* v. *Wilson* (1885) 12 R. 683; *Leyman* v. *Latimer* (1878) 3 Ex.D. 352.

which is injurious to the pursuer.[88] In particular, if the imputation contained two or more charges, both or all must be justified, or else the pursuer would be entitled to damages for any charge not justified.[89]

It is not, however, necessary to prove the truth of every word, but only to justify the gist or substance or the main charge made; it is not necessary to justify anything contained in an imputation which does not add to the sting of it.[90]

A counter-issue accordingly need not echo the very words of the pursuer's issue, but must meet the gist and substance of his complaint, so that, if made out, it takes the sting out of the charge made by the pursuer.[91] It will, however, be disallowed if it fails to do this.[92]

Similarly if the gist or substance of the imputation is shown to be true, the defence will not fail merely by reason of inaccuracy in one or more of the details,[93] so long as the inaccuracy does not make it a different imputation.[94] But any inaccuracy which changes the character of the main imputation or exaggerates or aggravates it must be proved true, or else the defence of *veritas* will fail.[95]

Multiple charges. Where the statement complained of contains several distinct charges, the defender may plead *veritas* in respect of any one or more, provided it or they can be separated from the rest of the statement.[96] But if particular charges are not severable from the rest of the statement which contains in substance one imputation, the plea of *veritas* must be taken, if at all, in respect of the whole statement.[97] A counter-issue which justifies only part of the pursuer's issue will be disallowed,[98] unless that part is severable.[99]

At common law a general plea of *veritas*, where the statement complained of contained several charges, had to succeed or fail as a whole, though partial success might have been reflected in minimised damages.

It is now provided by the Defamation Act, 1952, s. 5, that where there are " two or more distinct charges against the pursuer a defence of *veritas*

---

88 *Weaver* v. *Lloyd* (1824) 2 B. & C. 678; *Clarkson* v. *Lawson* (1829) 6 Bing. 266; *Goodburne* v. *Bowman* (1833) 9 Bing. 532; *Ingram* v. *Lawson* (1838) 5 Bing.N.C. 66; *Edsall* v. *Russell* (1842) 4 M. & G. 1090; *Smith* v. *Parker* (1844) 13 M. & W. 459.

89 *Clarke* v. *Taylor* (1836) 2 Bing.N.C. 654; *Clarkson* v. *Lawson, supra*; *Smith* v. *Parker* (1844) 13 M. & W. 459.

90 *Edwards* v. *Bell* (1824) 1 Bing. 403; *Clarke* v. *Taylor* (1836) 3 C.B. 95; *Morison* v. *Harmer* (1837) 4 C.B. 524; *Walker* v. *Brogden* (1865) 19 C.B.(N.S.) 65; *Sutherland* v. *Stopes* [1925] A.C. 49.

91 *Torrance* v. *Weddel* (1868) 7 M. 243; *Christie* v. *Craik* (1900) 2 F. 380; *Macleod* v. *Marshall* (1891) 18 R. 811; *Andrew* v. *Macara*, 1917 S.C. 247.

92 *Burnaby* v. *Robertson* (1848) 10 D. 855; *Bertram* v. *Pace* (1885) 12 R. 798; *Blasquez* v. *Lothians* (1889) 16 R. 893; *Milne* v. *Walker* (1893) 21 R. 155.

93 *Alexander* v. *N.E.Ry.* (1865) 6 B. & S. 340; *cf. Buchan* v. *N.B.Ry.* (1894) 21 R. 379.

94 *Gwynn* v. *S.E.Ry.* (1868) 18 L.T. 738.

95 *Weaver* v. *Lloyd* (1824) 2 B. & C. 678; *Cooper* v. *Lawson* (1838) 1 A. & E. 746; *Helsham* v. *Blackwood* (1851) 11 C.B. 111; *Walker* v. *Brogden* (1865) 19 C.B.(N.S.) 65.

96 *Clarkson* v. *Lawson* (1830) 4 Moo. & P. 356; *McGregor* v. *Gregory* (1843) 11 M. & W. 287; *O'Callaghan* v. *D. C. Thomson*, 1928 S.C. 532.

97 *Clarkson, supra*; *Eaton* v. *Johns* (1842) 1 Dowl.(N.S.) 602; *Davis* v. *Billing* (1891) 8 T.L.R. 58.

98 *British Workman* v. *Stewart* (1897) 24 R. 624; commented on in *O'Callaghan* v. *D. C. Thomson*, 1928 S.C. 532.

99 *McNeill* v. *Rorison* (1847) 10 D. 15.

shall not fail by reason only that the truth of every charge is not proved if the words not proved to be true do not materially injure the pursuer's reputation having regard to the truth of the remaining charges."

This can apply only to the case of severable charges, at least one of which has been proved true in all substantial and material respects. In such a case it is for the jury to consider whether the remaining charges materially injure the pursuer's reputation.

Counter-issue of veritas. If a defender pleads the truth of the statements complained of, or any part of them, in justification or in mitigation of damages or for any other purpose, he must table a counter-issue raising the defence.[1] Without this he cannot tender evidence of truth.[2] The counter-issue must meet the substance of the pursuer's issue [3] and not a part only of the issue,[4] though it need not repeat the words of the pursuer's issue to do so; it is enough if the counter-issue negatives the essence of the pursuer's complaint.[5] If there is an issue containing an innuendo, it is sufficient for a defender pleading *veritas* to put in a counter-issue facts which would justify the language complained of as explained in the innuendo, though they might not justify the language apart from the innuendo.[6]

If there are two or more separable charges in the issue, it is open to the defender to justify these charges either by separate counter-issues, or by a composite one which segregates the charges from one another.[7]

(8) *Proof that the statement was made in circumstances of absolute privilege*

The law recognises that on certain occasions individuals must be permitted, for reasons of public policy, to communicate matter which may be defamatory. These are recognised as privileged occasions, and the plea of privilege is accordingly a competent plea in defence to an action for defamation. It differs, however, from *veritas* in that a plea of privilege may be maintained independently of the truth of the imputation, and indeed the defence of privilege need be invoked only if the statement is, or may be, defamatory. Hence the defences of *veritas* and privilege can only be tabled alternatively, and not cumulatively, being mutually inconsistent.

Whether the statement complained of was or was not published in circumstances protected by privilege is a question of law, though facts

---

1 *Scott* v. *McGavin* (1821) 2 Mur. 484; *Hamilton* v. *Hope* (1826) 4 Mur. 222; *Greig* v. *Edmonstone* (1826) 4 Mur. 66; *Paterson* v. *Shaw* (1830) 5 Mur. 273; *Brodies* v. *Blair* (1835) 14 S. 267; *McNeill* v. *Rorison* (1848) 10 D. 15; *Torrance* v. *Weddel* (1868) 7 M. 243; *Craig* v. *Jex-Blake* (1871) 9 M. 973; *McIver* v. *McNeill* (1873) 11 M. 777; *Paul* v. *Jackson* (1884) 11 R. 460; *Bertram* v. *Pace* (1885) 12 R. 798; *Blasquez* v. *Lothians Racing Club* (1889) 16 R. 893; *Milne* v. *Walker* (1893) 21 R. 155; *Christie* v. *Craik* (1900) 2 F. 380.
2 *Scott* v. *Docherty* (1844) 6 D. 5; *McNeill, supra*; *Browne* v. *McFarlane* (1889) 16 R. 368.
3 *Bertram, supra*; *Milne, supra*; *British Workman's Assce. Co.* v. *Stewart* (1897) 24 R. 624.
4 *Ibid.*
5 *Ogilvy* v. *Paul* (1873) 11 M. 776; *Powell* v. *Long* (1896) 23 R. 534.
6 *Christie* v. *Craik* (1900) 2 F. 380.
7 *O'Callaghan* v. *Thomson*, 1928 S.C. 532.

may have to be elucidated to ascertain whether the circumstances give privilege; if privilege exists the action is irrelevant and the defender protected.

Two kinds of privilege. Privilege is of two kinds, absolute and qualified; the former confers complete immunity from legal liability on the maker of the statement complained of, irrespective of his state of mind; the latter confers immunity from liability on the maker of the statement complained of, provided the statement was made without any malicious or improper motive and in circumstances where an honest statement of belief is in the general interest, even if the facts stated to or of the pursuer should be defamatory of him.

It is an issue for the court, to be decided on relevancy, whether the circumstances entitle the maker of the statement to absolute or to qualified privilege. If any facts relating to the circumstances in which the statement was made are in dispute they must be elucidated by proof or the verdict of a jury, but it will then be for the court to rule whether the occasion was privileged.[8]

Absolute privilege. In circumstances to which absolute privilege attaches a person is under no liability whatever in damages for making a statement which is false and defamatory, irrespective of his state of mind. Not even averments of malice or express intent to harm the pursuer will make the statement actionable. The justification for this complete immunity is public policy, and it can apply only in cases where it is clearly in the public interest that such immunity should exist.

The list of occasions to which absolute privilege attaches is not fixed, but has been developed by the courts and may be further developed, but the immunity is such that the courts are unwilling to extend the list,[9] and will probably do so only in cases *ejusdem generis* with those already recognised.

Statements in Parliament. The civil courts cannot constitutionally take cognisance of anything said or done in either House of Parliament, and to do so would infringe the privilege of that House.[10] Apart from that it is in the public interest that members of either House should be permitted to speak freely; accordingly no action will lie against a member of either House for defamatory words uttered in the course of any parliamentary debate or proceeding,[11] nor for the report thereof in Hansard. But if a member has his speech printed and published for the interest of his constituents or others, only qualified, and not absolute, privilege attaches.[12] If he has his speech printed in a newspaper, and published

---

[8] *Hebditch* v. *McIlwain* [1894] 2 Q.B. 54; *cf. Hope* v. *I'Anson* (1901) 18 T.L.R. 201.
[9] *Royal Aquarium Society* v. *Parkinson* [1892] 1 Q.B. 431, 451, *per* Lopes L.J.
[10] Bill of Rights, 1688.
[11] *Ex parte Wason* (1869) L.R. 4 Q.B. 573; *Dillon* v. *Balfour* (1887) 20 L.R.Ir. 600; *Chenard* v. *Arissol* [1949] A.C. 127, 133.
[12] *Davison* v. *Duncan* (1857) 7 E. & B. 233; *Wason* v. *Walter* (1868) L.R. 4 Q.B. 95.

generally, no privilege at all attaches.[13] So too if he repeats orally outside the House what he said inside, qualified privilege at most will apply.

Absolute privilege attaches also to statements contained in a petition addressed to Parliament,[14] or to a Committee of either House thereof,[15] and to statements made under examination by any witness summoned to give evidence before a select committee of the House of Commons.[16] A letter from an M.P. to a Minister, allegedly defamatory of a third party, is not a " proceeding in Parliament " to which privilege attaches.[17]

Statements in reports published by either House of Parliament. All reports, papers, votes and proceedings published by, or under the authority of, either House of Parliament, are absolutely privileged.[18] Any proceedings for defamation brought in consequence thereof will be dismissed by the court on the defender's giving twenty-four hours' notice to the pursuer and producing to the court a certificate[19] under the hand of the Lord Chancellor, or of the Lord Keeper of the Great Seal, or of the Speaker or Clerk of the House of Commons, stating that the report or other paper was published by order or under the authority of one or other House.[20] If proceedings have been taken in respect of the publication of a copy, not of the original report, no certificate is necessary, but the defender may have the action dismissed on laying before the court the original, with an affidavit verifying the original and the correctness of the copy.[21] In an action based on the publication[22] of an extract from, or abstract of, a parliamentary report or other paper only qualified privilege attaches to the defender.[23] To impugn the validity of the report of a select committee of the House of Commons, particularly one accepted by the House and printed in the Commons Journal is contrary to the Bill of Rights, 1688.[24]

Statements between officers of state. Absolute privilege attaches to any official report or communication[25] made in the course of his duty by an officer of the forces to his superior officer,[26] or by an officer of state to his

---

[13] *Duncombe* v. *Daniell* (1838) 2 Jur. 32. *Cf. R.* v. *Creevey* (1813) 1 M. & S. 273.
[14] *Lake* v. *King* (1680) 1 Saund. 131.
[15] *Kane* v. *Mulvaney* (1866) Ir.R. 2 C.L. 402.
[16] *Goffin* v. *Donnelly* (1881) 50 L.J.Q.B. 303.
[17] H.C.Deb.Vol. 430, col. 208, discussing *Re Parliamentary Privilege Act*, 1770 [1958] A.C. 331 (summarised in [1958] C.L.Y. 2452–2453).
[18] Parliamentary Papers Act, 1840, s. 1, passed in consequence of, and overruling, *Stockdale* v. *Hansard* (1839) 9 A. & E. 1, where it had been held that an order of either House, authorising publication outside Parliament, did not give the publisher immunity from action for libel.
[19] Form of certificate in *Stockdale* v. *Hansard* (1840) 11 A. & E. 297.
[20] s. 1.
[21] *Ibid.* s. 2.
[22] Including broadcasting: Defamation Act, 1952, s. 9.
[23] *Ibid.* s. 3.
[24] *Dingle* v. *Associated Newspapers, Ltd.* [1960] 2 Q.B. 405.
[25] A private letter to a superior on service matters would have, at most, qualified privilege: *Dickson* v. *Earl of Wilton* (1859) 1 F. & F. 419; *Dickson* v. *Combermere* (1863) 3 F. & F. 527.
[26] *Home* v. *Bentinck* (1806) 2 B. & B. 130; *Dawkins* v. *Lord Paulet* (1869) L.R. 5 Q.B. 94.

departmental head,[27] even if it relates to a commercial rather than a political matter.[28]

In any event the report or other communication is unlikely to be ordered to be produced if the head of the department in question objected to its production as injurious to the public interest.[29] It is incompetent to seek to give secondary evidence of the contents of the report.[30]

Absolute privilege attaches to the official notification in the *London, Edinburgh,* or *Belfast Gazette* of an act of State, such as the removal of an officer's name from the pension list.[31]

Statements in judicial proceedings. The overriding public interest in free statement of facts, beliefs and opinions in the course of the administration of justice justifies absolute privilege for all statements made in judicial proceedings and complete immunity for the makers of such statements.[32] " The authorities establish beyond all question this: that neither party,[33] witness, counsel, jury nor judge can be put to answer civilly or criminally for words spoken in office; that no action for libel or slander lies whether against judges, counsel, witnesses, or parties for words spoken in the course of any proceeding before any court recognised by law and this although the words were written or spoken maliciously, without any justification or excuse, and from personal ill-will or anger against the party defamed." [34] This privilege exists for obvious reasons of public policy and to assist the free and honest discharge of duties in the administration of justice.[35]

The privilege applies whether the statements in question were made in open court or in chambers,[36] whether on an *ex parte* or undefended application or in a *lis inter partes,*[37] whether or not the court has jurisdiction to deal with the matter,[38] and whatever the stage of the proceedings.[39] Originally confined to recognised courts of justice the doctrine has been extended to tribunals exercising functions equivalent to those of an established court of justice and with similar attributes.[40]

---

[27] *Chatterton* v. *Secretary of State for India* [1895] 2 Q.B. 189. *Cf. Chenard* v. *Arissol* [1949] A.C. 127.
[28] *Isaacs, Ltd.* v. *Cook* [1925] 2 K.B. 391.
[29] *Glasgow Corporation* v. *Central Land Board,* 1956 S.C.(H.L.) 1; *cf. McKie* v. *Western S.M.T. Co.,* 1952 S.C. 206.
[30] *Ankin* v. *L.N.E.Ry.* [1930] 1 K.B. 527.
[31] *Grant* v. *Secretary of State for India* (1877) 2 C.P.D. 445, 464.
[32] *Royal Aquarium Society* v. *Parkinson* [1892] 1 Q.B. 431; *O'Connor* v. *Waldron* [1935] A.C. 76.
[33] In Scotland, a party has not absolute, but qualified, privilege: *Williamson* v. *Umphray* (1890) 17 R. 905, 910; *cf. Gordon* v. *British and Foreign Metaline Co.* (1886) 14 R. 75.
[34] *Royal Aquarium Society* v. *Parkinson* [1892] 1 Q.B. 431, 451, *per* Lopes L.J.; *cf. Dawkins* v. *Rokeby* (1873) L.R. 8 Q.B. 255; *More* v. *Weaver* [1928] 2 K.B. 520; *Hargreaves* v. *Bretherton* [1959] 1 Q.B. 45.
[35] *Garnett* v. *Ferrand* (1827) 6 B. & C. 611; *Kennedy* v. *Hilliard* (1859) 10 Ir.C.L.R. 195; *Fray* v. *Blackburn* (1863) 3 B. & S. 576; *Munster* v. *Lamb* (1883) 11 Q.B.D. 588; *McMurchy* v. *Campbell* (1887) 14 R. 745; *Bottomley* v. *Brougham* [1908] 1 K.B. 584; *Burr* v. *Smith* [1909] 2 K.B. 306.
[36] *Taafe* v. *Downes* (1812) 3 Moo.P.C. 47n.; *Pedley* v. *Morris* (1891) 61 L.J.Q.B. 21.
[37] *Bottomley* v. *Brougham* [1908] 1 K.B. 584, 588.
[38] *Usill* v. *Hales* (1878) 3 C.P.D. 319.
[39] *Bottomley, supra.*
[40] *O'Connor* v. *Waldron* [1935] A.C. 76, 81.

Persons protected. This absolute privilege protects judges of superior courts,[41] and of the sheriff court,[42] stipendiary magistrates and J.P.'s,[43] the president of a court-martial,[44] jurors,[45] counsel,[46] solicitors acting as procurators,[47] parties conducting their own cases,[48] and to witnesses,[49] both giving oral evidence and tendering affidavits or declarations,[50] and also when giving a precognition,[51] but not observations voluntarily made by persons in court who have no duty to make those statements.[52] It extends to written pleadings,[53] but not to solicitors' letters.[54]

In Scotland, differing in this respect from England, parties to an action enjoy only qualified privilege in their pleadings,[55] though it is of a high order if the statement is relevant to the action.[56] A party instructing his solicitor enjoys qualified privilege only.[57]

Absolute privilege also protects the Lord Advocate in his capacity as chief public prosecutor,[58] and probably also advocates-depute and procurators-fiscal acting as his deputies.[59]

---

[41] *Haggart's Trs.* v. *Lord President Hope* (1824) 2 Sh.App. 125; *McMurchy* v. *Campbell* (1887) 14 R. 725, 728; *cf. Fray* v. *Blackburn* (1863) 3 B. & S. 576 (High Court in England); *Taafe* v. *Downes* (1812) 3 Moo.P.C. 36n, (High Court in chambers); *Dicas* v. *Lord Brougham* (1833) 6 C. & P. 249 (High Court in bankruptcy); *Ex p. Fernandez* (1861) 30 L.J.C.P. 321 (*nisi prius*); *Anderson* v. *Gorrie* [1895] 1 Q.B. 668 (High Court of colony).

[42] *Harvey* v. *Dyce* (1876) 4 R. 265; *Primrose* v. *Waterston* (1902) 4 F. 783; *cf. Scott* v. *Stansfield* (1868) L.R. 3 Ex. 220; *Houlden* v. *Smith* (1850) 14 Q.B. 841 (English county court); *Ryalls* v. *Leader* (1856) L.R. 1 Ex. 296 (county court in bankruptcy); *R. v. Crossley* [1909] 1 K.B. 411 (county court judge as Workmen's Compensation arbitrator); *R.* v. *Skinner* (1772) Lofft. 55 (chairman of quarter sessions); *Hamond* v. *Howell* (1689) 2 Mod. 219 (recorder); *Thomas* v. *Churton* (1862) 2 B. & S. 475 (coroner).

[43] *Gibb* v. *Scott* (1740) Elchies, Public Officer, 9; *Gibsons* v. *Marr* (1823) 3 Mur. 271; *Primrose* v. *Waterston* (1902) 4 F. 783; *Law* v. *Llewellyn* [1906] 1 K.B. 487; *Allardice* v. *Robertson* (1830) 4 W. & Sh. 102, to a contrary effect, is unsound.

[44] *Jekyll* v. *Moore* (1806) 6 Esp. 63; *Dawkins* v. *Lord Rokeby* (1875) L.R. 7 H.L. 744.

[45] *R.* v. *Skinner* (1772) Lofft. 55.

[46] *Moodie* v. *Henderson* (1800) Mor. 360; *Williamson* v. *Umphray* (1890) 17 R. 905; *Rome* v. *Watson* (1898) 25 R. 733; *Clarke* v. *Haddon* (1893) 3 S.L.T. 85.

[47] *Mackay* v. *Ford* (1860) 5 H. & N. 792; *Munster* v. *Lamb* (1883) 11 Q.B.D. 588; see also *Stewart* v. *Kyd* (1870) 7 S.L.R. 577.

[48] *Trotman* v. *Dunn* (1815) 4 Camp. 211; *cf. Kennedy* v. *Hilliard* (1859) 10 Ir.C.L.R. 195; *Seaman* v. *Netherclift* (1876) 1 C.P.D. 540.

[49] *Mackintosh* v. *Weir* (1875) 2 R. 877; *A.B.* v. *C.D.* (1904) 7 F. 72, affd. *sub nom. Watson* v. *McEwan* (1905) 7 F.(H.L.) 109; *Slack* v. *Barr*, 1918, 1 S.L.T. 133; *cf. Dawkins* v. *Rokeby* (1875) L.R. 7 H.L. 744; *Seaman* v. *Netherclift* (1876) 2 C.P.D. 53; *Goffin* v. *Donnelly* (1881) 6 Q.B.D. 307; *Hargreaves* v. *Bretherton* [1959] 1 Q.B. 45; *Marrinan* v. *Vibart* [1962] 3 All E.R. 380. Older cases, such as *Watson* v. *Burnet* (1862) 24 D. 494 and *Rogers* v. *Dick* (1863) 1 M. 411, must be treated as disapproved.

[50] *Dawkins* v. *Rokeby, supra*; *Munster* v. *Lamb* (1883) 11 Q.B.D. 588; *Kennedy* v. *Hilliard* (1859) 10 Ir.C.L.R. 195.

[51] *Watson* v. *McEwan* (1905) 7 F.(H.L.) 109; *cf. Beresford* v. *White* (1914) 30 T.L.R. 591.

[52] *Wilson* v. *Collins* (1832) 5 C. & P. 373; *Delegal* v. *Highley* (1837) 3 Bing.N.C. 950; *Lynam* v. *Gowring* (1880) 6 L.R.Ir. 259; *Farmer* v. *Hyde* [1937] 1 K.B. 728.

[53] *Rome* v. *Watson* (1898) 25 R. 733.

[54] *Wilson* v. *Purvis* (1891) 18 R. 72 (qualified privilege provided acting within instructions).

[55] *Forteith* v. *Earl of Fife* (1821) 2 Mur. 463; *Ewing* v. *Cullen* (1833) 6 W. & Sh. 566; *Williamson* v. *Umphray* (1890) 17 R. 905; *Neill* v. *Henderson* (1901) 3 F. 387; *Slack* v. *Barr*, 1918, 1 S.L.T. 133.

[56] *Scott* v. *Turnbull* (1884) 11 R. 1131; *M.* v. *H.*, 1908 S.C. 1130; *Mitchell* v. *Smith*, 1919 S.C. 664; *McGillivray* v. *Davidson*, 1934 S.L.T. 45.   [57] *Williamson* v. *Umphray* [1890] 17 R. 905.

[58] *McMurchy* v. *Campbell* (1887) 14 R. 725, 728; *cf. Henderson* v. *Robertson* (1853) 15 D. 292; *Hester* v. *Macdonald,* 1961 S.C. 370.

[59] *Cf. Craig* v. *Peebles* (1876) 3 R. 441; in summary jurisdiction it may be that the privilege is absolute also; words used may not be covered by the protection of the Summary Jurisdiction (Scotland) Act, 1954, s. 75.

It matters not that the words were spoken maliciously, without reasonable or probable cause, or were entirely irrelevant to the matter under investigation in court, and no averments of any of these circumstances will justify inquiry.[60]

But absolute privilege applies only to statements by judges in their judicial capacity, and no privilege would attach to defamatory words spoken by a judge outside that capacity or after the business of the court is over.[61] The same doubtless applies to the privilege of counsel, and witnesses are protected only while acting as such.[62]

In English law it has been laid down that, in the case of judges of inferior courts, the judge is protected only if acting within his jurisdiction,[63] and not if acting *ultra vires*, provided that the plaintiff can show that the judge knew or ought to have known that he had no jurisdiction. In Scotland this distinction has not been drawn, and absolute privilege attaches equally to all judges when acting within their jurisdiction,[64] and equally may not protect any judge, of whatever rank, who is acting outwith his jurisdiction.[65]

Statements between solicitor and client in relation to the business underlying the relationship, such as instructions to the solicitor, enjoys qualified privilege only.[66] There is no privilege at all if the communication is not pertinent to the professional relationship.[67]

Statements in quasi-judicial proceedings. Absolute privilege similarly protects persons exercising functions comparable to those of judges of the ordinary courts of civil and criminal jurisdiction.[68] Thus it protects the president of a court-martial,[69] a county court judge sitting as an arbitrator under the former Workmen's Compensation Act,[70] a person holding an ecclesiastical inquiry,[71] the benchers of an Inn of Court considering a matter of professional misconduct,[72] the (English) Solicitors' Discipline Committee,[73] the General Medical Council Discipline Committee,[74] and a J.P. dealing with an application for the detention of a lunatic.[75]

---

[60] *Scott* v. *Stansfield* (1868) L.R. 3 Ex. 220; *McMurchy* v. *Campbell* (1887) 14 R. 745; *Anderson* v. *Gorrie* [1895] 1 Q.B. 668; *Tughan* v. *Craig* [1918] 1 Ir.R. 245; *More* v. *Weaver* [1928] 2 K.B. 520.

[61] *Seaman* v. *Netherclift* (1876) 1 C.P.D. 540; *Paris* v. *Levy* (1890) 9 C.B.(N.S.) 342.

[62] *Trotman* v. *Dunn* (1815) 4 Camp. 211; *Seaman* v. *Netherclift, supra*; *Hope* v. *Leng, Ltd.* (1907) 23 T.L.R. 243.

[63] *Miller* v. *Seare* (1777) 2 W.Bl. 1141; Gatley, 174.

[64] *Harvey* v. *Dyce* (1877) 4 R. 265; *Primrose* v. *Waterston* (1902) 4 F. 783.

[65] *Hamilton* v. *Anderson* (1856) 18 D. 1003.

[66] *Williamson* v. *Umphray* (1890) 17 R. 905; Lord Shand seems to have thought the privilege might be absolute. *Cf. Minter* v. *Priest* [1930] A.C. 558 (privilege, possibly qualified only, covering solicitor and prospective client), but *More* v. *Weaver* [1928] 2 K.B. 520, favours absolute privilege. [67] *Minter, supra.*

[68] *Royal Aquarium Society* v. *Parkinson* [1892] 1 Q.B. 431, 442, *per* Lord Esher M.R., approved in *O'Connor* v. *Waldron* [1935] A.C. 76, 81, *per* Lord Atkin.

[69] *Jekyll* v. *Sir John Moore* (1806) 6 Esp. 63; *Dawkins* v. *Rokeby* (1875) L.R. 7 H.L. 744.

[70] *R.* v. *Crossley* [1909] 1 K.B. 411. [71] *Barratt* v. *Kearns* [1905] 1 K.B. 504.

[72] *Lincoln* v. *Daniels* [1961] 3 All E.R. 740. *Cf. Marrinan* v. *Vibart* [1962] 3 All E.R. 380.

[73] *Lilley* v. *Roney* (1892) 61 L.J.Q.B. 727; *Addis* v. *Crocker* [1961] 1 Q.B. 11.

[74] *Leeson* v. *G.M.C.* (1889) 43 Ch.D. 366; *cf. Allbut* v. *G.M.C.* (1889) 23 Q.B.D. 400; *Thompson* v. *N.S.W. Branch B.M.A.* [1924] A.C. 764.

[75] *Hodson* v. *Pare* [1899] 1 Q.B. 455; *cf. Everett* v. *Griffiths* [1921] 1 A.C. 631.

The privilege does not, however, extend to persons or bodies who do not have recognised quasi-judicial functions. Thus it is inapplicable to a domestic tribunal, such as a club committee,[76] a medical referee,[77] and to bodies exercising administrative functions, even though in so doing they may have to hear witnesses and administer oaths, and to act with judicial impartiality, such as a meeting of a local authority to grant music and dancing licences,[78] a meeting of justices to deal with liquor licences,[79] a Court of Referees under the former Unemployment Insurance Act, 1920,[80] or an inspector appointed by the Industrial Assurance Commissioner.[81] The Bar Council in England has no judicial functions.[82]

It may be difficult to determine whether a person or body exercises judicial functions. That depends on the constitution, functions and procedure of the body in question.[83] It is, moreover, a condition for the existence of absolute privilege that the principles of natural justice are observed.[84]

The position of church courts is doubtful; there is authority for absolute privilege,[85] and also for only qualified privilege.[86] The courts of dissenting churches may have absolute privilege when acting within the jurisdiction conferred by the constitution of the church.[87] An elder speaking in the Kirk Session has qualified privilege only.[88]

Statements in documents in judicial or quasi-judicial proceedings. Absolute privilege attaches also to statements contained in written pleadings, even though they are introduced unnecessarily, are irrelevant, and have been inserted without instructions from the client and without any information from him which would justify them.[89] But there is no privilege at all if a litigant sends his pleading to a newspaper for publication, in which case, if the pleading is defamatory, the person sending in the pleading and the paper publishing it are both liable in damages.[90]

---

76   Hope v. I'Anson (1901) 18 T.L.R. 201; cf. Chapman v. Ellesmere [1932] 2 K.B. 431; Green v. Blake [1948] Ir.R. 242: Russell v. Norfolk [1949] 1 All E.R. 109.
77   Smith v. National Meter Co. [1945] K.B. 543.
78   Royal Aquarium Society v. Parkinson [1892] 1 Q.B. 431; R. v. L.C.C., re Empire Theatre (1894) 71 L.T. 638.
79   Attwood v. Chapman [1914] 3 K.B. 275; cf. Boulter v. Kent Justices [1897] A.C. 556; R. v. Sharman [1898] 1 Q.B. 578; R. v. Howard [1902] 2 K.B. 363.
80   Collins v. Whiteway [1927] 2 K.B. 378.
81   Hearts of Oak Assce. Co. v. Att.-Gen. [1932] A.C. 392.
82   Lincoln v. Daniels [1961] 3 All E.R. 740.
83   Copartnership Farms v. Harvey-Smith [1918] 2 K.B. 405; see also Hodson v. Pare [1899] 1 Q.B. 455; Barratt v. Kearns [1905] 1 K.B. 504.
84   Leeson v. G.M.C. (1889) 43 Ch.D. 366; Hodson, supra; G.M.C. v. Spackman [1943] A.C. 627.
85   Sturrock v. Greig (1849) 11 D. 1220; Robertson v. Preston (1780) Mor. 7465 (Kirk-Session); Porteous v. Izat (1781) Mor. 13937 (party to cause in General Assembly); cf. MacQueens v. Grant (1781) Mor. 7466; Adam v. Allan (1841) 3 D. 1058.
86   McDougal v. Campbell (1828) 6 S. 742 (Kirk-Session); Dunbar v. Presbytery of Auchterarder (1849) 12 D. 284.
87   Thallon v. Kinninmont (1856) 18 D. 27; Sturrock, supra. See also Edwards v. Begbie (1850) 12 D. 1134; McMillan v. Free Church of Scotland (1862) 24 D. 1282.
88   McDougal v. Campbell (1827) 6 S. 742.
89   Rome v. Watson (1898) 25 R. 733.
90   Richardson v. Wilson (1879) 7 R. 237; MacLeod v. Ross (1892) 20 R. 218. Cf. Gaskell & Chambers v. Hudson [1936] 2 K.B. 595.

Absolute privilege doubtless also covers statements in criminal indictments and complaints.[91]

Privilege attaches also to statements contained in affidavits or written declarations,[92] in interrogatories, and presumably in dying depositions, in precognitions,[93] in the judgment of the court,[94] record of court proceedings,[95] report by court-martial president in that capacity,[96] report by official receiver to the court or to the Board of Trade,[97] and a solicitor's account.[98]

The privilege covers also any document reasonably incidental to the initiation or conclusion of judicial or quasi-judicial proceedings, such as a letter of complaint against a solicitor forwarded to the Law Society with a view to disciplinary action,[99] or an application for an order for the detention of a mental patient,[1] or a solicitor's account, provided the statement is relevant and necessary and not gratuitously added.[2] It does not cover a letter to a judge relative to a matter due to come before him,[3] nor the publication of a summons which has been called,[4] nor a summary of an open or closed record not yet debated.[5] It covers also decrees of court, extracts thereof, and copies of entries in the Public Registers.[6]

Reports of judicial proceedings. The Law of Libel Amendment Act, 1888, as amended by the Defamation Act, 1952, s. 8, confers what has been understood to be absolute privilege on fair and accurate reports of proceedings publicly heard before courts exercising judicial authority within the United Kingdom, but these statutory provisions are not applicable to Scotland. In Scotland fair and accurate reports of judicial proceedings apparently enjoy absolute privilege in all cases at common law,[7] but comment on those proceedings enjoys only qualified privilege.[8] The report must be, and must if challenged be proved to be, fair and

---

91 But not the charge-sheet in a police-station: *Furniss* v. *Cambridge News, Ltd. (No. 2)* (1907) 23 T.L.R. 705.
92 *Henderson* v. *Broomhead* (1859) 28 L.J.Ex. 360; *Kennedy* v. *Hilliard* (1859) 10 Ir.C.L.R. 195; *Gompas* v. *White* (1890) 6 T.L.R. 20; *Lilley* v. *Roney* (1892) 61 L.J.Q.B. 725.
93 *Watson* v. *McEwan* (1905) 7 F.(H.L.) 109.
94 *Jekyll* v. *Sir John Moore* (1806) 6 Esp. 63; *Addis* v. *Crocker* [1960] 2 All E.R. 629; *Sturrock* v. *Greig* (1849) 11 D. 1220 (Kirk-Session judgment).
95 *MacCabe* v. *Joynt* [1901] 2 Ir.R. 115.
96 *Home* v. *Bentinck* (1820) 2 B. & B. 130; *Dawkins* v. *Prince Edward of Saxe-Weimar* (1876) 1 Q.B.D. 499.
97 *Bottomley* v. *Brougham* [1908] 1 K.B. 584; *Burr* v. *Smith* [1909] 2 K.B. 306.
98 *Bruton* v. *Downes* (1859) 1 F. & F. 668.
99 *Lilley* v. *Roney* (1892) 61 L.J.Q.B. 727.
1 *Hodson* v. *Pare* [1899] 1 Q.B. 455.
2 *Bruton* v. *Downes* (1859) 1 F. & F. 668; *More* v. *Weaver* [1928] 2 K.B. 520. Cf. *Minter* v. *Priest* [1930] A.C. 558.
3 *Gould* v. *Hume* (1829) 3 C. & P. 625.
4 *Richardson* v. *Wilson* (1879) 7 R. 237; cf. *Harper* v. *Provincial Newspapers*, 1937 S.L.T. 462.
5 *Macleod* v. *Justices of Lewis* (1892) 20 R. 218.
6 *Newton* v. *Fleming* (1848) 6 Bell 175.
7 *Drew* v. *Mackenzie* (1862) 24 D. 649, 656, per Lord Curriehill; *Richardson* v. *Wilson* (1880) 7 R. 237, 241, per L.P. Inglis; *Wright* v. *Outram* (1889) 16 R. 1004, 1006, per L.O. Kyllachy; *Macleod* v. *Justices of Lewis* (1893) 20 R. 218, 220, 221. As to proceedings in General Assembly, see *Porteous* v. *Izat* (1781) Mor. 13937; *sed quaere.*
8 *Drew, supra*; *Wright, supra.*

accurate; if inaccurate, incomplete, or biased, it loses privilege.[9] It need not be verbatim.[10] Correct copies of court decrees are entitled to privilege if published, as are accurate reports of criminal convictions.[11]

(9) *Proof that the statement was made in circumstances of qualified privilege*

The law confers a qualified privilege on the uttering of statements which may be defamatory in circumstances where, for reasons of public policy and overriding general benefit, plain speaking is justifiable and necessary, even at the risk of defaming another person. The justification for this protection has been said to be " the common convenience and welfare of society," [12] " because the amount of public inconvenience from the restriction of freedom of speech or writing would far out-balance that arising from the infliction of a private injury," [13] because " it is better for the general good that individuals should occasionally suffer than that freedom of communication between persons in certain relations should be in any way impeded," [14] or " because it is in the public interest that persons should be allowed to speak freely on occasion when it is their duty to speak, and to tell all they know or believe, or on occasions when it is necessary to speak in the protection of some common interest." [15] " The basis of the law as to privilege is that it is in the public interest that an individual who, on reasonable grounds and from a sense of duty, makes a prejudicial statement as to another, should not be deterred from doing so by the fear of an action of damages." [16]

" It may be unfortunate that a person against whom a charge that is not true is made should have no redress, but it would be contrary to public policy and the general interests of business and society that persons should be hampered in the discharge of their duty or the exercise of their rights by constant fear of actions for slander." [17]

" The proper meaning of a privileged communication is only this: that the occasion on which the communication was made rebuts the inference prima facie arising from a statement prejudicial to the character of the plaintiff, and puts it upon him to prove that there was malice in fact, that the defendant was actuated by motives of personal spite or ill-will, independent of the occasion on which the communication was made." [18]

When plea appropriate. The plea of privilege only arises where it has been relevantly averred that matter has been communicated which is actionable as being false and defamatory, either *ex facie* or as interpreted

9 *Wright, supra.*
10 *Andrews* v. *Chapman* (1853) 3 C. & K. 286.
11 *Buchan* v. *N.B.Ry.* (1894) 21 R. 379.
12 *Toogood* v. *Spyring* (1834) 1 C.M. & R. 181, 193; *cf. MacIntosh* v. *Dun* [1908] A.C. 390; *Perera* v. *Peiris* [1949] A.C. 1.
13 *Huntley* v. *Ward* (1859) 6 C.B.(N.S.) 514, 517.
14 *Bowen* v. *Hall* (1881) 6 Q.B.D. 333, 343.   15 *Gerhold* v. *Baker* [1918] W.N. 368, 369.
16 *Hayford* v. *Forrester-Paton*, 1927 S.C. 740, 762, *per* Lord Anderson. *Cf. Hamilton* v. *Hope* (1827) 4 Mur. 222, 232, 245.
17 *Dunnet* v. *Nelson*, 1926 S.C. 764, 769, *per* Lord Sands.
18 *Wright* v. *Woodgate* (1835) 2 C.M. & R. 573, 577, *per* Parke B., approved in *James* v. *Baird*, 1916 S.C. 510, 520, *per* Lord Johnston, and *Cochrane* v. *Young*, 1922 S.C. 696, 701.

by an innuendo. It is only if the statement is held capable of conveying a defamatory meaning that any question of privilege need, or can, be considered.[19] " The very essence of a privileged occasion is that it protects statements that are defamatory and false, when, apart from the protection, the very character of the statement itself carries with it the implication of malice." [20]

The privilege, where it applies, is qualified in that it is not absolute or a complete immunity from legal liability, but conditional on the statement having been made (a) in circumstances where for reasons of public policy the law permits plain, even if defamatory, speaking, and also (b) honestly and without any improper motive, not maliciously. The degree of untruth, the seriousness of the defamation, the extent of resultant injury are not relevant, and will not rebut the privilege if these conditions are satisfied. The sets of circumstances where plain speaking is justifiable and protected by qualified privilege are not finally settled nor is the list closed, and the circumstances must depend on changing social and business conditions.[21]

Where a plea of qualified privilege is upheld the person making allegedly defamatory statements incurs no legal liability for defamation at all; qualified privilege, if upheld, is a complete defence as much as is absolute privilege.[22] The only difference is that the plea may be rebutted by evidence of circumstances.

The presumption of malice which arises from the making of a defamatory statement is rebutted by the fact that the statement was made in circumstances held to entitle the speaker to qualified privilege and hence to immunity from liability. It is presumed, that is, that a statement made in circumstances of qualified privilege, albeit defamatory, was made honestly and without improper motive. This can, however, be rebutted, and the defence of qualified privilege countered, by express averment and proof that the statement was in fact malicious, and made from an improper motive. In brief, malice in the sense of dishonest motive must be proved, and if proved, overcomes the immunity arising from qualified privilege, and imposes liability. " The proper meaning of a privileged communication is only this: that the occasion on which the communication was made rebuts the inference [of malice] prima facie arising from a statement prejudicial to the character of the plaintiff, and puts it upon him to prove that there was malice in fact—that the defendant was actuated by motives of personal spite or ill-will, independent of the occasion on which the communication was made." [23] " The principle on which

---

[19] James v. Baird, 1916 S.C.(H.L.) 158, 162, 163.
[20] Lyal v. Henderson, 1916 S.C.(H.L.) 167, 175, per L.C. Buckmaster.
[21] Adam v. Ward [1917] A.C. 309.
[22] McPherson v. Daniels (1829) 10 B. & C. 270; Wason v. Walter (1868) L.R. 4 Q.B. 73; Watt v. Longsdon [1930] 1 K.B. 130.
[23] Wright v. Woodgate (1835) 2 C.M.& R. 573, 577, per Parke B. approved in Somerville v. Hawkins (1851) 10 C.B. 583; cf. Laughton v. Sodor and Man (1872) L.R. 4 P.C. 495; Jenoure v. Delmege [1891] A.C. 73; Adam v. Ward [1917] A.C. 309; Cochrane v. Young, 1922 S.C. 696, 701.

the law of qualified privilege rests is this: that where words are published which are both false and defamatory the law presumes malice on the part of the person who publishes them. The publication may, however, take place under circumstances which create a qualified privilege. If so the presumption of malice is rebutted by the privilege, and . . . the plaintiff has to prove express malice on the part of the person responsible for the publication. The effect of proving express malice is sometimes spoken of as defeating the privilege . . . Although the occasion remains a privileged occasion, the privilege afforded by the occasion ceases to be an effective weapon of defence . . . Qualified privilege is a defence only to the extent that it throws on the plaintiff the burden of proving express malice. Directly the plaintiff succeeds in doing this the defence vanishes, and it becomes immaterial that the publication was on a privileged occasion." [24]

" According to the Scottish practice, when the words are in themselves false and calumnious and are put in issue, general malice is assumed from the fact of their being false and calumnious, and that being so, there is no necessity upon either party to refer specifically to malice. But the necessity to insert specific reference to malice arises in this way, that although a slander or libel may be false and calumnious in its terms, nevertheless it may have been used on an occasion which was privileged, in the sense that the person who uttered it had the right, erroneously and even falsely, to make his statement. In such circumstances malice enters a Scottish record by way of a suggestion by the pursuer that the privilege which the defender pleads disappears in consequence of the special malice which is averred; and it has been the practice for many years . . . that if the record is in that state, namely, that the defender pleads privilege and the pursuer counters it by a special plea of specific malice, the case approaches the jury in this situation, that, if in the course of the inquiry before them it does appear that the occasion was privileged, then the pursuer is entitled to prove as matter of fact circumstances going to the malice which would rebut the privilege." [25]

The critical factor is accordingly the motive for making the statement complained of. " It is obviously right that a person should not be allowed to abuse a privileged occasion by making it the opportunity for indulging in some private spite, or for using the occasion for some indirect purpose or under the influence of some indirect motive." [26] " A man's motive for publishing a libel on a privileged occasion may be an improper one, even though he believes the statement to be true. He may be moved by hatred or dislike or a desire to injure the subject of the libel and may be using the occasion for that purpose, and if he is doing so the publication

---

[24] *Smith* v. *Streatfeild* [1913] 3 K.B. 764, 769, *per* Bankes L.J.
[25] *Langlands* v. *Leng*, 1916 S.C.(H.L.) 102, 109, *per* Lord Shaw. See also *Forteith* v. *Earl of Fife*, Nov. 18, 1819 F.C.; *McLean* v. *Fraser* (1823) 3 Mur. 353; *Adam* v. *Allan* (1841) 3 D. 1058; *Mackellar* v. *Duke of Sutherland* (1862) 24 D. 1124; *McBride* v. *Williams* (1869) 7 M. 427; *Auld* v. *Shairp* (1875) 2 R. 940.
[26] *Gerhold* v. *Baker* [1918] W.N. 368, 369, *per* Bankes L.J.

will be maliciously made even though he may believe the defamatory statements to be true." [27]

What is malice? Malice, actual or express or " in fact," includes not merely malevolence but all improper motives for making a defamatory communication, " animosity, ill-temper, love of scandal and gossip, or mere rash and thoughtless loquacity as induces a man to forget what is due to the fair fame of his neighbour," [28] " not only a bad motive but the want of any good motive; there need not be both because want of probable cause may be a good ground for inferring malice," [29] " a general temper of mind such as that here conceived by the defender, who had evidently lost all self-control," [30] " not a deep and deliberate desire to injure, but a reckless disregard of the comfort of others," [31] " gross recklessness and *culpa lata*," [32] " any indirect motive other than a sense of duty," [33] " not necessarily actual personal malice, but only such recklessness or gross carelessness and (it may be) ignorance as the law holds to be utterly inexcusable," [34] " every motive except the honest and pure wish fairly and sincerely to discharge a duty," [35] " any improper motive," [36] " an improper and malicious motive," [37] " [acting] from personal ill-will or from an indirect or improper motive," [38] that state of mind which leads the party to act not from a view of duty but of injury. [39]

Need for specific averment and proof. Actual malice must normally be specifically averred, not merely in general terms, but by setting out on record, and subsequently proving, facts and circumstances indicative of malice, or from which a jury may infer malice. [40] " If malice requires to be proved, then, as a general rule, a bare averment of malice will not be sufficient, for the simple reason that it does not afford to a defender adequate notice of the case which he will be called upon to meet." [41]

The requirement of specific averment of facts and circumstances is not invariable: " There are undoubtedly two classes of cases, in one of which a general allegation of malice is sufficient, while in the other the

---

[27] *Watt* v. *Longsdon* [1930] 1 K.B. 130, 154, *per* Greer L.J.
[28] *Adam* v. *Allan* (1841) 3 D. 1058, 1073.
[29] *Callendar* v. *Milligan* (1849) 11 D. 1174.
[30] *McDonald* v. *Fergusson* (1853) 15 D. 545.
[31] *Smith* v. *Green* (1854) 16 D. 549.
[32] *Cameron* v. *Hamilton* (1856) 18 D. 423.
[33] *Dickson* v. *Wilton* (1859) 1 F. & F. 419, 427.
[34] *Urquhart* v. *Grigor* (1865) 3 M. 283. *Cf. Bayne* v. *MacGregor* (1863) 1 M. 615.
[35] *Auld* v. *Shairp* (1875) 2 R. 940. *Cf. Adam, supra,* 1068, " violation of duty."
[36] *Suzor* v. *Buckingham,* 1914 S.C. 299, 304, 305; *cf. Scott* v. *Turnbull* (1884) 11 R. 1131, 1134.
[37] *Suzor* v. *McLachlan,* 1914 S.C. 306, 312.
[38] *Hayford* v. *Forrester-Paton,* 1927 S.C. 740, 747.
[39] *Hamilton* v. *Hope* (1827) 4 Mur. 222, 246.
[40] *Scott* v. *Turnbull* (1884) 11 R. 1131; *Gordon* v. *British & Foreign Metaline Co.* (1886) 14 R. 75; *Ingram* v. *Russell* (1893) 20 R. 771; *Sheriff* v. *Denholm* (1897) 5 S.L.T. 346; *Macdonald* v. *McColl* (1901) 3 F. 1082; *Lee* v. *Ritchie* (1904) 6 F. 642; *Campbell* v. *Cochrane* (1906) 8 F. 205; *M.* v. *H.,* 1908 S.C. 1130, 1135; *Dinnie* v. *Hengler,* 1910 S.C. 4; *Suzor* v. *McLachlan,* 1914 S.C. 306; *Cochrane* v. *Young,* 1922 S.C. 696, 705; *Dunnet* v. *Nelson,* 1926 S.C. 764; *Hayford* v. *Forrester-Paton,* 1927 S.C. 740.
[41] *Suzor* v. *McLachlan,* 1914 S.C. 306, 312, *per* L.P. Strathclyde.

more particular averments of malice . . . are required." [42] The matter is
one of degree rather than of distinct principles of relevancy.[43] " The
degree and character of the specification which is required for the purpose
of relevancy must vary with the circumstances of each case, but the
standard must always be such as to make the charge of malice prima facie
reasonable." [44]

Less specific averments are necessary where the circumstances appearing on record call for explanation on the defender's part,[45] and very
specific averments are required in the case of actions against public
officials [46] and actions for judicial slander, *i.e.*, slander by litigating
parties,[47] or instructions to counsel to make defamatory statements,[48]
and similarly where the alleged slander was in a report to the procurator-
fiscal.[49] The tendency is to widen the class of cases where specific averment is demanded,[50] and in *Rogers* v. *Orr* [51] it was said: " It may now be
regarded as settled in the practice of the court that, in all cases of privilege
alike, the pursuers' averments of malice must be supported by relative
(*sic*? relevant) averments of facts and circumstances, intrinsic or extrinsic,
which are relevant to infer malice on the part of the defender."

Extrinsic and intrinsic evidence of malice. The facts averred as affording evidence of malice are sometimes classified into extrinsic and intrinsic
circumstances.[52] Extrinsic circumstances are those outside the *res gestae*
and the terms of the statement or communication challenged as defamatory,[53] such as failure to make inquiry; intrinsic circumstances are those
which are parts of the *res gestae* and the statement or communication
challenged,[54] such as the language used and the incidents mentioned
therein. " If malice requires to be inferred from what have been called
extrinsic facts and circumstances, those extrinsic facts and circumstances
must be clearly set out upon the record. . . . But if, on the other hand,

[42] *Innes* v. *Adamson* (1889) 17 R. 11 approved by Lord Skerrington in *Suzor* v. *McLachlan*,
      1914 S.C. 306, 315, criticising the width of the dictum in *Macdonald* v. *McColl* (1901)
      3 F. 1082.
[43] *Ingram* v. *Russell* (1893) 20 R. 771.
[44] *Elder* v. *Gillespie*, 1923 S.L.T. 32.
[45] *Laidlaw* v. *Gunn* (1890) 17 R. 394; *Reid* v. *Moore* (1893) 20 R. 712; *Oliver* v. *Barnet*
      (1896) 3 S.L.T. 163; *Macdonald, supra*; contrast *Farquhar* v. *Neish* (1890) 17 R. 716;
      Sheriff v. *Denholm* (1897) 5 S.L.T. 346.
[46] *McMurchy* v. *Campbell* (1887) 14 R. 725; *Beaton* v. *Ivory* (1887) 14 R. 1057; *Innes* v.
      Adamson (1890) 17 R. 11; *Ingram, supra*; *Currie* v. *Weir* (1900) 2 F. 522; *cf. Buchanan* v.
      Glasgow Corpn. (1905) 7 F. 1001.
[47] *Scott* v. *Turnbull* (1884) 11 R. 1131; *Gordon* v. *British & Foreign Metaline Co.* (1887) 14 R.
      75; *Beaton* v. *Ivory* (1887) 14 R. 1062; *Adams* v. *Speedie* (1901) 8 S.L.T. 53; *Stevenson* v.
      Wilson (1903) 5 F. 309; *Campbell* v. *Cochrane* (1906) 8 F. 214; *M.* v. *H.*, 1908 S.C. 1130;
      Suzor, supra, 319; *Mitchell* v. *Smith*, 1919 S.C. 664, 673.
[48] *Williamson* v. *Umphray* (1890) 17 R. 905.
[49] *Urquhart* v. *Grigor* (1865) 3 M. 283.
[50] *Macdonald, supra*, but criticised in *Suzor, supra*.
[51] 1938 S.C. 121, 133, *per* Lord Moncrieff. *Cf.* L.P. Normand at p. 137.
[52] *Hamilton* v. *Hope*, 10 Mar. 1827, F.C.; 4 Mur. 244; *Torrance* v. *Leaf* (1834) 13 S. 1146;
      Hayford v. *Forrester-Paton*, 1927 S.C. 740, 763; *cf. Adam* v. *Allan* (1841) 3 D. 1058.
[53] *Nevill* v. *Fine Arts Co.* [1895] 2 Q.B. 156, 171.
[54] *Thomas* v. *Bradbury, Agnew* [1906] 2 K.B. 627, 637; *Adam* v. *Ward* [1917] A.C. 309, 318;
      Turner v. *M.G.M.* [1950] 1 All E.R. 449.

malice is to be inferred from the form of language used on the occasions complained of . . . then the language itself is the fact and circumstance from which malice must be inferred." [55] " If once the privilege be established, unless there be extrinsic evidence of malice, there must be something so extreme in the words used as to rebut the presumption of innocence and to afford evidence that there was a wrong, and an indirect, motive prompting the publication—*Spill* v. *Maule*.[56] " [57]

Direct evidence of malice. Direct evidence of malice may be provided by the nature of the defamatory words, in their nature alone affording evidence of express malice,[58] by antecedent dislike, quarrels or hatred,[59] refusal to make inquiry into the truth of accusations made against the pursuer or knowledge of their falsity,[60] repetition on several occasions,[61] or proof that the defender made the statement complained of in the knowledge that it was untrue.[62] " The fact that the defender knew the statement to be false is the best evidence of malice." [63] The bringing of unsuccessful actions against the pursuer also evidences malice,[64] as does an admission that the defender disapproved of music-hall performances, went to see if there was anything objectionable, and his object was to prevent a licence being granted.[65] In the case of judicial slander the irrelevance of the remarks may be evidence of malice.[66]

Malice inferred from circumstances. Malice has normally to be inferred from circumstances intrinsic to or extrinsic of the defamatory statement complained of. It may be inferred from a number of circumstances rather than from one single circumstance.[67] It has been said that the circumstances averred as showing malice must be of such proportion in relation to the slander as to make it reasonable to attribute the utterance complained of to the malice entertained,[68] but this has later been stated not to be taken as a general rule.[69] The evidence must be more consistent with malice than with an honest mind for the pursuer to succeed.[70]

Such an inference may be drawn if the statement was so violent as to afford evidence that it could not have been fairly and honestly made,[71]

55 *Suzor* v. *McLachlan,* 1914 S.C. 306, 312–313, *per* L.P. Strathclyde. *Cf. Boyd* v. *Reid* (1801) Hume 610.
56 (1869) L.R. 4 Ex. 232.
57 *Lyal* v. *Henderson,* 1916 S.C.(H.L.) 167, 175, *per* L.C. Buckmaster.
58 *Adam* v. *Ward* [1917] A.C. 309, 328, *per* Viscount Dunedin; *cf. Graeme* v. *Cunningham* (1765) Mor. 13923.
59 *Newlands* v. *Shaw* (1833) 12 S. 550; *Keay* v. *Wilsons* (1843) 5 D. 407; *cf. Dinnie* v. *Hengler* 1910 S.C. 4, 7; *A.B.* v. *X.Y.,* 1917 S.C. 15, 20; *Hayford* v. *Forrester-Paton,* 1927 S.C. 740, 758.
60 *Suzor* v. *McLachlan,* 1914 S.C. 306.
61 *Elder* v. *Gillespie,* 1923 S.L.T. 32.
62 *Hayford* v. *Forrester-Paton,* 1927 S.C. 740, 754.
63 *Mitchell* v. *Smith,* 1919 S.C. 664, 674, *per* Lord Sands.
64 *Gordon* v. *British and Foreign Metaline Co.* (1886) 14 R. 75, 84–85.
65 *Royal Aquarium Soc.* v. *Parkinson* [1892] 1 Q.B. 431.
66 *McIntosh* v. *Flowerdew* (1851) 13 D. 726, 728, 735; *Mackellar* v. *Duke of Sutherland* (1859) 21 D. 222, 226.
67 *Bell* v. *Black* (1866) 38 Sc.Jur. 412.
68 *Dunnet* v. *Nelson,* 1926 S.C. 764, 770, *per* Lord Sands.
69 *Rogers* v. *Orr,* 1939 S.C. 121.   70 *Turner* v. *M.G.M.* [1950] 1 All E.R. 449.
71 *Lyal* v. *Henderson,* 1916 S.C.(H.L.) 167, 175, *per* L.C. Buckmaster.

or there was something so extreme in the words used as to rebut the presumption of innocence and afford evidence that there was a wrong, and an indirect, motive prompting the publication,[72] or if there is an unexplained contradiction between the words used and those used previously in relation to the same matter,[73] or if the statement was admittedly made to further the defendant's chance of election and to harm the opponent's chance,[74] or from the defender's demeanour and whole conduct in relation to the action, though not necessarily from the refusal to apologise when requested to.[75]

Malice may be inferred from the absence of probable cause for making the statement complained of,[76] from the fact that the defender's statements were known to be false or that he had no reasonable ground for thinking them true,[76] from lying in the witness-box when giving evidence,[77] from absence of inquiry before making an accusation of embezzling, and from making the charge not privately but before other employees,[78] from a change in the defender's demeanour towards the pursuer, apparent jealousy and the levelling of unfounded accusations,[79] the use of improper or intemperate language,[80] from the intensity, violence, virulence or recklessness of the language used,[81] from recklessness of statement on the part of the defender,[82] from the reckless and intemperate nature of the language used,[83] so violent as to afford evidence that it could not have been fairly and honestly made,[84] or if it were made recklessly, careless whether it be true or false,[85] or grossly exaggerated,[86] or repeatedly [87] or too widely.[88] Malice need not be inferred from the inaccuracy of the statement alone,[89] but it may.[90]

---

[72] *Lyal, supra,* quoting *Spill* v. *Maule* (1869) L.R. 4 Ex. 232.
[73] *Macdonald* v. *McColl* (1901) 3 F. 1082; *cf. Hamilton of Dalzell* v. *Glasgow Dairy Co.,* 1931 S.C.(H.L.) 67.
[74] *Pankhurst* v. *Hamilton* (1887) 3 T.L.R. 500; *Braddock* v. *Bevins* [1948] 1 All E.R. 450.
[75] *Couper* v. *Balfour,* 1913 S.C. 492, 502, 506.
[76] *Anderson* v. *Wishart* (1818) 1 Mur. 429; *Black* v. *Brown* (1826) 5 S. 478; *Callendar* v. *Milligan* (1849) 11 D. 1174; *McDonald* v. *Fergusson* (1853) 15 D. 545; *Green* v. *Chalmers* (1879) 6 R. 318; *Shaw* v. *Morgan* (1888) 15 R. 865; *Macdonald* v. *Martin,* 1935 S.C. 621, 643; *Notman* v. *Commercial Bank of Scotland,* 1938 S.C. 522, 531.
[77] *Turner* v. *M.G.M. Pictures* [1950] 1 All E.R. 449.
[78] *Dinnie* v. *Hengler,* 1910 S.C. 4, 7. *Cf. Ingram* v. *Russell* (1893) 20 R. 771; *Golden* v. *Jeffers,* 1936 S.L.T. 388.
[79] *Suzor* v. *Buckingham,* 1914 S.C. 299, 304. *Cf. Auld* v. *Shairp* (1875) 2 R. 940.
[80] *Lee* v. *Ritchie* (1904) 6 F. 642. *Cf. Forteith* v. *Earl of Fife* (1821) 2 Mur. 477; *Denholm* v. *Thomson* (1881) 8 R. 31; *McKinlay* v. *Ritchie* (1904) 11 S.L.T. 628.
[81] *Gall* v. *Slessor,* 1907 S.C. 708; *Suzor* v. *McLachlan,* 1914 S.C. 306, 313.
[82] *Hayford* v. *Forrester-Paton,* 1927 S.C. 740, 755.
[83] *A.B.* v. *X.Y.,* 1917 S.C. 15, 20.
[84] *Lyal* v. *Henderson,* 1916 S.C.(H.L.) 167, 175.
[85] *Clark* v. *Molyneux* (1877) 3 Q.B.D. 237; *Royal Aquarium Soc.* v. *Parkinson* [1892] 1 Q.B. 431.
[86] *Cf. Clark* v. *Molyneux, supra.*
[87] *McDougal* v. *Campbell* (1827) 6 S. 742; *Logan* v. *Weir* (1872) 10 S.L.R. 22; *Ritchie* v. *Barton* (1883) 10 R. 813; *Stuart* v. *Moss* (1886) 13 R. 299; *Ingram* v. *Russell* (1893) 20 R. 771, 778; *Douglas* v. *Main* (1893) 20 R. 793; *Neill* v. *Henderson* (1901) 3 F. 387.
[88] *Douglas* v. *Main* (1893) 20 R. 793.
[89] *McLean* v. *Adam* (1889) 16 R. 175.
[90] *Martin and Starke* v. *Cruikshanks* (1896) 23 R. 874; *Kennedy* v. *Henderson* (1904) 11 S.L.T. 156; see also *McTernan* v. *Bennett* (1899) 1 F. 333; *Stevenson* v. *Wilson* (1903) 5 F. 309, 316.

When malice should not be inferred. Malice should not be too readily inferred. " To submit the language used on privileged occasions to a strict scrutiny, and to hold all excess beyond the actual exigencies of the occasion to be evidence of express malice, would greatly limit, if not altogether defeat, the protection which the law gives to statements so made. See *Laughton* v. *Bishop of Sodor and Man.*[91] " [92] There is no authority either for the view that mere inadequacy of inquiry made by a defender is sufficient to give rise to an inference of malice,[93] nor is an error of judgment.[94] Recklessness of conduct or of statement must be serious and indeed gross to indicate malicious motive where there is no allegation of personal ill-will.[95] Malice cannot be inferred from the seriousness of the charge [96] nor from the fact that the defender had pleaded *veritas*,[97] nor from the fact that the statement is proved untrue.[98]

Nor should malice necessarily be inferred because the defamatory statement has been published carelessly or negligently,[99] or made on record and not withdrawn when found to be false,[1] or made by reason of a mis-understanding,[2] nor if it appears that the defender honestly believed his statement to be true, even though it was not, and even though he did not have reasonable or sufficient grounds for believing it to be true,[3] unless indeed the grounds stated for belief were such that no sensible person could possibly have accepted them,[4] nor because the defender failed to make further inquiries [5] unless it amounted to deliberately ignoring contrary facts.[6]

Nor again should malice be inferred because the defender was hasty or stupid in coming to his conclusion [7] or without the sound judgment which prudence would dictate, so long as the action was taken bona fide.[8] Irrationality, stupidity or obstinacy do not constitute malice, though in an extreme case they may be some evidence of it.[9]

[91] (1872) L.R. 4 P.C. 495.
[92] *Lyal* v. *Henderson*, 1916 S.C.(H.L.) 167, 175, *per* L.C. Buckmaster, approved in *A.B.* v. *X.Y.*, 1917 S.C. 15; *Hayford, infra.*
[93] *Hayford* v. *Forrester-Paton*, 1927 S.C. 740, 755.
[94] *Ibid.* 756.
[95] *Ibid.* 763.
[96] *Lyal* v. *Henderson*, 1916 S.C.(H.L.) 167, 183; *Hayford* v. *Forrester-Paton*, 1927 S.C. 740, 748.
[97] *Hayford, supra*, 749, 756, 759.
[98] *Fountain* v. *Boodle* (1842) 3 Q.B. 5.
[99] *Capital and Counties Bank* v. *Henty* (1880) 5 C.P.D. 514.
[1] *McCaig* v. *Moscrip* (1872) 10 S.L.R. 140; contrast *Bell* v. *Black* (1866) 38 Sc.Jur. 412.
[2] *McLean* v. *Adam* (1888) 16 R. 175.
[3] *Clark* v. *Molyneux* (1877) 3 Q.B.D. 237; *Howe* v. *Jones* (1885) 1 T.L.R. 461; *Collins* v. *Cooper* (1902) 19 T.L.R. 118.
[4] *Brown* v. *Hawkes* [1891] 2 Q.B. 718; *White* v. *Credit Reform* [1905] 1 K.B. 653.
[5] *Clark, supra*; *Cooke* v. *Brogden* (1885) 1 T.L.R. 497; *Couper* v. *Balfour*, 1913 S.C. 492; *A.B.* v. *X.Y.*, 1917 S.C. 15.
[6] *Clark, supra*; *Lee* v. *Ritchie* (1904) 6 F. 642; *Dinnie* v. *Hengler*, 1910 S.C. 4; *Suzor* v. *McLachlan*, 1914 S.C. 306.
[7] *Clark, supra*; *Capital and Counties Bank* v. *Henty* (1880) 5 C.P.D. 514; *Brown* v. *Hawkes* [1891] 2 Q.B. 718.
[8] *Hayford, supra*, 755.
[9] *Turner* v. *M.G.M. Pictures* [1950] 1 All E.R. 449.

Malice and defamation by agents. The malice of an agent does not establish malice against the principal.[9a] It may be personal on his part, as where he has made a charge without instructions from his principal,[9b] or where he has identified himself with the charge made by him as agent for his principal.[10] An innocent servant is not liable to a defamed person if he publishes defamatory matter on an occasion of qualified privilege even though his employer was malicious.[11]

Malice and joint liability for defamation. Where two or more persons are responsible, and therefore jointly and severally liable, for defamation, malice on the part of one who alone is privileged does not infect the other or others so as to defeat their plea of derivative privilege,[12] but it would defeat a plea of fair comment.[13] And where one defender is held to be malicious that does not affect the privilege of the other or others if he or they have an independent privilege to publish the statement complained of.[14]

Malice and lack of probable cause. In pure defamation cases it is always sufficient, to rebut the plea of qualified privilege, to aver and prove actual or express malice. The pursuer never has to aver and prove malice and lack of probable cause.[15] " The cases clearly establish that, except in the three recognised categories [actions for abuse of process, actions for malicious prosecution or denunciation, and actions directed against public officers for words spoken or written, or acts done, in the discharge of their public duties [16]] ' want of probable cause ' has no place in issues of defamation. But this does not mean that in actions of defamation a defender may not prove probable cause as negativing or tending to negative malice, or that a pursuer may not prove want of probable cause as showing or tending to show malice." [17] Cases of the three categories mentioned may have defamatory implications and the defamation may be the most material ingredient in the injury suffered, but they are not pure actions for defamation and none of the cases thereon is authority for importing the element of lack of probable cause into an issue of pure defamation.[18]

Functions of court and jury in relation to privilege. The plea of qualified privilege must be tabled by the defender. It is a question of law for the

---

[9a] *Mackellar* v. *Duke of Sutherland* (1862) 24 D. 1124.
[9b] *Wilson* v. *Purvis* (1890) 18 R. 72; *Watson* v. *Ross* (1897) 5 S.L.T. 182. *Cf. Edmonson* v. *Cartner* (1905) 13 S.L.T. 78.
[10] *Crawford* v. *Adams* (1900) 2 F. 987.
[11] *Egger* v. *Viscount Chelmsford* [1964] 3 All E.R. 406.
[12] *Smith* v. *Streatfeild* [1913] 3 K.B. 764; *Adam* v. *Ward* [1917] A.C. 309; *Smith* v. *National Meter Co.* [1945] K.B. 543; *Eglantine Inn* v. *Smith* [1948] N.I. 29; *Egger* v. *Viscount Chelmsford* [1964] 3 All E.R. 406; *cf.* Defamation Act, 1952, s. 4 (6).
[13] *Thomas* v. *Bradbury, Agnew & Co.* [1906] 2 K.B. 627; *Egger, supra.*
[14] *Longdon Griffiths* v. *Smith* [1950] 2 All E.R. 662, distinguishing *Smith, supra,* and *Thomas supra.*
[15] *Webster* v. *Paterson,* 1910 S.C. 459, 468; *Macdonald* v. *Martin,* 1935 S.C. 621, 638, 643; *Notman* v. *Commercial Bank of Scotland,* 1938 S.C. 522, 531. See also *Rae* v. *R.S.S.P.C.C,* 1924 S.C. 102.
[16] *Notman, supra,* 531.
[17] *Notman, supra,* 535, *per* L.J.C. Aitchison, delivering judgment of Court of Seven Judges.
[18] *Notman, supra; cf. Robertson* v. *Keith,* 1936 S.C. 29.

court whether, if the statement is capable of a defamatory meaning, the concomitant circumstances alleged are such as to bring the case within any of the recognised classes of occasions protected by qualified privilege,[19] but this decision may not be capable of decision on relevancy and may have to await proof of the facts.[20]

Qualified privilege is conditional on the absence of indirect or ulterior motive for the communication, *i.e.*, absence of malice, in the sense of malevolence, spite or ill-will. The pursuer may therefore counter a defence of qualified privilege by a plea of actual malice, and the onus of proof of malice is on the pursuer, the defender being presumed, on a privileged occasion, to have acted in bona fide. If malice is relevantly averred the case must go to the jury. The presence or absence of malice in the circumstances is a question of fact. If the occasion is admitted or held to be privileged, the action is irrelevant unless actual malice on the defender's part be relevantly averred.[21]

" It is well settled that the question whether a defamatory statement has been published on a privileged occasion is for the judge and not for the jury. If the occasion is privileged, it is for the jury to say whether, in making the communication, the defender was actuated by malice. Before, however, the case reaches the jury, the judge who presides must be satisfied that facts have been proved from which an inference of malice may be drawn. In many, though perhaps not in all, cases of admitted privilege, the Court which approves of the issue must be satisfied that facts have been set forth from which an inference of express malice may be drawn." [22]

If the court holds the statement complained of to be incapable of conveying a defamatory meaning, the question of privilege falls. If the court holds the statement capable of conveying a defamatory meaning and not to have been made on a privileged occasion the question of malice falls.

Privilege belongs to occasions. Qualified privilege attaches to occasions, not to the persons who make communications, nor to kinds of statements. " The distinction must always be drawn between the communication and its occasion. It is the occasion which is privileged, not the communication; or only the communication through the occasion." [23] Any person may make a privileged communication, and any statement may be privileged, if the occasion is one to which in the circumstances qualified

19 *Torrance* v. *Leaf* (1834) 13 S. 1146; *Fenton* v. *Currie* (1843) 5 D. 705; *James* v. *Baird*, 1916 S.C. 510, 517; *cf. Toogood* v. *Spyring* (1834) 1 C.M. & R. 181; *Stuart* v. *Bell* [1891] 2 Q.B. 341; *Adam* v. *Ward* [1917] A.C. 309; *Hayford* v. *Forrester-Paton*, 1927 S.C. 740; *Minter* v. *Priest* [1930] A.C. 558.
20 *Hebditch* v. *MacIlwaine* [1894] 2 Q.B. 54, 58; *Smyth* v. *Mackinnon* (1897) 24 R. 1086; *McCallum* v. *McDiarmid* (1900) 2 F. 357; *Adam* v. *Ward* [1917] A.C. 309; *Hayford* v. *Forrester-Paton*, 1927 S.C. 740, 759.
21 *Chiene* v. *Archibald* (1868) 6 S.L.R. 62; *Barr* v. *Musselburgh Merchants Association*, 1912 S.C. 174.
22 *Hayford* v. *Forrester-Paton*, 1927 S.C. 740, 759, *per* Lord Hunter.
23 *James* v. *Baird*, 1916 S.C. 510, 520, *per* Lord Johnston.

privilege attaches by law. " The circumstances that constitute a privileged occasion can themselves never be catalogued and rendered exact. New arrangements of business, even new habits of life, may create unexpected combinations of circumstances which, though they differ from well known instances of privileged occasion, may none the less fall within the plain yet flexible language of the definition to which I have referred." [24]

The court has frequently held statements to be, at least on the pleadings, not privileged. Instances include a doctor stating to the patient's husband that the midwife had poisoned the patient [25]; a bank agent charging a customer with forgery [26]; a tradesman accusing an architect, who had condemned his work, of unfairness [27]; the members of a football committee censuring the conduct of a player and publishing their decision [28]; a newspaper publishing a false birth notice [29]; but in some such cases the possibility of the emergence of a case of privilege at the trial has been reserved, it being in such a case competent for the trial judge to take account of it and to direct the jury appropriately as to privilege and malice.

Privilege independent of seriousness of charge. If an occasion is privileged the defender enjoys the protection thereof, whether the defamation be trivial or serious, and the seriousness of the charge made is not by itself evidence of malice destroying privilege. [30]

Criterion of privilege objective. An occasion is not privileged because the defender thinks it is, but only if it is so in law. [31] Hence a communication addressed to the wrong person by a defender under a misapprehension in fact is not protected. [32] " I am unable to see how an occasion, which in point of fact is not privileged, can become privileged because the defender, in good faith and on grounds which commended themselves to her, considered that it was privileged. Her good faith, however strong its foundation, cannot convert a non-privileged occasion into a privileged occasion, although it may afford excellent evidence of the absence of malice." [33]

On what occasions does privilege attach? " In considering the question whether the occasion was an occasion of privilege, the court will regard

---

[24] *London Association for Protection of Trade* v. *Greenlands, Ltd.* [1916] 2 A.C. 15, *per* L.C. Buckmaster, referring to Baron Parke's opinion in *Toogood* v. *Spyring* (1834) 1 C.M. & R. 181, 193, and quoted in *Cochrane* v. *Young*, 1922 S.C. 696, 702, by Lord Hunter.

[25] *Reid* v. *Coyle* (1892) 19 R. 775.

[26] *Ingram* v. *Russell* (1893) 20 R. 771.

[27] *Crawford* v. *Adams* (1900) 2 F. 987.

[28] *Murdison* v. *Scottish Football Union* (1896) 23 R. 449.

[29] *Morrison* v. *Ritchie* (1902) 4 F. 645.

[30] *Lyal* v. *Henderson*, 1916 S.C.(H.L.) 167, 183; *Hayford* v. *Forrester-Paton*, 1927 S.C. 740, 748.

[31] *Hebditch* v. *MacIlwaine* [1894] 2 Q.B. 54, 60; *Stuart* v. *Bell* [1891] 2 Q.B. 341, 349, 357; *James* v. *Baird*, 1916 S.C. 510, 517, *per* L.P. Strathclyde; *Cochrane* v. *Young*, 1922 S.C. 696.

[32] *James, supra.*

[33] *James, supra.*

the alleged libel and will examine by whom it was published, to whom it was published, when, why and in what circumstances it was published, and will see whether these things establish a relation between the parties which gives rise to a social or moral right or duty, and the consideration of these things may involve the consideration of questions of public policy as had to be done in . . . *Macintosh* v. *Dun* [1908] A.C. 390, at p. 400." [34]

" A communication honestly made upon any subject in which a person has an interest, social or moral, or in reference to which he has a duty, is privileged if made to a person having a corresponding interest or duty. But, obviously, the duty or interest on which the privilege rests must exist in fact. It is not sufficient for the person who makes the communication honestly to believe that a duty or interest exists. The defence of privilege fails even though the person making the communication reasonably believed that the person to whom he made it had some duty or interest in the subject-matter, if none such really existed." [35]

(A) *Statements Made in the Discharge of Duty*

An occasion is privileged if the speaker, when communicating the matter complained of as defamatory, is acting " in the discharge of some public or private duty, whether legal or moral, or in the conduct of his own affairs, in matters where his interest is concerned. In such cases the occasion prevents the inference of malice, which the law draws from un-authorised communications, and affords a qualified defence depending on the absence of actual malice. If fairly warranted by any reasonable occasion or exigency, and honestly made, such communications are protected for the common convenience and welfare of society." [36] Another formulation has been expressed thus: " A communication made bona fide upon any subject-matter in which the party communicating has an interest, or in reference to which he has a duty, is privileged if made to a person having a corresponding interest or duty . . ." [37] Or again: " If the statement be made in the discharge of a duty or in the reasonable attention to a man's own business and affairs, which gives him legitimate cause to write or speak of his neighbour, the occasion displaces the presumption of malice and the presumption of falsehood, and he is only answerable if malice be shown to have existed in fact, and if the statement be untrue." [38]

[34] *James* v. *Baird*, 1916 S.C.(H.L.) 158, 163–164, *per* Earl Loreburn.
[35] *James* v. *Baird*, 1916 S.C. 510, 517–518, *per* L.P. Strathclyde; *cf. Harrison* v. *Bush* (1855) 5 E. & B. 344; *Stuart* v. *Bell* [1891] 2 Q.B. 349; *Hebditch* v. *MacIlwaine* [1894] 2 Q.B. 60; *Jenoure* v. *Delmege* [1891] A.C. 73.
[36] *Toogood* v. *Spyring* (1834) 1 C.M. & R. 181, 193, *per* Parke B., approved in *Stuart* v. *Bell* [1891] 2 Q.B. 341; *Macintosh* v. *Dun* [1908] A.C. 390; *Barr* v. *Musselburgh Merchants Assocn.*, 1912 S.C. 174, 180; *A.B.* v. *X.Y.*, 1917 S.C. 15; *Hayford* v. *Forrester-Paton*, 1927 S.C. 740; *cf. Shaw* v. *Morgan* (1888) 15 R. 865, 870.
[37] *Harrison* v. *Bush* (1855) 5 E. & B. 344, 348, *per* Lord Campbell, C.J. See also *Pullman* v. *Hill* [1891] 1 Q.B. 524; *Stuart* v. *Bell, supra*; *Adam* v. *Ward* [1917] A.C. 309.
[38] *Shaw* v. *Morgan* (1888) 15 R. 865, 870, *per* Lord Young.

The duty may be public, owed to the community, such as the duty to disclose a crime, or private, owed only to the hearer, such as the duty to report the conduct of a subordinate; it may be legal, such as the duty to disclose information to the police, or merely moral or social, such as the duty to warn one person against another. It may be difficult to define what kind of social or moral duty will justify disclosure.[39] Moral duty in this context has been said to mean " a duty recognised by English people of ordinary intelligence and moral principle, but at the same time not a duty enforceable by legal proceedings, whether civil or criminal. . . . Would the great mass of right-minded men in the position of the defendant have considered it their duty under the circumstances to make the communications? " [40]

By " interest " is meant not the interest a man might have in gossip or satisfying his curiosity, but interest in the sense of its being a matter of material concern, of substance or of importance to him, which may be a factor in his future conduct. It need not be financial.

Duty and interest must be actual. It is not sufficient for a defender to show that he made a statement honestly and reasonably believing that he was under a duty to make it, or that the hearer had an interest to receive the communication. If the duty and interest did not in fact exist, the occasion was not privileged.[40a] This is a protection against far-fetched pleas of duty and interest.

Circumstances where Duty and Interest Exist

(i) *Voluntary statements*

A voluntary statement made by one party to another of and concerning a third is protected by qualified privilege if there was a social, moral or legal duty to volunteer the information complained of as defamatory. A moral duty to volunteer information is probably harder to justify than is a duty to answer enquiries.[41]

" Though the fact that a communication is volunteered is material on the question of malice—was the defendant a fussy busybody acting ' ultroneously ' or a person discharging a genuine social duty?—it is not conversely true that the issue of privilege can generally turn on this circumstance. Privilege must depend on the relations of the parties, on the duty arising, and on the occasion which is used or abused, not on the mere accident who spoke first. When this is critical it is on account of the nature of the duty, the discharge of which may or may not be consistent with volunteering the statement. There is no general rule that statements which would be privileged if made in answer to an enquiry cease to be so when the informant has not waited to be asked." [42] A

---

[39] *Cf. Whiteley* v. *Adams* (1863) 15 C.B.(N.S.) 392, 418.
[40] *Stuart* v. *Bell* [1891] 2 Q.B. 341, 350, *per* Lindley L.J., applied in *Watt* v. *Longsdon* [1930] 1 K.B. 130.
[40a] *Hebditch* v. *MacIlwaine* [1894] 2 Q.B. 54; *cf. James* v. *Baird*, 1916 S.C.(H.L.) 158.
[41] *Toogood* v. *Spyring* (1834) 1 C.M. & R., 181, 193.
[42] *Greenlands, Ltd.* v. *Wilmshurst* [1913] 3 K.B. 507, 535, *per* Hamilton L.J.

perfectly general warning issued voluntarily may be privileged: " to protect those who are not able to protect themselves is a duty which everyone owes to society." [43]

(ii) *Statements to achieve the ends of justice*

Giving information or making complaint. Every citizen has a public duty to give information known to him, or reasonably believed by him, about the commission of crime, and is therefore entitled and indeed bound to communicate voluntarily what he knows, or reasonably believes, may be of use to the police and the procurator-fiscal.[44]

Such a statement enjoys qualified privilege and if the person states only what he knows and honestly believes, he cannot be subjected to an action of damages merely because it turns out that the person as to whom he has given the information is, after all, not guilty of the crime,[45] and this is so even though the charge is found to be without foundation,[46] or if proceedings in respect thereof are subsequently abandoned.[47]

To be protected by privilege, however, any such information or complaint must be made to a person who has some duty in the matter, or some jurisdiction to deal with the complaint, and not to a third party.[48] Nor is ultroneous repetition to members of the public of an accusation already made to the police privileged.[49] So, too, persons who signed a petition to the Lord Advocate craving that criminal proceedings should be taken against certain persons for conspiracy and perjury were privileged so far as concerned the signature of the document, but were not privileged in instigating the circulation of the document among the public with a view to securing further signatures.[50] Privilege does not protect where a charge of theft was made wholly unjustifiably, when the goods had been taken and were being retained in reliance on a claim of lien.[51] Nor will privilege protect if there is evidence that the report or complaint was motivated by malice or desire to obtain some collateral advantage,[52] or was made recklessly.[53]

[43] *Jenoure* v. *Delmege* [1891] A.C. 73, quoted in *Baird* v. *James*, 1916 S.C.(H.L.) 158, 161, *per* L.C. Buckmaster.
[44] *Ferguson* v. *Colquhoun* (1862) 24 D. 1428; *Thomson* v. *Adam* (1875) 4 R. 29; *Green* v. *Chalmers* (1878) 6 R. 318; *Lightbody* v. *Gordon* (1882) 9 R. 934; *Hassan* v. *Paterson* (1885) 12 R. 1164; *Croucher* v. *Inglis* (1889) 16 R. 774; *Buchanan* v. *Glasgow Corpn.* (1906) 13 S.L.T. 203; *Kufner* v. *Berstecher*, 1907 S.C. 797; *West* v. *Mackenzie*, 1917 S.C. 513. *Cf. Mills* v. *Kelvin & White*, 1913 S.C. 521.
[45] *Lightbody, supra*, 937, *per* L.P. Inglis; *cf. Green, supra*; *Rae* v. *R.S.S.P.C.C.*, 1924 S.C. 102.
[46] *McPherson* v. *Cattanach* (1850) 13 D. 287; *cf. Rankine* v. *Roberts* (1875) 1 R. 225; *Croucher* v. *Inglis* (1889) 16 R. 774.
[47] *Sheppeard* v. *Fraser* (1849) 11 D. 446; *McPherson* v. *Cattanach* (1851) 13 D. 287; *cf. Smith* v. *Green* (1853) 15 D. 549.
[48] *Wenman* v. *Ash* (1853) 13 C.B. 836; *Harrison* v. *Fraser* (1881) 29 W.R. 652; *Hebditch* v. *MacIlwaine* [1894] 2 Q.B. 54; *Sevenoaks* v. *Latimer* (1920) 54 Ir.L.T. 11. *Cf. Hassan* v. *Paterson* (1885) 12 R. 1164.
[49] *Walker* v. *Cumming* (1868) 6 M. 318.
[50] *Dowgray* v. *Gilmour* (1906) 14 S.L.T. 104.
[51] *Kennedy* v. *Henderson* (1903) 11 S.L.T. 156.
[52] *Douglas* v. *Main* (1893) 20 R. 793; *Currie* v. *Weir* (1900) 2 F. 522; *Brown* v. *Fraser* (1906) 8 F. 1000; *Shaw* v. *Burns*, 1911 S.C. 537; *cf. Hooper* v. *Truscott* (1836) 2 Bing.N.C. 457.
[53] *Denholm* v. *Thomson* (1880) 8 R. 31.

Taxing suspect with misconduct. Qualified privilege, in the interest of furthering justice, similarly protects statements made to a suspected individual when inquiries are being made of him as to his conduct and his explanation of apparent crime or irregularities,[54] even though the suspicions turn out to be unjustified.[55] Malice may, of course, rebut this privilege, but malice will not be inferred merely from the facts that the defender made his accusation harshly or hastily,[56] or because he had no reasonable grounds for believing that his accusation was justified,[57] or from the fact that third parties are accidentally present or hear the accusation,[58] though it may be inferred from the facts that the accusation is made before more persons than necessary [59] or more loudly or violently than necessary.[60]

The privilege covers not only taxing the suspect with his alleged default, but making inquiries of others who are reasonably believed to be possibly able to assist by giving further information.[61] Nor is the privilege elided by the fact that third parties are present and hear the question or the charge, so long as there is no unnecessary communication to them.[62]

Statements made in course of police inquiries. A statement made by one police officer in answer to another also engaged in making inquiries about a suspected crime is protected by privilege.[63]

Threats of prosecution. A threat of prosecution or of being reported to the police or the procurator-fiscal may be innuendoed as imputing dishonesty or criminality and hence may be defamatory; some such cases have been held not entitled to qualified privilege,[64] but others have.[65]

(iii) *Complaints against public officials*

Any citizen is entitled, in the interests of good public administration and the avoidance of injustice, inefficiency and dishonesty, voluntarily to bring to the notice of the proper authority, any misconduct, inefficiency

---

54   *Blackett* v. *Lang* (1854) 16 D. 989; *Henderson* v. *Patrick Thomson, Ltd.*, 1911, 1 S.L.T. 284; *cf. Padmore* v. *Lawrence* (1840) 11 A. & E. 380; *Wallace* v. *Carroll* (1860) 11 Ir.C.L.R. 485; *Force* v. *Warren* (1864) 15 C.B.(N.S.) 806; *Collins* v. *Cooper* (1902) 19 T.L.R. 118; *Chalmers* v. *Barclay, Perkins & Co.*, 1912 S.C. 521; *Rogers* v. *Orr*, 1939 S.C. 121.
55   *Padmore* v. *Lawrence, supra*; *Amann* v. *Damm* (1860) 8 C.B.(N.S.) 597; *Howe* v. *Jones* (1885) 1 T.L.R. 19, 461; *Collins* v. *Cooper, supra*.
56   *Amann* v. *Damm, supra*; *Todd* v. *Hawkins* (1837) 8 C. & P. 88; *Brown* v. *Hawkes* [1891] 2 Q.B. 718.
57   *Clark* v. *Molyneux* (1877) 3 Q.B.D. 237; *Collins* v. *Cooper, supra*.
58   *Toogood* v. *Spyring* (1834) 1 C.M. & R. 181; *Jones* v. *Thomas* (1885) 53 L.T. 678; *Hassan* v. *Paterson* (1885) 12 R. 1164; *Howe* v. *Jones, supra*; *Gray* v. *Maitland* (1896) 4 S.L.T. 38.
59   *Padmore* v. *Lawrence* (1840) 11 A. & E. 380; *Toogood* v. *Spyring, supra.* See also *Ingram* v. *Russell* (1893) 20 R. 771.
60   *Padmore* v. *Lawrence, supra*.
61   *Kine* v. *Sewell* (1838) 3 M. & W. 297; *Force* v. *Warren* (1864) 15 C.B.(N.S.) 806; *Collins* v. *Cooper, supra*.
62   *Toogood, supra*; *Padmore, supra*.
63   *Malcolm* v. *Duncan* (1897) 24 R. 747.
64   *Wilson* v. *Purvis* (1890) 18 R. 72; *Ramsay* v. *McLay* (1890) 18 R. 130; see also *Brown* v. *Fraser* (1906) 8 F. 1000; *Handasyde* v. *Hepworth* (1907) 15 S.L.T. 180.
65   *Cumming* v. *G.N.S.Ry.*, 1916, 1 S.L.T. 181.

or neglect of duty on the part of public officials or servants, and any such communication or complaint, if made bona fide to the proper authority, is protected by qualified privilege.[66]

This principle has been applied to such cases as a constituent writing to his M.P. seeking the latter's assistance in bringing to a Minister's notice a complaint against a public official,[67] a resident sending to the Home Secretary a memorial complaining of the conduct of a magistrate for that county,[68] a person writing to the Postmaster-General complaining of the conduct of a postmaster,[69] a person complaining to the Chief Constable of the conduct of a police sergeant,[70] a complaint to the bishop of the diocese regarding the conduct of a beneficed clergyman,[71] a complaint to the presbytery of the misconduct of a parish minister,[72] a complaint from the commanding officer of an army unit to his immediate superior as to the conduct of the colonel,[73] a complaint from a ratepayer to the watch committee as to the conduct of a police superintendent,[74] a complaint to the parish council about the parish medical officer,[75] and a complaint by an hotel guest to the management about the conduct of an hotel servant.[76]

Similarly the master of a ship has been held privileged in making an entry in the ship's log complaining of disobedience to orders by the pursuer, the chief officer.[77]

Where privilege lost. The privilege is, however, lost if it be shown that the complaint was not made bona fide but was motivated by ill-will or other oblique motive,[78] or was made public earlier or more widely than necessary.

It may also be lost if the complaint is made to the wrong person or body, as to a person having no authority over or responsibility for the acts of the person complained of, and no power to remedy the abuse.[79] This principle, if applied strictly, would in modern circumstances tend to stifle legitimate complaints because of the complex organisation of modern public administration and the consequent substantial danger of addressing a reasonable complaint to the wrong person or authority.

---

[66] *Couper* v. *Balfour*, 1913 S.C. 492; *cf. Harrison* v. *Bush* (1855) 5 E. & B. 344; *Woodward* v. *Lander* (1834) 6 C. & P. 548; *Proctor* v. *Webster* (1885) 16 Q.B.D. 112.
[67] *R.* v. *Rule* [1937] 2 K.B. 375.
[68] *Harrison* v. *Bush* (1855) 5 E. & B. 344.
[69] *Warren* v. *Falconer* (1771) Mor. 13933; *cf. Blake* v. *Pitfold* (1832) 1 Moo. & Rob. 198; *Woodward* v. *Lander* (1834) 6 C. & P. 548.
[70] *Cassidy* v. *Connochie*, 1907 S.C. 1112.
[71] *James* v. *Boston* (1845) 2 C. & K. 4.
[72] *A.* v. *B.* (1895) 22 R. 984; *Barclay* v. *Manuel* (1903) 10 S.L.T. 450.
[73] *Dickson* v. *Earl of Wilton* (1859) 1 F. & F. 419.
[74] *Bannister* v. *Kelty* (1895) 59 J.P. 793.
[75] *James* v. *Baird*, 1916 S.C.(H.L.) 158.
[76] *Reid* v. *Moore* (1893) 20 R. 712 (privilege rebutted by circumstances).
[77] *Hill* v. *Thomson* (1892) 19 R. 377.
[78] *James* v. *Boston* (1845) 2 C. & K. 4; *Harrison* v. *Bush* (1855) 5 E. & B. 344; *Dickson* v. *Earl of Wilton* (1859) 1 F. & F. 419.
[79] *Harwood* v. *Green* (1827) 3 C. & P. 141; *Blagg* v. *Sturt* (1847) 10 Q.B. 906; *Henderson* v. *Henderson* (1855) 17 D. 348; *Dickeson* v. *Hilliard* (1874) L.R. 9 Ex. 79; *Hebditch* v. *MacIlwaine* [1894] 2 Q.B. 54; *James* v. *Baird*, 1916 S.C.(H.L.) 158.

More recent cases suggest that if complaint be directed to the wrong person by honest unintentional mistake as to who is the proper person to deal with the complaint, the complainer will not lose his qualified privilege.[80]

(iv) Criticism of candidates for public office

Any citizen has the duty to communicate to persons promoting the candidature of a person for public office, or to those responsible for appointing to public office, any facts, known to or honestly believed by him, which reflect adversely on the capacity of the candidate for that office and which would, if the candidate were elected or appointed, undermine public confidence in his ability or integrity. Thus one elector is privileged in communicating to the others some matter as to the past life of the candidate which would, if true, render him unfit to represent the electors.[81] The matter must be relevant to the issue whether the candidate is or is not fit to be elected, and this principle is not a licence to introduce irrelevant discreditable matters.

Qualified privilege protects statements contained in the election address of one candidate concerning the opposing candidate.[82] The Defamation Act, 1952, s. 10, limits this privilege by providing that a defamatory statement published by or on behalf of a candidate in any election to a local government authority or to Parliament is not to be deemed to be published on a privileged occasion on the ground that it is material to a question in issue in the election, whether or not the person by whom it is published is qualified to vote at the election. This leaves it open to claim privilege on other grounds.

(B) Protection of Another's Interests

(i) Voluntary statements

One person may be justified in communicating to another, for the protection of that other's interests, what he knows, or honestly believes, about a third person, by the existence of a familial, fiduciary or confidential relationship with that other person, and communication made bona fide in such circumstances will be privileged. The existence of a social or moral duty to warn is sufficient.

Thus a relative or close friend may warn a youth as to the character of some associate,[83] or a young woman as to the character of her fiancé,[84] an employer may warn an employee as to a dismissed employee,[85] or an

---

[80] *Jenoure* v. *Delmege* [1891] A.C. 73; *cf. Watt* v. *Longsdon* [1930] 1 K.B. 130, 147, *per* Scrutton L.J.

[81] *Bruce* v. *Leisk* (1892) 19 R. 482; contrast *Anderson* v. *Hunter* (1891) 18 R. 467, where the communication was made by one who was not an elector for the constituency, and who was therefore held to have no duty of disclosure, and not to be privileged at all in doing so.

[82] *Braddock* v. *Bevins* [1948] 1 K.B. 580, modified by Defamation Act, 1952, s. 10.

[83] *Moffat* v. *Coats* (1906) 14 S.L.T. 392; *Nelson* v. *Irving* (1897) 24 R. 1054.

[84] *Todd* v. *Hawkins* (1837) 8 C. & P. 88 (where it was observed that a jury should take a liberal view of such a communication); *Adams* v. *Coleridge* (1884) 1 T.L.R. 84, *cf. Findlay* v. *Blaylock*, 1937 S.C. 21.

[85] *Somerville* v. *Hawkins* (1851) 10 C.B. 583; *Hunt* v. *G.N.Ry.* [1891] 2 Q.B. 189; *A. B.* v. *X.Y.*, 1917 S.C. 15.

associate,[86] a solicitor may warn a client of risk, even though not consulted on the matter,[87] a host may warn a guest against the latter's servant,[88] a person may warn a charitable committee about the bona fides of the beneficiary of the committee's efforts,[89] and the dean of a college may inform students that a thief has been found.[90]

But no privilege will attach if there is no moral duty, or no confidential or fiduciary relationship, and an ultroneous communication will not be protected merely because it is made privately.[91]

Protection of interests of stranger. It is in many cases doubtful whether there is any moral duty on an individual in particular circumstances to volunteer information to a stranger, to whom he stands in no familial, fiduciary or confidential relationship, for the protection of some interest of the latter.[91a] Is there any moral duty on a person to warn his neighbour against danger, material or financial? It has been suggested [92] that the true test is: Is the interest of the person receiving the communication of such a character as by its very nature to create a moral or social duty in the defendant in the circumstances to make the communication? If so, the occasion is privileged.

(ii) *Statements in reply to inquiries*

A statement about the character, credit, integrity or other quality of a person does not enjoy any privilege merely because it is given in response to an inquiry. It may, however, enjoy qualified privilege if an inquiry is made and the person asked honestly believes that the inquirer has some legitimate interest to obtain the desired information, as distinct from mere curiosity, so as to impose on the person asked a moral duty to answer to the best of his knowledge and belief, and if he does answer to the best of his knowledge and belief, in bona fide and without malice towards the subject of the inquiry.[93] Even a statement made in response to inquiries by a Minister of the Crown does not enjoy any higher than qualified privilege.[94]

To be protected by privilege the answer must be limited to matters relevant to the subject of the inquiry and no privilege will extend to the communication of irrelevant matters, or matters unnecessarily introduced

---

[86] *Milne* v. *Smith* (1892) 2. R. 95.
[87] *Davis* v. *Reeves* (1855) 5 Ir. C.L.R. 79; *Baker* v. *Carrick* [1894] 1 Q.B. 838.
[88] *Stuart* v. *Bell* [1891] 2 Q.B. 341.
[89] *Hayford* v. *Forrester-Paton*, 1927 S.C. 740.
[90] *Rogers* v. *Orr*, 1939 S.C. 121.
[91] *Picton* v. *Jackman* (1830) 4 C. & P. 257; *Brooks* v. *Blanshard* (1833) 1 Cr. & M. 779; *Watt* v. *Longsdon* [1930] 1 K.B. 130.
[91a] See, *e.g.*, *Rogers* v. *Clifton* (1803) 3 Bos. & P. 587; *Coxhead* v. *Richards* (1846) 2 C.B. 569; explained in *Watt* v. *Longdon* [1930] 1 K.B. 130.
[92] Gatley, 225.
[93] *Coxhead* v. *Richards* (1846) 2 C.B. 569; *Davis* v. *Reeves* (1855) 5 Ir.C.L.R. 79; *Owens* v. *Roberts* (1856) 6 Ir.C.L.R. 386; *Robshaw* v. *Smith* (1878) 38 L.T. 423; *Waller* v. *Loch* (1881) 7 Q.B.D. 615; *Greenlands, Ltd.* v. *Wilmshurst* [1913] 3 K.B. 507; *London Association* v. *Greenlands* [1916] 2 A.C. 15.
[94] *Notman* v. *Commercial Bank of Scotland*, 1938 S.C. 522.

into the answer, and that quite independently of malice.[95] It may be a narrow question in many cases whether matter is relevant or irrelevant, but the line is important, as relevant matter can be taken out of the protection of privilege only by allegations of malice, whereas irrelevant matter is unprivileged.

(iii) Inquiries as to financial credit

An honest answer to an inquiry, by a person or institution having a legitimate interest to know, such as a bank, regarding the financial standing, stability, solvency or credit-worthiness of some person or body is generally privileged.[96]

In the case of a bank, unless the customer authorises a reference to his bank, the bank is not privileged in answering such an inquiry, if the answer involves disclosure of information obtained by the bank from the customer's account, or is obtained during the existence of the relationship of banker and customer.[97]

In the case of trade associations or trade protection societies, information obtained about other traders, and supplied for reward to members or subscribers, is not privileged, even though supplied bona fide and in response to an inquiry from a member or subscriber having a legitimate interest to know.[98] The objection is to supplying of information for reward, and there seems no objection to mutual gratuitous exchange of such information among the legitimately interested members of a trade association.[99]

Inquiries as to business credit may be made through an agent employed for that purpose and that agent enjoys qualified privilege in communicating fairly and honestly anything he has discovered with regard to the credit of the person about whom he was retained to inquire.[1]

Information in reply to such an enquiry may be given by an agent, and the agent will be covered by privilege if the information is given honestly and in bona fide, but not if the principle were motivated by malice.[2]

Extent of protection conferred. The communication must not be any wider or more general than those matters covered by the legitimate interests of speaker and hearer.[3] No privilege protects any part of a communication which falls outwith these limits.[4]

---

95 *Nevill* v. *Fine Art Co.* [1895] 2 Q.B. 156; *Adam* v. *Ward* [1917] A.C. 309.
96 *Smith* v. *Thomas* (1835) 2 Bing.N.C. 372; *Storey* v. *Challands* (1837) 8 C. & P. 234; *Robshaw* v. *Smith* (1878) 38 L.T. 423; *Waller* v. *Loch* (1881) 7 Q.B.D. 615; *Ingram* v. *Russell* (1893) 20 R. 771; *London Association* v. *Greenlands, Ltd.* [1916] 2 A.C. 15.
97 *Tournier* v. *National Provincial Bank* [1924] 1 K.B. 461.
98 *Macintosh* v. *Dun* [1908] A.C. 390, impliedly overruling *Bayne* v. *Stubbs* (1901) 3 F. 408, but doubted in *London Association* v. *Greenlands* [1916] 2 A.C. 15, and *Watt* v. *Longsdon* [1930] 1 K.B. 120.
99 *London Association* v. *Greenlands, supra*; *Keith* v. *Lauder* (1905) 8 F. 356; *Barr* v. *Musselburgh*, 1912 S.C. 174.
1 *London Association* v. *Greenlands, Ltd.* [1916] 2 A.C. 15.
2 *London Association, supra*; *Adam* v. *Ward* [1917] A.C. 309.
3 *Warren* v. *Warren* (1834) 1 C.M. & R. 250; *Simmonds* v. *Dunne* (1871) Ir.R. 5 C.L. 358; *Adam* v. *Ward* [1917] A.C. 309.
4 *Warren* v. *Warren, supra*.

The privilege continues to protect the communication although on either or both sides it is transmitted through an agent, such as a solicitor, acting within the scope of his authority.[5]

(iv) Inquiries as to character of employees

Under this principle an honest reply made by a past or present employer to an inquiry by a prospective employer regarding the character, ability or other qualities of a potential employee will be privileged.[6] There is a moral duty on a former employer to answer enquiries to the best of his knowledge and belief.[7]

The privilege certainly covers an honest and true disclosure of ascertained facts, and probably also covers hearsay information honestly believed to be true. It probably also protects further information about the same subject subsequently disclosed,[8] or fresh information later discovered and disclosed in supplement or in correction of a previous reply.[9] It will also protect the converse case, where the later employer discovers something and warns the former employer in case he should again be asked for a testimonial,[10] or where an employer discharges an employee and informs other employees why he has done so,[11] or where he informs a guarantor of the employee's fidelity of his suspicions or knowledge of defalcations by the employee.[12]

Similarly an employer is privileged in stating, honestly and without malice, the reason for an employee's dismissal to a person or organisation which requests the reason or seeks the employee's reinstatement,[13] or in replying to a demand from the employee's solicitor for wages.[14]

A present or former employer will also be privileged in answering honestly inquiries by third parties, such as the police or criminal authorities, who have a legitimate interest to inquire.[15]

Privilege will also protect an expression of opinion, or other subjective appraisal of the employee's qualities, unless it can be shown that the opinion expressed was not honestly held. A person cannot complain if a

[5] *Toogood* v. *Spyring* (1834) 1 C.M. & R. 181; *Blackham* v. *Pugh* (1846) 2 C.B. 611; *Baker* v. *Carrick* [1894] 1 Q.B. 838; *Smith* v. *Streatfield* [1913] 3 K.B. 764; *Groom* v. *Crocker* [1939] 1 K.B. 194.
[6] *Weatherston* v. *Hawkins* (1786) 1 T.R. 110; *Kelly* v. *Partington* (1833) 4 B. & Ad. 700; *Fountain* v. *Boodle* (1842) 3 Q.B. 5; *Dickeson* v. *Hilliard* (1874) L.R. 9 Ex. 79; *Pullman* v. *Hill* [1891] 1 Q.B. 524.
[7] *Coxhead* v. *Richards* (1846) 2 C.B. 569.
[8] *Beatson* v. *Skene* (1860) 5 H. & N. 838.
[9] *Gardener* v. *Slade* (1849) 18 L.J.Q.B. 334.
[10] *Dixon* v. *Parsons* (1856) 1 F. & F. 24; *Fryer* v. *Kinnersley* (1863) 15 C.B.(N.S.) 422; *Farquhar* v. *Neish* (1890) 17 R. 716.
[11] *Somerville* v. *Hawkins* (1850) 10 C.B. 583; *Hunt* v. *G.N.Ry.* [1891] 2 Q.B. 189; *Bryant* v. *Edgar*, 1909 S.C. 1080; *A.B.* v. *X.Y.*, 1907 S.C. 15.
[12] *Dundas* v. *Livingstone* (1900) 3 F. 37.
[13] *Weatherston* v. *Hawkins* (1786) 1 T.R. 110; *Taylor* v. *Hawkins* (1851) 16 Q.B. 308; *Manby* v. *Witt* (1856) 18 C.B. 544; *Watson* v. *Burnet* (1862) 24 D. 494.
[14] *Laidlaw* v. *Gunn* (1890) 17 R. 394; *Sheriff* v. *Denholm* (1898) 5 S.L.T. 234, 346; *Hanton* v. *Hatje* (1907) 15 S.L.T. 531.
[15] *Kine* v. *Sewell* (1838) 3 M. & W. 297; *Cockayne* v. *Hodgkisson* (1833) 5 C. & P. 543; *Force* v. *Warren* (1864) 15 C.B.(N.S.) 806; *Nelson* v. *Irving* (1897) 24 R. 1054.

former employer, who has high, even unreasonable, standards, honestly criticises his former employee as not matching up to his standards.

A voluntary communication regarding a former employee, not made in reply to any inquiry, may be privileged if it were made not merely in honest belief in its truth but in the honest belief that there was in the circumstances a moral duty to warn a subsequent employer.[16] Similarly a communication volunteered to the registry from which a lady had obtained a servant, to the effect that she was incompetent, was held privileged.[17] A communication to employees of why a former employee had been discharged has been held privileged.[18] So too if an employer believes that an employee has been dishonest he is privileged in communicating this to anyone who has guaranteed the servant's fidelity.[19]

Privilege will not protect any reply which was not honestly believed to be true when it was made, or otherwise evidences malice. In *Macdonald* v. *McColl* [20] an unexplained contradiction between a good character given in one year and an unfavourable one in the following year was held to be a relevant averment of malice.

(C) *Communications Between Persons having Common Interest*

Principle. Qualified privilege attaches to communications between persons one of whom has a legitimate interest to make the statement and the other a corresponding interest or duty to receive it.[21]

The requisite interest must be reciprocal,[22] and this reciprocity must exist in fact and not merely be believed, mistakenly though honestly, to exist.[23] An occasion which in point of fact is not privileged cannot become privileged because the defender, in good faith and on grounds which commended themselves to him, considered it privileged. Good faith, however strong its foundation, cannot convert a non-privileged occasion into a privileged occasion, although it may afford excellent evidence of the absence of malice.[24] If the recipient of the statement had no duty or interest in respect of the subject-matter, there is no privilege.[25]

Nature of requisite interest. The interest existing between the parties must be a legitimate one, such that it is socially and morally right that the one should communicate the facts and that the other should receive

---

[16] *Rogers* v. *Clifton* (1803) 3 B. & P. 587; *Pattison* v. *Jones* (1828) 8 B. & C. 578.
[17] *Farquhar* v. *Neish* (1890) 17 R. 716.
[18] *A.B.* v. *X.Y.*, 1907 S.C. 15; *Bryant* v. *Edgar*, 1909 S.C. 1080; *Somerville* v. *Hawkins* (1850) 10 C.B. 583; *Hunt* v. *G.N.Ry.* [1891] 2 Q.B. 189.
[19] *Dundas* v. *Livingstone* (1900) 3 F. 37.
[20] (1901) 3 F. 1082.
[21] *Harrison* v. *Bush* (1855) 5 E. & B. 344; *Laughton* v. *Bishop of Sodor and Man* (1872) L.R. 4 C.P. 495; *Hunt* v. *G.N.Ry.* [1891] 2 Q.B. 189; *Stuart* v. *Bell* (1891) 2 Q.B. 341; *De Buse* v. *McCarthy* [1942] 1 K.B. 156.
[22] *James* v. *Baird*, 1916 S.C. 510; affd. 1916 S.C.(H.L.) 158; *Adam* v. *Ward* [1917] A.C. 309; *Watt* v. *Longsdon* [1930] 1 K.B. 130; *White* v. *Stone* [1939] 2 K.B. 827.
[23] *Whiteley* v. *Adams* (1863) 15 C.B.(N.S.) 392; *Stuart* v. *Bell* [1891] 2 Q.B. 341; *Hebditch* v. *McIlwaine* [1894] 2 Q.B. 54; *Davidson* v. *Barclays Bank* [1940] 1 All E.R. 316; *Winstanley* v. *Bampton* [1943] 1 K.B. 319.
[24] *James* v. *Baird*, 1916 S.C. 510, 517, 531; *cf. Cochrane* v. *Young*, 1922 S.C. 696.
[25] *Henderson* v. *Henderson* (1855) 17 D. 348; *James, supra.*

the communication.[26] The passing on of gossip or of news is not a legitimate interest for either party. Warnings as to character and complaints as to the defalcations or neglect of duty are among the commonest kinds of facts which have been held to constitute legitimate matters of interest between two parties.[27] In every case it will be a question of fact whether, in the circumstances of the case, any legitimate common interest exists.

If there is a legitimate common interest, the case can be taken out of the protection of privilege only by averments and proof of malice, but if there is no such legitimate interest, the communication is unprotected by privilege and averments of malice are unnecessary. Thus a clergyman will be protected by privilege when warning a parishioner about his son's conduct, but not when rebuking such conduct in his sermon.[28]

Privilege will also be defeated if the communication is made also to persons who have no interest or duty in receiving the information,[29] unless those persons received the information accidentally, the publication not being deliberately wider than necessary.[30] Hence publication in the press will defeat the plea of privilege.[31] But publication in the press or otherwise generally will be privileged if the matter is one of general public interest so that the whole community have a legitimate interest to know of it.[32]

Examples of common interest. The following are among the cases where the requisite legitimate common interest has been held to exist:

With regard to domestic relations. Communications between relatives as to the character of a suitor [33]; or by a landlord to a tenant as to inmates of the tenant's house [34]; by a tenant to the landlord as to the latter's gamekeeper [35]; by a tenant to the landlord's factor as to repairs [36]; by a person to his sister-in-law about the latter's son's companion.[37]

With regard to public persons and officials. Communications between a parishioner and his bishop as to the character of a clergyman [38]; between members of a congregation as to a prospective minister [39];

---

26 *London Association* v. *Greenlands* [1916] 2 A.C. 15, 35, 42.
27 *Shaw* v. *Morgan* (1888) 15 R. 865; *Cochrane* v. *Young*, 1922 S.C. 696.
28 *Dudgeon* v. *Forbes* (1833) 11 S. 1014; *Adam* v. *Allan* (1841) 3 D. 1058.
29 *Parsons* v. *Surgey* (1864) 4 F. & F. 247; *Simpson* v. *Downs* (1867) 16 L.T. 391; *Leitch* v. *Lyal* (1903) 11 S.L.T. 394; *Standen* v. *South Essex Recorders* (1934) 50 T.L.R. 365. Cf. *Rankine* v. *Roberts* (1873) 1 R. 230.
30 *Edmondson* v. *Birch* [1907] 1 K.B. 371; *Roff* v. *British and French, Ltd.* [1918] 2 K.B. 677; *Osborn* v. *Boulter* [1930] 2 K.B. 226.
31 *Duncombe* v. *Daniell* (1838) 2 Jur. 32; *Chapman* v. *Ellesmere* [1932] 2 K.B. 431; *Standen, supra.*
32 *Allbutt* v. *G.M.C.* (1889) 23 Q.B.D. 400; *Adam* v. *Ward* [1917] A.C. 309. Contrast *Chapman, supra.*
33 *Todd* v. *Hawkins* (1837) 8 C. & P. 88; *Adams* v. *Coleridge* (1884) 1 T.L.R. 84.
34 *Knight* v. *Gibbs* (1834) 1 A. & E. 43.
35 *Cockayne* v. *Hodgkisson* (1835) 5 C. & P. 543.
36 *Toogood* v. *Spyring* (1834) 1 C.M. & R. 181.
37 *Moffat* v. *Coats* (1906) 14 S.L.T. 392.
38 *James* v. *Boston* (1845) 2 C. & K. 4.
39 *Blackburn* v. *Blackburn* (1827) 4 Bing. 395.

between a minister and the presbytery about misconduct by another minister [40]; between a person and the chief constable as to the conduct of a police officer [41]; between parties to a litigation as to an alleged interference with the course of justice [42]; between a landlord and his tenant's commanding officer as to non-payment of rent [43]; between an aggrieved person and the discipline committee of a professional or similar body [44]; between one elector and others as to the life of the candidate [45]; between a member of a public body and others in relation to a matter of discussion [46]; between the principal of a college and the patron of a college chair as to the competence of a proposed presentee to the chair [47]; between a minister and a candidate for eldership as to a charge against the latter by a third party [48]; between a minister and the inspector of poor of another parish as to the pursuer's fitness to have charge of pauper children boarded with him [49]; between a member of a church congregation and the minister about the session clerk [50]; between a minister and his elders as to the conduct of the assistant minister [51]; between members of a parish church and the kirk session as to the pursuer's fitness to be ordained as an elder [52]; between a candidate for election and the electors about the opposition candidate, and between one elector and another about a candidate [53]; between the Stewards of the Jockey Club and the racing public about the qualification of a trainer.[54]

In ordinary cases an election address is now, by virtue of the Defamation Act, 1952, s. 10, no longer entitled to qualified privilege.[55]

With regard to professional services. Communications between friends as to the character of a doctor [56]; by an owner to a builder as to a schedule of quantities prepared by an architect [57]; by a doctor to a chemist as to a prescription dispensed by the latter.[58]

With regard to employees. Communications between friends as to the character of a servant in the employment of one [59]; between employer

40 *A.* v. *B.* (1895) 22 R. 984.
41 *McMurchy* v. *Campbell* (1887) 14 R. 745; *Cassidy* v. *Connochie*, 1907 S.C. 1112.
42 *Hines* v. *Davidson*, 1935 S.C. 30.
43 *Winstanley* v. *Bampton* [1943] K.B. 319.
44 *White* v. *Batey* (1892) 8 T.L.R. 698.
45 *Bruce* v. *Leisk* (1892) 19 R. 482.
46 *Craig* v. *Jex-Blake* (1871) 9 M. 973; *Chiene* v. *Archibald* (1868) 6 S.L.R. 62; *Shaw* v. *Morgan* (1888) 15 R. 865; *Neilson* v. *Johnston* (1890) 17 R. 442; *Teague* v. *Russell* (1900) 8 S.L.T. 253; *Campbell* v. *Weir*, 1924 S.L.T. 14.
47 *Auld* v. *Shairp* (1875) 2 R. 940.
48 *Murray* v. *Wylie*, 1916 S.C. 356.
49 *Croucher* v. *Inglis* (1889) 16 R. 774.
50 *Rankine* v. *Roberts* (1873) 1 R. 225.
51 *Barclay* v. *Manuel* (1902) 10 S.L.T. 450.
52 *Jack* v. *Fleming* (1891) 19 R. 1.
53 *Braddock* v. *Bevins* [1948] 1 K.B. 580.
54 *Russell* v. *Duke of Norfolk* [1949] 1 All E.R. 109.
55 *Plummer* v. *Charman* [1962] 3 All E.R. 823.
56 *Dixon* v. *Smith* (1860) 29 L.J.Ex. 125.
57 *Sadgrove* v. *Hole* [1901] 2 K.B. 1.
58 *Gall* v. *Slessor*, 1907 S.C. 708.
59 *Pattison* v. *Jones* (1828) 8 B. & C. 578.

and employee as to the character of a fellow servant [60]; between employee and employer on the same topic [61]; between employer and the employee's parent or guardian on his character and grounds for his dismissal [62]; by a second master to the headmaster as to misconduct of an assistant master [63]; by an employer to the employee's doctor as to his health [64]; by a former employer to the present employer about the employee's character [65]; by an employer to the insurance company who had guaranteed an employee's fidelity [66]; by a town councillor about the conduct of a burgh official [67]; by a chief constable to a subordinate about his conduct [68]; by a police inspector to the chief constable about the pursuer's misconduct while acting as a police officer [69]; by a police surgeon to the chief constable about the pursuer, a constable [70]; by the secretary of a co-operative society to the members about the society's foreman butcher [71]; by a ratepayer to the county council about the pursuer's conduct as matron of a local authority hospital [72]; by a railway inspector to his superiors as to the conduct of a clerk [73]; by an employer to the registry through which she had engaged the pursuer, a domestic servant [74]; by an employer to an employers' association about the misconduct of an employee [75]; by the chairman of a company to a fellow-director and an employee that the managing director had been guilty of immoral conduct with that employee.[76]

In business relations. Communications between a company chairman and directors, shareholders and the company's solicitor [77]; between a creditor in a bankruptcy and others [78]; between the convener of a town council committee and a contractor when in conversation about another contract [79]; between a local distress committee and a man of skill as to the condition of small holdings leased to tenants [80]; between the solicitor in an executry and the cautioners for the executrix as to the actings of

---

60 *Somerville* v. *Hawkins* (1851) 10 C.B. 583; *Manby* v. *Witt* (1856) 18 C.B. 544; *Masters* v. *Burgess* (1887) 3 T.L.R. 96; *Hunt* v. *G.N.Ry.* [1891] 2 Q.B. 189; *Newall* v. *Bennett* (1896) 3 S.L.T. 268; *Bryant* v. *Edgar*, 1909 S.C. 1080; *A.B.* v. *X.Y.*, 1917 S.C. 15.
61 *Scarll* v. *Dixon* (1864) 4 F. & F. 250; *Mead* v. *Hughes* (1891) 7 T.L.R. 291.
62 *Fowler* v. *Horner* (1812) 3 Camp. 294; *Watson* v. *Burnet* (1862) 24 D. 494; *Aberdein* v. *Macleay* (1893) 9 T.L.R. 539; *Dunnet* v. *Nelson*, 1926 S.C. 764.
63 *Hume* v. *Marshall* (1877) 42 J.P. 136; *Milne* v. *Bauchop* (1887) 5 R. 1114; *Gorlett* v. *Garment* (1897) 13 T.L.R. 391.
64 *Phelps* v. *Kemsley* (1942) 168 L.T. 18.
65 *McCallum* v. *McDiarmid* (1900) 2 F. 357; *Macdonald* v. *McColl* (1901) 3 F. 1082.
66 *Dundas* v. *Livingstone* (1900) 3 F. 37.
67 *Neilson* v. *Johnston* (1890) 17 R. 442; *Teague* v. *Russell* (1900) 8 S.L.T. 253.
68 *Innes* v. *Adamson* (1889) 17 R. 11.
69 *McMurchy* v. *Campbell* (1887) 14 R. 725.
70 *A.* v. *B.*, 1907 S.C. 1154.
71 *Williamson* v. *McCann* (1908) 16 S.L.T. 221.
72 *Couper* v. *Balfour of Burleigh*, 1914 S.C. 139.
73 *Martin* v. *Cruickshanks* (1896) 23 R. 874.
74 *Farquhar* v. *Neish* (1890) 17 R. 716.
75 *Keith* v. *Lauder* (1905) 8 F. 356.
76 *Fyvie* v. *Waddell*, 1923 S.L.T. 518 (repetitions not prima facie privileged).
77 *McGillivray* v. *Davidson*, 1934 S.L.T. 45.
78 *Oliver* v. *Barnet* (1895) 3 S.L.T. 163; *McCaig* v. *Moscrip* (1872) 10 S.L.R. 140.
79 *Reid* v. *Little* (1894) 2 S.L.T. 244 (no privilege at all because of occasion on which uttered).
80 *Cadzow* v. *Edinburgh Distress Cttee.*, 1914, 1 S.L.T. 493.

the executrix's son [81]; between an innkeeper and the shooting tenant of an estate as to a suspected poacher [82]; between a trade union secretary and the members in general meeting about the action of one branch [83]; between a football referee and the committee of a football union about the conduct of a player [84]; between a milkman and the customer about the latter's housekeeper who had accused the former of overcharging [85]; between the manager of a greyhound track and shareholders and others about the chairman of the company owning the track [86]; between a dismissed official and the president of a company about the company's manager in one area and his alleged interference with the course of justice there [87]; between the invigilator at an examination and the class about cheating by one member of the class.[88]

In connection with trade. Communication between friends as to the character of a tradesman with whom one is dealing [89]; by a school medical officer to the steward as to the quality of meat being supplied [90]; by a member of a trade protection society to the secretary thereof about another member [91]; by a customer to a tradesman as to the quality of goods supplied [92]; by a local association of traders to its members as to the credit-worthiness of persons named therein [93]; by the chairman of a local authority public health committee to that committee as to the source of a case of typhoid [94]; by an architect to a builder as to the plaintiff's paint.[95]

(D) *Statements in the Protection of the Defender's own Interests*

A statement made " in the reasonable attention to a man's own business and affairs, which gives him legitimate cause to write or speak of his neighbour, the occasion displaces the presumption of malice and the presumption of falsehood, and he is only answerable if malice be shewn to have existed in fact, and if the statement be untrue." [96] This head of privilege covers statements in reply to letters threatening legal proceedings,[97]

---

81 *Stewart* v. *Hannah* (1905) 8 F. 107.
82 *Nelson* v. *Irving* (1897) 24 R. 1054.
83 *Quigley* v. *Brown*, 1913, 2 S.L.T. 391.
84 *Murdison* v. *Scottish Football Union* (1896) 23 R. 449.
85 *Paton* v. *Edine* (1898) 6 S.L.T. 191.
86 *McGillivray* v. *Davidson*, 1934 S.L.T. 45.
87 *Hines* v. *Davidson*, 1935 S.C. 30.
88 *Bridgman* v. *Stockdale* [1953] 1 All E.R. 1166.
89 *Storey* v. *Challands* (1837) 8 C. & P. 234.
90 *Humphreys* v. *Stilwell* (1861) 2 F. & F. 590.
91 *White* v. *Batey* (1892) 8 T.L.R. 698.
92 *Oddy* v. *Paulet* (1865) 4 F. & F. 1009.
93 *Barr* v. *Musselburgh Merchants Assocn.*, 1912 S.C. 174, distinguishing *Macintosh* v. *Dun* (1908) A.C. 390, where similar information given for profit by commercial information agency.
94 *McLean* v. *Adam* (1888) 16 R. 175.
95 *Hall* v. *Bowden* (1953) C.P.L. 273.
96 *Shaw* v. *Morgan* (1888) 15 R. 865, 870, *per* Lord Young. *Cf. Toogood* v. *Spyring* (1834) 1 C.M. & R. 181.
97 *Laidlaw* v. *Gunn* (1890) 17 R. 394; *Sheriff* v. *Denholm* (1898) 5 S.L.T. 346; *Campbell* v. *Cochrane* (1905) 8 F. 205; *cf. Hanton* v. *Hatje* (1907) 15 S.L.T. 531.

statements in reply to defamatory accusations,[98] or attacks in the Press [99] or in defence of the interests of a principal or client,[1] and statements in the pleadings of an action in defence of the defender's interests.

Many instances have arisen of so-called judicial slander, i.e., statements made by a party in the pleadings in an action to which he is a party, complained of as defamatory by his opponent or a third party. The general principle is that a litigant is entitled to considerable freedom of speech in making statements on record in the defence of his own interests and may with impunity say many things which may be painful and injurious to his opponent or to third parties. But if he descends to false statements known to himself to be false, and makes these not for the legitimate purpose of maintaining his suit but for the gratification of his own spite and malice, he is liable to an action of damages.[2] To be privileged the statement must be pertinent to the matter in issue before the court or tribunal.[3]

The privilege may be rebutted by proof of malice, of which sufficiently specific averment of facts and circumstances yielding an inference of malice has been made.[4]

Malice may be disclosed by excessively violent language in the reply, though the court makes allowance for the defender's natural annoyance,[5] or by wholly unnecessary imputations going beyond a defence or reply.[6]

Under this head also fall cases of statements by employers to employees when dismissing them.[7] An accusation of misconduct then and there brought to the master's knowledge is privileged.[8] The mere expression of an opinion about the employee's incompetency does not justify an action of slander at all.[9] In any case such a statement is normally entitled to qualified privilege.[10] Similarly the manager of a theatre has qualified privilege in ejecting an alleged prostitute when there is in force a local authority by-law requiring the manager not to admit persons of bad fame,[11] a shopkeeper when a departmental manager challenges a person

---

98 *Coward* v. *Wellington* (1836) 7 C. & P. 531; *Hibbs* v. *Wilkinson* (1859) 1 F. & F. 608; *Hemmings* v. *Gasson* (1858) E.B. & E. 346.

99 *Gray* v. *S.S.P.C.A.* (1890) 17 R. 1185; *Hemmings, supra*; *Laughton* v. *Sodor and Man* (1872) L.R. 4 P.C. 495.

1 *Ramsay* v. *Nairne* (1833) 11 S. 1033; *Crawford* v. *Dunlop* (1900) 2 F. 987. *Cf. Wilson* v. *Purvis* (1890) 18 R. 72; *Baker* v. *Carrick* [1894] 1 Q.B. 838.

2 *Williamson* v. *Umphray* (1890) 17 R. 905.

3 *McCaig* v. *Moscrip* (1872) 10 S.L.R. 140; *Scott* v. *Turnbull* (1884) 11 R. 1131; *Selbie* v. *Saint* (1890) 18 R. 88; *Thomson* v. *Munro & Jamieson* (1900) 8 S.L.T. 327; *Neill* v. *Henderson* (1901) 3 F. 387; *Stevenson* v. *Wilson* (1903) 5 F. 309.

4 *Scott, supra*; *Gordon* v. *British and Foreign Metaline Co.* (1886) 14 R. 75; *Hay* v. *Cameron* (1898) 6 S.L.T. 48; *Selbie, supra*; *Douglas* v. *Ferguson* (1896) 4 S.L.T. 200; *Stevenson, supra*; *Campbell* v. *Cochrane* (1905) 8 F. 205; *M.* v. *H.*, 1908 S.C. 1130; *Webster* v. *Paterson*, 1910 S.C. 459; *Mitchell* v. *Smith*, 1919 S.C. 664. See also *Logan* v. *Weir* (1872) 10 S.L.R. 22.

5 *Laughton, supra*; *Gray* v. *S.S.P.C.A., supra*, 1200; *Adam* v. *Ward* [1917] A.C. 309.

6 *Milne* v. *Walker* (1898) 21 R. 155, 157.

7 e.g., *Hamilton* v. *Wright* (1895) 3 S.L.T. 10; *Suzor* v. *McLachlan*, 1914 S.C. 306.

8 *Cunningham* v. *Petherbridge* (1894) 2 S.L.T. 229; *A.B.* v. *X.Y.*, 1917 S.C. 15.

9 *Munro* v. *Mudie* (1901) 9 S.L.T. 91.

10 *Stuart* v. *Moss* (1885) 13 R. 299; *Sheriff* v. *Denholm* (1897) 5 S.L.T. 346; *Dinnie* v. *Hengler* 1910 S.C. 4; contrast *Adams* v. *Templeton*, 1913, 2 S.L.T. 241; *Suzor* v. *Buckingham*, 1914 S.C. 299.

11 *Finburgh* v. *Moss' Empires*, 1908 S.C. 928; *cf. Gorman* v. *Moss' Empires*, 1913 S.C. 1.

with theft or shoplifting,[12] an employer when dismissing a clerkess for theft of money,[13] and a landlord when instructing his solicitor to warn his tenant that her habits amounted to a nuisance.[14]

Fair retort. Where a statement is being made in reply to a previous attack somewhat greater latitude is allowed than would otherwise be, and an emphatic and indignant denial will not necessarily be actionable [15]: " publications in answer to a public attack, meeting that attack and vindicating the character of the person attacked, are not actionable; but . . . this privilege does not extend to charges unconnected with that reply or vindication." [16]   The view has been expressed [17] that a publication in a man's own defence against a public attack enjoys qualified privilege. The statements in the retort must be true, and the retort given the same publicity as, but no greater than, the attack,[18] and the retort must not go beyond the matters charged or attack the character of the original speaker.[19]   Thus where one trade union carried on a propaganda campaign, some of it defamatory, against the defenders and the latter retaliated, it was held to be published on a privileged occasion and justified as fair retort, so that the defenders were in the absence of proof of malice held entitled to absolvitor.[20]

(E) *Statements Made in Seeking Redress*

A statement is privileged if bona fide made in the course of making a complaint, requesting an inquiry, or otherwise seeking to have some grievance redressed,[21] so long as it is made to the proper body or person who has power to redress the grievance complained of,[22] contains nothing irrelevant to the alleged grievance [23] and is not actuated by malice. A letter to an M.P. is not privileged where the publication is not connected in any way with any parliamentary proceedings.[24]   An allegation of professional misconduct made to the Bar Council is privileged.[25]

Similarly an allegation of adultery made against a person in an action of divorce enjoys qualified privilege, and, moreover, of a high order.[26] " If a litigant makes a relevant averment in support of his case, he is not answerable in damages to a third party merely because that averment

---

12 *Henderson* v. *Patrick Thomson, Ltd.,* 1911, 1 S.L.T. 284; *cf. Neville* v. *C. & A. Modes,* 1945 S.C. 175.
13 *Dunnet* v. *Nelson,* 1926 S.C. 764.
14 *Gillie* v. *Labno* (1949) C.L.Y. 4792.
15 *Gray* v. *S.S.P.C.A.* (1890) 17 R. 1185; *Brodie* v. *Dowell* (1894) 2 S.L.T. 9.
16 *Milne* v. *Walker* (1893) 21 R. 155, 157, *per* Lord Kincairney.
17 *Gray, supra,* 1197, *per* Lord Shand.
18 *Hamilton* v. *Duncan* (1825) 4 S. 414.
19 *Monro* v. *Monro* (1803) Hume 616; *Milne, supra.*
20 *N.U. Bank Employees* v. *Murray,* 1949 S.L.T.(Notes) 26.
21 *Fairman* v. *Ives* (1822) 5 B. & Ald. 642; *cf. Macdonald* v. *Martin,* 1935 S.C. 621; *Winstanley* v. *Bampton* [1943] K.B. 319.
22 *Wenman* v. *Ash* (1853) 13 C.B. 836; *Hebditch* v. *MacIlwaine* [1894] 2 Q.B. 54.
23 *Adam* v. *Ward* [1917] A.C. 309.
24 *Rivlin* v. *Bilainkin* [1953] 1 Q.B. 485.
25 *Lincoln* v. *Daniels* [1960] 3 All E.R. 205.
26 *M.* v. *H.,* 1908 S.C. 1130.

may turn out to be inaccurate and to be injurious to the person complaining . . . but . . . he may be made liable if it can be shown that he made the averment complained of . . . with some indirect motive." [27]

A high order of privilege attaches to statements in written pleadings " for the protection of honest litigants, and to enable them freely to state their representation of the facts without incurring the risk of being exposed to an action of damages." [28] This protection extends to all statements in pleadings which are relevant, and also to those which are irrelevant unless they are not only plainly irrelevant but also impertinent to the case. [29]

(F) *Published Reports*

Qualified privilege also attaches to various categories of published reports on the ground of the overriding public interest that there should be generally available accurate reports of proceedings at which the public generally are entitled to be, but in fact cannot be, present, but in which they have a legitimate interest.

The privilege of newspaper in relation to reports is not a special privilege, but the privilege of anyone to report fairly and accurately public matters on which persons not present have a legitimate interest to obtain information. [30]

(i) *Reports of proceedings in Parliament*

Fair and accurate reports in newspapers or periodicals of the proceedings of either House of Parliament or any committee thereof enjoy qualified privilege. [31]

Extracts from, or abstracts of, any parliamentary report or paper, published by or under the authority of either House, [32] or broadcast, [33] enjoy similar privilege if it be proved by the defender that it was published bona fide and without malice. [32]

Similarly publication of a fair and accurate copy of, or extract from, a register maintained pursuant to any Act of Parliament and to which the public has access is privileged. [34] Such include registers of court decrees [35] and other sheriff court books. [36] But no privilege attaches to an incorrect copy or extract, [37] even if the mistake were made by a public official

[27] *M.* v. *H., supra,* 1137–1138, *per* Lord Kinnear. Counsel, pleading orally, and witnesses enjoy absolute privilege.
[28] *Mitchell* v. *Smith,* 1919 S.C. 664, 673, *per* Lord Sands.
[29] *Scott* v. *Turnbull* (1884) 11 R. 1131, 1134.
[30] *Wright & Greig* v. *Outram* (1890) 17 R. 596.
[31] *Wason* v. *Walter* (1868) L.R. 4 Q.B. 73.
[32] Parliamentary Papers Act, 1840, s. 3; *Bradlaugh* v. *Gossett* (1884) 12 Q.B.D. 271; *Mangena* v. *Lloyd* (1909) 99 L.T. 824, and see *Mangena* v. *Wright* [1909] 2 K.B. 958; *Dingle* v. *Associated Newspapers* [1960] 2 Q.B. 405.
[33] Defamation Act, 1952, s. 9.
[34] *Searles* v. *Scarlett* [1892] 2 Q.B. 56.
[35] *Russell* v. *Stubbs,* 1913 S.C.(H.L.) 14.
[36] *Fleming* v. *Newton* (1848) 1 H.L.Cas. 363.
[37] *Crabbe* v. *Stubbs* (1895) 22 R. 860; *Hunter* v. *Stubbs* (1903) 5 F. 920.

(though this is relevant in mitigation of damages), or to an extract so modified as to be capable of impugning an innocent party's credit.[38]

(ii) Reports of judicial proceedings

At common law a fair and accurate report of the proceedings in a public court of justice enjoys qualified privilege.[39] So long as the report is fair and accurate, the newspaper is not bound to verify the accuracy of the statements made by counsel, agent or witness, nor to consider whether the facts warranted the statements made.[40] The privilege is not confined to newspapers but extends to all persons desiring for a legitimate reason to acquaint the outside public with what those present in court heard.[39] If the report is not fair and accurate, (and the pursuer must prove this) the newspaper has no privilege at all.[39]

This is the position not only with newspapers but reports in periodicals, pamphlets and books, including legal books,[41] and presumably broadcast reports. The report need not be contemporaneous. The justification for the privilege is that the administration of justice is a matter of public concern and persons not in court are entitled to be informed of what has taken place.[42]

The privilege extends to the proceedings of every kind [43] of judicial and quasi-judicial [44] body, the sessions of which are open to the public,[45] but not to proceedings held behind closed doors,[46] nor to reports prohibited by statute,[47] nor to reports of matter, such as in a closed record, which has not been debated or referred to in public discussion in open court,[48] nor to reports which, even though accurate, are blasphemous or immoral,[49] nor to any case where the court requests or orders that a report should not be published if it would interfere with the administration of justice. It has been assumed in Scottish cases,[50] that qualified privilege also attaches to fair and accurate reports of foreign judicial proceedings. A railway company has been held entitled to post a bill stating accurately that certain persons had been convicted of travelling without paying the

---

38 Outram v. Reid (1852) 14 D. 577; Gordon v. Stubbs (1895) 3 S.L.T. 10.
39 Richardson v. Wilson (1879) 7 R. 237, 241, 243; Wright & Greig v. Outram (1890) 17 R. 596, 599; cf. Macleod v. Justices of Lewis (1892) 20 R. 218; Kimber v. Press Association [1893] 1 Q.B. 65.
40 Burnett & Hallamshire Fuel v. Sheffield Telegraph [1960] 2 All E.R. 157.
41 Blake v. Stevens (1864) 11 LT. 543.
42 Furniss v. Cambridge News, Ltd. (1907) 23 T.L.R. 705; Richardson, supra; Macleod, supra.
43 Usill v. Hales (1878) 3 C.P.D. 319; Thomson v. Munro (1900) 8 S.L.T. 327.
44 Allbutt v. G.M.C. (1889) 23 Q.B.D. 400.
45 Ryalls v. Leader (1866) L.R. 1 Ex. 296; Wason v. Walter (1868) L.R. 4 Q.B. 73; Kimber v. Press Association [1893] 1 Q.B. 65. See also Scott v. Scott [1913] A.C. 417, 440; McPherson v. McPherson [1936] A.C. 177.
46 Scott, supra, 452, per Lord Atkinson.
47 See Judicial Proceedings (Regulation of Reports) Act, 1926; Children and Young Persons (Scotland) Act, 1937, ss. 45–46, 52, 54. Cf. Children and Young Persons (Harmful Publications) Act, 1955.
48 Macleod v. Justices of Lewis (1892) 20 R. 218. Cf. Richardson v. Wilson, supra.
49 Steele v. Brannan (1872) L.R. 7 C.P. 261.
50 Riddell v. Clydesdale Horse Society (1885) 12 R. 976; Pope v. Outram, 1909 S.C. 230.

fare and other offences.[51]   A newspaper has been held entitled to rely, in support of a defence of fair comment, on judicial observations in other proceedings.[52]

A fair and accurate contemporaneous report of foreign judicial proceedings which contains a defamatory statement spoken in and germane to those proceedings is protected by qualified privilege if the statement concerned a subject-matter of legitimate and proper interest in this country, but not if the interest is due to mere idle curiosity or desire for gossip.[53]

Privilege conditional on fairness and accuracy.   The report must be fair and accurate,[54] though it may be abridged or summarised.[55]   Where a newspaper merely purports to report the result of a case, and does so with entire accuracy, it is not liable merely because it has failed to narrate the steps which led up to the judgment.[56]   " There is no duty on a reporter in a report of a law-suit to make his report exhaustive. It is, in my judgment, sufficient if the reporter gives the result of the litigation truly and correctly . . .   If a newspaper gives such a report . . . stating correctly the general conclusion arrived at by the court, I am of opinion that such a report is a fair report . . ." [57]   Slight inaccuracies do not destroy the privilege if the report is still substantially accurate,[58] but the privilege vanishes if the report is substantially inaccurate,[59] or if a witness's evidence is stated as fact and turns out to be false.[60]   An inaccurate representation of the case may be introduced by condensing a report or omitting some particulars,[61] by reporting criminal proceedings in a way which assumes guilt,[62] or misstating the effect of the judgment.[63]   A report may be published of the day's hearing though the case is not concluded.[64]   It may be defamatory by reason of the heading under which it is printed.[65]

The onus of proof that a report is fair and accurate is on the defender,[66] and the question whether it is or is not fair and accurate is one of

---

51 *Buchan* v. *N.B.Ry.* (1894) 21 R. 379.
52 *Waters* v. *Sunday Pictorial Newspapers* [1961] 2 All E.R. 758.
53 *Webb* v. *Times Publishing Co.* [1960] 2 Q.B. 535.
54 *Wright & Greig* v. *Outram* (1890) 17 R. 596, 599; *cf. Hunter* v. *Stubbs* (1903) 5 F. 920.
55 *Hoare* v. *Silverlock* (1850) 9 C.B. 20; *Andrews* v. *Chapman* (1853) 3 C. & K. 286; *Lewis* v. *Levy* (1858) E.B. & E. 537; *Turner* v. *Sullivan* (1862) 6 L.T.(N.S.) 130; *Macdougall* v. *Knight* (1886) 17 Q.B.D. 636; *Harper* v. *Provincial Newspapers*, 1937 S.L.T. 462.
56 *Duncan* v. *Associated Scottish Newspapers*, 1929 S.C. 14, 19.
57 *Ibid.* 21, *per* Lord Anderson.
58 *Andrews, supra*; *Alexander* v. *N.E.Ry.* (1865) 6 B. & S. 340; *Kimber* v. *Press Association* [1893] 1 Q.B. 65; *McLintock* v. *Stubbs, Ltd.* (1902) 5 F. 1; *Hope* v. *Leng, Ltd.* (1907) 23 T.L.R. 243.
59 *Hunter, supra*; *Crabbe & Robertson* v. *Stubbs* (1895) 22 R. 860; *Mitchell* v. *Hirst Kidd* [1936] 3 All E.R. 872; *Harper* v. *Provincial Newspapers*, 1937 S.L.T. 462.
60 *Grech* v. *Odhams Press, Ltd.* [1958] 2 Q.B. 275.
61 *Wright & Greig* v. *Outram* (1890) 17 R. 596; *cf. Lewis* v. *Walter* (1821) 4 B. & Ald. 605; *Lewis* v. *Levy* (1858) E.B. & E. 537; *Grech, supra*.
62 *R.* v. *Fisher* (1811) 2 Camp. 563; *Ashmore* v. *Borthwick* (1885) 2 T.L.R. 209.
63 *Hayward* v. *Hayward* (1886) 34 Ch.D. 198; *cf. Russell* v. *Stubbs*, 1913 S.C.(H.L.) 14.
64 *Kimber, supra*, 71.
65 *Lewis* v. *Levy, supra*; *Lewis* v. *Clement* (1822) 3 B. & B. 297.
66 *Wright & Greig, supra*; *Macdougall* v. *Knight* (1890) 25 Q.B.D. 1; *Harper* v. *Provincial Newspapers*, 1937 S.L.T. 462.

fact.[67] If the statement conveyed by the report is prima facie defamatory the pursuer need not anticipate and meet the defence of fair report in his summons [68]; otherwise he must impugn the accuracy of the report and table an innuendo.

Newspapers are not privileged in reporting words which, though deemed to have been uttered in the course of judicial proceedings, had no relation thereto.[69]

(iii) *Other Press or broadcast reports*

Qualified privilege also attaches at common law to a report of the proceedings of a public meeting, or of a body or authority if the public generally had a legitimate interest in the matter of discussion and the defender had a duty to make the information known to the public generally.[70]

The Defamation Act, 1952, s. 7 (as modified by s. 14 (*d*)), confers qualified privilege on the publication in a newspaper (as defined in s. 7 (5)) of any such report or other matter as is mentioned in the Schedule to the Act. The reports listed in Part I of the Schedule are privileged without explanation or contradiction, but those in Part II of the Schedule are privileged, but not (s. 7 (2)) " if it is proved that the defender has been requested by the pursuer to publish in the newspaper in which the original publication was made a reasonable letter or statement by way of explanation or contradiction,[71] and has refused or neglected to do so, or has done so in a manner not adequate or not reasonable having regard to all the circumstances." Reports of the latter class consequently enjoy qualified privilege " subject to explanation or contradiction." The defence of qualified privilege is in these cases not available if explanation or contradiction has been requested and unjustifiably not made.

This statutory protection may also be lost by proof of express or actual malice on the defender's part,[72] or that publication of the matter published was prohibited by law,[73] or was not of public concern and the publication thereof was not for the public benefit.[74] A defender seeking to rely on " publication . . . for the public benefit " must show that it was for the public benefit that the actual words complained of were published, not merely that the publication of the report as a whole was beneficial.[75] This has been held to be a question for the judge, not the jury, to decide.[76]

---

67 *Wright & Greig, supra.*
68 *Pope* v. *Outram,* 1909 S.C. 230.
69 *Thomson* v. *Munro & Jamieson* (1900) 8 S.L.T. 327.
70 *Allbutt* v. *G.M.C.* (1889) 23 Q.B.D. 400; *Adam* v. *Ward* [1917] A.C. 309.
71 A general demand for a full apology is not enough: the request should set out the terms of the letter or statement to be inserted or made: *Khan* v. *Ahmed* [1957] 2 Q.B. 149.
72 s. 7 (1).
73 s. 7 (3).
74 s. 7 (3). See *Kelly* v. *O'Malley* (1889) 6 T.L.R. 62; *Sharman* v. *Merritt* (1916) 32 T.L.R. 360.
75 *Pankhurst* v. *Sowler* (1887) 3 T.L.R. 193.
76 *Ponsford* v. *Financial Times, Ltd.* (1900) 16 T.L.R. 248.

ion to Meetings) Act, 1960, s. 1 (5) confers
nda of any meeting required by the Act
y of which is supplied to a member of the
supplied for the benefit of a newspaper.

t was to be Regarded as Fair Comment
er of Public Interest

tters of public interest is an element of
njoyed by all individuals,[77] and a person
, within the limits permitted by the law,
or reputation. The plea of fair comment
y accordingly be a valid defence to an
" It is the privilege of every citizen to
ing the public acts and utterances of
s said that everyone who occupies a
n, and it will not, I think, make the
rteous, or even offensive or vitupera-
g more than an expression of opinion

ce from *veritas* in that in the latter case
a defender must show .   amatory statement of fact and injurious
imputation is true in fact [79]; in fair comment the defender must show that
each statement of fact is true, that the matter is one of public interest, and
that the comment on the facts is " fair," as hereinafter defined. In *veritas*
actual malice is irrelevant; in fair comment it is relevant.

It differs as a defence from privilege in that in cases of privilege, both
absolute and qualified, a person is protected, if the statement was made in
defined circumstances only, from the consequences of having uttered what
would otherwise be actionably defamatory matter. Fair comment is a
liberty enjoyed equally by all persons.[80] Both defences can equally be rebutted by proof of actual malice.

The liberty of fair comment belongs equally to the Press and to individual citizens, and a newspaper has the same right as, and no higher or
greater right in this respect than, the ordinary citizen.[81] A newspaper
cannot plead privilege in respect of an anonymous letter or contribution
if it refuses to disclose the name of the writer.[82]

Requisites of defence. The requisites of the defence of fair comment
are that the statement in issue be shown to be (a) comment; (b) on a

[77] *Langlands* v. *Leng*, 1916 S.C.(H.L.) 102, 110; *Lyon* v. *Daily Telegraph* [1943] 1 K.B. 746, 753.
[78] *Godfrey* v. *Thomson* (1890) 17 R. 1108, 1114, *per* Lord McLaren; *cf. Gray* v. *S.S.P.C.A.* (1890) 17 R. 1185, 1200, *per* Lord McLaren.
[79] This is subject to the qualification of the Defamation Act, 1952, s. 5.
[80] *Merivale* v. *Carson* (1887) 20 Q.B.D. 275.
[81] *Langlands* v. *Leng*, 1916 S.C.(H.L.) 102, 110, *per* Lord Shaw; *cf. Campbell* v. *Spottiswoode* (1863) 3 B. & S. 769; *Arnold* v. *King-Emperor* (1914) 83 L.J.P.C. 299.
[82] *Brims* v. *Reid & Sons* (1885) 12 R. 1016; *McKerchar* v. *Cameron* (1892) 19 R. 383; *Morrison* v. *Smith* (1897) 24 R. 471.

matter of fact truly stated; (c) fairly and honestly made; (d) on a matter of public interest. These requisites are examined separately hereafter.

Provinces of judge and jury. It is for the judge to explain to the jury the requisites of the defence of fair comment, and for the jury to decide on the evidence whether the expressions complained of were statements of fact or comments on facts,[83] whether the facts stated as a basis for the comment were or were not truly stated [84] and if so whether the comment made thereon was fair,[85] but it is for the judge to decide whether the words are capable of being a statement of fact,[86] whether the matter of comment is of public interest or not,[87] and, if so, whether there is any sufficient evidence on which a reasonable jury could find the comment to be unfair.[88] If the court is satisfied that the statement complained of is comment on a matter of fact of public interest, truly stated, it may dismiss the action if satisfied that no reasonable jury could justifiably hold the statement to go beyond reasonable criticism. If the pursuer avers malice, the court must be satisfied that there are relevant averments thereof, and the presiding judge must explain what is meant by malice to the jury, who must decide, whether the statement is comment and whether it is fair or vitiated by malice and accordingly defamatory.

Onus of proof. The defender must, if the fact is challenged, prove that the matter commented on is of public interest, any facts stated as a basis for comment were truly stated,[89] and that the words complained of were fair comment thereon in the sense hereafter discussed.[89] The pursuer must prove that the words went beyond fair comment or were malicious. If the defender seeks to give evidence that he did not intend to refer to the pursuer, it is admissible for the pursuer to give evidence that the defender did intend to refer to him.[90]

(a) Comment

The statement relied on as fair comment must be truly comment, that is, an expression of appreciation, evaluation, criticism or opinion, and not a statement of fact. It is in every case a question of fact whether the statement in issue falls to be regarded as comment on facts or as a statement of fact.[91] If it falls to be regarded as a statement of fact the defence of fair comment is inapplicable, because it is defamation masquerading as comment.

---

[83] *Aga Khan* v. *Times Publishing Co.* [1924] 1 K.B. 675; *cf. Stopes* v. *Sutherland* (1924) 39 T.L.R. 677, 679.

[84] *Digby* v. *Financial News, Ltd.* [1907] 1 K.B. 502.

[85] *Hunt* v. *Star* [1908] 2 K.B. 309; *Dakhyl* v. *Labouchere* [1908] 2 K.B. 325.

[86] *McQuire* v. *Western Morning News* [1903] 2 K.B. 100; *Merivale* v. *Carson* (1887) 20 Q.B.D. 275; *Turner* v. *M.G.M.* [1950] 1 All E.R. 449.

[87] *South Hetton* v. *N.E. News* [1894] 1 Q.B. 133, 141.

[88] *South Hetton, supra; Sutherland* v. *Stopes* [1925] A.C. 47.

[89] *Digby* v. *Financial News* [1907] 1 K.B. 502; *Peter Walker, Ltd.* v. *Hodgson* [1909] 1 K.B. 239; *Wheatley* v. *Anderson*, 1927 S.C. 133; *Turner* v. *M.G.M.* [1950] 1 All E.R. 449.

[90] *Bridgmont* v. *Associated Newspapers, Ltd.* [1951] 2 K.B. 578.

[91] *Kemsley* v. *Foot* [1952] A.C. 345; *Jones* v. *Skelton* [1963] 3 All E.R. 952.

In many cases a statement conceals within it both a statement of fact and a comment thereon, as where it is said that X has disgraced his office by his misconduct; such a statement (a) imputes misconduct to X (fact) and says that he has disgraced his office thereby (comment).

The following have been held to be allegations of fact though in the guise of comment: that an individual had been motivated by disreputable motives [92]; that a public man has been guilty of particular acts of misconduct [93]; misdescription of a book or play in a criticism thereof.[94] Conversely words which appear to be an allegation of fact may be shown from their context to be an expression of opinion or of comment: thus an imputation of disgraceful motives for conduct may be comment if the context includes instances of conduct or other grounds from which such an inference can reasonably be drawn.[95] " The question in all cases is whether there is a sufficient substratum of fact stated or indicated in the words which are the subject-matter of the action." [96] " There is no privilege when, instead of commenting merely on the opinions in a publication, or arguing against them, an opponent takes occasion to calumniate the author." [97]

(b) On a matter of fact truly stated

The statement objected to must, if it is to fall within the defence of fair comment, be comment based on facts admitted or proved to be substantially true. " Proof of the authenticity of the facts upon which a comment is based is the first step to the successful establishment of the defence that it is fair." [98] An opinion or criticism based on inaccurate facts cannot give rise to a plea of fair comment.[99]

Prior to the Defamation Act, 1952, it was essential to prove, in so far as not admitted, that each and all of the allegations of fact in the statement complained of were true, and that the comment on these facts was fair and honest comment on a matter of public interest.[1] The defence accordingly failed if the truth of any of the allegations of fact was not established.

By the Defamation Act, 1952, s. 6, it is provided that: " In an action for defamation in respect of words consisting partly of allegations of fact and partly of expression of opinion, a defence of fair comment shall

92 Campbell v. Spottiswoode (1863) 3 B. & S. 769; Joynt v. Cycle Trade Co. [1904] 2 K.B. 292; Hunt v. Star [1908] 2 K.B. 309, 321; cf. Kemsley v. Foot [1952] A.C. 345; Jones, supra.

93 Cooper v. Lawson (1838) 8 A. & E. 746; Gathercole v. Miall (1846) 15 M. & W. 319; Popham v. Pickburn (1862) 7 H. & N. 891.

94 Merivale v. Carson (1887) 20 Q.B.D. 275.

95 Cooper v. Lawson (1838) 8 A. & E. 746; Popham v. Pickburn (1862) 7 H. & N. 891; Campbell v. Spottiswoode (1863) 3 B. & S. 769; Davis v. Shepstone (1886) 11 App.Cas. 187; O'Brien v. Salisbury (1889) 54 J.P. 215; Burton v. Board [1929] 1 K.B. 301; Kemsley v. Foot [1952] A.C. 345. Cf. Gray v. S.S.P.C.A. (1890) 17 R. 1185.

96 Kemsley v. Foot, supra, 356, per Lord Porter.

97 Adam v. Allan (1841) 3 D. 1058, 1064, per Lord Medwyn.

98 Wheatley v. Anderson, 1927 S.C. 133, 143, per L.J.C. Alness.

99 Merivale v. Carson (1887) 20 Q.B.D. 275; Broadway Approvals v. Odhams Press [1964] 2 All E.R. 904.

1 Sutherland v. Stopes [1925] A.C. 47; Burton v. Board [1929] 1 K.B. 301; Kemsley v. Foot [1952] A.C. 345.

not fail by reason only that the truth of every allegation of fact is not proved if the expression of opinion is fair comment having regard to such of the facts alleged or referred to in the words complained of as are proved."

Truth must be actual. It is not sufficient as a basis for fair comment to show that a state of facts was assumed to be true, or postulated as true, or even honestly believed to be true; the facts must be actually true.[2] Similarly criticism of a work of art or literature must not misrepresent the plot or other matter represented therein,[3] and criticism of judicial proceedings must not misstate the evidence, procedure, decision or other relevant facts.[4]

Where the facts are stated in a privileged document, such as a Parliamentary paper or judicial opinion, the defence of fair comment does not automatically fail because the facts are not correctly stated. If the comments are made *in gremio* of the privileged document the privilege protects comment on the facts thus stated. If the facts are thus misstated and another person comments on them he is entitled to the protection of the defence of fair comment, provided the comment would have been fair if the facts stated had been correctly stated.[5]

Though honest belief, on reasonable grounds, in the truth of facts stated as the basis for comment, does not justify reliance on the defence of fair comment if that belief was unfounded, it may mitigate damages.[6]

Comment and fact may be intermixed or separated. The allegations of fact and the comment thereon may be contained in the same letter, article or other statement, or they may be separated, as where comment is made in a newspaper leading article on facts reported on a news page. In the former case the statements of fact and the comments may be intermixed and difficult to separate, a fact which has given rise to the " rolled-up " plea [7]; in the latter case fact and comment are more readily distinguishable. This does not affect the law applicable, though the more fact and comment are intermixed the more likely readers are to regard it all as fact.[8]

The comments, moreover, to be within the defence, must be warranted by the facts stated in the writing complained of, in the sense that the facts

---

[2] *Campbell* v. *Spottiswoode* (1863) 3 B. & S. 769; *Joynt* v. *Cycle Trade Co.* [1904] 2 K.B. 292; *Digby* v. *Financial News* [1907] 1 K.B. 502; *Hunt* v. *Star, Ltd.* [1908] 2 K.B. 309; *Walker* v. *Hodgson* [1909] 1 K.B. 239; *Burton* v. *Board* [1929] 1 K.B. 301; *Kemsley* v. *Foot* [1952] A.C. 345.

[3] *Merivale* v. *Carson* (1887) 20 Q.B.D. 275.

[4] *Helsham* v. *Blackwood* (1857) 11 C.B. 111; *Hibbins* v. *Lee* (1864) 4 F. & F. 243.

[5] *Mangena* v. *Wright* [1909] 2 K.B. 958.

[6] *Campbell* v. *Spottiswoode* (1863) 3 B. & S. 769.

[7] *i.e.*, the plea that " In so far as the words complained of consist of statements of fact, they are true in substance and in fact; and in so far as the said words consist of expressions of opinion, they are bona fide and fair comment made in good faith and without malice on the said facts which are matter of public interest."

[8] *Hunt* v. *Star* [1908] 2 K.B. 309.

must afford a reasonable foundation for the comments. It is not legitimate for a defender, by averring further facts in his defences, to enlarge the range of inquiry.[9]

(c) Comment fairly and honestly made

The law will readily presume in favour of the commentator that his criticism is fairly and honestly made, and the onus of averment and proof to the contrary, that the criticism goes beyond reasonable criticism, or is not an opinion honestly held, is on the pursuer.

Comment must be fair, not in the sense of being reasonable, moderate or temperate, but of being an honest expression of what was bona fide believed.[10] It may still be fair comment, therefore, even though the views expressed be exaggerated, prejudiced, perverse, violent, or utterly extreme; it does not matter that no other critic takes a similar view. A commentator or critic is not obliged to moderate his condemnation of what he honestly believes to be bad.[11]

In judging of comment or criticism a jury must not apply the test of whether it thinks the criticism justified, or of whether it agrees with the criticism,[12] or of whether the critic expressed exaggerated or extreme views. The question for the jury is: Would any fair [13] man, however prejudiced he might be, or however exaggerated or obstinate his views, have written this criticism? [14]

Criticism may become abuse. While honest comment or criticism may with impunity be severe, it may not descend to invective or abuse, and an honest expression of view may cease to be fair comment on that account.[15] The view must be such that it can fairly be called criticism; if it is abuse rather than criticism it cannot be protected as fair comment.[15] Whether particular expressions fall to be considered as sharp criticism or as abuse is a question of fact in every case.

Nor may comment contain imputations against the person who is being criticised unless such imputations are justified by the facts.

But the presumption in favour of the fairness and honesty of comment may be rebutted by averment and proof of facts from which an inference can be drawn that the comment was motivated by actual malice or other oblique motive,[16] even though the language used does not otherwise exceed the limits of fair comment. Any motive for making the comment,

---

9 *Wheatley* v. *Anderson,* 1927 S.C. 133.
10 *Plymouth Mutual* v. *Traders' Association* [1906] 1 K.B. 403; *Turner* v. *M.G.M. Pictures* [1950] 1 All E.R. 449. *Cf. Wheatley* v. *Anderson,* 1927 S.C. 133, 145.
11 *McQuire* v. *Western Morning News* [1903] 2 K.B. 100; *Merivale* v. *Carson* (1887) 20 Q.B.D. 275.
12 *McQuire, supra.*
13 For this word Lord Porter in *Turner* v. *M.G.M.* [1950] 1 All E.R. 449, 461 would have substituted " honest."
14 *Merivale* v. *Carson* (1887) 20 Q.B.D. 275, 280, *per* Lord Esher M.R.; *Silkin* v. *Beaverbrook Newspapers* [1958] 2 All E.R. 516.
15 *McQuire* v. *Western Morning News* [1903] 2 K.B. 100.
16 *Thomas* v. *Bradbury, Agnew, Ltd.* [1906] 2 K.B. 627; *Lyle-Samuels* v. *Odhams, Ltd* [1920] 1 K.B. 135; *Sutherland* v. *Stopes* [1925] A.C. 47.

other than the honest expression of opinions genuinely held, will defeat the defence of fair comment.[17] Thus the unjustified imputation of sordid or wicked motive to a man is evidence of malice and renders the comment unfair.[18] Violent, extreme or exaggerated criticism does not by itself amount to evidence of malicious motive, but in extreme cases such facts may be evidence of malice.[19] Comment or criticism might be so extreme as to convince a jury that no honest critic could have taken such a view and to drive them to the view that there must have been a malicious motive.

(d) Matter of public interest

The liberty of fair comment may be exercised only in respect of matters of public interest. There is no comprehensive definition of public interest, but it is distinct from matters of private interest, of interest only to the persons concerned, and from matters of limited interest, of interest to a limited section of the community. Broadly speaking, anything which merits report in responsible newspapers might be said to be matter of public interest.

It is noteworthy that conduct which in one man or woman might be of public interest, might be of only private interest in the case of another person differently placed in the community. Statesmen, judges, leading sportsmen, film stars and others are so placed that practically anything they say or do may be regarded as of public interest; humbler folk must commit major crime before their doings are of any public interest.[20]

It is for the judge to decide, as a matter of law, whether particular matter is, or is not, a matter of public interest.[21]

Matters of public interest include:

(i) Affairs of State and Government

All aspects of the conduct of the government of the realm are of public interest, such as the policy of the Government, the sayings and doings of ministers and high officials, proceedings in Parliament and its committees, petitions to Parliament[22] and debates thereon,[23] reports issued by a department of State,[24] evidence before a Royal Commission[25] or a Select Committee of either House of Parliament,[26] the merits of any appointment to public office,[27] the qualifications and suitability of a person seeking such office,[28] and the administration of local authorities.[29]   A

---

17 *Merivale* v. *Carson* (1887) 20 Q.B.D. 275.
18 *Campbell* v. *Spottiswoode* (1863) 3 B. & S. 769; *Kemsley* v. *Foot* [1952] A.C. 345.
19 *Turner* v. *M.G.M.* [1950] 1 All E.R. 449.
20 *Cf. Kelly* v. *Sherlock* (1866) L.R. 1 Q.B. 686, 689, *per* Bramwell B.
21 *South Hetton Coal Co., Ltd.* v. *N.E. News Assocn.* [1894] 1 Q.B. 133, 141.
22 *Dunne* v. *Anderson* (1825) 3 Bing. 88.
23 *Wason* v. *Walter* (1868) L.R. 4 Q.B. 72.
24 *Henwood* v. *Harrison* (1872) L.R. 7 C.P. 606.
25 *Mulkern* v. *Ward* (1872) L.R. 13 Eq. 619.
26 *Hedley* v. *Barlow* (1865) 4 F. & F. 224.
27 *Turnbull* v. *Bird* (1861) 2 F. & F. 508; *Seymour* v. *Butterworth* (1862) 3 F. & F. 372.
28 *Auld* v. *Shairp* (1875) 2 R. 940; *cf. Anderson* v. *Hunter* (1891) 18 R. 467; *Bruce* v. *Leisk* (1892) 19 R. 482; *Christie* v. *Craik* (1899) 7 S.L.T. 67 (affd. (1900) 2 F. 380).
29 *Purcell* v. *Sowler* (1887) 2 C.P.D. 215; *cf. Langlands* v. *Leng*, 1916 S.C.(H.L.) 102.

public official " must expect criticism, such criticism as the law might not recognise as justified in the case of a merely private person, but readily admits when it is in the public interest that criticism should be brought to bear upon the conduct of public officials. When a person is in a public capacity, he may be criticised by the newspapers in the public interest; and that rebuts the presumption of malice in law which the court might otherwise make and leaves malice in fact to be found either in the special language of the article or in circumstances proved which point to some motive of enmity to the particular individual." [30]

(ii) *Administration of justice*

The administration of justice is undoubtedly a matter of public interest.[31] This includes the conduct of magistrates committing a prisoner for trial,[32] the proceedings at the trial, the evidence of witnesses given on oath in open court, the conduct of the judge, the jury verdict, the judge's decision,[33] and these may all be commented on once the trial is over. Comment on any of these matters while the trial is pending or in progress may be punished as contempt of court if in any way it tends to create bias, to influence jurors or witnesses, or in any other way prejudice the accused's right to a scrupulously fair trial.[34] It is also contempt of court to accuse a judge of unfairness or partiality in the exercise of his duties,[35] though criticism in good faith of his decision is permissible. Findings that the words complained of were defamatory and not a fair and accurate report of judicial proceedings, but that they were fair comment on a matter of public interest, are not necessarily inconsistent; comment may be fair even though founded on an inaccurate statement made by a witness at a trial.[36]

(iii) *The Church*

Matters of public interest include the proceedings and decisions of the General Assembly and of synods and presbyteries, and of corresponding bodies in other denominations, reports of committees of such bodies, pronouncements by leading churchmen on faith or morals, the manner of conducting public worship,[37] the substance of sermons preached,[38]

---

30 *Langlands, supra,* 107, *per* Viscount Haldane.
31 *Hibbins* v. *Lee* (1865) 4 F. & F. 243; *R.* v. *Sullivan* (1868) 11 Cox C.C. 44; *Woodgate* v. *Ridout* (1865) 4 F. & F. 202.
32 *Hibbins* v. *Lee, supra.*
33 *R.* v. *White* (1808) 1 Camp. 359n. But to impute partiality, unfairness or other misconduct is contempt of court: *R.* v. *Gray* [1900] 2 Q.B. 36; *Ambard* v. *Att.-Gen. for Trinidad* [1936] A.C. 322.
34 *Littler* v. *Thomson* (1839) 2 Beav. 129; *R.* v. *Gray* (1865) 10 Cox C.C. 184; *Tichborne* v. *Mostyn* (1867) L.R. 7 Eq. 55n.; *Daw* v. *Eley* (1868) L.R. 7 Eq. 49; *Re Cheltenham Ry.* (1869) L.R. 8 Eq. 580; *Bowden* v. *Russell* (1877) 46 L.J.Ch. 414; *Re T. P. O'Connor* (1896) 12 T.L.R. 291; *R.* v. *Payne* [1896] 1 Q.B. 577; *Re William Thomas Co.* [1930] 2 Ch. 368; *Ex p. McMahon* [1936] 2 All E.R. 1514; *Ex p. Gaskell and Chambers* [1936] 2 K.B. 595; *Stirling* v. *Associated Newspapers, Ltd.,* 1960 S.L.T. 5.
35 *R.* v. *Gray* [1900] 2 Q.B. 36; *Ambard* v. *Att.-Gen. for Trinidad* [1936] A.C. 322.
36 *Grech* v. *Odhams Press* [1957] 3 All E.R. 556; [1958] 2 Q.B. 275.
37 *Kelly* v. *Tinling* (1865) L.R. 1 Q.B. 699.
38 *Gathercole* v. *Miall* (1846) 15 M. & W. 319 (where it was held that management of a charitable society in the parish was not a matter of public interest). *Cf. Kelly* v. *Sherlock* (1866) L.R. 1 Q.B. 686.

the use to which church or vestry is put,[39] the conduct of clergymen in their capacity as holders of benefices, and the suitability of persons for election to the office of elder.[40]

(iv) *Conduct of persons in, or aspiring to, offices of public responsibility or trust*

The community has a public interest in the qualifications, ability and public conduct of public figures, who submit themselves to public scrutiny and criticism by seeking or attaining such posts,[41] but their private characters and conduct are not matters of public interest except in so far as they relate to or cast any light on their fitness for the office or position in question.[42] " Any gentleman who takes the position of architect under the School Board of Dundee is filling a capacity as a public official, and he must expect criticism, such criticism as the law might not recognise as justified in the case of a merely private person but readily admits when it is in the public interest that criticism should be brought to bear upon the conduct of public officials. When a person is in a public capacity, he may be criticised by the newspapers in the public interest; and that rebuts the presumption of malice in law which the courts might otherwise make, and leaves malice in fact to be proved, and malice in fact to be found either in the special language of the article or in circumstances proved which point to some motive of enmity to the particular individual." [43]

(v) *Management of public institutions*

The conduct and management of all institutions which serve the community generally, particularly where they are paid for largely or in part from national or local taxation, is a matter of public interest [44]; this includes the conduct at all levels of public corporations, all nationalised industries, the boards, committees and other groups which manage hospitals, harbours, radio and television services, universities and central institutions of higher education, and similar bodies.

Public interest probably attaches also to the doings of unofficial bodies acting in the general interest, such as the National Trust for Scotland and the Scottish History Society, but not to bodies of persons associated, as in clubs, for merely private purposes.[45]

Where the management is entirely in private hands, the conduct is not a matter of public interest unless the support or intervention of the public is in some way involved. Thus the management of a private

---

39 *Kelly* v. *Tinling, supra.*
40 *Jack* v. *Fleming* (1891) 19 R. 1; *Murray* v. *Wylie,* 1916 S.C. 356.
41 *Parmiter* v. *Coupland* (1840) 6 M. & W. 105; *Seymour* v. *Butterworth* (1862) 3 F. & F. 372; *Campbell* v. *Spottiswoode* (1863) 3 B. & S. 769; *Pankhurst* v. *Hamilton* (1887) 3 T.L.R. 500; *Langlands* v. *John Leng, Ltd.,* 1916 S.C.(H.L.) 102; *Lyle-Samuel* v. *Odhams, Ltd.* [1920] 1 K.B. 135.
42 *Gray* v. *S.S.P.C.A.* (1890) 17 R. 1185, 1200.
43 *Langlands, supra,* 106–107, *per* Viscount Haldane.
44 *Cox* v. *Feeney* (1863) 4 F. & F. 13.
45 *Gathercole* v. *Miall* (1846) 15 M. & W. 319.

company is not generally of public interest, though it apparently may become of public interest if considered sufficiently large and affecting a sufficiently large number of people.[46] Larger companies and businesses may become matters of public interest by reason of the economic implications for the community of their policy or management.

(vi) Administration of local government

The manner in which all local authorities work and administer their services is clearly matter of public interest.[47]

(vii) Literature and works of art

Persons who publish or otherwise bring before the public books,[48] plays,[49] newspapers,[50] advertisements,[51] music,[52] paintings,[53] sculpture,[54] architecture,[55] or other products of their skill and imagination, such as radio programmes,[56] or theatrical productions,[57] submit them thereby to public judgment and make them open to public comment. But books printed for private circulation, pictures exhibited privately, and buildings erected privately are not matters of public interest or open to public comment.[58]

The manner of the criticism is irrelevant, whether it takes the form of straight condemnation or sarcasm or ridicule,[59] but it must not misrepresent the contents or plot or other features of the book or other work,[60] or attack the character of the author or artist save in so far as that has been put in issue by the book itself, e.g., in autobiography,[61] or attack some person mentioned in the book.[62]

(viii) Public entertainments

Any form of entertainment which may be seen or heard by the public, whether admitted in person,[63] or hearing or viewing a broadcast

---

46 *South Hetton Coal Co.* v. *N.E. News* [1894] 1 Q.B. 133.
47 *Purcell* v. *Sowler* (1887) 2 C.P.D. 215; *cf. Langlands* v. *Leng*, 1916 S.C.(H.L.) 102.
48 *Carr* v. *Hood* (1808) 1 Camp. 355n.; *Strauss* v. *Francis* (1866) 4 F. & F. 1107; *Thomas* v. *Bradbury, Agnew & Co.* [1906] 2 K.B. 627; *Kemsley* v. *Foot* [1952] A.C. 345.
49 *Merivale* v. *Carson* (1887) 20 Q.B.D. 275; *McQuire* v. *Western Morning News* [1903] 2 K.B. 100.
50 *Heriot* v. *Stuart* (1796) 1 Esp. 437; *Stuart* v. *Lovell* (1817) 2 Stark. 93. But a newspaper's circulation is not a matter of general public interest: *Latimer* v. *Western Morning News* (1871) 25 L.T. 44.
51 *Paris* v. *Levy* (1860) 9 C.B.(N.S.) 342.
52 *Dibdin* v. *Swan* (1793) 1 Esp. 28.
53 *Thompson* v. *Shackell* (1828) Moo. & Mal. 187.
54 Gatley, 363.
55 *Soane* v. *Knight* (1827) Moo. & Mal. 74.
56 *Turner* v. *M.G.M.* [1950] 1 All E.R. 461, 463.
57 *McQuire* v. *Western Morning News* [1903] 2 K.B. 100.
58 *Gathercole* v. *Miall* (1846) 15 M. & W. 319; *Thomas* v. *Bradbury, Agnew & Co., supra.*
59 *Carr* v. *Hood, supra; Soane* v. *Knight, supra; McQuire* v. *Western Morning News* [1903] 2 K.B. 100.
60 *Carr* v. *Hood, supra; Merivale* v. *Carson* (1887) 20 Q.B.D. 275.
61 *Carr* v. *Wood, supra; Stuart* v. *Lovell* (1817) 2 Stark. 93; *Macleod* v. *Wakely* (1828) 3 C. & P. 311; *Fraser* v. *Berkley* (1836) 7 C. & P. 621; *Campbell* v. *Spottiswoode* (1863) 3 B. & S. 769; *Merivale* v. *Carson, supra; Joynt* v. *Cycle Trade Co.* [1904] 2 K.B. 292.
62 *Leyman* v. *Latimer* (1878) 47 L.J.Ex. 470.
63 *Green* v. *Chapman* (1837) 4 Bing.N.C. 92.

thereof,[64] is a matter of public interest. Thus performance at theatres,[65] music-halls,[66] concerts, football matches and other athletic spectacles are open to comment and criticism, but the private life or character of a performer is not a matter of public interest and not subject to comment.[67]

(ix) Public performances

The quality of the performance by any individual artiste in any public entertainment is similarly a matter of public interest and a fit subject of comment in the Press [68] or in the form of applause or hissing from the audience,[69] but his private life or character is not a matter of public interest.[70]

(x) Any matter brought before the public

A person who deliberately issues or brings anything before the public thereby subjects it, and himself in relation thereto, to criticism and comment, which, if honest and non-malicious, is entitled to protection as fair comment.

Thus the issue of an advertisement,[71] the prospectus of a company, an appeal for subscriptions in aid of some charity [72] or other project,[73] a claim to have invented or discovered [74] something, the putting on the market of some product,[75] the conduct of a newspaper,[76] the conduct of persons at a public meeting,[77] writing letters to the Press about some injustice, abuse or other matter,[78] all make the matter in question one within the general principle that anything which invites comment [79] or challenges public attention [80] or is brought before the public so as to invite criticism [81] is a proper subject of fair comment.

---

[64] Cf. Turner v. M.G.M. [1950] 1 All E.R. 449.
[65] McQuire v. Western Morning News [1903] 3 K.B. 100.
[66] Dibdin v. Swan (1793) 1 Esp. 28.
[67] Duplany v. Davis (1886) 3 T.L.R. 184.
[68] Cooney v. Ederain (1897) 14 T.L.R. 34.
[69] Clifford v. Brandon (1810) 2 Camp. 358; Gregory v. Duke of Brunswick (1844) 6 M. & G. 953.
[70] Duplany v. Davis (1886) 3 T.L.R. 184; cf. Langlands v. John Leng, Ltd., 1916 S.C.(H.L.) 105.
[71] Paris v. Levy (1860) 9 C.B.(N.S.) 342; Jenner v. A'Beckett (1871) L.R. 7 Q.B. 11.
[72] Boal v. Scottish Catholic Printing Co., 1907 S.C. 1120.
[73] Campbell v. Spottiswoode (1863) 3 B. & S. 769; Henwood v. Harrison (1872) L.R. 7 C.P. 396.
[74] Hunter v. Sharpe (1866) 4 F. & F. 983; Dakhyl v. Labouchere [1908] 2 K.B. 325n.
[75] Paris, supra.
[76] Kemsley v. Foot [1952] A.C. 345.
[77] Davis v. Duncan (1874) L.R. 9 C.P. 396.
[78] Koenig v. Ritchie (1862) 3 F. & F. 413; Odger v. Mortimer (1873) 28 L.T. 472; Murphy v. Halpin (1874) Ir.R. 8 C.L. 127; Nevin v. Roddy [1935] Ir.R. 397.
[79] Campbell v. Spottiswoode (1863) 3 B. & S. 769.
[80] Seymour v. Butterworth (1862) 3 F. & F. 372.
[81] Dwyer v. Esmonde (1877) Ir.R. 11 C.L. 243.

CHAPTER 24

INFRINGEMENTS OF THE INTEREST IN HONOUR AND REPUTATION—ABUSE OF LEGAL PROCESS

1. Civil Proceedings
2. Wrongful Diligence
3. Wrongfully initiating Criminal Proceedings
4. Administrative Proceedings

ALL individuals have free access to the civil courts and administrative tribunals for redress of their grievances, and the right, and indeed the duty, to report criminal conduct to the authorities with a view to the initiation of criminal proceedings. It is therefore not automatically a wrong for one person to initiate legal proceedings of any kind against another, even though the proceedings turn out to be mistaken, unfounded or unjustified. But exceptionally, however, the initiation of legal proceedings may be so unjustifiable as to be an abuse of legal process, and to amount to an actionable wrong against the other party to the proceedings, entitling him to damages for the trouble and annoyance, hurt to feelings and self-respect, and possibly also to public reputation and credit, resulting from the abuse of legal process.[1] Abuse of process is accordingly a wrong akin to defamation and giving rise to an *actio injuriarum*. " It is a wrong to anyone to use the diligence of the law against his estate without legal warrant, be the consequences of that illegal act what they may." [2] " The irregular execution of diligence is a civil wrong which might have consequences for the appellant far more important than the deprivation of the furniture, and which might, for example, be ruinous to his credit." [3]

It is not necessary to prove any actual loss; nominal loss will be presumed if the wrong be established. " It is of no consequence whether the pursuers have sustained any substantial damage. Suppose the damage to be such that one farthing is recovered, that will show that a wrong has been done by the defenders to the pursuers; and consequently, that this action is well founded." [4]

1. CIVIL PROCEEDINGS

Civil proceedings generally. No action will in general lie against a person who has brought any kind of civil proceedings against another, merely on the ground that the proceedings were incompetent or irrelevant,[5]

[1] *Cf. Borthwick* v. *Gilkison* (1863) 2 M. 125.
[2] *Meikle* v. *Sneddon* (1862) 24 D. 720, 723, *per* L.J.C. Inglis.
[3] *Brady* v. *Napier*, 1944 S.C. 18, 21, *per* L.P. Normand.
[4] *Meikle, supra; cf. McGregor* v. *McLaughlin* (1905) 8 F. 70.
[5] *Kennedy* v. *Fort William Commissioners* (1877) 5 R. 302, 307.

or were unfounded in fact,[6] or brought mistakenly[7] or against the wrong defender.[8] In bringing a civil action the pursuer merely exercises his legal right to try to obtain a remedy for what he conceives to be a just claim. The unsuccessful pursuer's only liability is to be found liable in the expenses of process,[9] which may afford very inadequate compensation to the successful defender for his trouble and outlays in defending the action. The defender's claim for expenses lies only against the pursuer or a *dominus litis*.[10]

Nor is there any liability if a party obtains a decree which turns out later to be a wrong decree and has to be recalled, as happens in every case of the reversal of a sheriff on appeal, or of a Lord Ordinary on a reclaiming motion, or of the Court of Session on an appeal to the House of Lords. That alone will not give rise to an action of damages.[11] Still less is a pursuer liable if he obtains decree under a principle of law subsequently altered, disapproved or overruled.[12]

Interim execution pending appeal. A pursuer may similarly take and enforce decree for interim execution without liability in damages even if the decree is reversed on appeal.[13]

Litigation affecting property. A mala fide possessor is not entitled to prolong his possession by litigation,[14] unless to obtain a decision between competing claimants.[15]

Malicious institution of civil proceedings. It is an open question whether an action would lie if it were expressly averred that the civil proceedings in question had been brought maliciously and out of actual spite. On principle such an action should certainly be relevant, as otherwise a person prepared to pay the expenses of process could cause another party immense trouble, worry, harm to reputation and credit, expense and waste of time by bringing a number of unfounded actions against him. Moreover, since litigants are presumed to, and usually do, litigate in good faith, considerable harm could be done by the making of untrue averments on record and even giving of inaccurate or exaggerated evidence, though such might fall short of defamation and give no remedy on that ground. In any event statements in pleadings enjoy absolute privilege.[16] But privilege does not protect a person in bringing an action. The protection given by the law to litigants initiating civil process should clearly

---

6 *Ormiston* v. *Redpath, Brown & Co.* (1866) 4 M. 488; *Kennedy, supra.*
7 *Ormiston, supra.*
8 *Kennedy, supra.*
9 *Ormiston* v. *Redpath, Brown* (1866) 4 M. 488; *Kennedy* v. *Fort William Commissioners* (1877) 5 R. 302, 307; *Harpers* v. *Greenwood* (1896) 4 S.L.T. 116.
10 *Cleland* v. *Laurie* (1848) 10 D. 1372; *Fraser* v. *Cameron* (1892) 19 R. 564; *Maxwell* v. *Young* (1901) 3 F. 638; *Picken* v. *Caledonian Ry.* (1901) 4 F. 39.
11 *McGregor* v. *McLaughlin* (1905) 8 F. 70; cf. *Clark* v. *Beattie*, 1909 S.C. 299.
12 *Re Waring* [1948] Ch. 221.
13 *Graham* v. *Dundas* (1829) 7 S. 876.
14 *Cleland* v. *Weir* (1848) 10 D. 924.
15 Cf. *Dougall* v. *National Bank* (1892) 20 R. 8.
16 *Rome* v. *Watson* (1898) 25 R. 733.

apply only to those who do so in good faith, even though mistakenly or without adequate foundation for their claims in fact or law; the mala fide litigant deserves no protection. It is thought that an action would lie if there were clear averments of malicious motive. In *Hallam* v. *Gye* [17] the Lord Ordinary refused an issue raising the question whether the defenders had maliciously and without probable cause raised and insisted in an action for payment against the pursuer, on the ground that the summons did not include any allegation that the defender had made claims on the pursuer " which he must or ought to have known to be unjust." This leaves open the relevancy of such a claim of damages if such knowledge had been averred, and does not settle that such a claim is wholly incompetent. In *Gordon* v. *Royal Bank* [18] Lord Justice-Clerk Boyle said: " There was nothing vexatious, improper, or malicious in their [*i.e.,* the Bank's] conduct, at least prior to the appeal; and it is only on grounds of such a nature that damages can be demanded on account of legal proceedings. After the appeal had been taken, however, and the Bank had determined to give up the case, they ought not to have let it still hang up in the House of Lords for two years. Here it is that I hesitate to say that there may not be a claim for damages." Lord Alloway said: " I know of no principle in law by which a party is to be subjected in damages for trying his rights in a court of law, merely because he has been unsuccessful. No doubt, if he act mala fide, an action of damages may arise, but only from his improper conduct and that without regard to whether he is pursuer or defender." Again in *McGregor* v. *McLaughlin* [19] where decree was taken against a defender invalidly cited, the action was held irrelevant in the absence of averments of malice; Lord Kinnear remarked that if a man " follows out *in good faith* the ordinary forms of process, he is not liable in damages, though he may be for costs, because he obtains a mistaken judgment in his favour."

Furthermore, there is the principle that a party utilising any remedy which he is entitled to use without the authority of the court is liable if he uses it maliciously and without probable cause.[20] There seems no good reason why this principle, well established in relation to interdict and the various kinds of diligence, should not also apply to ordinary actions for debt or damages. " A litigant using any legal right or remedy, to which he was absolutely entitled, and which he required to apply for no special warrant to enable him to use, could never be made liable for the consequences of its use, unless he was shown to have resorted to it maliciously and without probable cause." [21]

Malicious persistence in action. An action of damages, however, certainly lies against a person who raises, or persists in, an action in the

---

[17] (1835) 14 S. 199, 200.
[18] (1826) 5 S. 150, 152.
[19] (1905) 8 F. 70, 76.
[20] *Wolthekker* v. *Northern Agricultural Co.* (1862) 1 M. 211.
[21] *Wolthekker, supra*, 213, *per* L.J.C. Inglis.

full knowledge that he has no ground of action. It has to be shown in such a case that bringing or continuing the action was not negligent [22] or inadvertent,[23] but that decree was taken maliciously,[24] and without probable cause,[25] as where decree was taken in the knowledge that the sum due had been paid.[26] In cases of debt, a cheque effects payment conditional on its being honoured [27]; time should be allowed for it to be cashed,[28] but if it is dishonoured, it should be returned,[29] and decree may then be taken and diligence done. A creditor is not barred from taking decree by the debtor's tender of payment, unless that tender is of the whole sum sued for and also of the expenses of process incurred by the creditor.[30]

Taking decree in breach of agreement. It is sometimes an actionable wrong to take decree unjustifiably against a person. Where there has been an agreement not to take decree,[31] or to delay taking decree,[32] to act in breach of the agreement is a breach of contract [33] and actionable as such: in such cases malice is irrelevant.[34] A unilateral undertaking to a similar effect would have the same result if it amounted to an actionable promise; if it were *nudum pactum*, it would be only a breach of faith on the creditor's part. An intimation of intention to take proceedings in default of settlement within a specified time has been held, however, not to import any obligation to refrain from taking proceedings until that period had elapsed.[35] Where there was an agreement which included that the defender would not defend, the court declined to consider defences tendered by him.[36] In such a case it has been observed that the publication of the debtor's name in a " black list " might be one of the natural results flowing from such a decree being taken, and might therefore enter into the amount of damages to be awarded.[37]

Taking decree irregularly. " There can be no action of damages at the instance of a person against whom a decree has been regularly obtained . . . because no such decree can be obtained against a defender who has knowledge of the action and takes the proper steps to contest

---

[22] *Ormiston* v. *Redpath, Brown & Co.* (1866) 4 M. 488.
[23] *Rhind* v. *Kemp* (1893) 21 R. 275; see also *Davies* v. *Brown* (1867) 5 M. 842.
[24] *Pollock* v. *Goodwin's Trs.* (1898) 25 R. 1051; *Rhind* v. *Kemp* (1893) 21 R. 275; *McGregor* v. *McLaughlin* (1905) 8 F. 70.
[25] *Davies, supra.*
[26] *Ormiston* v. *Redpath, Brown, supra*; *Davies, supra*; *Rhind* v. *Kemp* (1893) 21 R. 275.
[27] *Leggatt* v. *Gray*, 1908 S.C. 67.
[28] *Macdougall* v. *Macnab* (1893) 21 R. 144.
[29] *Pollock* v. *Goodwin's Trs., supra.*
[30] *Pollock* v. *Goodwin's Trs., supra.*
[31] *MacRobbie* v. *MacLellan's Trs.* (1891) 18 R. 470, 475.
[32] *MacRobbie, supra.*
[33] *Robertson* v. *Ferguson* (1820) 2 Mur. 303; *Sturrock* v. *Welsh* (1890) 18 R. 109; *MacRobbie* v. *MacLellan's Trs.* (1891) 18 R. 470; *Gibson* v. *Anderson* (1897) 24 R. 556; *Gray* v. *Macintosh* (1906) 14 S.L.T. 403. The ordinary rules as to proof of the contract apply: *Turnbull* v. *Oliver* (1891) 19 R. 154.
[34] *MacRobbie, supra*, 745; *Gibson* v. *Anderson* (1896) 4 S.L.T. 48.
[35] *Mackersy* v. *Davis* (1895) 22 R. 368.
[36] *Central Cyclone Co.* v. *Low* (1900) 8 S.L.T. 280.
[37] *Gray* v. *Macintosh, supra.*

it." [38] But if a pursuer has deliberately or negligently failed to go through the necessary steps of procedure he may be liable in damages for taking decree irregularly. The decree must first be reduced on the ground of the irregularity, or otherwise set aside,[39] and there must be averments of malice.[40] A pursuer is, according to some authorities,[40] not liable for mere error or negligence in procedure. This seems anomalous, as procedural requirements are peremptory, and having regard to the analogy of cases where a party can do diligence without special application to the court, where there is liability if the diligence is not done regularly and in proper form.[41] On principle a pursuer should be strictly liable for errors in procedure, without proof of malice. In view of the difficulty of proving malice, the rule laid down [40] gives pursuers' agents liberty to be careless in serving summonses; the case of obtaining decree following on irregular procedure is quite different from obtaining a regular decree on wrong grounds of fact or law.[42] The law as stated in *McGregor* [43] seems therefore to require reconsideration. The question whether diligence has or has not been done on the decree is a separate one, and it seems wrong to say that an irregular decree is not wrongful so long as no diligence has followed thereon.[44] Harm to credit and reputation can easily be done though diligence has not followed, as where the fact of the decree being granted has been publicised in trade journals or otherwise.

A party is certainly not liable for the consequences of an innocent or inadvertent mistake in process on the part of a sheriff-officer who misserves a summons,[45] nor probably of a postman who misdelivers a copy summons sent by registered post or recorded delivery, such persons not being the agents or servants of the pursuer.

Personal bar. It is a condition of objecting to process as wrongful that the complainer took the normal steps to prevent decree passing in the action in which he was cited as defender. A party who does not choose to appear or defend cannot claim damages on a technicality.[46] Similarly he probably should exhaust all modes of appeal open to him and not rely on a plea of irregularity in some initial stage of process.

[38] *MacRobbie* v. *MacLellan's Trs.* (1891) 18 R. 470, 475, *per* Lord McLaren.
[39] In *McGregor* v. *McLaughlin* (1905) 8 F. 70 and *Clark* v. *Beattie*, 1909 S.C. 299, small debt decrees were recalled on rehearing; in *Crombie* v. *McEwan* (1861) 23 D. 333; *Gray* v. *Smart* (1892) 19 R. 692, and *Jackson* v. *Lillie & Russell* (1902) 10 S.L.T. 448, the decrees were small debt decrees which could not be reviewed by the Court of Session and had to be treated as regularly granted; see also *McDonald* v. *Grant* (1903) 11 S.L.T. 575.
[40] *MacRobbie, supra*; *McGregor, supra*, 76, 77.
[41] *Wolthekker* v. *Northern Agricultural Co.* (1863) 1 M. 211; *McGregor, supra*, 74.
[42] Lord Kinnear in *McGregor, supra*, seems to be in error in treating that case (where the defender had not been properly cited) as the same as a case of a pursuer obtaining decree on a mistaken ground.
[43] *McGregor, supra*, 76–77, where it was observed that a pursuer was entitled to rely on a sheriff-officer's execution of citation.
[44] As Gloag and Henderson interpret *McGregor's* case.
[45] *McGregor, supra*; *cf. Le Conte* v. *Douglas and Richardson* (1880) 8 R. 175; *Reid* v. *Clark*, 1913, 2 S.L.T. 330.
[46] *Bell* v. *Gunn* (1859) 21 D. 1009; *cf. Ormiston* v. *Redpath, Brown & Co.* (1866) 4 M. 488.

Vexatious litigation. A litigant who persists in raising frivolous actions may be required by the court to obtain the concurrence of a Lord Ordinary before being permitted to initiate proceedings.[47] This restriction, however, does not extend the rights of persons who have previously been cited as defenders by a vexatious litigant, nor the rights of persons whom the vexatious litigant may subsequently be permitted to sue, though if a defender is repeatedly and vexatiously pursued, that might be some evidence of malice. The fact that a pursuer had been pursuing a number of previous actions, some of them fruitless, has been taken into account in considering whether, the pursuer being notour bankrupt, he should be required to find caution.[48]

Malicious repetition of action. The plea of *res judicata* is an answer to the pursuer who brings the same action as one already heard by the court. But a pursuer may bring a further action and, by founding on a different legal ground, evade the defence of *res judicata*. In England it has been held that, even without reliance on the plea of *res judicata*, the court might dismiss as an abuse of process, and frivolous and vexatious, an action which in all substance and reality was the same charge as that brought against the defendants in an earlier unsuccessful action.[49] Such a case might well ground a claim for damages for malicious institution of unfounded proceedings, even though the principle of *res judicata* [50] does not justify the labelling of the later action as frivolous, vexatious or malicious.

Interdict. A petition for interdict, or an action with a conclusion for interdict, whether interim or perpetual, is a preventive proceeding directed against an alleged present violation, or imminent threat of infringement, of the petitioner's legal rights, and it operates by restraining the respondent from violating the petitioner's rights. Interdict is never granted as a matter of course, and should not be applied for or granted without strong, or, at least, reasonable grounds.[51]

A person no doubt has an absolute right to seek to interdict another, without incurring liability thereby, in the same way as to bring a petitory action against him, and doubtless incurs no liability if his petition is dismissed or not granted for any reason.[52]

It appears to be undecided whether malicious petitioning for interdict is actionable. By analogy with actions it should be so.

Obtaining interdict differs from securing a decree for payment of debt or damages in that the interdict once pronounced is immediately

---

[47] Vexatious Actions (Scotland) Act, 1898; *Lord Advocate* v. *Arnold*, 1951 S.C. 256; *Lord Advocate* v. *Rizza*, 1962 S.L.T.(Notes) 8. *Cf. Re Chaffers* (1897) 45 W.R. 365; *Re Vernazza* [1959] C.L.Y. 2668–2669.
[48] *Will* v. *Sneddon, Campbell & Munro*, 1931 S.C. 164.
[49] *Wright* v. *Bennett* [1948] 1 All E.R. 227.
[50] *e.g., Matuszczyk* v. *N.C.B.*, 1955 S.C. 418.
[51] *Hay's Trs.* v. *Young* (1877) 4 R. 398, 402; *Earl of Breadalbane* v. *Jamieson* (1877) 4 R. 667, 671.
[52] *Wilson* v. *Gilchrist* (1900) 2 F. 391.

enforceable to the effect of interfering with the respondent's present or proposed course of action. It is therefore a more serious matter than merely taking decree for payment against him, which by itself, does not affect his rights.

Wrongful interdict. A person seeking damages for an interdict having been granted against him wrongfully must, firstly, show that an operative decree of interdict, interim or permanent, was granted against him at the instance of the party now sued for damages. Thus he is not entitled to damages if interdict was granted subject to caution being found, and caution was not in fact found,[53] so that the interdict was never legally operative; if in such a case the respondent in the interdict proceedings has acted on the basis that the interdict was operative, his action was voluntary and any loss suffered is not attributable to the interdict.[54] Similarly, he can claim damages only for the period during which an interdict was operative, and not for any period after it has been recalled[55] or expired.[56]

Secondly, it must be shown that the interdict has now been recalled. So long as it is in force, it can be challenged only by way of appeal,[57] or petition for its recall on the ground of changed circumstances,[58] and not as wrongful. Its recall, unless on the ground of change of circumstances, is conclusive that it was obtained wrongfully.[59]

Thirdly, it must be shown that by reason of the interdict the pursuer had been prevented from exercising some legal right vested in him. If he had, or is held to have had, no legal right to do what he was interdicted from doing, he has no ground of complaint against the interdict and cannot recover damages. Thus a person interdicted from proceeding with a building was held not entitled to damages, even though the interdict had been recalled as not being the proper remedy in the circumstances, when it was found that he had no right to erect it.[60]

Again where a school board dismissed a master and obtained interdict against his continuing to act as such, and the interdict had to be recalled on the ground that the dismissal was irregular, but the school board then, in the exercise of statutory powers, validly suspended the master summarily, it was held that the master was not entitled to damages since the interdict, although wrongful, had not invaded any legal right of his or caused him any loss.[61] Or again where a tenant interdicted a firm of timber merchants from building a sawmill and the interdict was recalled on the ground that the tenant was not in possession of the site, the timber

---

[53] On caution see *Tasker* v. *Tasker*, 1952 S.L.T. 152.
[54] *Wilson* v. *Gilchrist* (1900) 2 F. 391.
[55] *Roberts* v. *Rosebery* (1825) 4 Mur. 1; *Buchanan* v. *Douglas* (1853) 15 D. 365.
[56] *Daw* v. *Eley* (1867) L.R. 3 Eq. 496; *Dudgeon* v. *Thomson* (1877) 4 R.(H.L.) 88.
[57] *Burn-Murdoch on Interdict*, para. 156.
[58] *Livingstone* v. *Presbytery of Hamilton* (1851) 13 D. 649; *Lord Lovat* v. *Macdonell* (1868) 6 M. 330.
[59] *Miller* v. *Hunter* (1865) 3 M. 740.
[60] *Jack* v. *Begg* (1875) 3 R. 35. *Cf. Mudie* v. *Miln* (1828) 6 S. 967.
[61] *Aird* v. *Tarbert School Board*, 1907 S.C. 305.

merchants' claim for damages for wrongful interdict was dismissed since they showed no legal right on their part to enter on the land in question and erect the sawmill.[62]

Lastly, it must be shown that loss was sustained, attributable to the interdict; damages cannot be given if the loss were caused by something else. Thus where building operations were interdicted, but during the subsistence of the interdict operations would have been at a standstill owing to hard frost, no damages were given.[63]

Again where the interdicted person suffered loss by his own neglect, he was held disentitled to damages.[64]

The loss, moreover, must have been directly caused by the wrongful interdict; it is not enough that the interdict was only the *causa sine qua non* of the loss.[65]

Interim interdict. Interim interdict may be granted by the court, if satisfied, on an *ex parte* statement by the applicant, that there is a prima facie case for making an order in the terms requested, to preserve the *status quo* pending the full investigation of the rights of parties. Since it is obtained on a prima facie case only, based on the truth of *ex parte* statements, it is held to be obtained *periculo petentis* and the mere want of success in having the interim interdict finally declared perpetual shows that it was obtained wrongfully, and the party interdicted is then entitled to damages if he can show that he was prevented by the interdict from exercising some right and has sustained some loss.[66] The mere circumstance that the applicant was misled, or sanguine, will not justify him if his interim interdict was unjustified. Malice need not be averred.[67]

Interim interdict is not, however, shown to have been wrongfully obtained if it is recalled by reason of changed circumstances, or the passing of the occasion which gave rise to the apprehension of interference with the petitioner's rights.

Interim interdict continuing possession. A person in bona fide possession of property on an apparently sufficient title, whose possession or enjoyment is challenged, is entitled to an interdict protecting his possession and stopping the other's encroachment, until the competing claims of the parties have been investigated: *spoliatus ante omnia restituendus est.*[68] There can be no question of wrongful interdict until it be proved that the challenger has the better title.[69] If in the result the possessor's title is found insufficient, so that he must yield possession to the claimant, he will be

---

[62] *Macdonald* v. *Lord Blythswood,* 1914 S.C. 930.
[63] *Macdonald* v. *Dunfermline Mags.,* 1879, reported only in *Glegg on Reparation* (4th ed.) 206.
[64] *Buchanan* v. *Douglas* (1853) 15 D. 365.
[65] *Arnot* v. *Dowie* (1863) 2 M. 119.
[66] *Wolthekker* v. *Northern Agricultural Co.* (1862) 1 M. 211, 213; *Kennedy* v. *Fort William Police Commrs.* (1877) 5 R. 302; *Fife* v. *Orr* (1895) 23 R. 8; *McGregor* v. *McLaughlin* (1905) 8 F. 70.
[67] *Abel's Exors.* v. *Edmond* (1863) 1 M. 1061.
[68] *Miller* v. *Hunter* (1865) 3 M. 740, 745.
[69] *Glasgow City Ry.* v. *Glasgow Coal Co.* (1885) 12 R. 1287, 1292.

liable in damages, but only if he be shown to have acted maliciously and without probable cause in thus seeking to protect his possession.[70] A general averment of malice is sufficient, the interdict being granted *ex parte*, and there need not be specific averments of facts and circumstances yielding an inference of malice.

Interim interdict inverting possession. In other cases the effect of interim interdict is to interfere with a party's continued possession of property or with the continued exercise of rights or otherwise to interfere with the *status quo.* In such cases the applicant for interdict is strictly liable for the truth of his *ex parte* statements and the grounds on which he obtains interdict, and is liable in damages for having obtained interdict wrongfully if for any reason the interdict turns out to be bad or unjustifiable. Its recall, or the court's refusal to make it perpetual, is conclusive, and there is no need to aver malice, mala fides, or anything similar to justify damages.[71] These principles have been applied where a local authority, having made an *ultra vires* order against a man building on his own ground, then interdicted him from doing so [72]; where proprietors of the solum interdicted a railway company from proceeding with the construction of its underground railway, although it had statutory powers to do so and was acting within them [73]; where the purchaser of certain articles from a company in liquidation interdicted the public sale of a large number of articles by the liquidator, it being ultimately ascertained that only a very few of those advertised for sale belonged to the petitioner [74]; where water trustees interdicted mineral owners from working minerals so as to injure their waterpipe, in a manner which, it was held, they were entitled to do.[75]

Interim interdict interfering with contract. Where the performance of a contract, as for building construction, is interfered with by interim interdict, the same principles apply and the party interdicting is liable in damages if the interdict should be found in the end to have been unjustifiable.[76]

Perpetual interdict. Perpetual interdict will be granted only after inquiry into the facts, or at least full opportunity having been given to the respondent to appear and show cause why it should not be granted. Accordingly to recover damages for the wrongful obtaining of perpetual interdict, it would seem necessary to have the interdict set aside on appeal (if appeal is still competent), or recalled on petition, or to be successful

---

[70] *Moir* v. *Hunter* (1832) 11 S. 32; *Buchanan* v. *Douglas* (1853) 15 D. 365; *Kennedy* v. *Fort William Police Commissioners* (1877) 5 R. 302; *Glasgow City Ry.* v. *Glasgow Coal Co.* (1885) 12 R. 1287.

[71] *Elibank* v. *Renton* (1833) 11 S. 238; *Wolthekker* v. *Northern Agricultural Co.* (1862) 1 M. 211; *Kennedy* v. *Fort William Police Commissioners* (1877) 5 R. 302.

[72] *Kennedy, supra.* [73] *Glasgow City Ry.* v. *Glasgow Coal Co.* (1885) 12 R. 1287.

[74] *Fife* v. *Orr* (1895) 23 R. 8.

[75] *Clippens Oil Co.* v. *Edinburgh & District Water Trs.*, 1907 S.C.(H.L.) 9.

[76] *Roberts* v. *Rosebery* (1825) 4 Mur. 1; *Reid* v. *Bruce* (1855) 17 D. 1100; *Abel's Exors.* v. *Edmonds* (1863) 1 M. 1061; *Robinson* v. *N.B.Ry.* (1864) 2 M. 841; *Glasgow City Ry.* v. *Glasgow Coal Co.* (1885) 12 R. 1287.

in a reduction of the decree of interdict on some such ground as that it had been obtained by misrepresentation to the court, before seeking to establish that it had been wrongfully granted. This could only happen if it could be specifically averred and proved that the petitioners had in some way deceived the court. Perpetual interdict granted after inquiry is unchallengeable; the petitioner is not liable because the court has chosen to exercise its discretion in his favour, even though that be unprecedented or proceed on a mistaken view of the facts.

It is thought that the mere expiry of an interdict by lapse of time,[77] or by reason of material change of circumstances, does not afford any justification for seeking damages for wrongful interdict.

Other forms of remedies. Where a landlord, in the belief that his tenant had deserted a farm without making proper provision for its management, had applied *ex parte* to the sheriff to appoint an interim manager, and this was granted, and the tenant subsequently brought a reduction of the decree, reserving his claim for damages, the court held the landlord's petition competent and assoilzied him.[78] Lord McLaren, however, thought the landlord's conduct wrongful and such as would have justified damages, had the tenant claimed such. " I conceive it to be a perfectly settled general rule of law that where an inhibitory order is obtained from a judge on an *ex parte* statement of the facts, the applicant is responsible for the truth of the statements on which he obtains the order. He cannot defend himself by alleging that he acted in good faith, or that the circumstances made his story reasonable or probable. I think that the cases relating to wrongous interdict establish this doctrine; and if this be the criterion of responsibility where a party is merely interdicted from making a particular use of his property, it must in principle apply to proceedings for taking the possession out of his hands altogether." It is submitted that this view is correct, that the tenant's proper remedy in the circumstances was to prosecute his claim of damages, in which he should have succeeded, and that the principle laid down by Lord McLaren is the proper one. If the landlord's fears were unjustified, the reasonableness of his fears and his good faith should have been no defence, when he had obtained his remedy *ex parte.*

Commissary proceedings. A claim of damages is competent for deliberately and fraudulently opposing the pursuer's attempts to obtain probate of a will, and intromitting wrongfully with the estate under an earlier will, but there must be relevant averments of malice and lack of probable cause.[79]

Wrongful application for lawburrows. Lawburrows is the process whereby a party who has, or thinks he has, reason to apprehend danger from another obliges the other to find caution not to trouble him.

---

[77] As where interdict against infringing a patent lapses when the patent-right expires.
[78] *Gibson* v. *Clark* (1895) 23 R. 294.
[79] *Cleland* v. *Laurie* (1848) 10 D. 1372.

Application for lawburrows must be made by petition to the sheriff court or J.P. court and is disposed of summarily. Caution may be ordered and it may further be ordered that if the defender fails to find caution he shall be imprisoned [80]; or the defender may be ordered to grant his own bond for implementing the terms of the order, failing which he may be imprisoned.[81] The decree may be reviewed by stated case.[82] The concurrence of the procurator-fiscal is required in actions of declarator of contravention of lawburrows.[83] An action of damages for assault, and for declarator of contravention of lawburrows, can be competently conjoined.[84]

No action of damages lies against an applicant for lawburrows merely on account of his not having a good cause for his fear of harm, but malice, or any oblique motive in making the application justifies damages.[85] In a suspension of lawburrows [86] (now superseded by appeal by stated case [87]) it was held that it was necessary to prove not merely that the diligence had been used maliciously, but also without probable cause. An averment of malice alone is insufficient.[88]

Wrongful petition for sequestration or liquidation. A petition for sequestration, (or for liquidation of a company), is an action which may be followed by stringent diligence.[89] A petitioning creditor is accordingly using a remedy which the law gives absolutely and without qualification and he is therefore under no liability for merely presenting a petition, even if it is refused, or the award of sequestration recalled on a technical point,[90] unless malice and lack of probable cause be also averred and proved.

It would be otherwise if the petition were presented by one who was not truly a creditor, or contained a statement of the debtor's notour bankruptcy which was unfounded in fact and known to be so.[91] Such a petition would be wrongful, illegal and unwarrantable and actionable without proof of malice, the objection being substantial and not merely technical; an example is where a petition was presented though notour bankruptcy had not been constituted.[92]

The same principle applies to petitioning for the winding up of a company [93]; malice and lack of probable cause must be averred, malice

---

[80] Maxima: six months, sheriff court; 14 days, J.P. court.
[81] Civil Imprisonment (Scotland) Act, 1882, s. 6.
[82] *Mackenzie* v. *Maclennan*, 1916 S.C. 617.
[83] Stair, I, 9, 30; *Robertson* v. *Ross* (1873) 11 M. 910.
[84] *Ball* v. *Longlands* (1834) 12 S. 934.
[85] *Sellars* v. *Anderson* (1778) Mor. 8042; *cf. Smith* v. *Baird* (1799) Mor. 8043.
[86] *Randall* v. *Johnston* (1867) 3 S.L.R. 322; *Brock* v. *Rankine* (1874) 1 R. 991; *cf. Gadois* v. *Baird* (1856) 28 Sc.Jur. 682; *Aitchison* v. *Thorburn* (1869) 6 S.L.R. 604.
[87] *Mackenzie* v. *Maclennan*, 1916 S.C. 617.
[88] *Barbour* v. *Hogg* (1825) 3 S. 647; *Baxter* v. *Ewart* (1827) 5 S. 813.
[89] *Kinnes* v. *Adam* (1882) 9 R. 698, 702.
[90] *Kinnes, supra.*
[91] *Kinnes, supra,* 702, 704. *Cf.* Bankruptcy (Scotland) Act, 1913, ss. 11–13; Companies Act, 1948, ss. 222–225.
[92] *Smith* v. *Taylor* (1882) 10 R. 291; *cf. Beaumont* v. *Watson* (1895) 2 S.L.T. 454.
[93] *Aitchison & Co.* (1903) 10 S.L.T. 501; *Seaspray S.S. Co.* v. *Tenant* (1908) 15 S.L.T. 874; *Cf. Re Kemp* (1841) 1 Mont.D. & De G. 657; *Farley* v. *Danks* (1855) 4 E. & B. 493; *Johnson* v. *Emerson* (1871) L.R. 6 Ex.329; *Quartz Hill Consolidated Gold Mining Co.* v. *Eyre* (1883) 11 Q.B.D. 674.

being relevantly averred if the petition appears to have been prompted " not by desire to benefit the shareholders but by an indirect motive." [94]

Wrongful conduct of sequestration. Once sequestration has been awarded and a trustee appointed, he may be liable to third parties for wrong done in the course of the sequestration, as by instructing the inventorying of property in the bankrupt's father's house.[95]

2. WRONGFUL DILIGENCE

In considering liability for the wrongful use of legal diligence, whether against the person of the debtor or against his property, heritable or moveable, the fundamental distinction drawn is between those kinds of diligence which a party is absolutely entitled to use, and which he can use without need to apply to court for special warrant or authority, and on the other hand those kinds of diligence where the party must apply to the court, and must make a statement or representation to the court to obtain the requisite authority to use that diligence.

In the former cases he is not answerable in damages merely because he fails to obtain judgment against the defender, but only if he can be shown to have resorted to it maliciously and without probable cause, or if there was some flaw in the steps of process. In the latter cases, where a party applies to the court for some special diligence or remedy and requires to make a statement or representation to the court to induce it to give the requisite authority, diligence is granted *periculo petentis*, and the pursuer is strictly answerable for the truth of the *ex parte* statement on the faith of which he obtains his warrant, and is liable in damages for the consequences of obtaining and using it unjustifiably, if his statement was inconsistent with fact, independently of good or bad faith.[96] He is equally answerable if his use of the warrant has been in any way irregular and disconform to procedural requirements.

Diligence which follows on a decree which is bad because of some intrinsic fault which makes it no decree at all, as where the summons was never properly served on the defender, is always wrongful and actionable as such, irrespective of malice.[97] Similarly it may be actionable to do diligence for inadequate cause, as where a cheque for rent was refused on the ground that it did not include the expenses of a decree obtained for the sum due but when the action was brought the landlord pled that the cheque was not legal tender, a plea which he was held to have waived in the first instance.[98]

---

[94] *Quartz Hill Co., supra,* 687, *per* Brett L.J.
[95] *Houlden* v. *Couper* (1871) 9 S.L.R. 169; contrast *McLachlan* v. *Bell* (1895) 23 R. 126; see also *Mackintosh* v. *Galbraith* (1900) 3 F. 66.
[96] *Wolthekker* v. *Northern Agricultural Co.* (1862) 1 M. 211, 212–213, *per* L.J.C. Inglis; *Kinnes* v. *Adam* (1882) 9 R. 698, 702; *McGregor* v. *McLaughlin* (1905) 8 F. 70.
[97] *MacRobbie* v. *MacLellan's Trs.* (1891) 18 R. 470; *Clark* v. *Beattie,* 1907 S.C. 299, 303.
[98] *Holt* v. *National Bank of Scotland,* 1927 S.L.T. 484.

Malice. Malice for this purpose is spite, oblique motive or malevolence, such as is required to rebut the defence of qualified privilege in actions of defamation.[99] A corporation may be guilty of malice in this sense,[1] but one person is not vicariously liable for the malice of another.[2]

It is possible to infer malice from absence of probable cause, from extrinsic facts, or from the manner in which the proceedings are carried out, if, for example, they were accompanied with harshness, discourtesy or inconsiderateness.[3]

Lack of probable cause. Malice and lack of probable cause are separate elements but not necessarily unrelated and independent. The absence of just cause may go to prove malice, and the presence of oblique or dishonest motive may go to show the absence of probable cause.[4] Probable cause really means provable cause, that is, excusable or just cause.[5]

Parties liable. The creditor in the obligation is liable for the wrongful use of diligence, as is also the agent who makes the actual blunder,[6] jointly and severally. The agent is probably liable only for his own acts or omissions,[7] not for those of officials whom he employs.[8]

A messenger-at-arms or sheriff-officer is not liable unless he knew, or should reasonably have known, that the diligence was irregular.[9]

(1) Diligence against the Person

(a) Meditatio fugae warrant

Where a creditor is in a position to make an oath or affirmation that his debtor is *in meditatione fugae* to avoid paying his debt, or has reasonable ground for apprehending that the debtor has such an intention, he may apply summarily to the sheriff court,[10] or to a magistrate who, if satisfied that there is a prima facie case, will grant a warrant [11] to apprehend the debtor for examination, and may grant warrant to imprison him until he finds caution *judicio sisti*, though not *judicatum solvi*.[12] It is merely an ancillary diligence which, by itself, has no effect in attaching

---

[99] *Young* v. *Leven* (1822) 1 Sh.App. 210; *Hallam* v. *Gye* (1835) 14 S. 199.
[1] *Gordon* v. *British & Foreign Metaline Co.* (1886) 14 R. 75.
[2] *Wilson* v. *Mackie* (1875) 3 R. 18.
[3] *Robertson* v. *Keith*, 1936 S.C. 29, 44, 47.
[4] *Robertson* v. *Keith*, 1936 S.C. 29, 47.
[5] *Ibid.* 48.
[6] *Stewart* v. *Macdonald* (1784) Mor. 13989; *Anderson* v. *Ormiston* (1750) Mor. 13949; *Pearson* v. *Anderson* (1833) 11 S. 1008; *Inglis* v. *McIntyre* (1861) 23 D. 1240; *Le Conte* v. *Douglas* (1880) 8 R. 175; *Smith* v. *Taylor* (1882) 10 R. 291; *Clark* v. *Beattie*, 1909 S.C. 299.
[7] *MacRobbie* v. *MacLellan's Trs.* (1891) 18 R. 470.
[8] *Henderson* v. *Rollo* (1871) 10 M. 104. See also *Taylor* v. *Rutherford* (1888) 15 R. 608.
[9] *Scot* v. *Weill* (1628) Mor. 6016; *Clark, supra*; *Reid* v. *Clark*, 1913, 2 S.L.T. 330. See also *Le Conte* v. *Douglas* (1880) 8 R. 175.
[10] See Dobie's *Sheriff Court Practice*, 35, and *McDermott* v. *Ramsay* (1876) 4 R. 217.
[11] The warrant may be reviewed by suspension in the Court of Session: *Goudie* v. *East Lothian Bank* (1822) 2 S. 56.
[12] Stair IV, 47, 23; Ersk. I, 2, 21; Bell, *Comm.* II, 449; Bell, *Prin.*, § 2318; Ross, *Lectures*, I, 345; Bell's *Law Dictionary*, s.v. *Meditatio fugae*; Graham Stewart on *Diligence*, 682–731.

property or transferring it to the creditor, and is unnecessary and indeed incompetent where other diligence could immediately be used.[13]

Though imprisonment for civil debt has been abolished in most cases,[14] the relevant Act does not affect or prevent apprehension or imprisonment under a *fugae* warrant,[15] but *fugae* warrants are now competent only in those cases [16] where imprisonment for debt is still competent,[17] and in cases of actions *ad factum praestandum*.[18] It seems to be no longer competent to arrest a debtor in an alimentary debt under a *fugae* warrant.[19] This diligence is accordingly almost obsolete.

Wrongful application for warrant. Though *fugae* warrants are almost obsolete, cases on the wrongful use of this diligence may still be useful illustrations of principles applicable elsewhere. The application for the warrant is made by the pursuer and, if granted, it is on the *ex parte* representations of the pursuer, and in respect of a debt not yet judicially constituted. It is therefore granted *periculo petentis* and the pursuer, and his solicitor, will be liable in damages if the warrant be found to be unnecessary or unfounded, even though sought in bona fide; there is no need to aver or prove malice or lack of probable cause,[20] nor to reduce the court's finding that the debtor was *in fuga*.[21]

The magistrate granting the warrant has also been held liable where the grant was wrongful in that the proceedings had been grossly irregular,[22] and an agent has been held liable for acting on an irregular warrant.[23] In another case issues were allowed against a creditor and his agent of " wrongfully " obtaining a warrant, and against the magistrate of granting it " maliciously and without probable cause." [24]

It is not enough to justify damages that the use of the warrant is said to be oppressive,[25] or that the debt is denied,[26] or that the creditor's belief that the debtor was going to abscond turns out to be wrong, so long as he had reasonable grounds for the belief.[27]

---

[13] *Kidd* v. *Hyde* (1882) 9 R. 803.
[14] Debtors (Scotland) Act, 1880.
[15] *Ibid.* s. 4.
[16] These are (a) decrees for death duties and purchase tax due to the Crown (1880 Act, as amended by Crown Proceedings Act, 1947, s. 49); (b) rates and assessments (1880 Act, s. 4); (c) wilful failure to pay an alimentary debt (Civil Imprisonment (Scotland) Act, 1882, ss. 3, 4).
[17] *Hart* v. *Anderson's Trs.* (1890) 18 R. 169; see also *Kidd* v. *Hyde* (1882) 9 R. 803.
[18] *McDermott* v. *Ramsay* (1876) 4 R. 217.
[19] *Glenday* v. *Johnston* (1905) 8 F. 24.
[20] *Hamilton* v. *Bryson*, 10 Mar. 1812, F.C.; *Clark* v. *Thomson* (1816) 1 Mur. 161, 180; *O'Reilly* v. *Innes* (1821) 2 Mur. 414; *Battersby* v. *Caldwell* (1828) 6 S. 667; *Swayne* v. *Fife Bank* (1835) 13 S. 1003; *Ford* v. *Muirhead* (1858) 20 D. 949; *Wolthekker* v. *Northern Agricultural Co.* (1862) 1 M. 211, 213; *Kennedy* v. *Fort William Police Commrs.* (1877) 5 R. 302, 305.
[21] *Maclean* v. *Colthart* (1865) 3 M. 719.
[22] *Laing* v. *Watson* (1789) Mor. 8555; (1791) 3 Paton, 219 (no oath as to debt); *Anderson* v. *Smith*, Nov. 26, 1814, F.C. (warrant signed after apprehension); *Milhollam* v. *Bertram* (1826) 5 S. 170; *Strachan* v. *Stoddart* (1828) 7 S. 4 (illegal and irregular warrants).
[23] *Cowan* v. *Watt* (1833) 11 S. 999 (debtor's name written on erasure.)
[24] *Carne* v. *Manuel* (1857) 13 D. 1253.   *Cf. McMeekin* v. *Russell* (1881) 8 R. 587.
[25] *Mantle* v. *Miller* (1856) 18 D. 395.
[26] *Cameron* v. *Russell* (1821) 1 S. 211.
[27] *Scudamore* v. *Lechmere* (1797) Mor. 8559; *Ford* v. *Muirhead* (1858) 20 D. 949.

(b) Imprisonment for civil debt

Civil imprisonment is now strictly limited [28] but the principles laid down in older cases, when it was a general civil remedy, are still applicable. Warrant must be applied for by the creditor and is therefore *periculo petentis*, subjecting to liability if sought unjustifiably. *A fortiori* there is liability if there is evidence of malice.[29]

If the procedure is in any way irregular, that is sufficient to render the diligence wrongful, and to justify damages.[30]

(c) Imprisonment for alimentary debts

Imprisonment is competent in the case only of wilful failure to pay sums decerned for aliment,[31] or such instalments of aliment as the court has appointed. Failure to pay is deemed to be wilful unless the debtor proves lack of means wherewith to pay.[32]

Warrant to commit to prison is sought by the creditor by petition to the sheriff, and the debtor must be cited to appear and the application heard and disposed of summarily. Warrant may be granted afresh under the same conditions at intervals of not less than six months.[32]

Since this diligence requires a warrant from the court granted on the faith of *ex parte* statements by the creditor, the creditor will be liable in damages if the diligence has been used " wrongfully," in that any statement made by him was inaccurate, and there is no need for the debtor to aver or prove malice and lack of probable cause.

Equally the diligence may be impugned as wrongful if there has been any irregularity in the procedure of obtaining or enforcing it, or any defect in the warrant of imprisonment, or if its use was unjustifiable in respect that the sum due had been paid.

But it is not rendered wrongful merely by bad motive, such as spite, if it is formally correct and legally justifiable.[33]

(d) Imprisonment on decrees ad factum praestandum

The court still has full power, notwithstanding the abolition of imprisonment for debt, to imprison for failure to implement a decree *ad factum praestandum*.[34] Not every obligation *ad factum praestandum* is suitable for enforcement in this way, such as obligations for personal services,[35]

---

28 It applies only to death duties and purchase tax (Debtors' (Scotland) Act, 1880, s. 4, as amended by Crown Proceedings Act, 1947, s. 49) rates and assessments (1880 Act, s. 4; Civil Imprisonment (Scotland) Act, 1882, s. 5) and wilful failure to pay an alimentary debt (Civil Imprisonment (Scotland) Act, 1882, ss. 3, 4).
29 *Cameron* v. *Mortimer* (1872) 10 M. 461; *MacIntosh* v. *Chalmers* (1883) 11 R. 8.
30 *Strachan* v. *Stoddart* (1828) 7 S. 4; *Pollock* v. *Clark* (1829) 8 S. 1, 7; *Frame* v. *Campbell* (1836) 14 S. 914; *Hart* v. *Frame* (1839) McL. & Rob. 595; *Smith* v. *Grant* (1858) 20 D. 1077. See also *Keene* v. *Aitken* (1875) 12 S.L.R. 308.
31 On the interpretation of this phrase, see Graham Stewart on *Diligence*, 728–729.
32 Civil Imprisonment Act, 1882, s. 4.
33 *Cameron* v. *Mortimer* (1872) 10 M. 461.
34 Debtors (Scotland) Act, 1880, s. 4.
35 *Hendry* v. *Marshall* (1878) 5 R. 687 (" The whole obligations of the lease "); *cf. McDougall* v. *Buchanan* (1867) 6 M. 120.

but such obligations as to deliver a thing,[36] execute a deed,[37] or to consign money,[38] are. No person can be imprisoned under decree of a Small Debt Court for the delivery of corporeal moveables unless it is found that his failure to comply with the decree has been wilful, and in such a case the period of imprisonment is limited to six weeks.[39] A similar provision now applies to all other decrees *ad factum praestandum*, with a maximum period of six months.[40]

The creditor in right of the decree may serve a charge *ad factum praestandum* and failing performance must apply to the court for warrant to imprison. This also is granted *periculo petentis* and subjects to liability if sought unjustifiably, or if there be any irregularity in the procedure employed.[41]

(e) Process—caption

This is a summary warrant for imprisonment to compel the return of a process borrowed from court, issued at the instance of the clerk in charge thereof or of a party wishing to borrow the process.[42] It subjects to liability both the client and his agent [43] if the application has been made unjustifiably,[44] or if there has been any irregularity in the procedure resulting in imprisonment. A judge or sheriff granting warrant to imprison is acting judicially and is not liable unless there are relevant averments of malice,[45] but clerks of court or others making application are liable if there is any misstatement to the court,[46] or irregularity in procedure.[47] No notice to the detainer need be given if he removed the process illegally,[47] but otherwise notice is customary.

(2)   Diligence against Property

(a) Arrestment

Arrestment on the dependence. Warrant to arrest moveables, debts and money on the dependence of the action may be obtained by completing appropriately the blank space in the printed form of summons and having the summons signeted,[48] or, in the sheriff court, by including a crave for warrant to arrest on the dependence. The same warrant or

---

[36] *Sibbald* v. *Alvas* (1678) Mor. 6074; *Ridpath* v. *Yair* (1674) Mor. 5996.
[37] *Ridpath, supra; Anderson* v. *Buchanan* (1775) Mor. 6081; *Chisholm* v. *Fraser* (1825) 3 S. 442; *Taylor* v. *Macdonald* (1854) 16 D. 378.
[38] *Mackenzie* v. *Balerno Paper Co.* (1883) 10 R. 1147.
[39] Hire-Purchase and Small Debt (Scotland) Act, 1932, s. 7, overruling *Rudman* v. *Jay*, 1908 S.C. 552.
[40] Law Reform (Misc. Prov.) (Scotland) Act, 1940, s. 1.
[41] *Stewart* v. *McDougall*, 1908 S.C. 315.
[42] See generally MacLaren's *Court of Session Practice*, 416; *Thomson* v. *Montrose Mags.* (1825) 3 S. 423; *Watt* v. *Ligertwood* (1874) 1 R.(H.L.) 21, 23.
[43] *Pearson* v. *Anderson* (1833) 11 S. 1008.
[44] *Hunter* v. *Kerr* (1842) 4 D. 1175.
[45] *Hamilton* v. *Anderson* (1858) 3 Macq. 363; *Watt* v. *Thomson* (1870) 8 M.(H.L.) 77.
[46] *Menzies* v. *Stevenson* (1839) MacF. 281; *Hunter, supra; Watt* v. *Thomson, supra.*
[47] *Watt* v. *Ligertwood* (1874) 1 R.(H.L.) 21.
[48] Personal Diligence Act, 1838, s. 16; Rules of Court, II, 103.

precept of arrestment entitles a pursuer to arrest money, goods, cattle or ships,[49] all or any of them,[50] though an arrestment of money must be of money in the hands of a third party.[51]

As the creditor has an absolute right to warrant for the use of arrestment on the dependence without inquiry by the court and without his making any representations to it, he will not be under any liability for wrongful use merely because it turns out that the diligence was unnecessary, or the claim wholly unfounded.[52] The debtor must aver in general terms, and prove, that arrestment was used maliciously and without probable cause.[53] It is not necessary to aver facts and circumstances from which malice may be inferred.[54]

Alternatively, arrestment may give rise to a claim if used " wrongfully," in which case no question of malice or want of probable cause arises, and they need not be averred. Arrestment is wrongful (a) if the warrant for arrestment is missing or defective,[55] or (b) if the arrestment has been executed in an irregular manner, or (c) if the arrestments are entirely without warrant.[56]

It is clearly wrongful and actionable to lay arrestments without any warrant at all,[56] or to seize goods before the arrestment is served,[57] or to use a defective warrant,[58] or to arrest a person's assets held in one capacity in an action against him in another capacity.[59]

It is similarly wrongful to execute arrestments in an illegal and unjustifiable manner, such as to remove a vessel from her anchorage before arrestments had been laid on[60] or to seize a vessel after she had sailed.[61]

No claim at all arises for a mere technical informality in service, or an error in the service copy or the certificate of execution of service, so long as the informality is such as would not vitiate the procedure in the action.

Arrestment in execution. Warrant is normally contained in an extract decree of court, or an extract decree proceeding on a clause of registration of a bond or deed for execution. The principles applicable to wrongful poinding seem to apply also to arrestment in execution.[62] Where

---

[49] See *Azcarate* v. *Iturrizaga*, 1938 S.C. 573.
[50] *Wolthekker* v. *Northern Agricultural Co.* (1862) 1 M. 211, 213.
[51] *Wolthekker, supra*, 213, per Lord Benholme.
[52] *Duff* v. *Bradberry* (1825) 4 S. 23; *Henning* v. *Hewetson* (1852) 14 D. 487; *Wolthekker* v. *Northern Agricultural Co.* (1862) 1 M. 211; *Wilson* v. *Mackie* (1875) 3 R. 18.
[53] Cases in last note and *Duffus* v. *Davidson* (1828) 4 Mur. 558; *Brodie* v. *Young* (1851) 13 D. 737; *Borthwick* v. *Gilkison* (1862) 2 M. 125; *Kennedy* v. *Fort William Police Commrs.* (1877) 5 R. 302; *Gordon* v. *British and Foreign Metaline Co.* (1886) 14 R. 75, 83; *Kerr* v. *Malcolm* (1906) 14 S.L.T. 191.
[54] *Baillie* v. *Hume* (1853) 16 D. 161.
[55] Cf. *MacTaggart* v. *MacKillop*, 1938 S.L.T. 100; 1939 S.L.T. 65.
[56] *Meikle* v. *Sneddon* (1862) 24 D. 720; *Borthwick* v. *Gilkison* (1863) 2 M. 125; *Wilson* v. *Mackie* (1875) 3 R. 18, 19. Cf. *Massarella* v. *Murray* (1897) 5 S.L.T. 68.
[57] *Petersen* v. *McLean* (1868) 6 M. 218.
[58] *Kennedy* v. *Fort William Police Commrs.* (1877) 5 R. 302.
[59] *Wilson* v. *Mackie* (1875) 3 R. 18. Cf. *Wilson* v. *Gloag* (1840) 2 D. 1233; *Macfarlane* v. *Sanderson* (1868) 40 Sc.Jur. 189.
[60] *Petersen* v. *McLean* (1868) 6 M. 218.
[61] *Carlberg* v. *Borjesson* (1877) 5 R. 188; 5 R.(H.L.) 215.
[62] *Taylor* v. *Rutherford* (1888) 15 R. 608.

an arrestment was laid by virtue of a summary warrant obtained on the *ex parte* certificate of a burgh collector of rates, *periculo petentis*, no averments of malice or lack of probable cause were held necessary.[63]

Action of furthcoming. Furthcoming, though in substance only a diligence completing the preference of an arrester, is in form an action in court to transfer to the arrester funds, or goods to be sold, to satisfy his claim against the common debtor. Since it proceeds in court on the basis of representations a debtor complaining of it as wrongful must aver and prove malice and lack of probable cause on the part of the creditor.[64]

(b) Inhibition

The principles applicable to arrestment on the dependence apply also to inhibition.[65]

(c) Charge for payment

A charge for payment is the first step of diligence,[66] and one which a creditor holding an extract decree is entitled to take without any further application to the court or special warrant therefrom, but as a matter of right. Accordingly service of a charge is actionable only if malice and want of probable cause be averred and proved.[67]

Alternatively, it may be actionable as being " wrongful," without any averment of malice or want of probable cause, if (a) the charge is given on an irregular warrant[68]; or (b) there is irregularity in the service of the charge[69]; or (c) the charge is used unjustifiably in the circumstances.[70]

It is undecided whether a creditor is liable in damages merely for serving a regular charge on an irregular or illegal warrant, without any further steps. Probably he is liable, because the expiry of the charge without payment renders the debtor notour bankrupt.[71] He is certainly liable if a charge founded on an illegal warrant has been followed by poinding[72] or imprisonment.[73] To be effectual a charge must contain the creditor's name and an address at which payment can be made.[74] In *McGregor* v. *McLaughlin*[75] a charge was served following on a small debt decree which had been irregularly obtained in that the defender was served with

[63] *Grant* v. *Airdrie Mags.*, 1939 S.C. 738.
[64] *Kinnes* v. *Adam* (1882) 9 R. 698.
[65] *Macleod* v. *Macleod* (1836) 15 S. 248; *Wolthekker* v. *Northern Agricultural Co.* (1862) 1 M. 211, 212; *Beattie* v. *Pratt* (1880) 7 R. 1171. See also *Herbertson* v. *Baxter* (1830) 8 S. 564; *Cox* v. *Urquhart* (1830) 8 S. 599.
[66] Personal Diligence Act, 1838; *Gibb* v. *Edinburgh Brewery* (1873) 11 M. 705; *Smith* v. *Taylor* (1882) 10 R. 291, 298.
[67] *Wolthekker* v. *Northern Agricultural Co.* (1862) 1 M. 211; *Gibb, supra*, is a mistaken decision.
[68] *Cf. Wilson* v. *Gorman*, 1924 S.L.T. 112.
[69] *Smith* v. *Taylor* (1882) 10 R. 291 (six days' *induciae* instead of fifteen).
[70] *Cf. Parkinson* v. *Bowen*, 1951 S.L.T. 393.
[71] Bankruptcy (Scotland) Act, 1913, s. 7.
[72] *Anderson* v. *Ormiston & Lorain* (1750) M. 13949; *Wilson* v. *Alexander* (1846) 9 D. 7.
[73] *Cook* v. *Wallace & Wilson* (1889) 16 R. 565.
[74] *Dunbar* v. *Mitchell*, 1928 S.L.T. 225.
[75] (1905) 8 F. 70.

the wrong summons. The decree was recalled on a rehearing, and the charge following thereon accordingly fell. No damage was averred to have resulted from the charge and the court held that no claim lay for the wrongful charge.

If there has been some irregularity in the service of a charge, such as a wrong *induciae*, the creditor is probably liable even where no further step has been taken. He is certainly liable where a further step has been taken, such as to petition for *cessio* of the debtor's estate on the incorrect narrative that notour bankruptcy had been constituted,[76] or a poinding been executed.[77]

If the charge has been used unjustifiably in the circumstances, as where the debt has been paid, the creditor is liable in damages for that wrongful diligence, even though no further procedure has followed,[78] and, *a fortiori*, if any further step has been taken.[79]

The claim of damages must be combined with an action for reduction of the diligence if the execution of the charge has been regular but the objection is to an error in the schedule of charge.[80]

(d) Personal Poinding

Poinding may be used by a creditor who holds an extract decree or an extract registered bond or notarial protest of a bill and has charged the debtor to pay, without any further application to the court or special warrant,[81] and it is therefore actionable by the debtor only if he can aver and prove that the creditor's use was malicious and without probable cause.[82]

Alternatively, poinding may be actionable as having been used " wrongfully," without any need to aver malice or lack of probable cause, if it has been used (a) on a defective warrant, or (b) proceeded with irregularly, or (c) used unjustifiably in the circumstances.

Poinding on a defective warrant may consist in proceeding on a defective extract decree, or in following on a charge invalid by reason of having been irregularly served, as where the charge had misstated the creditor's Christian name.[83]

A poinding carried through irregularly in any respect is wrongful so as to make the creditor liable in damages therefor. Thus a creditor has been held liable where goods were poinded to an excessive amount,[84]

---

76 *Smith* v. *Taylor* (1882) 10 R. 291.

77 *Beattie* v. *McLellan* (1846) 8 D. 930.

78 *Campbell* v. *Gordon* (1844) 1 Bell's App. 428; *Gibb* v. *Edinburgh Brewery* (1873) 11 M. 705; *Sturrock* v. *Welsh & Forbes* (1890) 18 R. 109 (decree and charge in face of agreement to hold claim as discharged); *MacRobbie* v. *MacLellan's Trs.* (1891) 18 R. 470; *Macdougall* v. *McNab* (1893) 21 R. 144; *Mackersy* v. *Davis* (1895) 22 R. 368.

79 *MacRobbie, supra* (application for *cessio*).

80 *Macdonell* v. *Bank of Scotland* (1835) 13 S. 701; *Brodie* v. *Smith* (1836) 14 S. 983; *Beattie* v. *McLellan* (1846) 8 D. 930; *Wilson* v. *Alexander* (1846) 9 D. 7; *Struthers* v. *Dykes* (1847) 9 D. 1437.

81 Debtors (Scotland) Act, 1838, s. 4.

82 *Wolthekker* v. *Northern Agricultural Co.* (1862) 1 M. 211.

83 *Struthers* v. *Dykes* (1847) 9 D. 1437; *cf. Brady* v. *Napier*, 1944 S.C. 18.

84 *McKinnon* v. *Hamilton* (1866) 4 M. 852; *Hamilton* v. *Emslie* (1868) 7 M. 173.

or where no attempt was made to appraise the poinded articles properly.[85] The inclusion of a third party's goods among those poinded is, however, *res inter alios* and not an irregularity entitling the debtor to damages.[86]

A poinding regular in all its procedure is wrongful if it was in the circumstances unjustifiable, as where it was executed although the debt had been discharged,[87] or partial payment had been accepted,[88] or the debtor had obtained and intimated a sist of diligence,[89] or payment had been made or tendered,[90] or the creditor had agreed to delay,[91] or was unfair and oppressive, as where a large number and variety of goods were lumped together at one sum and not properly valued,[92] or was done against the property of the debtor's wife.[93]

Sale of Poinded Effects. Sale of poinded effects requires warrant from the court proceeding on the report of the poinding, and is accordingly actionable, without question of malice, if inaccurate representations are made in obtaining the warrant or if the sale is carried through in any irregular or unjustifiable manner, as where due notice is not given.[94] So, too, sale may be wrongful if carried out oppressively, as where so conducted as to produce low prices,[95] or by selling much more than was necessary to satisfy the debt.[96]

The sale of poinded effects may raise questions with other than the debtor, as where the effects were held by the debtor under a hire-purchase contract. A poinding creditor cannot obtain a higher right to goods than the debtor had, and cannot therefore by virtue of poinding and sale retain against the true owners goods not belonging to the debtor; he is liable to return them to the true owners, or is liable in damages.[97] A more difficult issue arises where an owner has had property mistakenly, but in good faith and without negligence, poinded and sold for another person's debt and cannot recover them from the purchaser.

(e) Poinding of the ground

Poinding of the ground is in form an action in court, and a creditor employing this diligence will accordingly be liable only if the debtor can aver and prove malice and lack of probable cause on the creditor's part.[98] After decree, the procedure is generally as it is after the charge in a personal poinding.

---

[85] *MacKnight* v. *Green* (1835) 13 S. 342; *Le Conte* v. *Douglas* (1880) 8 R. 175.
[86] *Nelmes* v. *Gillies* (1883) 10 R. 890; *McLean* v. *Boyek* (1893) 10 S.L.R. 10.
[87] *Charters* v. *Wilson* (1838) MacF. 5; *Hutchison* v. *Innerleithen Mags.*, 1933 S.L.T. 52.
[88] *Robertson* v. *Ferguson* (1820) 2 Mur. 303; *Henderson* v. *Rollo* (1871) 10 M. 104.
[89] *Ritchie* v. *Dunbar* (1849) 11 D. 882; *Anderson* v. *Anderson* (1855) 17 D. 804.
[90] *Inglis* v. *McIntyre* (1861) 23 D. 1240.
[91] *Cameron* v. *Mortimer* (1872) 10 M. 461; *Macdougall* v. *McNab* (1893) 21 R. 144; *Mackersy* v. *Davis* (1895) 22 R. 368.
[92] *Le Conte* v. *Douglas* (1880) 8 R. 175.
[93] *Thompson* v. *A.G. für Glasindustrie*, 1917, 2 S.L.T. 266.
[94] *Le Conte* v. *Douglas* (1880) 8 R. 175; see also *Jack* v. *Waddell's Trs.*, 1918 S.C. 73.
[95] *Robertson* v. *Galbraith* (1857) 19 D. 1016.
[96] *Kennedy* v. *Creyk* (1887) 15 R. 118; see also *Ferguson* v. *Bothwell* (1882) 9 R. 687.
[97] *Hopkinson, Ltd.* v. *Napier*, 1953 S.C. 139.
[98] *Cf. Kinnes* v. *Adam* (1882) 9 R. 698.

As in the case of personal poinding, it will be sufficient to aver that the diligence has been used " wrongfully " (a) if the warrant for further proceedings is defective, or (b) if the poinding is carried out irregularly, or (c) if the proceedings were in the circumstances unjustifiable.[99] It is not actionable to poind and sell by mistake the goods of a stranger on the debtor's land.[1]

(f) Maills and duties

Maills and duties is an action in court, the effect of decree in which is to give the heritable creditor the rights the proprietor himself had for obtaining the rents of the subjects. Accordingly it will be actionable at the instance of a proprietor or tenant only if malice and lack of probable cause be averred.[2]

On principle it will be actionable merely as " wrongfully " used if the procedure is irregular, or if, though regular, the procedure was resorted to unjustifiably in the circumstances.

(g) Adjudication

Adjudication is in substance a diligence but in form an action in court and accordingly a debtor complaining of wrongful use must aver and prove malice and lack of probable cause on the part of the adjudging creditor.[3]

(h) Sequestration for rent

Warrant to sequestrate for rent due and unpaid is granted only on an *ex parte* statement of facts by the landlord, for the truth and accuracy of which he is strictly responsible, and accordingly it is sufficient, to justify an action of damages against the landlord, to aver that it was " wrongfully " used; malice and want of probable cause need not be averred.[4]

The wrongful use may consist in (a) irregularity in the warrant obtained or the procedure followed, or (b) using the diligence when in the circumstances it was unjustifiable.

Irregularity in the warrant or procedure may consist in including among sequestrated effects articles not covered by landlord's hypothec,[5] having goods inventoried,[6] or sold,[7] substantially in excess [8] of what is

---

99 See *McKinnon* v. *Hamilton* (1866) 4 M. 852; *Nelmes* v. *Gillies* (1883) 10 R. 890; *Kennedy* v. *Creyk* (1887) 15 R. 118.
1 *Nelmes, supra; MacLachlan* v. *Bell* (1895) 23 R. 126; *cf. Lindsay* v. *Wemyss* (1872) 10 M. 708.
2 *Kinnes* v. *Adam* (1882) 9 R. 698; *cf.* also *Sturrock* v. *Welsh & Forbes* (1890) 18 R. 109.
3 *Kinnes* v. *Adam* (1882) 9 R. 698, 702.
4 *Robertson* v. *Galbraith* (1857) 19 D. 1016; *Wolthekker* v. *Northern Agricultural Co.* (1862) 1 M. 211; *Watson* v. *McCulloch* (1878) 5 R. 843; *Gray* v. *Weir* (1891) 19 R. 25; *Alexander* v. *Campbell* (1903) 5 F. 634.
5 *Horn* v. *McLean* (1830) 8 S. 454; contrast *Lippe* v. *Colville* (1894) 1 S.L.T. 616.
6 *McLeod* v. *McLeod* (1829) 7 S. 396; *Oswald* v. *Graeme* (1851) 13 D. 1229; *Watson* v. *McCulloch* (1878) 5 R. 843.
7 *Cargill* v. *Baxter* (1829) 7 S. 662; *Robertson* v. *Galbraith* (1857) 19 D. 1016.
8 *Galloway* v. *Macpherson* (1830) 8 S. 539; *Robertson, supra; Kennedy* v. *Creyk* (1887) 15 R. 118; *Pollock* v. *Goodwin's Trs.* (1898) 25 R. 1051.

required to satisfy the landlord's claim, or in carrying through a sale under a sequestration in security before the term for payment had arrived.[9]

In a number of cases it has been held that sequestration for rent was wrongful as being unjustified in the circumstances. Such are cases where payment of rent had been already made,[10] or consigned,[11] tendered but refused,[12] where sequestration was for the whole rent though the tenant had possession of only part of the subjects,[13] where the rent had already been paid,[14] where the rent was consigned, or a payment made to account, but sequestration continued,[15] and where the payment due was due not under the lease but under another ancillary contract.[16]

It is not, however, a ground for damages that sequestration has been used harshly or unnecessarily, if in the circumstances it was legally competent and justifiable [17]: " harsh and vexatious procedure, without illegality, is not of itself a ground of action." [18]

A landlord may also be liable if he illegally and oppressively sells sequestrated effects in disregard of the tenant's interests and to his injury.[19]

In the case of sequestrations for rent brought in the Small Debt Court, since review of the decrees of these courts is limited, no damages can in general be recovered for irregularities in procedure or in the decree, but damages are recoverable for defects in the diligence following on decree.[20]

The warrant to carry back plenishing removed from the premises, which may be obtained as ancillary to warrant to sequestrate, may, exceptionally, be granted without intimation to the tenant, and in such a case, the landlord will be strictly responsible for obtaining it, and liable if it prove to have been obtained wrongfully, independently of malice.[21]

(i) Summary diligence

Summary diligence may be done on an extract registered protest for dishonour of a bill of exchange,[22] though not of a cheque,[23] by poinding

---

9 Wells v. Proudfoot (1800) Hume 225.

10 Samuel v. MacKenzie (1876) 4 R. 187, 190; Gilmour v. Craig (1908) 45 S.L.R. 362.

11 Oswald, supra; Alexander v. Campbell (1903) 5 F. 634.

12 Cameron v. Camerons (1820) 2 Mur. 232; Pollock v. Goodwin's Trs. (1898) 25 R. 1051.

13 McLeod v. McLeod (1829) 7 S. 396; Graham v. Gordon (1843) 5 D. 1207; Oswald, supra; Cumming v. Maxwell (1880) 17 S.L.R. 463; Murdoch v. McGeoghs (1888) 16 R. 93; Rebecca v. Corbet's Trs. (1886) 3 S.L.R. 161.

14 Houldsworth v. B.L.Co. (1850) 13 D. 376.   15 Oswald v. Graeme (1851) 13 D. 1229.

16 Catterns v. Tennent (1835) 1 Sh. & McL. 694; Clark v. Stewart (1872) 10 S.L.R. 152.

17 Cooper v. Campbell (1823) 2 S. 295; 1 W. & Sh. 131; Graham v. Dundas (1829) 7 S. 876; Robertson v. Galbraith (1857) 19 D. 1016; Riddle v. Mitchell (1870) 8 S.L.R. 140; Cameron v. Mortimer (1872) 10 M. 461; Turnbull v. Oliver (1891) 19 R. 154.

18 Robertson v. Galbraith, supra; Craig v. Harkness (1894) 2 S.L.T. 307. In McLeod v. McLeod (1829) 7 S. 396 and Oswald v. Graeme (1851) 13 D. 1229 there were irregularities. Rankine, Leases (3rd ed.) 406 takes a contrary view.   19 Robertson, supra.

20 Gray v. Smart (1892) 19 R. 692. Cf. Brown v. Halley (1895) 3 S.L.T. 22 (warrant to carry back); Scott v. Young (1897) 4 S.L.T. 324 (warrant to open lockfast places).

21 Johnston v. Young (1890) 18 R.(J.) 6; Gray v. Weir (1891) 19 R. 25; Gray v. Smart (1892) 19 R. 692; McLaughlan v. Reilly (1892) 20 R. 41; Jack v. Black, 1911 S.C. 691. See also Brown v. Halley (1895) 3 S.L.T. 22; McDonald v. Grant (1903) 11 S.L.R. 575; Shearer v. Nicoll, 1935 S.L.T. 313.

22 Bills of Exchange Act, 1681; Inland Bills Act, 1696; Bills of Exchange Act, 1772, ss. 42–43. As to bills granted to moneylenders see Murray v. McGuire, 1928 S.C. 647.

23 Glickman v. Linda, 1950 S.C. 18.

following on six days' charge, or arrestment, or petition for sequestration. Such diligence will be wrongful if there is any procedural irregularity; otherwise malice and want of probable cause must be averred.

(j) Ejection

A warrant of ejection is properly the executorial conclusion of an action of removing, brought after due warning given, at the expiry of a lease.[24] A decree in a summary removing [25] has the effect of a decree of removing and warrant of ejection.

Since it can be granted only as ancillary to a decree of removing, the obtaining or use of the warrant will be actionable only if the tenant shows that the landlord acted maliciously and without probable cause in obtaining the decree.

Alternatively, ejection may be actionable as wrongful if there is any irregularity in the procedure or if the warrant was used, or even obtained [26] unjustifiably in the circumstances. Thus a tenant recovered *solatium* and damages for injury to his furniture and for expenses incurred when he was summarily ejected without legal warrant and his furniture thrown into the roadway.[27] Ejection cannot legally be done during the night-time, and it is wrongful to do it then.[28]

A petition for summary ejection, as an independent substantive common-law process, is applicable in cases where a person possesses lands *vi, clam aut precario*, but has not, or never has had, a title to occupy the lands. Such are squatters, or persons in possession wholly without title.[29]

To justify damages as having been brought wrongfully it would be necessary to show that the landlord had acted maliciously and without probable cause, or that there had been some irregularity in the procedure or that the process was legally unjustifiable in the circumstances.[30]

Thus this remedy is unjustifiable where the possessor had a title of tenancy, even though obtained by fraud,[31] or where the landlord simply does not wish the property dilapidated, but justifiable where an employee who had a service tenancy has been dismissed.[32]

In the case of lands exceeding 2 acres in extent, not forming an agricultural holding, let for not less than a year, under a probative lease specifying a term of endurance, (a) if proper written notice to remove

---

[24] Sheriff Courts (Scotland) Act, 1907, s. 37. Contrast the action of ejection, on which see *Price* v. *Watson*, 1951 S.C. 359.
[25] *Ibid.* s. 38.
[26] *Bisset* v. *Whitson* (1842) 5 D. 5.
[27] *Douglas* v. *Walker* (1825) 3 S. 370.
[28] *Macgregor* v. *Viscount Strathallan* (1864) 2 M. 1339; *cf. Gordon* v. *Hope* (1703) Mor. 3739.
[29] *Hutchison* v. *Alexander* (1904) 6 F. 532; *cf. Macdonald* v. *Duchess of Leeds* (1860) 22 D. 1075; *Macdonald* v. *Watson* (1883) 10 R. 1079; *Gibson* v. *Gibson* (1899) 36 S.L.R. 522.
[30] *Fairbairn* v. *Cockburn's Trs.* (1878) 15 S.L.R. 705.
[31] *Brash* v. *Munro & Hall* (1903) 5 F. 1101. *Cf. Beresford's Trs.* v. *Gardner* (1877) 4 R. 885; affd. 5 R.(H.L.) 105.
[32] *Sinclair* v. *Tod*, 1907 S.C. 1038.

has been given, the lease or an extract thereof is sufficient warrant for ejection,[33] and (b) if the tenant grants a letter of removal, the letter is sufficient warrant for ejection.[34]

3. WRONGFULLY INITIATING CRIMINAL PROCEEDINGS

Information of crime. It is well settled that an individual who gives information to the procurator-fiscal or to the police, in consequence of which criminal proceedings are initiated against another person, is not liable to an action of damages at the instance of that other person merely because it turns out that the information was incorrect or the accusation unfounded. Giving information of suspected crime to the proper authorities is both a right and a public duty.[35] Such conduct is actionable only if averments are made and proved that the informer acted maliciously and without probable cause.[36] It is necessary to make more than a bare averment of malice and lack of probable cause, and to allege such facts and circumstances as, taken *pro veritate*, would rebut the presumption that a complainer has acted bona fide in giving information for a criminal charge,[37] though it has been doubted whether specific averments are necessary in every case.[38] The need for specific averments is at its highest in actions against officials giving information while acting in the course of their duties [39] where the presumption of bona fides is highest.

In this context it has been said that " in order to make out malice . . . it is necessary for the pursuer to prove that in making the statements or giving the information respecting the commission of the crime, the defender acted, not in discharge of his public duty, but from an illegitimate motive; and not only so, the pursuer must also prove that the statements were made or the information given without any reasonable grounds of belief,—in other words, without probable cause." [40]

Malice and lack of probable cause are not to be inferred merely because a thorough, or a more thorough, investigation was not made,[41] nor even because no investigation at all was made before the complaint

---

33 Sheriff Courts (Scotland) Act, 1907, s. 34.
34 *Ibid.* s. 35.
35 *Lightbody* v. *Gordon* (1882) 9 R. 934; *Urquhart* v. *McKenzie* (1887) 14 R. 18; *Chalmers* v. *Barclay Perkins & Co.*, 1912 S.C. 521.
36 *Arbuckle* v. *Taylor* (1815) 3 Dow. 160; *Young* v. *Leven* (1822) 1 Sh.App. 179; *Sheppeard* v. *Fraser* (1849) 11 D. 446; *Dallas* v. *Mann* (1853) 15 D. 746; *Henderson* v. *Robertson* (1853) 15 D. 292; *Thomson* v. *Adam* (1865) 4 M. 29; *Rae* v. *Linton* (1875) 2 R. 669; *Green* v. *Chalmers* (1878) 6 R. 318; *Lightbody* v. *Gordon* (1882) 9 R. 934; *Urquhart* v. *McKenzie* (1886) 14 R. 18; *Mills* v. *Kelvin & White*, 1913 S.C. 521. *Cf. Glinski* v. *McIver* [1962] A.C. 726. An informer for gain is not so protected: *Barnet* v. *Whyte* (1849) 11 D. 666.
37 *Lightbody* v. *Gordon* (1882) 9 R. 934; *Douglas* v. *Main* (1893) 20 R. 793.
38 *Currie* v. *Weir* (1900) 2 F. 522.
39 *McMurchy* v. *Campbell* (1887) 14 R. 725 (police inspector); *Buchanan* v. *Glasgow Corpn.* (1905) 7 F. 1001 (tramway inspector); *McCormack* v. *Glasgow Corpn.*, 1910 S.C. 562 (tramway conductor). *Cf. Chalmers* v. *Barclay Perkins & Co.*, 1912 S.C. 521, 532; *John Lewis & Co.* v. *Tims* [1952] A.C. 676 (store detectives).
40 *Lightbody, supra*, 938, per L.P. Inglis; *cf. Craig* v. *Peebles* (1876) 3 R. 441.
41 *Lightbody, supra*; *Rae* v. *Scottish S.P.C.C.*, 1924 S.C. 102.

was lodged.[42] But absence or inadequacy of inquiry is a factor to be considered, and prior ill-will,[42a] or recklessness in lodging a complaint, not caring whether it be true or false, are factors implying malice.[43] Knowledge of the falsity of the complaint clearly implies malice, and an informer, if he finds he has made a mistake, must communicate this, failing which he will lose his privilege.[44] The defender may prove the grounds for his complaints, though only one gave rise to prosecution.[45]

The court has in the past allowed the pursuer to recover from the procurator-fiscal, the Lord Advocate not objecting, the written information against the pursuer which the defender had presented to the procurator-fiscal.[46]

Information not volunteered. An informant who does not volunteer information but gives it in response to requests by the procurator-fiscal or the police is similarly protected. Similarly a person in possession of property is not liable if he surrenders the property to an officer of law and in consequence the complainer is prosecuted; nor is it the duty of the possessor in such a case to make a full inquiry into the authority of the officer of law to examine and seize the property in question.[47]

Action barred by conviction. An action of damages for wrongful information of crime can succeed only if (a) no criminal proceedings were taken, or (b) if any proceedings taken have failed, or were quashed on appeal, though satisfaction of these conditions does not by itself promise success in the action.[48] Standing a conviction, it is impossible for any civil court to hold that the information was given without probable cause, whether or not there was malice, and an action of damages must fail so long as a conviction stands; if it is contended that the conviction was incorrect, that should be, or have been, raised by way of appeal in the criminal proceedings, or by reduction of the conviction, and it cannot be investigated in civil proceedings. Similarly an action brought after fine paid or sentence has been served is plainly incompetent, notwithstanding averments that the fine or sentence was unjust or unwarranted, and notwithstanding averments of absence of probable cause for the information being given.[49] The fact of conviction does not, however, bar an action for wrongful arrest, because the arrest may have been unnecessary, oppressive and improper, even though the pursuer was rightly convicted,[50] nor for assault by a policeman immediately prior to the incident for which the pursuer was convicted.[51]

---

[42] *Hassan* v. *Paterson* (1885) 12 R. 1164; *Chalmers* v. *Barclay, Perkins & Co.*, 1912 S.C. 521.
[42a] *Shaw* v. *Burns*, 1911 S.C. 537.
[43] *Macdonald* v. *Fergusson* (1853) 15 D. 545; *Denholm* v. *Thomson* (1880) 8 R. 31; *Brown* v. *Fraser* (1906) 8 F. 1000.
[44] *Richmond* v. *Thomson* (1838) 16 S. 995; *Smith* v. *Green* (1853) 15 D. 549.
[45] *Kufner* v. *Berstecher*, 1907 S.C. 797.
[46] *Henderson* v. *Robertson* (1853) 15 D. 292.   [47] *Boswell* v. *N.B.Ry.* (1902) 4 F. 500.
[48] *Chalmers* v. *Barclay, Perkins & Co.*, 1912 S.C. 521.
[49] *Gilchrist* v. *Anderson* (1838) 1 D. 37; *Kennedy* v. *Wise* (1890) 17 R. 1036; *Hill* v. *Campbell* (1905) 8 F. 220.
[50] *Wood* v. *N.B.Ry.* (1899) 1 F. 562.   [51] *Wilson* v. *Bennett* (1904) 6 F. 269.

Liability for wrongful or malicious prosecution. Under Scottish criminal procedure a private individual is not normally responsible for initiating or conducting a prosecution, but only for giving information on which a prosecution may be brought.[52] Where a private individual prosecutes he has the same degree of privilege as the public prosecutor.[53] Any action for damages for wrongful subjection of the pursuer to prosecution, or for wrongful punishment, must therefore normally be directed against the Lord Advocate or the procurator-fiscal or other prosecutor in the public interest, or the judge or sheriff who dealt with the case. Since the Lord Advocate or procurator-fiscal exercise an independent discretion whether to prosecute or not on the basis of information given them,[54] an informer is not liable for a prosecution as being the natural and probable consequence of his having informed.[55]

Liability of Lord Advocate—solemn proceedings. The Lord Advocate, other Crown Counsel, and procurators-fiscal and their deputies acting on his authority and instructions, acting as public prosecutors under solemn criminal procedure, have absolute privilege in taking proceedings on indictment, and cannot be sued in any circumstances,[56] for latent irregularities in procedure,[57] or anything else. No amount of averments of malice and lack of probable cause will make a case relevant; the only remedy is through Parliament.

Liability of procurator-fiscal—summary proceedings. In summary criminal proceedings the procurator-fiscal acts on his own authority and in his own name. But at common law and under statute he enjoys substantial privilege and a large measure of immunity from liability.

At common law a procurator-fiscal is not liable unless it is specifically averred and clearly proved that he acted maliciously and without probable cause in prosecuting.[58]

The Summary Jurisdiction (Scotland) Act, 1954, s. 75 [59] provides:
" (1) No judge,[60] clerk of court, or prosecutor in the public interest[61] shall

---

52 See generally *J. & P. Coats* v. *Brown,* 1909 S.C.(J.) 29; *McBain* v. *Crichton,* 1961 J.C. 25; *cf. Mills* v. *Kelvin & White,* 1913 S.C. 521, 527.

53 In *Chalmers* v. *Barclay, Perkins & Co.,* 1912 S.C. 521, the defenders had, with the consent of the P.F., prosecuted the pursuer in Aberdeen Sheriff Court; the finding was Not Guilty. The pursuer then sued the defenders who were held free from liability unless malice and want of probable cause were proved.

54 *Cf. McBain* v. *Crichton,* 1961 J.C. 25.

55 As to liability for wrongful prosecution resulting in imprisonment see Chap. 20, *supra.*

56 *Henderson* v. *Robertson* (1853) 15 D. 292; *McMurchy* v. *Campbell* (1887) 14 R. 725; *Hester* v. *Macdonald,* 1961 S. C. 370.

57 *Hester, supra.*

58 *Arbuckle* v. *Taylor* (1815) 3 Dow 160; *Munro* v. *Taylor* (1845) 7 D. 500; *Henderson* v. *Robertson* (1853) 15 D. 292; *Craig* v. *Peebles* (1876) 3 R. 441. *Cf. Young* v. *Glasgow Mags.* (1891) 18 R. 825.

59 Replacing provisions in very similar terms in the Summary Procedure Act, 1864, ss. 30 and 35, and the Summary Jurisdiction (Scotland) Act, 1908, s. 59, and in effect superseding the Justices Protection Act, 1802 (damages limited to twopence); Circuit Courts (Scotland) Act, 1826, s. 26; Criminal Law (Scotland) Act, 1830, s. 13.

60 Not including sheriff: see subs. (4) *infra,* and *Harvey* v. *Dyce* (1876) 4 R. 265.

61 This covers procurators-fiscal and doubtless also such officials as factory inspectors who are specifically authorised to prosecute in the public interest.

be found liable by any court in damages for or in respect of any proceedings taken,[62] act done, or judgment, decree, or sentence pronounced
under this Act, [63] unless

    (a) the person suing has suffered imprisonment [64] in consequence; and

    (b) such proceeding, act, judgment, decree or sentence has been quashed; and

    (c) the person suing shall specifically aver and prove that such pro-
ceeding, act, judgment, decree or sentence was taken, done or pronounced maliciously and without probable cause.

(2) No such liability as aforesaid shall be incurred or found where
such judge, clerk of court, or prosecutor shall establish that the person
suing was guilty of the offence in respect whereof he had been convicted,
or on account of which he had been apprehended or had otherwise
suffered, and that he had undergone no greater punishment than was
assigned by law to such offence.

(3) No action to enforce such liability as aforesaid shall lie unless
it is commenced within two months after the proceeding, act, judgment,
decree or sentence founded on, or in the case where the Act under which
the action is brought fixes a shorter period, within that shorter period.[65]

(4) In this section 'judge' shall not include 'sheriff' and the
provisions of this section shall be without prejudice to the privileges and
immunities possessed by sheriffs."

To be entitled to this protection a prosecutor must have been proceeding " under this Act," so is not protected if he were acting outwith
the limit of his jurisdiction,[66] or proceeding without a warrant or on a
warrant from a judge who was not qualified to grant it,[67] or purporting
to prosecute on a charge which does not set forth any known offence
" but some indifferent or ludicrous act inferring no legal consequences
of any kind," [68] or proceeding under another Act, such as the Acts
regulating solemn procedure.[69]

A complaint framed in accordance with the Act then in force has
been held to be a complaint under the Act notwithstanding that one of
the penalties stated was incompetent.[70]

A procurator-fiscal has been held protected where a father, resident
in Midlothian, was arrested and detained in prison at the instance of the

---

62 On this see *Walker* v. *Brander*, 1920 S.C. 840.
63 The protection extends to summary jurisdiction only, not to sheriff and jury cases, tried
under solemn procedure.
64 The section does not apply to cases where only a fine was imposed, or a probation order
made: see also *Rae* v. *Strathern*, 1924 S.C. 147.
65 Cf. *Russell* v. *Lang* (1845) 7 D. 919; *Hill* v. *Dymock* (1857) 19 D. 955; *Swan* v. *Mackintosh*
(1867) 5 M. 599; *Ashley* v. *Rothesay Mags.* (1873) 11 M. 708; *Lundie* v. *MacBrayne* (1894)
21 R. 1085.
66 *McCrone* v. *Sawers* (1835) 13 S. 443; see also *Rae* v. *Strathern*, 1924 S.C. 147.
67 *Bell* v. *Black and Morrison* (1865) 3 M. 1026.
68 *Ferguson* v. *McNab* (1885) 12 R. 1083, 1089.
69 *Hester* v. *Macdonald*, 1961 S.C. 370.
70 *Hastings* v. *Henderson* (1890) 17 R. 1130 (under Summary Procedure Act, 1864).

procurator-fiscal of Lanarkshire, and tried in the Sheriff Court of Lanark-shire for neglecting his child in Glasgow. He was acquitted on the ground that the Act was not designed to compel payment of aliment, which was the matter really in issue. But the proceedings were held not to be *ultra vires* nor outwith the Act and there were no averments from which malice could be inferred. The court reserved its opinion on whether the pursuer had " suffered imprisonment " and whether the proceedings had been " quashed " within the meaning of the Act.[71]

Proceedings against a procurator-fiscal were also held to be excluded where the pursuer's averments amounted at most to averments of malicious prosecution, the proceedings were *ex facie* regular and compe-tent, and the pursuer had not suffered imprisonment nor had the pro-ceedings been quashed.[72]

The protection covers also persons employed by the procurator-fiscal in investigating or preparing a case. Thus a doctor has been held privi-leged, in the absence of averments of malice and lack of probable cause, for erroneously making a report which was defamatory.[73]

Private prosecutors. A private prosecutor initiating criminal proceed-ings for his own interest, as under the Day Trespass Act, 1832, is at common law free from liability in damages to a person whom he has prosecuted [74] unless it be specifically averred and proved that he acted maliciously and without probable cause.[75] He is not protected by the Summary Jurisdiction (Scotland) Act, 1954, s. 75.[76]

Liability of judges and sheriffs. By the Crown Proceedings Act, 1947, s. 2 (5), the Crown is not vicariously liable " in respect of anything done or omitted to be done by any person while discharging or purporting to discharge any responsibilities of a judicial nature vested in him, or any responsibilities which he has in connection with the execution of judicial process." This leaves open the possibility of personal liability of judges and sheriffs, which depends on common-law principles.

As in the case of judicial slander [77] it is thought that judges and sheriffs enjoy complete immunity from action for anything done in the exercise of their judicial office.[78] The only remedy is through Parliament.

Liability of magistrates. Stipendiary magistrates, judges of police and justices of the peace are within the ambit of the Summary Jurisdiction (Scotland) Act, 1954, s. 75.[79] The protection given will not cover a

---

71 *Rae* v. *Strathern,* 1924 S.C. 147.
72 *Graham* v. *Strathern,* 1924 S.C. 699.
73 *Urquhart* v. *Grigor* (1864) 3 M. 283.
74 *Bell* v. *Black and Morrison* (1865) 3 M. 1026, 1029.
75 *Cook* v. *Spence* (1897) 4 S.L.T. 295; *Chalmers* v. *Barclay, Perkins & Co.,* 1912 S.C. 521, 531.
76 *Secus* under the former Summary Procedure Act, 1864: see *Murray* v. *Allan* (1872) 11 M. 147; *Ferguson* v. *McNab* (1885) 12 R. 1083; *Lundie* v. *MacBrayne* (1894) 21 R. 1085.
77 *Hagart's Trs.* v. *Hope* (1824) 1 Sh.App. 125.
78 *McCreadie* v. *Thomson,* 1907 S.C. 1176, 1182.
79 See definition of " judge " in s. 77 of that Act.

magistrate who has acted *ultra vires*,[80] but he will possibly not be deprived of protection if he has merely honestly misinterpreted statutory provisions.[81] At common law a magistrate is liable for acting *ultra vires*, and it is not necessary to aver malice or want of probable cause.[82]

Other statutory protections. Similar statutory protection is conferred on persons prosecuting under other statutes.[83]

Abuse of powers of arrest or search. Misuse of the power to arrest for suspected crime has been mentioned elsewhere.[84] Search of the person of an accused prior to his apprehension is illegal and wrongful,[85] but warrant may be granted for the search of premises without apprehension of or charge made against the persons occupying the premises.[86]

If, however, the warrant granted and executed is essentially illegal, such as to search for papers which might indicate complicity in some criminal conduct, with which the person is not yet charged, an action lies.[87]

Search of premises without warrant is justifiable in cases of urgent necessity where an immediate search may recover material evidence and delay might defeat the purpose of a search.[88]

Examination of the person of a suspect prior to his arrest is not permissible,[89] and, where the accused's physical and mental condition are of the essence of the offence, if consent is refused to medical examination, only observation may be made.[90] Nor may fingerprints be taken of a person not apprehended.[91] After arrest fingerprints may be taken without consent[92] and physical examination made,[93] or search of clothing,[94] and specimen signatures obtained.[95]

4. ADMINISTRATIVE PROCEEDINGS

There appears to be no authority on the conditions under which the wrongful bringing of proceedings before an administrative tribunal can be made a ground of damages, but on principle, since such claims must be brought and orders issued in quasi-judicial form, it would seem that an averment of malice and lack of probable cause would be necessary to render wrongful proceedings actionable.

---

80 Ersk. I, 2, 32; *Pollock* v. *Clark* (1829) 8 S. 1; *Orr* v. *Currie* (1839) 1 D. 551; *Carne* v. *Manuel* (1851) 13 D. 1253.
81 *McPhee* v. *Macfarlane's Exor.*, 1933 S.C. 163; *cf. McCreadie* v. *Thomson*, 1907 S.C. 1176.
82 *McCreadie, supra.*
83 See Chap. 13, *supra.*
84 Chap. 20, *supra.*
85 *Jackson* v. *Stevenson* (1897) 24 R.(J.) 38; *Adair* v. *McGarry*, 1933 J.C. 72; *Bell* v. *Leadbetter*, 1934 J.C. 74.
86 *Stewart* v. *Roach*, 1950 S.C. 318.
87 *Bell* v. *Black and Morrison* (1865) 3 M. 1026. *Cf. H.M. Advocate* v. *Turnbull*, 1951 J.C. 96,
88 *H.M. Advocate* v. *McGuigan*, 1936 J.C. 16; *H.M. Advocate* v. *McKay*, 1961 J.C. 47.
89 *McGovern* v. *H.M. Advocate*, 1950 J.C. 33.
90 *Reid* v. *Nixon*, 1948 J.C. 68; *Farrell* v. *Concannon*, 1957 J.C. 12; *McKie* v. *H.M. Advocate*, 1958 J.C. 24.
91 *Adamson* v. *Martin*, 1916 S.C. 319; explained in *Adair, infra.*
92 *Adair* v. *McGarry*, 1933 J.C. 72.
93 *Forrester* v. *H.M. Advocate*, 1952 J.C. 28.
94 *Adair, supra.*
95 *Davidson* v. *H.M. Advocate*, 1951 J.C. 33.

CHAPTER 25

INFRINGEMENTS OF THE INTERESTS IN FREEDOM OF BELIEF, OPINION AND ACTION

" As an individual interest, the claim of the individual to believe what his own reason and conscience dictate and approve, and to express freely the opinions involved in such belief, is closely connected with the interest in the physical person. . . . But it is also closely connected with a social interest in free belief and free expression of opinion as guarantees of political efficiency and instruments of social progress. Except as interference with free belief and free expression of opinion takes the form of interference with freedom of the physical person, it is probable that the social interest is the more significant. In our bills of rights, however, individual free speech is always guaranteed, as an individual natural right. In other words, we have been accustomed to treat the matter from the standpoint of the individual interest. Undoubtedly there is such an interest, and there is the same social interest in securing it as in securing other individual interests of personality. The individual will fight for his beliefs no less than for his life and limb and for his honour.

" Hence the social interest in general security is involved in any interference with the former as well as in interference with the two latter. Moreover, free exercise of one's mental and spiritual faculties is a large part of life. As civilisation proceeds it may become the largest part. No one who is restrained in this respect may be said to live a full moral and social life." [1]

The Universal Declaration of Human Rights provides:

" *Article* 18: Everyone has the right to freedom of thought, conscience and religion; this right includes freedom to change his religion or belief, and freedom, either alone or in his community with others and in public or private, to manifest his religion or belief in teaching, practice, worship and observance.

Article 19: Everyone has the right to freedom of opinion and expression; this right includes freedom to hold opinions without interference and to seek, receive and impart information and ideas through any media and regardless of frontiers.

Article 20: 1. Everyone has the right to freedom of peaceful assembly and association.

2. No one may be compelled to belong to an association."

[1] Pound, " Interests of Personality," in *Selected Essays*, 87, 118. See also Pound, *Jurisprudence*, III, 63; Pollock, *Essays on Jurisprudence and Ethics*, 144–175; Mill, *On Liberty*, Chap. 2; Stephen, *Liberty, Equality, Fraternity*, Chap. 2.

The interests of the individual in freedom of speech, freedom of opinion, freedom of association, of meeting, and of procession, may, and frequently do, conflict with social interests in public peace and order, and in the preservation of existing institutions.[2]   These interests are in Britain today substantially conceded and protected but cannot be enforced wholly without reservation.[3] They exist, moreover, more in the form of liberties to act without liability to legal consequences or penalties, or as immunities from penal liability, save in defined circumstances, than in the form of rights arising *ex delicto* enforceable by civil process against anyone interfering with the freedom. Accordingly the cases which come before the courts usually do so in the form of actions of defamation for overstepping the liberty of free opinion and speech, or of prosecutions for breach of the peace, sedition, unlawful assembly, riot and kindred offences arising from exercising the liberty of free speech, association, procession or public meeting in an unsuitable place or in a manner likely to, or actually provoking a disturbance, than as actions for interference with a legally recognised liberty.

Interference with liberties of the subject as delicts.   The importance of the consideration of these constitutional liberties of the subject as interests of the individual is to ascertain whether the individual is entitled to recover damages from any person or body who or which interferes with his exercise of any of these liberties, unless that person or body can show legal justification for interference. In many cases there is justi-fication, as where there is genuine apprehension of breach of the peace resulting in public disorder with possible harm to individuals and damage to property. But, while there is a paucity of authority in some cases, it seems that at least some interferences with civil liberties could be action-able as delicts. In particular, there is no adequate Scottish authority on the question of recovering damages, at least nominal in amount, for the wrong of interfering with a public right or constitutional liberty.[4]

Freedom of speech.[5]   Every individual has full legal liberty to say or write whatever he chooses, provided he does not infringe the criminal law or the rights [6] or liberties [7] of others, by issuing treasonable, sedi-tious,[8] blasphemous,[9] obscene [10] or defamatory [11] matter, matter in

2 Pound, *op. cit.*, 119–121.
3 Stone, *Province and Function of Law*, 519–521.
4 *Cf. Ashby* v. *White* (1703) 2 Ld.Raym. 938 (interference with plaintiff's statutory right to vote, on which see now Representation of the People Act, 1949, s. 50 (2)).
5 See, generally, Dicey, *Law of the Constitution*, Chap. 6.
6 *e.g.*, the right to reputation.
7 *e.g.*, liberty of free passage along a street: *Aldred* v. *Miller*, 1924 J.C. 117.
8 *H.M.A.* v. *Grant* (1848) J. Shaw 17; *R.* v. *Burns* (1886) 2 T.L.R. 510.
9 To challenge the truth of Christian doctrines is not against public policy so long as it is done in the manner of serious controversy: *Bowman* v. *Secular Society* [1917] A.C. 406.
10 *McGowan* v. *Langmuir*, 1931 J.C. 10; *Galletly* v. *Laird*, 1953 J.C. 16; see also *McBain* v. *Crichton*, 1961 J.C. 25.
11 On defamation, see Chap. 23, *supra*.

contempt of court,[12] or matter inciting to mutiny or disaffection.[13] Is it civilly actionable to stifle a man's free expression of opinion? The matter seems undecided, probably because the only complete suppression of expression of opinion would be by government action; in most cases a defender, such as a publisher, would not be interfering with the pursuer's liberty of speech merely by declining for his own part and from his press to publish the matter in question, for economic or other reasons, nor do persons such as the police unjustifiably interfere with liberty of speech if they stop a meeting when they reasonably apprehend the resultant commission of some crime or the likelihood of a breach of the peace.[14] But magistrates might be liable for prohibiting a meeting where no disturbance was apprehended.[13] Police officers might be liable civilly if they were held to have had no adequate grounds for dispersing a meeting.[15] The question might also arise in the form of an action for conspiracy to injure, if the predominant motive of a combination of, *e.g.*, editors or publishers, was to injure the pursuer, which could happen by seeking to stifle his liberty of expression. But apart from that it is hard to envisage circumstances in which a civil action would lie.

Freedom of opinion. In the same way every individual has full freedom of opinion and conscience and may hold any views at all on any subject so long as he does not infringe the criminal law, or the civil liberties of other people, which can probably only happen if he seeks to express or apply or propagate the views. There seems to be no recorded attempt to bring an action against a person, party or organisation for attempting to interfere with a pursuer's freedom of belief and opinion, and it seems quite legitimate for persons holding one view on certain issues to seek to persuade others to their view, so long as they do so peaceably.

Where, however, the opinion gives rise to overt actings, such as rioting causing damage to property, there may, apart from criminal consequences, be liability on the wrongdoers and on the community to compensate for the harm done.[16] But this action is for the damage done not for holding the opinions which gave rise to the damage.

Freedom of public meeting. Individuals are freely entitled to come together in public meetings to discuss any matter of common interest, whether on private premises or in a public place, so long as they do not infringe the liberties of others or the rules of the criminal law for the maintenance of public order and the protection of life and property.[17]

---

[12] *Lawrie* v. *Roberts* (1882) 4 Coup. 606.

[13] *Cf. McAra* v. *Edinburgh Mags.*, 1913 S.C. 1059, 1073; see also Incitement to Disaffection Act, 1934. [14] *Thomas* v. *Sawkins* [1935] 2 K.B. 249; *Duncan* v. *Jones* [1936] 1 K.B. 218.

[15] If, for example, it was being held in a public place where such meetings have been customarily held (see *Aldred* v. *Langmuir*, 1932 J.C. 22) and no trouble or disturbance was reasonably to be apprehended.

[16] *Cf. Capaldi* v. *Greenock Mags.*, 1941 S.C. 110; *Coia* v. *Robertson*, 1942 S.C. 111; *Pompa's Trs.* v. *Edinburgh Mags.*, 1942 S.C. 119.

[17] Dicey, *Law of the Constitution*, Chap. 7; Goodhart, " Public Meetings and Processions " (1937) 6 Camb.L.J. 161; Wade, " The Law of Public Meetings " (1938) 2 M.L.R. 177; Ivamy, " The Right of Public Meeting," 1949 C.L.P. 183.

No person is liable to an action or prosecution merely by participation in a public meeting. On principle persons participating in a public meeting, not objectionable to the law on any ground, can recover damages from anyone who seeks to prevent or disturb or break up their meeting. In *Hendry* v. *Ferguson* [18] it was held to be a breach of the peace to create a noise and disturbance in a hall during a Salvation Army meeting (apparently open to the public) and it was observed that the real root of the offence was that it was an interference with the liberty of the subject to hold a lawful meeting in an orderly manner.

In *McAra* v. *Magistrates of Edinburgh* [19] a street orator sought declarator that the magistrates had no power to issue a proclamation, for breach of which he had been convicted, and that he was not bound to obey it. The proclamation prohibited the holding of meetings in certain streets of the city unless a licence to do so had been previously obtained. The court granted the declarator sought, holding that the Act relied on by the magistrates was in desuetude and that the magistrates were not empowered by common law or otherwise to issue such a proclamation. It is questionable whether he could have recovered damages for being prevented from exercising his right to hold a meeting. It was, however, observed that the defenders had powers to prohibit meetings in the street if they were likely to interfere with the liberty of citizens to use the streets for passage, or to prohibit certain meetings as likely to lead to a breach of the peace. In *McGiveran* v. *Auld* [20] causing an obstruction in the public street was held a relevant charge at common law.

In *Duncan* v. *Jones* [21] a woman, about to make a speech in the street, was arrested on a charge of obstructing a police officer in the course of his duty by attempting to hold the meeting after a police inspector, reasonably apprehending a breach of the peace, had told her not to do so.[22] In such circumstances she should have complied and sought to recover damages from the police for unjustified interference with her liberty of making a speech, to which she would have been entitled unless the police could have satisfied the court that they did reasonably apprehend a breach of the peace. If the police had had no reasonable apprehension of a breach of the peace occurring or of any other crime being committed, it is thought that their action in stopping the harangue would have been actionable. In the circumstances the inspector's apprehensions were probably reasonable and his interference justifiable.

Freedom of private meeting. In general, if a meeting is held on private property, it would be a trespass and wrongful for any person, including

---

[18] (1883) 10 R.(J.) 63; *cf. Marr* v. *McArthur* (1878) 5 R.(J.) 38; *Armour* v. *Macrae* (1886) 13 R.(J.) 41; *Whitchurch* v. *Millar* (1895) 23 R.(J.) 1.

[19] 1913 S.C. 1059.

[20] (1894) 21 R.(J.) 69.

[21] [1936] 1 K.B. 218; and see Wade, " Police Powers and Public Meetings " (1937) 6 Camb. L.J. 175.

[22] There was no allegation of obstruction of public passage in the street in question, which might have raised other complicating factors.

the police, to enter uninvited and prevent it or interfere with it. Of course the police may enter if it appears that offences, such as breach of the peace, are taking place, or if summoned to the premises.[23]

In *Thomas* v. *Sawkins* [24] the police were held to have a right to enter when there were grounds for believing that a breach of the peace might be committed or seditious speeches made, but in that case the meeting was advertised as open to the public, and the case is not an authority for the general liberty of the police to enter private premises uninvited where a meeting is being held.[25]

Freedom of procession. Individuals have prima facie liberty to use the highway for a procession, provided the passage of the procession does not cause a public nuisance [26] or otherwise involve breach of the criminal law, as by provoking a breach of the peace or a riot.[27] They are therefore not liable to an action merely by reason of forming or participating in a procession. Whether persons organising or taking part in a procession can sue a person who unjustifiably prevents or disperses their procession seems to be devoid of authority but on principle such an action would lie. A procession, otherwise lawful, does not become unlawful because it is known that it will, or may well, rouse opposition and even cause a breach of the peace.[28]

Claims *ex delicto* may arise where a meeting or procession is prevented or stopped without justification, or if force is used unnecessarily or in a degree disproportionate to the necessity of the situation. Thus in *Lynch* v. *Fitzgerald and Others* [29] damages were awarded to the father of a boy killed when civic guards fired, unjustifiably, it was found, on a group of demonstrators. So, too, a claim for wrongful arrest or imprisonment might arise in similar circumstances, or for wrongful seizure and detention of documents.[30]

Freedom of association. Persons have full liberty to associate themselves for any purpose, subject, in certain cases, to complying with certain legal restrictions,[31] provided the purpose does not involve infringing any rule of the criminal law,[32] and unless the predominant purpose is to damage another person and that damage actually results.[33] In particular, individuals, whether employers or employees, are freely entitled

---

[23] *Hendry* v. *Ferguson* (1883) 10 R.(J.) 63.
[24] [1935] 2 K.B. 249.
[25] *Cf. Davis* v. *Lisle* [1936] 2 K.B. 434.
[26] As in *Whitchurch* v. *Millar* (1895) 23 R.(J.) 1.
[27] *Deakin* v. *Milne* (1882) 10 R.(J.) 22, explained in *McAra* v. *Edinburgh Mags.*, 1913 S.C. 1059; *cf. Ferguson* v. *Carnochan* (1889) 16 R.(J.) 93; *Wise* v. *Dunning* [1902] 1 K.B. 167.
[28] *Beatty* v. *Gillbanks* (1882) 9 Q.B.D. 308.
[29] [1938] I.R. 382.
[30] *Pringle* v. *Bremner and Stirling* (1867) 5 M.(H.L.) 55; *Elias* v. *Pasmore* [1934] 2 K.B. 164; but see Wade, " Police Search " (1934) 50 L.Q.R. 354.
[31] *e.g.*, if the association supplies intoxicating liquor to its members, it must comply with the licensing acts; if formed to trade it must comply with the Partnership Act or the Companies Acts; *cf. Sykes* v. *Beadon* (1879) 11 Ch.D. 170.
[32] *e.g.*, to commit any crime in concert.
[33] *Crofter Co.* v. *Veitch*, 1942 S.C.(H.L.) 1.

to associate in trade associations or unions for the main purpose of bargaining collectively about wages, hours and other conditions of industrial employment,[34] and no person is liable to an action merely by reason of his association with others in such a body, though members of the group might commit the wrong of conspiracy to injure and be liable to an action therefor.[33]   Conversely, men associating probably have an action against anyone who unjustifiably seeks to prevent or break up their association or to penalise them for having associated in a union.[35]

Monopolies and " closed shops."   In some cases an individual is, by long-standing custom recognised as legally binding, obliged to join a professional body, such as the Faculty of Advocates, as a condition of exercising a particular profession.   If such a professional " closed shop " is legally recognised, the recalcitrant individual who is qualified to, but refuses to join, has no remedy against the body or its members if they refuse to concede to him the privilege of exercising the professional calling in question, or against the court for refusing to hear him.[36] " Such monopolies are only justified if they are so regulated as to promote the public interest.   Moreover, the weapon of expulsion from such a society is a step of the most extreme gravity . . ." [37]

In other cases, such as in medicine, a person with the appropriate qualifications may become registered,[38] but need not, though if he does not he suffers professional disabilities.[39]

Such monopolies are justified by the public interest in ensuring through the appropriate professional organisation that only persons of proven competence and subject to the code of professional discipline are permitted to hold themselves out as providing skilled professional services for others.   An action might lie if a properly qualified person's application for admission were rejected for an inadequate reason, or if he were expelled for an irrelevant reason.

An individual is in most cases, however, not legally obliged to join or remain a member of any association as a condition of working at a trade or holding employment, and may have an action against the members of an association who do him unlawful harm because he has left or will not voluntarily join their association, as by forcing his employer, by threat of a strike, to sack him.   If the individual alleges conspiracy he must aver and prove malicious motive and resulting damage. In *Huntley* v. *Thornton*,[40] the plaintiff, a member of a union, alleged that he had been unlawfully ordered to strike and that on his refusal the

---

34 Trade Union Act, 1871, ss. 2, 3.
35 *Cf. D. C. Thomson & Co.* v. *Deakin* [1952] Ch. 646, where a man dismissed for having joined a union appealed to the union, which called a strike.   A claim against the union officials for injunction and damages was dismissed.
36 *Cf. Equity and Law Life Assce. Soc., Ltd.* v. *Tritonia, Ltd.*, 1943 S.C.(H.L.) 88.
37 *Huntley* v. *Thornton* [1957] 1 All E.R. 234, 240, *per* Harman J.
38 Medical Act, 1956, s. 7.
39 *Ibid.* ss. 27–31.
40 [1957] 1 All E.R. 234.

defendants had expelled him from the union and conspired to injure him, by combining to prevent him obtaining or retaining work in his trade; he was awarded damages for conspiracy, with leave to move for an injunction if further intimidation occurred.   In *Rookes* v. *Barnard* [41] R was dismissed by his employers, under threat of strike action by the defendants, officials of a union from which R had resigned, thereby breaking the 100 per cent. union membership arrangement in force at his workplace between employers and union. The strike was a breach of a contract between employers and union that there would be no strikes, incorporated in the contract of service of each union member with the employers. His action against the union officials for wrongfully causing his dismissal, and for wrongfully conspiring to injure him, succeeded. The union officials' conduct towards the employers amounted to intimidation, and was not protected by the Trade Disputes Act, 1906.

It is equally or more clear that intimidation by threats of force or violence causing the employer to dismiss the plaintiff would have given him a right of action.[42]

A more difficult case is that of the liberty not to join a nominally voluntary association. If employees wish to maintain a " union shop " and employers are threatened with a strike if they take on a non-union man, they will probably not do so. Does such action by the union give any right to the man thereby prevented from obtaining employment? Probably yes, but it is difficult to be confident about the law on this matter in general terms.

The law on this matter is clearly heavily weighted against the individual as it is frequently difficult or impossible for him to establish that the loss caused him for his refusal to associate was " unlawful," the ordinary modes of union pressure on employers being lawful, and the individual's liberty to leave or not to join a union is not adequately secured by law.

Freedom from discrimination. A question of much difficulty is whether a member of a minority group, such as a Jew, a Mormon, or a coloured man, has any right of action against a person or group who discriminate against him, as by refusing him admission to certain premises. Probably he has not, such discrimination, however objectionable, being only a permissible exercise of the defender's liberty to impose conditions as to membership of their group or entry on their premises. But counter-action against the discrimination is not illegal either.[43]

Freedom of economic action. The liberty of the individual to engage in any economic activity he chooses, and in doing so to do business on whatever terms he can is being increasingly fettered. More and more professional activities are being regulated by requirements of obtaining qualifications, and businesses by the need to obtain a licence as a condition

[41] [1964] 1 All E.R. 367.
[42] *Cf. White* v. *Riley* [1921] 1 Ch. 1.
[43] *Cf. Scala Ballroom, Ltd.* v. *Ratcliffe* [1958] 3 All E.R. 220.

of carrying them on.   The nationalisation of basic industries, the requirements of town and country planning and distribution of industry regulation further limit the fields of economic activity, while the Restrictive Trade Practices Act, 1956, and the Resale Prices Act, 1964, place limits on the terms on which business may be done.   The only conceivable grounds for an action for wrongful interference with economic activity would seem to be the wrongful refusal of an authority, charged with licensing some restricted activity, to permit a pursuer to do business, and such an action would require the clearest averments and evidence of bad faith, malice or wrongful motive, not merely of mistaken exercise of discretion.   The law is still largely unexplored in this area.[44]

[44] See, however, *Sadler* v. *Sheffield Corpn.* [1924] 1 Ch. 483; *Short* v. *Poole Corpn.* [1926] Ch. 66; de Smith, *Judicial Review of Administrative Action*, Chap. 6.

CHAPTER 26

INFRINGEMENTS OF INTERESTS IN ECONOMIC RELATIONS

1. Fraud
2. Innocent Misrepresentation
3. Negligent Misrepresentation
4. Other Economic Loss Caused by Negligence
5. Malicious Falsehood (Verbal Injury)
6. Passing-Off
7. Breach of Confidence
8. Impersonation
9. Wrongful Refusal to Contract
10. Interference with Contract
11. Unlawful Price Maintenance by Contract
12. Enticement of Employees
13. Harbouring Another's Employee
14. Preventing Man from Obtaining Employment
15. Causing Consequential Loss of Services
16. Conspiracy to Injure
17. Deliberate Infliction of Loss of Business
18. Intimidation
19. Fomenting Strikes
20. Perjury

ECONOMIC relations are those legal relations between individuals which are prompted by business motives and have patrimonial consequences in that they involve actual or potential pecuniary advantages to at least one party. They include all kinds of commercial and industrial contracts, and the use of all personal and proprietary assets and advantages for gain. In many circumstances an individual has a claim *ex delicto* against another with whom he is in economic relations if the latter has deliberately or in breach of duty caused him economic loss.

1. FRAUD

Fraud is the principal ground for the recovery of damages for being overreached and induced to act to one's economic detriment. " Fraud is a machination or contrivance to deceive." [1] While it is a wrong wholly independent of contract, the commonest mode of fraudulently causing detriment to another is to induce him to enter into disadvantageous contractual relations and to incur loss thereby.

The essence of the wrong is in making a positive representation without honest belief in its truth, or concealing some fact which there

[1] Bell, *Prin.*, § 13; *cf.* Dig. IV, 3, 1; Voet, *ad loc.*; Stair, I, 9, 9; Ersk. III, 1, 16; IV, 1, 27.

was a duty to disclose,[2] intending thereby to induce in another a course of action, and actually inducing it and thereby causing him loss. Fraud consists in " a false representation made by the defendant knowingly, or without belief in its truth, or recklessly, careless whether it be true or false, with the intention that the plaintiff should act in reliance upon the representation, which causes damage to the plaintiff in consequence of his reliance upon it." [3]

Inducing person to contract by fraud. Where a party to a contract alleges that he has been induced to enter into the contract on the terms which he did by the fraud of the other contracting party he has both the remedies of rescinding the contract [4] and of claiming damages for the loss caused him by the contract. These remedies may be sought cumulatively or alternatively.[5] It is competent to affirm the contract, yet to claim damages *ex delicto* for the fraud which induced it.[6]

Where, however, the inducing fraud was not on the part of the other contracting party, as where A by fraudulent misrepresentation to B induces B to contract with C, the contract with C is not reducible by B on the ground of the fraudulent misrepresentation, unless, probably, it induced such essential error as to have entirely precluded consensus, and B's only remedy arises *ex delicto*, by way of claiming damages from A for the loss induced by his fraud.[7]

Whether the action is for rescission of the contract (the contractual remedy) or for damages for fraud (the delictual remedy) or for both, it seems that the pursuer has to aver and prove the same facts, namely, that the defender made a false representation of fact, knowingly or without belief in its truth or recklessly, that it was material to the contract, that he intended to induce, and actually did thereby induce the pursuer to make the contract on the terms on which he did, and that the pursuer suffered loss thereby.[8]

Where the contract is not being rescinded, a claim for damages for fraud which induced the contract cannot be proponed as a defence to an action for the contractual price, nor brought as a counter-claim, but must be brought as a separate action because it arises from a separate ground in law independent of and antecedent to the contract.[9]

---

[2] *Paul* v. *Old Shipping Co.* (1816) 1 Mur. 64; *Broatch* v. *Jenkins* (1866) 4 M. 1030; *Dempster* v. *Raes* (1873) 11 M. 843.

[3] *Derry* v. *Peek* (1889) 14 App.Cas. 337, 374, *per* Lord Herschell L.C.; *cf. Lees* v. *Tod* (1882) 9 R. 807, 853–854; *Boyd and Forrest* v. *G.S.W.Ry.*, 1912 S.C.(H.L.) 93; *Robinson* v. *National Bank of Scotland*, 1916 S.C.(H.L.) 154.

[4] The requisites for obtaining the contractual remedy of rescission are examined in books on Contract.

[5] *Kerr* v. *Duke of Roxburgh* (1822) 3 Mur. 141; *Amaan* v. *Handyside* (1865) 3 M. 526; *Smart* v. *Wilkinson*, 1928 S.C. 383; *Smith* v. *Sim*, 1954 S.C. 357.

[6] *Smith, supra.*

[7] *Thin & Sinclair* v. *Arrol* (1896) 24 R. 198, 206, *per* L.P. Robertson; *Aitken* v. *Pyper* (1900) 8 S.L.T. 258; *Gillies* v. *Campbell* (1902) 10 S.L.T. 289. *Cf.* Voet, IV, 3, 5.

[8] See averments narrated in *Smith* v. *Sim*, 1954 S.C. 357, 358–359. The elements of these averments are analysed in books on Contract.

[9] *Smart* v. *Wilkinson*, 1928 S.C. 383.

Inducing other injurious course of action by fraud. A claim based on fraud also lies where one person has by fraud induced another to enter upon a course of action which has naturally resulted in personal injuries. In *Langridge* v. *Levy* [10] the defendant sold a gun, fraudulently describing it as safe; he was held liable when it burst and injured the buyer. In *Burrows* v. *Rhodes* [11] B was induced by fraudulent misrepresentations to join the Jameson Raid into the Transvaal in which he suffered serious wounds; he was held entitled to damages for the injuries from the instigator of his participation. It is possible similarly to explain *Wilkinson* v. *Downton* [12] and *Janvier* v. *Sweeney* [13] as cases of personal injuries brought about by fraudulent misrepresentation.

Fraudulent advertisements. There seems no reason why a person should not recover damages if induced to act to his or her detriment by a fraudulent advertisement. The principal difficulties would be of proving the requisites of actionable fraud, and of showing that the statement complained of was seriously intended, as distinct from an unduly laudatory statement not designed to be taken literally.[14]

Fraudulent representation as to credit. Guarantees for any person and representations " as to the character, conduct, credit, ability, trade or dealings of any person, made or granted to the effect or for the purpose of enabling such person to obtain credit, money, goods, etc., postponement of payment of debt, or of any other obligation demandable from him, shall be in writing and shall be subscribed by the person undertaking such guarantee, security or cautionary obligation, or making such representations and assurances, or by some person duly authorised by him or them, otherwise the same shall have no effect ".[15] No action can accordingly be brought on merely oral representations.[16] Subject thereto, it is clearly actionable as fraud deliberately or recklessly to misrepresent a person's credit-worthiness, whereby another advances money and cannot obtain repayment, or for a purchaser, knowing of his insolvency, to represent to the seller that his credit was good and to get parties to whom he gave a reference to support the representation,[17] or to make fraudulent misrepresentations about the condition of a company in order to induce persons to subscribe additional capital to the company.[18]

Debts. The claim by one person to receive payment of a sum of money from another arising out of some past transaction such as a

---

[10] (1838) 2 M. & W. 519.
[11] [1899] 1 Q.B. 816.
[12] [1897] 2 Q.B. 57.
[13] [1919] 2 K.B. 316.
[14] *Cf. Carlill* v. *Carbolic Smoke-Ball Co.* [1893] 1 Q.B. 256.
[15] Mercantile Law (Scotland) Amendment Act, 1856, s. 6.
[16] *Clydesdale Bank, Ltd.* v. *Paton* (1896) 23 R.(H.L.) 22; see also *Union Bank* v. *Taylor*, 1925 S.C. 835.
[17] *Campbell, Robertson & Co.* v. *Shepherd* (1776) 2 Pat. 399.
[18] *Muir* v. *Burnside*, 1935 S.N. 46.

transfer of goods or services, may be interfered with by a third party
receiving payment on behalf of the creditor but without his authority
and granting a discharge which in the circumstances is a good discharge
to the debtor. In such a case the defrauded creditor has a claim *ex delicto*.
Thus if the debtor pays to a person whom he reasonably believes to be
the creditor, or to be an authorised agent of the creditor, or, where the
person is in a business which gives him ostensible authority to receive
payment for others, such as a solicitor,[19] and that person receives and
embezzles the money, the debt is held discharged,[20] but the creditor has
a claim against the receiver of the money on the ground of fraud and
breach of contract for the loss of the amount of the debt. If payment be
made to an unauthorised agent who embezzles the money, the debt is
not discharged, but the debtor may sue the embezzler, *quantum valeat*,
for the sum taken by him.[21]

In cases of mercantile agency, payment to an agent in possession of
the goods which he sells will be good in a question with the principal,
unless the debtor had actual notice that the agent had no authority to
receive payment.[22] Here again receipt by the agent and embezzlement can
give rise to a claim, by the creditor this time.

Negotiable Instruments. It is a species of fraud to do anything which
prevents a person entitled to payment under a negotiable instrument
from receiving payment according to the tenor of the instrument. Most
of the problems involve forgery of a signature and transacting with an
instrument by a person not entitled thereto.

A forged signature on a bill is wholly inoperative and no right to enforce payment can be acquired through or under that signature, unless
the party against whom it is sought to retain or enforce payment of the
bill is precluded from setting up the forgery for want of authority.[23]
Silence or delay on the part of the person whose signature has been forged
in objecting on discovery of the forgery does not necessarily imply adoption nor bar a repudiation of liability, unless the holder of the bill or
another party has been prejudiced by the silence or delay.[24]

Hence if the drawer of a bill forges the drawee's signature as acceptor
and the payee then endorses the bill to a fourth party who takes in good
faith, for value and without notice of the defect in the bill, the fourth
party will have no claim against the drawee whose signature was forged.[25]
His only remedy will be against the drawer for loss caused by the
forgery.

---

[19] *Smith* v. *N.B.Ry.* (1850) 12 D. 795; *Pearson* v. *Scott* (1878) 9 Ch.D. 198; contrast *Richardson* v. *McGeoch's Trs.* (1898) 1 F. 145; *Peden* v. *Graham* (1907) 15 S.L.T. 143; *Bowie's
Trs.* v. *Watson*, 1913 S.C. 326.

[20] Bell, *Prin.*, § 561; *International Sponge Importers* v. *Watt*, 1911 S.C.(H.L.) 57.

[21] *Peden* v. *Graham* (1907) 15 S.L.T. 143.

[22] *International Sponge Importers, supra.*

[23] Bills of Exchange Act, 1882, s. 24.

[24] *McKenzie* v. *British Linen Co.* (1881) 8 R. (H.L.)8; *British Linen Co.* v. *Cowan* (1906)
8 F. 704.

[25] *Smith* v. *Mercer* (1915) 6 Taunt. 76.

In such a case the drawee may bar himself from showing that his acceptance was forged if he had admitted that the acceptance was in his writing and had thereby given currency to the bill.[26] The onus of proving that a signature on a bill is genuine is on the holder of the bill.[27]

Where a firm of merchants, by letter to a bank, granted their manager authority to sign bills on behalf of the firm and, by procuration delivered to the bank, bound themselves to homologate his actings in their behalf, and the manager forged the names of various firms as acceptors of bills drawn by himself as procurator of his principals' firm, which he indorsed and discounted, appropriating the money to his own use, the bank was held entitled to recover the amount of the bills from the firm, there being no evidence of lack of due care on the bank's part.[28] The manager had defrauded his own firm by misusing but not going beyond the authority given him, and their remedy had to be against him personally.

In *Mackenzie* v. *British Linen Co.*[29] a bill purporting to be drawn by Mackenzie and Macdonald on Fraser and accepted by him was tendered to and discounted by the bank. It emerged that the signatures of both drawers were forged by Fraser. The bill became due, was dishonoured, and replaced by a second bill, indorsed by the drawers to the bank, with the signatures similarly forged. It was held that Mackenzie and Macdonald were not liable to the bank, whose only remedy, it seems, would have been against Fraser for the fraud by which he had cheated the bank.

In *Dickson* v. *Clydesdale Bank* [30] Mrs. D. drew a cheque in favour of Mrs. T; T presented it for payment but the bank refused, but they later paid it when T had by forgery substituted his own name as payee and altered the endorsement. It was held that the pursuer was entitled to declarator that her bank was not entitled to debit her account with the sum in the cheque, since the original presentation had not operated as an assignation of her funds, T not being a holder of the cheque, and the subsequent presentation was of a forged document and therefore of a nullity. In effect the bank was liable to repay her account and its remedy would be against T who had by his forgery deceived the bank into paying him.

Fraud facilitated by Banker's negligence. A banker is liable if by his negligence he permits a dishonest person to misappropriate payments made by cheque. Negligence is judged by reference to the standard of the practice of reasonable men in the world of banking and trying to act so as to protect themselves and others against fraud.[31] Thus where a farm manager received three cheques payable to him " for " the Marquess

---

26 *Leach* v. *Buchanan* (1802) 4 Esp. 226.
27 *B.L. Co., supra,* 706, *per* Lord Ardwall.
28 *Union Bank of Scotland* v. *Makin* (1873) 11 M. 499.
29 (1881) 8 R.(H.L.) 8.
30 1937 S.L.T. 585.
31 *Lloyds Bank* v. *Savory* [1933] A.C. 201; for examples see *Commrs. of Taxation* v. *English, Scottish and Australian Bank* [1920] A.C. 683; *Marquess of Bute* v. *Barclays Bank, Ltd.* [1954] 3 All E.R. 365.

of Bute, opened a personal account at the defendant bank therewith, and was permitted to draw thereon, the bank was held negligent and the Marquess held entitled to the sum in the cheques, with interest.[32] Where a cheque is stolen from the payee and the thief forges his endorsement thereon and pays it into a bank the bank may be protected by the Cheques Act, 1957, s. 4, so long as it has acted in good faith and without negligence.

Documents of title to goods. Where documents of title to goods are transferred outright or in security, the assignee may be liable if by failing to intimate the assignation he facilitates the removal of the goods from the custodier by an unauthorised person and their consequent loss. Thus in *Stiven* v. *Watson* [33] S arranged with W that tow should be delivered by A to W, to be held by W in security until A performed his obligations to S. The tow was consigned by rail to W, but he failed to intimate the delivery order to the railway company, so that A was able to remove the tow. A then became bankrupt. W was held liable in damages to S for failing to intimate the delivery order. Again in *Vickers* v. *Hertz* [34] an agent employed to find a purchaser for iron obtained by fraud from his principal a delivery order for the iron, which he endorsed and delivered to a third party in security of a loan. The third party thereby obtained possession of the iron and in a question with the defrauded principal, he was held entitled to retain it in security, the delivery order being a document of title under the Factors Act. The principal's only remedy was against the fraudulent agent for the sum which he required to pay to settle the loan and to obtain repossession of the iron.

Life Insurance Policies. It is wrongful for anyone to defraud the assured of the proceeds of a policy, as by stealing it and securing payment by representing that the assured had died. In such circumstances an action would lie against the fraudulent recipient of the sum assured. Similarly if an apparent owner produces the policy the insurers can safely pay him, provided they have had no notice intimated of an assignation to any third party, even though such assignation has been effected, and in such a case the assignee's only remedy would be against the assured, and such a remedy might well be barred if the failure to intimate the assignation were the fault of the assignee.[35]

Shares in companies. The ownership of shares in a company incorporated under the Companies Acts gives a claim to an ascertainable fraction of the company's assets, and the issue of a share certificate evidences this claim. When a company through its proper officers issues a share certificate to a person it represents that he is entitled to those shares, and is barred from denying that fact to anyone who has dealt

---

[32] *Marquess of Bute, supra.*
[33] (1874) 1 R. 412.
[34] (1871) 9 M.(H.L.) 65.
[35] *Williams* v. *Sorrell* (1799) 4 Ves. 389; *Kingdon* v. *Castleman* (1877) 46 L.J.Ch. 448.

with that person in reliance on the certificate, as by buying the shares or lending on security of them, and has suffered loss in consequence.[36] The company will be liable only if a false certificate were issued fraudulently or knowingly, or were issued innocently or negligently and the company has been in breach of duty to him, as where it has failed to register him as a member or to remove his name from the register. In such cases he may sue the company for damages for his loss.[37] The company is under no liability if the subsequent sale or mortgage were effected without reliance on the share certificate, as the company is then not barred from denying the seller's or mortgagor's title to the shares. Even if the company issues a new certificate to the buyer or mortgagee and thereby lets him continue to believe that he has acquired a good title to the shares, the loss was caused by the seller's or mortgagor's lack of title, not the action of the company.[38]

The company may, however, bar itself from denying the validity of the seller's or mortgagor's title by inducing him to act further on the basis that his title was good,[39] or by preventing him from pursuing a claim against the person who transferred the shares to him,[40] or by treating the seller or mortgagor as a shareholder, as by paying him dividends or offering him shares under a rights issue and inducing him to act on the faith of that implied representation and to suffer loss in consequence.[41]

If a company is barred from denying the validity of a person's title to shares, it can still remove his name from the register of members, as he has acquired no title to the shares, and that person's only remedy is to claim damages for the company's failure to register him or to remove his name from the register. Damages are measured by the value of the shares when registration was refused [42] or when his name was removed.[43]

Shareholder suffering loss by forged transfer. If a share transfer bearing to be signed by the true owner as transferor but in fact forged is presented for registration, it is a nullity and the company, if it has acted on the forged transfer, must restore the transferor's name to the register [44] and also pay damages to a person, such as a bona fide purchaser from the fraudulent transferee, who has incurred loss by acting on the faith of the share certificate issued to the fraudulent transferee.[45] The

36 *Clavering Son & Co.* v. *Goodwins, Jardine & Co.* (1891) 18 R. 652.
37 *Re Bahia and San Francisco Ry.* (1868) L.R. 3 Q.B. 584; *Re Ottos Kopje Diamond Mines, Ltd.* [1893] 1 Ch. 618.
38 *Foster* v. *Tyne Pontoon and Dry Docks Co. and Renwick* (1893) 63 L.J.Q.B. 50.
39 *Balkis Consolidated Co.* v. *Tomkinson* [1893] A.C. 396; *Hart* v. *Frontino and Bolivia South American Gold Mining Co., Ltd.* (1870) L.R. 5 Exch. 111.
40 *Dixon* v. *Kennaway & Co.* [1900] 1 Ch. 833; contrast *Foster* v. *Tyne Pontoon Co., supra.*
41 *Foster, supra.*
42 *Re Ottos Kopje Diamond Mines, Ltd.* [1893] 1 Ch. 618.
43 *Re Bahia and San Francisco Ry.* (1868) L.R. 3 Q.B. 584; *Hart* v. *Frontino and Bolivia South American Gold Mining Co.* (1870) L.R. 5 Exch. 111.
44 *Davis* v. *Bank of England* (1824) 2 Bing. 393; *Sloman* v. *Bank of England* (1845) 14 Sim. 475; *Barton* v. *L.N.W.Ry.* (1888) 38 Ch.D. 149; *Welch* v. *Bank of England* [1955] Ch. 508.
45 *Re Bahia and San Francisco Ry.* (1868) L.R. 3 Q.B. 584; *Balkis Consolidated Co.* v. *Tomkinson* [1893] A.C. 396; *Bloomenthal* v. *Ford* [1897] A.C. 156.

transferee's name may be removed from the register on discovery of the forgery.[46]

A person who acts under a forged transfer and has it registered and a fresh certificate issued is bound to indemnify the company, even though that person acted in good faith.[47]

The common practice of companies notifying the transferor that a transfer purporting to be signed by him has been presented for registration is a useful precaution but does not absolve the company, nor does failure to receive the notice or to reply bar a subsequent claim by the defrauded transferor.[48]

An owner of shares defrauded by a transfer on which his signature was forged may be barred by his own negligence from a remedy if that negligence has caused or facilitated the fraud,[49] or if he has ratified the registration of the forged transfer expressly or impliedly as by receiving the proceeds of sale or authorising the forger to deal with the proceeds of sale.[49]

Companies are empowered to pay compensation under the Forged Transfers Acts, 1891 and 1892, but these Acts do not give any person any right to compensation, but only empower its payment.

Unauthorised transfers. Where a transferor completes a transfer on his part and gives it, blank as to the transferee, along with the certificate, to an agent to whom he has given limited authority to deal with the shares and the agent completes the transfer in a way outside his authority, the transferor is barred from denying the agent's authority in a question with a third party who has purchased the shares in good faith,[50] and probably also in a question with the company. It is otherwise if the true owner was not responsible for creating the impression that the agent had authority to deal with the shares.[51]

Forger's or agent's liability. A person who by forging another's signature defrauds that other of the property in any shares is always personally liable to restore the shares or to pay damages in compensation for the loss sustained.[52] Thus where, as in *Welch* v. *Bank of England*,[53] one joint owner forges the signature of the other on transfers, sells the shares and pockets the proceeds of sale, the forger is liable to restore the shares or pay damages.

Similarly if an agent fraudulently or mistakenly assumes an authority he does not have and by so doing transfers his principal's shares to

46 *Simon* v. *Anglo-American Telegraph Co.* (1879) 5 Q.B.D. 188.
47 *Sheffield Corpn.* v. *Barclay* [1905] A.C. 392; *Welch* v. *Bank of England* [1955] Ch. 508; *cf. Starkey* v. *Bank of England* [1903] A.C. 114; *Oliver* v. *Bank of England* [1902] 1 Ch. 610.
48 *Barron* v. *L.N.W.Ry.* (1889) 24 Q.B.D. 77; *Welch, supra.*
49 *Welch* v. *Bank of England* [1955] Ch. 508.
50 *Colonial Bank* v. *Cody and Williams* (1890) 15 App.Cas. 267, 278; *Rimmer* v. *Webster* [1902] 2 Ch. 163; *Fuller* v. *Glyn, Mills, Currie & Co.* [1914] 2 K.B. 168.
51 *Swan* v. *North British Australasian Co.* (1863) 2 H. & C. 175.
52 *Cf. Robb* v. *Gow Bros. and Gemmell* (1905) 8 F. 90.
53 [1955] Ch. 508.

another person, who takes them in good faith, for value and without notice of the agent's lack of authority, the agent will be liable to his principal for having overstepped his authority to the extent of the value of the shares wrongfully sold by him.

Transferee's liability to company. A person who presents for registration by the company a transfer of shares in his own favour warrants that it is genuine.[54] In consequence, if it turns out to be forged or otherwise spurious, even though the transferee was unaware of this, the company may, without liability in damages, refuse to register him [55] or, even if it has done so and issued a fresh share certificate, remove his name from the register.[56] But a bona fide transferee or mortgagee from that person who relies on the share certificate issued to that person,[57] or on his registration as owner in the company's register of members will be entitled to damages if the company refuses to register the purchaser or mortgagee as a member.[58]

The person presenting a transfer also impliedly agrees to indemnify the company if the transfer is not in fact genuine,[59] even if he believed it to be genuine. Hence if the company has to pay damages to a purchaser of the shares from the person to whom they were transferred under a forged or unauthorised transfer, the company can claim against the presenter of that transfer.

Certification of share transfers. If only some of the shares or debentures vested in a registered owner and evidenced by his share or debenture certificate are being transferred the secretary of the company will certificate the transfer with a statement that a certificate in respect of the shares in the transfer has been lodged with the company and return it to the transferor, retaining the share certificate. A person who acts on the faith of a false certification, whether made deliberately or negligently, may recover from the company, provided that the person certifying was authorised by the company to do so.[60] A company secretary is not authorised *virtute officii* to certify.[61] If there was no authority the company will not be liable. It has to be presumed that a certification was signed by a duly authorised person, and the onus of proof of lack of authority is on the company. The representation made by the company by certificating a transfer is not that the transferor has any title to the shares but that the documents show a prima facie title to the shares [60]; hence the company is not liable if the transferor had in fact no title thereto, having obtained them by a forged transfer, or has presented a

---

[54] *Sheffield Corpn.* v. *Barclay* [1905] A.C. 392, 403.
[55] *Johnston* v. *Renton* (1870) L.R. 9 Eq. 181; *Simon* v. *Anglo-American Telegraph Co.* (1879) 5 Q.B.D. 188.
[56] *Johnston, supra; Simon, supra.*
[57] *Re Bahia and San Francisco Ry.* (1868) L.R. 3 Q.B. 584.
[58] *Foster* v. *Tyne Pontoon and Dry Docks Co. and Renwick* (1893) 63 L.J.Q.B. 50.
[59] *Sheffield Corpn.* v. *Barclay* [1905] A.C. 392, 403.
[60] Companies Act, 1948, s. 79.
[61] *Cf. Bishop* v. *Balkis Consolidated Co.* (1890) 25 Q.B.D. 512.

forged copy of a share certificate already sold. But it is liable if it certificates a transfer without demanding production of the share certificate and the transfer was forged; the company, by certificating the transfer, would have made it appear that the owner had authorised or ratified the transaction and a person deceived by the certified forged transfer would have an action if the company refused to register the transfer.

If a company certificates a transfer and by mistake returns the certificate to the transferor who, in fraud of the transferee, pledges the shares, the pledgee has no right of action against the company.[62]

The duty of certification may also be undertaken by Stock Exchanges, but in so doing, they do not act as agents for the companies, so that no claim lies against a company if a firm of brokers or a stock exchange fraudulently or negligently muddles a certification.

Deprivation of person of property by fraud. There is not much scope in Scots Law for fraudulently depriving another of his title to heritage. In *Rocca* v. *Catto's Trustees* [63] B was served heir to his deceased brother in 1819 and the subjects to which he became entitled passed through various hands into the hands of C's Trustees. In 1875 R brought a reduction of the decree of service, alleging herself to be granddaughter and heir of B's brother, and claimed to be entitled to possession. There were general averments of fraud, perjury and subornation of perjury. The action was dismissed on grounds of mora and taciturnity, and of the vicennial prescription of retours. The allegations of fraud were held to be too vague to be admitted to probation but it was indicated that even transmission to a singular successor would not prevent a true heir reducing the service of a false heir, nor doubtless from claiming damages if the decree of service had been obtained fraudulently.

Another possible case is where a piece of heritage is sold twice over. If A fraudulently sells Blackmoor almost simultaneously to X and to Y, the one who first records his disposition will have the preferable title and the other will have only a claim for repetition of the price paid and for damages for fraud and loss of the bargain. But if the title first recorded was recorded in bad faith, in the knowledge that there had been a previous purported sale and without adequate inquiry whether it was valid or not, the disposition will be reducible at the instance of the prior purchaser. Fraud need not then be alleged.[64]

In *Rodger (Builders), Ltd.* v. *Fawdry* [65] F contracted to sell an estate to R; the date for entry and payment having passed, the seller, having given an ultimatum and its period having expired, contracted to resell to B, and a disposition by the sellers in favour of the second purchaser's

[62] *Longman* v. *Bath Electric Tramways* [1905] 1 Ch. 646.
[63] (1876) 4 R. 70. *Cf. Fullarton* v. *Hamilton* (1825) 1 W. & S. 410; *Stobie* v. *Smith*, 1921 S.C. 894.
[64] *Petrie* v. *Forsyth* (1874) 2 R. 214; *Stodart* v. *Dalzell* (1876) 4 R. 236; *cf. Lang* v. *Dixon* (1813) 17 F.C. 412; *Marshall* v. *Hynd* (1828) 6 S. 384; *Morrison* v. *Sommerville* (1860) 23 D. 232.
[65] 1950 S.C. 483.

wife was executed, delivered and recorded. The court reduced the disposition holding that the second purchaser was not in the circumstances in bona fide, as he was aware of the prior contract and should have made enquiries and not relied on the seller's assurance that the prior contract was no longer in existence; the court in fact held that the prior contract was still in existence. Fraud did not require to be averred or proved.

Wills and settlements. A will or settlement is not by itself a document of title to property but once a will in favour of any person has been executed and the testator has died, the will has the effect of causing the property to be transmitted in accordance with the direction therein. If therefore X forges A's signature, as testator, to a will in X's or Y's favour, this will have the effect of cheating the heirs on intestacy, or the beneficiaries under any will revoked by the forged will, out of what they would otherwise have got, and they may not merely reduce the will as a forgery on discovering that defect, but claim restitution from X or Y of all he took under the will, or damages, in so far as restitution is impossible.[66] If X forged the will in Y's favour, the remedy, apart from reduction of the will, against X is surely damages for fraud, and against Y is restitution, failing which, damages, and that even though Y be innocent of complicity in the fraud and forgery.

In a case where a will is impetrated by circumvention of a weak and facile testator the remedy seems always to have been restricted to reduction of the will,[67] but if challenge were delayed until after the estate had been distributed, a claim of restitution, failing which, for damages, would seem obviously competent in addition.

Intestacy. In the same way if an individual succeeded in passing himself off on the death of the intestate as an heir *ab intestato*[68] or one of the next-of-kin, *e.g.*, by pretending successfully to be a long-lost child, he would be depriving the true heir of his inheritance, or those who would otherwise have been entitled on intestacy, of the greater share which they should have received, and the impostor seems clearly liable to an action for restitution, failing which, for damages, to the extent to which he had cheated the true heirs of their inheritance.

Rights in security over moveables. A right in security over corporeal moveables generally requires possession by the creditor, as security-holder, either actual or constructive, for its validity. An action doubtless lies against anyone who cheats or tricks him into parting with possession and thereby into the loss of his security-right, for restoration of the subject held in security or for damages.

---

[66] *Cf. Williamson* v. *Fyfe* (1796) 3 Pat. 478; *Scrimgeour* v. *Ker* (1836) 15 S. 245, especially at 248, where the defenders, who had made sales and granted feus on the faith of the settlement in their favour and now reduced, envisaged liability in damages to the purchasers and feuars, whose purchases and feus would have been reducible as granted *a non domino*.

[67] *Munro* v. *Strain* (1874) 1 R. 1039; *McCallum* v. *Graham* (1894) 21 R. 824.

[68] *Cf. Rocca* v. *Catto's Trs.* (1876) 4 R. 70; *Stobie* v. *Smith*, 1921 S.C. 894.

A security-holder, such as the holder of shares in security for a debt due to him, may be liable in damages for not taking reasonable care to preserve the security subjects, as for declining, without communication with the beneficial owners, to take up a scrip issue, and thereby causing them loss of profit.[69]

Right in security over heritage. In a number of cases agents have defrauded their clients of money secured over heritage, as by granting a forged discharge of a bond and embezzling the sum repaid.[70] Such a forged discharge is a nullity and the debtor in the bond is still liable to the creditor and has a claim against the agent for the sum embezzled.

Fraud by converting property to own use. Persons have frequently been defrauded of property by the double-dealing of a person to whom they entrusted the property in course of trade and other than by outright sale. Thus in *Brown* v. *Marr* [71] M obtained goods from S and other wholesale dealers on terms of sale or return, and pawned them. It was held that the title therein had passed to the fraudulent M and that he therefore had a title to pawn them. The only remedy open to S was therefore to sue M personally, if he could be found, for damages for fraud in obtaining the goods. Similarly in *Bryce* v. *Ehrmann*,[72] A, a retail jeweller, received a necklace from E, with power to sell and deliver on his own account, and, having pawned it with B, became bankrupt. E was held entitled to recover the necklace on repaying B what he had advanced. He would, then, have had a claim for fraud against A.

In *Gibbs* v. *British Linen Co.*[73] L who was indebted to the bank transferred to it certain shares *ex facie* absolutely but truly in partial security of a debt. He subsequently sold the shares to G and paid the bank, which executed transfers to the purchaser G, and gave a partial discharge of the debt. The purchaser sued the bank for rescission of the sale and repayment of the price on the ground of the seller's fraudulent misrepresentation, but it was held that although the debtor L had induced the sale by fraud the defenders were not parties thereto and not liable therefor.

2. INNOCENT MISREPRESENTATION

By " innocent misrepresentation " is meant the communication of an untrue statement of fact which was neither made fraudulently,[74] nor in circumstances raising a legal duty of care towards the complainer in

---

[69] *Waddell* v. *Hutton*, 1911 S.C. 575.
[70] See *Falconer* v. *Dalrymple* (1870) 9 M. 212; *Wallace's Trs.* v. *Port Glasgow Harbour Trs.* (1880) 7 R. 645; *Rose* v. *Spaven* (1880) 7 R. 925; *Dickson* v. *Scottish Provident Assoc. Co.* (1880) 18 S.L.R. 33; *Macdonald* v. *Warren* (1889) 27 S.L.R. 46; *Duncan* v. *Arthur* (1900) 7 S.L.T. 389; *Bowie's Trs.* v. *Watson*, 1913 S.C. 326; *Muir's Exors.* v. *Craig's Trs.*, 1913 S.C. 349.
[71] (1880) 7 R. 427.
[72] (1904) 7 F. 5.
[73] (1875) 4 R. 630.
[74] As defined in *Lees* v. *Tod* (1882) 9 R. 807; *Derry* v. *Peek* (1889) 14 App.Cas. 337; *Boyd and Forrest* v. *G.S.W.Ry.*, 1912 S.C.(H.L.) 93.

making statements. Such an innocent misrepresentation gives no ground of action *ex delicto*.[75] The distinction between negligent and innocent misrepresentation may be a narrow one in particular cases.

It seems now well established that where an innocent misrepresentation has induced a contract between representor and representee, the contract is reducible but no damages are recoverable,[76] nor any form of recompense which would have the same result.[77] The same result seems to follow where A represents some fact to B which induces C to act to his detriment, as by lending B money. If the misrepresentation were innocent A is not liable to C unless there was in the circumstances a breach of a duty of care such as to make the misrepresentation negligent.[78]

3. NEGLIGENT MISREPRESENTATION

It is a more difficult question whether damages are recoverable *ex delicto* for loss caused by a negligent misrepresentation. It is clear that they can be recovered *ex contractu*, as between parties bound by contract, where one owes the other a contractual duty not to cause him loss, and is in breach thereof. In *Candler* v. *Crane, Christmas & Co.*[79] the defendants, by their clerk, at a company's request, prepared the company's accounts and balance sheet which, to the clerk's knowledge, were intended to be put before the plaintiff to induce him to invest money in the company. The accounts had been carelessly prepared and did not give a true view of the company's affairs. Relying on the accuracy of the accounts the plaintiff invested £2,000, which he lost on the failure of the company, and for which he sued the defendants. It was admitted that the defendants had failed to use proper care and skill in the presentation of the accounts, but there was no fraud on their part. The plaintiff's claim was dismissed [80] on the ground that the defendants owed no duty to the plaintiff to exercise care in the preparation of the accounts. The majority held itself bound by *Le Lievre* v. *Gould* [81] and thought that the general doctrine of *Donoghue* v. *Stevenson* [82] did not extend to any means causing any kind of loss recognised by law, but had never been applied where the damage complained of was not physical. Denning L.J. thought that in the circumstances the defendants did owe a duty of care to the plaintiff, that *Le Lievre* was infected by two cardinal errors then current, the first that if a party to a contract performed it negligently, no third party injured thereby could sue, an error exposed by *Donoghue* v.

---

[75] *Manners* v. *Whitehead* (1898) 1 F. 171.
[76] *Stewart* v. *Kennedy* (1890) 17 R.(H.L.) 25; *Manners, supra*; *Robinson* v. *National Bank of Scotland*, 1916 S.C.(H.L.) 154.
[77] *Boyd and Forrest* v. *G.S.W.Ry.*, 1915 S.C.(H.L.) 20.
[78] *MacDonald* v. *Fyfe, Ireland and Dangerfield* (1895) 3 S.L.T. 124. *Cf. Hedley Byrne & Co.* v. *Heller and Partners, Ltd.* [1964] A.C. 465.
[79] [1951] 2 K.B. 164.
[80] Asquith and Cohen L.JJ., Denning L.J. dissenting.
[81] [1893] 1 Q.B. 491.
[82] 1932 S.C.(H.L.) 31.

Stevenson, and the second that, by reason of *Derry* v. *Peek* [83] no action ever lay for a negligent statement intended to be, and actually, acted on by a plaintiff to his loss, an error exposed by *Nocton* v. *Ashburton,*[84] which decided that an action did lie for a negligent statement where the circumstances disclosed a duty to be careful. Denning L.J. went on to suggest the circumstances in which a duty to use care in making a statement does exist, apart from contract: " first, what persons are under such duty? My answer is those persons, such as accountants, surveyors, valuers, and analysts, whose profession and occupation it is to examine books, accounts and other things, and to make reports on which other people—other than their clients—rely in the ordinary course of business. Their duty is not merely a duty to use care in their reports. They have also a duty to use care in their work which results in their reports. . . . Accountants. . . . are not liable, of course, for casual remarks made in the course of conversation, nor for other statements made outside their work, or not made in their capacity as accountants . . . but they are, in my opinion, in proper cases, apart from any contract in the matter, under a duty to use reasonable care in the preparation of their accounts and in the making of their reports.

" Secondly, to whom do these professional people owe this duty? . . . They owe the duty, of course, to their employer or client, to any third person to whom they themselves show the accounts, or to whom they know their employer is going to show the accounts so as to induce him to invest money or take some other action on them. I do not think, however, the duty can be extended still further so as to include strangers of whom they have heard nothing and to whom their employer without their knowledge may choose to show their accounts. . . . The test of proximity in these cases is: Did the accountants know that the accounts were required for submission to the plaintiff and used by him? . . .

" Thirdly, to what transactions does the duty of care extend? It extends, I think, only to those transactions for which the accountants know their accounts were required. . . . This distinction, that the duty only extends to the very transaction in mind at the time, is implicit in the decided cases. Thus a doctor, who negligently certifies a man to be a lunatic when he is not, is liable to him, although there is no contract in the matter, because the doctor knows that his certificate is required for the very purpose of deciding whether the man should be detained or not, but an insurance company's doctor owes no duty to the insured person because he makes his examination only for the purposes of the insurance company. . . . So, also, a Lloyd's surveyor who, in surveying for classification purposes, negligently passes a mast as sound when it is not, is not liable to the owner for damage caused by it breaking, because the surveyor makes his survey only for the purpose of classifying the ship for the Yacht Register and not otherwise: *Humphrey* v. *Bowers*

---

[83] (1889) 14 App.Cas. 337.
[84] [1914] A.C. 932.

(1929) 45 T.L.R. 297. Again a scientist or expert (including a marine hydrographer) is not liable to his readers for careless statements in his published works.[85] He publishes his work simply to give information, and not with any particular transaction in mind. When, however, a scientist or an expert makes an investigation and report for the very purpose of a particular transaction, then, in my opinion, he is under a duty of care in respect of that transaction. . . .

" In my opinion, accountants owe a duty of care not only to their own clients, but also to all those who they know will rely on their accounts in the transactions for which those accounts are prepared." [86]

This case caused considerable discussion and divergence of view,[87] but the dissenting view was upheld in *Hedley Byrne & Co.* v. *Heller & Partners, Ltd.*[88] H.B., having contracted on behalf of clients E, made enquiries of H as to the credit-worthiness of E. H gave satisfactory references which turned out to be unjustified and H.B. claimed for loss sustained by reliance thereon. The claim failed on the ground that, even if H. was in fact negligent (which was not decided), H had effectively disclaimed any assumption of a duty of care in the circumstances. But the House of Lords accepted that, apart from cases where a duty of care was imposed by a contractual or fiduciary relationship, a duty of care in the communicating of advice or information arose, in circumstances in which a reasonable man would know that he was being trusted, or his skill and judgment being relied on, to take such care as the circumstances require in making a reply. It was further indicated that, in the absence of circumstances requiring particular search and consideration by the bank, there was no legal duty on the replying bank beyond that of giving an honest answer.

Scottish View. Apart from the strong persuasive authority of *Hedley, Byrne & Co.* v. *Heller & Partners, Ltd.*,[89] the Scottish view of loss caused by negligent misrepresentation would, on principle, be that if the representor was so closely related to the ultimate representee that he should have realised that his representation was likely to be communicated to that representee, to be acted on, and, if incorrect, to cause loss, then he owes a duty to the ultimate representee to take reasonable care not to cause loss by misrepresentation. This is consistent with *Robinson* v. *National Bank of Scotland*,[90] where the bank was held not liable for

---

[85] This principle, it is hoped, applies to the author of a legal textbook.
[86] [1951] 2 K.B. 164.
[87] Notes in 67 L.Q.R. 173; 14 M.L.R. 345; Paton, " Liability in Tort for Negligent Statements " (1947) 25 Can.B.R. 123; Seavey, " Negligent Misrepresentation by Accountants " (1951) 67 L.Q.R. 466; Morison, " Liability in Negligence for False Statements " (1951) 67 L.Q.R. 212; Goodhart, " Liability for Negligent Misstatements " (1962) 78 L.Q.R. 107.
    On the U.S. case of *Ultramares Corpn.* v. *Touche* (1931) 174 N.E. 441, cited by the majority, see Seavey, " Mr. Justice Cardozo and The Law of Torts " (1939) 52 H.L.R. 372; 48 Yale L.J. 390; 39 Col.L.R. 20; *Torts, Selected Essays,* 72, and for notes on the case itself see 44 H.L.R. 134; 40 Yale L.J. 128; 30 Col.L.R. 1066; 29 Mich.L.R. 648. See also Prosser, 719–724.
[88] [1964] A.C. 465.   [89] [1964] A.C. 465. *Cf. Nocton* v. *Ashburton* [1914] A.C. 932.
[90] 1916 S.C.(H.L.) 154; see also *Salton & Co.* v. *Clydesdale Bank, Ltd.* (1898) 1 F. 110.

making representations as to credit-worthiness which were inaccurate and careless, when the relationship of parties in the circumstances imposed no special duty on the person making the representations to make sure that the information conveyed was accurate. The crucial question in each case is whether there was sufficient proximity between parties to impose the duty of care, and it is also relevant to consider whether the information was volunteered or requested, and whether what was sought was a general opinion or a carefully formulated view based on inquiry. " But when a mere inquiry is made by one banker of another, who stands in no special relation to him, then, in the absence of special circumstances from which a contract [91] to be careful can be inferred, I think there is no duty excepting the duty of common honesty to which I have referred." [92] Similarly in *Fortune* v. *Young* [93] a cautioner was held liable for financial loss sustained by the pursuer, since, though he had not addressed his letter of guarantee to the pursuer, he had contemplated that it would be shown to the pursuer in connection with the transaction which had caused the loss.

An important question in many cases will accordingly be whether the defender had owed the pursuer any duty to take care in reporting or communicating. Thus a banker owes no duty to a proposed cautioner to volunteer information about the state of the principal debtor's account,[94] but if asked he doubtless owes a duty to take reasonable care in answering. In another cautionry case [95] the failure of an employer to communicate to cautioners for the intromissions of an employee the previous detection of serious irregularities on the employee's part was said to amount to fraud. Today such failure could more readily be attributable to negligent misrepresentation.

Conditions of liability. Accepting that a duty of care, independent of contract, in making spoken or written statements, exists towards persons who, it is known, may rely on the statement, and in respect of transactions for the purposes of which the statements were made, it has further to be shown, before liability can be held established, that the statement was false and incorrect to a substantial extent, in a material respect, that the pursuer was induced to act as he did by that misstatement, and that he did so act to his detriment. These are the requirements for a remedy for fraudulent misrepresentation and it is thought that they would apply equally to negligent misrepresentation.

4. OTHER ECONOMIC LOSS CAUSED BY NEGLIGENCE

A professional adviser or employee is liable if he causes his client or employer economic loss by his negligence, that is by failure to possess or

---

[91] This should be " duty."
[92] *Robinson, supra,* 157, *per* Viscount Haldane.
[93] 1918 S.C. 1.
[94] *Young* v. *Clydesdale Bank* (1889) 17 R. 231; *cf. Aitken* v. *Pyper* (1900) 8 S.L.T. 258; *Russell* v. *Farrell* (1900) 2 F. 892.
[95] *French* v. *Cameron* (1893) 20 R. 966.

to use the standard of knowledge, skill, diligence and care reasonably to be expected of a normally competent member of his profession. In the case of economic losses, as distinct from personal injury, the duty to exercise care and diligence is primarily contractual, owed by virtue of a term implied into the contract of employment, and consequently a claim for loss caused by the breach of that duty is an action for breach of contract, not for delict. Thus it is settled that in general only the person who employed a solicitor can sue him for damages for loss caused by professional negligence.[96]

Similarly an employee owes his employer an implied contractual duty of care not to cause injury to a third party which may result in the employer being held liable, vicariously for the employee, in damages to the third party.[97]

5. MALICIOUS FALSEHOOD (VERBAL INJURY)

Harm done to a person in his business relations by written or oral false-hoods is today commonly called " verbal injury " in Scots law, though in truth this wrong is merely one species of the genus verbal injury [98] and like the other species, *convicium* and defamation, should have a distinctive name.[98] The most appropriate name is " injurious falsehood," or " malicious falsehood," [99] names used in English law, from which indeed the Scots law on this point seems to have been adopted entirely. Despite the use of the word " slander " in some of the cases this wrong is quite distinct from defamation, has different requisites, and may be committed without in any way impugning the pursuer's honour or character or hurting his self-esteem or feelings. It is an aspersion on his business or property.

The wrong consists in maliciously communicating written or oral falsehoods calculated in the ordinary course to produce, and in fact producing, actual damage.[1] The requisites of actionability are: (1) malicious communication: the pursuer must aver and prove not merely the malice presumed in defamation cases from the deliberate utterance of a false statement but malice in the sense of actual *animus injuriandi*, evidenced by spite or malevolence or other improper motive,[2] or intent to injure [3] or at least lack of honest belief in the truth of the statement made.[4] The

---

96 *Somerville* v. *Thomson*, May 19, 1815 F.C.; (1818) 6 Paton, 393; *Wilson* v. *Riddell* (1826) 4 S. 739; *Buchanan* v. *Pearson* (1840) 2 D. 1177; *Goldie* v. *Goldie* (1842) 4 D. 1489; *Robertson* v. *Fleming* (1861) 4 Macq. 167; *Williamson* v. *Begg* (1887) 14 R. 720; *Raes* v. *Meek* (1889) 16 R.(H.L.) 31; *Tully* v. *Ingram* (1891) 19 R. 65; *Auchincloss* v. *Duncan* (1894) 21 R. 1091.

97 *Semtex* v. *Gladstone* [1954] 2 All E.R. 206; *Lister* v. *Romford Ice Co.* [1957] A.C. 555.

98 See further discussion in Chap. 23, *supra*.

99 The term " malicious falsehood " is used in the Defamation Act, 1952, s. 3 (England only) for which s. 14 (*b*) substitutes a section for Scotland side-titled " Actions for verbal injury."

1 *Ratcliffe* v. *Evans* [1892] 2 Q.B. 524, 527.

2 *White* v. *Mellin* [1895] A.C. 154; *Balden* v. *Shorter* [1933] Ch. 427.

3 *Steward* v. *Young* (1870) L.R. 5 C.P. 122; *Montgomerie* v. *Paterson* (1894) R.P.C. 221, 237; affd., *ibid.* 633 (Inner Ho.).

4 *Greers, Ltd.* v. *Pearman and Corder, Ltd.* (1922) 39 R.P.C. 406.

communication must be made to persons other than the pursuer (because the essence of the wrong is the harm to the pursuer's business with others)[5]; (2) false statement: unlike the case of defamation, where the statement complained of, once challenged, is presumed false until *veritas* is proved by the defender, the statement in injurious falsehood must be proved to be false, and the onus of doing so is on the pursuer[6]; (3) damage: at common law the pursuer had to prove that some actual damage had been sustained by him,[7] but by statute [8] it is not now necessary for the pursuer to aver or prove special (*i.e.*, actual) damage if the words on which the action is founded are calculated to cause pecuniary damage to the pursuer. In cases not covered by this provision proof of actual damage will still be requisite [9] though evidence of a general loss of business is sufficient.[10] There is no damage if the loss arises from the pursuer being prevented from doing what he is not entitled to do.[11]

Defences. The defences of no malice, truth, and no damage suffered are obviously competent. The defence of absolute privilege is doubtless relevant and the defence of qualified privilege has been upheld.[12]

Classes of cases. The main classes of cases falling under the head of malicious falsehood (or " verbal injury ") are slander of title and slander of property, but other classes have been recognised, particularly in English cases.

Slander of title. Slander of title consists in making an unfounded imputation on the validity of the pursuer's title to certain property, heritable or moveable, hampering him in the use or disposal of the property. In cases of slander of title the words complained of impeach the pursuer's title to certain property. In *Philp* v. *Morton* [13] a notary protested, in the presence of those attending a displenishing sale at a farm, that the outgoing tenant was not entitled to sell the articles exposed for sale. The tenant recovered damages for the diminution in prices held to have resulted from the protest.

In *Yeo* v. *Wallace* [14] a tenant was selling his household furniture when representatives of the landlord intervened and stated, in the presence of the buyers, that if the auctioneer proceeded with the sale he did so at his own risk and purchasers would be responsible for anything they removed. The tenant claimed for loss by consequential lower prices. Lord Barcaple

---

5 *Malachy* v. *Soper* (1836) 3 Bing.N.C. 371; *Wilts United Dairies* v. *Robinson* [1957] R.P.C. 220; [1958] R.P.C. 94.
6 *Bruce* v. *Smith* (1898) 1 F. 327, 331; *Royal Baking Powder Co.* v. *Wright, Crossley & Co.* (1901) 18 R.P.C. 95, 99.
7 *McLean* v. *Adam* (1888) 16 R. 175; *Bruce* v. *Smith* (1898) 1 F. 327; *Thomson* v. *Fifeshire Advertiser*, 1936 S.N. 56.
8 Defamation Act, 1952, s. 14 (*b*), substituting Scottish section for s. 3 of main body of Act.
9 *Bree* v. *Marescaux* (1881) 7 Q.B.D. 434; *Joyce* v. *Motor Surveys* [1948] Ch. 252.
10 *Ratcliffe* v. *Evans* [1892] 2 Q.B. 524; *Hatchard* v. *Mège* (1887) 18 Q.B.D. 771.
11 *Royal Baking Powder Co.* v. *Wright, Crossley & Co.* (1901) 18 R.P.C. 95.
12 *McLean* v. *Adam* (1888) 16 R. 175.
13 (1816) Hume 865.
14 (1867) 5 S.L.R. 253.

dismissed the action, founding on English cases of slander of title which required proof of malice, which was not here averred, and on the ground that the landlord's representatives had merely made a statement with regard to the legal rights of the landlord in the circumstances, which was in no way false or erroneous.

In *Montgomerie* v. *Paterson* [15] circulars stating that another's patent was invalid might, it was held, amount to slander of title.

Finally, in *Harpers* v. *Greenwood & Batley* [16] H. sued G. for damage caused by G. having sought to interdict H. from infringing certain patents for machinery, and thereby maliciously caused them loss of trade. Lord Low held that it was settled in England, on grounds equally applicable, in his view, to Scotland, that an action for slander of title would lie only where special damage (sic.) was averred, and this had not been done. The ground of action was truly that G. had in effect falsely charged H. with being patent-infringers.

In *Serville* v. *Constance* [17] one boxer described himself as holding a title truly belonging to the other. An injunction was refused on the ground of passing-off but it was indicated [18] that an action for slander of title would have lain if malice had been established.

The principle was applied also where the defendant maintained, wrongly though honestly, that the plaintiff was not entitled to certain property on intestacy.[19]

Slander of property. Slander of property exists " where a defender disparages the pursuer's property to the pursuer's loss." [20] Some cases cited as instances of slander of property do not seem to justify that classification.

In *Hamilton* v. *Arbuthnot* [21] damages were awarded where a person spread a calumnious report against a merchant advertising a sale, that " the goods were an imposition and rotten and mildewed trash." This might be treated as much as a slander of the merchant, as being a cheat, as slander of property.

In *Broomfield* v. *Greig* [22] B. a baker, sued G, a doctor, for allegedly stating that B's bread was injurious to health and unfit for human food. This was held irrelevant, as amounting to no more than an opinion that the bread was unwholesome, though the court allowed an issue on the statement, supported by the innuendo that B kept adulterated bread and flour in his premises, as being an imputation of dishonesty. This seems to be simply a case of slander.[23]

[15] (1894) 11 R.P.C. 221, 237; affd., *ibid.* 633 (Inner House).
[16] (1896) 4 S.L.T. 116.
[17] [1954] 1 All E.R. 662.
[18] p. 664, *per* Harman J.
[19] *Loudon* v. *Ryder* (No. 2) [1953] Ch. 423.
[20] *Bruce* v. *Smith* (1898) 1 F. 327, 331, citing *Western Counties Manure Co.* v. *Chemical Manure Co.* (1874) L.R. 9 Ex. 218; *Ratcliffe* v. *Evans* [1892] 2 Q.B. 524; and *White* v. *Mellin* [1895] A.C. 154.
[21] (1750) Mor. 13923.   [22] (1868) 6 M. 563.
[23] *Cooper on Defamation*, p. 88, describes this case as a stumbling-block in the way of the development of this branch of law (*i.e.*, slander of property) in Scotland. The case seems clearly correct, but to have nothing to do with slander of property.

In *Macrae* v. *Wicks* [24] a hotel-proprietor sued a newspaper which had published a paragraph describing overcharging at the hotel. The court allowed an issue of slander by imputing overcharging, injurious to the hotel keeper in his trade. The case seems to have been treated as slander, but slander of property or of business seems more appropriate. [25]

In *McLean* v. *Adam* [26] M sued A for slander, for having stated falsely that a case of typhoid fever was probably to be traced to milk from M's dairy, and consequently having ruined M's business. The defender was held to have been privileged, to have acted in the discharge of his duty and in the honest belief that his statement was true, so that there was no malice, and Lord Young observed that the statement contains no imputation on M's character. The words " verbal injury " in the rubric seem to connote no more than defamation, and there is no mention of any special doctrine of slander of property. If slander there had been, it would have been ordinary slander, of M as being a dirty dairy-keeper.

In *Bruce* v. *Smith* [27] B, a builder, sued a newspaper for having published a paragraph that a building, being built by B, had collapsed but had been " run up again." In consequence the building could not be let and its selling value had been depreciated. The action was held relevant, Lord Moncreiff observing that this was not merely slander of property, but slander of the pursuer himself in connection with his trade as a builder. The judgment of the Lord Ordinary (Kincairney) contains the only clear acceptance in Scots law of a principle of slander of property, but he founds extensively [28] on English law and, having quoted Lords Bramwell and Bowen, says " I do not know of any established rule in the law of Scotland inconsistent with these apparently equitable opinions. I am therefore of opinion that it cannot be affirmed that our law denies a right of action in the case of slander of property, that is, where a defender disparages the pursuer's property to the pursuer's loss." The Inner House did not deal with this matter, and it must be asserted that Lord Kincairney's importation of English law (where the doctrines of slander of title and slander of property [29] are necessary, owing to the narrowness of the principles of libel and slander) was both unnecessary and unwarranted, and is moreover the sole clear authority for the doctrine in Scots law.

Merely to state that the defender's product is better than the pursuer's and to give reasons therefor is not slander of property, even though this involves disparaging the pursuer's goods, [30] but it may be otherwise if the defender is not a rival trader. [31]

---

24 (1886) 13 R. 732.
25 The pursuer's averments (p. 733) were that the paragraph " caused the business of the pursuer to deteriorate."
26 (1888) 16 R. 175.
27 (1898) 1 F. 327.
28 At pp. 330–331.
29 Grouped in some modern books as the tort of injurious falsehood.
30 *Evans* v. *Harlow* (1844) 5 Q.B. 624; *Young* v. *Macrae* (1862) 3 B. & S. 264; *White, supra*; *Hubbuck* v. *Wilkinson* [1899] 1 Q.B. 86.
31 This might be, in English terminology, slander of goods.

The property disparaged may be heritable or moveable, including patents,[32] trade marks,[33] trade names,[34] copyright [35] and shares in companies.[36]

Slander of goods (or trade libel). In one ill-reported Scottish case [37] a person was held liable in damages for having spread a calumnious report against a merchant advertising a sale, that the goods were an imposition and rotten and mildewed trash. This might be slander of goods or ordinary defamation. But a statement which disparages a man's goods does not necessarily cast any imputation on his personal character or his business reputation and will accordingly not necessarily be actionable as defamatory, but may be as trade libel.[38] To advertise that one's goods are better than any other is only advertisement and not actionable as disparagement of a rival's product.[39] Damages were awarded where a company which had not been awarded a subcontract informed the main contractor that the method of construction proposed by the successful tenderer was inadequate; this was false, malicious and productive of loss and inconvenience,[40] and an injunction was granted where there was a malicious suggestion that plaintiff's goods infringed a patent.[41] Other instances include selling canned milk manufactured by plaintiffs outwith the period of guarantee but representing it as recent [42] and issuing a trade manual criticising and denigrating the plaintiff's rival product.[43]

But letters written by a party in the same trade as the plaintiff in an endeavour to protect rights he believes he possesses rather than with a view to injuring the plaintiff are not a trade libel, there being no malice.[44]

Slander of business. English cases have extended the principle to liability for malicious falsehoods about a business calculated to produce, and in fact producing, actual damage. Instances include a false statement in the defendant's newspaper that the plaintiff had ceased to carry on business,[45] a false statement that the plaintiff's wife, who assisted him in his drapery business, had committed adultery in the shop,[46] the inclusion of the plaintiff's name as accompanist in the programme of a concert series after she had withdrawn therefrom,[47] a false statement that the plaintiff, a commercial traveller with whom the customer had formerly

---

[32] *Wren* v. *Weild* (1869) L.R. 4 Q.B. 730.
[33] *Greers, Ltd.* v. *Pearman and Corder, Ltd.* (1922) 39 R.P.C. 406.
[34] *Royal Baking Powder Co.* v. *Wright, Crossley & Co.* (1900) 18 R.P.C. 95.
[35] *Dicks* v. *Brooks* (1880) 15 Ch.D. 22.
[36] *Malachy* v. *Soper* (1836) 3 Bing.N.C. 371.
[37] *Hamilton* v. *Arbuthnot* (1750) Mor. 7682 and 13923.
[38] *Linotype Co.* v. *British Empire Typesetting Co.* (1899) 81 L.T. 331; *Alcott* v. *Millar's Karri Forests, Ltd.* (1905) 91 L.T. 722.
[39] *White* v. *Mellin* [1895] A.C. 154.
[40] *London Ferro Concrete Co.* v. *Justicz* (1951) 68 R.P.C. 261.
[41] *Mentmore Mfg. Co.* v. *Fomento* (1955) 72 R.P.C. 157.
[42] *Wilts United Dairies* v. *Robinson* [1958] R.P.C. 94.
[43] *Cellactite and British Uralite* v. *Robertson* [1957] C.L.Y. 1989.
[44] *Reuter* v. *Mulhens* [1953] 2 All E.R. 1160.
[45] *Ratcliffe* v. *Evans* [1892] 2 Q.B. 524.
[46] *Riding* v. *Smith* (1876) 1 Ex.D. 91.
[47] *Shapiro* v. *La Morta* (1923) 130 L.T. 622.

done business, was now employed by the defendant's firm,[48] a false statement to the Post Office and a manufacturers' association that the plaintiff was no longer in business at a particular address.[49] The principle was considered applicable to a newspaper report reflecting adversely on the pursuer's shop and business,[50] and would seem appropriate to the case where a newspaper published a paragraph, representing that the hotel-keeper grossly overcharged his guests.[51] This ground of action seems to have been tentatively tried in *Buchan* v. *Welch*,[52] where an action was founded on allegations that the defender falsely stated that the pursuers did not understand their business and that he was going to eject them from their premises and take over the business which they were giving up. There were no averments of malice and the action was dismissed.

6. PASSING-OFF

Independently of the statutory delicts constituted by infringing the interests created and protected by the statutory recognition of rights in copyright, registered designs, patents, trade marks and merchandise marks, and plant breeders' rights, it is at common law an actionable wrong based on misrepresentation for one party to represent his goods or services as being those of a competitor in such a way as to be calculated to deceive the public into thinking that the goods or services are truly the other's, and thereby to injure the other's business by obtaining for himself custom intended for the other.[53] The object of the action is to protect the goodwill of the complainer.[54] " One man is not entitled to sell his goods under such circumstances, by the name, or the packet, or the mode of making up the article, or in such a way as to induce the public to believe that they are the manufacture of someone else." [55] " The fundamental rule is that one man has no right to pass off his goods for sale as the goods of a rival trader." [56]

It is not absolutely essential that the parties be engaged in a common field of business or activity, but if they are not the possibility of deception and consequent damage is much reduced.[57]

---

[48] *Balden* v. *Shorter* [1933] Ch. 427.
[49] *Joyce* v. *Motor Surveys, Ltd.* [1948] Ch. 252.
[50] *Thompson* v. *Fifeshire Advertiser*, 1936 S.N. 56.
[51] *Macrae* v. *Wicks* (1886) 13 R. 732 (treated, rather inappropriately, as a case of ordinary slander).
[52] (1857) 20 D. 222.
[53] See Clive, " The Action for Passing Off," 1963 J.R. 117.
[54] *Spalding* v. *Gamage* (1915) 32 R.P.C. 273, 284; *Haig & Co.* v. *Forth Blending Co.*, 1954 S.C. 35, 37.
[55] *Haig & Co.* v. *Forth Blending Co.*, 1954 S.C. 35, 37, *per* Lord Hill Watson, citing *Cellular Clothing Co.* v. *Maxton and Murray* (1899) 1 F.(H.L.) 29, 30, 32; *Reddaway* v. *Banham* [1896] A.C. 199, 204, 209, 215; *Weingarten Bros.* v. *Bayer & Co.* (1905) 22 R.P.C. 341, 349. *Cf. Bile Bean Mfg. Co.* v. *Davidson* (1906) 8 F. 1181, 1199.
[56] *Leather Cloth Co.* v. *American Leather Cloth Co.* (1865) 11 H.L.C. 523, 538, *per* Lord Kingsdown.
[57] *Dunlop Pneumatic Tyre Co.* v. *Dunlop Motor Co.*, 1907 S.C.(H.L.) 15; *Scottish Union and National Insurance Co.* v. *Scottish National Insurance Co.*, 1909 S.C. 318; *cf. Dr. Barnardo's Homes* v. *Barnardo Amalgamated Industries* (1949) 66 R.P.C. 103; *McCulloch* v. *May* [1947] 2 All E.R. 845.

An action is competent even though no actual loss of business has been proved,[58] as it is assumed that the presence on the market of a quantity of deceptive goods will be detrimental to the plaintiff's business.[59] But only nominal damages can be awarded, unless there is proof of actual financial loss.[59]

Intention and Negligence. Deliberate intent to deceive the consumer need not be proved. The defender's conduct need not be fraudulent, and he need have had no intention of obtaining any benefit from his rival's reputation and goodwill. Nor need negligence be proved. Even if the similarity is entirely fortuitous and he be ignorant of his rival's product, he may be interdicted if the result of his actings is that the public are likely to be misled. " No trader, however honest his personal intentions, has a right to adopt, and use so much of his rival's established get-up as will enable any dishonest trader or retailer into whose hands the goods may come to sell them as the goods of his rival." [60] The absence of fraudulent intention may be a defence to a claim of damages for the past but will not prevent an interdict for the future.[61]

The court has to consider objectively whether the defender's conduct was likely to deceive [62]; evidence that members of the public were actually deceived is relevant but not essential[63]; regard must be had to the market,[64] and the possibility of deceiving the less wary. There can be less, or possibly no, likelihood of deception if the parties are not competing in the same line of business.[65]

Means of committing this wrong. There are numerous ways in which this wrong can be committed. Among the commonest are:

(1) To put on the market one's own goods described as those of another,[66] or goods described as made under the inspection of or by the authority of a person, though the latter was not a rival manufacturer,[67] or as goods with which the complainer is in some way associated,[68] or another's goods described as one's own.[69] This principle extends to such

---

[58] *Draper* v. *Trist* [1939] 3 All E.R. 513; *Procea Products, Ltd.* v. *Evans* (1951) 68 R.P.C. 210.

[59] *Draper, supra,* 526.

[60] *Haig* v. *Forth Blending Co.,* 1954 S.C. 35, 39–40, citing *Johnston* v. *Orr Ewing* (1882) 7 App.Cas. 219, 232; *Cellular Clothing Co.* v. *Maxton & Murray* (1899) 1 F.(H.L.) 29, 33; *Lever* v. *Goodwin* (1887) 36 Ch.D. 1, 3; *Star Cycle Co.* v. *Frankenburgs* (1907) 24 R.P.C. 405, 415; *Boord & Son* v. *Bagots, Hutton & Co.* [1916] A.C. 382, 391.

[61] *G.N.S.Ry.* v. *Mann* (1892) 19 R. 1035, 1041, *per* Lord McLaren.

[62] *Spalding* v. *Gamage* (1915) 84 L.J.Ch. 449; *Draper* v. *Trist* [1939] 3 All E.R. 513.

[63] *Draper, supra.*

[64] *Johnston* v. *Orr Ewing* (1882) 7 App.Cas. 219; *Singer Mfg. Co.* v. *Loog* (1882) 8 App.Cas. 15.

[65] *McCulloch* v. *Lewis A. May (Produce Distributors), Ltd.* [1947] 2 All E.R. 845. (Such facts might amount to fraud.)

[66] *Vokes, Ltd.* v. *Evans* (1931) 49 R.P.C. 140.

[67] *Wilkie* v. *McCulloch* (1823) 2 S. 369.

[68] *Samuelson* v. *Producers' Distributing Co.* [1932] 1 Ch. 201; *B.M.A.* v. *Marsh* (1931) 48 R.P.C. 565.

[69] *Henderson* v. *Munro* (1905) 13 S.L.T. 57.

" goods " as poems,[70] cartoons,[71] a musical act,[72] and a newspaper or periodical.[73]

(2) To imitate the " get-up " of another's goods. It is passing off to market goods whose labels, containers, packaging or other obvious features are likely to deceive salesmen or consumers into thinking that they are truly the goods of another, the " get-up " of which they resemble.[74] This principle does not prevent the marketing by a competitor of a similar product where the similarity is demanded by the purpose or function of the goods or is substantially common to all goods of that class.[75]

(3) To use another's trade mark. Apart from, or failing, an action under statute for infringement of trade mark,[76] a common-law action lies [77] for passing off by using the pursuer's trade mark.[78]

(4) To use the pursuer's name. If the defender engages in the same business as the pursuer and uses his own name, or one which he has assumed for a substantial time,[79] he is not thereby *per se* committing any wrong.[80] If customers mistakenly give him orders he is entitled to take advantage of this.[81] But he may commit the delict if he goes further and acts so as to give the impression that his goods are those of his competitor,[82] or if it appears that he is seeking to take advantage from the similarity of names to pass off his own goods as those of his competitor.[83] But it is clearly wrongful to trade under an assumed business name the same as that of a competitor, or so similar thereto as to be likely to be confusing.[84] For this reason the Board of Trade may prevent a company from having a registered name similar to that of an existing company.[85]

(5) To use the pursuer's trade name. It may be actionable to use the designation attached by the pursuer to his goods; this is so if the designation has acquired the customary connotation that the goods are the pursuer's,[86] but not if the designation is merely descriptive of the goods

70 *Lord Byron* v. *Johnston* (1816) 2 Mer. 29.
71 *Marengo* v. *Daily Sketch* [1948] 1 All E.R. 406.
72 *Hines* v. *Winnick* [1947] 2 All E.R. 517.
73 *Edinburgh Correspondent Newspaper* (1822) 1 S. 407; *Kark* v. *Odhams Press* [1962] 1 All E.R. 636, 639.
74 *Haig* v. *Forth Blending Co.*, 1954 S.C. 35 (whisky bottles of distinctive shape); *cf. Massam* v. *Thorley's Cattle Food Co.* (1880) 14 Ch.D. 748; *Bayer* v. *Baird* (1898) 25 R. 1142.
75 *Jamieson & Co.* v. *Jamieson* (1898) 14 T.L.R. 160; *J. B. Williams Co.* v. *Bromley & Co., Ltd.* (1909) 26 R.P.C. 765.
76 On which see Chap. 27, *infra*.
77 Trade Marks Act, 1938, s. 2.
78 *Singer Machine Manufrs.* v. *Wilson* (1877) 3 App.Cas. 376, 391; *cf. Melrose-Drover, Ltd.* v. *Heddle* (1901) 4 F. 1120.
79 *Jay's, Ltd.* v. *Jacobi* [1933] Ch. 411. Thus there could easily be two firms in a trade called John Smith and Son.
80 *Levy* v. *Walker* (1879) 10 Ch.D. 436; *Dunlop Pneumatic Tyre Co.* v. *Dunlop Motor Co.*, 1907 S.C.(H.L.) 15; *Cf. G.N.S.Ry.* v. *Mann* (1892) 19 R. 1035; *Cowan* v. *Millar* (1895) 22 R. 833; *Bayer* v. *Baird* (1898) 25 R. 1142; *Williamson* v. *Meikle*, 1909 S.C. 1272.
81 *Brinsmead* v. *Brinsmead and Waddington & Sons, Ltd.* (1913) 29 T.L.R. 237, 706.
82 *Sykes* v. *Sykes* (1824) 3 B. & C. 541; *Lee* v. *Haley* (1869) 5 Ch.App. 155.
83 *Dunlop Pneumatic Tyre Co.* v. *Dunlop Motor Co.*, 1907 S.C.(H.L.) 15.
84 *Boswell* v. *Mathie* (1884) 11 R. 1072; *G.N.S.Ry.*, v. *Mann* (1892) 19 R. 1035; *Williamson* v. *Meikle*, 1909 S.C. 1272.   85 Companies Act, 1948, ss. 17, 18.
86 *e.g., Powell* v. *Birmingham Vinegar Brewery Co.* [1896] 2 Ch. 54 (" Yorkshire Relish ") *Reddaway* v. *Banham* [1896] A.C. 199 (" camel-hair belting "); *Kinnell* v. *Ballantyne*, 1910 S.C. 246 (" Horse-Shoe " boilers).

or their function or some characteristic of them.[87] The onus is on the pursuer to show that the designation has acquired the connotation of being his manufacture, and this is easier where the designation incorporates the name of the place of manufacture.[88] The strongest cases are those where the pursuer has attached a made-up and not a descriptive name to his goods.[89]

(6) Selling pursuer's sub-standard goods without describing them as such. It is wrongful to sell a manufacturer's products which are substandard, defective, re-conditioned, part-worn, of discontinued pattern, or otherwise less than new and of the standard quality of current production without describing them as such, as this might lead purchasers to think that the manufacturer's normal quality was of this lower standard.[90] But there is no passing off if the goods are described as " seconds," " slightly imperfect," " discontinued lines " or otherwise identified. The same principle would probably apply to goods possibly damaged by fire or water, shop-soiled, or out of warranty.

(7) Deceptive advertisements. The exhibition or issue of advertising matter may amount to passing-off if it is so similar to the pursuer's advertisements as to be likely to confuse or lead the public to think that the defender's goods were those of the pursuer.[91] But apart from that, similarity of advertisement does not amount to passing off.[92]

(8) False attribution of manufacture. The selling by a retailer of goods of one manufacturer as being those of another, usually better known, manufacturer, is another form of passing off.[93]

(9) False attribution of approbation. It may amount to passing off falsely to say or to suggest that a person or body approves the defender's product or is advertising it.[94]

Remedies. Interdict is competent if the offending conduct is still in progress.[95] Damages are recoverable for loss of profits sustained by reason of the sale of the defender's products instead of the pursuer's, and for loss of goodwill [96] and damage to business reputation.[97] The

---

[87] *Cellular Clothing Co.* v. *Maxton and Murray* (1899) 1 F.(H.L.) 29 (" cellular clothing "); *British Vacuum Cleaner Co., Ltd.* v. *New Vacuum Cleaner Co., Ltd.* [1907] 2 Ch. 312 (" vacuum cleaner ").

[88] *e.g., Wotherspoon* v. *Currie* (1872) L.R. 5 H.L. 508; *Montgomery* v. *Thompson* [1891] A.C. 217; *Lecouturier* v. *Rey* [1910] A.C. 262.

[89] *Cf. Cellular Clothing Co.* v. *Maxton & Murray* (1899) 1 F.(H.L.) 29.

[90] *e.g., Gillette Safety Razor Co.* v. *Franks* (1924) 40 T.L.R. 606; *Spalding & Brothers* v. *Gamage, Ltd.* (1915) 84 L.J.Ch. 449; *Britains* v. *Morris* [1961] R.P.C. 217. Contrast *General Electric Co. and B.T.H. Co.* v. *Pryces Stores* (1933) 50 R.P.C. 232.

[91] *Masson Seeley & Co., Ltd.* v. *Embossotype Mfg. Co.* (1924) 41 R.P.C. 160. *Cf. Henderson* v. *Munro* (1905) 7 F. 636.

[92] *Wertheimer* v. *Stewart Cooper & Co.* (1906) 23 R.P.C. 481. There might, however, be a question of infringement of copyright.

[93] *Bass* v. *Laidlaw* (1886) 13 R. 898; *Thomson* v. *Robertson* (1888) 15 R. 880; *Thomson* v. *Dailly* (1897) 24 R. 1173; *Bass* v. *Laidlaw* (1908) 16 S.L.T. 660.

[94] *McCulloch* v. *May* [1947] 2 All E.R. 845; *Sim* v. *Heinz* [1959] 1 All E.R. 547; *cf. B.M.A.* v. *Marsh* (1931) 48 R.P.C. 565.

[95] *e.g., Johnston* v. *Orr Ewing* (1882) 7 App.Cas. 219; *Haig & Co.* v. *Forth Blending Co.,* 1954 S.C. 35.

[96] *Draper* v. *Trist* [1939] 3 All E.R. 513, 524; *A/B. Manus* v. *Fullwood and Bland, Ltd.* (1954) 71 R.P.C. 243.

[97] *Spalding and Brothers* v. *Gamage, Ltd.* (1918) 35 R.P.C. 101.

existence of fraudulent intent is irrelevant.[98] The pursuer is entitled to damages once it is proved that deceptive goods have been put on the market.

Business Names. If a man trades under his own name, or a business name, that name may, if applied or fixed to the goods in which he deals, be an ordinary trade mark and may be registrable as such. But even if not so used or registered, it may amount to passing off for another to use that name in connection with his goods, if the use is clearly calculated to deceive and is not the other trader's own name or a name under which he is entitled to trade.[99] Apart from these cases, " there is no right of exclusive property in a name, either a name under which a trader carries on his business or a name which he chooses to apply to his goods. The remedy which the law gives to a person who has used a particular name in trade is that he is entitled to prevent others from using the same name in such a way as is likely to mislead the public into thinking that the business or the goods so described is or are the business or the goods of the pursuer." [1]

The first user of a name descriptive of his business acquires no monopoly therein and no rights against a competitor in the same line of business who utilises the same descriptive name. A comparatively small difference in name will be held sufficient to avoid confusion and to permit both firms to use the ordinary descriptive name.[2]

Professional designations. In the same way a professional body or learned society can interdict non-members, or an association of non-members, from using a designation, or initials indicative of a professional designation, which is calculated to represent that the non-members are members of the pursuing body.[3]

A university can probably interdict a non-graduate from using a designation, or initials after his name, indicative of graduate status of that university, to which he is not entitled. Such a title as " Dr." by itself probably does not, however, amount to a claim to any particular degree or status, since it is applicable to several very different qualifications, particularly to holders of the Ph.D. or a higher doctorate such as D.Sc., but also to physicians, whether or not they hold the degree of M.D.[4]

---

[98] *Draper* v. *Trist* [1939] 3 All E.R. 513, 517.
[99] *Ainsworth* v. *Walmsley* (1866) L.R. 1 Eq. 518.
[1] *Williamson* v. *Meikle*, 1909 S.C. 1272; 26 R.P.C. 775, *per* Lord Skerrington. *Cf. Kinnell* v. *Ballantyne*, 1910 S.C. 246.
[2] *Office Cleaning Services, Ltd.* v. *Westminster Window and General Cleaners, Ltd.* (1946) 63 R.P.C. 39 (H.L.).
[3] *Society of Accountants in Edinburgh* v. *Corporation of Accountants* (1893) 20 R. 750; *Corporation of Accountants* v. *Society of Accountants in Edinburgh* (O.H.) 1903, 11 S.L.T. 424. *Cf. Walter* v. *Ashton* [1902] 2 Ch. 282; *Society of Accountants and Auditors* v. *Goodway* [1907] 1 Ch. 489; *Toner and Moore* v. *Merchant Service Guild, Ltd.* (1908) 25 R.P.C. 474; *A.G. and G.M.C.* v. *Barrett Proprietaries, Ltd.* (1933) 50 R.P.C. 48; *British Legion* v. *British Legion Club (Street), Ltd.* (1931) 48 R.P.C. 555; *The Clock, Ltd.* v. *The Clock House Hotel, Ltd.* (1931) 48 R.P.C. 269; *B.M.A.* v. *Marsh* (1931) 48 R.P.C. 571.
[4] *Younghusband* v. *Luftig* [1949] 2 K.B. 354.

It is similarly a criminal offence under various statutes to pretend to be, or take any name, title, addition or description implying that a person is qualified as a member of various professions.[5]

Trade Name of Pursuer's Goods. Though the trade name of the pursuer's goods is not registered as a trade mark, if it is in fact known in the trade as the distinctive name of the goods of a particular trader, it will amount to passing off for another to use that name for his or other goods. The right to complain arises only in respect of goods of the same kind for which the pursuer uses the name, or to which the known connection of goods and name extends. Thus the owners of the (Glasgow) *Evening Times* were held not entitled to interdict the publication of a (London) *Evening Times,* there being neither resemblance nor competition.[6]

The name may, however, be so identified with one trader that the use of it by another might induce the belief that his goods are the pursuer's,[7] or his business connected with,[8] or amalgamated with, or an extension or subsidiary of,[9] the pursuer's.

7. BREACH OF CONFIDENCE

Akin to infringement of privacy is the wrong done when a person, apart from possibly being in breach of contract, discloses to a third person or to the public generally some information which he should have withheld, which disclosure occasions distress to the complainer, whose secret thoughts or ideas are thereby published, and possibly also patrimonial loss.

" There may be cases in which if a person who stands in a confidential relation to another commits a breach of confidence in consequence of which injury results to the latter, the former will be liable in reparation if damages are relevantly averred and instructed." [10]   The difficulty is commonly to determine whether any relation of confidentiality exists, so as to make disclosure an actionable wrong. It is not enough that the disclosure was personally embarrassing to the pursuer, or acutely hurtful to his feelings, or his patrimonial interests. Thus no such confidential relationship existed between a person and his creditors as to make wrongful the publication, against his wishes, of a report of a meeting at which a composition contract was agreed upon.[11]   On the other hand a person employed in a professional capacity does stand in a confidential relationship

---

[5] *e.g.,* Veterinary Surgeons Acts, 1881, s. 17; 1900; 1950, s. 58; Architects (Registration) Acts, 1931, s. 17 and 1938, s. 4; Solicitors (Scotland) Act, 1933, ss. 36, 50; Midwives (Scotland) Act, 1951, ss. 9, 11; Nurses (Scotland) Act, 1951, s. 12; Pharmacy Act, 1954, s. 19; Medical Act, 1956, s. 31; Dentists Act, 1957, s. 35; Opticians Act, 1958, s. 22; Professions Supplementary to Medicine Act, 1960, ss. 6–7; see also *Younghusband* v. *Luftig* [1949] 2 K.B. 354.

[6] *Outram* v. *London Evening Newspapers Co.* (1911) 28 R.P.C. 308; *cf. Borthwick* v. *Evening Post* (1888) 37 Ch.D. 449; *Ridgeway Co.* v. *Amalgamated Press, Ltd.* (1912) 29 R.P.C. 130.

[7] *Warwick Tyre Co.* v. *New Motor and General Rubber Co.* (1910) 27 R.P.C. 161.

[8] *Manchester Brewery Co.* v. *North Cheshire and Manchester Brewery Co.* [1899] A.C. 83.

[9] *Eastman Photographic Material Co.* v. *John Griffiths Cycle Corpn.* (1898) 15 R.P.C. 105.

[10] *Mushets, Ltd.* v. *Mackenzie Bros.* (1899) 1 F. 756, 763, *per* Lord Moncreiff.

[11] *Fulton* v. *Stubbs, Ltd.* (1903) 5 F. 814.

to his client, so as to make it wrongful, quite apart from breach of contract, to disclose information,[12] unless under legal compulsion, or in other circumstances justifying disclosure. An employee is under an implied obligation to his employer not to disclose confidential information obtained in the employment.[13] It has been said too that " when a paper is entrusted by its owner to a person for a special purpose, any ultroneous use of it by him may expose him to a liability in damages to the owner apart from any question of contract." [14]

The circumstances may sometimes allow an alternative remedy [15]; thus an actress who proposes to publish the love letters written to her by a politician could be restrained on the ground of infringement of copyright. But " in Scotland the Court of Session is held to have jurisdiction by interdict to protect not property merely, but reputation and even private feelings, from outrage and invasion. . . . By the publication of such effusions—confidential, careless, unthinking of consequences—a man may be wounded in his tenderest part, his literary reputation hurt, his character traduced. It is accordingly the understood or implied condition of the communication—the implied limitation of the right conferred —that such communications are not to be published. With these natural feelings on the breach of epistolary confidence the determinations of the Court of Session have accorded." [16] But the court will not interdict if the receiver has a legitimate interest to publish and no harmful consequences can reasonably be contemplated.[17] Again the breach of confidence may be a breach of an express term of a contract of employment.[18]

Questions of breach of confidence are frequently raised in actions for defamation allegedly constituted by the communication of private knowledge of the character of a person. If the information is correct it is not defamatory, and even if it were so, the question whether it was wrongful to communicate it depends on the existence or not in the circumstances of any qualified privilege. Thus an employer may warn an employee about the character of an associate, and such a statement may be privileged.[19] But in such cases, there is usually no relationship between pursuer and defender which raised a duty of confidence, so that the question of breach of confidence can rarely arise.

---

12 *Whyte* v. *Smith* (1851) 14 D. 177 (doctor); *Brown's Trs.* v. *Hay* (1898) 25 R. 1112 (accountant); *A.B.* v. *C.D.* (1905) 7 F. 72 (doctor). A banker's duty of confidentiality rests on implied contract: *Tournier* v. *National Provincial and Union Bank of England* [1924] 1 K.B. 461.

13 *Merryweather* v. *Moore* [1892] 2 Ch. 518; *Robb* v. *Green* [1895] 2 Q.B. 315; *Kirchner* v. *Gruban* [1909] 1 Ch. 413; *Bents Brewery Co.* v. *Hogan* [1945] 2 All E.R. 570; *Cf. Cameron* v. *Gibb* (1867) 3 S.L.R. 282.

14 *Neuman & Co.* v. *Kennedy* (1905) 12 S.L.T. 763.

15 *Cf. Neuman & Co.* v. *Kennedy* (1905) 12 S.L.T. 763 (breach of confidence or breach of implied term of contract).

16 Bell, Comm. I, 111–112; *Cadell and Davies* v. *Stewart* (1804) Mor.Appx. Literary Property No. 4.

17 *White* v. *Dickson* (1881) 8 R. 896.

18 *Morson* v. *Rees* [1962] C.L.Y. 1130.

19 *Milne* v. *Smiths* (1892) 20 R. 95, 101; *Nelson* v. *Irving* (1897) 24 R. 1054; *Moffat* v. *Coats* (1906) 14 S.L.T. 392; 44 S.L.R. 20; *A.B.* v. *X.Y.*, 1917 S.C. 15.

Again, damages have been given against a party who bribed a clerk to disclose confidential matters relating to the pursuer's title.[20]

Existence of relationship of confidence. In many cases a relationship of trust or confidence has been held to exist independently of contract or proprietary right such as copyright, such as to entitle one party to restrain the other from disclosing or publishing something communicated subject to the cover of confidence.[21] The leading case is *Prince Albert* v. *Strange* [22] where the plaintiff, who had made some etchings for his private amusement, sent them to one Brown to have copies struck and a servant of Brown made extra copies which he sold to the defendant who advertised an exhibition thereof. A perpetual injunction was issued on the ground that defendant's possession had originated in a breach of trust or confidence by Brown's servant taking more impressions than were ordered.

Trade secrets and information. In the course of business individuals frequently obtain knowledge of matters of great commercial value to themselves as competitors, or to other competing traders, and the question may arise of whether the use or disclosure of such knowledge is wrongful. Sometimes the communication or use of secrets and information is restricted by restrictive covenant in a contract of employment or of the sale of a business.[23] Sometimes protection is given by way of patent, registration of industrial design, trade mark or copyright.

Such knowledge can be classified into ideas for industrial processes, or for literary or dramatic works, technical knowledge, including secret processes and lines of development, and information.

It is settled that one cannot prevent an employee who has left the pursuer's employment from using for his own benefit, or that of another employer, increased knowledge, ability or skill which he has gained in the pursuer's employment, because that is inseparable from the man himself. But one can prevent him using a secret process learned in the course of the employment.[24] Again, where plaintiffs disclosed confidential information to defendants to enable the latter to do work for the plaintiffs and the defendants misused the information for their own benefit, the plaintiffs were awarded damages for breach of confidence.[25] Where plaintiffs granted defendants an exclusive licence to manufacture their pattern of goods in the U.K. and the latter used the information given them to manufacture competing goods similar to those of the plaintiff's pattern, an order was made for an injunction, an account of profits and

[20] *Kerr* v. *Duke of Roxburgh* (1822) 3 Mur. 126. *Cf. Rutherford* v. *Boak* (1836) 14 S. 732.
[21] See *Morison* v. *Moat* (1851) 9 Hare 241, and cases discussed therein.
[22] (1849) 1 Mac. & G. 25; 1 H. & Tw. 1.
[23] The numerous cases on these points are collected and discussed in books on Contract.
[24] *Stevenson, Jordan & Harrison* v. *Macdonald & Evans* [1952] 1 T.L.R. 101; *Cranleigh Precision Engineering* v. *Bryant* [1964] 3 All E.R. 289; see further Turner, *Law of Trade Secrets*, p. 115 *et seq.*
[25] *Saltman Engineering Co.* v. *Campbell Engineering Co.* (1948) 65 R.P.C. 203. See also *Terrapin, Ltd.* v. *Builders' Supply Co.* [1960] R.P.C. 128.

delivery up of the imitative goods.[26] No interdict or injunction will be granted, however, if the secret has ceased to exist, as when it has been published in a patent application.[27]

Breach of confidence as proprietary wrong. " The injury to a tradeι resulting from publicity being given to the contents of his ledger, or his bank-book, lists of customers and the like . . . is at least not less real than the injury to feelings or reputation which may result from the indiscreet publication of private correspondence." [28] Thus an accountant who in the course of business obtained access to a client's papers was held to have no right to disclose the contents to the Inland Revenue or any third party, and the client was entitled to interdict and damages.[29] In such a case the wrong may be as much to the pursuer's business as to his feelings.

8. IMPERSONATION

Prima facie it is a species of fraud to represent oneself as being another living (but possibly not an imaginary) person, if that other suffers financial prejudice thereby.[30] Thus if A by representing himself to be B obtains money or goods from C an action will, it seems, lie against him at C's instance for restitution to C of the goods or money, failing which, if they are irrecoverable, for reparation for the loss. In such a case as *Morrison* v. *Robertson*,[31] where the innocent purchaser (Robertson) from the fraudulent person (Telford) had to restore the goods to the true owner (Morrison) when the first sale (Morrison to Telford) was declared void, Robertson doubtless had an action, *quantum valebat*, against Telford for the loss caused him by the fraud. Lord McLaren also there observed [32] that if there had been a valid first sale (instead of a contract wholly void for personation) the true owner might have had an action of damages against the person who obtained the goods by fraud, but that the subsale would then have been valid and the goods irrecoverable from the sub-purchaser.

If, however, a person represents himself to be a mythical or imaginary person, such as a judge of the High Court of Ruritania, he is liable for loss caused by the misrepresentation as an ordinary case of fraud, not of impersonation, as he has not personated anybody.

9. WRONGFUL REFUSAL TO CONTRACT

A refusal to contract with an offeror is an actionable wrong only in the exceptional cases of the common carrier and the innkeeper, who exercise a common calling and owe a continuing duty to the public to provide on

---

[26] *Peter Pan Mfg. Corpn.* v. *Corsets Silhouette, Ltd.* [1963] 3 All E.R. 402.
[27] *Mustad* v. *Allcock* (1928) reported at [1963] 3 All E.R. 416.
[28] *Brown's Trs.* v. *Hay* (1898) 25 R. 1112, 1118, *per* Lord McLaren.
[29] *Brown's Trs., supra.*
[30] *Cf. Phillips* v. *Brooks, Ltd.* [1919] 2 K.B. 243 (argued on contract only); *Serville* v. *Constance* [1954] 1 All E.R. 622.
[31] 1908 S.C. 332.
[32] p. 336.

request the service they hold themselves out as providing, unless they have a legally sufficient excuse. In all other cases a person incurs no delictual liability by refusing to contract with an offeror, and need assign no reason.

Common carriers. A common carrier is one who for hire undertakes the carriage of goods for any of the public indiscriminately from and to a certain place.[33] He may be a common carrier though he limits the class of goods carried or will carry certain goods only on certain conditions. A common carrier holds himself out as willing to carry for anyone who offers goods for carriage and may not refuse goods offered unless (a) they are not of a class which he professes to carry[34]; or (b) are dangerous or insufficiently packed[35]; or (c) have not been delivered to his departure point in sufficient time for loading before departure[36]; or (d) are consigned to a place to which he does not ply[37]; or (e) he has no room in his vehicle[38]; or (f) his charges have not been paid or offered to be paid[39]; nor, in the case of passengers, may he refuse to carry unless the passengers are not in a fit state to be carried. An unjustified refusal to carry is a ground for a claim of damages.[40]

Innkeepers. An innkeeper[41] is similarly liable in damages if, having accommodation, he declines unjustifiably to accept a guest who offers himself.[42] An inn or hotel (including a hydro or a temperance hotel)[43] is under an obligation to receive all members of the travelling public with their luggage, unless it is exceptional or dangerous, and to provide sleeping accommodation, food and drink, unless (a) the traveller, on request, gives no security to pay his bill; (b) is accompanied by an animal tending to cause alarm to other guests; (c) is not a traveller *in itinere*; (d) there is no available accommodation; (e) the traveller refuses to pay the ordinary tariff charges; (f) the traveller is an undesirable character, *i.e.*, physically disagreeable or dangerous or whose moral character would be objectionable to the other residents and prejudicial to the innkeeper's business.[44]

A public-house, *i.e.*, premises licensed for the sale of exciseable liquor, is possibly also an inn or hotel for these purposes; it is irrelevant that there is not sleeping accommodation for guests.[45]

---

33 Bell, *Prin.*, § 160.   34 *Johnson* v. *Midland Ry.* (1849) 4 Ex. 397.
35 *Bamfield* v. *Goole* [1910] 2 K.B. 94; *Batson, infra*; *cf. Wood* v. *Burns* (1893) 20 R. 602.
36 *Batson* v. *Donovan* (1820) 4 B. & Ald. 32.
37 *Johnson, supra*; *cf. Howey* v. *Lovell* (1826) 4 S. 752.
38 *Riley* v. *Horne* (1828) 5 Bing. 217.
39 *Batson, supra*; *Wyld* v. *Pickford* (1841) 8 M. & W. 443.
40 Bell, *Prin.*, § 159; *Crouch* v. *G.N.Ry.* (1856) 11 Ex. 742; *Garton* v. *Bristol and Exeter Ry.* (1861) 1 B. & S. 112.
41 This obligation probably does not extend to " Private Hotels," " Guest Houses " or " Boarding Houses " nor to premises offering " Accommodation " or " B and B." But see *May* v. *Wingate* (1694) Mor. 9236 (lodgings).
42 *Ewing* v. *Campbells* (1877) 5 R. 230, 233–234; *Constantine* v. *Imperial Hotels, Ltd.* [1944] K.B. 693; *cf. R.* v. *Ivens* (1835) 7 C. & P. 213.
43 *Ewing* v. *Campbells* (1877) 5 R. 230, 233–234.
44 *Rothfield* v. *N.B.Ry.*, 1920 S.C. 805, 811, per Lord Anderson. See also *Ewing* v. *Campbells* (1877) 5 R. 230; *Strathearn Hydropathic Co.* v. *Inland Revenue* (1881) 8 R. 798.
45 *Ewing* v. *Campbells* (1877) 5 R. 230, 234, per L.P. Inglis; *contra*, Lord Shand at p. 239.

10. INTERFERENCE WITH CONTRACT

It is an actionable delict for one person knowingly and unjustifiably to induce breach of a lawful contract existing between two other persons, thereby causing damage to one of them. The justification for this is that a violation of legal right (including a contractual right) committed knowingly is a cause of action.[46] " If C has an existing contract with A, and B is aware of it, and if B persuades or induces C to break the contract with resulting damage to A, this is, generally speaking, a tortious act for which B will be liable to A for the injury he has done him." [47] " Every person who knowingly and designedly entices or seduces such workmen to break their engagements and desert their employment to the injury of the master commits a wrongful act for which he is answerable in damages . . . ." [48] An injunction may be granted against conduct intended to cause strikes in breach of contract.[49]

Kinds of contracts affected. The principle, originally applied to contracts for personal service,[50] is not confined thereto [51] and has been applied to cases of a promise to marry,[52] a covenant restrictive of re-sale,[53] a contract to supply racing news,[54] and applies probably to any kind of commercial contract, probably even though voidable. It is not, however, actionable to interfere with a void contract.[55]

Defender's knowledge. The contract-breaker is liable only if he knew, or should reasonably have known in the circumstances, that the party induced was being induced to act in breach of a subsisting contract.[56] He is not liable if he reasonably believed that the party induced was legally free to act in the way he has been induced to do.[57] General knowledge of the existence of the contract is not enough; there must be knowledge, actual or constructive, of the term of the contract broken by the contract-breaker's interference.[58] Constructive knowledge may probably

---

[46] *Quinn* v. *Leathem* [1901] A.C. 495, 510, *per* Lord Macnaghten; *Jasperson* v. *Dominion Tobacco Co.* [1923] A.C. 709, 712, *per* Lord Haldane; *Exchange Telegraph Co.* v. *Giulianotti*, 1959 S.C. 19, 23, *per* Lord Guest.

[47] *Crofter Hand Woven Harris Tweed Co.* v. *Veitch*, 1942 S.C.(H.L.) 1, 8, *per* Viscount Simon L.C.; *cf. Findlay* v. *Blaylock*, 1937 S.C. 21, 25, *per* L.P. Normand.

[48] *Couper* v. *Macfarlane* (1879) 6 R. 683, 690, *per* Lord Ormidale; *cf.* Lord Gifford at pp. 693–694.

[49] *Cunard S.S. Co.* v. *Neary* [1960] C.L.Y. 3232.

[50] *Lumley* v. *Gye* (1853) 2 E. & B. 216; *Couper* v. *Macfarlane* (1879) 6 R. 683; *Read* v. *Friendly Society of Operative Stonemasons* [1902] 2 K.B. 732; *D.C. Thomson* v. *Deakin* [1952] Ch. 646.

[51] *B.M.T.A.* v. *Gray*, 1951 S.C. 586, 599, *per* L.P. Cooper; *D.C. Thomson* v. *Deakin*, *supra*.

[52] *Findlay* v. *Blaylock*, 1937 S.C. 21.

[53] *B.M.T.A.* v. *Gray*, 1951 S.C. 586; *cf. B.M.T.A.* v. *Salvadori* [1949] Ch. 556; *B.M.T.A.* v. *Naylor*, 1950, not reported, referred to in *B.M.T.A.* v. *Gray*, *supra*.

[54] *Exchange Telegraph Co.* v. *Giulianotti*, 1959 S.C. 19.

[55] *B.M.T.A.* v. *Gray*, *supra*, 604, *per* Lord Keith; *Shears* v. *Mendeloff* (1914) 30 T.L.R. 342; *Said* v. *Butt* [1920] 3 K.B. 497; *Lee* v. *Lord Dalmeny* [1927] 1 Ch. 300.

[56] The plaintiff in *Lumley* v. *Gye* (1853) 2 E. & B. 216, failed to prove knowledge.

[57] *British Industrial Plastics, Ltd.* v. *Ferguson* [1940] 1 All E.R. 479.

[58] *Long* v. *Smithson* (1918) 118 L.T. 678; *British Homophone, Ltd.* v. *Kunz* [1935] All E.R. Rep. 627.

be attached by " common knowledge about the way business is conducted," [59] or by the existence of a statute implying terms and conditions
into a contract.[60]

The defender's intention and motive. The defender will be liable if he
intended to, and did, cause breach of contract. It does not, however, matter
whether the defender had a malicious motive, *i.e.*, acted from ill-will or
malevolence.[61] Nor need the intention have been to cause any damage
by the breach, still less to have caused the precise kind or extent of harm
which in fact ensued.[62] It may even be that a defender is liable if, in the
knowledge of the existence of a contract, he does something, which has
as its direct consequence the breach of that contract.

Extent of breach. The defender is liable only if breach of contract has
occurred. It is probably not necessary that the breach which has been
induced should go to the root of the contract or be such as would justify
repudiation [63]; it is probably enough to have induced any breach, possibly
even one not actionable by the aggrieved party.[64] The breach induced
may be of any express term of the contract, or of any term implied into
the contract by law or custom.[65]

Methods of interference. The precise way in which the contract is
interfered with does not matter: it normally extends to persuasion, or
inducement by offer of reward. It might be effected by threats or any
other way of overcoming the will of the party in breach.

The method of interference used may be legal by itself, or illegal; it
does not need to be at all illegal or wrongful by itself to be actionable.
In *D. C. Thomson* v. *Deakin*,[66] D was an official of a trade union which
was in dispute with T, and D called a strike at T's works. D invited other
unions to help, and employees of B, which was in contractual relations
with T, intimated to B that they would not carry supplies to T. B accordingly informed T that for the present they would not implement their
contract with T. T sought an injunction to prevent D from procuring
breaches of contract by B. The Court of Appeal held that B's employees
were not in breach of contract, because B had broken their contract with

---

[59] *D.C. Thomson* v. *Deakin* [1952] Ch. 646, 687, *per* Lord Evershed M.R.

[60] *Cunard S.S. Co.* v. *Stacey* [1955] 1 Lloyds Rep. 247 (seamen's contract necessarily con-
forming to Merchant Shipping Act, 1894).

[61] *Quinn* v. *Leathem* [1901] A.C. 495, 510, Lord Macnaghten; *Glamorgan Coal Co.* v. *South
Wales Miners Federation* [1905] A.C. 239; *D. C. Thomson* v. *Deakin* [1952] Ch. 646, 676.

[62] *B.M.T.A.* v. *Salvadori* [1949] Ch. 556; *D. C. Thomson* v. *Deakin, supra,* 696–697, *per*
Jenkins L.J.

[63] This view, of Porter J., *obiter*, in *De Jetlay Marks* v. *Lord Greenwood* [1936] 1 All E.R.
863, 872 was doubted in *Thomson* v. *Deakin* [1952] Ch. 646, 689–690, *per* Lord Evershed
M.R.

[64] *National Phonograph Co., Ltd.* v. *Edison Bell Consolidated Phonograph Co., Ltd.* [1908]
1 Ch. 335.

[65] *Bent's Brewery Co., Ltd.* v. *Hogan* [1945] 2 All E.R. 570 (inducing employees to disclose
confidential information); *Hivac* v. *Park Royal Scientific Instruments, Ltd.* [1946] Ch.
169 (one firm inducing another's workmen to work for it in spare time: breach of implied
term of fidelity to true employer's business); *cf. Cameron* v. *Gibb* (1867) 3 S.L.R. 282.

[66] [1952] Ch. 646.

T. without having ordered their employees to perform it by carrying supplies to T; that there was no evidence that B's act was attributable to anything done by D; and that there was no proof that D knew of any contract between B and T. Injunction was therefore refused.

It seems implicit in the judgments delivered in this case that actionable interference with contract may be effected in at least five cases; these are:

(1) Where the defender applies direct persuasion or inducement to the party who breaks contract. This must have been more than advice, but such moral influence as to have caused the breach; was the breaking of the contract " fairly attributable to any such pressure, persuasion or procuration " on the part of the defender? [67] " Direct persuasion or procurement or inducement applied by the third party to the contract-breaker, with knowledge of the contract and the intention of bringing about its breach, is clearly to be regarded as a wrongful act in itself, and where this is shown a case of actionable interference in its primary form is made out." [68]

(2) Where the defender does any legally wrongful act which prevents the party from performing his part of the contract, *e.g.*, by placing restraint on him or by removing the only available essential tools or by kidnapping a necessary or irreplaceable servant.[69]

(3) Where the defender, having knowledge of the contract, interferes to do against the will of both and without the knowledge of either, what would have been a breach of contract if done by a contracting party himself.[70]

The contract-breaker may be a willing party to the breach, and (4) where the defender, " with knowledge of a contract between the contract-breaker and another, has dealings with the contract-breaker which the third party knows to be inconsistent with the contract, he has committed an actionable interference." [71] The inconsistent dealing may be commenced without knowledge of the contract, but if continued after the defender has notice of the contract, it becomes actionable interference.[72]

(5) Where the defender with knowledge of the contract causes the employees of a contracting party to break their contracts with him, and thereby disables that party from implementing his contract with the other contracting party.[73] Thus if A persuades all the pilots of an airline to refuse to fly, so that the airline cannot carry X as it has undertaken to do, A is liable to X.

In *Stratford* v. *Lindley* [73a] the W. union placed an embargo on their members handling barges of S., Ltd. and thereby caused them financial

---

[67] *Ibid.* 681, 686, *per* Evershed M.R. *Cf. Bent's Brewery Co., Ltd.* v. *Hogan* [1945] 2 All E.R. 570.

[68] *Ibid.* 694, *per* Jenkins L.J.

[69] *Ibid.* 678, *per* Evershed M.R.; 694–695, *per* Jenkins L.J.; 702, *per* Morris L.J.

[70] *Ibid.* 694, *per* Jenkins L.J., citing *G.W.K., Ltd.* v. *Dunlop Rubber Co.* (1926) 42 T.L.R. 376, 593.

[71] *Ibid.* 694, *per* Jenkins L.J. citing *British Industrial Plastics, Ltd.* v. *Ferguson* [1940] 1 All E.R. 479 (H.L.); *B.M.T.A.* v. *Salvadori* [1949] Ch. 556.

[72] *Ibid.* citing *De Francesco* v. *Barnum* (1890) 45 Ch.D. 430.

[73] *Ibid.* 682, *per* Evershed M.R.; 696–697, *per* Jenkins L.J.

[73a] [1964] 3 All E.R. 102.

loss, as a means of putting pressure on B., Ltd. (which was controlled by the same persons as S., Ltd.) to negotiate with the W. union as well as the T. union. S., Ltd. was held entitled to recover for the loss caused them thereby. The W. union had sufficient knowledge of the contracts with S., Ltd. to know that by putting on their embargo they were inducing a breach of contract.

Resultant damage. Some damage must have been caused before an action [74] for procurement of breach of contract can be raised.[75] Damage is of the essence of the wrong, but proof of specific damage is not required and some damage will readily be inferred. It is sufficient if the natural and probable consequence of the induced breach is that some damage will accrue to the pursuer.[76]

Justification for inducing breach. The delict is committed only if the breach is induced without legal justification. What will be justification in a particular case will always be a question of fact and it is submitted that the only general criterion of justification is whether a greater moral value will be maintained by the Court by its permitting the breach or by its upholding the sanctity of contract. In *Brimelow* v. *Casson*,[77] the defendants induced a theatre manager to break his contract with the plaintiff because the latter was paying such low wages to his chorus girls that some were compelled to resort to prostitution. The defendants' interest in maintaining standards in the theatrical profession was held to justify their having procured the breach. Again it was held sufficient justification that the contract-breaker was the parent of a minor son who had entered into an unsuitable engagement to marry, and that he was bona fide exercising parental guidance.[78] The self interest of the contract-breaker is not sufficient justification,[79] nor is it justifiable to induce breach of a contract between A and B because A was in breach of a prior contract with the defender.[80]

The only general guidance is the dictum [81] that " regard might be had to the nature of the contract broken; the position of the parties to the contract; the grounds for the breach; the means employed to procure the breach; the relation of the person procuring the breach to the person who breaks the contract; and . . . to the object of the person in procuring the breach."

---

[74] Including petition for interdict, as in *Exchange Telegraph Co.* v. *Giulianotti*, 1959 S.C. 19.
[75] *B.M.T.A.* v. *Gray*, 1951 S.C. 586.
[76] *Ibid.* p. 604, *per* Lord Keith; *cf. Exchange Telegraph Co.* v. *Gregory* [1896] 1 Q.B. 147; *Goldsoll* v. *Goldman* [1915] 1 Ch. 292; *Bent's Brewery Co.* v. *Hogan* [1945] 2 All E.R. 570; *Jones Brothers (Hunstanton), Ltd.* v. *Stevens* [1955] 1 Q.B. 275.
[77] [1924] 1 Ch. 302.
[78] *Findlay* v. *Blaylock*, 1937 S.C. 21; *cf. Muir* v. *Robbie* (1898) 6 S.L.T. 244; *Glamorgan Coal Co.* v. *South Wales Miners' Federation* [1903] 2 K.B. 545; [1905] A.C. 239; *Crofter Co.* v. *Veitch*, 1942 S.C.(H.L.) 1.
[79] *B.M.T.A.* v. *Gray*, 1957 S.C. 586, 600, *per* L. P. Cooper; 603, *per* Lord Russell.
[80] *Smithies* v. *National Assocn. of Operative Plasterers* [1909] 1 K.B. 310.
[81] *Glamorgan Coal Co.* v. *South Wales Miners' Federation* [1903] 2 K.B. 545; 574–575, *per* Romer L.J., approved in H.L. [1905] A.C. 239, 252.

Justification and malice. Justification is inconsistent with malicious motive in causing the breach of contract; to put it another way, a plea that causing breach of contract was justifiable may be rebutted by " clear and specific averments of facts and circumstances from which wrongful motive and malice may be inferred." [82]

Lawful but malicious act causing breach. If one party does what is quite lawful, such as buying up or hiring all available supplies, with the malicious motive of causing another party to break his contract with a third party, is such conduct actionable as amounting to interference with contract? On the analogy of cases of *aemulatio vicini*,[83] it is submitted that, if malice could be proved, such conduct would be actionable. A contrary view is suggested by *Thomson* v. *Deakin*,[84] in which case, however, excessive stress seems to have been placed on the need to prove an unlawful act on the part of the defendant; his act need not be intrinsically unlawful.

Making performance more onerous. It is also doubtful whether a person is liable if he does anything, rightful or wrongful, to one party to a contract which renders performance by the other party more onerous, difficult or expensive, even though not altogether impossible. If A, by operations *in suo*, withdraws subterranean water which gave hydrostatic support to B's land, at the time when C was building on B's land and causes C trouble, expense and waste of time, is A not liable on the principle of *aemulatio vicini*? [85] It is submitted that he is.

Statutory defence in trade disputes. In the special case of trade disputes, the Trade Disputes Act, 1906, s. 3 provides that " an act done by a person in contemplation or furtherance of a trade dispute [86] shall not be actionable on the ground only that it induces some other person to break a contract of employment or that it is an interference with the trade, business or employment of some other person, or with the right of some other person to dispose of his capital or his labour as he will." It has been doubted whether this defence applies where the contract breached by procurement from outside is other than a contract of employment.[87] This defence has been said to apply only where the defendant's act would not constitute any tort other than procurement of breach of contract,[88] and it has been held not to protect the inducement of breach of contract by intimidation or other tortious means,[89] nor to protect such inducement where the controversy was between one union and another.[90]

82 *Findlay* v. *Blaylock*, 1937 S.C. 21, 25–26, *per* L.P. Normand.
83 *Infra*, Chap. 27.
84 [1952] Ch. 646, 680, *per* Evershed M.R.
85 *Infra*, Chap. 27.
86 Defined s. 5 (3) and see *Larkin* v. *Long* [1915] A.C. 814.
87 *Brimelow*, *supra*, 314; *D. C. Thomson*, *supra*, 689, *per* Evershed M.R.
88 *Conway* v. *Wade* [1909] A.C. 506, 511–512, *per* Lord Loreburn.
89 *Rookes* v. *Barnard* [1964] 1 All E.R. 367.
90 *Stratford* v. *Lindley* [1964] 3 All E.R. 102.

11. Unlawful Price Maintenance by Contract

The Resale Prices Act, 1964, s. 1, makes it unlawful, save in exempted cases, to include in a contract a term or condition providing for the establishment of minimum resale prices for the goods in the United Kingdom. Indirect enforcement of minimum resale prices is also unlawful (s. 2) with certain exceptions (s. 3). The obligation to comply with these provisions is, by s. 4 (2), " a duty owed to any person who may be affected by a contravention of them, and any breach of that duty is actionable accordingly (subject to the defences and other incidents applying to actions for breach of statutory duty)." Compliance with these provisions is also enforceable by civil proceedings on behalf of the Crown for an interdict or other appropriate relief (s. 4 (3)).[90a]

12. Enticement of Employees

The enticement of employees to leave their existing employment, as by offering them better conditions of employment, is not an actionable wrong so long as there is no direct inducement to break existing contracts but only the offer of better alternative employment after the lawful termination of the existing contract. It is not even actionable to induce or persuade employees to terminate their existing contracts in lawful manner.[91] But " every master has a legal right and interest in the services of the workmen whom he has under engagement in his employment, and . . . every person who knowingly and designedly entices or seduces such workmen to break their engagements and desert their employment to the injury of the master, commits a wrongful act for which he is answerable in damages, it being always understood that the injury for which reparation is asked must be the natural and necessary consequence of the wrongful act complained of, and not merely remotely connected with it." [92]   In Couper v. Macfarlane [92] the judges emphasised the " illegal means " used to induce desertion from employment, but such means as threats, violence, false representations, promises and payments of money are not essential. The wrong could equally be committed by legal means such as an offer of greatly increased earnings. The essence of the wrong is not in the means but in the question whether the inducement was intended to, and did, draw the man from his job before he had given notice to terminate his employment in the proper way. It is particularly wrongful if the enticing employer persuades the employee to reveal secrets connected with his former employment.[93]

90a   *Cf.* Consumer Protection Act, 1961, s. 3.
91   *McManus* v. *Bowes* [1938] 1 K.B. 98.
92   *Couper & Sons* v. *Macfarlane* (1879) 6 R. 683, 690, *per* Lord Ormidale; *cf.* Lord Gifford at 693; see also Bell, *Prin.*, § 2033; *Dickson* v. *Taylor* (1816) 1 Mur. 141; *Kerr* v. *Duke of Roxburgh* (1822) 3 Mur. 126; *McGregor* v. *Mitchell* (1825) 4 S. 52; *Rutherford* v. *Boak* (1836) 14 S. 732; *Roxburgh* v. *McArthur* (1841) 3 D. 556; *Lumley* v. *Gye* (1853) 2 E. & Bl. 217; *Belmont Laundry Co.* v. *Aberdeen Steam Laundry Co.* (1898) 1 F. 45, and cases in Sheriff Court Reports.
93   *Kerr, Rutherford, Roxburgh, supra.*

13. HARBOURING ANOTHER'S EMPLOYEE

It is an actionable wrong knowingly to take into and retain in one's employment a person who is already under a contract of employment with another.[94] It is not necessary for this delict that the defender should have induced or contributed to the employee's breach of contract; it is sufficient if the employee has been taken on, having deserted or otherwise voluntarily broken his previous contract.[95] " The fact that A, knowing that B is under a contract of service with C, takes B into his service, or continues to employ him, during part of the period embraced in the contract of which C desires implement, constitutes " harbouring ", and is a legal wrong against the original employer." [96] The deserting employee is also, of course, liable in damages for breach of contract with his former employer. It does not matter for the purposes of this action that the court could not enforce implement of the former contract. It is possible that this action would lie against one employer who employed another's workmen in their spare time, unknown to him, certainly if the two employers are in direct competition and if the employees use for the benefit of one skill or knowledge derived from the true employer.[97] The deserted employer must have sustained some damage and cannot sue if the servant would not return to the former employer.[98]

14. PREVENTING MAN FROM OBTAINING EMPLOYMENT

There is no wrong in communicating to other employers or an association thereof unfavourable reports on an employee which result in his being unable to obtain employment, unless the reports were malicious, or slanderous,[99] or, probably, the circumstances amounted to conspiracy to injure the pursuer,[1] or some illegal means were employed.

Where " closed shops " are common or universal in a trade, a trade union may be liable for preventing a man from obtaining employment if it unjustifiably refuses to admit him to membership or unjustifiably expels him,[2] though by reason of the Trade Disputes Act, 1906, s. 4, the action could not be brought against the union for delict, but only for breach of contract.[3] The point arises most often in cases of alleged conspiracy to injure, as by procuring the pursuer's dismissal by threats of a strike at the employer's place of work,[4] but to claim damages for being prevented

---

[94] Bell, *Prin.*, § 2033; *Dickson* v. *Taylor* (1816) 1 Mur. 141; *Rose Street Foundry* v. *Lewis*, 1917 S.C. 341; see also *Cave* v. *Trench* [1949] C.L.Y. 1397.

[95] *Ibid.* 348, *per* L.J.C. Scott Dickson, citing *Lumley* v. *Gye* (1853) 2 E. & Bl. 216; 350, *per* Lord Salvesen.

[96] *Ibid.* 348, *per* L.J.C. Scott Dickson. See also *McGregor* v. *Mitchell* (1825) 4 S. 52; *Belmont Laundry Co., Ltd.* v. *Aberdeen Steam Laundry Co., Ltd.* (1898) 1 F. 45.

[97] *Cf. Hivac, Ltd.* v. *Park Royal Scientific Instruments, Ltd.* [1946] Ch. 169.

[98] *Jones Bros. (Hunstanton)* v. *Stevens* [1954] 3 All E.R. 677.

[99] *Keith* v. *Lauder* (1905) 8 F. 356 (qualified privilege obtains); *cf. Mushets, Ltd.* v. *Mackenzie* (1899) 1 F. 756.

[1] *Cf. Mackenzie* v. *Iron Trades Employers' Insurance Assocn., Ltd.*, 1910 S.C. 79.

[2] *Cf. Hewit* v. *Edinburgh Operative Lathsplitters* (1906) 14 S.L.T. 489.

[3] *Bonsor* v. *Musicians' Union* [1956] A.C. 104.

[4] *e.g.*, *Rookes* v. *Barnard* [1964] 1 All E.R. 367. See also Rideout, " Protection of the Right to Work " (1963) 25 M.L.R. 137.

from getting employment it would have to be shown that the prevention was complete, not merely from the particular factory or appointment from which the pursuer had been dismissed.

The point could also arise in the case of unjustifiable suspension or expulsion from membership of a professional society or institute, membership of which is a prerequisite of employment at anything more than clerical grade in many circumstances.

15. CAUSING CONSEQUENTIAL LOSS OF SERVICES

It is not an actionable wrong to cause a person indirect economic loss by injuring, or causing the death of, another person with whom the loser has contractual ties. Thus an employer has no claim where his employee is injured or killed by the fault of a third party,[5] nor has an employee where a third party has wrongfully injured or caused the death of his employer, nor has one partner where another partner has been injured or killed,[6] nor has a company for the loss of services of a director,[7] nor the owner of a business for the death of the manager,[8] nor a professional dancer for the death of his dancing partner (though he could claim in so far as he had lost a wife).[9]

The principle has been stated to be that the foresight of harmful consequences attributed to a wrongdoer does not extend to include the victim's contractual relationships; or it can be put that loss to a person in contractual relations with the injured person, occurring by reason of the injured person's incapacity, is too remote damage to the claimant to be recoverable from the wrongdoer.

English law on this matter is otherwise, and the competency of an action for loss of a servant's services is well settled.[10]

Similarly an injured person cannot competently include in his claim of damages a claim for loss caused to a company by his temporary incapacity and inability to act as director, manager and secretary, even though such loss would affect the pursuer financially in that he was also the principal shareholder in the company.[11]

16. CONSPIRACY TO INJURE

It has been stated in the House of Lords[12] that there is no material difference between conspiracy as a Scottish delict and as an English tort.

---

[5] *Allan* v. *Barclay* (1864) 2 M. 873; *Reavis* v. *Clan Line Steamers*, 1925 S.C. 725.
[6] *Gibson* v. *Glasgow Corpn.*, 1963 S.L.T.(Notes) 16.
[7] *Cf. Young* v. *Ormiston*, 1936 S.L.T. 79.
[8] *Quinn* v. *Greenock Tramways Co.*, 1926 S.C. 544.
[9] *Burgess* v. *Florence Nightingale Hospital* [1955] 1 Q.B. 349.
[10] The Law Reform Committee for Scotland (Eleventh Report, 1963, Cmnd. 1997) considered whether an employer should be enabled to recover damages for loss suffered in consequence of a wrong done to his employee by a third person and recommended no amendment of the law.
[11] *Young* v. *Ormiston*, 1936 S.L.T. 79.
[12] *Crofter Hand Woven Harris Tweed Co.* v. *Veitch*, 1942 S.C.(H.L.) 1, 2–3, *per* Viscount Simon L.C. This case proceeded in part on a consideration of purely English legal history.

This may well be questionable, but the law is now too settled to be disturbed by anything short of legislation.[13]

Conspiracy has been defined as consisting of an agreement of two or more to do an unlawful act or to do a lawful act by unlawful means [14]; to be actionable actual damage must have resulted. Most of the cases have dealt with trade rivalry, but the principle is not limited thereto.[15] Though sometimes combined with a claim for damage caused by interference with contract, a claim for damage caused by conspiracy is independent and does not necessarily involve inducing breach of contract.

It is quite clear that an act which is wrongful if done by one person, is equally if not more wrongful if done by two or more in combination. But in cases of conspiracy to injure " there are cases in which a combination of individuals to act in a certain way, resulting in deliberate damage to others, is actionable, even though the same thing, if done by a single individual without any element of combination, would not expose him to liability." [16] " A conspiracy to injure might give rise to civil liability even though the end were brought about by conduct and acts which by themselves and apart from the element of combination or concerted action could not be regarded as a legal wrong." [17] " The rule may seem anomalous, so far as it holds that conduct by two may be actionable if it causes damage, whereas the same conduct done by one, causing the same damage, would give no redress. In effect the plaintiff's right is that he should not be damnified by a conspiracy to injure him, and it is in the fact of the conspiracy that the unlawfulness resides. It is a different matter if the conspiracy is to do acts in themselves wrongful, such as to deceive or defraud, to commit violence, or to conduct a strike or lockout by means of conduct prohibited by the Conspiracy and Protection of Property Act, 1875 . . ." [18]

The wrong consists in the agreement or combination of two or more persons to use unlawful means, or to do an unlawful act, calculated to, and actually causing, damage to the pursuer's interests. Bare agreement is not civilly actionable and the wrong is committed only if the combination is put into effect and damage to the pursuer results.[19] There must be proved (a) agreement between the defenders; (b) to effect an unlawful purpose; and (c) resultant damage to the pursuers.[20] The onus is on the pursuers to prove all the essential ingredients of the wrong.[21]

13 See generally Friedman, *Law and Social Change in Contemporary Britain*, Chap. 6; Hughes, " The Tort of Conspiracy " (1952) 15 M.L.R. 209.
14 *Mulcahy* v. *R.* (1868) L.R. 3 E. and I.App. 306, 317, *per* Willes J., approved by Lord Dunedin in *Mackenzie* v. *Iron Trades Employers' Insce. Assocn., Ltd.*, 1910 S.C. 79, 83, and by Lord Wright in *Crofter Co., supra*, 22–23.
15 *Crofter Co., supra*, 11, *per* Viscount Simon; 36, *per* Lord Wright, citing *Gregory* v. *Duke of Brunswick* (1844) 6 M. & G. 953; *Thompson* v. *N.S.W. Branch of B.M.A.* [1924] A.C. 764.
16 *Crofter Co., supra*, 9, *per* Viscount Simon L.C.
17 *Quinn* v. *Leathem* [1901] A.C. 495, 510, *per* Lord Macnaghten, founding on Lord Watson in *Allen* v. *Flood* [1898] A.C. 1, 108, approved by Lord Wright in *Crofter Co., supra*, 23.
18 *Ibid.* 27, *per* Lord Wright.
19 *Mackenzie, supra*, 83; *Crofter Co., supra*, 5.
20 *Crofter Co., supra*, 6.
21 *Stratford* v. *Lindley* [1964] 3 All E.R. 102.

(a) *Combination.* There must be at least two defenders, averred to have acted in combination, and there must be some evidence of collaboration and joint action. Both or all defenders need not be of the same standing; it is sufficient if one or more be subordinates so long as they were not merely servants but had independent liberty of action and appreciated what they were about.[22] If servants or agents are employed that does not *per se* make them co-conspirators with their principal.[23]

Forms of combination. There is no limit to the kinds of combinations which may be attacked as actionable conspiracies. The principal instances have been: the combination of members of a theatre audience to hiss an actor off the stage [24]; of shipping firms to defeat the competition of a rival firm [25]; or trade union officials to compel an employer to dismiss a non-union employee [26]; of employees against their employer to compel him under threat of a strike to dismiss an employee belonging to another union [27]; of an employers' federation and a trade union against an employee who belonged to another union, in the interests of promoting collective bargaining [28]; of wholesalers and distributors against a retailer who was opposing their policy [29]; of trade union officials and employers against a rival employer in the interests of better conditions for union members [30]; of butchers to compel cattle salesmen to refuse to sell meat to cooperative societies [31]; of members of a trade association against a retailer to compel him to sell goods at their list price [32]; of officers of a trade union against a member of the union to enforce payment of a debt due from him to the union [33]; of trade union officials against the employer to secure the dismissal of a non-union man [34]; of trade union officials against an employer to make him concede negotiating rights to that union.[35]

(b) *Combination to effect an unlawful purpose.* In this branch of law a purpose or object becomes unlawful if its real or predominant purpose or motive is the infliction of injury on the complainer as distinguished from serving the bona fide and legitimate interests of those who combine.[36] " The test is not what is the natural result to the plaintiffs of such combined action, or what is the resulting damage which the defendants

---

22 *Crofter Co., supra,* 6, *per* Viscount Simon L.C.
23 *Ibid.* 28, *per* Lord Wright.
24 *Gregory* v. *Duke of Brunswick* (1844) 6 M. & G. 953 (action succeeded).
25 *Mogul S.S. Co.* v. *McGregor, Gow & Co.* [1892] A.C. 25.
26 *Quinn* v. *Leathem* [1901] A.C. 495 (action succeeded).
27 *White* v. *Riley* [1921] 1 Ch. 1.
28 *Reynolds* v. *Shipping Federation* [1924] 1 Ch. 28.
29 *Sorrell* v. *Smith* [1925] A.C. 700.
30 *Crofter Co.* v. *Veitch,* 1942 S.C.(H.L.) 1.
31 *S.C.W.S.* v. *Glasgow Fleshers' Trade Defence Assocn.* (1898) 5 S.L.T. 263.
32 *Ware and de Freville* v. *M.T.A.* [1921] 3 K.B. 40.
33 *Gibban* v. *Nat. Amalg. Labourers' Union* [1903] 2 K.B. 600 (action succeeded).
34 *Rookes* v. *Barnard* [1964] 1 All E.R. 367 (action succeeded).
35 *Stratford* v. *Lindley* [1964] 3 All E.R. 102 (action succeeded).
36 *Sorrell* v. *Smith,* [1925] A.C. 700, 711–712, *per* Lord Cave, L.C. approved in *Crofter Co., supra,* 7.

realise or should realise will follow, but what is in truth the object in the minds of the combiners when they acted as they did." [37] Liability depends on ascertaining the predominant purpose. " If that predominant purpose is to damage another person and damage results, that is tortious conspiracy. If the predominant purpose is the lawful protection or promotion of any lawful interest of the combiners (no illegal means being employed), it is not a tortious conspiracy, even though it causes damage to another person." [37] " Unless the real and predominant purpose is to advance the defendants' lawful interests in a matter where the defendants honestly believe that those interests would directly suffer if the action taken against the plaintiffs was not taken, a combination wilfully to damage a man in his trade is unlawful." [38]

Motive. In the leading case [39] most of the judges deliberately avoided the difficult word " motive," preferring to discuss the " purpose " or " object " of the defenders' conduct, and undoubtedly that word has been used carelessly in some of the previous cases. But in using the word " purpose " or " object " their Lordships were all essentially trying to convey what is properly understood by " motive," [40] bearing in mind that the motive need not be evil, in the form of spite or malevolence. But " to suppose that it follows from an absence of malice or ill-will that the true motive of the acts done in combination was to further the legitimate interests of the parties to the combination seems to me to be a *non sequitur.*" [41]

Motive is not the same as intention, and combined action is usually intentional, but may spring from one or more of many different motives. The fact that there was intention to injure does not mean that the conspiracy was actionable, because it leaves open the question: what was the real motive underlying, or predominant purpose of, the conduct which was intended to injure the pursuers?

Combination may have more than one purpose. Regard is had then to the predominant purpose of the combination, and if that is to injure, it is of no avail that a subsidiary purpose is to protect or further the defenders' own interests. Conversely, if the predominant purpose is to further the defenders' own legitimate interests, there is no actionable conspiracy merely because a subsidiary or incidental purpose is to injure the pursuers' interests.[42]

Interests which persons may legitimately combine to protect or further, even at the cost of doing harm to another's interests, include material interests which can be measured in money, such as maintenance

---

[37] *Crofter Co., supra,* 10, *per* Viscount Simon L.C.
[38] *Crofter Co., supra,* 11, *per* Viscount Simon L.C.
[39] *Crofter Co., supra.*
[40] *Cf.* Viscount Maugham at p. 15—" ' The real purpose ' or ' the true motive ' (which I think is the same thing) . . ."
[41] *Ibid.* 13, *per* Viscount Maugham, instancing the possible case of a trade union wishing to demonstrate its power.
[42] *Crofter Co., supra,* 10, 15.

or improvement of wages or working conditions,[43] or to develop the defenders' trade,[44] or to maintain a " closed shop," [45] or to achieve union recognition,[46] but also extends to purposes not financial but honestly believed to be desirable, and in fact supported by members, such as a boycott by musicians in opposition to colour discrimination among patrons of dance halls.[47]

The interests which the combining parties are seeking to promote may be of different kinds but it is sufficient if each is promoting a legitimate trade or business interest. It is doubtful if the defence of promoting self-interest would succeed if some of the combining parties were actuated merely by hate or vindictive spite with no just excuse at all.[48]

A conspiracy does not become actionable merely because the damage done is severe out of all proportion to the advantage sought to be gained.[49]

Nor does it become actionable because the defender's conduct was motivated by spite, hatred or malevolence unless that was the predominant motive (or the gratification of spite the predominant purpose). " Proof of malevolent feelings, coupled with proof that the combiners had in view no tangible benefit to themselves, would clearly, I think, be enough to show that the combination was wrongful. But it does not follow that malevolence is a necessary element to constitute the tort." [50] " Mere malevolence does not damage anyone. I cannot see how the pursuit of a legitimate practical object can be vitiated by glee at the adversary's expected discomfiture." [51]

Doubtful cases. If it is not clear what the predominant purpose is, or whether the protection of legitimate interests or the deliberate infliction of harm is predominant, it is doubtful whether the conspiracy is actionable. Probably in such cases the defenders would be entitled to absolvitor. More difficult is the question whether a conspiracy is actionable where the main purpose is not to do harm to the pursuer and yet not to further any interest of the defenders. Lord Porter left undecided [52] the problem whether it would be actionable to combine to compel the pursuer to subscribe to a charitable fund,[53] but Viscount Maughan thought [54] that a conspiracy the purpose of which was to show " a dislike of the religious views or the politics or the race or the colour of the plaintiff, or a mere

---

43 *Ibid.* 11.
44 *Mogul S.S. Co.* v. *McGregor Gow & Co.* [1892] A.C. 25.
45 *Rookes* v. *Barnard* [1964] 1 All E.R. 367.
46 *Stratford* v. *Lindley* [1964] 3 All E.R. 102.
47 *Scala Ballroom (Wolverhampton), Ltd.* v. *Ratcliffe* [1958] 3 All E.R. 220. See also *Mosley Publications* v. *Morrison* (1947) 1 C.L.C. 10032; *Byrne* v. *Kinematograph Renters Society* [1958] 1 W.L.R. 762.
48 *Crofter Co.*, *supra*, 16–17, *per* Viscount Maugham.
49 *Crofter Co.* v. *Veitch*, 1942 S.C.(H.L.) 1, 11–12, *per* Viscount Simon.
50 *Ibid.* 29, *per* Lord Wright.
51 *Crofter Co.*, *supra*, 31, *per* Lord Wright.
52 *Crofter Co.* v. *Veitch*, 1942 S.C.(H.L.) 1, 48.
53 It is submitted that it should be actionable in that benefit to the charity would be *res inter alios* as between the parties, but as between them the purpose was to impoverish the pursuer.
54 *Ibid.* p. 15; *cf. Huntley* v. *Thornton* [1957] 1 W.L.R. 321, 341.

demonstration of power by busybodies " would be actionable. Viscount Simon also indicated the view, *obiter*, that in the case before the House, he could not think that the union officials could have excused themselves, if they had been induced to take action to smash the weavers' trade by the promise from the millowners of a large subscription to trade union funds, merely by saying that the predominant purpose was thereby to benefit union funds.[55]

Combination to effect unlawful purpose: means unlawful. An alternative mode of combination to effect an unlawful purpose, is where the combining parties have agreed to do in combination what would be wrongful if done by any one of them alone by reason of the means employed, such as to deceive or defraud or to conduct a strike or lockout by means of conduct prohibited by the Conspiracy and Protection of Property Act, 1875.[56] If the means are unlawful the conduct is none the less actionable because done in combination.

(c) *Damage.* The requisite damage to business or other interests may be any kind of patrimonial loss, such as loss of business, loss of profits, or exclusion from a market, or exclusion from employment. In *Rookes* v. *Barnard*,[57] the plaintiff had lost his job, and could not recover it in that employment, nor possibly in any office in which the union he had left maintained a closed shop or even was powerful.

The defence of justification. The defence of justification in conspiracy is wider than in actions for inducing breach of contract, in that the furtherance of legitimate self-interest is a justification; it is abundantly clear from the cases that combination to promote an economic end such as to raise prices, extend business, increase profits, or cut off a rival's trade is accepted as justification.[58] " Any form of competition in trade is legitimate and lawful, that is, formed a just excuse, provided that illegal means are not used." [59]

The defence of privilege. This defence may also be applicable. If defenders enjoy privilege which would protect them in an action for defamation, it will also protect them from an action alleging conspiracy to injure.[60]

Statutory defence. The Conspiracy and Protection of Property Act, 1875, s. 3, as amended by the Trade Disputes Act, 1906, s. 1, provides that an act done in pursuance of an agreement or combination by two or more persons shall, if done in contemplation or furtherance of a trade dispute, not be actionable unless the act, if done without any such

---

[55] *Ibid.* 10.
[56] *Crofter Co., supra,* 23, *per* Lord Wright.
[57] [1964] 1 All E.R. 367.
[58] *Crofter Co., supra.*
[59] *Ibid.* 14, *per* Viscount Maugham, based on *Mogul* v. *McGregor* [1892] A.C. 25.
[60] *Marrinan* v. *Vibart* [1963] 1 Q.B. 234, 528.

agreement or combination, would be actionable. But this does not protect conduct, such as inducing a breach of contract, which would be actionable if done by one person acting alone.[61]

17. DELIBERATE INFLICTION OF LOSS OF BUSINESS

It is not wrongful, however deliberately, to cause a rival loss of business by any means which can reasonably be called competition in trade, such as offering lower prices or better service. It is, however, wrongful if the means used are unlawful, as where they involve infringement of statute,[62] frightening away customers from a rival,[63] or fraudulent misrepresentations about the pursuer's business,[64] or slander of title or property about the pursuer's wares.

18. INTIMIDATION

A person has a right of action if harm is caused him by actings on the part of himself or of another, prompted by threats on the part of a third party or by fear of what the third party may do. The basis is the Roman *actio quod metus causa*.[65] There is no action, however, if the actings threatened are wholly legal, such as to report a person's criminal conduct to the police or the procurator-fiscal, or to do diligence on a valid decree of court, or to dismiss an employee unless he resigned,[66] or to place a trader on a stop list.[67]

The fear requisite to ground an action must be reasonable, such fear as properly descends even upon a steadfast person.[68] It may be fear of any unpleasant consequences, such as violence,[69] illegal imprisonment,[70] or wrongful seizure of goods,[71] or loss of employment.[72]

Many cases have related to persons induced by fear to act to their detriment in respect of agreeing to a contract or settlement of some dispute. In such a case the contract is void, and reducible on proof of fear or duress,[73] but damages are also recoverable for the wrong of having induced the transaction and for the loss caused thereby. In *McIntosh* v. *Chalmers*[74] M was charged for payment under a bill and imprisoned.

---

[61] *Stratford* v. *Lindley* [1964] 3 All E.R. 102, 113.
[62] *Lyons* v. *Wilkins* [1899] 1 Ch. 255 (picketing contravening Conspiracy and Protection of Property Act, 1875, s. 7).
[63] *Tarleton* v. *McGawley* (1794) Peake 270.
[64] *Crofter Hand Woven Harris Tweed Co., Ltd.* v. *Veitch*, 1942 S.C.(H.L.) 1, 24. *Cf. National Phonograph Co., Ltd.* v. *Edison Bell Consolidated Phonograph Co., Ltd.* [1908] 1 Ch. 335.
[65] Dig. IV, 2; Voet, *ad loc*; *cf.* cases in Morison's Dictionary s.v. *Vis et Metus*.
[66] *Dumfriesshire Education Authy.* v. *Wright*, 1926 S.L.T. 217.
[67] *Thorne* v. *M.T.A.* [1937] A.C. 797.
[68] Voet, IV, 2, 11; Stair, I, 9, 8; *cf*, *Priestnell* v. *Hutcheson* (1857) 19 D. 495.
[69] *Gelot* v. *Stewart* (1871) 9 M. 957.
[70] *Stuart* v. *Whitefoord* (1677) Mor. 16489.
[71] *Wiseman* v. *Logie* (1700) Mor. 16505.
[72] *Gow* v. *Henry* (1899) 2 F. 48; contrast *Dumfriesshire Educn. Authy., supra.*
[73] Stair, I, 9, 8; Ersk., III, 1, 16; Bell, *Prin.*, § 12; *Comm.*, I, 314; *Willocks* v. *Callender* (1776) Mor. 1519; *Wightman* v. *Graham* (1787) Mor. 1521; *Foreman* v. *Sheriff* (1791) Mor. 16515; *Gelot* v. *Stewart* (1871) 9 M. 957.
[74] (1883) 11 R. 8; *cf. Wiseman* v. *Logie* (1700) Mor. 16505; *Arratt* v. *Wilson* (1718) Robertson 234; *Fraser* v. *Black*, Dec. 13, 1810, F.C.

While in prison he granted a letter of indemnity against any claim for damages for wrongful diligence as a condition of obtaining liberation. He was successful in a suspension of the diligence, and was held entitled to damages, even without reduction of the letter of indemnity.

An essential of actionable intimidation is that the complainer should have complied with the demand, *i.e.*, not merely been threatened, but have acted to the detriment of himself or another in compliance with and under the coercive influence of the threat.[75] A threat resisted is not actionable intimidation: " there must be a coercive threat to use unlawful means, so as to compel a person into doing something that he is unwilling to do, or not doing something that he wishes to do; and the party so threatened must comply with the demand rather than risk the threat being carried into execution. In such case, the party damnified by the compliance can sue for damages for intimidation." [76] Hence there is no intimidation if there is merely an actual or a statement of intention to commit a breach of contract.[77]

If there is a threat which is resisted, but is nevertheless carried into effect, the injured party's right of action is not for intimidation, but for the wrong committed by carrying the threat into effect, such as assault, or malicious damage, or inducing breach of contract, or otherwise as appropriate.[78]

Intimidation or threats takes two forms. The first is by threats causing the complainer himself to act to his detriment. This is not actionable if the conduct threatened is lawful, such as to take legal proceedings for the recovery of money owed, or to refuse further supplies until prior debts have been paid,[79] but is actionable if the conduct threatened is criminal or delictual, such as the threat of violence, or damage to property, or the threat, *e.g.*, not to renew a lease unless money is paid.[80] This is sometimes conveniently spoken of as duress.

The second form is the threat by one person to act towards a second person in such a way as to cause harm to a third person. " The relevant cause of action can be said shortly to be by C against A for A's intimidation of B with the object and effect of interfering with activities of C." [81] " It is a peculiar tort, because the plaintiff is only a secondary and indirect victim of the wrongdoing. A by intimidation of B causes B to act in such a way as to interfere with C's enjoyment of his land or exercise of his trade, business or employment or other lawful activity, whereby C suffers damage. Then C as plaintiff has a cause of action in tort against A as defendant." [82] The right of C which is infringed is the elementary right

---

[75] *Rookes* v. *Barnard* [1964] 1 All E.R. 367, 399, *per* Lord Devlin.
[76] *Stratford* v. *Lindley* [1964] 2 All E.R. 209, 216, *per* Lord Denning M.R.
[77] *Ibid.* 218.
[78] *Ibid.* 216.
[79] *Cf. Ware and de Freville* v. *M.T.A.* [1921] 3 K.B. 40.
[80] *Cf. Silverstein* v. *H.M. Advocate*, 1949 J.C. 160.
[81] *Rookes* v. *Barnard* [1962] 2 All E.R. 579, 608, *per* Pearson L.J. *Cf. Hewit* v. *Edinburgh Lathsplitters* (1906) 14 S.L.T. 489.
[82] *Rookes* v. *Barnard* [1962] 2 All E.R. 579, 603, *per* Pearson L.J.

to use his land and exercise his trade, business or employment and carry on any other lawful activity free from unlawful interference.[83] " Where the interference takes the form of some gross illegality (such as firing a cannon at a canoe manned by natives [84] or threatening death or dismemberment to tenants or customers or workmen) committed by A against B with the intention and effect of deterring B from trading or otherwise dealing with C, C has a cause of action against A for the interference with his right." [85]

It is intimidation actionable at the instance of P if X breaks, or, in concert with others, threatens to break, his own contract of employment with D, when resultant damage to P therefrom was foreseen or intended by X.[86]

There is, moreover, clearly a wrong if the defender has threatened to commit a wrongful act, e.g., assault, or, a fortiori, a crime.[87]

In some circumstances protection is given by the Trade Disputes Act, 1906, s. 3, whereby it is not actionable, in contemplation or furtherance of a trade dispute, to induce some other person to break his contract of employment, or to threaten the employer that he will induce some other person to break his contract of employment.[88] But s. 3, while protecting inducement, does not protect a person who breaks or threatens to break his own contract,[89] nor does it apply to disputes between one union and another.[90]

19. FOMENTING STRIKES

For a person to incite or encourage employees to come out on strike, is not usually a wrong actionable by the employer. The Trade Disputes Act, 1906, s. 3, provides that " an act done by a person in contemplation or furtherance of a trade dispute [91] shall not be actionable on the ground only that it induces some other person to break a contract of employment or that it is an interference with the trade, business or employment of some other person, or with the right of some other person to dispose of his capital or his labour as he wills." In Conway v. Wade [92] it was observed that this defence applied only where the act of the defendant would not also constitute some other tort than procurement of breach of contract.

---

[83] Ibid.
[84] A reference to Tarleton v. McGawley (1794) Peake 270.
[85] Rookes, supra, 604, per Pearson L.J.
[86] Connor v. Kent [1891] 2 Q.B. 545; White v. Riley [1921] 1 Ch. 1; Rookes v. Barnard [1964] 1 All E.R. 367; Stratford v. Lindley [1964] 2 All E.R. 209, 216.
[87] Ware and de Freville v. M.T.A. [1921] 3 K.B. 40; Thorne v. M.T.A. [1937] A.C. 797.
[88] Stratford v. Lindley [1964] 2 All E.R. 209, 216.
[89] Rookes v. Barnard [1964] 1 All E.R. 367, explained in Stratford, supra.
[90] Stratford v. Lindley [1964] 3 All E.R. 102, 113.
[91] Defined in section 5 (3) as " any dispute between employers and workmen, or between workmen and workmen, which is connected with the employment or non-employment, or the terms of the employment, or with the conditions of labour, of any person." This does not cover disputes between employer and employer's association: Larkin v. Long [1915] A.C. 814; nor workmen not employed in trade or industry: Smith v. Beirne (1955) 88 Ir.L.T. 24.
[92] [1909] A.C. 506, 511, per Lord Loreburn.

Also in *D. C. Thomson* v. *Deakin* [93] doubts were expressed whether this defence applied to contracts other than employment.

It is apparent, however, from the word " only " that the defence does not extend to cases where there is some ground of action as well as that persons have been induced to break their contracts of employment, or that trade has been interfered with, etc.

" If the plaintiff's only complaints are that the defendant did any one or more of the following things—namely (i) induced some other person . . . to break a contract of employment; (ii) interfered with the trade or business of some other person; (iii) interfered with some other person's employment; (iv) interfered with some other person's right to dispose of his capital as he wished; (v) interfered with some other person's right to dispose of his labour as he wished—then any cause of action which but for this section the plaintiff might have had is ruled out by this section. On the other hand, if the plaintiff can add some other material allegation, the question whether that gives him a valid cause of action has to be decided under the general law, and any cause of action so given is not ruled out by s. 3." [94]

Thus section 3 was no defence in one case [95] where the conduct of the trade union officers was not only a breach of contract of employment but a wrongful conversion of money; nor would it protect for inducing also a breach of statutory duty,[96] nor where there were unlawful threats or coercion,[97] or defamation,[98] or intimidation.[99] In short, section 3 is no defence if there are two or more grounds of action, and not all are among those listed in the section: if at least one is, say, conspiracy to injure, or intimidation, or inducing breach of contract (other than contract of employment).[1]

20. PERJURY

There seems to be no authority for the view that loss suffered in consequence of perjury allegedly committed by the defender in a previous case gives a right of action. There is express English authority against the competency of such an action.[2] If a witness enjoys absolute privilege for the evidence he gives in court, as he does,[3] it is highly undesirable to permit any court to give damages for loss allegedly resulting from that evidence. If, however, the witness has been successfully prosecuted for perjury, there has been a judicial finding that his evidence was untrue and an action for consequential loss might lie in such a case.

93 [1952] Ch. 646, 689, *per* Evershed M.R. *Cf. Brimelow* v. *Casson* [1924] 1 Ch. 302, 314, *per* Russell J.
94 *Rookes* v. *Barnard* [1962] 2 All E.R. 579, 602–603, *per* Pearson L.J.
95 *Royal London Mutual Insurance Soc., Ltd.* v. *Williamson* (1921) 37 T.L.R. 472.
96 *Milligan* v. *Ayr Harbour Trs.*, 1915 S.C. 937, 953.
97 *Conway, supra; Valentine* v. *Hyde* [1919] 2 Ch. 129.
98 *Dallimore* v. *Williams* (1912) 29 T.L.R. 67.
99 *Rookes* v. *Barnard* [1964] 1 All E.R. 367; see also *Stratford* v. *Lindley* [1964] 2 All E.R. 209.
1 *Stratford, supra*, 219.
2 *Hargreaves* v. *Bretherton* [1958] 3 All E.R. 122.
3 *Watson* v. *McEwan* (1905) 7 F.(H.L.) 109.

CHAPTER 27

INFRINGEMENTS OF INTERESTS IN HERITABLE PROPERTY

AN action for interdict or damages lies for any unjustifiable interference with or infringement of any interest which a person has in any heritable property. These interests are ownership, whether in superiority or in fee, and possession.

1. TITLE OF OWNERSHIP

The system of written titles and of registration of deeds evidencing title to land is such that questions of wrongfully depriving another of title to land rarely arise in Scotland as questions of delict in relation to property.[1] In *Stobie* v. *Smith* [2] the true heir-at-law of a deceased brought an action of reduction of a decree of special service whereby certain other relatives had been decerned heirs-at-law, in which capacity they had sold the heritage; the court reduced the decree of service and the disposition which followed thereon. There was no claim by the true heir-at-law for damages, but if there had been averments of fraud, there could have been, and even without such averments the true heir-at-law could surely have claimed damages for depreciation of the subjects or for any loss he had sustained in consequence of not having had them from the date of the succession. In this case also the purchasers from the heirs originally served would presumably, on being evicted, have had a claim against those heirs under the warrandice clause in the disposition to them.

---

[1] *Cf. Rodgers* v. *Fawdry*, 1950 S.C. 483.
[2] 1921 S.C. 894; *cf. Mackie* v. *Mackie* (1896) 4 S.L.T. 3.

2. EJECTION AND INTRUSION

Ejection as a delict is the unwarrantable entering on lands or other heritable subjects by forcibly casting out the person in actual possession, or the remaining in possession and refusing to remove when any title of occupancy has expired or been withdrawn.[3] Intrusion is entry *clam vel precario*, without violence, when the possessor holds *animo*.[4] The former possessor is entitled at once in either case to bring an action of ejection,[5] to have the ejector required to remove himself and to pay violent profits and other damages. The basis of the action is *spoliatus ante omnia restituendus*, and it is not a question of title. The former possessor who has been ejected or intruded upon need not aver on his part any title higher than possession,[6] and he may be owner or tenant or merely licensee or precarious possessor. His claim is merely not to be thrust out save by one with a better title to possess.

He may also, or separately, claim damages, by way of solatium, for the wrongful ejection.[7]

An owner kept out of possession by a tenant may claim damages for loss resulting from that person's failure to remove and wrongful retention of possession, and possibly also violent profits.[8]

Violent profits are penal damages instituted as a special deterrent against taking the law into one's own hands,[9] due by an intruder without colour of law.[10] By an old rule violent profits are valued at double the rent of houses within royal burghs, burghs of regality and major burghs of barony,[11] and in rural subjects at the greatest profit the pursuer can prove that he could have made if himself in possession.[12] They include all damages which the subjects may receive at the hands of the defender.[13]

Caution for violent profits may be required as a condition of being allowed to lodge defences.[14] Violent profits are not due if and so long as

---

[3] *Cf. Houldsworth* v. *Brand's Trs.* (1876) 3 R. 304; *Hendry* v. *Walker*, 1926 S.L.T. 678; *Mather* v. *Alexander*, 1926 S.C. 139; *Price* v. *Watson*, 1951 S.C. 359; *Macpherson* v. *Macpherson* (1950) 66 Sh.Ct.Rep. 125.

[4] Stair, I, 9, 25; IV, 28, 1; Bankt., IV, 24, 57; Hope, *Min.Prac.*, 10, 4; Ersk., IV, 1, 15; Rankine, *Landownership*, 21. *Cf. Mather* v. *Alexander*, 1926 S.C. 139.

[5] *Hally* v. *Lang* (1867) 5 M. 951, 954; *cf. Dickson* v. *Dickie* (1863) 1 M. 1157.

[6] Ersk., IV, 1, 47; *Ogilvie* v. *Restalrig* (1541) Mor. 14730; *Montgomery* v. *Hamilton* (1548) Mor. 14731; *Gadzeard* v. *Sheriff of Ayr* (1781) Mor. 14732. If he has a heritable title it should, of course, be averred, and it will be necessary if the ejector should exhibit a heritable title: *Macdonald* v. *Chisholm* (1860) 22 D. 1075.

[7] As in *Macdonald, supra*.

[8] *Houldsworth* v. *Brand's Trs.* (1876) 3 R. 304.

[9] Ersk., II, 6, 54.

[10] *Houldsworth* v. *Brand's Trs.* (1876) 3 R. 304, 310.

[11] Stair, I, 9, 27; II, 9, 44; IV, 29, 3; Bankt., I, 10, 133 and 147; Ersk, II, 6, 54; Bell, *Prin.*, § 1268 (c); *Weddell* v. *Buchan* (1611) Mor. 16460.

[12] Stair, II, 9, 44; Bankt., I, 10, 133; Ersk., II, 6, 54; Spottiswoode, *Prac.* 88; *Gardner* v. *Beresford's Trs.* (1877) 4 R. 1091.

[13] *Gardner, supra*.

[14] Ejection Caution Act, 1594, c. 217; Stair, IV, 28, 8; *Gardner, supra*. See also *Inglis's Trs.* v. *Macpherson*, 1910 S.C. 46; *Glasgow Lock Hospital* v. *Ashcroft*, 1949 S.L.T.(Sh.Ct.) 58; *Fife C.C.* v. *Hatten* (1950) 66 Sh.Ct.Rep. 38. As to uplifting consigned money, see *McDougal* v. *Blake* (1953) 69 Sht.Ct.Rep. 150.

the defender possessed in bona fide,[15] and not accordingly so long as a genuine issue of title to possess is being litigated.[16]

3. MOLESTATION

Molestation is a possessory action, now disused, for determining to which of two coterminous tenements some disputed part or pertinent pertains, so as to prevent the pursuer being further molested or troubled in his possession of the lands claimed.[17] The party in the wrong was obliged to compensate the party injured for loss caused, and to desist and cease from troubling in time coming. The modern remedy is by way of declarator and interdict.

4. TRESPASS

Trespass is an infringement of an occupier's right of exclusive possession, constituted by any temporary intrusion into or entry on the lands and heritage of another, without his permission or legal justification.[18]   A person who lodges in any premises or occupies or encamps on any land which is private property without permission or who encamps or lights a fire on or near any private road or enclosed or cultivated land, or in or near any plantation, or on or near any highway, is punishable criminally.[19] Trespass is also criminal on railway lines,[20] in pursuit of game [21] or fish.[22] These provisions are only exceptionally [23] exclusive of civil action.

Trespass is most commonly committed by simply entering on another's land on foot, on animal or in a vehicle,[24] but may equally be committed by dumping rubbish on his land, pasturing cattle on land,[25] swimming in a private loch, leaving vehicles on another's land,[26] exercising horses on the land,[27] and probably by putting or letting a dog into his land.[28]

In Scotland [29] damages are not recoverable for a simple trespass, particularly if innocent or unwitting, but only if some actual damage has been suffered.[30]

---

[15] *Queensberry's Exors.* v. *Symington* (1824) 2 Sh.App. 43, 80; *Carnegie* v. *Scott* (1830) 4 W. & Sh. 431; *Houldsworth* v. *Brand's Trs.* (1876) 3 R. 304.
[16] *Houldsworth, supra.*
[17] Stair, I, 9, 28; IV, 27, 1; Hope, *Min. Prac.,* 10, 6, 7; Bankt., I, 10, 150; IV, 24, 53; Ersk., IV, 1, 48.
[18] *Geils* v. *Thompson* (1872) 10 M. 327; *Stirling Craufurd* v. *Clyde Navigation Trs.* (1881) 8 R. 826; *cf. McAdam* v. *Laurie* (1876) 3 R.(J.) 20, 21.
[19] Trespass (Scotland) Act, 1865, s. 3; *cf. Paterson* v. *Robertson*, 1944 J.C. 166.
[20] Railway Regulation Acts, 1840, s. 16; 1868, s. 23; 1871, s. 14.
[21] Night Poaching Act, 1828, ss. 1, 9; Game (Scotland) Act, 1832, ss. 1, 2; Protection of Birds Act, 1954, s. 15 (2) .
[22] Salmon and Freshwater Fisheries (Protection) (Scotland) Act, 1951.
[23] As in Game (Scotland) Act, 1832, s. 16.
[24] *Matheson* v. *Stewart* (1872) 10 M. 704. *Cf. Perth General Station Committee* v. *Ross* (1896) 24 R.(H.L.) 44.
[25] *Macleod* v. *Davidson* (1886) 14 R. 92; *Robertson* v. *Wright* (1885) 13 R. 174. *Cf. Winans* v. *Macrae* (1885) 12 R. 1051.
[26] *Marsden* v. *Colnbrook* [1954] C.L.Y. 890.
[27] *Inverurie Mags.* v. *Sorrie*, 1956 S.C. 175.
[28] *Stoddart* v. *Stevenson* (1880) 7 R.(J.) 11; *cf. Wood* v. *Collins* (1890) 17 R.(J.) 55.
[29] In England any infringement of the owner's right justifies at least nominal damages: *Hickman* v. *Maisey* [1900] 1 Q.B. 752.
[30] *Graham* v. *Duke of Hamilton* (1868) 6 M. 965; *Lord Advocate* v. *Glengarnock Iron Co.,* 1909, 1 S.L.T. 15.

Interdict is competent [31] but the pursuer must show reasonable apprehension of the repetition of the same or a similar trespass.[32] Interdict is not competent against a right claimed but not being asserted.[33] Interdict and damages may be combined,[34] and declarator may be sought.[35] But trespass will not justify interdict if done in good faith,[36] or by permission and without any intention to establish any right against the owner,[37] or if there has been no loss and no apprehension of loss.[38]

Damages may be recovered if there is actual damage caused by the trespass, as to crops,[39] or if the trespass is combined with assault[40] or insult[41] to the landowner.

A trespasser may always be ordered or conducted off the premises,[42] so long as no greater force is used than is reasonably necessary in the circumstances. Violence against a trespasser is not justifiable, particularly if there is no actual interference with the use of property,[43] and the use of violence, even in a case of blatant trespass, may be an assault justifying a claim of damages against the landowner.[44] Moderate violence is justifiable if the trespasser threatens, or offers violence to, or causes reasonable apprehension of doing violence to, the landowner.[45]

Trespass in pursuit of animals. No person is entitled to trespass on the lands of another without his permission in pursuit of fish, animals or game.[46] This aspect of trespass is usually dealt with criminally as poaching. An exception, justified by necessity, exists in that farmers have been held justified in crossing the fields of a neighbour in pursuit of foxes, though liable in damages for any injury done.[47] Save by permission,

[31] *Stirling Craufurd* v. *Clyde Navigation Trs.* (1881) 8 R. 826; *Warrand* v. *Watson* (1905) 8 F. 253; *Inverurie Mags.* v. *Sorrie,* 1956 S.C. 175. See also *Johnson* v. *Grant,* 1923 S.C. 789; *Macleay* v. *Macdonald,* 1928 S.C. 776; 1929 S.C. 371.
[32] *Hay's Trs.* v. *Young* (1877) 4 R. 398; *Steuart* v. *Stephen* (1877) 4 R. 873; *Macleod* v. *Davidson* (1886) 14 R. 92; *Merryton Coal Co.* v. *Anderson* (1890) 18 R. 203; *Brocket Estates* v. *McPhee,* 1949 S.L.T.(Notes) 36.
[33] *Inverurie Mags., supra.*
[34] *Marquis of Tweeddale* v. *Dalrymple* (1778) Mor. 4992; *Earl of Breadalbane* v. *Livingstone* (1790) Mor. 4999; affd. (1791) 3 Paton 221.
[35] Cf. *Matheson* v. *Stewart* (1872) 10 M. 704.
[36] *Hay's Trs., supra; Macleod, supra; Behrens* v. *Richards* [1905] 2 Ch. 614.
[37] *Steuart* v. *Stephen* (1877) 4 R. 873; see also *Jolly* v. *Brown* (1828) 6 S. 872.
[38] *Winans* v. *Macrae* (1885) 12 R. 1051.
[39] *Hill* v. *Merricks* (1813) Hume 397; *Baird* v. *Thomson* (1825) 3 S. 447.
[40] *Grahame* v. *Mackenzie* (1810) Hume 641.
[41] *Cook* v. *Neville* (1798) Hume 602.
[42] *Wood* v. *N.B. Ry.* (1899) 2 F. 1; *MacLure* v. *MacLure,* 1911 S.C. 200; *Mather* v. *Alexander,* 1926 S.C. 139. Cf. *Lawrie* v. *Earl of Wemyss,* 1930 S.N. 120.
[43] *Wood* v. *N.B. Ry.* (1899) 2 F. 1.
[44] *Earl of Eglintoun* v. *Campbell* (1770) Maclaurin's *Crim. Tr.* 505; *Grahame* v. *Mackenzie* (1810) Hume 641; *Lord Advocate* v. *Kennedy* (1838) 2 Swin. 213; *Bell* v. *Shand* (1870) 7 S.L.R. 267.
[45] *Aitchison* v. *Thorburn* (1870) 7 S.L.R. 347.
[46] *Watson* v. *Earl of Errol* (1763) Mor. 4991; *Marquis of Tweeddale* v. *Dalrymple* (1778) Mor. 4992; 5 B.S. 475; *Earl of Breadalbane* v. *Livingstone* (1790) Mor. 4999; (1791) 3 Paton 221; *Baird* v. *Thomson* (1825) 3 S. 313; *Paul* v. *Summerhayes* (1879) 4 Q.B.D. 9; *Calvert* v. *Josling* (1889) 5 T.L.R. 185. See also *Sommerville* v. *Smith* (1860) 22 D. 279; *Montgomery* v. *Watson* (1861) 23 D. 635; *Thurlow* v. *Tait* (1893) 1 S.L.T. 62.
[47] *Colquhoun* v. *Buchanan* (1785) Mor. 4997.

persons other than the owner of lands may not ride over lands in the course of hunting foxes as a sport.[48]

Trespass by animals. According to Stair [49] there is no right for animals to take natural fruits of the soil in fields, or make promiscuous use of pasturage in winter, though they may graze at the roadside; nor may they be pastured on another's lands,[50] though interdict against trespass has been refused where it was not established that the defender had failed to take reasonable precautions to prevent their trespass [51] and where the trespass was trivial.[52]

A claim for damage done by animals trespassing on another's land is competent, on proof of failure by the owner to take reasonable care to keep the animals in, and of damage done by them.[53] There is probably no liability for bare trespass without any harm done, particularly by small animals which cause no appreciable damage.[54]

The right to poind or impound straying animals in security for damages seems to have existed at common law,[55] but is now regulated by statute. Under the Winter Herding Act, 1686,[56] proprietors of lands [57] must keep their animals herded the whole year so that they may not eat their neighbours' ground, woods, hedging or planting, contraveners to be liable for half a merk per beast trespassing " by and attour the damage done to the grass or planting." [58] This applies both to lands in exclusive possession and to land occupied by crofters as common pasture,[59] but not to intentional trespass under the erroneous belief that permission had been granted.[60]

It has been said that the Act should be construed more strictly than it has been in the past.[61] The Act has been held applicable to trespass on

[48] Ersk., II, 6, 6; *Watson* v. *Errol* (1763) Mor. 4991; *Marquis of Tweeddale* v. *Dalrymple* (1778) Mor. 4992; *Earl of Breadalbane* v. *Livingstone* (1790) Mor. 4999; affd. (1791) 3 Paton 221.

[49] II, 1, 7.

[50] *Macleod* v. *Davidson* (1886) 14 R. 92.

[51] *Robertson* v. *Wright* (1885) 13 R. 174.

[52] *Winans* v. *Macrae* (1885) 12 R. 1051.

[53] *Robertson* v. *Wright* (1885) 2 Sh.Ct.Rep. 60, sequel to 13 R. 174; see also *Porter* v. *Taylor* (1886) 2 Sh.Ct.Rep. 444; *Lindsay* v. *Somerville* (1902) 18 Sh.Ct.Rep. 230; *Stuart* v. *Gilmour* (1904) 19 Sh.Ct.Rep. 296; *Duncan* v. *Shaw* (1945) 61 Sh.Ct.Rep. 116. The English law of cattle-trespass is a branch of the strict liability doctrine of *Rylands* v. *Fletcher* (1868) L.R. 3 H.L. 330, and is not the law of Scotland.

[54] *Brown* v. *Giles* (1823) 1 C. & P. 118; *Read* v. *Edwards* (1864) 17 C.B.(N.S.) 245; *Sanders* v. *Teape* (1884) 51 L.T. 263.

[55] *Duncan* v. *Kids* (1676) Mor. 10514; Ersk., III, 6, 28; Bankt., IV, 41, 16. The Winter Herding Act, 1686, c. 11, has been said to be a reinforcement of the common law, which implies that a claim was competent.

[56] A.P.S., VIII, 595, c. 21; Act, 1686, c. 11. " Grass " includes corn: see *Govan* v. *Lang* (1794) Mor. 10499; *Loch* v. *Tweedie* (1799) Mor. 10501.

[57] Defined as heritors, liferenters, tenants, cottars, and other possessors of lands or houses; the term includes a seasonal grazing tenant: *Hill* v. *Burnett* (1954) 70 Sh.Ct.Rep. 328.

[58] In *Shaw and Mackenzie* v. *Ewart*, March 2, 1809, F.C., penalties and reparation for actual damage were both claimed.

[59] *Laurenson* v. *Bruce* (1893) 8 Sh.Ct.Rep. 338.

[60] *Camerons* v. *Miller* (1908) 23 Sh.Ct.Rep. 318.

[61] *MacArthur* v. *Jones* (1876) 6 R. 41.

all cultivated land, corn land as well as grass-land,[62] gardens,[63] highland sheep-farms,[64] and as between landlord and tenant.[65]

It is lawful, moreover, for the possessor of the ground to poind the trespassing beasts until paid the penalty and his expenses for keeping the beasts, but he must not use them under pain of being liable in a spuilzie.[66] They must be impounded. The Act does not expressly give the right of retention for the damage done but that has been continued from earlier practice.[67] The penalties are exigible even though the animals were not poinded,[68] and even though it is not alleged that damage has been done by the trespass.[69] The mere employment of a herd does not relieve the owner from liability; it must be such herding as secures and prevents the animals from straying.[70] The Act has been held not to apply to ground adjoining a drove-road which was unenclosed and unplanted, and it may apply only between coterminous occupiers,[71] and may not apply where the door of a house or shed situated in a field was sometimes left open.[72] Recovery of the penalties is competent only within the period permitted by the Summary Jurisdiction Acts.[73]

It has been held that the obligation to herd imports an absolute duty to keep cattle off a neighbour's land, so that it was no defence that a herd was kept by the neighbour also,[74] or that there were two herds and that a march fence had been erected at the joint expense of both neighbours.[75] Nor is liability elided by absence of proof that any actual damage had been suffered.[76]

So long as the trespassing cattle are actually on the neighbour's land they may be detained and poinded in security of payment of the penalty,[77] but the Act does not authorise their detention in security of damages. If the cattle escape there is no right to drive them back and detain them, though if they have been lawfully detained and escape they may be followed and recaptured.[78] Nor may they be detained after payment or tender of the statutory penalty for straying, and the expenses of keeping the detained animals,[79] nor may conditions be attached to their release,

---

[62] *Govan* v. *Lang*, Feb. 18, 1794, F.C.
[63] *MacArthur* v. *Miller* (1873) 1 R. 248.
[64] *Pringle* v. *MacRae* (1829) 4 Fac.Dec. 446.
[65] *Turnbull* v. *Couts*, Feb. 23, 1809, F.C.
[66] *Duncan* v. *Kids* (1676) Mor. 10514.
[67] Ersk., III, 6, 28; Bankt., IV, 41, 16.
[68] *Shaw and Mackenzie* v. *Ewart*, March 2, 1809, F.C.; *Mitchell* v. *McMillan* (1910) 25 Sh.Ct.Rep. 240.
[69] *Leith* v. *Ross* (1896) 11 Sh.Ct.Rep. 110.
[70] *Turnbull* v. *Couts*, Feb. 23, 1809, F.C.; *Shaw and Mackenzie, supra.*
[71] *Gordon* v. *Grant* (1870) 1 Guthrie Sel.Sh.Ct.Cas. 575; but see *Murphy* v. *Beckett* (1920) 36 Sh.Ct.Rep. 38.
[72] *Drysdale* v. *Saline Valley Coal Co.* (1897) 12 Sh.Ct.Rep. 59.
[73] *Grewer* v. *Wright* (1880) 2 Guthrie Sel.Sh.Ct.Cas. 412.
[74] *Turnbull* v. *Couts*, Feb. 23, 1809, F.C.; *Shaw* v. *Ewart*, March 2, 1809, F.C.
[75] *Loch* v. *Tweedie* (1799) Mor. 10501.
[76] *Pringle, supra; Shaw, supra.*
[77] *MacArthur* v. *Jones* (1878) 6 R. 41.
[78] *MacArthur, supra,* 43.
[79] *Fraser* v. *Smith* (1899) 1 F. 487.

nor may they be detained in security of penalties incurred in respect of other cattle previously poinded, which have escaped or been restored.[79]

Poinding the straying animals is not a prerequisite of recovering the penalty though it simplifies questions of proof.[80]

The Act does not inferentially impose any obligation to fence land so as to prevent animals from straying, but merely penalises the owner if they do. Similarly, there is no duty to prevent sheep straying on to the public road, so that no damages are recoverable by a road-user who collides with an animal on the road.[81]

Trespass by domestic animals is so trivial as to give no remedy, unless it is an element in sheep-worrying or destruction of poultry.[82]

The owner of an animal is probably also liable, though not under the Act of 1686, for foreseeable consequences of the trespass, as where a horse escaped into a neighbour's field and killed another horse there,[83] or cattle escaped into plaintiff's grounds and while she was trying in the dark to prevent them damaging her garden one knocked her down and injured her,[84] or otherwise where a trespassing animal does injury to person or beast, as by communicating infection to them.[85]

Licence. Trespass is elided by licence, which is " that consent which, without passing any interest in the property to which it relates, merely prevents the acts for which consent is given from being wrongful." [86] It is a merely personal permission, such as permission to camp for a week in a field, or to shoot over lands,[87] revocable at any time unless there has been a contractual agreement to maintain it for a period or for all time, and conferring no right *in rem* in the lands.

Justification. Trespass may be legally justifiable and therefore not actionable. Justification may arise from legal warrant, such as to search premises,[88] or standing legal authority, such as the authority given to many inspectors and others to enter on premises to see if the law is being complied with,[89] or as incidental to the office of constable.[90] Nor is it an actionable trespass to enter on land to execute a warrant or do diligence thereon. The court has refused to interdict police from entering club premises in disguise.[91]

---

80 *Shaw* v. *Ewart*, March 2, 1809, F.C.
81 *Fraser* v. *Pate*, 1923 S.C. 748; see also *Searle* v. *Wallbank* [1947] A.C. 341; *Wright* v. *Callwood* [1950] 2 K.B. 515; *Brock* v. *Richards* [1951] 1 K.B. 529.
82 Cf. *Arneil* v. *Paterson*, 1931 S.C.(H.L.) 117.
83 *Lee* v. *Riley* (1865) 18 C.B.(N.S.) 722.   84 *Wormald* v. *Cole* [1954] 1 Q.B. 614.
85 *Theyer* v. *Purnell* [1918] 2 K.B. 333; cf. *Robertson* v. *Connolly* (1851) 13 D. 779.
86 Pollock, *Torts*, 284. Cf. *Ashby* v. *Tolhurst* [1937] 2 K.B. 242.
87 *Inland Revenue* v. *Anderson*, 1922 S.C. 284.   88 *Stewart* v. *Roach*, 1950 S.C. 318.
89 Examples are: factory inspectors (Factories Act, 1961, s. 146); gas and electricity employees (Rights of Entry (Gas and Electricity Boards) Act, 1954, s. 1); medical officers of health and sanitary officials (Public Health (Scotland) Act, 1897, ss. 26, 28, 45, 82, 98, 109, 114); inspectors of mines (Mines and Quarries Act, 1954, s. 145); farm inspectors and sanitary inspectors (Agriculture (Safety, Health & Welfare Prov.) Act, 1956, ss. 10 (2), 11); local authority officers (Burgh Police (Scotland) Act, 1892, s. 118); inspectors of offices (Offices, Shops and Railway Premises Act, 1963, s. 53).
90 *R.* v. *Smith* (1833) 6 C. & P. 216; *Thomas* v. *Sawkins* [1935] 2 K.B. 249.
91 *Southern Bowling Club, Ltd.* v. *Ross* (1902) 4 F. 405.

It may also be justified by necessity, as, for example, need to rescue persons or animals from fire [92] or flood, to prevent the commission of a crime [93] or to apprehend a criminal, to escape from serious danger, to recover straying animals,[94] or kill predatory foxes,[95] or to enquire into a suspected contravention of the law.[96] " The exclusive right of a landowner yields whenever public interest or necessity requires that it should yield." [97] But trespass is not justified by a wrongful attempt to assert a right.[98] In such cases the question whether the necessity was such as to justify the trespass is one of fact in the circumstances of the case and depends on whether a greater moral value is sought to be preserved or maintained by the trespass than is implicit in the preservation of privacy of property.

Interference with air-space over land. In theory an occupier of land possesses it *a caelo usque ad centrum* [99] and can therefore object to any other person's property projecting over, being carried across, or passing over his property. But considerations of practical convenience have much modified this principle and it must probably now be understood as limited to such extent of air-space as is necessary for the effective enjoyment of the land.

Thus, it may be regarded as a wrong under this head for the branches of a tree growing on A's land to overhang B's land.[1] The primary remedy is to cut the overhanging branches, which may be done without notice if it is unnecessary to enter on the other's land to do so,[2] and damages will not be recoverable in the absence of proof of actual damage.[3]

Telephone and other wires cannot be carried across another's land without the owner's consent,[4] nor an advertising sign project from an adjacent building over the complainer's building.[5]

Shooting over the land of another is similarly an actionable nuisance because it is necessarily attended with some risk of harm.[6]

The question raised by the passage of aircraft over land is largely dealt with by the Civil Aviation Act, 1949, s. 10, which provides:

(1) No action shall lie in respect of trespass or in respect of nuisance, by reason only of the flight of an aircraft over any property at a height

---

[92] *Carter* v. *Thomas* [1893] 1 Q.B. 673; *Cope* v. *Sharpe* [1912] 1 K.B. 496.

[93] *Handcock* v. *Baker* (1800) 2 Bos. & P. 260.

[94] *Earl of Morton* v. *McMillan* (1893) 1 S.L.T. 92.

[95] *Colquhoun* v. *Buchanan* (1785) Mor. 4997.

[96] *Shepherd* v. *Menzies* (1900) 2 F. 443.

[97] Bell, *Prin.*, § 956. *Cf.* Hume, *Lect.* III, 206; Rankine, *Landownership*, 139.

[98] *Geils* v. *Thompson* (1872) 10 M. 327; *Matheson* v. *Stewart* (1872) 10 M. 704; *Merry & Cuninghame* v. *Aitken* (1895) 22 R. 247. *Cf. Merryton Coal Co.* v. *Anderson* (1890) 18 R. 203.

[99] On this maxim see McNair, *Law of the Air* (2nd ed.) Chap. 2 and App. 1.

[1] *Wedderburne* v. *Halkerston* (1781) Mor. 10495.

[2] *Lemmon* v. *Webb* [1895] A.C. 1.

[3] *Smith* v. *Giddy* [1904] 2 K.B. 448.

[4] *Wandsworth Board of Works* v. *United Telephone Co.* (1884) 13 Q.B.D. 904; *Finchley Electric Light Co.* v. *Finchley U.D.C.* [1903] 1 Ch. 437. *Cf.* also *Lancashire Telephone Co.* v. *Overseers of Manchester* (1884) 14 Q.B.D. 267; *Electric Telegraph Co.* v. *Overseers of Salford* (1885) 11 Ex.D. 181; *Stickland* v. *MacDonald* [1955] C.L.Y. 1944.

[5] *Kelsen* v. *Imperial Tobacco Co.* [1957] 2 Q.B. 334.

[6] *Clifton* v. *Viscount Bury* (1887) 4 T.L.R. 8.

above the ground, which, having regard to wind, weather and all the circumstances of the case is reasonable, or the ordinary incidents of such flight so long as the provisions of Part II [relating to the regulation of civil aviation] and this Part [Part IV, relating to liability for trespass, nuisance and surface damage caused by aircraft] of this Act and any Order in Council or order made under Part II or this Part of this Act are duly complied with.

Section 61 limits section 40 by providing in effect that it has no operation in the case of aircraft of any kind belonging to or exclusively employed in the service of Her Majesty, though the enactment may be applied to any such aircraft, with or without modification, by Order in Council. In the case of Crown aircraft the common law, subject to the Crown Proceedings Act, still applies.

5. ENCROACHMENT

Encroachment consists in the permanent usurpation by another of some portion of a man's lands, which deprives him of the free use of it for the future.[7] It may be constituted by a building projecting over the property of another [8] or a pipe through a neighbour's property,[9] or by trees over-hanging the neighbour's garden,[10] or by the roots of trees penetrating the ground beyond the boundary.[11] It could also be constituted by dump-ing rubbish on another's land,[12] or allowing material deposited on one's own land to subside or overflow on to the other's land, and probably also by driving piles into another's ground or resting shoring timbers for a wall on another's land.[13] Other modes of encroachment include carry-ing a new vent up through the wall of an upper floor, or attaching a flue to the outside of the gable,[14] or attaching a sign to another's building [15] or in a common entrance,[16] or constructing a road through the com-plainer's lands without authority.[17]

In such cases the invasion of the pursuer's exclusive rights in the property is sufficient to justify an action, and no damage or loss need be proved.[18]

Encroachment by mining or quarrying. It is a wrong for a mineral tenant or the owner of minerals to mine or quarry beyond the boundary

---

[7] Hume, *Lect.* III, 202.
[8] Ersk., II, 9, 9; Bell, *Prin.*, §§ 941, 967; Rankine, *Landownership*, 134; *Graham* v. *Greig* (1838) 1 D. 171; *McIntosh* v. *Scott* (1859) 21 D. 363; *Leonard* v. *Lindsay* (1886) 13 R. 958. *Cf. Sanderson* v. *Geddes* (1874) 1 R. 1198; (1883) 9 R.(H.L.) 92.
[9] *Galbreath* v. *Armour* (1845) 4 Bell 374; *cf. Hazle* v. *Turner* (1840) 2 D. 886.
[10] *Wedderburne* v. *Halkerston* (1781) Mor. 10495. *Cf. Geddes* v. *Hardie* (1806) Hume, *Lect.* III, 203; *Lemmon* v. *Webb* [1895] A.C. 1; *Hetherington* v. *Galt* (1905) 7 F. 706, 710.
[11] *Cf. Lemmon, supra*; *McCombe* v. *Reid* [1955] 2 Q.B. 429; *Davey* v. *Harrow Corpn.* [1957] 2 All E.R. 305; Rankine on *Landownership*, 636; Hume, *Lect.* III, 203.
[12] *Cf. Whitwham* v. *Westminster Brymbo Coal Co.* [1896] 1 Ch. 894.
[13] Rankine, *Landownership*, 139.
[14] *Walker* v. *Braidwood* (1797) Hume 512; *cf. Gellatly* v. *Arroll* (1863) 1 M. 592, 600.
[15] *Thomson* v. *Crombie* (1776) Mor. 13182; *Drysdale* v. *Lourie*, May 13, 1812, F.C.
[16] *Mackenzie* v. *Murray* (1812) Hume 520.
[17] *Fergusson Buchanan* v. *Dunbartonshire C.C.*, 1924 S.C. 42.
[18] *Ewing* v. *Colquhoun's Trs.* (1877) 4 R.(H.L.) 116, 126.

so as to abstract minerals truly belonging to another, or even to mine or quarry so close to the boundary as to damage the surface of the adjacent land or make it unworkable. The encroachment and abstraction of minerals may be done knowingly and intentionally, or negligently, mistakenly or accidentally, the difference being material on the computation of damages.

The intention of the wrongdoer is material to the quantum of damages. If the encroachment has been inadvertent [19] or by mistake [20] or done fairly and honestly [21] or under a bona fide belief in title [22] the damages will be measured by the value of the abstracted minerals under deduction of the whole expenses of severing and winning them and of raising them to the surface.[23]

On the other hand if the encroachment has been effected by fraud [24] or gross negligence,[25] wilfully,[26] furtively or in bad faith,[27] or in a manner wholly unauthorised and unlawful,[28] the damages will be the value of the abstracted minerals under deduction only of the expense of raising them to the surface, but not of severing and winning.[29] Accordingly there is a stricter standard where there has been mala fides,[30] though in each case the main consideration is the loss actually sustained.[31]

In special circumstances other ways of computing damages have been adopted,[31] and further damages may have to be awarded where there was a special and exceptional need for support by the minerals and this has been withdrawn.[32]

19 *Hilton* v. *Woods* (1867) L.R. 4 Eq. 432.
20 *United Merthyr Coal Co.* (1872) L.R. 15 Eq. 46; *Livingstone* v. *Rawyards Coal Co.* (1880) 7 R.(H.L.) 1.
21 *Wood* v. *Morewood* (1841) 3 Q.B. 440n.; *Trotter* v. *Maclean* (1879) 13 Ch.D. 574; *Townend* v. *Askern Coal Co.* [1934] Ch. 463.
22 *Jegon* v. *Vivian* (1871) L.R. 6 Ch. 742; *Ashton* v. *Stock* (1877) 6 Ch.D. 719; *Whitwham* v. *Westminster Brymbo Coal Co.* [1896] 2 Ch. 538.
23 *Hilton* v. *Woods* (1867) L.R. 4 Eq. 432; *Jegon* v. *Vivian* (1871) L.R. 6 Ch. 742; *Re United Merthyr Collieries* (1872) L.R. 15 Eq. 46; *Job* v. *Potton* (1875) L.R. 20 Eq. 84; *Ashton* v. *Stock* (1877) 6 Ch.D. 719; *Trotter* v. *Maclean* (1880) 13 Ch.D. 574; *Townend* v. *Askern Coal Co.* [1934] Ch. 463. *Cf. Livingstone, supra.*
24 *Fothergill* v. *Phillips* (1871) L.R. 6 Ch. 770; *Ecclesiastical Commrs.* v. *N.E.Ry.* (1877) 4 Ch.D. 45 (disapproved on another point in *Bulli Co.* v. *Osborne* [1899] A.C. 351); *Taylor* v. *Mostyn* (1886) 33 Ch.D. 226.
25 *Martin* v. *Porter* (1839) 5 M. & W. 352; *Wood* v. *Morewood* (1841) 3 Q.B. 440n.; *Morgan* v. *Powell* (1842) 3 Q.B. 278; *Wild* v. *Holt* (1842) 9 M. & W. 672; *Phillips* v. *Homfray* (1871) 6 Ch. 770.
26 *Martin, supra*; *Llynvi Co.* v. *Brogden* (1870) L.R. 11 Eq. 188; *Taylor* v. *Mostyn* (1886) 33 Ch.D. 226.
27 *Firmstone* v. *Wheelly* (1844) 2 D. & L. 203; *Durham* v. *Hood* (1871) 9 M. 474; *Ramsay* v. *Blair* (1876) 3 R.(H.L.) 41; *Wilsons* v. *Waddell* (1876) 4 R.(H.L.) 29; *Livingstone* v. *Rawyards Coal Co.* (1880) 7 R.(H.L.) 1; *Davidson's Trs.* v. *Caledonian Ry.* (1895) 23 R. 45; *Bulli Co.* v. *Osborne* [1899] A.C. 351. See also *Duke of Portland* v. *Wood's Trs.*, 1927 S.C.(H.L.) 1.
28 *Martin* v. *Porter* (1839) 5 M. & W. 352; *Wood* v. *Morewood* (1841) 3 Q.B. 440n.; *Trotter* v. *Maclean* (1880) 13 Ch.D. 574; *Joicey* v. *Dickinson* (1882) 45 L.T.(N.S.) 643; *Taylor* v. *Mostyn* (1886) 33 Ch.D. 226; *Re Barrington* (1886) 33 Ch.D. 523; *Peruvian Guano Co.* v. *Dreyfus* [1892] A.C. 166; *Townend* v. *Askern Coal Co.* [1934] Ch. 463.
29 *Re United Merthyr Collieries* (1872) L.R. 15 Eq. 46; *Townend, supra.*
30 *Holdsworth* v. *Brand's Trs.* (1876) 3 R. 304, 308 (Lord Curriehill), 310 (L.J.C. Moncreiff); *Livingstone* v. *Rawyards Coal Co.* (1880) 7 R.(H.L.) 1, 2 (L.Ch. Cairns); *Davidson's Trs.* v. *Caledonian Ry.* (1895) 23 R. 45 (Lord Stormonth-Darling), 47 (Lord Trayner); sequel [1903] A.C. 22.
31 *Livingstone, supra.*
32 *Livingstone, supra,* 3.

6. WITHDRAWAL OF OR INTERFERENCE WITH SUPPORT

It is wrongful so to conduct operations on one's land as to interfere with the support afforded to adjacent or superincumbent land or buildings, unless the liberty to withdraw support has been secured by contract.[33] Four sets of cases have to be distinguished.

(a) *Support by subjacent and adjacent land to surface unencumbered by buildings.* Where land is in its natural state, unencumbered by buildings, the owner is entitled to such support for it from the adjacent and subjacent land as is sufficient to maintain it in its natural state. This is not a right of the nature of a servitude but a " natural right "[34] or right inherent in and automatically appurtenant to the concept of a proprietary right in land.[35]

Accordingly, if the owner of adjacent or subjacent mineral strata abstracts them and thereby causes subsidence of the surface by withdrawal of the support, the surface-owner has a claim of damages against the owner of the minerals for the damage caused by the subsidence.[36] This rule applies generally, without reference to the nature of the strata, the difficulty of supporting the surface, or the comparative value of the surface and minerals. The right of support is not of reasonable support but an absolute right, a right that the land be kept securely at its ancient and natural level.[37] The right is infringed if support be withdrawn and subsidence results, whether there be negligence or not in the mining operations.[38] Threatened damage by removal of support may be prevented by interdict.[39]

Similarly, where minerals have been quarried on the surface, the workings must not be carried so close to the boundary of adjacent land, having regard to the stability of the surface and subsoil, as to cause lateral subsidence of the adjacent land.

The rights of parties are frequently further defined by contract, particularly where the owner of the land has disponed or feued the surface, reserving the minerals and liberty to work them,[40] or has disponed or leased the minerals to be worked by another.[41] " If A conveys minerals

[33] See Ersk., II, 1, 2; II, 9, 10; Bell, *Prin.*, § 965; and, *e.g.*, *Buchanan* v. *Andrew* (1873) 11 M.(H.L.) 13; *White* v. *Dixon* (1883) 10 R.(H.L.) 45; *Bank of Scotland* v. *Stewart* (1891) 18 R. 957; *Anderson* v. *McCracken Bros.* (1900) 2 F. 780.

[34] *Robertson* v. *Stewarts* (1872) 11 M. 189; *cf. N.B.Ry.* v. *Turners* (1904) 6 F. 900.

[35] *Humphries* v. *Brogden* (1848) 12 Q.B. 739, 744, *per* Lord Campbell; *Bonomi* v. *Backhouse* (1858) E.B. & E. 622, 644; 9 H.L.Cas. 503, 512, 513; *Rowbotham* v. *Wilson* (1860) 8 H.L.Cas. 348, 359, 367.

[36] *Livingstone* v. *Rawyards Coal Co.* (1880) 7 R.(H.L.) 1; *Gray* v. *Burns* (1894) 2 S.L.T. 187.

[37] Bell, *Prin.*, § 970; *Humphries* v. *Brogden* (1848) 12 Q.B. 739, 744; *Caledonian Ry.* v. *Sprot* (1856) 2 Macq. 449; *Bonomi* v. *Backhouse* (1861) 9 H.L.Cas. 503; *Elliott* v. *N.E.Ry.* (1863) 10 H.L.Cas. 333; *Davis* v. *Treharne* (1881) 6 App.Cas. 460; *Dalton* v. *Angus* (1881) 6 App.Cas. 740; *Pountney* v. *Clayton* (1883) 11 Q.B.D. 820; *White* v. *Dixon* (1883) 10 R.(H.L.) 45, 46; *Love* v. *Bell* (1884) 9 App.Cas. 286; *Att.-Gen.* v. *Conduit Colliery Co.* [1895] 1 Q.B. 301; *Hayles* v. *Peace* [1899] 1 Ch. 567.

[38] *Angus* v. *N.C.B.*, 1955 S.C. 175, 181–182.

[39] *Buchanan* v. *Andrew* (1872) 11 M.(H.L.) 13; *Siddons* v. *Short* (1877) 2 C.P.D. 572; *Mayor of Birmingham* v. *Allen* (1877) 6 Ch.D. 284.

[40] *e.g.*, *White* v. *Dixon* (1883) 10 R.(H.L.) 45; *White's Trs.* v. *Duke of Hamilton* (1887) 14 R. 597.

[41] *e.g.*, *Barr* v. *Baird* (1904) 6 F. 524; *Dryburgh* v. *Fife Coal Co.* (1905) 7 F. 1083.

to B reserving the property of the surface, or if A conveys the surface to B reserving the property of the minerals below it, A in the one case retains, and B in the other gets, a right to have the surface supported unless the contrary shall be expressly provided, or shall appear by plain implication from the terms of the conveyance." [42] A reserved right, subject to payment of " surface damages," has been held to import liability for damage to buildings on the surface caused by underground workings.[43] Right to work minerals may be reserved without any liability to compensate for surface damage at all.[44]

Where damages are recovered for subsidence damage, the pursuer may bring a further action if other and distinct damage occurs where there has been a fresh subsidence caused by the same workings,[45] or even though there has been no fresh subsidence if there has been damage to other ground.[46] It is immaterial that there has been no further mining.[47]

(b) *Support by land to land subsequently built upon.* Where minerals are disponed or leased when the surface is in its natural state, and buildings are subsequently erected on the surface and are later damaged by subsidence caused by the extraction of the minerals, the mineral owner is bound to compensate for surface damage, and is liable also for damage to the buildings, at least such as might fairly have been contemplated by the parties, though it might be otherwise if the ground had become covered with streets and buildings.[48] Where lands are conveyed for a specified purpose which contemplates building or other loading of the surface, the grant, in the absence of contrary intention appearing therein, carries by implication a right to reasonable and necessary support, from the adjacent lands and subjacent strata of the granter, for the purposes contemplated, and this right will transmit with the granter's lands to disponees from him.[49]

(c) *Support by land to land already encumbered with buildings.* Once land has been burdened with buildings the right of support is no longer a natural right attaching to the property, but is an acquired right of the nature of a positive servitude, separate from the right of ownership, and requiring to be constituted by express or implied grant,[50] of a nature similar to the Roman servitude *oneris ferendi.*[51]

---

[42] *White* v. *Dixon, supra,* 50, *per* Lord Watson.
[43] *Hallpenny* v. *Dewar* (1898) 25 R. 889; *cf. Gibson* v. *Farie,* 1918, 1 S.L.T. 404; see also *Taylor* v. *Auchinlea Coal Co.,* 1912, 2 S.L.T. 10; *Bain* v. *Duke of Hamilton* (1867) 6 M. 1.
[44] *Pringle* v. *Carron Co.* (1905) 7 F. 820; *cf. Buchanan* v. *Andrew* (1873) 11 M.(H.L.) 13; *Swanson* v. *Burnbank and Grongar Coal Co.,* 1926 S.N. 77.
[45] *Geddes* v. *Haldane* (1905) 13 S.L.T. 707.
[46] *Duke of Abercorn* v. *Merry & Cuninghame,* 1909 S.C. 750.
[47] *Darley Main Colliery* v. *Mitchell* (1886) 11 App.Cas. 127.
[48] *Neill's Trs.* v. *Dixon* (1880) 7 R. 741. *Cf. Barr* v. *Baird & Co.* (1904) 6 F. 524; *Dryburgh* v. *Fife Coal Co.* (1905) 7 F. 1083.
[49] *Aitken's Trs.* v. *Rawyards Colliery Co.* (1894) 22 R. 201; *N.B.Ry.* v. *Turners* (1904) 6 F. 900.
[50] Rankine on *Landownership* (4th ed.), 495; *Hide* v. *Thornborough* (1848) 2 C. & K. 250; *Wyatt* v. *Harrison* (1832) 3 B. & A. 871; *Partridge* v. *Scott* (1837) 3 M. & W. 220; *Humphries* v. *Brogden* (1850) 12 Q.B. 739; *Bonomi* v. *Backhouse* (1859) E.B. & E. 622; 9 H.L.Cas. 503.
[51] *Hamilton* v. *Turner* (1867) 5 M. 1086, 1090; *cf. Dalton* v. *Angus* (1881) 6 App.Cas. 793, 830.

This servitude right of support may be held to have been granted expressly,[52] but it may also be held to have been granted impliedly, as where the ownership of two subjects has been severed when the surface of the upper or of one had already been encumbered by buildings, or when the surface had been feued out or retained for the known purpose of being built upon.[53]

The right of support may also probably be constituted by the peaceable possession of a building supported by adjacent or subjacent soil in the ownership of another party for twenty years.[54]

The effect of the right is to make an adjacent owner take care in his operations not to damage the other's property by his operations.[55] " The pursuer having built upon his own ground, the defenders are liable for any damage wrongfully inflicted by their operations on the pursuer's property." [56]

This servitude right of support is additional to the common law natural right of support so that if buildings are erected and damage is caused by subsidence it will be presumed that the damage has been caused by the extra load on the surface, but if it can be proved that the extra weight had no connection with the subsidence and that it would have occurred in any case and caused damage even if no buildings had been put up, reparation will still be due,[57] and will be in respect of damage to the soil and to the buildings.[58]

The Mines (Working Facilities and Support) Act, 1925, s. 8, as amended, empowers the Minister of Fuel and Power to impose restrictions on working minerals in the interest of support for buildings or works. The Coal Mining (Subsidence) Act, 1950, s. 1, makes it the duty of the N.C.B. to carry out repairs and make payments in respect of subsidence damage, occurring to or affecting any dwelling-house to which the Act applies between 1946 and 1957. Notice must be given to the Board (s. 5). If the nature of the damage and the circumstances are such as to indicate that the damage may be subsidence damage, the onus is on the Board to disprove that presumption (s. 13). This statutory right is alternative to any other right to damages or compensation from the Board for subsidence damage (s. 14).

The Coal-Mining (Subsidence) Act, 1957, deals with subsidence damage, occurring after the passing of the Act, caused by coal-mining,

---

[52] Dunlop's Trs. v. Corbet, June 20, 1809, F.C.; Dryburgh v. Fife Coal Co. (1905) 7 F. 1083.
[53] Rankine on Landownership (4th ed.) 500; Simson v. Ker (1792) 3 Paton 238; Balds v. Alloa Coal Co. (1854) 16 D. 870; Hamilton v. Turner (1867) 5 M. 1086. See also Bain v. Duke of Hamilton (1867) 6 M. 1; Gibson v. Farie, 1918, 1 S.L.T. 404.
[54] Rankine on Landownership (4th ed.), 498–499; Dodd v. Holme (1834) 1 A. & E. 493; Partridge v. Scott (1837) 3 M. & W. 220; Hide v. Thornborough (1846) 2 C. & K. 250; Gayford v. Nicholls (1854) 9 Ex. 702; Rowbotham v. Wilson (1858) 8 E. & B. 123; Dalton v. Angus (1881) 6 App.Cas. 740.
[55] Hume, Lect. III, 208.
[56] Aitken's Trs. v. Rawyards Colliery Co. (1894) 22 R. 201, 207, per Lord Trayner.
[57] Hamilton v. Turner (1867) 5 M. 1086, 1099; Smith v. Thackerah (1866) L.R. 1 C.P. 564; cf. Dryburgh v. Fife Coal Co. (1905) 7 F. 1083.
[58] Brown v. Robins (1859) 4 H. & N. 186; Stroyan v. Knowles (1861) 6 H. & H. 454; Hunt v. Peake (1860) 29 L.J.Ch. 785.

to buildings and works on land and to land itself. The National Coal Board is bound to execute remedial works or pay the cost thereof. Notice must be given to the Board (s. 2). The Board may execute preventive works (s. 4). A claim for damage under the Act is alternative to a claim for damages or compensation apart from the Act (s. 6). Disputes are to be referred to the sheriff and the onus is on the Board to prove that damage which may be subsidence damage is not subsidence damage (s. 13).

The liability for damage caused by subsidence may include damage done by personal injury to a visitor in a house owned by the defenders and situated on the surface above coal seams being worked by them, not because of the defenders' ownership of the house (though this might make them liable in a question with their tenant) but as being neighbouring proprietors by whose operations the pursuer had been injured.[59]

Under the Coal-Mining (Subsidence) Act, 1957, s. 12, if a person dies or is seriously and permanently disabled as a result of an injury caused by subsidence damage and, apart from the section, no action lies for damages for the death or disablement, the Board is liable as if the death or disablement had been attributable to the negligence of the Board.

Other loadings on land. Similar principles apply where the surface is being loaded by the construction of roads,[60] railways,[61] reservoirs, oil tanks, water pipes,[62] gas pipes,[63] sewers,[64] possibly harbours on navigable rivers,[65] or other artificial constructions which impose a greater load on the surface.

In such cases the matter is commonly regulated also by statute, as under the Railways Clauses Consolidation (Scotland) Act, 1845,[66] the Harbours, Docks and Piers Clauses Act, 1847,[67] or special legislation.

Renunciation of rights. The natural right of support and the servitude right may both be lost by express renunciation.[68] Neither will be impliedly relinquished merely by a grant or lease or reservation of minerals with general power of working them.[69] Nor will either be extinguished by acquiescence, *mora* or the running of the negative prescription, though these may bar claims for particular items of damage suffered.[70]

[59] *McCormick* v. *Fife Coal Co.,* 1931 S.C. 19. See also *Angus* v. *N.C.B.,* 1955 S.C. 175.
[60] *Aitken's Trs.* v. *Rawyards Coal Co.* (1894) 22 R. 201.
[61] See *Caledonian Ry.* v. *Sprot* (1856) 2 Macq. 449; *Caledonian Ry.* v. *Lord Belhaven* (1857) 3 Macq. 56; *Caledonian Ry.* v. *Henderson* (1876) 4 R. 140; *Caledonian Ry.* v. *Dixon* (1880) 7 R.(H.L.) 117; *N.B.Ry.* v. *Turners* (1904) 6 F. 900.
[62] *Clippens Oil Co.* v. *Edinburgh and District Water Trs.* (1903) 6 F.(H.L.) 7.
[63] *Mid and East Calder Gas Light Co.* v. *Oakbank Oil Co.* (1891) 18 R. 788.
[64] *Midlothian C.C.* v. *N.C.B.,* 1960 S.C. 308.
[65] *Forth Conservancy Board* v. *Russell,* 1946 S.N. 85.
[66] ss. 16, 78–78D.
[67] s. 92.
[68] *Buchanan* v. *Andrew* (1873) 11 M.(H.L.) 13; *Bank of Scotland* v. *Stewart* (1891) 18 R. 957; *Anderson* v. *McCracken Bros.* (1900) 2 F. 780; *Rowbotham* v. *Wilson* (1861) 8 H.L.C. 348.
[69] *Harris* v. *Ryding* (1839) 5 M. & W. 60; *Smart* v. *Morton* (1856) 5 E. & B. 30; *Proud* v. *Bates* (1865) 34 L.J.Ch. 406; *Love* v. *Bell* (1884) 9 App.Cas. 286; *Gray* v. *Burns* (1894) 2 S.L.T. 187.
[70] Rankine on *Landownership,* 505.

Independently of the right of support, the right to recover compensation for damage caused by subsidence may be expressly or impliedly renounced or excluded in a particular case. Exclusion of the latter right does not import renunciation of the right to support, or of the liberty to complain or to check it by interdict.

(d) *Support of buildings to other buildings.* Where by express agreement between owners of adjacent building lots, or by contract implied from a feuing plan or from the special circumstances of the case, two proprietors build a common [71] gable, each proprietor becomes bound to maintain and repair the wall on his side at least so far as necessary to maintain it as an adequate gable for the other house.[72] Each building, that is, is burdened with a servitude right of support in favour of the other, and the one owner cannot demolish without regard to the support which his building furnishes to the other.[73]

In the case of tenement or flatted property, the relationship between the owners of upper and lower flats is that all are united by a common interest in maintaining the gables, walls and other common parts for the benefit of all, and this includes, but is wider than, a servitude right of support incumbent on the lower flat for the benefit of the upper flat which is enforceable at the instance of the upper flat.[74] A lower proprietor may be restrained therefore from doing anything to weaken a wall which *inter alia* supports a house above.[75] The onus is on the party proposing alterations to a lower floor to show that they can be carried out without apparent risk or any reasonable apprehension of danger to floors above.[76]

In several cases the court has held that reasonable apprehension of danger is sufficient to entitle a superior proprietor to object to material alterations.[77] If alterations are made which do weaken or endanger the integrity of the upper floors, the lower proprietor will be required to make them safe and secure, no matter what the expense.[78]

The duty of maintenance of the proprietor of a lower flat towards the proprietor of an upper to provide support is not absolute, but only to take the reasonable care expected of a *bonus paterfamilias*, to inspect periodically or when any premonitory signs of danger become apparent, and to repair in case of necessity.[79] But damages are due if there is negligence which results in damage.

---

[71] Frequently miscalled a " mutual " gable.
[72] Rankine, 655.
[73] Stair, II, 7, 6; Ersk., II, 9, 8; Bell, *Prin.*, § 1003; *Murray* v. *Brownhill* (1715) Mor. 14521.
[74] Stair, II, 7, 6. *Cf.* Ersk., II, 2, 11; Bankt, II, 7, 9; Bell, *Prin.*, § 1086; Rankine, 656.
[75] *Hall* v. *Corbet* (1698) Mor. 12775; *cf. Robertson* v. *Ranken* (1784) Mor. 14534; *Dennistoun* v. *Bell* (1824) 2 S. 649.
[76] *Gray* v. *Greig* (1825) 4 S. 105; *Murray* v. *Gullan* (1825) 3 S. 448; *Brown* v. *Boyd* (1841) 3 D. 1205.
[77] *Ferguson* v. *Marjoribanks*, Nov. 12, 1816, F.C.; *Pirnie* v. *Macritchie*, June 5, 1819, F.C.; *McKean* v. *Davidson* (1823) 2 S. 426; *Johnston* v. *White* (1877) 4 R. 721.
[78] *McNair* v. *McLauchlan* (1826) 4 S. 554.
[79] *Thomson* v. *St. Cuthbert's Cooperative Association*, 1958 S.C. 380; *cf. Smith* v. *Giuliani* 1925 S.C.(H.L.) 45.

7. ABSTRACTION OF WATER

Where subterranean water is present in old mine workings or other interstices in the earth and affords support to the surface by hydrostatic pressure, the removal of that support is a ground of action if it is followed by subsidence and damage to the surface.[80]

Underground water percolating naturally through the soil and not flowing in any known course can be appropriated by anyone sinking a well within the boundaries of his own property, and an adjacent proprietor has no claim if water is being thereby drained from his subsoil and abstracted therefrom.[81] Even enjoyment for the prescriptive period confers no title to the percolating water.[82] " Of the natural direction of underground drainage law can take no account." [83] If underground water flows into mine workings the mineowner may pump it up and dispose of it in whatever direction he pleases, so long as he does not act in aemulationem vicini,[84] but may not discharge it into a stream.[85]

Different considerations apply to water lying on the surface of the soil, as surface-water or in ponds or lochs, or flowing across the surface in a defined channel, whether natural or artificial.[86]

Water which collects on the surface of the soil after heavy rain, not forming a recognised pond or loch, can be allowed to drain away on to another person's land which lies lower without subjecting to any liability in damages, unless this draining has been done unnecessarily to the prejudice of the lower ground, in which case the court has a discretion in the matter.[87] The lower landowner has no ground of complaint if the flow of natural drainage is stopped and the water impounded or diverted.[88] Similar considerations apply to water which is not perennial and constitutes only a bog or morass.

Where water accumulates in a pond or loch, the loch and the water belong to the owner of the land which surrounds it, or, where two or more estates abut on it, to the owners of the several estates in common,[89] though this latter rule is only a presumption which may be rebutted,[90] and while the right to the water is one in common,[91] the rights to the

80 Balds v. Alloa Colliery Co. (1854) 16 D. 870.
81 Mags. of Linlithgow v. Elphinstone (1768) Mor. 12805; 5 B.S. 936; Acton v. Blundell (1843) 12 M. & W. 324; Irving v. Leadhills Mining Co. (1856) 18 D. 833; Chasemore v. Richards (1859) 7 H.L.C. 349; Blair v. Hunter, Finlay & Co. (1870) 9 M. 204; Rankine, Landownership, 513.
82 Chasemore, supra, at p. 385.
83 Irving, supra, 840, per L.J.C. Hope.
84 Irving, supra, 841; Blair, supra, 208.
85 Young v. Bankier Distillery Co. (1893) 20 R.(H.L.) 76.
86 Rankine, 531 et seq.
87 Ersk., II, 9, 2; Bankt., II, 7, 30; Bell, Prin., § 968; Campbell v. Bryson (1864) 3 M. 254.
88 Wood v. Waud (1848) 3 Exch. 748, 778; Greatrex v. Hayward (1853) 8 Exch. 291.
89 Stair, II, 3, 73; Bankt., II, 3, 165; Bell, Prin., §§ 651, 1110; Scott v. Lord Napier (1869) 7 M.(H.L.) 35.
90 Scot v. Lindsay (1635) Mor. 12771; Macdonald v. Farquharson (1836) 15 S. 259; Baird v. Robertson (1836) 14 S. 396; Cunninghame v. Dunlop (1838) 16 S. 1080; Stewart's Trs. v. Robertson (1874) 1 R. 334; Lord Blantyre v. Dumbarton Waterworks Commrs. (1888) 15 R.(H.L.) 56.
91 Menzies v. Macdonald (1854) 16 D. 827, 828, affd. (1856) 2 Macq. 463; 19 D.(H.L.) 1.

subjacent *solum* and underlying strata are exclusive to each proprietor so far as *ex adverso* of his lands and extending to the middle of the loch.[92]

In such circumstances a sole proprietor can use the loch as he thinks fit,[93] as by draining it or poisoning all the fish [94] or preventing all fishing.[95] In so far as the loch drains into a stream he may not divert or diminish the flow of water.[96]

Where there are several proprietors entitled to use the water in common no one may interfere with the water against the wishes of the other or others, and neither one nor all may interfere with the outflow of water into a stream.

In the case of water flowing in distinct channels, natural or artificial, except in the case where a stream rises, flows and falls into the sea entirely within the lands of one owner (in which case he may deal with it as he pleases),[97] the *solum* or *alveus* of the channel belongs to the riparian proprietors *ad medium filum* at all points *ex adverso* of their lands, and in the flowing water itself they all have a common interest but not any right of property. Each heritor has a right to the use of the water as it passes for ordinary domestic and agricultural purposes but beyond that must transmit it undiminished in quantity, unpolluted in quality and unaffected in force, natural direction and current to heritors lower down the stream.[98]

It follows that no riparian proprietor can withdraw water for other purposes, stop up or interfere with the channel in whole or in part or otherwise interfere with the natural flow of the water.

Interference by one riparian proprietor with the *alveus* in default of or in excess of agreement may be restrained by interdict, even though no damage be actually caused or clearly foreseen.[99]

So, too, diversion of the stream from its ordinary course without consent may be prevented, even without proof of damage or present loss of use of the water. This has covered throwing a weir across the river [1] diverting water by a lade,[2] extending a lade,[3] and using water for irrigation.[4]

But such interferences may be acquired in or erected into servitudes of aqueduct in which case objection is barred.

[92] *Cochrane* v. *Earl of Minto* (1815) 6 Paton 139.
[93] Stair, II, 3, 73; Bell, *Prin.*, §§ 651, 1110.
[94] *Mayor of Berwick* v. *Hayning* (1661) Mor. 12772; 2 B.S. 292.
[95] *Montgomery* v. *Watson* (1861) 23 D. 635.
[96] *Magistrates of Linlithgow* v. *Elphinstone* (1768) Mor. 12805; 5 B.S. 935.
[97] *Ferguson* v. *Shirreff* (1844) 6 D. 1363; *Lord Blantyre* v. *Dunn* (1848) 10 D. 509; *Morris* v. *Bicket* (1864) 2 M. 1082, 1092; affd. (1866) 4 M.(H.L.) 44.
[98] *Morris, supra.*
[99] *Duke of Gordon* v. *Duff* (1735) Mor. 12778; *Mags. of Aberdeen* v. *Menzies* (1748) Mor. 12787; *Menzies* v. *Earl of Breadalbane* (1826) 4 S. 783; 3 W. & Sh. 235; *Duke of Roxburghe* v. *Waldie* (1821) Hume 524; *Farquharson* v. *Farquharson* (1740) Mor. 12779; 5 B.S. 688; *King* v. *Hamilton* (1844) 6 D. 399; *Morris* v. *Bicket* (1864) 2 M. 1082; (1866) 4 M.(H.L.) 44.
[1] *Hay* v. *Feuers* (1677) Mor. 1818.
[2] *Johnstone* v. *Ritchie* (1822) 1 S. 304.
[3] *Lanark Twist Co.* v. *Edmonstone* (1810) Hume 520.
[4] *Beaton* v. *Ogilvie* (1670) Mor. 10912; *Wallace* v. *Morrison* (1761) Mor. 14511; see also *D'Eresby's Trs.* v. *Strathearn Hydropathic Co.* (1873) 1 R. 35.

As between upper and lower proprietors a lower proprietor may not by operations in the river-bed impede the natural flow of water away from the upper lands or cause it to be dammed up or to flow back to the actual or apprehended detriment of the upper proprietor's lands.[5] Thus a lower proprietor has been held entitled to restrain operations by an upper proprietor which may cause injury to the banks of the lower estate by increasing or diminishing the momentum of flow of the water [6] or deflecting its flow.[7] But impounding of water may be permitted if that is consistent with the reasonable rights of neighbours.[8]

Nor may an upper proprietor diminish the quantity of water passing downstream to lower proprietors except in so far as the water has been needed for the primary uses of drinking, cooling, washing and watering animals.[9] Thus a lessening of supply can be interdicted.[10]

Irrigation is a secondary use but the right to divert water for that purpose may be acquired by prescription [11] or permitted if it is reasonable in the circumstances and the surplus water is returned to the stream.[12]

Diversion of water for industrial use is wrongful if in the circumstances there is material injury to the lower proprietor's right to have the stream reach his land undiminished in quantity.[13]

8. INTERFERENCE WITH SERVITUDES

Servitudes are conventional real rights whereby the owner of one property, the dominant tenement, possesses as such owner certain privileges over another neighbouring property, the servient tenement.[14] The main servitudes recognised in Scots law are those of road or way, pasturage, fuel, feal and divot, bleaching and taking stone, slate or gravel, all connected with rural subjects, and of support for buildings, eavesdrop, and of light, air and prospect, all connected with urban subjects.

Interference with a servitude right frequently raises the disputed issue of the existence or not of the alleged servitude, which must be dealt with by declarator or by interdict against exercise of a claimed servitude right. But if the existence of the servitude right is undoubted or unchallenged interdict, with or without a claim of damages for loss sustained, is the normal remedy for being interfered with or obstructed in the exercise of

---

5 *Home* v. *Home* (1683) Mor. 11241, 11253; 3 B.S. 606; *Fairly* v. *Earl of Eglinton* (1744) Mor. 12780; *Gray* v. *Maxwell* (1762) Mor. 12800; *Burgess* v. *Brown* (1790) Hume 504; *Baillie* v. *Lady Saltoun* (1821) Hume 523; *Graham* v. *Loch* (1829) 5 Mur. 74; *Bridges* v. *Lord Saltoun* (1873) 11 M. 588.
6 *Lord Glenlee* v. *Gordon* (1804) Mor. 12834.
7 *Colquhoun's Trs.* v. *Orr-Ewing* (1877) 4 R.(H.L.) 116; *Murdoch* v. *Wallace* (1881) 8 R. 855; *Filshill* v. *Campbell* (1887) 14 R. 592.
8 *Abercorn* v. *Jamieson* (1791) Hume 510; *Hunter and Aitkenhead* v. *Aitken* (1880) 7 R. 510.
9 Bell, *Prin.*, § 1105; *Russell* v. *Haig*, Bell's Oct.Cas. 346; *Ogilvie* v. *Kincaid* (1791) Mor. 12824; *Johnstone* v. *Ritchie* (1822) 1 S. 363; *Hood* v. *Williamson* (1861) 23 D. 496; *Donaldson* v. *Earl of Strathmore* (1877) 24 S.L.R. 587; *Bonthrone* v. *Downie* (1878) 6 R. 324.
10 *Lord Melville* v. *Denniston* (1842) 4 D. 1231.
11 *Beaton* v. *Ogilvie* (1670) Mor. 10912.
12 *Kelso* v. *Boyds* (1768) Mor. 12807; *Mackenzie* v. *Woddrop* (1854) 16 D. 381.
13 Rankine, 543.
14 See, generally, Rankine on *Landownership* (4th ed.), 413–463.

the right. Thus a proprietor may not build over a lane which other proprietors have a right to use,[15] nor put a gate across a covered archway,[16] nor obstruct the free and reasonable use of a common access,[17] nor even substitute a different access if the passage is defined [18] or the diversion would cause inconvenience.[19] The servitude may be limited, but not extinguished, by acquiescence.[20]

Where a servitude right is interfered with by a third party, e.g., by a third party depositing rubbish on a road on A's land over which B has a servitude of way, it is a wrong both to the owner of the servient tenement, as an infringement of his right of property, and also to the owner of the dominant tenement as an infringement of his servitude right over another's property. Both may accordingly sue for injury to their several interests in the heritage concerned.[21]

9. NUISANCE

The term nuisance is used rather loosely to cover any use of property which causes trouble or annoyance to neighbours. Nuisances are divided in English law into public and private, according as they inconvenience a large section of the general public or only a few persons, and the former kind may give rise to prosecution as well as to an action in tort. This distinction is not drawn in Scots law where the only useful distinction is into common law nuisances, statutory nuisances and conventional nuisances.[22]

The Scots law of nuisance is based on the civilian maxim, *Sic utere tuo ut alienum non laedas*, and springs from the conflicting interests of adjacent landowners in the uses of their respective lands. Nuisances are not necessarily illegal in the sense of being contrary to law and punishable. If conduct amounts to a nuisance, then it is wrongful and to that extent illegal, but it is not a nuisance because it is illegal (*i.e.*, criminal). In *Duke of Buccleuch* v. *Cowan* [23] the court refused to insert in the issues for the trial of a river pollution case the word " wrongfully " holding that this was tautological, nuisance being a species of legal wrong.[24] Many nuisances indeed arise from the doing of what is undoubtedly lawful and, but for the inconvenience, unobjectionable. Indeed, apart from statute and possible criminal consequences, a nuisance may continue to be perpetrated so long as no person objects. Nor is it necessarily nuisance to make an unusual or unnatural use of land. The fact that the defender

---

15 *Bennett* v. *Playfair* (1877) 4 R. 321; *Argyllshire Commissioners of Supply* v. *Campbell* (1885) 12 R. 1255; *Shiel* v. *Young* (1895) 3 S.L.T. 171; *cf. Mackenzie* v. *Carrick* (1869) 7 M. 419.
16 *Oliver* v. *Robertson* (1869) 8 M. 137.
17 *Stewart, Pott & Co.* v. *Brown Brothers & Co.* (1878) 6 R. 35.
18 *Hill* v. *Maclaren* (1879) 6 R. 1363; *Moyes* v. *McDiarmid* (1900) 2 F. 918.
19 *Thomson's Trs.* v. *Findlay* (1898) 25 R. 407.
20 *Millar* v. *Christie*, 1961 S.C. 1.
21 *Cf. Stevenson* v. *Donaldson*, 1935 S.C. 551.
22 On the difference between Scots and English law see *Slater* v. *A. & J. McLellan*, 1924 S.C. 854, 858, *per* L.P. Clyde; *cf.* Bell, *Prin.*, § 973n.(*a*).
23 (1866) 4 M. 475, 482; sequel 5 M. 214.
24 So, too, in *Cooper and Wood* v. *N.B.Ry.* (1863) 1 M. 499.

is using his land in an unusual or " unnatural " way, if indeed any meaning can be attached to the latter phrase, is not evidence of nuisance.

Conversely it is no defence to an action founded on nuisance that the defender is making a legal or natural or normal use of his land.[25] " The mere fact that the business is quite a legitimate one does not prevent its being put a stop to, if it is conducted in an improper fashion, and it is in the power of anyone to apply to have it interdicted." [26] " If any person so uses his property as to occasion serious disturbance or substantial inconvenience to his neighbour or material damage to his neighbour's property, it is in the general case irrelevant as a defence for the defender to plead merely that he was making a normal and familiar use of his own property." [27]

" And to bring a thing under that character, and notion [i.e., nuisance], it is not necessary (so it is understood) that the matter in question be absolutely a noxious operation, or such as makes the neighbouring houses absolutely unwholesome or unsafe to dwell in. It is sufficient they are made (I do not say disagreeable or unpleasant) but materially uncomfortable, or noisome, subject in short to such a high degree of disturbance, vexation and annoyance, as encroaches on the free and reasonable use of them as dwelling places." [28]

" Whatever obstructs the public means of commerce and intercourse, whether in highways or navigable rivers; whatever is noxious or unsafe, or renders life uncomfortable to the public generally, or to the neighbourhood [29]; whatever is intolerably offensive to individuals in their dwellinghouses, or inconsistent with the comfort [30] of life, whether by stench (as the boiling of whale blubber[31]), by noise (as a smithy in an upper floor[32]), or by indecency (as a brothel next door) is a nuisance." [33]

Nuisance may be partly an infringement of interests in life and health and partly of interests in property. No distinction is drawn in the cases between the two and the same principles are applicable.[34] The distinction between harm to health and inconvenience in the use of property is in any event very narrow.

Nuisance always involves harm or inconvenience over a period of time. It is a continuing wrong; the occurrence on one or more isolated occasions of the subject of complaint is probably not nuisance, but continuous or repeated occurrences are prima facie actionable on the ground of nuisance. For this reason interdict is commonly the remedy sought in nuisance cases,

---

25 *Miller* v. *Stein* (1791) Mor. 12823; *Montgomerie* v. *Buchanan's Trs.* (1853) 15 D. 853; *Caledonian Ry.* v. *Baird* (1876) 3 R. 842; *Reinhardt* v. *Mentasti* (1889) 42 Ch.D. 685; *Wilsons* v. *Brydone* (1877) 14 S.L.R. 667.
26 *Manson* v. *Forrest* (1887) 14 R. 802, 808, *per* L.P. Inglis.
27 *Watt* v. *Jamieson*, 1954 S.C. 56, 58, *per* L.P. Cooper.
28 Hume, *Lect.* III, 214.
29 *Cf. Ogston* v. *Aberdeen Tramways Co.* (1896) 24 R.(H.L.) 8.
30 *Hislop* v. *Fleming* (1886) 13 R.(H.L.) 43.
31 *Cf. Fraser's Trs.* v. *Cran* (1879) 6 R. 451.
32 *Frame* v. *Cameron* (1864) 3 M. 290.
33 Bell, *Prin.*, § 974.
34 *Inglis* v. *Shotts Iron Co.* (1881) 8 R. 1006, 1021.

though damages may also be recovered for past harm and loss,[35] for necessarily continuing harm [36] or personal injuries.[37]

A person may object to conduct as amounting to nuisance as soon as it commences although his use of his own land has not actually been injuriously affected.[38] If he does not, his right to object may be cut off by prescription.[38]

Common law nuisances. At common law nuisance consists in the infringement by a neighbour of the natural rights incidental to ownership of land.[39] If any person so uses his property as to occasion serious disturbance or substantial inconvenience to his neighbour or material damage to his neighbour's property that is a nuisance.[40] " No one is entitled so to use his own property as to materially injure the health or materially affect or diminish the comfort of his neighbours as, *e.g.*, by the storing of offensive materials, or the carrying on of a business causing offensive smells or deleterious gases." [41] " What causes material discomfort and annoyance for the ordinary purposes of life to a man's house or to his property is to be restrained, subject, of course, to any findings which the particular circumstances of the particular case may raise." [42] " What makes life less comfortable and causes sensible discomfort and annoyance is a proper subject of injunction." [43] The fear or anticipation of harm in future does not make conduct, harmless so far, a nuisance, but proof that conduct will necessarily occasion a nuisance justifies interdict.[44]

The proper approach to a case of alleged nuisance is rather from the standpoint of the victim of the loss or inconvenience than from the standpoint of the alleged offender and in the general case it is irrelevant for the defender to plead merely that he was making a normal and familiar use of his own property. The balance in all such cases has to be held between the freedom of a proprietor to use his property as he pleases, and the duty of a proprietor not to inflict material loss or inconvenience on adjoining proprietors or adjoining property; and in every case the answer depends on considerations of fact and of degree.[45] To amount to nuisance the conduct complained of must cause material, not trivial, discomfort or harm,[46] and some actual damage must be proved.[47]

35 *e.g., Ewen* v. *Turnbull's Trs.* (1857) 19 D. 513; *Fleming* v. *Gemmill*, 1908 S.C. 340.
36 *Chalmers* v. *Dixon* (1876) 3 R. 461.
37 *Cleghorn* v. *Taylor* (1856) 18 D. 664.
38 *Harvie* v. *Robertson* (1903) 5 F. 338.
39 Bell, *Prin.,* § 974; Hume, *Lect.* III, 214; Rankine on *Landownership* (4th ed.), 399 *et seq.*
40 *Watt* v. *Jamieson*, 1954 S.C. 56, 57–58.
41 *Manson* v. *Forrest* (1881) 14 R. 802, 810, *per* Lord Shand.
42 *Fleming* v. *Hislop* (1886) 13 R.(H.L.) 43, 45; *per* Lord Selborne; 47 *per* Lord Bramwell; 48, *per* Lord Fitzgerald.
43 *Bamford* v. *Turnley* (1862) 31 L.J.Q.B. 286, cited in *Fleming, supra.*
44 *Trotter* v. *Fairnie* (1831) 5 W. & S. 655; *Arnot* v. *Brown* (1852) 1 Macq. 229; *Harvie* v. *Robertson* (1903) 5 F. 338.
45 *Watt, supra; cf. Inglis* v. *Shotts Iron Co.* (1881) 8 R. 1006, 1021.
46 *Hart* v. *Taylor* (1827) 4 Mur. 313; *Fraser's Trs.* v. *Cran* (1877) 4 R. 795; *cf. Walter* v. *Selfe* (1851) 4 De G. & S. 322; *Crump* v. *Lambert* (1867) L.R. 3 Eq. 413; *Fleming* v. *Hislop* (1886) 13 R.(H.L.) 43, 45, 47.
47 *Salvin* v. *North Brancepath Coal Co.* (1874) L.R. 9 Ch.App. 705; *Shotts Iron Co.* v. *Inglis* (1882) 9 R.(H.L.) 78, 89.

Strict liability for nuisance. Nuisance is a wrong of strict liability, so that it is not relevant to inquire whether the conduct alleged to be a nuisance is intentional or deliberate, or on the other hand negligent, careless or merely accidental. The sole questions are whether the defender has caused or permitted the happenings objected to, and whether they amounted in the circumstances to nuisance or not.[48] In supporting a claim based on nuisance it is not necessary to put fault or negligence in issue; " under an issue of nuisance the court has regard only to the fact of the event as having interfered with a natural right of property irrespective of the origin of any such interference." [49] Nor is it a defence to show that reasonable care has been taken to avoid the creation of a nuisance; the question is whether a nuisance has been created. Nor is the fact that the defender will suffer loss if he has to cease his operations relevant.

" It must be taken to be the law that if it is proved that the operations of the defenders cause real substantial injury to the property of the pursuer, he is entitled to have an interdict to protect him from that injury, even though it be impracticable to make use of the valuable minerals belonging to the defenders without doing such injury, so that the effect of the interdict is to prevent those minerals being used." [50]

In many cases both negligence and nuisance are averred [51] and in such cases fault is relevant on the first point but not on the second. Again there may be a narrow distinction between cases of nuisance and cases of strict liability for the escape of danger from one's land.[52]

Title to sue. The owner or tenant of property whose enjoyment thereof is substantially interfered with clearly has a title to sue; the owner of salmon fishing rights in the sea has a title.[53]

It has been contended that proprietors had no title to sue when they were not in occupation, even though the letting value of the premises was lowered, or likely to be lowered, by the defender's operations, but the opinion has been hazarded that such was a sufficient injury to confer a title to sue.[54]

A member of the general public may petition for interdict when the defender's conduct interferes with the exercise of a public right, as where the use of a rifle range restricted the use by the public of the foreshore for passage and recreation,[55] or a tramway company interfered with public

---

48 *Hart* v. *Taylor* (1827) 4 Mur. 307, 313; *Duke of Buccleuch* v. *Cowan* (1866) 5 M. 214, 216; *Elderslie Estates* v. *Gryfe Tannery, Ltd.,* 1959 S.L.T.(Notes) 71.

49 *Giblin* v. *Lanarkshire C.C.;* 1927 S.L.T. 563, 564, *per* Lord Moncrieff. *Cf. Jacobs* v. *L.C.C.* [1950] A.C. 361.

50 *Shotts Iron Co.* v. *Inglis* (1882) 9 R.(H.L.) 78, 88, *per* Lord Blackburn.

51 *Giblin* v. *Lanarkshire C.C.,* 1927 S.L.T. 563; *Slater* v. *McLellan,* 1924 S.C. 854. See also *Latham* v. *Johnson* [1913] 1 K.B. 398; *Jacobs* v. *L.C.C.* [1950] A.C. 361; *Bolton* v. *Stone* [1951] A.C. 850.

52 *Cf. Shotts Iron Co.* v. *Inglis* (1882) 9 R.(H.L.) 78.

53 *Duke of Richmond* v. *Lossiemouth Mags.* (1904) 12 S.L.T. 166.

54 *McEwan* v. *Steedman & McAlister,* 1912 S.C. 156, 163, *per* Lord Dundas, 164, *per* Lord Salvesen.

55 *Fergusson* v. *Pollok* (1901) 3 F. 1140.

use of the highway,[56] and the magistrates of a city, as representing and for behoof of the community, have been granted an interdict.[57]

The procurator-fiscal has been held to have a title to present a petition to have proprietors of a mill-lade fence it as being a nuisance and dangerous to the public,[58] and a householder has been held entitled to petition for the removal as a nuisance of a urinal erected by police commissioners.[59]

Liability to be called as defender. The occupier of the premises or other person actually causing what is complained of as nuisance is the obvious defender.

A landlord is liable along with his tenant for nuisance created by the tenant if the landlord has caused or permitted the tenant to commit the nuisance,[60] but not merely because his tenant has so misused the property let as to create a nuisance. He is not, that is, vicariously liable for the tenant.

If a third party complains of the operations of a local authority, such as its drainage functions, it is sufficient to call the local authority, and not necessary to proceed against individual inhabitants served by the drainage system.[61]

Local authorities and other public bodies have no immunity from action,[62] though they may have the defence of statutory authority.[63]

An occupier of premises is not liable for a nuisance not created by him or his use of the premises, unless he has continued or adopted the nuisance, or has failed to remedy it within a reasonable time after he came to know, or should reasonably have appreciated, that there was a nuisance.[64]

Remedies. Damages and interdict are both, together or separately, the usual remedies for nuisance, but declarator is sometimes combined with interdict.[65] In one case it was found that the defenders were not entitled to pollute a stream and that the pursuers were entitled to declarator to that effect even though the defenders had taken remedial measures which a man of skill reported were effectual in stopping the pollution.[66] The words of an interdict against causing a nuisance ought not to be formulated so as to exclude all scientific attempts to attain the desired end without causing a nuisance.[67] The court has power in interdict proceedings to make a declaratory finding and to suspend the operation

---

[56] *Ogston* v. *Aberdeen Tramways Co.* (1896) 24 R.(H.L.) 8.
[57] *Edinburgh Mags.* v. *Edinburgh, Leith and Granton Ry.* (1847) 19 S.Jur. 421.
[58] *Stevenson* v. *Hawick Mags.* (1871) 9 M. 753.
[59] *Adam* v. *Alloa Police Commrs.* (1874) 2 R. 143.
[60] *Robertson* v. *Stewart* (1872) 11 M. 189; *Caledonian Ry.* v. *Baird & Co.* (1876) 3 R. 839; *Scott* v. *Scott* (1881) 8 R. 851 (superior and vassal). *Cf. Mackay* v. *Greenhill* (1858) 20 D. 1251.
[61] *Barony Parochial Board* v. *Cadder Parochial Board* (1883) 10 R. 510.
[62] *Stevenson* v. *Hawick Mags.* (1871) 9 M. 753.
[63] *Infra*, p. 969.
[64] *Sedleigh-Denfield* v. *O'Callaghan* [1940] A.C. 880, 904; *B.R.S.* v. *Slater* [1964] 1 All E.R. 816.
[65] *Hume* v. *Young, Trotter & Co.* (1875) 2 R. 338; *White* v. *Dixon* (1875) 2 R. 904; *Fraser's Trs.* v. *Cran* (1877) 4 R. 794. See also *Mackenzie* v. *British Aluminium Co.* [1950] C.L.Y. 5123.
[66] *Dodd* v. *Hilson* (1874) 1 R. 527.
[67] *Fleming* v. *Hislop* (1886) 13 R.(H.L.) 43; *cf. Shotts Iron Co.* v. *Inglis* (1882) 9 R.(H.L.) 78.

thereof pending the progress of remedial measures.[68] Interdict will not
be granted against an anticipated nuisance unless the operations complained of will necessarily cause a nuisance. It is not enough if there is a
possibility of nuisance at some unpredictable future time.[69]

Nuisance largely a question of fact. Nuisance is in every case very much
a question of fact and of degree.[70] " The question of nuisance is to a great
extent one of circumstances and of neighbourhood." [71] " It is not every
slight pollution of a stream, nor every disagreeable odour, that is to be
dealt with as a nuisance, and put down by authority of law. The expression ' abatement of nuisance ' does not necessarily mean the entire and
absolute removal of all pollution of stream, and all disagreeable odour,
but such diminution of pollution and of smell as to render it such as
ought fairly and reasonably to be submitted to." [72] To amount to nuisance
the inconvenience must be material, and materiality is always a question
of circumstances.[73]

" The general rule is, that every one is bound so to use his property
as not to injure his neighbour. It is equally certain that this rule may
suffer modifications according to the varied considerations of social life.
Things which are forbidden in a crowded urban community may be permitted in the country. What is prohibited in enclosed land may be tolerated
in the open. Vicinity—close proximity—may make that a nuisance
which may cease to be so at a distance; and the habit and practice of the
neighbourhood has also some weight in cases of this kind. Nor, in
extreme cases, do I doubt that the comparative interests at stake may be
taken into view." [74]

The fitness of the locality does not prevent the carrying on of an
offensive trade from being an actionable nuisance but an action lies if the
annoyance is sufficiently great to amount to nuisance, having regard to
all the circumstances.[75]

A Dean of Guild court, in granting warrant for the alteration of
buildings and a change of use of them, may have to consider allegations
of probable nuisance arising out of the structural alterations or proposed
use of the buildings, and to do so may require to investigate the facts
relevant to the possibility of nuisance.[76]

Degree of protection justified. The degree of protection for property
which justifies the interdict of a neighbour's operations is such as is
reasonably required for ordinary and normal uses of the property in

[68] *Clippens Oil Co.* v. *Edinburgh & District Water Trs.* (1897) 25 R. 370, 383, *per* Lord Mc-
Laren, approved in *Ben Nevis Distillery* v. *British Aluminium Co.*, 1948 S.C. 592.
[69] *Steel* v. *Gourock Police Commrs.* (1872) 10 M. 954; *Gavin* v. *Ayr County Council*, 1950
S.C. 197.   [70] *Donald* v. *Humphrey* (1839) 1 D. 1184; *Swan* v. *Haliburton* (1830) 8 S. 637.
[71] *Manson* v. *Forrest* (1887) 14 R. 802, 810, *per* Lord Shand.
[72] *Robertson* v. *Stewarts* (1872) 11 M. 189, 198, *per* Lord Ardmillan.
[73] *Colls* v. *Home and Colonial Stores* [1904] A.C. 179, 185; *Maguire* v. *Charles McNeil, Ltd.*,
1922 S.C. 174, 186.
[74] *Inglis* v. *Shotts Iron Co.* (1881) 8 R. 1006, 1021, *per* L.J.C. Moncrieff.
[75] *Bamford* v. *Turnley* (1862) 31 L.J.Q.B. 286.
[76] *Buchan* v. *Stephen's Reps.*, 1946 S.C. 39.

question, not for any unusual use which requires an exceptional degree of freedom from noise, vibration, impure air or other interference. Operations which do not amount to a nuisance to ordinary habitation or use of property do not become a nuisance if the complainer's property is used as a nursing home or laboratory, or devoted to another use requiring specially high standards of freedom from disturbance.[77] Thus an injunction against noise and vibration emanating from the first floor of a building was refused where the plaintiff's profession of ophthalmic optician and oculist on the ground floor was held to be of a specially delicate character.[78]

Suitability of locality. The existence of a nuisance depends on *inter alia*, its locality [79] and it may be less objectionable if established in a district suitable for or long appropriated to the kind of use productive of the nuisance,[80] or necessarily inseparable from that kind of use.[81]

" The doctrine of locality is a concession made by the law to that social necessity which (particularly in towns) drives people into close neighbourhood, not only with each other, but also with the work by which they earn their living. The law of nuisance is designed to protect the use and enjoyment of property free from all interference and annoyance. But this plan has to be accommodated to the rule—inevitable in the nature of things—which requires considerable sacrifice of individual comfort to be made as the price of the advantages which close neighbourhood to others, and to remunerative employment, brings with it . . . The importance of locality, as a circumstance germane to the materiality of an annoyance complained of as occurring in it, is thus obvious . . . ' Locality ' in this connexion points to the immediate neighbourhood of which the complainer's property is the centre—' his immediate locality '—to use the words of Lord Chancellor Westbury in the *St. Helen's* case.[82] It is not to be understood in a sense so loose and extensive as to establish a parity between sources of nuisances sufficiently remote from the complainer's property as to make their effects comparatively little sensible there, and other sources of nuisance which may be established in such proximity as to destroy the comfortable occupation of it. To give the doctrine of locality so elastic an interpretation would in effect be to legalise the creation of nuisance at the will of any owner of property in the neighbourhood." [83]

---

[77] *Robinson* v. *Kilvert* (1889) 41 Ch.D. 88, 94.
[78] *Whycer* v. *Urry* [1955] C.L.Y. 1939.
[79] *Trotter* v. *Farnie* (1830) 9 S. 144, 145, 146; affd. (1831) 5 W. & S. 649.
[80] *Stewart* v. *Thomson*, Dec. 15, 1807, F.C.; *Rae* v. *Marshall*, March 3, 1809, F.C.; *Charity* v. *Riddle*, July 5, 1808, F.C.; *Glasgow Waterworks Co.* v. *Airds*, Dec. 20, 1814, F.C.; *Raeburn* v. *Kedslie* (1816) 1 Mur. 1; *Ballemy* v. *Comb*, Feb. 3, 1813, F.C.; *Arnott* v. *Whyte* (1826) 4 Mur. 149; 5 S. 517; *Colville* v. *Middleton*, May 27, 1817, F.C.; *cf. St. Helen's Smelting Co.* v. *Tipping* (1865) 11 H.L.Cas. 642. The zoning of areas in towns as residential or industrial may be relevant to this point.
[81] *e.g.*, shipyards must be at the water's edge or on a river bank.   [82] *Infra.*
[83] *Maguire* v. *Charles McNeil, Ltd.*, 1922 S.C. 174, 185, *per* L.P. Clyde, approving *Kinloch* v. *Robertson* (1756) Mor. 13163; *St. Helen's Smelting Co.* v. *Tipping* (1865) 11 H.L.Cas. 642; and *Rushmer* v. *Polsue and Alfieri* [1906] 1 Ch. 234.

"A building may be innocuous in one place and a nuisance in another."[84] The use of a building as a cattle mart was held not to be a nuisance because it made the adjacent roads crowded with cattle when the neighbourhood was a great resort for cattle. "The roads in the neighbourhood are not therefore in the same position as the streets of a district where there are none but dwelling houses."[85] The court has allowed defenders to prove that there already existed works of an offensive character in the neighbourhood of the pursuer's grounds which impaired the comfort of their occupation.[86]

Distinctions can be drawn broadly between urban and rural areas, and between residential, commercial and industrial districts in towns, and what is necessarily or reasonably incidental to one kind of area or district may be permitted there within reasonable limits though the same might be objectionable as a nuisance elsewhere.[87]

But suitability of locality confers no immunity, nor liberty to perpetrate a nuisance,[88] and even in an industrial district one party can complain if another introduces an element which is harmful to the industrial uses of the area.[89] "Suitable locality" is, in short, not a defence.[90] While clergymen, schoolmasters and other brain-workers working in an industrial area must accept greater discomfort than professional counterparts in more favourable areas they are not excluded from protection merely because ordinary wage-earners have resigned themselves to putting up with the nuisance.[91]

When right of action emerges. The right of action for nuisance emerges when the nuisance has been created, and particularly when appreciable harm or inconvenience has been caused, but it does not depend entirely on present injury to the lands. Future harm, and the prospect of the creation of an adverse right by the defender must be considered.[92] "So long as no pollution is produced [the pursuers] cannot complain of the existence of a manufactory. They have no title to complain of it. Their single title to complain is, that they are hurt, when the water in their own property is polluted by that means; and until they are so injured they cannot complain. But when the extent of the manufacture has

84 *Robertson* v. *Thomas* (1887) 14 R. 822, 826, *per* L.J.C. Moncrieff. *Cf. Ball* v. *Ray* (1873) L.R. 8 Ch. 467.
85 *Anderson* v. *Aberdeen Agricultural Hall Co.* (1879) 6 R. 901, 905, *per* L.P. Inglis.
86 *Cooper and Wood* v. *N.B.Ry.* (1863) 1 M. 499; but on this see also *Fleming* v. *Hislop* (1886) 13 R.(H.L.) 43, 49.
87 *Glasgow Waterworks Co.* v. *Airds*, Dec. 20, 1814, F.C.; *Colville* v. *Middleton*, May 27, 1817, F.C.; *Cooper* v. *N.B.Ry.* (1863) 1 M. 499; *Anderson* v. *Aberdeenshire Agricultural Hall Co.* (1879) 6 R. 901, 905.
88 *Bamford* v. *Turnley* (1862) 31 L.J.Q.B. 286, approved in *Shotts Iron Co.* v. *Inglis* (1882) 9 R.(H.L.) 78; *St. Helen's Smelting Co.* v. *Tipping* (1865) 11 H.L.Cas. 642; *Fraser's Trs.* v *Cran* (1877) 4 R. 795.
89 *Cooke* v. *Forbes* (1867) L.R. 5 Eq. 166; *McEwan* v. *Steedman & McAlister*, 1912 S.C. 156; *Maguire* v. *Charles McNeil, Ltd.*, 1922 S.C. 174. *Cf. Robinson* v. *Kilvart* (1889) 41 Ch.D. 88.
90 *Charity* v. *Riddle*, July 5, 1808, F.C.; *Dowie* v. *Oliphant*, Dec. 11, 1813, F.C.; *Walter* v. *Selfe* (1851) 4 De.G. & S. 315; *St. Helen's Smelting Co.*, *supra*; *Fraser's Trs.*, *supra*; *Fleming* v. *Hislop* (1886) 13 R.(H.L.) 49; *Maguire* v. *Charles McNeil, Ltd.*, 1922 S.C. 174.
91 *Maguire*, *supra*, 186.
92 *Harvie* v. *Robertson* (1903) 5 F. 338, 346, *per* Lord Kinnear.

become such as to produce pollution, then the title to complain arises, and for the first time.[93] " The right of action must begin when the nuisance begins, and the prescriptive user cannot begin at any earlier period. So long as what is done hurts nobody there is no nuisance, and there is no right of action to put a stop to operations which are *ex hypothesi* harmless." [94]

A complainer should not delay too long in bringing his action: " The pursuer, in my opinion, has hit upon the exact time when the nuisance was worst; he did not cry out before he was hurt, but was prompt to take steps when the nuisance became too offensive." [95]

A pursuer is not barred from taking action because he has himself been carrying on a nuisance and that so long as he has been so doing he has been *non valens agere*; and prescription will even in such circumstances run so as to bar his right to object to a neighbour's nuisance.[96]

A proprietor has an immediate title and interest to complain even though there is no present injury to his land.[97] " He is entitled to take into account not only the actual inconvenience and discomfort caused to people living on the ground by noxious fumes, but also the injury to the value of the property and the prospect of using it for advantageous purposes, other than those to which it is actually applied at the moment. It is enough that the enjoyment of property is interfered with by conduct which, if persisted in, will tend to create an adverse right." [98] Inhabitants of a district may be entitled to interdict against a local authority's operations if these would necessarily have the effect of creating a nuisance; they certainly can if a nuisance is actually created.[99]

Co-operating causes of harm. Nuisance, such as river pollution, may be caused by a number of co-operating causes. It is no defence for any one defender to show that others are contributing to the nuisance complained of,[1] but if nuisance is established each defender whose actings have contributed thereto is liable, jointly and severally [2] whether or not his own contribution by itself would have amounted to a nuisance.[3] But it is a defence to show that the pursuer himself is contributing to the creation of the nuisance.[4]

Adding to or varying nuisance. An increase of noise, pollution or other inconvenience may convert what was tolerable or trivial into what is material discomfort or interference and thereby make the operations a nuisance.[5]

---

[93] *Duke of Buccleuch* v. *Cowan* (1866) 5 M. 214, 217, *per* L.J.C. Inglis.
[94] *Harvie* v. *Robertson* (1903) 5 F. 338, 345–346, *per* Lord Kinnear.
[95] *Robertson* v. *Stewarts* (1872) 11 M. 189, 195, *per* L.P. Inglis.
[96] *Duke of Buccleuch* v. *Cowan* (1866) 5 M. 214; *Harvie* v. *Robertson* (1903) 5 F. 338.
[97] *Alison* v. *Watt* (1829) 7 S. 786.
[98] *Harvie, supra,* 346, *per* Lord Kinnear; *cf.* Lord Adam at p. 344.
[99] *Steel* v. *Gourock Police Commrs.* (1872) 10 M. 954. *Cf. Adam* v. *Alloa Police Commrs.* (1874) 2 R. 143; *Gavin* v. *Ayrshire C.C.*, 1950 S.C. 197.
[1] *Duke of Buccleuch* v. *Cowan* (1866) 5 M. 214, 218.   [2] *Fleming* v. *Gemmill*, 1908 S.C. 340.
[3] *Duke of Buccleuch, supra,* 228–229; *Fleming, supra.*
[4] *Colville* v. *Middleton*, May 27, 1817, F.C.
[5] *Jameson* v. *Hillcoats* (1800) Mor.Appx. Property, No. 4; *Balleny* v. *Comb*, Feb. 3, 1813, F.C.; *Trotter* v. *Farnie* (1830) 9 S. 144; (1831) 5 W. & Sh. 649; *Duke of Buccleuch* v. *Cowan* (1866) 5 M. 475; *Duke of Buccleuch* v. *Gilmerton Coal Co.* (1894) 31 S.L.R. 528.

If a defender is already committing one nuisance he may not vary it or substitute another for it, even though the substituted nuisance be less objectionable,[6] nor vary the mode of committing the same nuisance if the effect is to increase the harm done.[7] "A proprietor who has prescribed a right to pollute cannot in my opinion, use even his common law rights in such a way as to add to the pollution."[8]

Nature of nuisance. An actionable nuisance must be the work of man, by act or neglect, not a creation of nature. Thus if thistles naturally spread seeds to adjacent land that is not nuisance,[9] though it might be actionable on the ground of negligence, if it could be shown that in the circumstances there was any duty to have cut or stopped the growth of the weeds. Nor would the depredations of rabbits be a nuisance unless the defender had unreasonably encouraged them or failed to take reasonable steps to keep their numbers within bounds. And in some cases, such as the fall of leaves in autumn, a highway authority may be in fault if no action is taken to have the leaves removed. A tree growing on private land adjacent to the highway may be a nuisance if it interferes with ordinary use of the highway for passage, *a fortiori* if it falls on the highway and does harm there, though this latter class of harm is more appropriately considered as negligence.[10]

If a landowner is to be held liable for the depredations of wild and undomesticated animals naturally on his lands, such as birds, rabbits, foxes, rats and mice, it can only be for causing them to multiply [11] or not taking adequate steps to keep them down.[12] There can be no liability for a normal population of the kinds of creatures naturally on land.[13]

There may be liability for nuisance caused by conduct which attracts animals which do harm to a neighbour's property, as by dumping manure in unreasonable quantities and attracting flies [12] or rats.[14]

Modes of committing nuisance. There are endless modes and the following list cannot be complete or exclusive of new modes of commiting nuisance.

Nuisance by animals. The keeping of animals may amount to a nuisance. Thus it is a nuisance to keep dogs which cause unreasonable

---

6 *Clarke* v. *Somerset Drainage Commrs.* (1888) 4 T.L.R. 539, contrast *Baxendale* v. *Mac-Murray* (1867) L.R. 2 Ch. 790.
7 *MacIntyre* v. *MacGavin* (1890) 17 R. 818; (1893) 20 R.(H.L.) 49.
8 *MacIntyre, supra* (H.L.) 52, *per* Lord Watson.
9 *Cf. Giles* v. *Walker* (1890) 24 Q.B.D. 656 (doubted in *Davey* v. *Harrow Corpn.* [1957] 2 All E.R. 305). In *Giles* the thistles sprang up when the defendant ploughed up land; the case might have been otherwise if it had been found that he had done so and not taken steps against the natural consequences. *Cf. Forrest* v. *Irvine* (1953) 69 Sh.Ct.Rep. 203.
10 *Caminer* v. *Northern and London Investment Trust* [1951] A.C. 88; see also *Lambourn* v. *London Brick Co.* (1950) 156 E.G. 146; [1950] C.L.Y. 2738.
11 *Farrer* v. *Nelson* (1885) 15 Q.B.D. 258, 260.
12 *Bland* v. *Yates* (1914) 58 Sol.Jo. 612.
13 *Brady* v. *Warren* [1900] 2 I.R. 632; *Stearn* v. *Prentice* [1919] 1 K.B. 394.
14 *Stearn, supra.*

noise,[15] or horses which cause noise in the stable,[16] or cockerels which crow,[17] or pigs[18] or hens[19] or horses[20] which cause objectionable noise and smells, or to wash sheep after they had been dipped in a loch which supplied water to a town.[21] Similarly, it may be a nuisance to keep rabbits, pheasants, pigeons, bees, or other creatures which prey on the crops of another or do damage to his property to a material extent.[22] A tenant cannot shoot his landlord's pigeons as a way of abating the nuisance.[23]

Nuisance from noise. Unusual and excessive noise causing material inconvenience or injury may be a nuisance.[24] It is very much a question of degree.[25] It has been held to be a nuisance to work printing presses,[26] or to use an upper storey as a smithy,[27] to clang milk churns in a dairy,[28] to play music excessively,[29] to operate a saw-mill,[30] but not, in the circumstances, to use steam-hammers in an industrial district.[31]

The Civil Aviation Act, 1949, s. 40, providing that no action shall lie for, *inter alia,* nuisance by reason only of the flight of an aircraft over any property, absolves aircraft operators from liability for noise while in flight. Section 41 empowers an Order in Council to regulate the conditions under which noise and vibration may be caused by aircraft on aerodromes, and this may provide that no action shall lie for nuisance by reason only of noise and vibration.[32]

Nuisance from vibration. Vibration causing damage to property may also be a nuisance,[33] as where a room is used for dancing,[34] or steam hammers used in a foundry,[35] or pile-driving damages an adjacent

---

15 *Street* v. *Tugwell* (1800) 2 Selw.N.P. 1070; *Spider's Web* v. *Marchant* [1961] C.L.Y. 6359; *cf. Brown* v. *E. & M.Ry.* (1889) 22 Q.B.D. 391.
16 *Ball* v. *Ray* (1873) 8 Ch.App. 467; *Broder* v. *Saillard* (1876) 2 Ch.D. 692.
17 *Ireland* v. *Smith* (1895) 3 S.L.T. 180; *Leeman* v. *Montague* [1936] 2 All E.R. 1677.
18 *R.* v. *Wigg* (1705) 2 Salk. 460; *Digby* v. *West Ham Local Board* (1858) 22 J.P. 304; *cf. Att.-Gen.* v. *Squire* (1906) 5 L.G.R. 99.
19 *Ireland, supra.*
20 *Rapier* v. *London Tramways Co.* [1893] 2 Ch. 588; *cf. Benjamin* v. *Storr* (1874) L.R. 9 C.P. 400.
21 *Dumfries Water-works Commrs.* v. *McCulloch* (1874) 1 R. 975.
22 For English law see Williams, *Animals,* p. 238 *et seq.*
23 *Easton* v. *Longlands* (1832) 10 S. 542.
24 *Crump* v. *Lambert* (1867) L.R. 3 Eq. 413; *Broder* v. *Saillard* (1876) 2 Ch.D. 692; *Halsey* v. *Esso Petroleum Co.* [1961] 2 All E.R. 145.
25 *Gaunt* v. *Fynney* (1872) L.R. 8 Ch.App. 11; *Caradog-Jones* v. *Rose* [1961] C.L.Y. 6360; *Nelsovil* v. *Barnard* [1961] C.L.Y. 6361.
26 *Robertson* v. *Campbell,* Mar. 2 1802, F.C.; *cf. Johnston* v. *Constable* (1841) 3 D. 1263.
27 *Kinloch* v. *Robertson* (1756) Mor. 13163.
28 *Fanshawe* v. *London Dairy Co.* (1888) 4 T.L.R. 694; *Tinkler* v. *Aylesbury Dairy Co.* (1888) 5 T.L.R. 52.
29 *Walker* v. *Brewster* (1867) L.R. 5 Eq. 25; *Inchbald* v. *Barrington* (1869) L.R. 4 Ch.App. 388; *Winter* v. *Baker* (1887) 3 T.L.R. 569; *cf. Fleming* v. *Ure* (1750) Mor. 13159.
30 *Fergusson* v. *McCulloch,* 1953 S.L.T.(Sh.Ct.) 113.
31 *Maguire* v. *Charles McNeil, Ltd.,* 1922 S.C. 174.
32 See Air Navigation (General) Regulations, 1960 (S.I. No. 1069) for provisions.
33 *Scott* v. *Firth* (1865) 4 F. & F. 350; *Johnston* v. *Constable* (1841) 3 D. 1263. *Cf. Att.-Gen.* v. *P.Y.A. Quarries* [1961] C.L.Y. 6374.
34 *Jenkins* v. *Jackson* (1888) 40 Ch.D. 71.
35 *Maguire* v. *Charles McNeil, Ltd.,* 1922 S.C. 174.

building,[36] or vibration is caused by working a gas-engine,[37] or machinery used in a tenement.[38]

By the Noise Abatement Act, 1960, s. 1, noise or vibration which is a nuisance is a statutory nuisance under the Public Health (Scotland) Act, 1897, subject to the defence that the best practicable means have been used for preventing, or counteracting the effect of, noise or vibration.

Pollution of air. Occupiers of land have a common law right that the air which naturally reaches their lands shall be free from undue pollution and may therefore interdict those who emit into the surrounding atmosphere an unreasonable amount of impurities which cause perceptible unpleasantness or injury to health or property.[39] The means of pollution are immaterial, smells,[40] heat and fumes,[41] smoke,[42] chemical fumes,[43] sewage,[44] or infectious germs.[45]

In considering materiality of discomfort or harm it is relevant to consider the distance of the complainer from the source of pollution,[46] the locality, the prevailing direction of the wind and the degree of inconvenience or harm.

The Clean Air Act, 1956, makes it an offence, subject to certain defences, to emit dark smoke [47] from the chimney of any building,[48] and requires new furnaces to be, so far as practicable, smokeless.[49] Steps must also be taken to minimise the emission of grit and dust from furnace chimneys.[50] In areas designated smoke control areas it is, subject to certain exemptions and limitations, an offence to emit any smoke from a chimney of any building.[51] Smoke other than smoke from a private

---

36 *Hoare* v. *McAlpine* [1923] 1 Ch. 167.
37 *McEwan* v. *Steedman & McAlister*, 1912 S.C. 156.
38 *Robertson* v. *Campbell and Pillans*, Mar. 2, 1802, F.C.; *Neilson* v. *Waterstone* (1823) 2 S. 259; *Johnston* v. *Constable* (1841) 3 D. 1263.
39 *Dewar* v. *Fraser* (1767) Mor. 12803; *Ralston* v. *Pettigrew* (1768) Mor. 12808; *Russell* v. *Haig* (1791) Mor. 12823; *Steele* v. *Crocket* (1791) Mor. 12809; *Walter* v. *Selfe* (1851) De G. & S. 315; *Robertson* v. *Stewarts* (1872) 11 M. 189.
40 *Palmer* v. *Macmillan* (1794) Mor. 13188; *Farquhar* v. *Watson*, Jan. 19, 1813, F.C.; *Kelt* v. *Linday*, July 8, 1814, F.C.; *Swinton* v. *Pedie* (1839) McL. & R. 1018; *Scott* v. *Leith Commrs.* (1835) 13 S. 646; *Robertson, supra*; *Jameson* v. *Hillcoats* (1800) Mor.Appx. Property, No. 4; *Porteous* v. *Grieve* (1839) 1 D. 561; *Arnot* v. *Brown* (1852) 15 D.(H.L.) 10; *Chalmers* v. *Dixon* (1876) 3 R. 461; *Harvie* v. *Robertson* (1903) 5 F. 338.
41 *Wilson* v. *Brydone* (1877) 14 S.L.R. 667; *Wilson* v. *Gibb* (1903) 10 S.L.T. 293.
42 *Stewart* v. *Thomson*, Dec. 15, 1807, F.C.; *Heriot* v. *Faulds* (1804) Mor. 15255; *Laing* v. *Muirhead* (1822) 2 S. 73; *St. Helen's Smelting Co* v. *Tipping.* (1865) 11 H.L.Cas. 642.
43 *Ralston* v. *Pettigrew* (1768) Mor. 12808; *Hart* v. *Taylor* (1827) 4 Mur. 313; *Broadbent* v. *Imperial Gas Light Co.* (1859) 7 H.L.Cas. 600; *Fraser's Trs.* v. *Cran* (1877) 4 R. 794; *Shotts Iron Co.* v. *Inglis* (1882) 9 R.(H.L.) 78; *Fleming* v. *Hislop* (1886) 13 R.(H.L.) 43; *Ben Nevis Distillery (Fort William), Ltd.* v. *British Aluminium Co.*, 1948 S.C. 592; *Halsey* v. *Esso Petroleum Co.* [1961] 2 All E.R. 145.
44 *Mackay* v. *Greenhill* (1858) 20 D. 1251; *Fraser's Trs., supra*; *Hands* v. *Perth C.C.* (1959) 75 Sh.Ct.Rep. 173.
45 *Mutter* v. *Fyfe* (1848) 11 D. 303; *Metropolitan Asylum Board* v. *Hill* (1881) 6 App.Cas. 193; *Fleet* v. *Metropolitan Asylum Board* (1886) 2 T.L.R. 361; *Bendelow* v. *Worthy Union* (1887) 57 L.J.Ch. 762.
46 *Cf. Donald* v. *Humphrey* (1839) 1 D. 1184, 1186.
47 Defined by s. 24 (1) as including soot, ash, grit and gritty particles emitted in smoke, and by s. 34 (2) as being " as dark as or darker than " shade two on the Ringelmann Chart.
48 s. 1.   49 s. 3.
50 s. 5.
51 s. 11.

dwelling-house chimney or from a building or boiler-chimney is deemed a statutory nuisance if it is a nuisance to the inhabitants of the neighbourhood.[52] The owners of railway locomotive engines [53] and of vessels in specified waters [54] are prohibited from emitting dark smoke.

Pollution of water. The general principle is that no landowner may pollute the water which flows away from his lands in a non-navigable river so as to render it unfit for the use of man or beast, and that he may be restrained by interdict from doing so to any material extent by a heritor lower down the stream.[55]

No unnecessary or artificial impurity may be introduced into the water and it must be allowed to flow on in the same state as it was before.[56] The cause of the pollution is immaterial.[57] In considering whether the pollution causes material injury the size of the stream is relevant,[58] and also the quality of the water prior to the commencement of the pollution complained of. In a case where sheep after being dipped were washed in a loch from which a town drew its water it was said that there was pollution of the water even though it might not be sufficient to be deleterious to health.[59]

The right to pollute in a particular way and to a specified extent may be acquired by prescription and to that extent some or all of the rights of primary use of the water may be destroyed.[60] But in that event no upper heritor may increase the pollution or introduce a new kind of pollution if that would destroy an inferior heritor's use of the water for his secondary purpose.[61]

Similar principles apply to the pollution of inland lochs,[62] wells,[63] reservoirs,[64] canals,[65] mill-lades [66] and dry-ditches.[67] The irrigation of fields with water which, though used, is not polluted, is not a nuisance.[68]

---

[52] s. 16 and s. 31 (application).
[53] s. 19.
[54] s. 20.
[55] In *Duke of Richmond* v. *Lossiemouth* (1905) 12 S.L.T. 166 the discharge of sewage into the sea to the prejudice of salmon fishings was interdicted. See also *Gavin* v. *Ayrshire C.C.*, 1950 S.C. 197.
[56] *Miller* v. *Stein* (1791) Mor. 12823; *Russell* v. *Haig* (1791) Mor. 12823; *Millar* v. *Marshall* (1828) 5 Mur. 28; *Montgomerie* v. *Buchanan's Trs.* (1853) 15 D. 853; *Duke of Buccleuch* v. *Cowan* (1866) 5 M. 214; *Rigby & Beardmore* v. *Downie* (1872) 10 M. 568; *Robertson* v. *Stewarts* (1872) 11 M. 189; *Caledonian Ry.* v. *Baird & Co.* (1876) 3 R. 839; *McGavin* v. *McIntyre* (1890) 17 R. 818; *Fleming* v. *Gemmill*, 1908 S.C. 340.
[57] *Caledonian Ry.* v. *Baird & Co.* (1876) 3 R. 839, 842, 844, 847; *Scott* v. *Scott* (1881) 8 R. 851; *Dodd* v. *Hilson* (1874) 1 R. 527.
[58] *Dunn* v. *Hamilton* (1837) 15 S. 853, 860.
[59] *Dumfries Water-Works Commrs.* v. *McCulloch* (1874) 1 R. 975.
[60] *Downie* v. *Earl of Moray* (1824) 3 S. 107; (1825) 4 S. 169; *Russell* v. *Haig* (1791) Mor. 12823; 3 Paton 403; *Duke of Buccleuch* v. *Cowan* (1866) 5 M. 214. *Cf. Portobello Local Authy.* v. *Edinburgh Mags.* (1882) 10 R. 130.
[61] *Ewen* v. *Turnbull's Trs.* (1857) 19 D. 513; *cf. Russell* v. *Haig* (1791) Mor. 12823; (1792) 3 Paton 403.
[62] *Goldsmid* v. *Tunbridge Wells Commrs.* (1866) L.R. 1 Ch.App. 349.
[63] *Ballard* v. *Tomlinson* (1885) 29 Ch.D. 115.
[64] *Stockport Waterworks Co.* v. *Potter* (1861) 7 H. & N. 160.
[65] *Caledonian Ry.* v. *Baird & Co.* (1876) 3 R. 839.
[66] *Eyre* v. *Earl of Moray* (1827) 5 S. 912.
[67] *Scott* v. *Scott* (1881) 8 R. 851.
[68] *D'Eresby's Trs.* v. *Strathearn Hydropathic Establishment Co.* (1873) 1 R. 35.

The Rivers (Prevention of Pollution) (Scotland) Act, 1951, provides for the establishment of river purification boards to secure unified control of pollution from a river's source to the sea.[69] It makes it an offence to cause pollution of a river.[70] The Act is in supplement of and not in derogation of the common law and there is no authority on the point whether a breach of the statutory duty gives a civil remedy or not.

Under the Water (Scotland) Act, 1946, the local water authority may [71] make by-laws for preventing the pollution of water, and it is an offence to pollute water likely to be used for human consumption.[72]

There may be a right of action for pollution of public navigable waters adjacent to the pursuer's lands if the nuisance created affects the pursuer's use of his own lands. In *Esso Petroleum Co.* v. *Southport Corporation* [73] the appellants were held not liable either for nuisance or for negligence in having discharged oil to lighten a vessel which had grounded, which oil fouled the respondents' foreshore.

Misuse of highway as a nuisance. A person using the highway for passage, on foot or animal, or in a vehicle, is the neighbour for the purposes of nuisance of the occupiers of property fronting on that highway and if any road user uses the road in such a way as to interfere with other people's use of the road it is an encroachment on public right and also a nuisance to adjoining property. Thus damages were given for nuisance where the load on a trailer went on fire and the pursuer's garden was scorched and his house filled with smoke and dirt.[74] Interdict was granted against a tramway company's practice of piling snow, removed from the tram track, at the sides of the road and putting salt on the lines which caused injury to the feet of horses,[75] and against the use of a rifle range by volunteers when the noise of firing was a source of danger to horse traffic on an adjacent public road.[76] Issues were allowed in a claim for damages against the owner of a traction engine which by blowing off steam frightened the pursuer's horse, which upset the dog-cart and injured him.[77]

To leave a vehicle parked or broken down on or at the side of a highway may be a nuisance, if it hampers the public right of free passage, and may also amount to negligence if it creates a foreseeable risk of danger.

It may be nuisance for an occupier of premises to allow dense clouds of steam to be emitted periodically over the adjacent highway to the

---

[69] The Border Rivers (Prevention of Pollution) Act, 1951, provides for joint committees of river boards on either side of the border in respect of the Esk and the Tweed.
[70] s. 22. See also *Gavin* v. *Ayrshire C.C.*, 1950 S.C. 197.
[71] s. 61.
[72] s. 64; see also Sched. 4, s. 37.
[73] [1956] A.C. 218.
[74] *Slater* v. *A. & J. McLellan*, 1924 S.C. 854.
[75] *Ogston* v. *Aberdeen Tramways Co.* (1896) 24 R.(H.L.) 8. (It was indicated that the question would be a different one if the road authority had done the clearing and spreading of salt in the general community interest.)
[76] *Fergusson* v. *Pollok* (1901) 3 F. 1140.
[77] *Hay* v. *Leslie* (1896) 4 S.L.T. 124.

danger of passing traffic,[78] or to let smoke blow across the road,[79] or a branch of a tree project over the road and interfere with traffic.[80]

A person obstructing the highway is *versans in illicito* and liable for resultant harm, even though the precise accident is brought about by the intervention of another and subsequent conscious volition.[81] Something less than obstruction of the highway, such as a heap of slates in the gutter, may be a nuisance.[82] An unlighted vehicle left in the roadway at night may be a nuisance if it is a danger.[83]

Similarly interference with the liberty of members of the public to use the foreshore for passage and recreation may be interdicted.[84]

Where, however, the holding of an annual fair in the streets is sanctified by long usage, it has been held that there has been no actionable nuisance though there is congestion of the streets.[85]

Lawful games as a nuisance. The playing of lawful games such as cricket or golf imposes on the players duties of care for the safety of other persons, *i.e.*, may result in claims based on negligence,[86] but the management of the game by the club may be an actionable nuisance if, *e.g.*, balls are hit out of the ground with such frequency as to create material danger, or substantially to interfere with the use of an adjacent highway.[87]

Other nuisances. Among other uses of property held in the circumstances to amount to nuisances to neighbours have been dressing hides in public,[88] causing material discomfort by the heat from a boiler flue,[89] and the discharge from a water heater into a flue of vapour damaging to stonework,[90] using a thatched house as a smithy in proximity to other thatched houses in a burgh,[91] and having a mill lade adjacent to a public road or green.[92] The keeping of a brothel is a nuisance actionable at the instance of the neighbours.[93]

A monument in a churchyard to " martyrs of political reform " has been held not to be a nuisance, though such a monument might be an

---

[78] *Holling* v. *Yorkshire Traction Co.* [1948] 2 All E.R. 662.
[79] *Rollingson* v. *Kerr, Stammers and Warrell Morton & Co.* [1958] C.L.Y. 2427.
[80] *B.R.S.* v. *Slater* [1964] 1 All E.R. 816.
[81] *Reilly* v. *Greenfield Brick Co.*, 1909 S.C. 1328, 1338, citing *Clark* v. *Chambers* (1878) 3 Q.B.D. 327.
[82] *Almeroth* v. *Chivers* [1948] 1 All E.R. 53.
[83] *Parish* v. *Judd* [1960] 3 All E.R. 33.
[84] *Fergusson* v. *Pollok* (1900) 3 F. 1140.
[85] *Central Motors (St. Andrews)* v. *St. Andrews Mags.*, 1961 S.L.T. 290.
[86] *Ward* v. *Abraham*, 1910 S.C. 299; *McLeod* v. *St. Andrews Mags.*, 1924 S.C. 960.
[87] *Castle* v. *St. Augustine's Links, Ltd.* (1922) 38 T.L.R. 615; *cf. Bolton* v. *Stone* [1951] A.C. 850 (cricket).
[88] *Scott* v. *Cox*, July 5, 1810, F.C.
[89] *Wilson* v. *Brydone* (1877) 14 S.L.R. 667; *cf. Robertson* v. *Campbell*, Mar. 2 1802, F.C.; *Brunston* v. *Constable* (1841) 3 D. 1263.
[90] *Watt* v. *Jamieson*, 1954 S.C. 56.
[91] *Vary* v. *Thomson*, July 2, 1805, F.C.
[92] *Stevenson* v. *Hawick Mags.* (1871) 9 M. 753; *Lang* v. *Bruce* (1873) 11 M. 377.
[93] Bell, *Prin.*, § 974; *Thompson-Schwab* v. *Costaki* [1956] 1 All E.R. 652.

insult to common decency,[94] nor is the erection of a church in the back-green of a house,[95] and keeping cows within a burgh may be so conducted as not to be a nuisance.[96]

Statutory authority. The right to object to something as being a nuisance may be taken away if the offending conduct is being done under statutory authority. But any such statutory authority may permit the particular thing to be done, provided only that it can be done without interference with private rights.[97] Thus mere statutory authority to build a smallpox hospital[98] or sewage farm does not permit the commission of a nuisance thereby, nor does statutory duty absolve from the duty to take steps to avoid incidental nuisance.[99] But statutory authority may be conferred in terms wide enough to sanction even nuisances incidental to the operation of the authorised development and not caused by any negligence in the exercise of the power.[1] In *Lord Blantyre* v. *Clyde Navigation Trustees*[2] a riparian proprietor sued the statutory trustees of the river Clyde for having created a nuisance on his lands by their operations for improving navigation. He was held to have no remedy in that the trustees were not in breach of any obligation under their empowering Acts.

Prescriptive right to commit nuisance. A person commiting a nuisance may acquire a right to continue doing so if a complainer's right to object has not been exercised for forty (now twenty[3]) years and has accordingly prescribed,[4] *i.e.*, by the operation of the negative, not the positive, prescription.[5] The prescriptive period runs in the absence of complaint or interruption from the date when the complainer might first have taken action[6]; it is irrelevant that his complaint has only recently been worth making by reason of his own change of use of his premises, as from industrial to residential use.[7] It cannot run from a date earlier than his discovery of the ground of complaint.[8] Also prescription may cut off

---

94 *Paterson* v. *Beattie* (1845) 7 D. 561, 575.
95 *Cuming* v. *Stewart* (1850) 12 D. 1258.
96 *Manson* v. *Forrest* (1887) 14 R. 802.
97 *Pentland* v. *Henderson* (1855) 17 D. 542; *Cooper & Wood* v. *N.B.Ry.* (1863) 1 M. 499; *Ogston* v. *Aberdeen Tramways Co.* (1896) 24 R.(H.L.) 8.
98 *Metropolitan Asylum Board* v. *Hill* (1881) 6 App.Cas. 193, 201; *cf. Att.-Gen.* v. *Nottingham Corpn.* [1904] 1 Ch. 673; *Manchester Corpn.* v. *Farnworth* [1930] A.C. 171; *Edgington* v. *Swindon Corpn.* [1939] 1 K.B. 86; *East Suffolk Catchment Board* v. *Kent* [1941] A.C. 74; *Marriage* v. *East Norfolk Catchment Board* [1950] 1 K.B. 284.
99 *Lord Advocate* v. *N.B.Ry.* (1894) 2 S.L.T. 71; *cf. Adam* v. *Alloa Police Commrs.* (1874) 2 R. 143.
1 *Hammersmith Ry.* v. *Brand* (1869) L.R. 4 H.L. 171; *City of Glasgow Union Ry.* v. *Hunter* (1870) 8 M.(H.L.) 156; *L.B. & S.C.Ry.* v. *Truman* (1885) 11 App.Cas. 45; *Quebec Ry.* v. *Vandry* [1920] A.C. 662, 679.
2 (1871) 9 M.(H.L.) 6.
3 Conveyancing (Scotland) Acts, 1924, s. 17, and 1938, s. 4.
4 *Duncan* v. *Moray*, June 9, 1809, F.C.; *Collins* v. *Hamilton* (1837) 15 S. 902; *Robertson* v. *Stewart* (1872) 11 M. 198; *Rigby* v. *Downie* (1872) 10 M. 568, 573; *Fraser's Trs.* v.*Cran* (1877) 4 R. 795; *Midlothian C.C.* v. *Pumpherston Oil Co.* (1904) 6 F. 387, 397.
5 *Rigby* v. *Downie, supra; Harvie* v. *Robertson* (1903) 5 F. 338.
6 *Goldsmidt* v. *Tunbridge Wells Commrs.* (1866) L.R. 1 Ch.App. 349.
7 *Harvie* v. *Robertson* (1903) 5 F. 338; *Sturges* v. *Bridgman* (1879) 11 Ch.D. 852.
8 *Liverpool Corpn.* v. *Coghill* [1918] 1 Ch. 307.

the right of one adjacent owner to object without interfering with the right of another who has just come to the district. Also while prescription may cut off the right to object it is only the right to object to that particular nuisance, as it then existed, and it does not bar complaint about an extension or alteration or intensification of the nuisance,[9] or to a subsequent nuisance, such as a fresh abuse of the same stream.[10]

Acquiescence by an adjacent proprietor in the continuance of a nuisance, for a period less than the prescriptive period, confers no right to continue the nuisance unless there has been some act, expressing or implying sanction of it.[11] But a proprietor may be barred by acquiescence if, in the knowledge of a contravention of his rights, he permits the other party to undertake operations which would be expensive or difficult or impossible to undo,[12] or a fortiori, if he has approbated the operations.[13]

Licence. Similarly the grant of planning permission for the use of land in a particular way, or the licensing of particular premises for a certain use, as for betting or the sale of exciseable liquor or as a club, does not imply any permission to create a nuisance,[14] and indeed it is thought such permission or licence is subject to the implied condition that no greater nuisance of any kind will be caused than is naturally and necessarily incidental to the use for the purposes licensed.

The permission from burgh magistrates to use premises as a slaughterhouse has been held not to prevent a person, to whom the slaughterhouse was a nuisance, from seeking interdict.[15]

Plea of coming to the nuisance. It is sometimes alleged in defence to an action charging nuisance that the pursuer has no ground of complaint if he has acquired the premises affected, by universal or singular succession, after the commencment of the nuisance, and when either no person had been affected by the nuisance when it commenced or any affected person had taken no steps to have it abated or stopped, i.e. in effect that a person cannot complain if he has come to an established nuisance.

---

9 *Charity* v. *Riddle*, July 5, 1808, F.C.; *Baxendale* v. *MacMurray* (1867) L.R. 2 Ch. 790; *Clarke* v. *Somerset Drainage Commrs.* (1888) 57 L.J.M.C. 96; *MacIntyre* v. *MacGavin* (1890) 17 R. 818; (1893) 20 R.(H.L.) 49.

10 *Rigby* v. *Downie* (1872) 10 M. 568, 573.

11 *Colville* v. *Middleton*, May 27, 1817, F.C.; *Cowan* v. *Kinnaird* (1865) 4 M. 236, 241; *Duke of Buccleuch* v. *Cowan* (1866) 4 M. 475, 482; *Houldsworth* v. *Wishaw Mags.* (1887) 14 R. 920; cf. Bell, *Prin.*, § 946; *Bargaddie Coal Co.* v. *Wark* (1859) 3 Macq. 480; *Hill* v. *Dixon* (1850) 12 D. 811.

12 *Kinnoul* v. *Keir*, Jan. 18, 1814, F.C.; *Colville* v. *Middleton*, May 27, 1817, F.C.; *Abercorn* v. *Longmuir*, May 20, 1820, F.C.; *Stirling* v. *Haldane* (1829) 8 S. 131; *Bargaddie Coal Co.*, supra; *Hill* v. *Wood* (1863) 1 M. 360; *Muirhead* v. *Glasgow Highland Socy.* (1864) 2 M. 420; *Bicket* v. *Morris* (1866) 4 M.(H.L.) 49.

13 *Aytoun* v. *Douglas* (1800) Mor.Appx. Property, No. 5; *Aytoun* v. *Melville* (1801) Mor. Appx. Property, No. 6; *Hart* v. *Haylor* (1827) 4 Mur. 307.

14 Cf. Licensing (Scotland) Act, 1959, ss. 36 (grounds for objection to grant or transfer of certificate for licensed premises), and 174 (grounds for objection to grant or renewal of certificate of registration as a club); Betting and Gaming Act, 1960, s. 5 (conduct of licensed betting offices).

15 *Pentland* v. *Henderson* (1855) 17 D. 542.

Though raised in some older cases [16] it is now settled that a person is not obliged to put up with a nuisance merely because he has acquired his property after an adjacent proprietor had commenced to commit a nuisance, and an objector's rights are the same whether the nuisance commenced before or after he acquired his property.[17] " It is clear that whether the man went to the nuisance or the nuisance came to the man, the rights are the same." [18]

Public interest. The plea that the polluting premises were the means of employment for many has been repelled as a defence,[19] and it is equally irrelevant to allege that the operations creating the nuisance are for the public convenience or benefit.[20] But in the exercise of its discretion to grant or withhold interdict against a nuisance, the court may have to consider the public interest and whether the continuance of the nuisance is reasonably justified thereby.[21]

The court has jurisdiction in applications for interdict to make a declaratory finding, and to suspend the operation of that finding pending the progress of remedial measures; cases where this has been exercised are either cases where the granting of immediate interdict would be attended with consequences to the rights of the respondent as injurious, or possibly more so, than the wrong complained of, or because the effect of an immediate interdict would be to cause some great and immediate public inconvenience.[22]

In *Ben Nevis Distillery (Fort William), Ltd.* v. *British Aluminium Co.*[23] it was held inexpedient to interdict the major home producer of aluminium from continuing production at a time when currency problems made purchase abroad undesirable.

Loss to defender if operations stopped. It is in general no defence to allege that if the operations causing the nuisance are stopped the defender will suffer loss. The question has to be viewed from the angle of harm to the pursuers from continuation, not loss to the defenders from cessation.[24]

Where inconvenience trivial. If, having regard to the circumstances of place, district and time, the damage or inconvenience caused is regarded by the court as negligible, a remedy may be refused.[25] It has been held that a person must suffer without redress the amount of discomfort which

---

[16] *Miller* v. *Stein* (1791) Mor. 12823; *Jameson* v. *Hilcoats* (1800) Mor.Appx. Property, No. 4; *Duncan* v. *Earl of Moray*, June 9, 1809, F.C.; *Colville* v. *Middleton*, May 27, 1817, F.C.; *Arrott* v. *Whyte* (1826) 4 Mur. 159.

[17] *Chalmers* v. *Dixon* (1876) 3 R. 461; *Fleming* v. *Hislop* (1886) 13 R.(H.L.) 43.

[18] *Fleming, supra,* 49, per Lord Halsbury.

[19] *Farquhar* v. *Watson*, Jan. 19, 1813, F.C.

[20] *Arrott* v. *Whyte* (1826) 4 Mur. 158; *Duke of Buccleuch* v. *Cowan* (1866) 5 M. 214, 229; *Fraser's Trs.* v. *Cran* (1879) 6 R. 452.

[21] *Cf. Inglis* v. *Shotts Iron Co.* (1881) 8 R. 1006, 1021.

[22] *Clippens Oil Co.* v. *Edinburgh and District Water Trs.* (1897) 25 R. 370, 383, per Lord McLaren, approved in *Ben Nevis Distillery, infra,* at 598.

[23] 1948 S.C. 592.

[24] *Montgomerie* v. *Buchanan's Trs.* (1853) 15 D. 858; *Shotts Iron Co.* v. *Inglis* (1882) 9 R. (H.L.) 88; *Watt* v. *Jamieson*, 1954 S.C. 56.

[25] *Anderson* v. *Aberdeen Agricultural Hall Co.* (1879) 6 R. 901, 905.

arises from those acts necessary for the common and ordinary use and occupation of land and houses, if the acts are conveniently done.[26] The discomfort or annoyance founded on must be " material "; this excludes any sentimental, speculative, trivial discomfort or personal annoyance of the kind which the law can take no account of.[27]

Again there may be circumstances where a nuisance can be alleviated so that the complainer's rights would be adequately protected by mitigation reducing the nuisance to a point where the interposition of law is not appropriate.[28]

Where inconvenience temporary. Similarly acts which might be a nuisance if habitual or prolonged may be done with impunity if they are incidental to the ordinary use of the land and are merely occasional or temporary. Thus repairs, partial demolition and reconstruction are not nuisances so long as all reasonable skill and care is taken to avoid or minimise annoyance to neighbours in the process.[29] But such operations may be so prolonged as to justify interdict.[30]

Amelioration. If the defender pleads that he has taken or is taking remedial measures, the usual course has been to remit to a man of skill to report on the efficacy of the measures.[31] The court may in its discretion refuse interdict *in hoc statu* to permit the defender to take remedial action which will diminish or abate the nuisance yet allow him to continue his manufacture,[32] or may continue interim interdict pending an expert's report rather than make it perpetual.[33] Similarly an interdict may be refused where the defender has given undertakings, at least until it is seen whether his business can be carried on without creating a nuisance.[34] But interim interdict may be continued even though an expert has reported that, by reason of changed methods, no nuisance now existed,[35] and may eventually be made perpetual.[36] The opinion has been expressed [37] that even where a defender has put into operation remedial measures with apparent success the pursuer is still entitled to an interdict and that, unless the defender will submit to an interdict, the remedial works must be tested over a lengthy period by a neutral authority.

[26] *Fleming* v. *Hislop* (1886) 13 R.(H.L.) 43, 49; *Bamford* v. *Turnley* (1862) 31 L.J.Q.B. 286, 294.
[27] *Robertson* v. *Stewarts* (1872) 11 M. 189, 198.
[28] *Fleming, supra,* 45.
[29] *Ball* v. *Ray* (1873) L.R. 8 Ch. 467; *Harrison* v. *Southwark Water Co.* [1891] 2 Ch. 409, 413.
[30] *Bamford* v. *Turnley* (1862) 31 L.J.Q.B. 286; *Colwell* v. *St. Pancras B.C.* [1904] 1 Ch. 707.
[31] *Arnot* v. *Brown* (1852) 15 D.(H.L.) 10; *Duke of Buccleuch* v. *Brown* (1873) 1 R. 85, 1111; *Dodd* v. *Hilson* (1874) 1 R. 527; *Fraser's Trs.* v. *Cran* (1877) 4 R. 794; (1879) 6 R. 451. *McEwan* v. *Steedman & McAlister,* 1912 S.C. 156; 1913 S.C. 761.
[32] *Fleming* v. *Gemmill,* 1908 S.C. 340, 349; *McEwan* v. *Steedman & McAlister,* 1912 S.C. 156; 1913 S.C. 761.
[33] *Duke of Buccleuch* v. *Brown* (1873) 1 R. 85, 1111; *Fraser's Trs.* v. *Cran* (1877) 4 R. 794.
[34] *Manson* v. *Forrest* (1887) 14 R. 802.
[35] *Fraser's Trs., supra.*
[36] *Fraser's Trs.* v. *Cran* (1879) 6 R. 451.
[37] *Countess of Seafield* v. *Kemp* (1899) 1 F. 402.

Statutory nuisances. Under various statutes particular kinds of conduct are statutorily declared nuisances.

Under the Public Health (Scotland) Act, 1897, s. 17, it is the duty of each local authority to cause an inspection to be made of their district from time to time to ascertain what nuisances [38] exist calling for removal. Information of any nuisance may be given to the local authority by any person. The local authority may require the occupier or owner of the premises to remove the nuisance, or itself do so and take steps to prevent its recurrence. Under section 171 it is provided that other remedies are not affected by the statutory provisions, so that action for interdict and for damages by an aggrieved person appears not to be precluded.

Various other general and local Acts define particular kinds of conduct as amounting to nuisance and visit the commission with penalties.

Conventional nuisances. Feu contracts and similar deeds may impose conventional restrictions on the use of the land or buildings forbidding their use in such a way as to cause a nuisance, or restrictions on specified uses which are conventionally treated as being of the nature of a nuisance. [39] A provision dealing with conventional nuisance may provide that something shall be a nuisance though it might not be a nuisance at common law. [40] In each case such clauses may require reference to the common law of nuisance for interpretation.

The commission of an act which infringes a conventional prohibition of committing a nuisance does not necessarily give an aggrieved person a right of action since such restrictions are real burdens on the title of the vassal or tenant and will be enforceable only at the instance of the superior or landlord, not of a third party, unless he can show that he has a *jus quaesitum tertio* to enforce the prohibition. [41]

10. DAMAGE TO LAND BY ESCAPE OF DANGEROUS THINGS

Strict liability, based on an unusually high standard of care being demanded in the circumstances coupled with a judicial readiness to infer fault from the happening of an accident, attaches where a person has created or accumulated on his land something potentially dangerous which was not naturally there and has allowed it to escape therefrom and do harm to his neighbour's land. The defender is held liable unless he can bring himself within the principle of certain limited defences. [42]

---

[38] Defined by section 16. See also Coal Mines Refuse Act, 1952, s. 18 (5). An order for removal of a nuisance under the 1897 Act is civil not criminal, so that appeal does not lie to the High Court: *Wright* v. *Kennedy*, 1946 J.C. 142.

[39] Bell, *Prin.*, § 974; *Porteous* v. *Grieve* (1839) 1 D. 561; *Mutter* v. *Fyfe* (1848) 11 D. 303; *Frame* v. *Cameron* (1864) 3 M. 294; *Anderson* v. *Aberdeen Agricultural Hall Co.* (1879) 6 R. 907; *Manson* v. *Forrest* (1887) 14 R. 802. *Cf. Botanic Gardens Picture House* v. *Adamson*, 1924 S.C. 549; *Fergusson* v. *McCulloch*, 1953 S.L.T.(Sh.Ct.) 113.

[40] *Anderson, supra*, 904.

[41] *Hislop* v. *MacRitchie's Trs.* (1880) 8 R.(H.L.) 95; *N.B.Ry.* v. *Moore* (1891) 18 R. 1021.

[42] See also, generally, Thirteenth Report of Law Reform Committee for Scotland (Cmnd. 2348) recommending no change in the law.

Liability for escape of dangerous things differs from liability for nuisance in that in this case the thing on the defender's land is clearly potentially dangerous, and the escape is a single event rather than a continuing process. There may be liability on both grounds if there is repeated or periodical escape.

The requisites for liability are (a) that the defender has voluntarily brought on to or created on his own land some *novum opus* which had innovated on the natural state of things, and created a danger not naturally there, and which was obviously likely to cause serious harm to neighbours if precautions against risk of harm were found wanting, and (b) that they have been found wanting. Fault is readily presumed from the happening and the defender is liable without further proof of fault, but may rely on certain limited defences. His liability is strict, but not absolute. The underlying principle is *sic utere tuo ut alienum non laedas*; a proprietor must take great care that in using his lands he does not let something happen which damages a neighbour's property, and the justification lies in the inherent risk; the liability is for risk, not for fault, and liability arises if the risk of harm eventuates.

Development of the principle in Scotland. The principle of strict liability seems first to have been adumbrated in Scotland in *Henderson* v. *Stewart*,[43] where it was held that a tenant and not the landlord was liable where a dam which the tenant had been authorised to erect gave way, the water damaging an inferior heritor's property; it was argued that culpable negligence must be assumed, but this point was not decided. It was more clearly foreshadowed in *Samuel* v. *Edinburgh and Glasgow Ry.*,[44] where railway works had disturbed natural drainage and caused a burn to overflow after heavy rain and damage the pursuer's lands. The court sent the case to trial on an issue of whether inundation had been caused by the inadequacy of the defender's works for the purposes intended. Inglis for the pursuer seems to have contended for strict liability: if the railway had not been there no damage would have arisen; but the court was clearly hesitant. The case is equivocal authority.

There is also some foundation for the doctrine in *Cleghorn* v. *Taylor*,[45] where a chimney can, because of bad workmanship in putting it up, fell seventeen days later, fragments going through the skylight of an adjoining shop and damaging the stock. The proprietor was held liable for having his property in an insecure and insufficient state, his knowledge being held irrelevant. " It might not be proveable, in a great many cases, that the work had been at the first insufficiently executed . . . It is enough for the party injured that the can fell in consequence of being in an insecure and insufficient state." [46] It appears from the later cases of *Campbell* v.

---

[43] (1818) reported at 15 S. 868n.
[44] (1850) 13 D. 312.
[45] (1856) 18 D. 664.
[46] *Ibid.* 668, *per* L.J.C. Hope; *cf.* Lord Cowan at p. 671, founding on *sic utere tuo ut alienum non laedas*.

Kennedy [47] and *Laurent* v. *Lord Advocate* [48] that *Cleghorn* [49] should be understood as based on *culpa*.

The real genesis of this principle of liability is *Kerr* v. *Earl of Orkney*,[50] where the defender had erected a dam which had burst, the water sweeping away the pursuer's houses, mill and machinery. The pursuer alleged that the dam burst from the insufficiency of its construction or some other cause for which the defender was responsible, in substance an allegation of fault. The defence was that the dam had been carefully constructed but the flood which carried it away was of a most unprecedented character. The Lord Ordinary (Ardmillan) held [51] that " the respondent, in thus interfering with the course of the stream and the security of its banks by the erection of a *novum opus* at his own hand, was bound to be *peculiarly careful* in the construction of the work." The fact that the dam had burst within four months " must be held to throw on the respondent the burden of explaining the fact on some footing consistent with the strength and sufficiency of the work," and this the respondent had failed to do. In the Inner House Lord Justice-Clerk Hope stated [52] the general principle on which the view of the court was founded: " That principle is—that if a person chooses upon a stream to make a great operation for collecting and damming up the water for whatever purpose, he is bound, as the necessary condition of such an operation, to accomplish his object in such a way as to protect all persons lower down the stream from all danger: He must secure them against danger. It is not sufficient that he took all the pains which were thought at the time necessary and sufficient. They were exposed to no danger before the operation. He creates the danger, and he must secure them against the danger, so as to make them as safe notwithstanding his dam as they were before . . . A dam that gives way in a night's rain is not such as the maker was bound to erect. The fact that it gives way is a proof that his obligation was not fulfilled, and that the protection was not afforded which he was bound to provide."

" The court are quite agreed as to the general responsibility of any party who makes a *novum opus* to provide for the security of all who are liable to be affected by it, to make reparation for all damage occasioned by its inefficiency." [53]

The decision is substantially a piece of judicial legislation, and lightly based on liability for fault, in that fault was rather vaguely alleged and the court clearly thought that the circumstances were such as to demand not merely reasonable care, but a very high degree of skill and care, in view of the obvious potential dangers of the operation. But the liability, though strict, was not said to be absolute.

---

[47] (1864) 3 M. 121.
[48] (1869) 7 M. 607, 611.
[49] (1856) 18 D. 664.
[50] (1857) 20 D. 298.
[51] p. 301.
[52] p. 302.
[53] p. 304, *per* Lord Murray; Lords Wood and Cowan concurred on the principle of liability.

The court also clearly viewed the case as substantially one of *res ipsa loquitur*. " The Lord Ordinary is of opinion that the respondent has not instructed, nor even suggested, any intelligible explanation of the fact that the embankment burst, and the waters carried away the mill, on a footing which can protect him from liability." [54] " His dam was run up in a very short time . . . It gave way in four months. Its entire failure is proof that it was not constructed so as to afford, as it did not afford, the security against risk, which the maker was bound to provide." [55]

In the result the decision has established a principle of strict liability for all damage caused by the failure of a *novum opus*, or the escape of a dangerous thing started by the defender's operations, in that in such cases a high standard of care is demanded and fault is readily inferred from the occurrence of obviously possible harm.

Lord Justice-Clerk Hope's formulation of principle has been approved by the House of Lords [56]; in *Tennent* [56] Lord Chancellor Westbury stated the defender's duty in such a case as being " so to construct the work as to provide in an efficient manner, not only against usual occurrences and ordinary state of things, but also to provide against things which are unusual and extraordinary "; Lord Chelmsford said [57]: " He was bound, therefore, under those circumstances—interfering with the stream, and with another person's right over the stream—to provide against every contingency." In the *Caledonian Ry.* case [58] Lord Shaw said: " a person making an operation for collecting and damming up the water of a stream must so work as to make proprietors or occupants on a lower level as secure against injury as they would have been had nature not been interfered with. And this is so although the water accumulated suddenly, or the rainfall was extraordinary or even unprecedented in quantity. These are the general propositions of the law."

In *Mackintosh* v. *Mackintosh*,[59] where fire from heather burning spread to an adjacent estate and burned growing wood, it was said: " It appears to the Lord Ordinary to be settled in legal principle that wherever a proprietor performs on his own property an operation, which, though lawful, is in its nature attended with immediate peril to his neighbour, he is, in order to avoid responsibility, bound to use the utmost measure of precaution of which the case admits. *Tenet culpa levissima*. In working out this principle practically, it has been commonly held that the onus substantially lies on the person performing the operation to show that no precaution has been neglected, and that the damage arose from a cause over which he had not and could not have control—as an unexpected tempest or the like. If the operation is one which, in itself, is of

---

[54] p. 301, *per* Lord Ardmillan.
[55] p. 303, *per* L.J.C. Hope.
[56] *Tennant* v. *Earl of Glasgow* (1864) 2 M.(H.L.) 22, 26; *Caledonian Ry.* v. *Greenock Corpn.*, 1917 S.C.(H.L.) 56, 60, 63, 65.
[57] p. 28.
[58] *Supra*, 65–66.
[59] (1864) 2 M. 1357, 1361, *per* Lord Kinloch.

extreme danger to the adjoining property, the bare circumstance of danger occurring, or at least the slightest indication of neglect, will reasonably be sufficient to impose this onus." This is possibly going too far in the direction of liability entirely without fault. In the Inner House Lord Neaves [60] based his judgment on negligence, but " in all cases the amount of care which a prudent man will take must vary infinitely according to circumstances. No prudent man in carrying a lighted candle through a powder magazine would fail to take more care than if he was going through a damp cellar. The amount of care will be proportionate to the degree of risk run, and to the magnitude of the mischief that may be occasioned." Lord Cowan agreed with Lord Neaves and disagreed with the law laid down by the Lord Ordinary, as did Lord Justice-Clerk Inglis, who insisted [61] on the need for the complainer to prove negligence or *culpa*. The court held that the fire had been caused by the defender's negligence. Nevertheless the court's view was clearly that in such circumstances a higher standard of care than reasonable care was necessary and to that extent the case supports the principle of strict liability.

In *Tennent* v. *Earl of Glasgow* [62] one heritor replaced a hedge by a wall; flood water escaped from a burn, accumulated behind the wall until the wall fell, when the water escaped and damaged the pursuer's lands. The occurrence was held to be *damnum fatale* and the defender escaped liability. Lord Chancellor Westbury said: " If anything be done by an individual which interferes with natural occurrences . . . it is undoubtedly the duty of that individual so to construct the work as to provide in an efficient manner, not only against usual occurrences and ordinary state of things, but also to provide against things which are unusual and extraordinary." [63] Lord Chelmsford expressly stated his view that the pursuer was not entitled to recover " without showing some negligence or default upon his part which occasioned the injury."

Similarly in *Potter* v. *Hamilton and Strathaven Ry.*,[64] where a railway embankment diverted rainwater on to the pursuer's lands, it was said: " The railway . . . was, as regards these lands, a *novum opus* . . . The railway company . . . is in the position of persons who, in making a new work which intersects the natural flow of the water-courses, are bound to construct their works so as not to increase the accumulation of water, and so as to provide adequately for the escape of the water."

" A party who makes a new work is bound to protect those on a lower level from extraordinary as well as ordinary accumulations of water, provided they be not such as to amount to an unprecedented event, so improbable and unnatural as could not have been reasonably anticipated." [65] There were no averments or pleas of fault, but only of

[60] p. 1363.
[61] p. 1364.
[62] (1864) 2 M.(H.L.) 22.
[63] *Ibid.* 26, approved in *Potter* v. *Hamilton Ry.* (1864) 3 M. 83, 86.
[64] (1864) 3 M. 83, 85, *per* Lord Ardmillan, giving opinion of First Division.
[65] *Ibid.* 86.

damage caused by the *novum opus*, and the opinion contains no reference
to fault, save possibly that the court held that the injury was caused " by
the inadequacy of the provision made for the escape of the water," which
implies a measure of fault.

Shortly thereafter, in *Campbell* v. *Kennedy*,[66] the pursuer's goods were
damaged by water leaking from a defective pipe in the defender's superincumbent property. Strict liability was contended for, though negligence
had been alleged, but the judges all insisted that a finding of negligence
was essential for liability, and Lord Justice-Clerk Inglis observed [67]:
" no action for reparation of damage so caused can be relevant, unless
negligence or *culpa* of some description is averred . . . I cannot find any
example of a claim for reparation being allowed in any other case [than
breach of contract and of damage caused by delinquency] and . . . I know
of no trace of authority for a different doctrine." In his view, all the
foregoing cases must be understood as based on *culpa*, not on any principle
of liability entirely without fault.

In the later case of *Laurent* v. *Lord Advocate* [68] Inglis, now Lord President, again insisted that there must be fault, or delinquency or wrong, to
render the defender in an action of reparation liable in damages, while
recognising that there were cases where a defender was bound in more
exact diligence and would be answerable for any want of due care and
attention to the rights and interests of his neighbour.

Analogy with rule of Rylands v. *Fletcher.* In Anglo-American law
liability for damage caused by the escape of dangerous things is commonly
known as the " rule of *Rylands* v. *Fletcher* " from the case in which it
was first laid down generally. In that case [69] the defendants, employing
an independent contractor, constructed a reservoir on their lands; when
the water filled this it escaped through the disused mine-shaft of old
workings, which the contractors had not sealed off properly, into the
plaintiff's mine and flooded it. The plaintiffs brought an action on the
case alleging negligence [70] and it was found in fact that the contractors
had been negligent, though the defendant had not personally nor through
his servants been negligent. On appeal the question whether the defendant
was liable for his independent contractors was elided. Blackburn J.,
delivering the judgment of the Court of Exchequer Chamber, said [71]:
" The question of law therefore arises, what is the obligation which the
law casts on a person who, like the defendants, lawfully brings on his
land something which, though harmless while it remains there, will
naturally do mischief if it escapes out of his land. It is agreed on all
hands that he must take care to keep in that which he has brought on the

---

[66] (1864) 3 M. 121.
[67] p. 126, explaining *Cleghorn* v. *Taylor* (1856) 18 D. 664.
[68] (1869) 7 M. 607, 610–611.
[69] (1865) 3 H. & C. 774; revd. (1866) L.R. 1 Ex. 265; reversal affirmed (1868) L.R. 3 H.L. 330.
[70] The declaration, which contains three counts, all alleging negligence, is set out in the report in L.R. 1 Ex. 266.
[71] L.R. 1 Ex. 265, 279.

land and keeps there, in order that it may not escape and damage his neighbours, but the question arises whether the duty which the law casts upon him, under such circumstances, is an absolute duty to keep it in at his peril or is, as the majority of the Court of Exchequer have thought, merely a duty to take all reasonable and prudent precautions in order to keep it in, but no more. If the first be the law, the person who has brought on his land and kept there something dangerous, and failed to keep it in, is responsible for all the natural consequences of its escape. If the second be the limit of his duty, he would not be answerable except on proof of negligence, and consequently would not be answerable for escape arising from any latent defect which ordinary prudence and skill could not detect. . . . " We think that the true rule of law is, that the person who for his own purposes brings on his lands and collects and keeps there anything likely to do mischief if it escapes, must keep it in at his peril, and, if he does not do so, is prima facie answerable for all the damage which is the natural consequence of its escape. He can excuse himself by showing that the escape was owing to the plaintiff's default; or perhaps that the escape was the consequence of *vis major*, or the act of God; but as nothing of this kind exists here, it is unnecessary to enquire what excuse would be sufficient. The general rule, as above stated, seems on principle just. The person whose grain or corn is eaten down by the escaping cattle of his neighbour, or whose mine is flooded by the water from his neighbour's privy, or whose habitation is made unhealthy by the fumes and noisome vapours of his neighbour's alkali works, is damnified without any fault of his own; and it seems but reasonable and just that the neighbour, who has brought something on to his property which was not naturally there, harmless to others so long as it is confined to his own property, but which he knows to be mischievous if it gets on his neighbour's, should be obliged to make good the damage which ensues if he does not succeed in confining it to his own property. But for his act in bringing it there no mischief could have accrued, and it seems but just that he should at his peril keep it there, so that no mischief may accrue, or answer for the natural and anticipated consequences."

This general principle was approved in the House of Lords,[72] though Lord Chancellor Cairns distinguished between an accumulation of water present in the natural use of the land and non-natural use in the introduction to the land of what in its natural condition was not in or upon it. Lord Cranworth summed up the principle as follows: " If a person brings, or accumulates, on his land anything which, if it should escape, may cause damage to his neighbour, he does so at his peril. If it does escape and cause damage, he is responsible, however careful he may have been, and whatever precautions he may have taken to prevent the damage."

In *Read* v. *Lyons* [73] the House of Lords emphasised that the strict liability imposed by the principle was conditioned by two factors,

[72] (1868) L.R. 3 H.L. 330, 338–339.
[73] [1947] A.C. 156.

" escape " of something likely to do mischief if it escaped from premises of which the defendant had occupation or control to premises outside, and that the defendant had been making a " non-natural " use of the land. The House also declined to recognise any categories of things or operations dangerous in themselves, so as to subject persons dealing with them to strict liability.

The application of Rylands v. Fletcher to Scotland. The consonance of *Rylands* v. *Fletcher* with other principles of the English law of tort is here irrelevant, whether it is a generalisation covering the cases of medieval absolute liability which had survived the moralisation of the law and the shift to liability only for negligence,[74] or liability based on a presumption of negligence.[75] But it has been repeatedly referred to in Scotland, and in *East and South African Telegraph Co.* v. *Cape Town Tramways Co.*,[76] Lord Robertson said, *obiter*: " not only is the principle of *Rylands* v. *Fletcher* fully accepted in Scotland, but it had formed part of the law of Scotland before *Rylands* v. *Fletcher* was decided, and *Rylands* v. *Fletcher* has been treated as an authoritative exposition of law common to both countries." This dictum has been challenged even for South African law [77] and for Scots law is certainly incorrect. However in 1917 Lord Shaw [78] thought that there was no difference on this topic of liability for flooding between the law of Scotland and that of England. This may be true in result but is not so in legal principle. Again in *Miller* v. *Addie & Sons Collieries* [79] Lord Anderson thought that the rule of absolute obligation was part of the common law of Scotland.

But in other Scottish cases *Rylands* v. *Fletcher* has been treated with greater reserve and, though cited,[80] never seems to have been adopted as the sole basis of the decision. In *McLaughlan* v. *Craig* [81] Lord President Cooper warned against the danger of accepting the principle as Scots law, though there were cases in which there was little difference in the result between the application of the English rule of absolute liability and the Scottish rule of *culpa*, where the facts raised a presumption of negligence so compelling as to be practically incapable of being displaced. The

---

[74] Salmond (11th ed.) 643; Wigmore, " Responsibility for Tortious Acts—Its History " (1894) 7 H.L.R. 441; *Selected Essays*, at 77; *Essays in Anglo-American Legal History*, III, 518; Bohlen, *Studies*, 344; Holdsworth, *History of English Law*, VIII, 468–472; *Read* v. *Lyons* [1947] A.C. 156.

[75] Thayer, " Liability without Fault " (1916) 29 H.L.R. 801; *Selected Essays*, 599; Winfield, " The Myth of Absolute Liability " (1926) 42 L.Q.R. 37; *Select Legal Essays*, 15, and *Torts* (5th ed.) 487; Lawson, " Tort in the Civil Law ", 22 J.C.L. (3rd. ser.) 136, 146.

[76] [1902] A.C. 381, 394 (P.C.) quoted in *Reynolds* v. *Lanarkshire Tramways Co.* (1908) 16 S.L.T. 230, 232, *per* Lord Dundas; *Western Silver Fox Ranch* v. *Ross and Cromarty C.C.*, 1940 S.C. 601, 604, *per* Lord Patrick.

[77] Price (1953) 70 South African Law Jl., 381.

[78] *Caledonian Ry.* v. *Greenock Corpn.*, 1917 S.C.(H.L.) 56, 65.

[79] 1934 S.C. 150, 167.

[80] *e.g.*, in *Wilsons* v. *Waddell* (1876) 3 R. 288; *Chalmers* v. *Dixon* (1876) 3 R. 461; *Countess of Rothes* v. *Kirkcaldy Water Works Commrs.* (1879) 6 R. 974; (1882) 9 R.(H.L.) 108; *Miller* v. *Addie's Collieries*, 1934 S.C. 150; *Western Silver Fox Ranch* v. *Ross and Cromarty C.C.*, 1940 S.C. 601. It was ignored in *Pirie* v. *Magistrates of Aberdeen* (1871) 9 M. 412.

[81] 1948 S.C. 599, 611.

medieval rule of English common law that a man acts at his peril revived or surviving in the principle of *Rylands* v. *Fletcher* [82] " has never been part of our law."

The principle of *Rylands* v. *Fletcher* is ill-founded for application in Scotland. The analogies cited by Blackburn J., escaping cattle eating corn,[83] flooding a neighbour's land,[84] the escape of filth,[85] and the escape of fumes [86] have generally been held in Scotland to be based on negligence, albeit negligence may be presumed from the facts.

Conclusion. Reliance on *Rylands* v. *Fletcher* [87] is unnecessary in Scots law in that the corresponding principle of *Kerr* v. *Earl of Orkney*,[88] developed entirely in Scottish cases, is available. The native principle [89] seems capable of application to most, if not all, of the circumstances which seem to justify the imposition of a higher duty of care than normal.

Moreover, other modern systems which have, like Scots law, drawn heavily on Roman law, achieve the result by applying the notion of *culpa* coupled with a presumption of negligence in the circumstances.[90] The basis of the Scottish cases seems to be the imposition of a high standard of care and precaution in the case of innovations on the state of nature, coupled with a ready presumption of fault where harm has resulted. " In the class of cases which fall under what English lawyers call the principle of *Fletcher* v. *Rylands* (sic) negligence is still the ground of liability . . . the proprietor . . . is bound to observe a higher degree of diligence to prevent injury to his neighbour. Hence in such cases the mere occurrence of damage . . . is proof of negligence, and makes him prima facie answerable." [91] The standard is so different from that of merely taking reasonable care that the principle may fairly be regarded as one of risk-liability rather than of fault-liability, though it has developed out of fault-liability.

" *Non-natural* " *use.* The older Scottish cases contain no reference to this qualification on liability, which appeared first in the House of Lords' judgment in *Rylands* v. *Fletcher*,[92] but insist on the introduction of some *novum opus* which has innovated on the natural state of things. There is probably no substantial difference between the two phrases, but both are dangerously vague. What is a *novum opus*, or a non-natural use of

---

[82] (1868) L.R. 3 H.L. 330.
[83] *Robertson* v. *Wright* (1885) 13 R. 174; *Ramage* v. *Carswell*, 1918, 2 S.L.T. 62; 1919, 2 S.L.T. 268.
[84] *Kerr* v. *Earl of Orkney* (1857) 20 D. 298.
[85] *Weston* v. *Tailors of Potterrow* (1839) 1 D. 1218; *Fleming* v. *Gemmill*, 1908 S.C. 340; *N.B. Storage and Transit Co.* v. *Steele's Trs.*, 1920 S.C. 194.
[86] *Chalmers* v. *Dixon* (1876) 3 R. 461.
[87] (1868) L.R. 3 H.L. 330.
[88] (1857) 20 D. 298.
[89] *Kerr* v. *Earl of Orkney* (1857) 20 D. 298.
[90] McKerron (4th ed.) 286; Lawson, *Negligence in the Civil Law*, 43; French Code Civil, Art. 1384; *cf.* Elliott, " What is Culpa? " (1954) 66 J.R. 6.
[91] Bell, *Prin.*, § 970.
[92] (1868) L.R. 3 H.L. 330.

land? In *Chalmers* v. *Dixon*[93] Lord Justice-Clerk Moncreiff distinguished between " the ordinary uses of property, to which a neighbour is bound to submit, although they may cause incidental injury to him, and the construction of an *opus manufactum*, the bringing an article upon the land which creates a hazard which did not exist before." Lord Gifford[94] thought the distinction was between primary and ordinary uses of land, and other uses which were legal but exceptional or occasional, or required special erections upon or special preparation of the subject, and that it was this distinction which resolved the conflict between the two principles *sic utere tuo ut alienum non laedas* and that a man may use his property for any lawful purpose even though he thereby injure his neighbour.

It has been held that the introduction of a piped supply of gas into a house for domestic use is not a non-natural use,[95] and the same applies to domestic water[96] and electricity.[97] Similarly in England there was no strict liability for the fall of a branch of an apparently sound tree,[98] nor for the fall of rocks from an outcrop by natural weathering.[99]

In England[1] in *Rainham Chemical Works* v. *Belvedere Fish Guano Co.*[2] Lord Buckmaster called non-natural use " the use of land in an exceptional manner "; in *Rickards* v. *Lothian*[3] non-natural use was said to be " some special use bringing with it increased danger to others . . . not merely . . . the ordinary use of the land, or such a use as is proper for the general benefit of the community "; and in *Read* v. *Lyons*[4] Viscount Simon confessed " to finding this test of ' non-natural ' user (or of bringing on the land what was not ' naturally there,' which is not the same test) difficult to apply."

Scottish cases since 1868. In Scottish cases subsequent to the decision in *Rylands* v. *Fletcher*[5] that case has frequently been cited, along with the earlier Scottish cases, but rarely, if ever, seems to have been the sole basis of decision but only, at most, a supplementary authority. That case was relied on in *Wilsons* v. *Waddell*[6] but not on the point of strict liability.

---

[93] (1876) 3 R. 461, 464, approved in *Western Silver Fox Ranch* v. *Ross and Cromarty C.C.*, 1940 S.C. 601.

[94] *Ibid.* 467–468.

[95] *Miller* v. *Addie & Sons' Collieries*, 1934 S.C. 150; *McLaughlan* v. *Craig*, 1948 S.C. 599.

[96] *Campbell* v. *Kennedy* (1864) 3 M. 121; *Moffat* v. *Park* (1877) 5 R. 13; *Ross* v. *Fedden* (1872) L.R. 7 Q.B. 661; *Blake* v. *Woolf* [1898] 2 Q.B. 426; *Eastern and S. African Telegraph Co.* v. *Cape Town Tramways Co.* [1902] A.C. 381, 391; *Rickards* v. *Lothian* [1913] A.C. 263, 280; *Miller, supra,* 154, 157, 159.

[97] *Miller, supra,* 159; *McLaughlan, supra,* 611; *cf. Collingwood* v. *Home & Colonial Stores, Ltd.* (1936) 155 L.T. 550.

[98] *Noble* v. *Harrison* [1926] 2 K.B. 332.

[99] *Pontardawe R.D.C.* v. *Moore-Gwyn* [1929] 1 Ch. 656.

[1] See further Bohlen in *Studies in the Law of Torts*, 350; Stallybrass, 3 Camb.L.J. 376.

[2] [1921] 2 A.C. 465, 471.

[3] [1913] A.C. 263, 280, *per* Lord Moulton, an analysis described in *Read* v. *Lyons, infra,* as " of the first importance."

[4] [1947] A.C. 156 (questioned whether making munitions in war-time was non-natural use of land).

[5] (1868) L.R. 3 H.L. 330.

[6] (1876) 3 R. 288; 4 R.(H.L.) 29.

In *Chalmers* v. *Dixon*,[7] it was laid down that *opera manufacta* were only lawful where injury does not happen to neighbours and, though both *Rylands* v. *Fletcher* [5] and *Kerr* v. *Earl of Orkney* [8] were cited in terms suggesting absolute liability, the Lord Justice-Clerk went on to say that *culpa* did lie at the root of the matter. " If a man puts upon his land a new combination of materials, which he knows, or ought to know, are of a dangerous nature, then either care will prevent injury, in which case he is liable if injury occurs for not taking that due care, or else no precautions will prevent injury, in which case he is liable for his original act in placing the materials upon the ground." . . . " Then is it necessary that the danger should be known or anticipated? I think the man who brings new materials upon his land is bound to know the nature of these materials . . . it is not necessary to prove specific fault. Fault is necessarily implied in the result, and it is unnecessary to go further." [9] Lord Gifford also [10] thought that *culpa* was at the foundation of liability. " Much lighter fault may make a person liable in some circumstances than in others. Much greater liability attaches to a person who is using his property not for primary purposes, but for secondary, though lawful purposes, and by which his neighbours may be exposed to risks of damage. . . . A person making such a use of his property [with *opus manufactum* on the land] must take very extraordinary precautions to secure his neighbour against injury."

In *Moffat* v. *Park* [11] the defender's water pipe burst and the water damaged goods in the pursuer's warehouse. Liability was held established on the basis of fault, it being said [12] that *culpa* was essential to liability. " I am anxious to preserve entire the matter of principle, which is far more important than the particular case before us—the rule of law applicable to such cases. In all cases of damage for which reparation is sought I think it may be regarded as the leading principle that the damage or injury must be caused by the *culpa* or fault of the defender. The pursuer must shew that the defender is to blame, by himself or by some one whom he has authorised or allowed to act for him. No claim of damages arises merely from one man's property being injured by another's without *culpa*. There is no liability *ex dominio solo*. The mere fact of an accident occurring is not in itself evidence of *culpa* against anybody, although it may, according to its nature, raise certain inferences or presumptions. You must take an issue of *culpa*, and prove it. The fault, however, may be inferred from circumstances, sometimes from very

---

[7] (1876) 3 R. 461. This action could well have been treated as nuisance, and Nuisance is mentioned in the headnote.

[8] (1857) 20 D. 298.

[9] p. 465, *per* L.J.C. Moncreiff. All the judges were of the view that fault had been established.

[10] p. 468.

[11] (1877) 5 R. 13, following *Weston* v. *Tailors of Potterrow* (1839) 1 D. 1218; *Cleghorn* v. *Taylor* (1856) 18 D. 664; *Campbell* v. *Kennedy* (1864) 3 M. 121; *Reid* v. *Baird* (1876) 4 R. 234.

[12] 15, *per* Lord Ormidale.

slight circumstances, coupled with the fact of the occurrence of the accident, sometimes only from particular circumstances affording in themselves full and distinct evidence." [13]

In *Gemmill's Trs.* v. *Cross*,[14] where acid leaked from the defender's property and damaged the retaining wall of the pursuer's property, Lord Dundas founded directly and solely on *Rylands* v. *Fletcher* as authority for awarding damages.

In *Reynolds* v. *Lanarkshire Tramways Co.*[15] a passenger on an electric tramway car averred that he received an electric shock from a brass rod supporting the canopy of the platform at the end of the car, and that he fell off in consequence and was injured. The Lord Ordinary (Dundas) desiderated proof of fault. Pursuer's counsel founded on *Rylands* v. *Fletcher*, but the Lord Ordinary did not think the principle applicable; its place was in the branch of the law of property which had regard to the rights and liabilities of neighbourhood.

In *Miller* v. *Addie & Sons' Collieries* [16] it was doubted whether *Rylands* v. *Fletcher* had ever been treated in Scotland as a doctrine of absolute liability, and the view was expressed that in those cases to which the doctrine had been held to apply the obligation to take adequate precautions had been so onerous and imperative that the mere occurrence of damage and injury had of itself been sufficient to justify an inference of negligence.

In *Western Silver Fox Ranch* v. *Ross and Cromarty County Council* [17] Lord Patrick took the view that the doctrines of *Kerr* v. *Earl of Orkney* [18] and *Rylands* v. *Fletcher* [19] were the same, and that *Wilsons* [20] and *Chalmers* [21] were decided on the basis that *Rylands* [19] applied to Scotland, and, on the point there in issue, liability for harm caused by explosions, followed *Miles* v. *Forest Rock Granite Co.*,[22] but also held the defender liable on the ground of negligence. He said: " The cases and passages I have referred to above, in my opinion, amply justify the view I have expressed that any person who for his own purposes brings on land and there detonates such a dangerous thing as a considerable quantity of high explosive does so at his peril, and is liable for all the damage which is the natural consequence of the detonation. . . .[23] . . . If a quarrymaster using the utmost care fires a blast in his quarry whereby the skull of a

---

[13] p. 17, *per* Lord Gifford.
[14] (1906) 14 S.L.T. 576.
[15] (1908) 16 S.L.T. 230.
[16] 1934 S.C. 150, 154–155.
[17] 1940 S.C. 601. This case also contained a plea that the pursuers, silver fox farmers, had put their land to a non-natural use, which rests on a misapprehension; it is the *defenders'*, *not* the pursuers', non-natural use of land which is relevant. The true plea is that a pursuer cannot demand a higher standard of care towards him merely because he is using his property in an unusual way.
[18] (1857) 20 D. 298.
[19] (1868) L.R. 3 H.L. 330.
[20] (1876) 4 R.(H.L.) 29.
[21] (1876) 3 R. 461.
[22] (1918) 34 T.L.R. 500.
[23] p. 604.

neighbour is fractured, neither reason nor public policy nor, in my opinion, the law of Scotland dictates that his dependants should not recover damages from the quarrymaster, notwithstanding that they cannot prove the quarrymaster to have been guilty of negligence." [24] This latter passage is possibly questionable; the court would be justified in imposing liability in such a case, it is submitted, only if the circumstances were such as to justify an inference that there was some fault, that the harm was not inevitable, and that there was some precaution which the defender could, and should, have taken which would have avoided the harm.[25]

In *McLaughlan* v. *Craig* [26] the English principle was referred to, but distinguished as inapplicable and unsuitable to the circumstances.

In *Davie* v. *Edinburgh Magistrates* [27] a plea based on *Rylands* v. *Fletcher* was tabled, but not discussed.

Submission. In the result, it is submitted that the principle of strict liability formulated in *Rylands* v. *Fletcher* is not in accordance with the general Scottish principle of liability for *culpa* and has rarely, if ever, been adopted and applied as the sole ground of decision in any Scottish case, but that the principle of strict liability for risk created, formulated in *Kerr* v. *Earl of Orkney* and other Scottish cases, is the sound principle to rely on. This may be formulated as follows: a person who brings into being on his own land some innovation on the natural state of that land which has obvious dangerous potentialities is bound to take exceptional precautions to guard against the risk of its escape, is readily held to have been in fault if it escapes, and is liable for all the harm its escape does to a neighbour's lands. The defences are limited and to that extent the innovator acts at his peril, but his liability is not absolute, but only strict.

It is thought that, as much as in England, the conditions of " escape " and of " non-natural use " must be satisfied for liability to emerge, so that a person injured *on* the defender's property could not invoke the principle, there being no escape,[28] and a person claiming must establish that the use of land was " non-natural," [29] *i.e.* that there had been some innovation on the natural state of the land.

Applications of Scottish strict liability. The classes of cases to which strict liability, *i.e.*, more stringent liability than merely to take reasonable care, is applicable in Scots law are not settled, but are not closed and may be developed by analogy. The early cases all dealt with interferences

[24] p. 605.
[25] *Cf. Paterson* v. *Lindsay* (1885) 13 R. 261.
[26] 1948 S.C. 599.
[27] 1951 S.C. 720 (sequel 1953 S.C. 34).
[28] *Cf. Howard* v. *Furness Houlder Lines, Ltd.* [1936] 2 All E.R. 781; *Read* v. *Lyons* [1947] A.C. 156.
[29] *Miller* v. *Addie & Sons' Collieries*, 1934 S.C. 150; *McLaughlan* v. *Craig*, 1948 S.C. 599; *cf. Read* v. *Lyons* [1947] A.C. 156.

with the natural course of drainage,[30] or the escape of fire,[31] and the court declined to apply strict liability to a burst pipe in a building.[32] Later cases have related to the escape of smoke and fumes [33]; interference with natural drainage [34]; and the detonation of explosives [35]; the court has refused to apply the principle to escapes from domestic gas installations [36] or domestic water supplies.[37]

The *Rylands* v. *Fletcher* [38] principle has been applied in England to such " escapes " of things not naturally on the defendant's land as injury from a falling flagpole,[39] or a chair-o-plane,[40] or damage done by destructive caravan-dwellers.[41]   It is thought that such cases would fall outwith the scope of the corresponding Scottish principle and would be actionable only if negligence were proved.

Other English applications, such as the escape of water or gas being conducted in pipes under the highway,[42] electricity,[43] explosive matter,[44] seem to be cases to which the Scottish principle could be applied.

Some other English cases seem of doubtful value as precedents for the Scottish principle, such as escape of noxious fumes,[45] spoil from a colliery,[46] vibrations,[47] poisonous vegetation,[48] oil,[49] rusty wire from a fence [50]; such cases seem at least as much, if not more, appropriate to nuisance than to strict liability.

It has been indicated in England that the nationalised gas industry cannot fairly be said to collect and distribute gas " for its own purposes " within the rule in *Rylands* v. *Fletcher*, and is accordingly not liable under that rule for damage done by an escape.[51]

Application to moveable as well as heritable property.   It seems that the principle of strict liability applies to harm caused not only to the

---

30 *Samuel*; *Kerr*; *Tennent*; *Potter*; all *supra*; *Rothes* v. *Kirkcaldy Waterworks Commrs.* (1879) 6 R. 974; 9 R.(H.L.) 108.
31 *Mackintosh, supra.*
32 *Campbell, supra*; *Moffat* v. *Park* (1877) 5 R. 13.
33 *Chalmers, supra.*
34 *Caledonian Ry.* v. *Greenock Corpn.*, 1917 S.C.(H.L.) 56.
35 *Western Silver Fox Ranch* v. *Ross and Cromarty C.C.*, 1940 S.C. 601.
36 *Miller, supra*; *McLaughlan, supra.*
37 *Campbell, supra*; *Moffat* v. *Park* (1877) 5 R. 13.
38 (1868) L.R. H.L. 330.
39 *Shiffman* v. *Order of St. John* [1936] 1 All E.R. 557 (negligence also established).
40 *Hale* v. *Jennings Bros.* [1938] 1 All E.R. 579 (claim in negligence failed).
41 *Att.-Gen.* v. *Corke* [1933] Ch. 89.
42 *Charing Cross Electricity Supply Co.* v. *London Hydraulic Power Co.* [1913] 3 K.B. 442; *Northwestern Utilities, Ltd.* v. *London Guarantee Co., Ltd.* [1936] A.C. 108.
43 *National Telephone Co.* v. *Baker* [1893] 2 Ch. 180; *E. & S. African Telegraph Co., Ltd.* v. *Cape Town Tramways, Ltd.* [1902] A.C. 381.
44 *Miles* v. *Forest Rock Granite Co.* (1918) 34 T.L.R. 500; *Rainham Chemical Works* v. *Belvedere Fish Guano Co.* [1921] 2 A.C. 465.
45 *West* v. *Bristol Tramways Co.* [1908] 2 K.B. 14.
46 *Att.-Gen. & Cory Bros.* [1921] 1 A.C. 521.
47 *Hoare & Co.* v. *McAlpine* [1923] 1 Ch. 167.
48 *Crowhurst* v. *Amersham Burial Board* (1878) 4 Ex.D. 5; *Ponting* v. *Noakes* [1894] 2 Q.B. 281.   Contrast *Stewart* v. *Adams*, 1920 S.C. 129.
49 *Smith* v. *G.W.Ry.* (1926) 135 L.T. 122; [1926] All E.R.Rep. 242.
50 *Firth* v. *Bowling Iron Co.* (1878) 3 C.P.D. 254.
51 *Dunne* v. *N.W. Gas Board* [1963] 3 All E.R. 916.

pursuer's heritage such as buildings,[52] but to harm to his moveables on the heritage, such as loss of breeding animals,[53] or damage to vehicles.

Application to personal injuries or death. While there is no clear authority for the proposition, it would seem strange if, in an appropriate case, strict liability for the escape of a dangerous thing from one's land did not apply as much where the interest infringed was personal integrity as to damage to property.[54] *Reynolds* v. *Lanarkshire Tramways Co.*[55] is to a generally contrary effect, and English authorities are contradictory.[56]

Damage by fire. Liability for an escape of fire [57] is certainly strict, as where muirburn spread to an adjacent landowner's woods,[58] or plumbers used a blow-lamp to thaw pipes in the attic and set fire to the neighbour's house.[59]

Damage by flooding. Similar principles apply to flooding, as where a dam has given way,[60] a wall damming up flood water has given way,[61] a railway embankment dammed up and diverted rainwater on to the pursuer's lands,[62] or a culvert proved inadequate to carry away flood water.[63]

Engineering and other operations. Liability for damage caused by adjacent engineering or other operations depends on similar principles. Negligence is readily presumed from the occurrence of damage, provided it can be shown to have been reasonably foreseeable and causally connected with the operations. On this principle damages have been given where a house has been damaged by blasting not far away.[64]

Similar to this group are the cases where defect in one property causes damage to another, as where one house, being ruinous, fell and damaged a neighbouring tenement.[65]

Damage by atomic radiation. It may reasonably be assumed that damage caused by the escape of radio-active materials would fall under the principle. The Nuclear Installations (Licensing and Insurance) Act, 1959, imposes on the licensee of a nuclear site the duty (s. 4) of securing

---

[52] *e.g., Kerr* v. *Earl of Orkney* (1857) 20 D. 298.
[53] *Western Silver Fox Ranch* v. *Ross and Cromarty C.C.*, 1940 S.C. 601.
[54] See further Chap, 17, *supra.*
[55] (1908) 16 S.L.T. 230.
[56] See *Read* v. *Lyons* [1947] A.C. 156, and contrast *Miles* v. *Forest Rock Granite Co.* [1918] 34 T.L.R. 500; *Shiffman* v. *Order of St. John* [1936] 1 All E.R. 557.
[57] Damage by fire which occurs on and does not *escape from* the defender's land depends on ordinary standards of negligence: *Hutchison* v. *Davidson*, 1945 S.C. 395; *Malcolm* v. *Dickson*, 1951 S.C. 542; *Gilmour* v. *Simpson*, 1958 S.C. 477.
[58] *Mackintosh* v. *Mackintosh* (1864) 2 M. 1357.
[59] *Balfour* v. *Barty-King* [1957] 1 All E.R. 156.
[60] *Kerr* v. *Earl of Orkney* (1857) 20 D. 298; see also *Henderson* v. *Stewart* (1818) in 15 S. 868n.
[61] *Tennent* v. *Earl of Glasgow* (1864) 2 M.(H.L.) 22.
[62] *Potter* v. *Hamilton and Strathaven Ry.* (1864) 3 M. 83.
[63] *Caledonian Ry.* v. *Greenock Corpn.*, 1917 S.C.(H.L.) 56.
[64] *Turner* v. *Gibson* (1926) 42 Sh.Ct.Rep. 309; *cf. Davie* v. *Edinburgh Mags.*, 1951 S.C. 720; 1953 S.C. 34; *Western Silver Fox Ranch* v. *Ross and Cromarty C.C.*, 1940 S.C. 601.
[65] *Kay* v. *Littlejohn* (1666) 1 Stair's Dec. 358; Mor. 13974. *Cf. Douglas* v. *Monteith* (1826) 4 Mur. 130; *Callendar* v. *Eddington* (1826) 4 Mur. 108; *Chapman* v. *Parlane* (1825) 3 S. 585; sequel, *Parlane* v. *Binnie* (1825) 4 S. 122; *Cleghorn* v. *Taylor* (1856) 18 D. 664.

that no ionising radiations cause any hurt to any person or any damage to any property, whether that person or property is on the site or elsewhere. The licensee's liability must be covered by insurance (s. 5). Prima facie this is a strict, and may indeed be an absolute, liability, subject to the qualifications contained in the Act itself.[65a]

Liability for independent contractors. In cases to which strict liability applies the defender is liable for the acts and omissions not only of servants but of independent contractors. This was assumed in *Rylands* v. *Fletcher* [66] and has been applied in other cases.[67]

Exceptional sensitivity of pursuer's property. The exceptional sensitivity of the pursuer's use of his own land does not enhance the standard of care incumbent on the defender though it may increase the risk of harm. " A man cannot increase the liabilities of his neighbour by applying his own property to special uses, whether for business or pleasure." [68] This dictum was approved in *Western Silver Fox Ranch* v. *Ross and Cromarty C.C.* [69] but the issue was there confused by the statement [70] that " The ' special use ' of land by a neighbour to which the doctrine of *Rylands* v. *Fletcher* [71] will not apply must be a non-natural use, and I do not regard the use of land for the breeding of silver foxes as a non-natural use of land. . . . In my opinion the damage which occurred in this case was the natural consequence of the defenders' acts, as defined in *Rylands* v. *Fletcher* [71] and was not occasioned by a non-natural use of their land by the pursuers." This introduces a fundamental confusion by using the phrase " non-natural use " of the *pursuers*. This phrase expresses a condition of the defender's liability, but is wholly irrelevant as regards the pursuer; so far as concerns the pursuer the question is not whether his use of his land is " natural " or " non-natural " but whether it is such as to be peculiarly sensitive to harm from the escaping danger, such as scientific apparatus. Even if it is, that goes to damages, not to the defender's liability; as with negligence, strict liability depends so far as concerns culpability on an ordinary standard of sensitivity, but if there is liability for damages, it is for the damage actually suffered, foreseeable by the defender or not.

Exceptions. The principle does not apply to damage resulting from a natural use of land, as contrasted with a non-natural use. Thus if a natural loch on A's land is greatly swollen by very heavy rains and the outflow comes down in spate and damages B's land, A is not liable, having neither created nor accumulated the water, nor being under any duty to

---

[65a] See also Nuclear Installations (Amdt.) Act, 1965.
[66] (1868) L.R. 3 H.L. 330. *Cf. Stewart* v. *Adams*, 1920 S.C. 129.
[67] *Cleghorn* v. *Taylor* (1856) 18 D. 664.
[68] *E. & S. African Telegraph Co., Ltd.* v. *Cape Town Tramways* [1902] A.C. 381, 392, *per* Lord Robertson. *Cf. Hoare & Co.* v. *McAlpine* [1923] 1 Ch. 167.
[69] 1940 S.C. 601, 605.
[70] p. 606.
[71] (1868) L.R. 3 H.L. 330.

take precautions against its escape.[72] And on this ground the principle does not apply to water, gas or electricity in buildings for ordinary domestic purposes, as distinct from these elements in bulk, in mains or reservoirs.[73] It may even be a natural use of land in an industrial community in wartime to build a factory on the land and there manufacture explosives.[74]

Defences in case of strict liability. Strict liability for escape is not absolute and does not by any means exclude all defences. In cases to which the principle applies it is not, however, a relevant defence to show that reasonable precautions were taken to guard against foreseeable harms. That standard of care is not high enough.

The pursuer's own fault is a competent defence.[75] So also is it to establish that there was no " escape " from the defender's lands, or that the innovation was made for the common benefit of both parties [76] or that the pursuer had expressly or impliedly consented to the dangerous operation.[77]

Damnum fatale is a recognised defence [78]; *damnum fatale* connotes " circumstances which no human foresight can provide against, and of which human prudence is not bound to recognise the possibility, and which when they do occur, therefore, are calamities that do not involve the obligation of paying for the consequences that may result from them." [79] This does not cover a great rainfall or even a flood of extraordinary violence, because such must be anticipated from time to time.[80]

The defender is not strictly liable if the proximate cause of the escape and resulting harm is the malicious intervention of a third party,[81] or the negligent interference by a third party of a kind which could not have been foreseen and guarded against.[82] The defender's strict liability includes,

---

[72] *Cf. Smith* v. *Kenrick* (1849) 7 C.B. 515; *Baird* v. *Williamson* (1863) 15 C.B.(N.S.) 376 instanced in *Rylands* v. *Fletcher* (1868) L.R. 3 H.L. 330, 338–339, *per* L.C. Cairns.

[73] *Collingwood* v. *Home & Colonial Stores* [1936] 3 All E.R. 200; *Miller* v. *Addie & Sons' Collieries*, 1934 S.C. 150; *McLaughlan* v. *Craig*, 1948 S.C. 559. *Cf. Rickards* v. *Lothian* [1913] A.C. 263.

[74] *Read* v. *Lyons* [1947] A.C. 156, 169, 173, 187.

[75] *Wilsons* v. *Waddell* (1876) 3 R. 288; *cf. Rylands* v. *Fletcher* (1868) L.R. 3 H.L. 330; *Dunn* v. *Birmingham Canal Co.* (1872) L.R. 7 Q.B. 244; *Read* v. *Lyons* [1947] A.C. 156.

[76] *Carstairs* v. *Taylor* (1871) L.R. 6 Exch. 217; *Prosser* v. *Levy* [1955] 3 All E.R. 577.

[77] *Ross* v. *Fedden* (1872) L.R. 7 Q.B. 661; *Anderson* v. *Oppenheimer* (1880) 5 Q.B.D. 602; *Read, supra.*

[78] *Kerr* v. *Earl of Orkney* (1857) 20 D. 298; *Tennent* v. *Earl of Glasgow* (1864) 2 M.(H.L.) 22; *Potter* v. *Hamilton & Strathaven Ry.* (1864) 3 M. 83, criticised in *Caledonian Ry., infra,* at p. 66; *Pirie* v. *Aberdeen Mags.* (1871) 9 M. 412; *Chalmers* v. *Dixon* (1876) 3 R. 461, 464; *Caledonian Ry.* v. *Greenock Corpn.*, 1917 S.C.(H.L.) 56; *cf. Rylands* v. *Fletcher* (1868) L.R. 3 H.L. 330.

[79] *Tennent* v. *Earl of Glasgow* (1864) 2 M.(H.L.) 22, 26–27, *per* Lord Westbury, approved in *Caledonian Ry.* v. *Greenock Corpn.*, 1917 S.C.(H.L.) 56, 61, 66; *Chalmers, supra,* 465; *cf. Samuel* v. *Edinburgh & Glasgow Ry.* (1851) 13 D. 312, 314; *per* Lord Cockburn.

[80] *Potter, supra; Caledonian Ry., supra;* the defence succeeded in *Nichols* v. *Marsland* (1876) 2 Ex.D. 1, on which see *Caledonian Ry., supra,* at pp. 62–63, and in *Tennent* v. *Earl of Glasgow, supra;* see also *Rothes* v. *Kirkcaldy Waterworks Commrs.* (1879) 6 R. 974 (revd. 9 R.(H.L.) 108).

[81] *Box* v. *Jubb* (1879) 4 Ex.D. 76; *Rickards* v. *Lothian* [1913] A.C. 263.

[82] *Weston* v. *Tailors of Potterrow* (1839) 1 D. 1218.

however, liability for the foreseeable intervention of third parties, such as meddlesome small boys,[83] and for his own servants and invitees.

Statutory authority. Statutory authority to carry out the operation complained of may be a defence, depending on the precise terms of the statutory provision in question.[84] Even statutory powers, if granted after the Act, will not exonerate statutory undertakers from proceedings where damage or injury is caused by the escape of water from a reservoir constructed after the commencement of the Reservoirs (Safety Provisions) Act, 1930.[85]

Harm not caused by the defender's works. If the defender can satisfy the court that the flood or other harm would equally have injured the pursuer's lands even if the defender's works had not been erected he is entitled to escape liability. " The person who constructs an *opus manufactum* on the course of a stream or diverts its flow will be liable in damages, provided the injured proprietor can show—(1) that the *opus* has not been fortified by prescription—and (2) that but for it the phenomena would have passed him scathless." [86]

Fortification by prescription. A pursuer cannot complain if the *novum opus* has been fortified by prescription [87] which means [88] not " that the *opus* is protected by the actual prescription statutes, but that by analogy (as such analogy has been applied in the case of servitudes) the existence of a state of things for the period of the long prescription [89] may serve to prevent any person alleging that another state of things was the true state of nature." This may be the case, *e.g.*, where a stream has long been diverted into another channel, but it is difficult to see how, *e.g.*, a dam built across a stream, can ever be regarded as having become part of the true state of nature.

11. Damage by Game

Damage by game may give rise to claims of damages by tenant against landlord. An agricultural lease is not presumed to carry shooting rights.[90] A reasonable game population is a normal incident of open country and an agricultural tenant cannot complain of a reasonable quantity, though he can complain of an unreasonable amount or an unreasonable increase.[91] He cannot prevent the landlord shooting game, even when

---

[83] *Cf. Hughes* v. *Lord Advocate,* 1963 S.C.(H.L.) 31.
[84] *Cf. Port Glasgow & Newark Sailcloth Co.* v. *Caledonian Ry.* (1893) 20 R.(H.L.) 35; *Green* v. *Chelsea Waterworks Co.* (1894) 70 L.T. 547; *Charing Cross Electricity Co.* v. *Hydraulic Power Co.* [1914] 3 K.B. 772.
[85] s. 8.
[86] Rankine on *Landownership* (4th ed.), 376, approved in *Caledonian Ry.* v. *Greenock Corpn.,* 1917 S.C.(H.L.) 56, 61, 65.
[87] Rankine on *Landownership* (4th ed.), 376, approved in *Caledonian Ry., supra,* 61, 65.
[88] *Caledonian Ry., supra,* 65, *per* Lord Dunedin.
[89] Forty years at the time of this dictum; Qy?, now reduced to twenty years?
[90] *Earl of Hopetoun* v. *Wight,* Jan 17, 1810, F.C.; *Copland* v. *Maxwell* (1868) 9 M.(H.L.) 1.
[91] *Cf. Seligman* v. *Docker* [1948] 2 All E.R. 887.

there is no reservation of game in the lease,[92] nor can he capture them or scare them away,[93] though at common law he might shoot rabbits (which were not game) without consent,[94] unless the landlord has reserved that right [95] or granted it to a shooting tenant.[96] The Ground Game Acts 1880 and 1906, now give the tenant liberty to kill and take hares and rabbits concurrently with any other person entitled to the game on the same land, subject to certain limitations (s. 1).[97] The statutory right conferred on the occupier of the lands is inalienable (s. 2) and any agreement to the contrary is void (s. 3). A tenant has no claim for damage done when he might have prevented it by the exercise of his rights, e.g., to kill rabbits.[98]

A tenant has, however, a good claim for damages if the game population has been materially increased since the date of the lease, in consequence of the landlord's policy of preserving or encouraging game, or his failure to keep down the game,[99] or if the landlord has removed a fence separating the tenant's land from a landlord's plantation full of ground game.[1] It is doubtful whether a tenant or other occupier has a claim for damage to crops caused by an adjacent proprietor keeping an unreasonable stock of game.[2] The tenant's claim may be excluded by a clause in the lease, but such exclusion may be ineffective, if there has been systematic neglect of keeping game within limits or unreasonable encouragement of it.[3] So too a tenant who was entitled by his lease to kill rabbits was held disentitled to damages for damage done by rabbits to waygoing crops unless he could show that he had been prevented from killing them.[4] Exclusion clauses are strictly contrued [5] and a tenant must give sufficient and timeous notice.[6]

A tenant who alleged loss through game damage in seven successive years and made a specific claim for damages was held not barred from

---

[92] Ronaldson v. Ballantine (1804) Mor. 15270; Earl of Hopetoun v. Wight, Jan. 17, 1810, F.C.
[93] Wemyss v. Gulland (1847) 10 D. 204.
[94] Fraser v. Lawson (1882) 10 R. 396; Crawshay v. Duncan, 1915, 2 S.L.T. 13.
[95] Moncrieff v. Arnott (1828) 6 S. 530.
[96] North & George v. Cumming (1864) 3 M. 173.
[97] On failure to observe the conditions of the limitations see Jack v. Nairne (1887) 14 R.(J.) 20; Richardson v. Maitland (1897) 24 R.(J.) 32; Niven v. Renton (1888) 15 R.(J.) 42; Stuart v. Murray (1884) 12 R.(J.) 9; Bruce v. Prosser (1898) 25 R.(J.) 54; Duke of Bedford v. Kerr (1893) 20 R.(J.) 65; McDouall v. Cochrane (1901) 3 F.(J.) 71; Ferguson v. McNab (1885) 12 R. 1083.
[98] Wood v. Paton (1874) 1 R. 868.
[99] Drysdale v. Jamieson (1832) 11 S. 147; Wemyss v. Wilson (1847) 10 D. 194; Broadwood v. Hunter (1855) 17 D. 340, 1139; Morton v. Graham (1867) 6 M. 71; Kidd v. Byrne (1875) 3 R. 255; Cadzow v. Lockhart (1875) 3 R. 666. Cf. Syme v. Earl of Moray (1868) 5 S.L.R. 272. In Wemyss v. Gulland (1847) 10 D. 204, the question was raised whether a tenant could interdict his landlord against increasing the game beyond the average quantity on the farm when he took the lease. See also Seligman v. Docker [1948] 2 All E.R. 887.
[1] Cameron v. Drummond (1888) 15 R. 489. Cf. Ormston v. Hope (1917) 33 Sh.Ct.Rep. 128.
[2] Thomson v. Earl of Galloway, 1919 S.C. 611.
[3] Cadzow v. Lockhart (1876) 3 R. 666; contrast Morton v. Graham (1867) 6 M, 71.
[4] Wood v. Paton (1874) 1 R. 868.
[5] Morton v. Graham, supra; Cadzow, supra.
[6] Broadwood v. Hunter, supra; Emslie v. Young's Trs. (1894) 21 R. 710; Elliott's Trs. v. Elliott (1894) 21 R. 858.

insisting in his claim for the whole period, although he had paid his rent without deduction or reservation of his rights.[7]

Statutory compensation. Under the Agricultural Holdings (Scotland) Act, s. 15, where the tenant of an agricultural holding has sustained damage to his crops from game [*i.e.*, deer, pheasants, partridges, grouse and black game] the right to take and kill which is vested neither in him nor in anyone claiming under him other than the landlord and which the tenant has not permission in writing to kill,[8] he is entitled to compensation from his landlord for the damage if it exceeds one shilling per acre of the area over which it extends.[9] Notice in writing must be given within one month of the end of the calendar year [10] or other period of claim.[11] Failing agreement the amount of compensation is to be determined by arbitration. Where the right to kill and take game is vested in some person other than the landlord, the landlord is entitled to be indemnified by that other person against all claims for compensation under the section,[12] any dispute to be settled by arbitration. The corresponding section of an earlier Act was held applicable where damage was done by winged game which came over from a neighbouring proprietor's lands during a legal close season.[13] The agricultural tenant cannot claim directly against a shooting tenant nor can the latter be a party in his own name to an arbitration at the instance of the agricultural tenant against the landlord.[14]

A tenant is entitled to compensation for damage caused by deer if he has no permission in writing to kill deer.[15]

There appears to be nothing to prevent a tenant from claiming damages at common law from the proprietor of adjacent lands, but he would have to satisfy the court that the game damage he had sustained was, if not entirely, substantially the work of game coming from the adjacent lands, and that their numbers were greater than a normal and reasonable game population.[16] If the agricultural tenant is also tenant of the shooting rights he has no claim against the landlord.[17]

12. USE OF LAND IN AEMULATIONEM VICINI

In Scots law, following Roman law [18] and differing in this respect from English law, use of land which is otherwise lawful may be actionable as

---

[7] *Hardie* v. *Duke of Hamilton* (1878) 15 S.L.R. 329; *cf. Macdonald* v. *Johnstone* (1883) 10 R. 959; *Ramsay* v. *Howison*, 1908 S.C. 697.

[8] Permission to kill one of the enumerated kinds of game excludes a claim for damage by that kind: *Ross* v. *Watson*, 1943 S.C. 406.

[9] If damage exceeds this sum, the full amount may be claimed without deduction: *Roddan* v. *McCowan* (1890) 17 R. 1056.

[10] *Morton's Trs.* v. *McDougall*, 1944 S.C. 406.

[11] *Cf. Broadwood* v. *Hunter* (1855) 17 D. 340, 1139; 18 D. 574; *Elliott's Trs.* v. *Elliott* (1894) 21 R. 858.

[12] *Cf. Kidd* v. *Byrne* (1875) 3 R. 255.

[13] *Thomson* v. *Earl of Galloway*, 1919 S.C. 611.

[14] *Inglis* v. *Moir's Tutors* (1871) 10 M. 204.

[15] *Lady Auckland* v. *Dowie*, 1964 S.L.T.(Land Ct.) 20; 1965 S.L.T.(Notes) 2.

[16] *Cf. Inglis, supra*; *Cameron* v. *Drummond* (1888) 15 R. 489.

[17] *Sutherland* v. *Secretary of State for Scotland* (1942) 30 L.C. 26, 30.

[18] Dig. 39, 3, 1; Nov. 63, 1.

wrongful if the predominant motive for the use in question is the harm
of a neighbour, the gratification of spite, or other oblique motive. This
is known as the use of land *in aemulationem vicini.* " The chief restraint
imposed by law upon the use of property is, that the proprietor shall
not use it *in aemulationem vicini*—that is, that he shall not apply it to
any use which, without producing any substantial benefit to himself,
shall materially injure his neighbour." [19]   No one is entitled to act
wantonly, with the mere purpose of producing inconvenience and loss
to his neighbour; he may not act from mere spite or malice.[20]   The
principle has been accepted in the institutional writers [21] and many older
cases.[22] The doctrine applies only to active use by a proprietor and not
to his resistance to another.[23]

In *Young* v. *Bankier Distillery Co.*[24] *aemulatio vicini* was treated as a
qualification of the rule that an inferior heritor had to accept without
complaint the gravitational flow of water, on or below ground, from
higher ground.

In *Mayor of Bradford* v. *Pickles,*[25] however, where a landowner had
works done on his own land which diverted percolating water from
flowing to adjacent land from which a water authority drew water, and
it was held that his actings were not unlawful even if done with the sole
object of compelling the authority to acquire rights in his land and the
water thereunder, Lord Watson observed,[26] with reference to an argument
founding on Scots law, that he knew " of no case in which the act of a proprietor has been found to be illegal, or restrained as being *in aemulationem,*
where it was not attended with offence or injury to his neighbour. In
cases of nuisance a degree of indulgence has been extended to certain
operations, such as burning limestone, which in law are regarded as
necessary evils. If a landowner proceeded to burn limestone close to his
march, so as to cause annoyance to his neighbour, there being other
places on his property where he could conduct the operation with equal,
or greater convenience to himself, and without giving cause of offence,
the court would probably grant an interdict.[27] But the principle of
aemulatio has never been carried further. The law of Scotland, if it
differs in that, is in all other respects the same as the law of England.

---

[19] More, *Lect.,* I, 608–609.
[20] Bell, *Prin.,* § 964, 966.
[21] Bankt., I, 10, 40; II, 7, 15; IV, 45, 112; Ersk., II, 1, 2; Kames, *Equity,* 41–42; Bell, *Prin.,*
§ 964, 966. See also Hume, *Lect.,* III, 207; More, *Lect.,* I, 608.
[22] *Brodie* v. *Cadel* (1707) 4 B.S. 660; *Fairly* v. *Earl of Eglinton* (1744) Mor. 12780; *Trotter*
v. *Hume* (1757) Mor. 12798; *Gray* v. *Maxwell* (1762) Mor. 12800; *Dewar* v. *Fraser* (1767)
Mor. 12803; *Kelso* v. *Boyds* (1768) Mor. 12807; *Ralston* v. *Pettigrew* (1768) Mor. 12808;
Glasgow Mags. v. *Bell* (1776) 5 B.S. 598; *Hamilton* v. *Edington* (1793) Mor. 12824; *Glassford*
v. *Astley* (1808) Mor. Appx. Property, No. 7; *Ross* v. *Baird* (1829) 7 S. 361; *Ritchie* v.
Purdie (1832) 11 S. 771; *Irving* v. *Leadhills Mining Co.* (1856) 18 D. 833.
[23] *Graham* v. *Greig* (1838) 1 D. 171, 177.
[24] (1893) 20 R.(H.L.) 76, 77.
[25] [1895] A.C. 587, 597.
[26] Dissenting from the observations on Scots law made, *obiter,* by Lord Wensleydale in
Chasemore v. *Richards* (1859) 7 H.L.Cas. 349, 388.
[27] Did Lord Watson have in mind *Dewar* v. *Fraser* (1767) Mor. 12803?

No use of property which would be legal if due to a proper motive can become illegal because it is prompted by a motive which is improper, or even malicious." This passage in an English appeal, is *obiter* for Scots law and cannot be accepted as sound in face of the institutional and other authoritative writings. It is submitted that it is a misstatement of Scots law, and the case then before the House would properly have been decided otherwise in both Roman [28] and Scots [29] law. Moreover in *Campbell* v. *Muir* [30] the First Division held that a proprietor of salmon-fishings had acted *in aemulationem vicini*, in fishing so as to interfere with an angler fishing for salmon from the opposite bank, and that she was not entitled to do so and interdict was competent if she insisted in doing so. " I come to the result . . . that the defender was on the particular occasion acting *in aemulationem vicini* against his neighbour's right, and that that was a just ground for complaint."

To bring a case within the principle of *aemulatio vicini* it is necessary to show that the predominant, if not the sole, motive for the defender's conduct was not the protection or furtherance of his own legitimate interests but some other factor, [31] and that some loss to the pursuer has resulted. " The *animus* of the proprietor must be gathered, in every case, from its whole circumstances; and the rule shall apply, wherever the malicious and unsocial purpose is palpable, upon the whole, to common apprehension." [32]

Thus where a party erected certain buildings on his own land she was ordained to remove them to a different situation, [33] but where a limekiln could not without great inconvenience have been sited elsewhere it could not be complained of, whatever injury it might occasion to a neighbour or his property. [34] It is not objectionable under this principle to build a wall to protect the privacy of a garden against being overlooked by a neighbour's house. [35]

13. UNINTENTIONAL DAMAGE TO HERITAGE

Unintentional damage can be caused to heritage in countless ways, by trespass by persons or animals, by the negligent management of railways, road vehicles, [36] ships or aircraft, by fire [37] or flooding. [38] The basis of the

[28] Dig. 39, 3, 1.
[29] Kames, *Equity*, 1.
[30] 1908 S.C. 387, 393, *per* L.P. Dunedin. *Cf. MacInnes* v. *Macdonald* (1925) 42 Sh.Ct.Rep. 213.
[31] *Cf. Crofter Hand Woven Harris Tweed Co.* v. *Veitch*, 1942 S.C.(H.L.) 1. See also *Somerville* v. *Somerville* (1613) Mor. 12769.
[32] Hume, *Lect.*, III, 208.
[33] *Ralston* v. *Pettigrew* (1768) Mor. 12808; *Ross* v. *Baird* (1829) 7 S. 361.
[34] *Dewar* v. *Fraser* (1767) Mor. 12803.
[35] *Dunlop* v. *Robertson* (1803) Hume, 515; *Glassford* v. *Astley* (1808) Hume 516; *cf. Donald* v. *Esslemont & Macintosh*, 1923 S.C. 122.
[36] *Terras* v. *Alexander* (1952) 68 Sh.Ct.Rep. 225; *N. of Scotland Hydro-Electric Board* v. *Townsley* (1952) 68 Sh.Ct.Rep. 137.
[37] *Cf. Marshall* v. *R.O.P., Ltd.*, 1938 S.C. 773; *Gilmour* v. *Simpson*, 1958 S.C. 477.
[38] *Cf. Brownlie* v. *Barrhead Mags.*, 1925 S.C.(H.L.) 41; *Duke of Portland* v. *Wood's Trs.*, 1927 S.C.(H.L.) 1.

claim in every case is negligence, nuisance or strict liability, but certain special considerations attach to each of these kinds of unintentional damage. Structural injury to buildings by vibration, as distinct from nuisance to the comfortable enjoyment of premises, was alleged in *Maguire* v. *Charles McNeil, Ltd.*[39] but was held not established.

In *Cameron* v. *Fraser* [40] a shopkeeper was held entitled to damages where building operations were carried out on an adjacent tenement so as unnecessarily to cause substantial injury to the business of the shop. It is even clearer that there is liability where such operations have caused actual damage to the fabric of the pursuer's heritage.[41] " An operation carried on by a proprietor within burgh, which is either in its own nature unlawful, or which, though lawful in itself, is executed in a reckless, unskilful or negligent manner, whereby injury is done to his neighbour, is a wrong in law for which reparation is due. Nay, where the work is of a delicate or difficult description and likely to imperil the neighbour's tenement, the proprietor who undertakes it is bound in more exact diligence, and will be answerable for any want of due care and attention to the rights and interests of his neighbour which has been productive of damage, and the amount of care and attention required in the particular case, and the extent to which it has been neglected will always be a question for the jury on the evidence. But the principle is clear. There must be fault, or, in other words, delinquency or wrong, on the part of the defender of the action of reparation to render him liable to the pursuer in damages." [42]

Railways. A railway may be operated in such a way as to be a legal nuisance to persons occupying adjacent premises, or negligently, whereby damage befalls adjacent property, as where a wagon is derailed and runs into a building.

Railway fires. Damage is frequently done by fires caused by the escape of sparks from railway engines. At common law, where a railway is run under statutory authority, the railway authority's duty is to use the best possible type of spark arrester and it is not liable for sparks which the spark arrester has failed to catch.[43] The pursuer, that is, must prove negligence in the construction and use of the engine.[44]

Where the operation of the engines was not covered by statutory authority it has been held that inevitable accident was no defence to actions for fire-damage caused by sparks.[45]

[39] 1922 S.C. 174.
[40] (1881) 9 R. 26.
[41] *Laurent* v. *Lord Advocate* (1869) 7 M. 607.
[42] *Ibid.* 610–611, *per* L.P. Inglis, explaining *Callander* v. *Eddington* (1826) 4 Mur. 108; *Douglas* v. *Monteith* (1826) 4 Mur. 130; and *Cleghorn* v. *Taylor* (1856) 18 D. 664. See also *McIntosh* v. *Scott* (1859) 21 D. 368.
[43] *Vaughan* v. *Taff Vale Ry.* (1860) 5 H. & N. 679; *Murdoch* v. *G.S.W.Ry.* (1870) 8 M. 768; *Port Glasgow and Newark Sailcloth Co.* v. *Caledonian Ry.* (1893) 20 R.(H.L.) 35.
[44] *Parker* v. *L.N.E.Ry.* (1945) 175 L.T. 137; *Sellwood* v. *L.M.S.Ry.* (1945) 175 L.T. 366; see also *Campbell* v. *L.M.S.Ry.* [1948] C.L.Y. 4689.
[45] *Jones* v. *Festiniog Ry.* (1868) L.R. 3 QB. 733; *Powell* v. *Fall* (1880) 5 Q.B.D. 597 (traction engine); *Mansel* v. *Webb* [1918] 88 L.J.K.B. 323.

Under the Railway Fires Acts, 1905 and 1923, the railway authority is liable for damage caused to agricultural land, defined as including market-gardens, plantations and woods, orchards and fences, but not moorland or buildings, to an amount not exceeding £200 in each case, provided written notice of the fire and of the intention to claim is given within seven days of the damage and of the amount of claim within twenty-one days. In such a claim proof of the causal connection and of the extent of damage is required, but not of negligence on the part of the railway authority. A claim for common law negligence may be conjoined with a claim for statutory compensation.[46] Common law defences are probably open.[47]

Road vehicles. If heritable property is destroyed or damaged by a road vehicle, as where one runs off the road and damages the heritable property, liability depends on ordinary principles of negligence,[48] though where a vehicle runs off the road it raises a presumption of negligence in the management of the vehicle. Alternatively liability may be founded on nuisance.[49] In *Glasgow Corporation* v. *Barclay Curle & Co.*[50] the pursuers as road authority claimed at common law from the defenders the cost of repairing a street alleged to have been broken down by the defenders having run excessively heavy traffic over it. The claim failed as the evidence did not establish negligence on the defenders' part. But the competency of interdict or damages is undoubted, if the defender be shown to have been guilty of some negligence which resulted in destroying or restricting the public's right of passage on the highway.

Ships. A claim may be brought at common law for damage done to a harbour by a ship, but negligence must be proved.[51] Under the Harbours, Docks and Piers Clauses Act, 1847, s. 74, incorporated in special Harbour Acts, the owner of a vessel is liable to the harbour undertakers for any damage [52] done by such vessel or any person employed about her to the harbour, dock or pier or the quays or works connected therewith, independently of fault,[53] and the master, through whose wilful act or negligence any such damage is done, is also liable to make good the damage.[54] The harbour undertakers have a possessory lien under the same section over the vessel in respect of the damage done to the dock property.[55]

The owners were held not liable where the damage was occasioned by a vessel driven on to a pier by the extraordinary violence of a storm after the master and crew had had to abandon her and had consequently

---

[46] *Att.-Gen.* v. *G.W.Ry.* [1924] 2 K.B. 1; *Langlands (Swanley)* v. *B.T.C.* [1956] 2 All E.R. 702; see also *Gracey* v. *G.N.R.I.* (1950) 85 I.L.T. 179.

[47] *Groom* v. *G.W.Ry.* (1892) 8 T.L.R. 253, 256.

[48] *Grahamslaw* v. *Veitch's Trs.*, 1923 S.L.T. 162; *cf. Moss* v. *Christchurch R.D.C.* [1925] 2 K.B. 750; *Hutchison* v. *Davidson*, 1945 S.C. 395 (cottage burned by fire caused by passing traction engine).

[49] *Slater* v. *A. & J. McLellan*, 1924 S.C. 854.   [50] 1923 S.C.(H.L.) 78.

[51] *Clyde Navigation Trust* v. *Kelvin Shipping Co.*, 1927 S.C. 622, 626.

[52] Physical damage to the *opera manufacta* of the undertaking: *Workington Harbour Board* v. *Towerfield (Owners)* [1951] A.C. 112.

[53] *G.W.Ry.* v. *S.S. Mostyn* [1928] A.C. 57.

[54] *Cf. Baron Vernon* v. *Metagama*, 1927 S.C. 498.

[55] *The Countess* [1923] A.C. 345.

no control over the vessel,[56] nor in case of inevitable accident.[57] No liability attaches where the ship has been abandoned and is out of the control of its owners.[58] Liability is only for physical damage to harbour works, not for consequential loss of revenue.[59]

The sinking of a vessel in a lock or dock may cause an obstruction in a harbour without doing any physical damage; if so, the cost of removing it is recoverable, and possibly damages for loss of use of the dock, but not damages for injury thereto.[60]

Under the Merchant Shipping (Liability of Shipowners and Others) Acts, 1900 and 1958, the right of limiting liability for damages to vessels and goods under the Merchant Shipping Act, 1894, ss. 503–504, applies also to damage caused to property of any kind whether on land or water, and whether the liability arises at common law or under statute, and despite anything in the statute. Thus where a vessel had crashed through dock gates these provisions applied to limit liability.[61] The provisions for limiting liability formerly did not apply where there was merely an obstruction of the harbour and not injury thereto,[62] but now the 1958 Act, s. 2 (2) has provided that liability arising in connection with the raising, removal or destruction of any ship which is sunk, stranded or abandoned or of anything on board such a ship, or in respect of any damage however caused to harbour works, basins or navigable water-ways, is to be treated as a liability for damages, and it can accordingly now be limited as provided in the 1894 Act, ss. 503–504, as amended by the 1958 Act, ss. 1 and 2.

Aircraft. At common law there was doubtless liability for damage caused to property by the careless mismanagement of an aircraft, provided negligence could be established.[63] The principle of *res ipsa loquitur* seems applicable in most cases.

The Civil Aviation Act, 1949, s. 40 (2), provides that where material loss or damage is caused to any person or property on land or water by, or by a person in, or an article or person falling from, an aircraft while in flight, taking off or landing, then unless the loss or damage was caused or contributed to by the negligence of the person by whom it was suffered, damages in respect of the loss or damage shall be recoverable without proof of negligence or intention or other cause of action, as if the loss or damage had been caused by the wilful act, neglect or default of the owner of the aircraft.

---

[56] *River Wear Commissioners* v. *Adamson* (1877) 2 App.Cas. 743.
[57] *The Boucan* [1909] P. 163. But see *Dennis* v. *Tovell* (1872) L.R. 8 Q.B. 10.
[58] *G.W.Ry.* v. *S.S. Mostyn* [1928] A.C. 57.
[59] *Workington Harbour Board* v. *Towerfield (Owners), supra.*
[60] *The Stonedale No. 1* [1954] P. 338. See also *Greenock Harbour Trs.* v. *B.O.C.M., Ltd.,* 1944 S.C. 70 (crane falling into dock).
[61] *Mersey Docks and Harbour Board* v. *Hay* [1923] A.C. 345; *The City of Edinburgh* [1921. P. 274; *The Ruapehu* [1927] A.C. 523; [1929] P. 305; *Hamilton* v. *B.T.C.*, 1957 S.C. 300]
[62] *Clifton Steam Trawlers, Ltd.* v. *Duncan MacIver, Ltd.,* 1953 S.L.T. 230; *The Stonedale No. 1* [1956] A.C. 1.
[63] *Fosbroke-Hobbes* v. *Airwork, Ltd.* [1937] 1 All E.R. 108; *cf. Billings* v. *Reed* [1944] 2 All E.R. 415, 417.

By s. 61, as applied by s. 49 (3), this section is rendered inapplicable to aircraft belonging to or exclusively employed in the service of Her Majesty, though Her Majesty may by Order in Council apply these provisions to any such aircraft, with or without modification.

This statutory remedy appears to be applicable against all aircraft over which and whose owners the Scottish courts can exercise jurisdiction, independently of the nationality of the aircraft. The action lies against the owner but s. 40 (2) provides further that " where material loss or damage is caused as aforesaid in circumstances in which—(a) damages are recoverable in respect of the said loss or damage by virtue only of the foregoing provisions of this subsection; and (b) a legal liability is created in some person other than the owner to pay damages in respect of the said loss or damage; the owner shall be entitled to be indemnified by that other person against any claim in respect of the said loss or damage ". This appears to cover the case of a plane operated under charter, or on loan. By s. 49 (2), where an aircraft has been bona fide demised, let or hired out for longer than fourteen days and no operative member of the crew is in the employment of the owner, the provisions apply to the hirer as they would to the owner.

Insurance and limitation of liability. The Civil Aviation Act, 1949, s. 43, imposes on operators of aircraft an obligation to have in force a third-party insurance policy, and s. 42 provides for the limitation of a defender's liability unless it is proved that the loss or damage caused was attributable to wilful misconduct.

Special protection for certain kinds of property. Statute has conferred special protection on particular kinds of property.

The Telegraph Act, 1878, s. 8, gives the Postmaster-General a right to recover for destruction of or injury to any telegraphic line, in addition to the common law right to damages, though only one remedy may be utilised.[64]

The Electric Lighting Act, 1882, s. 17, imposes on electricity undertakings the duty of making compensation for all damage done by reason or in consequence of the exercise of the statutory powers.

The Gas Act, 1948, Sched. III, para. 29, provides that, apart from criminal sanctions, a Gas Board may recover the amount of any damage caused them by a person injuring any pipes, meter or fittings.

14. MALICIOUS DAMAGE TO LAND

Malicious damage to lands or buildings is more commonly dealt with criminally but is undoubtedly also delictual, damages being recoverable for the damage done. It is not necessary that the harm was actually intended or desired, so long as the conduct is deliberate and gives rise to actual, or reasonable apprehension of, harm to the pursuer's lands.

An owner of heritage is entitled to complain if the conduct of a neighbour is calculated to harm his lands and interfere with his use of them.

[64] See also *Lord Advocate* v. *Carmichael*, 1953 S.L.T.(Notes) 12.

Thus he has an action if his neighbour directs superfluous water onto his lands.[65]

In *Durham* v. *Hood*,[66] a mineral tenant deliberately sank a pit near his march and exploded charges of powder to get rid of water, which flooded the workings of a lower heritor; the latter was held entitled to interdict, the explosions being calculated to dislocate the coal strata and giving reasonable grounds for apprehension of flooding.

Riot damage. At common law no action lay against the magistrates of a burgh for damages in respect of injury to the property of an individual citizen caused by a riotous assembly [67] within the burgh. The only remedy would be against the individual rioters for the damage done by them. A statutory right of action for damages for loss caused by riot was introduced by the Riot Act, 1714.[68]

The Malicious Damage Act, 1812 [69]; the Malicious Damage (Scotland) Act, 1816 [70]; The Seditious Meetings Act, 1817 [71]; and the Riotous Assemblies (Scotland) Act, 1822,[72] make further similar provisions.[73] The statutory provisions must be closely followed [74] and the claim is competent only to the party injured or damnified, not to an insurer who has compensated the party who has suffered.[75]

The measure of damages is indicated in the statutory provisions as the full value of the property damaged, stolen or destroyed.[76] Loss of profits is probably consequential and too remote to be recoverable.[77]

15. MISUSE OF LAND LEASED

The relationship of landlord and tenant gives rise to a right on the landlord's part to recover damages from the tenant for any misuse of the land or premises leased by the tenant, whether the damage is caused intentionally or negligently.

Urban leases. A tenant is bound to take reasonable care of the subjects of let and not to damage them negligently.[78] If he does so he is

---

[65] Ersk., II, 9, 2; Bell, *Prin.*, § 968; Hume, *Lect.*, III, 209; *Montgomerie* v. *Buchanan's Trs.* (1853) 15 D. 853; *Campbell* v. *Bryson* (1864) 3 M. 254.

[66] (1871) 9 M. 474.

[67] As to such an assembly see also *Munday* v. *Metropolitan Police District Receiver* [1949] 1 All E.R. 337.   [68] s. 6 (repealed).

[69] ss. 3–4.

[70] ss. 2–3.

[71] s. 38.

[72] s. 10.

[73] Note that the limitations on the time within which actions for damages might be brought under these Acts have been removed by the Law Reform (Limitation of Actions) Act, 1954, s. 6 (4).

[74] *Scottish Plate Glass Insurance Corpn.* v. *Edinburgh Corpn.*, 1941 S.C. 115; *Capaldi* v. *Greenock Mags.*, 1941 S.C. 310; *Pompa's Trs.* v. *Edinburgh Mags.*, 1942 S.C. 119; *Coia* v. *Robertson*, 1942 S.C. 111.

[75] *Scottish Plate Glass Insurance Corpn.*, *supra*.

[76] *Coia*, *supra*, at p. 113; *Pompa's Trs.*, *supra*, at p. 120.   [77] *Capaldi*, *supra*, at p. 315.

[78] *Sutherland* v. *Robertson* (1736) Mor. 13979; *Hardie* v. *Black* (1768) Mor. 10133; *McLellan* v. *Ker* (1797) Mor. 10134; *Whitelaw* v. *Fulton* (1871) 10 M. 27; *Earl of Mansfield* v. *Caird* (1884) 21 S.L.R. 720; *Smith* v. *Henderson* (1897) 24 R. 1102; *Turner's Trs.* v. *Steel* (1900) 2 F. 363; *Mickel* v. *McCoard*, 1913 S.C. 896.

liable in damages measured by the damage to the value of the landlord's interest,[79] of which the cost of the repairs may be evidence.[80]

A tenant may be ejected from premises to which the Rent Acts apply without proof of suitable alternative accommodation if the condition of the house has been deteriorated by the tenant.[81] The Housing (Scotland) Act, 1950, s. 162, subjects to a penalty a person who wilfully or by culpable negligence damages or suffers to be damaged any house provided under that Act, without prejudice to any remedy for the recovery of the amount of damage.

Agricultural leases. An agricultural tenant must maintain fixed equipment of a farm in as good a state of repair (natural decay and fair wear and tear excepted) as when repaired, replaced or renewed by the landlord.[82] Compensation may be claimed on the tenant's quitting the holding or on the termination of the tenancy for any dilapidation or deterioration of, or damage to, any part of the holding,[83] and damages may be claimed for the tenant's failure to maintain the equipment in a proper state of repair.[84]

A claim may be brought at common law against a tenant for damages for miscropping during the currency of the lease; unlike an issue arising out of the termination of the tenancy this is a common law claim and does not fall to be referred to arbitration.[85] Such a claim may be barred by acquiescence.[86] A claim also lies under statute for compensation for deterioration.[87]

16. INCORPOREAL HERITABLE RIGHTS

Incorporeal rights of a heritable character may also require protection against infringement, usually by interdict. Thus interdict has been granted to restrain an infringement of the right of ferry.[88] Wrongfully assuming another's coat of arms is a real injury punishable by fine or imprisonment,[89] but there would seem no reason why it should not also be civilly actionable for interdict or damages.[90]

---

79 *Conquest* v. *Ebbetts* [1896] A.C. 490; *Gooderham* v. *C.B.C.* [1947] A.C. 66; *Smiley* v. *Townshend* [1950] 2 K.B. 311; see also *Whitelaw, supra*; *Campbell* v. *McLachlan's Exor.* (1944) 61 Sh.Ct.Rep. 86; *Jones* v. *Herxheimer* [1950] 2 K.B. 106.

80 *Campbell* v. *McLachlan's Exor.* (1944) 61 Sh.Ct.Rep. 86; see also *Whitelaw* v. *Fulton* (1871) 10 M. 27; *Hutchison* v. *Davidson*, 1945 S.C. 395.

81 Rent, etc., Restrictions Act, 1933, s. 3 and Sched. I, para. (*b*); *cf. Peach* v. *Lowe* [1947] 1 All E.R. 441; *Northampton Trs.* v. *Bond* [1950] C.L.Y. 3450; *Yates* v. *Morris* [1951] 1 K.B. 77.

82 Agricultural Holdings (Sc.) Act, 1949, s. 5 (2).

83 *Ibid.* s. 57 (1).

84 *Cf. Munro* v. *Fraser* (1858) 21 D. 103.

85 *Westwood* v. *Barnett*, 1925 S.C. 624.

86 *Taylor* v. *Duff's Trs.* (1869) 7 M. 351; *Baird* v. *Mount* (1874) 2 R. 101; *Lamb* v. *Mitchell's Trs.* (1883) 10 R. 640.

87 *Adam* v. *Smythe*, 1948 S.C. 446.

88 *L.M.S.Ry.* v. *McDonald*, 1924 S.C. 835.

89 Mack., *Works*, II, 170; Ersk., IV, 4, 81.

90 Ersk., *Prin.*, 752–754; Innes of Learney, *Scots Heraldry*, 230–231.

CHAPTER 28

INFRINGEMENTS OF INTERESTS IN CORPOREAL MOVEABLE PROPERTY

1. Spuilzie
2. Deliberate Damage to Goods
3. Unintentional Damage to Goods
4. Damage to Animals
5. Damage to Vehicles
6. Damage to Ships
7. Damage to Aircraft
8. Liability for Loss of Goods

CORPOREAL moveable property includes a wide range of things all of which have a corporeal tangible corpus capable of physical possession and the legal interests which may subsist in such things, ownership and possession, may be infringed in many different ways, by taking away from the legitimate owner or possessor, by withholding or failing to return, by selling by mistake, by damaging deliberately or carelessly, and so on.

1. SPUILZIE

The action of spuilzie, comparable to the Roman *actio vi bonorum raptorum* [1] lies where a person in lawful possession of goods has been unjustifiably dispossessed. [2] Spuilzie is " the taking away of moveables without consent of the owner or order of law, obliging to restitution of the things taken away, with all possible profits, or to reparation therefor according to the estimation of the injured made by his *juramentum in litem*. Thus, things stolen or robbed, though they might be criminally pursued for as theft or robbery, yet they may be also civilly pursued for as spuilzie." [3]

It is " the violent seizing, or unlawful taking possession of goods from another, without his consent or order of law, for lucre's sake." [4] It is said to be distinguished from theft by the goods being openly carried away under the pretence of some right or title, and not clandestinely or violently, as in the case of theft or robbery, [5] but conduct amounting criminally to theft would equally support a civil action of spuilzie. [6]

The action of damages for spuilzie is in substance a remedy for failure of a person who comes to be in possession of goods, the possession of

[1] Craig, *J.F.*, II, 11, 30; *cf.* II, 17, 25.
[2] More, *Lect.*, I, 358.
[3] Stair, I, 9, 16.
[4] Bankt., I, 10, 124; *cf.* Ersk., III, 7, 16; IV, 1, 15.
[5] More, *Lect.*, I, 359.
[6] *Kincaid* v. *Muirhead* (1682) Mor. 14752.

which he is not entitled to retain, to implement his quasi-contractual obligation to restore them to the person truly entitled thereto.[7]

The action seeks restitution of the thing spuilzied or damages measured by its value, and also violent profits, formerly estimated by the pursuer's oath *in litem*.[8] " When a spuilzie is committed, action lies against the delinquent, not only for restoring to the former possessor the goods or their value, but for all the profits he might have made of these goods had it not been for the spuilzie. These profits are estimated by the pursuer's own oath, and get the name of violent, because they are due in no other case than of violence or wrong." [9]

Spuilzie like theft attaches a *vitium reale* to goods concerned, so that they may be recovered from even bona fide purchasers.[10]

Pursuer's title. The pursuer need only prove lawful physical possession or custody, not necessarily ownership nor even any legal title to possess [11]; he " need prove no more than that he was in the lawful possession of the subject libelled, which gives him a right to be *ante omnia* restored to the possession; for the action is grounded on the plain principle, that no man is to be stripped of his possession but by the order of law." [12] Thus an executor, though unconfirmed, may recover the deceased's property.[13] The action may lie even against the true owner of goods, as where he has pledged goods and unwarrantably attempts to seize them from the pledgee.[14]

Requisites of action. The action lies *in solidum* [15] against any possessors [16] of the goods, or even a *bona fide* purchaser of spuilzied goods, because, like cases of theft, a *vitium reale* attaches to spuilzied goods which is not elided by such transfer.[17] Thus it lies against those taking delivery of or resetting or harbouring spuilzied goods.[18] But if the pursuer transacts with one of the guilty parties, all the rest are freed.[19]

---

[7] *Cf.* Bell, *Prin.*, § 527.

[8] More, I, 358. *Cf. Kelwood* v. *Cassillis* (1576) Mor. 14746; *Balmains* v. *Balvaird* (1583) Mor. 14746.

[9] Ersk., III, 7, 16; *cf.* Stair, I, 9, 16; *Lord Justice-Clerk* v. *Hume* (1668) Mor. 13985.

[10] Stair, *supra*; *Hay* v. *Leonard* (1677) Mor. 10286.

[11] Stair, I, 9, 17; IV, 26, 2; Ersk., IV, 1, 15; *Ogilvie* v. *Restalrig* (1541) Mor. 14730; *Dundas* v. *Hog* (1543) Mor. 14731; *Montgomery* v. *Hamilton* (1548) Mor. 14731; *Merchiston* v. *Napier* (1549) Mor. 14731; *Gadzeard* v. *Ayr* (1581) Mor. 14732; *Renton* v. *Her Son* (1629) Mor. 14733; *Maxwell* v. *Maxwell* (1676) Mor. 14729; *Falconer* v. *Burnet* (1724) Mor. 14734; *McDowal* v. *McDowal* (1822) 1 W. & Sh. 22. See also *Durie* v. *Duddingston* (1549) Mor. 14735; *Douglas* v. *Young* (1613) Mor. 14736; *Crawford* v. *Faill* (1614) Mor. 14737; *Mudiall* v. *Frissal* (1628) Mor. 14749.

[12] Ersk., IV, 1, 15.

[13] *Douglas* v. *McCubin* (1619) Mor. 14732; *Russel* v. *Kerse* (1626) Mor. 14733.

[14] Ersk., IV, 1, 15; More, *Lect.*, I, 358.

[15] Stair, I, 9, 17; IV, 30, 3; Ersk., IV, 1, 15; Bankt., I, 10, 130; *Douglas* v. *Young* (1613) Mor. 10507; *Strachan* v. *Morison* (1668) Mor. 14709; *Stove* v. *Colvin* (1831) 9 S. 633.

[16] *Cf. Maxwel* v. *Maxwels* (1676) Mor. 14729.

[17] Stair, I, 9, 16; Bankt., I, 10, 130; *Hay* v. *Leonard* (1677) Mor. 10286. *Cf. Todd* v. *Armour* (1882) 9 R. 901.

[18] *Cowgrane* (1609) Mor. 379, 14707; *Earl of Roxburgh* v. *Langtoun* (1628) Mor. 379.

[19] *Douglas* v. *Leich* (1611) cit. Stair, I, 9, 17; *Douglas* v. *Young* (1613) Mor. 14736.

The action lies for "unlawful meddling or accession thereto,"[20] or "intermeddling" with the goods,[21] excluding the owner from possession of them,[22] as where one co-proprietor carries away what belongs to all, by excluding a part-owner from a share in the proceeds of a captured whale,[23] poinding under an incompetent decree,[24] making an illegal though customary exaction for services rendered,[25] or eating and destroying growing corn.[26]

It has been held not to cover deliberately emptying corn from sacks on to the ground,[27] nor the conduct of liferenter in possession in cutting wood.[28]

Where action excluded. The action is excluded if the goods are restored, as good as when taken away, before action is brought,[29] but not if only part be restored,[30] or if the goods have been deteriorated,[31] or are not restored with all profits,[32] or if restoration is delayed.[33]

The lawful command or authority of a superior is a defence competent to a defender,[34] but not merely a father's instructions.[35]

The action is excluded by any legal or even colourable warrant,[36] or by good faith[37] such as sale under the powers of a trustee in bankruptcy's Act and Warrant,[38] certainly if immediate restitution be made,[39] or by voluntary delivery of the goods,[40] or by lawful poinding,[41] or by restitution of the goods.[42] The action prescribes as to the violent profits in three years,[43] but even thereafter an action lies for restitution.[44] It is

---

[20] Stair, I, 9, 17; *Cowgrane* (1609) Mor. 379, 14707; *Roxburgh* v. *Langtoun* (1628) Mor. 379.

[21] Ersk., III, 7, 16. Cf. *Dounie* v. *Graham* (1715) Mor. 14729.

[22] Bankt., I, 10, 124; *Lisk* v. *Scot* (1682) Falconer, No. 27. Cf. *Alison* v. *Trail* (1628) Mor. 14728.

[23] *Stove* v. *Colvin* (1831) 9 S. 633.

[24] *Brown* v. *Lamb* (1630) Mor. 14743; *Ballantyne* v. *Ross* (1821) 2 Mur. 329.

[25] *Brodie* v. *Watson* (1714) Mor. 14757.

[26] *Cultmalindie* v. *Oliphant* (1567) Mor. 14726.

[27] *Millar* v. *Killarnie* (1541) Mor. 14723.

[28] *Drummond* v. *Forrest* (1581) Mor. 14727.

[29] Stair, I, 9, 20; I, 9, 23; *Rollock* v. *Striviling* (1532) Mor. 14740; *Sym* v. *Ambrose* (1624) Mor. 14743.

[30] *Millar* v. *Lord Killairnie* (1541) Mor. 14741; —— v. *Lord Sinclair* (1580) Mor. 14726.

[31] —— v. *Foster* (1610) Mor. 14741; *Leslie* v. *Inglis* (1624) Mor. 14742.

[32] *Knows* v. *Learmonth* (1611) Mor. 14742.

[33] *Bethune* v. *Hume* (1679) Mor. 14751.

[34] *Scot* v. *Balfour* (1528) Mor. 14758; *Home* v. *Porteous* (1533) Mor. 14758; *Strathurd* v. *Seytoun* (1534) Mor. 14758; *Kilmure* v. *Williamson* (1610) Mor. 14761.

[35] *Glen* v. *Setoun* (1608) Mor. 14760; cf. *Marr* v. *Glencairn* (1586) Mor. 14759.

[36] Stair, I, 9, 19; *A Spaniard* v. *Tenant* (1551) Mor. 14725; *Rhind* v. *May* (1543) Mor. 14745; *Wauchope* v. *Borthwick* (1543) Mor. 14745; *Bastard's Exors.* v. *Douglas* (1543) Mor. 14747; *Scot* v. *Banks* (1628) Mor. 14749; *Thin* v. *Scot* (1683) Mor. 14753; *Muirhead* v. *Lawson* (1575) Mor. 14745; *Drummond* v. *Forrest* (1581) Mor. 14727; *Laird of Mertoun* v. *Town of Lauder* (1594) Mor. 14728; *Sinclair* v. *Dunbar* (1702) Mor. 14755; *Shaw* v. *Gray* (1732) Mor. 14757. See also *Gibb* v. *Doby* (1616) Mor. 14742; *Brown* v. *Lamb* (1630) Mor. 14743; *McKay* v. *Menzies* (1635) Mor. 14749.

[37] Stair, I, 9, 19, and cases there; *A.* v. *B.* (1637) Mor. 14750.

[38] *Mackintosh* v. *Galbraith* (1900) 3 F. 66.

[39] *Brown* v. *Huddlestone* (1625) Mor. 14748; *Shaw* v. *Gray* (1732) Mor. 14767.

[40] Stair, I, 9, 20.

[41] Stair, I, 9, 21.

[42] Stair, I, 9, 23.

[43] Prescription (Ejections) Act, 1579 (c. 81). See *Baillie* v. *Young* (1835) 13 S. 472, 475; Ersk., III, 7, 16.

[44] Stair, I, 9, 24; *Hay* v. *Kerr* (1627) Mor. 12131; Ersk, III, 7, 16.

not a defence that the pursuer had previously taken as much from the defender.[45]

If there is dispute as to the better title to possess, the rule is *spoliatus ante omnia restituendus*[46]; once restitution is made the dispute as to title may be resolved by declarator or action for delivery. If one party takes possession the former possessor may at once recover possession, forcibly if necessary, without committing any wrong.[47]

Stair[48] lays down that violent profits are recoverable where the things spuilzied have profits, such as farm animals or tools. But this has been limited to direct damage and not including indirect or consequential loss.[49]

Violent profits. The defender guilty of spuilzie is liable not only to make restitution of the thing spuilzied with all its natural profits, but liable for violent profits.[50] These are the highest profits the pursuer could have made from the subjects spuilzied,[51] and are determined in the first place by the pursuer's estimate made on his oath *in litem*. The pursuer's oath is conclusive as to the quantities lost, but his valuation is subject to modification by the court.[52]

Modern practice. While in modern practice the action of spuilzie *eo nomine* has fallen into disuse it remains competent and has in substance been applied in many modern cases. The essence of the wrong is to do any act in relation to goods which denies the complainer's title to own or possess them. Thus the buyer's right to damages under the Sale of Goods Act, 1893, s. 51 (1) for damages for non-delivery of goods bought, the property in which has passed to him, is in essence and origin an action of spuilzie.[53] A hire purchase company which repossesses goods on the hirer's default commits a spuilzie, unless the repossession is justified by the contract or judicial warrant has been obtained. A hotel-keeper who sells property left by a guest commits a spuilzie if he does not obtain judicial authority to sell. Many of the cases raise difficult issues of title to own or possess the goods in question.

Goods wrongfully removed. Where goods owned or possessed by one have been taken away by another, an action of restitution is competent

---

45 *More* v. *McPhaderick* (1678) Mor. 14729.
46 *Sommerville* v. *Hamilton* (1541) Mor. 14737; *Selkirk* v. *Kelso* (1541) Mor. 14738; *Brown, supra*; *Lady Renton* v. *Her Son* (1629) Mor. 14739; *Yeoman* v. *Oliphant* (1669) Mor. 14740; *A.* v. *B.* (1677) Mor. 14751.
47 *Haliburton* v. *Rutherford* (1541) Mor. 14723; *Douglas* v. *Boig* (1542) Mor. 14725.
48 Stair I, 9, 16.
49 *Ker* v. *Dunbar* (1706) Mor. 16460.
50 Stair, I, 9, 16; II, 9, 44; IV, 29, 1; IV, 30, 4; Bankt., I, 10, 124; Ersk., II, 6, 54; III, 7, 16; More, *Lect.*, I, 358; *Yester* v. *Hay* (1530) Balfour 467; *Huldie* v. *Steill* (1563) Balf. 467.
51 *Cowdenknows* v. *Didiston* (1551) Mor. 16457; *Clark* v. *Sinclair* (1580) Mor. 16458; *Damitson* v. *Linlithgow Mags.* (1582) Mor. 16459; *Ross* v. *Fowlis* (1595) Mor. 16459; *Balnagown* v. *Munro* (1610) Mor. 16460; *Weddell* v. *Buchan* (1611) Mor. 16460; *Ker* v. *Dunbar* (1706) Mor. 16460.
52 *Cf. Crawcour* v. *St. George S.P. Co.* (1842) 5 D. 10.
53 Similarly in English law such facts give rise to an action by the buyer in detinue or conversion; see, *e.g.*, *Whiteley* v. *Hilt* [1918] 2 K.B. 808; *Hollins* v. *Fowler* (1875) L.R. 7 H.L. 757.

so long as the goods are in the other's possession as well as a claim for their wrongful detention; thereafter only a claim of reparation for their loss can be brought.[54] If the thief has sold the goods, the true owner may reclaim them from the purchaser or any subsequent possessor, even if he be a bona fide purchaser for value who has taken without notice of the defect in title,[55] and it matters not at all in Scotland that the sale was in market overt.[56] The final purchaser, who has to restore the goods to the true owner, may recover from an intermediate seller the full sum paid him, not merely his profit on the transaction, on the basis of breach of the statutorily implied undertaking as to title,[57] and so in turn, claims may be made back through the chain of purchasers to the original thief, if he can be traced and is worth suing.[58] The true owner can recover damages from a bona fide intermediate purchaser only if the goods are irrecoverable and if he were *lucratus* by the transaction, and only to that extent.[59] The intermediate purchaser is not liable to the true owner for the whole value of the goods if they have not been recovered merely because they passed through his hands.

In the special case of money, banknotes and negotiable instruments, the *vitium reale* of theft is purged as soon as the money is transferred to a bona fide taker for value without notice of the giver's defective title, and in such a case the money is irrecoverable from him or any subsequent innocent receiver, and the only claim competent is an action of reparation against the thief.[60]

Another instance of wrongful removal is where goods have been delivered under a contract of sale and accepted, and possession has then been resumed by the seller on some ground connected with payment; such is a spuilzie for which damages have been given.[61]

Goods obtained by fraud. Where possession of goods is obtained by fraud the true owner can recover the goods from a third party, such as a pawnbroker, into whose hands they have come.[62] The third party is liable for spuilzie if he fails to make restitution, or is unable to do so, as where the goods have been consumed. The fraudulent person is possibly also liable for spuilzie, alternatively to a claim of damages for fraud.

---

[54] *Gorebridge Cooperative Soc.* v. *Turnbull* (1952) 68 Sh.Ct.Rep. 236; *cf. Walker & Watson* v. *Sturrock* (1897) 35 S.L.R. 26.

[55] *Cf. Morrisson* v. *Robertson*, 1908 S.C. 332.

[56] *Henderson* v. *Gibson* (1806) Mor.Appx. Moveables, No. 1; *Todd* v. *Armour* (1882) 9 R. 901; *cf. Veitch* v. *Cowie* (1947) 63 Sh.Ct.Rep. 53; Sale of Goods Act, 1893, s. 22 (3).

[57] Sale of Goods Act, 1893, s. 12 (1); *Mason* v. *Burningham* [1949] 2 K.B. 544; *cf. McDonald* v. *Provan* (*of Scotland Street*), 1960 S.L.T. 231.

[58] *Rowland* v. *Divall* [1923] 2 K.B. 500.

[59] Bell, *Prin.*, § 527; Bell, *Comm.*, I, 299; *Brown on Sale*, 460; *Scott* v. *Low* (1704) Mor. 9123; *Walker* v. *Spence and Carfrae* (1765) Mor. 12802; *Faulds* v. *Townsend* (1861) 23 D. 437; doubted in *Oliver & Boyd* v. *Marr* (1901) 9 S.L.T. 170; *Bunten* v. *Silverdale* (1951) 67 Sh.Ct.Rep. 62; *Jarvis* v. *Mansion* (1953) 69 Sh.Ct.Rep. 93; *Wilson* v. *Barclay* (1957) 73 Sh.Ct.Rep. 114. *Cf. International Banking Corpn.* v. *Ferguson, Shaw & Sons*, 1910 S.C. 182.

[60] Bell, *Prin.*, § 528; *Gorebridge Cooperative Soc.* v. *Turnbull* (1952) 68 Sh.Ct.Rep. 236.

[61] *Henry* v. *Dunlop* (1842) 5 D. 3.

[62] *Hart and Gemmell* v. *Panton & Co.* (1861) 1 Guthrie Sel.Cas. 439. *Cf. Muir Wood & Co.* v. *Moore and Kidd* (1876) *ibid.* 444.

Unwarranted seizure. The seizure, or detention, or other similar interference with a person's possession of moveables amounts to spuilzie if not authorised by law or warrant. Thus the detention of hotel guests' luggage for two days under an invalid claim of lien was held illegal, and justified damages.[63] Again actions have been held competent where two persons took possession of the goods in the pursuer's shop without any warrant,[64] and where a search of premises was made and some goods were removed under a warrant which was incompetent and illegal.[65]

If the defender avers a warrant this defence may be overcome by averments and proof that his conduct was malicious and without probable cause.[66] If the warrant was illegal or irregular, no such averments are necessary.[67]

Use in denial of another's right to possession. Where a manufacturer of goods sells them to the customer in a container which is contractually returnable,[68] such as a soda-water syphon or an oxygen cylinder, he retains ownership and *animus possidendi* thereof, transferring *corpus possidendi* only for the purpose of, and for the time necessary for, enabling the customer to abstract and use the contents. It is probably a spuilzie in such a case for the customer to fail to return the container, the claim being satisfied in practice in many cases by forfeiture of a deposit paid on the container along with the price of the contents. If the temporary possessor takes the container to a third party to have it refilled the latter is no party to the contract relative to the container and cannot be interdicted by the owner of the container.[69] It may even be a spuilzie for the customer to use the container for holding some other substance before returning it, particularly if that substance may contaminate the container and render it unfit for its intended use again, or to delay unreasonably in returning the container after consuming the contents. In the same way it is wrongful for one spouse to remove furniture from the matrimonial home and to deny the other a share in the possession and use thereof.[70]

Finding lost property. So long as the true possessor of property lost still has *animus possidendi*, which will be evidenced by his still making search or inquiries for what he has lost, he is still constructively in possession thereof, and a finder who has not taken reasonable steps to find the true possessor directly, or indirectly, as by handing the found

---

63 *Ferguson* v. *Peterkin* (1953) 69 Sh.Ct.Rep. 251.
64 *Paterson* v. *Walker* (1848) 11 D. 167; *Cleland* v. *Todd* (1849) 11 D. 1039; *Walker* v. *Cumming* (1868) 6 M. 318.
65 *Barret* v. *Whyte* (1849) 11 D. 666; *Bell* v. *Black and Morrison* (1865) 3 M. 1026. *Cf.* *H.M.A.* v. *Turnbull*, 1951 J.C. 96.
66 *Graham* v. *McLachlan* (1853) 15 D. 889; *Christie* v. *Thompson* (1858) 20 D. 1114.
67 *Snare* v. *Duff* (1850) 13 D. 286.
68 In most cases of tinned or packaged goods the price includes the container which becomes the property of the purchaser, and which he may therefore keep or throw away.
69 *Leitch & Co.* v. *Leydon*, 1931 S.C.(H.L.) 1.
70 *Aitken* v. *Aitken*, 1954 S.L.T.(Sh.Ct.) 60.

property to the police,[71] is in the position of a thief [72] and also doubtless liable to an action for spuilzie or for restitution at the instance of the true possessor.[73]

If the true possessor has lost physical possession and abandoned *animus possidendi* the finder may acquire a good title if the property is awarded to him by the police.[74] Failing that he at least has a possessory right superior to that of anyone other than the true owner and can therefore himself maintain possession against anyone other than the true owner and bring an action of spuilzie if dispossessed.[75] But apart from that he has as against the owner committed a spuilzie.[76]

The finder must also probably take the same reasonable care of found property so long as it is in his possession as a careful man would of his own.[77] He may well be liable if by his neglect the property is deteriorated or damaged.[78]

Abandoned property. If a possessor deliberately abandons property with no intention of transferring or reclaiming it it is no spuilzie for anyone to take possession of it.[79] But such abandonment is not readily presumed. In some cases, as of putting out articles to be collected by refuse collectors, the possessor relinquishes possession which passes into constructive and eventually actual possession of the cleansing authority, so that a person who appropriates possession is depriving the authority of possession and liable therefor.[80]

Conduct in breach of contract of loan, deposit, custody or hiring. Similar principles apply where the circumstances amount to breach of a contract of loan, of deposit, of custody or of hiring, though technically such are cases of damages for breach of contract rather than pure cases of reparation for delict where there has been no antecedent contract express or implied. Thus a borrower,[81] a depositary,[82] a custodier [83] and a hirer [84] are all liable to an action of restitution if they do not restore the goods at the expiry of the period fixed, or on request, and failing restitution are liable in damages for spuilzie.[85] They can escape liability

---

71 Burgh Police (Scotland) Act, 1892, s. 412; Lost Property (Scotland) Act, 1965.
72 *Lawson* v. *Heatley*, 1962 S.L.T. 53.
73 *Cf. Hamilton* v. *Liddle* (1930) 46 Sh.Ct.Rep. 249.
74 *Cf. Robertson* v. *Burns*, 1943 J.C. 1.
75 *Cf. Hogg* v. *Armstrong and Mowat* (1874) 1 Guthrie Sel.Sh.Ct.Cas. 438.
76 *Cf. Ellerman's Wilson Line* v. *Webster* [1952] 1 Lloyd's Rep. 179; *Digby* v. *Heelan* [1952] C.L.Y. 790; *R.* v. *Samuel* (1956) 40 Cr.App.R. 8; *Williams* v. *Phillips* (1957) 41 Cr.App.R. 5 (dustmen appropriating goods left in dust bins).
77 *Cf. Kolbin* v. *Kinnear*, 1931 S.C. (H.L.) 128.
78 *Cf. Newman* v. *Bourne & Hollingsworth* (1915) 31 T.L.R. 209; *Clayton* v. *Le Roy* [1911] 2 K.B. 1031.
79 *Cf. Ellerman's Wilson Line* v. *Webster* [1952] 1 Lloyd's Rep. 179.
80 *Cf. Digby* v. *Heelan* [1952] C.L.Y. 790; *Williams* v. *Phillips* (1957) 41 Cr.App.R. 5.
81 *Wilson* v. *Orr* (1879) 7 R. 266; *Bain* v. *Strang* (1888) 16 R. 186.
82 *Cf. Ballingall* v. *Dundee Ice Co.*, 1924 S.C. 238.
83 *Cf. Central Motors (Glasgow), Ltd.* v. *Cessnock Garage Co.*, 1925 S.C. 796.
84 *Cf. Gardner* v. *McDonald* (1792) Hume, 299; *Pullars* v. *Walker* (1858) 20 D. 1238; *Hinshaw* v. *Adam* (1870) 8 M. 933; *Seton* v. *Paterson* (1880) 8 R. 236.
85 *Shaw* v. *Symmons* [1917] 1 K.B. 799; *cf. Central Motors, supra*; *Russell* v. *Bose*, 1948 S.L.T.(Sh.Ct.) 54; *Strand Electric and Engineering Co.* v. *Brisford Entertainments* [1952] 2 Q.B. 246.

only by explaining the inability to restore the goods in a way which imports no fault to them.[86]

Wrongful retention of goods. The wrongful retention of goods from the party entitled to possession thereof is a spuilzie. Thus damages were given where A entrusted furniture to F for storage and then sold it to H. F delivered some furniture to H but refused to complete delivery until H settled an account due by him to F. A eventually cancelled their contract with H and called on F to deliver, which he declined to do save on conditions. A claimed damages for wrongful retention of the furniture by F, but not delivery, and the court indicated that the proper claim was for delivery, or alternatively for damages, but awarded damages for the deprivation of use, though without making it at all clear on what ground the award was made.[87] The proper ground is, it is submitted, spuilzie.

Sale by mistake. Where a custodier has by mistake sold goods to a third party, he is liable, failing restitution of the goods to the true owner, to an action of damages for reparation of the loss, which will be measured by the value of the goods sold. He is still liable for any profit made by him on the sale if the goods can be recovered from the third party who bought them.

If a sale has been concluded by mistake or without authority, no right of property can have passed to the buyer and the latter must restore the goods to the true owner and may claim damages from the seller on the basis of breach of warranty of authority to sell,[88] for the loss of the bargain and for outlays and expenses, or for repayment of the price on the basis of breach of the implied condition of title to sell,[89] or on the basis of the *condictio causa data, causa non secuta*, the consideration for the payment having totally failed.[90]

Where the buyer cannot be traced the goods obviously cannot be got back from him and the only remedy is against the seller, for reparation. The buyer's title is technically defective within the prescriptive period but unless he can be found and it can be challenged it will stand unimpugned, and, moreover, the buyer will be in good faith throughout.[91]

In *Lockhart*[92] McC gave a much valued mare to C to keep; C lent the mare to L who worked her and then sold her without C's knowledge to another party. C sought return of the mare or her value, reserving his claim for loss or damage; return being impossible damages were given, including something for *pretium affectionis*. In *MacIntyre v. Corson*,[93] lambs in transit by rail were penned in a yard, taken out by auctioneers

---

86 *Pullars, supra; Wilson, supra; Bain, supra.*
87 *Aarons* v. *Fraser*, 1934 S.C. 137; *cf. Thomas* v. *Greenslade* [1954] C.L.Y. 3421.
88 *Anderson* v. *Croall* (1903) 6 F. 153; *cf. Murdoch* v. *Greig* (1889) 16 R. 396.
89 Sale of Goods Act, 1893, s. 12 (1).
90 *Cantiere San Rocco* v. *Clyde Shipbuilding Co.*, 1923 S.C.(H.L.) 105.
91 *Cf. Webster* v. *General Accident Assurance Corpn.* [1953] 1 Q.B. 520.
92 *Lockhart* v. *Cunninghame* (1871) 8 S.L.R. 151.
93 (1906) 22 Sh.Ct.Rep. 331.

acting in bona fide mistake, and sold. The owner was held entitled, failing restitution, to the price at which he had bought them plus an allowance for his expected profit on them, as a fair measure of reparation for the loss sustained. In *Mackintosh* v. *Galbraith and Arthur*,[94] M deposited a car with C for repair and storage; G, trustee on C's sequestrated estates, sold all the stock-in-trade to A, who in turn sold it off, including the car by mistake. A was held liable to M in damages, measured by the value of the car as found by the court, since he had not taken sufficient care to exclude the car from the bankrupt's stock.

Statutory powers of sale. In many cases parties in possession of goods have a statutory power of sale of articles in their possession when certain conditions have not been implemented: the chief cases are:

(i) pawnbroker's right to sell unredeemed pledges [95];
(ii) innkeeper's right to sell goods left with him by person indebted to him [96];
(iii) warehousemen's right to sell imported goods on which they have incurred expenses [97];
(iv) where goods have been deposited for repair or other treatment and the depositor fails both to tender payment and to take delivery, the depositary is entitled to sell the goods, subject to certain conditions as to notice.[98]

In such cases sale warranted in the circumstances by the statute will not amount to a spuilzie, but a sale not statutorily warranted would be a spuilzie.

Use of another's goods by mistake. Where one person by mistake uses up another person's goods, as where A burns B's coal, the user is liable to the true owner for the value of the goods used, the use being a spuilzie, or for the value on the basis of recompense.

Where one person by mistake uses the goods of another, combined with those of his own into something new, or worked up by his skill and labour into something new, the property in the new substance vests in the creator of the new thing under the doctrine of *specificatio*, but the creator is liable in reparation to the owner of the goods used, measured by their market value.[99] If the goods used can be restored *in forma specifica*, as where they have been merely mixed, the true owner is entitled to recover his goods from the composite thing and the mixture must be sorted.[1] In that case no new right of property in the mixture arises.

No right of property in the new species arises, however, under the principle of *specificatio*, where part of the goods used were acquired from

94 (1900) 3 F. 66.
95 Pawnbrokers Acts, 1872, s. 19 and 1960, s. 3.
96 Innkeepers Act, 1878, s. 1.
97 Merchant Shipping Act, 1894, ss. 497–498.
98 Disposal of Uncollected Goods Act, 1952, s. 1.
99 *International Banking Corpn.* v. *Ferguson Shaw & Co.*, 1910 S.C. 182; *cf. McLaren* v. *Mann, Byars & Co.* (1935) 57 Sh.Ct.Rep. 57.
1 *Spence* v. *Union Marine Insce. Co.* (1868) L.R. 3 C.P. 437; *Harris* v. *Truman* (1881) 7 Q.B.D. 358.

the true owner thereof not by *bona fide* mistake, but by theft or otherwise *mala fide*. In such a case the *vitium reale* which taints the stolen goods affects the whole new thing, and a good title to it cannot be transferred, while the creator is liable to the true owner for the value of the thing taken and used on the basis of spuilzie, as well as liable criminally.[2]

2. DELIBERATE DAMAGE TO GOODS

Cases of deliberate damage to goods are normally prosecuted criminally but there is no doubt that a claim of damages lies for damage done in such a way.[3] Thus a thief may be sued for damage done to goods in the course of stealing their contents, as when he breaks open furniture. The deliberate killing of a dog or other animal may be justifiable in the circumstances [4] but if there is no, or inadequate, justification, the killer is clearly liable. Similarly deliberate damage to other goods may be justified by the need to save life or more valuable property from imminent danger. Thus if a ship carrying explosives catches fire, she may be scuttled to avoid an explosion which would damage docks and other vessels.

Deliberate damage to goods is not a spuilzie, as where defenders threw out corn from the pursuer's sacks on the sand.[5]

3. UNINTENTIONAL DAMAGE TO GOODS

Claims for loss of or damage to goods, such as personal belongings, clothing and furniture can frequently be brought under the head of breach of contract of carriage, but may arise independently thereof, as where belongings are lost or damaged in a vehicle accident or ship collision. The claim is based on negligence and is for the pre-loss value of the lost items, not their value when new,[6] or for the diminution in their value by reason of the damage, which may be measured by the cost of repair when they are readily repairable and repair can be reasonably contemplated as satisfactory. In the case of clothing repair is frequently inappropriate, even where feasible, and in *Lewis* [6] damages were awarded on the basis of prime cost less an allowance for depreciation and wear.

Consequential loss is in general not recoverable as being too remote; where property is stolen from an injured person [7] or from the scene of an accident there is probably *novus actus interveniens*. Where the pursuer, the manageress of an orchestra, lost in the sinking after collision of a steamship on which she had been travelling a quantity of music and manuscript orchestral settings, it was held that damages must be limited to the cost of replacement at ordinary market price or, failing that, to

---

[2] *McDonald* v. *Provan (of Scotland Street), Ltd.,* 1960 S.L.T. 231.
[3] *Cf. Graham* v. *Edinburgh and District Tramways Co.,* 1917 S.C. 7, 10, " No person is entitled deliberately to do damage to another person's property, even though that property is where it ought not to be, or has no right to be."
[4] See p. 1012, *infra.*
[5] *Millar* v. *Killarnie* (1541) Mor. 14723.
[6] *Lewis* v. *Laird Line,* 1925 S.L.T. 316, 320.
[7] *Cf. Cobb* v. *G.W.Ry.* [1894] A.C. 419.

the amount of payment to composers of that class of music, and that it was irrelevant that she might have earned profits from the publishing and performance of the music of which she had the sole performing rights, as she did not aver that she carried on a business of publishing or dealing in music and she had never been in use to make profits from royalties, publication or sale of music or from performing rights.[8]

A serious problem arises where there is, for example, lost in a hotel fire [9] the manuscript of a book on which the author has been working for years. It has a low intrinsic value, as paper, little or no market value, but an enormous value in terms of time and labour spent and possibly great potential value, both material and immaterial. But probably no damages can be given in respect of these elements.

Where goods have been lost or damaged by fire or flood the measure of damages is their market value, or the diminution of value of goods damaged, not the cost of effecting repairs or replacement.[10] Where sets of a thing are rendered incomplete or partially spoiled, the value of the whole set can be claimed.[11]

An employer is not, merely by reason of employing, under any duty to take reasonable care that his employee's goods are not stolen,[12] not even if he has to live on the employer's premises.[13]

4. Damage to Animals

Reparation is due where animals are injured or killed without justification. Liability depends on ordinary principles of negligence.[14] Thus an owner is liable for damage by one dog to another in a fight,[15] and a driver is liable if he negligently runs over a dog in the road.[16]

The Dogs Acts, 1906–28, make the owner of a dog liable in damages for injury done by that dog to any cattle,[17] defined [18] as including horses, mules, asses, sheep, goats and swine, or to poultry,[19] without proof of previous mischievous propensity in the dog, or the owner's knowledge

---

[8] *Reavis* v. *Clan Line Steamers*, 1925 S.C. 725; 1926 S.C. 215.
[9] *Cf.* the accidental burning of the MS. of Carlyle's *French Revolution* when he had lent it to J. S. Mill.
[10] *Weston* v. *Tailors of Potterrow* (1839) 1 D. 1218 (books in bookshop damaged by water from house above); *Campbell* v. *Kennedy* (1864) 3 M. 121; *Reid* v. *Baird* (1876) 4 R. 234; *Moffat* v. *Park* (1877) 5 R. 13; *McIntyre* v. *Gallacher* (1883) 11 R. 64; *Gilmour* v. *Simpson*, 1958 S.C. 477, 487.
[11] *Cleghorn* v. *Taylor* (1856) 18 D. 664.
[12] *Deyong* v. *Shenburn* [1946] K.B. 227.
[13] *Edwards* v. *West Herts. Hospital Cttee.* [1957] 1 All E.R. 541.
[14] *Barclay* v. *G.N.S.Ry.* (1882) 10 R. 144; *Wilson* v. *Wood* (1908) 24 Sh.Ct.Rep. 225; *Maxwell* v. *N.B.Ry.* (1921) 37 Sh.Ct.Rep. 280; *Balfour* v. *Duncan* (1950) 66 Sh.Ct.Rep. 40; *Riach* v. *Neish* (1950) 66 Sh.Ct.Rep. 286; *Beddie* v. *B.T.C.* (1958) 74 Sh.Ct.Rep. 130. *Cf. Robertson* v. *Connolly* (1851) 13 D. 779; 14 D. 315.
[15] *Flockhart* v. *Ferrier* (1958) 74 Sh.Ct.Rep. 175.
[16] *Graham* v. *Edinburgh & District Tramways Co.*, 1917 S.C. 7; *Burns* v. *Western S.M.T. Co.* (1955) 71 Sh.Ct.Rep. 232. But an engine driver's duty is to look out for signals only, not animals: *Beddie* v. *B.T.C., supra.*
[17] 1906, s. 1.
[18] 1906, s. 7.
[19] 1928, s. 1: " Poultry " in turn is defined by the Poultry Act, 1911. See also *Ives* v. *Brewer* (1951) 95 Sol.J. 286.

thereof, or proof that the injury was attributable to neglect on the part of the owner. The occupier of premises where the dog was kept or permitted to live is presumed to be the owner, and is to be liable unless he proves that he was not the owner at that time. A dog proved to have injured cattle or poultry or chased sheep may be dealt with as a dangerous dog.[20]

In cases of sheepworrying, if damage is done at various times by animals acting in concert belonging to different owners, both or all owners are liable jointly and severally for the whole damage.[21] Hence if only one of the dogs is identified his owner is liable for the whole damage.[22] If dogs make entirely separate raids but the actual damage done by each cannot be distinguished the owners will be liable equally [23] or *pro rata* where there is ground for holding that more damage is attributable to one than another. The liability in sheepworrying is for the value of the sheep killed, the diminution in value of any injured, and for such consequential losses as lost lambs. Similarly where cats kill poultry the owner of the cat is liable for the fair value of the poultry killed.[24]

In various miscellaneous cases of loss of or injury to animals reparation has been claimed on the basis of negligence. Such cases include: Where cows were served by a trespassing bull and dropped cross-bred calves [25]; where a horse was killed by falling into a hole in a field [26]; where a dog was hit by a careless shot [27]; where cattle died from eating yew cuttings,[28] or paint scrapings [29]; where a homing pigeon [30] or a dog [31] was lost in transit, or a pigeon shot [32]; or where vixens aborted and destroyed their cubs, having been frightened by blasting.[33] But the owners of a water-pipe running through a field were held not bound to have foreseen that a ram might get its horn entangled in an exposed part and die of suffocation.[34]

Justifiable killing of animals. Where a dog is worrying sheep or other animals it is justifiable to shoot the dog if that is the only way of preventing damage in the case of an actual attack, or if there is reason to

---

[20] 1906, s. 1 (4). The Dogs (Protection of Livestock) Act, 1953, makes further provision for criminal liability.
[21] *Murray* v. *Brown* (1881) 19 S.L.R. 253; *Smith* v. *Hewel* (1885) 1 Sh.Ct.Rep. 246; *Harrison* v. *White* (1892) 8 Sh.Ct.Rep. 318; *Arneil* v. *Paterson*, 1931 S.C.(H.L.) 117.
[22] *A.B.* v. *C.D.* (1911) 27 Sh.Ct.Rep. 212.
[23] *McIntyre* v. *Carmichael* (1870) 8 M. 570.
[24] *Allan* v. *Reekie* (1906) 22 Sh.Ct.Rep. 57; *Peden* v. *Charleton* (1906) 22 Sh.Ct.Rep. 91; *Turner* v. *Simpson* (1912) 29 Sh.Ct.Rep. 81; *Paterson* v. *Howith* (1913) 29 Sh.Ct.Rep. 216.
[25] *Harvie* v. *Turner* (1916) 32 Sh.Ct.Rep. 267; *Logan* v. *Rodger* (1953) 69 Sh.Ct.Rep. 3.
[26] *McLean* v. *Warnock* (1883) 10 R. 1052.
[27] *Davie* v. *Wilson* (1854) 16 D. 956.
[28] *Sloan* v. *Thomson* (1890) 7 Sh.Ct.Rep. 60; *cf. Millar* v. *Bonar* (1921) 38 Sh.Ct.Rep. 8; *Young* v. *Houston* (1924) 40 Sh.Ct.Rep. 118; contrast *King* v. *Lyon* (1910) 26 Sh.Ct.Rep. 75.
[29] *Stewart* v. *Adams*, 1920 S.C. 129.
[30] *McCrorie* v. *G.S.W.Ry.* (1890) 7 Sh.Ct.Rep. 65; *Hamps* v. *Darby* [1948] 2 K.B. 311.
[31] *Wales* v. *G.S.W.Ry.* (1890) 7 Sh.Ct.Rep. 144.
[32] *Muirhead* v. *Waugh* (1912) 28 Sh.Ct.Rep. 143.
[33] *Western Silver Fox Ranch* v. *Ross and Cromarty C.C.*, 1940 S.C. 601.
[34] *Smith* v. *N.C.B.*, 1954 S.L.T.(Notes) 55.

apprehend a renewal of the attack.[35] The onus is on the killer to establish the defence and he must prove actual attack or real and imminent danger, and also that there was no other practicable means of protecting his animals, or at least that he acted reasonably in regarding the shooting as necessary.[36] If the circumstances justify shooting, the killer is under no liability to the owner of the dog, but he will be liable if he shoots it without justification.[37] He is also liable if he shoots a dog or other trespassing animal under a mistaken view of his legal rights in the matter.[38]

In case of emergency, when a driver has to choose between killing or injuring an animal on the road, or pulling up so quickly as probably to injure some of his passengers or otherwise cause injury to humans, he must seek to preserve the humans from injury even at the cost of killing the animal, though he might still be liable to the owner of the animal if his driving were negligent vis-à-vis it.[39]

Animals on roads. There is in general no obligation on a landowner or agricultural tenant to fence his land so as to prevent his animals straying on to roads, and there are endless miles of unfenced roads, particularly in the north of Scotland, in sheep-grazing districts.[40] The owner of animals, such as sheep and cattle, is not therefore in fault if in such areas his beasts can stray on the road, nor if they get through any fence or hedge which there may be.[41] The same applies to a dog, but not if it is brought on to the road.[42] Animals may also legitimately be on the road when being taken from a field to the farm, or back again, or being driven to market, and other road users must foresee these possibilities and take reasonable care not to do animals harm.[43] But in these cases the owner must take reasonable care that the animals are driven and do not get out of control or do harm.[44]

It is an offence to cause or permit a dog to be on a " designated road " and not held on a lead.[45] The driver of a vehicle is liable if he injures or

[35] *Duncan* v. *Rodger* (1891) 7 Sh.Ct.Rep. 313; *Blackie* v. *Stewart* (1920) 37 Sh.Ct.Rep. 60; *Wilson* v. *Buchanan* (1943) 59 Sh.Ct.Rep. 54; *Leven* v. *Mitchell* (1949) 65 Sh.Ct.Rep. 225; *Farrell* v. *Marshall* (1962) 78 Sh.Ct.Rep. 128; *Mitchell* v. *Duncan* (1953) 69 Sh.Ct. Rep. 182; *Cope* v. *Sharpe* [1912] 1 K.B. 496; *Gott* v. *Measures* [1947] 2 All E.R. 609; *Cresswell* v. *Sirl* [1947] 2 All E.R. 730; *Goodway* v. *Becher* [1951] 2 All E.R. 349; *Eccles* v. *McBurney* [1959] N.I. 15.
[36] *Cresswell, supra,* 733. *Cf. Strachan* v. *Ross* (1925) 41 Sh.Ct.Rep. 212; *Thayer* v. *Newman* [1953] C.L.Y. 115; *Mitchell* v. *Duncan* (1953) 69 Sh.Ct.Rep. 182.
[37] *Workman* v. *Cowper* [1961] 2 Q.B. 143.
[38] *Clark* v. *Syme,* 1957 J.C. 1.
[39] *Sutherland* v. *Glasgow Corpn.,* 1951 S.C.(H.L.) 1; *Parkinson* v. *Liverpool Corpn.* [1950] 1 All E.R. 367.
[40] As to straying on to private ground and doing harm there, see *MacAtee* v. *Montgomery* (1949) 65 Sh.Ct.Rep. 79.
[41] *Heath's Garage, Ltd.* v. *Hodges* [1916] 2 K.B. 370; *Hughes* v. *Williams* [1943] 1 K.B. 574; *Searle* v. *Wallbank* [1947] A.C. 341; *cf. Milligan* v. *Henderson,* 1915 S.C. 1030; *Fraser* v. *Pate,* 1923 S.C. 748; *Sinclair* v. *Muir,* 1933 S.N. 62; *Brackenborough* v. *Spalding U.D.C.* [1942] A.C. 310; *Milne* v. *MacIntosh* (1952) 68 Sh.Ct.Rep. 301.
[42] *Ellis* v. *Johnstone* [1963] 2 Q.B. 8; *Gomberg* v. *Smith* [1963] 1 Q.B. 25.
[43] *Umphray* v. *Ganson,* 1917 S.C. 371.
[44] *Gilligan* v. *Robb,* 1910 S.C. 856; *Turner* v. *Coates* [1917] 1 K.B. 670; *Gayler & Pope* v. *Davies* [1924] 2 K.B. 75; *Deen* v. *Davies* [1935] 2 K.B. 282. See also *Wright* v. *Callwood* [1950] 2 K.B. 515; *Brock* v. *Richards* [1951] 1 K.B. 529.
[45] R.T.A., 1960, s. 220.

kills animals on the road by negligent driving; the question whether his driving was in the circumstances negligent depends on, *inter alia*, whether there were reasonable grounds for anticipating the presence of the animal or animals on, or coming onto, the road and what warning was given him of their possible presence. A driver must stop and give particulars if owing to the presence of a motor vehicle on a road an accident occurs whereby damage is caused to an animal (*i.e.*, horse, cattle, ass, mule, sheep, pig, goat or dog) other than one in or on the vehicle or its trailer.[46]

Animals on railway line. The Railways Clauses Consolidation (Scotland) Act, 1845, s. 60, imposes on the railway authority the duty to make and maintain, *inter alia*, fences for protecting the cattle of the owners of adjacent lands from straying thereout, and all necessary gates. If animals get onto the line by reason of defect in the fencing or gateway and are killed the authority is liable.[47]

5. DAMAGE TO VEHICLES

Railway vehicles. Since the whole railway undertakings of the British Transport Commission are one, claims arising from railway collisions will not now arise, and the only possible case is of damage to engines or rolling stock by outside persons, as by negligently leaving an obstruction on the lines. Any such claim, it seems, would be based on negligence. Thus where a train and a motor-car collided on a level crossing there was held to have been concurrent negligence of both drivers,[48] which implies possible liability to the railway authority for damage to its rolling stock.

Road vehicles. Where a vehicle is damaged in circumstances not arising out of a contract, *e.g.*, of hire, the basis of any claim of damages is negligence.[49] The negligence may take various forms in different circumstances. It has also been held in special circumstances that under the Locomotives Act, 1865, s. 12,[50] nuisance could found a claim apart from negligence.[51]

Thus claims are competent against road authorities for failing in their duty of keeping a road in a reasonably safe condition, or for failing to fence it,[52] failing to light and fence an open trench in the carriageway

---

46 R.T.A., 1960, s. 77.
47 See also *Dawson* v. *Railway Executive* (1951) 101 L.J. 541; *Saunders* v. *Railway Executive* [1951] C.L.Y. 2773.
48 *Smith* v. *L.M.S.Ry.*, 1948 S.C. 125.
49 *Cf. Central Motors (Glasgow), Ltd.* v. *Cessnock Garage*, 1925 S.C. 796; *Burns* v. *Royal Hotel (St. Andrews), Ltd.*, 1956 S.C. 463.
50 Now repealed.
51 *Hay* v. *Leslie* (1896) 4 S.L.T. 124.
52 *Harris* v. *Magistrates of Leith* (1881) 8 R. 613; *Johnstone* v. *Glasgow Magistrates* (1885) 12 R. 596; *Strachan* v. *Aberdeen District Committee* (1894) 21 R. 915. See also *Fraser* v. *Rothesay Mags.* (1892) 19 R. 817.

at night,[53] leaving a heap of road metal in the roadway,[54] or failing to light such an obstruction,[55] having such ruts in the road as to cause the breaking of an axle,[56] having an overhead bridge dangerously low,[57] allowing a tree to fall across the road,[58] allowing a road surface to be slippery and dangerous,[59] and failing to maintain a bridge, so that it collapsed under pressure of flood water.[60]

Similarly persons whose premises front on a road may be liable for causing ice to form on the roadway.[61]

Collisions between vehicles. The commonest cause of damage is in cases of collisions between moving vehicles, liability for which depends on proof of negligence, and on the same principles as govern liability for personal injury to persons in the other vehicle.[62] But equally damage may be caused by leaving another vehicle stationary in such a position as to be an obstruction, as where it is unlit.[63]

If the vehicle can be economically repaired the measure of damages is the cost of the repair, together with any consequential damage naturally and directly flowing from the wrongful act. If the vehicle is totally destroyed or cannot be economically repaired, the measure of damages is in general its immediately pre-accident value, together with consequential loss, as for hiring a substitute until a replacement can be obtained.[64] If the vehicle is out of use while undergoing repair damages may include awards in respect of depreciation, insurance and licence charges and a share of the overhead costs of the fleet of which it was a part.[65]

Damage caused by defective manufacture. The manufacturers of vehicles or parts thereof may be liable to the owner if the vehicle is damaged in consequence of the defective design of the vehicle or the negligent supply of a defective part, such as a tyre which bursts,[66] or a road spring which broke.[67]

---

[53] *Sanderson* v. *Paisley Burgh Commissioners* (1899) 7 S.L.T. 255.
[54] *Cromar* v. *Haddingtonshire County Council* (1902) 9 S.L.T. 437. *Cf. Nelson* v. *Lanarkshire Lower Ward Cttee.* (1891) 19 R. 311; *Barton* v. *Kinning Park Commissioners* (1892) 29 S.L.R. 329.
[55] *White* v. *McKean & Co.*, 1948 S.L.T. 210.
[56] *Blackie* v. *Magistrates of Leith* (1904) 12 S.L.T. 529.
[57] *McFee* v. *Broughty Ferry Police Commrs.* (1890) 17 R. 764.
[58] *Costello* v. *Midlothian C.C.*, 1946 S.N. 103.
[59] *W. Alexander & Sons* v. *Dundee Corpn.*, 1950 S.C. 123; *Western S.M.T. Co.* v. *Greenock Mags.*, 1958 S.L.T.(Notes) 50.
[60] *Dallas* v. *Ayr County Council* (1948) 64 Sh.Ct.Rep. 122. See also *Lanark C.C.* v. *N.C.B.*, 1948 S.C. 698.
[61] *Lambie* v. *Western S.M.T. Co.*, 1944 S.C. 415.
[62] *e.g., Pomphrey* v. *Cuthbertson*, 1951 S.C. 147.
[63] *Scott* v. *McIntosh*, 1935 S.C. 199; *Drew* v. *Western S.M.T. Co.*, 1947 S.C. 222; *West* v. *David Lawson, Ltd.*, 1949 S.C. 430.
[64] *Pomphrey, supra*; see also *Darbishire* v. *Warran* [1963] 3 All E.R. 310.
[65] *Galbraith's Stores* v. *Glasgow Corpn.* (1958) 74 Sh.Ct.Rep. 126.
[66] *Cf. Fraser* v. *Fraser* (1882) 9 R. 896; *Gavin* v. *Rogers* (1889) 17 R. 206; *Milne* v. *Townsend* (1892) 19 R. 830; *Elliot* v. *Young's Bus Service*, 1945 S.C. 445 (where fault not in original supplier but in subsequent failure to inspect).
[67] *Donnelly* v. *Glasgow Corpn.*, 1953 S.C. 107 (overruled in *Davie* v. *New Merton Board Mills* [1959] A.C. 604 on liability of operator of vehicle to employees injured in consequence). *Cf. Ross* v. *Glasgow Corpn.*, *ibid.* (liability to injured passenger).

In such cases it has to be shown that the defect was attributable to a fault in original manufacture, not discoverable by any reasonable subsequent inspection, and not attributable to old age, fair wear and tear, or insufficient maintenance.[66] There is apparently no liability on the supplier for the consequence of latent defect in a part if he obtained the part from a reputable supplier of parts of that kind and it contained a latent defect.[68]

6. DAMAGE TO SHIPS

Reparation may be claimed for damage caused to a ship by collision with another ship.[69] The ground of action is the negligent navigation [70] or management [71] of the other ship.[72] No liability is created by the mere fact of collision,[73] nor if a collision causes no damage,[74] or if it is not the effective cause of the damage,[75] or if damage is caused without negligence,[76] or by inevitable accident.[77] There is no difference between common law and Admiralty in the principle determining whether or not there has been negligence.[78]

Agony rule. While reasonable thought and foresight and ordinary skill and care in avoiding dangers may be expected of shipmasters, it is recognised that in a moment of great difficulty, strain or peril a master may omit to do something which would or might have averted damage, or may do something which causes or contributes to it. A false step thus taken in emergency, in the agony of danger, is not imputable as fault, whether the emergency is caused by negligence or not.[79] The questions are rather: which vessel was at fault in causing the emergency, if indeed either was? and: did the master have a reasonable chance to think and take avoiding action, or was he caught by sudden emergency?

---

68 *Davie, supra.*
69 See generally Marsden, *Collisions at Sea* (11th ed.).
70 Defined: *The Dundee* (1823) 1 Hag.Adm. 109, 120, *per* Lord Stowell. See also *The Voorwaarts and The Khedive* (1880) 5 App.Cas. 876; *The Highland Loch* [1912] A.C. 312.
71 See, *e.g.*, *The Merryweather* (1923) 16 Ll.L.Rep. 228; *The Neritina* (1946) 79 Ll.L.Rep. 531; *The Dageid* (1947) 80 Ll.L.Rep. 517; *The Norwalk Victory* (1949) 82 Ll.L.Rep. 539.
72 Until it was repealed in 1911 (Maritime Conventions Act, 1911, s. 4) there was a statutory presumption of fault, for breach of the duty to obey the Regulations for Preventing Collisions at Sea and to stand by a vessel after collision with her.
73 *The Margaret* (1881) 6 P.D. 76.
74 *The Adams* [1911] W.N. 200.
75 *The Tempus* [1913] P. 166, 172; *The Blue Ranger* (1942) 72 Ll.L.Rep. 97, 100.
76 *The Albert Edward* (1875) 44 L.J.Ad. 49.
77 *The Europa* (1850) 14 Jur. 627; *The Thomas Powell and The Cuba* (1866) 14 L.T. 603; *The Marpesia* (1872) L.R. 4 P.C. 212.
78 *Cayzer, Irvine & Co.* v. *Carron Co.* (1885) 13 R. 114; 9 App.Cas. 873; *The Heranger* [1939] A.C. 94; *S.S. Bogota* v. *S.S. Alconda*, 1924 S.C.(H.L.) 66. As to procedural differences between claim for injuries to crew and for damage to vessel, see *Laurel Crown* v. *Glencloy*, 1941 S.C. 609.
79 *The Jesmond and The Earl of Elgin* (1871) L.R. 4 P.C. 1, 7; *The Marpesia* (1872) L.R. 4 P.C. 212; *The C.M. Palmer and The Larnax* (1873) 2 Asp.M.C. 94; *The Nor* (1874) 2 Asp.M.C. 264; *The Sisters* (1876) 1 P.D. 117; *The Bywell Castle* (1879) 4 P.D. 219; *The William Frederick and the Byfoged Christiansen* (1879) 4 App.Cas. 669; *The Voorwaarts and The Khedive* (1880) 5 App.Cas. 876; *Laird Line* v. *United States Shipping Board*, 1924 S.C.(H.L.) 37; *Baron Vernon* v. *Metagama*, 1928 S.C.(H.L.) 21; *The Fagerstrand* (1929) 33 Ll.L.Rep. 67; *The La Plata* (1939) 64 Ll.L.Rep. 283.

Similarly a master is not to be held in fault if, placed in a dilemma, he chooses the course involving the lesser risk of harm, even though damage in fact results,[80] nor if he is misled or induced to take a wrong course of action by the improper or unusual navigation of the other vessel.[81]

But a master cannot be excused on the ground of peril or difficulty if his ship was responsible for that sudden difficulty,[82] nor if, having several possible courses of action, he takes the one which is certain to lead to collision.[83]

Effect of pilotage. The ship and her owners are liable for a collision caused by the fault or negligence of a pilot, whether voluntarily employed,[84] or employed where pilotage is compulsory.[85] The pilotage authority is not liable for the negligence of a licensed pilot,[86] but may be for an employee who acts as a pilot.[87] Under the Pilotage Act, 1913, s. 19, the grant of a licence to a pilot does not impose on the issuing authority any liability for loss occasioned by any act or default of the pilot. If the pilotage authority is the actual employer of pilots and thereby incurs vicarious liability, the Pilotage Authorities (Limitation of Liability) Act, 1936, provides, in the cases to which it applies, for limitation of liability, in the absence of actual fault or privity of the authority, to the sum of £100 multiplied by the number of pilots holding licences for the district. A pilot is personally liable for damage caused by his default but where he has given a bond his liability is limited to the amount of the bond together with the amount payable to him for pilotage in respect of the occasion when the liability arose.[88]

Breach of Statutory Regulations. The Merchant Shipping Act, 1894, s. 419 (1) provides that all owners and masters shall obey the Collisions Regulations,[89] and negligence may be constituted by the failure to obey

[80] *The Highland Loch* [1912] A.C. 312; *The Crown* v. *The Hessa* (1922) 10 Ll.L.Rep. 734.
[81] *The Rob Roy* (1849) 3 W.Rob. 190; *The Mary Hounsell* (1879) 4 P.D. 204; *The Redriff* (1921) 6 Ll.L.Rep. 348.
[82] *The Bywell Castle, supra*; *The Winona* (1944) 77 Ll.L.R. 156.
[83] *The Testbank* (1941) 70 Ll.L.R. 270, 276; (1942) 72 Ll.L.R. 6.
[84] *The Maria* (1839) 1 W.Rob. 95, 108; *The Eden* (1845) 2 W.Rob. 442.
[85] Pilotage Act, 1913, s. 15 (1). A compulsory pilot is a servant of the owners: *Thom* v. *J. & P. Hutchison*, 1925 S.C. 386, approved in *Workington Harbour and Dock Board* v. *Towerfield (Owners)* [1951] A.C. 112, 145. The owners were previously not liable for the negligence of a compulsory pilot. See also *The Waziristan* [1953] 2 All E.R. 1213; *The Hans Hoth* [1953] 1 All E.R. 218.
[86] *Shaw, Savill & Albion* v. *Timaru Harbour Board* (1889) 15 App.Cas. 429; *Fowles* v. *Eastern & Australian S.S. Co., Ltd.* [1916] 2 A.C. 556; see also *Parker* v. *N.B.Ry.* (1898) 25 R. 1059.
[87] *Holman* v. *Irvine Harbour Trs.* (1877) 4 R. 406; see also *Anchor Line* v. *Dundee Harbour Trust*, 1921 S.C. 547.
[88] Pilotage Act, 1913, s. 35.
[89] The Regulations now in force are the Collision Regulations (Ships and Seaplanes on the Water) and Signals of Distress (Ships) Order, 1953, which came into force on January, 1, 1954 (S.I. 1953, No. 1557). On the legal position at various earlier dates see Marsden, *Collisions at Sea* (11th ed.) 423 *et seq.* This is very material as to cases decided at earlier times, particularly prior to the Maritime Conventions Act, 1911, which abolished the presumption of fault where the Regulations had not been observed. The Regulations are set out and annotated in Marsden, pp. 479 *et seq.*

the regulations in any way.[90] It is a breach of duty not to obey an applicable regulation,[91] unless the departure from the prescribed course can be justified as being " necessary in order to avoid immediate danger." [92] Local rules are in force in addition in many areas, including the Clyde, and obedience to them is obligatory in the areas in which they are applicable.[93]

The Regulations apply to British ships everywhere but not to Her Majesty's ships to which, however, identical regulations are made applicable by the Admiralty.[94]

Departure from the Regulations. Departure from the course prescribed by the regulations is permissible, having due regard " to all dangers of navigation and collision, and to any special circumstances, including the limitations of the craft involved, which may render a departure from the Rules necessary in order to avoid immediate danger." [95] Departure from the regulations is accordingly neither conclusive nor presumptive of fault but may be perfectly justifiable, though it must be justified. Moreover, in a clear case of danger, there may even be a duty to depart from the regulations. This will be the case where the circumstances are such that a master of ordinary skill and intelligence must have seen quite clearly and almost certainly, that adherence to the Rules would cause a collision.[96] Nor is a vessel obliged to observe the regulations if, by so doing, she incurs some peril of the sea, such as danger of running ashore.[97]

Negligent damage without collision. Damage may be caused negligently without collision with another vessel, or even without the intervention of another vessel at all. Thus a ship has been held liable for sinking another vessel by the wash raised by her passage at excessive speed,[98] or for creating a situation of such imminent danger that a tug was compelled to cast off her tow which then ran aground,[99] or for being negligently aground in a fairway without a light so that another vessel, taking avoiding action, ran aground,[1] or for navigating so negligently that two other vessels, taking avoiding action, collided.[2] Ship repairers have been held liable for negligently causing cargo to catch fire and to damage the ship.[3]

---

[90] See, *e.g.*, *Clan Stuart* v. *Uskhaven*, 1928 S.C. 879; *Jolliffe* v. *L.N.E.Ry.*, 1938 S.L.T. 21.
[91] See, *e.g.*, *Grangemouth and Forth Towing Co.* v. *Wolk*, 1931 S.L.T. 394.
[92] Regs., Rule 27.
[93] See, *e.g.*, *Bogota* v. *Alconda*, 1924 S.C.(H.L.) 66; *Cameronia* v. *Hauk*, 1927 S.C. 518.
[94] See *The Truculent* [1952] P. 1; *The Albion* [1953] P. 117.
[95] Regs. Rule 27.
[96] *The Boanerges and The Anglo-India* (1865) 2 Mar.L.C.(O.S.) 239; *The Ida and The Wasa* (1866) 15 L.T. 103; *The Oostvorne* (1921) 6 Ll.L.Rep. 110.
[97] *The Lucia Janina* v. *The Mexican* (1864) Holt.Adm. 130. *Cf. The Concordia* (1866) L.R. 1 A. & E. 93.
[98] *The Batavier* (1854) 9 Moo.P.C. 286; *cf. The Royal Eagle* (1950) 84 Ll.L.Rep. 543; *The Royal Sovereign* (1950) 84 Ll.L.Rep. 549.
[99] *The Wheatsheaf* (1866) 13 L.T. 612.
[1] *The Industrie* (1871) L.R. 3 A. & E. 303.
[2] *The Umona and the Sirius* (1934) 49 Ll.L.Rep. 461.
[3] *Nautilus S.S. Co.* v. *D. & W. Henderson*, 1919 S.C. 605.

Contributory negligence. Contributory negligence in most ship collision cases is governed by the Maritime Conventions Act, 1911, under which, where damage or loss is caused by the fault of two or more vessels to one or more of them or their cargoes or freight, or to any property on board, the liability to make good damage or loss is in proportion to the degree in which each vessel was in fault; if different degrees of fault cannot be established liability is apportioned equally.[4] There is no difference between common law and Admiralty principles as to what amounts to contributory negligence.[5] In a case to which the 1911 Act is inapplicable [6] the Law Reform (Contributory Negligence) Act, 1945, applies.

If the court is not satisfied on the evidence on which side the fault lies, each ship must bear her own loss and no damages are recoverable.[7]

Limitation of Liability. The liability of shipowners is statutorily limited by reference to the tonnage of their ship, under the Merchant Shipping Act, 1894, s. 503, as amended, particularly by the Merchant Shipping (Liability of Shipowners and Others) Act, 1958. The amended section provides that the owners of a ship shall not be liable, so long as the occurrence [8] takes place without their actual fault or privity, for loss of life or personal injury,[9] or damage or loss to goods on board the ship, or loss of life or personal injury to a person not in the ship by the act or omission of a person in the ship, or in certain other circumstances, beyond 3100 gold francs per ton of the ship's tonnage (minimum 300 tons) in respect of loss of life or personal injury, and 1000 gold francs per ton in respect of loss of or damage to goods.

The limitation applies to loss caused to persons or goods in the owner's ship whether arising from improper navigation or another cause. The limitation applies to loss caused to persons or goods in other ships " in the navigation or management of the ship [10] . . . or through any other act or omission of any person on board the ship." [11] It does not cover liability arising from the need to remove a wreck caused by the petitioner's fault.[12] The limitation provisions apply to the Crown.[13] The benefits of the Acts may be excluded by contract.[14]

---

4 See also *Hay* v. *Le Neve* (1824) 2 Sh.App. 395; *Cayzer Irvine & Co.* v. *Carron Co.* (1884) 9 App.Cas. 873, 881; *The Eurymedon* [1938] P. 41. As to limitation of time for claiming see Chap. 13, *supra*; *Birkdale S.S. Co.*, 1922 S.L.T. 575; *Reresby* v. *Cobetas*, 1923 S.L.T. 492, 719; *Essien* v. *Clan Line Steamers*, 1925 S.N. 75.

5 *Boy Andrew* v. *St. Rognvald*, 1947 S.C.(H.L.) 70.

6 e.g., *The Sobieski* [1949] P. 313; *Stone Shipping, Ltd.* v. *The Admiralty* [1952] 1 Lloyd's Rep. 38, 104; [1953] 1 Lloyd's Rep. 239.

7 *The Olympic* v. *H.M.S. Hawke* [1913] P. 214, 247.

8 As to limitation in relation to distinct occurrences, see " *Lucullite* " v. " *R. Mackay*," 1929 S.C. 401.

9 Including injury to members of the crews: *Innes* v. *Ross*, 1957 S.L.T. 121.

10 *Cf. The Warkworth* (1884) 9 P.D. 145.

11 1894 Act, as amended, s. 503 (1) (c).

12 *Clifton Steam Trawlers, Ltd.* v. *Duncan MacIver, Ltd.*, 1953 S.L.T. 230.

13 Crown Proceedings Act, 1947, ss. 5, 7; *The Truculent* [1952] P. 1.

14 *The Satanita* [1897] A.C. 59; *The Kirknes* [1956] 2 Lloyd's Rep. 651.

The benefits are lost unless the occurrence took place " without his actual fault or privity," which phrase infers fault personal to the owner as distinct from constructive fault or vicarious liability.[15] The onus is on the owner to disprove actual fault or privity.

To obtain the benefit of limitation the owner must petition the Court of Session to determine the amount of the owner's liability and to distribute the amount rateably among the claimants.[16]

If an owner settles some claims against him and then limits his liability, he may take into account the sum already paid and the remaining claimants can claim only on the balance.[17]

By the Harbours Act, 1964, s. 25, harbour authorities administering a scheme for securing the safe movement of vessels in and about the harbour may limit their liability for loss or damage caused to any vessel or anything on board it without their actual fault or privity.

Damage to ship by foul berth. Shipowners may recover damages for damage done to a vessel by the failure of harbour authorities to take reasonable care to ensure that the berth assigned was in a safe condition for vessels using it. This is particularly relevant where the vessel may take the ground when the tide ebbs. The duty of harbour trustees is a heavy one but not amounting to insurance.[18] Similarly they may be liable for the fault of the harbourmaster in failing to point out a latent danger to the master of a ship.[19]

But the owners of a private wharf do not give any implied guarantee of its safety and are liable in damages only if they know, or ought to know, that the berth is dangerous and fail to warn the master of the condition of the berth.[20]

Damage to ship by failure to buoy channel. Damages have been awarded to shipowners for collisions with wrecks in the navigable channel leading to a port caused by having a misleading system of buoying to mark a wreck and in failing to have the pilot cutter in attendance to provide a pilot.[21] Similarly damages were awarded where a buoy had been displaced and a local pilot had not known of this.[22]

---

15 *Standard Oil Co.* v. *Clan Line*, 1924 S.C.(H.L.) 1; *Paterson Steamships, Ltd.* v. *Robin Hood Mills, Ltd.* (1937) 58 Ll.L.Rep. 33; *The Truculent* [1952] P. 1; *Beauchamp* v. *Turrell* [1952] 2 Q.B. 207; *The Empire Jamaica* [1955] 1 Lloyd's Rep. 50; [1955] 2 Lloyd's Rep. 109; *The Norman* [1960] 1 Lloyd's Rep. 1; *The Lady Gwendolen* [1965] 2 All E.R. 283. *Cf. Kidston* v. *McArthur* (1878) 5 R. 936.

16 M.S.A., 1894, s. 504.

17 *Rankine* v. *Raschen* (1877) 4 R. 725; *The Foscolino* (1886) 5 Asp.M.C. 420.

18 *Mersey Docks Trs.* v. *Gibbs* (1866) L.R. 1 E. & I.App. 93; *The Queen* v. *Williams* (1884) 9 App.Cas. 418; *Thomson* v. *Greenock Harbour Trs.* (1876) 3 R. 1194; *The Moorcock* (1888) 13 P.D. 157; *The Bearn* [1906] P. 48; *S.S. Fulwood* v. *Dumfries Harbour Commrs.*, 1907 S.C. 456; *Mair* v. *Aberdeen Harbour Commrs.*, 1909 S.C. 721; *Walker* v. *Duke of Buccleuch*, 1918, 1 S.L.T. 223; *Cormack* v. *Dundee Harbour Trs.*, 1930 S.C. 112. See also *Mackenzie* v. *Stornoway Pier Commrs.*, 1907 S.C. 435; *Renney* v. *Kirkcudbright Mags.* (1892) 19 R.(H.L.) 11; *Parker* v. *N.B.Ry.* (1898) 25 R. 1059.

19 *Robertson* v. *Portpatrick and Wigtownshire Joint Cttee.*, 1919 S.C. 293.

20 *Rix* v. *Carlingnose Granite Co.*, 1929 S.N. 62; *Firth Shipping Co.* v. *Morton's Trs.*, 1938 S.C. 177.

21 *Anchor Line* v. *Dundee Harbour Trs.*, 1922 S.C.(H.L.) 79. *Cf. Buchanan* v. *Clyde Lighthouses Trs.* (1884) 11 R. 531.   22 *A/S Forto* v. *Orkney Harbour Commrs.*, 1915 S.C. 743.

7. DAMAGE TO AIRCRAFT

Liability for damage to aircraft caused by collision over any part of the United Kingdom depends on negligence and in determining that issue, a fundamental issue is the observance or non-observance by the aircraft of the Air Navigation Order, 1960, and the Rules of the Air and Air Traffic Control Regulations, 1960 (S.I. 1960, No. 1070; 1961, Nos. 375, 527, 920) and any local aerodrome rules.

A departure from the rules may be made by the captain of an aircraft if necessary in order to avoid immediate danger. The rules do not exonerate from the consequences of neglect to use lights or signals or take precautions required by ordinary aviation practice or the special circumstances of the case.

Collision between an aircraft on the ground and one in flight, taking off or landing falls under the Civil Aviation Act, 1949, s. 40.[23] In the absence of contributory negligence damages are recoverable without proof of intention or negligence.

8. LIABILITY FOR LOSS OF GOODS

Strict liability exists for the loss of goods under the edict *nautae, caupones, stabularii*.[24]

Apart from that, liability exists for the loss of another's goods where that loss has been caused by negligence, or the failure to take reasonable precautions against a foreseeable risk.[25] Such cases can be explained as breaches of an implied term of a contract of loan or deposit.

---

[23] See also *Blankley* v. *Godley* [1952] 1 All E.R. 436.
[24] Chap. 8, *supra*.
[25] *Bonham-Carter* v. *Hyde Park Hotel* (1948) 64 T.L.R. 177; *Olley* v. *Marlborough Court* [1949] 1 K.B. 532.

CHAPTER 29

INFRINGEMENTS OF INTERESTS IN INCORPOREAL MOVEABLE PROPERTY

1. Commercial Goodwill
2. Patents
3. Trade Marks
4. Copyright
5. Registered Designs
6. Plant Breeders' Rights

INCORPOREAL moveable property includes all those kinds of proprietary rights which are not related to heritage or treated as heritable and consist in legal rights or claims only and confer no right to actual possession or control of any corporeal moveable subject. They include such kinds of property as claims of debt or damages, company shares, stock in public funds, life insurance policies, negotiable instruments, goodwill, patents, trade marks, literary copyright, copyright in industrial designs, and plant breeders' rights.

In many of these kinds of property the wrongs done to the person entitled to the property are truly those of causing economic loss by fraud or negligence.[1] In the last six cases the element of interference with proprietary right is stronger and only these are here considered.

1. COMMERCIAL GOODWILL

Goodwill is that most intangible asset of a business, its " connection," or the probability that the customers will continue to do business with it, arising from personality,[2] locality,[3] reputation and connection[4] which tend to give the business identity and permanence.[5]

In the absence of an enforcable restrictive covenant[6] limiting competition and seeking to preserve the goodwill of a business, it is not wrong for a former employee or seller of a business to set up in opposition and deliberately, or incidentally to the conduct of a competing business, to take away business and thus diminish the complainer's goodwill.[7] It is

---

[1] *Supra*, Chap. 26.
[2] *Drummond* v. *Leith Assessor* (1886) 13 R. 540.
[3] *Philp's Exor.* v. *Philp's Exor.* (1894) 21 R. 482.
[4] *Morrison* v. *Morrison* (1900) 2 F. 382; see also *Smith* v. *Macbride* (1888) 16 R. 36; *Cowan* v. *Millar* (1895) 22 R. 833.
[5] *Churton* v. *Douglas* (1859) John. 174; *Trego* v. *Hunt* [1896] A.C. 7; *cf. Wankie Coal Co.* v. *Inland Revenue* [1920] A.C. 66; *Barr* v. *Lions Ltd.*, 1956 S.C. 59.
[6] On the enforceability of such convenants see generally *Gloag on Contract* (2nd ed.) 571 *et seq.*; *Pollock on Contract* (13th ed.) 326 *et seq.*; *Chitty on Contract* (21st ed.), Vol. I, 481 *et seq.*
[7] *Re David & Matthews* [1899] 1 Ch. 378; *Quinn* v. *Leathem* [1901] A.C. 495.

undoubtedly not wrongful for a stranger to set up in competition, but merely an exercise of his liberty to trade as and where he wishes and, if he can, to develop a competing business.

Where a business has been sold and the goodwill assigned, the assignee has the exclusive right to carry on the business transferred, to use its name [8] and to represent himself as doing so,[9] and he may by interdict prevent the assignor from continuing to represent himself as carrying on the old business, and recover damages in so far as he has lost thereby,[10] but not in so far as there has been no misrepresentation or breach of agreement not to solicit, and customers have spontaneously gone to the assignor's new business.[11]

In such cases the matters are usually so dealt with by express agreements and restrictive covenants that most disputes will arise in the form of alleged breaches of contract [12] rather than in the form of interference with the proprietary right to the business name and connection.

It may, however, be a wrong of the nature of passing off to engage in the same line of business as the complainer and to use a similar name.[13] If the defender in so doing is using his own name or one under which he had traded for some time,[14] he commits no wrong in the absence of facts evidencing dishonest intention,[15] because he is entitled to take any advantage which may flow from using his own name in business.[16]

Malicious falsehood by way of trade libel. An action of damages may be brought if a rival manufacturer makes an untrue statement of and concerning the pursuer's product and thereby causes him actual damage in business or property.[17] An action lies for written or oral falsehoods, not actionable *per se* nor even defamatory, where they are maliciously published and are calculated in the ordinary course of things to produce, and where they do produce, actual damage.[18] It does not amount to trade libel for the rival to issue unduly laudatory advertisements about his own products, nor even to state that his products are superior to those of competitors, even if that is untrue and the cause of actual damage to the pursuer.[19] There is no need to prove express malice and that by itself will not make an advertisement actionable.[20]

[8] *Smith* v. *McBride & Smith* (1882) 16 R. 36; *Thynne* v. *Shove* (1890) 45 Ch.D. 577; *Burchell* v. *Wilde* [1900] 1 Ch. 551.
[9] *Walker* v. *Mottram* (1881) 19 Ch.D. 355, 363.
[10] *Walker, supra; Burrows* v. *Foster* (1862) 1 N.R. 156.
[11] *McKirdy* v. *Paterson* (1854) 16 D. 1013.
[12] See, *e.g., Dumbarton Steamboat Co.* v. *Macfarlane* (1899) 1 F. 993.
[13] *Tussaud* v. *Tussaud* (1890) 44 Ch.D. 678.
[14] *Jay's, Ltd.* v. *Jacobi* [1933] Ch. 411.
[15] *Sykes* v. *Sykes* (1824) 3 B. & C. 541.
[16] *Burgess* v. *Burgess* (1853) 3 De G.M. & G. 896; *John Brinsmead, Ltd.* v. *Brinsmead & Waddington & Sons, Ltd.* (1913) 29 T.L.R. 237, 706.
[17] *White* v. *Mellin* [1895] A.C. 154; *British Empire Type Co.* v. *Linotype Co.* (1898) 79 L.T. 8; *Royal Baking Powder Co.* v. *Wright, Crossley & Co.* (1901) 18 R.P.C. 95.
[18] *Ratcliffe* v. *Evans* [1892] 2 Q.B. 524; but see Defamation Act, 1952, s. 14.
[19] *Hubbuck* v. *Wilkinson* [1899] 1 Q.B. 86.
[20] *White, supra; Hubbuck, supra.*

To issue a misleading report of legal proceedings relative to a trade mark may amount to a trade libel [21]; the truth and accuracy of the report is a complete defence.[22] It is permissible and not libellous to publish an apology made by an infringer, even though it was extracted under pressure or by threat of an action for infringement.[23]

Imputations against goods may amount to an innuendo and thus be defamatory of the complainer personally, as where he is said to sell spurious [24] or worthless [25] goods.

Trade Secrets. There is no right of property in a trade secret, such as a particular formula or method of preparing or manufacturing some product, unless it is protected by a patent,[26] and anyone else who discovers the secret independently, or has it betrayed to him, can use it. Moreover if a trade mark or trade name is attached to the goods prepared by that formula, any person coming into possession of the formula may market his product under that trade mark or trade name.[27] The question which then may arise is whether the name is merely that descriptive of the goods, or is indicative of the particular goods made or sold by the original discoverer of the formula and his successors, that is, does, *e.g*,. " camel-hair belting" mean belting made of camel-hair by anyone, or only belting made by the plaintiffs and in fact made mostly of camel-hair.[28] Only if it bears the latter connotation does the name give the manufacturer any claim against anyone else who uses that name as descriptive of his goods.

Royal Warrants of Appointments. A Royal Warrant appointing a particular firm suppliers of goods of a specified kind to a member of the Royal Family [29] entitles the firm to design itself as such appointed supplier, and it is an offence falsely to represent that any goods are made by a person holding a Royal Warrant [30] or to use the Royal Arms in connection with any trade, business, calling or profession in a manner calculated to deceive,[31] and the use of the Royal Arms or any device, emblem or title [32] in a way calculated to deceive may be restrained by interdict at the instance of any person who is authorised to use such arms,

---

21 *Hayward & Co.* v. *Hayward & Sons* (1886) 34 Ch.D. 198; *Liebig's Extract of Meat Co.* v. *Anderson* (1887) 55 L.T. 206.
22 *Nahmaschinen Fabrik Co.* v. *Singer Mfg. Co.* (1893) 10 R.P.C. 310; *Coats* v. *Chadwick* [1894] 1 Ch. 347.
23 *Fisher* v. *Apollinaris Co.* (1875) L.R. 10 Ch. 297.
24 *Anderson* v. *Liebig's Extract of Meat Co.* (1881) 45 L.T. 757.
25 *British Empire Type Co., supra.*
26 *Cf. Hutchison, Main & Co.* v. *Pattullo Bros.* (1888) 15 R. 644, 650–651. If the secret is betrayed, the original manufacturer may have an action for breach of confidence against the person divulging the secret.
27 *James* v. *James* (1872) L.R. 13 Eq. 421; *Condy* v. *Mitchell* (1877) 37 L.T.(N.S.) 766; *Benbow* v. *Low* (1881) 44 L.T.(N.S.) 875; *Birmingham Vinegar Brewery Co.* v. *Powell* [1897] A.C. 710.
28 *Reddaway* v. *Banham* [1896] A.C. 199; *cf. Siegert* v. *Findlater* (1878) 7 Ch.D. 801; *Birmingham Vinegar Brewery Co.* v. *Powell* [1897] A.C. 710.
29 About 600 firms hold such warrants.
30 Merchandise Marks Act, 1887, s. 20.
31 Patents Act, 1949, s. 92.
32 *Royal Warrant Holders' Assocn.* v. *Lipman* (1934) 51 R.P.C. 155.

device, emblem or title, or is authorised by the Lord Chamberlain to take proceedings in that behalf.[33] The holding of a Royal Warrant is accordingly akin to a kind of property right.

2. PATENTS

A patent is the grant, by letters patent under the seal of the Patent Office, in the exercise of the royal prerogative, of an incorporeal right of property in the exclusive and monopoly privilege of exploiting an invention.[34] The monopoly privilege is to " make, use, exercise and vend the said invention " and it is given to the named patentee himself, his agents or licensees.[35] " The object of a patent is to give a monopoly or protection to the inventor. That means that it gives him a right to prohibit all other persons from doing what the inventor has protected by his patent." [36]

A prerequisite of obtaining a remedy for infringement is to establish that a valid patent right exists in respect of the invention, and many of the cases turn on the validity or otherwise of the patent. An objection that the patent is invalid in law is always open as a defence to proceedings for infringement.[37] An action for infringement is still competent after the expiry of the patent but only for infringements committed before that date.[38]

Infringement. The infringement of a patent is the doing, after the date of publication of the complete specification,[39] of that which the patent prohibits being done, namely, during the term of the patent directly or indirectly making use of or putting into practice the patented invention, or imitating it, without the consent, licence or agreement of the patentee, on pain of incurring penalties for contempt of the Royal command, and of being answerable to the patentee according to law for his damages thereby occasioned.[40] The prohibition is broken by making, using or selling the patented invention.

The defender's ignorance of the patent infringed is no excuse,[41] nor is his absence of intent to infringe,[42] but an innocent infringer will not be liable in damages if he satisfies the conditions of s. 59. Where there is an intention to infringe, or threat of doing so, an interdict to prevent infringement is competent.[43]

33 Trade Marks Act, 1938, s. 61; *cf. R.W.H. Assocn.* v. *Slade* (1908) 25 R.P.C. 245; *R.W.H. Assocn.* v. *Deane & Beal* [1912] 1 Ch. 10.
34 *Steers* v. *Rogers* (1893) 10 R.P.C. 245; *Edwards & Co.* v. *Picard* [1909] 2 K.B. 903. See also *Neilson* v. *Househill Coal Co.* (1842) 4 D. 470, 475.
35 See Form of Patent, in Patents Rules, 1958, Fourth Schedule.
36 *Hutchison, Main & Co.* v. *Pattullo Bros.* (1888) 15 R. 644, 657, *per* L.J.C. Moncreiff.
37 *Harrison* v. *Anderston Foundry Co.* (1875) 2 R. 857. But see also *Watson, Laidlaw & Co.* v. *Pott, Cassels & Williamson,* 1909 S.C. 1445.
38 *Paterson Engineering Co., Ltd.* v. *Candy Filter Co.* (1933) 50 R.P.C. 1.
39 Patents Act, 1949, s. 13 (4).
40 See Form of Patent in Patents Rules, 1958, Fourth Schedule.
41 *Proctor* v. *Bennis* (1888) 4 R.P.C. 333, 356.
42 *Stead* v. *Anderson* (1843) 2 W.P.C. 151; *Young* v. *Rosenthal* (1884) 1 R.P.C. 29, 39.
43 *Dowling* v. *Billington* (1890) 7 R.P.C. 191; *Bloom* v. *Shulman* (1934) 51 R.P.C. 708.

Whether or not there has been infringement in a particular case depends on the validity of the patent, the interpretation of the patent specification, determination of the scope of the monopoly granted, and ascertainment of whether the actings in question fall within or without the scope of the monopoly. The onus of proof is on the pursuer. Under s. 57 (2) it is a defence in proceedings for infringement to prove that at the time of the infringement there was in force a contract relating to that patent and containing a clause void under s. 57 (1). In an action for infringement particulars of the contravention alleged must be specified.[44]

Remedies for infringement. The form of letters patent used provides that infringers, apart from liability for contempt of the Royal command not to interfere with the patentee's monopoly rights, will be " answerable to the patentee according to law for his damages thereby occasioned," *i.e.*, by infringement. The 1949 Act provides (s. 59 (4)) that nothing in that section shall affect the power of the court to grant interdict in any proceedings for infringement of a patent.[45] This is merely declaratory of common law. S. 60 provides further that in an action for infringement of a patent the pursuer shall be entitled, at his option, to an accounting and payment of profits in lieu of damages. In addition a claim is commonly made for the delivery up to the pursuer or the destruction of all infringing articles in the defender's possession.[46]

Where a patentee alters his patent he cannot thereafter enforce an interdict which he obtained before the alteration, as the amended patent may be liable to objections which did not apply to the former patent and what would have been an infringement of the old might not be of the new.[47]

The grant of interdict may be justified by an express or implied threat, or indication of intent, to do some act which will violate the pursuer's right,[48] or by evidence of an actual past infringement from which the court will normally infer an intention to continue infringement, unless indeed there is clear intention not to do it again.[49] Interdict may be suspended on grounds of public convenience.[50]

The remedies of damages and an accounting and payment of profits are alternative, not cumulative.[51] If damages are chosen, the proper measure is such sum of money as restores the pursuer to the position he

---

[44] *Mica Insulator Co.* v. *Bruce Peebles & Co.* (1905) 7 F. 944.
[45] On the principles on which interlocutory injunctions (*i.e.*, interim interdict) are granted, see *Challender* v. *Royle* (1887) 36 Ch.D. 425; 4 R.P.C. 363. Grantees of an exclusive licence may seek interdict: *Scottish Vacuum Cleaner Co.* v. *Provincial Cinematograph Theatres*, 1915, 1 S.L.T. 389.
[46] *Cf. Incandescent Gas Light Co.* v. *McCulloch* (1897) 5 S.L.T. 180, 190.
[47] *Dudgeon* v. *Thomson* (1877) 4 R.(H.L.) 88.
[48] *Frearson* v. *Loe* (1878) 9 Ch.D. 48; *Adair* v. *Young* (1879) 12 Ch.D. 13; *Dowling* v. *Billington* (1890) 7 R.P.C. 191.
[49] *Losh* v. *Hague* (1837) 1 W.P.C. 200; see also *B.T.H. Co.* v. *Charlesworth Peebles & Co.*, 1922 S.C. 680.
[50] *Hopkinson* v. *St. James', etc., Electric Light Co.* (1893) 10 R.P.C. 46.
[51] 1949 Act, s. 60; *United Horse Shoe and Nail Co., infra. Cf. Neilson* v. *Betts* (1870) L.R. 5 H.L. 1.

would have been in but for the defender's wrongful conduct, including all direct and natural consequences of that wrong.[52] The profit made by the infringer is irrelevant; he is liable in damages even if he made no profits, and he is liable for only nominal damages if his infringing sales did not injure the patentee's trade, but he is liable to make full compensation for injury which his infringement and competition have occasioned even if he himself made little or no profit by doing so.[52] Damages may be awarded on the basis of a royalty on the selling price of the goods,[53] or of the amount the patentee would have charged for a licence to do what the defender has done.[54]

Restrictions on recovery of damages. It is provided [55] that in proceedings for infringement of a patent damages shall not be awarded against a defender who proves that at the date of the infringement he was not aware, and had no reasonable ground for supposing, that the patent existed; and a person is not to be deemed to have been aware or to have had reasonable grounds for supposing by reason only of the application to an article of the word " patent," " patented," or any word or words expressing or implying that a patent has been obtained for the article, unless the number of the patent accompanied the word or words in question.

In such proceedings the court may, if it thinks fit, refuse to award any damages in respect of any infringement committed after a failure to pay any renewal fee within the prescribed period and before any extension of that period.[56]

Where an amendment of a specification by way of disclaimer, correction or explanation has been allowed under the Act [57] after the publication of the specification, no damages shall be awarded in any proceeding in respect of the use of the invention before the date of the decision allowing the amendment, unless the court is satisfied that the specification as originally published was framed in good faith and with reasonable skill and knowledge.[58]

Nothing in s. 59, it is provided,[59] shall affect the power of the court to grant an interdict in any proceedings for infringement of a patent.

Accounting for profits. If the pursuer claims an accounting for profits instead of damages, he will be entitled to recover from the infringer the whole net profit made by the latter from the manufacture, sale and other dealing with the articles which infringe the pursuer's patent.[60]

---

[52] *United Horse Shoe and Nail Co.* v. *Stewart & Co.* (1888) 15 R.(H.L.) 45; 5 R.P.C. 266. See also *Watson, Laidlaw & Co.* v. *Pott, Cassels & Williamson,* 1914 S.C.(H.L.) 18.
[53] *B.T.H. Co.* v. *Charlesworth Peebles & Co.,* 1923 S.C. 599.
[54] *British Motor Syndicate* v. *Taylor* (1900) 17 R.P.C. 723; *B.T.H. Co.* v. *Naamlooze Vennootschap Pope's Metaaldraadlampenfabrik* (1923) 40 R.P.C. 119; *British United Shoe Machinery Co.* v. *Lambert Howarth* (1929) 46 R.P.C. 315.
[55] Patents Act, 1949, s. 59 (1).
[56] *Ibid.* s. 59 (2).
[57] *Ibid.* ss. 29–31.
[58] *Ibid.* s. 59 (3).
[59] *Ibid.* s. 59 (4).
[60] *Neilson* v. *Baird* (1843) 6 D. 51, 60; affd. 1 Bell's App. 219.

Delivery or destruction of infringing goods. A successful pursuer may obtain an order for the delivery up or destruction of infringing articles.[61]

Remedy for threats of infringement proceedings. Where a person, whether entitled to or interested in a patent or an application for a patent or not, by circulars, advertisements or otherwise threatens any other person with proceedings for infringement of a patent, any person aggrieved [62] thereby may bring an action against that person for (a) declarator that the threats are unjustifiable; (b) an interdict against the continuance of the threats; and (c) such damages, if any, as he has sustained thereby, and he is entitled to these remedies unless the defender proves that the acts in respect of which proceedings were threatened constitute or, if done, would constitute, an infringement of a patent or of rights arising from the publication of a complete specification in respect of a claim of the specification not shown by the pursuer to be invalid. A mere notification of the existence of a patent does not constitute a threat of proceedings within the meaning of this provision.[63]

It is immaterial that the threats were made in good faith and in the honest belief that the act complained of did infringe a valid patent,[64] and the manner of making the threats is also immaterial.[65] A solicitor's letter sent before initiating an action, or proposing a compromise, may be a threat, even if made in answer to enquiries,[66] if in substance it intimates an intention to take action for infringement,[67] and even if stated to be " without prejudice." [68] An oral statement may be a threat under the section.[69] A threat within the section may be made even though not communicated directly or indirectly to the person threatened; it is sufficient if the threat is expressed by any means and relates to the person who complains even though sent or published to other persons only.[70]

The threat may be made by implication, as where it is stated that something does infringe the complainer's patent,[71] though mere notification that a patent exists is not a threat.[72] Statements that acts expected to be done in the future will be an infringement amount to actionable threats.[73] A general warning may be an actionable threat if in the light of the circumstances it appears to have been directed only against some identifiable person or persons.[74]

---

[61] *Incandescent Gas Light Co.* v. *McCulloch* (1897) 5 S.L.T. 190.
[62] Not only the person threatened: this entitles a rival patentee to sue, if damage has accrued to him: *Johnson* v. *Edge* (1893) 9 R.P.C. 142.
[63] Patents Act, 1949, s. 65.
[64] *Skinner* v. *Perry* (1893) 10 R.P.C. 1.
[65] *Skinner, supra.*
[66] *Skinner, supra*; *H.V.E. Electric* v. *Cufflin Holdings* [1964] 1 All E.R. 674.
[67] *Douglass* v. *Pintsch's Patent Lighting Co., Ltd.* (1897) 13 R.P.C. 673; *Ellis & Sons, Ltd.* v. *Pogson* (1924) 40 R.P.C. 62; *Luna Advertising Co.* v. *Burnham & Co.* (1929) 45 R.P.C. 258.
[68] *Kurtz* v. *Spence* (1887) 5 R.P.C. 161, 173.
[69] *Kurtz, supra*; *Ellis, supra*; *Luna Advertising Co., supra*; *H.V.E. Electric, supra.*
[70] *John Summers & Sons, Ltd.* v. *The Cold Metal Process Co.* (1948) 65 R.P.C. 75.
[71] *Luna Advertising Co.* v. *Burnham & Co.* (1929) 45 R.P.C. 258.
[72] Act, s. 65 (3).
[73] Act, s. 65 (1) and (2); *Johnson* v. *Edge* (1893) 9 R.P.C. 142.
[74] *Challender* v. *Royle* (1888) 4 R.P.C. 363.

To bring the statutory action it is not necessary for the person aggrieved by the threat to prove any actual damage in order to ground his claim for relief.[75] Damages are measured by the natural and reasonable consequences of the threats,[76] and have been held to include the loss of a contract [77] or the breaking off of negotiations for a contract,[78] but do not cover any loss not due to the threats.

The onus is on the pursuer to prove the threat, then on the defender to prove that the acts in respect of which proceedings are threatened constitute an infringement. If the defender proves this, the onus reverts to the pursuer to prove invalidity if he can.[79]

Independently of the statutory provision a common-law claim of damages is competent if the defender's threat amounts to a malicious attempt to injure the pursuer by asserting a claim known to be unfounded and actual damage results from the threat.[80] The publication of circulars stating that a patent is invalid may be a good ground for an action of damages for malicious falsehood or " slander of title." [81]

3. TRADE MARKS

A trade mark is a symbol which is applied or attached to goods offered for sale in the market, so as to distinguish them from similar goods, and to identify them with a particular trader, or with his successors as the owners of a particular business, as being made, worked upon, imported, selected, certified or sold by him or them, or which has been registered under the Acts as the trade mark of a particular trader.[82] A mark includes a device, brand, heading, label, ticket, name, signature, word, letter, numeral or any combination thereof.[83] Legal protection is given on the basis that one trader is not entitled to represent that his goods are those of another. The association of a particular mark with a particular trader's goods may arise from business use and wont, or from registration. Registration in the Register of Trade Marks does not create a new right distinct from anything recognised at common law, but provides a new way of acquiring title to a trade mark, simplifies infringement actions, and is in general a prerequisite of an infringement action. It does not confer a proprietary right in a trade mark but only a right not to have another's goods confused with one's own. The registration relieves the pursuer of the onus incumbent on him at common law of

---

75 *John Summers & Sons, Ltd.* v. *The Cold Metal Process Co.* (1948) 65 R.P.C. 75. See also *Selsdon Fountain Pen Co.* v. *Miles Martin Pen Co.* (1948) 65 R.P.C. 365.
76 *Ungar* v. *Sugg* (1892) 9 R.P.C. 114.
77 *Skinner* v. *Perry* (1894) 11 R.P.C. 406.
78 *Solanite Signs, Ltd.* v. *Wood* (1933) 50 R.P.C. 315.
79 *Falk* v. *Jacobwitz* (1944) 61 R.P.C. 116.
80 *Wren* v. *Weild* (1868) L.R. 4 Q.B. 730; *Farr* v. *Weatherhead and Harding* (1933) 49 R.P.C. 262; *Carr* v. *Brand Light Syndicate, Ltd.* (1912) 28 R.P.C. 33.
81 *Montgomerie* v. *Paterson* (1894) 11 R.P.C. 221, 237; affd. *ibid.* 633.
82 *Kerly on Trade Marks* (8th ed.) 16. For statutory definition see Trade Marks Act, 1938, s. 68 (1) and (2). See also *Re Australian Wine Importers* (1889) 41 Ch.D. 278, 280, *per* Kay J.
83 Act, s. 68 (1).

proving that he had acquired a title to the mark by long use and association.[84] A trade mark must be registered in respect of particular goods or classes of goods.[85]

Rights conferred. The Trade Marks Register is divided into Parts A and B,[86] and the rights conferred by registration in the two parts differ. Registration in Part A [87] gives the proprietor the exclusive right to the use of the trade mark in relation to the goods in respect of which it is registered, which right shall be deemed to be infringed by any person who uses an identical mark or one so nearly resembling it as to be likely to deceive or cause confusion, but not if used outwith any conditions or limitations entered on the register or in certain other specified cases. Registration in Part B [88] gives similar rights save that in an action for infringement no interdict or other relief shall be granted if the defender establishes to the satisfaction of the court that the use of which the pursuer complains is not likely to deceive or cause confusion or to be taken as indicating a connection in the course of trade between the goods and some person having the right either as proprietor or as registered user to use the trade mark.

Infringement. Infringement may be constituted, firstly, under section 6, by the breach, in one or more of certain specified ways, of an obligation, entered into by contract in writing, between the proprietor or a registered user of a registered trade mark and a purchaser or owner of goods, not to do an act in relation to the goods to which the section applies. The breach, and consequent liability, may be by any person who is owner for the time being of the goods, unless he became owner in good faith, for value, and without notice of the obligation, or by virtue of a title derived through another who so became the owner thereof.

Secondly, infringement may be constituted by a person, not the proprietor or registered user of the trade mark, making, selling or otherwise handling goods marked with the proprietor's trade mark or with another mark which resembles it so as to be " likely to deceive or cause confusion." [89]

It is always a question of fact [90] whether the defender's goods are such that they are likely to deceive customers or to cause confusion with the pursuer's goods by reason of their deceptive resemblance in respect of the feature which is registered as the pursuer's trade mark. The degree of resemblance necessary to deceive or cause confusion is incapable of definition,[91] and previous cases are of little value save as examples.[92]

---

[84] *Boord & Son* v. *Thom & Cameron*, 1907 S.C. 1326, 1342.
[85] Trade Marks Rules, 1938, Sched. III and IV.
[86] 1938 Act, s. 1 (2). As to requisites for registration in Parts A and B respectively, see ss. 9 and 10 respectively.
[87] *Ibid.* s. 4.
[88] *Ibid.* s. 5.
[89] Act, ss. 11, 12 (1), 20 (4), 22 (4), 23 (2) and (5), 37 (3).
[90] *Rysta, Ltd.'s Application* (1943) 60 R.P.C. 87, 105, *per* Lord Greene M.R.
[91] *Seixo* v. *Provezende* (1865) L.R. 1 Ch.App. 192.
[92] *Johnston* v. *Orr-Ewing* (1882) 7 App.Cas. 219.

Resemblance has to be judged by reference to prospective purchasers of the goods on which the marks are used, assuming that they use ordinary care and intelligence, not merely by reference to strangers [93] or retail dealers buying for resale.[94] It cannot be assumed that careful examination will be made [95] and in certain markets the possibility that purchasers will be illiterate is material.[96]

All the facts and circumstances of the case have to be considered and the question is whether, as a whole, the mark alleged to infringe bears a deceptive similarity, or is materially different from that registered.[97] But regard has to be paid particularly to the dominant theme or idea of the mark and the overall impression it conveys, rather than to detailed points of difference.[98] There can be no infringement when the only resemblances between the two marks are in features which are common to the trade; the resemblance must be in some feature which is distinctive or peculiar to the pursuer's mark and which specially distinguishes his goods.[99]

Not only visual resemblance must be considered but resemblance in point of sound,[1] having regard to the possibility of orders by telephone,[2] and to careless pronunciation,[3] and to the appearance the marks would present in actual use when fairly and honestly used, including their size, colour, means of attachment, and the possibility of being blurred or defaced in transit or in use.[4]

Remedies. The successful pursuer in an infringement action is entitled to interdict against further infringement of his rights,[5] where there is some threat or probability of repeated or continued infringement, but it

[93] *Johnston* v. *Orr-Ewing* (1882) 7 App.Cas. 219; *Wilkinson* v. *Griffith* (1891) 8 R.P.C. 370; *Price's Patent Candle Co.* v. *Ogston and Tennant* (1909) 26 R.P.C. 797; *Andrew* v. *Kuchurich* (1913) 30 R.P.C. 93; *Société Anonyme Dubonnet's Application* (1915) 32 R.P.C. 241; *Bagots, Hutton & Co.'s Application* [1916] 2 A.C. 382; 33 R.P.C. 357.

[94] *Wilkinson, supra*; *Powell* v. *Birmingham Vinegar Brewery Co.* [1897] A.C. 710; *Edge* v. *Nicholls* [1911] A.C. 693.

[95] *Wotherspoon* v. *Currie* (1872) L.R. 5 H.L. 508; *Singer Mfg. Co.* v. *Loog* (1882) 8 App.Cas. 15; *Seixo* v. *Provezende* (1865) L.R. 1 Ch.App. 192; *Powell, supra*; *Payton* v. *Snelling* (1900) 17 R.P.C. 628.

[96] *Lever* v. *Goodwin* (1887) 36 Ch.D. 1; *Cowie* v. *Herbert* (1897) 24 R. 353; *Edge, supra*; *Singer Mfg. Co., supra*; *Scottish Union and National Insce. Co.* v. *Scottish National Insce. Co.*, 1909 S.C. 318; 26 R.P.C. 105; *Claudius Ash, Sons & Co.* v. *Invicta Mfg. Co.* (1911) 29 R.P.C. 465.

[97] *Pianotist Co., Ltd.'s Application* (1906) 23 R.P.C. 774.

[98] *Johnston* v. *Orr-Ewing* (1882) 7 App.Cas. 219; *Christiansen's T.M.* (1886) 3 R.P.C. 54; *Barchiera's T.M.* (1889) 5 T.L.R. 480; *Bale & Church, Ltd.* v. *Sutton Parsons & Sutton and Astrah Products, Ltd.* (1934) 51 R.P.C. 129; *Coca Cola Co. of Canada, Ltd.* v. *Pepsi Cola Co. of Canada, Ltd.* (1942) 59 R.P.C. 127.

[99] *Jamieson & Co.* v. *Jamieson* (1898) 15 R.P.C. 169; *Payton & Co., Ltd.* v. *Snelling* (1900) 17 R.P.C. 628; *Payton & Co., Ltd.* v. *Ward* (1900) 17 R.P.C. 58; *Marshall* v. *Sidebotham* (1901) 18 R.P.C. 43; *Alaska Packers' Association* v. *Crooks* (1901) 18 R.P.C. 129.

[1] *Magdalene Securities, Ltd.'s Application* (1931) 48 R.P.C. 477; *County Chemical Co.'s Application* (1937) 54 R.P.C. 182; *Fred Mellor (Huddersfield), Ltd.'s Application* (1948) 65 R.P.C. 238.

[2] *Magdalene Securities, supra*.

[3] *Rysta, Ltd.'s Application* (1943) 60 R.P.C. 87, 108.

[4] *Lyndon's T.M.* (1885) 3 R.P.C. 102; *Haines, Batchelor & Co.'s T.M.* (1885) 5 R.P.C. 669; *Lambert's T.M.* (1889) 6 R.P.C. 344; *Price's Patent Candle Co.* v. *Ogston and Tennant, Ltd.* (1909) 26 R.P.C. 797.

[5] *Kinnell* v. *Ballantine*, 1910 S.C. 246; see also *Montgomerie* v. *Young Bros.* (1904) 11 S.L.T. 298, 600; *Bass, Ratcliffe & Gratton* v. *Laidlaw* (1908) 16 S.L.T. 660.

may be withheld if an infringer, particularly an innocent one, gives undertakings.[6] Interdict may be granted where there is merely reasonable ground for apprehension of injury.[7]

The pursuer is further entitled to the delivery to him of goods bearing the offending marks for their destruction [8] or the erasure of the offending mark.[9]

The pursuer may also claim damages in respect of the past infringement, or alternatively (but not cumulatively), an accounting and payment of profits. Proof of a bare infringement justifies nominal damages,[10] and substantial damages are recoverable on proof of the loss which has actually been sustained. It is for the pursuer to prove what loss he has sustained by reason of the defender's conduct [11] and it cannot be assumed that the quantity of goods sold by the infringer under the offending mark would have been sold by the pursuer, had it not been for the defender's infringement.[12]

Damages extend to direct and natural consequences of the infringement, as where the sale of inferior goods under an infringing mark has damaged the pursuer's business reputation.[13] This raises difficult issues where stress of competition forces the pursuer to reduce prices to enable him to stay in the market.[14]

If the pursuer elects to take an accounting for profits and payment thereof, his claim is for the whole net profits made by the infringer by the use of the infringing trade mark.[15]

Limitations on remedies for unregistered trade mark. No person may seek interdict against or damages for the infringement of an unregistered trade mark, save by way of common-law action for passing-off.[16] In any such case it is necessary to prove all the requisites for success in a passing-off action.

Action for threats. In the case of trade marks [17] there is no special statutory right of action against a person who threatens another with an action for infringement. Hence the making by one person in good faith

---

6 *Cf. Smith & Wellstood* v. *Carron Co.* (1896) 3 S.L.T. 223; 13 R.P.C. 108.
7 *Singer Mfg. Co.* v. *Kimball & Morton* (1873) 11 M. 267.
8 *Farina* v. *Silverlock* (1858) 4 K. & J. 650.
9 *Dent* v. *Turpin* (1861) 2 J. & H. 139; *Upmann* v. *Elkan* (1872) L.R. 7 Ch. 130; *Slazenger* v. *Feltham* (1889) 5 T.L.R. 365.
10 *Blofield* v. *Payne* (1833) 4 B. & Ad. 410; *Daniel* v. *Whitehouse* (1898) 15 R.P.C. 134.
11 *Spalding & Bros.* v. *Gamage* (1915) 32 R.P.C. 273; 35 R.P.C. 101; see also *Thomson* v. *Dailly* (1897) 24 R. 1173.
12 *Leather Cloth Co.* v. *Hirschfeld* (1865) L.R. 1 Eq. 299; *cf. Magnolia Metal Co.* v. *Atlas Metal Co.* (1896) 14 R.P.C. 389 (passing-off); *United Horse Shoe and Nail Co.* v. *Stewart* (1888) 15 R.(H.L.) 45 (patent); *Kinnell* v. *Ballantine*, 1910 S.C. 246.
13 *Sykes* v. *Sykes* (1824) 3 B. & Cr. 541.
14 *American Braided Wire Co.* v. *Thomson* (1890) 7 R.P.C. 152; *United Horse Shoe and Nail Co., supra*; *Alexander* v. *Henry* (1895) 12 R.P.C. 360. See also *British Motor Syndicate* v. *Taylor* (1900) 17 R.P.C. 723; *Leeds Forge Co., Ltd.* v. *Deighton* (1908) 25 R.P.C. 209; *Wellman, Seaver & Head, Ltd.* v. *Burstinghaus & Co., Ltd.* (1911) 28 R.P.C. 326.
15 *Electrolux, Ltd.* v. *Electrix, Ltd.* (1953) 70 R.P.C. 158.
16 1938 Act, s. 2.
17 Contrast Patents Act, 1949, s. 65; Registered Designs Act, 1949, s. 26.

of a statement that another is infringing his trade mark, or a threat to take proceedings for infringement against the other, is not actionable.[18] This applies only to statements and warnings published in good faith and in the honest belief that they are justified, even though they may turn out to be mistaken [19] or unjustified,[20] and even though there is pending an action involving the right of the other party to use the trade mark or name he is using.[21]

Absence of good faith in making the statement complained of is essential; it is no proof of lack of good faith to show that the defender delayed bringing an action for infringement, certainly where the delay is reasonably explicable.[22]

But it is otherwise if the statements, warnings or threats are not made in good faith. If they amount to malicious or injurious falsehood or slander of title or to defamation of the other party they are actionable,[23] and the continued publication of the warnings after they have been proved, or have been held by the court, to be untrue may be checked by interdict.[24] Injunctions have also been granted where under pretence of issuing fair warning it has been alleged that another party's goods are spurious [25] or not genuine,[26] or inadequate.[27]

Even a warning or advertisement made in good faith and which is, or is found to be, justified may be a contempt of court if issued when proceedings are pending and if it in any way tends to prejudge the issue before the court or to interfere with the administration of justice.[28] The fact that an action is pending shows that the contention of infringement is not admitted, and it cannot therefore be publicly asserted as fact. Similarly a newspaper report of such an action might be a contempt if it goes beyond a fair and accurate report.

Merchandise Marks. The Merchandise Marks Acts, 1887 to 1953, deal with the criminal law of false marking of goods, and the application of false trade descriptions. There appears to be no authority for the grant of a civil remedy for loss caused by unjustified reliance on the marking or description of goods.

18 *Colley* v. *Hart* (1888) 44 Ch.D. 179; 6 R.P.C. 17; 7 R.P.C. 108; *cf. Ripley* v. *Arthur & Co.* (1901) 18 R.P.C. 82 (passing-off).
19 *Royal Baking Powder Co.* v. *Wright, Crossley & Co.* (1899) 16 R.P.C. 217; affd. 18 R.P.C. 95.
20 *Withers & Sons, Ltd.* v. *Withers & Co., Ltd.* (1927) 44 R.P.C. 19; *cf. Wren* v. *Weild* (1869) L.R. 4 Q.B. 730; *Helsey* v. *Brotherhood* (1881) 19 Ch.D. (both prior to introduction of patents threats action in 1883).
21 *Coats* v. *Chadwick* [1894] 1 Ch. 347.
22 *Incandescent Gas Light Co.* v. *Sunlight Incandescent Co.* (1897) 14 R.P.C. 180.
23 *Greers, Ltd.* v. *Pearman and Corder, Ltd.* (1922) 39 R.P.C. 406.
24 *Wren, supra.*
25 *Thorley's Cattle Food Co.* v. *Massam* (1880) 14 Ch.D. 763. *Cf. Coulson* v. *Coulson* (1887) 3 T.L.R. 740.
26 *Thomas* v. *Williams* (1880) 14 Ch.D. 864; *Liebig* v. *Anderson* (1887) 55 L.T. 206; *Cars* v. *Bland Light Syndicate, Ltd.* (1911) 28 R.P.C. 33.
27 *London Ferro-Concrete Co.* v. *Justicz* (1951) 68 R.P.C. 261.
28 *Coates* v. *Chadwick* [1894] 1 Ch. 347. See also *R.* v. *Payne* [1896] 1 Q.B. 577; *Re New Gold Coast Exploration Co.* [1901] 1 Ch. 860. *Cf. Goulard* v. *Lindsay* (1887) 4 R.P.C. 189.

4. COPYRIGHT

Copyright is the exclusive right, by virtue of and under the Copyright Act, 1956, personally or by an authorised person, to reproduce original literary, dramatic or musical work in any material form, publish it, perform it in public, broadcast it, cause it to be transmitted to subscribers to a diffusion service, make an adaptation of it or deal with the adaptation,[29] within fifty years from the end of the year in which the author died, or the work was first published, performed or broadcast.[30] Copyright extends also to reproducing in any material form, publishing, including in a television broadcast, or causing to be transmitted to subscribers to a diffusion service, a television programme which includes any artistic work, including paintings, drawings, and works of architecture.[31] It subsists also in sound recordings, cinematograph films, television and sound broadcasts, and separate editions of literary, dramatic or musical works.[32] The right of copyright exists only under and subject to the 1956 Act, so that all questions of infringement of copyright depend on the interpretation of that Act in the circumstances.

The Act provides in whom the ownership of copyright vests.[33] The copyright may be assigned to another, who thereupon becomes entitled to the rights and remedies of the owner, and transmitted as moveable property by testamentary disposition or by operation of law.[34]

Infringement. In relation to infringement it is material to remember that copyright protects the expression of thought or ideas and not the originality or substance of the thought or ideas. Infringement consists in unlawful copying of another's words or form of expression.

Infringement of copyright takes place when any person, not being the owner of the copyright and without the licence of the owner, does, or authorises any other person to do, any of the acts which the owner has the exclusive right of doing.[35] It is also constituted by import without licence, sale or other dealings with infringing material, *e.g.*, pirated editions.[36] Various kinds of dealing with a copyright work are, however, excepted from constituting infringement.[37]

Infringement is actionable [38] at the instance of the owner of the copyright and entitles him to the remedies of damages, interdict and accounts of profits,[39] to the recovery of infringing copies, plates, etc.[40]

---

[29] Copyright Act, 1956, ss. 1 (1), 2 (1) and (5). On the whole subject see *Copinger and Skone James on Copyright* (9th ed.).
[30] *Ibid.* s. 2 (2) and (3).
[31] *Ibid.* s. 3: " Artistic work " is defined in s. 3 (1).
[32] *Ibid.* ss. 12–15.
[33] *Ibid.* 4. As to anonymous and pseudonymous works and works of joint authorship, see s. 11. As to proof of ownership and other facts in a copyright action, see s. 20.
[34] *Ibid.* s. 36. As to copyright in unpublished work carried by bequest, see s. 38.
[35] *Ibid.* s. 1 (2).
[36] *Ibid.* ss. 5, 16.
[37] *Ibid.* ss. 6–10, 41.
[38] Certain infringements are also punishable as summary offences: s. 21.
[39] *Ibid.* s. 17 (1).
[40] *Ibid.* s. 18 (1).

and to damages for the intromission by the infringer with infringing copies, plates, etc.[41] Damages for infringement and for intromission with infringing copies are cumulative.[42]

Where an exclusive licence has been granted or is in force at the material time, the exclusive licensee has the same rights under section 17 as if the licence had been an assignation concurrently with the copyright owner's rights. Under section 18 the exclusive licensee has the same rights as if he had been an assignee and the copyright owner has no rights which he would not have had if the licence had been an assignation.[43]

In a case of infringement the quantity or proportion of matter copied from the work of another is a material factor, but more important is the matter of quality, whether the original author's work is substantially appropriated by the infringing publication.[44] In English cases injunctions have been granted where only a portion of the work complained of had been pirated, if that was inseparable from independent work.[45]

Damages under section 17. Where damages are sought for infringement they fall to be measured by the depreciation in the value of the author's copyright caused by the infringing publication.[46] Account must be taken in quantifying damages of any loss which the copyright owner has suffered by a diminution in the sales of his work, or loss of the profits which he might otherwise have made.[47] Some allowance may be made to cover the possibility that the copyright owner would not have sold quite so many copies as the infringing publication has done.[48] No account falls to be taken of any benefit which the infringer may have made from the use of the work.

Damages may be increased if it be shown that the infringing work has damaged the reputation of the original,[49] and where the design of the original had been vulgarised by the infringing copy it has been held competent, and an aggravation of damages, to withdraw the whole stock of the original work.[50]

The court has power under s. 17 (3) to award additional damages as it considers appropriate having regard to (a) the flagrancy of the infringement, and (b) any benefit shown to have accrued to the defender by reason of the infringement, if satisfied that an effective remedy would not otherwise be available to the pursuer, *e.g.*, where an interdict would not benefit the pursuer and the ordinary measure of damages would be inadequate.

---

41 *Ibid.* s. 18 (1) and (4); *Caxton Publishing Co.* v. *Sutherland Publishing Co.* [1939] A.C. 178.
42 *Caxton Publishing Co., supra.*
43 Act, s. 19 (2).
44 *Warne* v. *Seebohm* (1888) 39 Ch.D. 73.
45 *Mawman* v. *Tegg* (1826) 2 Russ. 385; *Lamb* v. *Evans* [1892] 3 Ch. 462.
46 *Sutherland Publishing Co.* v. *Caxton Publishing Co.* [1936] Ch. 323, 336.
47 *Birn* v. *Keen* [1918] 2 Ch. 281; *Fenning Film Service* v. *Wolverhampton Cinemas* [1914] 3 K.B. 1171.
48 *Birn, supra.*
49 *Hanfstaengl* v. *Smith* [1905] 1 Ch. 519; *Birn, supra.*
50 *Mansell* v. *Wesley*, Macg.Cop.Cas. (1938–9) 288.

Damages are not recoverable under section 17 if, even though an infringement was committed, at the time of the infringement the defender was not aware, and had no reasonable grounds for suspecting, that copyright subsisted in the work or other subject-matter to which the action relates, but in such a case the pursuer is still entitled to an account of profits, whether any other remedy is granted or not.[51]

Interdict is competent in lieu of or in addition to damages.

By section 17 (4), in an action for infringement of copyright in respect of the construction of a building, no interdict or other order shall be made (a) after the construction of the building has been made, so as to prevent it from being completed, or (b) so as to require the building, in so far as it has been constructed, to be demolished.

Accounting and payment of profits. The third possible remedy under section 17 is a claim for an accounting and payment of profits. Accounting can be claimed as well as interdict, but not as well as damages in respect that an accounting condones the infringement.[52] The profits recoverable are the net profits [53] made by publishing the infringing work. If there are obviously no profits an accounting will be refused,[54] in which case damages can be claimed.[55]

Remedies under section 18. Under section 18 the copyright owner is deemed to be the owner of any infringing copies and plates and other appliances used in making the infringing copies. He can accordingly treat the possessor thereof as intromitting with his property and is entitled to all such rights and remedies as he would be if he were the actual, and not merely the notional, owner thereof.

He may accordingly demand restitution and delivery of them to him, failing which damages measured by their wholesale value, not their retail price.[56] It has been held in England that a plaintiff was entitled as of right to an order for delivery though the alternative of damages does not appear to have been argued to the court.[57]

Independently of the statutory right there is a common law right to the delivery up of infringing copies, but only for their destruction or the cancellation of infringing parts.[58]

Where the infringing material is mixed with original work the order for delivery may apply only to the infringing part if it is physically separable,[59] but otherwise it must apply to the whole work.[60]

---

[51] Act, s. 17 (2).
[52] *Caxton Publishing Co.* v. *Sutherland Publishing Co.* [1939] A.C. 178, 198; *De Vitre* v. *Betts* (1873) L.R. 6 H.L. 319; *Colburn* v. *Simms* (1843) 2 Hare 543.
[53] *Delfe* v. *Delamotte* (1857) 3 K. & J. 587.
[54] *Colburn, supra*; *Powell* v. *Aikin* (1857) 4 K. & J. 343.
[55] *Mawman* v. *Tegg* (1826) 2 Russ. 385, 400.
[56] *Mansell* v. *Wesley*, Macg.Cop.Cas. (1938–1939) 288.
[57] *Boosey* v. *Whight* (No. 2) (1899) 81 L.T. 265.
[58] *Warne* v. *Seebohm* (1888) 39 Ch.D. 73; *Chappell* v. *Columbia Graphophone Co.* [1914] 2 Ch. 124, 745.
[59] *Warne, supra*; *Boosey, supra*.
[60] *Stevens* v. *Wildy* (1850) 19 L.J.Ch. 190.

Damages for wrongful intromission under section 18 are cumulative with damages for infringement under section 17, and not alternative thereto,[61] though damages should not be given under both sections in respect of the same head of loss.[62]

A pursuer is not, however, entitled by virtue of section 18 to any damages or other pecuniary remedy, except expenses, if it is proved or admitted that, at the time of the intromission in question—(a) the defender was not aware, and had no reasonable grounds for suspecting, that copyright subsisted in the work or other subject-matter to which the action relates, or (b) where the articles intromitted with were infringing copies, the defendant believed, and had reasonable grounds for believing, that they were not infringing copies, or (c) where the article intromitted with was a plate used or intended to be used for making any articles, the defender believed, and had reasonable grounds for believing, that the articles so made or intended to be made were not, or (as the case may be) would not be, infringing copies.[63]

Copyright in designs. Artistic work might be entitled to protection both under the Copyright Act, 1956, section 10, and the Registered Designs Act, 1949. Section 10 of the 1956 Act seeks to minimise this possibility by providing that an artistic work is not entitled to the protection of the 1956 Act if registered under the 1949 Act, and also if it is used as an industrial design but not registered as such under the 1949 Act.

5. REGISTERED DESIGNS

New or original designs [64] may be registered under the Registered Designs Act, 1949, in respect of any article or set of articles specified in the application by the person claiming to be the proprietor thereof.[65] The author is prima facie the proprietor of the design, but the design or the right to apply it to any article may be assigned or transmitted voluntarily or by operation of law to another person, who is treated as the proprietor.[66]

Registration under the Act gives the registered proprietor the copyright in the registered design, which is " the exclusive right in the United Kingdom and the Isle of Man to make or import for sale or for use for the purposes of any trade or business, or to sell, hire, or offer for sale or hire, any article in respect of which the design is registered, being an article to which the registered design or a design not substantially different from the registered design has been applied, and to make anything for enabling any such article to be made as aforesaid, whether in the United

---

[61] *Caxton Publishing Co.* v. *Sutherland Publishing Co.* [1939] A.C. 178.
[62] *Ibid.*
[63] Act, s. 18 (2). This subsection, unlike s. 17 (2) does not provide for an account of profits.
[64] Defined, Registered Designs Act, 1949, s. 1 (3).
[65] *Ibid.* s. 1.
[66] *Ibid.* s. 2.

Kingdom or the Isle of Man or elsewhere." [67] Copyright subsists for five years from the date of registration, but may be extended for two further periods of five years.[68]

Infringement. Infringement is constituted by the doing, by any person other than the registered proprietor of the design, of any of the things which the registered proprietor is declared to have the exclusive right of doing. Whether a design infringes another already registered in respect of similarity is a question of fact to be determined by visual inspection.[69]

Exceptions from infringement. In proceedings for the infringement of copyright in a registered design damages are not to be awarded against a defender who proves that at the date of the infringement he was not aware, and had no reasonable ground for supposing, that the design was registered; and a person is not to be deemed to have been aware or to have had reasonable grounds for supposing by reason only of the marking of an article with the word "registered" or any abbreviation thereof, or of any word or words expressing or implying that the design applied to the article had been registered, unless the number of the design accompanied the word or words or the abbreviation in question.[70] These provisions do not affect the power of the court to grant interdict in infringement proceedings.[71]

Certain other kinds of conduct are specially declared not to be infringement of copyright in designs by the Copyright Act, 1956, section 10.

Remedies. The remedies for infringement are provided by common law, not by the Act. They are suspension and interdict,[72] delivery up of the infringing designs,[73] and damages or an accounting for profits, but not both.

The basic measure of damages, as in patent and copyright cases, is the amount of profits which the pursuer has lost in consequence of the defender's infringement of his design, and which he would reasonably have made himself if he had sold the articles himself or obtained a royalty on them.[74]

Groundless threats of infringement proceedings. Where a person threatens any other person with proceedings for infringement of the

---

[67] *Ibid.* s. 7.
[68] *Ibid.* s. 8. There are provisions for cancelling registration (s. 11), keeping (s. 17), rectifying (ss. 20–21) and inspecting (s. 22) the Register of Designs, registration of assignations (s. 19), the issue of certificates of registration (s. 18), and the giving by the registrar of information whether a design is registered (s. 23).
[69] *Holdsworth* v. *McCrea* (1867) L.R. 2 H.L. 380, 386; *Staples* v. *Warwick* (1906) 23 R.P.C. 609.
[70] *Ibid.* s. 9 (1).
[71] *Ibid.* s. 9 (2).
[72] *Walker, Hunter & Co.* v. *Falkirk Iron Co.* (1887) 14 R. 1072; *Hutchison, Main & Co.* v. *St. Mungo Mfg. Co.* (1907) 24 R.P.C. 265.
[73] *Wallpaper Mfrs., Ltd.* v. *Derby Paper Staining Co.* (1924) 42 R.P.C. 449; *Dunlop Rubber Co.* v. *Booth* (1925) 43 R.P.C. 139.
[74] *United Horse Shoe and Nail Co.* v. *Stewart* (1886) 15 R.(H.L.) 45; 5 R.P.C. 260; *Pneumatic Tyre Co.* v. *Puncture Proof Pneumatic Tyre Co.* (1897) 16 R.P.C. 209.

copyright in a registered design, any person aggrieved thereby may claim (a) declarator that the threats are unjustifiable; (b) interdict against the continuance of the threats; and (c) such damages, if any, as he has sustained thereby, and he is entitled to these remedies unless the defender proves that the acts in respect of which proceedings were threatened constitute or, if done, would constitute an infringement of the copyright in a registered design, the registration of which is not shown by the pursuer to be invalid. A mere notification that a design is registered is not a threat of proceedings.[75] This section creates a purely statutory delict.

Where damages are awarded they are measured by fair compensation for the damage caused solely by the threats made and made known to third parties, but not for threats not authorised,[76] nor for consequences which go beyond the natural and reasonable consequences thereof.[77] Damage suffered by losing a contract[78] or the ending of negotiations for a contract[79] have been held recoverable.

Apart from the statutory claim an action at common law for verbal injury by way of malicious falsehood, slander of title or slander of goods remains competent.[80]

Unregistered designs. A design not registered under the 1949 Act may have the copyright therein protected under the Copyright Act, 1956, section 10, subject to the conditions set out therein.

6. PLANT BREEDERS' RIGHTS

The Plant Varieties and Seeds Act, 1964, empowers the Controller of the Plant Variety Rights Office thereby established[81] to grant rights known as plant breeders' rights in respect of plant varieties of the species or groups prescribed by a scheme under the Act[82] to persons qualified.[83] The rights are to be exercisable for not more than twenty-five years, as prescribed by a scheme under the Act, the controller having power to extend the period of protection up to twenty-five years, or to terminate it.[84] The right conferred is the exclusive right, personally or by authorising others, to sell the reproductive material of the plant variety, to reproduce it in Great Britain for sale, and to exercise certain other rights.[85] The exclusive rights may be exercised by others duly authorised, which authority may be conditional, limited or restricted, and are assignable like other kinds of proprietary rights.[86]

[75] *Ibid.* s. 26.
[76] *Ungar* v. *Sugg* (1891) 9 R.P.C. 113, 118.
[77] *Horne* v. *Johnston Bros.* (1921) 38 R.P.C. 366.
[78] *Skinner* v. *Perry* (1893) 11 R.P.C. 406.
[79] *Solanite* v. *Wood* (1933) 50 R.P.C. 315.
[80] *Wren* v. *Weild* (1869) L.R. 4 Q.B. 730; *Greers, Ltd.* v. *Pearman & Corder, Ltd.* (1922) 39 R.P.C. 406.
[81] s. 11.
[82] s. 1. As to protection of rights while application is pending, see Sched. 1.
[83] s. 2.
[84] s. 3.
[85] s. 4 (1).
[86] s. 4 (4).

Infringement. Infringement of plant breeders' rights is actionable at the instance of the holder of the rights, and in any proceedings for an infringement all such relief, by way of damages, injunction, interdict, account or otherwise, is available as it is in respect of infringements of other proprietary rights.[87] The purchase of reproductive material not in Great Britain at the time of sale is not, but its purchase and subsequent use in Great Britain as reproductive material together constitute, an infringement of the plant breeders' rights.[88]

Innocent infringement. There is no right to damages for an infringement of plant breeders' rights (a) if the person infringing the rights was not aware, and had no reasonable grounds for suspecting, that the plant variety in question was the subject of plant breeders' rights, or (b) in a case where the infringement consists of a breach of conditions attached to a licence, if that person had no notice of any of those conditions, but the person who would, but for these provisions, be entitled to damages is to be entitled to an account of profits in respect of the infringement and to payment of any amount found due on the account, independently of any other relief.[89]

[87] s. 4 (1).
[88] s. 4 (2).
[89] s. 4 (3).

CHAPTER 30

PERSONS PROFESSING SPECIAL SKILLS

1. GENERAL PRINCIPLES

IT is convenient to consider together breaches of duty by all kinds of persons professing special professional skills or abilities, though breach of those duties may infringe personal interests in some cases and in others interests of substance. A person who professes a skilled profession or trade thereby impliedly holds himself out as possessing the degree of skill and knowledge reasonably to be expected of a normally competent and skilled practitioner of that profession or trade. " The engagement here is to bestow attention, art and skill on the act to be performed; skill being presumed in all professional persons, according to the rule, ' *Spondet peritiam artis, et imperitia culpae annumeratur.*' " [1] " One not a professor of the art is liable only for the best exertion of his skill,

---

[1] Bell, *Prin.*, § 153. *Cf. Hinshaw* v. *Adam* (1870) 8 M. 933.

such as it may be." [2] " The public profession of an art is a representation and undertaking to all the world that the professor possesses the requisite ability and skill." [3] " I apprehend that any man who performs a service of art for another is responsible up to the limit of his own profession— that is, what he professes or announces to the employer. In the case of a registered practitioner—including the holder of a diploma, or licence, or other such badge of his art—it needs no announcement of his own; for in such cases the law assumes that he holds himself out as possessed of the ordinary skill and care of his profession." [4]

Contractual liability. A professional or skilled man owes an implied duty of care *ex contractu* but only to the person who has employed him [5] and not to any third party, except in possible special cases under the principle of *jus quaesitum tertio.* The precise standard of skill and care, failure to exhibit which would be a breach of contract, may be expressed in the contract,[6] but is normally left to be implied by law, and the standard which the law implies in that case is that the professional man will exhibit the standard of knowledge, skill and care to be expected of a reasonably competent member of his profession. So far as concerns contractual liability, a practitioner must follow his instructions. But " where express directions are given to such a person, slight deviations, within the fair limits of professional discretion, are justifiable." [7] In most cases, however, his instructions are general, and the method and details are left to his professional knowledge and discretion.

Delictual liability. Independently of contract a duty of care, not only to the employer but more generally to persons who might reasonably foreseeably be harmed by want of due care, may be owed by professional men in some cases. Thus a doctor owes a duty to his patient, whoever may have instructed him to treat that patient.[8] The standard of duty owed *ex delicto* is to show such knowledge and skill and to take such care and precautions as are reasonably expected of a normally skilled and competent member of the profession or trade in question, the same as that due *ex contractu.*

It was formerly thought, at least in England, that while in every case a professional man or skilled tradesman owed a duty of care *ex contractu* to his employer, he owed also, to the employer and to others within the ambit of the duty, a duty of care *ex delicto* only where the result of his failure to show the requisite degree of knowledge, skill and care was to

[2] *Ibid.,* § 154; *cf.* § 150, and *Comm.,* I, 489. *Cf. Philips* v. *Whiteley* [1938] 1 All E.R. 566.

[3] *Harmer* v. *Cornelius* (1858) 5 C.B.(N.S.) 236.

[4] *Dickson* v. *Hygienic Institute,* 1910 S.C. 352, 356, *per* Lord Dundas; *cf. Hart* v. *Frame* (1839) MacL. & Rob. 595.

[5] Advocates and barristers act under a mandate, not under a contract for services, still less a contract of service.

[6] *Dickson* v. *Hygienic Institute,* 1910 S.C. 352.

[7] Bell, *Prin.,* § 154 (3); *Burnett* v. *Clark* (1771) Mor. 8491; *Laing* v. *Lord Chief Baron* (1753) Elchies, Mandate, 4; *McAulay* v. *Ferguson* (1799) Hume 324.

[8] *Farquhar* v. *Murray* (1901) 3 F. 859; *Edgar* v. *Lamont,* 1914 S.C. 277. *Cf. Rosen* v. *Stephen* (1907) 14 S.L.T. 784.

cause physical damage to person or property, and not where it would merely cause economic loss. On this basis the duty of care *ex contractu* only was owed by, *e.g.*, accountants, bankers, solicitors and surveyors, but duties of care, both under contract and delict, were owed by, *e.g.*, builders, dentists, and physicians and surgeons. *Hedley Byrne & Co., Ltd.* v. *Heller & Partners, Ltd.*[9] settles, however, that a duty independent of contract may be owed in appropriate circumstances to take reasonable care not to cause economic loss.

In the discussion which follows, consideration is in general limited to those aspects of duty arising *ex delicto* and not those arising from breach of contract. A full consideration of professional negligence would involve also numerous matters of contract.

Standard of care demanded. The standard set is not one of insurance; the professional man does not guarantee the success of his advice or handling of the case committed to him, nor that it will be immune from criticism. It is liability for fault and breach of duty in every case. " If the act be difficult or complicated, want of success is not an absolute test of responsibility." [10] There is no fault in lack of success; but there may be fault in not giving care and attention, in inexperience or ignorance, in failing to consult one of greater experience, in failing to take precautions, in failing to warn the client of risks, or in other ways.

The standard of knowledge, skill and care has been described as " a reasonable degree of skill and care . . . a fair, reasonable and competent degree of skill." [11] But professional men should not be held liable for mere errors in judgment, but only for want of reasonable skill and diligence.[12] It has been said in a medical case: " We should be doing a disservice to the community at large if we were to impose liability for everything that happens to go wrong . . . We must insist on due care for the patient at every point, but we must not condemn as negligence that which is only a misadventure." [13]

Liability only within scope of profession. The standard of reasonable knowledge, skill and care can be expected only in matters which properly fall within the scope of the practitioner's profession, and only a lesser standard can be expected in matters akin to, but outwith the immediate scope of, the practitioner's profession, while clearly no special knowledge, skill or care at all can be expected in matters wholly outwith the scope of the practitioner's profession, if he should have in emergency to turn his hand to something outwith his own professional field.

Thus a bank has been held under no duty to advise a customer carefully, or indeed at all, on investment when they did not profess to be such

9 [1964] A.C. 465.
10 Bell, *Prin.*, § 154 (5).
11 *Lanphier* v. *Phipos* (1838) 8 C. & P. 475, *per* Tindal C.J.
12 *Hart* v. *Frame* (1839) MacL. & Rob. 595.
13 *Roe* v. *Ministry of Health* [1954] 2 Q.B. 66, 76, *per* Denning L.J.

advisers [14]; a jeweller, in piercing a lady's ears for ear-rings, could be expected to conform only to the standards of skill and care which might be expected of a jeweller, not of a surgeon.[15]

Scope of knowledge demanded. The requisite reasonable knowledge, skill and care includes not only the technicalities of the craft but such connected matters as a practical working knowledge of the law so far as relevant to the exercise of the profession,[16] or the maintenance of instruments used in a clean condition.[17] The requisite knowledge includes recent developments, new methods and up-to-date instruments, though a defender is not always or automatically in fault if he does not have or use particular apparatus.[18]

Standard set by others in same profession. Whether or not a professional man has measured up to the standard of knowledge, skill and care to be expected of a reasonably competent member of his profession is entirely a question of fact, and it must be judged by reference to the views and practice of persons of experience in the same profession.[19] The evidence supporting or condemning the alleged malpractice need not be unanimous, and probably will not be.

The standard must be set by reference to professional knowledge, methods and practice at the date of the alleged misconduct and not by reference to what may have subsequently come to be regarded as better or essential.[20]

A departure from normal and accepted professional practice is not necessarily evidence of negligence. But it may be so, if it is proved that there is a normal practice applicable to cases such as the one under consideration, that the defender did not adopt the normal practice, and that the course which he did adopt was one which no professional man of ordinary skill would have adopted if he had been taking ordinary care.[21] " A specific act is to be done according to rule, if a rule be fixed. When the rule is obscure, professional usage may excuse error." [22] " If the object be safely attainable by a known method, the professional man takes the risk of deviation from that method." [23] " A defendant charged with negligence can clear himself if he shows that he acted in accordance with general and approved practice." [24]

---

[14] *Banbury* v. *Bank of Montreal* [1918] A.C. 626; contrast *Woods* v. *Martins Bank, Ltd.* [1959] 1 Q.B. 55 (where bank held itself out as adviser on investments).
[15] *Philips* v. *William Whiteley, Ltd.* [1938] 1 All E.R. 566.
[16] *Jenkins* v. *Betham* (1855) 15 C.B. 168; *Lee* v. *Walker* (1872) L.R. 7 C.P. 121; *Re Republic of Bolivia Exploration Syndicate, Ltd.* [1914] 1 Ch. 139. *Cf. Turnbull* v. *Cruickshank & Fairweather* (1905) 7 F. 791.
[17] *Hales* v. *Kerr* [1908] 2 K.B. 601 (infection from barber's razor).
[18] *Whiteford* v. *Hunter* [1950] W.N. 553.
[19] *Chapman* v. *Walton* (1833) 10 Bing. 57.
[20] *Whiteford* v. *Hunter* [1950] W.N. 553 (H.L.) (failure to use diagnostic instrument then very rare); *Roe* v. *Minister of Health* [1954] 2 Q.B. 66.
[21] *Hunter* v. *Hanley*, 1955 S.C. 200.
[22] Bell, *Prin.,* § 154 (2).
[23] Bell, *Prin.,* § 154 (4).
[24] *Marshall* v. *Lindsey C.C.* [1935] 1 K.B. 516, 540, approved by H.L. in *Whiteford* v. *Hunter* [1950] W.N. 553.

The failure of the work undertaken may be some evidence of negligence [25] but is not at all conclusive; there is no room for automatic application of the maxim *res ipsa loquitur*.[26]

Higher standard for consultants. A higher standard may be expected from one who professes to be a specialist, consultant, or expert, in matters within the sphere of his special expertise, and what might not be professional negligence in a general practitioner of the profession in question may be professional negligence in a consultant. In such a case the question is whether the defender showed the standard of knowledge, skill and care reasonably to be expected of a competent specialist or consultant in the branch of professional knowledge he professes, rather than of a competent general practitioner of the profession or trade.

2. PARTICULAR PROFESSIONS

(1) *Accountants and auditors*

The duty to show the knowledge, skill and care expected of a reasonably competent and careful accountant and auditor is owed under contract, or in certain cases may be imposed by statute. A duty may be owed *ex delicto* to a person other than the employer, as where accounts were known to have been made up to show to this third person, who lost money by acting in reliance on them.[27] There can normally be no liability for failing to uncover some fraud or mistake not discoverable by an investigation within the scope of the employment.[28]

The requisite knowledge expected includes relevant rules of law, such as the provisions of the Companies Act [29] and the Bankruptcy Act. He must also take reasonable care of any documents entrusted to him by his client [30] and must not disclose any confidential information which has been communicated to him.[31]

Statutory duties. Companies formed under the Companies Acts must at each A.G.M. appoint auditors, who must be members of recognised bodies of accountants or authorised by the Board of Trade,[32] for the following year.[33] They must report to the members of the company

---

[25] *Cassidy* v. *Ministry of Health* [1951] 2 K.B. 343.
[26] *Mahon* v. *Osborne* [1939] 2 K.B. 14 (though Goddard L.J. was of contrary view); *Fish* v. *Kapur* [1948] 2 All E.R. 176.
[27] *Candler* v. *Crane, Christmas & Co.* [1951] 2 K.B. 164, overruled in *Hedley Byrne & Co.* v. *Heller & Partners* [1964] A.C. 465; *cf. De Savary* v. *Holden Howard* [1960] C.L.Y. 2112, also impliedly overruled by *Hedley Byrne's* case. See Morison, " Liability in Negligence for False Statements " (1952) 67 L.Q.R. 212; Seavey, " *Candler* v. *Crane, Christmas & Co.*: Negligent Misrepresentation by Accountants " (1952) 67 L.Q.R. 466.
[28] *Re London & General Bank* [1895] 2 Ch. 673; *Re Kingston Cotton Mill Co.* [1896] 2 Ch. 279; *Fox* v. *Morrish Grant & Co.* (1918) 35 T.L.R. 126; *Maritime Insurance Co.* v. *Fortune* (1931) 41 Ll.L.R. 16; *Henry Squire Cash Chemist, Ltd.* v. *Ball, Baker & Co.* (1911) 27 T.L.R. 269; affd. 28 T.L.R. 81.
[29] *Re Republic of Bolivia Exploration Syndicate, Ltd.* [1914] 1 Ch. 139; *Thomas* v. *Devonport Corpn.* [1900] 1 Q.B. 16.
[30] *Weld-Blundell* v. *Stephens* [1920] A.C. 956.
[31] *Fogg* v. *Gaulter* [1960] C.L.Y. 2500.
[32] Companies Act, 1948, s. 161.
[33] *Ibid.* s. 159.

on the accounts examined, and the report must contain statements as
to the matters contained in the Ninth Schedule to the Act,[34] and as to
directors' salaries, pensions, etc., and loans to officers if these are not
disclosed by the accounts.[35]   An auditor may be an " officer of the
company " and liable as such for defalcations.[36]

Auditors must qualify their report if the accounts are not correctly
kept or do not exhibit a true and fair view of the company's financial
position.   They should report matters on which they are not satisfied [37]
and must give information, not merely hints which may induce shareholders to inquire further.[38]   Their task is to act as " watchdogs not
bloodhounds," [39] to be careful but not unduly suspicious, and in pursuance of that task to take the skill, care and caution which a reasonably
competent, careful and cautious auditor would use.[40]   They do not
guarantee that the books correctly show the true position of the company's affairs, or even guarantee that the balance-sheet is accurate
according to the books of the company.[40]   They should satisfy themselves
that securities do in fact exist and are in safe custody.[41]

Auditors may be liable for negligence at common law if loss has been
caused by their failure to carry out their duties,[42] or may be liable to a
misfeasance summons,[43] under which an auditor, as an officer of the
company, may be liable for acts of misfeasance, or may be liable to
prosecution.[44]

An accountant acting as liquidator is liable for negligence in the
execution of his statutory duties to a creditor injured thereby,[45] and, by
means of a misfeasance summons, to the creditors in general.[46]

(2) *Advocates and barristers*

Advocates and barristers, by accepting instructions from a client, do not
enter into any express or implied contract, but take on themselves a
public duty to the client, the court and the public.[47]   They are accordingly
under no liability *ex contractu* for mistake, bad advice, mishandling of
the case, indiscretion, ignorance or error of judgment or of law.[48]

---

34 *Ibid.* s. 162.
35 *Ibid.* s. 196.
36 *R.* v. *Shacter* [1960] 2 Q.B. 252.
37 *Mead* v. *Ball, Baker & Co.* (1911) 28 T.L.R. 81.
38 *Re London & General Bank (No. 2)* [1896] 2 Ch. 673, 684–685.
39 *Re Kingston Cotton Mill Co. (No. 2)* [1896] 2 Ch. 279, 288; *cf. Maritime Insurance Co.,
   Ltd.* v. *Fortune & Son* (1931) 41 Ll.L.R. 16; *Fomento* v. *Selsdon Fountain Pen Co.* [1958]
   1 All E.R. 11.
40 *Re London & General Bank (No. 2)* [1896] 2 Ch. 673, 683. See also *Re City Equitable
   Fire Insurance Co.* [1925] Ch. 407.
41 *Re City Equitable Fire Insurance Co., supra.*
42 *Leeds Estate Building & Investment Co.* v. *Shepherd* (1887) 36 Ch.D. 787.
43 Companies Act, 1948, s. 333: misfeasance covers all kinds of breach of duty.
44 *Ibid.* s. 438.   *Cf. R.* v. *Kylsant* [1932] 1 K.B. 442.
45 *Pulsford* v. *Devenish* [1903] 2 Ch. 625.
46 *Re Windsor Coal Co.* [1929] 1 Ch. 151; *Re Home & Colonial Insce. Co.* [1930] 1 Ch. 102.
47 *Swinfen* v. *Lord Chelmsford* (1860) 5 H. & N. 890, 920, *per* Pollock C.B.
48 *Fell* v. *Brown* (1791) 1 Peake 131; *Purves* v. *Landell* (1845) 4 Bell 46; 12 Cl. & F. 91; *Burness*
   v. *Morris* (1849) 11 D. 1258; *Batchelor* v. *Pattison & Mackersey* (1876) 3 R. 914; *Swinfen*
   v. *Lord Chelmsford* (1860) 5 H. & N. 890.

Probable exceptions are if counsel has made an express undertaking, or if he has acted fraudulently or treacherously,[49] or otherwise dishonestly or not in good faith with a view to the interest of his client. Nor are they liable for acting outwith the scope of their authority in the conduct of a case.[50]

They possibly owe a duty of care *ex lege* to take care not to cause loss by misrepresentation to those who might foreseeably be harmed thereby.[51]

(3) Architects

An architect owes a contractual duty [52] to show the knowledge, skill and care expected of a reasonably competent architect, including knowledge of relevant law. He is therefore not liable for failing to discover defects in a building which would have been revealed only by a more detailed examination than he was instructed to make.[53]

But architects have been held liable for acting on unauthorised information and failing personally to measure the site, and in consequence preparing plans for a much smaller site,[54] for not properly superintending a building [55] (though not for details properly entrusted to a clerk of works) and for supplying plans which turned out to be useless.[56] They are possibly liable for negligence in issuing interim certificates,[57] and they are for issuing final certificates negligently,[58] but not for negligence in issuing a final certificate if they are acting as arbitrator between employer and building contractor.[59] There may be liability for not notifying damage as soon as possible, when in consequence of delay a claim was submitted too late.[60] Where matters are left to the architect's final decision he must act judicially.[61]

Failure of the building in some respect is evidence of want of skill or attention, unless the failure is in respect of some novelty in respect of which the architect had little experience, or which was largely experimental, for then failure may be quite consistent with skill.[62]

---

[49] *Swinfen, supra,* at pp. 920, 924; *cf. Harrison* v. *Rumsey* (1752) 2 Ves.Sen. 488.
[50] *R.* v. *Greenwich Cty. Ct. Registrar* (1885) 15 Q.B.D. 54; *cf. Swinfen* v. *Swinfen* (1856) 18 C.B. 485.
[51] *Hedley Byrne & Co.* v. *Heller & Partners* [1964] A.C. 465.
[52] *Le Lievre* v. *Gould* [1893] 1 Q.B. 491; *Bagot* v. *Stevens, Scanlan & Co.* [1964] 3 All E.R. 577. *Cf. Love* v. *Mack* (1905) 93 L.T. 352; *Armitage* v. *Palmer* [1960] C.L.Y. 326; *Grunwald* v. *Hughes,* 1965 S.L.T.(Notes) 18.
[53] *Sincock* v. *Bangs (Reading)* [1952] C.P.L. 562; *Philips* v. *Ward* [1956] 1 All E.R. 874. *Cf. Rayment* v. *Needham* [1954] C.L.Y. 334.
[54] *Columbus Co.* v. *Clowes* [1903] 1 K.B. 244.
[55] *Armstrong* v. *Jones* (1869) *Hudson's Building Contracts,* Vol. 2, 4th ed., 6; *Saunders & Collard* v. *Broadstairs L.B.* (1890) *ibid.* 164; *Rogers* v. *James* (1891) 8 T.L.R. 67; *Steljes* v. *Ingram* (1903) 19 T.L.R. 534; *Leicester Guardians* v. *Trollope* (1911) 75 J.P. 197.
[56] *Dalgleish* v. *Bromley Corpn.* [1953] C.P.L. 411.
[57] *Wisbech R.D.C.* v. *Ward* [1928] 2 K.B. 1.
[58] *Rogers* v. *James, supra; cf. Cotton* v. *Wallis* [1955] 3 All E.R. 373.
[59] *Stevenson* v. *Watson* (1879) 4 C.P.D. 148; *Tharsis Sulphur Co.* v. *Loftus* (1872) L.R. 8 C.P. 1; *Chambers* v. *Goldthorpe* [1901] 1 K.B. 624; *Boynton* v. *Richardson* (1924) 69 Sol.J. 107.
[60] *Ruback* v. *Braddock* [1952] C.L.Y. 351.
[61] *Hickman* v. *Roberts* [1913] A.C. 229; *Windsor R.D.C.* v. *Otterway and Try* [1954] 3 All E.R. 721.
[62] *Turner* v. *Garland* (1853) *Hudson's Building Contracts,* Vol. 2, 4th ed., 1.

When an architect has to require a builder to remedy defects, he is entitled to take into account the fact that the building is being put up cheaply.[63]

An architect may be sued for instructing an operation which is dangerous and causes harm to the workman who executes it,[64] or for passing as safe a wall which was not, and which shortly afterwards fell and caused injury.[65] He is not in general liable for siting a block of houses where another party's rights are infringed so that the client is liable in damages.[66]

(4) Auctioneers and valuators

Their duties probably arise *ex contractu* only, save that they may be liable for negligent misrepresentation of value to a third party under the principle of *Hedley Byrne & Co.* v. *Heller & Partners.*[67] They may be liable for negligently mis-valuing subjects of sale.[68]

(5) Bankers

A banker must exercise reasonable skill and care in connection with the business of banking. His duty is primarily contractual, based on the relationship of banker and customer,[69] but may also arise *ex lege.*[70] He is not necessarily under a duty to disclose to a prospective cautioner the extent of the debtor's indebtedness to the bank.[71] He is under a duty not unjustifiably to harm his customer's credit, as by wrongfully refusing payment of a cheque.[72]

As paying banker, he is bound to honour cheques drawn on the bank in proper form if he has available sufficient funds,[73] or if they are within the limits of any overdraft granted,[74] in the order in which they are presented.[75] The banker is under no liability if he, in good faith and without negligence, pays a bearer cheque on presentation,[76] or pays a crossed cheque in accordance with the crossing, notwithstanding any defect of title in the collecting banker or in the person from whom he

---

[63] *Cotton* v. *Wallis* [1955] 3 All E.R. 373.
[64] *Clayton* v. *Woodman* [1962] 2 Q.B. 533 (no liability in circumstances).
[65] *Clay* v. *Crump* [1963] 3 All E.R. 687.
[66] *Armitage* v. *Palmer* [1960] C.L.Y. 326.
[67] [1964] A.C. 465.
[68] *Woodley* v. *Newman* [1950] C.L.Y. 2693; *Bell Hotels* v. *Motion* [1952] C.L.Y. 194.
[69] *Marzetti* v. *Williams* (1830) 1 B. & A. 415; *King* v. *B.L. Co.* (1899) 1 F. 928.
[70] *Hedley Byrne & Co.* v. *Heller & Partners, Ltd.* [1964] A.C. 465. *Cf. Salton* v. *Clydesdale Bank* (1898) 1 F. 110; *Hockey* v. *Clydesdale Bank* (1898) 1 F. 119.
[71] *Royal Bank* v. *Greenshields*, 1914 S.C. 259; *Young* v. *Clydesdale Bank* (1889) 17 R. 231.
[72] *King* v. *B.L. Co.* (1899) 1 F. 928; *Plunkett* v. *Barclays Bank* [1936] 2 K.B. 107; *Davidson* v. *Barclays Bank* [1940] 1 All E.R. 316; *Wilson* v. *United Counties Bank, Ltd.* [1920] A.C. 102. See also *Gibb* v. *Lombank Scotland*, 1962 S.L.T. 288.
[73] *London Joint Stock Bank* v. *Macmillan and Arthur* [1918] A.C. 777; *Joachimson* v. *Swiss Bank Corpn.* [1921] 3 K.B. 110: The sum at credit probably must be able to honour the whole sum in the cheque: *Carew* v. *Duckworth* (1869) L.R. 4 Ex. 313.
[74] *Rouse* v. *Bradford Banking Co.* [1894] A.C. 586.
[75] *Kilsby* v. *Williams* (1822) 5 B. & A. 815; *Sednaoni* v. *Zariffa, Nahas & Co.* v. *Anglo-Austrian Bank* (1909) 30 Jl.Inst.Bankers, 413.
[76] *Charles* v. *Blackwell* (1877) 2 C.P.D. 151.

received it.[77] There is authority for the view that a banker is negligent if he fails to spot a forgery,[78] but it is unlikely that this would be so if the forgery were so clever as to make detection very difficult, or impossible without expert examination.[79]

As collecting banker, a banker is protected by the Bills of Exchange Act, 1882, s. 82, when he in good faith and without negligence receives payment for a customer of a cheque crossed generally or specially to himself and the customer has no title or a defective title thereto.[80] But he is liable if negligent, measured by the standard of the practice of reasonable men carrying on the business of bankers, and endeavouring to do so in such a manner as may be calculated to protect themselves and others against fraud.[81]

Advice as to investments is not part of the ordinary business of a banker, and a banker accordingly owes no duty to a customer or other person to take care in advising on investments, or to advise at all on such matters,[82] though he must take reasonable care if he undertakes to advise.[83]

If a banker receives an enquiry as to the financial position of a customer, he must answer honestly on the basis of the information available to him, but is not obliged to make further enquiries, and is not liable even though another banker might have expressed a contrary opinion on the same fact.[84] If the inquiry shows that the banker is being trusted, or his skill and judgment being relied on, he is under a legal duty to take reasonable care in giving advice or information, unless he clearly excludes responsibility.[85]

In allowing persons to deposit their papers and valuables in its vaults a bank acts as an onerous, or it may be, gratuitous depositary, and owes only the duties of care of such a depositary.

A bank acting as executor and/or trustee similarly owes the same duties of care as do ordinary persons acting in these capacities.

A bank which holds stock for behoof of certain customers may be liable in damages if it fails to take or to implement the customers' instructions in relation thereto.[86]

---

[77] Bills of Exchange Act, 1880, s. 80.
[78] *Smith* v. *Mercer* (1815) 6 Taunt. 76.
[79] *London and River Plate Bank* v. *Bank of Liverpool* [1896] 1 Q.B. 7. *Cf. Union Bank of Scotland* v. *Makin* (1873) 11 M. 499; *Wood* v. *Clydesdale Bank*, 1914 S.C. 397.
[80] *Capital and Counties Bank* v. *Gordon* [1903] A.C. 240. See also Bills of Exchange (Crossed Cheques) Act, 1906; *Commissioners of Taxation* v. *English Scottish and Australian Bank, Ltd.* [1920] A.C. 683.
[81] *Lloyds Bank, Ltd.* v. *Savory* [1933] A.C. 201, 221. See also *Motor Trades Guarantee Corpn. Ltd.* v. *Midland Bank, Ltd.* [1937] 4 All E.R. 90; *Penmount Estates, Ltd.* v. *National Provincial Bank, Ltd.* (1945) 173 L.T. 344; *Marquess of Bute* v. *Barclays Bank, Ltd.* [1954] 3 W.L.R. 741.
[82] *Banbury* v. *Bank of Montreal* [1918] A.C. 626.
[83] *Woods* v. *Martins Bank, Ltd.* [1959] 1 Q.B. 55.
[84] *Parsons* v. *Barclay & Co., Ltd.* (1910) 26 T.L.R. 628; *Robinson* v. *National Bank of Scotland*, 1916 S.C.(H.L.) 154; *Batts Combe Quarry Co.* v. *Barclays Bank Ltd* (1931) 48 T.L.R. 4.
[85] *Macken* v. *Munster and Leinster Bank* (1960) 95 I.L.T.R. 17; *Hedley Byrne & Co., Ltd.* v. *Heller & Partners, Ltd.* [1964] A.C. 465.
[86] *Dougall* v. *National Bank of Scotland* (1892) 20 R. 8.

(6) *Barbers and Hairdressers*

The duties of barbers and hairdressers are to show reasonable knowledge and take reasonable skill and care in the practice of their craft. This extends not merely to the avoidance of cuts and other physical injury but to keeping instruments clean so as not to communicate disease,[87] and to a duty to test hair for its reaction to proposed treatment, or at least to warn the customer of the risk which exists in the circumstances.[88] The precautions requisite in a particular case depend on what is good practice in the profession.[89]

It is a defence to show that the customer had an unusually sensitive skin, so as to be affected by chemicals or treatment which would not affect the normal person,[90] or to prove that the customer failed to disclose that she was, as she knew, allergic to hair-dye.[91]

(7) *Civil, mechanical and electrical engineers*

A professional engineer owes a duty to show reasonable knowledge, skill and care in the matters in respect of which he has been employed.[92] The duty is clearly a contractual one, but in view of the physical dangers to third parties which may result from incompetent or negligent work, a delictual duty may also be owed. When acting as arbitrator he must act judicially and seek to do justice between the parties.[93]

(8) *Company secretaries*

The duties of a company secretary are largely prescribed by his contract of employment and by statute. Any breach of duty or neglect on his part is a breach or contract actionable at the instance of the employing company only,[94] not by the shareholders or any third party damnified by his act or omission. Third parties may have a claim against the company if the secretary's conduct which injured them was in the course of his employment, on the ordinary principle of *respondeat superior*, and a secretary has been held personally liable where he omitted the word " Limited " from the name of the company on a bill of exchange.[95]

Every company formed under the Companies Acts must have a secretary,[96] and numerous statutory duties are imposed on him by the Act, either directly or by implication.[97] Default in these duties frequently imports criminal liability, but there is no authority for imposing civil liability on a secretary for breach of any of these statutory duties.

---

[87] *Hales* v. *Kerr* [1908] 2 K.B. 601.
[88] *Dobbin* v. *Waldorf Toilet Saloons, Ltd.* [1937] 1 All E.R. 331; *Parker* v. *Oxolo, Ltd.* [1937] 3 All E.R. 524; *Watson* v. *Buckley* [1940] 1 All E.R. 174; *Holmes* v. *Ashford* [1950] 2 All E.R. 76.   [89] *Little* v. *Giralt* (1949) 65 Sh.Ct.Rep. 113.
[90] *Griffiths* v. *Peter Conway, Ltd.* [1939] 1 All E.R. 685.
[91] *Ingham* v. *Emes* [1955] 2 Q.B. 366.
[92] *Cf. Moneypenny* v. *Hartland* (1824) 1 C. & P. 352.
[93] *Bristol Corpn.* v. *Aird* [1913] A.C. 241.
[94] See discussion of the position of the secretary *vis-a-vis* the company in Palmer's *Company Law* (20th ed.) 592; see also *Municipal Freehold Land Co.* v. *Pollington* (1890) 63 L.T. 238.
[95] *Penrose* v. *Martyr* (1858) E.B. & E. 499.
[96] Companies Act, 1948, s. 177.
[97] See Palmer's *Company Law* (20th ed.) 591 for a list of these.

A secretary sued for negligence, default, breach of duty or breach of trust may be relieved by the court, in whole or in part, from liability on such terms as the court thinks fit if it appears that he acted honestly and reasonably and that, having regard to the circumstances of the case, he ought fairly to be excused.[98] A secretary who apprehends proceedings may apply for relief.

(9) Dentists

Dentists are under a duty to show reasonable knowledge, skill and care in the treatment of patients.[99] The duty arises both *ex contractu* and *ex lege*. The fracturing of the jaw in the course of extracting a tooth is not *per se* evidence of negligence, even if part of the root of the tooth is still left in the jaw.[1] Nor is a dislocation negligence *per se*.[2] The choking of a patient by a swab calls for explanation, failing which the injured person is entitled to succeed,[3] and the dentist is not liable if he has consulted and relied on a doctor in respect of a post-operative condition.[4]

(10) Estate factors and agents

Persons acting as estate agents owe a duty of care and diligence to their principal *ex contractu*. Beyond that their duty depends very much on the circumstances of the case; it may include drawing attention to defects and difficulties in a course of action proposed by the principal, even though unasked, if this course of action is known to the agent.[5]

(11) Insurance brokers

The duty of insurance brokers arises *ex contractu* to show reasonable skill and care in effecting insurance in terms of their instructions. They will be liable for negligence, as by failing to ensure that declared risks are covered,[6] but not for delay to forward the cover note and consequent failure to warn the insured that the goods were not covered while at packers.[7] They may also incur liability *ex lege* for not taking proper care in tendering advice or answering questions on insurance if the circumstances indicate that their skill and judgment was being relied on.[8]

---

[98] Companies Act, 1948, s. 448. See *National Trustee Co. of Australasia* v. *General Finance Co.* [1905] A.C. 373; *Re Smith, Smith* v. *Thompson* (1902) 71 L.J.Ch. 411; *Re Turner, Barker* v. *Ivimey* [1897] 1 Ch. 536; *Re Second Dulwich Building Society* (1899) 68 L.J.Ch. 196; *Re Grindey, Clews* v. *Grindey* [1898] 2 Ch. 593; *Perrins* v. *Bellamy* [1899] 1 Ch. 797; *Re Lord de Clifford* [1900] 2 Ch. 707; and *cf.* Trusts (Scotland) Act, 1921, s. 32 and *Clarke* v. *Clarke's Trs.*, 1925 S.C. 693.

[99] *Edwards* v. *Mallan* [1908] 1 K.B. 1002; *Dickson* v. *Hygienic Institute*, 1910 S.C. 352.

[1] *Fish* v. *Kapur* [1948] 2 All E.R. 176; *Warner* v. *Payne* (1935), not reported, referred to in *Fish, supra*; *O'Neill* v. *Kelly* [1961] C.L.Y. 5977; *Lock* v. *Scantlebury* [1963] C.L.Y. 2415.

[2] *Stevenson* v. *Shafer* (1953) 69 Sh.Ct.Rep. 327.

[3] *Garner* v. *Morrell* [1953] C.L.Y. 2538.

[4] *Tanswell* v. *Nelson* [1959] C.L.Y. 2254.

[5] *Williams' Trs.* v. *Macandrew and Jenkins*, 1960 S.L.T. 246, distinguishing *Currors* v. *Walker's Trs.* (1889) 16 R. 355.

[6] *Coolee, Ltd.* v. *Wing, Heath & Co. and Others* (1930) 47 T.L.R. 78.

[7] *United Mills Agencies* v. *Harvey, Bray & Co.* [1952] 1 All E.R. 225, note.

[8] *Hedley Byrne & Co.* v. *Heller and Partners, Ltd.* [1964] A.C. 465.

(12) Nurses

The duty of a nurse is to show the knowledge, skill and care to be expected of a reasonably competent nurse towards patients under her charge. The duty may arise from express or implied contract, but arises also *ex lege*. A nurse privately employed is personally liable only, and if any nursing association which supplied her took reasonable care to supply a competent person, it is not liable for her negligence.[9]

It is now settled [10] that nurses employed in nationalised hospitals are servants of the hospital authority and render it vicariously liable for their fault, whether in a matter of professional skill and care or not. Whether or not the hospital employing her is liable, she is always personally liable.[11]

(13) Patent agents

Their duty is primarily contractual.[12] They must have an adequate knowledge of the relevant law; it may be negligence not to be aware of a recent legal decision.[13] They may be liable *ex lege* for incorrect information or advice where the circumstances would indicate that their skill and judgment was being relied on and they failed to take reasonable care in giving the information or advice.[14]

(14) Pharmacists

In this case the duty is both contractual and delictual, and is to show the knowledge, skill and care reasonably to be expected of a competent member of the profession.[15] An action has been held relevant on averments that a pharmaceutical chemist held himself out as competent to advise as to the use of drugs, and had advised a treatment which had been harmful, as he should have known it would.[16]

In the case of a pharmacist dispensing in hospital he should insist on his instructions being given according to the system in force in the hospital, such as a written prescription from a qualified person for any dangerous drug, and, if the order is for an unusually large quantity of a dangerous or poisonous drug, he should verify that there is no mistake in the order, or at least send up a note with the made-up prescription calling special attention to it.[17]

---

9 *Hall* v. *Lees* [1904] 2 K.B. 602.
10 *Macdonald* v. *Glasgow Western Hospitals*, 1954 S.C. 453, modifying principles laid down in *Lavelle* v. *Glasgow R.I.*, 1932 S.C. 245; and *Reidford* v. *Aberdeen Mags.*, 1933 S.C. 276; *Fox* v. *Glasgow S.W. Hospitals*, 1955 S.L.T. 337. See also Goodhart, " Hospitals and Trained Nurses " (1938) 54 L.Q.R. 553.
11 *Strangeways-Lesmere* v. *Clayton* [1936] 1 All E.R. 484; *Lavelle, supra.* See also *Craig* v. *McKendrick*, 1948 S.L.T.(Notes) 91; *Owen* v. *Garthdee Private Nursing Home, Ltd.*, 1949 S.L.T.(Notes) 34; *Cox* v. *Carshalton Group Hospital Cttee.* [1954] C.L.Y. 2248.
12 *Turnbull* v. *Cruickshank & Fairweather* (1905) 7 F. 791.
13 *Lee* v. *Walker* (1872) L.R. 7 C.P. 121.
14 *Cf. Hedley Byrne & Co.* v. *Heller and Partners, Ltd.* [1964] A.C. 465.
15 Beven, *Negligence*, II, 1361, quoting *Allen* v. *State Steamship Co.* (1892) 28 Am.St.R. 556. See also *Muir* v. *Stewart*, 1938 S.C. 590.
16 *Rosen* v. *Stephen* (1907) 14 S.L.T. 784.
17 *Collins* v. *Hertfordshire C.C.* [1947] K.B. 598.

(15) *Physicians and surgeons*

Physicians and surgeons directly employed by a patient owe him a duty of care both *ex contractu* and *ex delicto*. Where patients call in a doctor participating in the National Health Service these facts may raise a contract between them,[18] but there is certainly a separate delictual duty of care. A duty may be owed *ex contractu* to the person who employs the practitioner and a duty *ex delicto* to the patient for whom he is employed.[19] But a doctor called in at the instance of a third party to make an examination, and who has not undertaken the care and treatment of the patient, owes him no duty at all.[20]

The standard of the duty of care has frequently been laid down as a fair and reasonable standard of care and competence.[21] " If a person holds himself out as possessing special skill and knowledge and he is consulted, as possessing such skill and knowledge, by or on behalf of a patient, he owes a duty to the patient to use due caution in undertaking the treatment. If he accepts the responsibility and undertakes the treatment and the patient submits to his direction and treatment accordingly, he owes a duty to the patient to use diligence, care, knowledge, skill and caution in administering the treatment. No contractual relation is necessary, nor is it necessary that the service be rendered for reward . . . the law requires a fair and reasonable standard of care and competence. This standard must be reached in all the matters above mentioned. If the patient's death has been caused by the defendant's indolence or carelessness, it will not avail to show that he had sufficient knowledge; nor will it avail to prove that he was diligent in attendance, if the patient has been killed by his gross ignorance and unskilfulness . . . as regards cases where incompetence is alleged it is only necessary to say that the unqualified practitioner cannot claim to be measured by any lower standard than that which is applied to a qualified man. As regards cases of alleged recklessness juries are likely to distinguish between the qualified and the unqualified man. There may be recklessness in undertaking the treatment and recklessness in the conduct of it. It is, no doubt, conceivable that a qualified man may be held liable for recklessly undertaking a case which he knew, or should have known, to be beyond his powers, or for making his patient the subject of reckless experiment." [22]

" In the realm of diagnosis and treatment there is ample scope for genuine difference of opinion [23] and one man clearly is not negligent merely because his conclusion differs from that of other professional

---

[18] *Cf. Clarke* v. *Dunraven, The Satanita* [1897] A.C. 59.

[19] *Edgar* v. *Lamont*, 1914 S.C. 277.

[20] *Pimm* v. *Roper* (1862) 2 F. & F. 783 (injured person seen by railway surgeon to ascertain amount of compensation to be offered).

[21] *Lanphier* v. *Phipos* (1838) 8 C. & P. 475; *Harmer* v. *Cornelius* (1858) 5 C.B.(N.S.) 236; *Rich* v. *Pierpont* (1862) 3 F. & F. 35.

[22] *R.* v. *Bateman* (1925) 94 L.J.K.B. 791, approved in *Akerele* v. *The King* [1943] A.C. 255; followed in *Crawford* v. *Campbell*, 1948 S.L.T.(Notes) 91. As to duty owed by unqualified person giving treatment, see *Brogan* v. *Bennett* (1952) 86 I.L.T. 143.

[23] *Cf. Crivon* v. *Barnet Hospital Cttee.* [1958] C.L.Y. 2283.

men, nor because he has displayed less skill or knowledge than others would have shown. The true test for establishing negligence in diagnosis or treatment on the part of a doctor is whether he has been proved to be guilty of such failure as no doctor of ordinary skill would be guilty of if acting with ordinary care." [24] " In relation to professional negligence, I regard the phrase ' gross negligence ' only as indicating so marked a departure from the normal standard of conduct of a professional man as to infer a lack of that ordinary care which a man of ordinary skill would display. So interpreted, the words aptly describe what I consider the sound criterion in the matter, although, strictly viewed, they might give the impression that there are degrees of negligence." [25]

Standard flexible. The standard of skill and care is variable, depending on the circumstances. " Negligence in one man may be competent care in another. For instance a specialist consulted in his specialty would be liable for negligence in respect of treatment which in a junior and ordinary member of the profession would more than pass muster; and that might be negligence in a doctor of repute in the west of London which would yet come up to the highest warrantable expectations of the patient of the village doctor in remotest Kerry or Westmoreland." [26]

The standard is not affected by whether the treatment is onerous or gratuitous,[27] undertaken in emergency, or in pursuance of private employment, or under the facilities of the National Health Service, or whether the practitioner is qualified or not.[28]

A consultant or specialist must attain a higher standard in his own field than an ordinary practitioner. " Special profession involves higher duty; and the standard to be attained is that of the specialist among medical men, and not that of the general practitioner, and this includes proper instructions to the nurses and to the patient for their conduct in the intervals of the doctor's attendance." [29]

There is no absolute liability for failure to cure, nor even if the patient's post-treatment condition is worse than before, though such facts may raise a prima facie case of negligence.[30] Nor is there liability for harm resulting in the course of treatment from mischance or inevitable accident, which could not have been avoided by any such

---

[24] *Hunter* v. *Hanley*, 1955 S.C. 200, 204–205, *per* L.P. Clyde, approved in *Bolam* v. *Friern Hospital Cttee*. [1957] 2 All E.R. 118.

[25] *Ibid*. 206.

[26] Beven, *Negligence*, II, 1353.

[27] *Pippin* v. *Sheppard* (1822) 11 Pr. 400; *Everett* v. *Griffiths* [1920] 3 K.B. 193.

[28] The Medical Acts do not prohibit unqualified practice, but merely impose disabilities in respect of recovering fees, signing certificates, obtaining drugs, holding public posts, etc. A person holding himself out as qualified though not qualified, must show the skill and care of a qualified person: *Ruddock* v. *Lowe* (1865) 5 F. & F. 519; if the patient knows that the practitioner is unqualified, the latter is liable only if he fails to show the knowledge and skill of an ordinary person of common sense: *Shiells* v. *Blackburne* (1789) 1 H.Bl. 161.

[29] Beven, II, 1355.

[30] *Cassidy* v. *Ministry of Health* [1951] 2 K.B. 343; *Hatcher* v. *Black* [1954] C.L.Y. 2289; *White* v. *Westminster Hospital* [1961] C.L.Y. 5954.

precautions as a reasonable man could be expected to take, as where a needle broke in the course of an injection and was drawn into the patient's body.[31]

There may be liability for failure or refusal to recognise that a case is beyond the practitioner's skill, and for failure or refusal to call in a consultant, or take a second opinion, or to have the patient removed to hospital where greater skill and facilities are available.[32] There may be liability if the practitioner was himself physically unfit to perform the operation or give the requisite treatment.[33] A house surgeon is not liable if he has acted on the instructions of a consultant.[34]

Adherence to professional practice. Care and skill must normally be measured by the general and approved practice of the profession at the time of the alleged negligence, and to have acted in accordance with that practice will normally exculpate[35]; but refusal to follow or deviation from the general and approved practice is not necessarily evidence of negligence, but only if there is a normal practice for such cases, if it was not adopted, and if the course which was adopted was one which no professional man of ordinary skill would have adopted if he had been acting with ordinary care.[36] A practitioner is not negligent if he acts in accordance with a practice accepted as proper by a responsible body of skilled practitioners, merely because there is a body of opinion to the contrary[37]; he may be if he obstinately adheres to a practice condemned by substantially the whole of informed medical opinion.[38]

Warning patient of danger. It may be negligent to fail to warn the patient of the risks inherent in a proposed course of treatment, but only if proper practice is to give a warning in such circumstances and the patient would not have consented to the treatment.[39] It is relevant to inquire whether a doctor has told the patient that treatment involves no risk or has merely prevaricated to stop her worrying.[40] So too it may be negligent for a casualty surgeon in hospital not himself to communicate his findings to the patient's own doctor.[41]

Modes of negligence. Professional negligence can be committed by physicians and surgeons in countless ways, and the precise mode does

---

[31] *Roe* v. *Ministry of Health* [1954] 2 Q.B. 66; *Gerber* v. *Pines* (1934) Sol.J. 13. The doctor. was, however, held liable for not having told the patient at once of the accident; contrast *Daniels* v. *Heskin* [1954] C.L.Y. 2288.
[32] Cf. *Jones* v. *Manchester Corpn.* [1952] 2 Q.B. 852; *Payne* v. *St. Helier Hospital Cttee.* [1952] C.L.Y. 2442.
[33] *Nickolls* v. *Ministry of Health* [1955] C.L.Y. 1902.
[34] *Junor* v. *McNicol* [1959] C.L.Y. 2255.
[35] *Marshall* v. *Lindsey C.C.* [1935] 1 K.B. 516, 540, approved in *Whiteford* v. *Hunter* [1950] W.N. 553 (H.L.).
[36] *Hunter* v. *Hanley*, 1955 S.C. 200.
[37] *Bolam* v. *Friern Hospital Cttee.* [1957] 2 All E.R. 118.
[38] *Ibid.* 122.
[39] *Clarke* v. *Adams* [1950] 94 Sol.J. 599; *Bolam* v. *Friern Hospital Ctte.* [1957] 2 All E.R. 118.
[40] *Hatcher* v. *Black* [1954] C.L.Y. 2289.
[41] *Chapman* v. *Rix* [1958] C.L.Y. 2282; [1960] C.L.Y. 2186.

not affect the legal consequences, if the act or omission be held to be negligent in a professional respect.

The following are examples of conduct which may be, or has been held to be, professional negligence: making an inadequate examination [42]; making an incorrect diagnosis, by not using a particular kind of instrument [43]; failing to use due skill in diagnosis, so that wrong treatment is given [44]; administering an anaesthetic which was dangerous, having been kept in a dangerous manner [45]; administering one anaesthetic on top of another, so causing the patient's death [46]; leaving a swab or pack in the patient's body after an operation [47]; accidentally breaking the needle in the course of injection and not telling the patient that it was left in her body [48]; injecting the wrong drug [49]; neglecting to call to ascertain the patient's progress [50]; damaging a nerve in the course of an operation [51]; failing to cleanse wounds properly [52]; burning the patient by treatment which involved passing electrical current though her body [53]; performing an operation unnecessarily [54]; failing to make arrangements to receive messages from the patient in the event of bleeding taking place during the first two days after the operation [55]; failing to warn a patient of the risk of further pregnancy [56]; failure to give an anti-tetanus injection and to ascertain that one had not previously been given.[57]

Liability for issuing certificates. A medical practitioner must exercise reasonable skill and care in issuing certificates which enable action to be taken under statute, not merely to take reasonable care in ascertaining the necessary data, but to exercise reasonable professional skill in forming a conclusion from such data.[58] Thus liability is incurred for signing an untrue certificate of insanity, and without making the proper examination or inquiries which are required in the circumstances by a medical man using proper skill and care.[59] But liability is incurred only if the

---

42 *Wood* v. *Thurston* [1951] C.L.Y. 2361; *Newton* v. *Newtons Model Laundry* [1959] C.L.Y. 2256; see also *Chapman* v. *Rix* [1960] C.L.Y. 2186; *Ashingdon* v. *Tolleth* (1951) 101 L.J. 235 (osteopath).
43 *Whiteford* v. *Hunter* [1950] W.N. 553; *cf. Crivon* v. *Barnet H.M.C.* [1958] C.L.Y. 2283.
44 *Pudney* v. *Union Castle Mail S.S. Co.* [1953] 1 Lloyd's Rep. 73; *cf. McHardy* v. *Dundee Hospitals*, 1960 S.L.T.(Notes) 19; *McCormack* v. *Redpath Brown* [1961] C.L.Y. 5952.
45 *Roe* v. *Minister of Health* [1954] 2 Q.B. 66; *cf. Moore* v. *Lewisham Hospital Cttee.* [1959] C.L.Y. 2253.   46 *Jones* v. *Manchester Corpn.* [1952] 2 Q.B. 852.
47 *Dryden* v. *Surrey C.C.* [1936] 2 All E.R. 535; *Morris* v. *Winsbury-White* [1937] 4 All E.R. 494; *Mahon* v. *Osborne* [1939] 2 K.B. 14; *Hocking* v. *Bell* [1948] W.N. 21; *Cooper* v. *Nevill* [1961] C.L.Y. 5951.
48 *Gerber* v. *Pines* (1933) 79 Sol.J. 13; see also *Daniels* v. *Heskin* [1954] I.R. 73, where *Gerber* not followed; *Hunter* v. *Hanley*, 1955 S.C. 200.
49 *Collins* v. *Hertfordshire C.C.* [1947] K.B. 598.
50 *Farquhar* v. *Murray* (1901) 3 F. 859; *Corder* v. *Banks* [1960] C.L.Y. 2185.
51 *Hatcher* v. *Black* [1954] C.L.Y. 2289.
52 *Baron* v. *McNab* (1951) 67 Sh.Ct.Rep. 118; *Hayward* v. *Edinburgh R.I.* 1954 S.C. 453.
53 *Clarke* v. *Worboys* [1952] C.L.Y. 2443.
54 *Breen* v. *Baker* [1956] C.L.Y. 6013.
55 *Corder* v. *Banks* [1960] C.L.Y. 2185.
56 *Waters* v. *Park* [1961] C.L.Y. 5953.
57 *Coles* v. *Reading Hospital Cttee.* [1963] C.L.Y. 2356.
58 *Everett* v. *Griffiths* [1920] 3 K.B. 163, 216, *per* Atkin L.J.
59 *Hall* v. *Semple* (1862) 3 F. & F. 337; *Everett, supra*, affd. [1921] 1 A.C. 631; *Harnett* v. *Fisher* [1927] A.C. 574; *De Freville* v. *Dill* (1927) 96 L.J.K.B. 1056.

negligently issued certificate caused or permitted the wrongful detention, not if it were merely a prerequisite to the exercise by another of discretion, nor if it supervened on the decision by another to confine the alleged lunatic.

A measure of protection to medical practitioners against frivolous claims for damages for wrongful detention is afforded by the Mental Health (Scotland) Act, 1960, s. 107, which requires proof that the act complained of was done in bad faith or without reasonable care.[60]

(16) *Police officers*

There is some authority for the proposition that not only are police officers liable for wrongful arrest or imprisonment but they may be liable for negligent conduct. In *Simpson* v. *Dundee Mags*.[61] a man was taken ill in the street and was taken in charge and his condition attributed to drink. He died next day from coronary thrombosis. An action was held relevant on averments of failure to have realised that he was ill and not drunk, and to have summoned medical aid. In this, and in many other cases, the difficulty would be to prove that the loss had been caused by the breach of duty complained of. A possibility of saving the life in the case cited would not be enough to import liability, but it might be otherwise if the prompt summoning of aid would have saved the life.

(17) *Prison officers*

Prison governors and officers may be liable if by negligence they have allowed persons to do harm or damage; thus where a person's vehicle was damaged by youths who escaped from an " open " Borstal institution, damages were awarded, as there had been negligence in that one of the youths had escaped three times previously.[62] They may also be liable for failure to take precautions in prison workshops whereby prisoners are injured.[63]

(18) *Professions supplementary to medicine*

Persons practising any of the professions of chiropody, dietetics, medical laboratory technology, occupational therapy, physiotherapy, radiography and remedial gymnastics,[64] doubtless owe both a contractual duty to their employers and a delictual duty to their patients to show reasonable knowledge, skill and care in treating them. Thus a physiotherapist was held liable for not giving a patient adequate warning, in

---

[60] See Chap. 13, *supra*.
[61] 1928 S.N. 30.
[62] *Greenwell* v. *Prison Commissioners* (1951) 101 L.J. 486.
[63] *Cf. Pullin* v. *Prison Commrs.* [1957] 3 All E.R. 470; *Keatings* v. *Secretary of State for Scotland* (1961) 77 Sh.Ct.Rep. 113.
[64] These are the professions for which the Council for Professions Supplementary to Medicine and seven professional boards were set up under the Professions Supplementary to Medicine Act, 1960, to regulate their professional education, registration, and conduct.

consequence of which the plaintiff was burned,[65] and a radiographer for not taking proper precautions in consequence of which the patient was burned and disfigured.[66]

If employed by a hospital board or other authority, that authority is vicariously liable for the practitioner's negligence, even in a matter of professional skill.[67]

(19) Psychiatrists

In the absence of express authority to the contrary it is reasonable to assume that the psychiatrist owes to his patient duties of care, contractual and delictual, similar to those owed by physicians and surgeons.[68]

(20) School teachers

A school teacher owes a duty to take reasonable care for the safety and health of the children under his charge, and must exercise care and forethought, having regard to their age, inexperience, carelessness and high spirits and the nature and degree of danger, not to subject them to avoidable risks of harm. It is always a question of fact in the circumstances whether or not there was negligence.[69] The duty is of reasonable care, not of constant meticulous supervision.[70] It is not part of a school or teacher's duty to foresee every act of stupidity that might take place.[71]

Cases where the issue of such negligence has arisen for determination in particular circumstances include: where a girl of fourteen was told to go into the staff room to poke the fire and her apron caught fire[72]; where phosphorus was left lying about in a place to which boys had access, and one was injured[73]; where there has been inadequate supervision of children in the playground[74]; where a boy was told to carry an oil can from one room to another, and collided with another boy, injuring his eye with the oil can[75]; where building materials[76] or fuel[74] were delivered to the school and a pupil was injured by some of the stuff thrown by another; where a master allowed a boy to look through a telescope at an eclipse of the sun and the boy's eyes were injured[77]; where a teacher sent a child across the playground carrying milk bottles and she was

---

[65] Clarke v. Adams (1950) 94 Sol.J. 599.
[66] Gold v. Essex C.C. [1942] 2 K.B. 293; cf. Lavelle v. Glasgow R.I., 1932 S.C. 245; Crawford v. Campbell, 1948 S.L.T.(Notes) 91.
[67] Gold v. Essex C.C. [1942] 2 K.B. 293 (radiographer); Lavelle v. Glasgow R.I., 1932 S.C. 245 (where no negligence was proved) would now be decided differently on this point.
[68] In Bolam v. Friern Hospital Cttee. [1957] 2 All E.R. 118, there was no indication that the duties incumbent on a psychiatrist differed from those of other medical practitioners. Liability was held established in Landau v. Werner (1961) 105 Sol.J. 1008.
[69] Cf. Trevor v. Incorporated Froebel Educational Inst. [1954] C.L.Y. 2238.
[70] Clark v. Monmouthshire C.C. [1954] C.L.Y. 2240; Jeffery v. L.C.C. (1954) 52 L.G.R. 521.
[71] Perry v. King Alfred School Soc. [1961] C.L.Y. 5865.
[72] Smith v. Martin and Hull Corpn. [1911] 2 K.B. 775.
[73] Williams v. Eady (1893) 10 T.L.R. 41; cf. Suckling v. Essex C.C. [1955] C.L.Y. 1844.
[74] Rich v. L.C.C. [1953] 2 All E.R. 376; cf. Price v. Caernarvonshire C.C. [1960] C.L.Y. 2145; Newton v. East Ham Corpn. [1963] C.L.Y. 2426.
[75] Wray v. Essex C.C. [1936] 3 All E.R. 97.
[76] Jackson v. L.C.C. (1912) 28 T.L.R. 359; cf. Driscoll v. Gratton Wilson [1954] C.L.Y. 2239.
[77] Avery v. New Park School, 1949 S.L.T.(Notes) 7.

knocked down and injured [78]; where in the teacher's absence one pupil was injured in the eye by a pellet from a catapult [79]; where a child was injured doing gymnastics [80]; where a boy had his eye injured by scissors used by a classmate [81]; where a small boy was allowed to get out of the playground onto a highway where he caused a vehicle to swerve and the driver to be killed [82]; where a child was scalded by tea from the teacher's teacup [83]; where a deaf and dumb child was injured when deposited by a school bus.[84]

(21) Solicitors

A solicitor's duty is contractual and owed to his client only,[85] except in possible cases where a third party has acquired a *jus quaesitum tertio* under the contract of employment. There are numerous cases discussing possible breaches of his contractual duty.[86]

A solicitor, however, probably also owes a duty of care, *ex lege*, to third parties where information or advice is sought from him in circumstances in which a reasonable man would know that he was being trusted and his skill and judgment relied on by the third party, to take such care as the circumstances require in making a reply, and he will be liable in damages *ex delicto* if damage results from his failure to exercise that care.[87] This principle, it is thought, will not impose any liability merely because a client communicates information or advice from his solicitors to a friend, though it might if a client consults his solicitor expressly about his friend's problems. Where the circumstances indicate that the advice might be relied on by a third party, the advice may be qualified so as to exclude liability.[88]

(22) Stockbrokers

Stockbrokers are under a contractual liability to clients to show the knowledge, skill and care reasonably to be expected of a competent member of that profession.[89] They probably might incur delictual liability to third parties in circumstances similar to solicitors.

[78] *Hutchison* v. *Dumfries C.C.*, 1949 S.L.T.(Notes) 10; *cf. Cooper* v. *Manchester Corpn.* [1959] C.L.Y. 2260.
[79] *Henderson* v. *Edinburgh Corpn.*, 1950 S.L.T.(Notes) 63; *cf. Smith* v. *Hale* [1956] C.L.Y. 5940; *Harris* v. *Guest* [1960] C.L.Y. 2146.
[80] *Wright* v. *Cheshire C.C.* [1952] 2 All E.R. 789; *Baker* v. *Essex C.C.* [1952] C.L.Y. 2400; *Sutherland* v. *Glasgow Corpn.*, 1952 S.L.T.(Notes) 51; *Skinner* v. *Glasgow Corpn.*, 1961 S.L.T. 130.
[81] *Elsmere* v. *Middlesex C.C.* [1956] C.L.Y. 6025.
[82] *Carmarthenshire C.C.* v. *Lewis* [1955] A.C. 549.
[83] *Nicholson* v. *Westmorland C.C.* [1962] C.L.Y. 2087.
[84] *Ellis* v. *Sayers Confectioners* [1963] C.L.Y. 2347.
[85] *Groom* v. *Crocker* [1939] 1 K.B. 194; *Lake* v. *Bushby* [1949] 2 All E.R. 964; *Clark* v. *Kirby-Smith* [1964] 2 All E.R. 835.
[86] See, generally, *Begg on Law Agents* (2nd ed.), Chaps. 18–19, and cases of *Godefroy* v. *Dalton* (1830) 6 Bing. 460, 467; *Hart* v. *Frame* (1839) MacL. & Rob. 595; *Clark* v. *Kirby-Smith* [1964] 2 All E.R. 835.
[87] *Cf. Hedley Byrne & Co.* v. *Heller & Partners, Ltd.* [1964] A.C. 465.
[88] *Hedley Byrne & Co.*, *supra*.
[89] *Neilson* v. *James* (1882) 9 Q.B.D. 546; *cf. Jarvis* v. *Moy, Davies & Co.* [1936] 1 K.B. 399.

(23) Surveyors and valuers

Surveyors and valuers owe to their clients a contractual [90] duty to show the knowledge, skill and care reasonably to be expected of a competent member of the profession.[91] The knowledge demanded includes knowledge of the relevant law.[92]

Much depends on the terms of employment, whether a general or a detailed survey is required, but defects may be so serious that they should be discovered and reported on even in a general report,[93] or there may be indications which would have put a careful surveyor on his guard and led him to make a more thorough examination.[94]

In valuations defendants have been held liable for not properly utilising their knowledge and experience and hence making an undervaluation,[95] or for negligently making an overvaluation.[96]

They may probably also owe duties *ex lege* in circumstances similar to solicitors. An auctioneer is not liable to a person injured for the dangerous state of a house in which he conducts an auction sale.[97]

(24) University teachers

At common law the office of university professor was *munus publicum*, connoting that he owed duties to the public as well as to the university, and implying life appointment and irremovability except for fault.[98] In modern practice university teachers, including professors, by whomever appointed, are the servants of the University courts and must retire on attaining the age-limit.[99] But the office, certainly in the case of professors, is thought still to be of the nature of *munus publicum*, and the only remedy of students or members of the public for non-performance or mis-performance of the duties of the office is by way of complaint to the University court. There is no remedy in delict, nor in contract, the relationship between student and university not being contractual.

(25) Veterinary surgeons

Similar principles to those applicable to physicians are thought to apply to the veterinary surgeon,[1] whose liability arises normally out of

90 *Le Lievre* v. *Gould* [1893] 1 Q.B. 491; *Old Gate Estates* v. *Toplis* (1939) 161 L.T. 227; *Wooldridge* v. *Hicks* [1953] C.P.L. 700; *Eagle Star Insce. Co.* v. *Gale & Power* [1955] C.L.Y. 281; and on damages, see *Philips* v. *Ward* [1956] 1 All E.R. 874; *Stewart* v. *Brechin*, 1959 S.C. 306.
91 *Moneypenny* v. *Hartland* (1824) 1 C. & P. 352; *Parsons* v. *Way & Waller* [1952] C.P.L. 417.
92 *Jenkins* v. *Betham* (1855) 15 C.B. 168.
93 *Ker* v. *Allan*, 1949 S.L.T.(Notes) 20; *Sincock* v. *Bangs* (*Reading*) [1952] C.P.L. 562; *Philips* v. *Ward* [1956] 1 All E.R. 874; *Stewart*, *supra*; see also *Parsons* v. *Way and Waller* [1952] C.P.L. 417; *Tew* v. *Whitburn* [1952] C.P.L. 111; *Last* v. *Post* [1952] C.P.L. 255.
94 *Grove* v. *Jackman and Masters* (1950) 155 E.G. 182.
95 *Bell Hotels (1935), Ltd.* v. *Motion* [1952] C.P.L. 403.
96 *Baxter* v. *Gapp & Co., Ltd.* [1939] 2 K.B. 271.
97 *Grant* v. *Reid* (1949) 65 Sh.Ct.Rep. 230.
98 *Caird* v. *Sime* (1887) 14 R.(H.L.) 37, 43, 46, *per* Lord Watson. *Cf. Hastie* v. *McMurtrie* (1889) 16 R. 715.
99 *Cf. University Council of Vidyodaya University of Ceylon* v. *Linus Silva* (1964) 3 All E.R. 865.
1 *Cf.* Beven, *Negligence*, II, 1368, quoting *Barney* v. *Pinkham*, 26 Am.St.R. 389; *Chute Farms* v. *Curtis* [1961] C.L.Y. 5987.

contract with the owner of the animal only, but may be owed *ex lege* to the owner of any animal whom he treats.

(26) *Skilled tradesmen*

Similar principles apply to persons exercising a skilled trade, such as electricians, joiners, painters, motor mechanics, and plumbers. They owe a duty to show knowledge, skill and care from the contract of employment,[2] and also owe a duty *ex lege* in so far as failure to show the skill and care of a reasonably competent tradesman is foreseeably likely to cause physical or mental injury to a person who might foreseeably be injured by defective or careless workmanship. Thus electricians have been held to be under a duty to test both existing and any additional electrical installation for reversed polarity,[3] and may be under a duty to take care as to insulating wires.[4] Painters using a blowlamp must exercise great care[5] as a possible consequence of careless use thereof is the occurrence of personal injuries or death.[6] Joiners erecting a scaffolding for other workmen must take care in doing so.[7] Plasterers should not leave a heap of lime in the roadway.[8] Plumbers are liable for damage done by an insufficiently repaired pipe,[9] and a gasfitter for death caused by his unskilful workmanship.[10] They are not liable if acting in accordance with local trade practice, even though practice elsewhere is safer.[11] A motor-mechanic who repairs negligently may be liable for subsequent repairs to and loss of use of the vehicle.[12]

[2] *Hinshaw* v. *Adam* (1870) 8 M. 933. Cf. *Cleghorn* v. *Spittal's Trs.* (1856) 18 D. 664; *Campbell* v. *Kennedy* (1864) 3 M. 121; see also *McDonald* v. *Mackie* (1831) 5 W. & S. 462; *Sally* v. *Dunbar* (1899) 6 S.L.T. 322; *Terret* v. *Murphy* (1952) 68 Sh.Ct.Rep. 117.
[3] *Waddell's C.B.* v. *Lindsay*, 1960 S.L.T. 189.
[4] *Eccles* v. *Cross & McIlwham*, 1938 S.C. 697.
[5] *Gilmour* v. *Simpson*, 1958 S.C. 477.
[6] *Malcolm* v. *Dickson*, 1951 S.C. 542 (where death held in the circumstances too remote a consequence to impose any liability therefor).
[7] *Kettlewell* v. *Paterson* (1886) 24 S.L.R. 95; *Nicholson* v. *Macandrew* (1888) 15 R. 854; *Macdonald* v. *Wyllie* (1898) 1 F. 339. Cf. *Gardiner* v. *Main* (1894) 22 R. 100.
[8] *McLean* v. *Russell, MacNee & Co.* (1850) 12 D. 887.
[9] *McIntyre* v. *Gallacher* (1883) 11 R. 64.
[10] *McNamara* v. *Anderson Bros.* (1904) 11 S.L.T. 607.
[11] *McLaughlan* v. *Craig*, 1948 S.C. 599.
[12] *Brewis* v. *Stewart* (1962) 78 Sh.Ct.Rep. 95.

APPENDIX

Compensation for Victims of Crimes of Violence

It has been pointed out that a civil claim founded on delict may be brought where one person has harmed another in circumstances amounting to criminal violence. Thus an action lies for assault, rape, or robbery, and where a person is killed his relatives may pursue an assythment. But in many cases the wrongdoer may escape recognition, or he may not be worth suing.

Since the later 1950's it was increasingly urged that the State should accept liability for compensating the victims of violence, and various schemes were proposed.[1] In 1964 the Government announced its proposals.[2] It accepted the principle that victims of crimes of violence should be eligible for some compensation for personal injury at the public expense, but, having regard to the lack of experience in this and other countries of any scheme, proposed an experimental and non-statutory scheme of a flexible character which could be altered in the light of experience.

Compensation is payable on an *ex gratia* basis, as the Government did not accept that the State should be legally liable for injuries caused to people by the criminal acts of others. The scheme is administered by a body known as the Criminal Injuries Compensation Board, composed initially of a chairman and five members, all legally qualified, appointed by the Home Secretary and the Secretary of State for Scotland.[3] The Board is based on London but may establish offices elsewhere and may sit in London, Edinburgh and elsewhere as necessary. It must submit an annual report and accounts which may be debated in Parliament, and may at any time publish such information about the scheme and their decisions in individual cases as may assist intending applicants for compensation.[3a] The Board is solely and entirely responsible for determining the compensation payable in particular cases and its decisions will not be subject to appeal or ministerial review.[4]

Scope of compensation. The compensation scheme is limited to injuries arising on or after August 1, 1964, from offences committed in Great Britain or on British vessels or aircraft and triable in this country. No list of crimes, the victims of which may seek compensation,

---

[1] See " Compensation for Victims of Crimes of Violence " (1961, Cmnd. 1406), and a report by a Committee of " Justice " on " Compensation for Victims of Crimes of Violence " (1962), discussed in 1963 S.L.T.(News) 61.

[2] " Compensation for Victims of Crimes of Violence " (1964, Cmnd. 2323), discussed in 1964 S.L.T.(News) 109; the scheme, as amended, is printed in 1964 S.L.T.(News) 134. Requests for application forms and all enquiries should be addressed to: Criminal Injuries Compensation Board, Fourth Floor, 19–29 Woburn Place, London, W.C.1.

[3] Two members are members of the Scottish Bar.

[3a] See abbreviated reports of awards in *Current Law*, s.v. " Criminal Law ".

[4] Scheme, paras. 1–4.

is laid down. " Broadly speaking, however, applications are likely to arise either out of offences against the person, such as murder, manslaughter, assault and sexual offences; from offences against property accompanied by personal violence—principally robbery; or from personal injuries due to malicious damage to property, including arson." [5] It is not necessary that the offender have been convicted or been arrested or even be known.

Conditions of compensation. The Board entertains applications for *ex gratia* payment of compensation in cases where:

(a) the applicant, or, in the case of an application by a spouse or dependant, the deceased, suffered personal injury directly attributable either to a criminal offence or to an arrest or attempted arrest of an offender or suspected offender or to the prevention or attempted prevention of an offence or to the giving of help to any constable who is engaged in arresting or attempting to arrest an offender or suspected offender or preventing or attempting to prevent an offence, where such injury occurs in Great Britain or on a British vessel or aircraft;

(b) the injury was incurred after the commencement of the scheme [6];

(c) the injury gave rise to at least three weeks loss of earnings or is an injury for which not less than £50 compensation would be awarded;

(d) the circumstances of the injury have been reported to the police without delay or have been the subject of criminal proceedings in the courts; and

(e) the applicant is prepared to submit to such medical examination as the Board may require.[7]

The Board will scrutinise with particular care all applications in respect of sexual offences or offences arising out of a sexual relationship in order to determine whether there was any responsibility, by provocation or otherwise, on the part of the victim and have regard especially to any delay in submitting the application. Subject to the circumstances having been immediately reported to the police, the Board will consider applications for compensation arising out of rape and sexual assaults, in respect of pain, suffering and shock and in respect of loss of earnings due to pregnancy resulting from rape and of the expenses of childbirth if the victim is ineligible for National Insurance maternity grant, but compensation will not be payable for the maintenance of any child born as a result of a sexual offence.[8]

Crimes excluded. Offences committed against a member of the offender's household living with him at the time are excluded altogether, in view of the difficulty in establishing the facts and ensuring that the compensation does not benefit the offender.[9]

[5] White Paper, Para. 13.
[6] August 1, 1964.
[7] Scheme, Para. 5.
[8] Para. 6.
[9] Para. 7.

Motoring offences are also excluded, except where the motor-vehicle has been used as a weapon, in a deliberate attempt to run the victim down, on the basis that injuries caused by identified vehicles are covered by insurance and that it is usually difficult, where the vehicle has not been identified, to prove that an offence has occurred.[10]

Basis of compensation. Compensation is assessed on the basis of common law damages and in the form of a lump sum payment, though sometimes it may be necessary for more than one payment to be made, as where only a provisional medical assessment can be given in the first instance.[11] Where the victim is alive the compensation is limited in that:

(a) the rate of loss of earnings (and, where appropriate, of earning capacity) to be taken into account will not exceed twice the average (according to the age and sex of the victim) of industrial earnings [12] at the time that the injury was sustained;

(b) there will be no element comparable to exemplary or punitive damages.[13]

Fatal injury cases. Where the victim has died no compensation is payable for the benefit of his estate, but the Board may entertain claims from his spouse and dependants. For this purpose compensation will be payable to any person entitled to claim in England under the Fatal Accidents Acts, 1846 to 1959, or, in Scotland, under the corresponding Scottish law.[14] The amount of compensation will be governed by the same principles as under those provisions; the total income of the deceased, earned and unearned, to be taken into account being subject to the limit specified in para. 10 (a) above. Where the victim's funeral expenses are paid by a person who is ineligible for a death grant under the National Insurance Scheme, the Board may award that person a sum in compensation equivalent to the appropriate death grant.[15]

The Board has to consider whether, because of provocation or otherwise, the victim of the crime bears any share of responsibility for it, and, in accordance with its assessment of the share of responsibility, will reduce the amount of compensation or reject the claim altogether.[16]

Where applicable, the compensation will also be reduced by the amount of any payments from public funds accruing, as a result of the injury or death, to the benefit of the person to whom the award is made.[17]

The Board has discretion to make special arrangements for the administration of any sum payable to an infant.[18]

10 Para. 8; White Paper, Para. 18.
11 Para. 9.
12 *i.e.,* Average Weekly Earnings for Men (21 years and over) as published in the *Ministry of Labour Gazette.*
13 Para. 10.
14 Chap. 22, *supra.*
15 Para. 11.
16 Para. 12.
17 Para. 13.
18 Para. 14.

Procedure. Applications are made in writing to the Board as soon as possible after the event. The initial decision rejecting or allowing the claim and, in the latter case, fixing the amount of compensation is made by one member of the Board. A dissatisfied applicant is entitled to a hearing before three other members of the Board. This hearing is in private and as informal as is consistent with a proper determination of the application. The onus is on the applicant and he and a member of the Board's staff may call and examine witnesses. The Board has to reach its decision solely in the light of the evidence brought out at the hearing. The applicant may be assisted by a friend or legal adviser but the cost of legal representation is not admissible. The expenses of witnesses whose attendance was considered necessary are allowable.[19]

Interaction with claims founded on delict. It is not intended that if a person brings a civil action for common law damages for the injury he should obtain compensation from the Board in addition to a fully satisfied judgment in the action, and accordingly a person compensated by the Board will be required to undertake to repay them from any damages or settlement he may obtain by suing the offender.[20] There is, however, nothing to prevent a claim concurrently with a civil action, nor a claim being made in the event of the failure of a civil action, or a decree therein not being satisfied.

[19] Paras. 15–19.
[20] Para. 20.

INDEX

Abatement,
of nuisance, 456, 959
remedy not favoured, 457
Absolute liability,
aircraft, 554
based on risk, 49, 290
commercial practicability irrelevant, 326
continuing nature of, 326
distinct from strict liability, 213, 290, 325
for intentional wrongs, 173
loss essential for, 40
mental state irrelevant to, 50
precautions irrelevant, 213, 337
proof in cases of, 408
qualified, 323
qualified and limited, 324
requires proof of causation, 327
standard of, 324
under statute, 323, 658, 664
Absolute privilege,
difference from qualified privilege, 803, 811
difference from *veritas*, 802
effect of, 803
malice irrelevant to, 803, 807
occasions to which applies, 803–810
persons protected, 806
question of law, 802
See also Qualified privilege
Absolvitor,
extinguishes pursuer's claim, 429
what claims not barred by, 430
Abstention,
as element of harm, 5
as importing liability, 34, 36, 171
Abstraction of minerals,
damages for, 945
interdict against, 462, 944
Abuse, 767, 798
Abuse of process, 173, 851
administrative proceedings, 879
civil proceedings, 851
criminal proceedings, 874
diligence, 862
loss unnecessary in, 851
mistaken proceedings not wrong, 851
wrong akin to defamation, 851
See also: Wrongful civil proceedings;
Wrongful criminal proceedings;
Wrongful diligence;
Wrongful interdict;
Abuse of rights, 52
Abusive language, 495, 778, 797
Access, means of, 574, 659, 662

Accident,
aircraft, 551
defence to assault, 500
employment, 556
inevitable, no liability for, 35, 299, 301, 337, 500, 512, 522, 1054
liability for, 35
not an assault, 500
railway, 533
road, 509, 520
shipping, 546
skidding as, 522
Accountant,
acting in breach of confidence, 713
duties of, as auditor, 1046
duty of confidence, 917, 1045
preparing accounts negligently, 900
skill and care expected of, 900, 1045
statutory duties of, 1045
Accounting for profits,
remedy of, 1026, 1027, 1032, 1034, 1036, 1038, 1040
Acquiescence in nuisance, 970
Act,
as element of harm, 5
as importing liability, 33, 34, 36
justifiable, imposes no liability, 38
Act of God, *see damnum fatale*
Act of state, harm done by, 75, 99, 107
Actio de effusis vel dejectis, 20, 294, 641
Actio de pauperie, 643, 650
Actio injuriarum,
in Roman law, 19, 20, 735
in Scots law, 25, 487, 493, 503, 675, 676, 685, 717, 719, 735, 757, 787, 851
loss not essential in, 40, 468
requires *dolus*, 33, 717
requisites of, in Scots law, 32
See also Death of relative
Actio legis Aquiliae, 17–19, 20, 22, 25, 487, 493
extended use of, in Scots law, 725, 736, 788
in modern Roman law, 21–22
patrimonial loss essential in, 40, 469, 493, 736
remedy in, 19
requires *dolus* or *culpa*, 33, 788
requisites of, in Scots law, 32
Actio personalis moritur cum persona, 102, 409
Actio popularis, 104
Actio positi aut suspensi, 21, 292, 641
Actio quod metus causa, 697, 698, 932
Actio vi bonorum raptorum, 1001
Action,
bringing, in breach of agreement, 854

(*Volume 1 ends with page 484*)

(*Volume 1 ends with page 484*)

(Volume 1 ends with page 484)

(*Volume 1 ends with page 484*)

(*Volume 1 ends with page 484*)

(*Volume 1 ends with page 484*)

Course of the employment—*cont.*
Includes—*cont.*
    unauthorised act, 152
    work done improperly, 150
    work ordered, 150
  what outwith, 150
  what within, 149
Court, contempt of, 847
Court-martial, privilege of, 806, 807, 809
Cow,
  entering house, 268, 630, 631
  falling through floor, 268, 650
  trampling pedestrian, 631
Credit,
  fraudulent representation as to, 890
  imputations against, 781
  inquiries as to, 828
Cricket,
  as nuisance, 968
  injury from playing of, 36, 205, 616,
    639, 652, 968
Crime,
  assault in preventing, 501
  attempt, imputation of, 777
  compensation for victims of, 1062
  delict and, 7, 15, 22, 36
  imputation of, 777, 800
  person giving information of, 823, 874
  suspicion of, imputation of, 777, 800
  taxing suspect, 824
  trespass to prevent, 338
  victims of, compensation for, 1062
  wrongfully initiating proceedings for,
    874
Criticism as defamation, 784
Crown,
  as defender, 72
  as pursuer, 72
  exceptions from liability of, 73
  not bound by statutes, 75
  not liable for public corporations, 73
  personal liability, 72
  representation of, 76
  statutory duty, 73, 75
  vicarious liability of, 72, 133
Crown counsel, immunity of, 876
Culpa,
  allocation between joint wrongdoers,
    126
  different degrees of, 207
  generally required for liability, 116
  inadvertent breach of duty is, 186
  in Aquilian action, 18, 32, 33, 736, 788
  in defamation, 788
  limited by duty of care, 45, 176
  meanings of, 42, 47, 48
  negligence sometimes equals, 47, 176,
    177, 207
  presumption of, 641
  usages of term, 42, 48
  whether liability always requires, 49
Culpa lata aequiparatur dolo, 43, 173, 291,
    737, 788
Culpa tenet suos auctores, 116, 117, 489
  vicarious liability an exception to, 131,
    148, 291, 489

Culpability in contributory negligence,
    370
Culpability and compensation, 251, 252,
    259, 265, 270, 273, 275, 278, 285
Curator,
  ad litem, 94, 97
  bonis, title to sue of, 97
  may compromise claim, 434
  to minor, 94
Custodier, liability for not returning
    goods, 1007
Custody,
  interference with, 716
  liability for giving into, 136
Cyclists, duties of, 529

Dam bursting, 975
Damage,
  actionable only if due to breach of
    duty, 38
  consequential, *see* Remoteness of dam-
    age
  inseparable from duty and breach, 178
  need to prove, 329
  not ground of action alone, 38
  remoteness of, 65
Damage and interest, 24, 488
Damages,
  aggravated by greater loss, 467, 790
  appeals on questions of, 482
  as name for law of delict, 8
  assessed by Scottish practice, 466
  assessed once for all, 467
  awarded only for loss, 383
  compensatory, 466
  defined, 465
  destination of, 412
  determined by *lex fori,* 60, 66, 466
  evidence relevant to, 408
  exemplary, 466
  expenses recoverable in, 474
  factors aggravating or mitigating, 475
  factors for administration, 480
  factors irrelevant to, 476
  for,
    abstraction of minerals, 945
    abuse of process, 851
    adultery, 718
    affront, 481
    assault, 496
    damage to business, 472, 912
    damage to vehicle, 1015
    death, 469
    death of relative, 732
    defamation, 790
    destruction of property, 482
    infringement of,
      copyright, 1034
      patent, 1026
      plant breeders' rights, 1040
      registered design, 1038
      trade mark, 1032
    loss of,
      appointment, 472
      earnings, 472

(*Volume 1 ends with page 484*)

(*Volume 1 ends with page 484*)

(Volume 1 ends with page 484)

(*Volume 1 ends with page 484*)

(*Volume 1 ends with page 484*)

(Volume 1 ends with page 484)

(*Volume 1 ends with page 484*)

(*Volume 1 ends with page 484*)

(*Volume 1 ends with page 484*)

(*Volume 1 ends with page 484*)

(*Volume 1 ends with page 484*)

Level-crossing—*cont.*
duty of lookout at, 537, 538
duty to erect gates, 535, 536, 538
duty to whistle at, 536, 537
temporary, 537
vehicle at, 536
Lex Aquilia, 17, 18
culpa in, 18
dolus in, 18
remedy under, 19
Lex fori,
damages, evidence, pleading, procedure determined by, 60
requisite of actionability by, 58
Lex loci delicti,
must be proved as fact, 65
pursuer's rights determined by, 59, 61
requisite of actionability by, 58
Liability,
absolute, *see* Absolute liability
and responsibility, 33
anterior to measure of damage, 202
circumstances inferring, 33
civil, 15
common law and statutory, 327
conditions of, 33
consequential on breach of duty, 13
criminal, 15
degree of risk relevant to, 205
depends on normal susceptibility, 202
determined by foresight, 201
elements of, 178
employer's, 556
exclusion of, by contract, 341, 599
for agent, 134
for assythment, 724
for employee, 141
for independent contractor, 161
for intentional wrong, 171
for remote consequences, *see* Remoteness of damage
for risk, 49, 290
for unforeseen result, 258
founded on breach of duty, 13, 201
general exemptions from, 107
how elided, 178
if general type of harm foreseeable, 247
immunity from, 107, 334
inferred by,
intentional conduct, 33
negligent conduct, 33
inferred without fault, 33
joint and several, *see* Joint and several liability
limited by,
contract, 346
duty of care, 45
remoteness, 239
not *ex dominio solo*, 13
not for all resulting harm, 239
not for failure to attain ideal, 177
not *in vacuo*, 177
not without damage, 252
noxal, 21
personal, *see* Personal liability
personal, for contractor, 161

Liability—*cont.*
referable to *injuria* or *damnum injuria datum*, 32
remoteness and, 238
requires some harm, 177
several, *see* Several liability
statutory, *see* Statutory liability
strict, *see* Strict liability
summary of requisites for, 288
to be called as defender, 71
to contractor's employees, 581
transmission of,
on bankruptcy, 413
on death, 412
under praetorian edict, 295
vicarious, *see* Vicarious liability
where pursuer unforeseeable, 196, 203
without fault, 32, 33, 49, 50
wrongdoer always liable, 116
Libel, *see* Defamation
Liberty, interference with, 685, 881
Licensee, *see* Occupier's liability
Licensing, time for actions, 446
Life,
damages for shortening of, 733
duty to save, 16, 194, 228, 601
jettison of cargo to save, 338
trespass to save, 338
Life-saving appliances, 669
Lift,
duty of driver to person given, 514
landlord's responsibility for, 607
liability of installers of, 628
proper maintenance of, 597, 658, 662
Lifting apparatus, duty as to, 659, 662
Lights,
dazzle by, 517
dipping, 517
duty to carry, 516, 517
duty to provide, 566, 577, 599, 659
failure of, 516
failure to exhibit, 516
in common close, 607
on common stair, 671
on streets, 671
substitute, 517
Limitation of actions, statutory,
amendment of action, 452
defender must plead, 445
effect of, 445
extension of time, 452
interpretation in, 445
particular periods, 446–453
personal injuries claims, 449
terminus *a quo*, 450
where injury only later apparent, 451
where wrong continuing, 451
Limitation of liability,
by contract, 341, 553, 600
by statute, 548, 555, 997, 998, 1019
when statutorily excluded, 341, 601
Lion, dangerous animal, 648
Liquidation,
negligence of accountant in, 1046
wrongful petition for, 861
Literature, comment on, 849

(*Volume 1 ends with page 484*)

(*Volume 1 ends with page 484*)

(*Volume 1 ends with page 484*)

(Volume 1 ends with page 484)

(*Volume 1 ends with page 484*)

(*Volume 1 ends with page 484*)

(Volume 1 ends with page 484)

Reasonable care—*cont.*
  on roads, 510
  standard of, 206, 208, 209
  when inadequate, 213
Recklessness,
  elements of, 43
  equivalent to intention, 43, 173, 494
Reconditioning, defect from, 625
Record (open and closed) not privileged, 809, 838
Reduction, 697, 698
Reference, defamatory,
  mistaken, 751
  multiple, 752
Regiam Majestatem, 22
Register, statutory, extract from, privileged, 837
Registered designs,
  exceptions from infringement, 1038
  infringement of, 1038
  remedies for infringement, 1038
  rights by registration, 1037
  threats of infringement proceedings, 1038
Relative,
  expenses incurred for, 721
  injury to, 721
  loss of services by, 721
  slander of deceased, 734, 757
Relatives of deceased,
  action by, for solatium and loss of support, 725
  action by, or by executor, 102, 409–411, 471, 730
  family claim by, 473, 729
  for whose deaths claim competent, 727
  mental injury to, 721
  patrimonial loss to, 472
  physical injury to, 721
  single action only competent, 729
  solatium to, 471
Relief,
  action of, 128, 421
  against independent contractors, 169, 428
  between joint wrongdoers, 127, 423
  by action of damages, 426
  claim of, does not require assignation, 128
  contractual, 130, 421
  debt must be constituted, 128, 129, 423, 424
  in joint and several liability, 169, 423
  in vicarious liability, 158, 425
  third party procedure and, 129
  under statute, 130, 423
  where defender compromises claim, 423
Remedial gymnast, duty of care of, 1057
Remedies,
  civil and criminal, interaction of, 16
  civil, not suspended pending criminal trial, 16
  concurrent, 16
  determined by *lex fori*, 60
  generally, 454–484

Remedies—*cont.*
  given for infringed interest, 9
   See also Damages; Declarator; Interdict; Self-help; Solatium; Statutory remedies
Remoteness, 238, 251, 253, 286
  See also Remoteness of damage; Remoteness of injury
Remoteness of damage, 289
  authorities on, 254
  concerned with extent of liability, 238, 248
  conclusions on, 286
  consequences too remote from wrong, 238
  criterion of, 252
  determined by *lex loci delicti*, 65
  extends to direct consequences, 253
  extends to natural and probable consequences, 253
  formulae on, 253
  in contract, 276
  in intentional wrongs, 174, 286
  in negligent wrongs, 248
  in statutory duty cases, 329
  logically prior to measure of damages, 251
  logically subsequent to remoteness of injury, 250, 265
  no liability for all consequences, 248
  practice as to, 280
  problem of, 248
  question of compensation, 251
  relevant only where liability exists, 249
  verbal formulations of test of, 282
  verbal tests of, 253, 284
Remoteness of injury, 178, 289
  authorities on, 240
  concerned with existence of liability, 238
  criterion, 239–246
  foreseeable type of harm, 247
  harm of unforeseen kind, 248
  in causal connection, 238
  in statutory duty cases, 329
  logically prior to remoteness of damage, 250, 265
  problem of, 239
  question of culpability, 251
Repairs, damage from, 294, 625, 629
Reparation,
  as name for delict, 7, 8
  duty of, 3
  liability to make, 12
  natural obligation of, 6
  obligation of, 7, 13, 31
Repetition of defamation, 761, 762
  malice inferred from, 815
Report,
  blasphemous or immoral, 838
  broadcast, 837, 838
  careless communication of, 683
  fair, 837
  misleading, may be trade libel, 1025
  onus of proof of accuracy, 839

(Volume 1 ends with page 484)

Report—*cont.*
  privilege conditional on fairness and
    accuracy, 839
  prohibited by statute, 838
  repeating, 761
  when privileged, 837
Reputation, harm to, 736, 755, 851
  See also Defamation
Rescue, 224, 227–229, 356
Res dejectae vel effusae, 20
Res ipsa loquitur,
  absence of explanation, 402
  aircraft accident, 555, 556
  extent of application of, 402
  generally, 399
  inapplicable where event neutral, 402,
    403
  inapplicable where facts ascertainable,
    404
  in escape of danger cases, 976
  in surgical cases, 404, 1045, 1051, 1054
  prerequisites of, 401
  rebuttal of, 404
  tyre bursting, 523
Res judicata,
  as defence, 348
  between Ct. of Session and Shf. Ct., 430
  decree as, 429
  not inferred by dismissal, 430
  where action maliciously repeated, 856
Respondeat superior, 131, 148
Responsibility,
  allocation of, 4
  as answerability, 33
  as causative of harm, 33
  basis of apportionment in contributory
    negligence, 369
  diminished, 98
  essential of liability, 5
  liability and, 33
  moral, 33
Restitution,
  delict and obligation of, 15
  in integrum, 697, 698
  of goods, 455, 1002
Retailer of goods,
  contractual liability, 620
  delictual liability, 620
  duty to warn of danger, 621
  inadequate containers, 621
  liability for own fault, 621
  need for examination, 620
  selling dangerous goods, 621
Retaliation in assault, 500
Retort, angry, 797
Retort, fair, 836
Ridicule, 743, 849
Riding at person, 495
Right of way, action for defence of, 104
Right-thinking persons, 766
Rights,
  abuse of, 52
  correlative to duties, 12
  created by recognition of interests, 10
  duty correlative to, 180
  exercise of, not actionable, 185

Rights—*cont.*
  guaranteed, 10
  human, 9
  infringement of, whether actionable *per
    se*, 40
  natural, 9, 10
Riotous assemblies,
  damage done by, 999
  time for suing, 446
Risk,
  adjustment of, 5
  appreciable, 206
  area of, 31, 178, 195, 196, 198
  care proportioned to, 204, 210
  degree of, relevant to liability, 205
  foresight of, 197–204
  indifference to, is reckless, 43
  keeping animals at one's, 649
  liability for, 42, 49, 50, 290, 641, 653,
    974
  negligible, 192, 205
  some inevitable, 192
  voluntary assumption of, *see* Voluntary
    assumption of risk
  which has materialised, 191
River,
  operations in, 463
  pollution of, 966
Rixa, 778, 787, 794, 797
Road,
  accidents on, 509
  animals causing accidents on, 530, 1013
  animals straying onto, 520, 530
  damage by person not on road, 616
  dangerous, 610, 1014
  driving animals on, 520, 529, 631
  duty to erect walls, 609, 1014
  fencing, 609, 611, 1014
  following vehicle on, 521
  Highway Code, 511, 670
  junctions and roundabouts, 519
  keeping clear, 612
  lighting, 611
  maintenance of, 610, 1014
  major, 519
  obstruction in, 369, 517, 519, 531, 608,
    610, 1014
  overtaking vehicle, 521
  pedestrian crossings, 520
  persons crossing, 520
  private, 512, 609
  repair, 609, 610, 1014
  responsibility for, 608
  riding animal on, 532
  rule of,
    animals, 510
    pedestrians, 510
    vehicles, 510
  safety of, 608, 1014
  shutting up, 608
  smoke obscuring, 617
  statutes and orders relative to, 511, 670
  traffic signs, 512, 519
  trees, 609
  use of, by pedestrians, 532
  use of lights on, 517

(*Volume 1 ends with page 484*)

(*Volume 1 ends with page 484*)

(Volume 1 ends with page 484)

(Volume 1 ends with page 484)

Van der Linden, 702
Van Leeuwen, 488, 702
Vehicles,
  animals colliding with, 530
  brakes of, pulling violently, 513
  colliding with another vehicle, 521
  colliding with obstruction, 517
  collision damage to, 1015
  damage to, 1014, 1015
  defective condition of, 513, 523, 526
  defective steering, 513
  driver's signals, 517
  duty of driver of, 512, 525
  exemptions from speed limit, 515
  following, 521
  headlights, 517
  horn, 517
  horse-drawn, 528
  inspection of, 526
  latent defect in, 523, 526
  leaving unattended, 524, 528, 619, 620
  lights, 516, 524
  loading, 523
  meeting one another, 521
  mounting pavement, 523
  moving off from rest, 515
  obstructing roadway, 1015
  one following another, 521
  opening door of, 523
  overtaking, 517, 521
  overturning, 523
  parking, 523
  person falling from, 521
  person jumping off, 521
  public service, see Omnibus; Tramcar
  reversing, 515
  roadworthy, 526
  running away, 524
  safe driving of, 527
  skidding, 522
  speed of, 515
  stopping, 406, 513
  swerving, 406
  theft of parked, 523
  tyre bursting, 407, 513, 523
  wheel coming off, 513
    See also Omnibus; Tramcar
Ventilation, duty of, 577, 659
Verbal injuries, 172, 493, 494
Verbal injury,
  animus presumed, 737
  as generic term, 738, 904
  as name for species of wrong, 738
  bases of right of action, 735
  Defamation Act, 1952, and, 741
  in institutional writings, 736, 741
  modern misunderstanding of, 738, 741
  special damage in, 741
  true sense of, 738, 741, 904
    See also Convicium; Defamation;
    Malicious falsehood
Veritas,
  appearing from pleadings, 799
  as defence in defamation, 745, 798
  as to part of slander, 800

Veritas—cont.
  belief does not support plea, 800
  counter-issue of, 802
  difference from plea of fair comment,
    841
  difference from plea of privilege, 802
  exact truth to be proved, 800
  multiple charges, 802
  must justify defamation and inferences,
    799
  onus of proof on defender, 799
  part of charges, 801
  specific averments necessary, 799
  standard of proof, 799
  substance of charge to be justified, 801
  where several charges, 801
  whole imputation to be justified, 800
Veritas convicii non excusat, 745
Veterinary surgeon, duty of care of, 1060
Vexatious litigation, 856
Vibration, nuisance from, 964
Vicarious liability,
  casual negligence and, 580
  contribution in, 158
  deliberate wrong, 155
  does not exclude personal liability, 132,
    157, 580
  extent of, when it exists, 131
  for agent, 134
  for assault, 499
  for breach of statutory duty, 311
  for crime, 155
  for employee, 140
  for forbidden act, 135
  for independent contractor, 160
  for mandatory, 134
  for nurses, 637
  for partner, 138
  for physicians, 637
  for servant, 138, 140
  for surgeons, 637
  general principle of, 130
  indemnity in, 158, 580
  in Roman law, 26
  justification for, 131
  not co-extensive with personal liability,
    580
  not for extraneous acts, 150
  not for independent contractor, 160
  of chief constable, 105, 118, 144
  of child, 91
  of corporations, 78
  of Crown, 72, 114, 118, 133, 311
  of employee for employer, 116, 132
  of employer for employee, 132, 141,
    556, 579
  of firm for partner, 138
  of hirer, 116
  of husband for wife, 84, 89, 116
  of husband's employer to wife, 90
  of innkeeper, 160
  of landlord, 116, 958
  of mandant, 134
  of master for servant, 132, 141
  of official, 116
  of parent, 91, 94, 95, 116

(Volume 1 ends with page 484)

(Volume 1 ends with page 484)

(*Volume 1 ends with page 484*)